INTERNATIONAL AWARD WINNING
HARRIS REFERENCE
CATALOG

POSTAGE STAMP PRICES

UNITED STATES
UNITED NATIONS
CANADA & PROVINCES

Plus: Confederate States, U.S. Possessions,
U.S. Trust Territories,
Albums and Accessories,
Comprehensive U.S. Stamp Identifier

H.E. Harris & Co.®
Serving the Collector Since 1916

H.E. Harris & Company was founded by Henry Ellis Harris. Harris began the business in 1916 at an early age of fourteen and took advantage of free advertising in the Washington Post to begin his mail-order business. He built an enormously successful stamp company and garnered the support and confidence of the philatelic community. This annual US/BNA Catalog began publication in 1935 and was 64 pages.

Stock No. 0794823955
ISBN: 0-7948-2395-5

ABOUT OUR CATALOG PRICES

The prices quoted in this catalog are the prices for which H.E. Harris offers stamps for retail sale at the time of publication.

These prices are based on current market values as researched by our staff, but, more importantly, on our day-to-day buying and selling activities in the stamp market.

Although you may certainly use this catalog as a guide to current market prices, you must keep in mind the fact that prices can change in response to varying levels of collector demand, or dealer promotions, and/or special purchases. We are not responsible for typographical errors.

You should also remember that condition is always the key factor in determining the value and price of a given stamp or set of stamps. Unlike some other stamp catalogs, we price U.S. stamps issued up to 1935 in three different condition grades for unused and used examples. For these earlier issues, we have also shown the percentage premium that would apply to Never Hinged Mint examples.

Our illustrated definitions of condition grades are presented on pages X-XII.

We have not found it possible to keep every stamp in stock that is listed in this catalog, and we cannot guarantee that we can supply all of the stamps in all conditions that are listed.

However, we will search for any stamp in any condition that a customer may want if that stamp is not in our stock at the time the customer places an order for it.

H.E. Harris & Co.®
Serving the Collector Since 1916

INDEX

UNITED STATES STAMPS

UNITED STATES RELATED AREAS

UNITED NATIONS

CANADA & PROVINCES

OTHER FEATURES

A GUIDE FOR COLLECTORS

In this section we will attempt to define and explain some of the terms commonly used by stamp collectors. Instead of listing the terms in an alphabetical dictionary or glossary format, we have integrated them. In this way, you can see how an individual term fits within the total picture.

PRODUCTION

The manufacture of stamps involves a number of procedures. We will discuss the major steps here, with emphasis on their implications for stamp collectors. Although we present them separately, modern printing presses may combine one or more operations so that the steps tend to blend together. There also are steps in the process that we do not cover here. While they may be important to the production process, their direct implications for most collectors are minimal.

PLATE MAKING

Before anything can be printed, a printing plate must be made. Using the intaglio printing process (which is explained under **printing**) as an example, the steps involved in plate production are as follows:

- A **master die** is made. The design is recess engraved in a reverse mirror-image. Most master dies consist of only one impression of the design.
- The next step is to prepare a **transfer roll**. The soft steel of the transfer roll is rocked back and forth under pressure against the hardened master die and a series of multiple impressions, called **reliefs**, are created in the transfer roll. Note that the impression on the transfer roll will be raised above the surface, since the roll was pressed into the recesses of the master die.
- Once the transfer roll has been made and hardened, it is used to impress designs in to the soft steel of a **printing plate** that can fit up to 400 impressions of small, definitive-sized stamps or 200 impressions of large, commemorative-sized stamps. This time, the raised design on the transfer roll impresses a recessed design into the plate.

The process is much more complex than this, but these are the basics. Once the printing plate is hardened, it is almost ready to be used to create printed sheets of stamps. Depending on the printing equipment to be used, the printing plate will be shaped to fit around a cylinder for rotary press printing or remain flat for flat-bed press printing. In either form, the plate is then hardened and is ready for use in printing.

DESIGN VARIETIES

The complexity of the platemaking process can result in major or minor flaws. The inspection process will catch most of these flaws, but those that escape detection will result in **plate varieties**.

The early United States Classic issues have been examined in minute detail over the decades. Through **plating** studies, minor differences in individual stamps have been used to identify the position on the printing plate of each design variety. Sometimes called **"flyspeck philately"** because it involves the detection of minute "flyspeck" differences, such plating work has resulted in the identification of some of our greatest rarities. Compare the prices for the one cent blue issues of 1851 and 1857 (#s 5-9 and 18-24) and you will see the tremendous dollar difference that can result from minute design variations. (The Harris Stamp Identifier in this catalog explains the design differences.)

During the plate making or subsequent printing process, plate flaws that are detected will be corrected, sometimes incompletely or incorrectly. Corrections or revisions in an individual die impression or in all plate impressions include the following:

- **Retouching**—minor corrections made in a plate to repair damage or wear.
- **Recutting** or **re-engraving**—similar to, but more extensive than, retouching. Recutting usually applies to changes made before a plate has been hardened, while re-engraving is performed on a plate that has had to be tempered (softened) after hardening.
- **Redrawing**—the intentional creation of a slightly different design. The insertion of secret marks on the National Bank Notes plates when they were turned over to the Continental Bank Note Company in 1873 can be considered redrawings.
- **Reentry**—the reapplication of a design from a transfer roll to the plate, usually to improve a worn plate. If the reentry is not done completely, or if it is not done precisely on top of the previous design, a double transfer will result. Such double transfers will show on the printed stamp as an extra line at one or more points on the stamp.

Other design varieties may result from undetected plate flaws. A **plate crack** (caused by the hardened plate cracking under wear or pressure) or a **plate scratch** (caused by an object cutting into the plate) will show as an ink line on the printed stamp.

One other group that can be covered here to avoid possible confusion includes **reissues, reprints, special printings** and **reproductions**. None of these are design varieties that result from plate flaws, corrections or revisions. In fact, reissues, reprints and special printings are made from the same, unchanged plates as the originals. They show no differences in design and usually can be identified only by variations in paper, color or gum.

Reproductions (such as U.S. #3 and #4), on the other hand, are made from entirely new plates and, therefore, can be expected to show some variation from the originals.

ERRORS, FREAKS, ODDITIES

"EFOs", as they are called, are printed varieties that result from abnormalities in the production process. They are design varieties, but of a special nature because the result looks different from the norm. When you see them, you know something went wrong.

Basically, freaks and oddities can be loosely defined as minor errors. They include the following:

- **Misperforations**, that is, the placement of the perforations within the design rather than at the margins.
- **Foldovers**, caused by a sheet being turned, usually at a corner, before printing and/or perforating. The result is part of a design printed on the reverse of the sheet or placement of perforations at odd angles. Such freaks and oddities may be of relatively minor value, but they do make attractive additions to a collection. Truly major errors, on the other hand, can be of tremendous value. It would not be overstating the case to argue that many collectors are initially drawn to the hobby by the publicity surrounding discoveries of valuable errors and the hope that they might someday do the same. Major errors include the following:
- **Inverts.** These are the most dramatic and most valuable of all major errors and almost always result from printing processes that require more than one pass of a sheet through the presses. If the sheet inadvertently gets "flipped" between passes, the portion printed on the second pass will emerge inverted.

Two definitions we should introduce here are **"frame"** and **"vignette"**. The vignette is the central design of the stamp; the frame encloses the vignette and, at its outer edges, marks the end of the printed stamp design. Oftentimes, stamps described as inverted centers (vignettes) actually are inverted frames. The center was properly printed in the first pass and the frame was inverted in the second pass.

- **Color errors.** The most noticeable color errors usually involve one or more omitted colors. The sheet may not have made it through the second pass in a two-step printing process. In the past such errors were extremely rare because they were obvious enough to be noticed by inspectors. In modern multi-color printings, the chances of such errors escaping detection have increased. Nonetheless, they still qualify as major errors and carry a significant premium.

*Other color errors involve the use of an incorrect color. They may not seem as dramatic as missing colors, but the early issues of many countries include some very rare and valuable examples of these color errors.

Although technically not a color error, we can include here one of the most unusual of all errors, the United States 1917 5-cent stamps that are supposed to be blue, but are found in the carmine or rose color of the 2-cent stamps. The error was not caused by a sheet of the 5-centers being printed in the wrong color, as you might expect. Rather, because a few impressions on a 2-cent plate needed reentry, they were removed. But an error was made and the 5-cent design was entered. Thus it is a reentry error, but is described in most catalogs as a color error because that is the apparent result. Whatever the description, the 5-cent denomination surrounded by 2-cent stamps is a real showpiece.

- **Imperfs.** A distinction should be drawn here between imperforate errors and intentionally imperforate stamps. When the latter carry a premium value over their perforated counterparts, it is because they were printed in smaller quantities for specialized usages. They might have been intended, for example, for sale to vending machine manufacturers who would privately perforate the imperforate sheets

On the other hand, errors in which there is absolutely no trace of a perforation between two stamps that were supposed to be perforated carry a premium based on the rarity of the error. Some modern United States coil imperforate errors have been found in such large quantities that they carry little premium value. But imperforate errors found in small quantities represent tremendous rarities.

Be they intentional or errors, imperforate stamps are commonly collected in pairs or larger multiples because it can be extremely difficult—often impossible, to distinguish them from stamps that have had their perforations trimmed away in an attempt to pass them off as more valuable imperfs. Margin singles that show the stamp and a wide, imperforate selvage at one of the edges of the sheet are another collecting option.

PRINTING

There are three basic printing methods:

1. **Intaglio,** also known as **recess** printing. Line engraved below the surface of the printing plate (that is, in recess) accept the ink and apply it to damp paper that is forced into the recesses of the plate. Intaglio methods include **engraved** and **photogravure** (or **rotogravure**). Photogravure is regarded by some as separate from intaglio because the engraving is done by chemical etching and the finished product can be distinguished from hand or machine engraving.
2. **Typography.** This is similar to intaglio, in that it involves engraving, but the action is in reverse, with the design left at the surface of the plate and the portions to be unprinted cut away. Ink is then applied to the surface design, which is imprinted onto paper. **Typeset** letterpress printing is the most common form of typography.
3. **Lithography.** This method differs from the previous two in that it involves **surface printing**, rather than engraving. Based on the principle that oil and water do not mix, the design to be printed is applied with a greasy ink onto a plate that is then wet with a watery fluid. Printing ink run across the plate is accepted only at the greased (oiled) points. The ink applies the design to paper that is brought in contact with the plate. **Offset** printing, a modern lithographic method, involves a similar approach, but uses a rubber blanket to transfer the inked design to paper.

The printing method that was used to produce a given stamp can be determined by close inspection of that stamp.

1. Because the paper is pressed into the grooves of an intaglio plate, when viewed from the surface the design appears to be slightly raised. Running a fingernail lightly across the surface also will reveal this raised effect. When viewed from the back, the design will appear to be recessed (or pressed out toward the surface). Photogravure stamps have a similar appearance and feel, but when viewed under a magnifier, they reveal a series of dots, rather than line engravings.
2. Because the raised design on a plate is pressed into the paper when the typograph process is used, when viewed from the surface, the printing on the stamp does not have the raised effect of an intaglio product. On the other hand, when viewed from the reverse, a raised impression will be evident where the design was imprinted. Overprints often are applied by typography and usually show the raised effect on the back of the stamp.
3. Unlike either of the previous two methods, lithographed stamps look and feel flat. This dull, flat effect can be noticed on any of the United States 1918-20 offset printings, #s 525-536.

Overprints and **surcharges** are inscriptions or other markings added to printed stamps to adapt them to other uses. A **surcharge** is an overprint that changes or restates the value of the stamp. The United States Offices in China (K1-18) issues carry surcharges.

Some foreign semi-postal issues are stamps with a printed denomination that is applied to the postage fee and an overprinted surcharge that is applied to a specified charity.

Overprints can be applied for reasons other than to change their value. Examples would be for commemorative purposes (#s 646-648), to hinder the use of stolen stamps (#s 658-679 the Kansas-Nebraska issues), to change or designate the usage of the stamp (modern precancels), or to indicate usage in a distinct political unit (Canal Zone, Guam and Philippines overprints on United States stamps used during the early period of U.S. administration until new stamps could be printed).

Overprints can be applied by handstamp or even typewriter, but the most efficient and commonly used technique seen on stamps is typeset press printing.

WATERMARKS

This actually is one of the first steps in the stamp production process because it is part of paper manufacturing. A **watermark** is a slight thinning of the paper pulp, usually in the form of a relevant design. It is applied by devices attached to the rolls on papermaking machines. Without getting involved in the technical aspects, the result is a watermark that can sometimes be seen when held to the light, but more often requires watermark detector fluid.

A word of caution here. Such detector fluids may contain substances that can be harmful when inhaled. This is particularly true of lighter fluids that often are used by collectors in lieu of specially made stamp watermark detector fluids.

Watermarks are used to help detect counterfeits. Although it is possible to reproduce the appearance of a watermark, it is extremely difficult. The authorities have at times been able to identify a counterfeit by the lack of a watermark that should be present or by the presence of an incorrect watermark.

On the other hand, there are occasions when the incorrect or absent watermark did not indicate a counterfeit, but a printing error. The wrong paper may have been used or the paper may have been inserted incorrectly (resulting in an inverted or sideways watermark). The United States 30 cent orange red that is listed among the 1914-17 issues on unwatermarked paper (#467A) is an example of a printing error. It was produced on watermarked paper as part of the 1914-15 series, but a few sheets were discovered without watermarks.

Unfortunately, the difficulty encountered in detecting watermarks on light shades, such as orange or yellow, makes experts very reluctant to identify single copies of #476A. Although not visible, the watermark just might be there.

Because an examination of a full sheet allows the expert to examine the unprinted selvage and all stamps on that sheet at one time, positive identification is possible and most of the stamps that come down to us today as #476A trace back to such full sheets.

GUMMING

Gumming once was almost always applied after printing and before perforating and cutting of sheets into panes. Today, pregummed paper may be used, so the placement of this step in the process cannot be assured—nor is it the sequence of much significance.

The subject of gum will be treated more fully in the **Condition** section of this catalog. At this point, we will only note that certain stamps can be identified by their gum characteristics. Examples include the identification of rotary press stamps by the presence of gum breaker ridges or lines and the detection of the presence of original gum on certain stamps that indicates they can not be a rarer issue that was issued without gum, such as #s 40-47. Others, such as #s 102-111 can be identified in part by their distinctive white, crackly original gum.

PERFORATING

We have already discussed the absence of perforations in the **Errors** section. Here we will concentrate on the perforating process itself.

All perforating machines use devices to punch holes into the printed stamp paper. The holes usually are round and are known as perforations. When two adjacent stamps are separated, the semicircular cutouts are the **perforations**; the remaining paper between the perforations forms **perf tips**, or **"teeth"**.

Most perforations are applied by perforators that contain a full row of punches that are driven through the paper as it is fed through the perforating equipment. **Line Perforators** drive the punches up and down; **rotary perforators** are mounted on cylinders that revolve. There are other techniques, but these are the most common.

To clear up one point of confusion, the **perforation size** (for example, "perf 11") is not the size of the hole or the number of perforations on the side of a given stamp. Rather, it describes the number of perforations that could be fit within two centimeters.

A perf 8 stamp will have visibly fewer perforations than a perf 12 stamp, but it is much harder to distinguish between perf 11 and perf 10-1/2. **Perforation gauges** enable collectors to make these distinctions with relative ease.

TAGGING

Modern, high-speed, mechanical processing of mail has created the need for "tagging" stamps by coating them with a luminescent substance that could be detected under ultraviolet (U.V.) light or by printing them on paper that included such substances. When passed under a machine capable of detecting these substances, an envelope can be positioned and the stamp automatically cancelled, thereby eliminating time-consuming and tedious manual operations. The tagged varieties of certain predominantly untagged stamps, such as #s 1036 and C67, do carry modest premiums. There also are technical differences between phosphorescent and fluorescent types of luminescent substances. But these details are primarily of interest to specialists and will not be discussed in this general work.

PAPER

The fact that we have not devoted more attention to paper should not be an indication of any lack of interest or significance. Books have been written on this one subject alone, and a lack of at least a rudimentary knowledge of the subject can lead to mis-identification of important varieties and resultant financial loss.

The three most common categories of paper on which stamps are printed are **wove**, **laid**, and **India**. The most frequently used is machine-made **wove paper**, similar to that used for most books. The semiliquid pulp for wove paper is fed onto a fine wire screen and is processed much the same as cloth would be woven. Almost all United States postage stamps are printed on wove paper.

Laid paper is formed in a process that uses parallel wires rather than a uniform screen. As a result, the paper will be thinner where the pulp was in contact with the wires. When held to the light, alternating light and dark lines can be seen. Laid paper varieties have been found on some early United States stamps.

India paper is very thin and tough, without any visible texture. It is, therefore, more suited to obtaining the sharp impressions that are needed for printers' pre-production proofs, rather than to the high-volume printing of stamps.

Other varieties include **bluish** paper, so described because of the tone created by certain substances added to the paper, and silk paper, which contains threads or fibers of silk that usually can be seen on the back of the stamp. Many United States revenue stamps were printed on silk paper.

COLLECTING FORMATS

Whatever the production method, stamps reach the collector in a variety of forms. The most common is in sheet, or more correctly, pane form.

Sheets are the full, uncut units as they come from a press. Before distribution to post offices, these sheets are cut into **panes**. For United States stamps, most regular issues are printed in sheets of 400 and cut into panes of 100; most commemoratives are printed in sheets of 200 and cut into panes of 50. There are numerous exceptions to this general rule, and they are indicated in the mint sheet listings in this catalog.

Sheets also are cut in **booklet panes** for only a few stamps—usually four to ten stamps per pane. These panes are assembled in complete booklets that might contain one to five panes, usually stapled together between two covers. An intact booklet is described as **unexploded**; when broken apart it is described as exploded.

Coils are another basic form in which stamps reach post offices. Such stamps are wound into continuous coil rolls, usually containing from 100 to 5,000 stamps, the size depending on the volume needs of the expected customer. Almost all coils are produced with perforations on two opposite sides and straight edges on the remaining two sides.

Some serious collectors prefer collecting coils in pairs or strips—two or more adjacent stamps—as further assurance of genuineness. It is much easier to fake a coil single that shows only portions of each perforation hole than a larger unit that shows the complete perf hole.

A variation on this theme is the **coil line pair**—adjacent stamps that show a printed vertical line between. On rotary press stamps the line appears where the two ends of a printing plate meet on a rotary press cylinder. The joint is not complete, so ink falls between the plate ends and is transferred onto the printed coil. On flat plate stamps the guideline is the same as that created for sheet stamps, as described below.

Paste-up coil pairs are not as popular as line pairs. They were a necessary by-product of flat plate printings in which the coil strips cut from separate sheets had to be pasted together for continuous winding into roll form.

The modern collecting counterpart to coil line pairs is the plate **number strip**—three or five adjacent coil stamps with the plate number displayed on the middle stamp. Transportation coil plate strips have become particularly sought after. On most early coil rolls, the plate numbers were supposed to be trimmed off. Freaks in which the number remains are interesting, but do not carry large premiums since they are regarded as examples of miscut oddities rather than printing errors.

Miniature sheets and **souvenir sheets** are variations on one theme—small units that may contain only one or at most a much smaller quantity of stamps than would be found on the standard postal panes. Stamps may be issued in miniature sheet format for purposes of expedience, as for example the Bret Harte $5 issue (#2196), which was released in panes of 20 to accommodate the proportionately large demand by collectors for plate blocks rather than single stamps.

As the name implies, a souvenir sheet is a miniature sheet that was released as a souvenir to be saved, rather than postally used—although such sheets or the stamps cut out from them can be used as postage. Note: **souvenir cards** are created strictly for promotional and souvenir purposes. They contain stamp reproductions that may vary in size, color or design from the originals and are not valid for postal use.

Often, a common design may be produced in sheet, coil and booklet pane form. The common design is designated by collectors as one **type**, even though it may be assigned many different catalog numbers because of variations in color, size, perforations, printing method, denomination, etc. On the other hand, even minor changes in a basic design represent a new type.

Sheet stamps offer the greatest opportunity for format variation and collecting specialization. Using the following illustration for reference, the varieties that can be derived include the following:

Block (a)—this may be any unit of four stamps or more in at least 2 by 2 format. Unless designated as a different size, blocks are assumed to be blocks of four.

Specialized forms of blocks include:

Arrow block (b)—adjacent stamps at the margin of a sheet, showing the arrow printed in the margin for registration in the printing process, as, for example, in two-color printings. When the arrow designates the point at which a sheet is cut into panes, the result will appear as one leg of the arrow, or V, on each pane.

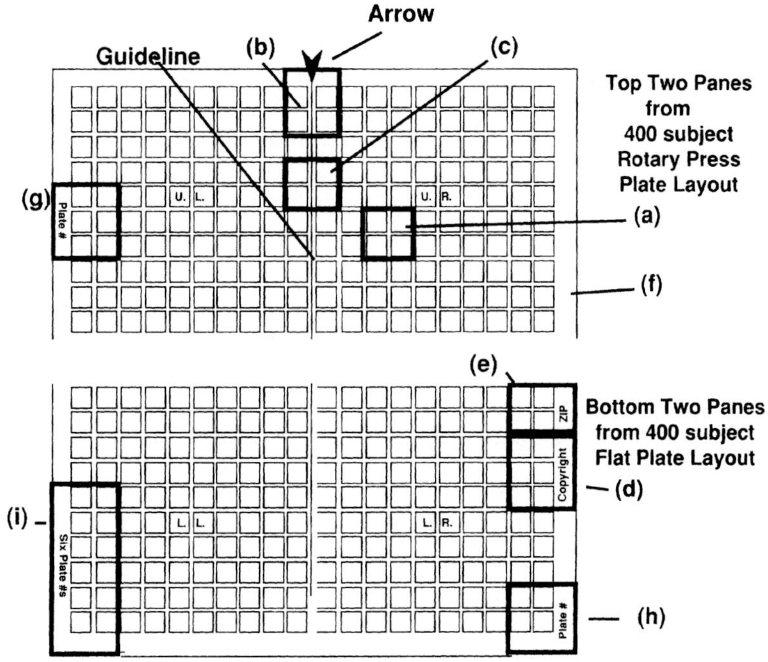

(This diagram is for placement purposes only, and is not an exact reproduction of margin markings)

Guideline block (c)—similar to arrow block, except that it can be any block that shows the registration line between two rows of two stamps each.

Gutter block—similar to guideline block, except that an uncolored gutter is used instead of a printed line. The best known United States gutter blocks are those cut from full-sheet "Farley printings". Pairs of stamps from adjacent panes on each side of the gutter form the gutter block.

Imprint, or **inscription blocks (d)**—include **copyright, mail early,** and **ZIP (e)** blocks. On most modern United States sheets, the **selvage**, that is, the margin that borders the outer rows of stamps **(f)**, includes one or more inscriptions in addition to the plate numbers. It may be a copyright protection notice or an inscription that encourages mail users to post their mail early or to use the ZIP code on their mail.

Because the inscription appears along the margin, rather than in one of the corners, it is customary to collect copyright blocks and mail early blocks in two rows of three stamps each, with the inscription centered in the margin. The ZIP inscription appears in one of the corners of each pane, so it is collected in corner margin blocks of four.

Plate number block—this is by far the most popular form of block collecting. On each sheet of stamps, a plate number (or numbers) is printed to identify the printing plate(s) used. Should a damage be discovered, the plate can easily be identified.

On flat plate sheets, where the plate number appeared along the margin, the format usually is in plate blocks of six, with the plate number centered in the margin **(g)**.

On rotary press and other sheets where a single plate number appears in one of the four corners of the margin, the customary collecting format is a corner margin block of four **(h)**. This also is true for plate blocks with two plate numbers in two adjacent corner stamps and for modern plates where single digits are used to designate each plate number and the complete series (containing one digit for each printing color) appears in the corner.

Before single digits were adopted for modern multi-color printings, the five-digit numbers assigned to each plate might run down a substantial portion of the sheet margin. **Plate strips** are collected in such instances. Their size is two rows times as many stamps as are attached to the margin area that shows all plate numbers **(i)**.

Because a sheet of stamps is cut into separate panes, printing plates include plate numbers that can be seen on each of the cut panes. On modern sheets the plate numbers would be located in each of the four corners of the uncut sheet. Once cut, each of the four panes would show the same plate number in one of its corners. The position of the plate number, which matches the position of the pane on the uncut sheet, is designated as upper left or right and lower left or right. Some specialists seek matched sets. A **matched set** is one of each of the four positions for a given plate number. A **complete matched set** is all positions of all plate numbers for a given issue.

Other definitions that relate in one way or another to the format in which stamps are produced include:

Se-tenant—from the French, meaning joined together. A pair, block, or larger multiple that contains different designs. The 1967 Space Twins issue is an example of a se-tenant pair in which the two different stamps are part of an integral design. The 1968 Historic Flags se-tenant strip contains ten separate designs, each of which can stand alone.

Tete-beche pair—from the French, meaning head-to-tail. Such pairs show adjacent stamps, one of which is upside down in relation to the other.

Proof—any trial impression used in the evaluation of prospective or final designs. **Final die proofs**—that is, those made from a completed die preparatory to its being used in the production of printing plates—are the standard proof collecting form.

Essay—a partial or complete illustration of a proposed design. In the strict philatelic sense, essays are printed in proof form.

Color trials—a preliminary proof of a stamp design in one or more colors. Trial color proofs are used to select the color in which the stamp will be printed.

Grill—a pattern of embossed cuts that break the stamp paper. See the information at the head of the 1861-67 Issue listings and the section of grills in the Harris Stamp Identifier.

POSTAL MARKINGS

The extensive subject of cancellations and postal markings on stamps and covers is too specialized to present in detail here. Volumes have been written on individual categories of markings—straight line markings, ship cancels, foreign mail cancels, flight covers, etc. In this section we will limit ourselves to the basic definitions related to the stamp and the manner in which it is cancelled, rather than the specialized usage of the envelope to which the stamp is affixed.

- **Manuscript**, or **pen cancels** were the earliest form of "killing" a stamp—that is, marking it to indicate it had been postally used.
- **Handstamps** were created shortly after the first stamps were issued. The early devices might only show a pattern such as a grid and often were carved from cork.
- **Fancy cancels** were an extension of the handstamp. Local postmasters carved cork cancelers that depicted bees, kicking mules, flowers, and hundreds of other figures. Stamps with clear strikes of such fancy cancels usually carry hefty premiums over those with standard cancels.
- **Machine cancels** are applied by mechanical rather than manual means.
- A stamp is **tied** to a cover (or piece) when the cancellation, whatever its form, extends beyond the margins of the stamp onto the cover. Such a tie is one indication of the authenticity of the cover.

Specialized cancellations include the following:

- **Cut cancel**—as the name implies, a cancel that actually cuts the stamp, usually in the form of a thin, straight incision. The most common usage of cut cancels on United States stamps is on Revenue issues.
- **Perfin**, or perforated initial—usually not a cancellation as such, but rather a privately administered punching into the stamp of one or more initials. Most often, the initials were those of a large firm that wished to prevent personal use of their stamps by employees.
- **Precancel**—a cancellation printed on stamps in advance of their sale. The primary purpose of precancels is for sale to large volume mailers, whose mail is delivered to post offices and processed in bulk without necessarily receiving further cancellation.
- **Non-contemporary cancel**—a cancellation applied to a stamp long after the normal period of use for that stamp. A stamp that is worth more used than unused or a damaged unused stamp that would be worth more on cover are examples of candidates for non-contemporary markings.
- **Cancel-to-order**, or **C.T.O.**—a cancel that is printed on a stamp by an issuing country to give it the appearance of having been used, or to render it invalid for postage in that country. Special fancy cancels or "favor cancels" have been applied at various times in the countries for philatelic reasons.

CATEGORIES

The number of specialized categories into which stamps can be slotted is limited only by the imagination of the individual collector. Some collectors have attempted to collect one of each and every stamp ever issued by every nation that ever existed. Other collectors have concentrated on all the possible varieties and usages of only one stamp. Between these two extremes, stamps can be divided into certain generally accepted categories, whether or not they are used as boundaries for a collection. These categories are as follows:

- **Definitives**, or **regulars**—stamps that are issued for normal, everyday postage needs. In the United States, they are put on sale for a period limited only by changing rate needs or infrequent issuance of a new definitive series. Post offices can requisition additional stocks of definitives as needed.
- **Commemoratives**—stamps issued to honor a specific event, anniversary, individual or group. They are printed in a predetermined quantity and are intended for sale during a limited period. Although they can be used indefinitely, once stocks are sold out at a local post office, commemoratives usually are not replenished unless the issue has local significance.
- **Pictorials**—stamps that depict a design other than the portrait of an individual or a static design such as a coat of arms or a flag. While some collectors think of these strictly as commemoratives (because most commemoratives are pictorials), some definitives also can be pictorials. Any number of definitives that depict the White House are examples.
- **Airmails**, or **air posts**—stamps issued specifically for airmail use. Although they do not have to bear a legend, such as "airmail", they usually do. Airmail stamps usually can be used to pay other postage fees.

When air flights were a novelty, airmail stamp collecting was an extremely popular specialty. Part of this popularity also can be ascribed to the fact that the first airmail stamps usually were given special attention by issuing postal administrations. Produced using relatively modern technology, they often were among the most attractive of a nation's issues.

- **Zeppelin stamps**—although these do not rate as a major category, they deserve special mention. Zeppelin issues were primarily released for specific use on Zeppelin flights during the 1920s and 1930s. They carried high face values and were issued during the Great Depression period, when most collectors could not afford to purchase them. As a result, most Zeppelin issues are scarce and command substantial premiums. United States "Zepps" are the Graf Zeppelins (C13-C15) and the Century of Progress issue (C18).
- **Back-of-the-book**—specialized stamps that are identified as "back-of-the-book" because of their position in catalogs following the listings of regular and commemorative postal issues. Catalogs identified them with a prefix letter.

Some collectors include airmail stamps in this category, in part because they carry a prefix letter (C) and are listed separately. Most collectors treat the airmails as part of a standard collection and begin the back-of-the-book section with semi-postals (B) or, for the United States, special deliveries (E).

Other frequently used "b-o-b" categories include postage dues (J), offices in China, or Shanghais (K), officials (O), parcel posts (Q), newspapers (PR), and revenues (R), the latter including "Duck" hunting permit stamps (RW).

Postal stationery and postal cards are the major non-stamp back-of-the-book categories. A complete envelope or card is called an **entire**; the cutout corner from such a piece, showing the embossed or otherwise printed design, is described as a **cut square**.

Some collecting categories do not relate to the intended use of the stamps. Examples include **topicals** (stamps collected by the theme of the design, such as sports, dance, paintings, space, etc.) and **first day covers**. Modern first day covers show a stamp or stamps postmarked in a designated first day city on the official first day of issue. The cancel design will relate to the issue and the cover may bear a privately-printed cachet that further describes and honors the subject of the stamp.

One of the oddities of the hobby is that **stampless covers** are an accepted form of "stamp" collecting. Such covers display a usage without a stamp, usually during the period before stamps were required for the payment of postage. They bear manuscript or handstamps markings such as "due 5," "PAID," etc. to indicate the manner in which postage was paid.

Although they do not constitute a postal marking, we can include **bisects** here for want of a better place. A bisect is a stamp cut in half and used to pay postage in the amount of one-half of the stamp's denomination. The 1847 ten cent stamp (#2) cut in half and used to pay the five cent rate is an example.

Bisects should be collected only on cover and properly tied. They also should reflect an authorized usage, for example, from a post office that was known to lack the proper denomination, and sould pay an amount called for by the usuage shown on the cover.

Not discussed in detail here is the vast subject of **covers**, or postal history. Envelopes, usually but not necessarily showing a postal use, are described by collectors as covers. Early "covers" actually were single letter sheets with a message on one side and folded into the form of an enclosing wrapper when viewed from the outside. The modern aerogramme or air letter is similar in design to these early folded letters.

H.E. Harris Pictorial Guide to Centering

Cat #	Very Fine	Fine	Average
1 to 293 1847 to 1898	 Perfs clear of design on all four sides. Margins may not be even.	 Perfs well clear of design on at least three sides. But may almost touch design on one side.	 Perfs cut into design on at least one side.
294 to 749 1901 to 1934	 Perfs clear of design. Margins relatively even on all four sides.	 Perfs clear of design. Margins not even on all four sides.	 Perfs touch design on at least one side.
750 to Date 1935 to Present	 Perfs clear of design. Centered with margins even on all four sides.	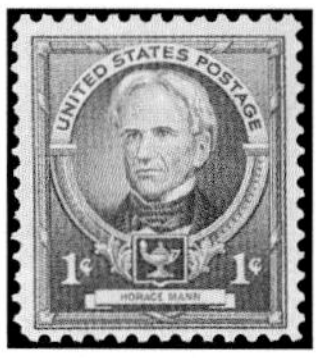 Perfs clear of design. Margins may be uneven.	 Perfs may touch design on at least one side.

Note: **Margins are the area from the edges of stamp to the design. Perfs are the serrations between stamps that aid in separating them.**

CENTERING

One major factor in the determination of a stamp's fair value is its **centering**, the relative balance of the stamp design within its margins. Whether the stamp has perforations or is imperforate, its centering can be judged. Because the stamp trade does not have an established system for grading or measuring centering, "eyeballing" has become the standard practice. As a result, one collector's definition may vary from another's. This can create some confusion, but the system seems to work, so it has remained in force.

Centering can range from poor to superb, as follows:

- **Poor**—so far off center that a significant portion of the design is lost because of bad centering. On a poorly centered perforated stamp, the perforations cut in so badly that even the perf tips may penetrate the design.
- **Average**—a stamp whose frame or design is cut slightly by the lack of margins on one or two sides. On a perforated stamp, the perf holes might penetrate the stamp, but some margin white space will show on the teeth. Average stamps are accepted by the majority of collectors for 19th century stamps and early 20th century stamps, as well as for the more difficult later issues.
- **Fine**—the perforations are clear of the design, except for those issues that are known to be extremely poorly centered, but the margins on opposite sides will not be balanced, that is, equal to each other. (Note: a stamp whose top and bottom margins are perfectly balanced may still be called fine if the left and right margins differ substantially from each other.)
- **Very fine**—the opposite margins may still appear to differ somewhat, but the stamp is closer to being perfectly centered than it is to being fine centered. Very fine stamps are sought by collectors who are particularly interested in high quality and who are willing to pay the premiums such stamps command.
- **Superb**— perfect centering. They are so scarce that no comprehensive price list could attempt to include a superb category. Superb stamps, when they are available, command very high premiums.
- **"Jumbo"**—an abnormal condition, in which the stamp's margins are oversized compared to those of the average stamp in a given issue. Such jumbos can occur in the plate making process when a design is cut into the printing plate and excessive space is allowed between that design and the adjacent stamps.

Note: Some collectors also define a "fine to very fine" condition, in which the margin balance falls into a mid-range between fine and very fine. In theory it may be an attractive compromise, but in practice the range between fine and very fine is too narrow to warrant a separate intermediate category.

Quality and Condition Definitions

In determining the value of a given stamp, a number of factors have to be taken into consideration. For mint stamps, the condition of the gum, whether or not it has been hinged, and the centering are all major factors that determine their value. For used stamps, the factors to consider are cancellation and centering. The following H.E. Harris guidelines will enable you to determine the quality standards you may choose from in acquiring stamps for your collection.

Mint Stamp Gum

Unused—A stamp that is not cancelled (used), yet has had all the original gum removed. On early U.S. issues this is the condition that the majority of mint stamps exist in, as early collectors often soaked the gum off their stamps to avoid the possibility of the gum drying and splitting.

Original Gum (OG)—A stamp that still retains the adhesive applied when the stamp was made, yet has been hinged or has had some of the gum removed. Mint stamps from #215 to date can be supplied in this condition.

Never Hinged (NH)—A stamp that is in "post office" condition with full gum that has never been hinged. For U.S. #215 to #1241 (1963), separate pricing columns or percentages are provided for "Never Hinged" quality. From #1242 (1964) to date, all stamps are priced as Never Hinged. Hinged Stamps 1964 to date are available at 20% off the NH price.

Cancellations

The cancellations on Used stamps range from light to heavy. A lightly cancelled stamp has the main design of the stamp clearly showing through the cancel, while a heavy cancel usually substantially obliterates the design elements of the stamp. In general it should be assumed that Very fine quality stamps will have lighter cancels than Average cancellation stamps.

Heavy Cancel

Light Cancel

GUM

The impact of the condition of the back of an unused stamp (i.e. the gum) upon that stamp's value in today's market needs careful consideration. The prices for 19th century stamps vary widely based on this element of condition.

Some traditional collectors feel that modern collectors pay too much attention to gum condition. Around the turn of the century, some collectors washed the gum off the stamps to prevent it from cracking and damaging the stamp themselves. But that generation has passed and the practice not only is no longer popular, it is almost unheard of.

To some extent the washing of gum is no longer necessary, since modern gums are not as susceptible to cracking. A more important development, however, has been the advent of various mounts that allow the collector to place a stamp in an album without the use of a hinge. With that development, "never hinged" became a premium condition that could be obtained on stamps issued from the 1930s to date. As a result, gum took on added significance, and its absence on 20th century stamps became unacceptable.

The standard definitions that pertain to gum condition are as follows:

- **Original gum**, or **o.g.**—the gum that was applied when the stamp was produced. There are gradations, from "full" original gum through "partial" original gum, down to "traces". For all intents and purposes, however, a stamp must have most of its original gum to be described as "o.g."
- **Regummed**— the stamp has gum, but it is not that which would have been applied when the stamp was produced. Many collectors will avoid regummed stamps because the gum may hide some repair work. At best, regumming may give the stamp an appearance of completeness, but a premium should not be paid for a stamp that lacks its original gum.
- **Unused**—while many collectors think of this as any stamp that is not used, the narrow philatelic definition indicates a stamp that has no gum or is regummed.
- **Unhinged**—as with "unused", the term has a specific meaning to collectors: a regumming that shows no traces of a hinge mark. Unfortunately, in their confusion some collectors purchase stamps described as "unused" and "unhinged" as if they bore original gum.
- **No gum**—the stamp lacks its gum, either because it was intentionally produced without gum (also described as **ungummed**) or had the gum removed at a later date. It is customary to find 19th century stamps without gum, and the condition is acceptable to all but the most fastidious collectors. On 20th century stamps, original gum is to be expected.

- **Hinged**—the gum shows traces of having been mounted with a hinge. This can range from **lightly hinged** (the gum shows traces, but none of the hinge remains) to **heavily hinged** (a substantial portion of one or more hinge remnants is stuck to the stamp, or a significant portion of the gum has been lost in the removal of a hinge).
- **Thinned**— not only has the gum been removed, but a portion of the stamp paper has been pulled away. A thin usually will show when the stamp is held to a light. One of the faults that may be covered over on regummed stamps is a thin that has been filled in.
- **Never hinged**—as the name implies, the stamp has its original gum in post office condition and has never been hinged. Although some collectors think of **"mint"** stamps as any form of unused, o.g. stamps, the more accepted "mint" definition is never hinged.

USED STAMPS

For used stamps, the presence of gum would be the exception, since it would have been removed when the stamp was washed from the envelope, so gum is not a factor on used stamps.

The centering definitions, on the other hand, would be the same as for unused issues. In addition, the cancellation would be a factor.

We should point out here that we are not referring to the type of cancellation, such as a fancy cancel that might add considerably to the value of a stamp, or a manuscript cancel that reduces its value. Rather, we are referring to the degree to which the cancellation covers the stamp.

A **lightly cancelled** used stamp, with all of the main design elements showing and the usage evidenced by an unobtrusive cancel, is the premier condition sought by collectors of used stamps. On the other hand, a stamp whose design has been substantially obliterated by a **heavy cancel** is at best a space filler that should be replaced by a moderate to lightly cancelled example.

PERFORATIONS

The condition of a stamp's perforations can be determined easily by visual examination. While not necessarily perfect, all perforations should have full teeth and clean perforation holes. A **blunt perf** is one that is shorter than it should be, while a **pulled perf** actually shows a portion of the margin or design having been pulled away. **Blind perfs** are the opposite: paper remains where the perforation hole should have been punched out.

One irony of the demand for perforation is that **straight edges**, that is, the normal sheet margin straight edge that was produced when flat-plate sheets were cut into panes, are not acceptable to many collectors. In fact, many collectors will prefer a reperforated stamp to a straight edge. (Technically, **"re"perforated** can only apply to a stamp that is being perforated again, as when a damaged or excessive margin has been cut away and new perforations are applied, but we will follow the common practice of including the perforation of normal straight edges in this category).

As a result of this preference, many straight edges no longer exist as such. When one considers that they were in the minority to start with (a pane of 100 flat plate stamps would include 19 straight edges) and that even fewer come down to us today, an argument could be made that they may someday be rarities...although it is hard to conceive of anyone paying a premium for straight edges.

FAKES, FAULTS, AND EXPERTIZING

Below the first quality level—stamps free of defects—a range of stamps can be found from attractive **"seconds"** that have barely noticeable flaws to **space fillers** that may have a piece missing and which ought to be replaced by a better copy—unless we are talking about great rarities which would otherwise be beyond the budget of most collectors.

The more common flaws include **thins**, **tears**, **creases**, **stains**, **pulled perfs**, **pinholes** (some dealers and collectors used to display their stamps pinned to boards), **face scuffs** or erasures, and **fading**.

Stamps with faults sometimes are **repaired**, either to protect them from further damage or to deceive collectors.

While the terms that are applied to stamps that are not genuine often are used interchangeably, they do have specific meaning, as follows:

- **fakes** (in French, faux; in German, falsch)—stamps that appear to be valuable varieties, but which were made from cheaper genuine stamps. Trimming away the perforations to create an imperforate is a common example of a fake.
- **bogus** stamps, **phantoms, labels**—outright fantasies, usually the product of someone's imagination, produced for amusement rather than deception.

While most stamps are genuine, and the average collector need not be concerned about the possibility of repairs, **expertizing** services do exist for collectors who are willing to pay a fee to obtain an independent opinion on their more valuable stamps.

UNITED STATES STAMP IDENTIFIER

Shows you how to distinguish between the rare and common U.S. stamps that look alike.

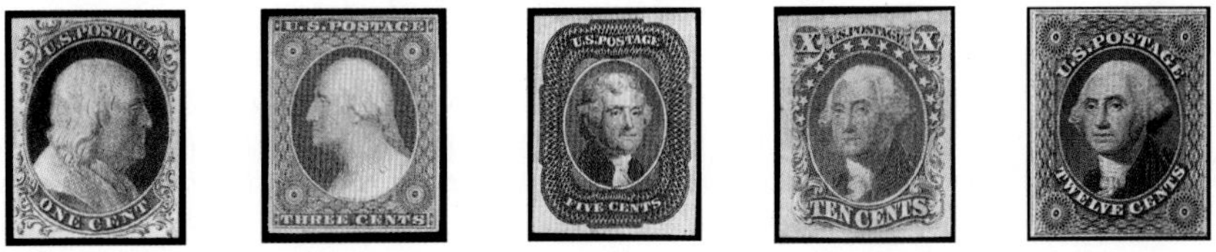

Types of 1¢ Franklin Design of 1851-60

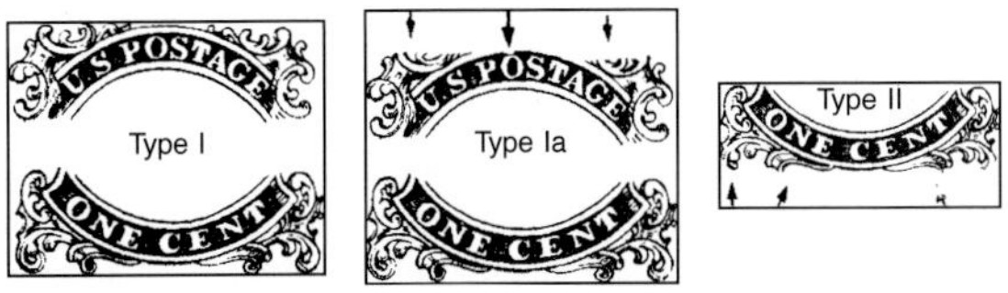

TYPE I has the most complete design of the various types of stamps. At top and bottom there is an unbroken curved line running outside the bands reading "U.S. POSTAGE" and "ONE CENT". The scrolls at bottom are turned under, forming curls. The scrolls and outer line at top are complete.

TYPE Ia is like Type I at bottom but ornaments and curved line at top are partly cut away.

TYPE Ib (not illustrated) is like Type I at top but little curls at bottom are not quite so complete nor clear and scroll work is partly cut away.

TYPE II has the outside bottom line complete, but the little curls of the bottom scrolls and the lower part of the plume ornament are missing. Side ornaments are complete.

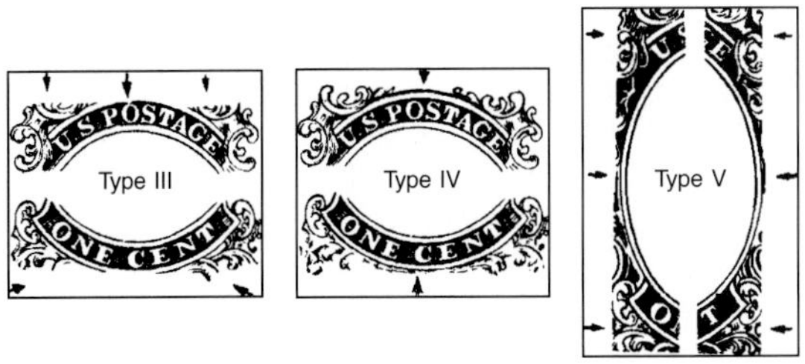

TYPE III has the outside lines at both top and bottom partly cut away in the middle. The side ormaments are complete.

TYPE IIIa (not illustrated) is similar to Type III with the outer line cut away at top or bottom, but not both.

TYPE IV is similar to Type II but the curved lines at top or bottom (or both) have been recut in several different ways, and usually appear thicker than Type IIs.

TYPE V is similar to Type III but has the side ormanents parlty cut away. Type V occurs only on perforated stamps.

Types of 3¢ Washington & 5¢ Jefferson Designs of 1851-60

3¢ WASHINGTON

TYPE I has a frame line around the top, bottom and sides.

TYPE II has the frame line removed at top and bottom, while the side frame lines are continuous from the top to bottom of the plate.

TYPE IIa is similar to Type II, but the side frame lines were recut individually, and therefore are broken between stamps.

5¢ JEFFERSON

TYPE I is a complete design with projections (arrow) at the top and bottom as well as at the sides.

TYPE II has the projections at the top or bottom partly or completely cut away.

Types of the 10¢ Washington Design of 1851-60

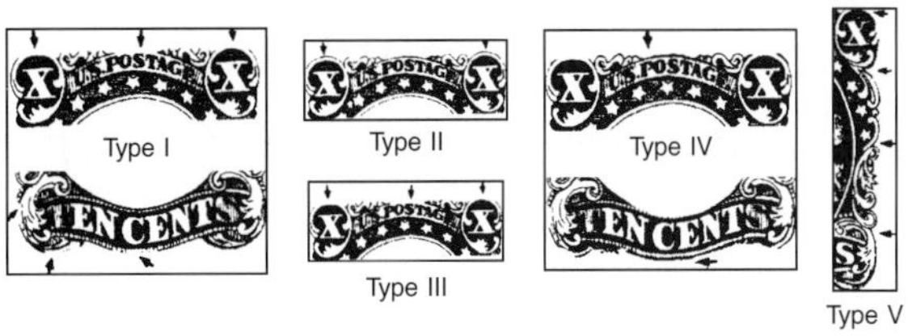

TYPE I has the "shells" at the lower corners practically complete, while the outer line below "TEN CENTS" is very nearly complete. At the top, the outer lines above "U.S. POSTAGE" above the "X" in each corner are broken.

TYPE II has the design complete at the top, but the outer line at the bottom is broken in the middle and the "shells" are partially cut away.

TYPE III has both top and bottom outer lines cut away; similar to Type I at the top and Type II at the bottom.

TYPE IV has the outer lines at the top or bottom of the stamp, or at both place, recut to show more strongly and heavily.

Types I, II, III and IV have complete ornaments at the sides and three small circles or pearls (arrow) at the outer edges of the bottom panel.

TYPE V has the side ornaments, including one or two of the small "pearls" partly cut away. Also, the outside line, over the "X" at the right top, has been partly cut away.

Types of the 12¢ Washington issues of 1851-60

PLATE 1 has stronger, more complete outer frame lines than does Plate 3. Comes imperforate (#17 or perf #36).

PLATE 3 has uneven or broken outer frame lines that are particularly noticeable in the corners. The stamps are perf 15. (#36b)

The REPRINT plate is similar to plate 1, but the Reprint stamps are greenish black and slightly taller than plate 1 stamps (25mm from top to bottom frame lines versus 24.5 mm) The paper is whiter and the perforations are 12 gauge.

UNITED STATES STAMP IDENTIFIER

Shows you how to distinguish between the rare and common U.S. stamps that look alike.

Types of the 1861 Issue, Grills & Re-Issues

Shortly after the outbreak of the Civil War in 1861, the Post Office demonitized all stamps issued up to that time in order to prevent their use by the Confederacy. Two new sets of designs, consisting of six stamps shown below plus 24¢ and 30¢ demonitized, were prepared by the American Bank Note Company. The first designs, except for the 10¢ and 24¢ values, were not regularly issued and are extremely rare and valuable. The second designs became the regular issue of 1861. The illustrations in the left column show the first (or unissued) designs, which were all printed on thin, semi- transparent paper. The second (or regular) designs are shown at right.

Types of the 1861 Issues

1st

SECOND DESIGN shows a small dash (arrow) under the tip of the ornaments at the right of the figure "1" in the upper left-hand corner of the stamp.

2nd

1st

SECOND DESIGN, 3¢ value, shows a small ball (arrow) at each corner of the design. Also, the ornaments at the corners are larger than in the first design.

2nd

1st

SECOND DESIGN, 5¢ value has a leaflet (arrow) projecting from the scrolled ornaments at each corner of the stamp.

2nd

1st

FIRST DESIGN has no curved line below the row of stars and there is only one outer line of the ornaments above them.
SECOND DESIGN has a heavy curved line below the row of stars (arrow); ornaments above the stars have double outer line.

2nd

1st

FIRST DESIGN has rounded corners. **SECOND DESIGN** has a oval and a scroll (arrow) in each corner of the design

2nd

Types of the 15¢ "Landing of Columbus" Design of 1869

Type I

Type II

TYPE I has the central picture without the frame line shown in Type II.
TYPE II has a frame line (arrows) around the central picture; also a diamond shaped ornament appears below the "T" of "Postage".
TYPE III (not illustrated) is like Type I except that the fringe of brown shading lines which appears around the sides and bottom of the picture on Types I and II has been removed.

IDENTIFIER CHART
1861-1867 Bank Notes

Description and Identifying Features				1¢	2¢	3¢	5¢	10¢	12¢	15¢	24¢	30¢	90¢
1861. National. First designs. Thin, semi-transparent paper. No grill.				55		56	57	58[1], 62B	59		60	61	62
1861-62. National. Modified designs[3]. Thicker, opaque paper. No grill.				63		64[2], 65[2], 66[2]	67	68	69		70[2]	71	72
1861-66. National. Thicker, opaque paper. No grill. a. New designs.					73					77			
b. Same designs, new shades.						74[2]	75[2], 76[2]				78[2]		
1867. National. Grills. All on thick, opaque paper.													
Grills	Pts. as seen from stamp face	Area of covered Horiz. x Vert.	# of rows of Pts.										
A	Up	All over	—			79	80					81	
B	Up	18 x 15 mm	22 x 18			82							
C	Up	c. 13 x 16 mm	16-17 x 18-21			83							
D	Down	c. 12 x 14 mm	15 x 17-18		84	85							
Z	Down	c. 11 x 14 mm	13-14 x 17-18	85A	85B	85C		85D	85E	85F			
E	Down	c. 11 x 13 mm	14 x 15-17	86	87	88		89	90	91			
F	Down	c. 9 x 13 mm	11-12 x 15-17	92	93	94	95	96	97	98	99	100	101
1875. National. Re-issues. Hard, white paper. White crackly gum. No grill.				102	103	104	105	106	107	108	109	110	111

FOOTNOTES:
1. #58 does not exist used. Unused, it cannot be distinguished from #62B.
2. Different from corresponding 1861-66 issues only in color.
3. See diagrams for design modification.

UNITED STATES STAMP IDENTIFIER

Shows you how to distinguish between the rare and common U.S. stamps that look alike.

Types of the 1870-71 Through 1887 Bank Notes

The stamps of the 1870-71 issue were printed by the National Bank Note Company. The similar issue of 1873 was printed by the Continental Bank Note Company. When Continental took over the plates previously used by National, they applied the so-called "secret marks" to the designs of the 1¢ through 15¢ denominations by which the two issues can be distinguished as shown below. The illustrations at the left show the original designs of 1870-71; those at the right show secret marks applied to the issue of 1873.

1¢ Secret mark is a small curved mark in the pearl at the left of the figure "1".

2¢ 1870-71 are red brown. The 1873 issue is brown and in some copies has a small diagonal line under the scroll at the left of the "U.S." (arrow).

3¢ Secret mark is the heavily shaded ribbon under the letters "RE".

6¢ Secret mark shows the first four vertical lines of shading in the lower part of the left ribbon greatly strengthened.

7¢ Secret mark is two tiny semicircles drawn around the end of the lines which outline the ball in the lower right-hand corner.

10¢ Secret mark is a small semicircle in the scroll at the right-hand side of the central design.

12¢ Secret mark shows the "balls" at the top and bottom on the figure "2" crescent-shaped (right) instead of nearly round as at the left.

15¢ Secret mark shows as strengthened lines (arrow) in the triangle in the upper left-hand corner, forming a "V".

IDENTIFIER CHART
1870-1887 Bank Notes

Description and Identifying Features	1¢	2¢	3¢	5¢	6¢	7¢	10¢	12¢	15¢	21¢	30¢	90¢
1870-71. National. No secret marks. White wove paper, thin to medium thick. With grills.	134	135	136		137	138	139	140	141	142	143	144
1870-71. National. As above, except without grills.	145	146	147		148	149	150	151	152	153	154[2]	155[2]
1873. Continental. White wove paper, thin to thick. No grills.												
a. With secret marks.	156	157	158		159	160	161	162	163			
b. No secret marks.											165[2]	166[2]
1875. Continental. Special Printing. Same designs as 1873 Continental. Hard, white wove paper. No gum.	167	168	169		170	171	172	173	174	175	176	177
1875. Continenal. New color or denomination. Hard yellowish, wove paper.		178		179								
1875. Continental. Special printing. Same designs as 1875 Continental. Hard, white wove paper. No gum.		180		181								
1879. American. Same designs as 1873-75. Continental. Soft, porous paper.	182	183[3]	184[3]	185	186[3]		188		189[3]		190[3]	191[3]
a. Without secret mark.							187[3]					
1880. American. Special printing. Same as 1879 issue. Soft, porous paper. No gum.	192	193, 203[3]	194[3]	204	195[3]	196	197[3]	198	199[3]	200	201[3]	202[3]
1881-82. American. Designs of 1873. Re-engraved[4]. Soft, porous paper.	206		207[5]		208		209					
1887. American. Same designs as 1881-82. New colors.		214[5]									217	218

FOOTNOTES:
1. See diagrams for secret marks.
2. Corresponding denominations differ from each other only in color.
3. Corresponding denominations differ from each other only in color and gum. The special printings are slightly deeper and richer. The lack of gum is not positive identifier because it can be washed from the 1879 issues.
4. See diagrams for re-engravings.
5. Corresponding denominations differ from each other in color.

UNITED STATES STAMP IDENTIFIER

Shows you how to distinguish between the rare and common U.S. stamps that look alike.

Re-Engraved Designs 1881-82

1¢ has strengthened vertical shading lines in the upper part of the stamp, making the background appear almost solid. Lines of shading have also been added to the curving ornaments in the upper corners.

3¢ has a solid shading line at the sides of the central oval (arrow) that is only about half the previous width. Also a short horizontal line has been cut below the "TS" of "CENTS".

6¢ has only three vertical lines between the edge of the panel and the outside left margin of the stamp. (In the preceding issues, there were four such lines.)

10¢ has only four vertical lines between the left side of the oval and the edge of the shield. (In the preceding issues there were five such lines.) Also, the lines in the background have been made much heavier so that these stamps appear more heavily linked than previous issues.

2¢ Washington Design of 1894-98

TYPE I has horizontal lines of the same thickness within and without the triangle.

TYPE II has horizontal lines which cross the triangle but are thinner within it than without.

TYPE III has thin lines inside the triangle and these do not cross the double frame line of the triangle.

2¢ Columbian "Broken Hat" Variety of 1893

231

As a result of a plate defect, some stamps of the 2¢ Columbian design show a noticeable white notch or gash in the hat worn by the third figure to the left of Columbus. This "broken hat" variety is somewhat less common than the regular 2¢ design.

Broken Hat variety, 231c

4¢ Columbian Blue Error

Collectors often mistake the many shades of the normal 4¢ ultramarine for the rare and valuable blue error. Actually, the "error" is not ultramarine at all, but a deep blue, similar to the deeper blue shades of the 1¢ Columbian.

$1 Perry Design of 1894-95

TYPE I shows circles around the "$1" are broken at point where they meet the curved line below "ONE DOLLAR" (arrows).

TYPE II shows these circles complete.

10¢ Webster design of 1898

TYPE I has an unbroken white curved line below the words "TEN CENTS".

TYPE II shows white line is broken by ornaments at a point just below the "E" in "TEN" and the "T" in "CENTS" (arrows).

2¢ Washington Issue of 1903

Die I
319, 319g, 320

The rounded inner frame line below and to the left "T" in "TWO" has a dark patch of color that narrows, but remains strong across the bottom.

Die II
319f, 320a

2¢ "cap of 2" Variety of 1890

Cap on left "2"

Plate defects in the printing of the 2¢ "Washington" stamp of 1890 accounts for the "Cap of left 2" and "Cap on both 2s" varieties illustrated.

Cap on right "2"

UNITED STATES STAMP IDENTIFIER

Shows you how to distinguish between the rare and common U.S. stamps that look alike.

FRANKLIN AND WASHINGTON ISSUES OF 1908-22

Perforation	Watermark	Other Identifying Features						 3¢ thru $1 denominations	 8¢ thru $1 denominations
PERF. 12	USPS	White paper		331	332			333-42	422-23
		Bluish gray paper		357	358			359-66	
	USPS	White paper		374	375	405	406	376-82, 407	414-21
COIL 12	USPS	Perf. Horizontal		348	349			350-51	
		Perf. Vertical		352	353			354-56	
	USPS	Perf. Horizontal		385	386				
		Perf. Vertical		387	388			389	
IMPERF.	USPS			343	344			345-47	
	USPS	Flat Plate		383	384	408	409		
		Rotary Press					459		
	Unwmkd.	Flat Plate				481	482-82A	483-85	
		Offset				531	532-34B	535	
COIL 8-1/2	USPS	Perf. Horizontal		390	391	410	411		
		Perf. Vertical		392	393	412	413	394-96	
PERF. 10	USPS								460
	USPS					424	425	426-30	431-40
	Unwmkd.	Flat Plate				462	463	464-69	470-78
		Rotary Press				543			
COIL 10	USPS	Perf. Horizontal	Flat			441	442		
			Rotary			448	449-50		
		Perf. Vertical	Flat			443	444	445-47	
			Rotary			452	453-55	456-58	
	Unwmkd.	Perf. Horizontal				486	487-88	489	
		Perf. Vertical				490	491-92	493-96	497
PERF. 11	USPS				519				
	USPS						461		
	Unwmkd.	Flat Plate				498	499-500	501-07	508-18
		Rotary Press				*544-45	546		
		Offset				525	526-28B	529-30	
Perf. 12-1/2	Unwkmd.	Offset				536			
11 x 10	Unwkmd.	Rotary				538	539-40	541	
10 x 11	Unwkmd.	Rotary				542			

* Design of #544 is 19 mm wide x 22-1/2 mm high. #545 is 19-1/2 to 20 mm wide x 22 mm high.

22mm

Size of Flat Plate Design

18-1/2 to 19mm

Stamps printed by rotary press are always slightly wider or taller on issues prior to 1954. Measurements do not apply to booklet singles.

HOW TO USE THIS IDENTIFICATION CHART

Numbers referred to herein are from Scott's Standard Postage Stamp Catalog. To identify any stamp in this series, first check the type by comparing it with the illustrations at the top of the chart. Then check the perforations, and whether the stamp is single or double line watermarked or unwatermarked. With this information you can quickly find out the Standard Catalog number by checking down and across the chart. For example, a 1¢ Franklin, perf. 12, single line watermark, must be Scott's #374.

UNITED STATES **STAMP IDENTIFIER**

Shows you how to distinguish between the rare and common U.S. stamps that look alike.

Types of The 2¢ Washington Design of 1912-20

Type I

Type I where the ribbon at left above the figure "2" has one shading line in the first curve, while the ribbon at the right has one shading line in the second curve. Bottom of toga has a faint outline. Top line of toga, from bottom to front of throat, is very faint. Shading lines of the face, terminating in front of the ear, are not joined. Type I occurs on both flat and rotary prcss printings.

Type Ia is similar to Type I except that all of the lines are stronger. Lines of the Toga button are heavy. Occurs only on flat press printings.

Type Ia

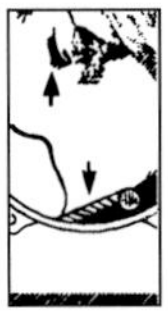

Type II

Type II has ribbons shaded as in Type I. Toga button and shading lines to left of it are heavy. Shading lines in front of ear are joined and end in a strong vertically curved line (arrow). Occurs only on rotary press printings.

Type III where ribbons are shaded with two lines instead of one; otherwise similar to Type II. Occurs on rotary press printings only.

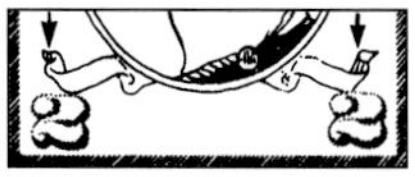

Type III

Type IV

Type IV where top line of toga is broken. Shading lines inside the toga bottom read "Did". The Line of color in the left "2" is very thin and usually broken. Occurs on offset printings only.

Type V in which top line of toga is complete. Toga button has five vertical shaded lines. Line of color in the left "2" is very thin and usually broken. Nose shaded as shown in illustration. Occurs on offset printings only.

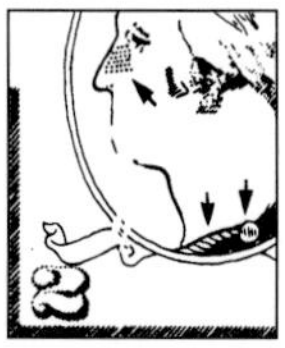

Type V

Type Va

Type Va is same as Type V except in shading dots of nose. Third row of dots from bottom has four dots instead of six. Also, the Overall height of Type Va is 1/3 millimeter less than Type V. Occurs on offset printings only.

Type VI is same as Type V except that the line of color in left "2" is very heavy (arrow). Occurs in offset printings only.

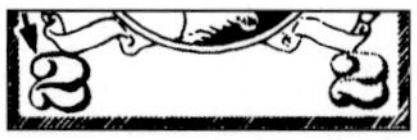

Type VI

Type VII

Type VII in which line of color in left "2" is clear and continuous and heavier than Types V or Va, but not as heavy as in Type VI. There are three rows of vertical dots (instead of two) in the shading of the upper lip, and additional dots have been added to hair at top of the head. Occurs on offset printings only.

Types of The 3¢ Washington Design of 1908-20

Type I

TYPE I in which the top line of the toga is weak, as are the top parts of the shading lines that join the toga line. The fifth shading line from the left (arrow) is partly cut away at the top. Also the line between the lips is thin. Occurs on flat and rotary press printings.

Type II

TYPE II where top line of toga is strong and the shading lines that join it are heavy and complete. The line between the lips is heavy. Occurs on flat and rotary press printings.

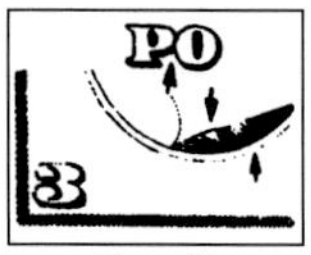

Type III

TYPE III in which top line of toga is strong, but the fifth shading line from the left (arrow) is missing. The center line of the toga button consists of two short vertical lines with a dot between them. The "P" and "O" of "POSTAGE" are separated by a small line of color. Occurs on offset printings only.

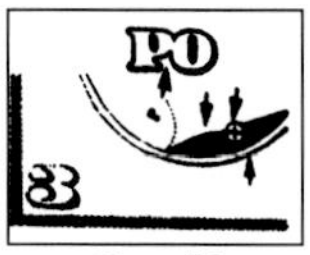

Type IV

TYPE IV in which the shading lines of the toga are complete. The center line of the toga button consists of a single unbroken vertical line running through the dot in the center. The "P" and the "O" of "POSTAGE" are joined. Type IV occurs only in offset printings.

Commemorative Identifier

The following handy identifier is a list of commemoratives organized alphabetically by key words on the stamp, which are the most prominent after "U.S. Postage," and matches the stamp with its corresponding Scott number.

GENERAL ISSUES

1847 – THE FIRST ISSUE
Imperforate

"For every single letter in manuscript or paper of any kind by or upon which information shall be asked or communicated in writing or by marks or signs conveyed in the mail, for any distance under three hundred miles, five cents; and for any distance over three hundred miles, ten cents . . . and every letter or parcel not exceeding half an ounce in weight shall be deemed a single letter, and every additional weight of half ounce, shall be charged with an additional single postage."

With these words, the Act of March 3, 1845, authorized, but not required, the prepayment of postage effective July 1, 1847, and created a need for the first United States postage stamps. Benjamin Franklin, as the first Postmaster General of the United States and the man generally regarded as the "father" of the postal system, was selected for the 5 cent stamp. As the first President of the United States, George Washington was designated for the 10 cent issue.

The 1847 stamps were released July 1, 1847, but were available only in the New York City post office on that date. The earliest known usages are July 7 for the 5 cent and July 2 for the 10 cent.

The best estimates are that 4,400,000 of the 5 cent and 1,050,000 of the 10 cent stamps reached the public. The remaining stocks were destroyed when the stamps were demonetized and could no longer be used for postage as of July 1, 1851.

Like most 19th century United States stamps, the first Issue is much more difficult to find unused than used. Stamps canceled by "handstamp" marking devices—usually carved from cork—are scarcer than those with manuscript, or "pen", cancels.

Issued without gum, the Reproductions of the 1847 issue were printed from entirely new dies for display at the 1876 Centennial Exposition and were not valid for postal use. The issue also was reproduced on a souvenir sheet issued in 1947 to celebrate the centenary of the First Issue. Differences between the 1847 issue, 1875 Reproductions and 1948 stamps are described in the Stamp Identifier at the front of this catalog.

1, 3, 948a
Franklin

2, 4, 948b
Washington

SCOTT NO.	DESCRIPTION	UNUSED VF	UNUSED F	UNUSED AVG	USED VF	USED F	USED AVG
	1847 Imperforate (OG + 100%)						
1	5¢ red brown	4250.00	3000.00	1900.00	825.00	595.00	395.00
1	— Pen cancel	....	....	....	525.00	350.00	275.00
2	10¢ black .	23650.00	16250.00	10000.00	1900.00	1350.00	875.00
2	— Pen cancel	....	....	....	950.00	725.00	575.00
	1875 Reprints of 1847 Issues, without gum						
3	5¢ red brown	1395.00	1050.00	850.00	....	....	....
4	10¢ black	1800.00	1200.00	1050.00	....	....	....

1851-61 – THE CLASSIC ISSUES

An act of Congress approved March 3, 1851, enacted new, reduced postage rates, introduced additional rates and made the prepayment of additional postage compulsory. Although the use of postage stamps was not required, the 1851 Act stimulated their use and paved the way for their required usage from July 1, 1855 on.

Under the Act of 1851, the basic prepaid single letter rate (defined as one-half ounce or less) was set at 3 cents. As this would be the most commonly used value, it was decided that a likeness of George Washington should grace the 3 cent stamp. Benjamin Franklin was assigned to the 1 cent stamp, which, among other usages, met the newspaper and circular rates.

Washington also appears on the 10, 12, 24 and 90 cent stamps and Franklin on the 30 cent value. Thomas Jefferson was selected for the new 5 cent stamp that was issued in 1856.

By 1857, improved production techniques and the increasing usage of stamps led to the introduction of perforated stamps that could be more easily separated. The result was the 1857-61 series whose designs are virtually identical to the 1851 set. The 1857-61 perforated stamps were set in the printing plates with very little space between each stamp. As a result, insufficient space was allowed to accommodate the perforations, which often cut into the design on these stamps. In fact, stamps with complete designs and wide margins on all four sides are the exception and command very substantial premiums.

The most fascinating—and most challenging—feature of the 1851-61 stamps is the identification of many major and minor types. An extremely slight design variation can mean a difference of thousands of dollars and collectors even today can apply their knowledge to discover rare, mis-identified types.

The various "Types", identified below by Roman numerals in parentheses, resulted from minor changes in the printing plates caused by wear or plate retouching. The 1851-57 one-cent blue stamp may be the most studied of all the United States issues and is found in seven major catalog-listed Types (14, if we count imperforate and perforated stamps separately), plus countless minor listed and unlisted varieties. A thorough explanation of the differences in the major types for all denominations of the 1857-61 series is contained in the Harris Stamp Identifier in this catalog.

Shortly after the outbreak of the Civil War, the 1851-61 stamps were demonetized to prevent Southern post offices from selling the stamps in the North to raise cash for the Confederate States. After the war, large supplies of unused 1857-61 stamps were located in Southern post offices and purchased by stamp dealers and collectors. This explains the relatively large supply of unused 1857-61 issues that still exist today. The short life and limited use of 90 cent high value, which was issued in 1860, and the 5 cent orange brown, released May 8, 1861, explains why those stamps sell for more used than unused.

5-9, 18-24, 40
Franklin

10, 11, 25, 26, 41
Washington

12, 27-30A, 42
Jefferson

13-16, 31-35, 43
Washington

17, 36, 44
Washington

SCOTT NO.	DESCRIPTION	UNUSED VF	UNUSED F	UNUSED AVG	USED VF	USED F	USED AVG
	1851-57 Imperforate (OG + 100%)						
5	1¢ blue (I)	....	....	....	36500.00	....	....
5A	1¢ blue (Ib)	8400.00	7000.00	5750.00	8000.00	5500.00	3800.00
6	1¢ dark blue (Ia)	24675.00	18750.00	13750.00	11500.00	8500.00	5500.00
7	1¢ blue (II)	900.00	625.00	475.00	250.00	195.00	150.00
8	1¢ blue (III)	7770.00	5000.00	3400.00	3500.00	2750.00	1700.00
8A	1¢ blue (IIIa)	5000.00	3400.00	2100.00	1175.00	850.00	650.00
9	1¢ blue (IV)	580.00	450.00	325.00	195.00	140.00	90.00
10	3¢ orange brown (I) . .	2500.00	2000.00	1600.00	200.00	125.00	75.00
11	3¢ deep claret (I)	250.00	175.00	125.00	18.50	10.50	9.00
12	5¢ red brown (I)	13650.00	10250.00	6750.00	1550.00	1150.00	875.00
13	10¢ green (I)	11050.00	8500.00	6000.00	1000.00	725.00	575.00
14	10¢ green (II)	2300.00	1750.00	1350.00	300.00	210.00	170.00
15	10¢ green (III)	2500.00	1800.00	1300.00	300.00	220.00	170.00
16	10¢ green (IV)	18900.00	12500.00	10000.00	1800.00	1350.00	1050.00
17	12¢ black	3250.00	2500.00	1750.00	500.00	395.00	295.00

NOTE: *For further details on the various types of similar appearing stamps please refer to our U.S. Stamp Identifier.*

37, 45
Washington

38, 46
Franklin

39, 47
Washington

SCOTT NO.	DESCRIPTION	UNUSED VF	UNUSED F	UNUSED AVG	USED VF	USED F	USED AVG
	1857-61 Same design as preceding Issue, Perf. 15-1/2 (†) (OG + 75%)						
18	1¢ blue (I)	1500.00	950.00	700.00	700.00	500.00	325.00
19	1¢ blue (Ia)	14200.00	10000.00	7250.00	9000.00	6000.00	3800.00
20	1¢ blue (II)	750.00	525.00	400.00	300.00	225.00	165.00
21	1¢ blue (III)	8150.00	5500.00	4200.00	3350.00	2150.00	1400.00
22	1¢ blue (IIIa)	1350.00	950.00	650.00	750.00	500.00	325.00
23	1¢ blue (IV)	4900.00	3400.00	2400.00	925.00	650.00	395.00
24	1¢ blue (V)	175.00	120.00	90.00	72.50	45.00	35.00
25	3¢ rose (I)	1750.00	1300.00	1000.00	165.00	110.00	70.00
26	3¢ dull red (II)	110.00	78.00	61.00	12.50	7.00	5.00
26a	3¢ dull red (IIa)	350.00	265.00	185.00	60.00	42.50	30.00
27	5¢ brick red (I)	14700.00	10500.00	7250.00	2000.00	1500.00	800.00
28	5¢ red brown (I)	2750.00	2200.00	1500.00	1350.00	900.00	550.00
28A	5¢ Indian red (I)	20500.00	14750.00	10500.00	3500.00	2700.00	1975.00
29	5¢ brown (I)	1400.00	975.00	725.00	450.00	340.00	225.00
30	5¢ orange brown (II)	925.00	650.00	500.00	1800.00	1200.00	675.00
30A	5¢ brown (II)	1250.00	975.00	650.00	325.00	275.00	180.00
31	10¢ green (I)	10500.00	7500.00	5500.00	1500.00	1100.00	650.00
32	10¢ green (II)	3200.00	2200.00	1650.00	350.00	275.00	180.00
33	10¢ green (III)	3200.00	2200.00	1650.00	350.00	275.00	180.00
34	10¢ green (IV)	21550.00	15000.00	12000.00	2600.00	2100.00	1650.00
35	10¢ green (V)	275.00	195.00	150.00	125.00	70.00	45.00
36	12¢ black, Plate I	925.00	675.00	500.00	395.00	275.00	175.00
36b	12¢ black, Plate III	550.00	380.00	250.00	200.00	175.00	125.00
37	24¢ gray lilac	950.00	700.00	475.00	380.00	350.00	220.00
38	30¢ orange	1250.00	850.00	600.00	750.00	375.00	265.00
39	90¢ blue	2150.00	1550.00	1200.00	6500.00	4950.00	3800.00
	1875 Reprints of 1857-61 Issue. Perf. 12 Without Gum						
40	1¢ bright blue	900.00	625.00	425.00	....	....	....
41	3¢ scarlet	3900.00	2600.00	1750.00	....	....	....
42	5¢ orange brown	1650.00	1100.00	700.00	....	....	....
43	10¢ blue green	3750.00	2500.00	1600.00	....	....	....
44	12¢ greenish black	4500.00	3000.00	2000.00	....	....	....
45	24¢ blackish violet	4875.00	3300.00	2200.00	....	....	....
46	30¢ yellow orange	4725.00	3200.00	2100.00	....	....	....
47	90¢ deep blue	7455.00	5000.00	3400.00	....	....	....

THE 1861-67 ISSUE

The 1861-66 Issue and its 1867 Grilled varieties are among the most interesting and controversial of all stamps. Born out of the need to demonetize previously-issued stamps in the possession of Southern post offices, they were rushed into service shortly after the outbreak of the Civil War.

The controversy begins with the "August Issues", catalog #s 55-62B. It is now generally accepted that all but the 10 and 24 cent values never were issued for use as postage. The set is more aptly described as "First Designs", because they were printed by the National Bank Note Company and submitted to the Post Office Department as fully gummed and perforated sample designs.

63, 85A, 86, 92, 102
Franklin

64-65, 79, 82, 83, 85, 85C, 88, 94, 104
Washington

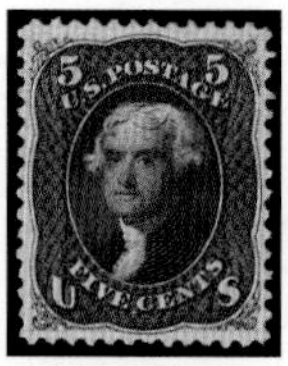
67, 75, 76, 80, 95, 105
Jefferson

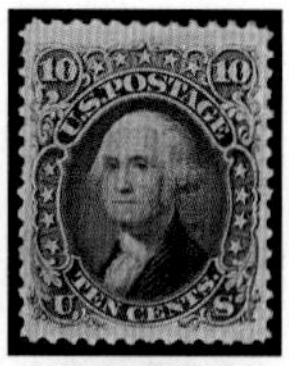
62B, 68, 85D, 89, 96, 106
Washington

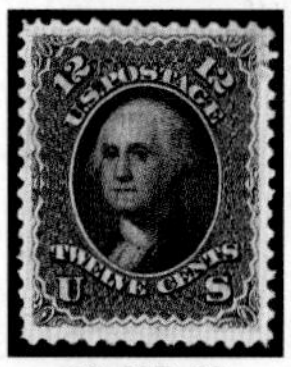
69, 85E, 90, 97, 107
Washington

70, 78, 99, 109
Washington

71, 81, 100, 110
Franklin

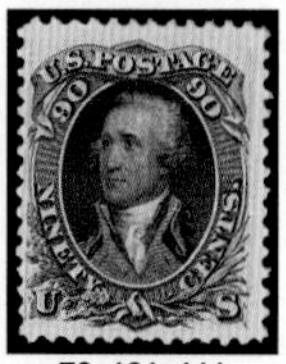
72, 101, 111
Washington

(†) means Issue is actually very poorly centered. Perforations may touch the design on "Fine" quality.

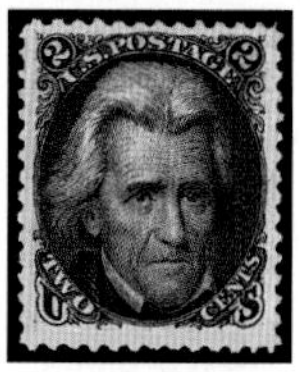
73, 84, 85B, 87, 93, 103
Jackson

77, 85F, 91, 98, 108
Lincoln

SCOTT NO.	DESCRIPTION	UNUSED VF	UNUSED F	UNUSED AVG	USED VF	USED F	USED AVG
	1861 First Design (†) Perf. 12 (OG + 75%)						
62B	10¢ dark green	5250.00	3400.00	2200.00	1750.00	1150.00	700.00
	1861-62 Second Design (†) Perf. 12 (OG + 75%)						
63	1¢ blue	225.00	150.00	110.00	55.00	35.00	24.00
64	3¢ pink	5460.00	3900.00	3100.00	800.00	600.00	425.00
64b	3¢ rose pink	325.00	250.00	190.00	165.00	115.00	90.00
65	3¢ rose	130.00	77.00	53.00	5.00	3.00	2.25
66	3¢ lake	2850.00	2100.00	1500.00	....	....	....
67	5¢ buff	11550.00	7250.00	5500.00	1100.00	800.00	550.00
68	10¢ yellow green	600.00	425.00	275.00	87.50	50.00	35.00
69	12¢ black	950.00	700.00	450.00	150.00	90.00	60.00
70	24¢ red lilac	1200.00	825.00	600.00	225.00	200.00	125.00
71	30¢ orange	1250.00	875.00	600.00	200.00	150.00	110.00
72	90¢ blue	2100.00	1500.00	1100.00	525.00	395.00	250.00
	1861-66 (†) (OG + 75%)						
73	2¢ black	275.00	200.00	125.00	115.00	75.00	45.00
74	3¢ scarlet	8190.00	5500.00	3700.00	....	....	....
75	5¢ red brown	2800.00	2200.00	1450.00	525.00	395.00	275.00
76	5¢ brown	775.00	550.00	425.00	180.00	125.00	95.00
77	15¢ black	1400.00	1000.00	650.00	210.00	160.00	100.00
78	24¢ lilac	900.00	675.00	395.00	235.00	140.00	95.00

From 1867 to 1870, grills were embossed into the stamp paper to break the fiber and prevent the eradication of cancellations. The first "A" grilled issues were grilled all over. When postal clerks found that the stamps were as likely to separate along the grill as on the perforations, the Post Office abandoned the "A" grill and tried other configurations, none of which proved to be effective. The Grilled Issues include some of our greatest rarities. The most notable is the 1 cent "Z", only two of which are known to exist. One realized $935,000 in a 1998 auction, making it the most valuable United States stamp. The grills are fully explained and identified in the Harris Stamp Identifier.

SCOTT NO.	DESCRIPTION	UNUSED VF	UNUSED F	UNUSED AVG	USED VF	USED F	USED AVG
	1867 Grill with Points Up A. Grill Covering Entire Stamp (†) (OG + 75%)						
79	3¢ rose	....	3600.00	3000.00	....	1375.00	950.00
80	5¢ brown	....	....	....	....	110000.00	....
81	30¢ orange	....	....	....	....	....	67500.00
	B. Grill about 18 x 15 mm. (OG + 75%)						
82	3¢ rose	....	....	....	....	170000.00	....
	C. Grill About 13 x 16 mm. (†) (OG + 75%)						
83	3¢ rose	3700.00	2700.00	1950.00	1000.00	775.00	575.00
	1867 Grill with Points Down D. Grill About 12 x 14 mm. (†) (OG + 75%)						
84	2¢ black	11550.00	9000.00	6500.00	4000.00	2750.00	1900.00
85	3¢ rose	3800.00	2600.00	1950.00	1050.00	750.00	575.00
	Z. Grill About 11 x 14 mm. (†) (OG + 75%)						
85A	1¢ blue	....	....	....	....	....	....
85B	2¢ black	5775.00	4200.00	2500.00	1350.00	1050.00	700.00
85C	3¢ rose	7350.00	5250.00	3700.00	3200.00	2750.00	1900.00
85D	10¢ green	....	....	....	110000.00	80000.00	....
85E	12¢ black	8400.00	6250.00	4700.00	1600.00	1200.00	950.00
85F	15¢ black	....	....	....	250000.00	....	....
	E. Grill About 11 x 13 mm. (†) (OG + 75%)						
86	1¢ blue	1900.00	1350.00	950.00	525.00	375.00	285.00
87	2¢ black	750.00	575.00	425.00	240.00	140.00	95.00
88	3¢ rose	495.00	375.00	250.00	32.50	22.50	14.50
89	10¢ green	2900.00	2200.00	1450.00	425.00	275.00	195.00
90	12¢ black	3000.00	2100.00	1200.00	450.00	275.00	195.00
91	15¢ black	5900.00	4200.00	3100.00	875.00	575.00	425.00

SCOTT NO.	DESCRIPTION	UNUSED VF	UNUSED F	UNUSED AVG	USED VF	USED F	USED AVG
	F. Grill About 9 x 13 mm. (†) (OG + 75%)						
92	1¢ blue	900.00	675.00	475.00	495.00	300.00	195.00
93	2¢ black	400.00	285.00	205.00	95.00	60.00	45.00
94	3¢ red	225.00	165.00	115.00	12.50	7.00	4.75
95	5¢ brown	1800.00	1400.00	950.00	950.00	650.00	395.00
96	10¢ yellow green	1550.00	1150.00	875.00	325.00	225.00	125.00
97	12¢ black	1800.00	1400.00	975.00	325.00	235.00	135.00
98	15¢ black	2100.00	1500.00	1100.00	425.00	285.00	200.00
99	24¢ gray lilac	3400.00	2400.00	2000.00	1250.00	750.00	475.00
100	30¢ orange	3750.00	2700.00	1950.00	1000.00	625.00	500.00
101	90¢ blue	7600.00	5000.00	3700.00	2000.00	1400.00	975.00

The Re-Issues of the 1861-66 Issue were issued with gum and, while scarce, are found used. They can be distinguished by their bright colors, sharp printing impressions, hard paper and white, crackly original gum.

SCOTT NO.	DESCRIPTION	UNUSED VF	UNUSED F	UNUSED AVG	USED VF	USED F	USED AVG
	1875. Re-Issue of 1861-66 Issue. Hard White Paper (OG + 75%)						
102	1¢ blue	650.00	550.00	450.00	1200.00	950.00	750.00
103	2¢ black	2100.00	1700.00	1400.00	5250.00	4250.00	3350.00
104	3¢ brown red	2600.00	2000.00	1650.00	5500.00	4850.00	3250.00
105	5¢ brown	1900.00	1600.00	1250.00	3250.00	2700.00	2200.00
106	10¢ green	2000.00	1700.00	1400.00	5250.00	4000.00	3200.00
107	12¢ black	2700.00	2100.00	1700.00	5750.00	4600.00	3500.00
108	15¢ black	2700.00	2200.00	1850.00	6000.00	4800.00	3750.00
109	24¢ deep violet	3200.00	2700.00	2250.00	8250.00	6600.00	5400.00
110	30¢ brownish orange	3400.00	2800.00	2350.00	9500.00	7600.00	6500.00
111	90¢ blue	4500.00	3600.00	3000.00	47500.00	37500.00	30000.00

THE 1869 PICTORIALS

As the first United States series to include pictorial designs, the 1869 issue is one of the most popular today. They were so unpopular that they were removed from sale less than a year after issue. Most protests were directed toward their odd size and the tradition-breaking pictorial designs.

The 1869 issue broke important new ground in the use of two color designs. Not only does this add to their attractiveness; it also is the source for the first United States "Inverted Centers". These inverted errors appear on the bi-colored 15, 24 and 30 cent values. The printing technology of the time required a separate printing pass for each color. On the first pass, the central designs, or vignettes, were printed. The second pass applied the frames.

In a very few instances, the sheets with their central designs already printed were passed upside down through the printing press. As a result, the frames were printed upside down. So the description "inverted center" for the 15 and 24 cent errors is technically incorrect, but the form in which these errors are photographed and displayed is with the center, rather than the frame, inverted.

Used copies of the 1869 Pictorials are not as scarce as might be expected. Any of the stamps above the 3 cent denomination were used on mail to Europe and were saved by collectors overseas. When stamp collecting became popular in the United States and Americans were able to purchase stamps abroad at relatively low prices, many of these used 1869 Pictorials found their way back to this country. On the other hand, because of the short life of the issue in post offices and their sudden withdrawal, unused stamps—particularly the high values—are quite rare.

All values of the 1869 Pictorials are found with the "G" grill. Ungrilled varieties are known on all values except the 6, 10, 12 and type II 15 cent stamps. (The Harris Stamp Identifier describes the difference in the three 15 cent types.)

The 1869 Pictorials were re-issued in 1875 in anticipation of the 1876 Centennial Exposition. Most collectors who had missed the original 1869 issue were delighted to have a second chance to purchase the stamps, which explains why the high value re-issues carry lower prices today than do the original 1869 pictorials. At the time, most collectors did not realize they were buying entirely different stamps. The same designs were used, but the re-issues were issued on a distinctive hard, white paper without grills.

The 1 cent stamp was re-issued a second time, in 1880. This re-issue can be distinguished by the lack of a grill and by the soft, porous paper used by the American Bank Note Company.

112, 123, 133,133a
Franklin

113, 124
Pony Express Rider

114, 125
Locomotive

115, 126
Washington

116, 127
Shield & Eagle

117, 128
S.S. Adriatic

118, 119, 129
Landing of Columbus

120, 130
Signing of Declaration

121, 131
Shield, Eagle & Flags

122, 132
Lincoln

SCOTT NO.	DESCRIPTION	UNUSED VF	UNUSED F	UNUSED AVG	USED VF	USED F	USED AVG
	1869 G. Grill measuring 9-1/2 x 9-1/2 mm. (†) (OG + 75%)						
112	1¢ buff	425.00	300.00	240.00	225.00	150.00	120.00
113	2¢ brown	425.00	300.00	240.00	140.00	75.00	50.00
114	3¢ ultramarine	235.00	185.00	145.00	27.00	20.00	15.00
115	6¢ ultramarine	1600.00	1200.00	850.00	300.00	195.00	150.00
116	10¢ yellow	1750.00	1350.00	1050.00	210.00	135.00	100.00
117	12¢ green	1500.00	1150.00	875.00	225.00	145.00	110.00
118	15¢ brown & blue (I)	4500.00	3500.00	2800.00	950.00	550.00	425.00
119	15¢ brown & blue (II)	2100.00	1350.00	1000.00	375.00	240.00	190.00
120	24¢ green & violet	4400.00	3000.00	2100.00	950.00	650.00	475.00
121	30¢ blue & carmine	4400.00	3000.00	2100.00	750.00	450.00	325.00
122	90¢ carmine & black	6300.00	4700.00	3700.00	2800.00	1950.00	1500.00
	1875 Re-Issue of 1869 Issue. Hard White Paper. Without Grill (OG + 75%)						
123	1¢ buff	500.00	350.00	250.00	375.00	275.00	195.00
124	2¢ brown	600.00	450.00	300.00	600.00	425.00	295.00
125	3¢ blue	4500.00	3000.00	2150.00	....	15000.00	....
126	6¢ blue	1200.00	800.00	550.00	1700.00	1050.00	650.00
127	10¢ yellow	1900.00	1300.00	950.00	1800.00	1250.00	875.00
128	12¢ green	2000.00	1500.00	1000.00	2850.00	1825.00	1075.00
129	15¢ brown & blue (III)	1800.00	1250.00	800.00	1100.00	700.00	450.00
130	24¢ green & violet	1800.00	1200.00	750.00	1425.00	875.00	550.00
131	30¢ blue & carmine	2500.00	1600.00	1100.00	2400.00	1600.00	975.00
132	90¢ carmine & black	4500.00	3500.00	2800.00	5800.00	4250.00	3200.00
	1880 Re-Issue. Soft Porous Paper, Issued Without Grill (†) (#133 OG +50%)						
133	1¢ buff	295.00	225.00	180.00	250.00	185.00	145.00
133a	1¢ brown orange (issued w/o gum)	325.00	195.00	150.00	250.00	185.00	145.00

THE 1870-88 BANK NOTE ISSUES

The "Bank Notes" are stamps that were issued between 1870 and 1888 by the National, Continental and American Bank Note Companies.

The myriad of varieties, secret marks, papers, grills, re-engravings and special printings produced by the three companies resulted in no less than 87 major catalog listings for what basically amounts to 16 different designs. For collectors, what seems to be the very difficult task of properly identifying all these varieties can be eased by following these guidelines:

1. The chronological order in which the three Bank Note companies produced stamps is their reverse alphabetical order: National, Continental, American.

2. "3, 6, 9" identifies the number of years each of the companies printed stamps within the 18-year Bank Note period. Starting in 1870, National continued its work for 3 more years, until 1873, when the Continental Company began printing stamps. That company served for the next 6 years, until 1879, when American took over the Continental company. Although American printed some later issues, the "Bank Note" period ended 9 years later, in 1888.

3. The first Bank Note issue, the Nationals of 1870-71, continued the practice of grilling stamps. Although some specialists contend there are grilled Continental stamps, for all intents and purposes, if a Bank Note stamp bears a genuine grill, it must be from the 1870-71 National issue.

4. The secret marks on values through the 12 cent, and possibly the 15 cent value, were added when the Continental Company took over. They enabled the government to distinguish between National's work and that of its successor. If a Bank Note stamp did not show a secret mark, the Post Office could identify it as the work of the National Bank Note Company. You can do the same.

5. The paper used by the National and Continental companies is similar, but that of the American Bank Note company is noticably different from the first two. When held to the light, the thick, soft American paper shows its coarse, uneven texture, while that of its two predecessors is more even and translucent. The American Bank Note paper also reveals a yellowish hue when held to the light, whereas the National and Continental papers are whiter.

6. Experienced collectors also apply a "snap test" to identify American Bank Note paper by gently flexing a Bank Note stamp at one of its corners. The American Bank Note paper will not "snap" back into place. The National and Continental stamps, on the other hand, often give off a noticeable sound when the flex is released.

7. By purchasing one Bank Note design put into use after 1882 (which can only be an American) and one early Bank Note stamp without the secret mark, (which can only be a National), the collector has a reference point against which to compare any other Bank Note stamp. If it is a soft paper, it is an American Bank Note issue; if a harder paper, it is either a National or a Continental—and these two can be classified by the absence (National) or presence (Continental) of the secret marks or other distinguishing features or colors. The Harris Stamp Identifier in this catalog provides illustrations of the secret marks and further information on the distinguishing features of the various Bank Notes. With two reference stamps, some practice and the use of the information in this catalog, collectors can turn the "job" of understanding the Bank Notes into a pleasant adventure.

134, 145, 156, 167, 182, 192, 206
Franklin

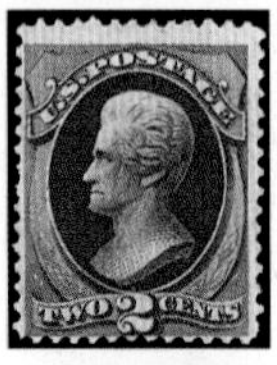
135, 146, 157, 168, 178, 180, 183, 193, 203
Jackson

136, 147, 158, 169, 184, 194, 207, 214
Washington

NOTE: For further details on the various types of similar appearing stamps please refer to our U.S. Stamp Identifier.

137, 148, 159, 170, 186, 195, 208
Lincoln

138, 149, 160, 171, 196
Stanton

139, 150, 161, 172, 187, 188, 197, 209
Jefferson

140, 151, 162, 173, 198
Clay

141, 152, 163, 174, 189, 199
Webster

142, 153, 164, 175, 200
Scott

143, 154, 165, 176, 190, 201, 217
Hamilton

144, 155, 166, 177, 191, 202, 218
Perry

1870 National Bank Note Co., without Secret Marks.
With H Grill about (10 x 12 mm. or 8-1/2 x 10 mm.) Perf 12. (†)
(OG +75%)

SCOTT NO.	DESCRIPTION	UNUSED VF	UNUSED F	UNUSED AVG	USED VF	USED F	USED AVG
134	1¢ ultramarine	1350.00	850.00	550.00	200.00	140.00	95.00
135	2¢ red brown	850.00	575.00	400.00	85.00	60.00	37.50
136	3¢ green	650.00	400.00	300.00	28.00	19.50	13.00
137	6¢ carmine	3500.00	1950.00	1200.00	700.00	475.00	295.00
138	7¢ vermillion	2500.00	1750.00	1050.00	550.00	340.00	225.00
139	10¢ brown	4000.00	2600.00	1750.00	900.00	550.00	350.00
140	12¢ dull violet	16800.00	11500.00	8250.00	3750.00	2400.00	1650.00
141	15¢ orange	4750.00	2700.00	1850.00	1450.00	925.00	575.00
142	24¢ purple	....	....	....	7100.00	5700.00	4100.00
143	30¢ black	10000.00	6750.00	4800.00	3500.00	2250.00	1500.00
144	90¢ carmine	12100.00	7250.00	4500.00	2000.00	1500.00	950.00

1870-71. National Bank Note Co., without Secret Marks.
Without Grill. Perf 12. (†)
(OG +75%)

SCOTT NO.	DESCRIPTION	UNUSED VF	UNUSED F	UNUSED AVG	USED VF	USED F	USED AVG
145	1¢ ultramarine	400.00	275.00	150.00	22.50	14.00	9.00
146	2¢ red brown	235.00	145.00	95.00	17.00	11.00	7.00
147	3¢ green	235.00	145.00	95.00	2.50	1.75	1.00
148	6¢ carmine	675.00	400.00	225.00	40.00	25.00	15.00
149	7¢ vermillion	700.00	450.00	250.00	125.00	70.00	42.50
150	10¢ brown	850.00	600.00	395.00	35.00	24.00	14.50
151	12¢ dull violet	1500.00	1000.00	600.00	225.00	150.00	95.00
152	15¢ bright orange	1500.00	1000.00	600.00	225.00	150.00	95.00
153	24¢ purple	1250.00	800.00	550.00	185.00	110.00	75.00
154	30¢ black	4000.00	2800.00	1600.00	275.00	190.00	110.00
155	90¢ carmine	3000.00	2000.00	1150.00	450.00	295.00	175.00

1873. Continental Bank Note Co.
Same designs as 1870-71, with Secret Marks, on thin hard grayish white paper. Perf 12 (†)
(OG + 75%)

SCOTT NO.	DESCRIPTION	UNUSED VF	UNUSED F	UNUSED AVG	USED VF	USED F	USED AVG
156	1¢ ultramarine	240.00	135.00	100.00	5.00	3.75	2.25
157	2¢ brown	340.00	195.00	110.00	25.00	17.50	10.00
158	3¢ green	110.00	60.00	35.00	1.25	.75	.50
159	6¢ dull pink	375.00	225.00	125.00	28.00	16.00	11.00
160	7¢ orange vermillion	900.00	600.00	375.00	100.00	70.00	45.00
161	10¢ brown	700.00	450.00	295.00	28.00	19.00	11.50
162	12¢ black violet	1600.00	1100.00	600.00	140.00	90.00	60.00
163	15¢ yellow orange	1600.00	1100.00	600.00	150.00	100.00	60.00
165	30¢ gray black	1950.00	1250.00	700.00	145.00	95.00	60.00
166	90¢ rose carmine	2200.00	1350.00	850.00	340.00	220.00	130.00

1875 Special Printing–On Hard White Wove Paper–Without Gum
Perf. 12

SCOTT NO.	DESCRIPTION	UNUSED VF	UNUSED F	UNUSED AVG	USED VF	USED F	USED AVG
167	1¢ ultramarine	17325.00	11500.00	6500.00	....	....	....
168	2¢ dark brown	7715.00	5000.00	3400.00	....	....	....
169	3¢ blue green	17850.00	12000.00	8000.00	....	....	....
170	6¢ dull rose	17850.00	12000.00	8000.00	....	....	....
171	7¢ reddish vermillion	4250.00	2800.00	1950.00	....	....	....
172	10¢ pale brown	17850.00	12000.00	8000.00	....	....	....
173	12¢ dark violet	6090.00	4000.00	2900.00	....	....	....
174	15¢ bright orange	17850.00	12000.00	8000.00	....	....	....
175	24¢ dull purple	4250.00	2800.00	1950.00	....	....	....
176	30¢ greenish black	14175.00	9500.00	6500.00	....	....	....
177	90¢ violet carmine	17325.00	11500.00	8000.00	....	....	....

179, 181, 185, 204
Taylor

205, 205C, 216
Garfield

SCOTT NO.	DESCRIPTION	UNUSED VF	UNUSED F	UNUSED AVG	USED VF	USED F	USED AVG
	1875 Continental Bank Note Co. Hard yellowish paper, Perf 12. (†) (OG + 50%)						
178	2¢ vermillion . . .	350.00	225.00	135.00	14.00	9.50	6.50
179	5¢ blue	450.00	325.00	200.00	25.00	19.00	11.00
	1875 Continental Bank Note Co., Special Printings. Same as 1875, on hard white paper, without gum. Perf 12.						
180	2¢ carmine vermillion	28875.00	10250.00	6250.00	....	....	....
181	5¢ bright blue . . .	46200.00	34,750.00	22,000.00	....	....	....
	1879 American Bank Note Co. Same designs as 1870-71 Issue (with Secret Marks) and 1875 Issue on soft, porous, coarse, yellowish paper. Perf 12. (†) (OG + 60%)						
182	1¢ dark ultramarine	200.00	135.00	75.00	4.75	3.00	2.00
183	2¢ vermilion	125.00	81.00	47.00	3.50	2.25	1.50
184	3¢ green	85.00	55.00	35.00	.95	.70	.50
185	5¢ blue	395.00	230.00	125.00	18.00	12.00	8.50
186	6¢ pink	650.00	425.00	280.00	30.00	22.00	13.00
187	10¢ brown (no secret mark)	1650.00	1100.00	600.00	30.00	22.00	13.00
188	10¢ brown (secret mark) . . .	1075.00	700.00	450.00	30.00	22.00	13.00
189	15¢ red orange .	300.00	165.00	100.00	28.00	21.00	12.50
190	30¢ full black . . .	800.00	475.00	275.00	90.00	60.00	40.00
191	90¢ carmine	1800.00	1150.00	725.00	375.00	240.00	175.00
	1880 American Bank Note Co., Special Printings. Same as 1879 Issue, on soft, porous paper, without gum. Perf 12.						
192	1¢ dark ultramarine	16800.00	10500.00	6250.00	....	....	....
193	2¢ black brown .	8135.00	5750.00	3700.00	....	....	....
194	3¢ blue green . . .	24675.00	15750.00	10000.00	....	....	....
195	6¢ dull rose	18375.00	11500.00	7000.00	....	....	....
196	7¢ scarlet vermillion	6825.00	4700.00	3200.00	....	....	....
197	10¢ deep brown .	16275.00	10500.00	6250.00	....	....	....
198	12¢ black purple	8925.00	6250.00	4200.00	....	....	....
199	15¢ orange	15065.00	9500.00	5750.00	....	....	....
200	24¢ dark violet . .	8925.00	6250.00	4200.00	....	....	....
201	30¢ greenish black	13385.00	8500.00	5000.00	....	....	....
202	90¢ dull carmine	13385.00	8500.00	5000.00	....	....	....
203	2¢ scarlet vermillion	30185.00	18500.00	11750.00	....	....	....
204	5¢ deep blue . . .	53815.00	33000.00	20250.00	....	....	....
	1882 American Bank Note Company Perf 12. (OG + 60%)						
205	5¢ yellow brown .	180.00	120.00	85.00	11.00	8.00	5.00
	1882 American Bank Note Co., Special Printing. Same as in 1882 Issue, on soft, porous Paper. Perf 12.						
205C	5¢ gray brown . .	....	29500.00	....	....	....	....

210, 211B, 213
Washington

211, 211D, 215
Jackson

212
Franklin

SCOTT NO.	DESCRIPTION	UNUSED VF	UNUSED F	UNUSED AVG	USED VF	USED F	USED AVG
	1881-82 American Bank Note Co. Same designs as 1873, Re-Engraved. On soft, porous paper. Perf 12. (†) (OG + 100%)						
206	1¢ gray blue	52.50	33.00	20.00	1.50	1.00	.70
207	3¢ blue green . . .	52.50	33.00	20.00	.80	.50	.35
208	6¢ rose	375.00	240.00	135.00	95.00	70.00	50.00
208a	6¢ brown red . . .	300.00	195.00	110.00	160.00	120.00	80.00
209	10¢ brown	150.00	105.00	68.00	6.50	5.00	3.00
209b	10¢ black brown	340.00	210.00	140.00	275.00	180.00	110.00
210	2¢ red brown . . .	45.00	29.00	19.00	.65	.45	.35
211	4¢ blue green . . .	170.00	110.00	75.00	25.00	17.50	12.50

SCOTT NO.	DESCRIPTION	UNUSED VF	UNUSED F	UNUSED AVG	USED VF	USED F	USED AVG
	1883 American Bank Note Co. Special Printing. Same design as 1883 Issue, on soft porous paper. Perf 12.						
211B	2¢ pale red brown	500.00	395.00	275.00	....	....	....
211D	4¢ deep blue green	26250.00	....	....	....	....	....
	1887 American Bank Note Co. New designs or colors. Perf 12. (OG + 60%)						
212	1¢ ultramarine . .	100.00	65.00	40.00	2.10	1.50	.95
213	2¢ green	37.50	23.00	15.00	.60	.40	.30
214	3¢ vermillion . . .	70.00	42.00	25.00	70.00	45.00	28.00

SCOTT NO.	DESCRIPTION	UNUSED O.G. VF	UNUSED O.G. F	UNUSED O.G. AVG	USED VF	USED F	USED AVG
	1888 American Bank Note Company. New Colors Perf 12. (NH + 100%)						
215	4¢ carmine	300.00	195.00	130.00	25.00	17.50	10.50
216	5¢ indigo	300.00	195.00	130.00	15.00	10.50	2.50
217	30¢ orange brown	575.00	375.00	225.00	145.00	100.00	60.00
218	90¢ purple	1450.00	950.00	525.00	300.00	210.00	125.00

THE 1890-93 SMALL BANK NOTE ISSUES

Unlike the complex Large Bank Notes, the 1890-93 series is the simplest of the 19th century definitive issues. They were printed by the American Bank Note Company and what few printing varieties there are can easily be determined by using the Harris Stamp Identifier.

The two major printing varieties are the 2 cent carmine with a "cap" on the left 2 (#219a) or both 2s (#219c).

The "cap" appears to be just that—a small flat hat just to the right of center on top of the denomination numeral 2. It was caused by a breakdown in the metal of the transfer roll that went undetected while it was being used to enter the designs into a few printing plates.

219
Franklin

219D, 220
Washington

221
Jackson

222
Lincoln

223
Grant

224
Garfield

225
Sherman

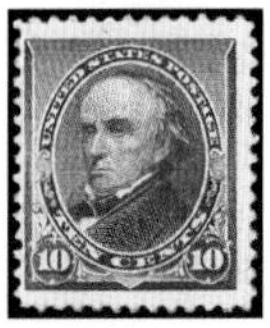

226
Webster

227
Clay

228
Jefferson

229
Perry

SCOTT NO.	DESCRIPTION	UNUSED O.G. VF	UNUSED O.G. F	UNUSED O.G. AVG	USED VF	USED F	USED AVG
	(NH +100%)						
219	1¢ dull blue	37.50	21.00	17.00	.60	.45	.25
219D	2¢ lake	300.00	175.00	125.00	2.00	1.40	.75
220	2¢ carmine	30.00	19.00	14.00	.55	.40	.30
220a	Cap on left "2" . .	195.00	110.00	70.00	10.00	6.50	4.50
220c	Cap on both "2"s	750.00	400.00	275.00	27.50	17.50	12.50
221	3¢ purple	95.00	60.00	45.00	10.00	6.00	4.50
222	4¢ dark brown . .	135.00	80.00	60.00	4.00	3.00	2.00
223	5¢ chocolate . . .	100.00	65.00	45.00	4.00	3.00	2.00
224	6¢ brown red . . .	95.00	60.00	45.00	27.50	18.00	12.50
225	8¢ lilac	80.00	55.00	40.00	16.00	9.75	7.00
226	10¢ green	225.00	145.00	100.00	5.00	3.25	2.00
227	15¢ indigo	350.00	210.00	150.00	27.50	19.50	12.50
228	30¢ black	475.00	300.00	210.00	35.00	22.50	14.00
229	90¢ orange	795.00	475.00	325.00	155.00	95.00	55.00

230
In Sight of Land

231
Landing of Columbus

232
Flagship

233
Fleet of Columbus

234
Soliciting Aid

235
At Barcelona

236
Restored To Favor

237
Presenting Natives

238
Discovery

239
At La Rábida

240
Recall of Columbus

241
Pledging Jewels

242
Columbus in Chains

243
Describing Third Voyage

244
Isabella & Columbus

245
Portrait of Columbus

THE COLUMBIANS

Perhaps the most glamorous of all United States issues is the 1893 Columbians set. Consisting of 16 denominations, the set was issued to celebrate the 1893 World's Columbian Exposition.

Even then, the Post Office Department was aware that stamps could be useful for more than just the prepayment of postage. We quote from an internal Post Office Department report of November 20, 1892:

"During the past summer the determination was reached by the Department to issue, during the progress of the Columbian Exposition at Chicago, a special series of adhesive postage stamps of such a character as would help to signalize the four hundredth anniversary of the discovery of America by Columbus. This course was in accordance with the practice of other great postal administrations on occasions of national rejoicing.

The collecting of stamps is deserving of encouragement, for it tends to the cultivation of artistic tastes and the study of history and geography, especially on the part of the young. The new stamps will be purchased in large quantities simply for the use of collections, without ever being presented in payment of postage; and the stamps sold in this way will, of course, prove a clear gain to the department."

As it turned out, the Columbians issue did sell well, being purchased in large quantities not only by collectors, but by speculators hoping to capitalize on the expected demand for the stamps and the fact that they were supposed to be on sale for only one year, from January 2 to December 31, 1893. (The 8 cent stamp was issued March 3,1893 to meet the new, reduced Registration fee.)

Although sales of the stamps were brisk at the Exposition site in Chicago, speculation proved less than rewarding. The hordes that showed up on the first day of sale in Chicago (January 3rd) and purchased large quantities of the issue ended up taking losses on most of the stamps.

The set was the most expensive postal issue produced to date by the Post Office. The lower denominations matched those of the previous, "Small" Bank Note issue and the 50 cent Columbian replaced the 90 cent Bank Note denomination. But the $1 through $5 denominations were unheard of at that time. The reason for their release was explained in the November 20, 1892 report: "...such high denominations having heretofore been called for by some of the principal post offices".

The Columbians were an instant success. Businesses did not like the wide size, but they usually could obtain the smaller Bank Note issue. Collectors enjoyed the new stamps, although at least one complained that some of the high values purchased by him had straight edges—and was quickly authorized to exchange "the imperfect stamps" for perfect ones.

The one major variety in this set is the 4 cent blue error of color. It is similar to, but richer in color than, the 1 cent Columbian and commands a larger premium over the normal 4 cent ultramarine color.

The imperforates that are known to exist for all values are proofs which were distributed as gifts and are not listed as postage stamps. The only exception, the 2 cent imperforate, is believed to be printers' waste that was saved from destruction.

SCOTT NO.	DESCRIPTION	UNUSED O.G. VF	F	AVG	USED VF	F	AVG
	1893 COLUMBIAN ISSUE (NH + 100%)						
230	1¢ deep blue . . .	33.00	21.00	14.00	.60	.40	.30
231	2¢ brown violet .	30.00	19.00	13.00	.30	.25	.20
231C	2¢ "broken hat" .	95.00	60.00	45.00	1.50	1.00	.60
232	3¢ green	85.00	50.00	40.00	18.00	13.00	9.00
233	4¢ ultramarine . .	110.00	70.00	45.00	11.00	7.25	4.50
234	5¢ chocolate . . .	125.00	75.00	50.00	11.00	7.25	4.50
235	6¢ purple	110.00	70.00	45.00	30.00	20.00	14.00
236	8¢ magenta	100.00	65.00	38.00	16.00	10.50	6.25
237	10¢ black brown	175.00	115.00	85.00	12.50	8.25	5.50
238	15¢ dark green .	375.00	240.00	150.00	110.00	65.00	42.50
239	30¢ orange brown	425.00	300.00	195.00	110.00	75.00	52.50
240	50¢ slate blue . .	825.00	575.00	400.00	210.00	135.00	95.00
241	$1 salmon	1900.00	1250.00	975.00	825.00	550.00	340.00
242	$2 brown red . . .	2000.00	1300.00	1000.00	825.00	550.00	340.00
243	$3 yellow green .	3350.00	2300.00	1550.00	1450.00	975.00	650.00
244	$4 crimson lake .	4650.00	3300.00	2300.00	1975.00	1325.00	850.00
245	$5 black	5650.00	3200.00	2300.00	2350.00	1400.00	925.00

246, 247, 264, 279
Franklin

248-252, 265-267, 279B
Washington

253, 268
Jackson

254, 269, 280
Lincoln

255, 270, 281
Grant

256, 271, 282
Garfield

257, 272
Sherman

258, 273, 282C, 283
Webster

259, 274, 284
Clay

260, 275
Jefferson

261, 261A, 276, 276A
Perry

262, 277
Madison

263, 278
Marshall

1894-98 THE FIRST BUREAU ISSUES

In 1894, the United States Bureau of Engraving and Printing replaced the American Bank Note Company as the contractor for all United States postage stamps. The "First" Bureau issues, as they are commonly known, actually consist of three series, as follows:

The 1894 Series. In order to expedite the transfer of production to the Bureau, the plates then being used by the American Bank Note Company for the 1890-93 Small Bank Notes were modified, small triangles being added in the upper corners. The 1 cent through 15 cent stamps are otherwise essentially the same as the 1890-93 issue although minor variations have been noted on some values. The 30 cent and 90 cent 1890-93 denominations were changed to 50 cents and $1, respectively, and new $2 and $5 denominations were added.

The 1895 Series. To protect against counterfeiting of United Sates stamps, the Bureau adopted the use of watermarked paper. (A scheme for counterfeiting 2 cent stamps had been uncovered around the same time the watermarked paper was being adopted. Some of these counterfeits are known postally used.) This series is almost exactly the same as the 1984 series except for the presence of watermarks. The watermarks can be difficult t detect on this series, particularly on the light-colored stamps, such as the 50 cent, and on used stamps. Since the 1894 unwatermarked stamps (with the exception of the 2 cent carmine type I) are worth more than the 1895 watermarked stamps, collectors will want to examine their 1894 stamps carefully. (Some collectors feel they can recognize the 1894 stamps by their ragged perforations, caused by difficulties the Bureau encountered when it first took over the produciton of postage stamps. This is not a reliable method.)

The 1898 "Color Changes." With the adoption of a Universal Postal Union code that recommended standard colors for international mail, the United States changed the colors for the lower values in the 1895 Series. The stamps were printed on the same watermarked paper as that used for the 1895 Series. Except for the 2 cent,which was changed from carmine to red, the colors of the 1898 Series are easily differentiated from the 1895 set. The 2 cent value is the most complicated of the First Bureau Issues. In addition to the color changes that took place, three different triangle types are known. The differences are attributed to the possibility that the work of engraving the triangles into the American Bank Note plates was performed by several Bureau engravers.

The 10 cent and $1 types I and II can be distinguished by the circles surrounding the numeral denominations. The Type IIs are identical to the circles of the 1890-93 Small Bank Notes.

All stamps in these series are perf. 12. The Harris Stamp Identifier at the front of this catalog provides additional information on the major types and watermarks of all three series.

SCOTT NO.	DESCRIPTION	UNUSED O.G. VF	UNUSED O.G. F	UNUSED O.G. AVG	USED VF	USED F	USED AVG
	1894 Unwatermarked (†) (NH + 100%)						
246	1¢ ultramarine . .	38.00	24.50	18.00	7.50	4.75	3.00
247	1¢ blue	85.00	50.00	35.00	4.00	2.50	1.75
248	2¢ pink (I)	35.00	22.00	16.00	8.50	5.50	3.50
249	2¢ carmine lake (I)	225.00	130.00	90.00	6.00	4.00	2.50
250	2¢ carmine (I) . .	35.00	23.00	16.00	1.25	.75	.50
251	2¢ carmine (II) . .	400.00	250.00	150.00	11.00	8.00	5.00
252	2¢ carmine (III) .	150.00	90.00	60.00	11.00	8.00	5.00
253	3¢ purple	145.00	85.00	60.00	14.00	8.00	5.50
254	4¢ dark brown . .	195.00	110.00	80.00	9.00	5.50	3.50
255	5¢ chocolate . . .	160.00	91.00	69.00	9.00	5.50	3.50
256	6¢ dull brown . . .	210.00	125.00	85.00	28.00	20.00	14.00
257	8¢ violet brown .	170.00	110.00	80.00	25.00	15.00	12.00
258	10¢ dark green .	325.00	210.00	140.00	19.50	10.00	7.00
259	15¢ dark blue . . .	375.00	240.00	180.00	75.00	45.00	30.00
260	50¢ orange	695.00	400.00	300.00	145.00	90.00	55.00
261	$1 black (I)	1300.00	800.00	550.00	400.00	240.00	165.00
261A	$1 black (II)	2700.00	1750.00	1200.00	825.00	550.00	375.00
262	$2 bright blue . . .	4000.00	2300.00	1850.00	1250.00	900.00	600.00
263	$5 dark green . .	6050.00	3700.00	2900.00	2800.00	2000.00	1400.00
	1895 Double Line Watermark "USPS" (†) (NH + 75%)						
264	1¢ blue	8.50	5.50	3.75	.50	.35	.25
265	2¢ carmine (I) . .	38.00	24.00	17.00	3.00	2.00	1.25
266	2¢ carmine (II) . .	42.00	27.00	19.00	5.00	3.50	2.25
267	2¢ carmine (III) .	6.50	4.00	3.00	.35	.30	.25
268	3¢ purple	45.00	28.00	20.00	2.25	1.50	1.00
269	4¢ dark brown . .	50.00	32.00	22.00	3.00	2.00	1.00
270	5¢ chocolate . . .	52.50	36.00	22.00	3.25	2.10	1.30
271	6¢ dull brown . . .	150.00	90.00	65.00	8.00	5.50	4.00
272	8¢ violet brown .	85.00	50.00	35.00	3.00	1.75	1.10
273	10¢ dark green .	110.00	70.00	50.00	2.25	1.40	.80
274	15¢ dark blue . . .	300.00	170.00	110.00	18.00	12.00	8.00
275	50¢ orange	350.00	210.00	150.00	35.00	25.00	15.00
276	$1 black (I)	750.00	425.00	300.00	110.00	70.00	45.00
276A	$1 black (II)	1700.00	1000.00	700.00	225.00	160.00	110.00
277	$2 bright blue . . .	1350.00	800.00	600.00	400.00	295.00	195.00
278	$5 dark green . .	3000.00	1800.00	1050.00	625.00	400.00	275.00
	1898 New Colors (NH + 75%)						
279	1¢ deep green . .	15.00	9.00	6.50	.50	.35	.25
279B	2¢ red (IV)	13.00	7.50	5.00	.40	.30	.25
279Bc	2¢ rose carmine (IV)	325.00	195.00	120.00	125.00	80.00	60.00
279Bd	2¢ orange red (IV)	17.50	10.00	7.00	.45	.35	.25
280	4¢ rose brown . .	40.00	27.00	18.00	3.00	2.00	1.25
281	5¢ dark blue	48.00	29.00	18.00	2.25	1.50	.85
282	6¢ lake	60.00	40.00	30.00	6.00	4.00	2.50
282C	10¢ brown (I) . . .	230.00	155.00	110.00	6.00	4.00	2.50
283	10¢ orange brown (II)	175.00	110.00	70.00	4.50	3.00	1.80
284	15¢ olive green .	180.00	110.00	75.00	13.00	8.00	5.50

1898 THE TRANS-MISSISSIPPI ISSUE

Issued for the Trans-Mississippi Exposition in Omaha, Nebraska, the "Omahas", as they also are known, did not receive the same welcome from collectors as that accorded the first commemorative set, the 1893 Columbians. Although the uproar was ascribed to the fact that collectors felt put upon by another set with $1 and $2 values, had the $1 to $5 values in the Columbian series appreciated in value, no doubt the protests would have been muted.

On the other hand, the public at large enjoyed the new issue. The Trans-Mississippi issues depict various works of art and are among the most beautiful stamps ever issued by the United States. The 8 and 10 cent values reproduce works by Frederic Remington and the $1 "Western Cattle in Storm", based on a work by J.A. MacWhirter, is regarded as one of our finest examples of the engraver's art.

As appealing as these stamps are in single colors, the set might have been even more beautiful. The original intent was to print each stamp with the vignette, or central design, in black and the frame in a distinctive second color that would be different for each denomination. That plan had to be dropped when the Bureau was called upon to produce large quantities of revenue stamps at the outbreak of the Spanish-American War.

285
Marquette on the Mississippi

286
Farming in the West

287
Indian Hunting Buffalo

288
Fremont on the Rocky Mountains

289
Troops Guarding Train

290
Hardships of Emigration

291
Western Mining Prospector

292
Western Cattle in Storm

293
Eads Bridge over Mississippi River

SCOTT NO.	DESCRIPTION	UNUSED O.G. VF	F	AVG	USED VF	F	AVG
	1898 Trans-Mississippi Exposition Issue (†) (NH + 100%)						
285	1¢ dark yellow green	45.00	30.00	21.00	9.75	6.50	4.00
286	2¢ copper red...........	35.00	23.00	18.00	3.00	2.00	1.25
287	4¢ orange..................	225.00	135.00	95.00	37.00	22.00	14.00
288	5¢ dull blue................	195.00	115.00	80.00	28.00	17.50	10.00
289	8¢ violet brown..........	250.00	160.00	100.00	52.50	34.00	20.00
290	10¢ gray violet...........	250.00	160.00	100.00	38.00	22.00	13.00
291	50¢ sage green.........	900.00	550.00	450.00	255.00	150.00	100.00
292	$1 black.....................	1900.00	1100.00	800.00	800.00	500.00	350.00
293	$2 orange brown.......	3000.00	1850.00	1300.00	1150.00	775.00	500.00

1901 THE PAN-AMERICAN ISSUE

Issued to commemorate the Pan-American Exposition in Buffalo, N.Y., this set depicts important engineering and manufacturing achievements. The beautiful engraving is showcased by the bicolored printing.

294, 294a
Fast Lake Navigation

295, 295a
Fast Express

296, 296a
Automobile

297
Bridge at Niagara Falls

298
Canal at Sault Ste. Marie

299
Fast Ocean Navigation

SCOTT NO.	DESCRIPTION	UNUSED O.G. VF	F	AVG	USED VF	F	AVG
	1901 Pan-American Issue (NH + 75%)						
294-99	1¢-10¢ (6 varieties, complete)	770.00	445.00	295.00	165.00	95.00	70.00
294	1¢ green & black.........	45.00	24.00	14.00	5.50	3.75	2.25
294a	same, center inverted	...	12500.00	...	...	6500.00	...
295	2¢ carmine & black.....	35.00	19.00	11.00	2.00	1.35	.75
295a	same, center inverted	...	37500.00	...	...	16000.00	...
296	4¢ deep red brown & black...	190.00	115.00	78.00	24.00	13.50	9.25
296a	same, center inverted	...	10000.00	...	...	...	...
296aS	same, center inverted (Specimen)	...	5500.00	...	...	...	...
297	5¢ ultramarine & black	135.00	80.00	48.00	23.00	13.00	9.25
298	8¢ brown violet & black	165.00	105.00	70.00	85.00	50.00	36.00
299	10¢ yellow brown & black.	240.00	125.00	90.00	37.50	22.00	15.25

	UNUSED PLATE BLOCKS OF 6 NH F	NH AVG	OG F	OG AVG	UNUSED ARROW BLOCKS NH F	NH AVG	OG F	OG AVG
294	400.00	285.00	240.00	180.00	160.00	105.00	72.50	57.50
295	400.00	285.00	235.00	180.00	160.00	100.00	65.00	50.00
296	3750.00	2750.00	2100.00	1650.00	825.00	575.00	375.00	315.00
297	4200.00	3250.00	2600.00	2000.00	825.00	550.00	400.00	325.00
298	7500.00	5500.00	4000.00	3200.00	1050.00	700.00	500.00	375.00
299	10500.00	8000.00	6000.00	4800.00	1500.00	900.00	695.00	500.00

THE 1902-03 SERIES

The Series of 1902-03 was the first regular issue designed and produced by the United States Bureau of Engraving and Printing, most of the work on the 1894-98 series having been performed by the American Bank Note Company. (When the Bureau was awarded the contract to produce the 1894 series, they added triangles in the upper corners of the American Bank Note designs.)

The new series filled a number of gaps and was the first United States issue to feature a woman—in this case Martha Washington, on the 8 cent value.

Modern collectors consider the 1902-03 issue one of the finest regular series ever produced by the Bureau.

The intricate frame designs take us back to a period when such work still was affordable. In its time, however, the 1902-03 set was looked upon with disdain. The 2 cent Washington, with its ornate frame design and unflattering likeness of George Washington, came in for particular scorn. Yielding to the clamor, in 1903, less than one year after its release, the Post Office recalled the much criticized 2 cent stamp and replaced it with an attractive, less ornate design that cleaned up Washington's appearance, particularly in the area of the nose, and used a shield design that was less ornate.

The issue marked the first time United States stamps were issued in booklet form, the 1 and 2 cent values being printed in panes of six stamps each. Also for the first time since perforating was adopted in 1857, United States stamps were once again deliberately issued in imperforate form for postal use. The intent was to have such stamps available in sheet and coil form for use in vending machines. The manufacturers of such machines could purchase the imperforate stamps and perforate them to fit their equipment. One of these imperforate issues, the 4 cent brown of 1908 (#314A), ranks as one of the great rarities of 20th century philately. It is found only with the private perforations of the Schermack Mailing Machine Company.

Coil stamps intended for use in stamp affixing and vending machines also made their inaugural appearance with this issue. Their availability was not widely publicized and few collectors obtained copies of these coils. All genuine coils from this series are very rare and extremely valuable. We emphasize the word "genuine" because most coils that are seen actually have been faked by trimming the perforated stamps or fraudulently perforating the imperfs.

The only major design types are found on the 1903 2 cent, catalog #s 319 and 320. Identified as Die I and Die II, the differences are described in the Harris Stamp Identifier.

300, 314, 316, 318
Franklin

301
Washington

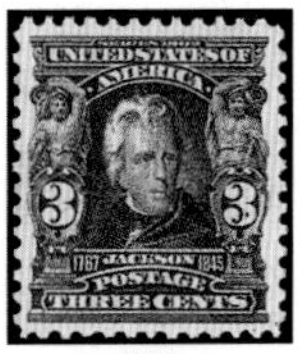
302
Jackson

303, 314A
Grant

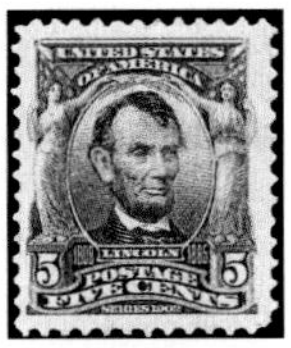
304, 315, 317
Lincoln

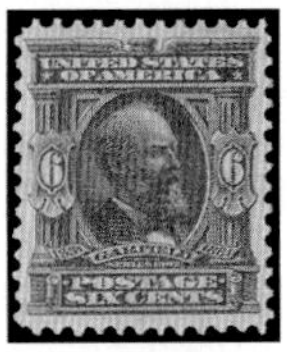
305
Garfield

306
Martha Washington

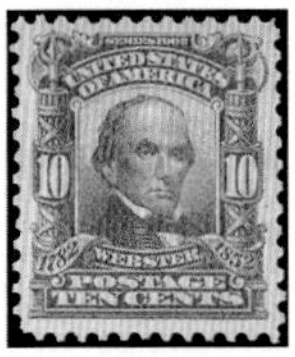
307
Webster

308
Harrison

309
Clay

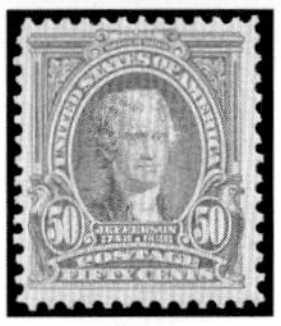
310
Jefferson

311
Farragut

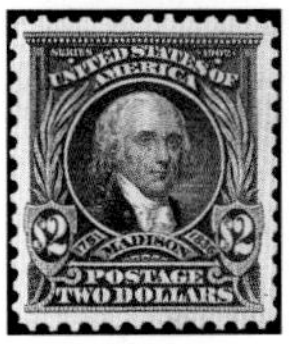
312, 479
Madison

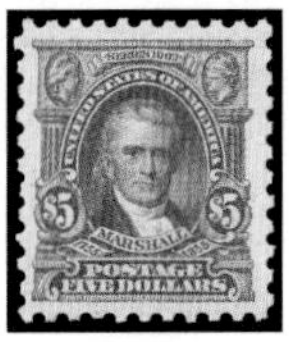
313, 480
Marshall

319-22
Washington

SCOTT NO.	DESCRIPTION	UNUSED O.G. VF	F	AVG	USED VF	F	AVG
	1902-03 Perf. 12 (†) (NH + 75%)						
300	1¢ blue green . . .	16.00	9.00	6.00	.35	.25	.20
300b	1¢ booklet pane of 6	....	550.00	375.00	....	....	....
301	2¢ carmine	18.00	12.00	7.50	.35	.25	.20
301c	2¢ booklet pane of 6	....	475.00	335.00	....	....	....
302	3¢ brown violet .	75.00	43.00	30.00	4.50	3.00	1.75
303	4¢ brown	75.00	43.00	30.00	2.50	1.50	1.00
304	5¢ blue	82.50	50.00	35.00	3.00	1.50	.75
305	6¢ claret	90.00	50.00	35.00	5.00	2.75	1.50
306	8¢ violet black . .	60.00	32.00	25.00	3.75	2.00	1.25
307	10¢ pale red brown	85.00	50.00	36.00	3.50	2.00	1.25
308	13¢ purple black	60.00	35.00	25.00	13.00	8.25	5.00
309	15¢ olive green .	195.00	120.00	85.00	10.00	6.25	4.00
310	50¢ orange	625.00	375.00	260.00	35.00	22.00	15.75
311	$1 black	925.00	500.00	350.00	90.00	55.00	35.00
312	$2 dark blue	1550.00	925.00	625.00	300.00	175.00	125.00
313	$5 dark green . .	3500.00	2200.00	1600.00	950.00	575.00	400.00
	1906 Imperforate (NH + 75%)						
	This and all subsequent imperforate issues can usually be priced as unused pairs at double the single price.						
314	1¢ blue green . . .	52.50	37.00	27.00	22.50	17.00	11.00
314A	4¢ brown	....	35000.00	....	....	26500.00	....
315	5¢ blue	695.00	500.00	320.00	800.00	600.00	450.00
	1908 Coil Stamps. Perf 12 Horizontally						
316	1¢ blue green, pair	....	....	....	....	....	....
317	5¢ blue, pair	....	5500.00	....	....	....	....
	1908 Coil Stamps. Perf 12 Vertically						
318	1¢ blue green, pair	....	5500.00	....	....	....	....
	1903. Perf. 12 (†) (NH + 60%)						
319	2¢ carmine, Die I	10.00	6.00	4.75	.45	.30	.20
319f	2¢ lake, Die II . . .	17.50	11.00	7.50	1.00	.70	.50
319g	2¢ carmine, Die I, booklet pane of 6	....	160.00	110.00	....	....	....
	1906 Imperforate (NH + 75%)						
320	2¢ carmine, Die I	30.00	22.00	15.00	28.00	16.00	11.00
320a	2¢ lake, Die I . . .	80.00	65.00	45.00	58.00	40.00	27.50
	1908 Coil Stamps. Perf 12 Horizontally						
321	2¢ carmine, pair .	....	....	....	....	....	....
	1908 Coil Stamps. Perf 12 Vertically						
322	2¢ carmine, pair .	....	5500.00	....	....	....	....

SCOTT NO.	UNUSED NH F	AVG	UNUSED OG F	AVG	SCOTT NO.	UNUSED NH F	AVG	UNUSED OG F	AVG
	PLATE BLOCKS OF 6					**CENTER LINE BLOCKS**			
300	280.00	160.00	175.00	110.00	314	300.00	200.00	180.00	145.00
301	325.00	170.00	180.00	120.00	320	305.00	210.00	175.00	145.00
314	375.00	250.00	230.00	170.00		**ARROW BLOCKS**			
319	175.00	120.00	95.00	70.00	314	235.00	185.00	140.00	110.00
320	415.00	290.00	225.00	175.00	320	210.00	175.00	120.00	95.00

1904 THE LOUISIANA PURCHASE ISSUE

Issued to commemorate the Louisiana Purchase Exposition held in St. Louis in 1904, these stamps were not well received. Collectors at the time did not purchase large quantities of the stamps, and the series was on sale for only seven months. As a result, well centered unused stamps are extremely difficult to locate.

323
Robert R. Livingston

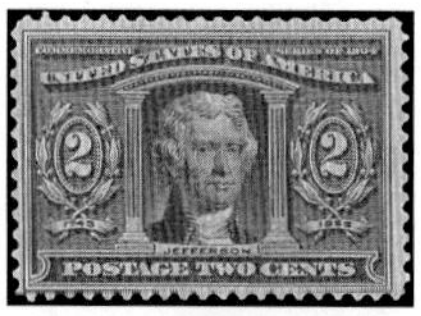

324
Jefferson

325
Monroe

326
McKinley

327
Map of Louisiana Purchase

SCOTT NO.	DESCRIPTION	UNUSED O.G. VF	F	AVG	USED VF	F	AVG
	1904 Louisiana Purchase Issue (NH + 75%)						
323-27	**1¢-10¢ (5 varieties, complete) .....**	**595.00**	**365.00**	**245.00**	**145.00**	**83.50**	**53.50**
323	1¢ green	57.50	30.00	21.00	8.50	5.00	3.00
324	2¢ carmine	44.50	25.00	18.00	2.50	2.00	1.00
325	3¢ violet	120.00	75.00	50.00	47.50	30.00	18.00
326	5¢ dark blue	150.00	85.00	55.00	36.00	19.00	14.00
327	10¢ red brown ..	260.00	170.00	115.00	56.00	32.00	20.00

1907 THE JAMESTOWN EXPOSITION ISSUE

This set may be the most difficult United States 20th century issue to find well centered. Issued in April, 1907 for the Jamestown Exposition at Hampton Roads, Virginia, the set was removed from sale when the Exposition closed on November 30th of that year. Very fine copies carry hefty premiums.

328
Capt. John Smith

329
Founding of Jamestown

330
Pocahontas

SCOTT NO.	DESCRIPTION	UNUSED O.G. VF	F	AVG	USED VF	F	AVG
	1907 Jamestown Exposition Issue (NH + 60%)						
328-30	**1¢-5¢ (3 varieties, complete) .....**	**295.00**	**225.50**	**153.00**	**76.00**	**33.00**	**17.50**
328	1¢ green	40.00	22.00	14.00	7.50	3.75	2.50
329	2¢ carmine	50.00	25.00	15.00	7.50	4.25	2.00
330	5¢ blue	210.00	100.00	60.00	65.00	27.50	14.00

SCOTT NO.	UNUSED PLATE BLOCKS OF 6 NH F	NH AVG	OG F	OG AVG	UNUSED ARROW BLOCKS NH F	NH AVG	OG F	OG AVG
323	395.00	300.00	200.00	160.00	200.00	120.00	130.00	85.00
324	400.00	300.00	210.00	160.00	160.00	100.00	95.00	65.00
325	1250.00	950.00	800.00	600.00	550.00	355.00	400.00	265.00
326	1450.00	950.00	800.00	700.00	675.00	380.00	375.00	250.00
327	3000.00	1950.00	1500.00	1150.00	1100.00	715.00	650.00	530.00
328	420.00	295.00	240.00	180.00	125.00	70.00	75.00	50.00
329	590.00	395.00	350.00	240.00	170.00	95.00	90.00	65.00
330	3600.00	2200.00	2000.00	1450.00	765.00	425.00	350.00	250.00

THE WASHINGTON-FRANKLIN HEADS

The Washington-Franklin Heads—so called because all stamps in the regular series featured the busts of George Washington and Benjamin Franklin—dominated the postal scene for almost two decades. Using a variety of papers, denominations, perforation sizes and formats, watermarks, design modifications and printing processes, almost 200 different major catalog listings were created from two basic designs.

The series started modestly, with the issuance of 12 stamps (#331-342) between November 1908 and January 1909. The modest designs on the new set replaced the ornate 1902-03 series. Their relative simplicity might have relegated the set to a secondary position in 20th century United States philately had it not been for the complexity of the varieties and the years of study the Washington-Franklin Heads now present to collectors.

The first varieties came almost immediately, in the form of imperforate stamps (#343-347) and coils, the latter being offered with horizontal (#348-351) or vertical (#352-356) perforations. The imperfs were intended for the fading vending machine technology that required private perforations while the coils were useful in standardized dispensers that were just coming into their own.

Then, in 1909, the Post Office began its experimentation. In this instance, it was the paper. As noted in our introduction to the 1909 Bluish Papers which follows, the Post Office Department and the Bureau of Engraving and Printing hoped that the new paper would reduce losses due to uneven shrinkage of the white wove paper used at the time. The experimental Washington-Franklin Bluish Papers (#357-66) are now among the most valuable in the series and the 8 cent Bluish Paper (#363) is the highest priced of the major listed items.

Attention was next directed to the double line watermark as the cause of the uneven shrinkage, as well as for weakness and thinning in the paper. As a result, a narrower, single line watermark was adopted for sheet stamps (#374-82), imperforates (#383-84), and coils with horizontal perfs (#385-86) and vertical perfs (#387-89).

Even as these experiments were being conducted, the perforation size was being examined to determine if a change was in order. Up until now, the perf 12 gauge had been used on all Washington-Franklin Heads.

The first perforation change was necessitated by the development of new coil manufacturing equipment. Under the increased pressure of the new equipment, the coil strips with the closely-spaced perf 12 gauge were splitting while being rolled into coils. To add paper between the holes, a perf 8-1/2 gauge was adopted for coil stamps and two new major varieties were created: with horizontal perfs (#390-91) and vertical perfs (#392-396).

Necessity was the driving force behind still more changes in 1912, when stamps with numeral denominations were issued to replace the "ONE CENT" and "TWO CENTS" stamps. This responded to the need for numeral denominations on foreign mail and created new sheets (#410-11) and vertically perforated (#412-13) coils. At the same time, a 7 cent value (#407) was issued to meet changing rate requirements.

In conjunction with the introduction of numerals on the 1 and 2 cent stamps, the design of the 1 cent was changed, with the bust of Washington replacing that of Franklin. Meanwhile, the bust of Franklin, which had been used only on the 1 cent stamp, was placed on all values from 8 cents to the $1 (#414-21) and a ribbon was added across their top to make the high value stamp even more noticeable to postal clerks.

As if to add just a little more variety while all the other changes were being made—but in actuality to use up a supply of old double-line watermark paper—50 cent and $1 issues with double-line watermarks (#422-23) were introduced.

The work with perforation changes on coil stamps carried over to sheet stamps in 1914 with the release of a perf 10 series (#424-40). The perf 10 size was then adapted to coils perforated horizontally (#441-42) and vertically (#443-47).

The transition to Rotary Press printing created new coils perforated 10 horizontally (#448-50) and vertically (#452-58). An imperforate Rotary coil (#459) for vending machine manufacturers also was produced.

A perf 10 double-line watermark $1 (#460) and a perf 11 two-cent sheet stamp (#461) added only slightly to the variety, but were followed by completely new runs on unwatermarked paper: perf 10 sheet stamps (#462-478) and imperforates (#481-84) were produced on the flat plate presses, while the Rotary press was used for coils perforated horizontally (#486-489) and vertically (#490-97).

While all this was taking place, the amazing 5 cent carmine error of color (#485) appeared on certain imperf 2 cent sheets. That same error (in rose, #505) was found when perf 11 sheet stamps (#498-518) were issued. The stamps turned out to be too hard to separate. Another strange issue, a 2 cent stamp on double-line watermark paper but perforated 11 (#519), came about when a small supply of old imperfs (#344) were discovered and put into the postal stream.

New $2 and $5 Franklins (#523-24), the former using an erroneous color, were released. To compensate for plate damage being caused by poor quality offset printings, perf 11 (#525-530) and imperforate (#531-535) were tried—and quickly resulted in a whole new series of "types" that had collectors spending more time with their magnifying glasses than with their families.

Odd perf sizes and printings (#538/546) came about as the Bureau cleaned out old paper stock. Then, in one final change, the Bureau corrected the color of the $2 from orange red and black to carmine and black. Almost 200 different stamps, all from two basic designs!

1909 THE BLUISH PAPERS

The Bluish Paper varieties are found on the 1 through 15 cent Washington-Franklin series of 1908-09 and on the 1909 Commemoratives. According to Post Office notices of the period, the experimental paper was a 30% rag stock that was intended to reduce paper waste. After being wet, a preliminary operation in the printing process, the standard white wove paper often would shrink so much that the perforators would cut into the designs. The rag paper did not solve the problem, the experiment was quickly abandoned and the 1909 Bluish Papers became major rarities.

The Harris Stamp Identifier provides further information on identifying the Washington-Franklin Heads.

331, 343, 348, 352, 357, 374, 383, 385, 387, 390, 392
Franklin

332, 344, 349, 353, 358, 375, 384, 386, 388, 391, 393
Washington

333, 345, 359, 376, 389, 394
Washington

334, 346, 350, 354, 360, 377, 395
Washington

335, 347, 351, 355, 361, 378, 396
Washington

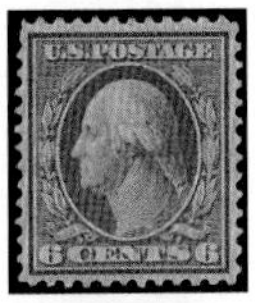
336, 362, 379
Washington

337, 363, 380
Washington

338, 356, 364, 381
Washington

339, 365
Washington

340, 366, 382
Washington

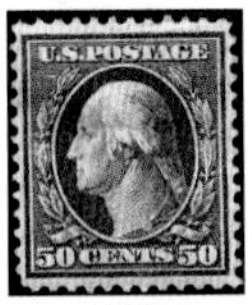
341
Washington

342
Washington

NOTE: *For further details on the various types of similar appearing stamps please refer to our U.S. Stamp Identifier.*

SCOTT NO.	DESCRIPTION	UNUSED O.G. VF	F	AVG	USED VF	F	AVG
	1908-09 Double Line Watermark "USPS" Perf. 12 (NH + 75%)						
331-42	**1¢-$1 (12 varieties, complete) .....**	**1580.00**	**940.00**	**605.00**	**205.00**	**140.00**	**82.50**
331	1¢ green	11.00	6.50	4.00	.35	.25	.20
331a	1¢ booklet pane of 6	200.00	145.00	95.00	......	......	......
332	2¢ carmine	11.25	7.00	4.25	.35	.25	.20
332a	2¢ booklet pane of 6	185.00	120.00	85.00	......	......	......
333	3¢ deep violet (I)	50.00	28.00	17.00	4.80	3.25	2.00
334	4¢ orange brown	55.00	34.00	22.00	1.80	1.20	.75
335	5¢ blue	72.00	40.00	24.00	3.25	2.25	1.45
336	6¢ red orange ..	80.00	50.00	30.00	8.50	5.00	3.15
337	8¢ olive green ..	60.00	38.00	24.00	5.00	3.00	2.00
338	10¢ yellow	80.00	55.00	40.00	3.00	1.60	1.00
339	13¢ blue green ..	60.00	34.00	23.00	32.00	20.00	11.50
340	15¢ pale ultramarine	82.00	50.00	35.00	12.00	8.00	5.00
341	50¢ violet	440.00	260.00	160.00	30.00	20.00	12.00
342	$1 violet brown .	675.00	400.00	260.00	115.00	80.00	50.00
	1908-09 Imperforate (NH + 75%)						
343-47	**1¢-5¢ (5 varieties, complete) .....**	**138.00**	**103.50**	**70.00**	**110.00**	**76.00**	**53.00**
343	1¢ green	18.50	13.00	9.50	6.00	4.50	3.00
344	2¢ carmine	27.50	22.00	14.00	5.75	4.00	2.75
345	3¢ deep violet (I)	67.50	52.00	39.00	27.00	19.00	12.50
346	4¢ orange brown	87.50	67.00	44.00	30.00	23.00	17.00
347	5¢ blue	110.00	80.00	53.00	47.00	30.00	21.00
	1908-10 Coil Stamps Perf. 12 Horizontally (NH + 75%)						
348	1¢ green	72.50	50.00	31.00	28.00	20.00	12.50
349	2¢ carmine	100.00	72.00	44.00	17.50	12.00	8.00
350	4¢ orange brown	285.00	185.00	135.00	170.00	120.00	80.00
351	5¢ blue	285.00	195.00	130.00	180.00	130.00	80.00

NOTE: **Counterfeits are common on #348-56 and #385-89**

SCOTT NO.	DESCRIPTION	UNUSED O.G. VF	F	AVG	USED VF	F	AVG
	1909 Coil Stamps Perf. 12 Vertically (NH + 75%)						
352	1¢ green	160.00	115.00	76.00	55.00	40.00	25.00
353	2¢ carmine	155.00	110.00	74.00	15.00	11.00	7.50
354	4¢ orange brown	375.00	285.00	195.00	115.00	85.00	55.00
355	5¢ blue	375.00	290.00	210.00	150.00	110.00	75.00
356	10¢ yellow	4750.00	3400.00	2100.00	2300.00	1800.00	1100.00

PLATE BLOCKS OF 6

SCOTT NO.	UNUSED NH F	AVG	UNUSED OG F	AVG
331	90.00	60.00	65.00	48.00
332	90.00	70.00	65.00	47.50
333	450.00	325.00	290.00	210.00
334	500.00	340.00	360.00	255.00
335	850.00	635.00	575.00	465.00
336	1250.00	900.00	700.00	495.00
337	700.00	495.00	375.00	275.00
338	950.00	750.00	700.00	450.00
339	700.00	575.00	400.00	300.00
343	125.00	115.00	80.00	60.00
344	160.00	130.00	140.00	100.00
345	330.00	250.00	320.00	240.00
346	400.00	300.00	310.00	260.00
347	525.00	425.00	450.00	325.00

CENTER LINE BLOCKS

SCOTT NO.	UNUSED NH F	AVG	UNUSED OG F	AVG
343	72.00	53.50	53.50	40.00
344	105.00	90.00	87.50	55.00
345	250.00	185.00	190.00	155.00
346	300.00	265.00	255.00	180.00
347	450.00	315.00	325.00	230.00

ARROW BLOCKS

SCOTT NO.	UNUSED NH F	AVG	UNUSED OG F	AVG
343	57.50	52.00	52.00	37.50
344	100.00	87.50	85.00	55.00
345	240.00	180.00	185.00	150.00
346	295.00	260.00	250.00	175.00
347	390.00	300.00	320.00	210.00

(NH + 75%)

	COIL LINE PAIRS UNUSED OG VF	F	AVG	COIL PAIRS UNUSED OG VF	F	AVG
348	350.00	225.00	155.00	150.00	100.00	65.00
349	600.00	400.00	275.00	215.00	130.00	95.00
350	1200.00	900.00	650.00	600.00	420.00	265.00
351	1200.00	900.00	650.00	600.00	370.00	230.00
352	700.00	500.00	350.00	340.00	235.00	165.00
353	700.00	500.00	350.00	330.00	230.00	165.00
354	1650.00	1100.00	775.00	800.00	535.00	395.00
355	1650.00	1100.00	775.00	800.00	625.00	445.00
356	15000.00	10000.00	7500.00	10000.00	6000.00	4500.00

SCOTT NO.	DESCRIPTION	UNUSED O.G. VF	F	AVG	USED VF	F	AVG
	1909 Bluish Gray paper Perf. 12 (NH + 75%)						
357	1¢ green	165.00	100.00	74.00	150.00	95.00	60.00
358	2¢ carmine	215.00	135.00	96.00	150.00	95.00	60.00
359	3¢ deep violet (I)	2750.00	1800.00	1300.00	4000.00	2800.00	2000.00
360	4¢ orange brown	......	16000.00	11000.00	......	......	......
361	5¢ blue	6050.00	3400.00	2400.00	12000.00	9000.00	7000.00
362	6¢ red orange ..	2000.00	1200.00	800.00	4000.00	2800.00	2000.00
363	8¢ olive green ..	......	19500.00	14000.00	......	......	......
364	10¢ yellow	2200.00	1300.00	950.00	5000.00	3500.00	2500.00
365	13¢ blue green ..	3500.00	2200.00	1500.00	2800.00	1900.00	1275.00
366	15¢ pale ultramarine	2000.00	1100.00	850.00	2000.00	1350.00	875.00

THE 1909 COMMEMORATIVES

After the 16-value Columbian commemorative set, the Post Office Department began gradually reducing the number of stamps in subsequent series. The 1909 commemoratives were the first to use the single-stamp commemorative approach that is now the common practice.

The Lincoln Memorial issue was released on the 100th anniversary of the birth of America's 16th President. The Alaska-Yukon was issued for the Alaska-Yukon Exposition held in Seattle to publicize the development of the Alaska territory. The Hudson-Fulton stamp commemorated Henry Hudson's 1609 discovery of the river that bears his name, the 1809 voyage of Robert Fulton's "Clermont" steamboat and the 1909 celebration of those two events.

As noted earlier, the 1909 Commemoratives were issued on experimental "bluish" paper in addition to the white wove standard. The stamps on white wove paper also were issued in imperforate form for private perforation by vending and stamp-affixing machine manufacturers.

367-369
Lincoln

370, 371
William H. Seward

372, 373
S.S. Clermont

SCOTT NO.	DESCRIPTION	UNUSED O.G. VF	F	AVG	USED VF	F	AVG
	1909 LINCOLN MEMORIAL ISSUE (NH + 50%)						
367	2¢ carmine, perf.	14.95	11.00	7.50	3.50	2.00	1.40
368	2¢ carmine, imperf.	50.00	39.00	28.00	30.00	18.00	12.00
369	2¢ carmine (bluish paper) . . .	300.00	180.00	130.00	300.00	210.00	120.00
	1909 ALASKA-YUKON ISSUE						
370	2¢ carmine, perf.	20.00	12.00	8.00	3.00	1.75	1.00
371	2¢ carmine, imperf.	60.00	44.00	35.00	32.00	22.00	14.00
	1909 HUDSON-FULTON ISSUE						
372	2¢ carmine, perf.	18.00	12.00	9.50	5.00	3.00	2.00
373	2¢ carmine, imperf	67.50	48.00	40.00	32.00	22.00	17.00
	1910-11 Single Line Watermark "USPS" Perf. 12 (NH + 50%)						
374-82	**1¢-15¢ (9 varieties, complete) . . . . .**	**760.00**	**475.00**	**290.00**	**52.00**	**33.00**	**19.75**
374	1¢ green	13.50	8.50	5.50	.30	.25	.20
374a	1¢ booklet pane of 6	200.00	130.00	90.00	......	......	......
375	2¢ carmine	14.50	9.00	6.00	.30	.25	.20
375a	2¢ booklet pane of 6	150.00	105.00	66.00	......	......	......
376	3¢ deep violet (I)	30.00	17.00	11.00	3.00	1.75	1.10
377	4¢ brown	40.00	24.00	18.00	1.20	.85	.55
378	5¢ blue	40.00	24.00	18.00	1.00	.75	.50
379	6¢ red orange . .	50.00	30.00	19.00	1.55	.90	.60
380	8¢ olive green . .	135.00	80.00	48.00	17.00	11.50	7.50
381	10¢ yellow	150.00	95.00	55.00	6.00	4.00	2.65
382	15¢ pale ultramarine	340.00	220.00	130.00	25.00	15.50	8.75
	1911 Imperforate						
383	1¢ green	11.00	8.50	5.00	3.50	2.50	1.50
384	2¢ carmine	20.00	17.00	9.50	3.00	2.00	1.00

SCOTT NO.	UNUSED NH F	AVG	UNUSED OG F	AVG
	PLATE BLOCKS OF 6			
367	175.00	120.00	125.00	85.00
368	300.00	210.00	240.00	175.00
370	320.00	220.00	220.00	150.00
371	390.00	275.00	280.00	190.00
372	380.00	240.00	280.00	190.00
373	430.00	300.00	300.00	200.00
374	100.00	65.00	70.00	50.00
375	105.00	65.00	75.00	50.00
376	210.00	140.00	150.00	100.00
377	250.00	170.00	185.00	120.00
378	300.00	225.00	225.00	140.00
383	80.00	55.00	50.00	36.00
384	210.00	150.00	140.00	95.00

SCOTT NO.	UNUSED NH F	AVG	UNUSED OG F	AVG
	CENTER LINE BLOCKS			
368	200.00	140.00	150.00	115.00
371	285.00	195.00	200.00	140.00
373	340.00	215.00	240.00	165.00
383	42.00	30.00	30.00	25.00
384	90.00	55.00	65.00	40.00
	ARROW BLOCKS			
368	180.00	130.00	120.00	110.00
371	235.00	190.00	180.00	135.00
373	265.00	200.00	200.00	160.00
383	42.00	30.00	30.00	20.00
384	50.00	45.00	45.00	36.00

Very Fine Plate Blocks from this period command premiums.

SCOTT NO.	DESCRIPTION	UNUSED O.G. VF	F	AVG	USED VF	F	AVG
	COIL STAMPS 1910 Perf. 12 Horizontally (NH + 75%)						
385	1¢ green	95.00	63.00	37.00	22.50	15.00	11.00
386	2¢ carmine	150.00	90.00	60.00	30.00	20.00	14.00
	1910-11 Perf. 12 Vertically (†)						
387	1¢ green	250.00	165.00	110.00	75.00	50.00	35.00
388	2¢ carmine	1500.00	950.00	725.00	500.00	350.00	240.00
389	3¢ deep violet (I)	......	58000.00	......	......	12400.00	......
	1910 Perf. 8-1/2 Horizontally						
390	1¢ green	11.50	6.50	4.75	7.50	5.50	4.00
391	2¢ carmine	67.50	45.00	27.00	18.00	12.00	8.00
	1910-13 Perf. 8-1/2 Vertically						
392	1¢ green	51.50	35.00	21.00	27.00	18.00	13.50
393	2¢ carmine	75.00	45.00	30.00	14.00	9.00	6.00
394	3¢ deep violet (I)	100.00	64.00	43.00	65.00	45.00	30.00
395	4¢ brown	105.00	68.00	45.00	65.00	45.00	30.00
396	5¢ blue	97.50	63.00	42.00	65.00	45.00	30.00

(NH + 75%)

SCOTT NO.	COIL LINE PAIRS UNUSED OG VF	F	AVG	COIL PAIRS UNUSED OG VF	F	AVG
385	450.00	300.00	195.00	200.00	125.00	87.50
386	1300.00	800.00	550.00	315.00	225.00	125.00
387	850.00	600.00	400.00	525.00	335.00	235.00
390	50.00	35.00	22.50	25.00	16.50	9.00
391	330.00	235.00	140.00	140.00	85.00	55.00
392	225.00	140.00	95.00	110.00	72.50	43.50
393	325.00	210.00	150.00	155.00	100.00	60.00
394	450.00	295.00	200.00	200.00	135.00	85.00
395	450.00	295.00	200.00	220.00	150.00	95.00
396	450.00	295.00	200.00	200.00	135.00	85.00

THE PANAMA-PACIFIC ISSUE

The Panama-Pacific stamps were issued to commemorate the discovery of the Pacific Ocean in 1513 and the opening of the 1915 Panama-Pacific Exposition that celebrated the completion of the Panama Canal. Released in perf 12 form in 1913, the set of four denominations was changed to perf 10 in 1914. Before the perf change, the 10 cent orange yellow shade was determined to be too light. It was changed to the deeper orange color that is found both perf 12 and perf 10.

Because many collectors ignored the perf 10 stamps when they were issued, these stamps are scarcer than their perf 12 predecessors. In fact, #404 is the rarest 20th century commemorative issue.

397, 401
Balboa

398, 402
Panama Canal

399, 403
Golden Gate

400, 400A, 404
Discovery of San Francisco Bay

SCOTT NO.	DESCRIPTION	UNUSED O.G. VF	F	AVG	USED VF	F	AVG
	1913 Perf. 12 (NH + 75%)						
397-400A	**1¢-10¢ (5 varieties, complete) . . .**	**660.00**	**350.00**	**230.00**	**76.00**	**42.00**	**26.00**
397	1¢ green	37.50	23.00	17.00	3.00	1.80	1.25
398	2¢ carmine . . .	36.50	20.00	13.00	1.10	.65	.50
399	5¢ blue	110.00	66.00	44.00	15.00	8.00	5.00
400	10¢ orange yellow	180.00	100.00	65.00	35.00	20.00	14.00
400A	10¢ orange . .	325.00	185.00	120.00	30.00	16.00	10.00
	1914-15 Perf. 10 (NH + 75%)						
401-04	**1¢-10¢ (4 varieties, complete) . . .**	**1600.00**	**1175.00**	**775.00**	**142.00**	**82.00**	**54.00**
401	1¢ green	46.00	26.00	18.00	9.00	6.50	4.00
402	2¢ carmine . . .	130.00	74.00	56.00	3.25	1.95	1.25
403	5¢ blue	255.00	135.00	95.00	28.00	18.00	12.00
404	10¢ orange . .	1250.00	1000.00	650.00	110.00	60.00	40.00

405/545
Washington

406/546
Washington

426/541
Washington

427, 446, 457, 465, 495, 503
Washington

428, 447, 458, 466, 467, 496, 504, 505
Washington

429, 468, 506
Washington

407, 430, 469, 507
Washington

414, 431, 470, 508
Franklin

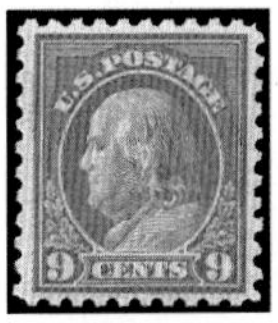

415, 432, 471, 509
Franklin

416, 433, 472, 497, 510
Franklin

434, 473, 511
Franklin

417, 435, 474 512
Franklin

513
Franklin

418, 437, 475, 514
Franklin

419, 438, 476, 515
Franklin

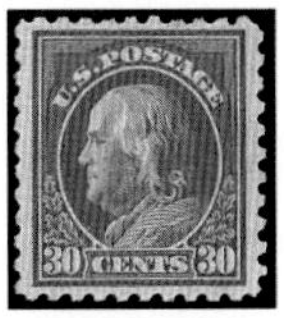

420, 439, 476A, 516
Franklin

421, 422, 440, 477, 517
Franklin

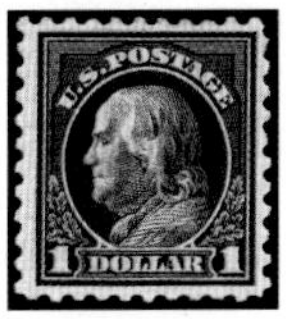

423, 478, 518
Franklin

SCOTT NO.	DESCRIPTION	UNUSED O.G. VF	F	AVG	USED VF	F	AVG
	1912-14 Single Line Watermark Perf. 12 (NH + 60%)						
405	1¢ green	16.50	9.50	5.50	.30	.25	.20
405b	1¢ booklet pane of 6	95.00	65.00	45.00	......	......	......
406	2¢ carmine (I)	9.00	5.50	3.50	.30	.25	.20
406a	2¢ booklet pane of 6	95.00	65.00	45.00	......	......	......
407	7¢ black	110.00	65.00	45.00	15.00	10.00	6.50
	1912 Imperforate						
408	1¢ green	2.75	2.00	1.50	.90	.60	.40
409	2¢ carmine (I)	3.95	3.00	2.00	1.00	.70	.50

PLATE BLOCKS OF 6

SCOTT NO.	UNUSED NH F	AVG	UNUSED OG F	AVG
397	195.00	135.00	145.00	95.00
398	325.00	260.00	215.00	150.00
401	425.00	250.00	275.00	195.00
405	140.00	70.00	90.00	60.00
406	160.00	120.00	100.00	70.00
408	32.00	24.00	19.00	14.00
409	56.00	40.00	36.00	25.00

SCOTT NO.	UNUSED NH F	AVG	UNUSED OG F	AVG
	CENTER LINE BLOCKS			
408	15.50	11.00	11.00	8.50
409	17.00	11.95	14.50	9.50
	ARROW BLOCKS			
408	10.00	9.00	7.50	6.00
409	12.00	10.00	10.00	8.00

SCOTT NO.	DESCRIPTION	UNUSED O.G. VF	F	AVG	USED VF	F	AVG
	COIL STAMPS 1912 Perf. 8-1/2 Horizontally (NH + 60%)						
410	1¢ green	8.50	5.00	3.50	6.00	3.50	2.10
411	2¢ carmine (I)	14.00	8.50	5.50	5.00	3.25	2.00
	1912 Perf. 8-1/2 Vertically						
412	1¢ green	32.00	22.00	15.00	8.00	5.00	3.50
413	2¢ carmine (I)	55.00	36.00	24.00	2.50	1.75	1.10

(NH + 60%)

SCOTT NO.	COIL LINE PAIRS UNUSED OG VF	F	AVG	COIL PAIRS UNUSED OG VF	F	AVG
410	48.00	29.00	18.00	19.00	12.50	8.00
411	70.00	45.00	30.00	30.00	20.00	12.50
412	150.00	100.00	65.00	80.00	60.00	40.00
413	295.00	200.00	135.00	135.00	95.00	65.00

SCOTT NO.	DESCRIPTION	UNUSED O.G. VF	F	AVG	USED VF	F	AVG
	1912-14 Perf. 12 Single Line Watermark (NH + 60%)						
414	8¢ pale olive green	67.50	44.00	28.00	2.35	1.30	1.00
415	9¢ salmon red	80.00	51.00	30.00	17.50	11.00	7.25
416	10¢ orange yellow	60.00	38.00	24.00	.75	.50	.35
417	12¢ claret brown	65.00	43.00	28.00	6.50	4.25	2.85
418	15¢ gray	125.00	77.00	50.00	5.60	3.50	2.40
419	20¢ ultramarine	275.00	185.00	115.00	24.00	14.00	10.00
420	30¢ orange red	160.00	105.00	65.00	24.00	14.00	10.00
421	50¢ violet	575.00	340.00	225.00	25.00	16.00	11.00
	1912 Double Line Watermark "USPS" Perf 12						
422	50¢ violet	350.00	225.00	150.00	28.00	18.00	12.00
423	$1 violet black	675.00	425.00	250.00	85.00	50.00	32.00
	1914-15 Single Line Watermark, "USPS" Perf. 10 (NH + 60%)						
424-40	**1¢-50¢ (16 varieties, complete) . . .**	**2120.00**	**1275.00**	**900.00**	**120.00**	**79.00**	**51.00**
424	1¢ green	6.50	4.00	2.50	.25	.20	.15
424d	1¢ booklet pane of 6	8.00	4.00	3.00	....	....	....
425	2¢ rose red . .	5.00	2.50	1.75	.25	.20	.15
425e	2¢ booklet pane of 6	30.00	23.00	16.00	....	....	....
426	3¢ deep violet (I)	32.50	20.00	13.00	2.65	1.50	1.00
427	4¢ brown	45.00	28.00	20.00	1.00	.65	.45
428	5¢ blue	40.00	28.00	20.00	1.00	.65	.45
429	6¢ red orange	70.00	45.00	30.00	2.75	1.75	1.00
430	7¢ black	135.00	79.00	59.00	8.00	5.00	3.00
431	8¢ pale olive green	60.00	39.00	24.00	2.95	2.10	1.40
432	9¢ salmon red	77.50	42.00	27.00	14.50	10.00	6.00
433	10¢ orange yellow	67.50	40.00	27.00	1.00	.75	.45
434	11¢ dark green	42.50	28.00	20.00	11.50	7.00	5.00
435	12¢ claret brown	40.00	26.00	18.00	10.00	7.00	4.00
437	15¢ gray	160.00	100.00	75.00	11.50	7.00	4.80
438	20¢ ultramarine	280.00	170.00	120.00	6.95	4.75	3.00
439	30¢ orange red	385.00	210.00	165.00	26.50	17.00	11.50
440	50¢ violet	800.00	500.00	325.00	28.00	18.00	12.00

UNUSED PLATE BLOCKS OF 6

SCOTT NO.	NH F	NH AVG	OG F	OG AVG
414	525.00	350.00	400.00	250.00
415	750.00	525.00	525.00	375.00
416	650.00	425.00	400.00	280.00
417	700.00	475.00	450.00	300.00
418	900.00	650.00	600.00	450.00
424 (6)	55.00	40.00	30.00	20.00
424 (10)	190.00	120.00	130.00	80.00
425 (6)	30.00	20.00	20.00	15.00
425 (10)	180.00	120.00	130.00	90.00
426	200.00	140.00	150.00	100.00
427	575.00	400.00	425.00	300.00
428	475.00	300.00	350.00	200.00
429	500.00	300.00	325.00	190.00
430	1200.00	850.00	800.00	550.00
431	500.00	395.00	400.00	280.00
432	800.00	575.00	600.00	425.00
433	800.00	575.00	600.00	425.00
434	275.00	180.00	200.00	115.00
435	355.00	200.00	240.00	150.00
437	1200.00	850.00	850.00	625.00
438	3850.00	2950.00	2500.00	1950.00
439	5250.00	3750.00	3250.00	2500.00
440	17000.00	11500.00	12500.00	9000.00

SCOTT NO.	DESCRIPTION	UNUSED O.G. VF	F	AVG	USED VF	F	AVG
	COIL STAMPS 1914 Perf. 10 Horizontally (NH + 60%)						
441	1¢ green	2.75	1.50	1.00	1.40	1.00	.65
442	2¢ carmine (I)	17.50	11.00	7.00	11.00	7.20	4.00
	1914 Perf.10 Vertically (NH + 60%)						
443	1¢ green	42.50	28.00	18.00	8.50	5.00	3.00
444	2¢ carmine (I)	47.50	28.00	17.00	2.75	1.95	1.20
445	3¢ violet (I) . . .	350.00	225.00	160.00	185.00	120.00	75.00
446	4¢ brown	210.00	140.00	105.00	70.00	42.00	30.00
447	5¢ blue	70.00	45.00	32.00	60.00	40.00	25.00

SCOTT NO.	DESCRIPTION	UNUSED O.G. VF	F	AVG	USED VF	F	AVG
	ROTARY PRESS COIL STAMPS 1915-16 Perf. 10 Horizontally (NH + 60%)						
448	1¢ green	9.50	7.00	4.00	5.00	3.50	2.25
449	2¢ red (I)	3500.00	2100.00	1450.00	550.00	425.00	260.00
450	2¢ carmine (III)	27.50	20.00	14.00	6.00	4.00	2.00
	1914-16 Perf. 10 Vertically (NH + 60%)						
452	1¢ green	22.50	16.00	12.00	3.50	2.50	1.75
453	2¢ carmine rose (I)	160.00	110.00	75.00	6.00	3.75	3.00
454	2¢ red (II)	145.00	100.00	65.00	16.00	9.00	6.00
455	2¢ carmine (III)	14.00	10.00	6.50	1.95	1.50	.75
456	3¢ violet (I) . . .	425.00	285.00	180.00	155.00	90.00	60.00
457	4¢ brown	55.00	28.00	20.00	32.00	20.00	12.00
458	5¢ blue.	45.00	30.00	20.00	32.00	20.00	12.00
	1914 Imperforate Coil (NH + 60%)						
459	2¢ carmine (I)	450.00	375.00	300.00	1100.00	800.00	....
	1915 Flat Plate Printing Double Line Watermark Perf. 10 (NH + 60%)						
460	$1 violet black	1250.00	750.00	525.00	135.00	80.00	55.00
	1915 Single Line Watermark "USPS" Perf. 11 (NH + 60%)						
461	2¢ pale carmine red (I)	200.00	115.00	65.00	400.00	210.00	125.00
	1916-17 Unwatermarked Perf. 10 (NH + 60%)						
462	1¢ green	13.50	9.50	6.00	.75	.40	.25
462a	1¢ booklet pane of 6	16.00	10.00	6.00	....	....	....
463	2¢ carmine (I)	7.95	5.50	3.50	.40	.30	.20
463a	2¢ booklet pane of 6	110.00	80.00	55.00	....	....	....
464	3¢ violet (I) . . .	120.00	65.00	48.00	21.50	14.00	9.00
465	4¢ orange brown	66.50	42.00	25.00	3.25	2.25	1.35
466	5¢ blue	120.00	65.00	40.00	3.25	2.25	1.35
467	5¢ carmine (error)	950.00	575.00	350.00	1000.00	650.00	450.00
468	6¢ red orange	140.00	75.00	45.00	12.50	7.00	4.00
469	7¢ black	180.00	100.00	68.00	20.00	12.00	7.00
470	8¢ olive green	110.00	62.00	41.00	10.50	6.00	4.00
471	9¢ salmon red	122.50	68.00	44.00	22.50	15.00	9.00
472	10¢ orange yellow	160.00	88.00	65.00	2.00	1.50	.90
473	11¢ dark green	67.50	43.00	25.00	30.00	17.00	11.50
474	12¢ claret brown	90.00	58.00	42.00	10.00	6.00	4.00
475	15¢ gray	250.00	175.00	100.00	20.00	11.00	8.00
476	20¢ light ultramarine	400.00	220.00	160.00	20.50	12.00	8.00
476A	30¢ orange red	....	4800.00	....	....	....	....
477	50¢ light violet	1600.00	950.00	625.00	110.00	70.00	45.00
478	$1 violet black.	1175.00	675.00	500.00	31.50	21.50	12.50
	Design of 1902-03						
479	$2 dark blue . .	450.00	310.00	225.00	74.50	42.00	33.50
480	$5 light green .	395.00	250.00	150.00	80.00	45.00	32.00
	1916-17 Imperforate (NH + 60%)						
481	1¢ green	2.50	1.75	.75	1.50	1.00	.50
482	2¢ carmine (I)	2.50	2.00	1.00	2.50	1.50	1.00
483	3¢ violet (I) . . .	35.00	25.00	17.00	10.00	8.00	6.00
484	3¢ violet (II) . .	22.50	19.00	13.00	6.75	5.25	4.00

(NH + 60%)

SCOTT NO.	COIL LINE PAIRS UNUSED OG VF	F	AVG	COIL PAIRS UNUSED OG VF	F	AVG
441	10.00	7.00	4.00	5.75	3.75	2.50
442	90.00	48.00	30.00	35.00	20.00	14.00
443	180.00	120.00	75.00	90.00	55.00	37.00
444	295.00	210.00	130.00	100.00	60.00	42.00
445	1600.00	900.00	600.00	740.00	495.00	350.00
446	900.00	500.00	350.00	445.00	275.00	155.00
447	325.00	185.00	127.00	175.00	110.00	75.00
448	62.00	39.00	25.00	32.00	18.00	12.00
450	90.00	65.00	40.00	58.00	40.00	25.00
452	115.00	65.00	40.00	47.50	35.00	20.00
453	850.00	500.00	350.00	400.00	250.00	160.00
454	750.00	425.00	325.00	350.00	200.00	140.00
455	90.00	50.00	35.00	32.00	18.00	12.00
456	1350.00	900.00	550.00	900.00	625.00	365.00
457	240.00	130.00	90.00	115.00	80.00	52.00
458	250.00	145.00	95.00	115.00	85.00	50.00
459	1800.00	1250.00	900.00	1050.00	850.00	500.00

***NOTE:** For further details on the various types of similar appearing stamps please refer to our U.S. Stamp Identifier.*

UNUSED PLATE BLOCKS OF 6

SCOTT NO.	NH F	NH AVG	OG F	OG AVG	SCOTT NO.	NH F	NH AVG	OG F	OG AVG
462	195.00	125.00	125.00	80.00	472	1600.00	1200.00	1200.00	800.00
463	155.00	100.00	100.00	60.00	473	450.00	325.00	300.00	200.00
464	1500.00	1100.00	1150.00	825.00	474	775.00	500.00	500.00	325.00
465	800.00	500.00	600.00	425.00	481	17.00	12.00	12.00	8.00
466	1100.00	850.00	950.00	565.00	482	35.00	22.00	22.50	17.00
470	675.00	500.00	545.00	320.00	483	200.00	160.00	160.00	110.00
471	850.00	675.00	595.00	400.00	484	140.00	90.00	115.00	80.00
	CENTER LINE BLOCKS					**ARROW BLOCKS**			
481	8.00	5.00	4.00	3.00	481	8.00	5.00	4.00	3.00
482	11.00	7.00	7.75	4.75	482	11.00	7.00	7.75	4.75
483	130.00	95.00	97.50	72.50	483	125.00	90.00	95.00	70.00
484	80.00	55.00	70.00	55.00	484	75.00	50.00	65.00	50.00

SCOTT NO.	DESCRIPTION	UNUSED O.G. VF	F	AVG	USED VF	F	AVG
	ROTARY PRESS COIL STAMPS 1916-19 Perf. 10 Horizontally (NH + 60%)						
486	1¢ green	1.75	1.00	.50	.40	.30	.20
487	2¢ carmine (II)	32.50	19.00	12.00	7.00	5.00	3.00
488	2¢ carmine (III)	5.95	3.75	2.50	2.40	1.75	1.00
489	3¢ violet (I) . . .	7.00	4.50	3.00	2.75	1.95	1.00
	1916-22 Perf. 10 Vertically (NH + 60%)						
490	1¢ green	1.00	.50	.50	.35	.25	.15
491	2¢ carmine (II)	2500.00	1600.00	1000.00	800.00	550.00	375.00
492	2¢ carmine (III)	16.00	9.00	6.00	.40	.25	.20
493	3¢ violet (I) . . .	37.50	21.00	16.00	5.00	3.00	2.00
494	3¢ violet (II) . .	22.50	13.00	8.50	1.40	.95	.75
495	4¢ orange brown	22.50	13.00	9.00	6.50	3.75	2.50
496	5¢ blue	7.00	4.00	3.00	1.60	1.00	.75
497	10¢ orange yellow	35.00	20.00	15.00	15.00	10.00	5.25

(NH + 60%)

SCOTT NO.	COIL LINE PAIRS UNUSED OG VF	F	AVG	COIL PAIRS UNUSED OG VF	F	AVG
486	6.50	4.50	3.50	3.25	2.00	1.25
487	160.00	105.00	75.00	67.50	42.00	25.00
488	28.00	18.00	12.00	12.50	9.00	5.75
489	40.00	30.00	24.00	16.00	10.00	7.00
490	6.00	3.75	1.90	2.50	1.50	.90
491	......	8000.00	4950.00	5450.00	3500.00	2250.00
492	70.00	50.00	35.00	36.00	20.00	14.00
493	160.00	100.00	70.00	78.75	60.00	35.00
494	90.00	60.00	48.00	47.00	35.00	19.50
495	100.00	75.00	55.00	47.00	35.00	19.25
496	40.00	28.00	19.50	15.00	9.00	7.00
497	160.00	115.00	75.00	75.00	45.00	35.00

1917-19 Flat Plate Printing Perf. 11 (NH + 60%)

SCOTT NO.	DESCRIPTION	UNUSED O.G. VF	F	AVG	USED VF	F	AVG
498/518	**(498-99, 501-04, 506-18) 19 varieties**	**640.00**	**395.00**	**265.00**	**35.00**	**22.25**	**16.95**
498	1¢ green	.80	.50	.50	.35	.25	.20
498e	1¢ booklet pane of 6	4.50	2.75	2.00	....	....	....
498f	1¢ booklet pane of 30	1300.00	800.00	550.00	....	....	....
499	2¢ rose (I) . . .	.80	.50	.25	.35	.25	.20
499e	2¢ booklet pane of 6	7.00	4.50	3.50	....	....	....
500	2¢ deep rose (Ia)	400.00	225.00	165.00	250.00	175.00	100.00
501	3¢ light violet (I)	20.00	12.00	8.00	.35	.25	.20
501b	3¢ booklet pane of 6	95.00	65.00	45.00	....	....	....
502	3¢ dark violet (II)	26.00	15.00	10.00	.80	.55	.35
502b	3¢ booklet pane of 6	80.00	45.00	30.00	....	....	....
503	4¢ brown	18.00	10.00	6.00	.50	.35	.20
504	5¢ blue	14.00	8.00	5.00	.55	.40	.25
505	5¢ rose (error)	680.00	400.00	275.00	700.00	475.00	300.00
506	6¢ red orange	22.00	13.00	8.00	.65	.50	.35
507	7¢ black	42.00	25.00	17.00	2.00	1.45	.80
508	8¢ olive bistre	17.00	10.00	6.00	1.45	1.20	.80
509	9¢ salmon red	24.00	14.00	9.00	3.65	2.30	1.65
510	10¢ orange yellow	28.00	16.00	10.00	.30	.25	.20
511	11¢ light green	14.00	8.00	3.00	5.60	3.50	2.40
512	12¢ claret brown	14.00	8.00	3.00	1.15	.65	.50
513	13¢ apple green	19.00	11.00	7.00	12.00	7.00	6.40
514	15¢ gray	64.00	38.00	26.00	1.60	1.00	.75
515	20¢ light ultramarine	85.00	46.00	34.00	.55	.35	.25
516	30¢ orange red	70.00	40.00	30.00	1.60	1.00	.85
517	50¢ red violet .	100.00	75.00	50.00	1.50	.80	.75
518	$1 violet black	95.00	65.00	45.00	3.00	2.00	1.25
	1917 Design of 1908-09 Double Line Watermark Perf. 11						
519	2¢ carmine . . .	700.00	375.00	250.00	1100.00	850.00	500.00

SCOTT NO.	NH F	NH AVG	OG F	OG AVG	SCOTT NO.	NH F	NH AVG	OG F	OG AVG
UNUSED PLATE BLOCKS OF 6									
498	19.50	14.75	14.00	12.00	511	200.00	110.00	150.00	90.00
499	19.50	14.75	14.00	12.00	512	185.00	110.00	130.00	85.00
501	170.00	128.00	140.00	100.00	513	185.00	105.50	145.00	85.00
502	190.00	175.00	165.00	128.00	514	835.00	465.00	595.00	385.00
503	190.00	150.00	135.00	115.00	515	975.00	565.00	675.00	425.00
504	165.00	100.00	135.00	80.00	516	750.00	440.00	600.00	350.00
506	230.00	155.00	180.00	125.00	517	2000.00	1350.00	1300.00	900.00
507	350.00	265.00	250.00	210.00	518	1500.00	925.00	1050.00	685.00
508	220.00	150.00	175.00	120.00	519	3500.00	1950.00	2500.00	1500.00
509	220.00	150.00	175.00	120.00	**ARROW BLOCK**				
510	260.00	215.00	165.00	125.00	518	450.00	280.00	300.00	225.00

523, 547
Franklin

524
Franklin

SCOTT NO.	DESCRIPTION	UNUSED O.G. VF	F	AVG	USED VF	F	AVG
1918 Unwatermarked (NH + 60%)							
523	$2 orange red & black.......	1250.00	850.00	600.00	350.00	240.00	150.00
524	$5 deep green & black......	425.00	305.00	215.00	50.00	35.00	20.00
1918-20 Offset Printing Perf. 11 (NH + 60%)							
525	1¢ gray green	6.00	4.00	2.50	1.25	.85	.50
526	2¢ carmine (IV)	42.50	30.00	16.00	6.00	4.25	2.75
527	2¢ carmine (V)	35.00	23.00	14.00	1.95	1.30	.75
528	2¢ carmine (Va)	17.00	11.00	8.00	.60	.50	.35
528A	2¢ carmine (VI)	70.00	53.00	35.00	2.00	1.50	1.00
528B	2¢ carmine (VII)	32.00	21.00	15.00	.60	.50	.35
529	3¢ violet (III). .	7.50	5.50	4.50	.45	.35	.25
530	3¢ purple (IV) .	2.50	1.75	1.25	.45	.30	.20
1918-20 Offset Printing Imperforate							
531	1¢ gray green	22.50	14.00	10.50	13.00	8.00	6.00
532	2¢ carmine rose (IV)	85.00	60.00	46.00	40.00	28.00	19.00
533	2¢ carmine (V)	345.00	260.00	190.00	125.00	90.00	65.00
534	2¢ carmine (Va)	37.50	33.00	19.00	10.00	7.50	5.00
534A	2¢ carmine (VI)	55.00	40.00	29.00	44.00	29.00	21.50
534B	2¢ carmine (VII)	2500.00	1800.00	1350.00	1050.00	925.00	600.00
535	3¢ violet (IV) .	18.50	13.00	9.00	10.00	6.50	4.00
1919 Offset Printing Perf. 12-1/2							
536	1¢ gray green	40.00	28.00	18.00	30.00	18.50	12.00

537
"Victory" and Flags

SCOTT NO.	DESCRIPTION	UNUSED O.G. VF	F	AVG	USED VF	F	AVG
1919 VICTORY ISSUE (NH + 50%)							
537	3¢ violet.....	18.50	10.50	6.50	6.50	4.00	2.50
1919-21 Rotary Press Printings—Perf. 11 x 10 (†) (NH + 50%)							
538	1¢ green	18.50	10.50	7.00	15.00	10.00	7.50
538a	Same, imperf. horizontally . .	80.00	50.00	36.00	....	....	....
539	2¢ carmine rose (II)	3300.00	2700.00	1800.00	....	3300.00	2300.00
540	2¢ carmine rose (III)	17.50	10.00	6.00	16.00	9.50	6.50
540a	Same, imperf. horizontally . .	75.00	45.00	36.00	....	....	....
541	3¢ violet (II) . .	60.00	36.00	28.00	52.00	30.00	22.50
Perf. 10 x 11							
542	1¢ green	17.00	11.00	7.00	1.60	1.00	.75
Perf. 10							
543	1¢ green	1.35	.75	.50	.65	.40	.20

SCOTT NO.	DESCRIPTION	UNUSED O.G. VF	F	AVG	USED VF	F	AVG
Perf. 11							
544	1¢ green (19 x 22-1/2mm)	....	18000.00	14200.00	....	3300.00	2500.00
545	1¢ green (19-1/2 x 22mm)	210.00	140.00	90.00	225.00	140.00	95.00
546	2¢ carmine rose (III)	145.00	95.00	60.00	245.00	150.00	100.00
1920 Flat Plate Printing Perf. 11							
547	$2 carmine & black	435.00	310.00	205.00	67.50	42.50	32.50

SCOTT NO.	NH F	NH AVG	OG F	OG AVG	SCOTT NO.	NH F	NH AVG	OG F	OG AVG
UNUSED PLATE BLOCKS OF 6					**UNUSED PLATE BLOCKS OF (—)**				
525 (6)	29.00	22.50	20.00	14.00	535 (6)	105.00	85.00	85.00	65.00
526 (6)	260.00	200.00	185.00	140.00	536 (6)	215.00	155.00	155.00	115.00
527 (6)	225.00	150.00	140.00	100.00	537 (6)	150.00	105.00	100.00	75.00
528 (6)	125.00	85.00	80.00	50.00	538 (4)	110.00	80.00	75.00	50.00
528A (6)	500.00	325.00	350.00	225.00	540 (4)	130.00	80.00	80.00	50.00
528B (6)	210.00	140.00	145.00	100.00	541 (4)	465.00	325.00	310.00	210.00
529 (6)	75.00	50.00	50.00	35.00	542 (6)	195.00	135.00	135.00	90.00
530 (6)	30.00	20.00	20.00	13.00	543 (4)	23.00	16.00	15.00	10.00
531 (6)	115.00	85.00	90.00	65.00	543 (6)	45.00	32.00	30.00	20.00
532 (6)	500.00	395.00	375.00	290.00	545 (4)	1200.00	800.00	950.00	675.00
533 (6)	2100.00	1800.00	1575.00	1175.00	546 (4)	1000.00	700.00	700.00	475.00
534 (6)	135.00	100.00	215.00	75.00	547 (8)	5250.00	4000.00	3800.00	2750.00
534A (6)	425.00	295.00	280.00	220.00	548 (6)	55.00	39.50	40.00	30.00
					549 (6)	84.00	58.75	60.00	45.00
					550 (6)	725.00	525.00	475.00	330.00
CENTER LINE					**ARROW BLOCKS**				
531	80.00	50.00	55.00	35.00	531	60.00	45.00	50.00	40.00
532	325.00	200.00	225.00	145.00	532	275.00	170.00	195.00	120.00
533	2000.00	1250.00	1000.00	650.00	533	1000.00	700.00	700.00	500.00
534	95.00	55.00	70.00	50.00	534	90.00	55.00	60.00	45.00
534A	275.00	200.00	185.00	125.00	534A	220.00	160.00	160.00	120.00
535	90.00	65.00	55.00	40.00	535	85.00	60.00	52.50	37.50
547	1400.00	975.00	1175.00	835.00	547	1275.00	900.00	1100.00	825.00

548
The "Mayflower"

549
Landing of the Pilgrims

550
Signing of the Compact

SCOTT NO.	DESCRIPTION	UNUSED O.G. VF	F	AVG	USED VF	F	AVG
1920 PILGRIM TERCENTENARY ISSUE (NH + 50%)							
548-50	**1¢-5¢ (3 varieties, complete) . . .**	**75.00**	**48.00**	**37.00**	**34.75**	**19.00**	**16.00**
548	1¢ green	9.50	6.50	4.75	5.50	3.00	2.00
549	2¢ carmine rose	11.00	7.00	4.00	3.50	2.00	1.60
550	5¢ deep blue .	65.00	40.00	32.00	27.50	15.00	13.50

FOR YOUR CONVENIENCE IN ORDERING, COMPLETE SETS ARE LISTED BEFORE SINGLE STAMP LISTINGS.

551, 653
Nathan Hale

552, 575, 578, 581, 594, 596, 597, 604, 632
Franklin

553, 576, 582, 598, 605, 631, 633
Harding

554, 577, 579, 583, 595, 599-99A, 606, 634-34A
Washington

555, 584, 600, 635
Lincoln

556, 585, 601, 636
Martha Washington

557, 586, 602, 637
Roosevelt

558, 587, 638, 723
Garfield

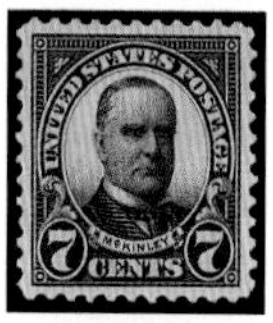
559, 588, 639
McKinley

560, 589, 640
Grant

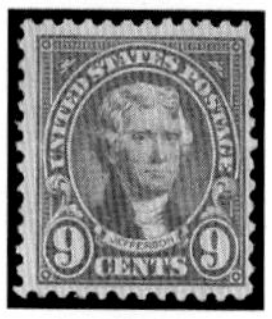
561, 590, 641
Jefferson

562, 591, 603, 642
Monroe

563, 692
Hayes

564, 693
Cleveland

565, 695
American Indian

566, 696
Statue of Liberty

567, 698
Golden Gate

568, 699
Niagara Falls

569,700
Bison

570, 701
Arlington Amphitheatre

571
Lincoln Memorial

572
U.S. Capitol

573
"America"

SCOTT NO.	DESCRIPTION	UNUSED O.G. VF	F	AVG	USED VF	F	AVG
	THE 1922-25 ISSUE Flat Plate Printings Perf. 11 (NH + 60%)						
551-73	**1/2¢-$5 (23 varieties, complete) . . .**	**1120.00**	**750.00**	**550.00**	**53.75**	**33.50**	**22.00**
551	1/2¢ olive brown (1925)	.60	.50	.25	.25	.20	.15
552	1¢ deep green (1923)	4.25	3.00	2.25	.25	.20	.15
552a	1¢ booklet pane of 6	9.00	6.50	4.50	....	....	....
553	1-1/2¢ yellow brown (1925)	5.25	3.25	2.50	.50	.35	.25
554	2¢ carmine (1923)	4.50	3.00	2.00	.25	.20	.15
554c	2¢ booklet pane of 6	11.00	8.00	5.00	....	....	....
555	3¢ violet (1923)	32.50	23.00	15.00	1.75	1.25	.85
556	4¢ yellow brown (1923)	33.50	24.00	15.00	.50	.35	.25
557	5¢ dark blue . .	33.50	24.00	15.00	.30	.20	.15
558	6¢ red orange	55.00	35.00	26.00	1.30	.80	.60
559	7¢ black (1923)	17.50	12.00	9.00	1.20	.70	.50
560	8¢ olive green (1923)	62.00	42.00	30.00	1.20	.80	.60
561	9¢ rose (1923)	26.50	16.00	10.50	2.45	1.40	1.00
562	10¢ orange (1923)	35.00	23.00	15.00	.30	.20	.15
563	11¢ light blue .	4.25	3.00	2.00	.75	.50	.30
564	12¢ brown violet (1923)	15.00	8.00	5.00	.30	.20	.15
565	14¢ blue (1923)	9.00	5.00	3.00	1.20	1.00	.60
566	15¢ gray	40.00	23.00	18.00	.25	.20	.15
567	20¢ carmine rose (1923)	40.00	25.00	20.00	.25	.20	.15
568	25¢ yellow green	33.50	21.00	15.00	1.00	.65	.50
569	30¢ olive brown (1923)	50.00	35.00	25.00	.80	.50	.35
570	50¢ lilac	85.00	50.00	40.00	.35	.20	.15
571	$1 violet black (1923)	67.50	45.00	34.00	.75	.50	.30
572	$2 deep blue (1923)	165.00	105.00	88.00	16.00	10.00	6.00
573	$5 carmine & blue (1923)	350.00	255.00	185.00	25.00	15.00	10.00
	1923-25 Imperforate						
575	1¢ green	16.50	12.00	9.00	7.75	4.50	3.00
576	1-1/2¢ yellow brown (1925)	3.25	2.00	1.25	3.00	1.60	1.25
577	2¢ carmine . . .	3.00	2.00	1.25	3.00	1.75	1.25
	Rotary Press Printings 1923 Perf. 11 x 10 (†) (NH + 60%)						
578	1¢ green	155.00	92.00	63.00	225.00	135.00	100.00
579	2¢ carmine . .	155.00	90.00	65.00	185.00	110.00	75.00
	1923-26 Perf. 10 (†)						
581-91	**1¢-10¢ (11 varieties, complete) . . .**	**285.00**	**175.00**	**122.00**	**25.00**	**16.25**	**10.75**
581	1¢ green	18.25	12.00	7.50	1.20	.85	.60
582	1-1/2¢ brown (1925)	6.00	4.00	3.00	1.20	.85	.60
583	2¢ carmine (1924)	4.00	2.00	1.25	.25	.20	.15
583a	2¢ booklet pane of 6 (1924)	110.00	70.00	50.00	....	....	....
584	3¢ violet (1925)	40.00	24.00	17.00	2.80	2.00	1.20
585	4¢ yellow brown (1925)	24.00	16.00	11.00	.80	.60	.40
586	5¢ blue (1925)	24.00	16.00	11.00	.45	.35	.20
587	6¢ red orange (1925)	18.50	10.00	6.50	1.00	.60	.40
588	7¢ black (1926)	25.00	16.00	10.50	9.00	6.00	4.00
589	8¢ olive green (1926)	40.00	24.00	15.00	5.00	3.25	2.00
590	9¢ rose (1926)	8.00	4.00	3.00	4.50	2.25	1.50
591	10¢ orange (1925)	90.00	55.00	42.00	.55	.45	.35
	Perf. 11 (†)						
594	1¢ green	....	19500.00	14500.00	....	5900.00	4750.00
595	2¢ carmine . . .	425.00	240.00	185.00	475.00	275.00	185.00
	Perf. 11						
596	1¢ green	....	....	....	....	70000.00	40000.00

SCOTT NO.		PLATE BLOCKS (6) UNUSED NH VF	F	AVG.	UNUSED OG VF	F	AVG.
551	1/2¢ olive brown (1923)	12.00	9.00	7.00	8.50	6.00	4.50
552	1¢ deep green (1923)	52.00	30.00	25.00	32.50	20.00	14.00
553	1-1/2¢ yellow brown (1923)	55.00	40.00	30.00	40.00	30.00	22.00
554	2¢ carmine (1923)	45.00	28.00	20.00	30.00	20.00	14.00
555	3¢ violet (1923)	350.00	225.00	180.00	195.00	150.00	110.00
556	4¢ yellow brown (1923)	350.00	225.00	180.00	195.00	150.00	110.00
557	5¢ dark blue	375.00	240.00	200.00	210.00	160.00	125.00
558	6¢ red orange	750.00	450.00	400.00	500.00	350.00	250.00
559	7¢ black (1923)	150.00	100.00	70.00	100.00	65.00	45.00
560	8¢ olive green (1923)........	1100.00	740.00	650.00	750.00	500.00	375.00
561	9¢ rose (1923)	340.00	225.00	160.00	195.00	160.00	130.00
562	10¢ orange (1923)	400.00	290.00	200.00	300.00	200.00	160.00
563	11¢ light blue	55.00	38.00	32.00	45.00	28.00	18.50
564	12¢ brown violet (1923)	170.00	100.00	70.00	145.00	80.00	70.00
565	14¢ blue (1923)	120.00	80.00	57.50	85.00	52.50	42.50
566	15¢ grey	500.00	350.00	240.00	350.00	225.00	175.00
567	20¢ carmine rose (1923) ..	475.00	320.00	240.00	400.00	220.00	190.00
568	25¢ yellow green	420.00	260.00	200.00	325.00	190.00	125.00
569	30¢ olive brown (1923)	550.00	375.00	295.00	325.00	225.00	160.00
570	50¢ lilac	1350.00	1000.00	750.00	850.00	600.00	450.00
571	$1 violet black (1923)	800.00	520.00	400.00	550.00	400.00	300.00
572	$2 deep blue (1923)	1750.00	1300.00	1000.00	1100.00	850.00	650.00
573	$5 carmine + blue (1923)..	5000.00	3750.00	2800.00	3500.00	2250.00	1750.00

SCOTT NO.		CENTER LINE BLOCKS F/NH	F/OG	AVG/OG	ARROW BLOCKS F/NH	F/OG	AVG/OG
571	$1 violet black	....	....	....	310.00	210.00	140.00
572	$2 deep blue	....	....	....	650.00	450.00	360.00
573	$5 carmine & blue	1050.00	900.00	750.00	1050.00	900.00	750.00
575	1¢ imperforate	58.00	50.00	40.00	55.00	47.50	38.00
576	1-1/2¢ imperforate	19.50	15.00	10.50	11.00	8.00	5.00
577	2¢ imperforate	22.50	17.50	12.00	12.00	9.00	7.00

SCOTT NO.		PLATE BLOCKS UNUSED NH VF	F	AVG.	UNUSED OG VF	F	AVG.
575 (6)	1¢ green	160.00	110.00	75.00	110.00	70.00	50.00
576 (6)	1-1/2¢ yellow brown (1925)	50.00	33.00	25.00	35.00	22.00	16.00
577 (6)	2¢ carmine	50.00	34.00	25.00	42.00	25.00	18.00
578	1¢ green	1350.00	875.00	675.00	1000.00	625.00	495.00
579	2¢ carmine	1100.00	700.00	525.00	695.00	450.00	350.00
581	1¢ green	225.00	140.00	100.00	160.00	100.00	70.00
582	1-1/2¢ brown (1925)	85.00	55.00	35.00	60.00	38.00	25.00
583	2¢ carmine (1923)	75.00	45.00	28.50	55.00	33.00	20.00
584	3¢ violet (1925)	400.00	260.00	190.00	260.00	190.00	150.00
585	4¢ yellow green (1925)	275.00	190.00	150.00	210.00	160.00	115.00
586	5¢ blue (1925)	375.00	240.00	170.00	275.00	170.00	120.00
587	6¢ red orange (1925)	200.00	130.00	85.00	140.00	90.00	60.00
588	7¢ black (1926)	250.00	155.00	100.00	175.00	110.00	70.00
589	8¢ olive green (1926)	400.00	260.00	190.00	275.00	190.00	125.00
590	9¢ rose (1926)	115.00	70.00	45.00	80.00	50.00	30.00
591	10¢ orange (1925)	1050.00	700.00	500.00	650.00	475.00	380.00

SCOTT NO.	DESCRIPTION	UNUSED VF	F	AVG	USED VF	F	AVG
	1923-29 Rotary Press Coil Stamps (NH + 50%)						
597/606	**597-99, 600-06 (10 varieties)**	**34.25**	**23.50**	**15.50**	**3.50**	**2.45**	**1.65**
	Perf. 10 Vertically						
597	1¢ green	.60	.25	.25	.25	.20	.15
598	1-1/2¢ deep brown (1925)	1.35	1.00	.75	.30	.20	.15
599	2¢ carmine (I) (1923)	.60	.50	.25	.25	.20	.15
599A	2¢ carmine (II) (1929)	200.00	110.00	70.00	22.00	13.50	8.50
600	3¢ violet (1924)	13.50	9.00	5.50	.35	.25	.15
601	4¢ yellow brown	8.00	5.50	4.00	1.00	.50	.30
602	5¢ dark blue (1924)	2.95	1.75	1.25	.40	.25	.15
603	10¢ orange (1924)	7.25	5.00	3.50	.35	.20	.15
	Perf. 10 Horizontally						
604	1¢ yellow green (1924)	.60	.50	.25	.25	.20	.15
605	1-1/2¢ yellow brown (1925)	.75	.50	.25	.45	.30	.20
606	2¢ carmine . . .	.65	.50	.25	.30	.20	.15

NOTE: For further details on the various types of similar appearing stamps please refer to our U.S. Stamp Identifier.

SCOTT NO.		UNUSED OG (NH + 40%) COIL LINE PAIRS VF	F	AVG.	COIL PAIRS VF	F	AVG.
597	1¢ green	2.55	1.95	1.40	1.10	.65	.45
598	1-1/2¢ brown (1925)	6.75	5.25	4.00	2.10	1.45	1.10
599	2¢ carmine (I)	2.15	1.65	1.20	1.25	.85	.55
599A	2¢ carmine (II) (1929)	850.00	575.00	385.00	425.00	225.00	150.00
600	3¢ deep violet (1924)	34.50	26.50	20.50	28.00	17.00	8.00
601	4¢ yellow brown	35.75	27.50	22.00	16.50	12.00	8.00
602	5¢ dark blue (1924)	11.75	9.00	6.00	6.25	4.25	2.75
603	10¢ orange (1924)	28.50	22.00	16.00	15.00	10.00	6.50
604	1¢ green (1924)	3.40	2.60	1.65	1.25	.75	.50
605	1-1/2¢ yellow brown (1925)	4.25	3.00	2.00	1.50	1.00	.75
606	2¢ carmine	2.75	2.00	1.35	1.25	.75	.50

610-613
Harding

SCOTT NO.	DESCRIPTION	UNUSED VF	F	AVG	USED VF	F	AVG
	1923 HARDING MEMORIAL ISSUE (NH + 50%)						
610	2¢ black, perf 11 flat	1.50	1.00	.75	.25	.20	.15
611	2¢ black, imperf	17.50	10.50	8.00	7.50	5.00	3.75
612	2¢ black, perf 10 rotary .	27.00	14.00	12.00	4.00	2.40	1.75
613	2¢ black perf 11 rotary	......	......	......	......	24000.00	19500.00

614
Ship "New Netherlands"

615
Landing at Fort Orange

616
Monument at Mayport, Fla.

SCOTT NO.	DESCRIPTION	UNUSED VF	F	AVG	USED VF	F	AVG
	1924 HUGUENOT-WALLOON ISSUE (NH + 40%)						
614-16	**1¢-5¢ (3 varieties, complete) . . .**	**69.00**	**49.00**	**36.00**	**30.00**	**21.00**	**15.00**
614	1¢ dark green	6.50	4.75	3.50	5.50	3.25	2.50
615	2¢ carmine rose	10.00	6.00	4.00	4.00	2.75	2.00
616	5¢ dark blue . .	57.50	45.00	35.00	21.00	16.00	11.00

617
Washington at Cambridge

618
Birth of Liberty

619
The Minute Man

SCOTT NO.	DESCRIPTION	UNUSED VF	F	AVG	USED VF	F	AVG
	1925 LEXINGTON-CONCORD SESQUICENTENNIAL (NH + 40%)						
617-19	**1¢-5¢ (3 varieties, complete) . . .**	**76.00**	**56.00**	**42.25**	**28.50**	**20.75**	**14.50**
617	1¢ deep green	8.75	5.50	4.75	4.00	2.50	1.75
618	2¢ carmine rose	13.50	9.00	6.00	6.00	4.50	3.50
619	5¢ dark blue . .	57.50	44.00	33.00	20.00	15.00	10.00

620
Sloop
"Restaurationen"

621
Viking Ship

1925 NORSE-AMERICAN ISSUE (NH + 40%)

SCOTT NO.	DESCRIPTION	UNUSED O.G. VF	F	AVG	USED VF	F	AVG
620-21	**2¢-5¢ (2 varieties, complete) . . .**	**45.00**	**28.50**	**19.25**	**21.25**	**14.25**	**10.00**
620	2¢ carmine & black	10.25	7.00	5.50	5.50	4.00	2.95
621	5¢ dark blue & black	37.50	23.00	15.00	17.00	11.00	7.75

622, 694
Harrison

623, 697
Wilson

6161925-26 Flat Plate Printings, Perf. 11

SCOTT NO.	DESCRIPTION	UNUSED O.G. VF	F	AVG	USED VF	F	AVG
622	13¢ green (1926)	24.00	15.00	11.00	1.35	.75	.60
623	17¢ black	28.00	17.00	13.00	.60	.40	.30

PLATE BLOCKS

SCOTT NO.		UNUSED NH VF	F	AVG.	UNUSED OG VF	F	AVG.
610 (6)	2¢ black perf 11 flat	45.00	30.00	22.00	33.00	23.00	18.00
611 (6)	2¢ black imperf.	210.00	140.00	90.00	160.00	105.00	80.00
611 (4)	2¢ black center line block .	110.00	85.00	60.00	77.50	60.00	45.00
611 (4)	2¢ black arrow block	58.00	45.00	32.50	45.00	35.00	25.00
612 (4)	2¢ black perf 10 rotary	500.00	370.00	300.00	390.00	275.00	210.00
614 (6)	1¢ dark green	80.00	54.00	40.00	60.00	39.00	25.00
615 (6)	2¢ carmine rose	150.00	90.00	65.00	110.00	75.00	55.00
616 (6)	5¢ dark blue	620.00	450.00	350.00	510.00	325.00	250.00
617 (6)	1¢ deep green	90.00	50.00	40.00	65.00	40.00	30.00
618 (6)	2¢ carmine rose	160.00	95.00	75.00	115.00	72.00	55.00
619 (6)	5¢ dark blue	510.00	395.00	300.00	410.00	315.00	220.00
620 (8)	2¢ carmine black	325.00	250.00	175.00	235.00	180.00	125.00
621 (8)	5¢ dark blue+black	1050.00	800.00	550.00	815.00	625.00	435.00
622 (6)	13¢ green (1926)	280.00	215.00	150.00	190.00	145.00	105.00
623 (6)	17¢ black	325.00	250.00	175.00	255.00	195.00	136.50

627
Liberty Bell

628
John Ericsson Statue

629, 630
Hamilton's Battery

1926-27 COMMEMORATIVES (NH + 40%)

SCOTT NO.	DESCRIPTION	UNUSED O.G. VF	F	AVG	USED VF	F	AVG
627/644	**627-29, 643-44 (5 varieties, complete) . . . . .**	**20.75**	**15.75**	**11.25**	**13.45**	**10.15**	**6.85**
	1926 COMMEMORATIVES						
627	2¢ Sesquicentennial	5.75	4.25	3.25	.85	.65	.45
628	5¢ Ericsson Memorial	15.50	12.00	8.50	5.25	3.85	2.75
629	2¢ White Plains	3.75	2.75	2.00	2.55	1.95	1.25
630	White Plains Sheet of 25	750.00	575.00	450.00	550.00	475.00	400.00
630V	2¢ Dot over "S" variety . . .	650.00	500.00	400.00	600.00	525.00	450.00
	Rotary Press Printings Designs of 1922-25 1926 Imperforate						
631	1-1/2¢ yellow brown	4.95	3.75	2.75	2.40	1.75	1.20
631	1-1/2¢ center line block	26.00	20.00	13.50	....	....	....
631	1-1/2¢ arrow block	12.25	9.50	6.50	....	....	....

SCOTT NO.	DESCRIPTION	UNUSED O.G. VF	F	AVG	USED VF	F	AVG
	1926-28 Perf. 11 x 10 1/2						
632/42	**1¢-10¢ (632-34, 635-42 11 varieties) . . .**	**40.25**	**30.75**	**23.25**	**2.60**	**2.10**	**1.55**
632	1¢ green (1927)	.50	.25	.25	.25	.20	.15
632a	1¢ booklet pane of 6	7.00	5.00	3.50	....	....	....
633	1-1/2¢ yellow brown (1927)	3.75	2.75	2.00	.25	.20	.15
634	2¢ carmine (I)	.40	.25	.25	.25	.20	.15
634	Electric Eye Plate	5.50	4.25	2.75	....	....	....
634d	2¢ booklet pane of 6	2.15	1.75	1.25	....	....	....
634A	2¢ carmine (II) (1928)	450.00	325.00	210.00	24.50	16.50	11.00
635	3¢ violet (1927)	1.00	.75	.50	.25	.20	.15
636	4¢ yellow brown (1927)	4.25	3.25	2.75	.25	.20	.15
637	5¢ dark blue (1927)	3.95	3.00	2.25	25	.20	.15
638	6¢ red orange (1927)	6.25	4.75	3.50	25	.20	.15
639	7¢ black (1927)	5.50	4.25	3.00	25	.20	.15
640	8¢ olive green (1927)	5.50	4.25	3.00	25	.20	.15
641	9¢ orange red (1931)	4.50	3.50	2.50	25	.20	.15
642	10¢ orange (1927)	6.75	5.50	4.00	.25	.20	.15

643

644

1927 COMMEMORATIVES

SCOTT NO.	DESCRIPTION	UNUSED O.G. VF	F	AVG	USED VF	F	AVG
643	2¢ Vermont . .	3.25	2.50	1.75	1.55	1.20	.85
644	2¢ Burgoyne .	6.95	5.50	3.75	3.95	3.00	1.95

645

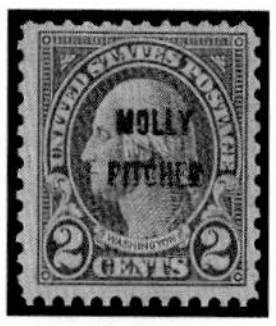

646

647

648

649

650

1928 COMMEMORATIVES (NH + 40%)

SCOTT NO.	DESCRIPTION	UNUSED O.G. VF	F	AVG	USED VF	F	AVG
645-50	**6 varieties, complete**	**36.00**	**25.75**	**18.00**	**32.50**	**23.50**	**16.00**
645	2¢ Valley Forge	2.50	2.00	1.50	.70	.55	.40
646	2¢ Molly Pitcher	2.35	2.00	1.50	1.40	1.10	.75
647	2¢ Hawaii	7.75	5.00	3.25	5.35	4.15	2.50
648	5¢ Hawaii	35.00	25.00	18.00	18.25	14.00	9.50
649	2¢ Aeronautics	3.50	2.25	1.75	1.75	1.00	.70
650	5¢ Aeronautics	12.50	8.50	6.50	7.25	4.00	3.00

651

654-656

657

1929 COMMEMORATIVES (NH + 40%)

SCOTT NO.	DESCRIPTION	UNUSED O.G. VF	F	AVG	USED VF	F	AVG
651/81	**651, 654-55, 657, 680-81 (6 varieties) .**	**10.25**	**8.25**	**5.25**	**5.00**	**3.70**	**2.75**
651	2¢ George R. Clark	2.25	1.25	1.25	1.00	.60	.50
	Same, arrow block of 4	4.50	3.35	2.35	....	....	....
	1929 Design of 1922-25 Rotary Press Printing Perf. 11x10-1/2						
653	1/2¢ olive brown	.60	.50	.50	.25	.20	.15

SCOTT NO.	DESCRIPTION	UNUSED O.G. VF	F	AVG	USED VF	F	AVG
	1929 COMMEMORATIVES						
654	2¢ Edison, Flat, Perf 11	2.15	1.75	1.25	1.15	.90	.65
655	2¢ Edison, Rotary, 11x10-1/2 . . .	1.50	1.25	1.00	.40	.30	.20
656	2¢ Edison, Rotary Press Coil, Perf. 10 Vertically	28.50	22.00	15.00	2.95	2.25	1.35
657	2¢ Sullivan Expedition	1.60	1.25	1.00	.85	.65	.50
	1929. 632-42 Overprinted Kansas (NH + 50%)						
658-68	**1¢-10¢ (11 varieties, complete) . . .**	**400.00**	**244.00**	**179.00**	**245.00**	**160.00**	**120.00**
658	1¢ green	5.00	3.00	2.25	4.00	2.50	1.75
659	1-1/2¢ brown .	6.50	4.50	2.75	5.00	3.00	2.75
660	2¢ carmine . . .	6.50	4.25	2.75	2.00	1.25	.80
661	3¢ violet	32.50	22.00	15.00	22.00	14.00	10.50
662	4¢ yellow brown	48.50	31.00	23.00	15.00	9.75	5.50
663	5¢ deep blue .	23.50	14.00	11.00	15.00	9.00	7.00
664	6¢ red orange	45.00	25.00	20.00	27.50	18.00	13.50
665	7¢ black	45.00	28.00	21.00	34.50	23.00	18.00
666	8¢ olive green	147.50	85.00	65.00	100.00	65.00	50.00
667	9¢ light rose . .	21.00	15.00	10.00	17.50	11.50	8.25
668	10¢ orange yellow	35.00	24.00	18.00	17.00	12.00	9.00
	1929. 632-42 Overprinted Nebraska (NH + 50%)						
669-79	**1¢-10¢, 11 varieties, complete. . . .**	**545.00**	**365.00**	**254.00**	**220.00**	**140.00**	**97.50**
669	1¢ green	6.00	4.00	2.50	3.00	1.90	1.35
670	1-1/2¢ brown .	6.00	3.75	2.25	3.50	1.95	1.35
671	2¢ carmine . . .	6.00	3.75	2.25	2.50	1.40	.90
672	3¢ violet	24.50	18.00	12.00	15.00	10.25	7.50
673	4¢ yellow brown	37.00	23.00	18.00	19.00	13.50	9.75
674	5¢ deep blue .	33.50	23.00	16.00	22.00	14.00	9.50
675	6¢ red orange	83.50	58.00	43.00	36.00	22.00	15.50
676	7¢ black	47.50	31.00	22.00	26.00	16.00	11.75
677	8¢ olive green	67.00	42.00	26.00	35.00	22.00	15.00
678	9¢ light rose . .	80.00	49.00	34.00	38.50	23.00	15.75
679	10¢ orange yellow	185.00	125.00	85.00	34.50	21.00	15.00

PLATE BLOCKS

SCOTT NO.		UNUSED NH VF	F	AVG.	UNUSED OG VF	F	AVG.
627 (6)	Sesquicentennial	65.00	50.00	35.00	49.50	38.00	26.00
628 (6)	5¢ Ericsson Memorial	145.00	110.00	77.50	110.00	85.00	60.00
629 (6)	2¢ White Plains	67.50	52.00	35.00	52.00	40.00	30.00
631	1-1/2¢ yellow brown	93.00	71.50	50.00	70.00	55.00	40.00
632	1¢ green	3.25	2.50	1.75	2.60	2.00	1.40
633	1-1/2¢ yellow brown (1927)	120.00	92.50	65.00	90.00	70.00	48.00
634	2¢ carmine (1)	2.60	1.95	1.40	2.10	1.70	1.25
635	3¢ violet	15.00	12.50	9.00	10.50	7.50	4.50
636	4¢ yellow brown (1927)	130.00	95.00	70.00	105.00	80.00	55.00
637	5¢ dark blue (1927)	29.50	22.50	15.75	22.75	17.50	12.75
638	6¢ red orange (1927)	29.50	22.50	15.75	22.75	17.50	12.75
639	7¢ black (1927)	29.50	22.50	15.75	22.75	17.50	12.75
640	8¢ olive green (1927)	29.50	22.50	15.75	22.75	17.50	12.75
641	9¢ orange red (1931)	30.00	23.00	16.00	23.00	18.00	13.00
642	10¢ orange (1927)	43.50	33.50	23.00	34.00	26.00	18.25
643 (6)	2¢ Vermont	65.00	50.00	35.00	58.00	42.00	28.00
644 (6)	2¢ Burgoyne	80.00	57.00	42.00	60.00	45.00	30.00
645 (6)	2¢ Valley Forge	58.00	40.00	28.00	41.00	30.00	19.50
646	2¢ Molly Pitcher	60.00	42.50	32.00	42.00	33.00	25.00
647	2¢ Hawaii	205.00	140.00	110.00	145.00	110.00	77.00
648	5¢ Hawaii	425.00	315.00	225.00	335.00	260.00	185.00
649 (6)	2¢ Aeronautics	24.00	18.00	12.00	19.50	14.00	10.00
650 (6)	5¢ Aeronautics	115.00	90.00	65.00	85.00	65.00	47.50
651 (6)	2¢ George R. Clark	19.50	15.00	10.00	14.50	11.00	7.50
653	1/2¢ olive brown	2.75	2.00	1.25	1.95	1.50	.95
654 (6)	2¢ Edison	51.00	39.50	28.00	40.00	31.50	22.50
655	2¢ Edison	70.00	55.00	40.00	58.00	45.00	30.50
657 (6)	2¢ Sullivan Expedition	45.00	35.00	26.50	39.50	30.00	22.50
	LINE PAIR						
656	2¢ Edison, coil	125.00	95.00	65.00	80.00	62.50	45.00

PLATE BLOCKS

SCOTT NO.		UNUSED NH VF	F	AVG.	UNUSED OG VF	F	AVG.
658	1¢ green	65.00	40.00	30.00	45.00	30.00	20.00
659	1-1/2¢ brown	80.00	50.00	35.00	60.00	38.00	25.00
660	2¢ carmine	80.00	50.00	35.00	60.00	38.00	25.00
661	3¢ violet	375.00	225.00	150.00	250.00	165.00	115.00
662	4¢ yellow brown	375.00	225.00	150.00	250.00	165.00	115.00
663	5¢ deep blue	275.00	165.00	125.00	185.00	120.00	90.00
664	6¢ red orange	850.00	550.00	400.00	525.00	325.00	225.00
665	7¢ black	850.00	550.00	400.00	525.00	325.00	225.00
666	8¢ olive green	1500.00	900.00	750.00	1000.00	625.00	475.00
667	9¢ light rose	450.00	300.00	200.00	295.00	200.00	125.00
668	10¢ orange yellow	650.00	425.00	295.00	425.00	285.00	195.00
669	1¢ green	85.00	50.00	40.00	55.00	35.00	25.00
670	1-1/2¢ brown	100.00	60.00	40.00	60.00	35.00	25.00
671	2¢ carmine	80.00	50.00	35.00	55.00	35.00	25.00
672	3¢ violet	350.00	200.00	140.00	225.00	135.00	95.00
673	4¢ yellow brown	475.00	300.00	200.00	325.00	200.00	140.00
674	5¢ deep blue	500.00	300.00	200.00	350.00	210.00	150.00
675	6¢ red orange	1000.00	550.00	450.00	650.00	375.00	265.00
676	7¢ black	550.00	325.00	225.00	335.00	215.00	155.00
677	8¢ olive green	750.00	450.00	315.00	475.00	350.00	250.00
678	9¢ light rose	1000.00	550.00	400.00	600.00	375.00	265.00
679	10¢ orange yellow	2000.00	1200.00	850.00	1200.00	750.00	550.00

680

681

SCOTT NO.	DESCRIPTION	UNUSED O.G. VF	F	AVG	USED VF	F	AVG
	1929 COMMEMORATIVES (NH + 30%)						
680	2¢ Fallen Timbers	2.50	2.00	1.25	1.05	.80	.55
681	2¢ Ohio River Canal	1.50	1.25	1.00	.85	.65	.50

682

683

684, 686

685, 687

1930-31 COMMEMORATIVES

SCOTT NO.	DESCRIPTION	UNUSED O.G. VF	F	AVG	USED VF	F	AVG
682/703	**(682-83, 688-90, 702-03) 7 varieties, complete**	**5.50**	**4.10**	**3.10**	**5.35**	**4.15**	**2.85**
	1930 COMMEMORATIVES						
682	2¢ Massachusetts Bay	1.50	1.25	1.00	.70	.60	.40
683	2¢ Carolina-Charleston	2.50	2.00	1.50	1.75	1.35	1.00
	1930 Rotary Press Printing Perf. 11 x 10-1/2 (NH + 30%)						
684	1-1/2¢ Harding	.75	.50	.50	.25	.20	.15
685	4¢ Taft	1.50	1.25	.75	.25	.20	.15
	1930 Rotary Press Coil Stamps Perf. 10 Vertically						
686	1-1/2¢ Harding	2.95	2.25	1.50	.25	.20	.15
687	4¢ Taft	4.75	3.75	2.50	.70	.55	.35

688

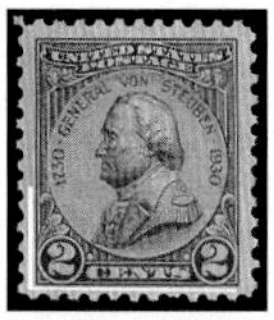

689

690

SCOTT NO.	DESCRIPTION	UNUSED O.G. VF	F	AVG	USED VF	F	AVG
	1930 COMMEMORATIVES						
688	2¢ Braddock's Field	1.95	1.50	1.00	1.45	1.00	.70
689	2¢ Von Steuben	1.10	1.00	.75	.70	.55	.40
	1931 COMMEMORATIVES						
690	2¢ Pulaski . . .	.75	.50	.50	.25	.20	.15

SCOTT NO.		PLATE BLOCKS UNUSED NH VF	F	AVG.	UNUSED OG VF	F	AVG.
680 (6)	2¢ Fallen Timbers	48.00	35.00	22.50	36.00	27.50	21.00
681 (6)	2¢ Ohio River Canal	33.75	25.00	15.75	26.00	20.00	12.00
682 (6)	2¢ Massachusetts Bay	58.50	40.00	27.00	39.00	30.00	18.00
683 (6)	2¢ Carolina-Charleston	85.00	60.00	40.00	64.50	49.50	36.00
684	1-1/2¢ Harding	3.65	2.50	1.70	2.90	2.25	1.65
685	4¢ Taft	17.00	12.00	9.00	13.00	10.00	6.00
688 (6)	3¢ Braddock's Field	71.50	47.50	33.00	52.00	40.00	24.00
689 (6)	2¢ Von Steuben	40.00	31.50	18.00	32.50	25.00	15.00
690 (6)	2¢ Pulaski	23.50	17.00	10.75	18.25	14.00	8.50
	LINE PAIR						
686	1-1/2¢ Harding	15.00	10.75	7.50	10.00	8.00	6.00
687	4¢ Taft	30.00	22.50	15.00	20.00	15.00	10.00

SCOTT NO.	DESCRIPTION	UNUSED VF	F	AVG	USED VF	F	AVG
	1931 Designs of 1922-26. Rotary Press Printing. (NH + 35%)						
692-701	11¢ to 50¢ (10 varieties, complete) . . .	184.00	140.00	105.00	3.25	2.50	1.80
	Perf. 11 x 10-1/2						
692	11¢ light blue .	5.50	4.25	3.50	.25	.20	.15
693	12¢ brown violet	10.50	8.00	5.50	.25	.20	.15
694	13¢ yellow green	4.00	3.00	2.25	.35	.25	.15
695	14¢ dark blue .	10.50	8.00	5.50	.90	.70	.50
696	15¢ gray	16.00	12.00	9.00	.25	.20	.15
	Perf. 10-1/2 x 11						
697	17¢ black	12.50	9.50	6.50	.45	.35	.25
698	20¢ carmine rose	16.50	13.00	9.00	.25	.20	.15
699	25¢ blue green	15.50	12.00	8.50	.25	.20	.15
700	30¢ brown . . .	36.50	28.00	21.00	.25	.20	.15
701	50¢ lilac	65.00	50.00	41.00	.25	.20	.15

702

703

1931 COMMEMORATIVES
(NH + 30%)

702	2¢ Red Cross	.50	.25	.25	.25	.20	.15
702	2¢ arrow block	1.50	1.00	.65	....	....	....
703	2¢ Yorktown .	.60	.50	.50	.60	.40	.30
703	2¢ center line block	3.00	2.15	1.75	....	....	....
703	2¢ arrow block	2.75	1.95	1.45	....	....	....

1932 WASHINGTON BICENTENNIAL ISSUE

Planning for this set, which celebrated the 200th anniversary of the birth of George Washington, began more than eight years before its release. Despite many suggestions that a pictorial series be created, the final set depicted 12 portraits of Washington at various stages of his life. For reasons of economy, the stamps were produced in single colors and in the same size as regular issues. Nevertheless, the set was an instant success and it was reported that more than a million covers were mailed from Washington, D.C. on January 1, 1932, the first day of issue.

704

705

706

707

708

709

710

711

712

713

714

715

SCOTT NO.	DESCRIPTION	UNUSED VF	F	AVG	USED VF	F	AVG
	(NH + 40%)						
704-15	1/2¢ to 10¢ (12 varieties, complete) . . .	55.75	41.00	30.00	4.00	3.05	2.40
704	1/2¢ olive brown	.35	.25	.25	.25	.20	.15
705	1¢ green	.40	.25	.25	.25	.20	.15
706	1-1/2¢ brown .	.75	.50	.25	.25	.20	.15
707	2¢ carmine rose	.40	.25	.25	.25	.20	.15
708	3¢ deep violet	1.15	1.00	.50	.25	.20	.15
709	4¢ light brown	.75	.50	.50	.25	.20	.15
710	5¢ blue.	4.50	3.50	2.50	.30	.20	.15
711	6¢ red orange	7.95	6.00	4.75	.25	.20	.15
712	7¢ black	.95	.75	.50	.35	.25	.20
713	8¢ olive bistre	9.50	6.00	4.75	1.20	.85	.75
714	9¢ pale red . .	7.15	5.00	3.50	.40	.30	.25
715	10¢ orange yellow	25.00	19.00	13.00	.25	.20	.15

716

717

718

719

1932 COMMEMORATIVES
(NH + 30%)

716/25	(716-19, 724-25) 6 varieties . . .	12.75	9.50	7.50	2.10	1.55	1.25
716	2¢ Winter Olympics	.95	.75	.50	.40	.30	.25
717	2¢ Arbor Day .	.40	.25	.25	.25	.20	.15
718	3¢ Summer Olympics	4.00	3.00	2.50	.25	.20	.15
719	5¢ Summer Olympics	6.00	4.50	3.50	.40	.30	.25

720-722

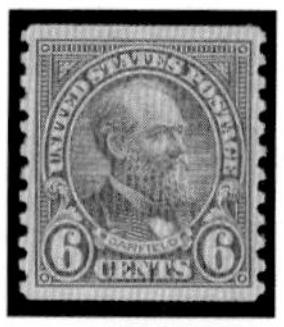
723

724

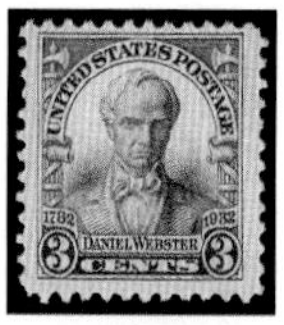
725

726

1932 Rotary Press

720	3¢ deep violet	.50	.25	.25	.25	.20	.15
720b	3¢ booklet pane of 6	60.00	40.00	28.00	....	....	....
721	3¢ deep violet coil perf 10 vertically	3.95	3.00	2.00	.25	.20	.15
722	3¢ deep violet coil perf 10 horizontally	2.95	2.25	1.50	1.00	.80	.65
723	6¢ Garfield, coil perf 10 vertically	17.50	13.00	9.00	.30	.25	.20
	1932 COMMEMORATIVES						
724	3¢ Penn	1.10	.75	.50	.35	.25	.20
725	3¢ Webster . .	1.30	.75	.50	.55	.40	.30

SCOTT NO.		UNUSED OG (NH + 30%) COIL LINE PAIRS VF	F	AVG.	COIL PAIRS VF	F	AVG.
686	1-1/2¢ Harding	10.00	8.00	5.50	4.50	3.50	2.25
687	4¢ Taft	20.00	15.00	10.00	9.00	7.00	4.75
721	3¢ deep violet perf 10 vertically	10.75	8.25	5.50	7.50	6.00	4.00
722	3¢ deep violet perf 10 horizontally	7.75	6.00	4.15	4.00	3.00	2.00
723	6¢ Garfield perf 10 vertically	71.50	55.00	33.00	27.50	21.00	14.00

727, 752

728, 730, 766

729, 731, 767

1933 COMMEMORATIVES (NH + 30%)

SCOTT NO.	DESCRIPTION	UNUSED VF	UNUSED F	UNUSED AVG	USED VF	USED F	USED AVG
726/34	**(726-29, 732-34) 7 varieties . . .**	**3.40**	**2.65**	**2.00**	**2.40**	**1.90**	**1.40**
726	3¢ Oglethorpe	1.30	.75	.75	.30	.25	.15
727	3¢ Washington's Headquarters .	.50	.50	.25	.25	.20	.15
728	1¢ Fort Dearborn	.60	.50	.25	.25	.20	.15
729	3¢ Federal Building	.80	.75	.50	.25	.20	.15

Special Printing for A.P.S. Convention
Imperforate: Without Gum

SCOTT NO.	DESCRIPTION	UNUSED VF	UNUSED F	UNUSED AVG	USED VF	USED F	USED AVG
730	1¢ yellow green, sheet of 25 . . .	....	42.50	....	....	42.50	....
730a	1¢ yellow green single	.85	.75	.45	.75	.60	.40
731	3¢ violet, sheet of 25	....	33.50	....	....	33.50	....
731a	3¢ violet, single	.65	.60	.45	.60	.50	.35

732

733, 735, 753, 768

734

736

SCOTT NO.	DESCRIPTION	UNUSED VF	UNUSED F	UNUSED AVG	USED VF	USED F	USED AVG
732	3¢ N.R.A	.40	.25	.25	.25	.20	.15
733	3¢ Byrd	1.50	1.25	1.00	.80	.60	.45
734	5¢ Kosciuszko	1.50	1.25	1.00	.45	.35	.25

1934 NATIONAL PHILATELIC EXHIBITION
Imperforate Without Gum

SCOTT NO.	DESCRIPTION	UNUSED VF	UNUSED F	UNUSED AVG	USED VF	USED F	USED AVG
735	3¢ dark blue, sheet of 6	....	18.50	....	....	15.00	....
735a	3¢ dark blue, single	3.50	3.25	....	2.75	2.10	....

737, 738, 754

739, 755

1934 COMMEMORATIVES (NH + 30%)

SCOTT NO.	DESCRIPTION	UNUSED VF	UNUSED F	UNUSED AVG	USED VF	USED F	USED AVG
736-39	**4 varieties . . .**	**1.95**	**1.45**	**.85**	**1.15**	**.90**	**.75**
736	3¢ Maryland . .	.55	.50	.25	.30	.25	.20
737	3¢ Mother's Day, rotary, perf 11 x 10-1/2	.50	.25	.25	.30	.25	.20
738	3¢ Mother's Day, flat, perf 11	.60	.50	.25	.30	.25	.20
739	3¢ Wisconsin .	.60	.50	.25	.30	.25	.20

FOR YOUR CONVENIENCE IN ORDERING, COMPLETE SETS ARE LISTED BEFORE SINGLE STAMP LISTINGS.

740, 751, 756, 769

741, 757

742, 750, 758, 770

743, 759

744, 760

745, 761

746, 762

747, 763

748, 764

749, 765

1934 NATIONAL PARKS ISSUE (NH + 30%)

SCOTT NO.	DESCRIPTION	UNUSED VF	UNUSED F	UNUSED AVG	USED VF	USED F	USED AVG
740-49	**1¢-10¢ (10 varieties, complete) . . .**	**22.25**	**16.00**	**12.75**	**9.25**	**7.10**	**4.80**
740	1¢ Yosemite .	.30	.25	.25	.25	.20	.15
741	2¢ Grand Canyon	.30	.25	.25	.25	.20	.15
742	3¢ Mt. Rainier	.50	.25	.25	.25	.20	.15
743	4¢ Mesa Verde	1.60	1.25	1.00	.60	.45	.30
744	5¢ Yellowstone	1.75	1.25	1.00	.85	.65	.45
745	6¢ Crater Lake	3.35	2.25	1.75	1.45	1.10	.70
746	7¢ Acadia . . .	1.75	1.25	1.00	1.15	.90	.60
747	8¢ Zion	4.50	3.50	2.50	2.75	2.10	1.45
748	9¢ Glacier . . .	4.25	3.00	2.50	.85	.65	.45
749	10¢ Great Smoky Mountains	5.00	3.75	3.00	1.30	1.00	.65

Special Printing for the A.P.S. Convention & Exhibition of Atlantic City
Imperforate Souvenir Sheet
(NH + 30%)

SCOTT NO.	DESCRIPTION	UNUSED VF	UNUSED F	UNUSED AVG	USED VF	USED F	USED AVG
750	3¢ deep violet, sheet of 6	....	45.00	....	....	40.00	....
750a	3¢ deep violet, single	6.50	5.50	....	6.00	5.00	....

Special Printing for Trans-Mississippi Philatelic Exposition and Convention at Omaha
Imperforate Souvenir Sheet
(NH + 30%)

SCOTT NO.	DESCRIPTION	UNUSED VF	UNUSED F	UNUSED AVG	USED VF	USED F	USED AVG
751	1¢ green, sheet of 6	....	16.50	....	....	16.00	....
751a	1¢ green, single	2.75	2.25	....	2.75	2.25	....

SCOTT NO.		PLATE BLOCKS UNUSED NH VF	F	AVG.	UNUSED OG VF	F	AVG.
692	11¢ light blue	22.50	16.50	10.00	16.50	12.75	9.50
693	12¢ brown violet	47.50	32.50	20.00	33.00	25.00	19.75
694	13¢ yellow green	21.50	16.50	10.00	16.50	12.75	9.50
695	14¢ dark blue	42.00	28.00	18.00	30.00	20.00	12.50
696	15¢ grey	65.00	50.00	35.00	46.75	36.00	27.00
697	17¢ black	47.50	35.00	22.50	34.50	26.50	18.00
698	20¢ carmine rose	75.00	55.00	40.00	55.00	43.00	30.00
699	25¢ blue green	75.00	60.00	40.00	55.00	45.00	30.00
700	30¢ brown	145.00	100.00	75.00	105.00	75.00	55.00
701	50¢ lilac	350.00	275.00	155.00	250.00	195.00	115.00
702	2¢ Red Cross	4.00	3.00	2.00	3.00	2.50	1.75
703	2¢ Yorktown (4)	5.75	4.00	2.70	4.25	3.35	2.65
704-15	Washington Bicentennial	590.00	435.00	290.00	445.00	335.00	248.50
704	1/2¢ olive brown	7.50	5.00	3.50	5.50	4.00	3.00
705	1¢ green	7.50	5.00	3.50	5.75	4.50	3.25
706	1-1/2¢ brown	34.50	23.50	17.00	25.00	18.00	13.25
707	2¢ carmine rose	3.00	2.00	1.25	2.25	1.60	1.10
708	3¢ deep violet	25.00	18.50	12.50	21.00	15.00	10.50
709	4¢ light brown	11.50	8.00	6.00	8.50	6.00	4.50
710	5¢ blue	30.00	22.00	16.00	23.50	18.00	14.00
711	6¢ red orange	105.00	80.00	49.50	78.00	60.00	46.50
712	7¢ black	12.00	8.50	6.00	9.00	7.00	5.50
713	8¢ olive bistre	105.00	80.00	49.50	78.00	60.00	40.00
714	9¢ pale red	80.00	55.00	40.00	57.50	42.50	30.00
715	10¢ orange yellow	200.00	150.00	100.00	155.00	115.00	90.00
716 (6)	2¢ Winter Olympics	22.00	16.00	11.00	16.95	13.00	9.50
717	2¢ Arbor Day	14.00	10.50	6.50	10.75	8.25	6.00
718	3¢ Summer Olympics	30.00	22.50	15.00	21.00	15.00	11.00
719	5¢ Summer Olympics	45.00	35.00	25.00	35.00	28.00	20.00
720	3¢ deep violet	2.95	2.00	1.40	2.15	1.65	1.10
724 (6)	3¢ Penn	20.00	14.00	9.50	14.00	11.00	9.00
725 (6)	3¢ Daniel Webster	35.75	26.00	14.00	28.00	22.00	16.00
726 (6)	3¢ Oglethorpe	23.50	16.50	11.00	18.00	14.00	10.00
727	3¢ Washington Hdqrs	10.00	7.00	4.50	7.95	6.00	4.50
728	1¢ Fort Dearborn	3.55	2.75	1.65	2.95	2.25	1.65
729	3¢ Federal Building	6.00	4.00	2.75	4.25	3.35	2.25
732	3¢ N.R.A.	2.95	2.00	1.40	2.55	1.95	1.40
733 (6)	3¢ Byrd	27.50	20.00	13.00	21.00	16.00	13.00
734 (6)	5¢ Kosciuszko	60.00	45.00	28.00	42.95	33.00	25.00
736 (6)	3¢ Maryland	17.50	12.50	8.25	13.00	10.00	8.25
737	3¢ Mother's Day, rotary perf. 11 x 10-1/2	2.95	2.00	1.30	2.40	1.75	1.40
738 (6)	3¢ Mother's Day, flat, perf. 11	8.50	6.50	3.95	6.50	5.00	3.85
739 (6)	3¢ Wisconsin	9.50	7.50	5.00	7.00	5.50	4.00
740-49	10 varieties complete	210.00	160.00	96.50	160.00	125.00	94.00
740 (6)	1¢ Yosemite	2.55	1.80	1.15	2.00	1.55	1.10
741 (6)	2¢ Grand Canyon	2.65	1.95	1.25	2.15	1.65	1.20
742 (6)	3¢ Mt. Rainier	3.50	2.75	1.65	3.00	2.30	1.55
743 (6)	4¢ Mesa Verde	15.50	12.00	7.25	13.00	10.00	7.00
744 (6)	5¢ Yellowstone	19.50	15.00	9.00	14.00	11.00	8.25
745 (6)	6¢ Crater Lake	33.50	26.00	15.50	26.50	20.50	15.50
746 (6)	7¢ Acadia	21.50	16.50	10.00	17.25	13.25	10.00
747 (6)	8¢ Zion	33.50	26.00	15.50	26.50	20.50	15.50
748 (6)	9¢ Glacier	33.50	26.00	15.50	26.50	20.50	15.50
749 (6)	10¢ Great Smoky Mountains	53.50	41.25	24.75	39.00	30.00	23.50

SELECTED U.S. COMMEMORATIVE MINT SHEETS

SCOTT NO.	F/NH SHEET	SCOTT NO.	F/NH SHEET
610 (100)	145.00	709 (100)	40.00
614 (50)	255.00	710 (100)	235.00
615 (50)	450.00	711 (100)	490.00
617 (50)	335.00	712 (100)	40.00
618 (50)	520.00	713 (100)	500.00
620 (100)	865.00	714 (100)	400.00
627 (50)	230.00	715 (100)	1750.00
628 (50)	595.00	716 (100)	67.50
629 (100)	300.00	717 (100)	26.00
643 (100)	285.00	718 (100)	195.00
644 (50)	290.00	719 (100)	305.00
645 (100)	235.00	724 (100)	50.00
646 (100)	220.00	725 (100)	82.50
647 (100)	675.00	726 (100)	55.00
648 (100)	2625.00	727 (100)	22.00
649 (50)	130.00	728 (100)	15.00
650 (50)	465.00	729 (100)	22.00
651 (50)	70.00	732 (100)	14.00
654 (100)	175.00	733 (50)	50.00
655 (100)	145.00	734 (100)	110.00
657 (100)	140.00	736 (100)	33.00
680 (100)	200.00	737 (50)	9.00
681 (100)	125.00	738 (50)	15.00
682 (100)	135.00	739 (50)	15.00
683 (100)	220.00	740-49 set	665.00
688 (100)	175.00	740 (50)	6.50
689 (100)	100.00	741 (50)	9.00
690 (100)	65.00	742 (50)	13.00
702 (100)	37.50	743 (50)	33.50
703 (50)	28.00	744 (50)	55.00
704-15 set	4500.00	745 (50)	85.00
704 (100)	25.00	746 (50)	46.50
705 (100)	30.00	747 (50)	120.00
706 (100)	71.50	748 (50)	115.00
707 (100)	30.00	749 (50)	215.00
708 (100)	95.00		

THE FARLEY PERIOD

The 1933-35 period was one of great excitement for the hobby. With a stamp collector in the White House, in the person of President Franklin Delano Roosevelt, it was a period during which special Souvenir Sheets were issued for the A.P.S. Convention in 1933 (catalog #730) and the National Philatelic Exhibition in 1934 (#735). Collectors gloried in the limelight.

But there was a darker side, in the form of rare imperforate sheets that were being released to then Postmaster General James A. Farley, President Roosevelt himself, and a few other prominent personages. The protests against the practice grew to unmanageable proportions when word got around that one of the imperforate sheets of the 1934 Mother's Day issue had been offered to a stamp dealer for $20,000. Adding insult to injury, it was learned shortly thereafter that not only were there individual sheets floating around, but full, uncut sheets also had been presented as gifts to a fortunate few.

The outcry that followed could not be stifled. Congress had become involved in the affair and the demands were mounting that the gift sheets be recalled and destroyed. This being deemed impractical or undesirable, another solution was found—one that comes down to us today in the form of "The Farleys".

The solution was to let everyone "share the wealth", so to speak. Instead of recalling the few sheets in existence, additional quantities of the imperforates were issued in the same full sheet form as the gift sheets. Naturally, this step substantially reduced the value of the original, very limited edition, but it satisfied most collectors and left as its legacy "The Farley Issues".

The Farleys were issued March 15, 1935, and consisted of reprints of 20 issues. They remained on sale for three months, a relatively short time by most standards, but more than enough time for collectors who really cared. Although purists felt then—and some still do now—that President Roosevelt would have saved collectors a considerable sum by having the first few sheets destroyed, the issue has provided us with a wondrous selection of Gutters and Lines, arrow blocks, single sheets and full panes.

The collector on a limited budget can fill the spaces in an album with single imperforates. But the Farleys are such an interesting study that owning and displaying at least one of each variety of any one issue is a must. We illustrate here one of the full sheets of the 1 cent Century of Progress Farley Issue. The full sheets consisted of nine panes of 25 stamps each. The individual panes were separated by wide horizontal **(A)** or vertical **(B)** gutters and the gutters of four adjacent sheets formed a cross gutter **(C)**.

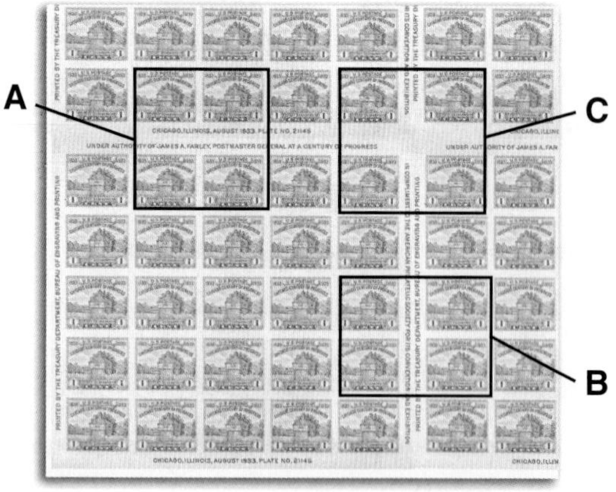

NOTE: For #s 753-765 and 771, lines separated the individual panes. The lines ended in arrows at the top, bottom and side margins.

1935 "FARLEY SPECIAL PRINTINGS"
Designs of 1933-34 Imperforate (#752, 753 Perf.) Without Gum

SCOTT NO.		PLATE BLOCK	CENTER LINE BLOCK	ARROW BLOCK T OR B	ARROW BLOCK L OR R	PAIR WITH V. LINE	PAIR WITH H. LINE	FINE UNUSED	FINE USED
752-71	**20 varieties, complete .**	....	**470.00**	....	....	**135.00**	**91.50**	**35.00**	**29.75**
752	3¢ Newburgh	22.50	50.00	16.50	9.50	7.50	4.50	.45	.20
753	3¢ Byrd . . .	(6)19.00	95.00	90.00	4.00	42.50	1.65	.75	.75
754	3¢ Mother's Day	(6)19.00	9.50	4.00	4.25	1.65	1.75	.75	.65
755	3¢ Wisconsin	(6)19.00	9.50	4.00	4.25	1.65	1.75	.75	.65
756-65	**1¢-10¢ Parks (10 varieties, complete)**	**295.00**	**150.00**	**140.00**	**140.00**	**42.25**	**43.50**	**19.50**	**17.00**
756	1¢ Yosemite	(6) 5.00	4.00	1.40	1.10	.60	.50	.30	.25
757	2¢ Grand Canyon . . .	(6) 6.50	5.50	1.55	1.45	.65	.85	.40	.30
758	3¢ Mt. Rainier	(6)16.50	6.50	3.60	4.00	1.55	1.75	.75	.65
759	4¢ Mesa Verde	(6)22.00	11.00	6.00	7.00	2.50	3.10	1.50	1.35
760	5¢ Yellowstone	(6)27.50	16.50	12.00	10.50	5.25	4.75	2.50	2.00
761	6¢ Crater Lake	(6)45.00	22.00	15.00	16.50	6.50	7.50	3.00	2.75
762	7¢ Acadia .	(6)36.00	18.00	10.50	12.25	4.50	5.50	2.25	2.00
763	8¢ Zion . . .	(6)45.00	20.00	14.50	12.00	6.25	5.35	2.75	2.25
764	9¢ Glacier .	(6)50.00	22.00	13.00	5.75	5.75	6.50	3.00	2.50
765	10¢ Great Smoky Mountains	(6)57.50	33.00	25.00	22.00	11.00	10.00	5.00	4.25
766a-70a	**5 varieties, complete .**	....	**95.00**	....	....	**40.00**	**35.50**	**9.45**	**7.75**
766a	1¢ Fort Dearborn	....	20.00	....	....	9.00	6.50	.75	.45
767a	3¢ Federal Building . .	....	21.50	....	....	9.00	6.50	.75	.45
768a	3¢ Byrd . . .	....	19.00	....	....	7.75	6.50	3.00	2.75
769a	1¢ Yosemite	....	12.00	....	....	5.25	5.00	1.85	1.50
770a	3¢ Mt. Rainier	....	28.00	....	....	11.50	13.00	3.60	3.05
771	16¢ Air Post Special Delivery . .	(6)80.00	82.50	15.00	16.50	6.75	7.50	3.50	3.20

U.S. FARLEY ISSUE COMPLETE MINT SHEETS

SCOTT NO.	F/NH SHEET	SCOTT NO.	F/NH SHEET
752-71 set	7500.00	761 (200)	650.00
752 (400)	400.00	762 (200)	500.00
753 (200)	635.00	763 (200)	550.00
754 (200)	190.00	764 (200)	600.00
755 (200)	190.00	765 (200)	1000.00
756-65 set	4100.00	766 (225)	400.00
756 (200)	67.50	767 (225)	400.00
757 (200)	75.00	768 (150)	550.00
758 (200)	160.00	769 (120)	240.00
759 (200)	280.00	770 (120)	600.00
760 (200)	450.00	771 (200)	725.00

772, 778a

773, 778b

774

775, 778c

1935-36 COMMEMORATIVES

SCOTT NO.	DESCRIPTION	FIRST DAY COVERS SING	FIRST DAY COVERS PL. BLK.	MINT SHEET	PLATE BLOCK F/NH	UNUSED F/NH	USED F
772/84	(772-77, 782-84) 9 varieties.......		....	....	....	3.60	1.70
772	3¢ Connecticut	12.00	19.50	16.50 (50)	2.25	.40	.20
773	3¢ San Diego	12.00	19.50	16.50 (50)	1.85	.40	.20
774	3¢ Boulder Dam	12.00	19.50	16.50 (50)	(6)2.75	.40	.20
775	3¢ Michigan	12.00	19.50	16.50 (50)	1.85	.40	.20

776, 778d

777

1936 COMMEMORATIVE

SCOTT NO.	DESCRIPTION	FIRST DAY COVERS SING	FIRST DAY COVERS PL. BLK.	MINT SHEET	PLATE BLOCK F/NH	UNUSED F/NH	USED F
776	3¢ Texas	15.00	25.00	16.50 (50)	1.85	.40	.20
777	3¢ Rhode Island	12.00	19.50	25.00 (50)	3.00	.60	.20

778

782

783

784

1936 THIRD INTERNATIONAL PHILATELIC EXHIBITION "TIPEX" Imperforate Souvenir Sheet
Designs of 772, 773, 775, 776

SCOTT NO.	DESCRIPTION	FIRST DAY COVERS SING	FIRST DAY COVERS PL. BLK.	MINT SHEET	PLATE BLOCK F/NH	UNUSED F/NH	USED F
778	red violet, sheet of 4 . . .	16.50	....	....	....	4.00	4.00
778a	3¢ Connecticut	....	....	....	....	1.00	.95
778b	3¢ San Diego	....	....	....	....	1.00	.95
778c	3¢ Michigan	....	....	....	....	1.00	.95
778d	3¢ Texas	....	....	....	....	1.00	.95
782	3¢ Arkansas Statehood	12.00	19.50	20.00 (50)	1.95	.60	.20
783	3¢ Oregon Territory	12.00	19.50	14.50 (50)	1.75	.40	.20
784	3¢ Suffrage for Women .	12.00	19.50	30.00 (100)	1.75	.40	.20

FIRST DAY COVERS:

First Day Covers are envelopes cancelled on the "First Day of Issue" of the stamp used on an envelope. Usually they also contain a picture (cachet) on the left side designed to go with the theme of the stamp. From 1935 to 1949, prices listed are for cacheted, addressed covers. From 1950 to date, prices are for cacheted, unaddressed covers.

785

786

787

788

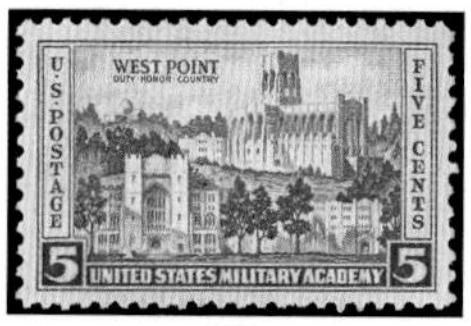

789

1936-37 ARMY AND NAVY ISSUE

SCOTT NO.	DESCRIPTION	FIRST DAY COVERS SING	FIRST DAY COVERS PL. BLK.	MINT SHEET	PLATE BLOCK F/NH	UNUSED F/NH	USED F
785-94	**10 varieties, complete**	57.50	......	......	59.00	5.50	2.30

ARMY COMMEMORATIVES

SCOTT NO.	DESCRIPTION	FIRST DAY COVERS SING	FIRST DAY COVERS PL. BLK.	MINT SHEET	PLATE BLOCK F/NH	UNUSED F/NH	USED F
785	1¢ green	6.00	12.00	15.00 (50)	1.60	.40	.20
786	2¢ carmine	6.00	12.00	15.00 (50)	1.60	.40	.20
787	3¢ purple	6.00	12.00	25.00 (50)	2.75	.60	.20
788	4¢ gray	6.00	14.50	40.00 (50)	12.00	.60	.30
789	5¢ ultramarine	7.00	14.50	50.00 (50)	13.50	1.00	.30

790

791

792

793

794

NAVY COMMEMORATIVES

SCOTT NO.	DESCRIPTION	FIRST DAY COVERS SING	FIRST DAY COVERS PL. BLK.	MINT SHEET	PLATE BLOCK F/NH	UNUSED F/NH	USED F
790	1¢ green	6.00	12.00	9.00 (50)	1.40	.25	.20
791	2¢ carmine	6.00	12.00	14.00 (50)	1.60	.35	.20
792	3¢ purple	6.00	12.00	18.50 (50)	2.50	.50	.20
793	4¢ gray	6.00	14.50	45.00 (50)	12.00	.75	.30
794	5¢ ultramarine	7.00	14.50	50.00 (50)	13.50	1.00	.35

795

796

1937 COMMEMORATIVES

SCOTT NO.	DESCRIPTION	FIRST DAY COVERS SING	FIRST DAY COVERS PL. BLK.	MINT SHEET	PLATE BLOCK F/NH	UNUSED F/NH	USED F
795/802	**(795-96, 798-802) 7 varieties**	......	......	......	......	**3.00**	**1.40**
795	3¢ Northwest Ordinance	8.50	16.00	16.50 (50)	1.80	.45	.20
796	5¢ Virginia Dare	8.50	16.00	25.00 (48)	10.00(6)	.45	.30

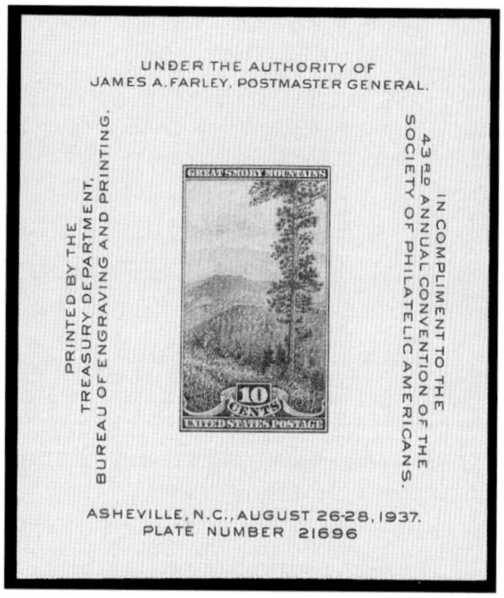

797

1937 S.P.A. CONVENTION ISSUE
Design of 749 Imperforate Souvenir Sheet

SCOTT NO.	DESCRIPTION	FIRST DAY COVERS SING	FIRST DAY COVERS PL. BLK.	MINT SHEET	PLATE BLOCK F/NH	UNUSED F/NH	USED F
797	10¢ blue green	8.50	......	......	......	1.10	.80

798

799

800

801

802

SCOTT NO.	DESCRIPTION	FIRST DAY COVERS SING	FIRST DAY COVERS PL. BLK.	MINT SHEET	PLATE BLOCK F/NH	UNUSED F/NH	USED F
798	3¢ Constitution	10.00	16.00	37.50 (50)	4.00	.95	.20
799	3¢ Hawaii	10.00	16.00	12.50 (50)	1.85	.35	.20
800	3¢ Alaska	10.00	16.00	12.50 (50)	1.85	.35	.20
801	3¢ Puerto Rico	10.00	16.00	12.50 (50)	1.85	.35	.20
802	3¢ Virgin Islands	10.00	16.00	12.50 (50)	1.85	.35	.20

1938 Presidential Series

In 1938 a new set of definitive stamps was issued honoring the first 29 presidents, Ben Franklin, Martha Washington, and the White House. These were regular issues that effectively replaced the previous definitive issues of the 1922-25 series.

The "Presidential Series" contained 32 denominations ranging from 1/2¢-$5.00. It is an interesting series because various printing methods were employed. The 1/2¢-50¢ values were printed in single colors on rotary presses using both normal and "electric eye" plates. The $1.00 to $5.00 values were printed in two colors on flat plate presses.

The $1.00 value was reprinted twice, once in 1951 on revenue paper watermarked "USIR" (#832b) and again in 1954. The 1954 issue was "dry printed" on thick white paper, with an experimental colorless gum (832c).

This series in regular and coil form was used for 16 years until it was replaced by the new definitive issues of 1954.

803

804, 839, 848

805, 840, 849

806, 841, 850

807, 842, 851

808, 843

809, 844

810, 845

811, 846

812

813

814

815, 847

816

817

818

819

820

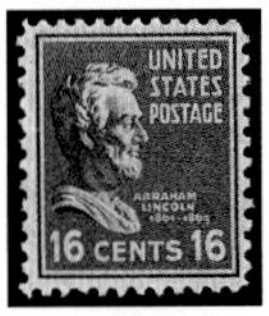

821

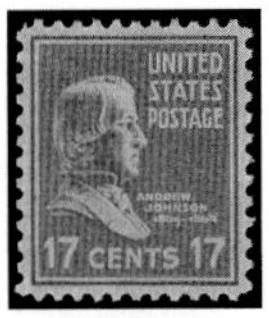

822

823

824

825

826

827

828

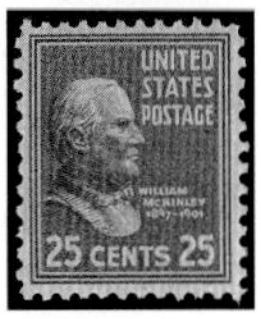

829

830

831

832

833

834

SCOTT NO.	DESCRIPTION	FIRST DAY COVERS SING	PL. BLK.	MINT SHEET	PLATE BLOCK F/NH	UNUSED F/NH	USED F
	1938 PRESIDENTIAL SERIES						
803-34	**1/2¢-$5, 32 varieties, complete ....**	**520.00**	....	....	**900.00**	**200.00**	**17.50**
803-31	**1/2¢-50¢, 29 varieties**	**110.00**	....	....	**225.00**	**50.00**	**5.90**
803	1/2¢ Franklin	2.50	5.50	15.00(100)	1.00	.20	.15
804	1¢ G. Washington ..	2.50	5.50	20.00(100)	1.00	.25	.15
804b	1¢ booklet pane of 6	14.00	....	....	....	2.25	....
805	1-1/2¢ M. Washington	2.50	5.50	20.00(100)	1.00	.25	.15
806	2¢ J. Adams	2.50	5.50	20.00(100)	1.00	.25	.15
806	E.E. Plate Block of 10	....	....	....	7.00	....	....
806b	2¢ booklet pane of 6	14.00	....	....	....	4.50	....
807	3¢ Jefferson	2.50	5.50	20.00(100)	1.00	.25	.15
807	E.E. Plate Block of 10	....	....	....	50.00	....	....
807a	3¢ booklet pane of 6	14.00	....	....	....	8.25	....
808	4¢ Madison	2.50	5.50	110.00(100)	5.25	1.10	.15
809	4-1/2¢ White House	2.50	5.50	25.00(100)	1.60	.30	.20
810	5¢ J. Monroe	2.50	5.50	30.00(100)	1.75	.35	.15
811	6¢ J.Q. Adams	2.50	5.50	47.50(100)	2.25	.55	.15
812	7¢ A. Jackson	2.50	5.50	47.50(100)	3.00	.55	.15
813	8¢ Van Buren	2.50	5.50	47.50(100)	2.35	.55	.15
814	9¢ Harrison	2.50	5.50	50.00(100)	2.50	.55	.15
815	10¢ Tyler	2.50	5.50	50.00(100)	2.00	.45	.15
816	11¢ Polk	3.75	6.75	55.00(100)	3.00	1.00	.15
817	12¢ Taylor	3.75	6.75	130.00(100)	7.00	2.00	.15
818	13¢ Fillmore	3.75	6.75	185.00(100)	8.50	2.00	.15
819	14¢ Pierce	3.75	6.75	130.00(100)	7.00	2.00	.15
820	15¢ Buchanan	3.75	6.75	65.00(100)	3.50	.75	.15
821	16¢ Lincoln	4.50	8.25	140.00(100)	8.25	2.00	.55
822	17¢ Johnson	4.50	8.25	140.00(100)	7.00	2.00	.20
823	18¢ Grant	4.50	8.25	240.00(100)	13.00	2.50	.20
824	19¢ Hayes	4.50	8.25	210.00(100)	9.00	2.50	.75
825	20¢ Garfield	4.75	11.25	110.00(100)	5.50	1.25	.15
826	21¢ Arthur	5.25	11.25	250.00(100)	12.00	2.75	.25
827	22¢ Cleveland	5.25	11.25	165.00(100)	13.50	2.00	.75
828	24¢ B. Harrison	6.25	11.25	550.00(100)	22.00	6.00	.25
829	25¢ McKinley	6.25	13.75	130.00(100)	5.50	1.20	.20
830	30¢ T. Roosevelt ...	8.50	13.75	650.00(100)	32.50	7.50	.20
831	50¢ Taft	15.00	30.00	950.00(100)	45.00	10.00	.20
	Flat Plate Printing Perf. 11						
832	$1 Wilson	70.00	150.00	1150.00(100)	55.00	12.00	.20
832	$1 center line block .	....	....	....	55.00	....	....
832	$1 arrow block	....	....	....	50.00	....	....
832b	$1 Watermarked "USIR"	....	....	....	....	325.00	70.00
832c	$1 dry print thick paper (1954)	35.00	75.00	725.00(100)	32.50	8.00	.20
833	$2 Harding	135.00	275.00	....	140.00	26.00	6.50
833	$2 center line block .	....	....	....	115.00	....	....
833	$2 arrow block	....	....	....	110.00	....	....
834	$5 Coolidge	225.00	400.00	....	525.00	120.00	6.00
834	$5 center line block .	....	....	....	525.00	....	....
834	$5 arrow block	....	....	....	500.00	....	....

835

836

837

838

1938-39 COMMEMORATIVES

SCOTT NO.	DESCRIPTION	FIRST DAY COVERS SING	FIRST DAY COVERS PL. BLK.	MINT SHEET	PLATE BLOCK F/NH	UNUSED F/NH	USED F
835-58	**(835-38, 852-58) 11 varieties, complete**	....	....	....	....	**7.00**	**2.15**
835	3¢ Ratification	10.00	14.00	35.00(50)	6.00	.80	.20
836	3¢ Swedes-Finns . .	10.00	14.00	14.00(48)	(6)4.00	.35	.20
837	3¢ Northwest Territory	10.00	14.00	35.00(100)	11.50	.35	.20
838	3¢ Iowa Territory . . .	10.00	14.00	24.00(50)	8.50	.60	.20

1939 PRESIDENTIALS ROTARY PRESS COIL

SCOTT NO.	DESCRIPTION	FIRST DAY COVERS SING	LINE PAIR	MINT SHEET	LINE PAIR	UNUSED F/NH	USED F
839-51	**13 varieties, complete**	**67.50**	**120.00**	....	**148.50**	**36.75**	**5.30**
	Perforated 10 Vertically						
839	1¢ G. Washington . .	5.00	8.50	....	1.40	.40	.15
840	1-1/2¢ M. Washington	5.00	8.50	....	1.65	.40	.15
841	2¢ J. Adams	5.00	8.50	....	1.75	.40	.15
842	3¢ T. Jefferson	5.00	8.50	....	2.00	.70	.15
843	4¢ J. Madison	5.75	10.50	....	32.50	8.00	.75
844	4-1/2¢ White House	5.75	10.50	....	6.25	.70	.50
845	5¢ J. Monroe	5.75	11.00	....	30.00	5.50	.50
846	6¢ J.Q. Adams	5.75	11.00	....	8.00	1.75	.20
847	10¢ J. Tyler	8.50	16.00	....	50.00	12.00	.90
	Perforated 10 Horizontally						
848	1¢ G. Washington . .	5.00	8.50	....	3.75	1.10	.25
849	1-1/2¢ M. Washington	5.00	8.50	....	5.00	1.50	.65
850	2¢ J. Adams	5.00	8.50	....	7.50	2.50	.75
851	3¢ T. Jefferson	5.00	8.50	....	7.00	2.75	.75

852

853

854

855

856

1939 COMMEMORATIVES

SCOTT NO.	DESCRIPTION	FIRST DAY COVERS SING	FIRST DAY COVERS PL. BLK.	MINT SHEET	PLATE BLOCK F/NH	UNUSED F/NH	USED F
852	3¢ Golden Gate	12.00	19.50	20.00(50)	2.00	.40	.20
853	3¢ World's Fair	12.00	19.50	18.00(50)	2.75	.40	.20
854	3¢ Inauguration	12.00	19.50	55.00(50)	(6)8.00	.90	.20
855	3¢ Baseball	37.50	60.00	150.00(50)	14.00	3.00	.30
856	3¢ Panama Canal . .	17.50	25.00	25.00(50)	(6)5.00	.60	.20

857

858

1939 COMMEMORATIVES

SCOTT NO.	DESCRIPTION	FIRST DAY COVERS SING	FIRST DAY COVERS PL. BLK.	MINT SHEET	PLATE BLOCK F/NH	UNUSED F/NH	USED F
857	3¢ Printing	12.00	19.50	14.00(50)	1.75	.35	.20
858	3¢ Four States	10.00	14.50	18.00(50)	2.00	.35	.20

859

860

861

862

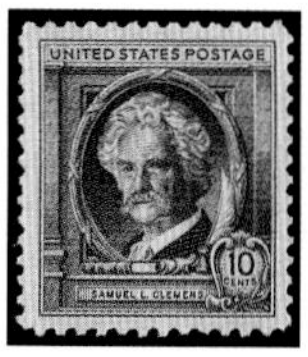

863

1940 FAMOUS AMERICANS ISSUES

SCOTT NO.	DESCRIPTION	FIRST DAY COVERS SING	FIRST DAY COVERS PL. BLK.	MINT SHEET	PLATE BLOCK F/NH	UNUSED F/NH	USED F
859-93	**35 varieties, complete**	**130.00**	....	....	**500.00**	**50.00**	**23.50**
	American Authors						
859	1¢ Washington Irving	3.00	4.00	20.00(70)	1.75	.35	.20
860	2¢ James F. Cooper	3.00	4.00	20.00(70)	1.75	.35	.20
861	3¢ Ralph W. Emerson	3.00	4.00	22.50(70)	1.85	.35	.20
862	5¢ Louisa May Alcott	4.00	6.00	40.00(70)	13.00	.50	.35
863	10¢ Samuel L. Clemens	7.50	13.50	180.00(70)	52.50	2.50	2.00

864

865

866

867

868

American Poets

SCOTT NO.	DESCRIPTION	FIRST DAY COVERS SING	FIRST DAY COVERS PL. BLK.	MINT SHEET	PLATE BLOCK F/NH	UNUSED F/NH	USED F
864	1¢ Henry W. Longfellow	3.00	4.00	20.00(70)	2.75	.35	.20
865	2¢ John Whittier . . .	3.00	4.00	20.00(70)	2.75	.35	.20
866	3¢ James Lowell . . .	3.00	4.00	22.50(70)	3.25	.35	.20
867	5¢ Walt Whitman . .	4.00	6.00	50.00(70)	15.00	.80	.35
868	10¢ James Riley . . .	7.50	11.50	225.00(70)	60.00	3.50	2.50

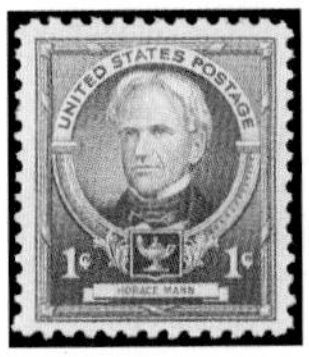
869
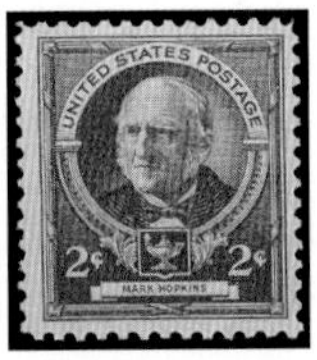
870

871

872

873

American Educators

SCOTT NO.	DESCRIPTION	FIRST DAY COVERS SING	FIRST DAY COVERS PL. BLK.	MINT SHEET	PLATE BLOCK F/NH	UNUSED F/NH	USED F
869	1¢ Horace Mann . . .	3.00	4.00	20.00(70)	3.50	.35	.20
870	2¢ Mark Hopkins . . .	3.00	4.00	20.00(70)	1.75	.35	.20
871	3¢ Charles W. Eliot .	3.00	4.00	22.50(70)	4.00	.40	.20
872	5¢ Frances Willard .	4.00	6.00	55.00(70)	17.50	.75	.35
873	10¢ Booker T. Washington	9.50	13.50	200.00(70)	42.50	3.50	2.00

874

875

876

877

878

American Scientists

SCOTT NO.	DESCRIPTION	FIRST DAY COVERS SING	FIRST DAY COVERS PL. BLK.	MINT SHEET	PLATE BLOCK F/NH	UNUSED F/NH	USED F
874	1¢ John J. Audubon	3.00	4.00	20.00(70)	1.75	.35	.20
875	2¢ Dr. Crawford Long	3.00	4.00	20.00(70)	1.75	.35	.20
876	3¢ Luther Burbank .	3.00	4.00	22.50(70)	1.85	.40	.20
877	5¢ Dr. Walter Reed .	4.00	6.00	35.00(70)	9.00	.45	.35
878	10¢ Jane Addams . .	6.00	11.50	145.00(70)	30.00	2.25	1.60

879

880

881

882

883

American Composers

SCOTT NO.	DESCRIPTION	FIRST DAY COVERS SING	FIRST DAY COVERS PL. BLK.	MINT SHEET	PLATE BLOCK F/NH	UNUSED F/NH	USED F
879	1¢ Stephen Foster .	3.00	4.00	20.00(70)	1.75	.35	.20
880	2¢ John Philip Sousa	3.00	4.00	20.00(70)	1.75	.35	.20
881	3¢ Victor Herbert . . .	3.00	4.00	20.00(70)	1.75	.35	.20
882	5¢ Edward A. MacDowell	4.00	6.00	47.50(70)	14.00	.75	.35
883	10¢ Ethelbert Nevin	6.00	11.50	370.00(70)	50.00	6.00	2.10

884

885

886

887

888

American Artists

SCOTT NO.	DESCRIPTION	FIRST DAY COVERS SING	FIRST DAY COVERS PL. BLK.	MINT SHEET	PLATE BLOCK F/NH	UNUSED F/NH	USED F
884	1¢ Gilbert Stuart . . .	3.00	4.00	20.00(70)	1.75	.40	.20
885	2¢ James Whistler .	3.00	4.00	20.00(70)	1.75	.35	.20
886	3¢ A. Saint-Gaudens	3.00	4.00	22.50(70)	1.75	.40	.20
887	5¢ Daniel C. French	4.00	6.00	55.00(70)	12.50	1.00	.35
888	10¢ Frederic Remington	6.00	11.50	195.00(70)	40.00	3.00	2.00

889

890

891

892

893

American Inventors

SCOTT NO.	DESCRIPTION	FIRST DAY COVERS SING	FIRST DAY COVERS PL. BLK.	MINT SHEET	PLATE BLOCK F/NH	UNUSED F/NH	USED F
889	1¢ Eli Whitney	3.00	4.00	35.00(70)	3.00	.40	.20
890	2¢ Samuel Morse . .	3.00	4.00	35.00(70)	3.00	.40	.20
891	3¢ Cyrus McCormick	3.00	4.00	32.50(70)	2.50	.55	.15
892	5¢ Elias Howe	4.00	6.00	120.00(70)	20.00	1.75	.45
893	10¢ Alexander G. Bell	8.00	20.00	1150.00(70)	105.00	18.00	3.50

894

895

1940 COMMEMORATIVES

SCOTT NO.	DESCRIPTION	FIRST DAY COVERS SING	FIRST DAY COVERS PL. BLK.	MINT SHEET	PLATE BLOCK F/NH	UNUSED F/NH	USED F
894-902	**9 varieties, complete**	....	....	....	....	**3.80**	**1.45**
894	3¢ Pony Express . . .	7.00	11.00	24.00(50)	4.50	.60	.25
895	3¢ Pan Am Union . .	5.00	11.00	24.00(50)	4.50	.45	.20

MINT SHEETS: From 1935 to date, we list prices for standard size Mint Sheets in Fine, Never Hinged condition. The number of stamps in each sheet is noted in ( ).

FAMOUS AMERICANS: Later additions to the Famous American series include #945 Edison, #953 Carver, #960 White, #965 Stone, #975 Rogers, #980 Harris, #986 Poe, and #988 Gompers.

896

897

898

1940 COMMEMORATIVES

SCOTT NO.	DESCRIPTION	FIRST DAY COVERS SING	FIRST DAY COVERS PL. BLK.	MINT SHEET	PLATE BLOCK F/NH	UNUSED F/NH	USED F
896	3¢ Idaho Statehood	6.00	11.00	20.00(50)	3.00	.60	.20
897	3¢ Wyoming Statehood	6.00	11.00	20.00(50)	2.25	.50	.20
898	3¢ Coronado Expedition	6.00	11.00	20.00(52)	2.25	.40	.20

899

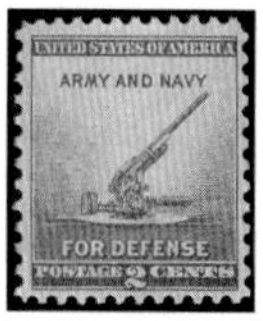

900

901

902

NATIONAL DEFENSE ISSUE

SCOTT NO.	DESCRIPTION	FIRST DAY COVERS SING	FIRST DAY COVERS PL. BLK.	MINT SHEET	PLATE BLOCK F/NH	UNUSED F/NH	USED F
899	1¢ Liberty	4.00	7.00	20.00(100)	.90	.30	.15
900	2¢ Gun	4.00	7.00	20.00(100)	.90	.30	.15
901	3¢ Torch	4.00	7.00	22.50(100)	.90	.30	.15
902	3¢ Emancipation . . .	9.00	11.00	27.50(50)	4.75	.60	.35

903

1941-43 COMMEMORATIVES

SCOTT NO.	DESCRIPTION	FIRST DAY COVERS SING	FIRST DAY COVERS PL. BLK.	MINT SHEET	PLATE BLOCK F/NH	UNUSED F/NH	USED F
903-08	**3¢-5¢ six varieties .**	....	....	....	....	**3.40**	**1.00**

1941 COMMEMORATIVES

SCOTT NO.	DESCRIPTION	FIRST DAY COVERS SING	FIRST DAY COVERS PL. BLK.	MINT SHEET	PLATE BLOCK F/NH	UNUSED F/NH	USED F
903	3¢ Vermont	7.00	10.75	32.00(50)	4.00	.60	.20

904

905

906

1942 COMMEMORATIVES

SCOTT NO.	DESCRIPTION	FIRST DAY COVERS SING	FIRST DAY COVERS PL. BLK.	MINT SHEET	PLATE BLOCK F/NH	UNUSED F/NH	USED F
904	3¢ Kentucky	5.00	10.75	18.00(50)	1.85	.35	.20
905	3¢ Win The War . . .	4.50	7.50	24.00(100)	1.20	.30	.15
906	5¢ China Resistance	12.00	20.00	60.00(50)	20.00	1.75	.35

907

908

1943 COMMEMORATIVES

SCOTT NO.	DESCRIPTION	FIRST DAY COVERS SING	FIRST DAY COVERS PL. BLK.	MINT SHEET	PLATE BLOCK F/NH	UNUSED F/NH	USED F
907	2¢ Allied Nations . . .	6.00	7.50	15.00(100)	1.00	.30	.15
908	1¢ Four Freedoms .	6.00	10.50	15.00(100)	1.00	.30	.15

909

910

911

912

913

914

915

916

917

918

919

920

921

1943-44 OVERRUN COUNTRIES SERIES

SCOTT NO.	DESCRIPTION	FIRST DAY COVERS SING	FIRST DAY COVERS PL. BLK.	MINT SHEET	PLATE BLOCK F/NH	UNUSED F/NH	USED F
909-21	**13 varieties, complete**	**50.00**	....	....	**72.50**	**6.50**	**3.25**
909	5¢ Poland	5.00	10.00	21.50(50)	9.00	.40	.25
910	5¢ Czechoslovakia .	5.00	10.00	17.50(50)	4.00	.40	.25
911	5¢ Norway	5.00	10.00	15.00(50)	2.75	.40	.25
912	5¢ Luxembourg	5.00	10.00	15.00(50)	1.85	.40	.25
913	5¢ Netherlands	5.00	10.00	15.00(50)	1.85	.40	.25
914	5¢ Belgium	5.00	10.00	15.00(50)	1.85	.40	.25
915	5¢ France	5.00	10.00	15.00(50)	1.85	.40	.25
916	5¢ Greece	5.00	10.00	45.00(50)	17.50	1.10	.40
917	5¢ Yugoslavia	5.00	10.00	27.50(50)	8.00	.60	.30
918	5¢ Albania	5.00	10.00	25.00(50)	8.00	.60	.30
919	5¢ Austria	5.00	10.00	20.00(50)	6.00	.60	.30
920	5¢ Denmark	5.00	10.00	27.50(50)	8.00	.60	.30
921	5¢ Korea (1944) . . .	5.00	10.00	17.50(50)	7.00	.60	.30

922

923

924

925

926

927

1944 COMMEMORATIVES

SCOTT NO.	DESCRIPTION	FIRST DAY COVERS SING	FIRST DAY COVERS PL. BLK.	MINT SHEET	PLATE BLOCK F/NH	UNUSED F/NH	USED F
922-26	5 varieties	....	....	....	....	1.90	1.00
922	3¢ Railroad	9.00	12.00	20.00(50)	2.25	.40	.25
923	3¢ Steamship	9.00	12.00	20.00(50)	2.25	.40	.25
924	3¢ Telegraph	9.00	12.00	15.00(50)	1.75	.40	.20
925	3¢ Corregidor	9.00	12.00	17.50(50)	1.75	.40	.25
926	3¢ Motion Picture ..	9.00	12.00	20.00(50)	1.75	.40	.20

928

929

1945-46 COMMEMORATIVES

SCOTT NO.	DESCRIPTION	FIRST DAY COVERS SING	FIRST DAY COVERS PL. BLK.	MINT SHEET	PLATE BLOCK F/NH	UNUSED F/NH	USED F
927-38	1¢-5¢ (12 varieties, complete)		....	....	....	4.00	2.25
927	3¢ Florida	10.00	15.00	32.00(50)	3.00	.75	.20
928	5¢ Peace Conference	10.00	15.00	15.00(50)	1.00	.30	.20
929	3¢ Iwo Jima	17.00	20.00	20.00(50)	3.50	.50	.20

930

931

932

933

SCOTT NO.	DESCRIPTION	FIRST DAY COVERS SING	FIRST DAY COVERS PL. BLK.	MINT SHEET	PLATE BLOCK F/NH	UNUSED F/NH	USED F
930	1¢ FDR & Hyde Park	4.00	6.00	6.00(50)	1.00	.30	.20
931	2¢ FDR & "Little White House"	4.00	6.00	8.50(50)	1.00	.30	.20
932	3¢ FDR & White House	4.00	6.00	10.00(50)	1.25	.30	.20
933	5¢ FDR & Globe (1946)	4.00	6.00	15.00(50)	1.25	.35	.20

934

935

936

937

938

SCOTT NO.	DESCRIPTION	FIRST DAY COVERS SING	FIRST DAY COVERS PL. BLK.	MINT SHEET	PLATE BLOCK F/NH	UNUSED F/NH	USED F
934	3¢ Army	10.00	14.00	12.50(50)	1.25	.30	.20
935	3¢ Navy	10.00	14.00	15.00(50)	1.25	.30	.20
936	3¢ Coast Guard	10.00	14.00	12.00(50)	1.25	.30	.20
937	3¢ Al Smith	10.00	14.00	22.00(100)	1.25	.30	.20
938	3¢ Texas Statehood	10.00	14.00	18.00(50)	1.75	.50	.20

939

940

941

942

943

944

1946-47 COMMEMORATIVES

SCOTT NO.	DESCRIPTION	FIRST DAY COVERS SING	FIRST DAY COVERS PL. BLK.	MINT SHEET	PLATE BLOCK F/NH	UNUSED F/NH	USED F
939/52	(939-47, 949-52) 13 varieties	....	....	....	....	4.50	1.95
939	3¢ Merchant Marine	10.00	12.00	10.00(50)	1.30	.30	.15
940	3¢ Honorable Discharge	10.00	12.00	22.00(100)	1.30	.30	.15
941	3¢ Tennessee Statehood	3.00	5.00	15.00(50)	1.30	.30	.15
942	3¢ Iowa Statehood .	3.00	5.00	12.50(50)	1.50	.40	.15
943	3¢ Smithsonian Institute	3.00	5.00	12.50(50)	1.50	.40	.15
944	3¢ Kearny Expedition	3.00	5.00	12.00(50)	1.50	.40	.15

945

946

947

1947 COMMEMORATIVES

SCOTT NO.	DESCRIPTION	FIRST DAY COVERS SING	FIRST DAY COVERS PL. BLK.	MINT SHEET	PLATE BLOCK F/NH	UNUSED F/NH	USED F
945	3¢ Thomas A. Edison	3.00	5.00	17.50(70)	1.25	.30	.15
946	3¢ Joseph Pulitzer .	3.00	5.00	12.50(50)	1.25	.30	.15
947	3¢ Stamp Centenary	3.00	5.00	10.00(50)	1.25	.30	.15

NEVER HINGED: From 1888 to 1935, Unused OG or Unused prices are for stamps with original gum that have been hinged. If you desire Never Hinged stamps, refer to the NH listings.

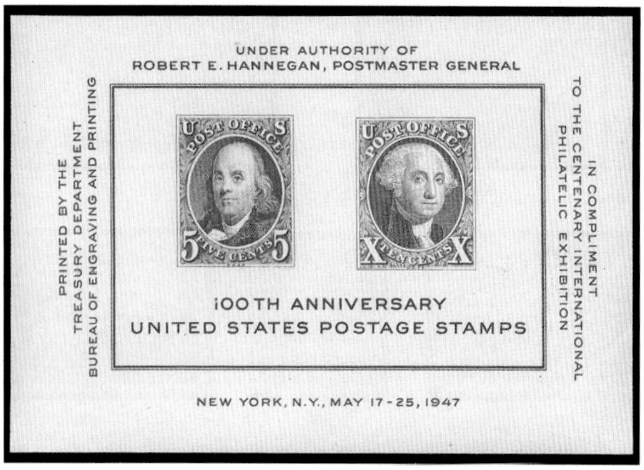

"CIPEX" SOUVENIR SHEET

SCOTT NO.	DESCRIPTION	FIRST DAY COVERS SING	FIRST DAY COVERS PL. BLK.	MINT SHEET	PLATE BLOCK F/NH	UNUSED F/NH	USED F
948	5¢ & 10¢ Sheet of 2	4.00	....	....	....	1.50	1.00
948a	5¢ blue, single stamp	....	....	....	....	.65	.50
948b	10¢ brown orange, single stamp	....	....	....	....	.65	.50

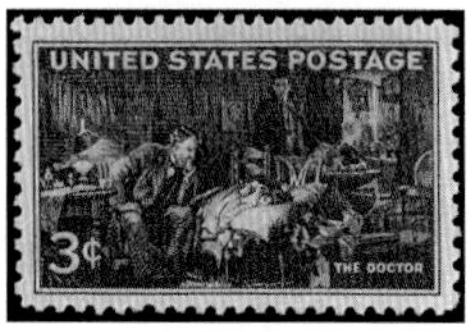

949

950

951

952

953

SCOTT NO.	DESCRIPTION	FIRST DAY COVERS SING	FIRST DAY COVERS PL. BLK.	MINT SHEET	PLATE BLOCK F/NH	UNUSED F/NH	USED F
949	3¢ Doctors	8.00	12.00	10.00(50)	1.00	.30	.20
950	3¢ Utah Centennial .	3.00	5.00	15.00(50)	1.50	.30	.20
951	3¢ "Constitution" . . .	8.00	12.00	10.00(50)	1.00	.30	.20
952	3¢ Everglades National Park	4.00	6.00	18.00(50)	2.00	.45	.20

954

955

956

957

1948 COMMEMORATIVES

SCOTT NO.	DESCRIPTION	FIRST DAY COVERS SING	FIRST DAY COVERS PL. BLK.	MINT SHEET	PLATE BLOCK F/NH	UNUSED F/NH	USED F
953-80	**3¢-5¢ (28 varieties, complete)**	....	....	....	....	**9.25**	**5.25**
953	3¢ George Washington Carver	6.00	10.00	19.00(70)	1.60	.35	.20
954	3¢ Gold Rush	2.40	5.00	18.00(50)	1.60	.35	.20
955	3¢ Mississippi Territory	2.40	5.00	18.00(50)	1.60	.35	.20
956	3¢ Chaplains	3.00	5.00	18.00(50)	1.60	.35	.20
957	3¢ Wisconsin Statehood	2.40	5.00	18.00(50)	1.60	.35	.20

958

959

960

961

962

963

SCOTT NO.	DESCRIPTION	FIRST DAY COVERS SING	FIRST DAY COVERS PL. BLK.	MINT SHEET	PLATE BLOCK F/NH	UNUSED F/NH	USED F
958	5¢ Swedish Pioneer	2.40	5.00	12.50(50)	1.25	.35	.20
959	3¢ Women's Progress	2.40	5.00	18.00(50)	1.75	.40	.20
960	3¢ William White . . .	2.40	5.00	18.00(70)	1.25	.35	.20
961	3¢ U.S.-Canada Friendship	2.40	5.00	12.50(50)	1.25	.35	.20
962	3¢ Francis S. Key . .	2.40	5.00	12.50(50)	1.25	.35	.20
963	3¢ Salute to Youth .	2.40	5.00	12.50(50)	1.25	.35	.20

964

965

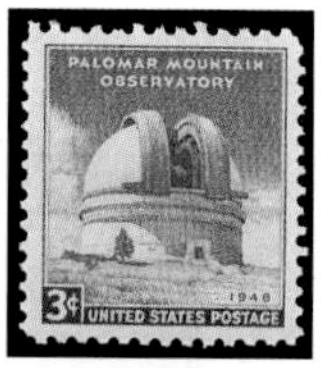

966

967

968

969

970

SCOTT NO.	DESCRIPTION	FIRST DAY COVERS SING	FIRST DAY COVERS PL. BLK.	MINT SHEET	PLATE BLOCK F/NH	UNUSED F/NH	USED F
964	3¢ Oregon Territory .	2.40	5.00	20.00(50)	2.00	.50	.20
965	3¢ Harlan Stone . . .	2.40	5.00	12.50(70)	1.25	.35	.20
966	3¢ Mt. Palomar	3.00	5.00	20.00(70)	1.80	.35	.20
967	3¢ Clara Barton	3.00	5.00	12.50(50)	1.25	.35	.20
968	3¢ Poultry	2.40	5.00	12.50(50)	1.25	.35	.20
969	3¢ Gold Star Mothers	2.40	5.00	12.50(50)	1.25	.35	.20
970	3¢ Fort Kearny	2.40	5.00	12.50(50)	1.60	.35	.20

PLATE BLOCKS: are portions of a sheet of stamps adjacent to the number(s) indicating the printing plate number used to produce that sheet. Flat plate issues are usually collected in plate blocks of six (number opposite middle stamp) while rotary issues are normally corner blocks of four.

971

972

973

974

SCOTT NO.	DESCRIPTION	FIRST DAY COVERS SING	FIRST DAY COVERS PL. BLK.	MINT SHEET	PLATE BLOCK F/NH	UNUSED F/NH	USED F
971	3¢ Volunteer Firemen	5.00	7.00	15.00(50)	1.50	.45	.20
972	3¢ Indian Centennial	2.40	5.00	15.00(50)	1.50	.35	.20
973	3¢ Rough Riders . . .	2.40	5.00	12.50(50)	1.50	.35	.20
974	3¢ Juliette Low	7.00	10.00	12.50(50)	1.50	.35	.20

975

976

977

978

979

980

SCOTT NO.	DESCRIPTION	FIRST DAY COVERS SING	FIRST DAY COVERS PL. BLK.	MINT SHEET	PLATE BLOCK F/NH	UNUSED F/NH	USED F
975	3¢ Will Rogers	2.40	5.00	20.00(50)	1.25	.35	.20
976	3¢ Fort Bliss	2.40	5.00	20.00(50)	2.20	.50	.20
977	3¢ Moina Michael . .	2.40	5.00	12.50(50)	1.25	.35	.20
978	3¢ Gettysburg Address	3.00	5.00	12.50(50)	1.25	.35	.20
979	3¢ American Turners	2.40	5.00	12.50(50)	1.25	.35	.20
980	3¢ Joel C. Harris . . .	2.40	5.00	20.00(70)	1.25	.35	.20

981

982

983

984

1949-50 COMMEMORATIVES

SCOTT NO.	DESCRIPTION	FIRST DAY COVERS SING	FIRST DAY COVERS PL. BLK.	MINT SHEET	PLATE BLOCK F/NH	UNUSED F/NH	USED F
981-97	**17 varieties, complete**	....	....	....	....	**5.70**	**3.20**
981	3¢ Minnesota Territory	2.40	4.25	20.00(50)	2.00	.50	.20
982	3¢ Washington & Lee University	2.40	4.25	12.50(50)	1.25	.35	.20
983	3¢ Puerto Rico	3.00	4.25	12.50(50)	1.25	.35	.20
984	3¢ Annapolis	3.00	4.25	12.50(50)	1.25	.35	.20

985

986

SCOTT NO.	DESCRIPTION	FIRST DAY COVERS SING	FIRST DAY COVERS PL. BLK.	MINT SHEET	PLATE BLOCK F/NH	UNUSED F/NH	USED F
985	3¢ G.A.R.	3.00	4.25	12.50(50)	1.25	.35	.20
986	3¢ Edgar A. Poe . . .	3.00	4.25	25.00(70)	1.75	.45	.20

987

988

989

1950 COMMEMORATIVES

SCOTT NO.	DESCRIPTION	FIRST DAY COVERS SING	FIRST DAY COVERS PL. BLK.	MINT SHEET	PLATE BLOCK F/NH	UNUSED F/NH	USED F
987	3¢ Bankers Association	2.40	4.25	17.50(50)	1.75	.40	.20
988	3¢ Samuel Gompers	2.40	4.25	15.00(70)	1.25	.35	.20
989	3¢ Statue of Freedom	2.40	4.25	12.50(50)	1.25	.35	.20

990

991

992

993

994

995

996

997

SCOTT NO.	DESCRIPTION	FIRST DAY COVERS SING	FIRST DAY COVERS PL. BLK.	MINT SHEET	PLATE BLOCK F/NH	UNUSED F/NH	USED F
990	3¢ Executive Mansion	2.40	4.25	12.50(50)	1.25	.35	.20
991	3¢ Supreme Court .	2.40	4.25	12.50(50)	1.25	.35	.20
992	3¢ United States Capitol	2.40	4.25	12.50(50)	1.25	.35	.20
993	3¢ Railroad	4.00	5.25	12.50(50)	1.25	.35	.20
994	3¢ Kansas City	2.40	4.25	15.00(50)	1.60	.35	.20
995	3¢ Boy Scouts	7.00	10.00	12.50(50)	1.25	.35	.20
996	3¢ Indiana Territory .	2.40	4.25	15.00(50)	1.50	.50	.20
997	3¢ California Statehood	2.40	4.25	25.00(50)	3.00	.70	.20

998

999

1000

1001

1002

1003

1951-52 COMMEMORATIVES

SCOTT NO.	DESCRIPTION	FIRST DAY COVERS SING	FIRST DAY COVERS PL. BLK.	MINT SHEET	PLATE BLOCK F/NH	UNUSED F/NH	USED F
998-1016	19 varieties, complete	....	....	....	....	6.40	3.50
998	3¢ Confederate Veterans	3.00	4.25	17.50(50)	1.75	.40	.20
999	3¢ Nevada Settlement	2.00	4.25	19.00(50)	1.75	.35	.20
1000	3¢ Landing of Cadillac	2.00	4.25	17.00(50)	1.50	.35	.20
1001	3¢ Colorado Statehood	2.00	4.25	17.00(50)	1.50	.35	.20
1002	3¢ Chemical Society	2.00	4.25	12.50(50)	1.25	.35	.20
1003	3¢ Battle of Brooklyn	2.00	4.25	12.50(50)	1.25	.35	.20

1004

1005

1006

1007

1008

1009

1010

1952 COMMEMORATIVES

SCOTT NO.	DESCRIPTION	FIRST DAY COVERS SING	FIRST DAY COVERS PL. BLK.	MINT SHEET	PLATE BLOCK F/NH	UNUSED F/NH	USED F
1004	3¢ Betsy Ross	2.50	5.50	12.00(50)	1.20	.40	.20
1005	3¢ 4-H Club	6.00	10.00	17.50(50)	1.75	.50	.20
1006	3¢ B. & O. Railroad .	4.00	6.50	17.50(50)	2.50	.40	.20
1007	3¢ AAA	2.00	4.25	14.00(50)	1.60	.40	.20
1008	3¢ NATO	2.00	4.25	17.50(100)	1.25	.35	.20
1009	3¢ Grand Coulee Dam	2.00	4.25	12.50(50)	1.25	.35	.20
1010	3¢ Lafayette	2.00	4.25	17.50(50)	1.50	.40	.20

NOTE: **To determine the VF price on stamps issued from 1941 to date, add 20% to the F/NH or F (used) price. All VF unused stamps from 1941 to date will be NH.**

1011

1012

1013

1014

1015

1016

SCOTT NO.	DESCRIPTION	FIRST DAY COVERS SING	FIRST DAY COVERS PL. BLK.	MINT SHEET	PLATE BLOCK F/NH	UNUSED F/NH	USED F
1011	3¢ Mt. Rushmore . .	2.00	4.25	17.50(50)	1.75	.45	.20
1012	3¢ Civil Engineers . .	2.00	4.25	12.50(50)	1.25	.35	.20
1013	3¢ Service Women .	2.25	4.25	12.50(50)	1.25	.35	.20
1014	3¢ Gutenburg Press	2.00	4.25	12.50(50)	1.25	.35	.20
1015	3¢ Newspaper Boys	2.00	4.25	12.50(50)	1.25	.35	.20
1016	3¢ Red Cross	3.00	6.25	12.50(50)	1.25	.35	.20

1017

1018

1019

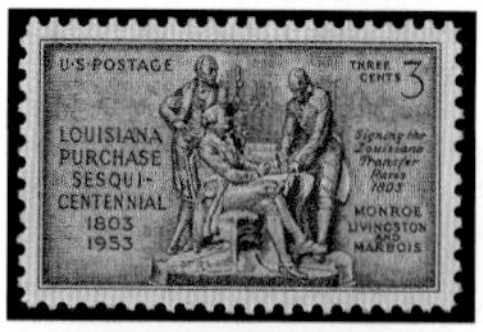

1020

1021

1022

1953-54 COMMEMORATIVES

SCOTT NO.	DESCRIPTION	FIRST DAY COVERS SING	FIRST DAY COVERS PL. BLK.	MINT SHEET	PLATE BLOCK F/NH	UNUSED F/NH	USED F
1017/63	(1017-29, 1060-63) 17 varieties, complete	....	....	....	....	5.55	3.20
1017	3¢ National Guard . .	2.00	4.25	12.50(50)	1.25	.35	.20
1018	3¢ Ohio Statehood .	2.00	4.25	17.50(70)	1.25	.35	.20
1019	3¢ Washington Territory	2.00	4.25	12.50(50)	1.25	.35	.20
1020	3¢ Louisiana Purchase	4.00	6.00	12.50(50)	1.25	.35	.20
1021	5¢ Opening of Japan	3.00	4.25	14.00(50)	1.50	.40	.20
1022	3¢ American Bar Association	5.00	6.25	17.50(50)	1.50	.40	.20

1023

1024

1025

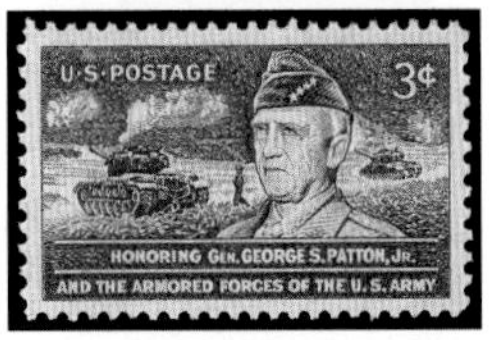

1026

1027

1028

SCOTT NO.	DESCRIPTION	FIRST DAY COVERS SING	FIRST DAY COVERS PL. BLK.	MINT SHEET	PLATE BLOCK F/NH	UNUSED F/NH	USED F
1023	3¢ Sagamore Hill . .	2.00	4.25	12.50(50)	1.25	.35	.20
1024	3¢ Future Farmers .	2.00	4.25	12.50(50)	1.25	.35	.20
1025	3¢ Trucking Industry	2.50	4.50	12.50(50)	1.25	.35	.20
1026	3¢ Gen. George S. Patton	3.00	4.75	12.50(50)	1.25	.35	.20
1027	3¢ New York City . .	2.00	4.25	12.50(50)	1.25	.35	.20
1028	3¢ Gadsden Purchase	2.00	4.25	17.00(50)	1.60	.35	.20

1029

1954 COMMEMORATIVE

SCOTT NO.	DESCRIPTION	FIRST DAY COVERS SING	FIRST DAY COVERS PL. BLK.	MINT SHEET	PLATE BLOCK F/NH	UNUSED F/NH	USED F
1029	3¢ Columbia University	2.00	4.25	12.50(50)	1.25	.35	.20

1030

1031, 1054

1031A, 1054A

1032

1033, 1055

1034, 1056

1035, 1057, 1075a

1036, 1058

1037, 1059

1038

1039

1040

1041, 1075b

1042

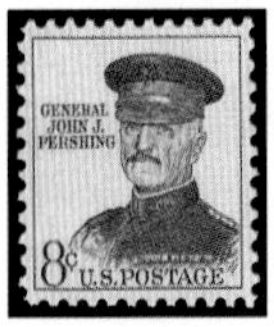

1042A

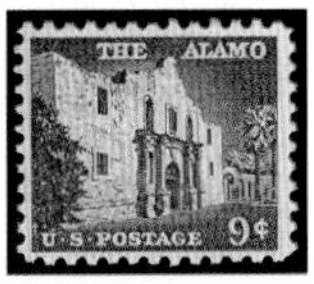

1043

1044

1044A

1045

1046

1047

1048, 1059A

1049

1050

1051

1052

1053

1954-68 LIBERTY SERIES

SCOTT NO.	DESCRIPTION	FIRST DAY COVERS SING	FIRST DAY COVERS PL. BLK.	MINT SHEET	PLATE BLOCK F/NH	UNUSED F/NH	USED F
1030-53	**1/2¢-$5, 27 varieties, complete . . . .**	**110.00**	**235.00**	**.......**	**525.00**	**120.00**	**14.50**
1030-51	**1/2¢-50¢, 25 varieties**	**55.00**	**115.00**	**.......**	**70.00**	**17.25**	**3.50**
1030	1/2¢ Benjamin Franklin (1955)	2.00	4.25	9.25(100)	.80	.25	.15
1031	1¢ George Washington	2.00	4.25	8.00(100)	.80	.25	.15
1031A	1-1/4¢ Palace of Governors (1960) . .	2.00	4.25	8.00(100)	.80	.25	.15
1032	1-1/2¢ Mount Vernon	2.00	4.25	22.00(100)	2.50	.25	.15
1033	2¢ Thomas Jefferson	2.00	4.25	14.00(100)	.80	.25	.15
1034	2-1/2¢ Bunker Hill (1959)	2.00	4.25	22.00(100)	1.00	.25	.15
1035	3¢ Statue of Liberty .	2.00	4.25	13.50(100)	.80	.25	.15
1035a	3¢ booklet pane of 6	3.50	....	....	....	5.00	....
1036	4¢ Abraham Lincoln	2.00	4.25	27.00(100)	.80	.25	.15
1036a	4¢ booklet pane of 6	3.00	....	....	....	3.50	....
1037	4-1/2¢ Hermitage (1959)	2.00	4.25	27.00(100)	1.35	.30	.15
1038	5¢ James Monroe . .	2.00	4.25	27.00(100)	1.35	.30	.15
1039	6¢ T. Roosevelt (1955)	2.00	4.25	40.00(100)	2.10	.60	.15
1040	7¢ Woodrow Wilson (1956)	2.00	4.25	30.00(100)	1.60	.40	.15
1041	8¢ Statue of Liberty (flat plate)	2.00	4.25	35.00(100)	2.50	.40	.15
1041B	8¢ Statue of Liberty .	2.00	4.25	50.00(100)	4.00	.60	.15
1042	8¢ Liberty re-engraved (1958)	2.00	4.25	35.00(100)	1.60	.40	.15
1042A	8¢ John J. Pershing (1961)	2.25	5.00	35.00(100)	1.60	.40	.15
1043	9¢ Alamo (1956) . . .	2.25	5.00	55.00(100)	2.25	.50	.15
1044	10¢ Independence Hall (1956)	2.25	5.00	45.00(100)	2.25	.50	.15
1044A	11¢ Statue of Liberty (1961)	2.25	5.00	45.00(100)	2.25	.50	.15
1045	12¢ Benjamin Harrison (1959)	2.25	5.00	60.00(100)	2.25	.60	.15
1046	15¢ John Jay (1958)	2.50	5.25	120.00(100)	4.95	1.10	.15
1047	20¢ Monticello (1956)	2.50	5.25	90.00(100)	4.00	.95	.15
1048	25¢ Paul Revere (1958)	2.50	5.25	175.00(100)	9.00	2.10	.15
1049	30¢ Robert E. Lee (1955)	3.75	6.00	175.00(100)	79.00	2.00	.15
1050	40¢ John Marshall (1955)	3.75	7.00	295.00(100)	12.50	3.00	.15
1051	50¢ Susan B. Anthony (1955)	5.50	8.50	225.00(100)	10.50	3.00	.15
1052	$1 Patrick Henry (1955)	9.25	17.50	....	32.50	7.50	.25
1053	$5 Alexander Hamilton (1956)	50.00	110.00	....	500.00	105.00	12.50

1954-65 COIL STAMPS
Perf. 10 Vertically or Horizontally

SCOTT NO.	DESCRIPTION	FIRST DAY COVERS SING	LINE PAIR	MINT SHEET	LINE PAIR	UNUSED F/NH	USED F
1054-59A	**1¢-25¢ (8 varieties, complete) . . . .**	**16.00**	**29.75**	**.......**	**29.75**	**4.65**	**2.40**
1054	1¢ George Washington	2.00	3.75	....	1.25	.30	.15
1054A	1-1/4¢ Palace of Governors(1960) . . .	2.00	3.75	....	3.00	.30	.15
1055	2¢ Thomas Jefferson(1957)	2.00	3.75	....	.75	.30	.15
1056	2-1/2¢ Bunker Hill Mon. (1959)	2.00	3.75	....	5.50	.45	.30
1057	3¢ Statue of Liberty(1956)	2.00	3.75	....	.85	.25	.15
1058	4¢ Abraham Lincoln (1958)	2.00	3.75	....	.85	.25	.15
1059	4-1/2¢ Hermitage (1959)	2.00	3.75	....	18.00	3.00	2.00
1059A	25¢ Paul Revere (1965)	2.50	5.00	....	3.00	.95	.20

NOTE: **Pairs of the above can be priced at two times the single price.**

1060

1061

1062

1063

1954 COMMEMORATIVES

SCOTT NO.	DESCRIPTION	FIRST DAY COVERS SING	PL. BLK.	MINT SHEET	PLATE BLOCK F/NH	UNUSED F/NH	USED F
1060	3¢ Nebraska Territory	2.00	4.25	16.00(50)	1.50	.35	.20
1061	3¢ Kansas Territory.	2.00	4.25	20.00(50)	2.00	.50	.20
1062	3¢ George Eastman	2.00	4.25	15.00(70)	1.50	.35	.20
1063	3¢ Lewis & Clark . . .	4.00	6.00	25.00(50)	2.50	.60	.20

1064

1065

1066

1067

1068

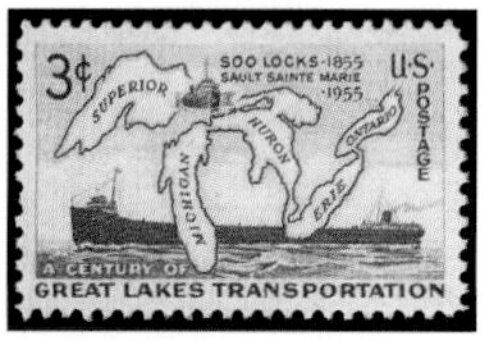

1069

1068

1955 COMMEMORATIVES

SCOTT NO.	DESCRIPTION	FIRST DAY COVERS SING	PL. BLK.	MINT SHEET	PLATE BLOCK F/NH	UNUSED F/NH	USED F
1064-72	**3¢-8¢ (9 varieties, complete)**	....	....	....	....	**2.95**	**1.50**
1064	3¢ Pennsylvania Academy	2.00	4.25	15.00(50)	1.75	.40	.20
1065	3¢ Land Grant Colleges	2.50	4.50	22.00(50)	2.00	.50	.20
1066	8¢ Rotary International	5.00	7.00	27.00(50)	2.75	.70	.20
1067	3¢ Armed Forces Reserve	2.00	4.25	12.50(50)	1.25	.35	.20
1068	3¢ Great Stone Face	2.00	4.25	15.00(50)	1.75	.40	.20
1069	3¢ Soo Locks	2.00	4.25	18.00(50)	1.50	.50	.20

1070

1071

1072

SCOTT NO.	DESCRIPTION	FIRST DAY COVERS SING	PL. BLK.	MINT SHEET	PLATE BLOCK F/NH	UNUSED F/NH	USED F
1070	3¢ Atoms for Peace	2.00	4.25	12.50(50)	1.25	.35	.20
1071	3¢ Fort Ticonderoga	2.00	4.25	12.50(50)	1.25	.35	.20
1072	3¢ Andrew Mellon . .	2.00	4.25	22.50(70)	1.75	.40	.20

1073

1074

1075

1956 COMMEMORATIVES

SCOTT NO.	DESCRIPTION	FIRST DAY COVERS SING	PL. BLK.	MINT SHEET	PLATE BLOCK F/NH	UNUSED F/NH	USED F
1073/85	**(1073-74, 1076-85) 12 varieties. . . . . . .**	....	....	....	....	**3.80**	**2.00**
1073	3¢ Benjamin Franklin	2.00	4.25	14.00(50)	1.40	.35	.20
1074	3¢ Booker T. Washington	3.50	5.50	14.00(50)	1.40	.35	.20
1075	3¢ & 8¢ FIPEX Sheet of 2	6.00	....	....	....	3.25	3.25
1075a	3¢ deep violet, single	....	....	....	....	1.25	1.05
1075b	8¢ violet blue & carmine, single	....	....	....	....	1.75	1.25

1076

1077

1078

1079

SCOTT NO.	DESCRIPTION	FIRST DAY COVERS SING	PL. BLK.	MINT SHEET	PLATE BLOCK F/NH	UNUSED F/NH	USED F
1076	3¢ FIPEX	2.00	4.25	12.50(50)	1.25	.35	.20
1077	3¢ Wild Turkey	2.75	4.50	12.50(50)	1.25	.35	.20
1078	3¢ Antelope	2.75	4.50	12.50(50)	1.25	.35	.20
1079	3¢ Salmon	2.75	4.50	16.00(50)	1.50	.35	.20

PLATE BLOCKS: are portions of a sheet of stamps adjacent to the number(s) indicating the printing plate number used to produce that sheet. Flat plate issues are usually collected in plate blocks of six (number opposite middle stamp) while rotary issues are normally corner blocks of four.

1080

1081

1082

SCOTT NO.	DESCRIPTION	FIRST DAY COVERS SING	FIRST DAY COVERS PL. BLK.	MINT SHEET	PLATE BLOCK F/NH	UNUSED F/NH	USED F
1080	3¢ Pure Food & Drug Act	2.00	4.25	13.50(50)	1.35	.35	.20
1081	3¢ "Wheatland"	2.00	4.25	13.50(50)	1.35	.35	.20
1082	3¢ Labor Day	2.00	4.25	13.50(50)	1.35	.35	.20

1083

1084

1085

SCOTT NO.	DESCRIPTION	FIRST DAY COVERS SING	FIRST DAY COVERS PL. BLK.	MINT SHEET	PLATE BLOCK F/NH	UNUSED F/NH	USED F
1083	3¢ Nassau Hall	2.00	4.25	13.50(50)	1.35	.35	.20
1084	3¢ Devil's Tower . . .	2.00	4.25	15.00(50)	1.50	.35	.20
1085	3¢ Children of the World	2.00	4.25	15.00(50)	1.50	.35	.20

1086

1087

1088

1089

1090

1091

1957 COMMEMORATIVES

SCOTT NO.	DESCRIPTION	FIRST DAY COVERS SING	FIRST DAY COVERS PL. BLK.	MINT SHEET	PLATE BLOCK F/NH	UNUSED F/NH	USED F
1086-99	14 varieties, complete	....	....	....	....	4.35	2.65
1086	3¢ Alexander Hamilton	2.00	4.25	12.50(50)	1.25	.35	.20
1087	3¢ Polio	2.25	4.50	12.50(50)	1.25	.35	.20
1088	3¢ Coast & Geodetic Survey	2.00	4.25	12.50(50)	1.25	.35	.20
1089	3¢ Architects	2.00	4.25	12.50(50)	1.25	.35	.20
1090	3¢ Steel Industry . . .	2.00	4.25	12.50(50)	1.25	.35	.20
1091	3¢ International Naval Review	2.00	4.25	12.50(50)	1.25	.30	.20

1092

1093

1094

1095

1096

1097

SCOTT NO.	DESCRIPTION	FIRST DAY COVERS SING	FIRST DAY COVERS PL. BLK.	MINT SHEET	PLATE BLOCK F/NH	UNUSED F/NH	USED F
1092	3¢ Oklahoma Statehood	2.00	4.25	12.50(50)	1.25	.35	.20
1093	3¢ School Teachers	2.25	4.50	12.50(50)	1.25	.35	.20
1094	4¢ 48-Star Flag	2.00	4.25	12.50(50)	1.25	.35	.20
1095	3¢ Shipbuilding Anniversary	2.00	4.25	20.00(70)	1.25	.35	.20
1096	8¢ Ramon Magsaysay	2.50	4.25	14.00(48)	1.40	.35	.20
1097	3¢ Birth of Lafayette	2.00	4.25	12.50(50)	1.25	.35	.20

1098

1099

1100

SCOTT NO.	DESCRIPTION	FIRST DAY COVERS SING	FIRST DAY COVERS PL. BLK.	MINT SHEET	PLATE BLOCK F/NH	UNUSED F/NH	USED F
1098	3¢ Whooping Cranes	2.25	4.50	12.50(50)	1.25	.35	.20
1099	3¢ Religious Freedom	2.00	4.25	12.50(50)	1.25	.35	.20

1104

1105

1106

1107

1958 COMMEMORATIVES

SCOTT NO.	DESCRIPTION	FIRST DAY COVERS SING	FIRST DAY COVERS PL. BLK.	MINT SHEET	PLATE BLOCK F/NH	UNUSED F/NH	USED F
1100-23	21 varieties, complete	....	....	....	....	7.00	4.00
1100	3¢ Gardening & Horticulture	2.00	4.25	12.50(50)	1.25	.35	.20
1104	3¢ Brussels Exhibition	2.00	4.25	12.50(50)	1.25	.35	.20
1105	3¢ James Monroe . .	2.00	4.25	18.00(70)	1.25	.35	.20
1106	3¢ Minnesota Statehood	2.00	4.25	18.00(50)	1.70	.35	.20
1107	3¢ Int'l. Geophysical Year	2.00	4.25	12.50(50)	1.25	.35	.20

1108

1109

1110, 1111

1112

SCOTT NO.	DESCRIPTION	FIRST DAY COVERS SING	FIRST DAY COVERS PL. BLK.	MINT SHEET	PLATE BLOCK F/NH	UNUSED F/NH	USED F
1108	3¢ Gunston Hall . . .	2.00	4.25	12.50(50)	1.25	.35	.20
1109	3¢ Mackinac Bridge	2.00	4.25	18.00(50)	1.75	.40	.20
1110	4¢ Simon Bolivar . . .	2.00	4.25	14.00(70)	1.25	.35	.20
1111	8¢ Simon Bolivar . . .	2.00	4.50	19.50(72)	1.85	.35	.20
1112	4¢ Atlantic Cable Centenary	2.00	4.25	12.50(50)	1.25	.35	.20

1113

1114

1115

1116

SCOTT NO.	DESCRIPTION	FIRST DAY COVERS SING	FIRST DAY COVERS PL. BLK.	MINT SHEET	PLATE BLOCK F/NH	UNUSED F/NH	USED F
1113	1¢ Abraham Lincoln (1959)	2.00	4.25	5.00(50)	.75	.30	.20
1114	3¢ Bust of Lincoln (1959)	2.00	4.25	15.00(50)	1.75	.40	.20
1115	4¢ Lincoln-Douglas Debates	2.00	4.25	17.50(50)	1.75	.40	.25
1116	4¢ Statue of Lincoln (1959)	2.00	4.25	15.00(50)	1.75	.40	.25

1117, 1118

1119

1120

SCOTT NO.	DESCRIPTION	FIRST DAY COVERS SING	FIRST DAY COVERS PL. BLK.	MINT SHEET	PLATE BLOCK F/NH	UNUSED F/NH	USED F
1117	4¢ Lajos Kossuth . .	2.00	4.25	14.00(70)	1.25	.35	.20
1118	8¢ Lajos Kossuth . .	2.00	4.50	19.50(72)	1.60	.35	.20
1119	4¢ Freedom of Press	2.00	4.25	12.50(50)	1.25	.35	.20
1120	4¢ Overland Mail . . .	2.00	4.25	12.50(50)	1.25	.35	.20

Plate blocks will be blocks of 4 stamps unless otherwise noted.

1121

1122

1123

SCOTT NO.	DESCRIPTION	FIRST DAY COVERS SING	FIRST DAY COVERS PL. BLK.	MINT SHEET	PLATE BLOCK F/NH	UNUSED F/NH	USED F
1121	4¢ Noah Webster . .	2.00	4.25	14.00(70)	1.25	.35	.20
1122	4¢ Forest Conservation	2.00	4.25	12.50(50)	1.25	.35	.20
1123	4¢ Fort Duquesne . .	2.00	4.25	12.50(50)	1.25	.35	.20

1124

1125, 1126

1127

1128

1129

1959 COMMEMORATIVES

SCOTT NO.	DESCRIPTION	FIRST DAY COVERS SING	FIRST DAY COVERS PL. BLK.	MINT SHEET	PLATE BLOCK F/NH	UNUSED F/NH	USED F
1124-38	**4¢-8¢, 15 varieties .**	......	....	....	....	**4.95**	**2.85**
1124	4¢ Oregon Statehood	2.00	4.25	20.00(50)	2.20	.35	.20
1125	4¢ José de San Martin	2.00	4.25	14.00(70)	1.25	.35	.20
1126	8¢ José de San Martin	2.00	4.25	19.50(72)	1.40	.35	.20
1127	4¢ NATO	2.00	4.25	12.50(70)	1.25	.35	.20
1128	4¢ Arctic Exploration	2.00	4.25	12.50(50)	1.25	.35	.20
1129	8¢ World Peace & Trade	2.00	4.25	16.00(50)	1.75	.40	.20

1130

1131

1132

1133

1134

1135

1136, 1137

1138

SCOTT NO.	DESCRIPTION	FIRST DAY COVERS SING	FIRST DAY COVERS PL. BLK.	MINT SHEET	PLATE BLOCK F/NH	UNUSED F/NH	USED F
1130	4¢ Silver Centennial	2.00	4.25	16.00(50)	1.60	.35	.20
1131	4¢ St. Lawrence Seaway	2.00	4.25	12.50(50)	1.25	.35	.20
1132	4¢ 49-Star Flag	2.00	4.25	12.50(50)	1.25	.35	.20
1133	4¢ Soil Conservation	2.00	4.25	12.50(50)	1.25	.35	.20
1134	4¢ Petroleum	2.00	4.25	15.00(50)	1.25	.40	.20
1135	4¢ Dental Health . . .	5.00	7.00	15.00(50)	1.40	.40	.20
1136	4¢ Ernst Reuter	2.00	4.25	14.00(70)	1.25	.35	.20
1137	8¢ Ernst Reuter	2.00	4.25	19.50(72)	1.50	.35	.20
1138	4¢ Dr. Ephraim McDowell	2.00	4.25	19.50(70)	1.50	.35	.20

1139

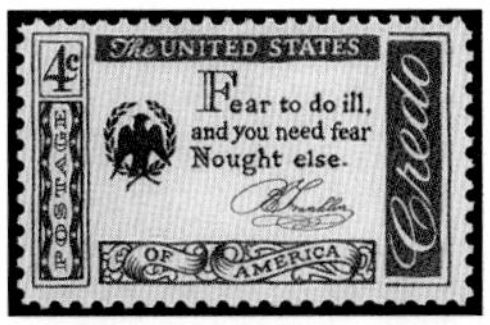

1140

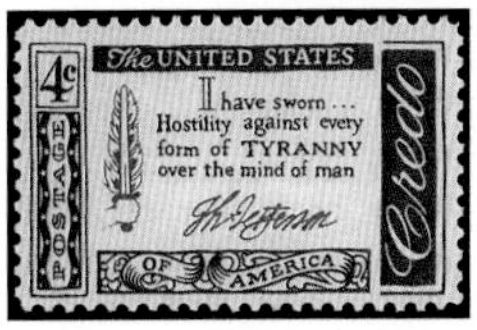

1141

1142

1143

1144

1960-61 CREDO OF AMERICA SERIES

SCOTT NO.	DESCRIPTION	FIRST DAY COVERS SING	FIRST DAY COVERS PL. BLK.	MINT SHEET	PLATE BLOCK F/NH	UNUSED F/NH	USED F
1139-44	**6 varieties, complete**	....	....	....	....	**1.85**	**1.15**
1139	4¢ Credo—Washington	2.00	4.25	12.50(50)	1.25	.35	.20
1140	4¢ Credo—Franklin .	2.00	4.25	12.50(50)	1.25	.35	.20
1141	4¢ Credo—Jefferson	2.00	4.25	12.50(50)	1.25	.35	.20
1142	4¢ Credo—Key	2.00	4.25	12.50(50)	1.25	.35	.20
1143	4¢ Credo—Lincoln .	2.00	4.25	12.50(50)	1.25	.35	.20
1144	4¢ Credo—Henry (1961)	2.00	4.25	12.50(50)	1.25	.35	.20

1145

1146

1147, 1148

1149

1150

1151

1152

1153

1960 COMMEMORATIVES

SCOTT NO.	DESCRIPTION	FIRST DAY COVERS SING	FIRST DAY COVERS PL. BLK.	MINT SHEET	PLATE BLOCK F/NH	UNUSED F/NH	USED F
1145-73	**4¢-8¢, 29 varieties .**	....	....	....	....	**8.85**	**5.25**
1145	4¢ Boy Scouts	8.50	10.50	17.50(50)	1.75	.40	.20
1146	4¢ Winter Olympics .	2.00	4.25	12.50(50)	1.00	.35	.20
1147	4¢ Thomas Masaryk	2.00	4.25	14.00(70)	1.00	.35	.20
1148	8¢ Thomas Masaryk	2.00	4.25	21.00(72)	1.40	.40	.20
1149	4¢ World Refugee Year	2.00	4.25	12.50(50)	1.00	.35	.20
1150	4¢ Water Conservation	2.00	4.25	12.50(50)	1.00	.35	.20
1151	4¢ SEATO	2.00	4.25	14.00(70)	1.00	.35	.20
1152	4¢ American Women	2.00	4.25	12.50(50)	1.00	.35	.20
1153	4¢ 50-Star Flag	2.00	4.25	12.50(50)	1.00	.35	.20

1154

1155

1156

1157

1158

1159, 1160

1161

1162

1163

SCOTT NO.	DESCRIPTION	FIRST DAY COVERS SING	FIRST DAY COVERS PL. BLK.	MINT SHEET	PLATE BLOCK F/NH	UNUSED F/NH	USED F
1154	4¢ Pony Express . . .	2.00	4.25	19.50(50)	2.00	.45	.20
1155	4¢ Employ the Handicapped	2.00	4.25	12.00(50)	1.25	.30	.20
1156	4¢ World Forestry Congress	2.00	4.25	12.00(50)	1.25	.30	.20
1157	4¢ Mexican Independence	2.00	4.25	12.00(50)	1.25	.30	.20
1158	4¢ U.S.-Japan Treaty	2.00	4.25	12.00(50)	1.25	.30	.20
1159	4¢ Ignacy Paderewski	2.00	4.25	17.00(70)	1.75	.30	.20
1160	8¢ Ignacy Paderewski	2.00	4.25	19.50(72)	1.75	.35	.20
1161	4¢ Robert A. Taft . .	2.00	4.25	19.00(70)	1.75	.30	.20
1162	4¢ Wheels of Freedom	2.00	4.25	17.00(50)	1.75	.30	.20
1163	4¢ Boys' Club of America	2.25	4.25	15.00(50)	1.75	.30	.20

SCOTT NO.	DESCRIPTION	FIRST DAY COVERS SING	PL. BLK.	MINT SHEET	PLATE BLOCK F/NH	UNUSED F/NH	USED F

1164

1165, 1166

1167

1168, 1169

1170

1171

1172

1173

SCOTT NO.	DESCRIPTION	FIRST DAY COVERS SING	PL. BLK.	MINT SHEET	PLATE BLOCK F/NH	UNUSED F/NH	USED F
1164	4¢ Automated Post Office	2.00	4.25	20.00(50)	1.75	.45	.20
1165	4¢ Gustaf Mannerheim	2.00	4.25	14.00(70)	1.00	.30	.20
1166	8¢ Gustaf Mannerheim	2.00	4.25	19.50(72)	1.40	.35	.20
1167	4¢ Camp Fire Girls .	5.00	7.25	23.00(50)	2.50	.60	.20
1168	4¢ Giuseppe Garibaldi	2.00	4.25	14.00(70)	1.00	.30	.20
1169	8¢ Giuseppe Garibaldi	2.00	4.25	19.50(72)	1.40	.35	.20
1170	4¢ Walter George . .	2.00	4.25	29.00(70)	2.50	.75	.20
1171	4¢ Andrew Carnegie	2.00	4.25	17.50(70)	1.25	.35	.20
1172	4¢ John Foster Dulles	2.00	4.25	17.50(70)	1.25	.35	.20
1173	4¢ "ECHO I" Satellite	3.00	6.50	15.00(50)	1.40	.70	.20

1174, 1175

1176

1177

1961 COMMEMORATIVES

SCOTT NO.	DESCRIPTION	FIRST DAY COVERS SING	PL. BLK.	MINT SHEET	PLATE BLOCK F/NH	UNUSED F/NH	USED F
1174/90	**(1174-77, 1183-90) 12 varieties . . . . . .**	....	....	....	....	**4.00**	**2.25**
1174	4¢ Mahatma Gandhi	2.00	4.25	16.00(70)	1.25	.50	.20
1175	8¢ Mahatma Gandhi	2.00	4.25	19.50(72)	1.75	.50	.20
1176	4¢ Range Conservation	2.00	4.25	17.00(50)	1.75	.50	.20
1177	4¢ Horace Greeley .	2.00	4.25	20.00(70)	1.75	.50	.20

1178

1179

1180

1181

1182

1183

1961-65 CIVIL WAR CENTENNIAL SERIES

SCOTT NO.	DESCRIPTION	FIRST DAY COVERS SING	PL. BLK.	MINT SHEET	PLATE BLOCK F/NH	UNUSED F/NH	USED F
1178-82	**4¢-5¢, 5 varieties, complete . . . .**	....	....	....	....	**2.75**	**.80**
1178	4¢ Fort Sumter	7.50	10.00	27.50(50)	2.50	.60	.20
1179	4¢ Shiloh (1962) . . .	7.50	10.00	17.50(50)	1.75	.40	.20
1180	5¢ Gettysburg (1963)	7.50	10.00	17.50(50)	1.75	.60	.20
1181	5¢ Wilderness (1964)	7.50	10.00	17.50(50)	1.75	.55	.20
1181	Zip Code Block	....	....	....	1.40	....	....
1182	5¢ Appomattox (1965)	7.50	10.00	40.00(50)	4.00	.75	.20
1182	Zip Code Block	....	....	....	3.50	....	....

1184

1185

1186

1187

1188

1189

1190

1961 COMMEMORATIVES

SCOTT NO.	DESCRIPTION	FIRST DAY COVERS SING	PL. BLK.	MINT SHEET	PLATE BLOCK F/NH	UNUSED F/NH	USED F
1183	4¢ Kansas Statehood	2.00	4.25	30.00(50)	2.75	.60	.20
1184	4¢ George W. Norris	2.00	4.25	12.00(50)	1.30	.35	.20
1185	4¢ Naval Aviation . .	2.00	4.25	12.00(50)	1.30	.35	.20
1186	4¢ Workmen's Compensation	2.00	4.25	18.00(50)	1.75	.35	.20
1187	4¢ Frederic Remington	2.00	4.25	15.00(50)	1.30	.35	.20
1188	4¢ Sun Yat-sen	6.00	10.00	15.00(50)	1.30	.35	.20
1189	4¢ Basketball	9.00	12.00	15.00(50)	1.30	.75	.20
1190	4¢ Nursing	13.50	20.00	15.00(50)	1.30	.75	.20

NOTE: To determine the VF price on stamps issued from 1941 to date, add 20% to the F/NH or F (used) price (minimum .03 per item). All VF unused stamps from 1941 date priced as NH.

1191

1192

1193

1194

1962 COMMEMORATIVES

SCOTT NO.	DESCRIPTION	FIRST DAY COVERS SING	FIRST DAY COVERS PL. BLK.	MINT SHEET	PLATE BLOCK F/NH	UNUSED F/NH	USED F
1191-1207	**17 varieties . . . .**	....	....	....	....	**5.40**	**3.40**
1191	4¢ New Mexico Statehood	1.75	4.00	17.00(50)	1.25	.40	.20
1192	4¢ Arizona Statehood	1.75	4.00	14.00(50)	1.25	.30	.20
1193	4¢ Project Mercury	5.00	7.50	14.00(50)	1.25	.30	.20
1194	4¢ Malaria Eradication	1.75	4.00	14.00(50)	1.25	.30	.20

1195

1196

1197

SCOTT NO.	DESCRIPTION	FIRST DAY COVERS SING	FIRST DAY COVERS PL. BLK.	MINT SHEET	PLATE BLOCK F/NH	UNUSED F/NH	USED F
1195	4¢ Charles Evans Hughes	2.00	4.00	13.00(50)	1.25	.30	.20
1196	4¢ Seattle World's Fair	2.00	4.00	13.00(50)	1.25	.30	.20
1197	4¢ Louisiana Statehood	2.00	4.00	17.00(50)	1.50	.40	.20

1198

1199

1200

1201

1202

1203

1205

1206

1207

SCOTT NO.	DESCRIPTION	FIRST DAY COVERS SING	FIRST DAY COVERS PL. BLK.	MINT SHEET	PLATE BLOCK F/NH	UNUSED F/NH	USED F
1198	4¢ Homestead Act	2.00	4.00	14.00(50)	1.25	.35	.20
1199	4¢ Girl Scouts . . .	7.00	10.00	14.00(50)	1.25	.35	.20
1200	4¢ Brien McMahon	2.00	4.00	14.00(50)	1.25	.35	.20
1201	4¢ Apprenticeship	2.00	4.00	14.00(50)	1.25	.35	.20
1202	4¢ Sam Rayburn .	2.00	4.00	17.00(50)	1.50	.35	.20
1203	4¢ Dag Hammarskjold	2.00	4.00	10.00(50)	1.00	.35	.20
1204	same, yellow inverted	5.00	10.25	10.00(50)	1.50	.35	.20
1205	4¢ Christmas 1962	2.00	4.00	17.00(50)	1.00	.35	.20
1206	4¢ Higher Education	2.00	4.00	10.00(50)	1.00	.35	.20
1207	4¢ Winslow Homer	2.00	4.00	12.50(50)	1.25	.35	.20

1208

1209, 1225

1213, 1229

1962-66 REGULAR ISSUE

SCOTT NO.	DESCRIPTION	FIRST DAY COVERS SING	FIRST DAY COVERS PL. BLK.	MINT SHEET	PLATE BLOCK F/NH	UNUSED F/NH	USED F
1208	5¢ Flag & White House (1963)	2.00	4.25	27.50(100)	1.35	.30	.15
1209	1¢ Andrew Jackson (1963)	2.00	4.00	10.00(100)	.75	.20	.15
1213	5¢ Washington . .	2.00	4.00	27.50(100)	1.35	.30	.15
1213a	5¢ b. pane of 5—Slog. I	2.50	....	....	....	6.50	....
1213a	5¢ b. pane of 5—Slog. II (1963)	....	....	....	....	20.00	....
1213a	5¢ b. pane of 5—Slog. III (1964)	....	....	....	....	3.50	....
1213c	5¢ Tagged pane of 5 Slogan II (1963).......	....	....	....	....	90.00	....
1213c	5¢ b. p. of 5—Slog. III (1963)	....	....	....	....	2.50	....

Slogan I—Your Mailman Deserves Your Help · Keep Harmful Objects Out of...
Slogan II—Add Zip to Your Mail · Use Zone Numbers for Zip Code.
Slogan III—Add Zip to Your Mail · Always Use Zip Code.

1962-66 COIL STAMPS Perf. 10 Vertically

SCOTT NO.	DESCRIPTION	FIRST DAY COVERS SING	LINE PAIRS	MINT SHEET	LINE PAIRS	UNUSED F/NH	USED F
1225	1¢ Andrew Jackson (1963)	2.00	3.00	....	3.00	.20	.15
1229	5¢ George Washington	2.00	3.00	....	3.25	1.25	.15

1230

1231

1232

1233

1963 COMMEMORATIVES

SCOTT NO.	DESCRIPTION	FIRST DAY COVERS SING	FIRST DAY COVERS PL. BLK.	MINT SHEET	PLATE BLOCK F/NH	UNUSED F/NH	USED F
1230-41	**12 varieties . . . .**	....	....	....	....	**3.85**	**2.00**
1230	5¢ Carolina Charter	2.00	4.00	14.00(50)	1.50	.40	.20
1231	5¢ Food for Peace	2.00	4.00	12.00(50)	1.25	.30	.20
1232	5¢ West Virginia Statehood	2.00	4.00	20.00(50)	2.00	.50	.20
1233	5¢ Emancipation Proclamation	4.00	6.00	12.50(50)	1.25	.35	.20

1234

1235

1236

1237

1238

1239

1240

1241

1242

1243

1963 COMMEMORATIVES

SCOTT NO.	DESCRIPTION	FIRST DAY COVERS SING	FIRST DAY COVERS PL. BLK.	MINT SHEET	PLATE BLOCK F/NH	UNUSED F/NH	USED F
1234	5¢ Alliance for Progress	2.00	4.00	10.00(50)	1.00	.30	.20
1235	5¢ Cordell Hull . .	2.00	4.00	17.50(50)	1.75	.40	.20
1236	5¢ Eleanor Roosevelt	2.00	4.00	12.50(50)	1.25	.35	.20
1237	5¢ The Sciences .	2.00	4.00	10.00(50)	1.00	.30	.20
1238	5¢ City Mail Delivery	2.00	4.00	10.00(50)	1.00	.30	.20
1239	5¢ International Red Cross	2.00	4.00	10.00(50)	1.00	.30	.20
1240	5¢ Christmas 1963	2.00	4.00	25.00(100)	1.50	.35	.20
1241	5¢ John J. Audubon	2.00	4.00	10.00(50)	1.00	.30	.20

1244

1245

1964 COMMEMORATIVES

SCOTT NO.	DESCRIPTION	FIRST DAY COVERS SING	FIRST DAY COVERS PL. BLK.	MINT SHEET	PLATE BLOCK	UNUSED F/NH	USED
1242-60	19 varieties	....	....	....	....	6.95	3.50
1242	5¢ Sam Houston . . .	4.00	6.00	25.00(50)	2.75	.70	.20
1243	5¢ Charles M. Russell	2.00	4.00	17.50(50)	1.75	.35	.20
1244	5¢ New York World's Fair	2.00	4.00	12.50(50)	1.25	.35	.20
1245	5¢ John Muir	2.00	4.00	20.00(50)	2.00	.50	.20

1246

1247

SCOTT NO.	DESCRIPTION	FIRST DAY COVERS SING	FIRST DAY COVERS PL. BLK.	MINT SHEET	PLATE BLOCK	UNUSED F/NH	USED
1246	5¢ John F. Kennedy	2.50	5.00	25.00(50)	2.50	.75	.20
1247	5¢ New Jersey Tercentenary	1.75	4.00	15.00(50)	1.25	.35	.20

1248

1249

1250

1251

1252

SCOTT NO.	DESCRIPTION	FIRST DAY COVERS SING	FIRST DAY COVERS PL. BLK.	MINT SHEET	PLATE BLOCK	UNUSED F/NH	USED
1248	5¢ Nevada Statehood	2.00	4.00	17.00(50)	1.50	.35	.20
1249	5¢ Register and Vote	2.00	4.00	12.00(50)	1.20	.30	.20
1250	5¢ Shakespeare . . .	2.00	4.00	12.00(50)	1.20	.30	.20
1251	5¢ Mayo Brothers . .	5.00	7.00	25.00(50)	2.75	.60	.20
1252	5¢ American Music .	2.00	4.00	12.00(50)	1.20	.30	.20

1253

1254

1255

1256

1257

SCOTT NO.	DESCRIPTION	FIRST DAY COVERS SING	FIRST DAY COVERS PL. BLK.	MINT SHEET	PLATE BLOCK	UNUSED F/NH	USED
1253	5¢ Homemakers . . .	2.00	4.00	12.00(50)	1.20	.30	.20
1254-57	5¢ Christmas, 4 varieties, attached	5.25	7.50	42.00(100)	2.50	2.00	1.50
1254	5¢ Holly	2.75	....	....	....	.40	.20
1255	5¢ Mistletoe	2.75	....	....	....	.40	.20
1256	5¢ Poinsettia	2.75	....	....	....	.40	.20
1257	5¢ Pine Cone	2.75	....	....	....	.40	.20

COMMEMORATIVES: Commemorative stamps are special issues released to honor or recognize persons, organizations, historical events or landmarks. They are usually issued in the current first class denomination to supplement regular issues.

1258

1259

1260

SCOTT NO.	DESCRIPTION	FIRST DAY COVERS SING	FIRST DAY COVERS PL. BLK.	MINT SHEET	PLATE BLOCK	UNUSED F/NH	USED
1258	5¢ Verrazano-Narrows Bridge	2.00	4.00	12.50(50)	1.25	.35	.20
1259	5¢ Modern Art	2.00	4.00	12.00(50)	1.20	.30	.20
1260	5¢ Radio Amateurs	8.00	10.00	25.00(50)	2.50	.60	.20

1261

1262

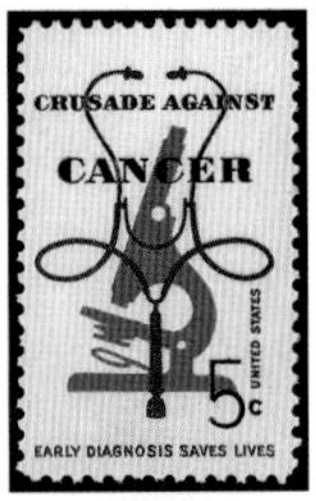

1263

1264

1265

1965 COMMEMORATIVES

SCOTT NO.	DESCRIPTION	FIRST DAY COVERS SING	FIRST DAY COVERS PL. BLK.	MINT SHEET	PLATE BLOCK	UNUSED F/NH	USED
1261-76	**5¢-11¢, 16 varieties**	....	....	....	....	**5.15**	**3.00**
1261	5¢ Battle of New Orleans	2.00	4.00	22.50(50)	2.25	.50	.20
1262	5¢ Physical Fitness	2.00	4.00	12.00(50)	1.20	.30	.20
1263	5¢ Crusade Against Cancer	4.00	6.00	12.00(50)	1.20	.30	.20
1264	5¢ Winston Churchill	2.00	4.00	17.50(50)	1.75	.40	.20
1265	5¢ Magna Carta	2.00	4.00	8.00(50)	1.20	.30	.20

1266

1267

1268

1269

1270

1271

1272

1273

SCOTT NO.	DESCRIPTION	FIRST DAY COVERS SING	FIRST DAY COVERS PL. BLK.	MINT SHEET	PLATE BLOCK	UNUSED F/NH	USED
1266	5¢ International Cooperation Year	2.00	4.00	12.50(50)	1.25	.30	.20
1267	5¢ Salvation Army	3.00	4.00	12.50(50)	1.25	.30	.20
1268	5¢ Dante Alighieri	2.00	4.00	12.50(50)	1.25	.30	.20
1269	5¢ Herbert Hoover	2.00	4.00	18.00(50)	1.75	.50	.20
1270	5¢ Robert Fulton	2.00	4.00	12.00(50)	1.20	.45	.20
1271	5¢ Florida Settlement	2.00	4.00	18.00(50)	1.75	.40	.20
1272	5¢ Traffic Safety	2.00	4.00	18.00(50)	1.75	.40	.20
1273	5¢ John S. Copley	2.00	4.00	18.00(50)	1.75	.30	.20

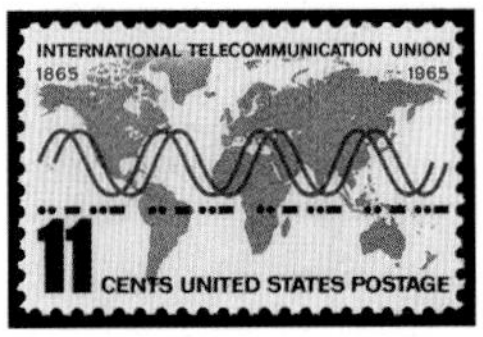

1274

1275

1276

SCOTT NO.	DESCRIPTION	FIRST DAY COVERS SING	FIRST DAY COVERS PL. BLK.	MINT SHEET	PLATE BLOCK	UNUSED F/NH	USED
1274	11¢ Telecommunication	2.00	4.00	30.00(50)	7.00	.75	.40
1275	5¢ Adlai Stevenson	2.00	4.00	12.00(50)	1.20	.30	.15
1276	5¢ Christmas 1965	2.00	4.00	22.00(100)	1.20	.30	.15

Stamp History

Thatcher Ferry Bridge

In 1962, during the regular course of business H.E. Harris purchases, at their 4 cent face value, a pane of 50 stamps honoring the Canal Zone's Thatcher Ferry Bridge. Due to a printing error, the silver bridge has been omitted. Harris discovers that his is the only pane from the sheet of 200 printed that has reached the public. Because a recent error in a Dag Hammerskjold stamp prompted the U.S. Postal Service to reprint thousands in order to make the error worthless, Harris questions how the Canal Zone will handle the bridge error. Flooding the market, he insists, would blunt the fun and excitement of stamp collecting. When the Canal Zone says it will reprint the error, Harris sues.

March 25, 1965, The Federal District Court in Washington rules in Harris' favor, stopping the Canal Zone authorities from reprinting the stamp error. Viewed as a precendent-setting event in philately, the effort won Harris the respect and awards of his fellow collectors.

1278, 1299

1279

1280

1281, 1297

1282, 1303

1283, 1304

1283B, 1304C

1284, 1298

1285

1286

1286A

1287

1288, 1288B, 1288d, 1305E, 1305Ei

1289

1290

1291

1292

1293

1294, 1305C

1295

1305

1965-78 PROMINENT AMERICAN SERIES

SCOTT NO.	DESCRIPTION	FIRST DAY COVERS SING	FIRST DAY COVERS PL. BLK.	MINT SHEET	PLATE BLOCK	UNUSED F/NH	USED
1278-95	**1¢-$5, 20 varieties, complete (No #1288B or 1288d)**	**91.50**	....	....	**150.00**	**32.50**	**7.75**
1278	1¢ T. Jefferson (1968)	1.75	4.00	8.00(100)	.75	.20	.15
1278a	1¢ bklt.pane of 8	2.50	....	....	....	1.00	....
1278ae	1¢ test gum	90.00	....	....	....	2.00	....
1278b	1¢ bklt pane of 4 (1971)	18.00	....	....	....	1.00	....
1279	1¼¢ A. Gallatin (1967)	1.75	4.00	20.00(100)	12.00	.20	.15
1280	2¢ F.L. Wright (1966)	1.75	4.00	8.00(100)	.90	.20	.15
1280a	2¢ bklt pane of 5 (1968)	2.50	....	....	....	1.00	....
1280c	2¢ bklt pane of 6 (1971)	18.00	....	....	....	1.00	....
1280ce	2¢ test gum	125.00	....	....	....	1.00	....
1281	3¢ F. Parkman (1967)	1.75	4.00	14.00(100)	.95	.25	.15
1282	4¢ A. Lincoln	1.75	4.00	29.00(100)	.95	.25	.15
1283	5¢ G. Washington (1966)	1.75	4.00	19.00(100)	.95	.25	.15
1283B	5¢ Washington, ... redrawn (1967)	1.75	4.00	18.00(100)	1.00	.30	.15
1284	6¢ F. D. Roosevelt(1966)	1.75	4.00	29.00(100)	1.10	.35	.15
1284b	6¢ bklt pane of 8 (1967)	3.00	....	....	....	1.75	....
1284c	6¢ bklt pane of 5 (1968)	150.00	....	....	....	1.60	....
1285	8¢ A. Einstein (1966)	4.00	6.00	45.00(100)	2.25	.50	.15
1286	10¢ A. Jackson (1967)	2.00	4.25	45.00(100)	2.25	.50	.15
1286A	12¢ H. Ford (1968) ..	2.00	4.25	45.00(100)	2.25	.50	.15
1287	13¢ J.F. Kennedy (1967)	2.50	4.50	67.50(100)	3.50	.70	.20
1288	15¢ O.W. Holmes, die I (1968)	2.25	4.50	55.00(100)	2.25	.60	.15
1288d	15¢ Holmes, die II (1979)	....	....	90.00(100)	14.00	1.10	.15
1288B	same, from bklt pane (1978).......	2.25	....	....	....	.60	.15
1288Bc	15¢ bklt pane of 8 ..	3.75	....	....	....	4.75	....
1289	20¢ G.C. Marshall (1967)	2.25	4.50	80.00(100)	5.00	.70	.15
1290	25¢ F. Douglass (1967)	5.00	6.00	95.00(100)	5.00	1.20	.15
1291	30¢ J. Dewey (1968)	2.50	5.00	125.00(100)	5.50	1.25	.15
1292	40¢ T. Paine (1968)	2.50	5.00	125.00(100)	6.00	1.50	.15
1293	50¢ L. Stone (1968)	3.75	7.25	200.00(100)	8.00	2.00	.20
1294	$1 E. O'Neil (1967) .	6.00	12.50	325.00(100)	17.00	5.00	.15
1295	$5 J. B. Moore (1966)	50.00	115.00	....	60.00	16.00	5.00

BOOKLET PANE SLOGANS

Slogan IV : Mail Early in the Day.
Slogan V: Use Zip Code.

#1278b–Slogans IV and V
#1280a, 1284c–Slogans IV or V

1966-81 COIL STAMPS

SCOTT NO.	DESCRIPTION	FIRST DAY COVERS SING	LINE PAIR	MINT SHEET	LINE PAIR	UNUSED F/NH	USED
1297-1305C	**1¢-$1, 9 varieties, (No #1305Ei)** ...	....	....	....	**15.00**	**6.80**	**2.75**
	Perf. 10 Horizontally						
1297	3¢ F. Parkman (1975)	1.75	2.75	....	.70	.20	.15
1298	6¢ F.D. Roosevelt (1967)	1.75	2.75	....	1.55	.40	.15
	Perf. 10 Vertically						
1299	1¢ T. Jefferson (1968)	1.75	2.75	....	.45	.60	.15
1303	4¢ A. Lincoln	1.75	2.75	....	.70	1.00	.15
1304	5¢ G. Washington ...	1.75	2.75	....	.55	2.30	.15
1304C	5¢ Washington, redrawn (1981)	1.75	2.75	....	1.15	.25	.15
1305	6¢ F.D. Roosevelt (1968)	1.75	2.75	....	.85	.40	.15
1305E	15¢ O.W. Holmes, die I (1978)	2.00	3.25	....	1.40	.50	.15
1305Ei	15¢ O.W. Holmes, die II (1979)	....	....	....	3.00	.80	.30
1305C	$1 E. O'Neil (1973) ..	5.00	9.50	....	8.50	3.95	1.50

1306

1307

1308

1309

1310

1312

1313

1314

1966 COMMEMORATIVES

SCOTT NO.	DESCRIPTION	FIRST DAY COVERS SING	FIRST DAY COVERS PL. BLK.	MINT SHEET	PLATE BLOCK	UNUSED F/NH	USED
1306/22	**(1306-10, 1312-22) 16 varieties**	....	....	....	....	**5.10**	**3.00**
1306	5¢ Migratory Bird Treaty	2.00	4.25	12.50(50)	1.20	.35	.20
1307	5¢ A.S.P.C.A.	2.00	4.00	12.50(50)	1.20	.35	.20
1308	5¢ Indiana Statehood	2.00	4.00	19.50(50)	2.25	.35	.20
1309	5¢ American Circus . .	3.00	4.25	20.00(50)	2.25	.35	.20
1310	5¢ SIPEX (single) ...	2.00	4.00	12.50(50)	1.20	.35	.20
1311	5¢ SIPEX, Imperf Souvenir Sheet	2.00	....		....	.35	.20
1312	5¢ Bill of Rights	2.25	4.00	12.50(50)	1.20	.35	.20
1313	5¢ Polish Millennium .	2.00	4.00	12.50(50)	1.20	.35	.20
1314	5¢ National Park Service	2.00	4.00	12.50(50)	1.20	.35	.20

1315

1316

1317

1318

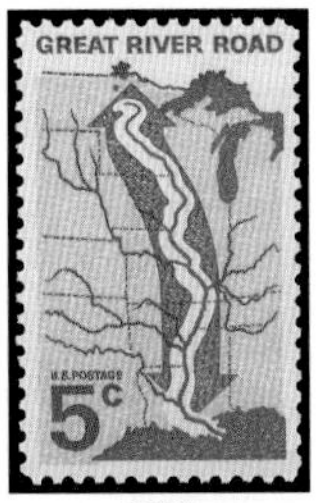

1319

1320

SCOTT NO.	DESCRIPTION	FIRST DAY COVERS SING	FIRST DAY COVERS PL. BLK.	MINT SHEET	PLATE BLOCK	UNUSED F/NH	USED
1315	5¢ Marine Corps Reserve...........	2.00	4.00	12.50(50)	1.25	.30	.20
1316	5¢ Women's Clubs ..	2.00	4.00	12.50(50)	1.25	.30	.20
1317	5¢ Johnny Appleseed	2.00	4.00	17.50(50)	1.50	.40	.20
1318	5¢ Beautification	2.00	4.00	12.50(50)	.80	.30	.20
1319	5¢ Great River Road .	2.00	4.00	21.00(50)	2.10	.40	.20
1320	5¢ Servicemen– Bonds	2.00	4.00	12.50(50)	1.20	.30	.20

1321

1322

1323

SCOTT NO.	DESCRIPTION	FIRST DAY COVERS SING	FIRST DAY COVERS PL. BLK.	MINT SHEET	PLATE BLOCK	UNUSED F/NH	USED
1321	5¢ Christmas 1966 ..	1.75	4.00	24.00(100)	1.50	.30	.20
1322	5¢ Mary Cassatt	1.75	4.00	12.00(50)	1.20	.30	.20

1324

1325

1326

1327

1967 COMMEMORATIVES

SCOTT NO.	DESCRIPTION	FIRST DAY COVERS SING	FIRST DAY COVERS PL. BLK.	MINT SHEET	PLATE BLOCK	UNUSED F/NH	USED
1323-37	**15 varieties, complete ....**	....	....	....	....	**7.50**	**3.20**
1323	5¢ National Grange ..	2.00	4.00	12.00(50)	1.25	.35	.20
1324	5¢ Canada Centennial	2.00	4.00	12.00(50)	1.25	.30	.20
1325	5¢ Erie Canal	2.00	4.00	12.00(50)	1.25	.30	.20
1326	5¢ Search for Peace .	2.00	4.00	12.00(50)	1.25	.30	.20
1327	5¢ Henry D. Thoreau	2.00	4.00	17.50(50)	1.50	.40	.20

1328

1329

1330

SCOTT NO.	DESCRIPTION	FIRST DAY COVERS SING	FIRST DAY COVERS PL. BLK.	MINT SHEET	PLATE BLOCK	UNUSED F/NH	USED
1328	5¢ Nebraska Statehood	2.00	4.00	17.00(50)	1.50	.30	.20
1329	5¢ Voice of America .	4.00	6.00	12.00(50)	1.00	.30	.20
1330	5¢ Davy Crockett ...	2.50	4.25	17.50(50)	1.50	.50	.20

1331 1332

SCOTT NO.	DESCRIPTION	FIRST DAY COVERS SING	FIRST DAY COVERS PL. BLK.	MINT SHEET	PLATE BLOCK	UNUSED F/NH	USED
1331-32	5¢ Space, attached, 2 varieties	12.50	25.00	60.00(50)	5.75	3.75	1.80
1331	5¢ Astronaut	4.00	....	....	....	1.50	.40
1332	5¢ Gemini 4 Capsule	4.00	....	....	....	1.50	.40

1333

1334

SCOTT NO.	DESCRIPTION	FIRST DAY COVERS SING	FIRST DAY COVERS PL. BLK.	MINT SHEET	PLATE BLOCK	UNUSED F/NH	USED
1333	5¢ Urban Planning ..	2.00	4.00	12.00(50)	1.20	.30	.20
1334	5¢ Finland Independence	2.00	4.00	12.00(50)	1.20	.30	.20

1335

1336

1337

SCOTT NO.	DESCRIPTION	FIRST DAY COVERS SING	FIRST DAY COVERS PL. BLK.	MINT SHEET	PLATE BLOCK	UNUSED F/NH	USED
1335	5¢ Thomas Eakins ..	2.00	4.00	12.00(50)	1.20	.30	.20
1336	5¢ Christams 1967 ..	2.00	4.00	12.00(50)	1.20	.30	.20
1337	5¢ Mississippi Statehood	2.00	4.00	22.50(50)	2.25	.50	.20

FOR YOUR CONVENIENCE IN ORDERING, COMPLETE SETS ARE LISTED BEFORE SINGLE STAMP LISTINGS.

1338, 1338A, 1338D

1338F, 1338G

SCOTT NO.	DESCRIPTION	FIRST DAY COVERS SING	FIRST DAY COVERS PL. BLK.	MINT SHEET	PLATE BLOCK	UNUSED F/NH	USED
	GIORI PRESS 1868 Design size: 18½ x 22 mm Perf.11						
1338	6¢ Flag & White House	1.75	4.00	24.00(100)	1.20	.30	.15
	HUCK PRESS Design size: 18 x 21 mm 1969 Coil Stamp Perf. 10 Vertically						
1338A	6¢ Flag & White House	1.75	....	....	....	.30	.15
	1970 Perf. 11 x 10½						
1338D	6¢ Flag & White House	2.00	4.25	17.00(100)	4.00(20)	.30	.15
	1971 Perf. 11 x 10½						
1338F	8¢ Flag & White House	2.00	4.25	21.50(100)	4.75(20)	.30	.15
	Coil Stamp Perf. 10 Vertically						
1338G	8¢ Flag & White House	2.00	....	....	....	.30	.15

1339

1340

1968 COMMEMORATIVES

SCOTT NO.	DESCRIPTION	FIRST DAY COVERS SING	FIRST DAY COVERS PL. BLK.	MINT SHEET	PLATE BLOCK	UNUSED F/NH	USED
1339/64	**(1339-40, 1342-64) 25 varieties ....**	....	....	....	....	**12.45**	**6.95**
1339	6¢ Illinois Statehood .	2.00	4.00	22.50(50)	2.25	.50	.20
1340	6¢ Hemisfair '68	2.00	4.00	12.00(50)	1.20	.30	.20

1341

SCOTT NO.	DESCRIPTION	FIRST DAY COVERS SING	FIRST DAY COVERS PL. BLK.	MINT SHEET	PLATE BLOCK	UNUSED F/NH	USED
1341	$1 Airlift to Servicemen	8.50	17.50	175.00(50)	15.00	3.95	2.75

1342

1343

1344

SCOTT NO.	DESCRIPTION	FIRST DAY COVERS SING	FIRST DAY COVERS PL. BLK.	MINT SHEET	PLATE BLOCK	UNUSED F/NH	USED
1342	6¢ Support our Youth	2.00	4.00	12.00(50)	1.20	.30	.20
1343	6¢ Law and Order . . .	4.00	6.00	19.50(50)	2.25	.50	.20
1344	6¢ Register and Vote	2.00	4.00	12.00(50)	1.20	.30	.20

1345

1346

1347

1348

1349

1350

1351

1352

1353

1354

1968 HISTORIC AMERICAN FLAGS

SCOTT NO.	DESCRIPTION	FIRST DAY COVERS SING	FIRST DAY COVERS PL. BLK.	MINT SHEET	PLATE BLOCK	UNUSED F/NH	USED
1345-54	**10 varieties, complete, attached . . . .**	**10.00**	....	**25.00(50)**	**12.00**	**6.00**	....
1345-54	**Same, set of singles**	**57.50**	....	....	....	**5.25**	**4.25**
1345	6¢ Fort Moultrie Flag .	6.00	....	....	....	.55	.45
1346	6¢ Fort McHenry Flag	6.00	....	....	....	.55	.45
1347	6¢ Washington's Cruisers	6.00	....	....	....	.55	.45
1348	6¢ Bennington Flag . .	6.00	....	....	....	.55	.45
1349	6¢ Rhode Island Flag	6.00	....	....	....	.55	.45
1350	6¢ First Stars & Stripes	6.00	....	....	....	.55	.45
1351	6¢ Bunker Hill Flag . .	6.00	....	....	....	.55	.45
1352	6¢ Grand Union Flag	6.00	....	....	....	.55	.45
1353	6¢ Philadelphia Light Horse	6.00	....	....	....	.55	.45
1354	6¢ First Navy Jack . .	6.00	....	....	....	.55	.45

NOTE: All ten varieties of 1345-54 were printed on the same sheet; therefore, plate and regular blocks are not available for each variety separately. Plate blocks of four will contain two each of #1346, with number adjacent to #1345 only; Zip blocks will contain two each of #1353 and #1354, with inscription adjacent to #1354 only; Mail Early blocks will contain two each of #1347-49 with inscription adjacent to #1348 only. A plate strip of 20 stamps, with two of each variety will be required to have all stamps in plate block form and will contain all marginal inscription.

1355

1356

1357

1358

1359

1360

1361

1968 COMMEMORATIVES

SCOTT NO.	DESCRIPTION	FIRST DAY COVERS SING	FIRST DAY COVERS PL. BLK.	MINT SHEET	PLATE BLOCK	UNUSED F/NH	USED
1355	6¢ Walt Disney	40.00	50.00	55.00(50)	5.00	1.50	.30
1356	6¢ Father Marquette .	2.00	4.00	19.50(50)	2.25	.50	.20
1357	6¢ Daniel Boone	2.00	4.00	17.50(50)	1.50	.50	.20
1358	6¢ Arkansas River . . .	2.00	4.00	29.00(50)	2.25	.60	.20
1359	6¢ Leif Erikson	2.00	4.00	12.00(50)	1.25	.50	.20
1360	6¢ Cherokee Strip . . .	2.00	4.00	14.00(50)	1.25	.40	.20
1361	6¢ Trumbull Art	4.00	6.00	17.50(50)	1.50	.50	.20

1362

1363

1364

SCOTT NO.	DESCRIPTION	FIRST DAY COVERS SING	FIRST DAY COVERS PL. BLK.	MINT SHEET	PLATE BLOCK	UNUSED F/NH	USED
1362	6¢ Waterfowl Conservation	2.00	4.00	17.50(50)	1.75	.40	.20
1363	6¢ Christmas 1968 . .	2.00	....	12.00(50)	2.10(10)	.30	.20
1364	6¢ Chief Joseph	2.00	4.00	20.00(50)	2.25	.50	.20

1365 1366

1367 1368

1969 COMMEMORATIVES

SCOTT NO.	DESCRIPTION	FIRST DAY COVERS SING	FIRST DAY COVERS PL. BLK.	MINT SHEET	PLATE BLOCK	UNUSED F/NH	USED
1365-86	**22 varieties, complete**	....	....	....	....	**13.00**	**4.50**
1365-68	Beautification, 4 varieties, attached	6.00	8.50	32.50(50)	4.25	3.75	3.00
1365	6¢ Azaleas & Tulips .	3.00	....	....	....	1.00	.25
1366	6¢ Daffodils	3.00	....	....	....	1.00	.25
1367	6¢ Poppies	3.00	....	....	....	1.00	.25
1368	6¢ Crabapple Trees .	3.00	....	....	....	1.00	.25

1369

1370

1371

SCOTT NO.	DESCRIPTION	FIRST DAY COVERS SING	FIRST DAY COVERS PL. BLK.	MINT SHEET	PLATE BLOCK	UNUSED F/NH	USED
1369	6¢ American Legion .	2.00	4.00	12.00(50)	1.20	.30	.20
1370	6¢ Grandma Moses .	2.00	4.00	12.00(50)	1.20	.30	.20
1371	6¢ Apollo 8 Moon Orbit	2.50	5.00	18.00(50)	1.75	.50	.20

1372

1373

1374

1375

SCOTT NO.	DESCRIPTION	FIRST DAY COVERS SING	FIRST DAY COVERS PL. BLK.	MINT SHEET	PLATE BLOCK	UNUSED F/NH	USED
1372	6¢ W.C. Handy–Musician	3.50	5.00	18.00(50)	1.75	.50	.20
1373	6¢ California Settlement	2.00	4.00	18.00(50)	1.75	.30	.20
1374	6¢ Major J.W. Powell	2.00	4.00	17.50(50)	1.75	.40	.20
1375	6¢ Alabama Statehood	2.00	4.00	17.50(50)	1.75	.40	.20

1376 1377

1378 1379

SCOTT NO.	DESCRIPTION	FIRST DAY COVERS SING	FIRST DAY COVERS PL. BLK.	MINT SHEET	PLATE BLOCK	UNUSED F/NH	USED
1376-79	Bontanical Congress, 4 varieties, attached .	7.00	9.50	35.00(50)	4.50	3.75	3.00
1376	6¢ Douglas Fir	3.00	....	....	....	1.00	.25
1377	6¢ Lady's-slipper	3.00	....	....	....	1.00	.25
1378	6¢ Ocotillo	3.00	....	....	....	1.00	.25
1379	6¢ Franklinia	3.00	....	....	....	1.00	.25

AVERAGE QUALITY: From 1935 to date, deduct 20% from the Fine price to determine the price for an Average quality stamp.

MINT SHEETS: From 1935 to date, we list prices for standard size Mint Sheets in Fine, Never Hinged condition. The number of stamps in each sheet is noted in ( ).

1380

1381

1382

1383

SCOTT NO.	DESCRIPTION	FIRST DAY COVERS SING	FIRST DAY COVERS PL. BLK.	MINT SHEET	PLATE BLOCK	UNUSED F/NH	USED
1380	6¢ Dartmouth College	2.00	4.00	17.50(50)	1.75	.40	.20
1381	6¢ Professional Baseball	16.00	25.00	65.00(50)	6.50	1.50	.20
1382	6¢ College Football . .	7.00	13.50	27.50(50)	2.25	.75	.20
1383	6¢ Eisenhower	2.00	4.00	12.00(32)	1.75	.40	.20

1384

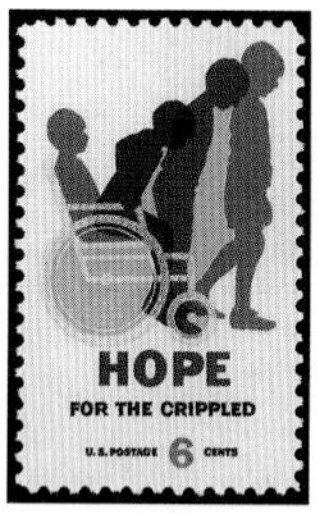

1385

1386

SCOTT NO.	DESCRIPTION	FIRST DAY COVERS SING	FIRST DAY COVERS PL. BLK.	MINT SHEET	PLATE BLOCK	UNUSED F/NH	USED
1384	6¢ Christmas 1969 . .	2.00	....	14.00(50)	3.50(10)	.30	.20
1384a	6¢ precancelled set of 4 cities	....	....	225.00(50)	125.00(10)	3.00	....
1385	6¢ Rehabilitation	2.00	4.00	12.00(50)	1.20	.30	.20
1386	6¢ William M. Harnett	2.00	4.00	8.00(32)	1.20	.30	.20

1387

1388

1389

1390

1391

1392

1970 COMMEMORATIVES

SCOTT NO.	DESCRIPTION	FIRST DAY COVERS SING	FIRST DAY COVERS PL. BLK.	MINT SHEET	PLATE BLOCK	UNUSED F/NH	USED
1387/1422	**(1387-92, 1405-22) 24 varieties, (No precancels) . .**	....	....	....	....	**11.85**	**5.75**
1387-90	Natural History, 4 varieties, attached .	5.00	7.00	12.00(32)	2.25	1.95	1.50
1387	6¢ Bald Eagle	2.50	....	....	....	.50	.20
1388	6¢ Elephant Herd . . .	2.50	....	....	....	.50	.20
1389	6¢ Haida Canoe	2.50	....	....	....	.50	.20
1390	6¢ Reptiles	2.50	....	....	....	.50	.20
1391	6¢ Maine Statehood .	2.00	4.00	17.50(50)	1.75	.40	.20
1392	6¢ Wildlife–Buffalo . .	2.00	4.00	17.50(50)	1.75	.40	.20

1393, 1401

1393D

1394

1395, 1402

1396

1397

1398

1399

1400

1970-74 REGULAR ISSUE

SCOTT NO.	DESCRIPTION	FIRST DAY COVERS SING	FIRST DAY COVERS PL. BLK.	MINT SHEET	PLATE BLOCK	UNUSED F/NH	USED
1393/1400	**6¢-21¢, 8 varieties, complete (No #1395)**	....	....	....	....	**3.85**	**1.30**
1393	6¢ D. Eisenhower . . .	1.75	4.00	20.00(100)	1.50	.30	.15
1393a	6¢ bklt pane of 8	2.75	....	....	....	1.95	....
1393ae	6¢ test gum	90.00	....	....	....	1.90	....
1393b	6¢ bklt pane of 5– Slogan IV or V	3.75	....	....	....	1.75	....
1393D	7¢ B. Franklin (1972)	1.75	4.00	25.00(100)	1.50	.30	.15
1394	8¢ Ike–black, blue, red (1971)	1.75	4.00	29.00(100)	1.50	.30	.15
1395	same, deep claret bklt single (1971) . . .	2.50	....	....	....	.45	.15
1395a	8¢ bklt pane of 8	2.50	....	....	....	2.40	....
1395b	8¢ bklt pane of 6	2.25	....	....	....	1.90	....
1395c	8¢ bklt pane of 4, VI & VII (1972)	2.00	....	....	....	1.70	....
1395d	8¢ bklt pane of 7 II or V (1972)	2.50	....	....	....	2.50	....
1396	8¢ Postal Service Emblem (1971)	1.75	4.00	34.00(100)	3.25(12)	.35	.15
1397	14¢ F. LaGuardia (1972)	1.75	4.00	50.00(100)	3.50	.75	.15
1398	16¢ E. Pyle (1971) . .	2.50	4.50	85.00(100)	4.50	.75	.15
1399	18¢ E. Blackwell (1974)	2.00	4.25	60.00(100)	3.50	.75	.20
1400	21¢ A.P. Giannini (1973)	2.50	4.50	70.00(100)	3.75	.75	.30

1970-71 COIL STAMPS–Perf. 10 Vertically

SCOTT NO.	DESCRIPTION	FIRST DAY COVERS SING	LINE PAIR	MINT SHEET	LINE PAIR	UNUSED F/NH	USED
1401	6¢ D. Eisenhower . . .	1.75	2.75	....	.65	.30	.15
1402	8¢ Eisenhower, claret (1971)	1.75	2.75	....	.80	.35	.15

1405

1406

1407

1408

1409

1970 COMMEMORATIVES

SCOTT NO.	DESCRIPTION	FIRST DAY COVERS SING	FIRST DAY COVERS PL. BLK.	MINT SHEET	PLATE BLOCK	UNUSED F/NH	USED
1405	6¢ E.L. Master–Poet .	2.00	4.00	17.50(50)	1.75	.40	.20
1406	6¢ Woman Suffrage .	2.00	4.00	12.00(50)	1.20	.30	.20
1407	6¢ South Carolina Tercentenary	2.00	4.00	20.00(50)	2.25	.50	.20
1408	6¢ Stone Mountain Memorial	2.00	4.00	15.00(50)	1.50	.50	.20
1409	6¢ Fort Snelling	2.00	4.00	22.00(50)	2.25	.55	.20

1412 1413

1410 1411

SCOTT NO.	DESCRIPTION	FIRST DAY COVERS SING	FIRST DAY COVERS PL. BLK.	MINT SHEET	PLATE BLOCK	UNUSED F/NH	USED
1410-13	Anti-Pollution, 4 varieties, attached .	5.00	7.00	20.00(50)	6.00(10)	3.00	2.40
1410	6¢ Globe & Wheat . .	2.50	....	....	....	.75	.25
1411	6¢ Globe & City	2.50	....	....	....	.75	.25
1412	6¢ Globe & Bluegill . .	2.50	....	....	....	.75	.25
1413	6¢ Globe & Seagull . .	2.50	....	....	....	.75	.25

1414

SCOTT NO.	DESCRIPTION	FIRST DAY COVERS SING	FIRST DAY COVERS PL. BLK.	MINT SHEET	PLATE BLOCK	UNUSED F/NH	USED
1414	6¢ Nativity	1.75	....	12.00(50)	1.75(8)	.30	.20

FIRST DAY COVERS: First Day Covers are envelopes cancelled on the "First Day of Issue" of the stamp used on the envelope. Usually they also contain a picture (cachet) on the left side designed to go with the theme of the stamp. From 1935 to 1949, prices listed are for cacheted, addressed covers. From 1950 to date, prices are for cacheted, unaddressed covers.

1415 1416

1417 1418

SCOTT NO.	DESCRIPTION	FIRST DAY COVERS SING	FIRST DAY COVERS PL. BLK.	MINT SHEET	PLATE BLOCK	UNUSED F/NH	USED
1415-18	Christmas Toys, 4 varieties, attached .	5.50	....	30.00(50)	6.25(8)	3.00	2.25
1415	6¢ Locomotive	3.00	....	....	....	1.00	.25
1416	6¢ Horse	3.00	....	....	....	1.00	.25
1417	6¢ Tricycle	3.00	....	....	....	1.00	.25
1418	6¢ Doll Carriage	3.00	....	....	....	1.00	.25

Precancelled

SCOTT NO.	DESCRIPTION	FIRST DAY COVERS SING	FIRST DAY COVERS PL. BLK.	MINT SHEET	PLATE BLOCK	UNUSED F/NH	USED
1414a	6¢ Nativity (precancelled)	4.00	....	14.00(50)	2.75(8)	.30	.15
1415a-18a	Christmas Toys, precancelled, 4 varieties attached	45.00	....	45.00(50)	9.50(8)	4.25	3.75
1415a	6¢ Locomotive	7.00	....	....	....	1.50	.20
1416a	6¢ Horse	7.00	....	....	....	1.50	.20
1417a	6¢ Tricycle	7.00	....	....	....	1.50	.20
1418a	6¢ Doll Carriage	7.00	....	....	....	1.50	.20

NOTE: Unused precancels are with original gum, while used are without gum.

1419

1420

SCOTT NO.	DESCRIPTION	FIRST DAY COVERS SING	FIRST DAY COVERS PL. BLK.	MINT SHEET	PLATE BLOCK	UNUSED F/NH	USED
1419	6¢ U.N. 25th Anniversary	2.00	4.00	12.00(50)	1.20	.30	.20
1420	6¢ Pilgrim Landing . .	2.00	4.00	12.00(50)	1.20	.30	.20

1421 1422

SCOTT NO.	DESCRIPTION	FIRST DAY COVERS SING	FIRST DAY COVERS PL. BLK.	MINT SHEET	PLATE BLOCK	UNUSED F/NH	USED
1421-22	D.A.V. Servicemen, 2 varieties, attached .	3.00	5.00	15.00(50)	2.25	.60	.35
1421	6¢ Disabled Veterans	2.00	....	....	....	.30	.20
1422	6¢ Prisoners of War .	2.00	....	....	....	.30	.20

SE-TENANTS: Beginning with the 1964 Christmas issue (#1254-57), the United States has issued numerous Se-Tenant stamps covering a wide variety of subjects. Se-Tenants are issues where two or more different stamp designs are produced on the same sheet in pair, strip or block form. Mint stamps are usually collected in attached blocks, etc.; used are generally saved as single stamps.

1423

1424

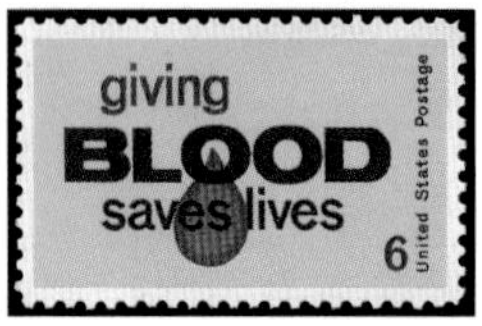

1425

1426

1971 COMMEMORATIVES

SCOTT NO.	DESCRIPTION	FIRST DAY COVERS SING	FIRST DAY COVERS PL. BLK.	MINT SHEET	PLATE BLOCK	UNUSED F/NH	USED
1423-45	**6¢-8¢, 23 varieties complete**	....	....	....	....	**8.75**	**4.95**
1423	6¢ Sheep	1.75	4.00	20.0050)	2.00	.50	.20
1424	6¢ General D. MacArthur	1.75	4.00	24.00(50)	2.25	.50	.20
1425	6¢ Blood Donors	1.75	4.00	12.00(50)	1.20	.30	.20
1426	8¢ Missouri Statehood	1.75	4.00	20.00(50)	5.75(12)	.50	.20

1427 1428

1429 1430

SCOTT NO.	DESCRIPTION	FIRST DAY COVERS SING	FIRST DAY COVERS PL. BLK.	MINT SHEET	PLATE BLOCK	UNUSED F/NH	USED
1427-30	Wildlife Conservation, 4 varieties, attached	5.00	9.00	12.50(32)	2.50	2.00	1.50
1427	8¢ Trout	2.50	....	....	....	.40	.25
1428	8¢ Alligator	2.50	....	....	....	.40	.25
1429	8¢ Polar Bear	2.50	....	....	....	.40	.25
1430	8¢ Condor	2.50	....	....	....	.40	.25

1431

1432

1433

SCOTT NO.	DESCRIPTION	FIRST DAY COVERS SING	FIRST DAY COVERS PL. BLK.	MINT SHEET	PLATE BLOCK	UNUSED F/NH	USED
1431	8¢ Antarctic Treaty	2.00	4.00	11.50(50)	1.25	.35	.20
1432	8¢ American Revolution	2.00	4.00	11.50(50)	1.40	.40	.20
1433	8¢ John Sloan–Artist	2.00	4.00	11.50(50)	1.25	.35	.20

1434 1435

SCOTT NO.	DESCRIPTION	FIRST DAY COVERS SING	FIRST DAY COVERS PL. BLK.	MINT SHEET	PLATE BLOCK	UNUSED F/NH	USED
1434-35	Space Achievements, 2 varieties, attached	3.50	4.50	13.50(50)	1.75	.75	.55
1434	8¢ Moon, Earth, Sun & Landing Craft	2.00	....	....	....	.45	.30
1435	8¢ Lunar Rover	2.00	....	....	....	.45	.30

1436

1437

1438

1439

SCOTT NO.	DESCRIPTION	FIRST DAY COVERS SING	FIRST DAY COVERS PL. BLK.	MINT SHEET	PLATE BLOCK	UNUSED F/NH	USED
1436	8¢ Emily Dickinson	2.00	4.00	17.50(50)	1.75	.40	.20
1437	8¢ San Juan	2.00	4.00	17.50(50)	1.75	.35	.20
1438	8¢ Drug Addiction	2.00	4.00	11.25(50)	1.75(6)	.35	.20
1439	8¢ CARE	2.00	4.00	11.25(50)	2.20(8)	.35	.20

1440 1441

1442 1443

SCOTT NO.	DESCRIPTION	FIRST DAY COVERS SING	FIRST DAY COVERS PL. BLK.	MINT SHEET	PLATE BLOCK	UNUSED F/NH	USED
1440-43	Historic Preservation 4 varieties, attached	5.00	6.00	12.50(32)	2.00	1.75	1.00
1440	8¢ Decatur House	2.50	....	....	....	.40	.25
1441	8¢ Whaling Ship	2.50	....	....	....	.40	.25
1442	8¢ Cable Car	2.50	....	....	....	.40	.25
1443	8¢ Mission	2.50	....	....	....	.40	.25

1444

1445

SCOTT NO.	DESCRIPTION	FIRST DAY COVERS SING	FIRST DAY COVERS PL. BLK.	MINT SHEET	PLATE BLOCK	UNUSED F/NH	USED
1444	8¢ Christmas Nativity	2.00	4.00	11.25(50)	3.00(12)	.35	.20
1445	8¢ Christmas Patridge	2.00	4.00	11.25(50)	3.00(12)	.35	.20

1446

1447

1972 COMMEMORATIVES

SCOTT NO.	DESCRIPTION	FIRST DAY COVERS SING	FIRST DAY COVERS PL. BLK.	MINT SHEET	PLATE BLOCK	UNUSED F/NH	USED
1446/74	**29 varieties, complete**	....	....	....	....	**10.15**	**5.50**
1446	8¢ Sidney Lanier–Poet	2.00	4.00	17.50(50)	2.25	.50	.20
1447	8¢ Peace Corps	2.00	4.00	12.50(50)	1.80(6)	.35	.20

1448 1449

1450 1451

1452

1454

1453

1972 NATIONAL PARKS CENTENNIAL

SCOTT NO.	DESCRIPTION	FIRST DAY COVERS SING	FIRST DAY COVERS PL. BLK.	MINT SHEET	PLATE BLOCK	UNUSED F/NH	USED
1448-54	**2¢-15¢, 7 varieties, complete**	....	....	....	....	**2.50**	**1.50**
1448-51	Cape Hatteras, 4 varieties, attached	6.00	7.00	11.00(100)	1.00	1.00	.65
1448	2¢ Ship's Hull	....	....	....	....	.25	.15
1449	2¢ Lighthouse	....	....	....	....	.25	.15
1450	2¢ Three Seagulls	....	....	....	....	.25	.15
1451	2¢ Two Seagulls	....	....	....	....	.25	.15
1452	6¢ Wolf Trap Farm Park	2.00	4.00	15.00(50)	1.75	.40	.20
1453	8¢ Yellowstone Park	2.00	4.00	12.00(32)	1.50	.40	.20
1454	15¢ Mount McKinley	2.00	4.00	25.00(50)	2.75	.60	.35

1455

1972 COMMEMORATIVES

SCOTT NO.	DESCRIPTION	FIRST DAY COVERS SING	FIRST DAY COVERS PL. BLK.	MINT SHEET	PLATE BLOCK	UNUSED F/NH	USED
1455	8¢ Family Planning	2.00	4.00	11.25(50)	1.25	.35	.20

1456 1457

1458 1459

SCOTT NO.	DESCRIPTION	FIRST DAY COVERS SING	FIRST DAY COVERS PL. BLK.	MINT SHEET	PLATE BLOCK	UNUSED F/NH	USED
1456-59	Colonial Craftsmen, 4 varieties, attached	3.75	4.75	15.00(50)	1.75	1.50	1.20
1456	8¢ Glassmaker	2.25	....	....	....	.45	.25
1457	8¢ Silversmith	2.25	....	....	....	.45	.25
1458	8¢ Wigmaker	2.25	....	....	....	.45	.25
1459	8¢ Hatter	2.25	....	....	....	.45	.25

1460

1461

1462

SCOTT NO.	DESCRIPTION	FIRST DAY COVERS SING	FIRST DAY COVERS PL. BLK.	MINT SHEET	PLATE BLOCK	UNUSED F/NH	USED
1460	6¢ Olympics–Cycling	2.10	4.25	12.00(50)	2.50(10)	.30	.20
1461	8¢ Olympics–Bob Sled Racing	2.10	4.25	12.25(50)	2.80(10)	.35	.20
1462	15¢ Olympics–Foot Racing	2.10	4.25	22.00(50)	4.75(10)	.50	.45

1463

SCOTT NO.	DESCRIPTION	FIRST DAY COVERS SING	FIRST DAY COVERS PL. BLK.	MINT SHEET	PLATE BLOCK	UNUSED F/NH	USED
1463	8¢ Parent Teacher Association	2.00	4.00	17.50(50)	1.50	.40	.20
1463a	Same, Reversed Plate Number	2.00	4.00	11.75(50)	1.40	....	....

1464 1465

1466 1467

SCOTT NO.	DESCRIPTION	FIRST DAY COVERS SING	FIRST DAY COVERS PL. BLK.	MINT SHEET	PLATE BLOCK	UNUSED F/NH	USED
1464-67	Wildlife Conservation, 4 varieties, attached .	4.00	6.00	9.00(32)	1.75	1.50	1.10
1464	8¢ Fur Seal	2.00	....	....	....	.45	.25
1465	8¢ Cardinal	2.00	....	....	....	.45	.25
1466	8¢ Brown Pelican . . .	2.00	....	....	....	.45	.25
1467	8¢ Bighorn Sheep . . .	2.00	....	....	....	.45	.25

1468

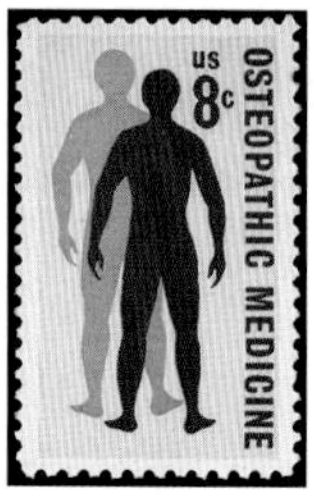

1469

1470

SCOTT NO.	DESCRIPTION	FIRST DAY COVERS SING	FIRST DAY COVERS PL. BLK.	MINT SHEET	PLATE BLOCK	UNUSED F/NH	USED
1468	8¢ Mail Order Business	2.00	4.00	17.50(50)	4.50(12)	.40	.20
1469	8¢ Osteopathic Medicine	2.00	4.25	20.00(50)	2.75(6)	.50	.20
1470	Tom Sawyer–Folklore	2.00	4.00	20.00(50)	2.25	.50	.20

1471

1472

1473

SCOTT NO.	DESCRIPTION	FIRST DAY COVERS SING	FIRST DAY COVERS PL. BLK.	MINT SHEET	PLATE BLOCK	UNUSED F/NH	USED
1471	8¢ Christmas–Virgin Mother	1.75	4.00	14.00(50)	3.50(12)	.35	.20
1472	8¢ Christmas–Santa . Claus	1.75	4.00	14.00(50)	3.50(12)	.40	.20
1473	8¢ Pharmacy	8.00	10.00	19.50(50)	2.25(4)	.50	.20

1474

1475

SCOTT NO.	DESCRIPTION	FIRST DAY COVERS SING	FIRST DAY COVERS PL. BLK.	MINT SHEET	PLATE BLOCK	UNUSED F/NH	USED
1474	8¢ Stamp Collecting .	2.00	4.25	9.50(40)	1.25(4)	.35	.20

1476

1477

1478

1479

1973 COMMEMORATIVES

SCOTT NO.	DESCRIPTION	FIRST DAY COVERS SING	FIRST DAY COVERS PL. BLK.	MINT SHEET	PLATE BLOCK	UNUSED F/NH	USED
1475-1508	**34 varieties, complete**	....	....	....	....	**12.00**	**7.25**
1475	8¢ "Love"	2.25	5.00	12.00(50)	1.50(6)	.35	.20
	COLONIAL COMMUNICATIONS						
1476	8¢ Pamphlet Printing	2.00	4.00	15.00(50)	1.75	.40	.20
1477	8¢ Posting Broadside	2.00	4.00	15.00(50)	1.75	.40	.20
1478	8¢ Colonial Post Rider	2.00	4.00	15.00(50)	1.75	.40	.20
1479	8¢ Drummer & Soldiers	2.00	4.00	15.00(50)	1.75	.40	.20

1480 1481

1482 1483

SCOTT NO.	DESCRIPTION	FIRST DAY COVERS SING	FIRST DAY COVERS PL. BLK.	MINT SHEET	PLATE BLOCK	UNUSED F/NH	USED
1480-83	Boston Tea Party, 4 varieties, attached .	4.50	6.50	17.00(50)	1.75	1.50	1.10
1480	8¢ Throwing Tea	2.25	....	....	....	.45	.25
1481	8¢ Ship	2.25	....	....	....	.45	.25
1482	8¢ Rowboats	2.25	....	....	....	.45	.25
1483	8¢ Rowboat & Dock .	2.25	....	....	....	.45	.25

1484

1485

1488

1486

1487

AMERICAN ARTS

SCOTT NO.	DESCRIPTION	FIRST DAY COVERS SING	FIRST DAY COVERS PL. BLK.	MINT SHEET	PLATE BLOCK	UNUSED F/NH	USED
1484	8¢ George Gershwin–Composer	2.00	4.00	10.25(40)	3.75(12)	.35	.20
1485	8¢ Robinson Jeffers–Poet.	2.00	4.00	10.25(40)	3.75(12)	.35	.20
1486	8¢ Henry O. Tanner–Artist	5.00	6.00	10.25(40)	3.75(12)	.35	.20
1487	8¢ Willa Cather–Novelist	2.00	4.00	15.00(40)	5.00(12)	.50	.20
1488	8¢ Nicolaus Copernicus	2.00	4.00	12.25(40)	1.50	.35	.20

1489

1490

1491

1492

1493

1494

1495

1496

1497

1498

1973 POSTAL SERVICE EMPLOYEES

SCOTT NO.	DESCRIPTION	FIRST DAY COVERS SING	FIRST DAY COVERS PL. BLK.	MINT SHEET	PLATE BLOCK	UNUSED F/NH	USED
1489-98	**10 varieties, complete, attached .**	**6.50**	....	**18.00(50)**	**9.00(20)**	**4.50**	**3.50**
1489-98	**Set of singles, complete**	**22.00**	....	....	....	**4.25**	**2.50**
1489	8¢ Window Clerk	2.25	....	....	....	.45	.25
1490	8¢ Mail Pickup	2.25	....	....	....	.45	.25
1491	8¢ Conveyor Belt . . .	2.25	....	....	....	.45	.25
1492	8¢ Sacking Parcels . .	2.25	....	....	....	.45	.25
1493	8¢ Mail Cancelling . .	2.25	....	....	....	.45	.25
1494	8¢ Manual Sorting . . .	2.25	....	....	....	.45	.25
1495	8¢ Machine Sorting . .	2.25	....	....	....	.45	.25
1496	8¢ Loading Truck . . .	2.25	....	....	....	.45	.25
1497	8¢ Letter Carrier	2.25	....	....	....	.45	.25
1498	8¢ Rural Delivery . . .	2.25	....	....	....	.45	.25

1499

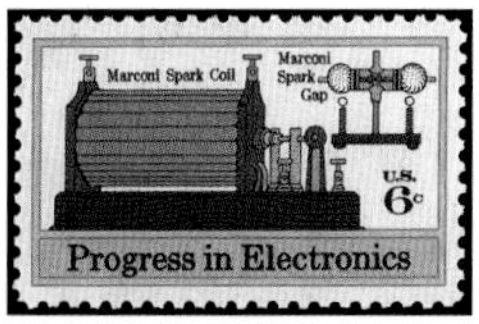

1500

1501

1502

1503

1973 COMMEMORATIVES

SCOTT NO.	DESCRIPTION	FIRST DAY COVERS SING	FIRST DAY COVERS PL. BLK.	MINT SHEET	PLATE BLOCK	UNUSED F/NH	USED
1499	8¢ Harry S. Truman .	2.00	4.00	14.00(32)	2.25	.50	.20
1500	6¢ Electronics	2.00	4.00	12.00(50)	1.20	.35	.20
1501	8¢ Electronics	2.00	4.00	11.50(50)	1.25	.35	.20
1502	15¢ Electronics	2.00	4.00	25.00(50)	2.50	.60	.40
1503	8¢ Lyndon B. Johnson	2.00	4.00	15.00(32)	5.50(12)	.50	.20

1504

1505

1506

1973-74 RURAL AMERICA

SCOTT NO.	DESCRIPTION	FIRST DAY COVERS SING	FIRST DAY COVERS PL. BLK.	MINT SHEET	PLATE BLOCK	UNUSED F/NH	USED
1504	8¢ Angus Cattle	2.00	4.00	17.00(50)	1.75	.35	.20
1505	10¢ Chautauqua (1974)	2.00	4.00	14.00(50)	1.50	.35	.20
1506	10¢ Winter Wheat (1974)	2.00	4.00	21.00(50)	2.00	.35	.20

1507

1508

1973 CHRISTMAS

SCOTT NO.	DESCRIPTION	FIRST DAY COVERS SING	FIRST DAY COVERS PL. BLK.	MINT SHEET	PLATE BLOCK	UNUSED F/NH	USED
1507	8¢ Madonna	2.25	3.25	14.50(50)	3.50(12)	.35	.20
1508	8¢ Christmas Tree . .	2.25	3.25	14.50(50)	3.50(12)	.35	.20

1509, 1519

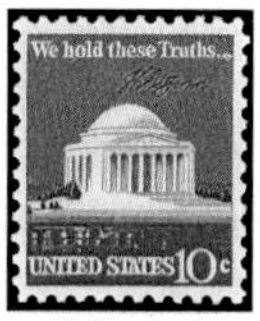

1510, 1520

1511

1518

1973-74 REGULAR ISSUES

SCOTT NO.	DESCRIPTION	FIRST DAY COVERS SING	FIRST DAY COVERS PL. BLK.	MINT SHEET	PLATE BLOCK	UNUSED F/NH	USED
1509	10¢ Crossed Flags . .	2.25	4.00	33.25(100)	7.25(20)	.35	.15
1510	10¢ Jefferson Memorial	2.25	4.00	30.00(100)	1.50	.35	.15
1510b	10¢ bklt pane of 5– Slogan VIII	2.25	....	....	....	1.85	....
1510c	10¢ bklt pane of 8 . . .	2.25	....	....	....	2.50	....
1510d	10¢ bklt pane of 6 (1974)	2.25	....	....	....	8.75	....
1511	10¢ Zip Code Theme (1974)	2.25	4.00	29.50(100)	2.75(8)	.35	.15

BOOKLET PANE SLOGANS

VI–Stamps in This Book.... VII– This Book Contains 25.... VIII–Paying Bills....

COIL STAMPS Perf.10 Vertically

SCOTT NO.	DESCRIPTION	FIRST DAY COVERS SING	LINE PAIR	MINT SHEET	LINE PAIR	UNUSED F/NH	USED
1518	6.3¢ Liberty Bell	2.25	2.75	....	.70	.40	.25
1519	10¢ Crossed Flags . .	2.25	....	....	....	.40	.15
1520	10¢ Jefferson Memorial	2.25	2.75	....	1.00	.35	.15

1525

1527

1526

1528

1529

1974 COMMEMORATIVES

SCOTT NO.	DESCRIPTION	FIRST DAY COVERS SING	FIRST DAY COVERS PL. BLK.	MINT SHEET	PLATE BLOCK	UNUSED F/NH	USED
1525-52	**28 varieties, complete . . . .**	....	....	....	....	**11.00**	**6.00**
1525	10¢ Veterans of Foreign Wars	2.25	4.00	14.00(50)	1.40	.35	.20
1526	10¢ Robert Frost	2.25	4.00	21.00(50)	2.00	.35	.20
1527	10¢ Environment– EXPO '74	2.25	4.00	14.00(40)	4.00(12)	.35	.20
1528	10¢ Horse Racing . . .	2.25	4.00	19.50(50)	5.00(12)	.50	.20
1529	10¢ Skylab Project . .	2.25	4.00	14.25(50)	1.40	.35	.20

1530

1531

1532

1533

1534

1535

1536

1537

1974 UNIVERSAL POSTAL UNION

SCOTT NO.	DESCRIPTION	FIRST DAY COVERS SING	FIRST DAY COVERS PL. BLK.	MINT SHEET	PLATE BLOCK	UNUSED F/NH	USED
1530-37	**8 varieties, attached**	**6.00**	....	**15.00(32)**	**7.50(16)**	**3.50(8)**	**2.95**
1530-37	**Set of singles, complete**	**17.50**	....	....	....	**3.25**	**2.25**
1530	10¢ Raphael	2.75	....	....	....	.50	.35
1531	10¢ Hokusai	2.75	....	....	....	.50	.35
1532	10¢ J.F. Peto	2.75	....	....	....	.50	.35
1533	10¢ J.E. Liotard	2.75	....	....	....	.50	.35
1534	10¢ G. Terborch	2.75	....	....	....	.50	.35
1535	10¢ J.B.S. Chardin . .	2.75	....	....	....	.50	.35
1536	10¢ T. Gainsborough	2.75	....	....	....	.50	.35
1537	10¢ F. de Goya	2.75	....	....	....	.50	.35

1538

1540

1539

1541

1974 COMMEMORATIVES

SCOTT NO.	DESCRIPTION	FIRST DAY COVERS SING	FIRST DAY COVERS PL. BLK.	MINT SHEET	PLATE BLOCK	UNUSED F/NH	USED
1538-41	Mineral Heritage, 4 varieties, attached .	3.50	5.00	17.50(48)	2.00	1.75	1.25
1538	10¢ Petrified Wood . .	2.25	....	....	....	.50	.25
1539	10¢ Tourmaline	2.25	....	....	....	.50	.25
1540	10¢ Amethyst	2.25	....	....	....	.50	.25
1541	10¢ Rhodochrosite . .	2.25	....	....	....	.50	.25

1542

SCOTT NO.	DESCRIPTION	FIRST DAY COVERS SING	PL. BLK.	MINT SHEET	PLATE BLOCK	UNUSED F/NH	USED
1542	10¢ Fort Harrod Bicentennial	2.25	4.00	20.00(50)	2.00	.60	.20

1543 1544

1545 1546

SCOTT NO.	DESCRIPTION	FIRST DAY COVERS SING	PL. BLK.	MINT SHEET	PLATE BLOCK	UNUSED F/NH	USED
1543-46	Continental Congress, 4 varieties, attached .	4.50	6.00	18.00(50)	2.00	1.75	1.25
1543	10¢ Carpenter's Hall .	2.25	....	....	....	.50	.20
1544	10¢ Quote–First Congress	2.25	....	....	....	.50	.20
1545	10¢ Quote–Declaration– of Independence	2.25	....	....	....	.50	.20
1546	10¢ Independence Hall	2.25	....	....	....	.50	.20

1547

1548

1549

SCOTT NO.	DESCRIPTION	FIRST DAY COVERS SING	PL. BLK.	MINT SHEET	PLATE BLOCK	UNUSED F/NH	USED
1547	10¢ Energy Conservation	2.25	4.00	21.00(50)	2.00	.45	.20
1548	10¢ Sleepy Hollow ..	2.25	4.00	15.00(50)	1.50	.40	.20
1549	10¢ Retarded Children	2.25	4.00	15.00(50)	1.50	.40	.20

1550

1551

1552

SCOTT NO.	DESCRIPTION	FIRST DAY COVERS SING	PL. BLK.	MINT SHEET	PLATE BLOCK	UNUSED F/NH	USED
1550	10¢ Christmas–Angel	2.25	4.00	14.00(50)	4.00(10)	.35	.15
1551	10¢ Christmas–Currier & Ives	2.25	4.00	14.00(50)	4.50(12)	.35	.15
1552	10¢ Christams– Dove of Peace	2.25	4.00	20.00(50)	9.00(20)	.40	.30
1552	same	....	....	....	4.75(12)	....	....

1553

1554

1555

1975 COMMEMORATIVES

SCOTT NO.	DESCRIPTION	FIRST DAY COVERS SING	PL. BLK.	MINT SHEET	PLATE BLOCK	UNUSED F/NH	USED
1553-80	**8¢-10¢, 28 varieties, complete**	....	....	....	....	**12.00**	**5.25**
1553	10¢ Benjamin West– Arts	2.25	4.00	20.00(50)	5.00(10)	.45	.20
1554	10¢ Paul Dunbar–Arts	2.25	4.00	20.00(50)	5.00(10)	.45	.20
1555	10¢ D.W. Griffith–Arts	2.25	4.00	20.00(50)	2.00	.45	.20

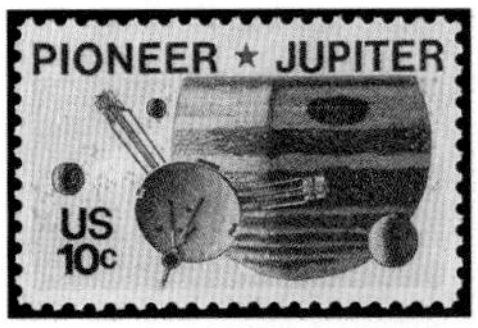

1556

1557

1558

SCOTT NO.	DESCRIPTION	FIRST DAY COVERS SING	PL. BLK.	MINT SHEET	PLATE BLOCK	UNUSED F/NH	USED
1556	10¢ Pioneer 10	2.25	4.00	17.00(50)	2.00	.45	.20
1557	10¢ Mariner 10	2.25	4.00	17.00(50)	2.00	.45	.20
1558	10¢ Collective Bargaining	2.25	4.00	14.50(50)	3.00(8)	.40	.20

1559

1560

1561

1562

SCOTT NO.	DESCRIPTION	FIRST DAY COVERS SING	PL. BLK.	MINT SHEET	PLATE BLOCK	UNUSED F/NH	USED
1559	8¢ Sybil Ludington ..	2.25	4.00	14.00(50)	4.00(10)	.35	.20
1560	10¢ Salem Poor	2.25	4.00	20.00(50)	5.00(10)	.45	.20
1561	10¢ Haym Salomon .	2.25	4.00	20.00(50)	5.00(10)	.45	.20
1562	18¢ Peter Francisco .	2.25	4.00	27.50(50)	7.50(10)	.70	.40

1563

1564

SCOTT NO.	DESCRIPTION	FIRST DAY COVERS SING	PL. BLK.	MINT SHEET	PLATE BLOCK	UNUSED F/NH	USED
1563	10¢ Lexington-Concord	2.25	4.00	15.00(40)	5.50(12)	.45	.20
1564	10¢ Battle of Bunker Hill	2.25	4.00	15.00(40)	5.50(12)	.45	.20

1565

1566

1567

1568

SCOTT NO.	DESCRIPTION	FIRST DAY COVERS SING	FIRST DAY COVERS PL. BLK.	MINT SHEET	PLATE BLOCK	UNUSED F/NH	USED
1565-68	Military Uniforms, 4 varieties, attached .	4.00	6.00	15.00(50)	5.00(12)	1.75	1.30
1565	10¢ Continental Army	2.25	....	....	....	.50	.20
1566	10¢ Continental Navy	2.25	....	....	....	.50	.20
1567	10¢ Continental Marines	2.25	....	....	....	.50	.20
1568	10¢ American Militia .	2.25	....	....	....	.50	.20

1569

1570

SCOTT NO.	DESCRIPTION	FIRST DAY COVERS SING	FIRST DAY COVERS PL. BLK.	MINT SHEET	PLATE BLOCK	UNUSED F/NH	USED
1569-70	Apollo-Soyuz Mission, 2 varieties, attached .	3.00	4.50	8.00(24)	5.00(12)	.95	.55
1569	10¢ Docked	2.25	....	....	....	.50	.20
1570	10¢ Docking	2.25	....	....	....	.50	.20

1571

SCOTT NO.	DESCRIPTION	FIRST DAY COVERS SING	FIRST DAY COVERS PL. BLK.	MINT SHEET	PLATE BLOCK	UNUSED F/NH	USED
1571	10¢ International Women's Year	2.25	4.00	14.00(50)	2.10(6)	.35	.20

1572 1573

1574 1575

SCOTT NO.	DESCRIPTION	FIRST DAY COVERS SING	FIRST DAY COVERS PL. BLK.	MINT SHEET	PLATE BLOCK	UNUSED F/NH	USED
1572-75	Postal Service Bicentennial, 4 varieties, attached .	4.00	5.00	15.00(50)	5.00(12)	1.85	1.50
1572	10¢ Stagecoach & Trailer	2.25	....	....	....	.50	.20
1573	10¢ Locomotives	2.25	....	....	....	.50	.20
1574	10¢ Airplanes	2.25	....	....	....	.50	.20
1575	10¢ Satellite	2.25	....	....	....	.50	.20

1576

1577 1578

SCOTT NO.	DESCRIPTION	FIRST DAY COVERS SING	FIRST DAY COVERS PL. BLK.	MINT SHEET	PLATE BLOCK	UNUSED F/NH	USED
1576	10¢ World Peace through Law	2.25	4.00	18.00(50)	2.00	.45	.20
1577-78	Banking & Commerce, 2 varieties, attached .	2.50	3.75	18.00(40)	2.00	1.00	.70
1577	10¢ Banking	2.25	....	....	....	.60	.20
1578	10¢ Commerce	2.25	....	....	....	.60	.20

1579

1580

SCOTT NO.	DESCRIPTION	FIRST DAY COVERS SING	FIRST DAY COVERS PL. BLK.	MINT SHEET	PLATE BLOCK	UNUSED F/NH	USED
1579	(10¢) Madonna	2.25	4.00	18.00(50)	5.00(12)	.45	.20
1580	(10¢) Christams Card	2.25	4.00	18.00(50)	5.00(12)	.45	.20
1580b	(10¢) Christmas Card, perf. $10^1/2$ x 11	....	....	48.50(50)	15.00(12)	1.00	.50

1581, 1811

1582

1584

1585

1590, 1591, 1616

1592, 1617

1593

1594, 1816

1595, 1618

1596

1597, 1598, 1618C

1599, 1619

1603

1604

1605

1606

1608

1610

1611

1612

1975-81 AMERICANA ISSUE

SCOTT NO.	DESCRIPTION	FIRST DAY COVERS SING	FIRST DAY COVERS PL. BLK.	MINT SHEET	PLATE BLOCK	UNUSED F/NH	USED
1581/1612	**1¢-$5, (No #1590, 1590a, 1595, or 1598) 19 varieties, complete**	**51.50**	**........**	**........**	**155.00**	**33.50**	**6.95**
1581	1¢ Inkwell & Quill (1977)	2.25	4.00	7.00(100)	.70	.20	.15
1582	2¢ Speaker's Stand (1977)	2.25	4.00	8.25(100)	.70	.20	.15
1584	3¢ Ballot Box (1977)	2.25	4.00	11.50(100)	.70	.20	.15
1585	4¢ Books & Eyeglasses (1977)	2.25	4.00	13.00(100)	.85	.20	.15
1590	9¢ Capitol, from bklt pane (1977)	15.00	....	....	....	1.25	1.00
1590a	same, perf 10 (1977)	....	....	....	....	31.50	....
1590,1623	Attached pair, from bklt pane	....	....	....	....	1.75	....
1590a, 1623b	Attached pair, perf. 10	....	....	....	....	35.00	....
1591	9¢ Capitol, grey paper	2.25	4.00	30.00(100)	1.50	.40	.15
1592	10¢ Justice (1977)	2.25	4.00	32.00(100)	1.50	.40	.15
1593	11¢ Printing Press	2.25	4.00	40.00(100)	1.75	.50	.15
1594	12¢ Torch (1981)	2.25	4.00	42.50(100)	2.25	.50	.15
1595	13¢ Liberty Bell from bklt pane	2.25	....	....	....	.50	.15
1595a	13¢ bklt pane of 6	2.25	....	....	....	3.25	....
1595b	13¢ bklt pane of 7–Slogan VIII	2.50	....	....	....	3.50	....
1595c	13¢ bklt pane of 8	2.50	....	....	....	3.50	....
1595d	13¢ bklt pane of 5–Slogan IX (1976)	2.25	....	....	....	3.50	....
	VIII–Paying Bills... IX–Collect Stamps...						
1596	13¢ Eagle & Shield	2.25	4.00	45.00(100)	6.00(12)	.50	.15
1597	15¢ Fort McHenry Flag (1978)	2.25	4.00	43.00(100)	9.50(20)	.50	.15
1598	same, from bklt pane (1978)	2.25	....	....	....	.90	.15
1598a	15¢ bklt pane of 8	3.00	....	....	....	8.50	....
1599	16¢ Statue of Liberty (1978)	2.25	4.00	70.00(100)	3.25	.85	.35
1603	24¢ Old North Church	2.25	4.00	80.00(100)	4.00	.95	.20
1604	28¢ Fort Nisqually (1978)	2.25	4.00	90.00(100)	5.00	1.10	.20
1605	29¢ Lighthouse (1978)	2.25	4.00	100.00(100)	5.00	1.20	.50
1606	30¢ School House (1979)	2.25	4.00	100.00(100)	5.00	1.20	.20
1608	50¢ "Betty" Lamp (1979)	2.50	5.25	180.00(100)	8.25	2.00	.30
1610	$1 Rush Lamp (1979)	3.50	17.50	350.00(100)	14.50	3.50	.20
1610c	Same, candle flame inverted	....	....	....	....	14500.00	....
1611	$2 Kerosene Lamp (1978)	7.00	14.50	600.00(100)	27.00	6.25	.70
1612	$5 Conductor's Lantern (1979)	15.00	31.50	1400.00(100)	70.00	15.00	3.00

1613

1614

1615

1615C

1975-79 COIL STAMPS Perforated Vertically

SCOTT NO.	DESCRIPTION	FIRST DAY COVERS SING	FIRST DAY COVERS PL. BLK.	MINT SHEET	LINE PR.	UNUSED F/NH	USED
1613-19	**3.1¢-16¢, 9 varieties, complete**	**........**	**........**	**........**	**12.50**	**3.75**	**1.80**
1613	3.1¢ Guitar (1979)	2.25	2.75	....	1.20	.45	.20
1614	7.7¢ Saxhorns (1976)	2.25	2.75	....	1.30	.60	.40
1615	7.9¢ Drum (1976)	2.25	2.75	....	1.20	.60	.40
1615C	8.4¢ Piano (1978)	2.25	2.75	....	3.75	.60	.40
1616	9¢ Capitol (1976)	2.25	2.75	....	1.30	.60	.40
1617	10¢ Justice (1977)	2.25	2.75	....	1.10	.50	.20
1618	13¢ Liberty Bell	2.25	2.75	....	1.00	.60	.30
1618C	15¢ Fort McHenry Flag (1978)	2.25	....	....	....	.65	.20
1619	16¢ Statue of Liberty (1978)	2.25	2.75	....	2.50	.75	.60

COIL LINE PAIRS: are two connected coil stamps with a line the same color as the stamps printed between the two stamps. This line usually appears every 20 to 30 stamps on a roll depending on the issue.

1622, 1625

1623, 1623b

1975-77 REGULAR ISSUES

SCOTT NO.	DESCRIPTION	FIRST DAY COVERS SING	FIRST DAY COVERS PL. BLK.	MINT SHEET	PLATE BLOCK	UNUSED F/NH	USED
1622	13¢ Flag & Independence Hall, 11 x 10½	2.25	4.00	48.00(100)	12.00(20)	.55	.15
1622c	same, perf. 11 (1981)	....	....	180.00(100)	90.00(20)	1.20	....
1623	13¢ Flag & Capitol from bklt pane, perf 11 x 10½ (1977)	3.00	....	....	....	.50	.50
1623a	bklt pane of 8 (one–1590, seven–1623)	30.00	....	....	....	3.75	3.75
1623b	13¢ Flag & Capitol from bklt pane, perf. 10	2.25	....	....	....	.90	.75
1623c	bklt pane of 8 (one–1590a, seven–1623b)	17.00	....	....	....	40.00	....
	1975 COIL STAMP						
1625	13¢ Flag & Independence Hall	2.25	....	....	3.75	.55	.15

1629 1630 1631

1632

1976 COMMEMORATIVES

SCOTT NO.	DESCRIPTION	FIRST DAY COVERS SING	FIRST DAY COVERS PL. BLK.	MINT SHEET	PLATE BLOCK	UNUSED F/NH	USED
1629/1703	**(1629-32, 1683-85, 1690-1703) 21 varieties**	**........**	**........**	**........**	**........**	**12.80**	**3.50**
1629-31	Spirit of '76, 3 varieties, attached	3.00	6.00	19.00(50)	6.00(12)	1.75	1.25
1629	13¢ Boy Drummer	2.00	....	....	....	.50	.20
1630	13¢ Older Drummer	2.00	....	....	....	.50	.20
1631	13¢ Fifer	2.00	....	....	....	.50	.20
1632	13¢ Interphil	2.25	4.00	18.75(50)	1.75	.45	.20

1633

1682

1976 BICENTENNIAL STATE FLAGS
Complete Set Printed in One Sheet of 50 Stamps

1633 *Delaware*
1634 *Pennsylvania*
1635 *New Jersey*
1636 *Georgia*
1637 *Connecticut*
1638 *Massachusetts*
1639 *Maryland*
1640 *South Carolina*
1641 *New Hampshire*
1642 *Virginia*
1643 *New York*
1644 *North Carolina*
1645 *Rhode Island*
1646 *Vermont*
1647 *Kentucky*
1648 *Tennessee*
1649 *Ohio*
1650 *Louisiana*
1651 *Indiana*
1652 *Mississippi*
1653 *Illinois*
1654 *Alabama*
1655 *Maine*
1656 *Missouri*
1657 *Arkansas*
1658 *Michigan*
1659 *Florida*
1660 *Texas*
1661 *Iowa*
1662 *Wisconsin*
1663 *California*
1664 *Minnesota*
1665 *Oregon*
1666 *Kansas*
1667 *West Virginia*
1668 *Nevada*
1669 *Nebraska*
1670 *Colorado*
1671 *North Dakota*
1672 *South Dakota*
1673 *Montana*
1674 *Washington*
1675 *Idaho*
1676 *Wyoming*
1677 *Utah*
1678 *Oklahoma*
1679 *New Mexico*
1680 *Arizona*
1681 *Alaska*
1682 *Hawaii*

1976 BICENTENNIAL STATE FLAGS
Complete Set Printed in One Sheet of 50 Stamps
Continued

SCOTT NO.	DESCRIPTION	FIRST DAY COVERS SING	FIRST DAY COVERS PL. BLK.	MINT SHEET	PLATE BLOCK	UNUSED F/NH	USED
1633-82	13¢ State Flags, 50 varieties, attached	....	....	27.50(50)	....	27.50	....
	Set of 50 singles	95.00	....	....	....	....	18.75
	Singles of above	2.50	....	....	....	.75	.50

1683

1684

1685

SCOTT NO.	DESCRIPTION	FIRST DAY COVERS SING	FIRST DAY COVERS PL. BLK.	MINT SHEET	PLATE BLOCK	UNUSED F/NH	USED
1683	13¢ Telephone	2.25	4.00	20.00(50)	2.10	.60	.20
1684	13¢ Aviation	2.25	4.00	20.00(50)	5.50(10)	.60	.20
1685	13¢ Chemistry	2.25	4.00	25.00(50)	7.50(12)	.60	.20

1686

1687

1976 BICENNTENNIAL SOUVENIR SHEETS

SCOTT NO.	DESCRIPTION	FIRST DAY COVERS SING	FIRST DAY COVERS PL. BLK.	MINT SHEET	PLATE BLOCK	UNUSED F/NH	USED
1686-89	4 varieties, complete	32.50	....	....	....	30.00	27.00
1686	13¢ Cornwallis Surrender	6.00	....	....	....	5.00	4.75
1686a-e	13¢ singles, each	3.50	....	....	....	1.20	1.10
1687	18¢ Independence	7.50	....	....	....	7.00	6.50
1687a-e	18¢ singles, each	3.75	....	....	....	1.60	1.50
1688	24¢ Washington Crossing Delaware	9.50	....	....	....	8.75	8.25
1688a-e	24¢ singles, each	4.25	....	....	....	1.90	1.80
1689	31¢ Washington at Valley Forge	11.50	....	....	....	11.00	10.50
1689a-e	31¢ singles, each	5.25	....	....	....	2.40	2.30

1690

1691 1692 1693 1694

SCOTT NO.	DESCRIPTION	FIRST DAY COVERS SING	FIRST DAY COVERS PL. BLK.	MINT SHEET	PLATE BLOCK	UNUSED F/NH	USED
1690	13¢ Benjamin Franklin	2.25	4.00	24.00(50)	2.20	.50	.20
1691-94	Declaration of Independence, 4 varieties, attached	5.00	10.00	36.00(50)	14.50(16)	4.00	3.00
1691	13¢ Delegation members	2.25	....	....	....	1.10	.25
1692	13¢ Adams, etc.	2.25	....	....	....	1.10	.25
1693	13¢ Jefferson, Franklin, etc.	2.25	....	....	....	1.10	.25
1694	13¢ Hancock, Thomson, etc.	2.25	....	....	....	1.10	.25

1695

1696

1697

1698

SCOTT NO.	DESCRIPTION	FIRST DAY COVERS SING	FIRST DAY COVERS PL. BLK.	MINT SHEET	PLATE BLOCK	UNUSED F/NH	USED
1695-98	Olympic Games, 4 varieties, attached	4.00	6.00	23.50(50)	6.75(12)	2.40	1.95
1695	13¢ Diving	2.25	....	....	....	.75	.25
1696	13¢ Skiing	2.25	....	....	....	.75	.25
1697	13¢ Running	2.25	....	....	....	.75	.25
1698	13¢ Skating	2.25	....	....	....	.75	.25

1699

1700

SCOTT NO.	DESCRIPTION	FIRST DAY COVERS SING	FIRST DAY COVERS PL. BLK.	MINT SHEET	PLATE BLOCK	UNUSED F/NH	USED
1699	13¢ Clara Maass	2.25	4.00	20.00(40)	7.00(12)	.60	.20
1700	13¢ Adolph S. Ochs	2.25	4.00	16.00(32)	2.25	.60	.20

1701

1702, 1703

SCOTT NO.	DESCRIPTION	FIRST DAY COVERS SING	FIRST DAY COVERS PL. BLK.	MINT SHEET	PLATE BLOCK	UNUSED F/NH	USED
1701	13¢ Nativity	2.25	....	20.00(50)	6.00(12)	.55	.20
1702	13¢ "Winter Pastime" (Andreati)	2.25	....	20.00(50)	5.25(10)	.55	.20
1703	13¢ "Winter Pastime" (Gravure Int.)	2.25	....	20.00(50)	10.00(20)	.55	.20

1704

1705

1977 COMMEMORATIVES

SCOTT NO.	DESCRIPTION	FIRST DAY COVERS SING	FIRST DAY COVERS PL. BLK.	MINT SHEET	PLATE BLOCK	UNUSED F/NH	USED
1704-30	**27 varieties, complete**	....	....	....	....	**13.00**	**5.00**
1704	13¢ Princeton	2.25	4.00	20.00(40)	5.50(10)	.60	.20
1705	13¢ Sound Recording	2.25	4.00	25.00(50)	2.25	.60	.20

1708 1709

1706 1707

SCOTT NO.	DESCRIPTION	FIRST DAY COVERS SING	FIRST DAY COVERS PL. BLK.	MINT SHEET	PLATE BLOCK	UNUSED F/NH	USED
1706-09	Pueblo Art, 4 varieties, attached .	4.00	....	18.00(40)	5.75(10)	3.00	2.50
1706	13¢ Zia	2.25	....	....	....	.75	.25
1707	13¢ San Ildefonso . . .	2.25	....	....	....	.75	.25
1708	13¢ Hopi	2.25	....	....	....	.75	.25
1709	13¢ Acoma	2.25	....	....	....	.75	.25

1710

1711

SCOTT NO.	DESCRIPTION	FIRST DAY COVERS SING	FIRST DAY COVERS PL. BLK.	MINT SHEET	PLATE BLOCK	UNUSED F/NH	USED
1710	13¢ Transatlantic Flight	3.00	5.00	28.00(50)	7.50(12)	.60	.20
1711	13¢ Colorado Statehood	2.25	4.00	28.00(50)	7.50(12)	.60	.20

1712

1713

MINT SHEETS: From 1935 to date, we list prices for standard size Mint Sheets in Fine, Never Hinged condition. The number of stamps in each sheet is noted in ( ).

1714

1715

1716

SCOTT NO.	DESCRIPTION	FIRST DAY COVERS SING	FIRST DAY COVERS PL. BLK.	MINT SHEET	PLATE BLOCK	UNUSED F/NH	USED
1712-15	Butterflies, 4 varieties, attached .	4.00	6.00	18.75(50)	5.75(12)	2.00	1.75
1712	13¢ Swallowtail	2.25	....	....	....	.60	.20
1713	13¢ Checkerspot	2.25	....	....	....	.60	.20
1714	13¢ Dogface	2.25	....	....	....	.60	.20
1715	13¢ Orange-Tip	2.25	....	....	....	.60	.20
1716	13¢ Lafayette	2.25	6.00	17.00(40)	1.90	.50	.20

1717 1718

1719 1720

SCOTT NO.	DESCRIPTION	FIRST DAY COVERS SING	FIRST DAY COVERS PL. BLK.	MINT SHEET	PLATE BLOCK	UNUSED F/NH	USED
1717-20	Skilled Hands, 4 varieties, attached .	4.00	....	18.75(50)	5.75(12)	2.00	1.75
1717	13¢ Seamstress	2.25	....	....	....	.60	.20
1718	13¢ Blacksmith	2.25	....	....	....	.60	.20
1719	13¢ Wheelwright	2.25	....	....	....	.60	.20
1720	13¢ Leatherworker . .	2.25	....	....	....	.60	.20

1721

1722

1723

1724

SCOTT NO.	DESCRIPTION	FIRST DAY COVERS SING	FIRST DAY COVERS PL. BLK.	MINT SHEET	PLATE BLOCK	UNUSED F/NH	USED
1721	13¢ Peace Bridge . . .	2.25	4.00	20.00(50)	1.90	.50	.20
1722	13¢ Herkimer at Oriskany	2.25	4.00	17.50(40)	4.75(10)	.50	.20
1723-24	Energy, 2 varieties, attached .	2.50	....	15.50(40)	5.25(12)	1.10	.85
1723	13¢ Conservation . . .	2.25	....	....	....	.60	.20
1724	13¢ Development . . .	2.25	....	....	....	.60	.20

1725

1726

1727

1728

1729

1730

SCOTT NO.	DESCRIPTION	FIRST DAY COVERS SING	FIRST DAY COVERS PL. BLK.	MINT SHEET	PLATE BLOCK	UNUSED F/NH	USED
1725	13¢ Alta California . .	2.25	4.00	20.00(50)	1.90	.50	.20
1726	13¢ Articles of Confederation	2.25	4.00	20.00(50)	1.90	.50	.20
1727	13¢ Talking Pictures .	2.25	4.00	20.00(50)	1.90	.50	.20
1728	13¢ Surrender at Saratoga	2.25	....	17.50(40)	4.75(10)	.50	.20
1729	13¢ Washington, Christmas	2.50	....	42.50(100)	9.00(20)	.50	.20
1730	13¢ Rural Mailbox, Christmas	2.50	....	42.50(100)	4.75(10)	.50	.20

1731

1732

1733

1978 COMMEMORATIVES

SCOTT NO.	DESCRIPTION	FIRST DAY COVERS SING	FIRST DAY COVERS PL. BLK.	MINT SHEET	PLATE BLOCK	UNUSED F/NH	USED
1731/69	**(1731-33, 1744-56, 1758-69) 28 varieties**	....	....	....	....	**19.50**	**7.00**
1731	13¢ Carl Sandburg . .	2.25	4.00	28.00(50)	2.75	.60	.20
1732-33	Captain Cook, 2 varieties, attached .	2.00	....	24.00(50)	12.00(20)	1.50	1.20
1732	13¢ Captain Cook (Alaska)	2.25	4.00	....	1.90	.55	.20
1733	13¢ "Resolution" (Hawaii)	2.25	4.00	....	1.90	.55	.20

NOTE: The Plate Block set includes #1732 & 1733 Plate Blocks of four.

1734

1735, 1736, 1743

1737

1978-80 DEFINITIVES

SCOTT NO.	DESCRIPTION	FIRST DAY COVERS SING	FIRST DAY COVERS PL. BLK.	MINT SHEET	PLATE BLOCK	UNUSED F/NH	USED
1734	13¢ Indian Head Penny	2.25	4.00	62.50(150)	2.25	.50	.15
1735	(15¢) "A" Defintive (Gravure)	2.25	4.00	47.50(100)	2.25	.50	.15
1736	same (Intaglio), from bklt pane	2.25	....	....	....	.50	.15
1736a	15¢ "A" bklt pane of 8	3.50	....	....	....	3.85	....
1737	15¢ Roses	2.25	....	....	....	.50	.15
1737a	same, bklt pane of 8 .	4.00	....	....	....	3.85	....

1738 1739 1740 1741 1742

SCOTT NO.	DESCRIPTION	FIRST DAY COVERS SING	FIRST DAY COVERS PL. BLK.	MINT SHEET	PLATE BLOCK	UNUSED F/NH	USED
1738-42	Windmills, strip of 5, attached (1980)	5.00	....	....	....	3.00	2.25
1738	15¢ Virginia Windmill	2.25	....	....	....	.70	.20
1739	15¢ Rhode Island Windmill	2.25	....	....	....	.70	.20
1740	15¢ Massachusetts Windmill	2.25	....	....	....	.70	.20
1741	15¢ Illinois Windmill .	2.25	....	....	....	.70	.20
1742	15¢ Texas Windmill . .	2.25	....	....	....	.70	.20
1742a	Same, bklt pane of 10	6.00	....	....	....	5.75	....

1978 COIL STAMP

SCOTT NO.	DESCRIPTION	FIRST DAY COVERS SING	LINE PR.	MINT SHEET	LINE PR.	UNUSED F/NH	USED
1743	(15¢) "A" Definitive	2.25	2.75	....	1.20	.50	.15

1745

1744

1746

1747

1748

SCOTT NO.	DESCRIPTION	FIRST DAY COVERS SING	FIRST DAY COVERS PL. BLK.	MINT SHEET	PLATE BLOCK	UNUSED F/NH	USED
1744	13¢ Harriet Tubman .	5.00	7.00	28.00(50)	7.50(12)	.65	.20
1745-48	Quilts, 4 varieties, attached	3.50	....	19.50(48)	5.50(12)	3.00	2.00
1745	13¢ Flowers	2.25	....	....	....	.75	.25
1746	13¢ Stars	2.25	....	....	....	.75	.25
1747	13¢ Stripes	2.25	....	....	....	.75	.25
1748	13¢ Plaid	2.25	....	....	....	.75	.25

1750

1749

1752

1751

SCOTT NO.	DESCRIPTION	FIRST DAY COVERS SING	FIRST DAY COVERS PL. BLK.	MINT SHEET	PLATE BLOCK	UNUSED F/NH	USED
1749-52	American Dance, 4 varieties, attached .	5.00	....	19.50(48)	5.50(12)	3.00	2.25
1749	13¢ Ballet	2.25	....	....	....	.75	.25
1750	13¢ Theater	2.25	....	....	....	.75	.25
1751	13¢ Folk	2.25	....	....	....	.75	.25
1752	13¢ Modern	2.25	....	....	....	.75	.25

1753

1754

1755

1756

SCOTT NO.	DESCRIPTION	FIRST DAY COVERS SING	FIRST DAY COVERS PL. BLK.	MINT SHEET	PLATE BLOCK	UNUSED F/NH	USED
1753	13¢ French Alliance .	2.25	4.00	15.50(40)	1.90	.50	.20
1754	13¢ Dr. Papanicolaou	2.25	4.00	24.00(50)	2.25	.60	.20
1755	13¢ Jimmie Rodgers .	2.25	4.00	27.50(50)	8.00(12)	.75	.25
1756	15¢ George M. Cohan	2.25	4.00	35.00(50)	9.50(12)	.75	.20

1757

1978 CAPEX SOUVENIR SHEET

SCOTT NO.	DESCRIPTION	FIRST DAY COVERS SING	FIRST DAY COVERS PL. BLK.	MINT SHEET	PLATE BLOCK	UNUSED F/NH	USED
1757	$1.04 CAPEX	4.25	....	20.00(6)	4.00	4.00	3.25
1757a	13¢ Cardinal	2.25	....	....	....	.55	.50
1757b	13¢ Mallard	2.25	....	....	....	.55	.50
1757c	13¢ Canada Goose . .	2.25	....	....	....	.55	.50
1757d	13¢ Blue Jay	2.25	....	....	....	.55	.50
1757e	13¢ Moose	2.25	....	....	....	.55	.50
1757f	13¢ Chipmunk	2.25	....	....	....	.55	.50
1757g	13¢ Red Fox	2.25	....	....	....	.55	.50
1757h	13¢ Raccoon	2.25	....	....	....	.55	.50

1758

1759

SCOTT NO.	DESCRIPTION	FIRST DAY COVERS SING	FIRST DAY COVERS PL. BLK.	MINT SHEET	PLATE BLOCK	UNUSED F/NH	USED
1758	15¢ Photography . . .	2.25	4.00	17.00(40)	6.25(12)	.50	.20
1759	15¢ Viking Mission . .	2.25	4.00	21.00(50)	2.10	.50	.20

1760

1761

1762

1763

SCOTT NO.	DESCRIPTION	FIRST DAY COVERS SING	FIRST DAY COVERS PL. BLK.	MINT SHEET	PLATE BLOCK	UNUSED F/NH	USED
1760-63	American Owls, 4 varieties, attached	5.00	6.00	22.00(50)	2.50	2.25	1.75
1760	15¢ Great Gray	2.25	....	....	....	.70	.25
1761	15¢ Saw-Whet	2.25	....	....	....	.70	.25
1762	15¢ Barred Owl	2.25	....	....	....	.70	.25
1763	15¢ Great Horned . . .	2.25	....	....	....	.70	.25

1764 1765

1766 1767

SCOTT NO.	DESCRIPTION	FIRST DAY COVERS SING	FIRST DAY COVERS PL. BLK.	MINT SHEET	PLATE BLOCK	UNUSED F/NH	USED
1764-67	Trees, 4 varieties, attached	5.00	....	18.00(40)	6.25(12)	2.25	1.75
1764	15¢ Giant Sequoia . .	2.25	....	....	....	.70	.25
1765	15¢ Pine	2.25	....	....	....	.70	.25
1766	15¢ Oak	2.25	....	....	....	.70	.25
1767	15¢ Birch	2.25	....	....	....	.70	.25

1768

1769

SCOTT NO.	DESCRIPTION	FIRST DAY COVERS SING	FIRST DAY COVERS PL. BLK.	MINT SHEET	PLATE BLOCK	UNUSED F/NH	USED
1768	15¢ Madonna, Christmas	2.25	4.00	40.00(100)	6.25(12)	.50	.15
1769	15¢ Hobby Horse, Christmas	2.25	4.00	40.00(100)	6.25(12)	.50	.15

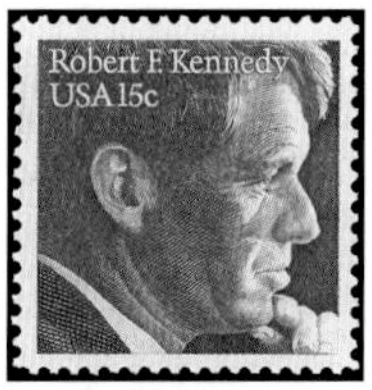

1770

1771

1979 COMMEMORATIVES

SCOTT NO.	DESCRIPTION	FIRST DAY COVERS SING	FIRST DAY COVERS PL. BLK.	MINT SHEET	PLATE BLOCK	UNUSED F/NH	USED
1770/1802	**(1770-94, 1799-1802) 29 varieties, complete**	....	....	....	....	**17.50**	**6.00**
1770	15¢ Robert F. Kennedy	2.25	4.00	25.00(48)	2.75	.65	.20
1771	15¢ Martin L. King, Jr.	3.00	5.00	32.50(50)	8.50(12)	.75	.20

1772

1773

1774

SCOTT NO.	DESCRIPTION	FIRST DAY COVERS SING	FIRST DAY COVERS PL. BLK.	MINT SHEET	PLATE BLOCK	UNUSED F/NH	USED
1772	15¢ International Year of the Child	2.25	4.00	23.50(50)	2.75	.65	.20
1773	15¢ John Steinbeck .	2.25	4.00	28.00(50)	2.75	.65	.20
1774	15¢ Albert Einstein . .	3.00	5.00	28.00(50)	2.75	.65	.20

U.S. BICENTENNIAL: The U.S.P.S. issued stamps commemorating the 200th anniversary of the struggle for independence from 1775 through 1783. These include numbers: 1432, 1476-83, 1543-46, 1559-68, 1629-31, 1633-82, 1686-89, 1691-94, 1704, 1716-20, 1722, 1726, 1728-29, 1753, 1789, 1826, 1937-38, 1941, 2052 and C98.

1775 1776

1777 1778

SCOTT NO.	DESCRIPTION	FIRST DAY COVERS SING	FIRST DAY COVERS PL. BLK.	MINT SHEET	PLATE BLOCK	UNUSED F/NH	USED
1775-78	Pennsylvania Toleware, 4 varieties, attached .	5.00	....	20.00(40)	5.50(10)	2.50	2.00
1775	15¢ Coffee Pot	2.25	....	....	....	.75	.20
1776	15¢ Tea Caddy	2.25	....	....	....	.75	.20
1777	15¢ Sugar Bowl	2.25	....	....	....	.75	.20
1778	15¢ Coffee Pot	2.25	....	....	....	.75	.20

1779 1780

1781 1782

SCOTT NO.	DESCRIPTION	FIRST DAY COVERS SING	FIRST DAY COVERS PL. BLK.	MINT SHEET	PLATE BLOCK	UNUSED F/NH	USED
1779-82	Architecture, 4 varieties, attached	5.00	6.00	30.00(48)	4.00	3.50	2.75
1779	15¢ Virginia Rotunda	2.25	....	....	....	1.00	.25
1780	15¢ Baltimore Cathedral	2.25	....	....	....	1.00	.25
1781	15¢ Boston State House	2.25	....	....	....	1.00	.25
1782	15¢ Philadelphia Exchange	2.25	....	....	....	1.00	.25

1783

1784

1785

1786

SCOTT NO.	DESCRIPTION	FIRST DAY COVERS SING	FIRST DAY COVERS PL. BLK.	MINT SHEET	PLATE BLOCK	UNUSED F/NH	USED
1783-86	Endangered Flora, 4 varieties, attached .	5.00	....	25.00(50)	7.50(12)	2.75	1.70
1783	15¢ Trillium	2.25	....	....	....	.75	.20
1784	15¢ Broadbean	2.25	....	....	....	.75	.20
1785	15¢ Wallflower	2.25	....	....	....	.75	.20
1786	15¢ Primrose	2.25	....	....	....	.75	.20

1787

1788

1789, 1789a

1790

SCOTT NO.	DESCRIPTION	FIRST DAY COVERS SING	FIRST DAY COVERS PL. BLK.	MINT SHEET	PLATE BLOCK	UNUSED F/NH	USED
1787	15¢ Guide Dog	2.25	....	28.00(50)	11.50(20)	.70	.20
1788	15¢ Special Olympics	2.25	....	28.00(50)	6.00(10)	.65	.20
1789	15¢ John Paul Jones perf. 11 x 12	2.25	....	28.00(50)	6.00(10)	.65	.20
1789a	same, perf. 11	2.25	....	40.00(50)	9.00(10)	1.00	.30

NOTE: #1789a may be included in year date sets and special offers and not 1789.

SCOTT NO.	DESCRIPTION	FIRST DAY COVERS SING	FIRST DAY COVERS PL. BLK.	MINT SHEET	PLATE BLOCK	UNUSED F/NH	USED
1790	10¢ Summer Olympics, Javelin Thrower	2.25	4.00	14.50(50)	5.00(12)	.40	.20

1791 1792

1793 1794

SCOTT NO.	DESCRIPTION	FIRST DAY COVERS SING	FIRST DAY COVERS PL. BLK.	MINT SHEET	PLATE BLOCK	UNUSED F/NH	USED
1791-94	Summer Olympics, 4 varieties, attached .	5.00	....	22.50(50)	7.00(12)	2.50	2.00
1791	15¢ Runners	2.25	....	....	....	.70	.25
1792	15¢ Swimmers	2.25	....	....	....	.70	.25
1793	15¢ Rowers	2.25	....	....	....	.70	.25
1794	15¢ Equestrian	2.25	....	....	....	.70	.25

1795 1796

1797 1798

1980

SCOTT NO.	DESCRIPTION	FIRST DAY COVERS SING	FIRST DAY COVERS PL. BLK.	MINT SHEET	PLATE BLOCK	UNUSED F/NH	USED
1795-98	Winter Olympics, 4 varieties, attached .	5.00	....	22.50(50)	7.00(12)	2.50	2.00
1795	15¢ Skater	2.25	....	....	....	.70	.25
1796	15¢ Downhill Skier . .	2.25	....	....	....	.70	.25
1797	15¢ Ski Jumper	2.25	....	....	....	.70	.25
1798	15¢ Hockey	2.25	....	....	....	.70	.25
1795a-98a	same, perf. 11, attached	....	....	49.50(50)	15.00(12)	4.50	....
1795a	15¢ Skater	....	....	....	....	1.20	....
1796a	15¢ Downhill Skier . .	....	....	....	....	1.20	....
1797a	15¢ Ski Jumper	....	....	....	....	1.20	....
1798a	15¢ Hockey	....	....	....	....	1.20	....

1799

1800

1979 COMMEMORATIVES

SCOTT NO.	DESCRIPTION	FIRST DAY COVERS SING	FIRST DAY COVERS PL. BLK.	MINT SHEET	PLATE BLOCK	UNUSED F/NH	USED
1799	15¢ Christmas–Madonna	2.25	....	42.00(100)	6.25(12)	.55	.15
1800	15¢ Christmas–Santa Claus	2.25	....	42.00(100)	6.25(12)	.55	.15

1801

1802

SCOTT NO.	DESCRIPTION	FIRST DAY COVERS SING	FIRST DAY COVERS PL. BLK.	MINT SHEET	PLATE BLOCK	UNUSED F/NH	USED
1801	15¢ Will Rogers.....	3.00	....	25.00(50)	7.00(12)	.55	.20
1802	15¢ Vietnam Veterans	3.00	5.25	30.00(50)	7.00(10)	.55	.75

1803

1804

1980 COMMEMORATIVES

SCOTT NO.	DESCRIPTION	FIRST DAY COVERS SING	FIRST DAY COVERS PL. BLK.	MINT SHEET	PLATE BLOCK	UNUSED F/NH	USED
1795/1843	**(1795-98, 1803-10, 1821-43) 35 varieties, complete**	....	....	....	....	**21.50**	**6.80**
1803	15¢ W.C. Fields	2.25	4.00	25.00(50)	6.50(12)	.55	.20
1804	15¢ Benjamin Banneker	2.25	4.00	35.00(50)	9.50(12)	.85	.20

1805

1806, 1808, 1810

1807

1809

SCOTT NO.	DESCRIPTION	FIRST DAY COVERS SING	FIRST DAY COVERS PL. BLK.	MINT SHEET	PLATE BLOCK	UNUSED F/NH	USED
1805-10	6 varieties, attached .	4.50	....	26.00(60)	24.00(36)	4.25	2.75
1805-06	2 varieties, attached .	2.50	....	....	....	....	....
1807-08	2 varieties, attached .	2.50	....	....	....	....	....
1809-10	2 varieties, attached .	2.50	....	....	....	....	....
1805	15¢ "Letters Preserve Memories".........	2.25	....	....	....	.75	.25
1806	15¢ claret & multicolor	2.25	....	....	....	.75	.25
1807	15¢ "Letters Lift Spirits"	2.25	....	....	....	.75	.25
1808	15¢ green & multicolor	2.25	....	....	....	.75	.25
1809	15¢ "Letters Shape Opinions"	2.25	....	....	....	.75	.25
1810	15¢ red, white & blue	2.25	....	....	....	.75	.25

1813

1818, 1819, 1820

1980-81 Coil Stamps, Perf. 10 Vertically

SCOTT NO.	DESCRIPTION	FIRST DAY COVERS SING	FIRST DAY COVERS LINE PR.	MINT SHEET	LINE PR.	UNUSED F/NH	USED
1811	1¢ Inkwell & Quill ...	2.25	2.75	....	.50	.20	.15
1813	3.5¢ Two Violins	2.25	2.75	....	1.40	.30	.25
1816	12¢ Torch (1981) ...	2.25	2.75	....	2.25	.50	.40
1818	(18¢) "B" definitive...	2.50	3.50	47.50(100)	2.25	.70	.15
1819	(18¢) "B" definitive, from bklt pane......	2.25	....	....	....	1.00	.15
1819a	(18¢) "B" bklt pane of 8	4.00	....	....	....	7.00	....

1981 Coil Stamp Perf. Vertically

SCOTT NO.	DESCRIPTION	FIRST DAY COVERS SING	FIRST DAY COVERS LINE PR.	MINT SHEET	LINE PR.	UNUSED F/NH	USED
1820	(18¢) "B" definitive...	2.25	2.75	....	2.00	.75	.15

1821

1822

1823

1824

1825

1826

SCOTT NO.	DESCRIPTION	FIRST DAY COVERS SING	FIRST DAY COVERS PL. BLK.	MINT SHEET	PLATE BLOCK	UNUSED F/NH	USED
1821	15¢ Frances Perkins .	2.25	4.00	25.00(50)	2.50	.60	.20
1822	15¢ Dolley Madison .	2.25	4.00	70.00(150)	2.50	.60	.20
1823	15¢ Emily Bissell....	2.25	4.00	25.00(50)	2.50	.60	.20
1824	15¢ Helen Keller & Anne Sullivan	2.25	4.00	35.00(50)	3.25	.80	.20
1825	15¢ Veterans Administration	2.25	4.00	25.00(50)	2.50	.60	.20
1826	15¢ General Bernardo deGalvez..........	2.25	4.00	37.00(50)	3.50	.60	.20

1827

1828

1829

1830

SCOTT NO.	DESCRIPTION	FIRST DAY COVERS SING	FIRST DAY COVERS PL. BLK.	MINT SHEET	PLATE BLOCK	UNUSED F/NH	USED
1827-30	Coral Reefs, 4 varieties, attached .	5.00	....	22.50(50)	7.00(12)	2.50	2.00
1827	15¢ Brain Coral, Virgin Is.	2.25	....	....	....	.80	.20
1828	15¢ Elkhorn Coral, Florida	2.25	....	....	....	.80	.20
1829	15¢ Chalice Coral, American Samoa ...	2.25	....	....	....	.80	.20
1830	15¢ Finger Coral, Hawaii	2.25	....	....	....	.80	.20

1831

1832

1833

SCOTT NO.	DESCRIPTION	FIRST DAY COVERS SING	FIRST DAY COVERS PL. BLK.	MINT SHEET	PLATE BLOCK	UNUSED F/NH	USED
1831	15¢ Organized Labor	2.25	4.00	25.00(50)	6.50(12)	.65	.20
1832	15¢ Edith Wharton ..	2.25	4.00	27.50(50)	2.75	.65	.20
1833	15¢ Education......	2.25	4.00	30.00(50)	3.75(6)	.65	.20

1834 1835 1836 1837

SCOTT NO.	DESCRIPTION	FIRST DAY COVERS SING	PL. BLK.	MINT SHEET	PLATE BLOCK	UNUSED F/NH	USED
1834-37	American Folk Art, 4 varieties, attached .	5.00	....	27.00(40)	9.00(10)	3.25	2.00
1834	15¢ Bella Bella Tribe .	2.25	....	....	....	1.00	.20
1835	15¢ Chilkat Tlingit Tribe	2.25	....	....	....	1.00	.20
1836	15¢ Tlingit Tribe	2.25	....	....	....	1.00	.20
1837	15¢ Bella Coola Tribe	2.25	....	....	....	1.00	.20

1838 1839 1840 1841

SCOTT NO.	DESCRIPTION	FIRST DAY COVERS SING	PL. BLK.	MINT SHEET	PLATE BLOCK	UNUSED F/NH	USED
1838-41	American Architecture, 4 varieties, attached .	4.00	5.00	25.00(40)	3.50	3.00	2.00
1838	15¢ Smithsonian Inst.	2.25	....	....	....	.90	.20
1839	15¢ Trinity Church . . .	2.25	....	....	....	.90	.20
1840	15¢ Penn Academy . .	2.25	....	....	....	.90	.20
1841	15¢ Lyndhurst	2.25	....	....	....	.90	.20

1842

1843

SCOTT NO.	DESCRIPTION	FIRST DAY COVERS SING	PL. BLK.	MINT SHEET	PLATE BLOCK	UNUSED F/NH	USED
1842	15¢ Madonna	2.25	4.00	22.50(50)	6.50(12)	.55	.15
1843	15¢ Christmas Wreath & Toy	2.25	4.00	23.50(50)	11.75(20)	.55	.15

SE-TENANTS: Beginning with the 1964 Christmas issue (#1254-57), the United States has issued numerous Se-Tenant stamps covering a wide variety of subjects. Se-Tenants are issues where two or more different stamp designs are produced on the same sheet in pair, strip or block form. Mint stamps are usually collected in attached blocks, etc.; used are generally saved as single stamps.

1844

1845

1846

1847

1848

1849

1850

1851

1852

1853

1854

1855

1856

1857

1858

1859

1860

1861

1862

1863

1864

1865

1866

1867

1868

1869

1980-85 GREAT AMERICANS

SCOTT NO.	DESCRIPTION	FIRST DAY COVERS SING	PL. BLK.	MINT SHEET	PLATE BLOCK	UNUSED F/NH	USED
1844-69	**1¢-50¢, 26 varieties, complete . . . .**	....	....	....	....	**16.50**	**5.40**
1844	1¢ Dorothea Dix (1983)	2.25	4.00	10.00(100)	3.25(20)	.25	.20
1844a	same, Bullseye perf. .	....	....	....	2.25(20)	.25	....
1845	2¢ Igor Stravinsky (1982)	2.25	4.00	10.00(100)	.80	.25	.20
1846	3¢ Henry Caly (1983)	2.25	4.00	11.25(100)	.80	.25	.20
1847	4¢ Carl Schurz (1983)	2.25	4.00	15.00(100)	.80	.25	.20
1848	5¢ Pearl Buck (1983)	2.25	4.00	32.00(100)	1.60	.40	.20
1849	6¢ Walter Lippmann (1985)	2.25	4.00	17.50(100)	3.75(20)	.25	.25
1850	7¢ Abraham Baldwin (1985)	2.25	4.00	30.00(100)	5.50(20)	.60	.20
1851	8¢ Henry Knox (1985)	2.25	4.00	23.50(100)	1.25	.30	.20
1852	9¢ Sylvanus Thayer (1985)	2.25	4.00	35.00(100)	7.00(20)	.40	.25
1853	10¢ Richard Russell (1984)	2.25	4.00	50.00(100)	8.50(20)	.60	.20
1854	11¢ Partridge (1985) .	2.25	4.00	60.00(100)	3.00	.45	.20
1855	13¢ Crazy Horse (1982)	2.25	4.00	45.00(100)	3.00	.50	.40
1856	14¢ Sinclair Lewis (1985)	2.25	4.00	57.00(100	13.00(20)	.60	.20
1857	17¢ Rachel Carson (1981)	2.25	4.00	50.00(100)	2.50	.60	.20
1858	18¢ George Mason (1981)	2.25	4.00	48.50(100)	3.75	.60	.20
1859	19¢ Sequoyah	2.25	4.00	65.00(100)	3.50	.75	.40
1860	20¢ Ralph Bunche (1982)	2.25	4.00	70.00(100)	4.00	.80	.20
1861	20¢ T. H. Gallaudet (1983)	2.25	4.00	70.00(100)	4.25	1.00	.20

SCOTT NO.	DESCRIPTION	FIRST DAY COVERS SING	FIRST DAY COVERS PL. BLK.	MINT SHEET	PLATE BLOCK	UNUSED F/NH	USED
1862	20¢ Harry Truman (1984)	2.25	4.00	65.00(100)	15.00(20)	.80	.20
1862a	same, Bullseye perf	....	....	....	4.50	.80	....
1863	22¢ J. Audubon (1985)	2.25	4.00	75.00(100)	16.00(20)	.80	.20
1863a	same, Bullseye perf	....	....	....	5.50	.80	....
1864	30¢ F.C. Laubach (1984)	2.25	4.00	90.00(100)	20.00(20)	1.00	.20
1864a	same, Bullseye perf	....	....	....	5.00	1.00	....
1865	35¢ Charles Drew (1981)	2.25	4.50	125.00(100)	6.00	1.20	.40
1866	37¢ Robert Millikan (1982)	2.25	4.50	125.00(100)	6.00	1.20	.20
1867	39¢ Grenville Clark(1985)	2.25	4.50	125.00(100)	24.00(20)	1.20	.20
1867a	same, Bullseye perf	....	....	....	6.25	1.20	....
1868	40¢ Lillian Gilbreth (1984)	2.25	4.50	110.00(100)	25.00(20)	1.35	.20
1868a	same, Bullseye perf	....	....	....	6.25	1.35	....
1869	50¢ Chester Nimitz (1985)	2.25	4.50	145.00(100)	10.00	1.60	.20
1869a	same, Bullseye perf	....	....	....	10.00	1.60	....

1874

1875

1981 COMMEMORATIVES

SCOTT NO.	DESCRIPTION	FIRST DAY COVERS SING	FIRST DAY COVERS PL. BLK.	MINT SHEET	PLATE BLOCK	UNUSED F/NH	USED
1874/1945	(1874-79, 1910-45) 42 varieties, complete	....	....	....	....	32.00	8.75
1874	15¢ Everett Dirksen .	2.25	4.00	22.00(50)	2.10	.55	.20
1875	15¢ Whitney Moore Young	2.25	4.00	22.00(50)	2.10	.55	.20

1876 1877

1878 1879

SCOTT NO.	DESCRIPTION	FIRST DAY COVERS SING	FIRST DAY COVERS PL. BLK.	MINT SHEET	PLATE BLOCK	UNUSED F/NH	USED
1876-79	Flowers, 4 varieties, attached .	5.00	6.00	32.50(48)	3.50	3.25	2.60
1876	18¢ Rose	2.25	....	....	....	.80	.25
1877	18¢ Camellia	2.25	....	....	....	.80	.25
1878	18¢ Dahlia	2.25	....	....	....	.80	.25
1879	18¢ Lily	2.25	....	....	....	.80	.25

1880

1881

1882

1883

1884

1885

1886

1887

1888

1889

1981 WILDLIFE DEFINITIVES

SCOTT NO.	DESCRIPTION	FIRST DAY COVERS SING	FIRST DAY COVERS PL. BLK.	MINT SHEET	PLATE BLOCK	UNUSED F/NH	USED
1880-89	Wildlife, set of singles	17.00	....	....	....	10.50	1.90
1880	18¢ Bighorned Sheep	2.25	....	....	....	1.10	.20
1881	18¢ Puma	2.25	....	....	....	1.10	.20
1882	18¢ Seal	2.25	....	....	....	1.10	.20
1883	18¢ Bison	2.25	....	....	....	1.10	.20
1884	18¢ Brown Bear	2.25	....	....	....	1.10	.20
1885	18¢ Polar Bear	2.25	....	....	....	1.10	.20
1886	18¢ Elk	2.25	....	....	....	1.10	.20
1887	18¢ Moose	2.25	....	....	....	1.10	.20
1888	18¢ White-tailed Deer	2.25	....	....	....	1.10	.20
1889	18¢ Pronghorned Antelope	2.25	....	....	....	1.10	.20
1889a	Wildlife, bklt pane of 10	6.50	....	....	....	11.25	....

1890

1891

1892

1893

1894, 1895, 1896

1981 FLAG AND ANTHEM ISSUE

SCOTT NO.	DESCRIPTION	FIRST DAY COVERS SING	FIRST DAY COVERS PL. BLK.	MINT SHEET	PLATE BLOCK	UNUSED F/NH	USED
1890	18¢ "Waves of Grain"	2.25	4.00	67.00(100)	14.50(20)	.75	.15
	1981 Coil Stamp Perf. 10 Vertically						
			PLATE# STRIP 3		PLATE# STRIP 3		
1891	18¢ "Shining Sea" . . .	2.25	....	....	6.00	.60	.15
	1981						
1892	6¢ Stars, from bklt pane	2.25	....	....	....	1.75	1.25
1893	18¢ "Purple Mountains" from bklt pane	2.25	....	....	....	.75	.15
1892-93	6¢ & 18¢ as above, attached pair	....	....	....	....	2.75	....
1893a	2-1892, 6-1893 bklt pane of 8	5.25	....	....	....	7.50	....
			PLATE BLOCK		PLATE BLOCK		
1894	20¢ Flag & Supreme Court	2.25	4.00	110.00(100)	22.50(20)	1.10	.15
			PLATE# STRIP 3		PLATE# STRIP 3		
1895	20¢ Flag & Supreme Court	2.25	5.00	....	4.50	.65	.15
1896	20¢ Flag & Supreme Court, from bklt pane	2.25	....	....	....	.80	.15
1896a	20¢ bklt pane of 6 . . .	3.50	....	....	....	4.25	....
1896b	20¢ bklt pane of 10 . .	5.50	....	....	....	7.00	....

Note: **For plate number strips of 5, see page 149**

1897

1897A

1898

1898A

1899

1900

1901

1902

1903

1904

1905

1906

1907

1908

NOTE: #1898A—"Stagecoach 1890s" is 19-1/2 mm long.

1981-84 Perf. 10 Vertically TRANSPORTATION COILS

SCOTT NO.	DESCRIPTION	FIRST DAY COVERS SING	PLATE# STRIP 3	MINT SHEET	PLATE# STRIP 3	UNUSED F/NH	USED
1897-1908	1¢-20¢, 14 varieties, complete	29.50	....	....	....	4.25	2.60
1897	1¢ Omnibus (1983) . .	2.25	17.50	....	.70	.20	.20
1897A	2¢ Locomotive (1982)	2.25	25.00	....	.75	.20	.20
1898	3¢ Handcar (1983) . .	2.25	25.00	....	1.05	.20	.20
1898A	4¢ Stagecoach (1982)	2.25	22.50	....	1.80	.20	.20
1899	5¢ Motorcycle (1983)	2.25	25.00	....	1.25	.20	.20
1900	5.2¢ Sleigh (1983) . .	2.25	37.50	....	7.00	.30	.20
1901	5.9¢ Bicycle (1982) . .	2.25	37.50	....	8.00	.50	.40
1902	7.4¢ Baby Buggy (1984)	2.25	25.00	....	9.50	.50	.40
1903	9.3¢ Mail Wagon	2.25	42.50	....	9.00	.30	.20
1904	10.9¢ Hansom Cab (1982)	2.25	40.00	....	17.00	.75	.40
1905	11¢ Caboose (1984) .	2.25	40.00	....	4.00	.40	.20
1906	17¢ Electric Car	2.25	37.50	....	3.75	.60	.20
1907	18¢ Surrey	2.25	55.00	....	4.00	.65	.20
1908	20¢ Fire Pumper	2.25	55.00	....	3.75	.65	.20

NOTE: Plate # Strips of 3 and 5 have plate number under center stamp. Some issues have lines between two of the stamps.

PRECANCELLED COILS

The following are for precancelled, unused, never hinged stamps. Stamps without gum sell for less.

SCOTT NO.		PL# STRIP 3	UNUSED
1895b	20¢ Supreme Court	90.00	1.00
1898Ab	4¢ Stagecoach	8.50	.35
1900a	5.2¢ Sleigh	14.00	.30
1901a	5.9¢ Bicycle	50.00	.45
1902a	7.4¢ Baby Buggy	6.25	.40
1903a	9.3¢ Mail Wagon	4.50	.40
1904a	10.9¢ Hansom Cab	40.00	.50
1905a	11¢ Caboose	4.50	.45
1906a	17¢ Electric Car	6.00	.55

1909

1983 EXPRESS MAIL BOOKLET SINGLE

SCOTT NO.	DESCRIPTION	FIRST DAY COVERS SING	PL. BLK.	MINT SHEET	PLATE BLOCK	UNUSED F/NH	USED
1909	$9.35 Eagle & Moon .	75.00	....	....	....	35.00	27.00
1909a	$9.35 bklt pane of 3 .	200.00	....	....	....	95.00	....

1910

1911

1981 COMMEMORATIVES (Continued)

SCOTT NO.	DESCRIPTION	FIRST DAY COVERS SING	PL. BLK.	MINT SHEET	PLATE BLOCK	UNUSED F/NH	USED
1910	18¢ American Red Cross	2.25	4.00	27.75(50)	3.25	.60	.20
1911	18¢ Savings & Loans Assoc.	2.25	4.00	25.75(50)	2.75	.60	.20

1912

1913

1914

1915

1916

1917

1918

1919

SCOTT NO.	DESCRIPTION	FIRST DAY COVERS SING	PL. BLK.	MINT SHEET	PLATE BLOCK	UNUSED F/NH	USED
1912-19	Space Achievement, 8 varieties, attached .	6.00	9.00	34.5048)	7.00(8)	5.00	5.50
1912-19	same, set of singles .	15.50	....	....	....	....	1.80
1912	18¢ Exploring the Moon	2.00	....	....	....	.80	.25
1913	18¢ Releasing Boosters	2.00	....	....	....	.80	.25
1914	18¢ Cooling Electric Systems	2.00	....	....	....	.80	.25
1915	18¢ Understanding the Sun	2.00	....	....	....	.80	.25
1916	18¢ Probing the Planets	2.00	....	....	....	.80	.25
1917	18¢ Shuttle and Rockets	2.00	....	....	....	.80	.25
1918	18¢ Landing	2.00	....	....	....	.80	.25
1919	18¢ Comprehending the Universe	2.00	....	....	....	.80	.25

1920

SCOTT NO.	DESCRIPTION	FIRST DAY COVERS SING	PL. BLK.	MINT SHEET	PLATE BLOCK	UNUSED F/NH	USED
1920	18¢ Professional Management	2.25	4.00	26.50(50)	2.75	.60	.20

1921

1922

1923

1924

SCOTT NO.	DESCRIPTION	FIRST DAY COVERS SING	PL. BLK.	MINT SHEET	PLATE BLOCK	UNUSED F/NH	USED
1921-24	Wildlife Habitats, 4 varieties, attached .	5.00	6.00	30.00(50)	3.50	3.25	2.50
1921	18¢ Blue Heron	2.25	....	....	....	.90	.25
1922	18¢ Badger	2.25	....	....	....	.90	.25
1923	18¢ Grizzly Bear	2.25	....	....	....	.90	.25
1924	18¢ Ruffled Grouse . .	2.25	....	....	....	.90	.25

1925

1926

1927

SCOTT NO.	DESCRIPTION	FIRST DAY COVERS SING	FIRST DAY COVERS PL. BLK.	MINT SHEET	PLATE BLOCK	UNUSED F/NH	USED
1925	18¢ Disabled Persons	2.25	4.00	26.00(50)	2.75	.75	.20
1926	18¢ Edna St. Vincent Millay	2.25	4.00	26.00(50)	2.75	.75	.20
1927	18¢ Alcoholism	4.50	7.00	60.00(50)	47.50(20)	.75	.20

1928 1929

1930 1931

SCOTT NO.	DESCRIPTION	FIRST DAY COVERS SING	FIRST DAY COVERS PL. BLK.	MINT SHEET	PLATE BLOCK	UNUSED F/NH	USED
1928-31	American Architecture, 4 varieties, attached .	5.00	6.00	32.50(40)	4.25	3.75	3.00
1928	18¢ New York Univ. Library	2.25	....	....	....	1.00	.25
1929	18¢ Biltmore House .	2.25	....	....	....	1.00	.25
1930	18¢ Palace of the Arts	2.25	....	....	....	1.00	.25
1931	18¢ National Farmers Bank	2.25	....	....	....	1.00	.25

1932

1933

SCOTT NO.	DESCRIPTION	FIRST DAY COVERS SING	FIRST DAY COVERS PL. BLK.	MINT SHEET	PLATE BLOCK	UNUSED F/NH	USED
1932	18¢ Babe Zaharias . .	12.00	15.00	38.00(50)	4.50	.90	.30
1933	18¢ Bobby Jones . . .	15.00	18.00	80.00(50)	8.25	1.75	.30

1934

1935

1936

1937 1938

SCOTT NO.	DESCRIPTION	FIRST DAY COVERS SING	FIRST DAY COVERS PL. BLK.	MINT SHEET	PLATE BLOCK	UNUSED F/NH	USED
1934	18¢ Coming Through the Rye	2.25	4.50	38.00(50)	3.75	.80	.20
1935	18¢ James Hoban . . .	2.25	4.00	26.00(50)	2.75	.60	.20
1936	20¢ James Hoban . . .	2.25	4.00	26.00(50)	3.00	.60	.20
1937-38	Yorktown/Virginia Capes, 2 varieties, attached .	2.00	4.00	29.00(50)	3.35	1.75	1.25
1937	18¢ Yorktown	2.25	....	....	....	1.00	.30
1938	18¢ Virginia Capes . .	2.25	....	....	....	1.00	.30

1939

1940

1941

SCOTT NO.	DESCRIPTION	FIRST DAY COVERS SING	FIRST DAY COVERS PL. BLK.	MINT SHEET	PLATE BLOCK	UNUSED F/NH	USED
1939	(20¢) Madonna & Child	2.25	4.00	52.00(100)	2.75	.60	.15
1940	(20¢) Christmas Toy .	2.25	4.00	27.00(50)	2.75	.60	.15
1941	20¢ John Hanson . . .	2.25	4.00	29.50(50)	3.00	.70	.15

1943

1942 1944 1945

SCOTT NO.	DESCRIPTION	FIRST DAY COVERS SING	FIRST DAY COVERS PL. BLK.	MINT SHEET	PLATE BLOCK	UNUSED F/NH	USED
1942-45	Desert Plants, 4 varieties, attached .	5.00	6.00	32.50(40)	4.00	3.75	3.00
1942	20¢ Barrel Cactus . . .	2.25	....	....	....	1.00	.25
1943	20¢ Agave	2.25	....	....	....	1.00	.25
1944	20¢ Beavertail Cactus	2.25	....	....	....	1.00	.25
1945	20¢ Saguaro	2.25	....	....	....	1.00	.25

1946, 1947, 1948

1949

1981-1982 Regular Issues

SCOTT NO.	DESCRIPTION	FIRST DAY COVERS SING	FIRST DAY COVERS PL. BLK.	MINT SHEET	PLATE BLOCK	UNUSED F/NH	USED
1946	(20¢) "C" Eagle, 11x10$^{1/2}$	2.25	4.00	54.00(100)	2.75	.60	.15
			LINE PAIR		LINE PAIR		
1947	(20¢) "C" Eagle, coil .	2.25	2.75	....	2.25	.80	.15
1948	(20¢) "C" Eagle, from pane	2.25	....	....	....	.80	.15
1948a	same, bklt pane of 10	6.00	....	....	....	7.50	....
1949	20¢ Bighorned Sheep, blue, from bklt pane (1982)	2.25	....	....	....	.75	.15
1949a	same, bklt pane of 10	6.00	....	....	....	7.50	....
1949c	Type II, from bklt pane	....	....	....	....	1.75	.40
1949d	same, bklt pane of 10	....	....	....	....	16.00	....

1950

1951

1952

1982 COMMEMORATIVES

SCOTT NO.	DESCRIPTION	FIRST DAY COVERS SING	FIRST DAY COVERS PL. BLK.	MINT SHEET	PLATE BLOCK	UNUSED F/NH	USED
1950/2030	(1950-52, 2003-04, 2006-30) 30 varieties	....	....	....	....	24.00	5.75
1950	20¢ Franklin D. Roosevelt	2.25	4.00	30.50(48)	2.90	.80	.20
1951	20¢ LOVE, perf. 11 . .	1.85	4.25	30.50(50)	2.90	.65	.20
1951a	same, perf. 11x 10½ . .	....	....	51.75(50)	5.50	1.10	.35

NOTE: **Perforations will be mixed on Used #1951.**

SCOTT NO.	DESCRIPTION	FIRST DAY COVERS SING	FIRST DAY COVERS PL. BLK.	MINT SHEET	PLATE BLOCK	UNUSED F/NH	USED
1952	20¢ George Washington	2.25	4.00	30.50(50)	2.95	.65	.20

1982 STATE BIRDS AND FLOWERS

1953

1973

1953	*Alabama*	1978	*Montana*
1954	*Alaska*	1979	*Nebraska*
1955	*Arizona*	1980	*Nevada*
1956	*Arkansas*	1981	*New Hampshire*
1957	*California*	1982	*New Jersey*
1958	*Colorado*	1983	*New Mexico*
1959	*Connecticut*	1984	*New York*
1960	*Delaware*	1985	*North Carolina*
1961	*Florida*	1986	*North Dakota*
1962	*Georgia*	1987	*Ohio*
1963	*Hawaii*	1988	*Oklahoma*
1964	*Idaho*	1989	*Oregon*
1965	*Illinois*	1990	*Pennsylvania*
1966	*Indiana*	1991	*Rhode Island*
1967	*Iowa*	1992	*South Carolina*
1968	*Kansas*	1993	*South Dakota*
1969	*Kentucky*	1994	*Tennessee*
1970	*Louisiana*	1995	*Texas*
1971	*Maine*	1996	*Utah*
1972	*Maryland*	1997	*Vermont*
1973	*Massachusetts*	1998	*Virginia*
1974	*Michigan*	1999	*Washington*
1975	*Minnesota*	2000	*West Virginia*
1976	*Mississippi*	2001	*Wisconsin*
1977	*Missouri*	2002	*Wyoming*

1966

2002

Perf. 10½ x 11

SCOTT NO.	DESCRIPTION	FIRST DAY COVERS SING	FIRST DAY COVERS PL. BLK.	MINT SHEET	PLATE BLOCK	UNUSED F/NH	USED
1953-2002	20¢, 50 varieties, attached.......	....	....	45.00(50)	....	45.00	....
	set of singles	86.00	....	....	....	....	25.00
	singles of above . . .	2.00	....	....	....	1.10	.65
1953a-2002a	same, perf. 11	....	....	47.50(50)	....	47.50	....
	singles of above . . .	....	....	....	....	1.25	....

NOTE: **Used singles will not be sorted by perf. sizes.**

2003

2004

2005

SCOTT NO.	DESCRIPTION	FIRST DAY COVERS SING	FIRST DAY COVERS PL. BLK.	MINT SHEET	PLATE BLOCK	UNUSED F/NH	USED
2003	20¢ USA/Netherlands	2.25	4.00	34.50(50)	17.00(20)	.70	.20
2004	20¢ Library of Congress	2.25	4.00	28.00(50)	2.75	.60	.20
			PLATE# STRIP 3		PLATE# STRIP 3		
2005	20¢ Consumer Education, Coil	2.25	60.00	....	28.50	1.20	.15

2006 2007 2008 2009

SCOTT NO.	DESCRIPTION	FIRST DAY COVERS SING	FIRST DAY COVERS PL. BLK.	MINT SHEET	PLATE BLOCK	UNUSED F/NH	USED
2006-09	World's Fair, 4 varieties, attached .	5.00	6.00	42.50(50)	4.50	4.00	2.00
2006	20¢ Solar Energy . . .	2.25	....	....	....	1.00	.20
2007	20¢ Synthetic Fuels .	2.25	....	....	....	1.00	.20
2008	20¢ Breeder Reactor	2.25	....	....	....	1.00	.20
2009	20¢ Fossil Fuels	2.25	....	....	....	1.00	.20

2010

2011

2012

SCOTT NO.	DESCRIPTION	FIRST DAY COVERS SING	FIRST DAY COVERS PL. BLK.	MINT SHEET	PLATE BLOCK	UNUSED F/NH	USED
2010	20¢ Horatio Alger . . .	2.25	4.00	27.00(50)	2.75	.60	.20
2011	20¢ Aging Together .	2.25	4.00	27.00(50)	2.75	.60	.20
2012	20¢ Barrymores	2.25	4.00	30.00(50)	2.75	.60	.20

2013

2014

2015

SCOTT NO.	DESCRIPTION	FIRST DAY COVERS SING	FIRST DAY COVERS PL. BLK.	MINT SHEET	PLATE BLOCK	UNUSED F/NH	USED
2013	20¢ Dr. Mary Walker .	2.25	4.00	29.50(50)	3.00	.60	.20
2014	20¢ Peace Garden . .	2.25	4.00	42.00(50)	4.00	.85	.20
2015	20¢ America's Libraries	2.25	4.00	27.00(50)	2.75	.60	.20

2016

2017

2018

SCOTT NO.	DESCRIPTION	FIRST DAY COVERS SING	FIRST DAY COVERS PL. BLK.	MINT SHEET	PLATE BLOCK	UNUSED F/NH	USED
2016	20¢ Jackie Robinson	7.00	13.50	110.00(50)	11.00	2.50	.20
2017	20¢ Touro Synagogue	3.00	4.00	40.00(50)	18.00(20)	.85	.20
2018	20¢ Wolf Trap Farm .	2.25	4.00	27.00(50)	2.50	.60	.20

PLATE BLOCKS: are portions of a sheet of stamps adjacent to the number(s) indicating the printing plate number used to produce that sheet. Flat plate issues are usually collected in plate blocks of six (number opposite middle stamp) while rotary issues are normally corner blocks of four.

2019 2020

2021 2022

SCOTT NO.	DESCRIPTION	FIRST DAY COVERS SING	FIRST DAY COVERS PL. BLK.	MINT SHEET	PLATE BLOCK	UNUSED F/NH	USED
2019-22	American Architecture, 4 varieties, attached .	5.00	6.00	35.00(40)	4.50	4.00	3.25
2019	20¢ Fallingwater Mill Run	2.25	....	....	....	1.25	.25
2020	20¢ Illinois Inst. Tech	2.25	....	....	....	1.25	.25
2021	20¢ Gropius House . .	2.25	....	....	....	1.25	.25
2022	20¢ Dulles Airport . . .	2.25	....	....	....	1.25	.25

2023

2024

2025

2026

SCOTT NO.	DESCRIPTION	FIRST DAY COVERS SING	FIRST DAY COVERS PL. BLK.	MINT SHEET	PLATE BLOCK	UNUSED F/NH	USED
2023	20¢ St. Francis of Assisi	2.25	4.00	30.00(50)	3.00	.65	.20
2024	20¢ Ponce de Leon . .	2.25	4.00	47.00(50)	21.00(20)	1.00	.20
2025	13¢ Kitten & Puppy, Christmas	2.25	4.00	19.50(50)	2.25	.50	.20
2026	20¢ Madonna & Child, Christmas	2.25	4.00	30.00(50)	16.50(20)	.65	.20

2027 2028

2029 2030

SCOTT NO.	DESCRIPTION	FIRST DAY COVERS SING	FIRST DAY COVERS PL. BLK.	MINT SHEET	PLATE BLOCK	UNUSED F/NH	USED
2027-30	Winter Scenes, Christmas, 4 varieties, attached .	4.00	5.00	43.00(50)	5.00	4.25	3.50
2027	20¢ Sledding	2.25	....	....	....	1.25	.20
2028	20¢ Snowman	2.25	....	....	....	1.25	.20
2029	20¢ Skating	2.25	....	....	....	1.25	.20
2030	20¢ Decorating	2.25	....	....	....	1.25	.20

2031

1983 COMMEMORATIVES

SCOTT NO.	DESCRIPTION	FIRST DAY COVERS SING	FIRST DAY COVERS PL. BLK.	MINT SHEET	PLATE BLOCK	UNUSED F/NH	USED
2031-65	**13¢-20¢, 35 varieties, complete . . . .**	....	....	....	....	**28.40**	**7.50**
2031	20¢ Science & Industry	2.25	4.00	27.00(50)	2.75	.60	.20

2033

2032 2034 2035

SCOTT NO.	DESCRIPTION	FIRST DAY COVERS SING	FIRST DAY COVERS PL. BLK.	MINT SHEET	PLATE BLOCK	UNUSED F/NH	USED
2032-35	20¢ Ballooning, 4 varieties, attached .	5.00	6.00	27.00(40)	3.75	3.25	2.50
2032	20¢ Intrepid	2.25	....	....	....	1.10	.25
2033	20¢ Red, white, & blue balloon	2.25	....	....	....	1.10	.25
2034	20¢ Yellow, gold & green balloon	2.25	....	....	....	1.10	.25
2035	20¢ Explorer II	2.25	....	....	....	1.10	.25

2036

2037

2038

SCOTT NO.	DESCRIPTION	FIRST DAY COVERS SING	FIRST DAY COVERS PL. BLK.	MINT SHEET	PLATE BLOCK	UNUSED F/NH	USED
2036	20¢ USA/Sweden . . .	2.25	4.00	27.00(50)	2.75	.65	.20
2037	20¢ Civilian Conservation Corps	2.25	4.00	27.00(50)	2.75	.65	.20
2038	20¢ Joseph Priestley	2.25	4.00	27.00(50)	2.75	.65	.20

2039

2040

2041

SCOTT NO.	DESCRIPTION	FIRST DAY COVERS SING	FIRST DAY COVERS PL. BLK.	MINT SHEET	PLATE BLOCK	UNUSED F/NH	USED
2039	20¢ Volunteerism . . .	2.25	4.00	34.50(50)	18.00(20)	.65	.20
2040	20¢ German Immigrants	2.25	4.00	27.00(50)	2.75	.65	.20
2041	20¢ Brooklyn Bridge .	3.00	5.00	30.00(50)	2.75	.65	.20

2042

2043

2044

SCOTT NO.	DESCRIPTION	FIRST DAY COVERS SING	FIRST DAY COVERS PL. BLK.	MINT SHEET	PLATE BLOCK	UNUSED F/NH	USED
2042	20¢ Tennessee Valley Authority	2.25	4.00	34.50(50)	18.00(20)	.65	.80
2043	20¢ Physical Fitness .	2.25	4.00	34.50(50)	18.00(20)	.65	.80
2044	20¢ Scott Joplin	2.25	4.00	35.00(50)	3.00	.75	1.00

2045

2046

2047

SCOTT NO.	DESCRIPTION	FIRST DAY COVERS SING	FIRST DAY COVERS PL. BLK.	MINT SHEET	PLATE BLOCK	UNUSED F/NH	USED
2045	20¢ Medal of Honor .	6.00	8.00	30.00(40)	3.75	.85	.20
2046	20¢ Babe Ruth	8.00	16.00	110.00(50)	10.00	2.50	.20
2047	20¢ Nathaniel Hawthorne	2.25	4.00	32.50(50)	3.25	.75	.20

2048 2049

2050 2051

SCOTT NO.	DESCRIPTION	FIRST DAY COVERS SING	FIRST DAY COVERS PL. BLK.	MINT SHEET	PLATE BLOCK	UNUSED F/NH	USED
2048-51	Olympics, 4 varieties, attached .	5.00	6.00	30.00(50)	4.00	3.50	2.75
2048	13¢ Discus	2.25	....	....	....	1.00	.30
2049	13¢ High Jump	2.25	....	....	....	1.00	.30
2050	13¢ Archery	2.25	....	....	....	1.00	.30
2051	13¢ Boxing	2.25	....	....	....	1.00	.30

2052

2053

2054

SCOTT NO.	DESCRIPTION	FIRST DAY COVERS SING	FIRST DAY COVERS PL. BLK.	MINT SHEET	PLATE BLOCK	UNUSED F/NH	USED
2052	20¢ Treaty of Paris ..	2.25	4.00	24.00(40)	3.00	.65	.20
2053	20¢ Civil Service	2.25	4.00	34.50(50)	18.00(20)	.65	.20
2054	20¢ Metropolitan Opera	2.25	4.00	30.00(50)	3.00	.65	.20

MINT SHEETS: From 1935 to date, we list prices for standard size Mint Sheets in Fine, Never Hinged condition. The number of stamps in each sheet is noted in ( ).

2055 2056

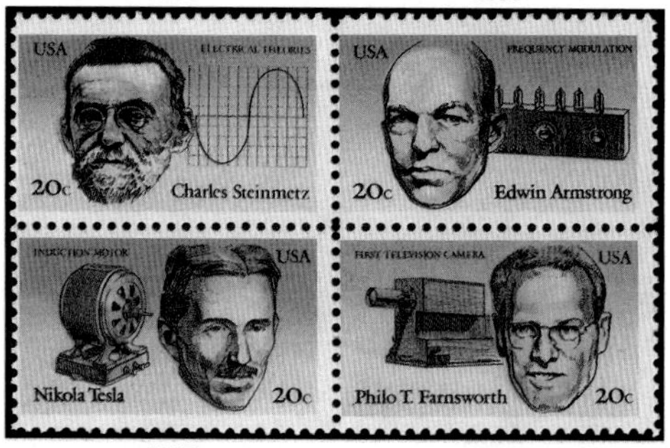

2057 2058

SCOTT NO.	DESCRIPTION	FIRST DAY COVERS SING	FIRST DAY COVERS PL. BLK.	MINT SHEET	PLATE BLOCK	UNUSED F/NH	USED
2055-58	Inventors, 4 varieties, attached .	5.00	6.00	47.50(50)	5.75	5.00	3.50
2055	20¢ Charles Steinmetz	2.25	....	....	....	1.35	.25
2056	20¢ Edwin Armstrong	2.25	....	....	....	1.35	.25
2057	20¢ Nikola Tesla	2.25	....	....	....	1.35	.25
2058	20¢ Philo T. Farnsworth	2.25	....	....	....	1.35	.25

2059 2060

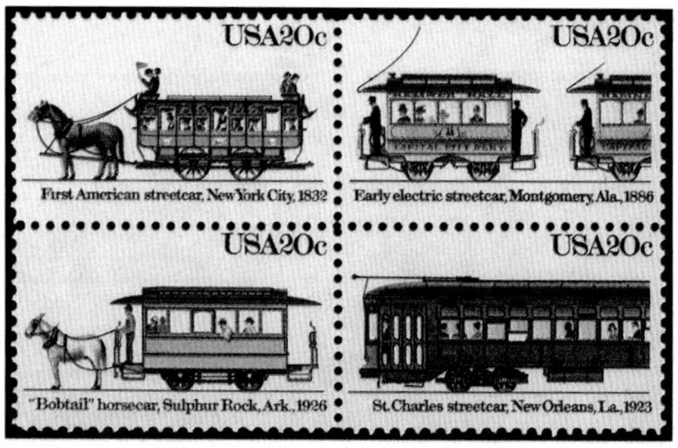

2061 2062

SCOTT NO.	DESCRIPTION	FIRST DAY COVERS SING	FIRST DAY COVERS PL. BLK.	MINT SHEET	PLATE BLOCK	UNUSED F/NH	USED
2059-62	Streetcars, 4 varieties, attached .	5.00	6.00	37.50(50)	4.75	4.00	3.00
2059	20¢ First Streetcar ..	2.25	....	....	....	1.25	.25
2060	20¢ Electric Trolley ..	2.25	....	....	....	1.25	.25
2061	20¢ "Bobtail"	2.25	....	....	....	1.25	.25
2062	20¢ St. Charles Streetcar	2.25	....	....	....	1.25	.25

2063

2064

SCOTT NO.	DESCRIPTION	FIRST DAY COVERS SING	FIRST DAY COVERS PL. BLK.	MINT SHEET	PLATE BLOCK	UNUSED F/NH	USED
2063	20¢ Madonna	2.25	4.00	27.00(50)	2.75	.60	.20
2064	20¢ Santa Claus	2.25	4.00	34.50(50)	18.00(20)	.60	.20

2065

SCOTT NO.	DESCRIPTION	FIRST DAY COVERS SING	FIRST DAY COVERS PL. BLK.	MINT SHEET	PLATE BLOCK	UNUSED F/NH	USED
2065	20¢ Martin Luther ...	2.25	4.00	27.00(50)	2.75	.60	.20

2066

1984 COMMEMORATIVES

SCOTT NO.	DESCRIPTION	FIRST DAY COVERS SING	FIRST DAY COVERS PL. BLK.	MINT SHEET	PLATE BLOCK	UNUSED F/NH	USED
2066-2109	44 varieties, complete	....	....	....	....	37.50	9.30
2066	20¢ Alaska Statehood	2.25	4.00	27.00(50)	3.00	1.00	.20

2067 2068 2069 2070

SCOTT NO.	DESCRIPTION	FIRST DAY COVERS SING	FIRST DAY COVERS PL. BLK.	MINT SHEET	PLATE BLOCK	UNUSED F/NH	USED
2067-70	Winter Olympics, 4 varieties, attached .	5.00	6.00	39.00(50)	4.50	4.00	3.00
2067	20¢ Ice Dancing	2.25	....	....	....	1.10	.30
2068	20¢ Downhill Skiing . .	2.25	....	....	....	1.10	.30
2069	20¢ Cross Country Skiing	2.25	....	....	....	1.10	.30
2070	20¢ Hockey	2.25	....	....	....	1.10	.30

2071 2072 2073 2074

SCOTT NO.	DESCRIPTION	FIRST DAY COVERS SING	FIRST DAY COVERS PL. BLK.	MINT SHEET	PLATE BLOCK	UNUSED F/NH	USED
2071	20¢ Federal Deposit Insurance Corporation	2.25	4.00	27.00(50)	2.75	.75	.20
2072	20¢ Love	1.95	4.00	34.50(50)	18.00(20)	.75	.20
2073	20¢ Carter G. Woodson	3.00	4.00	30.00(50)	2.00	.75	.20
2074	20¢ Conservatiion . . .	2.25	4.00	27.00(50)	2.00	.75	.20

2076

2075

2077

2078

2079

SCOTT NO.	DESCRIPTION	FIRST DAY COVERS SING	FIRST DAY COVERS PL. BLK.	MINT SHEET	PLATE BLOCK	UNUSED F/NH	USED
2075	20¢ Credit Union	1.95	4.50	27.00(50)	2.75	.60	.20
2076-79	Orchids, 4 varieties, attd.	4.00	5.00	34.00(48)	3.75	3.25	2.75
2076	20¢ Wildpink	2.25	....	....	....	.95	.25
2077	20¢ Lady's-slipper . . .	2.25	....	....	....	.95	.25
2078	20¢ Spreading Pogonia	2.25	....	....	....	.95	.25
2079	20¢ Pacific Calypso .	2.25	....	....	....	.95	.25

2080

2081

SCOTT NO.	DESCRIPTION	FIRST DAY COVERS SING	FIRST DAY COVERS PL. BLK.	MINT SHEET	PLATE BLOCK	UNUSED F/NH	USED
2080	20¢ Hawaii Statehood	2.25	4.00	30.00(50)	3.00	.70	.20
2081	20¢ National Archives	2.25	4.00	30.00(50)	3.00	.70	.20

2082 2083 2084 2085

SCOTT NO.	DESCRIPTION	FIRST DAY COVERS SING	FIRST DAY COVERS PL. BLK.	MINT SHEET	PLATE BLOCK	UNUSED F/NH	USED
2082-85	Olympics, 4 varieties, attached	5.00	6.00	51.75(50)	6.00	5.50	4.75
2082	20¢ Men's Diving . . .	2.25	....	....	....	1.50	.25
2083	20¢ Long Jump	2.25	....	....	....	1.50	.25
2084	20¢ Wrestling	2.25	....	....	....	1.50	.25
2085	20¢ Women's Kayak .	2.25	....	....	....	1.50	.25

2086 2087 2088

SCOTT NO.	DESCRIPTION	FIRST DAY COVERS SING	FIRST DAY COVERS PL. BLK.	MINT SHEET	PLATE BLOCK	UNUSED F/NH	USED
2086	20¢ Louisiana Exposition	2.25	4.00	37.50(40)	4.25	.95	1.20
2087	20¢ Health Research	2.25	4.00	32.00(50)	3.50	.70	.20
2088	20¢ Douglas Fairbanks	2.25	4.00	36.50(50)	20.00(20)	.70	1.50

2089 2090 2091

SCOTT NO.	DESCRIPTION	FIRST DAY COVERS SING	FIRST DAY COVERS PL. BLK.	MINT SHEET	PLATE BLOCK	UNUSED F/NH	USED
2089	20¢ Jim Thorpe	4.50	8.00	40.00(50)	4.75	1.00	.30
2090	20¢ John McCormack	3.00	4.00	30.00(50)	3.00	.65	.20
2091	20¢ St. Lawrence Seaway	3.00	4.00	30.00(50)	3.00	.65	.20

SE-TENANTS: Beginning with the 1964 Christmas issue (#1254-57), the United States has issued numerous Se-Tenant stamps covering a wide variety of subjects. Se-Tenants are issues where two or more different stamp designs are produced on the same sheet in pair, strip or block form. Mint stamps are usually collected in attached blocks, etc.—Used are generally saved as single stamps. Our Se-Tenant prices follow in this collecting pattern.

2092

2093

SCOTT NO.	DESCRIPTION	FIRST DAY COVERS SING	PL. BLK.	MINT SHEET	PLATE BLOCK	UNUSED F/NH	USED
2092	Preserving Wetlands .	1.95	4.00	45.00(50)	5.00	1.10	.20
2093	Roanoke Voyages . .	2.25	4.00	40.00(50)	4.00	1.00	.20

2094

2095

2096

2097

SCOTT NO.	DESCRIPTION	FIRST DAY COVERS SING	PL. BLK.	MINT SHEET	PLATE BLOCK	UNUSED F/NH	USED
2094	20¢ Herman Melville .	2.25	4.00	27.00(50)	2.75	.70	.20
2095	20¢ Horace Moses . .	2.25	4.00	40.00(50)	19.00(20)	1.20	.20
2096	20¢ Smokey Bear . . .	2.25	4.00	34.00(50)	3.50	1.20	.20
2097	20¢ Roberto Clemente	12.00	20.00	140.00(50)	13.50	2.00	.50

2098 2099

2100 2101

SCOTT NO.	DESCRIPTION	FIRST DAY COVERS SING	PL. BLK.	MINT SHEET	PLATE BLOCK	UNUSED F/NH	USED
2098-2101	American Dogs, 4 varieties, attached	5.00	6.00	37.50(40)	5.25	4.50	3.75
2098	20¢ Beagle, Boston Terrier	2.25	....	....	....	1.10	.25
2099	20¢ Chesapeake Bay Retriever, Cocker Spaniel	2.25	....	....	....	1.10	.25
2100	20¢ Alaskan Malamute, Collie	2.25	....	....	....	1.10	.25
2101	20¢ Black & Tan Coonhound, American Foxhound .	2.25	....	....	....	1.10	.25

2102

2103

2104

SCOTT NO.	DESCRIPTION	FIRST DAY COVERS SING	PL. BLK.	MINT SHEET	PLATE BLOCK	UNUSED F/NH	USED
2102	20¢ Crime Prevention	2.25	4.00	27.00(50)	2.75	.60	.20
2103	20¢ Hispanic Americans	3.00	4.00	22.00(40)	2.75	.60	.20
2104	20¢ Family Unity	2.25	4.00	45.00(50)	22.00(20)	1.25	.20

2105

2106

2107

SCOTT NO.	DESCRIPTION	FIRST DAY COVERS SING	PL. BLK.	MINT SHEET	PLATE BLOCK	UNUSED F/NH	USED
2105	20¢ Eleanor Roosevelt	2.25	4.00	26.00(40)	3.00	.70	.20
2106	20¢ Nation of Readers	2.25	4.00	37.50(50)	4.00	1.10	.30
2107	20¢ Madonna & Child	2.25	4.00	27.00(50)	2.75	.60	.20

2108

2109

SCOTT NO.	DESCRIPTION	FIRST DAY COVERS SING	PL. BLK.	MINT SHEET	PLATE BLOCK	UNUSED F/NH	USED
2108	20¢ Santa Claus	1.35	4.00	27.00(50)	2.75	.60	.15
2109	20¢ Vietnam Veterans	5.00	4.00	45.00(40)	5.50	1.50	.30

2110

1985 COMMEMORATIVES

SCOTT NO.	DESCRIPTION	FIRST DAY COVERS SING	PL. BLK.	MINT SHEET	PLATE BLOCK	UNUSED F/NH	USED
2110/2166	(2110, 2137-47, 2152-66) 27 varieties	....	....	....	....	41.45	8.25
2110	22¢ Jerome Kern . . .	2.25	4.00	32.00(50)	3.25	.70	.20

2111-2113

2114, 2115

2116

1985 REGULAR ISSUES

SCOTT NO.	DESCRIPTION	FIRST DAY COVERS SING	PL. BLK.	MINT SHEET	PLATE BLOCK	UNUSED F/NH	USED
2111	(22¢) "D" Eagle	2.25	4.00	100.00(100)	35.00(20)	.90	.15
			PLATE# STRIP 3		PLATE# STRIP 3		
2112	(22¢) "D" Eagle, coil .	2.25	21.00	....	6.75	.75	.15
2113	(22¢) "D" Eagle from bklt pane	2.25	....	....	....	1.25	.15
2113a	same, bklt pane of 10	7.50	....	....	....	12.00	....
			PLATE BLOCK		PLATE BLOCK		
2114	22¢ Flag over Capitol	2.25	4.00	75.00(100)	4.00	.80	.15
			PLATE# STRIP 3		PLATE# STRIP 3		
2115	22¢ Flag over Capitol, coil	2.25	27.50	....	3.75	.70	.15
2115b	22¢ Flag "T" coil (1985-87)	2.90	....	....	5.50	.80	.15
2116	22¢ Flag over Capitol from bklt pane	2.25	....	....	....	1.00	.20
2116a	same, bklt pane of 5 . .	2.90	....	....	....	4.75	....

2117

2118

2119

2120

2121

1985 SEASHELLS FROM BOOKLET PANE

SCOTT NO.	DESCRIPTION	FIRST DAY COVERS SING	PL. BLK.	MINT SHEET	PLATE BLOCK	UNUSED F/NH	USED
2117-21	Shells, strip of 5, attached	3.00	....	....	....	4.25	4.00
2117	22¢ Frilled Dogwinkle	2.25	....	....	....	.90	.20
2118	22¢ Reticulated Helmet	2.25	....	....	....	.90	.20
2119	22¢ New England Neptune	2.25	....	....	....	.90	.20
2120	22¢ Calico Scallop . .	2.25	....	....	....	.90	.20
2121	22¢ Lightning Whelk .	2.25	....	....	....	.90	.20
2121a	22¢ Seashells, bklt pane of 10	7.50	....	....	....	8.00	6.50

2122

1985 EXPRESS MAIL STAMP FROM BOOKLET PANE

SCOTT NO.	DESCRIPTION	FIRST DAY COVERS SING	PL. BLK.	MINT SHEET	PLATE BLOCK	UNUSED F/NH	USED
2122	$10.75 Eagle & Moon	65.00	....	....	....	32.50	15.00
2122a	same, bklt pane of 3 .	160.00	....	....	....	95.00	....
2122b	Type II, from bklt pane	....	....	....	....	45.00	20.00
2122c	same, bklt pane of 3 .	....	....	....	....	135.00	....

2123

2124

2125

2126

2127

2128

2129

2130

2131

2132

2133

2134

2135

2136

TRANSPORTATION COILS 1985-87 PERF. 10

SCOTT NO.	DESCRIPTION	FIRST DAY COVERS SING	PLATE# STRIP 3	MINT SHEET	PLATE# STRIP 3	UNUSED F/NH	USED
2123	3.4¢ School Bus	2.00	11.50	....	1.35	.25	.30
2124	4.9¢ Buckboard	2.00	14.00	....	1.25	.25	.30
2125	5.5¢ Star Route Truck (1986)	2.00	15.00	....	2.50	.25	.30
2126	6¢ Tricycle	2.00	14.00	....	2.00	.25	.30
2127	7.1¢ Tractor (1987) . .	2.00	15.00	....	3.15	.35	.30
2128	8.3¢ Ambulance	2.00	14.00	....	1.95	.35	.30
2129	8.5¢ Tow Truck (1987)	2.00	12.50	....	3.45	.35	.30
2130	10.1¢ Oil Wagon	2.00	12.50	....	2.75	.40	.30
2131	11¢ Stutz Bearcat . . .	2.00	18.00	....	1.75	.40	.30
2132	12¢ Stanley Steamer	2.00	15.00	....	2.35	.60	.30
2133	12.5¢ Pushcart	2.00	15.00	....	3.00	.40	.30
2134	14¢ Iceboat	2.00	15.00	....	2.30	.40	.30
2135	17¢ Dog Sled (1986) .	2.00	12.50	....	3.25	.70	.30
2136	25¢ Bread Wagon (1986)	2.00	15.00	....	4.00	.80	.20

Note: **For plate number strips of 5, see page 149**

PRECANCELLED COILS

The following are for precancelled, unused, never hinged stamps.
Stamps without gum sell for less.

SCOTT NO.		PL# STRIP 3	UNUSED
2123a	3.4¢ School Bus	7.50	.35
2124a	4.9¢ Buckboard	2.35	.35
2125a	5.5¢ Star Route Truck	2.35	.35
2126a	6¢ Tricycle	2.30	.35
2127a	7.1¢ Tractor	4.00	.35
2127b	7.1¢ Tractor, precancel (1989)	2.75	.35
2128a	8.3¢ Ambulance	1.75	.35
2129a	8.5¢ Tow Truck	4.00	.35
2130a	10.1¢ Oil Wagon	3.25	.35
2130b	10.1¢ Oil Wagon, red precancel (1988)	3.00	.35
2132a	12¢ Stanley Steamer	3.00	.60
2132b	12¢ Stanley Steamer "B" Press	28.00	1.85
2133a	12.5¢ Pushcart	4.00	.40

2137

1985 COMMEMORATIVES (continued)

SCOTT NO.	DESCRIPTION	FIRST DAY COVERS SING	PL. BLK.	MINT SHEET	PLATE BLOCK	UNUSED F/NH	USED
2137	22¢ Mary Bethune . .	2.25	4.00	42.50(50)	4.25	.95	.20

2138 2139

2140 2141

SCOTT NO.	DESCRIPTION	FIRST DAY COVERS SING	PL. BLK.	MINT SHEET	PLATE BLOCK	UNUSED F/NH	USED
2138-41	Duck Decoys, 4 varieties, attached .	5.00	6.00	100.00(50)	14.00	10.00	7.95
2138	22¢ Broadbill	2.25	....	....	....	2.75	2.00
2139	22¢ Mallard	2.25	....	....	....	2.75	2.00
2140	22¢ Canvasback	2.25	....	....	....	2.75	2.00
2141	22¢ Redhead	2.25	....	....	....	2.75	2.00

2142

2143

2144

2145

SCOTT NO.	DESCRIPTION	FIRST DAY COVERS SING	FIRST DAY COVERS PL. BLK.	MINT SHEET	PLATE BLOCK	UNUSED F/NH	USED
2142	22¢ Winter Special Olympics	2.25	4.00	26.00(40)	3.00	1.00	.20
2143	22¢ "LOVE"	1.95	4.00	34.00(50)	3.25	1.00	.20
2144	22¢ Rural Electricity .	2.25	....	56.00(50)	35.00(20)	1.00	.20
2145	22¢ Ameripex '86 ...	2.25	4.00	29.00(48)	2.80	1.00	.20

2146

2147

SCOTT NO.	DESCRIPTION	FIRST DAY COVERS SING	FIRST DAY COVERS PL. BLK.	MINT SHEET	PLATE BLOCK	UNUSED F/NH	USED
2146	22¢ Abigail Adams ..	2.25	4.00	30.00(50)	3.75	.85	.20
2147	22¢ Frederic Bartholdi	2.25	4.00	29.00(50)	3.00	.65	.20

2149

2150

1985 REGULAR ISSUE COILS

SCOTT NO.	DESCRIPTION	FIRST DAY COVERS SING	PLATE# STRIP 3	MINT SHEET	PLATE# STRIP 3	UNUSED F/NH	USED
2149	18¢ George Washington	2.25	50.00	....	4.50	.85	.30
2149a	18¢ George Washington, precancel	....	....	....	4.25	.60	....
2150	21.1¢ Envelope	2.25	32.50	....	4.50	1.00	.75
2150a	21.1¢ Envelope, precancel	....	....	....	4.85	.75	.50

2152

2153

2154

SCOTT NO.	DESCRIPTION	FIRST DAY COVERS SING	FIRST DAY COVERS PL. BLK.	MINT SHEET	PLATE BLOCK	UNUSED F/NH	USED
2152	22¢ Korean War Veterans	3.00	4.00	41.50(50)	5.00	1.00	.20
2153	22¢ Social Security ..	2.25	4.00	29.00(50)	3.50	1.00	.20
2154	22¢ World War I Veterans	3.00	4.00	41.50(50)	5.00	1.00	.20

2155 2156

2157 2158

SCOTT NO.	DESCRIPTION	FIRST DAY COVERS SING	FIRST DAY COVERS PL. BLK.	MINT SHEET	PLATE BLOCK	UNUSED F/NH	USED
2155-58	American Horses, 4 varieties, attached .	5.00	6.00	125.00(40)	16.00	15.00	10.00
2155	22¢ Quarter Horse ..	2.25	....	....	....	3.50	.75
2156	22¢ Morgan	2.25	....	....	....	3.50	.75
2157	22¢ Saddlebred	2.25	....	....	....	3.50	.75
2158	22¢ Appaloosa	2.25	....	....	....	3.50	.75

2160

2159

2161

2162

2163

SCOTT NO.	DESCRIPTION	FIRST DAY COVERS SING	FIRST DAY COVERS PL. BLK.	MINT SHEET	PLATE BLOCK	UNUSED F/NH	USED
2159	22¢ Public Education	2.25	4.00	60.00(50)	6.00	1.50	.20
2160-63	Youth Year, 4 varieties, attached .	5.00	6.00	61.00(50)	8.00	6.00	4.50
2160	22¢ YMCA	2.25	....	....	....	1.75	.40
2161	22¢ Boy Scouts	2.25	....	....	....	1.75	.40
2162	22¢ Big Brothers & Big Sisters	2.25	....	....	....	1.75	.40
2163	22¢ Camp Fire	2.25	....	....	....	1.75	.40

2164

2165

2166

2167

SCOTT NO.	DESCRIPTION	FIRST DAY COVERS SING	FIRST DAY COVERS PL. BLK.	MINT SHEET	PLATE BLOCK	UNUSED F/NH	USED
2164	22¢ Help End Hunger	2.25	4.00	32.75(50)	3.00	.70	.20
2165	22¢ Madonna & Child	2.25	4.00	29.00(50)	3.00	.60	.15
2166	22¢ Poinsettia	2.25	4.00	29.00(50)	3.00	.60	.15
2167	22¢ Arkansas Statehood	2.25	4.00	65.00(50)	6.00	1.20	.20

2168

2169

2170

2171

2172

2173

2175

2176

2177

2178

2179

2180

2181

2182, 2197

2183

2184

2185

2186

2187

2188

2189

2190

2191

2192

2193

2194

2195

2196

1986-93 GREAT AMERICANS

SCOTT NO.	DESCRIPTION	FIRST DAY COVERS SING	PL. BLK.	MINT SHEET	PLATE BLOCK	UNUSED F/NH	USED
2168	1¢ Margaret Mitchell .	5.00	6.00	10.00(100)	.75	.20	.15
2169	2¢ Mary Lyon (1987) .	2.25	4.00	10.00(100)	.75	.20	.15
2170	3¢ Dr. Paul D. White .	2.25	4.00	12.50(100)	.75	.20	.15
2171	4¢ Father Flanagan . .	2.25	4.00	14.00(100)	.75	.20	.15
2172	5¢ Hugo L. Black . . .	2.25	4.00	35.00(100)	2.00	.50	.15
2173	5¢ Luis Muñoz Marin (1990)	2.25	4.00	18.00(100)	1.10	.30	.15
2175	10¢ Red Cloud (1987)	2.25	4.00	45.00(100)	2.50	.40	.15
2176	14¢ Julia Ward Howe (1987)	2.25	4.00	50.00(100)	2.75	1.00	.20
2177	15¢ Buffalo Bill Cody (1988)	2.25	4.00	70.00(100)	4.50	1.00	.20
2178	17¢ Belva Ann Lockwood	2.25	4.00	50.00(100)	3.00	1.00	.20
2179	20¢ Virginia Apgar (1994)	2.25	4.00	50.00(100)	3.10	1.00	.20
2180	21¢ Chester Carlson (1988)	2.25	4.00	60.00(100)	3.50	1.00	.50
2181	23¢ Mary Cassatt (1988)	2.25	4.00	65.00(100)	4.00	1.00	.20
2182	25¢ Jack London (1988)	2.25	4.00	70.00(100)	4.00	1.00	.20
2182a	as above bklt pane of 10	8.00	....	....	....	7.00	....
2183	28¢ Sitting Bull (1989)	2.25	....	120.00(100)	7.00	1.30	.50
2184	29¢ Earl Warren (1992)	2.25	4.00	90.00(100)	5.00	1.00	.20
2185	29¢ Thomas Jefferson (1993)	2.25	4.75	90.00(100)	4.00(4)	1.00	.20
2185b	same, Plate Block of 8	....	....	....	8.00(8)	....	....
2186	35¢ Dennis Chavez (1991)	2.25	4.00	100.00(100)	6.00	1.20	.50
2187	40¢ Claire Lee Chenault (1990)	3.00	5.00	120.00(100)	6.75	1.35	.25
2188	45¢ Dr. Harvey Cushing (1988)	1.85	4.25	130.00(100)	6.75	1.50	.25

SCOTT NO.	DESCRIPTION	FIRST DAY COVERS SING	PL. BLK.	MINT SHEET	PLATE BLOCK	UNUSED F/NH	USED
2189	52¢ Hubert Humphrey (1991)	2.00	4.50	160.00(100)	9.00	1.75	.25
2190	56¢ John Harvard . . .	3.00	4.50	160.00(100)	9.00	1.75	.25
2191	65¢ H.H. Arnold (1988)	3.00	4.25	170.00(100)	9.50	2.00	.25
2192	75¢ Wendell Willkie (1992)	2.75	5.50	190.00(100)	10.00	2.00	.25
2193	$1 Dr. Bernard Revel	5.00	10.00	375.00(100)	19.00	4.00	.50
2194	$1 John Hopkins (1989)	5.00	10.00	60.00(20)	13.50	3.75	.50
2195	$2 William Jennings Bryan	8.00	10.00	525.00(100)	22.50	5.50	.80
2196	$5 Bret Harte (1987) .	17.50	28.50	250.00(20)	52.50	15.00	5.00
2197	25¢ Jack London, bklt single (1988) . . .	2.25	....	....	....	.90	.15
2197a	as above bklt pane (6), perf.10	5.00	....	....	....	5.25	....

2198

2199

2200

2201

1986 COMMEMORATIVES

SCOTT NO.	DESCRIPTION	FIRST DAY COVERS SING	PL. BLK.	MINT SHEET	PLATE BLOCK	UNUSED F/NH	USED
2167/2245	**(2167, 2202-04, 2210-11, 2220-24, 2235-45) 22 varieties . . . . . .**		....	....	....	23.30	5.75
2198	22¢ Cover & Handstamp	2.25	....	....	....	.90	.40
2199	22¢ Collector with Album	2.25	....	....	....	.90	.40
2200	22¢ No. 836 under magnifier	2.25	....	....	....	.90	.40
2201	22¢ President sheet .	2.25	....	....	....	.90	.40
2201a	Stamp Collecting bklt pane, 4 varieties, attached .	6.00	....	....	....	3.50	2.60

2202

2203

2204

SCOTT NO.	DESCRIPTION	FIRST DAY COVERS SING	PL. BLK.	MINT SHEET	PLATE BLOCK	UNUSED F/NH	USED
2202	22¢ LOVE	1.95	4.25	39.00(50)	4.00	1.00	.20
2203	22¢ Sojourner Truth .	3.00	4.00	40.00(50)	4.25	1.00	.20
2204	22¢ Texas Republic .	3.00	4.00	57.00(50)	6.00	1.25	.20

BOOKLET PANE SINGLES: Traditionally, booklet panes have been collected only as intact panes since, other than the straight edged sides, they were identical to sheet stamps. However, starting with the 1971 8¢ Eisenhower stamp, many issues differ from the comparative sheet stamp or may even be totally different issues (e.g. #1738-42 Windmills). These newer issues are now collected as booklet singles or panes—both methods being acceptable.

2205

2206

2207

2208

2209

SCOTT NO.	DESCRIPTION	FIRST DAY COVERS SING	FIRST DAY COVERS PL. BLK.	MINT SHEET	PLATE BLOCK	UNUSED F/NH	USED
2205	22¢ Muskellunge	2.25	....	....	....	2.50	.25
2206	22¢ Altantic Cod	2.25	....	....	....	2.50	.25
2207	22¢ Largemouth Bass	2.25	....	....	....	2.50	.25
2208	22¢ Bluefin Tuna	2.25	....	....	....	2.50	.25
2209	22¢ Catfish	2.25	....	....	....	2.50	.25
2209a	Fish, bklt pane, 5 varieties, attached	6.50	....	....	....	12.50	9.00

2210

2211

SCOTT NO.	DESCRIPTION	FIRST DAY COVERS SING	FIRST DAY COVERS PL. BLK.	MINT SHEET	PLATE BLOCK	UNUSED F/NH	USED
2210	22¢ Public Hospitals .	2.25	4.00	34.00(50)	3.50	.75	.20
2211	22¢ Duke Ellington . .	4.00	6.00	35.00(50)	4.00	.85	.20

1986 PRESIDENTS MINIATURE SETS

Complete set printed on 4 miniature sheets of 9 stamps each.

2216a *Washington*
2216b *Adams*
2216c *Jefferson*
2216d *Madison*
2216e *Monroe*
2216f *J.Q. Adams*
2216g *Jackson*
2216h *Van Buren*
2216i *W.H. Harrison*
2217a *Tyler*
2217b *Polk*
2217c *Taylor*
2217d *Fillmore*
2217e *Pierce*
2217f *Buchanan*
2217g *Lincoln*
2217h *A. Johnson*
2217i *Grant*
2218a *Hayes*
2218b *Garfield*
2218c *Arthur*
2218d *Cleveland*
2218e *B. Harrison*
2218f *McKinley*
2218g *T. Roosevelt*
2218h *Taft*
2218i *Wilson*
2219a *Harding*
2219b *Coolidge*
2219c *Hoover*
2219d *F.D. Roosevelt*
2219e *White House*
2219f *Truman*
2219g *Eisenhower*
2219h *Kennedy*
2219i *L.B. Johnson*

2216

1986 AMERIPEX '86 MINIATURE SHEETS

SCOTT NO.	DESCRIPTION	FIRST DAY COVERS SING	FIRST DAY COVERS PL. BLK.	MINT SHEET	PLATE BLOCK	UNUSED F/NH	USED
2216-19	22¢ 36 varieties complete in 4 minature sheets . . .	29.95	....	....	....	38.00	28.00
2216a-19i	set of 36 singles . . .	70.00	....	....	....	....	22.50

2220 2221

2222 2223

1986 COMMEMORATIVES

SCOTT NO.	DESCRIPTION	FIRST DAY COVERS SING	FIRST DAY COVERS PL. BLK.	MINT SHEET	PLATE BLOCK	UNUSED F/NH	USED
2220-23	Explorers, 4 varieties, attached .	6.00	7.00	62.00(50)	7.50	6.75	5.00
2220	22¢ Elisha Kent Kane	2.50	....	....	....	1.75	.50
2221	22¢ Adolphus W. Greely	2.50	....	....	....	1.75	.50
2222	22¢ Vilhjalmur Stefansson	2.50	....	....	....	1.75	.50
2223	22¢ R.E. Peary, M. Henson	2.50	....	....	....	1.75	.50

2224

SCOTT NO.	DESCRIPTION	FIRST DAY COVERS SING	FIRST DAY COVERS PL. BLK.	MINT SHEET	PLATE BLOCK	UNUSED F/NH	USED
2224	22¢ Statue of Liberty .	4.00	6.00	40.00(50)	4.00	.80	.20

2225

2226

2228

1986-91 TRANSPORTATION COILS–"B" Press
Perf. 10 Vertically

SCOTT NO.	DESCRIPTION	FIRST DAY COVERS SING	PLATE# STRIP 3	MINT SHEET	PLATE# STRIP 3	UNUSED F/NH	USED
2225	1¢ Omnibus	2.25	6.50	....	.85	.20	.15
2225a	1¢ Omnibus, untagged (1991)	....	....	....	1.25	.20	.15
2226	2¢ Locomotive (1987)	2.25	6.50	....	1.00	.20	.15
2226a	2¢ Locomative, untagged (1994)	....	....	....	1.10	.20	.15
2228	4¢ Stagecoach	....	....	....	1.75	.20	.15
2228a	same, overall tagging (1990)	....	....	....	15.00	.75	.30
2231	8.3¢ Ambulance precancelled (1986) .	....	....	....	8.50	2.00	.60

Note: **For plate number strips of 5, see page 149**
#2225—"¢" sign eliminated. #1897 has "1¢".
#2226—inscribed "2 USA". #1897A inscribed "USA 2¢".
#2228—"Stagecoach 1890s" is 17 mm long.

2235

2236

2237

2238

1986 COMMEMORATIVES (continued)

SCOTT NO.	DESCRIPTION	FIRST DAY COVERS SING	FIRST DAY COVERS PL. BLK.	MINT SHEET	PLATE BLOCK	UNUSED F/NH	USED
2235-38	Navajo Art, 4 varieties, attached	4.00	5.00	60.00(50)	6.50	6.00	4.50
2235	22¢ Navajo Art	2.25	....	....	....	1.75	.25
2236	22¢ Navajo Art	2.25	....	....	....	1.75	.25
2237	22¢ Navajo Art	2.25	....	....	....	1.75	.25
2238	22¢ Navajo Art	2.25	....	....	....	1.75	.25

2239

SCOTT NO.	DESCRIPTION	FIRST DAY COVERS SING	FIRST DAY COVERS PL. BLK.	MINT SHEET	PLATE BLOCK	UNUSED F/NH	USED
2239	22¢ T.S. Eliot	2.25	4.00	55.00(50)	5.50	1.20	.20

2240

2241

2242

2243

SCOTT NO.	DESCRIPTION	FIRST DAY COVERS SING	FIRST DAY COVERS PL. BLK.	MINT SHEET	PLATE BLOCK	UNUSED F/NH	USED
2240-43	Woodcarved Figurines, 4 varieties, attached	4.00	5.00	45.00(50)	5.00	4.25	3.50
2240	22¢ Highlander Figure	2.25	....	....	....	1.10	.30
2241	22¢ Ship Figurehead	2.25	....	....	....	1.10	.30
2242	22¢ Nautical Figure	2.25	....	....	....	1.10	.30
2243	22¢ Cigar Store Figure	2.25	....	....	....	1.10	.30

2244

2245

SCOTT NO.	DESCRIPTION	FIRST DAY COVERS SING	FIRST DAY COVERS PL. BLK.	MINT SHEET	PLATE BLOCK	UNUSED F/NH	USED
2244	22¢ Madonna	2.25	4.00	58.00(100)	3.00	.65	.15
2245	22¢ Village Scene	2.25	4.00	58.00(100)	3.00	.65	.15

2246

2247

2248

2249

2250

2251

1987 COMMEMORATIVES

SCOTT NO.	DESCRIPTION	FIRST DAY COVERS SING	FIRST DAY COVERS PL. BLK.	MINT SHEET	PLATE BLOCK	UNUSED F/NH	USED
2246/2368	(2246-51, 2275, 2336-38, 2349-54, 2360-61, 2367-68) 20 varieties	....	....	....	....	19.40	5.00
2246	22¢ Michigan Statehood	2.25	4.00	65.00(50)	6.50	1.00	.20
2247	22¢ Pan American Games	2.25	4.00	30.00(50)	3.00	.80	.20
2248	22¢ LOVE	3.00	4.50	57.00(100)	3.00	.80	.20
2249	22¢ Jean Baptiste Pointe du Sable	2.25	4.00	33.00(50)	3.50	.80	.20
2250	22¢ Enrico Caruso	2.25	4.00	33.00(50)	3.50	.80	.20
2251	22¢ Girls Scouts	2.25	4.00	35.00(50)	3.50	.80	.20

2252

2253

2254

2255

2256

2257

2258

2259

2260

2261

2262

2263

2264

2265

2266

1987-93 TRANSPORTATION COILS

SCOTT NO.	DESCRIPTION	FIRST DAY COVERS SING	PLATE# STRIP 3	MINT SHEET	PLATE# STRIP 3	UNUSED F/NH	USED
2252	3¢ Conestoga Wagon (1988)	2.25	9.00	....	1.25	.20	.20
2252a	same, untagged (1992)	....	9.00	....	1.75	.25	.20
2253	5¢ Milk Wagon	2.25	9.00	....	1.90	.25	.20
2254	5.3¢ Elevator, precancel ('88)	2.25	9.00	....	1.90	.40	.20
2255	7.6¢ Carreta, precancel ('88)	2.25	9.00	....	3.25	.40	.20
2256	8.4¢ Wheel Chair, precancel (1988)	2.25	9.00	....	3.25	.40	.20
2257	10¢ Canal Boat	2.25	9.00	....	3.25	.40	.20
2257a	same, overall tagging (1993)	....	9.00	....	3.75	.40	.20
2258	13¢ Police Wagon, precancel (1988)	2.25	9.00	....	6.50	.80	.25
2259	13.2¢ Railroad Coal Car, precancel (1988)	2.25	9.00	....	3.50	.40	.20
2260	15¢ Tugboat (1988)	2.25	9.00	....	3.50	.50	.20
2260a	same, overall tagging (1990)	....	9.00	....	5.25	.75	.20
2261	16.7¢ Popcorn Wagon, precancel (1988)	2.25	9.00	....	4.25	.50	.20
2262	17.5¢ Racing Car	2.25	9.00	....	4.75	.70	.35
2262a	17.5¢ Racing Car, precancel (1988)	2.25	9.00	....	5.25	.70	.20
2263	20¢ Cable Car (1988)	2.25	9.00	....	4.50	.70	.20
2263b	same, overall tagging (1990)	....	9.00	....	10.00	1.25	.20
2264	20.5¢ Fire Engine, precancel (1988)	2.25	9.00	....	8.00	1.25	.45
2265	21¢ Railroad Mail Car, precancel (1988)	2.25	9.00	....	5.50	.70	.45
2266	24.1¢ Tandem Bicycle, precancel (1988)	2.25	9.00	....	5.50	.85	.45

2267

2268

2269

2270

2271

2272

2273

2274

1987 SPECIAL OCCASIONS BOOKLET PANE

SCOTT NO.	DESCRIPTION	FIRST DAY COVERS SING	FIRST DAY COVERS PL. BLK.	MINT SHEET	PLATE BLOCK	UNUSED F/NH	USED
2267	22¢ Congratulations!	2.25	....	....	....	2.25	.40
2268	22¢ Get Well!	2.25	....	....	....	2.25	.40
2269	22¢ Thank You!	2.25	....	....	....	2.25	.40
2270	22¢ Love You, Dad!	2.25	....	....	....	2.25	.40
2271	22¢ Best Wishes!	2.25	....	....	....	2.25	.40
2272	22¢ Happy Birthday!	2.25	....	....	....	2.25	.40
2273	22¢ Love You, Mother!	2.25	....	....	....	2.25	.40
2274	22¢ Keep in Touch!	2.25	....	....	....	2.25	.40
2274a	Special Occasions bklt pane of 10, attached	17.00	....	....	....	18.50	....

NOTE: **#2274a contains 1 each of #2268-71, 2273-74 and 2 each of #2267 and 2272.**

2275

1987 COMMEMORATIVES (continued)

SCOTT NO.	DESCRIPTION	FIRST DAY COVERS SING	FIRST DAY COVERS PL. BLK.	MINT SHEET	PLATE BLOCK	UNUSED F/NH	USED
2275	22¢ United Way	2.25	4.00	29.00(50)	3.00	1.00	.20

2276, 2276A

2277, 2279, 2282, 2282a

2278, 2285A, 2285Ac

1987-88 REGULAR ISSUE

SCOTT NO.	DESCRIPTION	FIRST DAY COVERS SING	FIRST DAY COVERS PL. BLK.	MINT SHEET	PLATE BLOCK	UNUSED F/NH	USED
2276	22¢ Flag & Fireworks	2.25	4.00	58.00(100)	3.25	1.00	.15
2276a	bklt pane of 20	12.50	....		....	13.50	....
2277	(25¢) "E" Earth (1988)	2.25	4.00	85.00(100)	4.25	.95	.15
2278	25¢ Flag with Clouds (1988)	2.25	4.00	70.00(100)	3.50	1.00	.15

2280

2281

2283, 2283a

2284

2285, 2285b

SCOTT NO.	DESCRIPTION	FIRST DAY COVERS SING	FIRST DAY COVERS PL. BLK. / PLATE # STRIP 3	MINT SHEET	PLATE BLOCK / PLATE# STRIP 3	UNUSED F/NH	USED
2279	(25¢) "E" Earth coil (1988)	2.25	7.50	....	4.50	.75	.15
2280	25¢ Flag over Yosemite, coil (1988)	2.25	7.50	....	4.50	.85	.15
2280a	25¢ Flag over Yosemite, phosphor (1989)	2.25	....	....	5.00	.95	.15
2281	25¢ Honey Bee, coil (1988)	2.25	7.50	....	4.00	.85	.15
2282	(25¢) "E" Earth, bklt single (1988)	2.25	....	....	....	.85	.20
2282a	(25¢) "E" Earth, bklt pane of 10	7.25	....	....	....	8.00	....
2283	25¢ Pheasant bklt single (1988)	2.25	....	....	....	.85	.15
2283a	25¢ Pheasant, bklt pane of 10	7.25	....	....	....	8.00	....
2283b	25¢ Pheasant, (red omitted) bklt single	....	....	....	....	10.00	....
2283c	25¢ Pheasant, (red omitted) bklt pane of 10	....	....	....	....	95.00	....
2284	25¢ Grosbeak, bklt single (1988)	2.25	....	....	....	1.00	.15
2285	25¢ Owl bklt single	2.25	....	....	....	1.00	.15
2285b	25¢ Owl/Grosbeck, bklt pane of 10	7.25	....	....	....	7.00	....
2285A	25¢ Flag with Clouds, bklt single	2.25	....	....	....	.90	.15
2285Ac	as above, bklt pane of 6 (1988)	4.00	....	....	....	5.75	....

2286

2310

2335

1987 AMERICAN WILDLIFE

2286	*Barn Swallow*	**2303**	*Red-winged Blackbird*	**2320**	*Bison*
2287	*Monarch Butterfly*	**2304**	*American Lobster*	**2321**	*Snowy Egret*
2288	*Bighorn Sheep*	**2305**	*Black-tailed Jack Rabbit*	**2322**	*Gray Wolf*
2289	*Broad-tailed Hummingbird*	**2306**	*Scarlet Tanager*	**2323**	*Mountain Goat*
2290	*Cottontail*	**2307**	*Woodchuck*	**2324**	*Deer Mouse*
2291	*Osprey*	**2308**	*Roseate Spoonbill*	**2325**	*Black-tailed Prairie Dog*
2292	*Mountain Lion*	**2309**	*Bald Eagle*	**2326**	*Box Turtle*
2293	*Luna Moth*	**2310**	*Alaskan Brown Bear*	**2327**	*Wolverine*
2294	*Mule Deer*	**2311**	*Iiwi*	**2328**	*American Elk*
2295	*Gray Squirrel*	**2312**	*Badger*	**2329**	*California Sea Lion*
2296	*Armadillo*	**2313**	*Pronghorn*	**2330**	*Mockingbird*
2297	*Eastern Chipmunk*	**2314**	*River Otter*	**2331**	*Raccoon*
2298	*Moose*	**2315**	*Ladybug*	**2332**	*Bobcat*
2299	*Black Bear*	**2316**	*Beaver*	**2333**	*Black-footed Ferret*
2300	*Tiger Swallowtail*	**2317**	*White-tailed Deer*	**2334**	*Canada Goose*
2301	*Bobwhite*	**2318**	*Blue Jay*	**2335**	*Red Fox*
2302	*Ringtail*	**2319**	*Pika*		

SCOTT NO.	DESCRIPTION	FIRST DAY COVERS SING	FIRST DAY COVERS PL. BLK.	MINT SHEET	PLATE BLOCK	UNUSED F/NH	USED
2286-2335	22¢, 50 varieties, attached	70.00	....	70.00(50)	....	70.00	....
	set of singles	86.00	....	....	....	....	30.00
	singles of above, each	2.00	....	....	....	....	1.00

2336

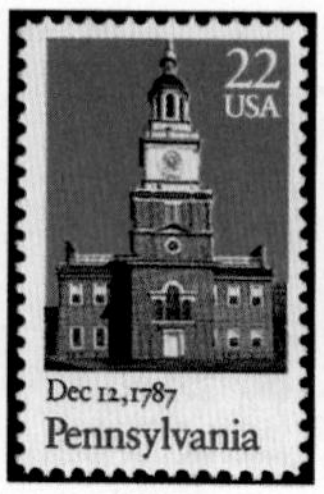

2337

2338

2339

2340

2341

2342

2343

2344

2345

2346

2347

2348

1987-90 COMMEMORATIVES

SCOTT NO.	DESCRIPTION	FIRST DAY COVERS SING	FIRST DAY COVERS PL. BLK.	MINT SHEET	PLATE BLOCK	UNUSED F/NH	USED
2336	22¢ Delaware Statehood	2.25	4.00	60.00(50)	6.50	1.50	.25
2337	22¢ Pennsylvania Statehood	2.25	4.00	60.00(50)	6.50	1.50	.25
2338	22¢ New Jersey Statehood	2.25	4.00	60.00(50)	6.50	1.50	.25
2339	22¢ Georgia Statehood (1988)	2.25	4.00	60.00(50)	6.50	1.50	.40
2340	22¢ Connecticut Statehood (1988)	2.25	4.00	60.00(50)	6.50	1.50	.25
2341	22¢ Massachusetts Statehood (1988) . . .	2.25	4.00	60.00(50)	6.50	1.50	.60
2342	22¢ Maryland Statehood (1988)	2.25	4.00	60.00(50)	6.50	1.50	.40
2343	25¢ South Carolina Statehood (1988) . . .	2.25	4.00	60.00(50)	6.50	1.50	.25
2344	25¢ New Hampshire Statehood (1988) . . .	2.25	4.00	60.00(50)	6.50	1.50	.25
2345	25¢ Virginia Statehood (1988)	2.25	4.00	60.00(50)	6.50	1.50	.25
2346	25¢ New York Statehood (1988)	2.25	4.00	60.00(50)	6.50	1.50	.25
2347	25¢ North Carolina Statehood (1989) . . .	2.25	4.00	60.00(50)	6.50	1.50	.25
2348	25¢ Rhode Island Statehood (1990)	2.25	9.00	60.00(50)	6.50	1.50	.25

2349

2350

SCOTT NO.	DESCRIPTION	FIRST DAY COVERS SING	FIRST DAY COVERS PL. BLK.	MINT SHEET	PLATE BLOCK	UNUSED F/NH	USED
2349	22¢ Morocco	2.25	4.00	35.00(50)	3.50	.75	.20
2350	22¢ William Faulkner	2.25	4.00	50.00(50)	5.50	1.25	.20

2351 2352

2353 2354

SCOTT NO.	DESCRIPTION	FIRST DAY COVERS SING	FIRST DAY COVERS PL. BLK.	MINT SHEET	PLATE BLOCK	UNUSED F/NH	USED
2351-54	Lacemaking, 4 varieties, attached	4.00	5.00	40.00(40)	5.50	5.00	4.00
2351	22¢ Lace, Ruth Maxwell	2.25	....	....	....	1.25	.30
2352	22¢ Lace, Mary McPeek	2.25	....	....	....	1.25	.30
2353	22¢ Lace, Leslie K. Saari	2.25	....	....	....	1.25	.30
2354	22¢ Lace, Trenna Ruffner	2.25	....	....	....	1.25	.30

2355

2356

2357

2358

2359

SCOTT NO.	DESCRIPTION	FIRST DAY COVERS SING	FIRST DAY COVERS PL. BLK.	MINT SHEET	PLATE BLOCK	UNUSED F/NH	USED
2355	22¢ "The Bicentennial"	2.25	....	....	....	1.50	.30
2356	22¢ "We the people" .	2.25	....	....	....	1.50	.30
2357	22¢ "Establish justice"	2.25	....	....	....	1.50	.30
2358	22¢ "And secure" . . .	2.25	....	....	....	1.50	.30
2359	22¢ "Do ordain"	2.25	....	....	....	1.50	.30
2359a	Drafting of Constitution bklt pane, 5 varieties, attached	4.60	....	....	....	7.50	6.50

2360

2361

SCOTT NO.	DESCRIPTION	FIRST DAY COVERS SING	FIRST DAY COVERS PL. BLK.	MINT SHEET	PLATE BLOCK	UNUSED F/NH	USED
2360	22¢ Signing of U.S. Constitution	2.25	4.00	55.00(50)	5.50	1.25	.20
2361	22¢ Certified Public Accountants	12.00	15.00	170.00(50)	15.00	3.50	.20

2362

2363

2364

2365

2366

LOCOMOTIVES ISSUE

SCOTT NO.	DESCRIPTION	FIRST DAY COVERS SING	FIRST DAY COVERS PL. BLK.	MINT SHEET	PLATE BLOCK	UNUSED F/NH	USED
2362	22¢ "Strourbridge Lion, 1829"	2.25	....	....	....	1.25	.25
2363	22¢ "Best Friend of Charleston, 1830" . . .	2.25	....	....	....	1.25	.25
2364	22¢ "John Bull, 1831"	2.25	....	....	....	1.25	.25
2365	22¢ "Brother Jonathan, 1832"	2.25	....	....	....	1.25	.25
2366	22¢ "Gowan + Marx, 1839"	2.25	....	....	....	1.25	.25
2366a	Locomotives, bklt pane, 5 varieties, attached .	4.60	....	....	....	6.00	4.75

2367

2368

SCOTT NO.	DESCRIPTION	FIRST DAY COVERS SING	FIRST DAY COVERS PL. BLK.	MINT SHEET	PLATE BLOCK	UNUSED F/NH	USED
2367	22¢ Madonna	2.25	4.00	58.00(100)	3.00	.90	.15
2368	22¢ Ornament	2.25	4.00	58.00(100)	3.00	.90	.15

2369

2370

2371

2372 2373

2374 2375

2376

2377

2378

1988 COMMEMORATIVES

SCOTT NO.	DESCRIPTION	FIRST DAY COVERS SING	FIRST DAY COVERS PL. BLK.	MINT SHEET	PLATE BLOCK	UNUSED F/NH	USED
2339/2400	**(2339-46, 2369-80, 2386-93, 2399-2400) 30 varieties**	....	....	....	....	**34.25**	**7.50**
2369	22¢ Winter Olympics .	2.25	4.00	40.00(50)	3.75	.85	.20
2370	22¢ Australia Bicentennial	2.25	4.00	25.00(50)	3.00	.65	.20
2371	22¢ James Weldon Johnson	2.25	4.00	32.00(50)	3.25	1.00	.30
2372-75	Cats, 4 varieties, attached	8.00	12.00	40.00(40)	6.50	5.00	4.00
2372	22¢ Siamese, Exotic Shorthair	2.25	....	....	....	1.50	.60
2373	22¢ Abyssinian, Himalayan	2.25	....	....	....	1.50	.60
2374	22¢ Maine Coon, Burmese	2.25	....	....	....	1.50	.60
2375	22¢ American Shorthair, Persian	2.25	....	....	....	1.50	.60
2376	22¢ Knute Rockne . .	4.00	6.00	45.00(50)	4.75	1.20	.50
2377	25¢ Francis Ouimet . .	8.00	10.00	60.00(50)	7.00	1.25	.30
2378	25¢ LOVE	2.25	4.00	68.00(100)	3.50	.75	.20

2379

2380

SCOTT NO.	DESCRIPTION	FIRST DAY COVERS SING	FIRST DAY COVERS PL. BLK.	MINT SHEET	PLATE BLOCK	UNUSED F/NH	USED
2379	45¢ LOVE	2.25	4.00	67.50(50)	7.00	1.50	.25
2380	25¢ Summer Olympics	2.25	4.00	40.00(50)	3.75	1.00	.20

2381

2382

2383

2384

2385

SCOTT NO.	DESCRIPTION	FIRST DAY COVERS SING	FIRST DAY COVERS PL. BLK.	MINT SHEET	PLATE BLOCK	UNUSED F/NH	USED
2381	25¢ Locomobile	2.25	....	....	....	2.25	.25
2382	25¢ Pierce-Arrow . . .	2.25	....	....	....	2.25	.25
2383	25¢ Cord	2.25	....	....	....	2.25	.25
2384	25¢ Packard	2.25	....	....	....	2.25	.25
2385	25¢ Duesenberg	2.25	....	....	....	2.25	.25
2385a	Classic Automobiles bklt pane , 5 varieties, attached	4.60	....	....	....	12.00	8.00

BOOKLET PANE SINGLES: Traditionally, booklet panes have been collected only as intact panes since, other than the straight edged sides, they were identical to sheet stamps. However, starting with the 1971 8¢ Eisenhower stamp, many issues differ from the comparative sheet stamp or may even be totally different issues (e.g. #1738-42 Windmills). These newer issues are now collected as booklet singles or panes—both methods being acceptable.

SCOTT NO.	DESCRIPTION	FIRST DAY COVERS SING	FIRST DAY COVERS PL. BLK.	MINT SHEET	PLATE BLOCK	UNUSED F/NH	USED

2386 2387

2388 2389

SCOTT NO.	DESCRIPTION	FIRST DAY COVERS SING	FIRST DAY COVERS PL. BLK.	MINT SHEET	PLATE BLOCK	UNUSED F/NH	USED
2386-89	Antarctic Explorers, 4 varieties, attached .	4.00	5.00	57.50(50)	6.75	5.75	4.50
2386	25¢ Nathaniel Palmer	2.25	....	....	....	1.50	.40
2387	25¢ Lt. Charles Wilkes	2.25	....	....	....	1.50	.40
2388	25¢ Richard E. Byrd .	2.25	....	....	....	1.50	.40
2389	25¢ Lincoln Ellsworth	2.25	....	....	....	1.50	.40

2390

2391

2392

2393

SCOTT NO.	DESCRIPTION	FIRST DAY COVERS SING	FIRST DAY COVERS PL. BLK.	MINT SHEET	PLATE BLOCK	UNUSED F/NH	USED
2390-93	Carousel Animals, 4 varieties, attached .	4.00	5.00	57.50(50)	6.75	6.00	4.75
2390	25¢ Deer	2.25	....	....	....	1.60	.30
2391	25¢ Horse	2.25	....	....	....	1.60	.30
2392	25¢ Camel	2.25	....	....	....	1.60	.30
2393	25¢ Goat	2.25	....	....	....	1.60	.30

2394

SCOTT NO.	DESCRIPTION	FIRST DAY COVERS SING	FIRST DAY COVERS PL. BLK.	MINT SHEET	PLATE BLOCK	UNUSED F/NH	USED
2394	$8.75 Express Mail . .	32.00	70.00	495.00(20)	120.00	27.00	12.00

2395

2396

2397

2398

SCOTT NO.	DESCRIPTION	FIRST DAY COVERS SING	FIRST DAY COVERS PL. BLK.	MINT SHEET	PLATE BLOCK	UNUSED F/NH	USED
2395-2398	Special Occasions, bklt singles	7.00	....	....	....	4.50	1.20
2396a	Bklt pane (6) with gutter 3–#2395 + 3–#2396 .	4.60	....	....	....	6.00	5.00
2398a	Bklt pane (6) with gutter 3–#2397 + 3–#2398 .	4.60	....	....	....	6.00	5.00

2399

2400

SCOTT NO.	DESCRIPTION	FIRST DAY COVERS SING	FIRST DAY COVERS PL. BLK.	MINT SHEET	PLATE BLOCK	UNUSED F/NH	USED
2399	25¢ Madonna and Child	2.25	4.00	32.00(50)	3.25	1.00	.15
2400	25¢ One Horse Sleigh	2.25	4.00	32.00(50)	3.25	1.00	.15

2401

2402

1989 COMMEMORATIVES

SCOTT NO.	DESCRIPTION	FIRST DAY COVERS SING	FIRST DAY COVERS PL. BLK.	MINT SHEET	PLATE BLOCK	UNUSED F/NH	USED
2347/2437	**(2347, 2401-04, 2410-14, 2416-18, 2420-28, 2434-37) 26 varieties . . . . . .**	....	....	....	....	**27.70**	**5.75**
2401	25¢ Montana Statehood	2.25	4.00	52.00(50)	5.00	1.20	.20
2402	25¢ A.P. Randolph . .	3.00	4.00	41.00(50)	4.00	1.10	.20

2403

2404

SCOTT NO.	DESCRIPTION	FIRST DAY COVERS SING	FIRST DAY COVERS PL. BLK.	MINT SHEET	PLATE BLOCK	UNUSED F/NH	USED
2403	25¢ North Dakota Statehood	2.25	4.00	52.00(50)	5.00	1.50	.20
2404	25¢ Washington Statehood	2.25	4.00	52.00(50)	5.00	1.50	.20

2405

2406

2407

2408

2409

SCOTT NO.	DESCRIPTION	FIRST DAY COVERS SING	FIRST DAY COVERS PL. BLK.	MINT SHEET	PLATE BLOCK	UNUSED F/NH	USED
2405	25¢ "Experiment,1788-90"	2.25	....	....	....	1.40	.25
2406	25¢ "Phoenix, 1809" .	2.25	....	....	....	1.40	.25
2407	25¢ "New Orleans, 1812"	2.25	....	....	....	1.40	.25
2408	25¢ "Washington, 1816"	2.25	....	....	....	1.40	.25
2409	25¢ "Walk in the Water,1818"	2.25	....	....	....	1.40	.25
2409a	Steamboat, bklt pane, 5 varieties, attached .	6.00	....	....	....	6.50	5.00
2409av	same, bklt pane, unfolded	....	....	....	....	10.00	....

2410

2411

SCOTT NO.	DESCRIPTION	FIRST DAY COVERS SING	FIRST DAY COVERS PL. BLK.	MINT SHEET	PLATE BLOCK	UNUSED F/NH	USED
2410	25¢ World Stamp Expo '89	2.25	4.00	35.00(50)	3.75	1.00	.20
2411	25¢ Arturo Toscanini .	2.25	4.00	35.00(50)	3.75	1.00	.20

2412

2413

2414

2415

SCOTT NO.	DESCRIPTION	FIRST DAY COVERS SING	FIRST DAY COVERS PL. BLK.	MINT SHEET	PLATE BLOCK	UNUSED F/NH	USED
2412	25¢ U.S. House of Representatives	2.25	4.00	45.00(50)	4.50	1.00	.20
2413	25¢ U.S. Senate	2.25	4.00	57.00(50)	5.00	1.00	.20
2414	25¢ Executive Branch	2.25	4.00	45.00(50)	5.00	1.00	.20
2415	25¢ U.S. Supreme Court (1990)	2.25	4.00	45.00(50)	4.75	1.00	.20

2416

SCOTT NO.	DESCRIPTION	FIRST DAY COVERS SING	FIRST DAY COVERS PL. BLK.	MINT SHEET	PLATE BLOCK	UNUSED F/NH	USED
2416	25¢ South Dakota Statehood	2.25	4.00	55.00(50)	5.00	1.00	.20

2417

2418

SCOTT NO.	DESCRIPTION	FIRST DAY COVERS SING	FIRST DAY COVERS PL. BLK.	MINT SHEET	PLATE BLOCK	UNUSED F/NH	USED
2417	25¢ Lou Gehrig	5.00	8.00	55.00(50)	6.00	1.20	.30
2418	25¢ Ernest Hemingway	2.25	4.00	42.50(50)	4.50	1.00	.20

2419

SCOTT NO.	DESCRIPTION	FIRST DAY COVERS SING	FIRST DAY COVERS PL. BLK.	MINT SHEET	PLATE BLOCK	UNUSED F/NH	USED
2419	$2.40 Moon Landing .	7.50	15.75	160.00(20)	40.00	12.00	7.50

2420

2421

SCOTT NO.	DESCRIPTION	FIRST DAY COVERS SING	FIRST DAY COVERS PL. BLK.	MINT SHEET	PLATE BLOCK	UNUSED F/NH	USED
2420	25¢ Letter Carriers . .	2.25	4.00	26.00(50)	3.25	1.00	.20
2421	25¢ Bill of Rights	2.25	4.00	55.00(50)	5.75	1.25	.20

2422 2423

2424 2425

SCOTT NO.	DESCRIPTION	FIRST DAY COVERS SING	FIRST DAY COVERS PL. BLK.	MINT SHEET	PLATE BLOCK	UNUSED F/NH	USED
2422-25	Prehistoric Animals, 4 attached	5.00	7.00	52.50(40)	6.25	6.25	4.50
2422	25¢ Tyrannosaurus Rex	2.50	....	....	....	1.50	.25
2423	25¢ Pteranodon	2.50	....	....	....	1.50	.25
2424	25¢ Stegosaurus	2.50	....	....	....	1.50	.25
2425	25¢ Brontosaurus . . .	2.50	....	....	....	1.50	.25

2426

SCOTT NO.	DESCRIPTION	FIRST DAY COVERS SING	FIRST DAY COVERS PL. BLK.	MINT SHEET	PLATE BLOCK	UNUSED F/NH	USED
2426	25¢ Kachina Doll	2.25	4.00	40.00(50)	5.00	1.00	.20

2427

2428, 2429

2431

SCOTT NO.	DESCRIPTION	FIRST DAY COVERS SING	FIRST DAY COVERS PL. BLK.	MINT SHEET	PLATE BLOCK	UNUSED F/NH	USED
2427	25¢ Madonna & Child	1.75	4.00	32.00(50)	3.25	1.00	.15
2427a	same, bklt pane of 10	7.25	....	....	....	9.00	....
2427av	same, bklt pane, unfolded	....	....	....	....	10.00	....
2428	25¢ Sleigh full of Presents	2.25	4.00	32.00(50)	3.25	.75	.15
2429	25¢ Sleigh full of Presents, bklt single	2.25	....	....	....	.90	.20
2429a	same, bklt pane of 10	7.25	....	....	....	8.00	....
2429av	same, bklt pane, unfolded	....	....	....	....	21.00	....
2431	25¢ Eagle & Shield, self-adhesive	1.95	....	....	....	1.25	.75
2431a	same, bklt pane of 18	32.00	....	....	....	19.50	....
2431	same, coil	....	....	....	3.00(3)	.85	....

2433

SCOTT NO.	DESCRIPTION	FIRST DAY COVERS SING	PL. BLK.	MINT SHEET	PLATE BLOCK	UNUSED F/NH	USED
2433	$3.60 World Stamp Expo, Imperf. Souvenir Sheet	15.00	....	....	....	25.00	20.00

2434 2435

2436 2437

SCOTT NO.	DESCRIPTION	FIRST DAY COVERS SING	PL. BLK.	MINT SHEET	PLATE BLOCK	UNUSED F/NH	USED
2434-37	Classic Mail Delivery, 4 attached	5.00	7.00	45.00(40)	6.25	5.50	4.00
2434	25¢ Stagecoach	2.25	....	....	....	1.50	.40
2435	25¢ Paddlewheel Steamer	2.25	....	....	....	1.50	.40
2436	25¢ Biplane	2.25	....	....	....	1.50	.40
2437	25¢ Automobile	2.25	....	....	....	1.50	.40
2438	$1.00 Classic Mail Delivery Imperf. Souvenir Sheet	4.50	....	....	....	8.00	5.00

2439

2440, 2441

2442

1990 COMMEMORATIVES

SCOTT NO.	DESCRIPTION	FIRST DAY COVERS SING	PL. BLK.	MINT SHEET	PLATE BLOCK	UNUSED F/NH	USED
2348/2515	**(2348, 2415, 2439-40, 2442, 2444-49, 2496-2500, 2506-15, 26 varieties . . . . . .**	....	....	....	....	**32.55**	**5.75**
2439	25¢ Idaho Statehood	2.25	4.00	52.00(50)	5.00	1.50	.20
2440	25¢ LOVE	2.25	4.00	32.00(50)	3.25	1.50	.20
2441	25¢ LOVE, bklt single	2.25	....	....	....	1.25	.20
2441a	25¢ LOVE bklt pane of 10	8.65	....	....	....	12.00	....
2441av	same, bklt pane, unfolded	....	....	....	....	50.00	....
2442	25¢ Ida B. Wells	3.00	4.00	70.00(50)	7.00	1.50	.20

2443

2444

2445

2446

2449

2447

2448

SCOTT NO.	DESCRIPTION	FIRST DAY COVERS SING	PL. BLK.	MINT SHEET	PLATE BLOCK	UNUSED F/NH	USED
2443	15¢ Umbrella, bklt single	2.25	....	....	....	.70	.25
2443a	15¢ Umbrella, bklt pane of 10	5.75	....	....	....	5.00	3.40
2443av	same, bklt pane, unfolded	....	....	....	....	9.00	....
2444	25¢ Wyoming Statehood	8.00	10.00	55.00(50)	5.00	1.10	.20
2445-48	Classic Films, 4 varieties, attached .	8.00	7.00	87.00(40)	12.00	10.00	7.50
2445	25¢ Wizard of OZ . . .	4.00	....	....	....	2.75	.25
2446	25¢ Gone with the Wind	4.00	....	....	....	2.75	.25
2447	25¢ Beau Geste	4.00	....	....	....	2.75	.25
2448	25¢ Stagecoach	4.00	....	....	....	2.75	.25
2449	25¢ Marianne Craig Moore	2.25	4.00	55.00(50)	5.00	1.75	.20

2451

2452, 2452B, 2452D

2453, 2454

2457, 2458

2463

2464

2466

2468

1990-95 TRANSPORTATION COILS

SCOTT NO.	DESCRIPTION	FIRST DAY COVERS SING	PLATE# STRIP 3	MINT SHEET	PLATE# STRIP 3	UNUSED F/NH	USED
2451	4¢ Steam Carriage (1991)	2.25	6.50	....	1.50	.20	.15
2451b	4¢ Steam Carriage, untagged......		....	....	1.50	.20	.15
2452	5¢ Circus Wagon	2.25	6.50	....	1.75	.20	.15
2452a	5¢ Circus Wagon, untagged........		....	....	1.85	.20	.20
2452B	5¢ Circus Wagon, Gravure (1992)	2.25	6.50	....	1.85	.20	.20
2452D	5¢ Circus Wagon, coil (Reissue, 1995 added)	3.00	10.00	....	1.85	.20	.20
2453	5¢ Canoe, precancel, brown (1991)	2.25	6.50	....	1.85	.20	.15
2454	5¢ Canoe, precancel, red (1991)	2.25	6.50	....	2.50	.20	.20
2457	10¢ Tractor Trailer (1991)	2.25	6.50	....	2.75	.45	.25
2458	10¢ Tractor Trailer, Gravure (1994)	2.25	6.50	....	3.25	.45	.25
2463	20¢ Cog Railway Car, coil.	1.95	10.00	....	5.00	.50	.15
2464	23¢ Lunch Wagon (1991)	2.25	6.50	....	4.50	.75	.15
2466	32¢ Ferryboat, coil . .	1.95	10.00	....	7.00	1.00	.15
2468	$1 Seaplane, coil . . .	3.00	10.00	....	13.00	3.00	1.00

NOTE: **For plate number strips of 5, see page 149**

2470 2471 2472 2473 2474

SCOTT NO.	DESCRIPTION	FIRST DAY COVERS SING	FIRST DAY COVERS PL. BLK.	MINT SHEET	PLATE BLOCK	UNUSED F/NH	USED
2470	25¢ Admiralty Head Lighthouse	2.25	....	....	....	2.25	.25
2471	25¢ Cape Hatteras Lighthouse	2.25	....	....	....	2.25	.25
2472	25¢ West Quoddy Head Lighthouse	2.25	....	....	....	2.25	.25
2473	25¢ American Shoals Lighthouse	2.25	....	....	....	2.25	.25
2474	25¢ Sandy Hook Lighthouse	2.25	....	....	....	2.25	.25
2474a	Lighthouse, bklt pane, 5 varieties	4.60	....	....	....	9.00	7.00
2474av	Same, bklt pane, unfolded	....	....	....	....	14.50	....

2475

SCOTT NO.	DESCRIPTION	FIRST DAY COVERS SING	FIRST DAY COVERS PL. BLK.	MINT SHEET	PLATE BLOCK	UNUSED F/NH	USED
2475	25¢ ATM Plastic Stamp, single	2.25	....	....	....	2.00	1.25
2475a	Same, pane of 12 . . .	20.00	....	....	....	13.00	....

2476 2477 2478 2479

2480 2481 2482 2483

1990-95 REGULAR ISSUE

SCOTT NO.	DESCRIPTION	FIRST DAY COVERS SING	FIRST DAY COVERS PL. BLK.	MINT SHEET	PLATE BLOCK	UNUSED F/NH	USED
2476	1¢ Kestrel (1991) . . .	2.25	4.00	6.00(100)	.75	.20	.15
2477	1¢ Kestrel (redesign 1¢, 1995)	2.25	4.00	6.00(100)	.75	.20	.15
2478	3¢ Bluebird (1993) . .	2.25	4.00	15.00(100)	1.50	.20	.15
2479	19¢ Fawn (1993)	2.25	4.00	55.00(100)	5.00	.75	.15
2480	30¢ Cardinal (1993) .	2.25	4.00	85.00(100)	5.00	1.00	.80
2481	45¢ Pumpkinseed Sunfish (1992)	2.00	4.50	135.00(100)	7.00	1.25	.75
2482	$2 Bobcat	6.00	14.00	105.00(20)	25.00	5.50	1.00
2483	20¢ Blue Jay, bklt single (1991)	1.95	....	....	....	.85	.30
2483a	same, bklt pane of 10	9.00	....	....	....	8.25	....
2483av	same, bklt pane, unfolded	....	....	....	....	9.00	....

2484, 2485 2486 2487, 2493, 2495 2488, 2494, 2495A

2489 2490 2491 2492

SCOTT NO.	DESCRIPTION	FIRST DAY COVERS SING	FIRST DAY COVERS PL. BLK.	MINT SHEET	PLATE BLOCK	UNUSED F/NH	USED
2484	29¢ Wood Duck, bklt single (BEP) (1991)	2.25	....	....	....	.95	.20
2484a	same, bklt pane of 10 (BEP)	9.00	....	....	....	8.00	....
2484av	same, bklt pane, unfolded	....	....	....	....	11.00	....
2485	29¢ Wood Duck, bklt single (KCS) (1991)	2.25	....	....	....	1.00	.20
2485a	same, bklt pane of 10 (KCS)	9.00	....	....	....	9.75	....
2485av	same, bklt pane, unfolded	....	....	....	....	12.50	....
2486	29¢ African Violet, bklt single	2.25	....	....	....	1.10	.20
2486a	same, bklt pane of 10	9.00	....	....	....	8.75	....
2486av	same, bklt pane, unfolded	....	....	....	....	9.75	....
2487	32¢ Peach, bklt single	1.95	....	....	....	1.00	.25
2488	32¢ Pear, bklt single .	1.95	....	....	....	1.00	.25
2488a	32¢ Peach & Pear, bklt pane of 10	7.25	....	....	....	9.50	....
2488av	same, bklt pane, unfolded	....	....	....	....	10.75	....
2489	29¢ Red Squirrel, self-adhesive (1993) .	2.25	....	....	....	.95	.45
2489a	same, bklt pane of 18	13.50	....	....	....	15.00	....
2489v	same, coil	....	....	....	3.00(3)	.95	....
2490	29¢ Rose, self-adhesive (1993)	2.25	....	....	....	.95	.40
2490a	same, bklt pane of 18	13.50	....	....	....	15.00	....
2491	29¢ Pine Cone, self-adhesive	2.25	....	....	....	.95	.40
2491a	same, bklt pane of 18	13.50	....	....	....	15.00	....
2492	32¢ Pink Rose, self-adhesive	1.95	....	....	....	.95	.30
2492a	same, bklt pane of 20	14.50	....	....	....	16.00	....
2492b	same, bklt pane of 15	11.50	....	....	....	13.00	....
2493	32¢ Peach, self-adhesive	1.95	....	....	....	.95	.30
2494	32¢ Pear, self-adhesive	1.95	....	....	....	.95	.30
2494a	32¢ Peach & Pear, self-adhesive, bklt pane of 20	14.50	....	....	....	16.00	....
2495	32¢ Peach, self-adhesive coil (1993)	1.95	....	....	7.00(3)	3.00	....
2495A	32¢ Pear, self-adhesive coil	1.95	....	....	....	3.00	....

2496 2497

2498 2499

2500

SCOTT NO.	DESCRIPTION	FIRST DAY COVERS SING	FIRST DAY COVERS PL. BLK.	MINT SHEET	PLATE BLOCK	UNUSED F/NH	USED
2496-2500	Olympians, strip of 5, attached	7.50	10.00	38.00(35)	13.00(10)	7.00	5.00
2496	25¢ Jesse Owens . .	2.40	....	....	....	1.75	.50
2497	25¢ Ray Ewry	2.40	....	....	....	1.75	.50
2498	25¢ Hazel Wightman	2.40	....	....	....	1.75	.50
2499	25¢ Eddie Eagan . . .	2.40	....	....	....	1.75	.50
2500	25¢ Helene Madison .	2.40	....	....	....	1.75	.50

2501

2502

2503

2504

2505

SCOTT NO.	DESCRIPTION	FIRST DAY COVERS SING	FIRST DAY COVERS PL. BLK.	MINT SHEET	PLATE BLOCK	UNUSED F/NH	USED
2501	25¢ Assiniboine	2.40	....	....	....	2.00	.25
2502	25¢ Cheyenne	2.40	....	....	....	2.00	.25
2503	25¢ Comanche	2.40	....	....	....	2.00	.25
2504	25¢ Flathead	2.40	....	....	....	2.00	.25
2505	25¢ Shoshone	2.40	....	....	....	2.00	.25
2505a	25¢ bklt pane of 10 . .	7.85	....	....	....	13.00	....
2505av	same, bklt pane, unfolded	....	....	....	....	20.00	....

2506 2507

SCOTT NO.	DESCRIPTION	FIRST DAY COVERS SING	FIRST DAY COVERS PL. BLK.	MINT SHEET	PLATE BLOCK	UNUSED F/NH	USED
2506-07	Micronesia + Marshall Islands 2 varieties, attached .	5.00	6.00	48.00(50)	5.00	2.00	1.30
2506	25¢ Micronesia	2.50	....	....	....	1.00	.25
2507	25¢ Marshall Islands .	2.50	....	....	....	1.00	.25

2508 2509

2510 2511

1990 REGULAR ISSUES

SCOTT NO.	DESCRIPTION	FIRST DAY COVERS SING	FIRST DAY COVERS PL. BLK.	MINT SHEET	PLATE BLOCK	UNUSED F/NH	USED
2508-11	Sea Creatures, ... 4 varieties, attached .	5.00	6.00	40.00(40)	6.00	5.50	4.00
2508	25¢ Killer Whales . . .	2.50	....	....	....	1.25	.25
2509	25¢ Northern Sea Lions	2.50	....	....	....	1.25	.25
2510	25¢ Sea Otter	2.50	....	....	....	1.25	.25
2511	25¢ Common Dolphin	2.50	....	....	....	1.25	.25

2512

2513

2514

2515, 2516

SCOTT NO.	DESCRIPTION	FIRST DAY COVERS SING	FIRST DAY COVERS PL. BLK.	MINT SHEET	PLATE BLOCK	UNUSED F/NH	USED
2512	25¢ Americas Issue (Grand Canyon)	2.25	4.00	40.00(50)	4.25	1.25	.20
2513	25¢ Dwight D. Eisenhower	2.25	4.00	43.00(40)	6.00	1.25	.20
2514	25¢ Madonna & Child–Antonello	2.25	4.00	32.50(50)	3.25	.85	.15
2514a	same, bklt pane of 10	6.50	....	....	....	8.00	....
2514av	same, bklt pane, unfolded	....	....	....	....	15.00	....
2515	25¢ Christmas Tree .	2.25	4.00	32.50(50)	3.25	.75	.15
2516	25¢ Christmas Tree bklt single	2.25	....	....	....	1.50	.15
2516a	same, bklt pane of 10	6.00	....	....	....	12.00	....
2516av	same, bklt pane, unfolded	....	....	....	....	19.50	....

2517- 2519, 2520

1991 REGULAR ISSUES

SCOTT NO.	DESCRIPTION	FIRST DAY COVERS SING	FIRST DAY COVERS PL. BLK.	MINT SHEET	PLATE BLOCK	UNUSED F/NH	USED
2517	(29¢) 'F' Flower.	2.25	4.25	85.00(100)	4.25	.95	.15
			PLATE # STRIP 3		PLATE# STRIP 3		
2518	(29¢) "F" Flower, coil .	2.25	10.00	....	4.25	.85	.15
2519	(29¢) "F" Flower, bklt single (BEP)	2.25	....	....	....	1.00	.15
2519a	same, bklt pane of 10 (BEP)	6.50	....	....	....	10.00	....
2520	(29¢) "F" Flower, bklt single (KCS)	3.00	....	....	....	3.50	.70
2520a	same, bklt pane of 10 (KCS)	6.50	....	....	....	27.50	....

2521

2522

SCOTT NO.	DESCRIPTION	FIRST DAY COVERS SING	FIRST DAY COVERS PL. BLK.	MINT SHEET	PLATE BLOCK	UNUSED F/NH	USED
2521	(4¢) "F" Make-up Rate	2.25	4.25	15.00(100)	1.00	.20	.15
2522	(29¢) "F" ATM Plastic Stamp, single	2.25	....	....	....	1.75	.50
2522a	same, pane of 12 . . .	9.00	....	....	....	18.00	....

2523, 2523A

SCOTT NO.	DESCRIPTION	FIRST DAY COVERS SING	PLATE# STRIP 3	MINT SHEET	PLATE# STRIP 3	UNUSED F/NH	USED
2523	29¢ Flag over Mt. Rushmore, coil.	2.25	10.00	....	6.00	1.20	.15
2523A	29¢ Falg over Mt. Rushmore, photogravure coil . .	2.25	10.00	....	6.00	1.20	1.00

NOTE: **For plate number strips of 5, see page 149**

2524-27

SCOTT NO.	DESCRIPTION	FIRST DAY COVERS SING	FIRST DAY COVERS PL. BLK.	MINT SHEET	PLATE BLOCK	UNUSED F/NH	USED
2524	29¢ Flower	2.25	4.25	77.50(100)	4.50	1.00	.15
2524A	29¢ Flower, perf. 13 .	....	....	100.00(100)	6.00	1.20	.50
			PLATE# STRIP 3		PLATE# STRIP 3		
2525	29¢ Flower, coil rouletted	2.25	10.00	....	5.50	1.00	.20
2526	29¢ Flower, coil, perf (1992)	2.25	10.00	....	5.50	1.00	.25
2527	29¢ Flower, bklt single	2.25	....	....	....	1.00	.20
2527a	same, bklt pane of 10	6.50	....	....	....	9.50	....
2527av	same, bklt pane, unfolded	....	....	....	....	9.75	....

2528

2529, 2529C

2530

2531

2531A

SCOTT NO.	DESCRIPTION	FIRST DAY COVERS SING	PLATE# STRIP 3	MINT SHEET	PLATE# STRIP3	UNUSED F/NH	USED
2528	29¢ Flag with Olympic Rings, bklt single	2.25	....	....	....	1.00	.15
2528a	same, bklt pane of 10	6.50	....	....	....	10.00	....
2528av	same, bklt pane, unfolded	....	....	....	....	9.00	....
2529	19¢ Fishing Boat Type I	2.25	10.00	....	4.50	.60	.15
2529a	same, Type II (1993) .	....	....	....	4.50	.60	.40
2529C	19¢ Fishing Boat (reengraved)	2.25	10.00	....	7.00	1.10	.40
2530	19¢ Hot-Air Balloon bklt single	2.25	....	....	....	.60	.25
2530a	same, bklt pane of 10	10.00	....	....	....	5.50	.20
2530av	same, bklt pane, unfolded	....	....	....	....	7.00	....
2531	29¢ Flags on Parade	2.25	4.25	95.00(100)	5.00	1.00	.20
2531A	29¢ Liberty Torch ATM Stamp	2.25	....	....	....	1.10	.30
2531Ab	same, pane of 18 . . .	15.00	....	....	....	20.00	....

2532

1991 COMMEMORATIVES

SCOTT NO.	DESCRIPTION	FIRST DAY COVERS SING	FIRST DAY COVERS PL. BLK.	MINT SHEET	PLATE BLOCK	UNUSED F/NH	USED
2532/2579	**(2532-35, 2537-38, 2550-51, 2553-61, 2567, 2578-79) 29 varieties . . . . . .**	**........**	**........**	**........**	**........**	**30.50**	**11.50**
2532	50¢ Switzerland	2.25	5.00	65.00(40)	7.50	1.75	.40

2533

2534

2535, 2536

2537

2538

2539

SCOTT NO.	DESCRIPTION	FIRST DAY COVERS SING	FIRST DAY COVERS PL. BLK.	MINT SHEET	PLATE BLOCK	UNUSED F/NH	USED
2533	29¢ Vermont Statehood	2.25	4.25	70.00(50)	7.50	1.50	.20
2534	29¢ Savings Bonds . .	2.25	4.25	45.00(50)	4.50	1.00	.20
2535	29¢ Love	2.25	4.25	38.00(50)	4.00	1.00	.20
2536	29¢ Love, bklt single	2.25	....	....	....	1.00	.20
2536a	same, bklt pane of 10	6.50	....	....	....	8.50	....
2536av	same, bklt pane, unfolded	....	....	....	....	9.50	....
2537	52¢ Love	2.25	5.00	80.00(50)	7.00	1.50	.35
2538	29¢ William Saroyan .	2.25	4.25	37.00(50)	3.75	1.00	.20
2539	$1 USPS/Olympic Rings	3.00	6.50	55.00(20)	12.75	2.75	1.50

2540

SCOTT NO.	DESCRIPTION	FIRST DAY COVERS SING	FIRST DAY COVERS PL. BLK.	MINT SHEET	PLATE BLOCK	UNUSED F/NH	USED
2540	$2.90 Eagle and Olympic Rings	10.00	16.50	185.00(20)	40.00	12.00	5.50

2541

2542

SCOTT NO.	DESCRIPTION	FIRST DAY COVERS SING	FIRST DAY COVERS PL. BLK.	MINT SHEET	PLATE BLOCK	UNUSED F/NH	USED
2541	$9.95 Express Mail . .	27.00	50.00	500.00(20)	120.00	27.00	11.00
2542	$14.00 Express Mail .	35.00	67.50	650.00(20)	140.00	35.00	22.00

2543

2544

2544A

SCOTT NO.	DESCRIPTION	FIRST DAY COVERS SING	FIRST DAY COVERS PL. BLK.	MINT SHEET	PLATE BLOCK	UNUSED F/NH	USED
2543	$2.90 Space Vechicle, priority mail	8.00	17.50	375.00(40)	45.00	10.00	2.75
2544	$3 Challenger Shuttle, priority mail (1995) . .	8.00	17.50	140.00(20)	32.50	7.50	3.00
2544A	$10.75 Endeavour Shuttle, express mail (1995) .	27.50	57.50	575.00(20)	130.00	30.00	10.00

2545

2546

2547

2548

2549

SCOTT NO.	DESCRIPTION	FIRST DAY COVERS SING	FIRST DAY COVERS PL. BLK.	MINT SHEET	PLATE BLOCK	UNUSED F/NH	USED
2545	29¢ "Royal Wulff" . . .	2.25	....	....	....	2.00	.25
2546	29¢ "Jock Scott"	2.25	....	....	....	2.00	.25
2547	29¢ "Apte Tarpon" . . .	2.25	....	....	....	2.00	.25
2548	29¢ "Lefty's Deceiver"	2.25	....	....	....	2.00	.25
2549	29¢ "Muddler Minnow"	2.25	....	....	....	2.00	.25
2549a	Fishing Flies, bklt pane, 5 varieties, attached .	4.50	....	....	....	11.00	9.00
2549av	same, bklt pane, unfolded	....	....	....	....	16.00	....

2550

2551, 2552

SCOTT NO.	DESCRIPTION	FIRST DAY COVERS SING	FIRST DAY COVERS PL. BLK.	MINT SHEET	PLATE BLOCK	UNUSED F/NH	USED
2550	29¢ Cole Porter	2.25	4.25	50.00(50)	4.50	1.10	.25
2551	29¢ Desert Storm . . .	2.25	4.25	50.00(50)	4.50	1.10	.25
2552	29¢ Desert Storm, bklt single	2.25	....	....	....	2.50	.25
2552a	same, bklt pane of 5 .	4.75	....	....	....	5.50	....
2552av	same, bklt pane, unfolded	....	....	....	....	7.50	....

2553

2554

2555

2556

2557

2558

SCOTT NO.	DESCRIPTION	FIRST DAY COVERS SING	FIRST DAY COVERS PL. BLK.	MINT SHEET	PLATE BLOCK	UNUSED F/NH	USED
2553-57	Summer Olympics, 5 varieties, attached .	4.50	....	35.00(40)	10.50(10)	5.00	4.00
2553	29¢ Pole Vault	2.25	....	....	....	1.10	.30
2554	29¢ Discus	2.25	....	....	....	1.10	.30
2555	29¢ Sprinters	2.25	....	....	....	1.10	.30
2556	29¢ Javelin	2.25	....	....	....	1.10	.30
2557	29¢ Hurdles	2.25	....	....	....	1.10	.30
2558	29¢ Numismatics . . .	2.25	4.25	45.00(50)	4.50	1.00	.30

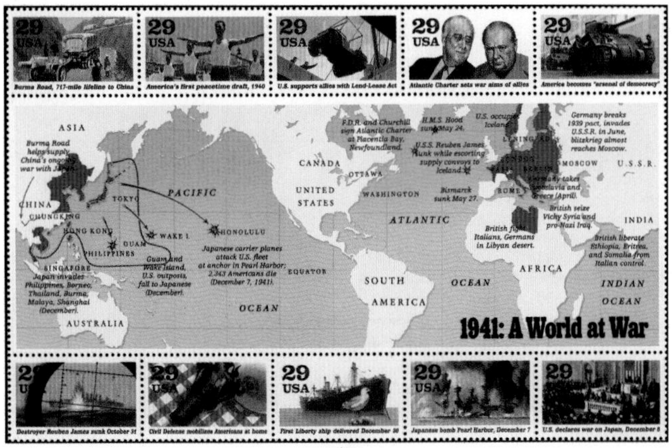

2559

SCOTT NO.	DESCRIPTION	FIRST DAY COVERS SING	FIRST DAY COVERS PL. BLK.	MINT SHEET	PLATE BLOCK	UNUSED F/NH	USED
2559	$2.90 World War II, 1941, souvenir sheet of 10 .	14.00	....	27.00(20)	....	13.50	11.00
2559a	29¢ Burma Road	3.00	....	....	....	1.35	.75
2559b	29¢ Peacetime Draft .	3.00	....	....	....	1.35	.75
2559c	29¢ Lend-Lease Act .	3.00	....	....	....	1.35	.75
2559d	29¢ Atlantic Charter .	3.00	....	....	....	1.35	.75
2559e	29¢ "Arsenal of Democracy"	3.00	....	....	....	1.35	.75
2559f	29¢ Destroyer "Reuben James"	3.00	....	....	....	1.35	.75
2559g	29¢ Civil Defense . . .	3.00	....	....	....	1.35	.75
2559h	29¢ Liberty Ship	3.00	....	....	....	1.35	.75
2559i	29¢ Pearl Harbor . . .	3.00	....	....	....	1.35	.75
2559j	29¢ Declaration of War on Japan	3.00	....	....	....	1.35	.75

2560

SCOTT NO.	DESCRIPTION	FIRST DAY COVERS SING	FIRST DAY COVERS PL. BLK.	MINT SHEET	PLATE BLOCK	UNUSED F/NH	USED
2560	29¢ Basketball	3.00	4.50	48.00(50)	4.75	1.50	.25

2561

SCOTT NO.	DESCRIPTION	FIRST DAY COVERS SING	FIRST DAY COVERS PL. BLK.	MINT SHEET	PLATE BLOCK	UNUSED F/NH	USED
2561	29¢ District of Columbia	2.25	4.25	36.00(50)	3.75	1.00	.25

2562

2563

2564

2565

2566

SCOTT NO.	DESCRIPTION	FIRST DAY COVERS SING	FIRST DAY COVERS PL. BLK.	MINT SHEET	PLATE BLOCK	UNUSED F/NH	USED
2562	29¢ Laurel and Hardy	2.25	....	....	....	1.00	.35
2563	29¢ Bergen and McCarthy	2.25	....	....	....	1.00	.35
2564	29¢ Jack Benny	2.25	....	....	....	1.00	.35
2565	29¢ Fanny Brice	2.25	....	....	....	1.00	.35
2566	29¢ Abbott and Costello	2.25	....	....	....	1.00	.35
2566a	Comedians, bklt pane of 10	8.00	....	....	....	10.00	8.00
2566av	same, bklt pane, unfolded	....	....	....	....	12.50	....

2567

SCOTT NO.	DESCRIPTION	FIRST DAY COVERS SING	FIRST DAY COVERS PL. BLK.	MINT SHEET	PLATE BLOCK	UNUSED F/NH	USED
2567	29¢ Jan Matzeliger . .	2.25	4.25	40.00(50)	4.75	1.20	.25

2568

2569

2570

2571

2572

2573

2574

2575

2576

2577

SCOTT NO.	DESCRIPTION	FIRST DAY COVERS SING	FIRST DAY COVERS PL. BLK.	MINT SHEET	PLATE BLOCK	UNUSED F/NH	USED
2568	29¢ Mercury and Mariner 10	2.25	....	....	....	2.00	.40
2569	29¢ Venus and Mariner 2	2.25	....	....	....	2.00	.40
2570	29¢ Earth and Landsat	2.25	....	....	....	2.00	.40
2571	29¢ Moon and Lunar Orbiter	2.25	....	....	....	2.00	.40
2572	29¢ Mars and Viking Orbiter	2.25	....	....	....	2.00	.40
2573	29¢ Jupiter and Pioneer 11	2.25	....	....	....	2.00	.40
2574	29¢ Saturn and Voyager 2	2.25	....	....	....	2.00	.40
2575	29¢ Uranus and Voyager 2	2.25	....	....	....	2.00	.40
2576	29¢ Neptune and Voyager 2	2.25	....	....	....	2.00	.40
2577	29¢ Pluto, "Not Yet Explored" . .	2.25	....	....	....	2.00	.40
2577a	Space Explorations, bklt pane of 10	9.00	....	....	....	17.00	12.00
2577av	same, bklt pane, unfolded	....	....	....	....	19.00	....

2578

2579-81

2582

2583

2584

2585

SCOTT NO.	DESCRIPTION	FIRST DAY COVERS SING	FIRST DAY COVERS PL. BLK.	MINT SHEET	PLATE BLOCK	UNUSED F/NH	USED
2578	(29¢) Christmas– Traditional	2.25	4.25	40.00(50)	4.00	1.00	.20
2578a	same, bklt pane of 10	7.00	....	....	....	8.00	....
2578av	same, bklt pane, unfolded	....	....	....	....	10.50	....
2579	(29¢) Christmas– Contemporary	2.25	4.25	40.00(50)	4.00	.80	.20
2580-85	(29¢) Santa & Chimney set of 6 singles	12.00	....	....	....	12.50	3.00
2581b-85a	same, bklt pane of 4	....	....	....	....	25.00	....
2581-85av	same, bklt pane of 4, unfolded	20.00	....	....	....	32.50	....

NOTE: **The far left brick from the top row of the chimney is missing from Type II, No. 2581**

2587

2590

1992-95 Regular Issues

SCOTT NO.	DESCRIPTION	FIRST DAY COVERS SING	FIRST DAY COVERS PL. BLK.	MINT SHEET	PLATE BLOCK	UNUSED F/NH	USED
2587	32¢ James K. Polk (1995)	1.95	4.75	80.00(100)	4.50	1.00	.25
2590	$1 "Surrender at Saratoga" (1994)	4.00	6.50	50.00(20)	12.50	3.00	1.00

2592

SCOTT NO.	DESCRIPTION	FIRST DAY COVERS SING	FIRST DAY COVERS PL. BLK.	MINT SHEET	PLATE BLOCK	UNUSED F/NH	USED
2592	$5 Washington & Jackson (1994)	22.00	30.00	275.00(20)	60.00	14.00	4.00

2593, 2594

SCOTT NO.	DESCRIPTION	FIRST DAY COVERS SING	FIRST DAY COVERS PL. BLK.	MINT SHEET	PLATE BLOCK	UNUSED F/NH	USED
2593	29¢ Pledge of Allegiance (black) bklt single . . .	2.25	....	....	....	1.00	.15
2593a	same, bklt pane of 10	7.00	....	....	....	9.50	....
2593av	same, bklt pane, unfolded	....	....	....	....	10.50	....
2594	29¢ Pledge of Allegiance (red) bklt single (1993)	2.25	....	....	....	1.50	.15
2594a	same, bklt pane of 10	7.00	....	....	....	15.00	....
2594av	same, bklt pane, unfolded	....	....	....	....	10.50	....

2595-97

2598

2599

1992-94 Self-Adhesive Stamps

SCOTT NO.	DESCRIPTION	FIRST DAY COVERS SING	FIRST DAY COVERS PL. BLK.	MINT SHEET	PLATE BLOCK	UNUSED F/NH	USED
2595	29¢ Eagle & Shield (brown) bklt single . . .	2.25	....	....	....	1.20	.30
2595a	same, bklt pane of 17	12.00	....	....	....	16.50	....
2595v	same, coil	2.50	....	....	....	1.20	.30
2596	29¢ Eagle & Shield (green) bklt single . . .	1.75	....	....	....	1.20	.30
2596a	same, bklt pane of 17	12.00	....	....	....	16.50	....
2596v	same, coil	2.50	....	....	....	1.20	.30
2597	29¢ Eagle & Shield (red) bklt single	2.25	....	....	....	1.20	.30
2597a	same, bklt pane of 17	12.00	....	....	....	16.50	....
2597v	same, coil	2.50	....	....	....	1.20	.30
2598	29¢ Eagle (1994) . . .	2.25	....	....	....	1.20	.30
2598a	same, bklt pane of 18	13.50	....	....	....	16.50	....
2598v	29¢ Eagle, coil	2.50	....	....	5.00(3)	1.20	....
2599	29¢ Statue of Liberty (1994)	2.25	....	....	....	1.20	.30
2599a	same, bklt pane of 18	13.50	....	....	....	16.50	....
2599v	29¢ Statue of Liberty, coil	2.50	....	....	5.00(3)	1.20	....

2602

2603, 2604

2605

2606-08

2609

1991-93 Regular Issue

SCOTT NO.	DESCRIPTION	FIRST DAY COVERS SING	PLATE# STRIP 3	MINT SHEET	PLATE# STRIP 3	UNUSED F/NH	USED
2602	(10¢) Eagle, Bulk-Rate coil	2.25	10.00	....	3.75	.30	.20
2603	(10¢) Eagle, Bulk-Rate coil (orange-yellow) (BEP)	2.25	10.00	....	4.25	.30	.20
2604	(10¢) Eagle, Bulk-Rate coil (Stamp Ventures) (gold) (1993)	2.25	10.00	....	3.00	.40	.20
2605	23¢ Flag, Presort First-Class	2.25	10.00	....	5.00	.70	.30
2606	23¢ USA, Presort First-Class (ABN) (1992)	2.25	10.00	....	5.75	.70	.30
2607	23¢ USA, Presort First-Class (BEP) (1992)	2.25	10.00	....	5.75	.75	.30
2608	23¢ USA, Presort First-Class (Stamp Ventures) (1993)	2.25	10.00	....	5.75	1.00	.30
2609	29¢ Flag over White House, coil (1992)	2.25	10.00	....	6.00	1.20	.15

NOTE: **For plate number strips of 5, see page 149**

2611

2612

2613

2614

2615

1992 COMMEMORATIVES

SCOTT NO.	DESCRIPTION	FIRST DAY COVERS SING	FIRST DAY COVERS PL. BLK.	MINT SHEET	PLATE BLOCK	UNUSED F/NH	USED
2611/2720	**(2611-23, 2630-41, 2697-2704, 2710-14, 2720) 48 varieties . . . . . .**	....	....	....	....	**50.00**	**16.50**
2611-15	Winter Olympics, 5 varieties, attached .	6.00	....	36.00(35)	10.50(10)	5.00	4.00
2611	29¢ Hockey	2.25	....	....	....	1.30	.25
2612	29¢ Figure Skating . .	2.25	....	....	....	1.30	.25
2613	29¢ Speed Skating . .	2.25	....	....	....	1.30	.25
2614	29¢ Skiing	2.25	....	....	....	1.30	.25
2615	29¢ Bobsledding	2.25	....	....	....	1.30	.25

2616

2617

SCOTT NO.	DESCRIPTION	FIRST DAY COVERS SING	FIRST DAY COVERS PL. BLK.	MINT SHEET	PLATE BLOCK	UNUSED F/NH	USED
2616	29¢ World Columbian Expo	2.25	4.25	42.00(50)	4.50	1.50	.25
2617	29¢ W.E.B. Du Bois .	3.00	4.25	50.00(50)	5.50	1.50	.25

2618

2619

SCOTT NO.	DESCRIPTION	FIRST DAY COVERS SING	FIRST DAY COVERS PL. BLK.	MINT SHEET	PLATE BLOCK	UNUSED F/NH	USED
2618	29¢ Love	2.25	4.25	37.50(50)	3.75	.85	.25
2619	29¢ Olympic Baseball	3.75	5.50	57.50(50)	5.50	1.25	.25

2620 2621

2622 2623

SCOTT NO.	DESCRIPTION	FIRST DAY COVERS SING	FIRST DAY COVERS PL. BLK.	MINT SHEET	PLATE BLOCK	UNUSED F/NH	USED
2620-23	First Voyage of Columbus	4.00	5.00	37.50(40)	5.25	4.25	4.00
2620	29¢ Seeking Isabella's Support	2.25	....	....	....	1.25	.25
2621	29¢ Crossing the Atlantic	2.25	....	....	....	1.25	.25
2622	29¢ Approaching Land	2.25	....	....	....	1.25	.25
2623	29¢ Coming Ashore .	2.25	....	....	....	1.25	.25

2624

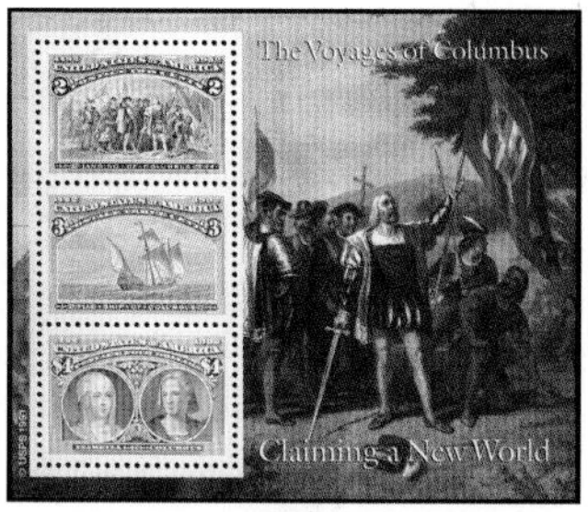

2625

2626

2627

2628

2629

SCOTT NO.	DESCRIPTION	FIRST DAY COVERS SING	FIRST DAY COVERS PL. BLK.	MINT SHEET	PLATE BLOCK	UNUSED F/NH	USED
2624-29	1¢-$5 Columbian Souvenir Sheets (6) .	55.00	....	....	....	45.00	40.00
2624a-29a	same, set of 16 singles	105.00	....	....	....	42.00	37.00

2630

SCOTT NO.	DESCRIPTION	FIRST DAY COVERS SING	FIRST DAY COVERS PL. BLK.	MINT SHEET	PLATE BLOCK	UNUSED F/NH	USED
2630	29¢ NY Stock Exchange	4.00	6.00	28.50(40)	3.75	.75	.25

2631 2632 2633 2634

SCOTT NO.	DESCRIPTION	FIRST DAY COVERS SING	FIRST DAY COVERS PL. BLK.	MINT SHEET	PLATE BLOCK	UNUSED F/NH	USED
2631-34	Space, US/Russian Joint Issue	4.00	5.00	45.00(50)	5.50	5.00	3.50
2631	29¢ Cosmonaut & Space Shuttle	2.50	....	....	....	1.30	.30
2632	29¢ Astronaut & Mir Space Station	2.50	....	....	....	1.30	.30
2633	29¢ Apollo Lunar Module & Sputnik	2.50	....	....	....	1.30	.30
2634	29¢ Soyuz, Mercury & Gemini Space Craft . .	2.50	....	....	....	1.30	.30

2635

2636

SCOTT NO.	DESCRIPTION	FIRST DAY COVERS SING	FIRST DAY COVERS PL. BLK.	MINT SHEET	PLATE BLOCK	UNUSED F/NH	USED
2635	29¢ Alaska Highway .	2.25	4.75	37.50(50)	3.75	1.20	.25
2636	29¢ Kentucky Statehood	2.25	4.75	37.50(50)	3.75	1.20	.25

2637

2638

2639

2640

2641

2642

2643

2644

2645

2646

SCOTT NO.	DESCRIPTION	FIRST DAY COVERS SING	FIRST DAY COVERS PL. BLK.	MINT SHEET	PLATE BLOCK	UNUSED F/NH	USED
2637-41	Summer Olympics, 5 varieties, attached .	5.50	....	32.50(35)	10.50(10)	5.00	3.50
2637	29¢ Soccer	2.25	....	....	....	1.30	.50
2638	29¢ Women's Gymnastics	2.25	....	....	....	1.30	.50
2639	29¢ Volleyball	2.25	....	....	....	1.30	.50
2640	29¢ Boxing	2.25	....	....	....	1.30	.50
2641	29¢ Swimming	2.25	....	....	....	1.30	.50
2642	29¢ Ruby-throated Hummingbird	2.25	....	....	....	1.30	.50
2643	29¢ Broad-billed Hummingbird	2.25	....	....	....	1.30	.50
2644	29¢ Costa's Hummingbird	2.25	....	....	....	1.30	.50
2645	29¢ Rufous Hummingbird	2.25	....	....	....	1.30	.50
2646	29¢ Calliope Hummingbird	2.25	....	....	....	1.30	.50
2646a	29¢ Hummingbirds, bklt pane, 5 vareities, attached .	5.00	....	....	....	5.00	....
2646av	same, bklt pane, unfolded	....	....	....	....	6.00	....

2647

2648

2649

1992 WILDFLOWERS

2647 *Indian Paintbrush*
2648 *Fragrant Water Lily*
2649 *Meadow Beauty*
2650 *Jack-in-the-Pulpit*
2651 *California Poppy*
2652 *Large-Flowered Trillium*
2653 *Tickseed*
2654 *Shooting Star*
2655 *Stream Violet*
2656 *Bluets*
2657 *Herb Robert*
2658 *Marsh Marigold*
2659 *Sweet White Violet*
2660 *Claret Cup Cactus*
2661 *White Mountain Avens*
2662 *Sessile Bellwort*
2663 *Blue Flag*
2664 *Harlequin Lupine*
2665 *Twinflower*
2666 *Common Sunflower*
2667 *Sego Lily*
2668 *Virginia Bluebells*
2669 *Ohi'a Lehua*
2670 *Rosebud Orchid*
2671 *Showy Evening Primrose*
2672 *Fringed Gentian*
2673 *Yellow Lady's Slipper*
2674 *Passionflower*
2675 *Bunchberry*
2676 *Pasqueflower*
2677 *Round-lobed Hepatica*
2678 *Wild Columbine*
2679 *Fireweed*
2680 *Indian Pond Lily*
2681 *Turk's Cap Lily*
2682 *Dutchman's Breeches*
2683 *Trumpet Honeysuckle*
2684 *Jacob's Ladder*
2685 *Plains Prickly Pear*
2686 *Moss Campion*
2687 *Bearberry*
2688 *Mexican Hat*
2689 *Harebell*
2690 *Desert Five Spot*
2691 *Smooth Solomon's Seal*
2692 *Red Maids*
2693 *Yellow Skunk Cabbage*
2694 *Rue Anemone*
2695 *Standing Cypress*
2696 *Wild Flax*

SCOTT NO.	DESCRIPTION	FIRST DAY COVERS SING	FIRST DAY COVERS PL. BLK.	MINT SHEET	PLATE BLOCK	UNUSED F/NH	USED
2647-96	29¢ Wildflowers, 50 varieties, attached	70.00	....	60.00(50)	....	60.00	....
	set of singles	86.00	....	....	....	....	27.50
	singles of above, each	1.75	....	....	....	1.50	.75

2697

SCOTT NO.	DESCRIPTION	FIRST DAY COVERS SING	FIRST DAY COVERS PL. BLK.	MINT SHEET	PLATE BLOCK	UNUSED F/NH	USED
2697	$2.90 World War II (1942) Souvenir Sheet of 10	12.00	....	27.00(20)	....	13.50	11.00
2697a	29¢ Tokyo Raid	2.50	....	....	....	1.35	.75
2697b	29¢ Commodity Rationing	2.50	....	....	....	1.35	.75
2697c	29¢ Battle of Coral Sea	2.50	....	....	....	1.35	.75
2697d	29¢ Fall of Corregidor	2.50	....	....	....	1.35	.75
2697e	29¢ Japan Invades Aleutians	2.50	....	....	....	1.35	.75
2697f	29¢ Allies Break Codes	2.50	....	....	....	1.35	.75
2697g	29¢ USS Yorktown Lost	2.50	....	....	....	1.35	.75
2697h	29¢ Women Join War Effort	2.50	....	....	....	1.35	.75
2697i	29¢ Marines on Guadalcanal	2.50	....	....	....	1.35	.75
2697j	29¢ Allies Land in North Africa	2.50	....	....	....	1.35	.75

2698

2699

SCOTT NO.	DESCRIPTION	FIRST DAY COVERS SING	FIRST DAY COVERS PL. BLK.	MINT SHEET	PLATE BLOCK	UNUSED F/NH	USED
2698	29¢ Dorothy Parker . .	2.25	4.75	40.00(50)	4.00	1.50	.25
2699	29¢ Dr. T. von Karman	2.25	4.75	40.00(50)	4.00	1.50	.25

2700

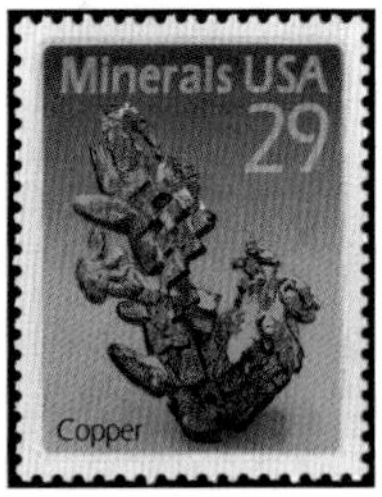

2701

2704

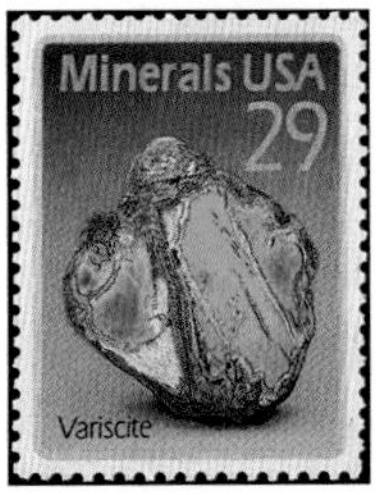

2702

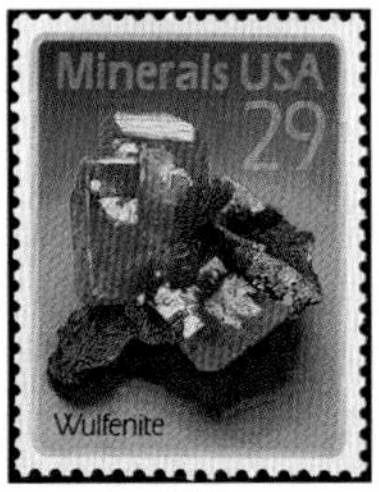

2703

SCOTT NO.	DESCRIPTION	FIRST DAY COVERS SING	FIRST DAY COVERS PL. BLK.	MINT SHEET	PLATE BLOCK	UNUSED F/NH	USED
2700-03	Minerals, 4 varieties, attached .	5.00	4.00	38.00(40)	4.75	4.25	3.00
2700	29¢ Azurite	2.25	....	....	....	1.20	.30
2701	29¢ Copper	2.25	....	....	....	1.20	.30
2702	29¢ Variscite	2.25	....	....	....	1.20	.30
2703	29¢ Wulfenite	2.25	....	....	....	1.20	.30
2704	29¢ Juan Rodriguez Cabrillo	2.25	4.75	36.00(50)	3.75	1.00	.25

2705

2706

2707

2708

2709

SCOTT NO.	DESCRIPTION	FIRST DAY COVERS SING	FIRST DAY COVERS PL. BLK.	MINT SHEET	PLATE BLOCK	UNUSED F/NH	USED
2705	29¢ Giraffe	2.25	....	....	....	1.10	.25
2706	29¢ Giant Panda	2.25	....	....	....	1.10	.25
2707	29¢ Flamingo	2.25	....	....	....	1.10	.25
2708	29¢ King Penguins . .	2.25	....	....	....	1.10	.25
2709	29¢ White Bengal Tiger	2.25	....	....	....	1.10	.25
2709a	29¢ Wild Animals, bklt pane of 5	5.00	....	....	....	5.00	4.50
2709av	same, bklt pane , unfolded	....	....	....	....	6.75	....

2710

SCOTT NO.	DESCRIPTION	FIRST DAY COVERS SING	FIRST DAY COVERS PL. BLK.	MINT SHEET	PLATE BLOCK	UNUSED F/NH	USED
2710	29¢ Christmas–Traditional	2.25	4.75	36.00(50)	3.75	1.00	.20
2710a	same, bklt pane of 10	9.00	....	....	....	7.75	....
2710av	same, bklt pane, unfolded	....	....	....	....	9.50	....

2711, 2715 2712, 2716, 2719

2713, 2717 2714, 2718

SCOTT NO.	DESCRIPTION	FIRST DAY COVERS SING	FIRST DAY COVERS PL. BLK.	MINT SHEET	PLATE BLOCK	UNUSED F/NH	USED
2711-14	Christmas Toys, 4 varieties, attached .	4.00	5.00	55.00(50)	4.75	5.50	4.50
2711	29¢ Hobby Horse . . .	2.25	....	....	....	1.50	.20
2712	29¢ Locomotive	2.25	....	....	....	1.50	.20
2713	29¢ Fire Engine	2.25	....	....	....	1.50	.20
2714	29¢ Steamboat	2.25	....	....	....	1.50	.20
2715	29¢ Hobby Horse (gravure) bklt single	2.25	....	....	....	1.50	.20
2716	29¢ Locomotive (gravure) bklt single	2.25	....	....	....	1.50	.20
2717	29¢ Fire Engine (gravure) bklt single	2.25	....	....	....	1.50	.20
2718	29¢ Steamboat (gravure) bklt single	2.25	....	....	....	1.50	.20
2718a	29¢ Christmas Toys (gravure) bklt pane of 4	9.00	....	....	....	6.50	5.50
2718av	same, bklt pane, unfolded	....	....	....	....	7.00	....
2719	29¢ Locomotive ATM, self-adhesive	2.25	....	....	....	1.20	.75
2719a	same, bklt pane of 18	13.50	....	....	....	21.00	....

2720

SCOTT NO.	DESCRIPTION	FIRST DAY COVERS SING	FIRST DAY COVERS PL. BLK.	MINT SHEET	PLATE BLOCK	UNUSED F/NH	USED
2720	29¢ Happy New Year	3.00	4.75	22.50(20)	5.50	1.20	.20

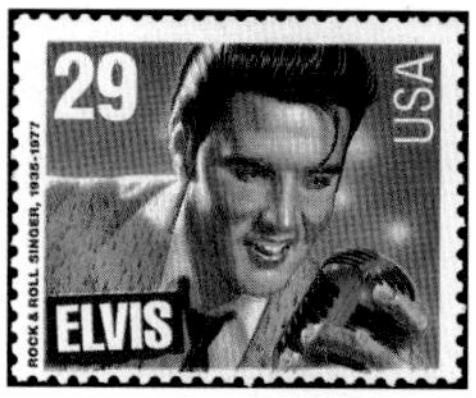

2721

2722

2723

1993 COMMEMORATIVES

SCOTT NO.	DESCRIPTION	FIRST DAY COVERS SING	FIRST DAY COVERS PL. BLK.	MINT SHEET	PLATE BLOCK	UNUSED F/NH	USED
2721/2806	**(2721-30, 2746-59, 2765-66, 2771-74, 2779-89, 2791-94, 2804-06) 57 varieties**	....	....	....	....	**68.50**	**21.50**
2721	29¢ Elvis Presley . . .	2.00	5.00	35.00(40)	4.50	1.00	.25
2722	29¢ "Oklahoma!"	2.25	4.75	28.50(40)	3.75	.85	.25
2723	29¢ Hank Williams . .	2.25	4.75	60.00(40)	7.00	2.00	.25
2723a	29¢ Hank Williams, perf. 11.2 x 11.4	....	....	950.00(40)	150.00	25.00	15.00

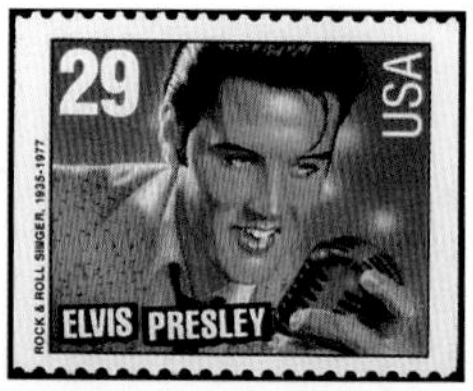

2724, 2731

2725, 2732

2726, 2733

2727, 2734

2728, 2735

2729, 2736

2730, 2737

SCOTT NO.	DESCRIPTION	FIRST DAY COVERS SING	FIRST DAY COVERS PL. BLK.	MINT SHEET	PLATE BLOCK	UNUSED F/NH	USED
2724-30	Rock & Roll/Rhythm & Blues, 7 varieties, attached .	12.00	....	45.00(35)	12.00(8)	10.00	7.50
2724-30	same, Top Plate Block of 10	....	....	....	16.00(10)	....	....
2724	29¢ Elvis Presley . . .	3.00	....	....	....	1.50	.50
2725	29¢ Bill Haley	3.00	....	....	....	1.50	.50
2726	29¢ Clyde McPhatter	3.00	....	....	....	1.50	.50
2727	29¢ Ritchie Valens . .	3.00	....	....	....	1.50	.50
2728	29¢ Otis Redding . . .	3.00	....	....	....	1.50	.50
2729	29¢ Buddy Holly	3.00	....	....	....	1.50	.50
2730	29¢ Dinah Washington	3.00	....	....	....	1.50	.50
2731	29¢ Elvis Presley, bklt single	3.00	....	....	....	1.25	.40
2732	29¢ Bill Haley, bklt single	3.00	....	....	....	1.25	.40
2733	29¢ Clyde McPhatter, bklt single	3.00	....	....	....	1.25	.40
2734	29¢ Ritchie Valens, bklt single	3.00	....	....	....	1.25	.40
2735	29¢ Otis Redding, bklt single	3.00	....	....	....	1.25	.40
2736	29¢ Buddy Holly, bklt single	3.00	....	....	....	1.25	.40
2737	29¢ Dinah Washington, bklt single	3.00	....	....	....	1.25	.40
2737a	same, bklt pane of 8 .	10.00	....	....	....	7.00	....
2737av	same, bklt pane, unfolded	....	....	....	....	9.00	....
2737b	same, bklt pane of 4 .	5.00	....	....	....	5.00	....
2737bv	same, bklt pane, unfolded	....	....	....	....	5.50	....

2741

2742

2743

2744

2745

SCOTT NO.	DESCRIPTION	FIRST DAY COVERS SING	FIRST DAY COVERS PL. BLK.	MINT SHEET	PLATE BLOCK	UNUSED F/NH	USED
2741	29¢ Saturn & 3 Rockets	2.25	....	....	....	1.00	.30
2742	29¢ 2 Flying Saucers	2.25	....	....	....	1.00	.30
2743	29¢ 3 Rocketeers . . .	2.25	....	....	....	1.00	.30
2744	29¢ Winged Spaceship	2.25	....	....	....	1.00	.30
2745	29¢ 3 Space Ships . .	2.25	....	....	....	1.00	.30
2745a	29¢ Space Fantasy, bklt pane of 5	4.50	....	....	....	4.75	4.00
2745av	same, bklt pane, unfolded	....	....	....	....	6.00	....

2746

2747

2748

2749

2752 2753

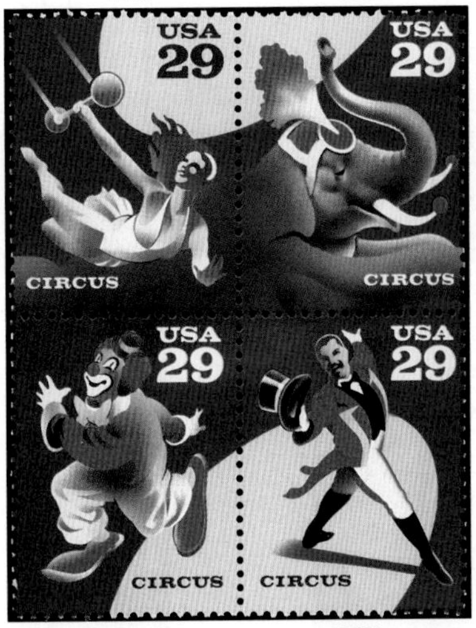

2750 2751

SCOTT NO.	DESCRIPTION	FIRST DAY COVERS SING	FIRST DAY COVERS PL. BLK.	MINT SHEET	PLATE BLOCK	UNUSED F/NH	USED
2746	29¢ Percy Lavon Julian	3.00	4.75	55.00(50)	5.00	1.00	.25
2747	29¢ Oregon Trail	2.25	4.75	60.00(50)	6.00	1.70	.25
2748	29¢ World University Games	2.25	4.75	38.00(50)	3.75	.85	.25
2749	29¢ Grace Kelly	3.00	4.75	38.00(50)	3.75	.85	.25
2750-53	Circus, 4 varieties, attached	5.00	6.00	42.50(40)	8.00(6)	5.00	4.00
2750	29¢ Clown	2.25	....	....	....	1.35	.30
2751	29¢ Ringmaster	2.25	....	....	....	1.35	.30
2752	29¢ Trapeze Artist . . .	2.25	....	....	....	1.35	.30
2753	29¢ Elephant	2.25	....	....	....	1.35	.30

2754

2755

SCOTT NO.	DESCRIPTION	FIRST DAY COVERS SING	FIRST DAY COVERS PL. BLK.	MINT SHEET	PLATE BLOCK	UNUSED F/NH	USED
2754	29¢ Cherokee Strip . .	2.25	4.75	15.50(20)	3.75	1.10	.25
2755	29¢ Dean Acheson . .	2.25	4.75	38.00(50)	3.75	1.10	.25

2756 2757

2758 2759

SCOTT NO.	DESCRIPTION	FIRST DAY COVERS SING	FIRST DAY COVERS PL. BLK.	MINT SHEET	PLATE BLOCK	UNUSED F/NH	USED
2756-59	Sporting Horses, 4 varieties, attached .	7.50	4.75	38.00(40)	5.00	4.50	3.50
2756	29¢ Steeplechase . . .	3.00	....	....	....	1.25	.60
2757	29¢ Thoroughbred . .	3.00	....	....	....	1.25	.60
2758	29¢ Harness	3.00	....	....	....	1.25	.60
2759	29¢ Polo	3.00	....	....	....	1.25	.60

2760

2761

2762

2763

2764

SCOTT NO.	DESCRIPTION	FIRST DAY COVERS SING	FIRST DAY COVERS PL. BLK.	MINT SHEET	PLATE BLOCK	UNUSED F/NH	USED
2760	29¢ Hyacinth	2.25	....	....	....	1.05	.30
2761	29¢ Daffodil	2.25	....	....	....	1.05	.30
2762	29¢ Tulip	2.25	....	....	....	1.05	.30
2763	29¢ Iris	2.25	....	....	....	1.05	.30
2764	29¢ Lilac	2.25	....	....	....	1.05	.30
2764a	Garden Flowers, bklt pane of 5	4.50	....	....	....	4.95	4.00
2764av	same, bklt pane, unfolded	....	....	....	....	6.00	....

2765

SCOTT NO.	DESCRIPTION	FIRST DAY COVERS SING	FIRST DAY COVERS PL. BLK.	MINT SHEET	PLATE BLOCK	UNUSED F/NH	USED
2765	$2.90 World War II, 1943, Souvenir Sheet of 10	12.00	....	27.00(20)	....	13.50	11.00
2765a	29¢ Allies battle U-boats	2.50	....	....	....	1.35	.75
2765b	29¢ Medics treat wounded	2.50	....	....	....	1.35	.75
2765c	29¢ Allies attack Sicily	2.50	....	....	....	1.35	.75
2765d	29¢ B-24's hit Ploesti refineries	2.50	....	....	....	1.35	.75
2765e	29¢ V-Mail	2.50	....	....	....	1.35	.75
2765f	29¢ Italy invaded by Allies	2.50	....	....	....	1.35	.75
2765g	29¢ Bonds and Stamps help	2.50	....	....	....	1.35	.75
2765h	29¢ "Willie and Joe" .	2.50	....	....	....	1.35	.75
2765i	29¢ Gold Stars	2.50	....	....	....	1.35	.75
2765j	29¢ Marines assault Tarawa	2.50	....	....	....	1.35	.75

2766

SCOTT NO.	DESCRIPTION	FIRST DAY COVERS SING	FIRST DAY COVERS PL. BLK.	MINT SHEET	PLATE BLOCK	UNUSED F/NH	USED
2766	29¢ Joe Louis	5.00	6.00	50.00(50)	5.50	1.50	.25

2767

2768

2769

2770

SCOTT NO.	DESCRIPTION	FIRST DAY COVERS SING	FIRST DAY COVERS PL. BLK.	MINT SHEET	PLATE BLOCK	UNUSED F/NH	USED
2767	29¢ "Show Boat"	2.50	....	....	....	1.75	.30
2768	29¢ "Porgy & Bess" . .	2.50	....	....	....	1.75	.30
2769	29¢ "Oklahoma!"	2.50	....	....	....	1.75	.30
2770	29¢ "My Fair Lady" . .	2.50	....	....	....	1.75	.30
2770a	Broadway Musicals, bklt pane of 4	6.00	....	....	....	7.50	....
2770av	same, bklt pane, unfolded	....	....	....	....	8.50	....

2771, 2775

2772, 2777

2773, 2776

2774, 2778

SCOTT NO.	DESCRIPTION	FIRST DAY COVERS SING	FIRST DAY COVERS PL. BLK.	MINT SHEET	PLATE BLOCK	UNUSED F/NH	USED
2771-74	Country Music, 4 varieties, attached .	6.00	7.00	25.00(20)	7.00	6.50	4.00
2771	29¢ Hank Williams . .	2.50	....	....	....	1.50	.35
2772	29¢ Patsy Cline	2.50	....	....	....	1.50	.35
2773	29¢ The Carter Family	2.50	....	....	....	1.50	.35
2774	29¢ Bob Wills	2.50	....	....	....	1.50	.35
2775	29¢ Hank Williams, bklt single	2.50	....	....	....	1.20	.30
2776	29¢ The Carter Family, bklt single	2.50	....	....	....	1.20	.30
2777	29¢ Patsy Cline, bklt single	2.50	....	....	....	1.20	.30
2778	29¢ Bob Wills, bklt single	2.50	....	....	....	1.20	.30
2778a	Country Music, bklt pane of 4	5.00	....	....	....	4.50	....
2778av	same, bklt pane, unfolded	....	....	....	....	5.00	....

2779 2780

2781 2782

2783

2784

SCOTT NO.	DESCRIPTION	FIRST DAY COVERS SING	FIRST DAY COVERS PL. BLK.	MINT SHEET	PLATE BLOCK	UNUSED F/NH	USED
2779-82	National Postal Museum, 4 varieties, attached .	4.00	5.00	25.00(20)	7.00	6.00	4.50
2779	29¢ Ben Franklin	2.25	....	....	....	1.50	.50
2780	29¢ Soldier & Drum . .	2.25	....	....	....	1.50	.50
2781	29¢ Lindbergh	2.25	....	....	....	1.50	.50
2782	29¢ Stamps & Bar Code	2.25	....	....	....	1.50	.50
2783-84	American Sign Language/ Deaf Communication, 2 varieties, attached .	2.50	4.75	17.00(20)	4.25	2.00	1.25
2783	29¢ Mother/Child . . .	2.25	....	....	....	1.10	.25
2784	29¢ Hand Sign	2.25	....	....	....	1.10	.25

2785 2786

2787 2788

SCOTT NO.	DESCRIPTION	FIRST DAY COVERS SING	FIRST DAY COVERS PL. BLK.	MINT SHEET	PLATE BLOCK	UNUSED F/NH	USED
2785-88	Youth Classics, 4 varieties, attached .	5.00	6.00	50.00(40)	7.00	6.00	4.50
2785	29¢ Rebecca of Sunnybrook Farm	2.25	....	....	....	1.60	.30
2786	29¢ Little House on the Prairie	2.25	....	....	....	1.60	.30
2787	29¢ Adventures of Huckleberry Finn	2.25	....	....	....	1.60	.30
2788	29¢ Little Women . . .	2.25	....	....	....	1.60	.30

2789, 2790

2791, 2798, 2801

2792, 2797, 2802

2793, 2796, 2799, 2803

2794, 2795, 2800

SCOTT NO.	DESCRIPTION	FIRST DAY COVERS SING	FIRST DAY COVERS PL. BLK.	MINT SHEET	PLATE BLOCK	UNUSED F/NH	USED
2789	29¢ Christmas–Traditional	2.25	4.75	36.00(50)	3.75	1.00	.20
2790	29¢ Christmas–Traditional, bklt single	2.25	....	....	....	1.00	.20
2790a	same, bklt pane of 4 .	3.00	....	....	....	3.50	....
2790av	same, bklt pane, unfolded	....	....	....	....	5.25	....
2791-94	Christmas–Contemporary, 4 varieties, attached .	3.00	4.75	47.50(50)	5.00	4.25	3.00
2791	29¢ Jack-in-the-Box .	2.25	....	....	....	1.10	.20
2792	29¢ Red-Nosed Reindeer	2.25	....	....	....	1.10	.20
2793	29¢ Snowman	2.25	....	....	....	1.10	.20
2794	29¢ Toy Soldier Blowing Horn	2.25	....	....	....	1.10	.20
2795	29¢ Toy Soldier Blowing Horn, bklt single	2.25	....	....	....	1.25	.20
2796	29¢ Snowman, bklt single	2.25	....	....	....	1.25	.20
2797	29¢ Red-Nosed Reindeer, bklt single	2.25	....	....	....	1.25	.20
2798	29¢ Jack-in-the-Box, bklt single	2.25	....	....	....	1.25	.20
2798a	same, bkle pane of 10	7.00	....	....	....	9.75	....
2798av	same, bklt pane, unfolded	....	....	....	....	12.00	....
2799-2802v	29¢ Christmas–Contemporary, coil	....	....	....	11.00(8)	5.50(4)	....
2799	29¢ Snowman, self-adhesive (3 buttons)	2.25	....	....	....	1.20	.50
2800	29¢ Toy Soldier Blowing Horn, self-adhesive . .	2.25	....	....	....	1.20	.50
2801	29¢ Jack-in-the-Box, self-adhesive	2.25	....	....	....	1.20	.50
2802	29¢ Red-Nosed Reindeer, self-adhesive	2.25	....	....	....	1.20	.50
2802a	same, bklt pane of 12	9.00	....	....	....	13.00	....
2803	29¢ Snowman, self-adhesive (2 buttons)	2.25	....	....	....	1.20	.50
2803a	same, bklt pane of 18	13.50	....	....	....	20.00	....

2804

2805

2806

SCOTT NO.	DESCRIPTION	FIRST DAY COVERS SING	FIRST DAY COVERS PL. BLK.	MINT SHEET	PLATE BLOCK	UNUSED F/NH	USED
2804	29¢ Commonwealth of North Mariana Islands	2.25	4.75	20.00(20)	5.00	1.00	.25
2805	29¢ Columbus Landing in Puerto Rico	2.25	4.75	60.00(50)	4.00	1.20	.25
2806	29¢ AIDS Awareness	2.25	4.75	41.00(50)	4.50	1.20	.25
2806a	29¢ AIDS Awareness, bklt single	2.25	....	....	....	1.00	.25
2806b	same, bklt pane of 5 .	9.00	....	....	....	4.75	....
2806bv	same, bklt pane, unfolded	....	....	....	....	6.00	....

2807

2808

2809

2810

2811

1994 COMMEMORATIVES

SCOTT NO.	DESCRIPTION	FIRST DAY COVERS SING	FIRST DAY COVERS PL. BLK.	MINT SHEET	PLATE BLOCK	UNUSED F/NH	USED
2807/76	(2807-12, 2814C-28, 2834-36, 2838-39, 2841a, 2848-68, 2871-72, 2876) 60 varieties........	....		....	....	78.00	25.50
2807-11	Winter Olympics, 5 varieties, attached .	5.00	....	22.00(20)	12.00(10)	7.00	6.00
2807	29¢ Alpine Skiing . . .	2.25	....	....	....	1.50	.50
2808	29¢ Luge	2.25	....	....	....	1.50	.50
2809	29¢ Ice Dancing	2.25	....	....	....	1.50	.50
2810	29¢ Cross Country Skiing	2.25	....	....	....	1.50	.50
2811	29¢ Ice Hockey	2.25	....	....	....	1.50	.50

2813

2812

2815

2814

1994 COMMEMORATIVES (continued)

SCOTT NO.	DESCRIPTION	FIRST DAY COVERS SING	FIRST DAY COVERS PL. BLK.	MINT SHEET	PLATE BLOCK	UNUSED F/NH	USED
2812	29¢ Edward R. Murrow	2.25	4.75	38.00(50)	3.75	.85	.25
2813	29¢ Love (sunrise), self-adhesive	2.25	....	....	....	1.10	.30
2813a	same, bklt pane of 18	13.50	....	....	....	17.50	....
2813v	29¢ Love (sunrise), self-adhesive coil . . .	2.50	....	....	7.00(3)	1.40	....
2814	29¢ Love (dove), bklt single	2.25	....	....	....	1.10	.30
2814a	same, bklt pane of 10	7.00	....	....	....	10.00	....
2814av	same, bklt pane, unfolded	....	....	....	....	11.00	....
2814C	29¢ Love (dove)	2.25	4.75	45.00(50)	4.75	1.10	.20
2815	52¢ Love (dove)	2.00	4.50	70.00(50)	7.00(4)	1.50	.40
....	same, plate block of 10	....	....	....	16.00(10)	....	....

2816

2817

2818

SCOTT NO.	DESCRIPTION	FIRST DAY COVERS SING	FIRST DAY COVERS PL. BLK.	MINT SHEET	PLATE BLOCK	UNUSED F/NH	USED
2816	29¢ Allison Davis . . .	2.25	4.75	20.00(20)	5.00	1.20	.25
2817	29¢ Chinese New Year of the Dog	2.25	4.75	32.50(20)	9.00	2.25	.25
2818	29¢ Buffalo Soldiers .	4.00	5.00	16.00(20)	6.50	1.50	.25

2819

2820

2821

2822

2823

2824

2825

2826

2827

2828

SCOTT NO.	DESCRIPTION	FIRST DAY COVERS SING	FIRST DAY COVERS PL. BLK.	MINT SHEET	PLATE BLOCK	UNUSED F/NH	USED
2819	29¢ Rudolph Valentino	2.25	....	....	....	2.00	.75
2920	29¢ Clara Bow	2.25	....	....	....	2.00	.75
2821	29¢ Charlie Chaplin .	2.25	....	....	....	2.00	.75
2822	29¢ Lon Chaney	2.25	....	....	....	2.00	.75
2823	29¢ John Gilbert	2.25	....	....	....	2.00	.75
2824	29¢ Zasu Pitts	2.25	....	....	....	2.00	.75
2825	29¢ Harold Lloyd	2.25	....	....	....	2.00	.75
2826	29¢ Keystone Cops . .	2.25	....	....	....	2.00	.75
2827	29¢ Theda Bara	2.25	....	....	....	2.00	.75
2828	29¢ Buster Keaton . .	2.25	....	....	....	2.00	.75
2819-28	Silent Screen Stars, 10 varieties, attached	7.00	....	55.00(40)	20.00(10)	18.00	15.00

2829

2830

2831

2832

2833

SCOTT NO.	DESCRIPTION	FIRST DAY COVERS SING	FIRST DAY COVERS PL. BLK.	MINT SHEET	PLATE BLOCK	UNUSED F/NH	USED
2829	29¢ Lily	2.25	....	....	....	1.25	.30
2830	29¢ Zinnia	2.25	....	....	....	1.25	.30
2831	29¢ Gladiola	2.25	....	....	....	1.25	.30
2832	29¢ Marigold	2.25	....	....	....	1.25	.30
2833	29¢ Rose	2.25	....	....	....	1.25	.30
2833a	Summer Garden Flowers, bklt pane of 5	4.50	....	....	....	7.00	6.00
2833av	same, bklt pane, unfolded	....	....	....	....	7.00	....

2834

2835

2836

2837

SCOTT NO.	DESCRIPTION	FIRST DAY COVERS SING	FIRST DAY COVERS PL. BLK.	MINT SHEET	PLATE BLOCK	UNUSED F/NH	USED
2834	29¢ World Cup Soccer	2.25	4.75	20.00(20)	4.25	1.00	.50
2835	40¢ World Cup Soccer	2.25	4.75	25.00(20)	5.50	1.50	.75
2836	50¢ World Cup Soccer	2.25	5.50	34.50(20)	6.50	2.00	1.00
2837	29¢-50¢ World Cup Soccer Souvenir Sheet	3.50	....		....	6.00	4.00

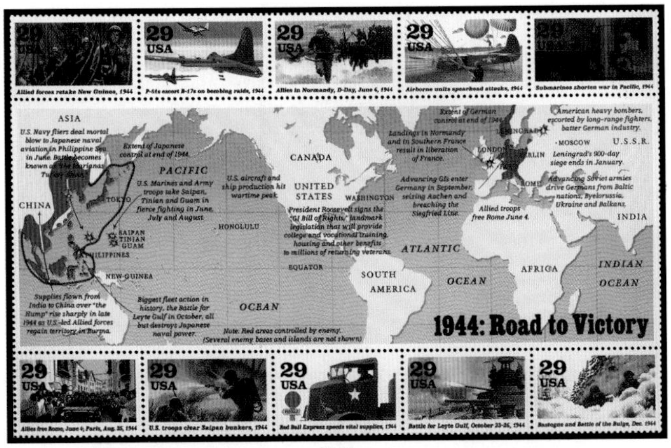

2838

SCOTT NO.	DESCRIPTION	FIRST DAY COVERS SING	FIRST DAY COVERS PL. BLK.	MINT SHEET	PLATE BLOCK	UNUSED F/NH	USED
2838	$2.90 World War II, 1944, Souvenir Sheet of 10	12.00	....	35.00(20)	....	22.50	20.00
2838a	29¢ Allied forces retake New Guinea	2.50	....	....	....	2.00	1.00
2838b	29¢ P-51s escort B-17s on bombing raids	2.50	....	....	....	2.00	1.00
2838c	29¢ Allies in Normandy, D-Day, June 6	2.50	....	....	....	2.00	1.00
2838d	29¢ Airborne units spearhead attacks . .	2.50	....	....	....	2.00	1.00
2838e	29¢ Submarines shorten war in Pacific	2.50	....	....	....	2.00	1.00
2838f	29¢ Allies free Rome, June 4; Paris , August 25	2.50	....	....	....	2.00	1.00
2838g	29¢ U.S. troops clear Saipan bunkers	2.50	....	....	....	2.00	1.00
2838h	29¢ Red Ball Express speeds vital supplies .	2.50	....	....	....	2.00	1.00
2838i	29¢ Battle for Leyte Gulf, October, 23-26	2.50	....	....	....	2.00	1.00
2838j	29¢ Bastogne and Battle of the Bulge, December	2.50	....	....	....	2.00	1.00

2839

2840

SCOTT NO.	DESCRIPTION	FIRST DAY COVERS SING	FIRST DAY COVERS PL. BLK.	MINT SHEET	PLATE BLOCK	UNUSED F/NH	USED
2839	29¢ Norman Rockwell	1.75	4.75	45.00(50)	4.50	1.75	.75
2840	50¢ "Four Freedoms" Souvenir Sheets	5.00	....	....	....	7.50	6.00

2841

SCOTT NO.	DESCRIPTION	FIRST DAY COVERS SING	FIRST DAY COVERS PL. BLK.	MINT SHEET	PLATE BLOCK	UNUSED F/NH	USED
2841	29¢ Moon Landing 25th Anniversary, Sheet of 12	12.00	....	....	....	15.00	....
2841a	29¢ Moon Landing 25th Anniversary, single stamp	1.75	....	....	....	1.50	.50

2842

SCOTT NO.	DESCRIPTION	FIRST DAY COVERS SING	FIRST DAY COVERS PL. BLK.	MINT SHEET	PLATE BLOCK	UNUSED F/NH	USED
2842	$9.95 Moon Landing Express Mail Stamp	27.00	50.00	675.00(20)	150.00	35.00	12.50

2843

2844

2845

2846

2847

SCOTT NO.	DESCRIPTION	FIRST DAY COVERS SING	FIRST DAY COVERS PL. BLK.	MINT SHEET	PLATE BLOCK	UNUSED F/NH	USED
2843	29¢ Hudson's General	2.25	....	....	....	1.10	.30
2844	29¢ McQueen's Jupiter	2.25	....	....	....	1.10	.30
2845	29¢ Eddy's No. 242 . .	2.25	....	....	....	1.10	.30
2846	29¢ Ely's No. 10	2.25	....	....	....	1.10	.30
2847	29¢ Buchanan's No. 999	2.25	....	....	....	1.10	.30
2847a	Locomotives, bklt pane of 5	4.50	....	....	....	5.50	4.25
2847av	same, bklt pane, unfolded	....	....	....	....	6.50	....

2848

SCOTT NO.	DESCRIPTION	FIRST DAY COVERS SING	FIRST DAY COVERS PL. BLK.	MINT SHEET	PLATE BLOCK	UNUSED F/NH	USED
2848	29¢ George Meany . .	1.75	4.75	45.00(50)	4.50	1.00	.25

2849

2850

2851

2852

2853

SCOTT NO.	DESCRIPTION	FIRST DAY COVERS SING	FIRST DAY COVERS PL. BLK.	MINT SHEET	PLATE BLOCK	UNUSED F/NH	USED
2849-53	Popular Singers, 5 varieties, attached	8.00	....	30.00(20)	12.00(6)	7.75	6.00
2849	29¢ Al Jolson	3.00	....	....	....	1.75	.75
2850	29¢ Bing Crosby	3.00	....	....	....	1.75	.75
2851	29¢ Ethel Waters	3.00	....	....	....	1.75	.75
2852	29¢ Nat "King" Cole	3.00	....	....	....	1.75	.75
2853	29¢ Ethel Merman	3.00	....	....	....	1.75	.75
....	same, Plate Block of 12	....	....	....	18.00(12)	....	....

2854

2855

2856

2857

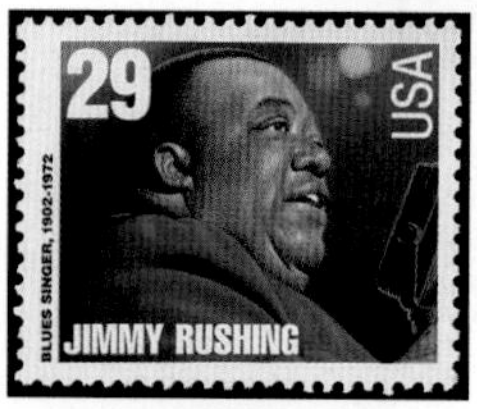

2858

2859

2860

2861

SCOTT NO.	DESCRIPTION	FIRST DAY COVERS SING	FIRST DAY COVERS PL. BLK.	MINT SHEET	PLATE BLOCK	UNUSED F/NH	USED
2854-61	Blues & Jazz Singers, 8 varieties, attached	12.00	....	45.00(35)	14.50(10)	13.50	7.50
....	same, Horizontal Plate Block of 10 w/Top Label	....	....	....	15.50(10)	....	....
2854	29¢ Bessie Smith	3.00	....	....	....	1.75	.50
2855	29¢ Muddy Waters	3.00	....	....	....	1.75	.50
2856	29¢ Billie Holiday	3.00	....	....	....	1.75	.50
2857	29¢ Robert Johnson	3.00	....	....	....	1.75	.50
2858	29¢ Jimmy Rushing	3.00	....	....	....	1.75	.50
2859	29¢ "Ma" Rainey	3.00	....	....	....	1.75	.50
2860	29¢ Mildred Bailey	3.00	....	....	....	1.75	.50
2861	29¢ Howlin' Wolf	3.00	....	....	....	1.75	.50

2862

SCOTT NO.	DESCRIPTION	FIRST DAY COVERS SING	FIRST DAY COVERS PL. BLK.	MINT SHEET	PLATE BLOCK	UNUSED F/NH	USED
2862	29¢ James Thurber	1.75	4.75	38.00(50)	5.00	1.00	.25

2863 2864

2865 2866

SCOTT NO.	DESCRIPTION	FIRST DAY COVERS SING	FIRST DAY COVERS PL. BLK.	MINT SHEET	PLATE BLOCK	UNUSED F/NH	USED
2863-66	Wonders of the Sea, 4 varieties, attached	5.00	6.00	27.50(24)	5.25	5.50	4.50
2863	29¢ Diver & Motorboat	2.25	....	....	....	1.20	.30
2864	29¢ Diver & Ship	2.25	....	....	....	1.20	.30
2865	29¢ Diver & Ship's Wheel	2.25	....	....	....	1.20	.30
2866	29¢ Diver & Coral	2.25	....	....	....	1.20	.30

2867 2868

SCOTT NO.	DESCRIPTION	FIRST DAY COVERS SING	FIRST DAY COVERS PL. BLK.	MINT SHEET	PLATE BLOCK	UNUSED F/NH	USED
2867-68	Cranes	4.00	5.00	19.50(20)	5.00	2.25	1.50
2867	29¢ Black-Necked Crane	3.00	....	....	....	1.15	.25
2868	29¢ Whooping Crane	3.00	....	....	....	1.15	.25

2869

Legends of the West

2869a	*Home on the Range*	**2869k**	*Nellie Cashman*
2869b	*Buffalo Bill Cody*	**2869l**	*Charles Goodnight*
2869c	*Jim Bridger*	**2869m**	*Geronimo*
2869d	*Annie Oakley*	**2869n**	*Kit Carson*
2869e	*Native American Culture*	**2869o**	*Wild Bill Hickok*
2869f	*Chief Joseph*	**2869p**	*Western Wildlife*
2869g	*Bill Pickett*	**2869q**	*Jim Beckwourth*
2869h	*Bat Masterson*	**2869r**	*Bill Tilghman*
2869i	*John Fremont*	**2869s**	*Sacagawea*
2869j	*Wyatt Earp*	**2869t**	*Overland Mail*

2869g

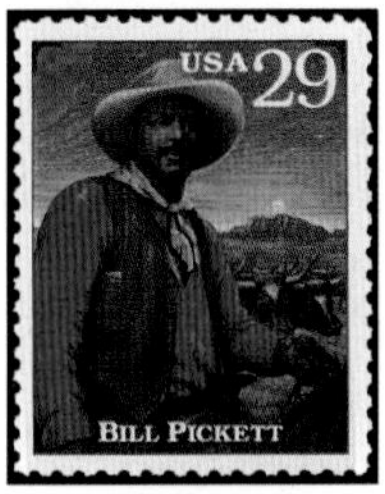

2870g

SCOTT NO.	DESCRIPTION	FIRST DAY COVERS SING	FIRST DAY COVERS PL. BLK.	MINT SHEET	PLATE BLOCK	UNUSED F/NH	USED
2869	Legends of the West, 20 varieties, attached	....	....	27.50(20)	....	27.50	25.00
....	set of singles	31.50	....	....	....	....	15.00
....	singles of above, each	....	....	....	....	....	.85
2869v	same as above, uncut sheet of 120 (6 panes)	....	....	100.00(120)	....	100.00	....
....	block of 40 with vertical or horizontal, gutter between (2 panes)	....	....	27.50(40)	....	27.50	....
....	block of 24 with vertical gutter.....	....	....	20.75(24)	....	20.75	....
....	block of 25 with horizontal gutter	....	....	21.50(25)	....	21.50	....
....	cross gutter block of 20	....	....	....	....	31.00	....
....	cross gutter block of 4	....	....	....	....	17.00	....
....	vertical pair with horizontal gutter	....	....	....	....	2.75	....
....	horizontal pair with vertical gutter	....	....	....	....	2.75	....
2870	Legends of the West, (Recallled), 20 varieties, attached	....	....	475.00(20)	....	475.00	....

2871

2872

2873

2874

SCOTT NO.	DESCRIPTION	FIRST DAY COVERS SING	FIRST DAY COVERS PL. BLK.	MINT SHEET	PLATE BLOCK	UNUSED F/NH	USED
2871	29¢ Christmas–Traditional	2.25	4.75	37.00(50)	3.75	1.25	.20
2871a	29¢ Christmas–Traditional bklt single	2.25	....	....	....	1.10	.20
2871b	same, bklt pane of 10	9.00	....	....	....	10.50	....
2871bv	same, bklt pane, unfolded	....	....	....	....	11.50	....
2872	29¢ Christmas Stocking	2.25	4.75	37.00(50)	3.75	1.25	.20
2872v	29¢ Christmas Stocking, bklt single	2.25	....	....	....	1.25	.20
2872a	same, bklt pane of 20	....	....	....	....	17.00	....
2872av	same, bklt pane, unfolded	....	....	....	....	20.00	....
2873	29¢ Santa Claus, self-adhesive	2.25	....	....	....	1.20	.25
2873a	same, bklt pane of 12	9.00	....	....	....	13.50	....
2874	29¢ Cardinal in Snow, self-adhesive	2.25	....	....	....	1.50	1.20
2874a	same, bklt pane of 18	13.50	....	....	....	20.00	....

2875

SCOTT NO.	DESCRIPTION	FIRST DAY COVERS SING	FIRST DAY COVERS PL. BLK.	MINT SHEET	PLATE BLOCK	UNUSED F/NH	USED
2875	$2 B.E.P. Souvenir Sheet of 4 (Madison)	25.00	....	....	....	27.50	25.00
2875a	single from above ($2 Madison)	6.00	....	....	....	7.50	6.00

2876

2877, 2878

SCOTT NO.	DESCRIPTION	FIRST DAY COVERS SING	FIRST DAY COVERS PL. BLK.	MINT SHEET	PLATE BLOCK	UNUSED F/NH	USED
2876	29¢ Year of the Boar .	3.00	4.75	22.50(20)	5.75	1.25	.25
2877	(3¢) "G" Make-up Rate (ABN, bright blue) ...	2.25	4.75	10.00(100)	1.00	.20	.15
2878	(3¢) "G" Make-up Rate (SVS, dark blue)	2.25	4.75	15.00(100)	1.25	.25	.15

2879, 2880

2881-85, 2889-92

2886, 2887

2888

SCOTT NO.	DESCRIPTION	FIRST DAY COVERS SING	FIRST DAY COVERS PL. BLK.	MINT SHEET	PLATE BLOCK	UNUSED F/NH	USED
2879	(20¢) "G" Old Glory Postcard Rate (BEP, black "G")	2.25	4.75	65.00(100)	6.00	.75	.20
2880	(20¢) "G" Old Glory Postcard Rate (SVS, red "G") .	2.25	4.75	75.00(100)	9.50	.75	.20
2881	(32¢) "G" Old Glory (BEP, black "G")	2.25	4.75	105.00(100)	80.00	1.75	.35
2882	(32¢) "G" Old Glory (SVS, red "G")	2.25	4.75	84.00(100)	5.25	1.00	.25
2883	(32¢) "G" Old Glory, bklt single (BEP, black "G")	2.25	....	....	....	1.10	.25
2883a	same, bklt pane of 10	7.25	....	....	....	11.00	....
2884	(32¢) "G" Old Glory, bklt single (ABN, blue "G")	2.25	....	....	....	1.25	.25
2884a	same, bklt pane of 10	7.25	....	....	....	12.50	....
2885	(32¢) "G" Old Glory, bklt single (KCS, red "G")	2.25	....	....	....	1.50	.25
2885a	same, bklt pane of 10	7.25	....	....	....	15.00	....
2886	(32¢) "G", self-adhesive	2.25	....	....	....	1.10	.30
2886a	same, bklt pane of 18	13.50	....	....	....	18.50	....
2887	(32¢) "G" Old Glory, self-adhesive (blue shading)	2.25	....	....	....	1.40	.40
2887a	same, bklt pane of 18	13.50	....	....	....	22.00	....

SCOTT NO.	DESCRIPTION	FIRST DAY COVERS SING	PLATE# STRIP 3	MINT SHEET	PLATE# STRIP 3	UNUSED F/NH	USED
2888	(25¢) Old Glory First-Class Presort, coil	2.25	10.00	....	6.25	1.10	.35
2889	(32¢) "G" Old Glory, coil (BEP, black "G")	2.25	10.00	....	12.50	2.00	.35
2890	(32¢) "G" Old Glory, coil (ABN, blue "G") . .	2.25	10.00	....	6.25	1.10	.20
2891	(32¢) "G" Old Glory, coil (SVS, red "G") . . .	2.25	10.00	....	11.00	2.00	.40
2892	(32¢) "G" Old Glory, coil (SVS, red "G") rouletted	2.25	10.00	....	10.00	1.25	.20

2893

2897, 2913-16, 2920, 2921

2902, 2902B

2903, 2904, 2904A, 2904B

2905, 2906

2907

2908-10

2911, 2912, 2912A, 2912B

1995-97 Regular Issues

SCOTT NO.	DESCRIPTION	FIRST DAY COVERS SING	FIRST DAY COVERS PL. BLK.	MINT SHEET	PLATE BLOCK	UNUSED F/NH	USED
2893	(5¢) "G" Old Glory, Nonprofit, coil	1.95	10.00	....	2.50	.50	.40
2897	32¢ Flag over Porch .	1.95	4.75	80.00(100)	4.75	1.00	.20

1995-97 Regular Issue Coils

SCOTT NO.	DESCRIPTION	FIRST DAY COVERS SING	PLATE# STRIP 3	MINT SHEET	PLATE# STRIP 3	UNUSED F/NH	USED
2902	(5¢) Butte, Nonprofit, coil	1.95	10.00	....	2.00	.30	.20
2902B	(5¢) Butte, self-adhesive coil	1.95	....	....	2.75	.30	.20
2903	(5¢) Mountain, (BEP, violet 1996)	2.25	10.00	....	2.00	.30	.20
2904	(5¢) Mountain (SVS, blue 1996)	2.25	10.00	....	2.00	.30	.20
2904A	(5¢) Mountain, self-adhesive coil . . .	2.25	....	....	2.75	.30	.20
2904B	(5¢) Mountain, self-adhesive coil (1997)	2.25	....	....	2.75	.30	.20
2905	(10¢) Automobile, Bulk Rate, coil	2.25	10.00	....	2.75	.30	.35
2906	(10¢) Automobile, self-adhesive coil . . .	2.25	....	....	2.75	.30	.20
2907	(10¢) Eagle, bulk-rate, coil (1996)	2.25	....	....	4.00	.60	.35

SCOTT NO.	DESCRIPTION	FIRST DAY COVERS SING	PLATE# STRIP 3	MINT SHEET	PLATE# STRIP 3	UNUSED F/NH	USED
2908	(15¢) Auto Tail Fin, Presorted First-Class Card, coil (BEP)	2.25	10.00	....	3.50	.50	.30
2909	(15¢) Auto Tail Fin, Presorted First-Class Card, coil (SVS)	2.25	10.00	....	3.50	.50	.30
2910	(15¢) Auto Tail Fin, self-adhesive coil . .	2.25	....	....	3.75	.55	.30
2911	(25¢) Juke Box, Presorted First-Class, coil (BEP)	2.25	10.00	....	5.75	.80	.40
2912	(25¢) Juke Box, Presorted First-Class, coil (SVS)	2.25	10.00	....	5.75	.80	.40
2912A	(25¢) Juke Box, self-adhesive coil . .	2.25	....	....	5.75	.80	.45
2912B	(25¢) Juke Box, self-adhesive coil (1997)	2.25	....	....	5.75	.80	.30
2913	32¢ Flag over Porch, coil (BEP, red date) .	2.25	10.00	....	6.00	1.00	.25
2914	32¢ Flag over Porch, coil (SVS, blue date) . . .	2.25	10.00	....	6.00	1.00	.25
2915	32¢ Flag over Porch, self-adhesive coil (Die Cut 8.7)	2.25	....	....	14.00	1.00	.30
2915A	32¢ Flag over Porch, self-adhesive coil (1996, Die Cut 9.8)	2.25	....	....	8.00	1.20	.30
2915B	32¢ Flag over Porch, self-adhesive coil (1996, Die Cut 11.5)	2.25	....	....	14.00	1.20	.25
2915C	32¢ Flag over Porch, self-adhesive coil (1996, Die Cut 10.9)	10.00	....	....	25.00	2.50	1.00
2915D	32¢ Flag over Porch, self adhesive coil (1997)	2.25	....	....	14.00	1.85	1.00

Note: **For plate number strips of 5, see page 149**

2919

1995-97 Booklet Panes

SCOTT NO.	DESCRIPTION	FIRST DAY COVERS SING	FIRST DAY COVERS PL. BLK.	MINT SHEET	PLATE BLOCK	UNUSED F/NH	USED
2916	32¢ Flag over Porch, bklt single	2.25	....	....	....	1.10	.20
2916a	same, bklt pane of 10	7.25	....	....	....	10.75	....
2916av	same, bklt pane, unfolded	....	....	....	....	1.00	....
2919	32¢ Flag over Field self-adhesive	2.25	....	....	....	1.10	.30
2919a	same, bklt pane of 18	13.50	....	....	....	17.00	....
2920	32¢ Flag over Porch, self-adhesive (large "1995")	2.25	....	....	....	1.10	.30
2920a	same, bklt pane of 20	14.50	....	....	....	21.00	....
2920b	32¢ Flag over Porch, self-adhesive (small "1995")	10.00	....	....	....	7.50	.80
2920c	same, bklt pane of 20	50.00	....	....	....	145.00	....
2920D	32¢ Flag over Porch ("1996" date) self-adhesive	2.25	....	....	....	2.00	1.00
2920e	same, Bklt pane of 10	9.00	....	....	....	10.75	....
2921	32¢ Flag over Porch, self-adhesive (Red 1996, Die Cut 9.8)	2.25	....	....	....	1.10	.30
2921a	same, bklt pane of 10	7.00	....	....	....	10.75	....
2921av	same, bklt pane, unfolded	....	....	....	....	11.50	....
2921b	32¢ Flag over Porch, (Red 1997)	2.25	....	....	....	1.50	.30
2921c	same, bklt pane of 10	6.95	....	....	....	10.75	....
2921d	same, bklt pane of 5	5.50	....	....	....	5.50	....

2933

2934

2935

2936

2938

2940

2941

2942

2943

1995-99 GREAT AMERICANS

SCOTT NO.	DESCRIPTION	FIRST DAY COVERS SING	FIRST DAY COVERS PL. BLK.	MINT SHEET	PLATE BLOCK	UNUSED F/NH	USED
2933	32¢ Milton S. Hershey	2.25	4.75	80.00(100)	4.75	1.00	.30
2934	32¢ Carl Farley (1996)	2.25	4.75	80.00(100)	4.75	1.00	.50
2935	32¢ Henry R. Luce (1998)	2.25	4.75	16.00(20)	4.75	1.00	.50
2936	32¢ Lila & DeWitt Wallace (1998)	2.25	4.75	16.00(20)	4.75	1.00	.50
2938	46¢ Ruth Benedict . .	2.25	5.00	110.00(100)	6.50	2.00	.90
2940	55¢ Alice Hamilton . .	2.25	5.00	120.00(100)	7.00	2.00	.35
2941	55¢ Justin Morrill (1999)	2.25	5.00	25.00(20)	7.00	2.00	1.25
2942	77¢ Mary Breckenridge (1998)	2.25	5.50	35.00(20)	8.50	2.50	.50
2943	78¢ Alice Paul	2.25	5.50	200.00(100)	10.00	2.50	.50

2948

2949

2950

1995 COMMEMORATIVES

SCOTT NO.	DESCRIPTION	FIRST DAY COVERS SING	FIRST DAY COVERS PL. BLK.	MINT SHEET	PLATE BLOCK	UNUSED F/NH	USED
2948/3023	**(2948, 2950-58, 2961-68, 2974, 2976-92, 2998-99, 3001-07, 3019-23) 50 varieties . . . . . .**	....	....	....	....	**70.00**	**25.75**
2948	(32¢) Love (Cherub) .	2.25	4.75	40.00(50)	4.25	.95	.25
2949	(32¢) Love (Cherub), self-adhesive	2.25	....	....	....	1.10	.25
2949a	same, bklt pane of 20	14.50	....	....	....	20.00	....
2950	32¢ Florida Statehood	2.25	4.75	35.00(20)	8.00	1.20	.25

2951 2952

2953 2954

SCOTT NO.	DESCRIPTION	FIRST DAY COVERS SING	FIRST DAY COVERS PL. BLK.	MINT SHEET	PLATE BLOCK	UNUSED F/NH	USED
2951-54	Kids Care About Environment, 4 varieties, attached	4.00	4.75	16.50(16)	5.00	4.50	3.50
2951	32¢ Earth in a Bathtub	2.25	....	....	....	1.20	.35
2952	32¢ Solar Energy . . .	2.25	....	....	....	1.20	.35
2953	32¢ Tree Planting . . .	2.25	....	....	....	1.20	.35
2954	32¢ Beach Clean-Up	2.25	....	....	....	1.20	.35

2955

2956

2957, 2959

2958

2960

SCOTT NO.	DESCRIPTION	FIRST DAY COVERS SING	FIRST DAY COVERS PL. BLK.	MINT SHEET	PLATE BLOCK	UNUSED F/NH	USED
2955	32¢ Richard M. Nixon	2.25	4.75	55.00(50)	5.50	1.50	.25
2956	32¢ Bessie Coleman .	2.25	4.75	42.50(50)	4.50	1.50	.25
2957	32¢ Love (Cherub) . .	2.25	4.75	40.00(50)	3.95	.90	.25
2958	55¢ Love (Cherub) . .	2.50	5.00	68.00(50)	6.75	1.75	.60
2959	32¢ Love (Cherub), bklt single	2.25	....	....	....	1.00	.25
2959a	same, bklt pane of 10	7.25	....	....	....	9.75	....
2959av	same, bklt pane, unfolded	....	....	....	....	10.50	....
2960	55¢ Love (Cherub), self-adhesive	2.50	....	....	....	1.75	.70
2960a	same, bklt pane of 20	23.50	....	....	....	28.50	....

2961

2962

2963

2964

2965

SCOTT NO.	DESCRIPTION	FIRST DAY COVERS SING	FIRST DAY COVERS PL. BLK.	MINT SHEET	PLATE BLOCK	UNUSED F/NH	USED
2961-65	Recreational Sports, 5 varieties, attached .	7.00	....	21.00(20)	12.00(10)	5.50	4.00
2961	32¢ Volleyball	3.00	....	....	....	1.20	.50
2962	32¢ Softball	3.00	....	....	....	1.20	.50
2963	32¢ Bowling	3.00	....	....	....	1.20	.50
2964	32¢ Tennis	3.00	....	....	....	1.20	.50
2965	32¢ Golf	3.00	....	....	....	1.20	.50

2966

2967

2968

SCOTT NO.	DESCRIPTION	FIRST DAY COVERS SING	FIRST DAY COVERS PL. BLK.	MINT SHEET	PLATE BLOCK	UNUSED F/NH	USED
2966	32¢ POW & MIA	3.00	4.00	16.00(20)	3.95	1.20	.25
2967	32¢ Marilyn Monroe .	4.00	5.00	26.50(20)	6.50	2.00	.25
2967v	same as above, uncut sheet of 120 (6 panes)	....	....	180.00(120)	....	....	....
....	block of 8 with vertical gutter	....	....	....	....	50.00	....
....	cross gutter block of 8	....	....	....	....	65.00	....
....	vertical pair with horizontal gutter	....	....	....	....	5.50	....
....	horizontal pair with vertical gutter	....	....	....	....	9.50	....
2968	32¢ Texas Statehood	3.00	4.75	28.00(20)	6.50	1.50	.25

2969

2970

2971

2972

2973

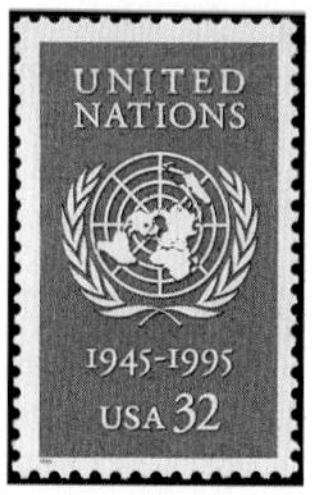

2974

SCOTT NO.	DESCRIPTION	FIRST DAY COVERS SING	FIRST DAY COVERS PL. BLK.	MINT SHEET	PLATE BLOCK	UNUSED F/NH	USED
2969	32¢ Split Rock Lighthouse	2.25	....	....	....	1.50	.35
2970	32¢ St. Joseph Lighthouse	2.25	....	....	....	1.50	.35
2971	32¢ Spectacle Reef Lighthouse	2.25	....	....	....	1.50	.35
2972	32¢ Marblehead Lighthouse	2.25	....	....	....	1.50	.35
2973	32¢ Thirty Mile Point Lighthouse	2.25	....	....	....	1.50	.35
2973a	Great Lakes Lighthouses, bklt pane of 5	5.50	....	....	....	8.00	6.00
2973av	same, bklt pane, unfolded	....	....	....	....	9.00	....
2974	32¢ United Nations . .	1.75	4.75	16.00(20)	3.95	.90	.25

2975

CIVIL WAR

2975a *Monitor-Virginia*
2975b *Robert E. Lee*
2975c *Clara Barton*
2975d *Ulysses S. Grant*
2975e *Shiloh*
2975f *Jefferson Davis*
2975g *David Farragut*
2975h *Frederick Douglass*
2975i *Raphael Semmes*
2975j *Abraham Lincoln*
2975k *Harriet Tubman*
2975l *Stand Watie*
2975m *Joseph E. Johnston*
2975n *Winfield Hancock*
2975o *Mary Chestnut*
2975p *Chancellorsville*
2975q *William T. Sherman*
2975r *Phoebe Pember*
2975s *"Stonewall" Jackson*
2975t *Gettysburg*

SCOTT NO.	DESCRIPTION	FIRST DAY COVERS SING	FIRST DAY COVERS PL. BLK.	MINT SHEET	PLATE BLOCK	UNUSED F/NH	USED
2975	32¢ Civil War, 20 varieties, attached	....	....	40.00(20)	....	40.00	30.00
....	set of singles	35.00	....	....	....	....	15.00
....	singles of above, each	....	....	....	....	....	1.00
2975v	32¢ Civil War, uncut sheet of 120 (6 panes)	....	....	150.00(120)	....	150.00	....
....	cross gutter block of 20	....	....	....	....	55.00	....
....	cross gutter block of 4	....	....	....	....	27.50	....
....	vertical pair with horizontal gutter	....	....	....	....	6.00	....
....	horizontal pair with vertical gutter	....	....	....	....	6.00	....

2976

2977

2978

2979

SCOTT NO.	DESCRIPTION	FIRST DAY COVERS SING	FIRST DAY COVERS PL. BLK.	MINT SHEET	PLATE BLOCK	UNUSED F/NH	USED
2976-79	Carousel Horses, 4 varieties, attached .	4.00	4.75	21.50(20)	5.25	4.75	3.75
2976	32¢ Palamino	2.25	....	....	....	1.20	.30
2977	32¢ Pinto Pony	2.25	....	....	....	1.20	.30
2978	32¢ Armored Jumper	2.25	....	....	....	1.20	.30
2979	32¢ Brown Jumper . .	2.25	....	....	....	1.20	.30

2980

SCOTT NO.	DESCRIPTION	FIRST DAY COVERS SING	FIRST DAY COVERS PL. BLK.	MINT SHEET	PLATE BLOCK	UNUSED F/NH	USED
2980	32¢ Women's Suffrage	1.95	4.75	30.00(40)	3.95	.90	.25

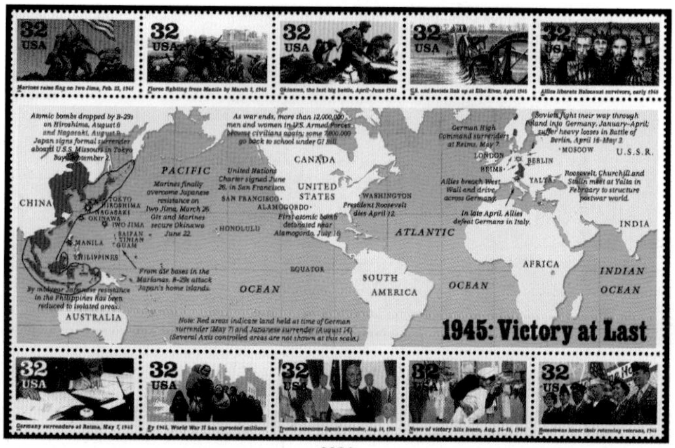

2981

SCOTT NO.	DESCRIPTION	FIRST DAY COVERS SING	FIRST DAY COVERS PL. BLK.	MINT SHEET	PLATE BLOCK	UNUSED F/NH	USED
2981	$3.20 World War II (1945) Souvenir Sheet of 10	8.25	....	28.00(20)	....	22.50	20.00
2981a	32¢ Marines raise flag on Iwo Jima	2.25	....	....	....	2.00	1.00
2981b	32¢ Fierce fighting frees Manila	2.25	....	....	....	2.00	1.00
2981c	32¢ Okinawa, the last big battle	2.25	....	....	....	2.00	1.00
2981d	32¢ U.S. & Soviets link up at Elbe River	2.25	....	....	....	2.00	1.00
2981e	32¢ Allies liberate Holocaust survivors	2.25	....	....	....	2.00	1.00
2981f	32¢ Germany surrenders at Reims	2.25	....	....	....	2.00	1.00
2981g	32¢ By 1945, World War II has uprooted millions	2.25	....	....	....	2.00	1.00
2981h	32¢ Truman announces Japan's surrender . . .	2.25	....	....	....	2.00	1.00
2981i	32¢ News of victory hits home	2.25	....	....	....	2.00	1.00
2981j	32¢ Hometowns honor their returning veterans . . .	2.25	....	....	....	2.00	1.00

2982

SCOTT NO.	DESCRIPTION	FIRST DAY COVERS SING	PL. BLK.	MINT SHEET	PLATE BLOCK	UNUSED F/NH	USED
2982	32¢ Louis Armstrong .	1.95	4.75	30.00(20)	6.00	1.50	.50

2983 2984

2985 2986

2987 2988

2989 2990

2991 2992

SCOTT NO.	DESCRIPTION	FIRST DAY COVERS SING	PL. BLK.	MINT SHEET	PLATE BLOCK	UNUSED F/NH	USED
2983-92	Jazz Musicians, 10 varieties attached . . .	8.25	....	35.00(20)	19.00(10)	17.00	15.00
2983	32¢ Coleman Hawkins	2.25	....	....	....	2.00	1.00
2984	32¢ Louis Armstrong .	2.25	....	....	....	2.00	1.00
2985	32¢ James P. Johnson	2.25	....	....	....	2.00	1.00
2986	32¢ "Jelly Roll" Morton	2.25	....	....	....	2.00	1.00
2987	32¢ Charlie Parker . .	2.25	....	....	....	2.00	1.00
2988	32¢ Eubie Blake	2.25	....	....	....	2.00	1.00
2989	32¢ Charles Mingus .	2.25	....	....	....	2.00	1.00
2990	32¢ Thelonius Monk .	2.25	....	....	....	2.00	1.00
2991	32¢ John Coltrane . .	2.25	....	....	....	2.00	1.00
2992	32¢ Erroll Garner . . .	2.25	....	....	....	2.00	1.00

2993 2994 2995 2996

2997

2998

2999

SCOTT NO.	DESCRIPTION	FIRST DAY COVERS SING	PL. BLK.	MINT SHEET	PLATE BLOCK	UNUSED F/NH	USED
2993	32¢ Aster	2.25	....	....	....	1.25	.25
2994	32¢ Chrysanthemum	2.25	....	....	....	1.25	.25
2995	32¢ Dahlia	2.25	....	....	....	1.25	.25
2996	32¢ Hydrangea	2.25	....	....	....	1.25	.25
2997	32¢ Rudbeckia	2.25	....	....	....	1.25	.25
2997a	Fall Garden Flowers, bklt pane of 5	5.50	....	....	....	5.25	4.00
2997av	same, bklt pane, unfolded	....	....	....	....	6.00	....
2998	60¢ Eddie Rickenbacker	2.25	5.00	80.00(50)	7.00	1.85	.40
2998a	same, large date (1999)	2.25	5.00	70.00(50)	7.25	1.50	.40
2999	32¢ Republic of Palau	2.25	4.75	38.00(50)	3.75	1.20	.25

3000
COMIC STRIPS

3000a *The Yellow Kid*
3000b *Katzenjammer Kids*
3000c *Little Nemo*
3000d *Bringing Up Father*
3000e *Krazy Kat*
3000f *Rube Goldberg*
3000g *Toonerville Folks*
3000h *Gasoline Alley*
3000i *Barney Google*
3000j *Little Orphan Annie*
3000k *Popeye*
3000l *Blondie*
3000m *Dick Tracy*
3000n *Alley Oop*
3000o *Nancy*
3000p *Flash Gordon*
3000q *Li'l Abner*
3000r *Terry and the Pirates*
3000s *Prince Valiant*
3000t *Brenda Starr*

SCOTT NO.	DESCRIPTION	FIRST DAY COVERS SING	PL. BLK.	MINT SHEET	PLATE BLOCK	UNUSED F/NH	USED
3000	32¢ Comic Strips, 20 varieties, attached	....	....	21.00(20)	....	21.00	15.00
....	set of singles	50.00	....	....	....	....	12.50
....	single of above, each	....	....	....	....	....	.75

SCOTT NO.	DESCRIPTION	FIRST DAY COVERS SING	FIRST DAY COVERS PL. BLK.	MINT SHEET	PLATE BLOCK	UNUSED F/NH	USED
	COMIC STRIPS (continued)						
3000v	32¢ Comic Strips, uncut sheet of 120 (6 panes)	....	....	120.00(120)	....	120.00	....
....	cross gutter block of 20	....	....	....	....	40.00	....
....	cross gutter block of 4	....	....	....	....	18.50	....
....	vertical pair with horizontal gutter	....	....	....	....	4.50	....
....	horizontal pair with vertical gutter	....	....	....	....	4.50	....

3001

3002

SCOTT NO.	DESCRIPTION	FIRST DAY COVERS SING	FIRST DAY COVERS PL. BLK.	MINT SHEET	PLATE BLOCK	UNUSED F/NH	USED
3001	32¢ Naval Academy .	2.25	4.75	18.00(20)	4.50	1.00	.25
3002	32¢ Tennessee Williams	2.25	4.75	25.00(20)	5.00	1.50	.40

3003

3004, 3010, 3016

3005, 3009, 3015

3006, 3011, 3017

3007, 3008, 3014

3012, 3018

SCOTT NO.	DESCRIPTION	FIRST DAY COVERS SING	FIRST DAY COVERS PL. BLK.	MINT SHEET	PLATE BLOCK	UNUSED F/NH	USED
3003	32¢ Madonna & Child	2.25	4.75	38.00(50)	3.75	.80	.20
3003a	32¢ Madonna & Child, bklt single	2.25	....	....	....	1.10	.20
3003b	same, bklt pane of 10	7.25	....	....	....	10.50	....
3003bv	same, bklt pane, unfolded	....	....	....	....	11.50	....
3004-07	Santa & Children with Toys, 4 varieties, attached .	4.00	4.75	60.00(50)	6.00	5.00	4.00
3004	32¢ Santa at Chimney	2.25	....	....	....	1.30	.25
....	same, bklt single	2.25	....	....	....	1.30	.25
3005	32¢ Girl holding Jumping Jack	2.25	....	....	....	1.30	.25
....	same, bklt single	2.25	....	....	....	1.30	.25
3006	32¢ Boy holding Toy Horse	2.25	....	....	....	1.30	.25
....	same, bklt single	2.25	....	....	....	1.30	.25
3007	32¢ Santa working on Sled	2.25	....	....	....	1.30	.25
....	same, bklt single	2.25	....	....	....	1.30	.25
3007b	32¢ Santa & Children with Toys, bklt pane of 10 (3 each of 3004-05) . .	7.25	....	....	....	11.50	....
....	same, bklt pane unfolded	....	....	....	....	12.50	....
3007c	32¢ Santa & Children with Toys, bklt pane of 10 (3 each of 3006-07) . .	7.25	....	....	....	11.50	....
....	same, bklt pane, unfolded	....	....	....	....	12.50	....
3008	32¢ Santa working on Sled, self-adhesive	2.25	....	....	....	1.25	.40
3009	32¢ Girl holding Jumping Jack, self-adhesive . .	2.25	....	....	....	1.25	.40
3010	32¢ Santa at Chimney, self-adhesive	2.25	....	....	....	1.25	.40
3011	32¢ Boy holding Toy Horse, self-adhesive	2.25	....	....	....	1.25	.40
3011a	32¢ Santa & Children with Toys, self-adhesive, pane of 20	14.50	....	....	....	22.50	....
3012	32¢ Midnight Angel, self-adhesive	2.25	....	....	....	1.25	.45
3012a	same, bklt pane of 20	14.50	....	....	....	22.50	....

3013

SCOTT NO.	DESCRIPTION	FIRST DAY COVERS SING	FIRST DAY COVERS PL. BLK.	MINT SHEET	PLATE BLOCK	UNUSED F/NH	USED
3013	32¢ Children Sledding, self-adhesive	2.25	....	....	....	1.25	.50
3013a	same, bklt pane of 18	13.00	....	....	....	20.00	....
3014-17	Santa & Children with Toys, self-adhesive, coil strip of 4	....	....	....	....	5.50	....
3014	32¢ Santa working on Sled, self-adhesive coil . . .	2.25	....	....	....	1.75	1.00
3015	32¢ Girl holding Jumping Jack, self-adhesive coil	2.25	....	....	....	1.75	1.00
3016	32¢ Santa at Chimney, self-adhesive coil . . .	2.25	....	....	....	1.75	1.00
3017	32¢ Boy holding Toy Horse, self-adhesive coil . . .	2.25	....	....	....	1.75	1.00
3018	32¢ Midnight Angel, self-adhesive coil . . .	3.00	....	....	....	1.75	1.00

3019

3020

3021

3022

3023

SCOTT NO.	DESCRIPTION	FIRST DAY COVERS SING	FIRST DAY COVERS PL. BLK.	MINT SHEET	PLATE BLOCK	UNUSED F/NH	USED
3019-23	Antique Automobiles, 5 varieties, attached .	5.50	....	30.00(25)	15.00(10)	7.50	6.50
3019	32¢ 1893 Duryea . . .	2.25	....	....	....	1.50	.90
3020	32¢ 1894 Haynes . . .	2.25	....	....	....	1.50	.90
3021	32¢ 1898 Columbia . .	2.25	....	....	....	1.50	.90
3022	32¢ 1899 Winton	2.25	....	....	....	1.50	.90
3023	32¢ 1901 White	2.25	....	....	....	1.50	.90

3024

3025

3026

3027

3028

3029

1996 COMMEMORATIVES

SCOTT NO.	DESCRIPTION	FIRST DAY COVERS SING	FIRST DAY COVERS PL. BLK.	MINT SHEET	PLATE BLOCK	UNUSED F/NH	USED
3024/3118	(3024, 3030, 3058-67, 3069-70, 3072-88, 3090-3104, 3106-11, 3118) 53 varieties........	....		....	....	60.00	16.00
3024	32¢ Utah Statehood .	2.25	4.75	60.00(50)	5.00	1.25	.25
3025	32¢ Crocus	2.25	....	....	....	1.20	.25
3026	32¢ Winter Aconite . .	2.25	....	....	....	1.20	.25
3027	32¢ Pansy	2.25	....	....	....	1.20	.25
3028	32¢ Snowdrop	2.25	....	....	....	1.20	.25
3029	32¢ Anemone	2.25	....	....	....	1.20	.25
3029a	Winter Garden Flowers, bklt pane of 5	5.50	....	....	....	5.50	4.00
3029av	same, bklt pane, unfolded	....	....	....	....	6.50	....

3030

3031, 3031A, 3044

3032, 3045

3033

3036, 3036a

3048, 3053

3049, 3054

3050, 3051, 3055

3052, 3052E

SCOTT NO.	DESCRIPTION	FIRST DAY COVERS SING	FIRST DAY COVERS PL. BLK.	MINT SHEET	PLATE BLOCK	UNUSED F/NH	USED
3030	32¢ Love (Cherub), self-adhesive	2.25	....	....	....	1.10	.20
3030a	same, bklt pane of 20	14.50	....	....	....	20.00	....
3030b	same, bklt pane of 15	11.50	....	....	....	15.00	....
3031	1¢ Kestrel, self-adhesive	2.25	....	5.00(50)	.75	.20	.20
3031A	1¢ Kestrel, self-adhesive (2000)	1.95	....	5.00(50)	.75	.20	.20
3032	2¢ Red-headed Woodpecker	2.25	4.75	11.00(100)	1.20	.20	.20
3033	3¢ Eastern Bluebird (redesign 3¢)	2.25	4.75	12.00(100)	1.30	.20	.20
3036	$1 Red Fox, self-adhesive	5.00	10.00	50.00(20)	10.00	2.25	.75
3036a	$1 Red Fox, 11.75 X 11(2002)	....	....	43.00(20)	10.00	2.25	.75
3044	1¢ Kestrel, coil	2.25	5.00	....	1.00	.20	.20
3044a	1¢ Kestrel, large date, coil(1999)	2.25	5.00	....	1.00	.20	.20
3045	2¢ Red-headed Wood-pecker, coil	2.25	....	....	1.00	.20	.20
3048	20¢ Blue Jay, self-adhesive	2.25	....	....	....	.75	.20
3048a	same, bklt pane of 10	8.00	....	....	....	7.25	....
3049	32¢ Yellow Rose, self-adhesive	2.25	....	....	....	1.10	.20
3049a	same, bklt pane of 20	14.50	....	....	....	19.50	....
3050	20¢ Ring-necked Pheasant, self-adhesive	2.25	....	....	....	.70	.20
3050a	same, bklt pane of 10	9.00	....	....	....	6.75	....
3050b	20¢ Pheasant, die cut 11	2.25	....	....	....	.70	.20
3050c	same, bklt pane of 10	5.50	....	....	....	6.75	....
3051	20¢ Ring-necked Pheasant, die cut 10 1/2 x 11, self-adhesive	2.25	....	....	....	1.00	.30
3051a	same, sideways, die cut 10 1/2	2.25	....	....	....	6.50	1.50
3051b	same, bklt pane of 5, (4 #3051, 1 #3051a) .	3.50	....	....	....	8.50	....
3052	33¢ Coral Pink Rose, self-adhesive	2.25	....	....	....	1.35	.30
3052a	same, bklt pane of 4 .	3.00	....	....	....	5.25	....
3052b	same, bklt pane of 5 .	3.75	....	....	....	6.50	....
3052c	same, bklt pane of 6 .	4.50	....	....	....	7.50	....
3052d	same, bklt pane of 20	14.50	....	....	....	22.50	....
3052E	33¢ Coral Pink Rose, die-cut 10.75 x 10.5, self-adhesive (2000) .	2.25	....	....	....	1.00	.30
3052Ef	same, bklt pane of 20	14.50	....	....	....	18.00	....
3053	20¢ Blue Jay, self-adhesive, coil (1996)	2.25	....	....	6.00	1.00	.20
3054	32¢ Yellow Rose, self-adhesive coil (1997)	2.25	....	....	7.50	1.00	.20
3055	20¢ Ring-necked Pheasant, self-adhesive coil (1998)	2.25	....	....	5.00	.75	.20

3058

3059

3060

SCOTT NO.	DESCRIPTION	FIRST DAY COVERS SING	FIRST DAY COVERS PL. BLK.	MINT SHEET	PLATE BLOCK	UNUSED F/NH	USED
3058	32¢ Ernest Just	3.00	4.75	19.50(20)	5.00	1.20	.25
3059	32¢ Smithsonian Institution	2.25	4.75	19.50(20)	5.00	1.20	.25
3060	32¢ Year of the Rat . .	2.25	4.75	22.00(20)	5.50	1.40	.25

3061

3062

3063

3064

SCOTT NO.	DESCRIPTION	FIRST DAY COVERS SING	FIRST DAY COVERS PL. BLK.	MINT SHEET	PLATE BLOCK	UNUSED F/NH	USED
3061-64	Pioneers of Communication, 4 varieties, attached .	4.00	4.75	18.00(20)	4.75	4.25	3.25
3061	32¢ Eadweard Muybridge	2.25	....	....	....	1.40	.50
3062	32¢ Ottmar Mergenthaler	2.25	....	....	....	1.40	.50
3063	32¢ Frederic E. Ives .	2.25	....	....	....	1.40	.50
3064	32¢ William Dickson .	2.25	....	....	....	1.40	.50

3065

SCOTT NO.	DESCRIPTION	FIRST DAY COVERS SING	FIRST DAY COVERS PL. BLK.	MINT SHEET	PLATE BLOCK	UNUSED F/NH	USED
3065	32¢ Fulbright Scholarships	2.25	4.75	85.00(50)	8.00	1.50	.25

3066

3067

SCOTT NO.	DESCRIPTION	FIRST DAY COVERS SING	FIRST DAY COVERS PL. BLK.	MINT SHEET	PLATE BLOCK	UNUSED F/NH	USED
3066	50¢ Jacqueline Cochran	2.25	5.00	60.00(50)	5.75	1.50	.50
3067	32¢ Marathon	3.00	4.75	17.00(20)	4.00	1.00	.25

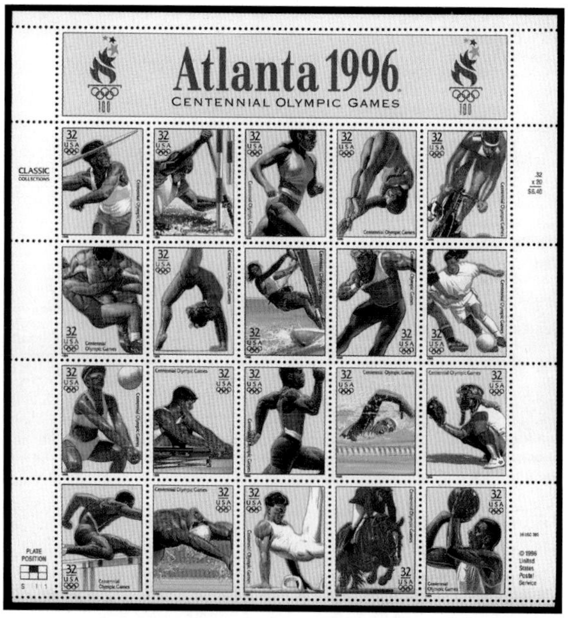

3068

1996 SUMMER OLYMPIC GAMES

3068a	*Decathlon*	**3068k**	*Beach volleyball*
3068b	*Men's canoeing*	**3068l**	*Men's rowing*
3068c	*Women's running*	**3068m**	*Men's sprints*
3068d	*Women's diving*	**3068n**	*Women's swimming*
3068e	*Men's cycling*	**3068o**	*Women's softball*
3068f	*Freestyle wrestling*	**3068p**	*Men's hurdles*
3068g	*Women's gymnastics*	**3068q**	*Men's swimming*
3068h	*Women's sailboarding*	**3068r**	*Men's gymnastics*
3068i	*Men's shot put*	**3068s**	*Equestrian*
3068j	*Women's soccer*	**3068t**	*Men's basketball*

SCOTT NO.	DESCRIPTION	FIRST DAY COVERS SING	FIRST DAY COVERS PL. BLK.	MINT SHEET	PLATE BLOCK	UNUSED F/NH	USED
3068	32¢ Centennial Olympic Games, 20 varieties, attached	....	....	20.00(20)	....	25.00	16.00
....	set of singles	35.00	....	....	....	....	14.00
....	single of above, each	....	....	....	....	....	.90
3068v	same as above, uncut sheet of 120 (6 panes)	....	....	135.00(120)	....	135.00	....
....	cross gutter block of 20	....	....	....	....	35.00	....
....	cross gutter block of 4	....	....	....	....	19.50	....
....	vertical pair with horizontal gutter	....	....	....	....	4.50	....
....	horizontal pair with vertical gutter	....	....	....	....	4.50	....

3069

3070, 3071

SCOTT NO.	DESCRIPTION	FIRST DAY COVERS SING	FIRST DAY COVERS PL. BLK.	MINT SHEET	PLATE BLOCK	UNUSED F/NH	USED
3069	32¢ Georgia O'Keeffe	2.25	....	17.50(15)	5.50	1.50	.25
3070	32¢ Tennessee Statehood	2.25	4.75	38.00(50)	4.00	.80	.25
3071	32¢ Tennessee Statehood, self-adhesive	2.25	....	....	....	1.10	.40
3071a	same, bklt pane of 20	14.50	....	....	....	20.00	....

3072

3073

3074

3075

3076

SCOTT NO.	DESCRIPTION	FIRST DAY COVERS SING	FIRST DAY COVERS PL. BLK.	MINT SHEET	PLATE BLOCK	UNUSED F/NH	USED
3072-76	American Indian Dances, 5 varieties, attached	5.50	....	30.00(20)	18.00(10)	8.00	7.00
3072	32¢ Fancy Dance	2.25	....	....	....	1.25	.50
3073	32¢ Butterfly Dance	2.25	....	....	....	1.25	.50
3074	32¢ Traditional Dance	2.25	....	....	....	1.25	.50
3075	32¢ Raven Dance	2.25	....	....	....	1.25	.50
3076	32¢ Hoop Dance	2.25	....	....	....	1.25	.50

3077 3078

3079 3080

SCOTT NO.	DESCRIPTION	FIRST DAY COVERS SING	FIRST DAY COVERS PL. BLK.	MINT SHEET	PLATE BLOCK	UNUSED F/NH	USED
3077-80	Prehistoric Animals, 4 varieties, attached	4.00	4.75	30.00(20)	6.50	5.00	3.00
3077	32¢ Eohippus	2.25	....	....	....	1.25	.40
3078	32¢ Woolly Mammoth	2.25	....	....	....	1.25	.40
3079	32¢ Mastodon	2.25	....	....	....	1.25	.40
3080	32¢ Saber-tooth Cat	2.25	....	....	....	1.25	.40

3081

3082

SCOTT NO.	DESCRIPTION	FIRST DAY COVERS SING	FIRST DAY COVERS PL. BLK.	MINT SHEET	PLATE BLOCK	UNUSED F/NH	USED
3081	32¢ Breast Cancer Awareness	2.25	4.75	20.00(20)	5.00	1.10	.25
3082	32¢ James Dean	3.00	4.75	24.00(20)	6.00	1.25	.25
3082v	same as above, uncut sheet of 120 (6 panes)	....	....	175.00(120)	....	175.00(120)	....
....	block of 8 with vertical gutter	....	....	....	....	29.00	....
....	cross gutter block of 8	....	....	....	....	37.50	....
....	vertical pair with horizontal gutter	....	....	....	....	4.50	....
....	horizontal pair with vertical gutter	....	....	....	....	7.00	....

3083

3084

3085

3086

SCOTT NO.	DESCRIPTION	FIRST DAY COVERS SING	FIRST DAY COVERS PL. BLK.	MINT SHEET	PLATE BLOCK	UNUSED F/NH	USED
3083-86	Folk Heroes, 4 varieties, attached .	4.00	4.75	20.00(20)	5.25	4.75	3.50
3083	32¢ Mighty Casey . . .	2.25	....	....	....	1.50	.50
3084	32¢ Paul Bunyan . . .	2.25	....	....	....	1.50	.50
3085	32¢ John Henry	2.25	....	....	....	1.50	.50
3086	32¢ Pecos Bill	2.25	....	....	....	1.50	.50

3087

3088, 3089

SCOTT NO.	DESCRIPTION	FIRST DAY COVERS SING	FIRST DAY COVERS PL. BLK.	MINT SHEET	PLATE BLOCK	UNUSED F/NH	USED
3087	32¢ Olympic Discus Thrower	2.25	4.75	27.50(20)	7.00	1.50	.25
3088	32¢ Iowa Statehood .	2.25	4.75	70.00(50)	7.00	1.25	.25
3089	32¢ Iowa Statehood, self-adhesive	2.25	....	....	....	1.25	.30
3089a	same, bklt pane of 20	14.50	....	....	....	21.00	....

3090

SCOTT NO.	DESCRIPTION	FIRST DAY COVERS SING	FIRST DAY COVERS PL. BLK.	MINT SHEET	PLATE BLOCK	UNUSED F/NH	USED
3090	32¢ Rural Free Delivery	2.25	4.75	17.50(20)	5.00	1.25	.25

3091

3092

3093

3094

3095

SCOTT NO.	DESCRIPTION	FIRST DAY COVERS SING	FIRST DAY COVERS PL. BLK.	MINT SHEET	PLATE BLOCK	UNUSED F/NH	USED
3091-95	Riverboats, 5 varieties, attached .	6.50	....	25.00(20)	12.50(10)	6.00	5.00
3091	32¢ Robt. E. Lee	2.25	....	....	....	1.20	.35
3092	32¢ Sylvan Dell	2.25	....	....	....	1.20	.35
3093	32¢ Far West	2.25	....	....	....	1.20	.35
3094	32¢ Rebecca Everingham	2.25	....	....	....	1.20	.35
3095	32¢ Bailey Gatzert . .	2.25	....	....	....	1.20	.35
3091-95b	32¢ Riverboats, special die cutting, 5 attached . .	....	....	....	170.00(10)	82.50	....
3095b	same, as above, pane of 20	....	....	325.00(20)	....	325.00	....

3098 3099

3096 3097

SCOTT NO.	DESCRIPTION	FIRST DAY COVERS SING	FIRST DAY COVERS PL. BLK.	MINT SHEET	PLATE BLOCK	UNUSED F/NH	USED
3096-99	Big Band Leaders, 4 varieties, attached .	6.00	7.00	27.00(20)	7.00	5.50	4.50
3096	32¢ Count Basie	2.25	....	....	....	1.50	.50
3097	32¢ Tommy & Jimmy Dorsey	2.25	....	....	....	1.50	.50
3098	32¢ Glenn Miller	2.25	....	....	....	1.50	.50
3099	32¢ Benny Goodman	2.25	....	....	....	1.50	.50

3102 3103

3100 3101

SCOTT NO.	DESCRIPTION	FIRST DAY COVERS SING	FIRST DAY COVERS PL. BLK.	MINT SHEET	PLATE BLOCK	UNUSED F/NH	USED
3100-03	Songwriters, 4 varieties, attached .	6.00	7.00	27.00(20)	7.00	5.50	4.50
3100	32¢ Harold Arlen	2.25	....	....	....	1.50	.50
3101	32¢ Johnny Mercer . .	2.25	....	....	....	1.50	.50
3102	32¢ Dorothy Fields . .	2.25	....	....	....	1.50	.50
3103	32¢ Hoagy Carmichael	2.25	....	....	....	1.50	.50

3104

SCOTT NO.	DESCRIPTION	FIRST DAY COVERS SING	FIRST DAY COVERS PL. BLK.	MINT SHEET	PLATE BLOCK	UNUSED F/NH	USED
3104	23¢ F. Scott Fitzgerald	2.25	4.75	48.00(50)	5.00	1.00	.25

SE-TENANTS: Beginning with the 1964 Christmas issue (#1254-57), the United States has issued numerous Se-Tenant stamps covering a wide variety of subjects. Se-Tenants are issues where two or more different stamp designs are produced on the same sheet in pair, strip or block form. Mint stamps are usually collected in attached blocks, etc.—Used are generally saved as single stamps. Our Se-Tenant prices follow in this collecting pattern.

3105

ENDANGERED SPECIES

3105a	*Black-footed ferret*	**3105i**	*California condor*
3105b	*Thick-billed parrot*	**3105j**	*Gila trout*
3105c	*Hawaiian monk seal*	**3105k**	*San Francisco garter snake*
3105d	*American crocodile*	**3105l**	*Woodland caribou*
3105e	*Ocelot*	**3105m**	*Florida panther*
3105f	*Schaus swallowtail butterfly*	**3105n**	*Piping plover*
3105g	*Wyoming toad*	**3105o**	*Florida manatee*
3105h	*Brown pelican*		

SCOTT NO.	DESCRIPTION	FIRST DAY COVERS SING	FIRST DAY COVERS PL. BLK.	MINT SHEET	PLATE BLOCK	UNUSED F/NH	USED
3105	32¢ Endangered Species, 15 varieties, attached	15.00	....	22.00(15)	....	20.00	15.00
....	set of singles	27.50	....	....	....	....	12.00
....	singles of above, each	....	....	....	....	....	1.00

3106

3107, 3112

SCOTT NO.	DESCRIPTION	FIRST DAY COVERS SING	FIRST DAY COVERS PL. BLK.	MINT SHEET	PLATE BLOCK	UNUSED F/NH	USED
3106	32¢ Computer Technology	2.25	4.75	35.00(40)	4.00	1.00	.25
3107	32¢ Madonna & Child	2.25	4.75	38.00(50)	4.25	1.00	.20

3108, 3113

3109, 3114

3110, 3115

3111, 3116

SCOTT NO.	DESCRIPTION	FIRST DAY COVERS SING	FIRST DAY COVERS PL. BLK.	MINT SHEET	PLATE BLOCK	UNUSED F/NH	USED
3108-11	Christmas Family Scenes, 4 varieties, attached	4.00	4.75	50.00(50)	5.50	5.00	4.00
3108	32¢ Family at Fireplace	2.25	....	....	....	1.25	.30
3109	32¢ Decorating Tree	2.25	....	....	....	1.25	.30
3110	32¢ Dreaming of SantaClaus	2.25	....	....	....	1.25	.30
3111	32¢ Holiday Shopping	2.25	....	....	....	1.25	.30
3112	32¢ Madonna & Child, self-adhesive	2.25	....	....	....	1.00	.30
3112a	same, bklt pane of 20	14.50	....	....	....	18.00	....
3113	32¢ Family at Fireplace, self-adhesive	2.25	....	....	....	1.20	.30
3114	32¢ Decorating Tree, self-adhesive	2.25	....	....	....	1.20	.30
3115	32¢ Dreaming of Santa Claus, self-adhesive	2.25	....	....	....	1.20	.30
3116	32¢ Holiday Shopping, self-adhesive	2.25	....	....	....	1.20	.30
3116a	Christams Family Scenes, self-adhesive, bklt pane of 20	14.50	....	....	....	18.00	....

3117

3118

SCOTT NO.	DESCRIPTION	FIRST DAY COVERS SING	FIRST DAY COVERS PL. BLK.	MINT SHEET	PLATE BLOCK	UNUSED F/NH	USED
3117	32¢ Skaters, self-adhesive	2.25	....	....	....	1.10	.40
3117a	same, bklt pane of 18	13.00	....	....	....	18.50	....
3118	32¢ Hanukkah, self-adhesive	2.25	....	17.00(20)	4.50	1.00	.25

3119

SCOTT NO.	DESCRIPTION	FIRST DAY COVERS SING	FIRST DAY COVERS PL. BLK.	MINT SHEET	PLATE BLOCK	UNUSED F/NH	USED
3119	50¢ Cycling, sheet of 2	4.00	....	....	....	3.25	3.00
3119a-b	same, set of 2 singles	5.00	....	....	....	3.00	2.50

3120

3121

1997 COMMEMORATIVES

SCOTT NO.	DESCRIPTION	FIRST DAY COVERS SING	FIRST DAY COVERS PL. BLK.	MINT SHEET	PLATE BLOCK	UNUSED F/NH	USED
3120/75	**(3120-21, 3125, 3130-31, 3134-35, 3141, 3143-50, 3152-75) 40 varieties**	....	....	....	....	**43.50**	**15.00**
3120	32¢ Year of the Ox . .	3.00	....	24.00(20)	5.00	1.20	.25
3121	32¢ Benjamin O. Davis, Sr.	3.00	4.75	24.00(20)	4.50	1.10	.25

3122

SCOTT NO.	DESCRIPTION	FIRST DAY COVERS SING	FIRST DAY COVERS PL. BLK.	MINT SHEET	PLATE BLOCK	UNUSED F/NH	USED
3122	32¢ Statue of Liberty, self-adhesive (1997)	2.25	....	....	....	1.35	.25
3122a	same, bklt pane of 20	14.50	....	....	....	20.00	....
3122b	same, bklt pane of 4	4.75	....	....	....	5.00	....
3122c	same, bklt pane of 5	5.00	....	....	....	6.00	....
3122d	same, bklt pane of 6	5.75	....	....	....	7.00	....
3122E	32¢ Statue of Liberty, die cut 11.5 x 11.8 .	....	....	....	....	2.00	1.00
3122Ef	same, bklt pane of 20	....	....	....	....	40.00	....
3122Eg	same, bklt pane of 6	....	....	....	....	11.00	....

3123

3124

SCOTT NO.	DESCRIPTION	FIRST DAY COVERS SING	FIRST DAY COVERS PL. BLK.	MINT SHEET	PLATE BLOCK	UNUSED F/NH	USED
3123	32¢ Swans, self-adhesive	2.25	....	....	....	1.10	.35
3123a	same, bklt pane of 20	14.50	....	....	....	19.50	....
3124	55¢ Swans, self-adhesive	2.50	....	....	....	2.00	.60
3124a	same, bklt pane of 20	19.75	....	....	....	33.50	....

3125

SCOTT NO.	DESCRIPTION	FIRST DAY COVERS SING	FIRST DAY COVERS PL. BLK.	MINT SHEET	PLATE BLOCK	UNUSED F/NH	USED
3125	32¢ Helping Children Learn	2.25	4.75	19.50(20)	5.00	1.10	.25

3126, 3128

3127, 3129

SCOTT NO.	DESCRIPTION	FIRST DAY COVERS SING	FIRST DAY COVERS PL. BLK.	MINT SHEET	PLATE BLOCK	UNUSED F/NH	USED
3126	32¢ Citron, Moth, Larvae, Pupa, Beetle, self-adhesive (Die Cut 10.9 x 10.2) .	2.25	....	....	....	1.10	.35
3127	32¢ Flowering Pineapple, Cockroaches, self-adhesive (Die Cut 10.9 x 10.2) .	2.25	....	....	....	1.10	.35
3127a	same, bklt pane of 20 (10–#3126, 10–#3127)	14.50	....	....	....	19.50	....
3128	32¢ Citron, Moth, Larvae, Pupa, Beetle, self-adhesive (Die Cut 11.2 x 10.8) .	2.25	....	....	....	1.75	.60
3128a	same, stamp sideways	2.25	....	....	....	5.00	1.00
3128b	same, bklt pane of 5 (2–#3128 & #3129, 1–#3128a)	5.50	....	....	....	10.00	....
3129	32¢ Flowering Pineapple, Cockroaches, self-adhesive (Die Cut 11.2 x 10.8) .	2.25	....	....	....	1.75	.60
3129a	same, stamp sideways	2.25	....	....	....	10.00	2.00
3129b	same, bklt pane of 5 (2–#3128 & #3129, 1–#3129a)	5.50	....	....	....	15.00	....

3130

3131

SCOTT NO.	DESCRIPTION	FIRST DAY COVERS SING	FIRST DAY COVERS PL. BLK.	MINT SHEET	PLATE BLOCK	UNUSED F/NH	USED
3130-31	32¢ Stagecoach & Ship, (Pacific '97) 2 varieties, attached	3.00	4.75	16.50(16)	5.00	2.25	2.00
3130	32¢ Ship	2.25	....	....	....	1.20	.35
3131	32¢ Stagecoach	2.25	....	....	....	1.20	.35
3130-31v	same, as above, uncut sheet of 96 (6 panes)	....	....	110.00(96)	....	110.00	....
....	block of 32 with vertical or horizontal gutter between (2 panes)	....	....	37.50(32)	....	37.50	....
....	cross gutter block of 16	....	....	....	....	30.00	....
....	vertical pairs with horizontal gutter	....	....	....	....	10.00	....
....	horizontal pairs with vertical gutter	....	....	....	....	8.00	....

3132

SCOTT NO.	DESCRIPTION	FIRST DAY COVERS SING	FIRST DAY COVERS PL. BLK.	MINT SHEET	PLATE BLOCK	UNUSED F/NH	USED
3132	(25¢) Juke Box, self-adhesive linerless coil	2.25	....	....	10.00	2.00	1.00
3133	32¢ Flag Over Porch, self-adhesive, linerless coil	2.25	....	....	10.00	1.30	1.00

3134

3135

SCOTT NO.	DESCRIPTION	FIRST DAY COVERS SING	FIRST DAY COVERS PL. BLK.	MINT SHEET	PLATE BLOCK	UNUSED F/NH	USED
3134	32¢ Thornton Wilder .	2.25	4.75	17.50(20)	4.50	1.10	.25
3135	32¢ Raoul Wallenberg	3.00	4.75	17.50(20)	4.50	1.10	.25

3136

DINOSAURS

3136a	*Ceratosaurus*	**3136f**	*Stegosaurus*	**3136k**	*Daspletosaurus*
3136b	*Camptosaurus*	**3136g**	*Allosaurus*	**3136l**	*Palaeosaniwa*
3136c	*Camarasaurus*	**3136h**	*Opisthias*	**3136m**	*Corythosaurus*
3136d	*Brachiosaurus*	**3136i**	*Edmontonia*	**3136n**	*Ornithominus*
3136e	*Goniopholis*	**3136j**	*Einiosaurus*	**3136o**	*Parasaurolophus*

SCOTT NO.	DESCRIPTION	FIRST DAY COVERS SING	FIRST DAY COVERS PL. BLK.	MINT SHEET	PLATE BLOCK	UNUSED F/NH	USED
3136	32¢ Dinosaurs, 15 varieties, attached	11.50	....	....	....	20.00	18.00
....	set of singles	26.50	....	....	....	....	10.00
....	singles of above, each	....	....	....	....	....	.75

3137, 3138

SCOTT NO.	DESCRIPTION	FIRST DAY COVERS SING	FIRST DAY COVERS PL. BLK.	MINT SHEET	PLATE BLOCK	UNUSED F/NH	USED
3137	32¢ Bugs Bunny, self-adhesive, pane of 10	9.50	....	....	....	12.50	....
3137a	same, single from pane	2.50	....	....	....	1.25	.35
3137b	same, pane of 9 (#3137a)	....	....	....	....	7.00	....
3137c	same, pane of 1 (#3137a)	....	....	....	....	2.50	....
3137v	same, top press sheet (6 panes) ...		....	525.00	....	525.00	....
3137v	same, bottom press w/ plate# (6 panes)		....	800.00	....	800.00	....
....	pane of 10 from press sheet	....	....	95.00	....	95.00	....
....	pane of 10 from press sheet w/ plate#		....	500.00	....	500.00	....

1997 COMMEMORATIVES (continued)

SCOTT NO.	DESCRIPTION	FIRST DAY COVERS SING	FIRST DAY COVERS PL. BLK.	MINT SHEET	PLATE BLOCK	UNUSED F/NH	USED
3138	32¢ Bug Bunny, self-adhesive, Die Cut, pane of 10 . .	....	....	....	....	200.00	....
3138a	same, single from pane	....	....	....	....	....	....
3138b	same, pane of 9 (#3138a)	....	....	....	....	....	....
3138c	same, pane of 1 (#3138a)	....	....	....	....	190.00	....

3139

3140

SCOTT NO.	DESCRIPTION	FIRST DAY COVERS SING	FIRST DAY COVERS PL. BLK.	MINT SHEET	PLATE BLOCK	UNUSED F/NH	USED
3139	50¢ Benjamin Franklin, Souvenir Sheet of 12 (Pacific '97)	25.00	....	....	....	20.00	....
3139a	same, single from sheet	5.00	....	....	....	1.60	1.50
3140	60¢ George Washington, Souvenir Sheet of 12 (Pacific '97)	25.00	....	....	....	22.00	....
3140a	same, single from sheet	5.00	....	....	....	1.85	1.50

3141

SCOTT NO.	DESCRIPTION	FIRST DAY COVERS SING	FIRST DAY COVERS PL. BLK.	MINT SHEET	PLATE BLOCK	UNUSED F/NH	USED
3141	32¢ Marshall Plan . . .	1.95	4.75	17.50(20)	4.25	1.00	.25

3142

CLASSIC AMERICAN AIRCRAFT

3142a	*Mustang*	**3142k**	*Flying Fortress*
3142b	*Model B*	**3142l**	*Stearman*
3142c	*Cub*	**3142m**	*Constellation*
3142d	*Vega*	**3142n**	*Lightning*
3142e	*Alpha*	**3142o**	*Peashooter*
3142f	*B-10*	**3142p**	*Tri-Motor*
3142g	*Corsair*	**3142q**	*DC-3*
3142h	*Stratojet*	**3142r**	*314 Clipper*
3142i	*GeeBee*	**3142s**	*Jenny*
3142j	*Staggerwing*	**3142t**	*Wildcat*

SCOTT NO.	DESCRIPTION	FIRST DAY COVERS SING	FIRST DAY COVERS PL. BLK.	MINT SHEET	PLATE BLOCK	UNUSED F/NH	USED
3142	32¢ Classic American Aircraft, 20 varieties, attached	....	....	18.50(20)	....	20.00	15.00
....	set of singles	35.00	....	....	....	....	12.00
	singles of above, each	....	....	....	....	....	.75
3142v	same as above, uncut sheet of 120 (6 panes)	....	....	125.00(120)	....	125.00	....
....	cross gutter block of 20	....	....	....	....	28.00	....
....	cross gutter block of 4	....	....	....	....	18.50	....
....	vertical pair with horizontal gutter	....	....	....	....	3.50	....
....	horizontal pair with vertical gutter	....	....	....	....	3.50	....

3143, 3148   3144, 3149

3145, 3147   3146, 3150

SCOTT NO.	DESCRIPTION	FIRST DAY COVERS SING	FIRST DAY COVERS PL. BLK.	MINT SHEET	PLATE BLOCK	UNUSED F/NH	USED
3143-46	Legendary Football Coaches, 4 varieties, attached .	4.00	4.75	19.50(20)	7.00	5.00	4.00
3143	32¢ Paul "Bear" Bryant	2.25	....	....	....	1.30	.80
3144	32¢ Glenn "Pop" Warner	2.25	....	....	....	1.30	.80
3145	32¢ Vince Lombardi .	2.25	....	....	....	1.30	.80
3146	32¢ George Halas . . .	2.25	....	....	....	1.30	.80
3147	32¢ Vince Lombardi .	2.25	4.75	19.50(20)	7.00	1.30	.80
3148	32¢ Paul "Bear" Bryant	2.25	4.75	19.50(20)	7.00	1.30	.80
3149	32¢ Glenn "Pop" Warner	2.25	4.75	19.50(20)	7.00	1.30	.80
3150	32¢ George Halas . . .	2.25	4.75	19.50(20)	7.00	1.30	.80

3151

CLASSIC AMERICAN DOLLS

3151a	*"Alabama Baby," and doll by Martha Chase*	**3151i**	*"Babyland Rag"*
3151b	*"Columbian Doll"*	**3151j**	*"Scootles"*
3151c	*Johnny Gruelle's "Raggedy Ann"*	**3151k**	*Doll by Ludwig Greiner*
3151d	*Doll by Martha Chase*	**3151l**	*"Betsy McCall"*
3151e	*"American Child"*	**3151m**	*Percy Crosby's "Skippy"*
3151f	*"Baby Coos"*	**3151n**	*"Maggie Mix-up"*
3151g	*Plains Indian*	**3151o**	*Dolls by Albert Schoenhut*
3151h	*Doll by Izannah Walker*		

SCOTT NO.	DESCRIPTION	FIRST DAY COVERS SING	FIRST DAY COVERS PL. BLK.	MINT SHEET	PLATE BLOCK	UNUSED F/NH	USED
3151	32¢ Classic American Dolls, 15 varieties, attached	....	....	20.00(15)	....	22.00	18.00
....	set of singles	30.00	....	....	....	....	12.00
....	singles of above. each	....	....	....	....	....	.80

3152

SCOTT NO.	DESCRIPTION	FIRST DAY COVERS SING	FIRST DAY COVERS PL. BLK.	MINT SHEET	PLATE BLOCK	UNUSED F/NH	USED
3152	32¢ Humphrey Bogart	3.00	....	25.00(20)	5.00	1.10	.25
3152v	same, as above, uncut sheet of 120 (6 panes)	....	....	125.00(120)	....	125.00	....
....	block of 8 with vertical gutter	....	....	....	....	18.00	....
....	cross gutter block of 8	....	....	....	....	21.00	....
....	vertical pair with horizontal gutter	....	....	....	....	3.50	....
....	horizontal pair with vertical gutter	....	....	....	....	5.00	....

3153

SCOTT NO.	DESCRIPTION	FIRST DAY COVERS SING	FIRST DAY COVERS PL. BLK.	MINT SHEET	PLATE BLOCK	UNUSED F/NH	USED
3153	32¢ "The Stars & Stripes Forever"	2.25	4.75	45.00(50)	5.50	1.00	.25

3154

3155

3156

3157

SCOTT NO.	DESCRIPTION	FIRST DAY COVERS SING	FIRST DAY COVERS PL. BLK.	MINT SHEET	PLATE BLOCK	UNUSED F/NH	USED
3154-57	Opera Singers, 4 varieties, attached .	4.00	4.75	21.50(20)	5.25	4.75	4.00
3154	32¢ Lily Pons	2.25	....	....	....	1.25	1.00
3155	32¢ Richard Tucker . .	2.25	....	....	....	1.25	1.00
3156	32¢ Lawrence Tibbett	2.25	....	....	....	1.25	1.00
3157	32¢ Rosa Ponselle . .	2.25	....	....	....	1.25	1.00

3158

3159

3160

3161

3162

3163

3164

3165

SCOTT NO.	DESCRIPTION	FIRST DAY COVERS SING	FIRST DAY COVERS PL. BLK.	MINT SHEET	PLATE BLOCK	UNUSED F/NH	USED
3158-65	Composers and Conductors, 8 varieties, attached .	7.00	....	23.50(20)	12.00(8)	10.00	9.00
3158	32¢ Leopold Stokowski	2.25	....	....	....	1.50	1.00
3159	32¢ Arthur Fiedler . . .	2.25	....	....	....	1.50	1.00
3160	32¢ George Szell . . .	2.25	....	....	....	1.50	1.00
3161	32¢ Eugene Ormandy	2.25	....	....	....	1.50	1.00
3162	32¢ Samuel Barber . .	2.25	....	....	....	1.50	1.00
3163	32¢ Ferde Grofé	2.25	....	....	....	1.50	1.00
3164	32¢ Charles Ives	2.25	....	....	....	1.50	1.00
3165	32¢ Louis Moreau Gottschalk	2.25	....	....	....	1.50	1.00

3166

3167

SCOTT NO.	DESCRIPTION	FIRST DAY COVERS SING	FIRST DAY COVERS PL. BLK.	MINT SHEET	PLATE BLOCK	UNUSED F/NH	USED
3166	32¢ Padre Félix Varela	2.25	4.75	17.00(20)	4.00	1.00	.50
3167	32¢ U.S. Air Force 50th Anniversary	4.00	6.00	17.00(20)	4.00	1.25	.30

3168

3169

3170

3171

3172

SCOTT NO.	DESCRIPTION	FIRST DAY COVERS SING	FIRST DAY COVERS PL. BLK.	MINT SHEET	PLATE BLOCK	UNUSED F/NH	USED
3168-72	Movie Monster, 5 varieties, attached .	10.00	....	25.00(20)	14.00(10)	7.00	5.00
3168	32¢ Lon Chaney as The Phantom of the Opera	2.25	....	....	....	1.50	.75
3169	32¢ Bela Lugosi as Dracula	2.25	....	....	....	1.50	.75
3170	32¢ Boris Karloff as Frankenstein's Monster	2.25	....	....	....	1.50	.75
3171	32¢ Boris Karloff as The Mummy	2.25	....	....	....	1.50	.75
3172	32¢ Lon Chaney Jr. as The Wolfman	2.25	....	....	....	1.50	.75
3168-72v	same as above, uncut sheet of 180 (9 panes)	....	....	225.00(180)	....	225.00	....
....	block of 8 with vertical gutter	......	....	....	....	14.00	....
....	block of 10 with horizontal gutter	....	....	....	....	17.50	....
....	cross gutter block of 8	....	....	....	....	22.50	....
....	vertical pair with horizontal gutter	....	....	....	....	4.00	....
....	horizontal pair with vertical gutter	....	....	....	....	4.00	....

3173

SCOTT NO.	DESCRIPTION	FIRST DAY COVERS SING	FIRST DAY COVERS PL. BLK.	MINT SHEET	PLATE BLOCK	UNUSED F/NH	USED
3173	32¢ First Supersonic Flight, 50th Anniversary	3.00	4.75	17.50(20)	4.25	1.00	.25

3174

SCOTT NO.	DESCRIPTION	FIRST DAY COVERS SING	FIRST DAY COVERS PL. BLK.	MINT SHEET	PLATE BLOCK	UNUSED F/NH	USED
3174	32¢ Women in Military Service	3.00	4.75	17.50(20)	4.25	1.00	.25

3175

SCOTT NO.	DESCRIPTION	FIRST DAY COVERS SING	FIRST DAY COVERS PL. BLK.	MINT SHEET	PLATE BLOCK	UNUSED F/NH	USED
3175	32¢ Kwanzaa	3.00	4.75	42.00(50)	5.00	1.00	.25
....	same, as above, uncut sheet of 250 (5 panes)	....	....	725.00(250)	....	....	....

3176

3177

SCOTT NO.	DESCRIPTION	FIRST DAY COVERS SING	FIRST DAY COVERS PL. BLK.	MINT SHEET	PLATE BLOCK	UNUSED F/NH	USED
3176	32¢ Madonna & Child, self-adhesive	2.25	....	....	....	1.00	.20
3176a	same, bklt pane of 20	14.50	....	....	....	17.50	....
3177	32¢ American Holly, self-adhesive	2.25	....	....	....	1.00	.20
3177a	same, bklt pane of 20	14.50	....	....	....	17.50	....
3177b	same, bklt pane of 4 .	3.00	....	....	....	4.50	....
3177c	same, bklt pane of 5 .	3.75	....	....	....	5.50	....
3177d	same, bklt pane of 6 .	4.50	....	....	....	6.50	....

3178

SCOTT NO.	DESCRIPTION	FIRST DAY COVERS SING	FIRST DAY COVERS PL. BLK.	MINT SHEET	PLATE BLOCK	UNUSED F/NH	USED
3178	$3 Mars Rover Sojourner, Souvenir Sheet	14.00	....	....	....	10.00	9.00
....	same, as above, uncut sheet of 18 souvenir sheets	....	....	195.00(18)	....	195.00	....
3178v	single souvenir sheet from uncut sheet of 18		....	....	....	15.00	....

3179

1998 COMMEMORATIVES

SCOTT NO.	DESCRIPTION	FIRST DAY COVERS SING	FIRST DAY COVERS PL. BLK.	MINT SHEET	PLATE BLOCK	UNUSED F/NH	USED
3179/3252	**(3179-81, 3192-3203, 3206, 3211-27, 3230-35, 3237-43, 3249-52) 50 varieties**	....	....	....	....	**57.25**	**17.00**
3179	32¢ Year of the Tiger	3.00	4.75	22.50(20)	5.50	1.20	.25

3180

3181

SCOTT NO.	DESCRIPTION	FIRST DAY COVERS SING	FIRST DAY COVERS PL. BLK.	MINT SHEET	PLATE BLOCK	UNUSED F/NH	USED
3180	32¢ Alpine Skiing . . .	2.25	4.75	18.50(20)	4.50	1.00	.25
3181	32¢ Madam C.J. Walker	3.00	4.75	18.50(20)	5.00	1.25	.25

3182

CELEBRATE THE CENTURY 1900's

3182a *Model T Ford*
3182b *Theodore Roosevelt*
3182c *"The Great Train Robbery" 1903*
3182d *Crayola Crayons, introduced, 1903*
3182e *St. Louis World's Fair, 1904*
3182f *Pure Food & Drug Act, 1906*
3182g *Wright Brothers first flight, 1903*
3182h *Boxing match in painting*
3182i *Immigrants arrive.*
3182j *John Muir, preservationist*
3182k *"Teddy" bear created*
3182l *W.E.B. DuBois, social activist*
3182m *Gibson Girl*
3182n *First baseball World Series, 1903*
3182o *Robie House, Chicago*

SCOTT NO.	DESCRIPTION	FIRST DAY COVERS SING	FIRST DAY COVERS PL. BLK.	MINT SHEET	PLATE BLOCK	UNUSED F/NH	USED
3182	32¢ Celebrate the Century 1900's, 15 varieties, attached	17.50	....	15.00(15)	....	15.00	12.00
....	set of singles	32.00	....	....	....	....	9.00
....	singles of above, each	....	....	....	....	....	.75
3182v	same as above, uncut sheet of 60 (4 panes)	....	....	70.00(4)	....	70.00	....

3183

CELEBRATE THE CENTURY 1910's

3183a *Charlie Chaplin as the Little Tramp*
3183b *Federal Reserve system created, 1913*
3183c *George Washington Carver*
3183d *Avant-garde art, 1913*
3183e *First-Transcontinental telephone line, 1914*
3183f *Panama Canal opens, 1914*
3183g *Jim Thorpe wins decathlon, 1912*
3183h *Grand Canyon National Park, 1913*
3183i *United States enters WWI*
3183j *Boy Scouts, 1910*
3183k *Woodrow Wilson*
3183l *First crossword puzzle, pub., 1913*
3183m *Jack Dempsey wins title, 1919*
3183n *Construction toys*
3183o *Child labor reform*

SCOTT NO.	DESCRIPTION	FIRST DAY COVERS SING	FIRST DAY COVERS PL. BLK.	MINT SHEET	PLATE BLOCK	UNUSED F/NH	USED
3183	32¢ Celebrate the Century 1910's, 15 varieties, attached	17.50	....	15.00(15)	....	15.00	12.00
....	set of singles	32.00	....	....	....	....	9.00
....	singles of above, each	....	....	....	....	....	.75
3183v	same as above, uncut sheet of 60 (4 panes)	....	....	70.00(4)	....	70.00	....

3184

CELEBRATE THE CENTURY 1920's

3184a *Babe Ruth*
3184b *The Gatsby style*
3184c *Prohibition enforced*
3184d *Electric toy trains*
3184e *19th Ammendment*
3184f *Emily Post's Etiquette*
3184g *Margaret Mead, anthropologist*
3184h *Flappers do the Charleston*
3184i *Radio entertains America*
3184j *Art Deco style (Chrysler Building)*
3184k *Jazz flourishes*
3184l *Four Horsemen of Notre Dame*
3184m *Lindbergh flies the Atlantic*
3184n *American realism*
3184o *Stock Market crash, 1929*

SCOTT NO.	DESCRIPTION	FIRST DAY COVERS SING	FIRST DAY COVERS PL. BLK.	MINT SHEET	PLATE BLOCK	UNUSED F/NH	USED
3184	32¢ Celebrate the Century 1920's, 15 varieties, attached	17.50	....	15.00(15)	....	15.00	12.00
....	set of singles	32.00	....	....	....	....	9.00
....	singles of above, each	....	....	....	....	....	.75
3184v	same, as above, uncut sheet of 60 (4 panes)	....	....	70.00(4)	....	70.00	....

3185

CELEBRATE THE CENTURY 1930's

3185a *Franklin D. Roosevelt*
3185b *Empire State Building*
3185c *1st Issue of Life Magazine*
3185d *Eleanor Roosevelt*
3185e *FDR's New Deal*
3185f *Superman arrives*
3185g *Household conveniences*
3185h *"Snow White and the Seven Dwarfs"*
3185i *"Gone with the Wind"*
3185j *Jesse Owens*
3185k *Streamline design*
3185l *Golden Gate Bridge*
3185m *America survives the Depression*
3185n *Bobby Jones wins Grand Slam*
3185o *The Monopoly Game*

SCOTT NO.	DESCRIPTION	FIRST DAY COVERS SING	FIRST DAY COVERS PL. BLK.	MINT SHEET	PLATE BLOCK	UNUSED F/NH	USED
3185	32¢ Celebrate the Century 1930's, 15 varieties, attached	17.50	....	15.00(15)	....	15.00	12.00
....	set of singles	32.00	....	....	....	....	9.00
....	singles of above, each	....	....	....	....	....	.75
3185v	same as above, uncut sheet of 60 (4 panes)	....	....	70.00(4)	....	70.00	....

3186

CELEBRATE THE CENTURY 1940's

3186a	*World War II*	**3186i**	*GI Bill, 1944*
3186b	*Antibiotics save lives*	**3186j**	*Big Band Sounds*
3186c	*Jackie Robinson*	**3186k**	*Intl. Style of Architecture*
3186d	*Harry S. Truman*	**3186l**	*Postwar Baby Boom*
3186e	*Women support war effort*	**3186m**	*Slinky, 1945*
3186f	*TV entertains America*	**3186n**	*"A Streetcar Named Desire" 1947*
3186g	*Jitterbug sweeps nation*	**3186o**	*Orson Welles' "Citizen Kane"*
3186h	*Jackson Pollock, Abstract Expressionism*		

SCOTT NO.	DESCRIPTION	FIRST DAY COVERS SING	FIRST DAY COVERS PL. BLK.	MINT SHEET	PLATE BLOCK	UNUSED F/NH	USED
3186	33¢ Celebrate the Century 1940's, 15 varieties, attached	17.50	....	15.00(15)	....	15.00	12.00
....	set of singles	32.00	....	....	....	....	10.00
....	singles of above, each	....	....	....	....	....	.85
3186v	same as above, uncut sheet of 60 (4 panes)	....	....	70.00(4)	....	70.00	....

3187

CELEBRATE THE CENTURY 1950's

3187a	*Polio vaccine developed*	**3187i**	*Drive-in movies*
3187b	*teen fashions*	**3187j**	*World series rivals*
3187c	*The "Shot Heard Round the World"*	**3187k**	*Rocky Marciano, undefeated*
3187d	*US launches satellites*	**3187l**	*"I Love Lucy"*
3187e	*Korean War*	**3187m**	*Rock 'n Roll*
3187f	*Desegregation public schools*	**3187n**	*Stock car racing*
3187g	*Tail fins, chrome*	**3187o**	*Movies go 3-D*
3187h	*Dr. Seuss "The Cat in the Hat"*		

SCOTT NO.	DESCRIPTION	FIRST DAY COVERS SING	FIRST DAY COVERS PL. BLK.	MINT SHEET	PLATE BLOCK	UNUSED F/NH	USED
3187	33¢ Celebrate the Century 1950's, 15 varieties, attached	17.50	....	15.00(15)	....	15.00	12.00
....	set of singles	32.00	....	....	....	....	10.00
....	singles of above, each	....	....	....	....	....	.85
3187v	same as above, uncut sheet of 60 (4 panes)	....	....	70.00(4)	....	70.00	....

3188

CELEBRATE THE CENTURY 1960's

3188a	*"I Have a Dream" Martin Luther King*	**3188i**	*Barbie Doll*
3188b	*Woodstock*	**3188j**	*The Integrated Circuit*
3188c	*Man Walks on the Moon*	**3188k**	*Lasers*
3188d	*Green Bay Packers*	**3188l**	*Super Bowl I*
3188e	*Star Trek*	**3188m**	*Peace Symbol*
3188f	*The Peace Corps*	**3188n**	*Roger Maris, 61 in '61*
3188g	*The Vietnam War*	**3188o**	*The Beatles "Yellow Submarine"*
3188h	*Ford Mustang*		

SCOTT NO.	DESCRIPTION	FIRST DAY COVERS SING	FIRST DAY COVERS PL. BLK.	MINT SHEET	PLATE BLOCK	UNUSED F/NH	USED
3188	33¢ Celebrate the Century 1960's, 15 varieties, attached	17.50	....	15.00(15)	....	15.00	12.00
....	set of singles	32.00	....	....	....	....	10.00
....	singles of above, each	....	....	....	....	....	.85
3188v	same as above, uncut sheet of 60 (4 panes)	....	....	70.00(4)	....	70.00	....

3189

CELEBRATE THE CENTURY 1970's

3189a	*Earth Day Celebrated*	**3189i**	*Pioneer 10*
3189b	*"All in the Family", TV Series*	**3189j**	*Women's Rights Movement*
3189c	*Sesame Street*	**3189k**	*1970's Fashion*
3189d	*Disco Music*	**3189l**	*Monday Night Football*
3189e	*Steelers Win Four Super Bowls*	**3189m**	*America Smiles*
3189f	*U.S. Celebrates 200th Birthday*	**3189n**	*Jumbo Jets*
3189g	*Secretariat Wins Triple Crown*	**3189o**	*Medical Imaging*
3189h	*VCR's Transform Entertainment*		

SCOTT NO.	DESCRIPTION	FIRST DAY COVERS SING	FIRST DAY COVERS PL. BLK.	MINT SHEET	PLATE BLOCK	UNUSED F/NH	USED
3189	33¢ Celebrate the Century 1970's, 15 varieties, attached	17.50	....	15.00(15)	....	15.00	12.00
....	set of singles	32.00	....	....	....	....	10.00
....	singles of above, each	....	....	....	....	....	.85
3189v	same as above, uncut sheet of 60 (4 panes)	....	....	70.00(4)	....	70.00	....

3190

CELEBRATE THE CENTURY 1980's

- **3190a** *Space Shuttle program*
- **3190b** *Cats, Musucal Smash*
- **3190c** *San Francisco 49ers*
- **3190d** *Hostages Come Home*
- **3190e** *Figure Skating*
- **3190f** *Cable TV*
- **3190g** *Vietnam Veterans Memorial*
- **3190h** *Compact Discs*
- **3190i** *Cabbage Patch Kids*
- **3190j** *"The Cosby Show", Hit Comedy*
- **3190k** *Fall of the Berlin Wall*
- **3190l** *Video Games*
- **3190m** *"E.T. The Extra-Terrestrial"*
- **3190n** *Personal Computers*
- **3190o** *Hip-hop Culture*

SCOTT NO.	DESCRIPTION	FIRST DAY COVERS SING	FIRST DAY COVERS PL. BLK.	MINT SHEET	PLATE BLOCK	UNUSED F/NH	USED
3190	33¢ Celebrate the Century 1980's, 15 varieties, attached	17.50	....	15.00(15)	....	15.00	12.00
....	set of singles	32.00	....	....	....	....	10.00
....	singles of above, each	....	....	....	....	....	.85
3190v	same as above, uncut sheet of 60 (4 panes)	....	....	70.00(4)	....	70.00	....

3191

CELEBRATE THE CENTURY 1990's

- **3191a** *New Baseball Records*
- **3191b** *Gulf War*
- **3191c** *"Seinfield" Sitcom Sensation*
- **3191d** *Extreme Sports*
- **3191e** *Improving Education*
- **3191f** *Computer Art and Graphics*
- **3191g** *Recovering Species*
- **3191h** *Return to Space*
- **3191i** *Special Olympics*
- **3191j** *Virtual Reality*
- **3191k** *"Jurassic Park"*
- **3191l** *"Titanic" Blockbuster Film*
- **3191m** *Sport Utility Vehicles*
- **3191n** *World Wide Web*
- **3191o** *Cellular Phones*

SCOTT NO.	DESCRIPTION	FIRST DAY COVERS SING	FIRST DAY COVERS PL. BLK.	MINT SHEET	PLATE BLOCK	UNUSED F/NH	USED
3191	33¢ Celebrate the Century 1990's, 15 varieties, attached	17.50	....	15.00(15)	....	15.00	12.00
....	set of singles	32.00	....	....	....	....	10.00
....	singles of above, each	....	....	....	....	....	.85
3191v	same as above, uncut sheet of 60 (4 panes)	....	....	70.00(4)	....	70.00	....

3192

SCOTT NO.	DESCRIPTION	FIRST DAY COVERS SING	FIRST DAY COVERS PL. BLK.	MINT SHEET	PLATE BLOCK	UNUSED F/NH	USED
3192	32¢ "Remember the Maine"	3.00	4.75	19.50(20)	5.00	1.10	.25

3193

3194

3195

3196

3197

SCOTT NO.	DESCRIPTION	FIRST DAY COVERS SING	FIRST DAY COVERS PL. BLK.	MINT SHEET	PLATE BLOCK	UNUSED F/NH	USED
3193-97	Flowering Trees, self-adhesive, 5 varieties, attached	5.75	....	19.50(20)	12.00(10)	5.00	4.50
3193	32¢ Southern Magnolia	2.25	....	....	....	1.10	.35
3194	32¢ Blue Paloverde .	2.25	....	....	....	1.10	.35
3195	32¢ Yellow Poplar . .	2.25	....	....	....	1.10	.35
3196	32¢ Prairie Crab Apple	2.25	....	....	....	1.10	.35
3197	32¢ Pacific Dogwood	2.25	....	....	....	1.10	.35

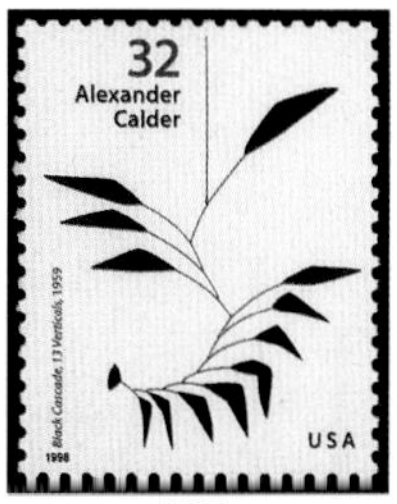

3198

3199

3200

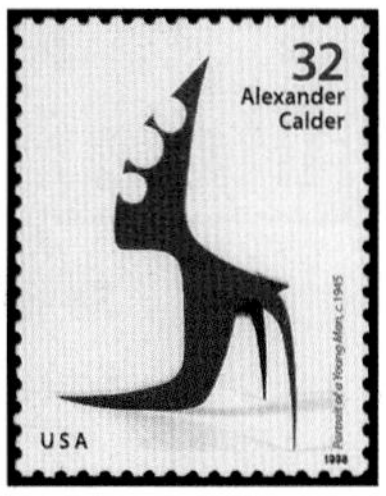

3201

3202

SCOTT NO.	DESCRIPTION	FIRST DAY COVERS SING	FIRST DAY COVERS PL. BLK.	MINT SHEET	PLATE BLOCK	UNUSED F/NH	USED
3198-3202	Alexander Calder, 5 varieties, attached	5.75	....	19.50(20)	10.5010)	6.50	5.50
3198	32¢ Black Cascade, 13 Verticals, 1959 . .	1.95	....	....	....	1.50	.75
3199	32¢ Untitled, 1965 . .	1.95	....	....	....	1.50	.75
3200	32¢ Rearing Stallion, 1928	1.95	....	....	....	1.50	.75
3201	32¢ Potrait of a Young Man, c. 1945	1.95	....	....	....	1.50	.75
3202	32¢ Un Effet du Japonais, 1945	1.95	....	....	....	1.50	.75
3198-3202v	same, as above, uncut sheet of 120 (6 panes) . . .	....	....	140.00(120)	....	....	....

3203

SCOTT NO.	DESCRIPTION	FIRST DAY COVERS SING	FIRST DAY COVERS PL. BLK.	MINT SHEET	PLATE BLOCK	UNUSED F/NH	USED
3203	32¢ Cinco De Mayo, self-adhesive	2.25	4.75	19.50(20)	5.00	1.10	.25
3203v	same as above, uncut sheet of 180 (9 panes)	....	....	180.00(180)	....	180.00	....
....	cross gutter block of 4	....	....	....	....	16.00	....
....	vertical pair with horizontal gutter	....	....	....	....	3.00	....
....	horizontal pair with vertical gutter	....	....	....	....	3.00	....

3204, 3205

SCOTT NO.	DESCRIPTION	FIRST DAY COVERS SING	FIRST DAY COVERS PL. BLK.	MINT SHEET	PLATE BLOCK	UNUSED F/NH	USED
3204	32¢ Sylvester & Tweety, self-adhesive, pane of 10	12.00	....	....	....	9.00	....
3204a	same, single from pane	2.25	....	....	....	1.00	.35
3204b	same, pane of 9 (#3204a)	....	....	....	....	6.50	....
3204c	same, pane of 1 (#3204a)	7.00	....	....	....	2.75	....
....	same, top press sheet of 60 (6 panes)	....	....	100.00(60)	....	100.00	....
....	same, bottom press sheet of 60 (6 panes)	....	....	175.00(60)	....	175.00	....
....	same, pane of 10 from press sheet	....	....	....	....	17.50	....
....	same, pane of 10 from press sheet w/ plate #	....	....	....	....	80.00	....
....	vert. pair with horiz. gutter	....	....	....	....	10.00	....
....	horiz pair with vert. gutter	....	....	....	....	20.00	....
3205	32¢ Sylvester & Tweety, self-adhesive, Die-Cut, pane of 10	20.00	....	....	....	18.00	....
3205a	same, single from pane	....	....	....	....	1.75	....
3205b	same, pane of 9 (#3205a)	....	....	....	....	14.00	....
3205c	same, pane of 1, imperf.	12.00	....	....	....	6.00	....

3206

SCOTT NO.	DESCRIPTION	FIRST DAY COVERS SING	FIRST DAY COVERS PL. BLK.	MINT SHEET	PLATE BLOCK	UNUSED F/NH	USED
3206	32¢ Wisconsin, self-adhesive	1.95	4.75	17.50(20)	4.25	1.20	.25

3207, 3207a

3208, 3208a

SCOTT NO.	DESCRIPTION	FIRST DAY COVERS SING	PLATE# STRIP 3	MINT SHEET	PLATE# STRIP 3	UNUSED F/NH	USED
3207	(5¢) Wetlands, Nonprofit, coil	2.25	10.00	....	2.00	.20	.20
3207A	same, self-adhesive coil	2.25	....	....	2.00	.20	.20
....	same, plate strip of 5	....	....	....	....	2.50	....
3208	(25¢) Diner, Presorted First-Class, coil	1.95	10.00	....	6.00	1.00	.50
3208a	same, self-adhesive coil, die cut 9.7	1.95	....	....	6.00	1.00	.50
....	same, plate strip of 5	....	....	....	....	5.75	....

3209

SCOTT NO.	DESCRIPTION	FIRST DAY COVERS SING	FIRST DAY COVERS PL. BLK.	MINT SHEET	PLATE BLOCK	UNUSED F/NH	USED
3209	1¢-$2 Trans-Mississippi, Souvenir Sheet of 9 .	12.00	....	....	....	12.00	10.00
....	same, set of 9 singles	18.00	....	....	....	9.25	7.25
3209v	block of 9 with horiz. gutter	....	....	....	....	60.00	....
3209v	vert. pair with horiz. gutter	....	....	....	....	12.50	....

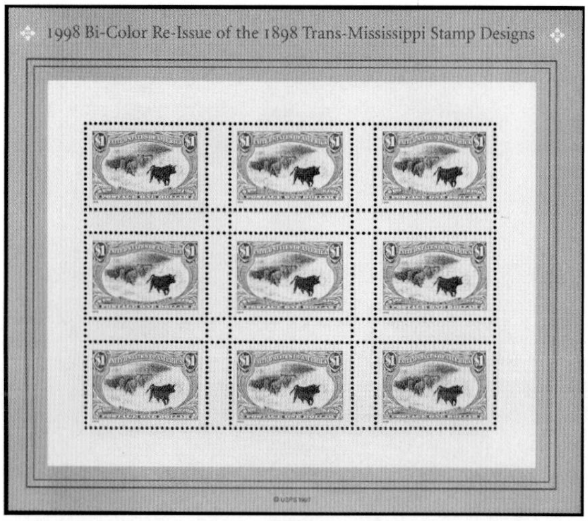

3210

SCOTT NO.	DESCRIPTION	FIRST DAY COVERS SING	FIRST DAY COVERS PL. BLK.	MINT SHEET	PLATE BLOCK	UNUSED F/NH	USED
3210	$1 Cattle in Storm, Souvenir Sheet of 9 .	17.50	....	....	....	25.00	23.00
....	same, single stamp . .	....	....	....	....	3.00	2.25
3209-10	same, press sheet of 54 (6 panes, 3–#3209 & 3–#3210)	....	....	175.00(54)	....	175.00	....
3210v	cross gutter block of 12	....	....	....	....	85.00	....
3210v	vert. pair with horiz. gutter	....	....	....	....	12.50	....
3210v	horiz. pair with vert. gutter	....	....	....	....	12.50	....

3211

SCOTT NO.	DESCRIPTION	FIRST DAY COVERS SING	FIRST DAY COVERS PL. BLK.	MINT SHEET	PLATE BLOCK	UNUSED F/NH	USED
3211	32¢ Berlin Airlift, 50th Anniversary	1.95	4.75	17.50(20)	4.25	1.00	.25

3212 3213

3214 3215

SCOTT NO.	DESCRIPTION	FIRST DAY COVERS SING	FIRST DAY COVERS PL. BLK.	MINT SHEET	PLATE BLOCK	UNUSED F/NH	USED
3212-15	Folk Musicains, 4 varieties, attached .	12.00	14.00	24.00(20)	6.00	5.00	4.00
3212	32¢ Huddie "Leadbelly" Ledbetter	3.00	....	....	....	1.25	.50
3213	32¢ Woody Guthrie . .	3.00	....	....	....	1.25	.50
3214	32¢ Sonny Terry	3.00	....	....	....	1.25	.50
3215	32¢ Josh White	3.00	....	....	....	1.25	.50

3217 3216

3218 3219

SCOTT NO.	DESCRIPTION	FIRST DAY COVERS SING	FIRST DAY COVERS PL. BLK.	MINT SHEET	PLATE BLOCK	UNUSED F/NH	USED
3216-19	Gospel Singers, 4 varieties, attached	12.00	14.00	24.00(20)	6.00	5.00	4.00
3216	32¢ Mahalia Jackson	3.00	....	....	....	1.25	.50
3217	32¢ Roberta Martin . .	3.00	....	....	....	1.25	.50
3218	32¢ Clara Ward	3.00	....	....	....	1.25	.50
3219	32¢ Sister Rosetta Tharpe	3.00	....	....	....	1.25	.50

3220

3221

SCOTT NO.	DESCRIPTION	FIRST DAY COVERS SING	FIRST DAY COVERS PL. BLK.	MINT SHEET	PLATE BLOCK	UNUSED F/NH	USED
3220	32¢ Spanish Settlement of the Southwest	2.25	4.75	18.50(20)	4.50	1.00	.25
3221	32¢ Stephen Vincent Benet	2.25	4.75	18.50(20)	4.50	1.00	.25

3222 3223

3224 3225

SCOTT NO.	DESCRIPTION	FIRST DAY COVERS SING	FIRST DAY COVERS PL. BLK.	MINT SHEET	PLATE BLOCK	UNUSED F/NH	USED
3222-25	Tropical Birds, 4 varieties, attached .	5.00	6.00	22.00(20)	7.00	6.00	5.00
3222	32¢ Antillean Euphonia	2.25	....	....	....	1.25	.75
3223	32¢ Green-throated Carib	2.25	....	....	....	1.25	.75
3224	32¢ Crested Honeycreeper	2.25	....	....	....	1.25	.75
3225	32¢ Cardinal Honeyeater	2.25	....	....	....	1.25	.75

3226

SCOTT NO.	DESCRIPTION	FIRST DAY COVERS SING	FIRST DAY COVERS PL. BLK.	MINT SHEET	PLATE BLOCK	UNUSED F/NH	USED
3226	32¢ Alfred Hitchcock	2.25	....	23.00(20)	5.00	1.20	.25
3226v	same as above, uncut sheet of 120 (6 panes) . . .	....	....	120.00(120)	....	120.00	....
....	block of 8 with vertical gutter.....		....	....	....	18.00	....
....	cross gutter block of 8	....	....	....	....	25.00	....
....	vertical pair with horizontal gutter		....	....	....	4.50	....
....	horizontal pair with vertical gutter	....	....	....	....	6.00	....

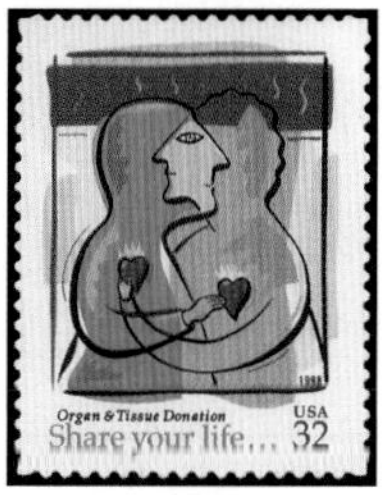

3227

3228, 3229

SCOTT NO.	DESCRIPTION	FIRST DAY COVERS SING	FIRST DAY COVERS PL. BLK.	MINT SHEET	PLATE BLOCK	UNUSED F/NH	USED
3227	32¢ Organ & Tissue Donation, self-adhesive	2.25	....	19.50(20)	4.00	1.20	.25
3228	(10¢) Modern Bicycle, self-adhesive coil, die cut 9.8	2.25	....	....	3.75	.40	.20
....	same, plate strip of 5		....	....	....	4.50	....
3229	(10¢) Modern Bicycle, coil	2.25	10.00	....	3.75	.40	.20
....	same, plate strip of 5	....	....	....	....	4.50	....

3230

3231

3232

3233

1998 COMMEMORATIVES (continued)

3234

SCOTT NO.	DESCRIPTION	FIRST DAY COVERS SING	PL. BLK.	MINT SHEET	PLATE BLOCK	UNUSED F/NH	USED
3230-34	Bright Eyes, self-adhesive, 5 varieties, attached	12.00	....	37.00(20)	19.00(10)	8.00	7.00
3230	32¢ Bright Eyes Dog	3.00	....	....	....	1.50	.40
3231	32¢ Bright Eyes Fish	3.00	....	....	....	1.50	.40
3232	32¢ Bright Eyes Cat	3.00	....	....	....	1.50	.40
3233	32¢ Bright Eyes Parakeet	3.00	....	....	....	1.50	.40
3234	32¢ Bright Eyes Hamster	3.00	....	....	....	1.50	.40

3235

SCOTT NO.	DESCRIPTION	FIRST DAY COVERS SING	PL. BLK.	MINT SHEET	PLATE BLOCK	UNUSED F/NH	USED
3235	32¢ Klondike Gold Rush	2.25	....	18.50(20)	4.50	1.20	.25

3236

AMERICAN ART

3236a *"Portrait of Richard Mather," by John Foster*
3236b *"Mrs. Elizabeth Freake and Baby Mary," by The Freake Limner*
3236c *"Girl in Red Dress with Cat and Dog," by Ammi Phillips*
3236d *"Rubens Peale with Geranium," by Rembrandt Peale*
3236e *"Long-billed Curlew, Numenius Longrostris," by John James Audubon*
3236f *"Boatmen on the Missouri," by George Caleb Bingham*
3236g *"Kindred Spirits," by Asher B. Durand*
3236h *"The Westwood Children," by Joshua Johnson*
3236i *"Music and Literature," by William Harnett*
3236j *"The Fog Warning," by Winslow Homer*
3236k *"The White Cloud, Head Chief of the Iowas," by George Catlin*
3236l *"Cliffs of Green River," by Thomas Moran*
3236m *"The Last of the Buffalo," by Alfred Bierstadt*
3236n *"Niagara," by Frederic Edwin Church*
3236o *"Breakfast in Bed," by Mary Cassatt*
3236p *"Nighthawks," by Edward Hopper*
3236q *"American Gothic," by Grany Wood*
3236r *"Two Against the White," by Charles Sheeler*
3236s *"Mahoning," by Franz Kline*
3236t *"No. 12," by Mark Rothko*

SCOTT NO.	DESCRIPTION	FIRST DAY COVERS SING	PL. BLK.	MINT SHEET	PLATE BLOCK	UNUSED F/NH	USED
3236	32¢ American Art, 20 varieties, attached	....	....	30.00(20)	....	30.00	25.00
....	set of singles	35.00	....	....	....	....	15.00
....	same as above, uncut sheet of 120 (6 panes)	....	....	175.00(120)	....	175.00	....
....	block of 24 with vert. gutter	....	....	....	....	27.50	....
....	block of 25 with horiz. gutter	....	....	....	....	32.50	....
....	cross gutter block of 20	....	....	....	....	40.00	....
....	vert. pair with horiz. gutter	....	....	....	....	7.00	....

AMERICAN ART (continued)

SCOTT NO.	DESCRIPTION	FIRST DAY COVERS SING	PL. BLK.	MINT SHEET	PLATE BLOCK	UNUSED F/NH	USED
....	horiz. pair with vert. gutter	....		....	....	9.00	....
....	horiz. blk of 8 with vert. gutter	....		....	....	....	....
....	vert. blk of 10 with horiz. gutter	....		....	....	....	....

3237

SCOTT NO.	DESCRIPTION	FIRST DAY COVERS SING	PL. BLK.	MINT SHEET	PLATE BLOCK	UNUSED F/NH	USED
3237	32¢ Ballet	1.95	....	25.00(20)	6.00	1.50	.25
....	same,uncut sheet of 120 (6 panes)	....	....	115.00(120)	....	115.00	....
....	cross gutter blk of 4 .	....	....	....	....	13.00	....
....	vert. pair with horiz. gutter	....	....	....	....	3.00	....
....	horiz. pair with vert. gutter	....	....	....	....	3.00	....

3238

3239

3240

3241

3242

SCOTT NO.	DESCRIPTION	FIRST DAY COVERS SING	PL. BLK.	MINT SHEET	PLATE BLOCK	UNUSED F/NH	USED
3238-42	Space Discovery, 5 varieties, attached	5.75	11.00	22.00(20)	12.00(10)	7.50	6.50
3238	32¢ Space City	2.25	....	....	....	1.50	1.00
3239	32¢ Space ship landing	2.25	....	....	....	1.50	1.00
3240	32¢ Person in space suit	2.25	....	....	....	1.50	1.00
3241	32¢ Space Ship taking off	2.25	....	....	....	1.50	1.00
3242	32¢ Large domed structure	2.25	....	....	....	1.50	1.00
3238-42v	same, uncut sheet of 180 (9 panes)	....	....	185.00(180)	....	185.00	....
....	cross gutter blk of 10	....	....	....	....	27.50	....
....	vert. blk of 10 with horiz. gutter	....	....	....	....	20.00	....
....	horiz. pair with vert. gutter	....	....	....	....	3.50	....
....	vert. pair with horiz. gutter	....	....	....	....	3.50	....

3243

3244

SCOTT NO.	DESCRIPTION	FIRST DAY COVERS SING	PL. BLK.	MINT SHEET	PLATE BLOCK	UNUSED F/NH	USED
3243	32¢ Giving and Sharing, self-adhesive	2.25	4.75	20.00(20)	5.00	1.20	.30
3244	32¢ Madonna & Child, self-adhesive	2.25	....	....	....	.90	.20
3244a	same, booklet pane of 20	14.50	....	....	....	21.00	....

3245, 3249

3246, 3250

3247, 3251

3248, 3252

SCOTT NO.	DESCRIPTION	FIRST DAY COVERS SING	FIRST DAY COVERS PL. BLK.	MINT SHEET	PLATE BLOCK	UNUSED F/NH	USED
3245	32¢ Evergreen Wreath, self-adhesive	2.25	....	....	....	2.00	1.00
3246	32¢ Victorian Wreath, self-adhesive	2.25	....	....	....	2.00	1.00
3247	32¢ Chili Pepper Wreath, self-adhesive	2.25	....	....	....	2.00	1.00
3248	32¢ Tropical Wreath, self-adhesive	2.25	....	....	....	2.00	1.00
3248a	32¢ Christmas Wreaths, self-adhesive, bklt pane of 4	4.00	....	....	....	30.00	....
3248b	same, bklt pane of 5	5.00	....	....	....	37.50	....
3248c	same, bklt pane of 6	5.50	....	....	....	45.00	....
3249-52	32¢ Christmas Wreaths, self-adhesive, 4 varieties, attached	4.00	4.75	22.50(20)	7.50	7.50	5.00
3249	32¢ Evergreen Wreath, self-adhesive	2.25	....	....	....	1.50	.25
3250	32¢ Victorian Wreath, self-adhesive	2.25	....	....	....	1.50	.25
3251	32¢ Chili Pepper Wreath, self-adhesive	2.25	....	....	....	1.50	.25
3252	32¢ Tropical Wreath, sel-adhesive	2.25	....	....	....	1.50	.25
3252b	same, bklt pane of 20	14.50	....	....	....	25.00	....

3257, 3258

3259, 3263

3260, 3264, 3265, 3266, 3267, 3268, 3269,

3261

3262

SCOTT NO.	DESCRIPTION	FIRST DAY COVERS SING	FIRST DAY COVERS PL. BLK.	MINT SHEET	PLATE BLOCK	UNUSED F/NH	USED
3257	(1¢) Weather Vane (white USA)	2.25	3.50	7.50(50)	1.10	.20	.20
3258	(1¢) Weather Vane (pale blue USA)	2.25	3.50	3.75(50)	1.10	.20	.20
3259	22¢ Uncle Sam, self-adhesive	2.25	4.75	9.50(20)	2.50	.55	.20
3260	(33¢) Uncle Sam's Hat	2.25	4.75	45.00(50)	4.50	1.00	.20
3261	$3.20 Space Shuttle Landing, self-adhesive	7.50	26.50	145.00(20)	35.00	10.00	5.00
3262	$11.75 Piggyback Space Shuttle, self-adhesive	28.50	95.00	500.00(20)	110.00	27.50	15.00
3263	22¢ Uncle Sam, self adhesive coil	2.25	....	....	5.50	.75	.25
....	same, plate strip of 5	....	....	....	....	6.50	....
3264	(33¢) Uncle Sam's Hat, coil	2.25	10.00	....	8.00	1.00	.50
....	same, plate strip of 5	....	....	....	....	9.50	....
3265	(33¢) Uncle Sam's Hat, self-adhesive coil, die cut 9.9	2.25	....	....	10.00	1.00	.30
....	same, plate strip of 5	....	....	....	....	11.00	....
3266	(33¢) Uncle Sam's Hat, self-adhesive coil, die cut 9.7	2.25	....	....	8.00	2.00	1.00
....	same, plate strip of 5	....	....	....	....	10.00	....
3267	(33¢) Uncle Sam's Hat, self-adhesive, die cut 9.9	2.25	....	....	....	1.10	.30
3267a	same, bklt pane of 10	7.25	....	....	....	11.00	....
3268	(33¢) Uncle Sam's Hat, self-adhesive, die cut 11.2 x 11.1	2.25	....	....	....	1.10	.30
3268a	same, bklt pane of 10	7.25	....	....	....	11.00	....
3268b	same, bklt pane of 20	14.50	....	....	....	21.50	....
3269	(33¢) Uncle Sam's Hat, self-adhesive, die cut 8	2.25	....	....	....	1.10	.30
3269a	same, bklt pane of 18	13.50	....	....	....	19.50	....

3270, 3271

SCOTT NO.	DESCRIPTION	FIRST DAY COVERS SING	FIRST DAY COVERS PL. BLK.	MINT SHEET	PLATE BLOCK	UNUSED F/NH	USED
3270	(10¢) Eagle, Presorted Std. coil	2.25	....	....	4.00	.35	.25
....	same, plate strip of 5	....	....	....	....	4.50	....
3271	(10¢) Eagle, Presorted Std., self-adhesive coil	2.25	....	....	4.00	.40	.25
....	same, plate strip of 5	....	....	....	....	4.50	....

3272

3273

1999 COMMEMORATIVES

SCOTT NO.	DESCRIPTION	FIRST DAY COVERS SING	FIRST DAY COVERS PL. BLK.	MINT SHEET	PLATE BLOCK	UNUSED F/NH	USED
3272/3369	**(3272-73, 3276, 3286-92, 3308-09, 3314-3350, 3352, 3354, 3356-59, 2368-69) 56 varieties . . . . . .**	....	....	....	....	**59.50**	**19.25**
3272	33¢ Year of the Rabbit	2.25	4.75	21.50(20)	5.00	1.25	.25
3273	33¢ Malcolm X, Civil Rights, self-adhesive	2.25	4.75	19.50(20)	6.00	1.35	.25

3274

3275

SCOTT NO.	DESCRIPTION	FIRST DAY COVERS SING	FIRST DAY COVERS PL. BLK.	MINT SHEET	PLATE BLOCK	UNUSED F/NH	USED
3274	33¢ Love, self-adhesive	2.25	....	....	....	1.10	.25
3274a	same, bklt pane of 20	14.50	....	....	....	20.00	....
3275	55¢ Love, self-adhesive	2.50	....	28.50(20)	6.50	1.50	.50

3276

3277, 3278, 3279, 3280, 3281, 3282

3283

SCOTT NO.	DESCRIPTION	FIRST DAY COVERS SING	FIRST DAY COVERS PL. BLK.	MINT SHEET	PLATE BLOCK	UNUSED F/NH	USED
3276	33¢ Hospice Care, self-adhesive	2.25	4.75	16.50(20)	4.00	1.00	.25
3277	33¢ Flag and City . .	2.25	4.75	80.00(100)	4.50	1.00	.75
3278	33¢ Flag and City, self-adhesive, die cut 11.1	1.95	4.75	16.50(20)	4.00	1.00	.20
3278a	same, bklt pane of 4	4.00	....	....	....	4.50	....
3278b	same, bklt pane of 5	5.00	....	....	....	5.25	....
3278c	same, bklt pane of 6	5.50	....	....	....	6.75	....
3278d	same, bklt pane of 10	7.25	....	....	....	9.00	....
3278e	same, bklt pane of 20	14.50	....	....	....	17.50	....
3278F	33¢ Flag and City, self-adhesive, die cut 11.5x11.75	2.25	....	....	....	1.10	.50
3278Fg	same, bklt pane of 20	14.50	....	....	....	20.00	....
3278i	Flag and City, die cut 11.25	2.25	....	....	....	.90	.20
3278j	same, bklt pane of 10	7.25	....	....	....	8.50	....
3279	33¢ Flag and City, self-adhesive, die cut 9.8	2.25	....	....	....	1.25	.30
3279a	same, bklt pane of 10	7.25	....	....	....	10.50	....
3280	33¢ Flag and City, coil	2.25	....	....	4.50	1.00	.25
....	same, plate srtip of 5	....	....	....	....	6.50	....
3281	33¢ Flag and City, self-adhesive coil (square corners) large date	2.25	....	....	7.50	1.00	.25
....	same, plate strip of 5	....	....	....	....	9.00	....
3281c	same, small date . . .	2.25	....	....	9.00	2.00	.25
....	same, plate strip of 5	....	....	....	....	12.50	....

SCOTT NO.	DESCRIPTION	FIRST DAY COVERS SING	FIRST DAY COVERS PL. BLK.	MINT SHEET	PLATE BLOCK	UNUSED F/NH	USED
3282	33¢ Flag and City, self-adhesive coil (round corners)	2.25	....	....	8.00	1.10	.50
....	same, plate strip of 5	....	....	....	....	10.00	....
3283	33¢ Flag and Chalkboard, self-adhesive	2.25	....	....	....	1.20	.50
3283a	same, bklt pane of 18	13.50	....	....	....	17.00	....

3286

3287

SCOTT NO.	DESCRIPTION	FIRST DAY COVERS SING	FIRST DAY COVERS PL. BLK.	MINT SHEET	PLATE BLOCK	UNUSED F/NH	USED
3286	33¢ Irish Immigration	2.25	4.75	20.00(20)	4.00	1.20	.25
3287	33¢ Alfred Lunt & Lynn Fontanne, Actors . .	2.25	4.75	20.00(20)	4.00	1.20	.25

3288

3289

3290

3291

3292

SCOTT NO.	DESCRIPTION	FIRST DAY COVERS SING	FIRST DAY COVERS PL. BLK.	MINT SHEET	PLATE BLOCK	UNUSED F/NH	USED
3288-92	Arctic Animals, 5 varieties, attached	12.00	....	16.50(15)	12.50(10)	6.00	5.00
3288	33¢ Arctic Hare	2.25	....	....	....	1.30	.40
3289	33¢ Arctic Fox	2.25	....	....	....	1.30	.40
3290	33¢ Snowy Owl	2.25	....	....	....	1.30	.40
3291	33¢ Polar Bear	2.25	....	....	....	1.30	.40
3292	33¢ Gray Wolf	2.25	....	....	....	1.30	.40

3293
SONORAN DESERT

3293a *Cactus wren, brittlebush, teddy bear cholla*
3293b *Desert tortoise*
3293c *White-winged dove, prickly pear*
3293d *Gambel quail*
3293e *Saquaro cactus*
3293f *Desert mule deer*
3293g *Desert cottontail, hedgehog cactus*
3293h *Gila monster*
3293i *Western diamondback rattlesnake, cactus mouse*
3293j *Gila woodpecker*

SCOTT NO.	DESCRIPTION	FIRST DAY COVERS SING	FIRST DAY COVERS PL. BLK.	MINT SHEET	PLATE BLOCK	UNUSED F/NH	USED
3293	33¢ Sonoran Desert, 10 varieties, attached, self-adhesive	....	....	9.00(10)	....	10.00	9.00
....	set of singles	18.50	....	....	....	....	6.00
3293v	same, uncut sheet of 60 (6 panes)	....	....	60.00(60)	....	60.00	....

3294, 3298, 3302

3295, 3299, 3303

3296, 3300, 3304

3297, 3301, 3305

SCOTT NO.	DESCRIPTION	FIRST DAY COVERS SING	FIRST DAY COVERS PL. BLK.	MINT SHEET	PLATE BLOCK	UNUSED F/NH	USED
3294	33¢ Blueberries, self-adhesive, die cut 11.2 x 11.7	2.25	....	....	....	1.10	.30
3294a	same, dated "2000" .	2.25	....	....	....	1.10	.30
3295	33¢ Raspberries, self-adhesive, die cut 11.2 x 11.7	2.25	....	....	....	1.10	.30
3295a	same, dated "2000" .	2.25	....	....	....	1.10	.30
3296	33¢ Strawberries, self-adhesive, die cut 11.2x 11.7	2.25	....	....	....	1.10	.30
3296a	same, dated "2000" .	2.25	....	....	....	1.10	.30
3297	33¢ Blackberries, self-adhesive, die cut 11.2 x 11.7	2.25	....	....	....	1.10	.30
3297a	same, bklt pane of 20 (3294-97 x 5 of each)	14.50	....	....	....	20.00	....
3297c	same, dated "2000" .	2.25	....	....	....	1.10	.20
3297d	same, bklt pane of 20	14.50	....	....	....	20.00	....
3297e	same, block of 4, (#3294a-96a, 3297c)	4.00	....	....	....	4.25	....
3298	33¢ Blueberries, self-adhesive, die cut 9.5 x 10	2.25	....	....	....	1.20	.35
3299	33¢ Strawberries, self-adhesive, die cut 9.5 x 10	2.25	....	....	....	1.20	.35
3300	33¢ Raspberries, self-adhesive, die cut 9.5 x 10	2.25	....	....	....	1.20	.35
3301	33¢ Blackberries, self-adhesive, die cut 9.5 x 10	2.25	....	....	....	1.20	.35
3301a	same, bklt pane of 4 (3298-3301 x 1)	4.00	....	....	....	7.00	....
3301b	same, bklt pane of 5, (3298, 3299, 3301, 3300 x 2)	5.00	....	....	....	8.00	....
3301c	same, bklt pane of 6, (3300, 3301, 3298 x 2, 3299)	6.00	....	....	....	10.00	....
3302-05	33¢ Berries, self-adhesive coil, strip of 4, attached	4.00	....	....	....	7.00	....
3302	33¢ Blueberries, self-adhesive coil . .	2.25	....	....	....	1.50	.40
3303	33¢ Raspberries, self-adhesive coil . .	2.25	....	....	....	1.50	.40
3304	33¢ Blackberries, self-adhesive coil . .	2.25	....	....	....	1.50	.40
3305	33¢ Strawberries, self-adhesive coil . .	2.25	....	....	....	1.50	.40
3302-05	33¢ Berries, self-adhesive coil, pl# strip of 5 (3302 x 2, 3303-05 x 1)	10.00	....	....	....	7.00	....

3306, 3307

3308

SCOTT NO.	DESCRIPTION	FIRST DAY COVERS SING	FIRST DAY COVERS PL. BLK.	MINT SHEET	PLATE BLOCK	UNUSED F/NH	USED
3306	33¢ Daffy Duck, self-adhesive, pane of 10	12.00	....	....	....	12.00	....
3306a	same, single from pane	2.25	....	....	....	1.10	.35
3306b	same, pane of 9 (3306a)	....	....	....	....	7.50	....
3306c	same, pane of 1 (3306a)	7.00	....	....	....	2.25	....
3306v	same, top press sheet of 60 (6 panes)	....	....	80.00(60)	....	80.00	....
....	same, bottom press sheet of 60 w/ plate # (6 panes)	....	....	110.00(60)	....	110.00	....
....	same, pane of 10 from press sheet	....	....	....	....	15.00	....
....	same, pane of 10 from press sheet with plate # . .	....	....	....	....	85.00	....
....	vert. pair with horiz. gutter	....	....	....	....	5.00	....
....	horiz. pair with vert. gutter	....	....	....	....	10.00	....
3307	33¢ Daffy Duck, self-adhesive, die cut, pane of 10	15.00	....	....	....	14.00	....
3307a	same, single from pane	....	....	....	....	1.10	....
3307b	same, pane of 9 (3307a)	....	....	....	....	10.00	....
3307c	same, pane of 1, imperf.	12.00	....	....	....	5.00	....
3308	33¢ Ayn Rand	2.25	4.75	16.40(20)	4.00	.90	.25

3309

SCOTT NO.	DESCRIPTION	FIRST DAY COVERS SING	FIRST DAY COVERS PL. BLK.	MINT SHEET	PLATE BLOCK	UNUSED F/NH	USED
3309	33¢ Cinco De Mayo, self-adhesive	2.25	4.75	16.50(20)	4.00	1.10	.25

3310

3311

3312

3313

SCOTT NO.	DESCRIPTION	FIRST DAY COVERS SING	FIRST DAY COVERS PL. BLK.	MINT SHEET	PLATE BLOCK	UNUSED F/NH	USED
3310-13	33¢ Tropical Flowers, self-adhesive, 4 varieties, attached	8.00	....	....	....	5.50	5.00
3310	33¢ Bird of Paradise, self-adhesive	2.25	....	....	....	1.25	.30
3311	33¢ Royal Poinciana, self-adhesive	2.25	....	....	....	1.25	.30
3312	33¢ Gloriosa Lily, self-adhesive	2.25	....	....	....	1.25	.30
3313	33¢ Chinese Hibiscus, self-adhesive	2.25	....	....	....	1.25	.30
3313a	same, bklt pane of 20 (3310-13 x 5)	....	....	....	....	17.50	....

3314

3315

3316

SCOTT NO.	DESCRIPTION	FIRST DAY COVERS SING	FIRST DAY COVERS PL. BLK.	MINT SHEET	PLATE BLOCK	UNUSED F/NH	USED
3314	33¢ John & William Bartram, Botanists	2.25	4.75	16.50(20)	4.00	1.10	.25
3315	33¢ Prostate Cancer Awareness	2.25	4.75	16.50(20)	4.00	1.10	.25
3316	33¢ California Gold Rush	2.25	4.75	16.50(20)	4.00	1.10	.25

3317

3318

3319

3320

SCOTT NO.	DESCRIPTION	FIRST DAY COVERS SING	FIRST DAY COVERS PL. BLK.	MINT SHEET	PLATE BLOCK	UNUSED F/NH	USED
3317-20	Aquarium Fish, self-adhesive, 4 varieties, attached	8.00	....	20.00(20)	11.00(8)	6.50	6.00
3317	33¢ Yellow fish, red fish, cleaner shrimp	2.25	....	....	....	1.35	.30
3318	33¢ Fish, thermometer	2.25	....	....	....	1.35	.30
3319	33¢ Red fish, blue fish	2.25	....	....	....	1.35	.30
3320	33¢ Fish, heater . . .	2.25	....	....	....	1.35	.30

3321

3322

3323

3324

SCOTT NO.	DESCRIPTION	FIRST DAY COVERS SING	FIRST DAY COVERS PL. BLK.	MINT SHEET	PLATE BLOCK	UNUSED F/NH	USED
3321-24	Xtreme Sports, self-adhesive, 4 varieties, attached	8.00	....	20.00(20)	5.00	4.50	4.00
3321	33¢ Skateboarding .	2.25	....	....	....	1.25	.35
3322	33¢ BMX biking	2.25	....	....	....	1.25	.35
3323	33¢ Snowboarding .	2.25	....	....	....	1.25	.35
3324	33¢ Inline skating . .	2.25	....	....	....	1.25	.35

3325

3326

3327

3328

SCOTT NO.	DESCRIPTION	FIRST DAY COVERS SING	FIRST DAY COVERS PL. BLK.	MINT SHEET	PLATE BLOCK	UNUSED F/NH	USED
3325-28	American Glass, 4 varieties, attached	10.00	....	18.00(15)	....	6.00	5.00
3325	33¢ Freeblown glass	3.00	....	....	....	1.30	.40
3326	33¢ Mold-blown glass	3.00	....	....	....	1.30	.40
3327	33¢ Pressed glass .	3.00	....	....	....	1.30	.40
3328	33¢ Art glass	3.00	....	....	....	1.30	.40

3329

SCOTT NO.	DESCRIPTION	FIRST DAY COVERS SING	FIRST DAY COVERS PL. BLK.	MINT SHEET	PLATE BLOCK	UNUSED F/NH	USED
3329	33¢ James Cagney .	1.95	4.75	20.00(20)	6.00	1.20	.25

3330

3331

3332

SCOTT NO.	DESCRIPTION	FIRST DAY COVERS SING	FIRST DAY COVERS PL. BLK.	MINT SHEET	PLATE BLOCK	UNUSED F/NH	USED
3330	55¢ General William "Billy" Mitchell, self-adhesive	2.50	....	32.00(20)	7.00	1.75	.75
3331	33¢ Honoring Those Who Served, self-adhesive	2.25	....	16.50(20)	4.00	.90	.25
3332	45¢ Universal Postal Union	2.25	5.00	23.50(20)	6.00	1.25	.75

3333

3334

3335

3336

3337

SCOTT NO.	DESCRIPTION	FIRST DAY COVERS SING	FIRST DAY COVERS PL. BLK.	MINT SHEET	PLATE BLOCK	UNUSED F/NH	USED
3333-37	33¢ Famous Trains, 5 varieties, attached	10.00	15.00	22.00(20)	12.00(8)	6.00	5.00
3333	33¢ Daylight	3.00	....	....	....	1.20	.40
3334	33¢ Congressional .	3.00	....	....	....	1.20	.40
3335	33¢ 20th Century Limited	3.00	....	....	....	1.20	.40
3336	33¢ Hiawatha	3.00	....	....	....	1.20	.40
3337	33¢ Super Chief . . .	3.00	....	....	....	1.20	.40
3333-37v	same, uncut sheet of 120 (6 panes)	....	....	175.00(120)	....	175.00	....
....	block of 8 with horiz. gutter	....	....	....	....	22.50	....
....	block of 10 with vert. gutter	....	....	....	....	23.50	....
....	cross gutter block of 8	....	....	....	....	25.00	....
....	horiz. pair with vert. gutter	....	....	....	....	4.00	....
....	vert. pair with horiz. gutter	....	....	....	....	4.00	....

3338

SCOTT NO.	DESCRIPTION	FIRST DAY COVERS SING	FIRST DAY COVERS PL. BLK.	MINT SHEET	PLATE BLOCK	UNUSED F/NH	USED
3338	33¢ Frederick Law Olmstead, Landscape Architect	1.95	4.75	19.00(20)	5.00	1.10	.25

3339 3340

3341

3342

3343 3344

SCOTT NO.	DESCRIPTION	FIRST DAY COVERS SING	FIRST DAY COVERS PL. BLK.	MINT SHEET	PLATE BLOCK	UNUSED F/NH	USED
3339-44	33¢ Hollywood Composers, 6 varieties, attached	12.00	17.00	25.00(20)	9.50(6)	7.50	6.50
....	same, plate block of 8	....	....	....	8.00	....	....
3339	33¢ Max Steiner . . .	3.00	....	....	....	1.25	.60
3340	33¢ Dimitri Tiomkin .	3.00	....	....	....	1.25	.60
3341	33¢ Bernard Herrmann	3.00	....	....	....	1.25	.60
3342	33¢ Franz Waxman .	3.00	....	....	....	1.25	.60
3343	33¢ Alfred Newman	3.00	....	....	....	1.25	.60
3344	33¢ Erich Wolfgang Korngold	3.00	....	....	....	1.25	.60

3345 3346

3347

3348

3349 3350

SCOTT NO.	DESCRIPTION	FIRST DAY COVERS SING	FIRST DAY COVERS PL. BLK.	MINT SHEET	PLATE BLOCK	UNUSED F/NH	USED
3345-50	33¢ Broadway Songwriters, 6 varieties, attached	12.00	17.00	25.00(20)	9.50(6)	7.50	6.50
....	same, plate block of 8	....	....	....	8.00	....	....
3345	33¢ Lra & George Gershwin	3.00	....	....	....	1.25	.60
3346	33¢ Lerner & Loewe	3.00	....	....	....	1.25	.60
3347	33¢ Lorenz Hart . . .	3.00	....	....	....	1.25	.60
3348	33¢ Rodgers & Hammer-stein	3.00	....	....	....	1.25	.60
3349	33¢ Meredith Willson	3.00	....	....	....	1.25	.60
3350	33¢ Frank Loesser .	3.00	....	....	....	1.25	.60

3351

INSECTS & SPIDERS

- **3351a** *Black Widow*
- **3351b** *Elderberry longhorn*
- **3351c** *Lady beetle*
- **3351d** *Yellow garden spider*
- **3351e** *Dogbane beetle*
- **3351f** *Flower fly*
- **3351g** *Assassin bug*
- **3351h** *Ebony jewelwing*
- **3351i** *Velvet ant*
- **3351j** *Monarch caterpillar*
- **3351k** *Monarch butterfly*
- **3351l** *Eastern hercules beetle*
- **3351m** *Bombardier beetle*
- **3351n** *Dung beetle*
- **3351o** *Spotted water beetle*
- **3351p** *True Katydid*
- **3351q** *Spinybacked spider*
- **3351r** *Periodical cicada*
- **3351s** *Scorpionfly*
- **3351t** *Jumping spider*

SCOTT NO.	DESCRIPTION	FIRST DAY COVERS SING	FIRST DAY COVERS PL. BLK.	MINT SHEET	PLATE BLOCK	UNUSED F/NH	USED
	INSECTS & SPIDERS (continued)						
3351	33¢ Insects & Spiders, 20 varieties, attached	....	....	18.50(20)	....	20.00	19.00
....	set of singles	37.50	....	....	....	....	12.50
....	same, uncut sheet of 80 (4 panes)	....	....	80.00(80)	....	80.00	....
....	same, block of 10 with vert. gutter	....	....	....	....	20.00	....
....	same, block of 8 with horiz. gutter	....	....	....	....	20.00	....
....	same, cross gutter block of 20	....	....	....	....	35.00	....
....	same, vert. pair with horiz. gutter	....	....	....	....	3.00	....
....	same, horiz. pair with vert. gutter	....	....	....	....	3.00	....

3352

SCOTT NO.	DESCRIPTION	FIRST DAY COVERS SING	FIRST DAY COVERS PL. BLK.	MINT SHEET	PLATE BLOCK	UNUSED F/NH	USED
3352	33¢ Hanukkah, self-adhesive	2.25	4.75	16.50(20)	4.00	1.10	.25

3353

SCOTT NO.	DESCRIPTION	FIRST DAY COVERS SING	FIRST DAY COVERS PL. BLK.	MINT SHEET	PLATE BLOCK	UNUSED F/NH	USED
3353	22¢ Uncle Sam, coil	1.95	....	....	5.00	.70	.50
....	same, plate strip of 5	....	....	....	....	6.00	....

3354

3355

SCOTT NO.	DESCRIPTION	FIRST DAY COVERS SING	FIRST DAY COVERS PL. BLK.	MINT SHEET	PLATE BLOCK	UNUSED F/NH	USED
3354	33¢ NATO, 50th Anniv.	2.25	4.75	16.50(20)	4.00	1.10	.25
3355	33¢ Madonna & Child, self-adhesive	2.25	....	....	....	1.20	.20
3355a	same, bklt pane of 20	14.50	....	....	....	20.00	....

3356, 3360, 3364

3357, 3361, 3365

3358, 3362, 3366

3359, 3363, 3367

SCOTT NO.	DESCRIPTION	FIRST DAY COVERS SING	FIRST DAY COVERS PL. BLK.	MINT SHEET	PLATE BLOCK	UNUSED F/NH	USED
3356-59	33¢ Christmas Deer, self-adhesive	4.00	....	20.00(20)	7.00	6.00	....
3356	33¢ Christmas Deer, gold & red, self-adhesive	2.25	....	....	....	1.50	.50
3357	33¢ Christmas Deer, gold & blue, self-adhesive	2.25	....	....	....	1.50	.50
3358	33¢ Christmas Deer, gold & purple, self-adhesive	2.25	....	....	....	1.50	.50
3359	33¢ Christmas Deer, gold & green, self-adhesive	2.25	....	....	....	1.50	.50
3360	33¢ Christmas Deer, gold & red, bklt single, self-adhesive	2.25	....	....	....	1.50	.30
3361	33¢ Christmas Deer, gold & blue, bklt single, self-adhesive	2.25	....	....	....	1.50	.30
3362	33¢ Christmas Deer, gold & purple, bklt single, self-adhesive	2.25	....	....	....	1.50	.30
3363	33¢ Christmas Deer, gold & green, bklt single, self-adhesive	2.25	....	....	....	1.50	.30
3363a	same, bklt pane of 20	14.50	....	....	....	30.00	....
3364	33¢ Christmas Deer, gold & red, bklt single, (21x19mm), self-adhesive	2.25	....	....	....	2.50	.40
3365	33¢ Christmas Deer, gold & blue, bklt single, (21x19mm), self-adhesive	2.25	....	....	....	2.50	.40
3366	33¢ Christmas Deer, gold & purple, bklt single (21x19mm), self-adhesive	2.25	....	....	....	2.50	.40
3367	33¢ Christmas Deer, gold & green, bklt single, (21x19mm), self-adhesive	2.25	....	....	....	2.50	.40
3367a	same, bklt pane of 4 (3364-67 x 1)	4.00	....	....	....	10.50	....
3367b	same, bklt pane of 5 (3364, 3366, 3367, 3365 x 2)	5.00	....	....	....	13.00	....
3367c	same, bklt pane of 6 (3365, 3367, 3364 x 2, 3366)	6.00	....	....	....	16.00	....

3368

3369

SCOTT NO.	DESCRIPTION	FIRST DAY COVERS SING	FIRST DAY COVERS PL. BLK.	MINT SHEET	PLATE BLOCK	UNUSED F/NH	USED
3368	33¢ Kwanzaa, self-adhesive	2.25	....	18.00(20)	5.00	1.10	.25
3369	33¢ Baby New Year, self-adhesive	2.25	....	20.00(20)	5.00	1.10	.25

3370

3371

3372

2000 COMMEMORATIVES

SCOTT NO.	DESCRIPTION	FIRST DAY COVERS SING	FIRST DAY COVERS PL. BLK.	MINT SHEET	PLATE BLOCK	UNUSED F/NH	USED
3370/3446	**(3370-72, 3379-90, 3393-3402 3414-17, 3438-46) 38 varieties . . . . .**	....	....	....	....	**38.00**	**11.00**
3370	33¢ Year of the Dragon	2.25	4.75	25.00(20)	6.00	1.20	.25
3371	33¢ Patricia Roberts Harris, self-adhesive	2.25	....	25.00(20)	6.00	1.00	.25
3372	33¢ Los Angeles Class Submarine (microprint USPS)	2.25	4.75	25.00(20)	6.00	1.00	.25

3373

3374

3375

3376

3377

SCOTT NO.	DESCRIPTION	FIRST DAY COVERS SING	FIRST DAY COVERS PL. BLK.	MINT SHEET	PLATE BLOCK	UNUSED F/NH	USED
3373	22¢ S Class Submarine	2.25	....	....	....	2.00	1.50
3374	33¢ Los Angeles Class Submarine (no microprint)	2.25	....	....	....	3.00	1.50
3375	55¢ Ohio Class Submarine	2.50	....	....	....	5.00	2.00
3376	60¢ USS Holland Submarine	2.50	....	....	....	5.00	3.00
3377	$3.20 Gato Class Submarine	7.50	....	....	....	15.00	9.50
3377a	same, bklt pane of 5, (#3373-77)	12.00	....	....	....	42.50	....
....	same, complete booklet of 2 panes	....	....	....	....	50.00	....

3378

PACIFIC COAST RAIN FOREST

3378a *Harlequin duck*
3378b *Dwarf oregongrape, snail-eating ground beetle*
3378c *American dipper*
3378d *Cutthroat trout*
3378e *Roosevelt elk*
3378f *Winter wren*
3378g *Pacific giant salamander, Rough-skinned newt*
3378h *Western tiger swallowtail*
3378i *Douglas squirrel, foliose lichen*
3378j *Foliose lichen, banana slug*

SCOTT NO.	DESCRIPTION	FIRST DAY COVERS SING	FIRST DAY COVERS PL. BLK.	MINT SHEET	PLATE BLOCK	UNUSED F/NH	USED
3378	33¢ Pacific Coast Rain Forest, 10 varieties, attached, self-adhesive	....	....	14.00(10)	....	12.00	10.00
....	set of singles	25.00	....	....	....	....	6.00
3378v	same, uncut sheet of 60 (6 panes)	....	....	60.00(60)	....	60.00	....

3379

3380

3381

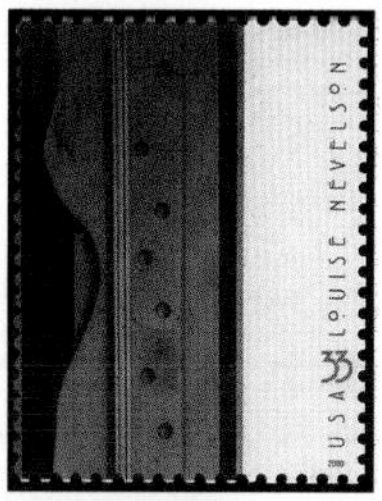

3382

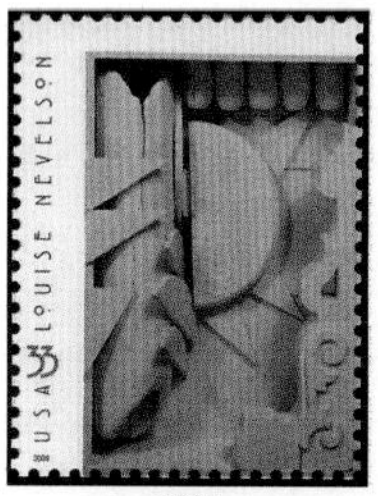

3383

SCOTT NO.	DESCRIPTION	FIRST DAY COVERS SING	FIRST DAY COVERS PL. BLK.	MINT SHEET	PLATE BLOCK	UNUSED F/NH	USED
3379-83	33¢ Louise Nevelson, (1899-1988), Sculptor, 5 varieties, attached	10.00	15.00	22.50(20)	11.00(10)	5.00	4.00
3379	33¢ Silent Music I . .	2.25	....	....	....	1.20	.40
3380	33¢ Royal Tide I . . .	2.25	....	....	....	1.20	.40
3381	33¢ Black Chord . . .	2.25	....	....	....	1.20	.40
3382	33¢ Nightsphere-Light	2.25	....	....	....	1.20	.40
3383	33¢ Dawn's Wedding Chapel I.	2.25	....	....	....	1.20	.40

3384

3385

3386

3387

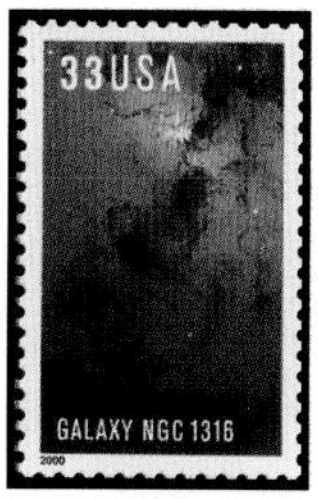

3388

SCOTT NO.	DESCRIPTION	FIRST DAY COVERS SING	FIRST DAY COVERS PL. BLK.	MINT SHEET	PLATE BLOCK	UNUSED F/NH	USED
3384-88	33¢ Hubble Space Telescope Images, 5 varieties, attached	10.00	15.00	22.50(20)	11.00(10)	5.00	4.00
3384	33¢ Eagle Nebula . .	3.00	....	....	....	1.20	.40
3385	33¢ Ring Nebula . . .	3.00	....	....	....	1.20	.40
3386	33¢ Lagoon Nebula	3.00	....	....	....	1.20	.40
3387	33¢ Egg Nebula . . .	3.00	....	....	....	1.20	.40
3388	33¢ Galaxy NGC1316	3.00	....	....	....	1.20	.40

3389

3390

SCOTT NO.	DESCRIPTION	FIRST DAY COVERS SING	FIRST DAY COVERS PL. BLK.	MINT SHEET	PLATE BLOCK	UNUSED F/NH	USED
3389	33¢ American Samoa	2.25	4.75	17.50(20)	4.50	1.00	.25
3390	33¢ Library of Congress	2.25	4.75	17.50(20)	4.50	1.00	.25

3391, 3392

SCOTT NO.	DESCRIPTION	FIRST DAY COVERS SING	FIRST DAY COVERS PL. BLK.	MINT SHEET	PLATE BLOCK	UNUSED F/NH	USED
3391	33¢ Road Runner & Wile E. Coyote, self-adhesive, pane of 10	12.00	....	....	....	9.50	....
3391a	same, single from pane	2.25	....	....	....	1.10	.35
3391b	same, pane of 9 (3391a)	....	....	....	....	7.00	....
3391c	same, pane of 1 (3391a)	7.00	....	....	....	2.75	....
....	same, top press sheet of 60 (6 panes) w/ plate #	....	....	80.00(60)	....	80.00	....
....	same, bottom press sheet of 60 (6 panes) w/ plate #	....	....	95.00(60)	....	95.00	....
....	same, pane of 10 from press sheet	....	....	....	....	15.00	....
....	same, pane of 10 with plate # on front .	....	....	....	....	65.00	....
....	vert. pair with horiz. gutter	....	....	....	....	4.00	....
....	horiz. pair with vert. gutter	....	....	....	....	8.00	....
3392	33¢ Road Runner & Wile E. Coyote, self-adhesive, die cut, pane of 10 .	15.00	....	....	....	11.00	....
3392a	same, single from pane	....	....	....	....	1.10	....
3392b	same, pane of 9 (3392a)	....	....	....	....	9.00	....
3392c	same, pane of 1, imperf.	12.00	....	....	....	3.00	....

3393 3394 3395 3396

SCOTT NO.	DESCRIPTION	FIRST DAY COVERS SING	FIRST DAY COVERS PL. BLK.	MINT SHEET	PLATE BLOCK	UNUSED F/NH	USED
3393-96	33¢ Distinguished Soldiers, 4 varieties, attached	8.00	12.00	20.00(20)	5.00	4.50	4.00
3393	33¢ Major General John L. Hines (1868-1968) .	2.25	....	....	....	1.25	.35
3394	33¢ General Omar N. Bradley (1893-1981)	2.25	....	....	....	1.25	.35
3395	33¢ Sergeant Alvin C. York (1887-1964) . .	2.25	....	....	....	1.25	.35
3396	33¢ Second Lieutenant Audie L. Murphy (1924-71)	2.25	....	....	....	1.25	.35

3397

3398

SCOTT NO.	DESCRIPTION	FIRST DAY COVERS SING	FIRST DAY COVERS PL. BLK.	MINT SHEET	PLATE BLOCK	UNUSED F/NH	USED
3397	33¢ Summer Sports	2.25	4.75	17.50(20)	4.50	1.00	.25
3398	33¢ Adoption, self-adhesive	2.25	....	17.50(20)	4.50	1.00	.25

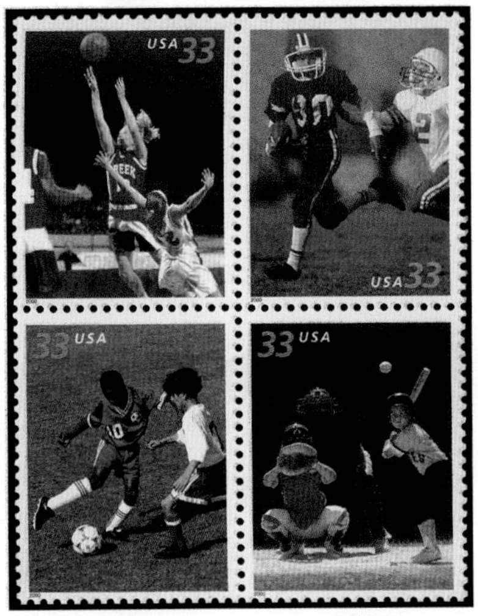

3399 3400 3401 3402

SCOTT NO.	DESCRIPTION	FIRST DAY COVERS SING	FIRST DAY COVERS PL. BLK.	MINT SHEET	PLATE BLOCK	UNUSED F/NH	USED
3399-3402	33¢ Youth Team Sports, 4 varieites, attached	8.00	12.00	20.00(20)	5.00	4.50	3.50
3399	33¢ Basketball	3.00	....	....	....	1.25	.40
3400	33¢ Football	3.00	....	....	....	1.25	.40
3401	33¢ Soccer	3.00	....	....	....	1.25	.40
3402	33¢ Baseball	3.00	....	....	....	1.25	.40

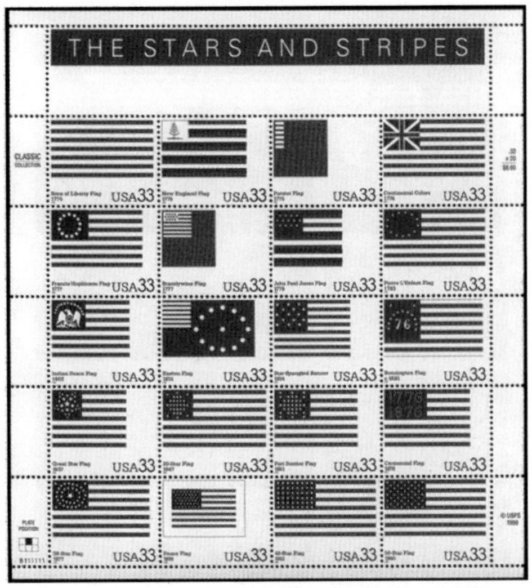

3403

THE STARS AND STRIPES

3403a *Sons of Liberty Flag, 1775*
3403b *New England, 1775*
3403c *Forster Flag, 1775*
3403d *Continental Colors, 1776*
3403e *Francis Hopkinson Flag, 1777*
3403f *Brandywine Flag, 1777*
3403g *John Paul Jones Flag, 1779*
3403h *Pierre L'Enfant Flag, 1783*
3403i *Indian Peace Flag, 1803*
3403 j *Easton Flag, 1814*
3403k *Star-Spangled Banner, 1814*
3403l *Bennington Flag, c.1820*
3403m *Great Star Flag, 1837*
3403n *29-Star Flag, 1847*
3403o *Fort Sumter Flag, 1861*
3403p *Centennial Flag, 1876*
3403q *38-Star Flag*
3403r *Peace Flag, 1891*
3403s *48-Star Flag, 1912*
3403t *50-Star Flag, 1960*

SCOTT NO.	DESCRIPTION	FIRST DAY COVERS SING	FIRST DAY COVERS PL. BLK.	MINT SHEET	PLATE BLOCK	UNUSED F/NH	USED
3403	33¢ The Stars & Stripes, 20 varieties, attached, self-adhesive	....	....	19.50(20)	....	19.50	15.00
....	set of singles	37.50	....	....	....	....	10.00
3403v	same, uncut sheet of 120 (6 panes)	....	....	120.00(120)	....	120.00	....
....	same, block of 8 with horiz. gutter . . .	....	....	....	....	18.00	....
....	same, block of 10 with vert. gutter	....	....	....	....	20.00	....
....	same, cross gutter block of 20	....	....	....	....	40.00	....
....	vert. pair with horiz. gutter	....	....	....	....	4.50	....
....	horiz. pair with vert. gutter	....	....	....	....	4.50	....

3404

3405

3406

3407

SCOTT NO.	DESCRIPTION	FIRST DAY COVERS SING	FIRST DAY COVERS PL. BLK.	MINT SHEET	PLATE BLOCK	UNUSED F/NH	USED
3404	33¢ Blueberries, self-adhesive linerless coil	2.25	....	....	....	2.00	.50
3405	33¢ Strawberries, self-adhesive linerless coil	2.25	....	....	....	2.00	.50
3406	33¢ Blackberries, self-adhesive linerless coil	2.25	....	....	....	2.00	.50
3407	33¢ Raspberries, self-adhesive linerless coil	2.25	....	....	....	2.00	.50
3404-07	33¢ Berries, self-adhesive linerless coil, strip of 4	5.00	....	....	....	9.00	....
....	same, pl# strip of 5 .	....	....	....	....	15.00	....

3408

LEGENDS OF BASEBALL

3408a	*Jackie Robinson*	**3408k**	*Lefty Grove*
3408b	*Eddie Collins*	**3408l**	*Tris Speaker*
3408c	*Christy Mathewson*	**3408m**	*Cy Young*
3408d	*Ty Cobb*	**3408n**	*Jimmie Foxx*
3408e	*George Sisler*	**3408o**	*Pie Traynor*
3408f	*Rogers Hornsby*	**3408p**	*Satchel Paige*
3408g	*Mickey Cochrane*	**3408q**	*Honus Wagner*
3408h	*Babe Ruth*	**3408r**	*Josh Gibson*
3408i	*Walter Johnson*	**3408s**	*Dizzy Dean*
3408 j	*Roberto Clemente*	**3408t**	*Lou Gehrig*

SCOTT NO.	DESCRIPTION	FIRST DAY COVERS SING	FIRST DAY COVERS PL. BLK.	MINT SHEET	PLATE BLOCK	UNUSED F/NH	USED
3408	33¢ Legends of Baseball, 20 varieties, attached, self-adhesive	....	....	19.50(20)	....	19.50	15.00
....	set of singles	37.50	....	....	....	....	12.00
3408v	same, uncut sheet of 120 (6 panes)	....	....	135.00(120)	....	135.00	....
....	cross gutter block of 20	....	....	....	....	40.00	....
....	block of 8 with vert. gutter	....	....	....	....	22.50	....
....	block of 10 with horiz. gutter	....	....	....	....	22.50	....
....	vert. pair with horiz. gutter	....	....	....	....	3.50	....
....	horiz. pair with vert. gutter	....	....	....	....	4.50	....

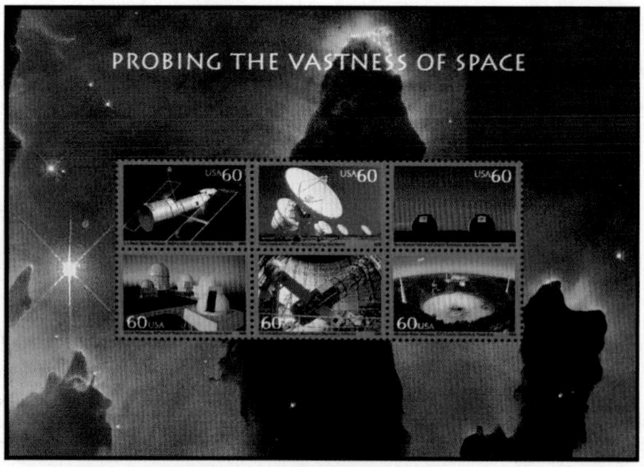

3409

SCOTT NO.	DESCRIPTION	FIRST DAY COVERS SING	FIRST DAY COVERS PL. BLK.	MINT SHEET	PLATE BLOCK	UNUSED F/NH	USED
3409	60¢ Probing the Vastness of Space, souvenir sheet of 6	15.00	....	....	....	25.00	20.00
3409a	60¢ Hubble Space Telescope	3.00	....	....	....	4.00	2.00
3409b	60¢ National Radio Astronomy Observatory	3.00	....	....	....	4.00	2.00
3409c	60¢ Keck Observatory	3.00	....	....	....	4.00	2.00
3409d	60¢ Cerro Tololo Inter-American Observatory	3.00	....	....	....	4.00	2.00
3409e	60¢ Mt. Wilson Observatory	3.00	....	....	....	4.00	2.00
3409f	60¢ Arecibo Observatory	3.00	....	....	....	4.00	2.00

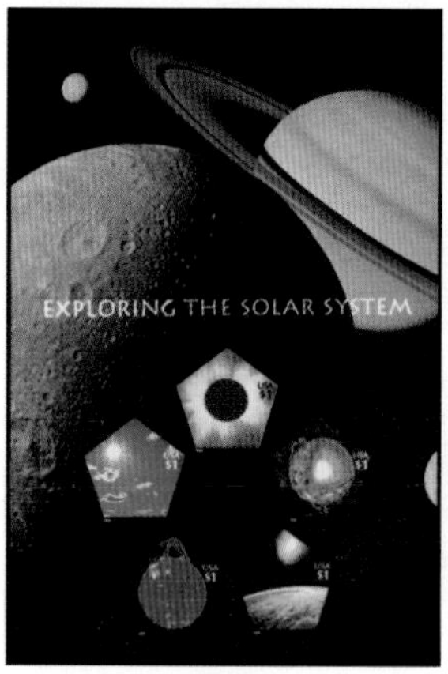

3410

3411

SCOTT NO.	DESCRIPTION	FIRST DAY COVERS SING	FIRST DAY COVERS PL. BLK.	MINT SHEET	PLATE BLOCK	UNUSED F/NH	USED
3410	$1 Exploring the Solar System, souvenir sheet of 5	13.50	....	....	....	22.50	20.00
3410a	$1 Solar eclipse . . .	3.50	....	....	....	4.50	4.00
3410b	$1 Cross-section of sun	3.50	....	....	....	4.50	4.00
3410c	$1 Sun and Earth . .	3.50	....	....	....	4.50	4.00
3410d	$1 Sun & solar flare	3.50	....	....	....	4.50	4.00
3410e	$1 Sun with clouds .	3.50	....	....	....	4.50	4.00
3411	$3.20 Escaping the Gravity of Earth hologram, souvenir sheet of 2 .	16.50	....	....	....	22.50	20.00
3411a	$3.20 International Space Station hologram, from souvenir sheet	7.50	....	....	....	11.25	7.50
3411b	$3.20 Astronauts Working hologram, from souvenir sheet	7.50	....	....	....	11.25	7.50

3412

SCOTT NO.	DESCRIPTION	FIRST DAY COVERS SING	FIRST DAY COVERS PL. BLK.	MINT SHEET	PLATE BLOCK	UNUSED F/NH	USED
3412	$11.75 Space Achievement and Exploration hologram, souvenir sheet of 1 .	27.50	....	....	....	40.00	35.00

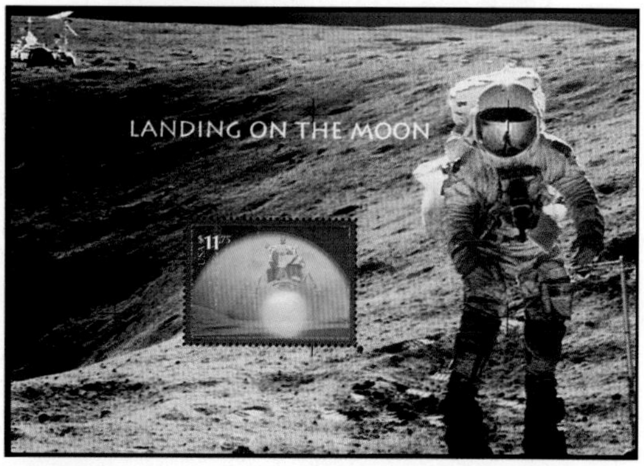

3413

SCOTT NO.	DESCRIPTION	FIRST DAY COVERS SING	FIRST DAY COVERS PL. BLK.	MINT SHEET	PLATE BLOCK	UNUSED F/NH	USED
3413	$11.75 Landing on the Moon hologram, souvenir sheet of 1	27.50	....	....	....	40.00	35.00

3414

3415

3416

3417

SCOTT NO.	DESCRIPTION	FIRST DAY COVERS SING	FIRST DAY COVERS PL. BLK.	MINT SHEET	PLATE BLOCK	UNUSED F/NH	USED
3414-17	33¢ Stampin' the Future, 4 varieties, attached	8.00	10.00	20.00(20)	9.50(8)	4.50	3.50
3414	33¢ Designed by Zachary Canter	2.25	....	....	....	1.25	.40
3415	33¢ Designed by Sarah Lipsey	2.25	....	....	....	1.25	.40
3416	33¢ Designed by Morgan Hill	2.25	....	....	....	1.25	.40
3417	33¢ Designed by Ashley Young	2.25	....	....	....	1.25	.40

3420

3422, 3436

3426

3427

3428

3430

3431, 3432

3433, 3434

3435

2000-2007 DISTINGUISHED AMERICANS

SCOTT NO.	DESCRIPTION	FIRST DAY COVERS SING	FIRST DAY COVERS PL. BLK.	MINT SHEET	PLATE BLOCK	UNUSED F/NH	USED
3420	10¢ Joseph W. Stilwell	2.25	4.00	5.00(20)	1.50	.25	.20
3422	23¢ Wilma Rudolph, self-adhesive, die cut 11.25 x 10.75	2.25	4.75	10.00(20)	2.75	.60	.20
3426	33¢ Claude Pepper .	2.25	4.75	17.50(20)	4.50	1.00	.25
3427	58¢ Margaret Chase Smith, self-adhesive (2007)	2.25	5.50	28.00(20)	6.00	1.50	.50
3428	63¢ Dr. Jonas Salk (2006)	2.25	6.00	28.00(20)	6.00	1.40	.40
3430	75¢ Harriett Beecher Stowe, self-adhesive (2007)	2.95	6.00	33.50(20)	8.00	2.50	.60
3431	76¢ Hattie W. Caraway, die cut 11	2.95	5.50	33.50(20)	8.00	2.50	.60
3432	76¢ Hattie W. Caraway, die cut 11.5 x 11 . . .	....	....	75.00(20)	18.50	4.00	4.00
3433	83¢ Edna Ferber, die cut 11 x 11.5 . . .	2.95	5.50	38.00(20)	9.00	1.95	.75
3434	83¢ Edna Ferber, die cut 11.25 (2003)	2.95	5.50	38.00(20)	9.00	2.50	.75
3435	87¢ Dr. Albert Sabin (2006)	2.95	5.50	38.00(20)	9.00	1.95	.75
3436	23¢ Wilma Rudolph, self-adhesive, die cut 11.25 x 10.75	2.25	....	....	....	.60	.20
3436a	same, bklt pane of 4	3.00	....	....	....	2.75	....
3436b	same, bklt pane of 6	4.00	....	....	....	3.75	....
3436c	same, bklt pane of 10	6.75	....	....	....	6.50	....

3438

SCOTT NO.	DESCRIPTION	FIRST DAY COVERS SING	FIRST DAY COVERS PL. BLK.	MINT SHEET	PLATE BLOCK	UNUSED F/NH	USED
3438	33¢ California Statehood, self-adhesive	2.25	....	22.50(20)	5.50	1.20	.25

3439

3440

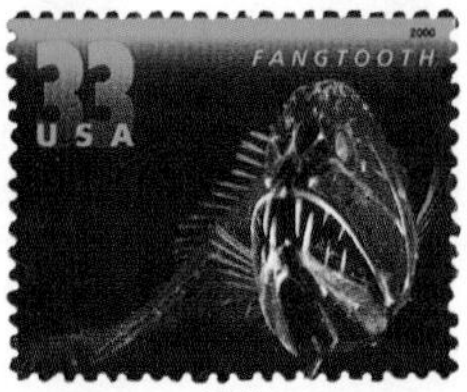

3441

3442

3443

SCOTT NO.	DESCRIPTION	FIRST DAY COVERS SING	FIRST DAY COVERS PL. BLK.	MINT SHEET	PLATE BLOCK	UNUSED F/NH	USED
3439-43	33¢ Deep Sea Creatures, 5 varieities attached	5.75	11.00	17.50(20)	....	5.00	4.00
3439	33¢ Fanfin Anglerfish	2.25	....	....	....	1.20	.35
3440	33¢ Sea Cucumber .	2.25	....	....	....	1.20	.35
3441	33¢ Fangtooth	2.25	....	....	....	1.20	.35
3442	33¢ Amphipod	2.25	....	....	....	1.20	.35
3443	33¢ Medusa	2.25	....	....	....	1.20	.35

3444

3445

3446

SCOTT NO.	DESCRIPTION	FIRST DAY COVERS SING	FIRST DAY COVERS PL. BLK.	MINT SHEET	PLATE BLOCK	UNUSED F/NH	USED
3444	33¢ Thomas Wolfe .	2.25	4.75	17.50(20)	4.50	1.00	.25
3445	33¢ White House . .	2.25	4.75	22.50(20)	5.25	1.20	.25
3446	33¢ Edward G. Robinson	2.25	4.75	26.00(20)	6.50	1.50	.50
....	same, uncut sheet of 120 (6 panes)	....	....	175.00(120)	....	175.00	....
....	cross gutter block of 8	....	....	....	....	35.00	....
....	block of 8 with vert. gutter	....	....	....	....	24.00	....
....	horiz. pair with vert. gutter	....	....	....	....	6.00	....
....	vert. pair with horiz. gutter	....	....	....	....	4.50	....

3447

3448, 3449, 3450,

3451, 3452, 3453

SCOTT NO.	DESCRIPTION	FIRST DAY COVERS SING	FIRST DAY COVERS PL. BLK.	MINT SHEET	PLATE BLOCK	UNUSED F/NH	USED
3447	10¢ New York Public Library Lion, coil	2.25	....	....	4.00	.50	.20
....	same, pl# strip of 5 .	....	....	....	....	5.00	....
3447a	10¢ New York Public Library, self-adhesive, coil, die cut 11.5	2.25		....	....	.50	.05
....	same, pl# strip of 5 .	....	....	....	....	4.00	....
3448	(34¢) Flag over Farm	2.25	4.75	25.00(20)	6.00	1.30	.60
3449	(34¢) Flag over Farm, self-adhesive	2.25	4.75	25.00(20)	6.00	1.30	.30
3450	(34¢) Flag over Farm, self-adhesive	2.25	....	....	....	1.25	.25
3450a	same, bklt pane of 18	14.00	....	....	....	21.50	....
3451	(34¢) Statue of Liberty, self-adhesive	2.25	....	....	....	1.20	.30
3451a	same, bklt pane of 20	14.50	....	....	....	18.50	....
3451b	same, bklt pane of 4	4.00	....	....	....	5.00	....
3451c	same, bklt pane of 6	5.50	....	....	....	7.00	....
3452	(34c) Statue of Liberty, coil	2.25	....	....	7.00	1.00	.20
....	same, pl# strip of 5 .	....	....	....	....	9.00	....
3453	(34c) Statue of Liberty, self-adhesive coil . .	1.95	....	....	10.00	1.00	.20
....	same, pl# strip of 5 .	....	....	....	....	12.00	....

3454, 3458, 3465 — 3455, 3459, 3464 — 3456, 3460, 3463 — 3457, 3461, 3462

SCOTT NO.	DESCRIPTION	FIRST DAY COVERS SING	FIRST DAY COVERS PL. BLK.	MINT SHEET	PLATE BLOCK	UNUSED F/NH	USED
3454-57	(34¢) Flowers, self-adhesive, 4 varieties attached .	4.25	....	....	....	6.00	....
3454	(34¢) Fressia, self-adhesive, die cut 10.25 x 10.75	2.25	....	....	....	1.50	.30
3455	(34¢) Symbidium Orchid, self-adhesive, die cut 10.25 x 10.75	2.25	....	....	....	1.50	.30
3456	(34¢) Longiflorum Lily, self-adhesive, die cut 10.25 x 10.75	2.25	....	....	....	1.50	.30
3457	(34¢) Asian Hydrid, self-adhesive, die cut 10.25 x 10.75	2.25	....	....	....	1.50	.30
3457b	same, bklt pane of 4 (3454-57)	4.00	....	....	....	6.00	....
3457c	same, bklt pane of 6 (3456, 3457, 3454 x 2 3455 x 2)	5.50	....	....	....	9.00	....
3457d	same, bklt pane of 6 (3454, 3455, 3456 x 2 3457 x 2)	5.50	....	....	....	9.00	....
3457e	(34¢) Flowers, bklt pane of 20, self-adhesive (5 each 3457a + label)	14.50	....	....	....	20.00	....
3458-61	(34¢) Flowers, self-adhesive, 4 varieties attached .	4.25	....	....	....	12.50	....
3458	(34¢) Fressia, bklt single, self-adhesive, die cut 11.5 x 11.75	2.25	....	....	....	3.25	.50
3459	(34¢) Symbidium Orchid, bklt single, self-adhesive, die cut 11.5 x 11.75 .	2.25	....	....	....	3.25	.50
3460	(34¢) Longiflorum Lily, bklt single, self-adhesive, die cut 11.5 x 11.75 .	2.25	....	....	....	3.25	.50
3461	(34¢) Asian Hybrid Lily, bklt single, self-adhesive, die cut 11.5 x 11.75 .	2.25	....	....	....	3.25	.50
3461b	same, bklt pane of 20, self-adhesive (2 each 3461a, 3 each 3457a)	14.50	....	....	....	38.00	....
3461c	same, bklt pane of 20, self-adhesive (2 each 3457a, 3 each 3461a)	14.50	....	....	....	50.00	....
3462	(34¢) Longiflorum Lily, self-adhesive coil . .	2.25	....	....	....	4.00	.50
3463	(34¢) Asian Hybrid Lily, self-adhesive coil . .	2.25	....	....	....	4.00	.50
3464	(34¢) Symbidium Orchid, self-adhesive coil . .	2.25	....	....	....	4.00	.50
3465	(34¢) Fressia, self-adhesive coil . .	2.25	....	....	....	4.00	.50
3462-65	(34¢) Flowers, self- adhesive coil, strip of 4	4.25	....	....	....	16.50	....
....	same, pl# strip of 5 .	....	....	....	....	21.50	....

3466, 3476, 3477, 3485

3467, 3468, 3475, 3484, 3484A

3468A, 3475A

3469, 3470

3471

3471A

2001 REGULAR ISSUES

SCOTT NO.	DESCRIPTION	FIRST DAY COVERS SING	FIRST DAY COVERS PL. BLK.	MINT SHEET	PLATE BLOCK	UNUSED F/NH	USED
3466	34¢ Statue of Liberty, self-adhesive coil, die cut 9.75 (round corners)	2.25	....	....	7.00	1.30	.50
....	same, pl# strip of 5 .	....	....	....	....	9.00	....
3467	21¢ Buffalo	2.25	4.75	60.00(100)	8.00	1.50	.75
3468	21¢ Buffalo. self-adhesive	2.25	4.75	12.00(20)	3.00	.65	.75
3468A	23¢ George Washington, self-adhesive	2.25	4.75	12.00(20)	2.75	.65	.75
3469	34¢ Flag over Farm .	2.25	4.75	85.00(100)	10.00	1.00	.35
3470	34¢ Flag over Farm, self-adhesive	2.25	4.75	17.50(20)	4.50	1.00	.50
3471	55¢ Eagle, self-adhesive	2.50	5.00	27.50(20)	7.00	1.50	.50
3471A	57¢ Eagle, self-adhesive	2.50	5.00	27.50(20)	7.00	1.50	.50

3472

3473

SCOTT NO.	DESCRIPTION	FIRST DAY COVERS SING	FIRST DAY COVERS PL. BLK.	MINT SHEET	PLATE BLOCK	UNUSED F/NH	USED
3472	$3.50 Capitol Dome, self-adhesive	8.00	30.00	175.00(20)	45.00	10.00	5.00
3473	$12.25 Washington Monument, self-adhesive	30.00	98.50	650.00(20)	150.00	30.00	11.00
3475	21¢ Buffalo, self-adhesive coil . .	2.25	....	....	5.00	.65	.30
....	same, pl# strip of 5 .	....	....	....	....	6.00	....
3475A	23¢ George Washington, self-adhesive coil . .	2.25	....	....	....	1.00	.30
....	same, pl# strip of 5 .	....	....	....	....	6.00	....
3476	34¢ Statue of Liberty, coil	2.25	....	....	6.00	1.00	.40
....	same, pl# strip of 5 .	....	....	....	....	7.50	....
3477	34¢ Statue of Liberty, self-adhesive coil die cut 9.75 (square corners)	2.25	....	....	6.00	1.00	.20
....	same, pl# strip of 5 .	....	....	....	....	7.50	....

3478, 3489 — 3479, 3490 — 3480, 3488 — 3481, 3487

SCOTT NO.	DESCRIPTION	FIRST DAY COVERS SING	FIRST DAY COVERS PL. BLK.	MINT SHEET	PLATE BLOCK	UNUSED F/NH	USED
3478	34¢ Longiflorum, self-adhesive coil . .	2.25	....	....	....	1.50	.40
3479	34¢ Asain Hybrid Lily, self-adhesive coil . .	2.25	....	....	....	1.50	.40
3480	34¢ Symbidium Orchid, self-adhesive coil . .	2.25	....	....	....	1.50	.40
3481	34¢ Fressia, self-adhesive coil . .	2.25	....	....	....	1.50	.40
3478-81	34¢ Flowers, self-adhesive, coil, strip of 4	4.25	....	....	....	6.00	....
....	same, pl# strip of 5 .	....	....	....	....	10.00	....

3482, 3483

3491, 3493

3492, 3494

3495

SCOTT NO.	DESCRIPTION	FIRST DAY COVERS SING	FIRST DAY COVERS PL. BLK.	MINT SHEET	PLATE BLOCK	UNUSED F/NH	USED
3482	20¢ George Washington, self-adhesive, die cut 11.25	2.25	....	....	....	1.00	.30
3482a	same, bklt pane of 10	5.50	....	....	....	8.00	....
3482b	same, bklt pane of 4, die cut 11.25 x 11 . .	3.00	....	....	....	3.00	....
3482c	same, bklt pane of 6, die cut 11.25 x 11 . .	4.00	....	....	....	5.00	....
3483	20¢ George Washington, self-adhesive, die cut 10.5 x 11.25	2.25	....	....	....	5.00	1.00
3483a	same, bklt pane of 4 (2 each 3482-3483) .	3.00	....	....	....	15.00	....
3483b	same, bklt pane of 6 (3 each 3482-3483) .	4.00	....	....	....	22.00	....
3483c	same, bklt pane of 10, die cut 10.5 x 11 (3482 x 5 at L, 3483 x 5 at R) .	5.50	....	....	....	16.50	....
3483d	same, bklt pane of 4 (2 each 3482-3483), die cut 11.25 x 11 . .	....	....	....	....	17.00	....
3483e	same, bklt pane of 6 (2 each 3482-3483), die cut 11.25 x 11 . .	....	....	....	....	22.00	....
3483f	same, bklt pane of 10 (5 each 3482-3483), die cut 11.25 x 11 . .	....	....	....	....	16.50	....
3483g	pair, 3482 at left, 3483 at right	....	....	....	....	3.50	....
3483h	pair 3483 at left, 3482 at right	....	....	....	....	3.50	....
3484	21¢ Buffalo, self-adhesive, die cut 11.25	2.25	....	....	....	1.00	.50
3484b	same, bklt pane of 4	3.00	....	....	....	3.25	....
3484c	same, bklt pane of 6	4.00	....	....	....	4.75	....
3484d	same, bklt pane of 10	5.50	....	....	....	8.00	....
3484A	21¢ Buffalo, self-adhesive, die cut 10.5 X 11.25	2.25	....	....	....	4.00	.50
3484Ae	same, bklt pane of 4 (3484 x 2 at L, 3484A x 2 at R)	....	....	....	....	8.50	....
3484Af	same, bklt pane of 6 (3484 x 3 at L, 3484A x 3 at R)	....	....	....	....	12.00	....
3484Ag	same, bklt pane of 10 (3484 x 5 at L, 3484A x 5 at R)	....	....	....	....	13.50	....
3484Ah	same, bklt pane of 4 (3484A x 2 at L, 3484 x 2 at R)	....	....	....	....	8.50	....
3484Ai	same, bklt pane of 6 (3484A x 3 at L, 3484 x 3 at R)	....	....	....	....	12.00	....
3484Aj	same, bklt pane of 10 (3484A x 5 at L, 3484 x 5 at R)	....	....	....	....	13.50	....
3484Ak	same, pair (3484 at L, 3484A at R)	....	....	....	....	3.50	....
3484Al	same, pair (3484A at L, 3484 at R)	....	....	....	....	3.50	....
3485	34¢ Statue of Liberty, self-adhesive	2.25	....	....	....	1.40	.20
3485a	same, bklt pane of 10	7.25	....	....	....	13.50	....
3485b	same, bklt pane of 20	14.50	....	....	....	27.00	....
3485c	same, bklt pane of 4	4.00	....	....	....	4.50	....
3485d	same, bklt pane of 6	5.50	....	....	....	6.50	....
3487-90	34¢ Flowers, self-adhesive 4 varieties attached .	4.25	....	....	....	4.50	2.50
3487	34¢ Fressia, self-adhesive, die cut 10.25 x 10.75	2.25	....	....	....	1.20	.25
3488	34¢ Symbidium Orchid, self-adhesive, die cut 10.25 x 10.75	2.25	....	....	....	1.20	.25
3489	34¢ Longiflorum Lily, self-adhesive, die cut 10.25 x 10.75	2.25	....	....	....	1.20	.25
3490	34¢ Asian Hybrid Lily, self-adhesive, die cut 10.25 x 10.75	2.25	....	....	....	1.20	.25
3490b	same, bklt pane of 4 (3487-90 x 1)	4.00	....	....	....	5.00	....
3490c	same, bklt pane of 6 (3489-3490, 3487 x 2, 3488 x 2)	5.50	....	....	....	7.50	....
3490d	same, bklt pane of 6 (3487-3488, 3498 x 2 3490 x 2)	5.50	....	....	....	7.50	....
3490e	same, bklt pane of 20 (3487-90 x 5 + label)	14.50	....	....	....	22.50	....
3491	34¢ Apple, self-adhesive	2.25	....	....	....	1.75	.25
3492	34¢ Orange, self-adhesive	2.25	....	....	....	1.75	.25
3491-92	34¢ Apple & Orange, Pair	2.50	....	....	....	2.00	....
3492b	34¢ Apple & Orange, bklt pane of 20, self-adhesive	14.50	....	....	....	19.50	....
3493	34¢ Apple, self-adhesive, die cut 11.5 x 10.75 .	2.25	....	....	....	1.50	.50
3494	34¢ Orange, self-adhesive, die cut 11.5 x 10.75 .	2.25	....	....	....	1.50	.50
3493-94	34¢ Apple & Orange, Pair	2.50	....	....	....	3.50	....
3494b	same, bklt pane of 4 (3493 x 2, 3494 x 2)	4.00	....	....	....	2.00	....
3494c	same, bklt pane of 6 (3493 x 3, 3494 x 3) (3493 at UL)	5.50	....	....	....	12.00	....
3494d	same, bklt pane of 6 (3493 x 3, 3494 x 3) (3494 at UL)	5.50	....	....	....	12.00	....
3495	34¢ Flag over Farm, self-adhesive	1.95	....	....	....	1.00	.40
3495a	same, ATM bklt pane of 18	14.00	....	....	....	17.50	....

3496

3497, 3498

3499

SCOTT NO.	DESCRIPTION	FIRST DAY COVERS SING	FIRST DAY COVERS PL. BLK.	MINT SHEET	PLATE BLOCK	UNUSED F/NH	USED
3496	(34¢) LOVE, self-adhesive, die cut 11.75	2.25	....	....	....	1.10	.25
3496a	same, bklt pane of 20	14.50	....	....	....	21.50	....
3497	34¢ LOVE, self-adhesive, die cut 11.25	2.25	....	....	....	1.10	.25
3497a	same, bklt pane of 20	14.50	....	....	....	19.50	....
3498	34¢ LOVE, self-adhesive, die cut 11.5 x 10.75 .	2.25	....	....	....	1.10	.25
3498a	same, bklt pane of 4	4.00	....	....	....	4.50	....
3498b	same, bklt pane of 6	5.50	....	....	....	6.50	....
3499	55¢ LOVE, self-adhesive	2.50	5.00	32.00(20)	7.50	1.50	.50

3500

3501

2001 COMMEMORATIVES

SCOTT NO.	DESCRIPTION	FIRST DAY COVERS SING	FIRST DAY COVERS PL. BLK.	MINT SHEET	PLATE BLOCK	UNUSED F/NH	USED
3500/3548	**(3500-01, 3503-04, 3507-19, 3521, 3523-33, 3536-40, 3545-48) 38 varieties . . . . .**	....	....	....	....	**38.40**	**13.50**
3500	34¢ Year of the Snake	2.25	4.75	26.00(20)	6.00	1.35	.30
3501	34¢ Roy Wilkins, self-adhesive	2.25	4.75	24.00(20)	5.50	1.25	.25

3502

AMERICAN ILLUSTRATORS

3502a *Marine Corps poster*
3502b *"Interlude (The Lute Players)"*
3502c *Advertisement for Arrow Collars and Shirts*
3502d *Advertisement for Carrier Corp. Refrigeration*
3502e *Advertisement for Luxite Hosiery*
3502f *Illustration for correspondence school lesson*
3502g *"Br'er Rabbit"*
3502h *"An Attack on a Galleon"*
3502i *Kewpie and Kewpie Doodle Dog*
3502 j *Illustration for cover of True Magazine*
3502k *"Galahad's Departure"*
3502l *"The First Lesson"*
3502m *Illustration for cover of McCall's*
3502n *"Back Home for Keeps"*
3502o *"Something for Supper"*
3502p *"A Dash for the Timber"*
3502q *Illustration for "Moby Dick"*
3502r *"Captain Bill Bones"*
3502s *Illustration for The Saturday Evening Post*
3502t *"The Girl He Left Behind"*

AMERICAN ILLUSTRATORS (Continued)

SCOTT NO.	DESCRIPTION	FIRST DAY COVERS SING	FIRST DAY COVERS PL. BLK.	MINT SHEET	PLATE BLOCK	UNUSED F/NH	USED
3502	34¢ American Illustrators, 20 varieties, attached, self-adhesive	....	....	27.50(20)	....	27.50	25.00
....	set of singles	37.50	....	....	....	....	15.00
3502v	same, uncut sheet of 80 (4 panes)	....	....	120.00(80)	....	120.00	....
....	cross gutter block of 20	....	....	....	....	60.00	....
....	block of 8 with horiz. gutter	....	....	....	....	40.00	....
....	block of 10 with vert. gutter	....	....	....	....	40.00	....
....	vert. pair with horiz. gutter	....	....	....	....	7.00	....
....	horiz. pair with vert. gutter	....	....	....	....	7.00	....

3503

3504

SCOTT NO.	DESCRIPTION	FIRST DAY COVERS SING	FIRST DAY COVERS PL. BLK.	MINT SHEET	PLATE BLOCK	UNUSED F/NH	USED
3503	34¢ Diabetes Awareness	2.25	4.75	17.50(20)	4.50	1.00	.25
3504	34¢ Nobel Prize Centenary	2.25	4.75	17.50(20)	4.50	1.00	.25

3505

SCOTT NO.	DESCRIPTION	FIRST DAY COVERS SING	FIRST DAY COVERS PL. BLK.	MINT SHEET	PLATE BLOCK	UNUSED F/NH	USED
3505	1¢-80¢ Pan-American Expo. Invert Souvenir Sheet of 7	10.00	....	....	....	15.00	12.00
....	same, uncut sheet of 28 (4 panes)	....	....	....	....	75.00	....

3506

GREAT PLAINS PRAIRIE

3506a *Pronghorns, Canada geese*
3506b *Burrowing owls, American buffalos*
3506c *American buffalo, Black-tailed prairie dogs, wild alfalfa*
3506d *Black-tailed prairie dogs, American Buffalo*
3506e *Painted lady butterfly, American buffalo, prairie coneflowers, prairie wild roses*
3506f *Western Meadowlark, camel cricket, prairie coneflowers, prairie wild flowers*
3506g *Badger, Harvester ants*
3506h *Eastern short-horned lizard, plains gopher*
3506i *Plains spadefoot, dung beetle, prairie roses*
3506j *Two-striped grasshopper, Ord's kangaroo rat*

SCOTT NO.	DESCRIPTION	FIRST DAY COVERS SING	FIRST DAY COVERS PL. BLK.	MINT SHEET	PLATE BLOCK	UNUSED F/NH	USED
3506	34¢ Great Plains Prairie, 10 varieties, attached, self-adhesive	....	....	15.00(10)	....	13.00	7.50
....	set of singles	19.50	....	....	....	....	6.00
3506v	same, uncut sheet of 60 (6 panes)	....	....	60.00(60)	....	60.00	....

3509

3507

3508

SCOTT NO.	DESCRIPTION	FIRST DAY COVERS SING	FIRST DAY COVERS PL. BLK.	MINT SHEET	PLATE BLOCK	UNUSED F/NH	USED
3507	34¢ Peanuts, self-adhesive	2.25	4.75	20.00(20)	5.00	1.25	.25
3508	34¢ US Veterans, self-adhesive	2.25	4.75	17.50(20)	4.50	1.25	.25
3509	34¢ Frida Kahlo	2.25	4.75	17.50(20)	4.50	1.00	.25

3510 3511

3512 3513

3514 3515

3516 3517

3518 3519

BASEBALL'S LEGENDARY PLAYING FIELDS

3510	*Ebbets Field*	3515	*Forbes Field*
3511	*Tiger Stadium*	3516	*Fenway Field*
3512	*Crosley Field*	3517	*Comiskey Park*
3513	*Yankee Stadium*	3518	*Shibe Park*
3514	*Polo Grounds*	3519	*Wrigley Field*

SCOTT NO.	DESCRIPTION	FIRST DAY COVERS SING	FIRST DAY COVERS PL. BLK.	MINT SHEET	PLATE BLOCK	UNUSED F/NH	USED
3510-19	34¢ Baseball's Legendary Playing Fields, 10 varieties, self-adhesive	7.25	....	19.50(20)	11.00(10)	10.00	8.50
....	set of singles	25.00	....	....	....	....	6.00
3510-19v	same, uncut sheet of 160 (8 panes)	....	....	160.00(160)	....	160.00	....
....	cross gutter block of 12	....	....	....	....	25.00	....
....	block of 10 with vert. gutter	....	....	....	....	15.00	....
....	block of 4 with horiz. gutter	....	....	....	....	7.50	....
....	vert. pair with horiz. gutter	....	....	....	....	3.50	....
....	horiz. pair with vert. gutter	....	....	....	....	3.50	....

3520

3521

3522

SCOTT NO.	DESCRIPTION	FIRST DAY COVERS SING	FIRST DAY COVERS PL. BLK.	MINT SHEET	PLATE BLOCK	UNUSED F/NH	USED
3520	(10¢) Atlas Statue, coil self-adhesive, die cut 8.5	2.25	....	....	4.00	.30	.25
....	same, pl# strip of 5 .	....	....	....	....	4.50	....
3521	34¢ Leonard Bernstein	2.25	4.75	17.50(20)	4.50	1.00	.25
3522	(15¢) Woody Wagon, self-adhesive coil . .	2.25	....	....	4.00	.50	.30
....	same, pl# strip of 5 .	....	....	....	....	5.00	....

3523

SCOTT NO.	DESCRIPTION	FIRST DAY COVERS SING	FIRST DAY COVERS PL. BLK.	MINT SHEET	PLATE BLOCK	UNUSED F/NH	USED
3523	34¢ Lucille Ball, self-adhesive	2.25	4.75	23.50(20)	6.00	1.25	.25
3523v	same, uncut sheet of 180 (9 panes)	....	....	185.00(180)	....	185.00	....
....	cross gutter block of 8	....	....	....	....	30.00	....
....	block of 8 with vert. gutter	....	....	....	....	22.50	....
....	vert. pair with horiz. gutter	....	....	....	....	3.00	....
....	horiz. pair with vert. gutter	....	....	....	....	4.00	....

3524 3525

3526 3527

SCOTT NO.	DESCRIPTION	FIRST DAY COVERS SING	FIRST DAY COVERS PL. BLK.	MINT SHEET	PLATE BLOCK	UNUSED F/NH	USED
3524-27	34¢ Amish Quilts, 4 varieties attached .	4.25	5.25	20.00(20)	5.00	4.50	4.00
3524	34¢ Diamond in the Square	2.25	....	....	....	1.20	.40
3525	34¢ Lone Star	2.25	....	....	....	1.20	.40
3526	34¢ Sunshine and Shadow	2.25	....	....	....	1.20	.40
3527	34¢ Double Ninepatch Variation	2.25	....	....	....	1.20	.40

3528

3529

3530

3531

SCOTT NO.	DESCRIPTION	FIRST DAY COVERS SING	FIRST DAY COVERS PL. BLK.	MINT SHEET	PLATE BLOCK	UNUSED F/NH	USED
3528-31	34¢ Carnivorous Plants, 4 varieties attached .	4.25	5.25	20.00(20)	5.00	4.50	4.00
3528	34¢ Venus Flytrap . .	2.25	....	....	....	1.20	.40
3529	34¢ Yellow Trumpet	2.25	....	....	....	1.20	.40
3530	34¢ Cobra	2.25	....	....	....	1.20	.40
3531	34¢ English Sundew	2.25	....	....	....	1.20	.40

3532

3533

3534, 3535

SCOTT NO.	DESCRIPTION	FIRST DAY COVERS SING	FIRST DAY COVERS PL. BLK.	MINT SHEET	PLATE BLOCK	UNUSED F/NH	USED
3532	34¢ "Eid Mubarak", self-adhesive	2.25	4.75	17.50(20)	4.50	1.00	.25
3533	34¢ Enrico Fermi, self-adhesive	2.25	4.75	17.50(20)	4.50	1.00	.25
3534	34¢ That's All Folks, self-adhesive, pane of 10	12.50	....	....	....	9.50	....
3534a	same, single from pane	2.50	....	....	....	1.10	.25
3534b	same, pane of 9 (3534a)	....	....	....	....	9.00	....
3534c	same, pane of 1 (3534a)	7.25	....	....	....	2.75	....
....	same, top press sheet of 60 (6 panes) w/ pl# .	....	....	80.00(60)	....	80.00	....
....	same, bottom press sheet of 60 (6 panes) w/ pl#	....	....	95.00(60)	....	95.00	....
....	same, pane of 10 from press sheet	....	....	....	....	15.00	....
....	same, pane of 10 w/ pl# on front	....	....	....	....	70.00	....
....	vert. pair with horiz. gutter	....	....	....	....	4.00	....
....	horiz. pair with vert. gutter	....	....	....	....	7.50	....
3535	34¢ That's All Folks, die cut, self-adhesive, pane of 10	15.00	....	....	....	40.00	....
3535a	same, single form pane	....	....	....	....	3.00	....
3535b	same, pane of 9 (3435a)	....	....	....	....	25.00	....
3535c	same, pane of 1, imperf.	12.50	....	....	....	12.00	....

3536

SCOTT NO.	DESCRIPTION	FIRST DAY COVERS SING	FIRST DAY COVERS PL. BLK.	MINT SHEET	PLATE BLOCK	UNUSED F/NH	USED
3536	34¢ Madonna and Child, self-adhesive	2.25	....	....	....	1.00	.20
3536a	same, bklt pane of 20	14.50	....	....	....	18.50	....

3537, 3537a, 3541

3538, 3538a, 3542

3539, 3539a, 3543

3540, 3540a, 3544

SCOTT NO.	DESCRIPTION	FIRST DAY COVERS SING	FIRST DAY COVERS PL. BLK.	MINT SHEET	PLATE BLOCK	UNUSED F/NH	USED
3537-40	34¢ Santas, self-adhesive, 4 varieties attach, large date	4.25	5.25	20.00(20)	5.00	4.50	4.00
3537	34¢ Santa w/ horse, large date	2.25	....	....	....	1.20	.40
3538	34¢ Santa w/ horn, large date	2.25	....	....	....	1.20	.40
3539	34¢ Santa w/ drum, large date	2.25	....	....	....	1.20	.40
3540	34¢ Santa w/ dog, large date	2.25	....	....	....	1.20	.40

SCOTT NO.	DESCRIPTION	FIRST DAY COVERS SING	FIRST DAY COVERS PL. BLK.	MINT SHEET	PLATE BLOCK	UNUSED F/NH	USED
3537a-40a	34¢ Santas, self-adhesive, 4 varieties attach, small date	4.25	5.25	....	....	4.50	4.00
3537a	34¢ Santa w/ horse, small date	2.25	....	....	....	1.20	.40
3538a	34¢ Santa w/ horn, small date	2.25	....	....	....	1.20	.40
3539a	34¢ Santa w/ drum, small date	2.25	....	....	....	1.20	.40
3540a	34¢ Santa w/ dog, small date	2.25	....	....	....	1.20	.40
3540d	same, bklt pane of 20, 3537a-40a x 5 + label	14.50	....	....	....	20.00	....
3537b-40e	34¢ Santas, self-adhesive, 4 varieties attach, large date	4.25	5.25	....	....	4.50	4.00
3537b	34¢ Santa w/ horse, large date	2.25	....	....	....	1.20	.40
3538b	34¢ Santa w/ horn, large date	2.25	....	....	....	1.20	.40
3539b	34¢ Santa w/ drum, large date	2.25	....	....	....	1.20	.40
3540e	34¢ Santa w/ dog, large date	2.25	....	....	....	1.20	.40
3540g	same, bklt pane of 20, 3537b-40e x 5 + label	14.50	....	....	....	20.00	....
3541-44	34¢ Santas, self-adhesive, 4 varieties attach, green denom.	4.25	....	....	....	4.50	....
3541	34¢ Santa w/ horse, green denom	2.25	....	....	....	1.20	.30
3542	34¢ Santa w/ horn, green denom	2.25	....	....	....	1.20	.30
3543	34¢ Santa w/ drum, green denom.	2.25	....	....	....	1.20	.30
3544	34¢ Santa w/ dog, green denom	2.25	....	....	....	1.20	.30
3544b	same, bklt pane of 4 (3541-3544)	4.00	....	....	....	4.50	....
3544c	same, bklt pane of 6 (3543-44, 3541-42 x 2)	5.50	....	....	....	6.00	....
3544d	same, bklt pane of 6 (3541-42, 3543-44 x 2)	5.50	....	....	....	6.00	....

3545

SCOTT NO.	DESCRIPTION	FIRST DAY COVERS SING	FIRST DAY COVERS PL. BLK.	MINT SHEET	PLATE BLOCK	UNUSED F/NH	USED
3545	34¢ James Madison	2.25	4.75	17.50(20)	4.50	1.00	.30
3545v	same, uncut sheet of 120 (6 panes)	....	....	110.00(120)	....	110.00	....
....	cross gutter block of 4	....	....	....	....	11.00	....
....	horiz. pair with vert. gutter	....	....	....	....	4.50	....
....	vert. pair with horiz. gutter	....	....	....	....	3.50	....

3546

3547

3548

SCOTT NO.	DESCRIPTION	FIRST DAY COVERS SING	FIRST DAY COVERS PL. BLK.	MINT SHEET	PLATE BLOCK	UNUSED F/NH	USED
3546	34¢ We Give Thanks, self-adhesive	2.25	4.75	17.50(20)	4.50	1.00	.25
3547	34¢ Hanukkah, self-adhesive	2.25	4.75	17.50(20)	4.50	1.00	.25
3548	34¢ Kwanzaa, self-adhesive	2.25	4.75	17.50(20)	4.50	1.00	.25

3549, 3549B, 3550, 3550A

3551

SCOTT NO.	DESCRIPTION	FIRST DAY COVERS SING	FIRST DAY COVERS PL. BLK.	MINT SHEET	PLATE BLOCK	UNUSED F/NH	USED
3549	34¢ United We Stand, self-adhesive	2.25	....	....	....	1.20	.25
3549a	same, bklt pane of 20	14.50	....	....	....	22.50	....
3549B	34¢ United We Stand, die cut 10.5 x 10.75 on 2 or 3 sides	2.25	....	....	....	1.30	.25
3549Bc	same, bklt pane of 4	4.00	....	....	....	4.50	....
3549Bd	same, bklt pane of 6	5.50	....	....	....	6.50	....
3549Be	same, bklt pane of 20 (double-sided)	....	....	....	....	18.50	....
3550	34¢ United We Stand, self-adhesive coil (square corners) . . .	2.25	....	....	....	1.00	.20
....	same, pl# strip of 5 .	....	....	....	....	8.00	....
3550A	34¢ United We Stand, self-adhesive coil, (round corners)	2.25	....	....	....	1.00	.40
....	same, pl# strip of 5 .	....	....	....	....	9.00	....
3551	57¢ Love, self-adhesive	2.50	5.00	27.50(20)	7.00	1.50	.50

3554 3555

3552 3553

2002 COMMEMORATIVES

SCOTT NO.	DESCRIPTION	FIRST DAY COVERS SING	FIRST DAY COVERS PL. BLK.	MINT SHEET	PLATE BLOCK	UNUSED F/NH	USED
3552/3695	**(3552-60, 3650-56, 3658-74, 3676-79, 3692, 3695) 39 varieties**	....	....	....	....	**43.75**	**12.25**
3552-55	34¢ Winter Olympics, self-adhesive, 4 varieties attached	4.25	5.25	20.00(20)	5.00	4.50	3.50
3552	34¢ Ski Jumping . . .	2.25	....	....	....	1.20	.40
3553	34¢ Snowboarding .	2.25	....	....	....	1.20	.40
3554	34¢ Ice Hockey	2.25	....	....	....	1.20	.40
3555	34¢ Figure Skating .	2.25	....	....	....	1.20	.40
3552-55v	same, uncut sheet of 180 (9 panes)	....	....	185.00(180)	....	185.00	....
....	cross gutter block of 8	....	....	....	....	25.00	....
....	block of 4 with vert. gutter	....	....	....	....	8.00	....
....	block of 8 with horiz. gutter	....	....	....	....	11.50	....
....	vert. pair with horiz. gutter	....	....	....	....	3.00	....
....	horiz. pair with vert. gutter	....	....	....	....	2.00	....

3556

3557

3558

SCOTT NO.	DESCRIPTION	FIRST DAY COVERS SING	FIRST DAY COVERS PL. BLK.	MINT SHEET	PLATE BLOCK	UNUSED F/NH	USED
3556	34¢ Mentoring a Child, self-adhesive	2.25	4.75	17.50(20)	4.50	1.00	1.20
3557	34¢ Langston Hughes, self-adhesive	2.25	4.75	17.50(20)	4.50	1.00	1.20
3558	34¢ Happy Birthday, self-adhesive	2.25	4.75	17.50(20)	4.50	1.00	1.20

3559

3560

SCOTT NO.	DESCRIPTION	FIRST DAY COVERS SING	FIRST DAY COVERS PL. BLK.	MINT SHEET	PLATE BLOCK	UNUSED F/NH	USED
3559	34¢ Year of the Horse, self-adhesive	2.25	4.75	30.00(20)	7.00	1.50	.25
3560	34¢ Military Academy Bicentennial, self-adhesive	2.25	4.75	17.50(20)	5.00	1.00	.25

3561

3610

GREETINGS FROM AMERICA

3561	*Alabama*	**3578**	*Louisiana*	**3595**	*Ohio*
3562	*Alaska*	**3579**	*Maine*	**3596**	*Oklahoma*
3563	*Arizona*	**3580**	*Maryland*	**3597**	*Oregon*
3564	*Arkansas*	**3581**	*Massachusetts*	**3598**	*Pennsylvania*
3565	*California*	**3582**	*Michigan*	**3599**	*Rhode Island*
3566	*Colorado*	**3583**	*Minnesota*	**3600**	*South Carolina*
3567	*Connecticut*	**3584**	*Mississippi*	**3601**	*South Dakota*
3568	*Delaware*	**3585**	*Missouri*	**3602**	*Tennessee*
3569	*Florida*	**3586**	*Montana*	**3603**	*Texas*
3570	*Georgia*	**3587**	*Nebraska*	**3604**	*Utah*
3571	*Hawaii*	**3588**	*Nevada*	**3605**	*Vermont*
3572	*Idaho*	**3589**	*New Hampshire*	**3606**	*Virginia*
3573	*Illinois*	**3590**	*New Jersey*	**3607**	*Washington*
3574	*Indiana*	**3591**	*New Mexico*	**3608**	*West Virginia*
3575	*Iowa*	**3592**	*New York*	**3609**	*Wisconsin*
3576	*Kansas*	**3593**	*North Carolina*	**3610**	*Wyoming*
3577	*Kentucky*	**3594**	*North Dakota*		

SCOTT NO.	DESCRIPTION	FIRST DAY COVERS SING	FIRST DAY COVERS PL. BLK.	MINT SHEET	PLATE BLOCK	UNUSED F/NH	USED
3561-3610	34¢ Greetings from America, self-adhesive, 50 varieties attached	....	....	45.00(50)	....	45.00	....
....	set of singles	120.00	....	....	....	....	30.00

3611

LONGLEAF PINE FOREST

3611a	*Bachman's sparrow*	**3611g**	*Gray Fox, gopher tortoise*
3611b	*Northern bobwhite, yellow pitcher plants*	**3611h**	*Blind click beetle, sweetbay, pine woods freefrog*
3611c	*Fox squirrel, red-bellied woodpecker*	**3611i**	*Rosebuds orchid, pipeworts, southern toad, yellow pitcher plants*
3611d	*Brown-headed nuthatch*	**3611j**	*Grass-pink orchid, yellow-sided skimmer, pipeworts*
3611e	*Broadhead skink, yellow pitcher plants, pipeworts*		
3611f	*Eastern towhee, yellow pitcher plants, meadow beauties, toothache grass*		

SCOTT NO.	DESCRIPTION	FIRST DAY COVERS SING	FIRST DAY COVERS PL. BLK.	MINT SHEET	PLATE BLOCK	UNUSED F/NH	USED
3611	34¢ Longleaf Pine Forest, 10 varieties, attached, self-adhesive	....	....	12.00(10)	....	12.00	10.00
....	set of singles	25.00	....	....	....	....	7.00
3611v	same, uncut sheet of 90 (9 panes)	....	....	100.00(90)	....	100.00	....

3612

3613, 3614, 3615

3616, 3617, 3618, 3619

3620, 3621, 3622, 3623, 3624, 3625

SCOTT NO.	DESCRIPTION	FIRST DAY COVERS SING	FIRST DAY COVERS PL. BLK.	MINT SHEET	PLATE BLOCK	UNUSED F/NH	USED
3612	5¢ Toleware coffee pot, coil	2.25	....	....	....	.25	.20
....	same, pl# strip of 5 .	....	....	....	....	2.25	....
3613	3¢ Lithographed Star (year at LL)	2.25	4.75	4.50(50)	.75	.20	.20
3614	3¢ Photogravure Star (year of LR)	2.25	4.75	4.50(50)	.75	.20	.20
3615	3¢ Star, coil	2.25	....	....	....	.20	.20
....	same, pl# strip of 5 .	....	....	....	....	2.00	....
3616	23¢ George Washington	2.25	4.75	60.00(100)	5.00	.75	.20
3617	23¢ George Washington, self-adhesive coil ..	2.25	....	....	....	.75	.20
....	same pl# strip of 5 ..	....	....	....	....	5.00	....
3618	23¢ George Washington, self-adhesive die cut 11.25	2.25	....	....	....	.75	.20
3618a	same, bklt pane of 4	3.00	....	....	....	3.00	....
3618b	same, bklt pane of 6	4.00	....	....	....	4.50	....
3618c	same, bklt pane of 10	6.75	....	....	....	7.25	....
3619	23¢ George Washington, self-adhesive, die cut 10.5 x 11.25	1.95	....	....	....	3.00	.50
3619a	same, bklt pane of 4 (3619 x 2 at L, 3618 x 2 at R)........		....	....	....	8.50	....
3619b	same, bklt pane of 6 (3619 x 3 at L, 3618 x 3 at R)........		....	....	....	13.00	....
3619c	same, bklt pane of 4 (3618 x 2 at L, 3619 x 2 at R)........		....	....	....	8.50	....
3619d	same, bklt pane of 6 (3618 x 3 at L, 3619 x 3 at R)		....	....	....	13.00	....
3619g	same, pair (3619 at L, 3618 at R)	....	....	....	....	4.00	....
3619h	same, pair (3618 at L, 3619 at R)	....	....	....	....	3.00	....
3620	(37¢) Flag	2.25	4.75	90.00(100)	12.00	1.00	.20
3621	(37¢) Flag, self-adhesive	2.25	4.75	17.50(20)	4.50	1.00	.20
3622	(37¢) Flag, self-adhesive coil	2.25	....	....	....	1.00	.20
....	same, pl# strip of 5 .	....	....	....	....	6.75	....
3623	(37¢) Flag, self-adhesive, die cut 11.25	2.25	....	....	....	1.00	.20
3623a	same, bklt pane of 20	....	....	....	....	19.50	....
3624	(37¢) Flag, self-adhesive, die cut 10.5 x 10.75.	2.25	....	....	....	1.00	.20
3624a	same, bklt pane of 4	4.00	....	....	....	4.25	....
3624b	same, bklt pane of 6	5.50	....	....	....	6.00	....
3624c	same, bklt pane of 20	15.00	....	....	....	19.50	....
3625	(37¢) Flag, self-adhesive, die cut 8	2.25	....	....	....	1.20	.25
3625a	same, ATM bklt pane of 18	15.00	....	....	....	17.50	....

3626

3627

3628

3629

SCOTT NO.	DESCRIPTION	FIRST DAY COVERS SING	FIRST DAY COVERS PL. BLK.	MINT SHEET	PLATE BLOCK	UNUSED F/NH	USED
3626	(37¢) Toy mail wagon, self-adhesive	2.25	....	....	....	1.20	.35
3627	(37¢) Toy locomotive, self-adhesive	2.25	....	....	....	1.20	.35
3628	(37¢) Toy taxicab, self-adhesive	2.25	....	....	....	1.20	.35
3629	(37¢) Toy fire pumper, self-adhesive	2.25	....	....	....	1.20	.35
3626-29	(37¢) Antique Toys, self-adhesive, 4 varieties attached .	4.25	....	....	....	4.50	3.50
3629b	same, bklt pane of 4 (3626-29 x 1)	4.25	....	....	....	4.50	....
3629c	same, bklt pane of 6 (3627, 3629, 3626 x 2, 3628 x 2)	5.50	....	....	....	6.50	....
3629d	same, bklt pane of 6 (3626, 3628, 3627 x 2, 3629 x 2)	5.50	....	....	....	6.25	....
3629e	same, bklt pane of 20	15.00	....	....	....	19.50	....
3629F	37¢ Flag	2.25	4.75	100.00(100)	9.00	1.50	.75

3638, 3643

3629F, 3630, 3631, 3632, 3632A, 3632C, 3633, 3633A, 3635, 3636, 3636D, 3637

3639, 3642

3640, 3645

3641, 3644

SCOTT NO.	DESCRIPTION	FIRST DAY COVERS SING	FIRST DAY COVERS PL. BLK.	MINT SHEET	PLATE BLOCK	UNUSED F/NH	USED
3630	37¢ Flag, self-adhesive	2.25	4.75	18.50(20)	4.50	1.20	.20
3631	37¢ Flag, coil	2.25	....	....	....	1.20	.30
....	same, pl# strip of 5 .	....	....	....	....	8.00	....
3632	37¢ Flag, self-adhesive coil, die cut 10 vert.	2.25	....	....	....	1.20	.30
....	same, pl# strip of 5 .	....	....	....	....	8.00	....
3632A	37¢ Flag coil, die cut 10, flag lacking star point	2.25	....	....	....	1.20	.40
....	same, pl# strip of 5 .	....	....	....	....	8.00	....
3632C	37¢ Flag, self-adhesive coil, die cut 11.75 (2004)	2.25	....	....	....	1.20	.40
....	same, pl# strip of 5 .	....	....	....	....	8.00	....
3633	37¢ Flag, self-adhesive coil, die cut 8.5 vert.	2.25	....	....	....	1.20	.40
....	same, pl# strip of 5 .	....	....	....	....	8.00	....

SCOTT NO.	DESCRIPTION	FIRST DAY COVERS SING	FIRST DAY COVERS PL. BLK.	MINT SHEET	PLATE BLOCK	UNUSED F/NH	USED
3633A	37¢ Flag coil, die cut 8.5, right angel corners .	1.95	....	....	....	2.00	.50
....	same, pl# strip of 5 .	....	....	....	....	15.00	....
3633B	37¢ Flag coil, die cut 9.5 (dated 2005)	2.25	....	....	....	1.00	.30
....	same, plt. strip of 5 .	....	....	....	....	8.00	....
3634	37¢ Flag, self-adhesive, die cut 11	2.25	....	....	....	1.20	.40
3634a	same, bklt pane of 10	....	....	....	....	9.50	....
3634b	same, self-adhesive, bklt single, dated 2003 .	2.25	....	....	....	1.00	.50
3634c	same, bklt pane of 4 (3634b)	4.25	....	....	....	4.25	....
3634d	same, bklt pane of 6 (3634b)	5.50	....	....	....	5.75	....
3635	37¢ Flag, self-adhesive, die cut 11.25	2.25	....	....	....	1.20	.50
3635a	same, bklt pane of 20	....	....	....	....	19.50	....
3636	37¢ Flag, self-adhesive, die cut 10.5 x 10.75.	2.25	....	....	....	1.20	.50
3636c	same, bklt pane of 20	....	....	....	....	19.50	....
3636D	37¢ Flag, die cut 11.25 x 11, self-adhesive	2.25	....	....	....	.85	.50
3636De	same, bklt pane of 20	....	....	....	....	19.50	....
3637	37¢ Flag, self-adhesive, die cut 8	2.25	....	....	....	1.00	.50
3637a	same, ATM bklt pane of 18	15.00	....	....	....	17.50	....
3638	37¢ Toy locomotive, self-adhesive coil, die cut 8.5 horiz.	2.25	....	....	....	1.50	.50
3639	37¢ Toy mail wagon, self-adhesive coil, die cut 8.5 horiz.	2.25	....	....	....	1.50	.50
3640	37¢ Toy fire pumper, self-adhesive coil, die cut 8.5 horiz.	2.25	....	....	....	1.50	.50
3641	37¢ Toy taxicab, self-adhesive coil, die cut 8.5 horiz.	2.25	....	....	....	1.50	.50
3638-41	37¢ Antique Toys, self-adhesive coil, strip of 4	4.25	....	....	....	6.00	5.00
....	same, pl# strip of 5 .	....	....	....	....	12.50	....
3642	37¢ Toy mail wagon, self-adhesive, die cut 11	2.25	....	....	....	1.20	.30
3642a	same, die cut 11x11.25, 2003	2.25	....	....	....	1.20	.30
3643	37¢ Toy locomotive, self-adhesive, die cut 11	2.25	....	....	....	1.20	.30
3643a	same, die cut 11x11.25, 2003	2.25	....	....	....	1.20	.30
3644	37¢ Toy taxicab, self-adhesive, die cut 11	2.25	....	....	....	1.20	.30
3644a	same, die cut 11x11.25, 2003	2.25	....	....	....	1.20	.30
3645	37¢ Toy fire pumper, self-adhesive, die cut 11	2.25	....	....	....	1.20	.30
3645f	same, die cut 11x11.25, 2003	2.25	....	....	....	1.20	.30
3642-45	37¢ Antique Toys, self-adhesive, 4 varieties attach.	4.25	....	....	....	4.50	3.50
3645b	same, bklt pane of 4 (3642-45 x 1)	4.25	....	....	....	7.00	....
3645c	same, bklt pane of 6 (3643, 3645, 3642 x 2, 3644 x 2)	5.50	....	....	....	7.00	....
3645d	same, bklt pane of 6 (3642, 3644, 3642 x 2, 3645 x 2)	5.50	....	....	....	7.00	....
3645e	same, bklt pane of 20	15.00	....	....	....	19.50	....
3645g	37¢ Antique Toys, self-adhesive, blk of 4 (3642a, 3643a, 3644a, 3645f)	4.25	....	....	....	4.25	....
3645h	same, bklt pane of 20	15.00	....	....	....	16.00	....

3646

3648

3647

SCOTT NO.	DESCRIPTION	FIRST DAY COVERS SING	FIRST DAY COVERS PL. BLK.	MINT SHEET	PLATE BLOCK	UNUSED F/NH	USED
3646	60¢ Coverlet Eagle, self-adhesive	2.75	5.50	24.50(20)	6.25	1.35	6.00
3647	$3.85 Jefferson Memorial, self-adhesive	8.75	35.00	165.00(20)	39.50	8.75	6.00
3647A	same, die cut 11x10.75, dated 2003	8.75	35.00	165.00(20)	39.50	8.75	4.50
3648	$13.65 Capitol Dome, self-adhesive	35.00	105.00	550.00(20)	125.00	29.00	12.00

MASTERS OF AMERICAN PHOTOGRAPHY

3649a *Albert Sands Southworth & Josiah Johnson Hawes*
3649b *Timothy H. O'Sullivan*
3649c *Carleton E. Watkins*
3649d *Getrude Kasebier*
3649e *Lewis W. Hine*
3649f *Alvin Langdon Coburn*
3649g *Edward Steichen*
3649h *Alfred Steiglitz*
3649i *Man Ray*
3649j *Edward Weston*
3649k *James VanDerZee*
3649l *Dorothea Lange*
3649m *Walker Evans*
3649n *Eugene Smith*
3649o *Paul Strand*
3649p *Ansel Adams*
3649q *Imogen Cunningham*
3649r *Andre Kertesz*
3649s *Garry Winogrand*
3649t *Minor White*

3649

SCOTT NO.	DESCRIPTION	FIRST DAY COVERS SING	FIRST DAY COVERS PL. BLK.	MINT SHEET	PLATE BLOCK	UNUSED F/NH	USED
3649	37¢ Masters of American Photography, self-adhesive, 20 varieties attached	....	....	19.50(20)	....	19.50	15.00
....	same, set of singles	50.00	....	....	....	....	12.00

3650

3652

3651

SCOTT NO.	DESCRIPTION	FIRST DAY COVERS SING	FIRST DAY COVERS PL. BLK.	MINT SHEET	PLATE BLOCK	UNUSED F/NH	USED
3650	37¢ John James Audubon, self-adhesive	2.25	4.75	17.50(20)	4.50	1.25	.30
3651	37¢ Harry Houdini, self-adhesive	2.25	4.75	17.50(20)	4.50	1.25	.30
3652	37¢ Andy Warhol, self-adhesive	2.25	4.75	17.50(20)	4.50	1.25	.30

3653 3654

3655 3656

SCOTT NO.	DESCRIPTION	FIRST DAY COVERS SING	FIRST DAY COVERS PL. BLK.	MINT SHEET	PLATE BLOCK	UNUSED F/NH	USED
3653-56	37¢ Teddy Bears, self-adhesive, 4 varieties attached	5.00	6.00	27.00(20)	6.00	6.00	5.00
3653	37¢ Bruin Teddy Bear	2.25	....	....	....	1.50	.40
3654	37¢ Stick Teddy Bear	2.25	....	....	....	1.50	.40
3655	37¢ Gund Teddy Bear	2.25	....	....	....	1.50	.40
3656	37¢ Ideal Teddy Bear	2.25	....	....	....	1.50	.40

3657

3658

3659

SCOTT NO.	DESCRIPTION	FIRST DAY COVERS SING	FIRST DAY COVERS PL. BLK.	MINT SHEET	PLATE BLOCK	UNUSED F/NH	USED
3657	37¢ Love, self-adhesive	2.25	....	....	....	1.20	.25
....	same, bklt pane of 20	15.00	....	....	....	19.50	....
3658	60¢ Love, self-adhesive	2.75	5.50	27.50(20)	7.00	2.20	.75
3659	37¢ Ogden Nash, self-adhesive	2.25	4.75	17.50(20)	4.50	1.00	.25

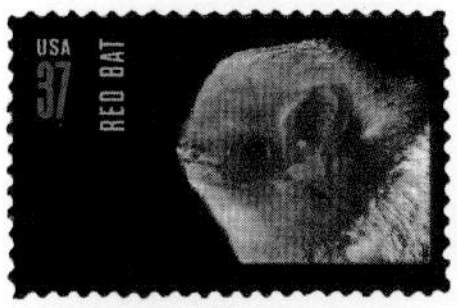

3661

3660

3662

3663

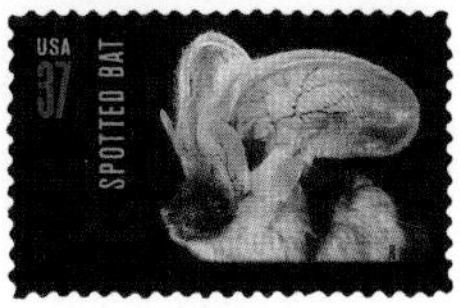

3664

SCOTT NO.	DESCRIPTION	FIRST DAY COVERS SING	FIRST DAY COVERS PL. BLK.	MINT SHEET	PLATE BLOCK	UNUSED F/NH	USED
3660	37¢ Duke Kahanamoku, self-adhesive	2.25	4.75	17.50(20)	4.50	1.00	.30
3661-64	37¢ American Bats, self-adhesive, 4 varieties attached	4.25	4.75	20.00(20)	6.00	4.50	3.50
3661	37¢ Red Bat	2.25	....	....	....	1.20	.35
3662	37¢ Leaf-nosed Bat .	2.25	....	....	....	1.20	.35
3663	37¢ Pallid Bat	2.25	....	....	....	1.20	.35
3664	37¢ Spotted Bat . . .	2.25	....	....	....	1.20	.35

3665 3666

3667 3668

SCOTT NO.	DESCRIPTION	FIRST DAY COVERS SING	FIRST DAY COVERS PL. BLK.	MINT SHEET	PLATE BLOCK	UNUSED F/NH	USED
3665-68	37¢ Women In Journalism, self-adhesive, 4 varieties attached	6.00	7.00	25.00(20)	6.00	5.00	4.00
3665	37¢Nellie Bly	2.25	....	....	....	1.50	.40
3666	37¢ Ida M. Tarbel . .	2.25	....	....	....	1.50	.40
3667	37¢ Ethel L. Payne .	2.25	....	....	....	1.50	.40
3668	37¢ Marguerite Higgins	2.25	....	....	....	1.50	.40

3669

SCOTT NO.	DESCRIPTION	FIRST DAY COVERS SING	FIRST DAY COVERS PL. BLK.	MINT SHEET	PLATE BLOCK	UNUSED F/NH	USED
3669	37¢ Irving Berlin, self-adhesive	2.25	4.75	25.00(20)	5.50	1.25	.25

3670 3671

SCOTT NO.	DESCRIPTION	FIRST DAY COVERS SING	FIRST DAY COVERS PL. BLK.	MINT SHEET	PLATE BLOCK	UNUSED F/NH	USED
3670-71	37¢ Neuter and Spay, self-adhesive, 2 varieites attached	4.00	4.75	22.50(20)	5.50	2.50	2.00
3670	37¢ Kitten	2.25	....	....	....	1.20	.30
3671	37¢ Puppy	2.25	....	....	....	1.20	.30

3672

3673

3674

SCOTT NO.	DESCRIPTION	FIRST DAY COVERS SING	FIRST DAY COVERS PL. BLK.	MINT SHEET	PLATE BLOCK	UNUSED F/NH	USED
3672	37¢ Hanukkah, self-adhesive	2.25	4.75	17.50(20)	4.50	1.20	.30
3673	37¢ Kwanzaa, self-adhesive	2.25	4.75	17.50(20)	4.50	1.20	.30
3674	37¢ EID, self-adhesive	2.25	4.75	17.50(20)	4.50	1.20	.30

3675

SCOTT NO.	DESCRIPTION	FIRST DAY COVERS SING	FIRST DAY COVERS PL. BLK.	MINT SHEET	PLATE BLOCK	UNUSED F/NH	USED
3675	37¢ Madonna & Child, self-adhesive	2.25	4.75	17.50(20)	4.50	1.20	.30
....	same, bklt pane of 20	15.00	....	....	....	16.00	....

3676, 3683, 3684, 3688

3677, 3680, 3685, 3689

3678, 3681, 3686, 3690

3679, 3682, 3687, 3691

SCOTT NO.	DESCRIPTION	FIRST DAY COVERS SING	FIRST DAY COVERS PL. BLK.	MINT SHEET	PLATE BLOCK	UNUSED F/NH	USED
3676-79	37¢ Snowmen, self-adhesive, 4 varieties attached .	6.00	7.00	20.00(20)	5.00	4.50	3.50
3676	37¢ Snowman with red and green scarf	2.25	....	....	....	1.20	.40
3677	37¢ Snowman with blue scarf	2.25	....	....	....	1.20	.40
3578	37¢ Snowman with pipe	2.25	....	....	....	1.20	.40
3679	37¢ Snowman with top hat	2.25	....	....	....	1.20	.40
3680	37¢ Snowman with blue scarf, self-adhesive coil	2.25	....	....	....	1.20	.50
3681	37¢ Snowman with pipe, self-adhesive coil . .	2.25	....	....	....	1.20	.50
3682	37¢ Snowman with top hat, self-adhesive coil . .	2.25	....	....	....	1.20	.50
3683	37¢ Snowman with red and green scarf, self-adhesive coil	2.25	....	....	....	1.20	.50
3680-83	37¢ Snowmen, self-adhesive coil, strip of 4	4.25	....	....	....	6.00	....
....	same, pl# strip of 5 .	....	....	....	....	9.00	....
3684	37¢ Snowman with red and green scarf, large design	2.25	....	....	....	1.20	.40
3685	37¢ Snowman with blue scarf, large design .	2.25	....	....	....	1.20	.40
3686	37¢ Snowman with pipe, large design	2.25	....	....	....	1.20	.40
3687	37¢ Snowman with top hat, large design	2.25	....	....	....	1.20	.40
3684-87	37¢ Snowman, self-adhesive, 4 varieties attached .	4.25	....	....	....	4.50	3.50
3687b	same, bklt pane of 20 (3684-87 x 5 + label)	15.00	....	....	....	21.50	....
3688	37¢ Snowman with red and green scarf, small design	2.25	....	....	....	1.20	.50
3689	37¢ Snowman with blue scarf, small design .	2.25	....	....	....	1.20	.50
3690	37¢ Snowman with pipe, small design	2.25	....	....	....	1.20	.50
3691	37¢ Snowman with top hat, small design	2.25	....	....	....	1.20	.50
3688-91	37¢ Snowmen , self-adhesive, 4 varieties attached .	4.25	....	....	....	4.50	3.50
3691b	same, bklt pane of 4, (3688-91)	4.25	....	....	....	4.50	....
3691c	same, bklt pane of 6 (3690-91, 3688-89 x 2)	5.50	....	....	....	6.00	....
3691d	same, bklt pane of 6 (3688-89, 3690-91 x 2)	5.50	....	....	....	6.00	....

3693, 3775, 3785

3692

3695

SCOTT NO.	DESCRIPTION	FIRST DAY COVERS SING	FIRST DAY COVERS PL. BLK.	MINT SHEET	PLATE BLOCK	UNUSED F/NH	USED
3692	37¢ Cary Grant, self-adhesive	2.25	4.75	25.00(20)	5.00	1.20	.30
3693	(5¢) Sea Coast coil, self-adhesive	2.25	....	....	....	.25	.20
....	same, pl# strip of 5 .	....	....	....	....	2.50	....

3694

SCOTT NO.	DESCRIPTION	FIRST DAY COVERS SING	FIRST DAY COVERS PL. BLK.	MINT SHEET	PLATE BLOCK	UNUSED F/NH	USED
3694	37¢ Hawaiian Missionary, self-adhesive, souvenir sheet of 4	5.00	....	....	....	5.25	4.00
3694a	37¢ Hawaii 2¢ of 1851	2.25	....	....	....	1.20	.75
3694b	37¢ Hawaii 5¢ of 1851	2.25	....	....	....	1.20	.75
3694c	37¢ Hawaii 13¢ of 1851	2.25	....	....	....	1.20	.75
3694d	37¢ Hawaii 13¢ of 1852	2.25	....	....	....	1.20	.75
3695	37¢ Happy Birthday, self-adhesive	2.25	4.75	17.50(20)	4.50	1.00	.25

3696

3745

GREETINGS FROM AMERICA

3696	*Alabama*	**3713**	*Louisiana*	**3730**	*Ohio*
3697	*Alaska*	**3714**	*Maine*	**3731**	*Oklahoma*
3698	*Arizona*	**3715**	*Maryland*	**3732**	*Oregon*
3699	*Arkansas*	**3716**	*Massachusetts*	**3733**	*Pennsylvania*
3700	*California*	**3717**	*Michigan*	**3734**	*Rhode Island*
3701	*Colorado*	**3718**	*Minnesota*	**3735**	*South Carolina*
3702	*Connecticut*	**3719**	*Mississippi*	**3736**	*South Dakota*
3703	*Delaware*	**3720**	*Missouri*	**3737**	*Tennessee*
3704	*Florida*	**3721**	*Montana*	**3738**	*Texas*
3705	*Georgia*	**3722**	*Nebraska*	**3739**	*Utah*
3706	*Hawaii*	**3723**	*Nevada*	**3740**	*Vermont*
3707	*Idaho*	**3724**	*New Hampshire*	**3741**	*Virginia*
3708	*Illinois*	**3725**	*New Jersey*	**3742**	*Washington*
3709	*Indiana*	**3726**	*New Mexico*	**3743**	*West Virginia*
3710	*Iowa*	**3727**	*New York*	**3744**	*Wisconsin*
3711	*Kansas*	**3728**	*North Carolina*	**3745**	*Wyoming*
3712	*Kentucky*	**3729**	*North Dakota*		

SCOTT NO.	DESCRIPTION	FIRST DAY COVERS SING	FIRST DAY COVERS PL. BLK.	MINT SHEET	PLATE BLOCK	UNUSED F/NH	USED
3696-3745	37¢ Greetings from America, self-adhesive, 50 varieties attached	....	....	45.00(50)	....	45.00	....
....	set of singles	120.00	....	....	....	....	30.00

3747

3748

2003 COMMEMORATIVES

SCOTT NO.	DESCRIPTION	FIRST DAY COVERS SING	FIRST DAY COVERS PL. BLK.	MINT SHEET	PLATE BLOCK	UNUSED F/NH	USED
3746/3824	**(3746-48, 3771, 3773-74, 3781-82, 3786-91, 3803, 3808-18, 3821-24) 30 varieties . . . . .**	**........**	**........**	**........**	**........**	**33.00**	**10.50**
3746	37¢ Thurgood Marshall, self-adhesive	2.25	4.75	25.00(20)	5.00	1.20	.30
3747	37¢ Year of the Ram, self-adhesive	2.25	4.75	25.00(20)	5.00	1.20	.30
3748	37¢ Zora Neale Hurston, self-adhesive	2.25	4.75	25.00(20)	5.00	1.20	.30

3749, 3758

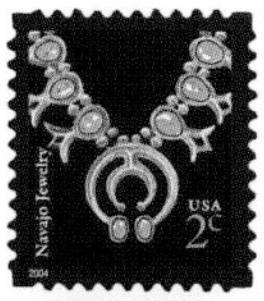

3750, 3751, 3752, 3753

3754, 3759

3755, 3761

3756

3757, 3762

AMERICAN DESIGN SERIES

SCOTT NO.	DESCRIPTION	FIRST DAY COVERS SING	FIRST DAY COVERS PL. BLK.	MINT SHEET	PLATE BLOCK	UNUSED F/NH	USED
3749	1¢ Tiffany Lamp, self-adhesive (2007) . . .	2.25	4.75	2.25(20)	.50	.20	.20
3750	2¢ Navajo Necklace, self-adhesive	2.25	4.75	2.25(20)	.50	.20	.15
3751	same, self-adhesvie, die cut 11.25 X 11.5	2.25	4.75	2.25(20)	.50	.20	.20
3752	same, w/ USPS micro-printing, self-adhesive, die cut 11.25 X 11 . .	2.25	4.75	2.25(20)	.50	.20	.20
3753	same, die cut 11.5 X 11, (2007 date)	2.25	4.75	2.25(20)	.50	.20	.20
3754	3¢ Silver Coffeepot, self-adhesive (2007) . . .	2.25	4.75	2.25(20)	.50	.20	.20
3755	4¢ Chippendale Chair, self-adhesive (2004)	2.25	4.75	4.50(20)	.75	.20	.15
3756	5¢ Toleware, self-adhesive	2.25	4.75	4.50(20)	.85	.25	.15
3757	10¢ American Clock, self-adhesive	2.25	4.75	4.75(20)	1.35	.30	.15
3758	1¢ Tiffany Lamp, coil	2.25	....	....	....	.25	.15
....	same, pl# strip of 5 .	....	....	....	....	2.25	....
3759	3¢ Silver Coffeepot, coil	2.25	....	....	....	.20	.20
....	same, pl# strip of 5 .	....	....	....	....	8.00	....
3761	4¢ Chippendale Chair, coil (2007)	2.25	....	....	....	.25	.20
....	same, pl# strip of 5 .	....	....	....	....	3.00	.20
3762	10¢ American Clock, coil	2.25	....	....	....	.30	.20
....	same, pl# strip of 5 .	....	....	....	....	3.00	....

3766

3769

3770

SCOTT NO.	DESCRIPTION	FIRST DAY COVERS SING	FIRST DAY COVERS PL. BLK.	MINT SHEET	PLATE BLOCK	UNUSED F/NH	USED
3766	$1 Wisdom, self-adhesive	3.50	7.50	43.00(20)	10.00	2.25	.60
3769	(10¢) New York Library Lion, perf. 10 vert. . .	2.25	....	....	2.00	.30	.20
....	same, pl# strip of 5 .	....	....	....	....	2.75	....
3770	(10¢) Atlas Statue, self-adhesive coil, die cut 11 dated 2003	2.25	....	....	....	.30	.25
....	same, pl# strip of 5 .	....	....	....	....	3.00	....

3771

SCOTT NO.	DESCRIPTION	FIRST DAY COVERS SING	FIRST DAY COVERS PL. BLK.	MINT SHEET	PLATE BLOCK	UNUSED F/NH	USED
3771	80¢ Special Olympics, self-adhesive	3.00	7.00	37.50(20)	8.50	1.95	1.00

3772

AMERICAN FILM MAKING

3772a	*Screenwriting*	**3772d**	*Music*	**3772g**	*Cinematography*
3772b	*Directing*	**3772e**	*Make-up*	**3772h**	*Film editing*
3772c	*Costume design*	**3772f**	*Art Direction*	**3772i**	*Special effects*
				3772j	*Sound*

SCOTT NO.	DESCRIPTION	FIRST DAY COVERS SING	FIRST DAY COVERS PL. BLK.	MINT SHEET	PLATE BLOCK	UNUSED F/NH	USED
3772	37¢ American Film Making, self-adhesive, 10 varieties attached	....	....	8.00(10)	....	16.00	12.50
....	set of singles	25.00	....	....	....	....	6.00

3773

3774

3781

3782

SCOTT NO.	DESCRIPTION	FIRST DAY COVERS SING	FIRST DAY COVERS PL. BLK.	MINT SHEET	PLATE BLOCK	UNUSED F/NH	USED
3773	37¢ Ohio Statehood, self-adhesive	2.25	4.75	25.00(20)	5.00	1.20	.30
3774	37¢ Pelican Island National Wildlife Refuge, self-adhesive	2.25	4.75	25.00(20)	5.00	1.20	.30
3775	(5¢) Sea Coast coil, perf. 9.75 vert.	2.25	....	....	....	.20	.15
....	same, pl# strip of 5 .	....	....	....	....	2.00	....

3776

3777

3778

3779

3780

3783

3784, 3784A

3786

SCOTT NO.	DESCRIPTION	FIRST DAY COVERS SING	FIRST DAY COVERS PL. BLK.	MINT SHEET	PLATE BLOCK	UNUSED F/NH	USED
3776	37¢ Uncle Sam on Bicycle	2.25	....	....	....	1.50	.50
3777	37¢ 1888 Pres. Campaign badge	2.25	....	....	....	1.50	.50
3778	37¢ 1893 Silk bookmark	2.25	....	....	....	1.50	.50
3779	37¢ Modern hand fan	2.25	....	....	....	1.50	.50
3780	37¢ Carving of woman with flag & sword . . .	2.25	....	....	....	1.50	.50
3776-80	37¢ Old Glory, self-adhesive, 5 varieties attached .	5.00	....	....	....	7.00	....
3780b	same, complete booklet of 2 panes	....	....	....	....	25.00	....
3781	37¢ Cesar E. Chavez, self-adhesive	2.25	4.75	25.00(20)	6.00	1.20	.30
3782	37¢ Louisiana Purchase, self-adhesive	2.25	4.75	25.00(20)	6.00	1.20	.30

SCOTT NO.	DESCRIPTION	FIRST DAY COVERS SING	FIRST DAY COVERS PL. BLK.	MINT SHEET	PLATE BLOCK	UNUSED F/NH	USED
3783	37¢ First Flight of the Wright Brothers, self-adhesive	2.25	....	12.00(10)	....	1.20	.30
3783a	same, bklt pane of 9	....	....	....	....	9.00	....
3783b	same, bklt pane of 1	7.00	....	....	....	2.00	....
3784	37¢ Purple Heart, self-adhesive	2.25	4.75	25.00(20)	5.00	1.20	.30
3784A	37¢ Purple Heart, self-adhesive, die cut 10.75 x 10.25	2.25	4.75	25.00(20)	5.00	1.20	.50
3785	(5¢) Sea Coast coil, four-side die cuts	2.25	....	....	....	.25	.20
....	same, pl# strip of 5 .	....	....	....	....	2.25	....
3786	37¢ Audrey Hepburn, self-adhesive	2.25`	4.75	25.00(20)	6.00	1.20	.30

3787

3788

3789

3790

3792–3801, 3792a–3801a

3791

SCOTT NO.	DESCRIPTION	FIRST DAY COVERS SING	FIRST DAY COVERS PL. BLK.	MINT SHEET	PLATE BLOCK	UNUSED F/NH	USED
3787-91	37¢ Southern Lighthouses, self-adhesive, 5 varieties attached	5.00	....	39.50(20)	....	10.00	9.00
3787	37¢ Old Cape Henry, Virginia	2.25	....	....	....	2.00	.50
3788	37¢ Cape Lookout, North Carolina	2.25	....	....	....	2.00	.50
3788a	same, dropped denomination.......		....	....	....	....	....
3789	37¢ Morris Island, South Carolina	2.25	....	....	....	2.00	.50
3790	37¢ Tybee Island, Georgia	2.25	....	....	....	2.00	.50
3791	37¢ Hillsboro Inlet, Florida	2.25	....	....	....	2.00	.50
3791b	same, strip of 5 (3787, 3788a, 3789-91)	....	....	....	....	....	....
3792	(25¢) Eagle, gray with gold eagle, coil	2.25	....	....	....	.75	.40
3792a	same, serpentine die cut 11.5(2005)	2.25	....	....	....	.75	.40
3793	(25¢) Eagle, gold with red eagle, coil	2.25	....	....	....	.75	.40
3793a	same, serpentine die cut 11.5(2005)	2.25	....	....	....	.75	.40
3794	(25¢) Eagle, dull blue with gold eagle, coil	2.25	....	....	....	.75	.40
3794a	same, serpentine die cut 11.5(2005)	2.25	....	....	....	.75	.40
3795	(25¢) Eagle, gold with Prussian blue eagle, coil	2.25	....	....	....	.75	.40
3795a	same, serpentine die cut 11.5(2005)	2.25	....	....	....	.75	.40
3796	(25¢) Eagle, green with gold eagle, coil	2.25	....	....	....	.75	.40
3796a	same, die cut 11.5(2005)	2.25	....	....	....	.75	.40
3797	(25¢) Eagle, gold with gray eagle, coil	2.25	....	....	....	.75	.40
3797a	same, die cut 11.5(2005)	2.25	....	....	....	.75	.40
3798	(25¢) Eagle, Prussian blue with gold eagle, coil	2.25	....	....	....	.75	.40
3798a	same, die cut 11.5(2005)	2.25	....	....	....	.75	.40
3799	(25¢) Eagle, gold with dull blue eagle, coil .	2.25	....	....	....	.75	.40
3799a	same, die cut 11.5(2005)	2.25	....	....	....	.75	.40
3800	(25¢) Eagle, red with gold eagle, coil	2.25	....	....	....	.75	.40
3800a	same, die cut 11.5(2005)	2.25	....	....	....	.75	.40
3801	(25¢) Eagle, gold with green eagle, coil . . .	2.25	....	....	....	.75	.40
3801a	same, die cut 11.5(2005)	2.25	....	....	....	.75	.40
3792-3801	(25¢) Eagle, self-adhesive coil, strip of 10	6.00	....	....	....	6.00	....
....	same, pl# strip of 11	....	....	....	....	8.50	....
3792a-3801a	same, self-adhesive, coil strip of 10, serpentine die cut 11.5(dated 2005)	6.00	....	....	....	8.00	....
....	same, plt. strip of 11	....	....	....	....	10.00	....

3802
ARCTIC TUNDRA

3802a	*Gyrfalcon*	**3802f**	*Caribou & willow ptarmigans*
3802b	*Gray wolf*	**3802g**	*Arctic ground squirrel*
3802c	*Common raven*	**3802h**	*Willow ptarmigan & bearberry*
3802d	*Musk oxen & caribou*	**3802i**	*Arctic grayling*
3802e	*Grizzly bears & caribou*	**3802j**	*Singing vole, thin-legged spider, lingonberry, Labrador tea*

SCOTT NO.	DESCRIPTION	FIRST DAY COVERS SING	FIRST DAY COVERS PL. BLK.	MINT SHEET	PLATE BLOCK	UNUSED F/NH	USED
3802	37¢ Arctic Tundra, 10 varieties, attached, self-adhesive	....	....	8.00(10)	....	10.00	8.00
....	set of singles	25.00	....	....	....	....	5.00

3803

SCOTT NO.	DESCRIPTION	FIRST DAY COVERS SING	FIRST DAY COVERS PL. BLK.	MINT SHEET	PLATE BLOCK	UNUSED F/NH	USED
3803	37¢ Korean War Veterans, Memorial, self-adhesive	2.25	4.75	20.00(20)	5.00	1.20	.30

3804

3805

3806

3807

SCOTT NO.	DESCRIPTION	FIRST DAY COVERS SING	FIRST DAY COVERS PL. BLK.	MINT SHEET	PLATE BLOCK	UNUSED F/NH	USED
3804	37¢ Young Mother .	2.25	....	....	....	1.20	.35
3805	37¢ Children Playing	2.25	....	....	....	1.20	.35
3806	37¢ On a Balcony . .	2.25	....	....	....	1.20	.35
3807	37¢ Child in Straw Hat	2.25	....	....	....	1.20	.35
3804-07	37¢ Mary Cassatt Paintings, self-adhesive, 4 varieties attached	4.25	....	....	....	5.00	4.00
3807b	same, bklt pane of 20 (3804-07 x 5)	15.00	....	....	....	20.00	....

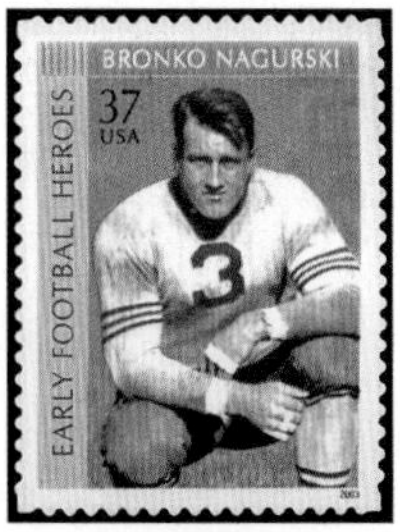

3808

3809

3810

3811

SCOTT NO.	DESCRIPTION	FIRST DAY COVERS SING	FIRST DAY COVERS PL. BLK.	MINT SHEET	PLATE BLOCK	UNUSED F/NH	USED
3808-11	37¢ Early Football Heroes, self-adhesive, 4 varieties attached	4.25	4.75	25.00(20)	6.00	6.00	5.00
3808	37¢ Bronko Nagurski	2.25	....	....	....	1.50	.40
3809	37¢ Ernie Nevers . .	2.25	....	....	....	1.50	.40
3810	37¢ Walter Camp . .	2.25	....	....	....	1.50	.40
3811	37¢ Red Grange . . .	2.25	....	....	....	1.50	.40

3812

3813

SCOTT NO.	DESCRIPTION	FIRST DAY COVERS SING	FIRST DAY COVERS PL. BLK.	MINT SHEET	PLATE BLOCK	UNUSED F/NH	USED
3812	37¢ Roy Acuff, self-adhesive	2.25	4.75	16.00(20)	4.00	1.20	.30
3813	37¢ District of Columbia, self-adhesive	2.25	4.75	13.00(16)	4.00	1.50	.40

3814

3815

3816

3817

3818

3819

3820

SCOTT NO.	DESCRIPTION	FIRST DAY COVERS SING	FIRST DAY COVERS PL. BLK.	MINT SHEET	PLATE BLOCK	UNUSED F/NH	USED
3814-18	37¢ Reptiles & Amphibians, self-adhesive, 5 varieties attached	5.00	10.50	20.00(20)	11.50	6.00	5.00
3814	37¢ Scarlet Kingsnake	2.25	....	....	....	1.25	.50
3815	37¢ Blue-Spotted Salamander	2.25	....	....	....	1.25	.50
3816	37¢ Reticulate Lizard	2.25	....	....	....	1.25	.50
3817	37¢ Ornate Chorus Frog	2.25	....	....	....	1.25	.50
3818	37¢ Ornate Box Turtle	2.25	....	....	....	1.25	.50
3819	23¢ George Washington, self-adhesive, die cut 11	2.25	4.75	18.00(20)	3.50	1.00	.50
3820	37¢ Madonna & Child, self-adhesive (2003)	2.25	....	....	....	1.20	.50
3820a	same, bklt pane of 20	....	....	....	....	20.00	....

3821, 3825 3822, 3826 3823, 3827 3824, 3828

SCOTT NO.	DESCRIPTION	FIRST DAY COVERS SING	FIRST DAY COVERS PL. BLK.	MINT SHEET	PLATE BLOCK	UNUSED F/NH	USED
3821-24	37¢ Christmas Music Makers, self-adhesive, 4 varieties attached	4.25	4.75	20.00(20)	6.00	5.00	4.00
3821	37¢ Reindeer with Pipes	2.25	....	....	....	1.20	.50
3822	37¢ Santa Claus with Drum	2.25	....	....	....	1.20	.50
3823	37¢ Santa Claus with Trumpet	2.25	....	....	....	1.20	.50
3824	37¢ Reindeer with Horn	2.25	....	....	....	1.20	.50
3842b	same, bklt pane of 20, (3821-24 x 5 + label)	15.00	....	....	....	20.00	....
3825	37¢ Reindeer with Pipes, die cut 10.5 x 10.75.	2.25	....	....	....	1.20	.50
3826	37¢ Santa Claus with Drum, die cut 10.5 x 10.75.	2.25	....	....	....	1.20	.50
3827	37¢ Santa Claus with Trumpet die cut 10.5 x 10.75.	2.25	....	....	....	1.20	.50
3828	37¢ Reindeer with Horn, die cut 10.5 x 10.75.	2.25	....	....	....	1.20	.50
3825-28	37¢ Christmas Music Makers, self-adhesive, 4 varieties attached, die cut 10.5 x 10.75	4.25	....	....	....	5.00	4.00
3828b	same, bklt pane of 4 (3825-28)	4.25	....	....	....	5.00	....
3828c	same, bklt pane of 6 (3827-28, 3825-26 x 2)	5.50	....	....	....	6.00	....
3828d	same, bklt pane of 6 (3825-26, 3827-28 x 2)	5.50	....	....	....	6.00	....

3829, 3829A, 3830, 3830D

SCOTT NO.	DESCRIPTION	FIRST DAY COVERS SING	FIRST DAY COVERS PL. BLK.	MINT SHEET	PLATE BLOCK	UNUSED F/NH	USED
3829	37¢ Snowy Egret, self-adhesive coil, die cut 8.5	1.95	....	....	....	1.20	.40
....	same, pl# strip of 5 .	....	....	....	....	10.00	....
3829A	37¢ Snowy Egret, self-adhesive coil, die cut 9.5	1.95	....	....	....	1.20	.25
....	same, pl# strip of 5 .	....	....	....	....	10.00	....

3831
PACIFIC CORAL REEF

3831a	*Emperor angelfish, blue & mound coral*	**3831f**	*Pink anemonefish, sea anemone*
3831b	*Humphead wrasse, Moorish idol*	**3831g**	*Snowflake moray eel, Spanish dancer*
3831c	*Bumphead parrotfish*	**3831h**	*Lionfish*
3831d	*Black-spotted puffer, threadfin butterflyfish*	**3831i**	*Triton's trumpet*
3831e	*Hawksbill turtle, palette surgeonfish*	**3831j**	*Oriental sweetlips, bluestreak cleaner wrasse, mushroom coral*

2004 COMMEMORATIVES AND REGULAR ISSUES

SCOTT NO.	DESCRIPTION	FIRST DAY COVERS SING	FIRST DAY COVERS PL. BLK.	MINT SHEET	PLATE BLOCK	UNUSED F/NH	USED
3830	37¢ Snowy Egret, self adhesive	2.25	....	....	....	.85	.20
3830a	same, bklt pane of 20	....	....	....	....	16.00	....
3830D	37¢ Snowy Egret, w/ USPS microprinting.	2.25	....	....	....	.85	.20
....	same, plt strip of 11 .	....	....	....	....	16.00	....
3831	37¢ Pacific Coral Reef, 10 varieties, attached, self-adhesive	....	....	10.00(10)	....	10.00	8.00
....	set of singles	25.00	....	....	....	....	5.75

3832 3834 3835

SCOTT NO.	DESCRIPTION	FIRST DAY COVERS SING	FIRST DAY COVERS PL. BLK.	MINT SHEET	PLATE BLOCK	UNUSED F/NH	USED
3832	37¢ Year of the Monkey, self-adhesive	2.25	4.75	20.00(20)	5.00	1.20	.30
3833	37¢ Candy Hearts, self-adhesive	2.25	....	....	....	1.20	.25
3833a	same, bklt pane of 20	....	....	....	....	20.00	....
3834	37¢ Paul Robeson, self-adhesive	2.25	4.75	20.00(20)	5.00	1.20	.30
3835	37¢ Theodore Seuss Geisel (Dr. Seuss) self-adhesive	2.25	4.75	20.00(20)	5.00	1.20	.25

3833

3836 3837

SCOTT NO.	DESCRIPTION	FIRST DAY COVERS SING	FIRST DAY COVERS PL. BLK.	MINT SHEET	PLATE BLOCK	UNUSED F/NH	USED
3836	37¢ White Lilacs and Pink Roses, self-adhesive	2.25	....	....	....	1.20	.25
3836a	same, bklt pane of 20	....	....	....	....	20.00	....
3837	60¢ Five varieties of Pink Roses, self-adhesive	2.75	5.50	30.00(20)	7.50	2.00	1.00

3838 3839

SCOTT NO.	DESCRIPTION	FIRST DAY COVERS SING	FIRST DAY COVERS PL. BLK.	MINT SHEET	PLATE BLOCK	UNUSED F/NH	USED
3838	37¢ United States Air Force Academy, self-adhesive	2.25	4.75	20.00(20)	5.00	1.20	.30
3839	37¢ Henry Mancini, self-adhesive	2.25	4.75	20.00(20)	5.00	1.20	.30

3841 3840

3842 3843

SCOTT NO.	DESCRIPTION	FIRST DAY COVERS SING	FIRST DAY COVERS PL. BLK.	MINT SHEET	PLATE BLOCK	UNUSED F/NH	USED
3840-43	37¢ American Choreographers, self-adhesive, 4 varieties attached	4.25	4.75	20.00(20)	5.00	4.50	4.00
3840	37¢ Martha Graham	2.25	....	....	....	.85	.50
3841	37¢ Alvin Ailey	2.25	....	....	....	.85	.50
3842	37¢ Agnes de Mille .	2.25	....	....	....	.85	.50
3843	37¢ George Balanchine	2.25	....	....	....	.85	.50

3844, 3845, 3846, 3847, 3848, 3849, 3850, 3851, 3852, 3853

SCOTT NO.	DESCRIPTION	FIRST DAY COVERS SING	FIRST DAY COVERS PL. BLK.	MINT SHEET	PLATE BLOCK	UNUSED F/NH	USED
3844-3853	(25¢) Eagle, water activated coil, strip of 10, perf. 9.75	6.00	....	....	....	8.00	....
....	same, pl# strip of 11	....	....	....	....	12.00	....
3844	(25¢) Eagle, gray with gold eagle, coil, perf. 9.75	2.25	....	....	....	1.00	.50
3845	(25¢) Eagle, gold with green eagle, coil, perf. 9.75	2.25	....	....	....	1.00	.50
3846	(25¢) Eagle, red with gold eagle, coil, perf. 9.75	2.25	....	....	....	1.00	.50
3847	(25¢) Eagle, gold with dull blue eagle, coil, perf. 9.75	2.25	....	....	....	1.00	.50
3848	(25¢) Eagle, Prussian blue with gold eagle, coil, perf. 9.75	2.25	....	....	....	1.00	.50
3849	(25¢) Eagle, gold with gray eagle, coil, perf. 9.75	2.25	....	....	....	1.00	.50
3850	(25¢) Eagle, Prussian green with gold eagle, coil, perf. 9.75	2.25	....	....	....	1.00	.50
3851	(25¢) Eagle, gold with Prussian blue eagle, coil, perf. 9.75	2.25	....	....	....	1.00	.50
3852	(25¢) Eagle, dull blue with gold eagle, coil, perf. 9.75	2.25	....	....	....	1.00	.50
3853	(25¢) Eagle, gold with red eagle, coil, perf. 9.75	2.25	....	....	....	1.00	.50

3855

3854

3856

SCOTT NO.	DESCRIPTION	FIRST DAY COVERS SING	FIRST DAY COVERS PL. BLK.	MINT SHEET	PLATE BLOCK	UNUSED F/NH	USED
3854	37¢ Lewis & Clark Bicentennial, self-adhesive	2.25	4.75	24.00(20)	5.00	1.50	.40
3855	37¢ Lewis & Clark Bicentennial, Lewis booklet single	2.25	....	....	....	1.50	.40
3856	37¢ Lewis & Clark Bicentennial, Clark booklet single .	2.25	....	....	....	1.50	.40
3855-56	37¢ Lewis & Clark, pair	5.00	....	....	....	3.50	....
3856b	37¢ Lewis & Clark: The Corps of Discovery, 1804-06, self-adhesive, bklt pane of 10........		....	....	....	25.00	....

3857

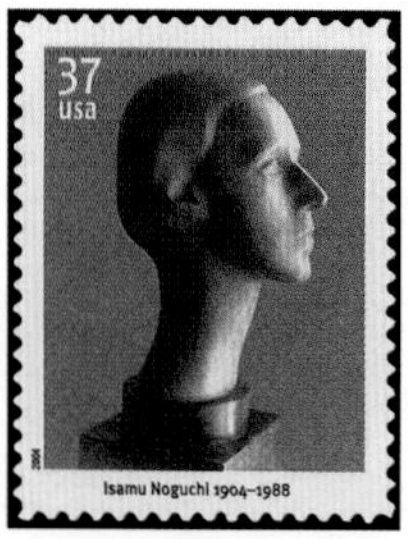

3858

3859

3860

3861

SCOTT NO.	DESCRIPTION	FIRST DAY COVERS SING	FIRST DAY COVERS PL. BLK.	MINT SHEET	PLATE BLOCK	UNUSED F/NH	USED
3857-61	37¢ Isamu Noguchi, self-adhesive, 5 varieties attached	5.00	9.50	20.00(20)	10.00(10)	5.00	4.00
3857	37¢ Akari 25N	2.25	....	....	....	1.20	.35
3858	37¢ Margaret La Farge Osborn	2.25	....	....	....	1.20	.35
3859	37¢ Black Sun	2.25	....	....	....	1.20	.35
3860	37¢ Mother and Child	2.25	....	....	....	1.20	.35
3861	37¢ Figure (detail) . .	2.25	....	....	....	1.20	.35

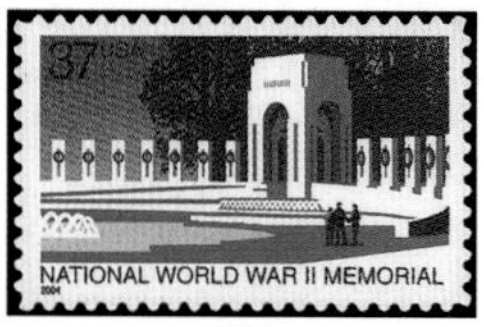

3862

3864, 3874, 3874a, 3875

3863

SCOTT NO.	DESCRIPTION	FIRST DAY COVERS SING	FIRST DAY COVERS PL. BLK.	MINT SHEET	PLATE BLOCK	UNUSED F/NH	USED
3862	37¢ National WWII Memorial, self-adhesive	2.25	4.75	20.00(20)	5.00	1.20	.30
3863	37¢ 2004 Olympic Games, Athens, Greece, self-adhesive	2.25	4.75	20.00(20)	5.00	1.20	.30
3864	(5¢) Sea Coast, coil, perf. 9.75 vert.	2.25	....	....	....	.25	.20
....	same, pl # strip of 5 .	....	....	....	....	1.50	....

3865 3866

3867 3868

SCOTT NO.	DESCRIPTION	FIRST DAY COVERS SING	FIRST DAY COVERS PL. BLK.	MINT SHEET	PLATE BLOCK	UNUSED F/NH	USED
3865-68	37¢ Art of Disney: Friendship, self-adhesive, 4 varieties attached	4.25	4.75	20.00(20)	5.00	4.00	3.50
3865	37¢ Goofy, Mickey Mouse, Donald Duck	2.25	....	....	....	1.20	.35
3866	37¢ Bambi, Thumper	2.25	....	....	....	1.20	.35
3867	37¢ Mufasa, Simba .	2.25	....	....	....	1.20	.35
3868	37¢ Jiminy Cricket, Pinocchio	2.25	....	....	....	1.20	.35

3869

3870

SCOTT NO.	DESCRIPTION	FIRST DAY COVERS SING	FIRST DAY COVERS PL. BLK.	MINT SHEET	PLATE BLOCK	UNUSED F/NH	USED
3869	37¢ U.S.S. Constellation, self-adhesive	2.25	4.75	20.00(20)	5.00	1.20	.30
3870	37¢ R. Buckminster Fuller, self-adhesive	2.25	4.75	20.00(20)	5.00	1.20	.30

3871

3872

SCOTT NO.	DESCRIPTION	FIRST DAY COVERS SING	FIRST DAY COVERS PL. BLK.	MINT SHEET	PLATE BLOCK	UNUSED F/NH	USED
3871	37¢ James Baldwin, self-adhesive	2.25	4.75	20.00(20)	5.00	1.20	.30
3872	37¢ Giant Magnolias, self-adhesive	2.25	....	....	....	1.20	.30
3872a	same, bklt pane of 20	....	....	....	....	22.00	....

3873

ART OF THE AMERICAN INDIAN

3873a	*Mimbres bowl*	**3873f**	*Mississippian dffigy*
3873b	*Kutenai parfleche*	**3873g**	*Acoma pot*
3873c	*Tlingit sculptures*	**3873h**	*Navajo weaving*
3873d	*Ho-Chunk bag*	**3873i**	*Seneca carving*
3873e	*Seminole doll*	**3873j**	*Luiseno basket*

SCOTT NO.	DESCRIPTION	FIRST DAY COVERS SING	FIRST DAY COVERS PL. BLK.	MINT SHEET	PLATE BLOCK	UNUSED F/NH	USED
3873	37¢ Art of the American Indian, 10 varieties attached	....	....	8.00(10)	....	12.00	10.00
....	set of singles	25.00	....	....	....	....	6.00
3874	(5¢) Sea Coast, coil, perf. 10 vert., self-adhesive	2.25	....	....	....	.25	.20
....	same, pl# strip of 5 .	....	....	....	....	2.25	....
3874a	(5¢) Sea Coast with small date, coil, die cut 10 vert., self-adhesive	2.25	....	....	....	.25	.20
....	same, pl# strip of 5 .	....	....	....	....	2.25	....
3875	(5¢) Sea Coast, coil, perf. 11.5 vert., self-adhesive	2.25	....	....	....	.25	.20
....	same, pl# strip of 5 .	....	....	....	....	2.25	....

3876

3877

SCOTT NO.	DESCRIPTION	FIRST DAY COVERS SING	FIRST DAY COVERS PL. BLK.	MINT SHEET	PLATE BLOCK	UNUSED F/NH	USED
3876	37¢ John Wayne . . .	2.25	4.75	20.00(20)	5.00	1.20	.30
....	same, uncut sheet of 120	....	....	120.00(20)	....	120.00	....
....	cross gutter block of 8	....	....	....	....	21.00	....
....	block of 8 with vert. gutter	....	....	....	....	13.50	....
....	horizontal pair with vertical gutter	....	....	....	....	4.00	....
....	vertical pair with horizontal gutter . . .	....	....	....	....	3.00	....
3877	37¢ Sickle Cell Disease Awareness	2.25	4.75	20.00(20)	5.00	1.20	.30

3878

CLOUDSCAPES

3878a	*Cirrus radiatus*	**3878i**	*Altocumulus castellanus*
3878b	*Cirrostratus fibratus*	**3878j**	*Alotcumulus lenticularis*
3878c	*Cirrocumulus undulatus*	**3878k**	*Stratocumulus undulatus*
3878d	*Cumulonimbus mammatus*	**3878l**	*Stratus opacus*
3878e	*Cumulonimbus incus*	**3878m**	*Cumulus humilis*
3878f	*Alocumulus stratiformis*	**3878n**	*Cumulus congestus*
3878g	*Altostratus translucidus*	**3878o**	*Cumulonimbus with tornado*
3878h	*Altocumulus undulatus*		

SCOTT NO.	DESCRIPTION	FIRST DAY COVERS SING	FIRST DAY COVERS PL. BLK.	MINT SHEET	PLATE BLOCK	UNUSED F/NH	USED
3878	37¢ Cloudscapes, 15 varieties attached	35.00	....	20.00(15)	....	20.00	18.00
....	set of singles	35.00	....	....	....	....	12.00

3879

3880

SCOTT NO.	DESCRIPTION	FIRST DAY COVERS SING	FIRST DAY COVERS PL. BLK.	MINT SHEET	PLATE BLOCK	UNUSED F/NH	USED
3879	37¢ Madonna & Child, self-adhesive, die cut 10.75 x 11	2.25	....	....	....	1.20	.30
3879a	same, bklt pane of 20	....	....	....	....	22.00	....
3880	37¢ Hanukkah-Dreidel, self-adhesive	2.25	4.75	16.00(20)	4.00	1.20	.30

3881

3882

SCOTT NO.	DESCRIPTION	FIRST DAY COVERS SING	FIRST DAY COVERS PL. BLK.	MINT SHEET	PLATE BLOCK	UNUSED F/NH	USED
3881	37¢ Kwanzaa-People in Robes, self-adhesive	2.25	4.75	20.00(20)	5.00	1.20	.30
3882	37¢ Moss Hart, self-adhesive	2.25	4.75	20.00(20)	5.00	1.20	.30

3883, 3887, 3892

3884, 3888, 3891

3885, 3889, 3894

3886, 3890, 3893

SCOTT NO.	DESCRIPTION	FIRST DAY COVERS SING	FIRST DAY COVERS PL. BLK.	MINT SHEET	PLATE BLOCK	UNUSED F/NH	USED
3883-86	37¢ Santa Christmas Ornaments, self-adhesive, 4 attached	4.25	4.75	20.00(20)	5.00	4.50	3.50
3883	37¢ Purple Santa Ornament	2.25	....	....	....	1.20	.40
3884	37¢ Green Santa Ornament	2.25	....	....	....	1.20	.40
3885	37¢ Blue Santa Ornament	2.25	....	....	....	1.20	.40
3886	37¢ Red Santa Ornament	2.25	....	....	....	1.20	.40
3886b	same, bklt pane of 20	....	....	....	....	20.00	....
3887	37¢ Purple Santa Ornament, die cut 10.25 x 10.75	2.25	....	....	....	1.20	.40
3888	37¢ Green Santa Ornament, die cut 10.25 x 10.75	2.25	....	....	....	1.20	.40
3889	37¢ Blue Santa Ornament, die cut 10.25 x 10.75	2.25	....	....	....	1.20	.40
3890	37¢ Red Santa Ornament, die cut 10.25 x 10.75	2.25	....	....	....	1.20	.40
3887-90	37¢ Santa Christmas Ornaments, self-adhesive, 4 attached die cut 10.25 x 10.75	4.25	....	....	....	3.75	2.75
3890b	same, bklt pane of 4	4.25	....	....	....	4.25	....
3890c	same, bklt pane of 6 (3889-90, 3887-88 x 2)	5.50	....	....	....	5.75	....
3890d	same, bklt pane of 6 (3887-88, 3889-90 x 2)	5.50	....	....	....	5.75	....
3891	37¢ Green Santa Ornament, die cut 8	2.25	....	....	....	1.20	.50
3892	37¢ Purple Santa Ornament, die cut 8	2.25	....	....	....	1.20	.50
3893	37¢ Red Santa Ornament, die cut 8	2.25	....	....	....	1.20	.50
3894	37¢ Blue Santa Ornament, die cut 8	2.25	....	....	....	1.20	.50
3891-94	37¢ Christmas Ornaments, self-adhesive, 4 attached, die cut 8	4.25	....	....	....	4.50	3.50
3894b	same, bklt pane of 18	15.00	....	....	....	20.00	....

2005 COMMEMORATIVES AND REGULAR ISSUES

3895

CHINESE NEW YEAR TYPES OF 1992-2004

3895a	*Rat*	**3895g**	*Horse*
3895b	*Ox*	**3895h**	*Ram*
3895c	*Tiger*	**3895i**	*Rooster*
3895d	*Rabbit*	**3895j**	*Dog*
3895e	*Dragon*	**3895k**	*Boar*
3895f	*Snake*	**3895l**	*Monkey*

SCOTT NO.	DESCRIPTION	FIRST DAY COVERS SING	FIRST DAY COVERS PL. BLK.	MINT SHEET	PLATE BLOCK	UNUSED F/NH	USED
3895	37¢ Chinese New Year, self-adhesive, 24 varieties attached	....	....		....	25.00	....
....	set of singles	23.50	....	....	....	....	7.50

3896

3897

3898

SCOTT NO.	DESCRIPTION	FIRST DAY COVERS SING	FIRST DAY COVERS PL. BLK.	MINT SHEET	PLATE BLOCK	UNUSED F/NH	USED
3896	37¢ Marian Anderson, self-adhesive	3.00	4.75	20.00(20)	5.00	1.20	.30
3897	37¢ Ronald Reagan, self-adhesive	3.00	4.75	20.00(20)	5.00	1.20	.30
....	same, uncut sheet of 120	....	....	120.00(120)	....	120.00	....
....	cross gutter block of 4	....	....	....	....	9.50	....
....	horiz. pair with vert. gutter	....	....	....	....	4.00	....
....	vert. pair with horiz. gutter	....	....	....	....	3.00	....
3898	37¢ Love-Hand and Flower Bouquet, self-adhesive	3.00	....	....	....	1.20	.30
3898a	same, bklt pane of 20	....	....	....	....	19.50	....

3899

NORTHEAST DECIDUOUS FOREST

3899a	*Eastern buckmouth*	**3899f**	*Long-tailed weasel*
3899b	*Red-shouldered hawk*	**3899g**	*Wild turkey*
3899c	*Eastern red bat*	**3899h**	*Ovenbird*
3899d	*White-tailed deer*	**3899i**	*Red eft*
3899e	*Black bear*	**3899j**	*Eastern chipmunk*

SCOTT NO.	DESCRIPTION	FIRST DAY COVERS SING	FIRST DAY COVERS PL. BLK.	MINT SHEET	PLATE BLOCK	UNUSED F/NH	USED
3899	37¢ Northeast Deciduous Forest, self-adhesive, 10 varieties attached	....	....	12.00(10)	....	12.00	....
....	set of singles	25.00	....	....	....	....	5.00

3900

3901

3902

3903

SCOTT NO.	DESCRIPTION	FIRST DAY COVERS SING	FIRST DAY COVERS PL. BLK.	MINT SHEET	PLATE BLOCK	UNUSED F/NH	USED
3900	37¢ Hyacinth	3.00	....	....	....	1.20	.30
3901	37¢ Daffodil	3.00	....	....	....	1.20	.30
3902	37¢ Tulip	3.00	....	....	....	1.20	.30
3903	37¢ Iris	3.00	....	....	....	1.20	.30
3900-03	37¢ Spring Flowers, self-adhesive, 4 varieties attached .	4.25	....	....	....	19.50	....
3903b	same, bklt pane of 20	....	....	....	....	19.50	....

3904

3905

SCOTT NO.	DESCRIPTION	FIRST DAY COVERS SING	FIRST DAY COVERS PL. BLK.	MINT SHEET	PLATE BLOCK	UNUSED F/NH	USED
3904	37¢ Robert Penn Warren, self-adhesive	3.00	4.75	20.00(20)	5.00	1.20	.30
3905	37¢ Yip Harburg, self-adhesive	3.00	4.75	20.00(20)	5.00	1.20	.30

3906 3907

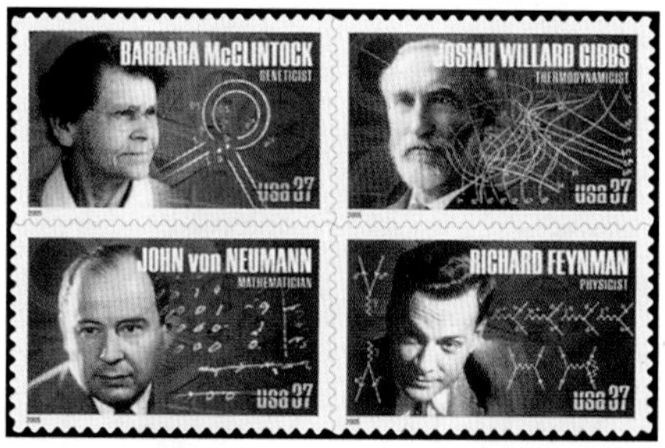

3908 3909

SCOTT NO.	DESCRIPTION	FIRST DAY COVERS SING	FIRST DAY COVERS PL. BLK.	MINT SHEET	PLATE BLOCK	UNUSED F/NH	USED
3906-09	37¢ American Scientists, self-adhesive, 4 attached	4.25	4.75	20.00(20)	5.00	4.50	3.50
3906	37¢ Barbara McClintock	3.00	....	....	....	1.20	.30
3907	37¢ Josiah Willard Gibbs	3.00	....	....	....	1.20	.30
3908	37¢ John von Neuman	3.00	....	....	....	1.20	.30
3909	37¢ Richard Feynman	3.00	....	....	....	1.20	.30
....	same, plate blk of 8 with Top Label	....	....	....	8.00(8)	....	....

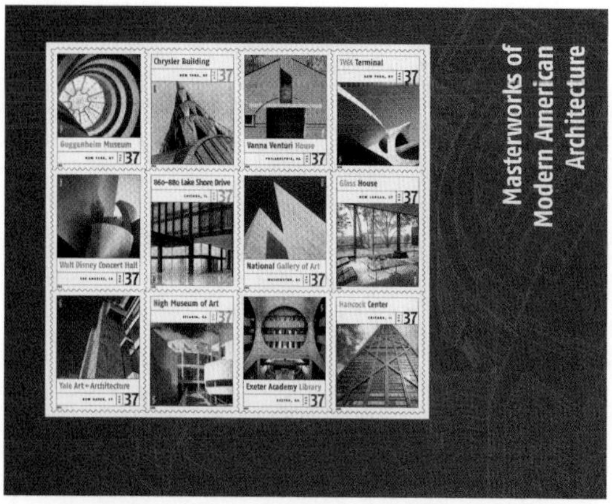

3910

MODERN AMERICAN ARCHITECTURE

3910a	*Guggenheim Museum*	**3910g**	*National Gallery of Art*
3910b	*Chrysler Building*	**3910h**	*Glass House*
3910c	*Vanna Venturi House*	**3910i**	*Yale Art and Architecture Bldg.*
3910d	*TWA Terminal*	**3910j**	*High Museum of Atlanta*
3910e	*Walt Disney Concert Hall*	**3910k**	*Exeter Academy Library*
3910f	*860-880 Lake Shore Drive*	**3910l**	*Hancock Center*

SCOTT NO.	DESCRIPTION	FIRST DAY COVERS SING	FIRST DAY COVERS PL. BLK.	MINT SHEET	PLATE BLOCK	UNUSED F/NH	USED
3910	37¢ Modern American Architecture, self-adhesive, 12 varieties attached	....	....	15.00(12)	....	15.00	....
....	set of singles	....	....	....	....	....	7.50

3911

SCOTT NO.	DESCRIPTION	FIRST DAY COVERS SING	PL. BLK.	MINT SHEET	PLATE BLOCK	UNUSED F/NH	USED
3911	37¢ Henry Fonda, self-adhesive	3.00	4.75	20.00(20)	5.00	1.20	.30
....	same, uncut sheet of 180	....	....	180.00(180)	....	180.00	....
....	cross gutterblk of 8 .	....	....	....	....	19.00	....
....	blk of 8 w/ vert. gutter	....	....	....	....	12.00	....
....	horiz. pair w/ vert. gutter	....	....	....	....	4.00	....
....	vert. pair w/ horiz. gutter	....	....	....	....	3.00	....

3912 3913

3914 3915

SCOTT NO.	DESCRIPTION	FIRST DAY COVERS SING	PL. BLK.	MINT SHEET	PLATE BLOCK	UNUSED F/NH	USED
3912-15	37¢ Disney Characters, self-adhesive, 4 attached	4.25	4.75	20.00(20)	5.00	4.50	3.50
3912	37¢ Pluto, Mickey Mouse	3.00	....	....	....	.85	.20
3913	37¢ Mad Hatter, Alice	3.00	....	....	....	.85	.20
3914	37¢ Flounder, Ariel .	3.00	....	....	....	.85	.20
3915	37¢ Snow White, Dopey	3.00	....	....	....	.85	.20

3916

3917

3918

3919

3920

3921

3922

3923

3924

3925

ADVANCES IN AVIATION

3916	*Boeing 247*	**3921**	*Lockheed P80 Shooting Star*
3917	*Consolidated PBY Catalina*	**3922**	*Consolidated B24 Liberator*
3918	*Grumman F6F*	**3923**	*Boeing B29 Superfortress*
3919	*Republic P47 Thunderbolt*	**3924**	*Beechcraft 35 Bonanza*
3920	*E & R Corp. Ercoupe 415*	**3925**	*Northrop YB-49 Flying Wing*

SCOTT NO.	DESCRIPTION	FIRST DAY COVERS SING	PL. BLK.	MINT SHEET	PLATE BLOCK	UNUSED F/NH	USED
3916-25	37¢ Advances in Aviation, self-adhesive, 10 attached	25.00	....	20.00(20)	10.00(10)	9.00	8.00
....	set of singles	....	....	....	....	....	6.00

3926

3927

3928

3929

SCOTT NO.	DESCRIPTION	FIRST DAY COVERS SING	PL. BLK.	MINT SHEET	PLATE BLOCK	UNUSED F/NH	USED
3926	37¢ Blanket w/ yellow, orange, and red stripes	3.00	....	....	....	1.20	.40
3927	37¢ Blanket w/ black, orange red, and yellow	3.00	....	....	....	1.20	.40
3928	37¢ Blanket w/ yellow and black diamonds	3.00	....	....	....	1.20	.40
3929	37¢ Blanket w/ zigzag diamonds	3.00	....	....	....	1.20	.40
3926-29	37¢ Rio Grande Blankets, self-adhesive, 4 attached	4.25	....	....	....	4.00	3.50
3929b	same, bklt pane of 20	15.00	....	....	....	20.00	....

3930

3931

3936

3932

3933

3934

3935

SCOTT NO.	DESCRIPTION	FIRST DAY COVERS SING	FIRST DAY COVERS PL. BLK.	MINT SHEET	PLATE BLOCK	UNUSED F/NH	USED
3930	37¢ Presidential Libraries Act, 50th Anniv., self-adhesive	3.00	4.75	20.00(20)	5.00	1.20	.30
3931	37¢ 1953 Studebaker Starliner.	3.00	....	....	....	1.50	.30
3932	37¢ 1954 Kaiser Darren	3.00	....	....	....	1.50	.30
3933	37¢ 1953 Chevrolet Corvette	3.00	....	....	....	1.50	.30
3934	37¢ 1952 Nash Healey	3.00	....	....	....	1.50	.30
3935	37¢ 1955 Ford Thunderbird	3.00	....	....	....	1.50	.30
3931-35	37¢ Sporty Cars of the 1950's, self-adhesive, 5 attached	5.00	....	....	....	5.00	4.00
3935b	same, bklt pane of 20	15.00	....	....	....	20.00	....
3936	37¢ Arthur Ashe, self-adhesive	3.00	4.75	16.00(20)	4.00	1.20	.30

3937

TO FORM A MORE PERFECT UNION

3937a	*1948 Executive Order 9981*	**3937f**	*1961 Freedom Riders*
3937b	*1965 Voting Rights Act*	**3937g**	*1964 Civil Rights Act*
3937c	*1960 Lunch Counter Sit-Ins*	**3937h**	*1963 March on Washington*
3937d	*1957 Litte Rock Nine*	**3937i**	*1965 Selma March*
3937e	*1955 Montgomery Bus Boycott*	**3937j**	*1954 Brown vs. Board of Education*

SCOTT NO.	DESCRIPTION	FIRST DAY COVERS SING	FIRST DAY COVERS PL. BLK.	MINT SHEET	PLATE BLOCK	UNUSED F/NH	USED
3937	37¢ To Form A More Perfect Union, self-adhesive, 10 attached .	15.00	....	12.00(10)	....	12.00	7.50
....	set of singles	....	....	....	....	....	6.00

3938

3939

3943

3940

3941

3942

SCOTT NO.	DESCRIPTION	FIRST DAY COVERS SING	FIRST DAY COVERS PL. BLK.	MINT SHEET	PLATE BLOCK	UNUSED F/NH	USED
3938	37¢ Child Health, self-adhesive	3.00	4.75	20.00(20)	5.00	1.20	.30
3939-42	37¢ Let's Dance, self-adhesive, 4 attached	4.25	4.75	20.00(20)	5.00	4.00	3.50
3939	37¢ Merengue	3.00	....	....	....	1.20	.30
3940	37¢ Salsa	3.00	....	....	....	1.20	.30
3941	37¢ Cha Cha Cha . .	3.00	....	....	....	1.20	.30
3942	37¢ Mambo	3.00	....	....	....	1.20	.30
3943	37¢ Greta Garbo, self-adhesive	3.00	4.75	20.00(20)	5.00	1.20	.30

3944

JIM HENSON AND THE MUPPETS

3944a	*Kermit the Frog*	**3944g**	*Animal*
3944b	*Fozzie Bear*	**3944h**	*Dr. Brunsen Honeydew and Beaker*
3944c	*Sam the Eagle and flag*	**3944i**	*Rowlf the Dog*
3944d	*Miss Piggy*	**3944j**	*The Great Gonzo and Camilia*
3944e	*Statler and Waldorf*	**3944k**	*Jim Henson*
3944f	*The Swedish Chef and fruit*		

SCOTT NO.	DESCRIPTION	FIRST DAY COVERS SING	FIRST DAY COVERS PL. BLK.	MINT SHEET	PLATE BLOCK	UNUSED F/NH	USED
3944	37¢ Jim Henson and the Muppets, self-adhesive, 11 varieties attached	12.00	....	15.00(11)	....	9.35	6.50
....	set of singles	30.00	....	....	....	....	7.00

3945

3946

3947

3948

SCOTT NO.	DESCRIPTION	FIRST DAY COVERS SING	FIRST DAY COVERS PL. BLK.	MINT SHEET	PLATE BLOCK	UNUSED F/NH	USED
3945-48	37¢ Constellations, self-adhesive, 4 attached	4.25	4.75	20.00(20)	5.00	4.50	4.00
3945	37¢ Leo	3.00	....	....	....	1.20	.30
3946	37¢ Orion	3.00	....	....	....	1.20	.30
3947	37¢ Lyra	3.00	....	....	....	1.20	.30
3948	37¢ Pegasus	3.00	....	....	....	1.20	.30

3949, 3953, 3957

3950, 3954, 3958

3951, 3955, 3959

3952, 3956, 3960

SCOTT NO.	DESCRIPTION	FIRST DAY COVERS SING	FIRST DAY COVERS PL. BLK.	MINT SHEET	PLATE BLOCK	UNUSED F/NH	USED
3949-52	37¢ Christmas Cookies, self-adhesive, 4 attached	4.25	4.75	20.00(20)	5.00	4.50	4.00
3949	37¢ Santa Claus cookie	3.00	....	....	....	1.20	.30
3950	37¢ Snowmen cookie	3.00	....	....	....	1.20	.30
3951	37¢ Angel cookie . .	3.00	....	....	....	1.20	.30
3952	37¢ Elves cookie . . .	3.00	....	....	....	1.20	.30
3953	37¢ Santa Claus cookie, die cut 10.75 X 11 . .	3.00	....	....	....	1.20	.30
3954	37¢ Snowmen cookie, die cut 10.75 X 11 . .	3.00	....	....	....	1.20	.30
3955	37¢ Angel cookie, die cut 10.75 X 11 . .	3.00	....	....	....	1.20	.30
3956	37¢ Elves cookie, die cut 10.75 X 11 . .	3.00	....	....	....	1.20	.30
3953-56	37¢ Christmas cookies, self-adhesive, 4 attached, die cut 10.75 X 11 . .	4.25	....	....	....	4.50	4.00
3956b	same, bklt pane of 20	....	....	....	....	19.50	....

SCOTT NO.	DESCRIPTION	FIRST DAY COVERS SING	FIRST DAY COVERS PL. BLK.	MINT SHEET	PLATE BLOCK	UNUSED F/NH	USED
3957	37¢ Santa Claus cookie, die cut 10.5 X 10.75	3.00	....	....	....	1.20	.40
3958	37¢ Snowmen cookie, die cut 10.5 X 10.75	3.00	....	....	....	1.20	.40
3959	37¢ Angel cookie, die cut 10.5 X 10.75	3.00	....	....	....	1.20	.40
3960	37¢ Elves cookie, die cut 10.5 X 10.75	3.00	....	....	....	1.20	.40
3957-60	37¢ Christmas Cookies, self-adhesvie, 4 attached die cut 10.5 X 10.75	4.25	....	....	....	4.50	4.00
3960b	same, booklet pane of 4	4.25	....	....	....	5.00	....
3960c	same, bklt pane of 6 (3959-60, 3957-58 X 2)	5.50	....	....	....	10.00	....
3960d	same, bklt pane of 6 (3957-58, 3959-60 X 2)	5.50	....	....	....	10.00	....

3961 3962

3963 3964

SCOTT NO.	DESCRIPTION	FIRST DAY COVERS SING	FIRST DAY COVERS PL. BLK.	MINT SHEET	PLATE BLOCK	UNUSED F/NH	USED
3961-64	37¢ Distinguished Marines, self-adhesive, 4 attached	4.25	4.75	20.00(20)	5.00	4.50	4.00
....	same, plate block of 8	....	....	....	10.00(8)	....	....
3961	37¢ Lt. General John A. Lejeune . . .	3.00	....	....	....	.85	.20
3962	37¢ Lt. General Lewis B. Puller	3.00	....	....	....	.85	.20
3963	37¢ Sgt. John Basilone	3.00	....	....	....	.85	.20
3964	37¢ Sgt. Major Daniel J. Daly	3.00	....	....	....	.85	.20

3965-3975

3976

3978, 3979, 3980

SCOTT NO.	DESCRIPTION	FIRST DAY COVERS SING	FIRST DAY COVERS PL. BLK.	MINT SHEET	PLATE BLOCK	UNUSED F/NH	USED
3965	(39¢) Flag and Statue of Liberty	3.00	4.75	85.00(100)	4.50	1.30	.25
3966	(39¢) Flag and Statue of Liberty, self-adhesive	3.00	4.75	16.75(20)	4.50	1.30	.25
3967	(39¢) Flag and Statue of Liberty, coil	3.00	....	....	....	1.20	.25
....	same, pl# strip of 5 .	....	....	....	....	6.75	....
3968	(39¢) Flag and Statue of Liberty, self-adhesive coil, die cut 8.5	3.00	....	....	....	1.20	.25
....	same, pl# strip of 5 .	....	....	....	....	6.75	....
3969	(39¢) Flag and Statue of Liberty, coil, die cut 10.25	3.00	....	....	....	1.20	.25
....	same, pl# strip of 5 .	....	....	....	....	6.75	....
3970	(39¢) Flag and Statue of Liberty, self-adhesive coil, die cut 9.5	3.00	....	....	....	1.20	.25
....	same, pl# strip of 5 .	....	....	....	....	6.75	....
3971	(39¢) Flag and Statue of Liberty, self-adhesive die cut 11.25 X 11 . .	3.00	....	....	....	1.20	.25
....	same, bklt pane of 20	16.00	....	....	....	18.00	....
3972	(39¢) Flag and Statue of Liberty, self-adhesive die cut 11.25 X 10.75	3.00	....	....	....	1.20	.25
....	same, bklt pane of 20	16.00	....	....	....	18.00	....
3973	(39¢) Flag and Statue of Liberty, self-adhesive die cut 10.25 X 10.75	3.00	....	....	....	1.20	.25
....	same, bklt pane of 20	16.00	....	....	....	18.00	....
3974	(39¢) Flag and Statue of Liberty, self-adhesive die cut 11.25 X 11 . .	3.00	....	....	....	1.20	.25
....	same, bklt pane of 4	4.50	....	....	....	3.75	....
....	same, bklt pane of 6	6.00	....	....	....	5.50	....
3975	(39¢) Flag and Statue of Liberty, self-adhesive die cut 8	3.00	....	....	....	1.20	.25
....	same, bklt pane of 18	16.00	....	....	....	16.25	....

2006 COMMEMORATIVES AND REGULAR ISSUES

SCOTT NO.	DESCRIPTION	FIRST DAY COVERS SING	FIRST DAY COVERS PL. BLK.	MINT SHEET	PLATE BLOCK	UNUSED F/NH	USED
3976	(39¢) Birds	3.00	....	....	....	1.20	.30
....	same, bklt pane of 20	16.00	....	....	....	18.00	....
3978	39¢ Flag and Statue of Liberty, self-adhesive die cut 11.25 X 10.75	3.00	4.75	16.75(20)	4.50	1.20	.30
3978a	same, bklt pane of 10	....	....	....	....	9.00	....
3978b	same, bklt pane of 20	....	....	....	....	18.00	....
3979	39¢ Flag and Statue of Liberty, coil, perf 10	3.00	....	....	....	1.20	.30
....	same, pl# strip of 5 .	....	....	....	....	6.75	....
3980	same, self-adhesive coil, die cut 11	3.00	....	....	....	1.20	.30
....	same, pl# strip of 5 .	....	....	....	....	7.50	....
3981	same, self-adhesive coil w/ USPS micro die cut 9.5	3.00	....	....	....	1.20	.30
....	same, pl# strip of 5 .	....	....	....	....	7.50	....
3982	same, self-adhesive coil, die cut 10 vertical . .	3.00	....	....	....	1.20	.30
....	same, pl# strip of 5 .	....	....	....	....	7.50	....
3983	same, self-adhesive coil, die cut 8.5	3.00	....	....	....	1.20	.30
....	same, pl# strip of 5 .	....	....	....	....	7.50	....
3985	39¢ Flag and Statue of Liberty, self-adhesive, die cut 11.25 X 10.75 on 2 or 3 sides	3.00	....	....	....	1.20	.30
3985a	same, bklt pane of 20	....	....	....	....	18.00	....
3985b	same, die cut 11.1 on 2 or 3	3.00	....	....	....	1.20	.30
3985c	same, bklt pane of 4	....	....	....	....	3.75	....
3985d	same, bklt pane of 6	....	....	....	....	5.50	....

3987 3988 3989 3990

3991 3992 3993 3994

FAVORITE CHILDREN'S BOOK ANIMALS

3987	*The Very Hungry Caterpillar*	**3991**	*Wild Thing*
3988	*Wilbur*	**3992**	*Curious George*
3989	*Fox in Socks*	**3993**	*Olivia*
3990	*Maisy*	**3994**	*Frederick*

SCOTT NO.	DESCRIPTION	FIRST DAY COVERS SING	FIRST DAY COVERS PL. BLK.	MINT SHEET	PLATE BLOCK	UNUSED F/NH	USED
3987-94	39¢ Children's Book Animals, self-adhesive 8 attached	10.00	....	14.50(16)	7.50(8)	7.25	5.00
....	set of singles	....	....	....	....	....	4.00
....	same, uncut sheet of 96	....	....	90.00(96)	....	90.00	....
....	cross gutter block of 8	....	....	....	....	17.50	....
....	blk of 8 w/ horiz. gutter	....	....	....	....	10.00	....
....	blk of 8 w/ vert. gutter	....	....	....	....	9.00	....
....	horz. pair w/ vert. gutter	....	....	....	....	2.50	....
....	vert. pair w/ horz. gutter	....	....	....	....	2.50	....

3995

3996

SCOTT NO.	DESCRIPTION	FIRST DAY COVERS SING	FIRST DAY COVERS PL. BLK.	MINT SHEET	PLATE BLOCK	UNUSED F/NH	USED
3995	39¢ 2006 Winter Olympic games, Turin, Italy, self-adhesive	3.00	4.75	20.00(20)	5.00	1.20	.50
3996	39¢ Hattie McDaniel, self-adhesive	3.00	4.75	20.00(20)	5.00	1.20	.50

CHINESE NEW YEAR TYPES OF 1992-2004

3997a	*Rat*	**3997g**	*Horse*
3997b	*Ox*	**3997h**	*Ram*
3997c	*Tiger*	**3997i**	*Monkey*
3997d	*Rabbit*	**3997j**	*Rooster*
3997e	*Dragon*	**3997k**	*Dog*
3997f	*Snake*	**3997l**	*Boar*

SCOTT NO.	DESCRIPTION	FIRST DAY COVERS SING	FIRST DAY COVERS PL. BLK.	MINT SHEET	PLATE BLOCK	UNUSED F/NH	USED
3997	39¢ Chinese New Year self-adhesive, 12 varieties attached . .	....	....	10.75(12)	....	10.75	....
....	set of singles	32.00	....	....	....	....	7.50

3998

4000, 4001, 4002

3999

SCOTT NO.	DESCRIPTION	FIRST DAY COVERS SING	FIRST DAY COVERS PL. BLK.	MINT SHEET	PLATE BLOCK	UNUSED F/NH	USED
3998	39¢ Wedding Doves, Dove Facing Left, self-adhesive	3.00	....	....	....	.90	.30
3998a	same, bklt pane of 20	16.00	....	....	....	18.00	....
3999	63¢ Wedding Doves, Dove Facing Right, self-adhesive	3.00	....	....	....	1.40	1.00
3999a	same, bklt pane of 40	....	....	....	....	46.00	....
4000	24¢ Common Buckeye butterfly	3.00	4.75	55.00(100)	2.75	.60	.30
4001	24¢ Common Buckeye butterfly self-adhesive, die cut 11	3.00	4.75	11.00(20)	2.75	.60	.30
4001a	same, single from bklt. pane, die cut 10.75 X11.25	3.00	....	....	....	.60	.30
4001b	same, bklt pane of 10 (4001a)	....	....	....	....	6.00	....
4001c	same, bklt pane of 4 (4001a)	....	....	....	....	2.40	....
4001d	same, bklt pane of 6 (4001a)	....	....	....	....	3.60	....
4002	24¢ Common Buckeye butterfly, self-adhesive, coil, die cut 8.5	3.00	....	....	....	.60	.30
....	same, pl# strip of 5 .	....	....	....	....	4.25	....

4003, 4008, 4013

4004, 4009, 4014

4005, 4010, 4015

4006, 4011, 4016

4007, 4012, 4017

SCOTT NO.	DESCRIPTION	FIRST DAY COVERS SING	FIRST DAY COVERS PL. BLK.	MINT SHEET	PLATE BLOCK	UNUSED F/NH	USED
4003	39¢ Chili Peppers, self-adhesive, coil . .	3.00	....	....	....	.90	.30
4004	39¢ Beans, self-adhesive, coil	3.00	....	....	....	.90	.30
4005	39¢ Sunflower and Seeds self-adhesive, coil . .	3.00	....	....	....	.90	.30
4006	39¢ Squashes, self-adhesive, coil	3.00	....	....	....	.90	.30
4007	39¢ Corn, self-adhesive, coil	3.00	....	....	....	.90	.30
4003-07	39¢ Crops of the Americas, coil, strip of 5	5.00	....	....	....	4.50	3.50
....	same, pl# strip of 5 .	....	....	....	....	6.75	....
....	same, pl# strip of 11	....	....	....	....	13.00	....
4008	39¢ Chili Peppers, self-adhesive, bklt single, die cut 10.75 X 11.25	3.00	....	....	....	.90	.30
4009	39¢ Beans, self-adhesive bklt single, die cut 10.75 X 11.25	3.00	....	....	....	.90	.30
4010	39¢ Sunflower and Seeds self-adhesive, bklt single, die cut 10.75 X 11.25	3.00	....	....	....	.90	.30
4011	39¢ Squashes, self-adhesive, bklt single die cut 10.75 X 11.25	3.00	....	....	....	.90	.30
4012	39¢ Corn, self-adhesive bklt single, die cut 10.75 X 11.25	3.00	....	....	....	.90	.30
4008-12	39¢ Crops of the Americas, strip of 5	5.00	....	....	....	4.50	3.50
4012b	same, bklt pane of 20	....	....	....	....	18.00	....
4013	39¢ Chili Peppers, self-adhesive, bklt single, die cut 10.75 X 10.5	3.00	....	....	....	.90	.30
4014	39¢ Beans, self-adhesive bklt single, die cut 10.75 X10.5	3.00	....	....	....	.90	.30
4015	39¢ Sunflower and Seeds self-adhesive, bklt single, die cut 10.75 X10.5 .	3.00	....	....	....	.90	.30
4016	39¢ Squashes, self-adhesive, bklt single die cut 10.75 X 10.5	3.00	....	....	....	.90	.30
4016a	same, bklt pane of 4	....	....	....	....	3.60	....
4017	39¢ Corn, self-adhesive bklt single, die cut 10.75 X 10.5	3.00	....	....	....	.90	.30
4013-17	39¢ Crops of the Americas strip of 5	5.00	....	....	....	4.50	3.50
4017b	same, bklt pane of 4	....	....	....	....	3.60	....
4017c	same, bklt pane of 6 (4013-16, 4017 X 2)	....	....	....	....	5.40	....
4017d	same, bklt pane of 6 (4013-15, 4017, 4016 X2)	....	....	....	....	5.40	....

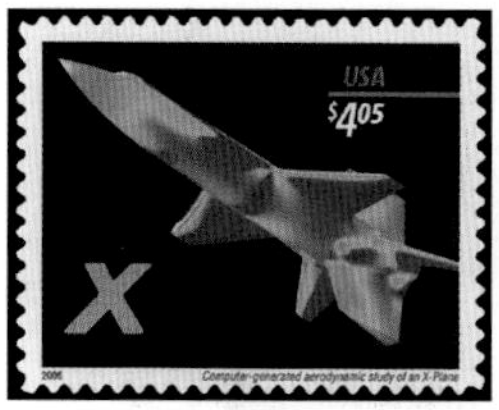

4018

4020

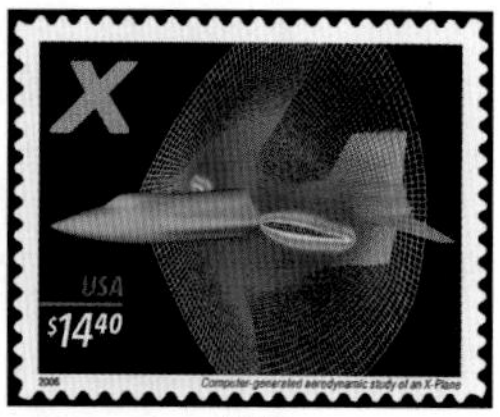

4019

SCOTT NO.	DESCRIPTION	FIRST DAY COVERS SING	FIRST DAY COVERS PL. BLK.	MINT SHEET	PLATE BLOCK	UNUSED F/NH	USED
4018	$4.05 X-Plane, self-adhesive	9.00	25.00	175.00(20)	45.00	9.00	6.00
4019	$14.40 X-Plane, self-adhesive	30.00	75.00	575.00(20)	150.00	30.00	16.50
4020	39¢ Sugar Ray Robinson, self-adhesive	3.00	4.75	16.75(20)	4.50	1.00	.25

4021 4022

4023 4024

SCOTT NO.	DESCRIPTION	FIRST DAY COVERS SING	FIRST DAY COVERS PL. BLK.	MINT SHEET	PLATE BLOCK	UNUSED F/NH	USED
4021-24	39¢ Benjamin Franklin (1706-90), self-adhesive 4 attached	4.25	4.75	16.75(20)	4.50	3.75	....
4021	39¢ Benjamin Franklin Statesman	3.00	....	....	....	1.00	.30
4022	39¢ Benjamin Franklin Scientist	3.00	....	....	....	1.00	.30
4023	39¢ Benjamin Franklin Printer	3.00	....	....	....	1.00	.30
4024	39¢ Benjamin Franklin Postmaster	3.00	....	....	....	1.00	.30

4025 4026

4027 4028

SCOTT NO.	DESCRIPTION	FIRST DAY COVERS SING	FIRST DAY COVERS PL. BLK.	MINT SHEET	PLATE BLOCK	UNUSED F/NH	USED
4025-28	39¢ Disney Characters, self-adhesive, 4 attached	4.25	4.75	16.75(20)	4.50	3.75	....

SCOTT NO.	DESCRIPTION	FIRST DAY COVERS SING	FIRST DAY COVERS PL. BLK.	MINT SHEET	PLATE BLOCK	UNUSED F/NH	USED
4025	39¢ Mickey and Minnie Mouse	3.00	....	....	....	.90	.40
4026	39¢ Cinderella and Prince Charming	3.00	....	....	....	.90	.40
4027	39¢ Beauty and the Beast	3.00	....	....	....	.90	.40
4028	39¢ Lady and the Tramp	3.00	....	....	....	.90	.40

4029

4030

SCOTT NO.	DESCRIPTION	FIRST DAY COVERS SING	FIRST DAY COVERS PL. BLK.	MINT SHEET	PLATE BLOCK	UNUSED F/NH	USED
4029	39¢ Lovebirds, self-adhesive	3.00	....	....	....	.90	.30
....	same, bklt pane of 20	....	....	....	....	18.00	....
4030	39¢ Katherine Anne Porter self-adhesive	3.00	4.75	16.75(20)	4.50	.90	.30

4031

4032

SCOTT NO.	DESCRIPTION	FIRST DAY COVERS SING	FIRST DAY COVERS PL. BLK.	MINT SHEET	PLATE BLOCK	UNUSED F/NH	USED
4031	39¢ Amber Alert, self-adhesive	3.00	4.75	16.75(20)	4.50	.90	.30
4032	39¢ Purple Heart, self-adhesive	3.00	4.75	16.75(20)	4.50	.90	.30

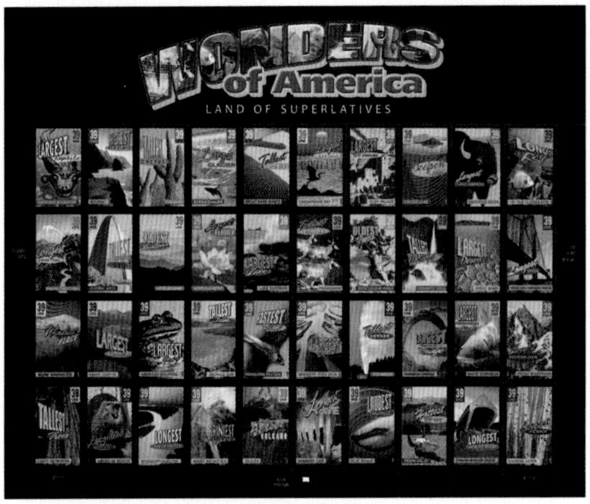

4033-4072

WONDERS OF AMERICA

4033 *American Alligator*
4034 *Moloka'i*
4035 *Saguaro*
4036 *Bering Glacier*
4037 *Great Sand Dunes*
4038 *Chesapeake Bay*
4039 *Cliff Palace*
4040 *Crater Lake*
4041 *American Bison*
4042 *Off the Florida Keys*
4043 *Pacific Crest Trail*
4044 *Gateway Arch*
4045 *Appalachians*
4046 *American Lotus*
4047 *Lake Superior*
4048 *Pronghorn*
4049 *Bristlecone Pines*
4050 *Yosemite Falls*
4051 *Great Basin*
4052 *Verrazano-Narrows Bridge*
4053 *Mount Washington*
4054 *Grand Canyon*
4055 *American Bullfrog*
4056 *Oroville Dam*
4057 *Peregrine Falcon*
4058 *Mississippi River Delta*
4059 *Steamboat Geyser*
4060 *Rainbow Bridge*
4061 *White Sturgeon*
4062 *Rocky Mountains*
4063 *Coast Redwoods*
4064 *American Beaver*
4065 *Mississippi-Missouri*
4066 *Mount Wai'ale'ale*
4067 *Kilauea*
4068 *Mammoth Cave*
4069 *Blue Whale*
4070 *Death Valley*
4071 *Cornish-Windsor Bridge*
4072 *Quaking Aspen*

SCOTT NO.	DESCRIPTION	FIRST DAY COVERS SING	FIRST DAY COVERS PL. BLK.	MINT SHEET	PLATE BLOCK	UNUSED F/NH	USED
4033-72	39¢ Wonders of America, self-adhesive, 40 attached	....	....	33.50(40)	....	33.50	....
....	same, set of singles	....	....	....	....	....	30.00

4073, 4074a

SCOTT NO.	DESCRIPTION	FIRST DAY COVERS SING	FIRST DAY COVERS PL. BLK.	MINT SHEET	PLATE BLOCK	UNUSED F/NH	USED
4073	39¢ Samuel de Champlain, self-adhesive	3.00	4.75	16.75(20)	4.50	1.00	.50
4074	39¢ Samuel de Champlain, souvenir sheet of 4 (joint issue,4074a x 2 and Canada 2156a x 2)	....	....	....	....	4.50	....
4074a	same, single from s/s	....	....	....	....	....	.50

4075

SCOTT NO.	DESCRIPTION	FIRST DAY COVERS SING	FIRST DAY COVERS PL. BLK.	MINT SHEET	PLATE BLOCK	UNUSED F/NH	USED
4075	$1-$5 Washington 2006 World Exhibition, souvenir sheet of 3 .	....	....	....	....	16.00	....
4075a	$1 Lincoln Memorial	4.50	....	....	....	2.00	.75
4075b	$2 U.S. Capitol	7.50	....	....	....	4.00	1.50
4075c	$5 "America"	15.00	....	....	....	10.00	3.50

4076

SCOTT NO.	DESCRIPTION	FIRST DAY COVERS SING	FIRST DAY COVERS PL. BLK.	MINT SHEET	PLATE BLOCK	UNUSED F/NH	USED
4076	39¢ Distinguished American Diplomats, self-adhesive, souvenir sheet of 6 .	15.00	....	....	....	5.50	....
4076a	39¢ Robert D. Murphy	3.00	....	....	....	.90	.30
4076b	39¢ Frances E. Willis	3.00	....	....	....	.90	.30
4076c	39¢ Hiram Bingham IV	3.00	....	....	....	.90	.30
4076d	39¢ Philip C. Habib .	3.00	....	....	....	.90	.30
4076e	39¢ Charles E. Bohlen	3.00	....	....	....	.90	.30
4076f	39¢ Clifton R. Wharton Sr.	3.00	....	....	....	.90	.30

4077

4078

SCOTT NO.	DESCRIPTION	FIRST DAY COVERS SING	FIRST DAY COVERS PL. BLK.	MINT SHEET	PLATE BLOCK	UNUSED F/NH	USED
4077	39¢ Judy Garland, self-adhesive	3.00	4.75	16.75(20)	4.50	.90	.30
....	same, uncut sheet of 120	....	....	120.00(120)	....	120.00	....
....	block of 8 with vert. gutter	....	....	....	....	10.50	....
....	cross gutter block of 8	....	....	....	....	18.00	....
....	horiz. pair with vert. gutter	....	....	....	....	4.00	....
....	vert. pair with horiz. gutter	....	....	....	....	3.00	....
4078	39¢ Ronald Reagan, self-adhesive	3.00	4.75	16.75(20)	4.50	.90	.30

4079

SCOTT NO.	DESCRIPTION	FIRST DAY COVERS SING	FIRST DAY COVERS PL. BLK.	MINT SHEET	PLATE BLOCK	UNUSED F/NH	USED
4079	39¢ Happy Birthday, Self-adhesive	3.00	4.75	16.75(20)	4.50	.90	.30

4080 4081

4082 4083

SCOTT NO.	DESCRIPTION	FIRST DAY COVERS SING	FIRST DAY COVERS PL. BLK.	MINT SHEET	PLATE BLOCK	UNUSED F/NH	USED
4080-83	39¢ Baseball Sluggers, self-adhesive, 4 attached	4.25	4.75	16.75(20)	4.50	3.75	....
4080	39¢ Roy Campanella	3.00	....	....	....	.90	.30
4081	39¢ Hank Greenberg	3.00	....	....	....	.90	.30
4082	39¢ Mel Ott	3.00	....	....	....	.90	.30
4083	39¢ Mickey Mantle .	3.00	....	....	....	.90	.30
....	same, uncut sheet of 120	....	....	120.00(120)	....	120.00	....
....	cross gutter blk of 8 .	....	....	....	....	18.00	....
....	blk of 8 with vert. gutter	....	....	....	....	10.50	....
....	horz. pair with vert. gutter	....	....	....	....	4.00	....
....	vert. pair with horz. gutter	....	....	....	....	4.00	....

4084

D.C. COMICS SUPER HEROES

4084a	*Superman*	**4084k**	*Superman Cover*
4084b	*Green Lantern*	**4084l**	*Green Lantern Cover*
4084c	*Wonder Woman*	**4084m**	*Wonder Woman Cover*
4084d	*Green Arrow*	**4084n**	*Green Arrow Cover*
4084e	*Batman*	**4084o**	*Batman Cover*
4084f	*The Flash*	**4084p**	*The Flash Cover*
4084g	*Plastic Man*	**4084q**	*Plastic Man Cover*
4084h	*Aquaman*	**4084r**	*Aquaman Cover*
4084i	*Supergirl*	**4084s**	*Supergirl Cover*
4084j	*Hawkman*	**4084t**	*Hawkman Cover*

SCOTT NO.	DESCRIPTION	FIRST DAY COVERS SING	FIRST DAY COVERS PL. BLK.	MINT SHEET	PLATE BLOCK	UNUSED F/NH	USED
4084	39¢ D.C. Comics Super Heroes, self-adhesive, 20 varieties attached	....	....	16.75(20)	....	16.75	....
....	same, uncut sheet of 80	....	....	75.00(80)	....	75.00	....
....	cross gutter block of 20	....	....	....	....	25.00	....
....	horz. pair w/ vert. gutter	....	....	....	....	4.00	....
....	vert. pair w/ horz. gutter	....	....	....	....	4.00	....
....	set of singles	....	....	....	....	....	16.00

4085 4086

4087 4088

SCOTT NO.	DESCRIPTION	FIRST DAY COVERS SING	FIRST DAY COVERS PL. BLK.	MINT SHEET	PLATE BLOCK	UNUSED F/NH	USED
4085-88	39¢ Motorcycles, self-adhesive, 4 attached	4.25	4.75	16.75(20)	4.50	3.75	....
4085	39¢ 1940 Indian Four	3.00	....	....	....	.90	.30
4086	39¢ 1918 Cleveland	3.00	....	....	....	.90	.30
4087	39¢ 1970 Chopper .	3.00	....	....	....	.90	.30
4088	39¢ 1965 Harley Davidson Electa-Glide	3.00	....	....	....	.90	.30

4089

4096

SCOTT NO.	DESCRIPTION	FIRST DAY COVERS SING	FIRST DAY COVERS PL. BLK.	MINT SHEET	PLATE BLOCK	UNUSED F/NH	USED
4089-98	39¢ Quilts of Gee's Bend, Alabama, self-adhesive, 10 attached	....	....	....	....	9.00	....
4089	39¢ House Variation by Mary Lee Bendolph .	3.00	....	....	....	.90	.30
4090	39¢ Pig in a Pen Medallion by Minnie Sue Coleman	3.00	....	....	....	.90	.30
4091	39¢ Nine Patch by Ruth P. Mosely	3.00	....	....	....	.90	.30
4092	39¢ Housetop Four Block Half Log Cabin by Lottie Mooney	3.00	....	....	....	.90	.30
4093	39¢ Roman Stripes Variation by Loretta Pettway .	3.00	....	....	....	.90	.30
4094	39¢ Chinese Coins Variation by Arlonzia Pettway	3.00	....	....	....	.90	.30
4095	39¢ Blocks and Strips by Annie Mae Young ..	3.00	....	....	....	.90	.30
4096	39¢ Medallion by Loretta Pettway	3.00	....	....	....	.90	.30
4097	39¢ Bars and String-pierced Columns by Jessie T. Pettway	3.00	....	....	....	.90	.30
4098	39¢ Medallion with Checkerboard Center by Patty Ann Williams	3.00	....	....	....	.90	.30
4098a	same, bklt pane of 20 (4089-4098 x 2)	....	....	....	....	18.00	....

4099

SOUTHERN FLORIDA WETLANDS

4099a	*Snail Kite*	**4099f**	*Roseate Spoonbills*
4099b	*Wood Storks*	**4099g**	*Everglades Mink*
4099c	*Florida Panther*	**4099h**	*Cape Sable Seaside Sparrow*
4099d	*Bald Eagle*	**4099i**	*American Alligator*
4099e	*American Crocodile*	**4099j**	*White Ibis*

SCOTT NO.	DESCRIPTION	FIRST DAY COVERS SING	FIRST DAY COVERS PL. BLK.	MINT SHEET	PLATE BLOCK	UNUSED F/NH	USED
4099	39¢ Southern Florida Wetlands, self-adhesive, 10 attached	....	....	8.00(10)	....	8.00	....
....	set of singles	20.00	....	....	....	....	5.00

4100

SCOTT NO.	DESCRIPTION	FIRST DAY COVERS SING	FIRST DAY COVERS PL. BLK.	MINT SHEET	PLATE BLOCK	UNUSED F/NH	USED
4100	39¢ Madonna and Child, self-adhesive	3.00	....	....	....	.90	.30
4100a	same, bklt pane of 20	....	....	....	....	18.00	....

4101, 4105, 4109, 4113

4102, 4106, 4110, 4115

4103, 4107, 4111, 4114

4104, 4108, 4112, 4116

SCOTT NO.	DESCRIPTION	FIRST DAY COVERS SING	FIRST DAY COVERS PL. BLK.	MINT SHEET	PLATE BLOCK	UNUSED F/NH	USED
4101-04	39¢ Snowflakes, self-adhesive, die cut 11.25 x 11, 4 attached	4.25	4.75	16.75(20)	4.50	3.75	....
4101	39¢ Spindly Arms and Branches	3.00	....	....	....	.90	.30
4102	39¢ Leafy Arms	3.00	....	....	....	.90	.30
4103	39¢ Large Center . .	3.00	....	....	....	.90	.30
4104	39¢ Arms w/ Wide Centers	3.00	....	....	....	.90	.30
4105-08	39¢ Snowflakes, self-adhesive, die cut 11.25 x 11.5, 4 attached	4.25	....	....		3.75	....
4105	39¢ Spindly Arms and Branches	3.00	....	....	....	.90	.30
4106	39¢ Leafy Arms	3.00	....	....	....	.90	.30
4107	39¢ Large Center . .	3.00	....	....	....	.90	.30
4108	39¢ Arms w/ Wide Centers	3.00	....	....	....	.90	.30
4108b	same, bklt pane of 20 (4105-08 x 5)	....	....	....	....	18.00	....
4109-12	39¢ Snowflakes, self-adhesive, die cut 11.25 x 11, 4 attached	4.25	....	....	....	3.75	....
4109	39¢ Spindly Arms and Branches	3.00	....	....	....	.90	.30
4110	39¢ Leafy Arms	3.00	....	....	....	.90	.30
4111	39¢ Large Center . .	3.00	....	....	....	.90	.30
4112	39¢ Arms w/ Wide Centers	3.00	....	....	....	.90	.30
4112b	same, bklt pane of 4 (4109-12)	....	....	....	....	3.60	....
4112c	same, bklt pane of 6 (4111-4112, 4109-4110 x 2)	....	....	....	....	5.40	....
4112d	same, bklt pane of 6 (4109-4110, 4111-4112 x 2)	....	....	....	....	5.40	....
4113-16	39¢ Snowflakes, die cut 8, self-adhesive, 4 attached	4.25	....	....	....	3.75	....
4113	39¢ Spindly Arms and Branches	3.00	....	....	....	.90	.30
4114	39¢ Large Center . . .	3.00	....	....	....	.90	.30
4115	39¢ Leafy Arms	3.00	....	....	....	.90	.30
4116	39¢ Arms w/ Wide Centers	3.00	....	....	....	.90	.30
4116b	same, bklt pane of 18 (4113 x 5, 4114 x 4, 4115 x 5, 4116 x 4)	....	....	....	....	16.00	....

4117

4118

4119

SCOTT NO.	DESCRIPTION	FIRST DAY COVERS SING	FIRST DAY COVERS PL. BLK.	MINT SHEET	PLATE BLOCK	UNUSED F/NH	USED
4117	39¢ EID, self-adhesive	3.00	4.75	16.75(20)	4.50	.90	.30
4118	39¢ Hanukkah-Dreidal, self-adhesive	3.00	4.75	16.75(20)	4.50	.90	.30
4119	39¢ Kwanzaa-People self-adhesive	3.00	4.75	16.75(20)	4.50	.90	.30

4120

4121

2007 COMMEMORATIVES AND REGULAR ISSUES

SCOTT NO.	DESCRIPTION	FIRST DAY COVERS SING	FIRST DAY COVERS PL. BLK.	MINT SHEET	PLATE BLOCK	UNUSED F/NH	USED
4120	39¢ Ella Fitzgerald, self-adhesive	3.00	4.75	16.75(20)	4.50	.90	.30
4121	39¢ Oklahoma Statehood self-adhesive	3.00	4.75	16.75(20)	4.50	.90	.30

4122

SCOTT NO.	DESCRIPTION	FIRST DAY COVERS SING	FIRST DAY COVERS PL. BLK.	MINT SHEET	PLATE BLOCK	UNUSED F/NH	USED
4122	39¢ Hershey's Kiss, self-adhesive	3.00	4.75	16.75(20)	4.50	.90	.30
4122a	same, bklt pane of 20	....	....	....	....	18.00	....

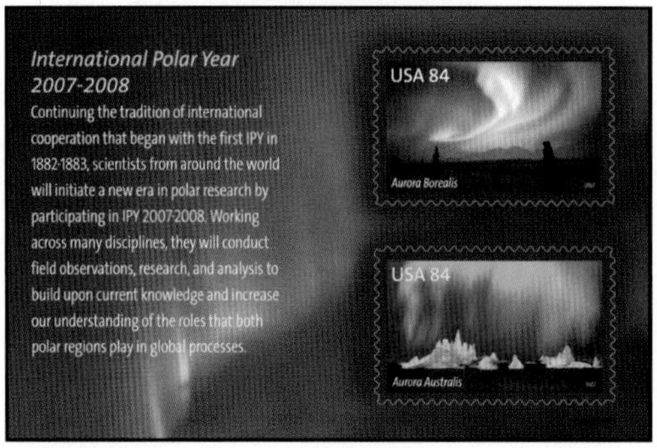

4123

SCOTT NO.	DESCRIPTION	FIRST DAY COVERS SING	FIRST DAY COVERS PL. BLK.	MINT SHEET	PLATE BLOCK	UNUSED F/NH	USED
4123	84¢ International Polar Year, self-adhesive, souvenir sheet of 2 .	....	....	....	....	3.50	....
4123a	84¢ Aurora Borealis	4.00	....	....	....	1.75	.75
4123b	84¢ Aurora Australis	4.00	....	....	....	1.75	.75

4124

4125, 4126, 4127, 4128

SCOTT NO.	DESCRIPTION	FIRST DAY COVERS SING	FIRST DAY COVERS PL. BLK.	MINT SHEET	PLATE BLOCK	UNUSED F/NH	USED
4124	39¢ Henry Wadsworth Longfellow, self-adhesive	3.00	4.75	16.75(20)	4.50	.90	.30
4125	(41¢) Forever Liberty Bell, self-adhesive, large micro print	3.50	....	....	....	.95	.35
4125a	same, bklt pane of 20	....	....	....	....	19.00	....
4126	(41¢) Forever, Liberty Bell, self-adhesive, small micro print	3.50	....	....	....	.95	.35
4126a	same, bklt pane of 20	....	....	....	....	.95	.35
4127	(41¢) Forever Liberty Bell, self-adhesive, medium micro print	3.50	....	....	....	.95	.35
4127a	same, bklt pane of 20	....	....	....	....	19.00	....
4127b	same, bklt pane of 4	....	....	....	....	3.80	....
4127c	same, bklt pane of 6	....	....	....	....	5.70	....
4128	(41¢) Forever Liberty Bell, self-adhesive, ATM .	3.50	....	....	....	.95	.35
4128a	same, bklt pane of 18	....	....	....	....	17.00	....

4129, 4130, 4132, 4133, 4134, 4135

SCOTT NO.	DESCRIPTION	FIRST DAY COVERS SING	FIRST DAY COVERS PL. BLK.	MINT SHEET	PLATE BLOCK	UNUSED F/NH	USED
4129	(41¢) American Flag, die cut 11.25	3.50	5.00	17.50(20)	4.75	.95	.35
4130	(41¢) American Flag, self-adhesive, 11.25 x 10.75	3.50	5.00	17.50(20)	4.75	.95	.35

SCOTT NO.	DESCRIPTION	FIRST DAY COVERS SING	FIRST DAY COVERS PL. BLK.	MINT SHEET	PLATE BLOCK	UNUSED F/NH	USED
4131	(41¢) American Flag, coil, die cut 9.75 . . .	3.50	....	....	....	.95	.35
....	same, pl# strip of 5 .	....	....	....	....	7.00	....
4132	(41¢) American Flag, coil, self-adhesive, die cut 9.5	3.50	....	....	....	.95	.35
....	same, pl# strip of 5 .	....	....	....	....	7.00	....
4133	(41¢) American Flag, coil, self-adhesive, die cut 11	3.50	....	....	....	.95	.35
....	same, pl# strip of 5 .	....	....	....	....	7.00	....
4134	(41¢) American Flag, coil, self-adhesive, die cut 8.5	3.50	....	....	....	.95	.35
....	same, pl# strip of 5 .	....	....	....	....	7.00	....
4135	(41¢) American Flag, coil, self-adhesive, rounded corners, die cut 11 .	3.50	....	....	....	.95	.35
....	same, pl# strip of 5 .	....	....	....	....	7.00	....

4136

SCOTT NO.	DESCRIPTION	FIRST DAY COVERS SING	FIRST DAY COVERS PL. BLK.	MINT SHEET	PLATE BLOCK	UNUSED F/NH	USED
4136	41¢ Settlement of Jamestown, self-adhesive .	3.50	5.00	17.50(20)	4.75	.95	.35

4137, 4139, 4141, 4142

4138, 4140

SCOTT NO.	DESCRIPTION	FIRST DAY COVERS SING	FIRST DAY COVERS PL. BLK.	MINT SHEET	PLATE BLOCK	UNUSED F/NH	USED
4137	26¢ Florida Panther, water-activated, ...	3.00	4.75	10.00(20)	2.75	.60	.20
4138	17¢ Big Horn Sheep, self-adhesive	3.00	4.00	8.00(20)	1.75	.40	.15
4139	26¢ Florida Panther, self-adhesive	3.00	4.75	10.00(20)	2.75	.60	.20
4140	17¢ Big Horn Sheep, self-adhesive, coil . .	3.00	....	....	....	.40	.15
....	same, pl# strip of 5 .	....	....	....	....	3.00	....
4141	26¢ Florida Panther, self-adhesive, coil . .	3.00	....	....	....	.60	.20
....	same, pl# strip of 5 .	....	....	....	....	4.00	....
4142	26¢ Florida Panther, self-adhesive	3.00	....	....	....	.60	.20
4142a	same, bklt pane of 10	....	....	....	....	6.00	....

4143

STAR WARS

4143a	*Darth Vader*	**4143h**	*Queen Padme Amidala*
4143b	*Millennium Falcon*	**4143i**	*Obi-Wan Kenobi*
4143c	*Emperor Palpatine*	**4143j**	*Boba Fett*
4143d	*Anakin Skywalker and Obi-Wan Kenobi*	**4143k**	*Darth Maul*
		4143l	*Chewbacca and Han Solo*
4143e	*Luke Skywalker*	**4143m**	*X-wing Starfighter*
4143f	*Princess Leia & R2-D2*	**4143n**	*Yoda*
4143g	*C-3PO*	**4143o**	*Stormtroopers*

SCOTT NO.	DESCRIPTION	FIRST DAY COVERS SING	FIRST DAY COVERS PL. BLK.	MINT SHEET	PLATE BLOCK	UNUSED F/NH	USED
4143	41¢ Star Wars, self-adhesive, 15 attached	....	....	14.00(15)	....	14.00	....
....	same, set of singles	....	....	....	....	....	12.00

4144

4145

SCOTT NO.	DESCRIPTION	FIRST DAY COVERS SING	FIRST DAY COVERS PL. BLK.	MINT SHEET	PLATE BLOCK	UNUSED F/NH	USED
4144	$4.60 Air Force One, self-adhesive	10.00	30.00	195.00(20)	50.00	10.00	6.50
4145	$16.25 Marine One, self-adhesive	35.00	80.00	650.00(20)	160.00	35.00	18.00

4146 4147 4148 4149 4150

SCOTT NO.	DESCRIPTION	FIRST DAY COVERS SING	FIRST DAY COVERS PL. BLK.	MINT SHEET	PLATE BLOCK	UNUSED F/NH	USED
4146-50	41¢ Pacific Lighthouses, self-adhesive, 5 attached	5.50	8.00	17.50(20)	....	4.75	....
4146	41¢ Diamond Head .	3.50	....	....	....	.95	.35
4147	41¢ Five Finger	3.50	....	....	....	.95	.35
4148	41¢ Grays Harbor . .	3.50	....	....	....	.95	.35
4149	41¢ Umpqua River .	3.50	....	....	....	.95	.35
4150	41¢ St. George Reef	3.50	....	....	....	.95	.35

4151

4152

SCOTT NO.	DESCRIPTION	FIRST DAY COVERS SING	FIRST DAY COVERS PL. BLK.	MINT SHEET	PLATE BLOCK	UNUSED F/NH	USED
4151	41¢ Wedding Hearts, self-adhesive	3.50	....	....	....	.95	.35
4151a	same, bklt pane of 20	....	....	....	....	19.00	....
4152	58¢ Wedding Hearts, self-adhesive	4.00	5.50	28.00(20)	6.00	1.50	.50

4153 4154

4155 4156

SCOTT NO.	DESCRIPTION	FIRST DAY COVERS SING	FIRST DAY COVERS PL. BLK.	MINT SHEET	PLATE BLOCK	UNUSED F/NH	USED
4153-56	41¢ Pollination, self-adhesive, 4 attached	4.50	....	....	....	4.00	....
4153	41¢ Purple Nightshade and Morrison's Bumblebee, type I, straight edge at left .	3.50	....	....	....	.95	.35
4153a	same, type II, straight edge at right	3.50	....	....	....	.95	.35
4154	41¢ Hummingbird Trumpet and Calliope Hummingbird, type I, straight edge at right	3.50	....	....	....	.95	.35
4154a	same, type II, straight edge at left	3.50	....	....	....	.95	.35
4155	41¢ Saguaro and Lesser Long-nosed Bat, type I, straight edge at left .	3.50	....	....	....	.95	.35
4155a	same, type II, straight edge at right	3.50	....	....	....	.95	.35
4156	41¢ Prairie Ironweed and Southern Dogface Butterfly, type I, straight edge at right	3.50	....	....	....	.95	.35
4156a	same, type II, straight edge at left	3.50	....	....	....	.95	.35
4156b	same, blk of 4 (4153-4156)	4.50	....	....	....	4.00	....
4156c	same, blk of 4 (4153a-4156a)	4.50	....	....	....	4.00	....
4156d	same, bklt pane of 20 (4153-4156 x 3, 4153a-4156a x 2)	4.50	....	....	....	19.00	....

4157, 4158

SCOTT NO.	DESCRIPTION	FIRST DAY COVERS SING	FIRST DAY COVERS PL. BLK.	MINT SHEET	PLATE BLOCK	UNUSED F/NH	USED
4157	(10¢) Patriotic Banner, self-adhesive, round corners	....	....	....	....	.30	.20
....	same, pl# strip of 5 .	....	....	....	....	3.00	....
4158	(10¢) Patriotic Banner, self-adhesive, straight corners	....	....	....	....	.30	.20
....	same, pl# strip of 5 .	....	....	....	....	3.00	....

4159

MARVEL COMICS SUPER HEROES

4159a	*Spider-Man*	**4159k**	*Spider-Man Cover*
4159b	*The Incredible Hulk*	**4159l**	*The Incredible Hulk Cover*
4159c	*Sub-Mariner*	**4159m**	*Sub-Mariner Cover*
4159d	*The Thing*	**4159n**	*Fantastic Four Cover*
4159e	*Captain America*	**4159o**	*Captain America Cover*
4159f	*Silver Surfer*	**4159p**	*Silver Surfer Cover*
4159g	*Spider-Woman*	**4159q**	*Spider-Woman Cover*
4159h	*Iron Man*	**4159r**	*Iron Man Cover*
4159i	*Elektra*	**4159s**	*Elektra Cover*
4159j	*Wolverine*	**4159t**	*X-Men Cover*

SCOTT NO.	DESCRIPTION	FIRST DAY COVERS SING	FIRST DAY COVERS PL. BLK.	MINT SHEET	PLATE BLOCK	UNUSED F/NH	USED
4159	41¢ Marvel Comics Super Heroes, self-adhesive, 20 varieties attached	....	17.50(20)	....	17.50	....	
....	same, set of singles	....	....	....	....	....	16.75
....	41¢ Vintage Mahogany Speedboats, self-adhesive, 4 attached	4.50	6.50	17.50(20)	5.00	4.00	....
....	41¢ Purple Heart, self-adhesive	3.50	5.00	17.50(20)	4.75	.95	.35
....	41¢ Louis Comfort Tiffany, self-adhesive	3.50	....	....	....	.95	.35
....	same, bklt pane of 20	....	....	....	....	19.00	....

SEMI-POSTAL

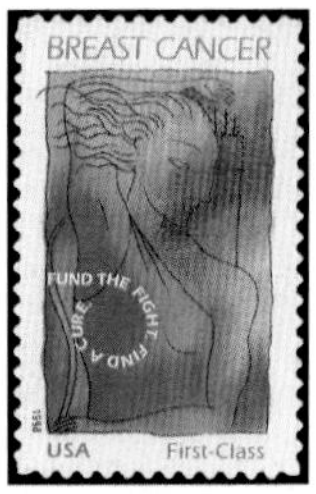

B1

B2

B3

SCOTT NO.	DESCRIPTION	FIRST DAY COVERS SING	FIRST DAY COVERS PL. BLK.	MINT SHEET	PLATE BLOCK	UNUSED F/NH	USED
			1998				
B1	(32¢ + 8¢) Breast Cancer	2.25	5.50	22.50(20)	5.50	1.25	.70
			2002				
B2	(34¢ + 11¢)Heroes of 2001	2.50	5.50	30.00(20)	7.50	1.50	.70
			2003				
B3	(37¢ + 8¢)Stop Family Violence	2.50	5.50	22.50(20)	5.50	1.25	.50

PLATE NUMBER STRIPS OF 5

SCOTT NO.	UNUSED F/NH	SCOTT NO.	UNUSED F/NH
1891	7.50	2451	1.60
1895	6.00	2451b	1.60
1897	.95	2452	3.00
1897A	.85	2452a	3.00
1898	1.20	2452B	3.00
1898A	2.00	2452D	2.50
1899	1.60	2453	2.75
1900	15.00	2454	2.75
1901	19.00	2457	3.25
1902	13.25	2458	5.00
1903	20.00	2463	7.00
1904	50.00	2464	5.50
1905	5.50	2466	9.00
1906	4.00	2468	21.50
1907	5.25	2495Ab	20.00
1908	5.00	2518	5.50
1898Ab	10.00	2523	8.00
1900A	16.50	2523A	6.50
1901A	67.50	2525	8.00
1902A	7.00	2526	8.00
1903A	5.25	2529	5.00
1904A	42.00	2529a	5.00
1905A	5.25	2529c	11.50
1906A	7.00	2598b	10.00
2005	165.00	2599b	10.00
2112	10.00	2602	4.25
2115	5.50	2603	4.50
2115b	6.75	2604	4.50
2123	2.00	2605	5.25
2124	1.80	2606	6.25
2125	2.75	2607	7.50
2126	2.40	2608	8.00
2127	3.50	2609	6.75
2128	2.75	2802b	14.00
2129	5.00	2813b	12.00
2130	3.50	2886b	20.00
2131	3.00	2888	8.00
2132	4.50	2889	16.50
2133	4.75	2890	9.50
2134	3.50	2891	14.00
2135	6.00	2892	12.00
2136	6.50	2893	3.00
2123A	7.00	2902	2.00
2124A	2.50	2902B	2.75
2125A	3.50	2903	2.50
2126A	3.00	2904	2.95
2127A	4.50	2904A	2.75
2127Av	3.25	2904B	2.75
2128A	3.00	2905	3.50
2129A	4.50	2906	3.75
2130A	3.50	2907	6.00
2130Av	3.25	2908	4.00
2132A	4.50	2909	4.00
2132B	35.00	2910	4.00
2133A	4.50	2911	7.50
2149	5.50	2912	7.50
2149A	5.00	2912A	8.75
2150	5.50	2912B	8.75
2150A	5.25	2913	8.00
2225	1.20	2914	9.00
2225a	1.50	2915	20.00
2226	1.10	2915A	10.00
2226a	1.35	2915B	16.50
2228	2.00	2915C	23.00
2228a	16.00	2915D	23.00
2231	13.00	3017a	35.00
2252	1.40	3018	13.50
2252a	1.90	3044	1.00
2253	2.50	3045	1.25
2254	2.50	3053	8.50
2255	3.50	3054	10.00
2256	3.50	3055	8.00
2257	4.50	3132	15.00
2257a	18.00	3133	10.00
2258	7.50	3207	3.00
2259	5.00	3207A	3.00
2260	4.00	3208	7.25
2260a	6.25	3208A	7.25
2261	4.75	3228	4.00
2262	8.00	3229	5.00
2262a	8.00	3263	7.50
2263	5.00	3264	10.00
2263b	12.00	3265	12.50
2264	10.00	3266	13.50
2265	7.50	3270	5.00
2266	6.00	3271	5.00
2279	5.00	3280	9.00
2280	5.00	3281	12.00
2280a	6.00	3282	12.00
2281	6.00	3305A	11.00

AIR POST

C1-C3
Curtiss Jenny Biplane

C4
Airplane Propeller

C5
Badge of Air Service

C6
Airplane

1918 (C1-6 NH + 75%)

SCOTT NO.	DESCRIPTION	UNUSED O.G. VF	F	AVG	USED VF	F	AVG
C1-3	**6¢-24¢, 3 varieties, complete**	**360.00**	**270.00**	**187.50**	**151.00**	**105.00**	**74.75**
C1	6¢ orange	100.00	75.00	52.50	42.00	30.00	21.00
C2	16¢ green	140.00	105.00	72.50	52.00	38.50	25.75
C3	24¢ carmine rose & blue	140.00	105.00	72.50	65.00	42.00	32.00
C3a	same, center inverted	....	140000.00	....	....	....	....

SCOTT NO.		CENTER LINE BLOCKS F/NH	F/OG	A/OG	ARROW BLOCKS F/NH	F/OG	A/OG
C1	6¢ orange	495.00	280.00	225.00	450.00	240.00	190.00
C2	16¢ green	795.00	400.00	325.00	695.00	360.00	285.00
C3	24¢ carmine rose & blue	795.00	400.00	325.00	650.00	350.00	275.00

1923

SCOTT NO.	DESCRIPTION	UNUSED O.G. VF	F	AVG	USED VF	F	AVG
C4-6	**8¢-24¢, 3 varieties, complete**	**320.00**	**237.00**	**160.00**	**98.50**	**69.50**	**47.50**
C4	8¢ dark green	40.00	29.50	20.50	20.50	15.00	10.00
C5	16¢ dark blue	142.00	105.00	71.50	42.00	28.00	19.50
C6	24¢ carmine	155.00	115.00	77.50	41.25	30.50	20.50

C7-C9
Map of U.S. and Airplanes

1926-30 (C7-12 NH + 50%)

SCOTT NO.	DESCRIPTION	UNUSED O.G. VF	F	AVG	USED VF	F	AVG
C7-9	**10¢-20¢, 3 varieties, complete**	**19.95**	**15.25**	**7.60**	**6.95**	**5.00**	**3.45**
C7	10¢ dark blue	4.00	3.05	2.20	.55	.40	.25
C8	15¢ olive brown...	4.75	3.60	2.75	3.50	2.50	1.75
C9	20¢ yellow green (1927)	14.00	9.75	6.50	3.25	2.25	1.65

C10
Lindbergh's Airplane "Spirit of St. Louis"

1927 LINDBERGH TRIBUTE ISSUE

SCOTT NO.	DESCRIPTION	UNUSED O.G. VF	F	AVG	USED VF	F	AVG
C10	10¢ dark blue	10.75	8.25	5.50	2.85	2.20	1.40
C10a	same, bklt pane of 3	125.00	95.00	67.50	....	....	....

C11
Beacon and Rocky Mountains

C12, C16, C17, C19
Winged Globe

1928 BEACON

SCOTT NO.	DESCRIPTION	UNUSED O.G. VF	F	AVG	USED VF	F	AVG
C11	5¢ carmine & blue .	7.00	4.75	3.00	1.00	.65	.35

1930 Flat Plate Printing, Perf.11

SCOTT NO.	DESCRIPTION	UNUSED O.G. VF	F	AVG	USED VF	F	AVG
C12	5¢ violet	15.00	12.00	8.50	.70	.55	.40

C13
Graf Zeppelin

C14

C15

1930 GRAF ZEPPELIN ISSUE (NH + 50%)

SCOTT NO.	DESCRIPTION	UNUSED O.G. VF	F	AVG	USED VF	F	AVG
C13-15	**65¢-$2.60, 3 varieties, complete**	**2350.00**	**1975.00**	**1480.00**	**1825.00**	**1450.00**	**1050.00**
C13	65¢ green	400.00	300.00	260.00	325.00	240.00	175.00
C14	$1.30 brown	850.00	725.00	500.00	650.00	500.00	340.00
C15	$2.60 blue	1300.00	1050.00	800.00	950.00	750.00	575.00

1931-32 Rotary Press Printing. Perf. $10^1/2$ x 11, Designs as #C12 (C16-C24 NH + 40%)

SCOTT NO.	DESCRIPTION	UNUSED O.G. VF	F	AVG	USED VF	F	AVG
C16	5¢ violet	10.00	7.50	5.50	.80	.55	.35
C17	8¢ olive bistre	3.95	3.25	2.15	.55	.40	.30

C18
Graf Zeppelin

1933 CENTURY OF PROGRESS ISSUE

SCOTT NO.	DESCRIPTION	UNUSED O.G. VF	F	AVG	USED VF	F	AVG
C18	50¢ green	125.00	100.00	75.00	100.00	80.00	60.00

1934 DESIGN OF 1930

SCOTT NO.	DESCRIPTION	UNUSED O.G. VF	F	AVG	USED VF	F	AVG
C19	6¢ dull orange	4.50	3.25	2.00	.40	.30	.20

C20-22
China Clipper

1935 TRANS-PACIFIC ISSUE

SCOTT NO.	DESCRIPTION	UNUSED O.G. VF	F	AVG	USED VF	F	AVG
C20	25¢ blue	1.80	1.40	1.05	1.40	1.00	.70

1937. Type of 1935 Issue, Date Omitted

SCOTT NO.	DESCRIPTION	UNUSED O.G. VF	F	AVG	USED VF	F	AVG
C21	20¢ green	13.00	9.75	7.50	2.00	1.65	1.25
C22	50¢ carmine	12.00	10.25	7.75	5.40	4.50	3.50

C23
Eagle

1938

SCOTT NO.	DESCRIPTION	UNUSED O.G. VF	F	AVG	USED VF	F	AVG
C23	6¢ dark blue & carmine	.65	.55	.45	.30	.25	.20

C24
Winged Globe

1939 TRANS-ATLANTIC ISSUE

SCOTT NO.	DESCRIPTION	UNUSED O.G. VF	F	AVG	USED VF	F	AVG
C24	30¢ dull blue	14.00	12.00	10.50	1.70	1.40	1.10

AIR POST PLATE BLOCKS #C1-C24

SCOTT NO.		UNUSED NH VF	F	AVG	UNUSED O.G. VF	F	AVG
C1(6)	6¢ orange	1550.00	1150.00	925.00	1115.00	825.00	550.00
C2(6)	16¢ green	2665.00	1975.00	1575.00	2000.00	1485.00	1100.00
C3(12)	24¢ carmine rose & blue	3100.00	2300.00	1825.00	2450.00	1815.00	1250.00
C4(6)	8¢ dark green ...	610.00	450.00	360.00	445.00	330.00	260.00
C5(6)	16¢ dark blue....	3845.00	2850.00	2250.00	2975.00	2200.00	1650.00
C6(6)	24¢ carmine.....	4790.00	3550.00	2825.00	3700.00	2750.00	2100.00
C7(6)	10¢ dark blue....	71.50	55.00	44.00	54.00	41.50	27.50
C8(6)	15¢ olive brown ..	85.00	66.00	52.75	65.00	50.00	33.00
C9(6)	20¢ yellow green .	200.00	155.00	125.00	145.00	110.00	85.00
C10(6)	10¢ dark blue ...	265.00	205.00	165.00	195.00	150.00	110.00
C11(6)	5¢ carmine & blue	82.00	63.25	50.00	60.00	46.50	31.50
C12(6)	5¢ violet	285.00	220.00	175.00	215.00	165.00	120.00
C13(6)	65¢ green	4500.00	3500.00	2500.00	3100.00	2475.00	1950.00
C14(6)	$1.30 brown.....	12000.00	9500.00	5700.00	8000.00	6750.00	5000.00
C15(6)	$2.60 blue	18500.00	14000.00	11000.00	12000.00	10000.00	8000.00
C16(4)	5¢ violet	175.00	135.00	105.00	125.00	95.00	65.00
C17(4)	8¢ olive bistre ...	58.50	45.00	36.00	40.00	30.00	24.00
C18(4)	5¢ green	1500.00	1150.00	800.00	1050.00	795.00	635.00
C19(4)	6¢ dull orange ...	39.50	33.00	26.00	30.00	25.00	20.00
C20(6)	25¢ blue........	33.00	27.50	22.00	26.50	22.00	17.50
C21(6)	20¢ green	185.00	155.00	122.50	150.00	125.00	100.00
C22(6)	50¢ carmine.....	180.00	150.00	115.00	145.00	120.00	90.00
C23(4)	6¢ dark blue & carmine	14.00	10.50	8.00	9.50	8.00	6.00
C24(6)	30¢ dull blue	250.00	210.00	160.00	200.00	165.00	130.00

C25-C31

1941-44 TRANSPORT ISSUE

SCOTT NO.	DESCRIPTION	FIRST DAY COVERS SING	PL. BLK.	MINT SHEET	PLATE BLOCK	UNUSED F/NH	USED
C25-31	**6¢-50¢, 7 varieties, complete ....**	....	....	....	**127.50**	**23.95**	**5.60**
C25	6¢ Transport Plane ..	7.00	10.00	9.50(50)	1.05	.20	.20
C25a	same, bklt pane of 3 .	30.00		....	....	4.25	....
C26	8¢ Transport Plane ..	6.00	11.25	11.50(50)	2.20	.25	.20
C27	10¢ Transport Plane .	8.00	15.00	82.50(50)	10.50	1.65	.20
C28	15¢ Transport Plane .	8.00	15.00	150.00(50)	13.95	3.50	.40
C29	20¢ Transport Plane .	10.00	20.00	125.00(50)	12.65	2.60	.35
C30	30¢ Transport Plane .	20.00	30.00	140.00(50)	14.00	3.00	.40
C31	50¢ Transport Plane .	28.50	68.75	625.00(50)	80.00	14.00	4.25

C32

1946

SCOTT NO.	DESCRIPTION	FIRST DAY COVERS SING	PL. BLK.	MINT SHEET	PLATE BLOCK	UNUSED F/NH	USED
C32	5¢ DC-4 Skymaster..	2.00	4.25	8.00(50)	.75	.20	.20

C33, C37, C39, C41

C34

C35

C36

1947

SCOTT NO.	DESCRIPTION	FIRST DAY COVERS SING	PL. BLK.	MINT SHEET	PLATE BLOCK	UNUSED F/NH	USED
C33-36	**5¢-25¢, 4 varieties, complete ....**	....	....	....	....	**2.10**	**.70**
C33	5¢ DC-4 Skymaster..	2.00	4.25	17.00(100)	.75	.20	.20
C34	10¢ Pan American Bldg.	2.00	4.25	14.00(50)	1.50	.30	.20
C35	15¢ New York Skyline	2.00	4.25	22.50(50)	1.85	.50	.20
C36	25¢ Plane over Bridge	2.00	5.00	55.00(50)	6.00	1.25	.20

1948
Rotary Press Coil–Perf. 10 Horiz.

SCOTT NO.	DESCRIPTION	FIRST DAY COVERS SING	LINE PR.	MINT SHEET	LINE PR.	UNUSED F/NH	USED
C37	5¢ DC-4 Skymaster. . .	2.00	4.25	....	9.50	1.40	1.00

C38

C40

SCOTT NO.	DESCRIPTION	FIRST DAY COVERS SING	PL. BLK.	MINT SHEET	PLATE BLOCK	UNUSED F/NH	USED
C38	5¢ New York Jubliee .	2.00	4.25	20.00(100)	5.75	.25	.20

1949

SCOTT NO.	DESCRIPTION	FIRST DAY COVERS SING	PL. BLK.	MINT SHEET	PLATE BLOCK	UNUSED F/NH	USED
C39	6¢ DC-4 Skymaster (as #C33)	2.00	4.25	20.00(100)	.75	.25	.20
C39a	same, bklt pane of 6 .	10.00	....	....	....	11.50	....
C40	6¢ Alexandria, Virginia	2.00	4.25	11.00(50)	.95	.25	.20

Rotary Press Coil–Perf. 10 Horiz.

SCOTT NO.	DESCRIPTION	FIRST DAY COVERS SING	LINE PR.	MINT SHEET	LINE PR.	UNUSED F/NH	USED
C41	6¢ DC-4 Skymaster (as#C37)	2.00	4.25	....	15.00	3.50	.20

NOTE: Unused Air Mail coil pairs can be supplied at two times the single price.

C42

C43

C44

1949 U.P.U. ISSUES

SCOTT NO.	DESCRIPTION	FIRST DAY COVERS SING	PL. BLK.	MINT SHEET	PLATE BLOCK	UNUSED F/NH	USED
C42-44	**10¢-25¢, 3 varieties, complete ....**	....	....	....	....	**1.90**	**1.05**
C42	10¢ Post Office	2.00	4.25	17.50(50)	1.70	.40	.30
C43	15¢ Globe & Doves . .	3.00	5.00	25.00(50)	1.50	.60	.35
C44	25¢ Plane & Globe . .	4.00	6.25	42.00(50)	7.25	1.00	.50

C45

C46

C47

1949-58

SCOTT NO.	DESCRIPTION	FIRST DAY COVERS SING	PL. BLK.	MINT SHEET	PLATE BLOCK	UNUSED F/NH	USED
C45-51	**7 varieties, complete**	....	....	....	....	**9.00**	**2.30**
C45	6¢ Wright Brothers (1949)	2.00	4.25	25.00(50)	2.00	.50	.25
C46	80¢ Hawaii (1952) . . .	15.00	35.00	350.00(50)	35.00	8.00	2.00
C47	6¢ Powered Flight (1953)	2.00	4.25	9.25(50)	.75	.25	.20

SCOTT NO.	DESCRIPTION	FIRST DAY COVERS SING	FIRST DAY COVERS PL. BLK.	MINT SHEET	PLATE BLOCK	UNUSED F/NH	USED

C48, C50

1949-58 (continued)

SCOTT NO.	DESCRIPTION	FDC SING	FDC PL. BLK.	MINT SHEET	PLATE BLOCK	UNUSED F/NH	USED
C48	4¢ Eagle (1954) . . .	2.00	4.25	16.50(100)	1.95	.25	.15

C49

C51, C52, C60, C61

SCOTT NO.	DESCRIPTION	FDC SING	FDC PL. BLK.	MINT SHEET	PLATE BLOCK	UNUSED F/NH	USED
C49	6¢ Air Force (1957) .	2.00	4.25	10.00(50)	.75	.25	.20
C50	5¢ Eagle (1958) . . .	2.00	4.25	19.50(100)	1.85	.25	.20
C51	7¢ Silhouette of Jet, blue (1958)	2.00	4.25	19.50(100)	1.00	.25	.20
C51a	same, bklt pane of 6	8.00	....	....	....	12.00	....

Rotary Press Coil–Perf. 10 Horiz.

SCOTT NO.	DESCRIPTION	FDC SING	LINE PR.	MINT SHEET	LINE PR.	UNUSED F/NH	USED
C52	7¢ Silhouette of Jet, blue	2.00	3.25	....	20.00	2.50	.20

C53

C54

1959

SCOTT NO.	DESCRIPTION	FDC SING	FDC PL. BLK.	MINT SHEET	PLATE BLOCK	UNUSED F/NH	USED
C53-56	**4 varieties, complete**	....	....	....	....	**1.50**	**.85**
C53	7¢ Alaska Statehood .	2.00	4.25	14.00(50)	1.25	.30	.20
C54	7¢ Balloon Jupiter . . .	2.00	4.25	20.00(50)	1.60	.45	.20

C55

C56

SCOTT NO.	DESCRIPTION	FDC SING	FDC PL. BLK.	MINT SHEET	PLATE BLOCK	UNUSED F/NH	USED
C55	7¢ Hawaii Statehood	2.00	4.25	14.00(50)	1.25	.30	.20
C56	10¢ Pan-Am Games	2.00	4.25	25.00(50)	2.75	.55	.30

C57

C58, C63

C59

C62

1959-66 REGULAR ISSUES

SCOTT NO.	DESCRIPTION	FDC SING	FDC PL. BLK.	MINT SHEET	PLATE BLOCK	UNUSED F/NH	USED
C57/63	**(C57-60, C62-63) 6 varieties........**		....	....	....	**3.90**	**1.90**

1959-66

SCOTT NO.	DESCRIPTION	FDC SING	FDC PL. BLK.	MINT SHEET	PLATE BLOCK	UNUSED F/NH	USED
C57	10¢ Liberty Bell (1960)	2.00	4.25	85.00(50)	8.00	1.75	1.00
C58	15¢ Statue of Liberty .	2.00	4.25	22.50(50)	1.95	.45	.25
C59	25¢ Abraham Lincoln (1960)	2.00	4.25	40.00(50)	4.00	.90	.20

1960. Design of 1958

SCOTT NO.	DESCRIPTION	FDC SING	FDC PL. BLK.	MINT SHEET	PLATE BLOCK	UNUSED F/NH	USED
C60	7¢ Jet Plane, carmine	2.00	4.25	22.50(100)	1.25	.30	.20
C60a	same, bklt pane of 6 .	9.00	....	....	....	15.00	....

Rotary Press Coil–Perf. 10 Horiz.

SCOTT NO.	DESCRIPTION	FDC SING	LINE PR.	MINT SHEET	LINE PR.	UNUSED F/NH	USED
C61	7¢ Jet Plane, carmine	2.00	3.25		45.00	5.00	.35

1961-67

SCOTT NO.	DESCRIPTION	FDC SING	FDC PL. BLK.	MINT SHEET	PLATE BLOCK	UNUSED F/NH	USED
C62	13¢ Liberty Bell	2.00	4.25	21.50(50)	2.10	.45	.20
C63	15¢ Statue re-drawn .	2.00	4.25	27.50(50)	2.60	.60	.20

C64, C65

1962-64

SCOTT NO.	DESCRIPTION	FDC SING	FDC PL. BLK.	MINT SHEET	PLATE BLOCK	UNUSED F/NH	USED
C64/69	**(C64, C66-69) 5 varieties**	....	....	....	....	**2.00**	**1.25**

1962

SCOTT NO.	DESCRIPTION	FDC SING	FDC PL. BLK.	MINT SHEET	PLATE BLOCK	UNUSED F/NH	USED
C64	8¢ Plane & Capitol . .	2.00	4.25	23.00(100)	1.20	.25	.15
C64b	same, bklt pane of 5, Slogan I	1.95	....	....	....	6.25	....
C64b	bklt pane of 5, Slogan II, (1963)	....	....	....	....	75.00	....
C64b	bklt pane of 5, Slogan III (1964)	....	....	....	....	13.00	....
C64c	bklt pane of 5 tagged, Slogan III (1964)	....	....	....	....	1.85	....

SLOGAN I–Your Mailman Deserves Your Help... **SLOGAN II–Use Zone Numbers..**

SLOGAN III–Always Use Zip Code....

Rotary Press Coil–Perf. 10 Horiz.

SCOTT NO.	DESCRIPTION	FDC SING	LINE PR.	MINT SHEET	LINE PR.	UNUSED F/NH	USED
C65	8¢ Plane & Capitol . .	2.00	3.25	....	5.75	.45	.20

C66

C67

C68

1963

SCOTT NO.	DESCRIPTION	FDC SING	FDC PL. BLK.	MINT SHEET	PLATE BLOCK	UNUSED F/NH	USED
C66	15¢ Montgomery Blair	2.00	4.25	33.50(50)	4.00	.75	.60
C67	6¢ Bald Eagle	2.00	4.25	16.50(100)	2.25	.20	.15
C68	8¢ Amelia Earhart . . .	2.00	4.25	18.50(50)	1.80	.40	.20

C69

1964

SCOTT NO.	DESCRIPTION	FDC SING	FDC PL. BLK.	MINT SHEET	PLATE BLOCK	UNUSED F/NH	USED
C69	8¢ Dr. Robert H. Goddard	2.00	5.00	23.75(50)	2.25	.50	.20

C70

C71

C72, C73

1967-69

SCOTT NO.	DESCRIPTION	FIRST DAY COVERS SING	FIRST DAY COVERS PL. BLK.	MINT SHEET	PLATE BLOCK	UNUSED F/NH	USED
C70/76	**(C70-72, C74-76) 6 varieties........**		**........**	**........**	**........**	**2.95**	**1.00**

1967-68

SCOTT NO.	DESCRIPTION	FIRST DAY COVERS SING	FIRST DAY COVERS PL. BLK.	MINT SHEET	PLATE BLOCK	UNUSED F/NH	USED
C70	8¢ Alaska Purchase .	2.00	4.25	16.50(50)	1.95	.35	.20
C71	20¢ "Columbia Jays" .	2.00	4.25	48.00(50)	4.50	1.00	.20
C72	10¢ 50-Stars (1968) .	2.00	4.25	32.50(100)	1.75	.40	.15
C72b	same, bklt pane of 8 .	3.00	....	....	....	2.50	....
C72c	same, bklt pane of 5, Slogan IV or V	140.00	....	....	....	4.00	....

SLOGAN IV–Mail Early in the Day... **SLOGAN V–Use Zip Code...**

1968 Rotary Press Coil–Perf. 10 Vert.

SCOTT NO.	DESCRIPTION	FIRST DAY COVERS SING	LINE PR.	MINT SHEET	LINE PR.	UNUSED F/NH	USED
C73	10¢ 50-Star	2.00	3.25	....	2.25	.35	.20

C74

C75

SCOTT NO.	DESCRIPTION	FIRST DAY COVERS SING	FIRST DAY COVERS PL. BLK.	MINT SHEET	PLATE BLOCK	UNUSED F/NH	USED
C74	10¢ Air Mail Anniversary	2.00	4.25	15.00(50)	3.10	.30	.20
C75	20¢ "USA" & Plane . .	2.00	4.25	28.00(50)	2.50	.55	.20

C76

1969

SCOTT NO.	DESCRIPTION	FIRST DAY COVERS SING	FIRST DAY COVERS PL. BLK.	MINT SHEET	PLATE BLOCK	UNUSED F/NH	USED
C76	10¢ Man on the Moon	6.00	14.50	15.00(32)	2.25	.50	.20

C77

C78, C82

C79, C83

1971-73

SCOTT NO.	DESCRIPTION	FIRST DAY COVERS SING	FIRST DAY COVERS PL. BLK.	MINT SHEET	PLATE BLOCK	UNUSED F/NH	USED
C77-81	**9¢-21¢, 5 varieties, complete . . . .**	**........**	**........**	**........**	**........**	**1.95**	**.80**
C77	9¢ Delta Winged Plane	2.00	4.25	25.00(100)	1.30	.30	.25
C78	11¢ Silhouette of Plane	2.00	4.25	35.00(100)	1.60	.40	.15
C78b	same, precanceled . .	....	....	....	....	....	.50
C78a	11¢ bklt pane of 4 . . .	2.25	....	....	....	1.20	....
C79	13¢ Letter (1973) . . .	2.00	4.25	35.00(100)	1.60	.40	.15
C79b	same, precanceled . .	....	....	....	....	....	.60
C79a	13¢ bklt pane of 5 . . .	2.25	....	....	....	1.50	....

C80

SCOTT NO.	DESCRIPTION	FIRST DAY COVERS SING	FIRST DAY COVERS PL. BLK.	MINT SHEET	PLATE BLOCK	UNUSED F/NH	USED
C80	17¢ Liberty Head . . .	2.00	4.25	22.50(50)	2.25	.50	.20
C81	21¢ "USA" & Plane . .	2.00	4.25	27.00(50)	2.25	.50	.20

Rotary Press Coils–Perf. 10 Vert.

SCOTT NO.	DESCRIPTION	FIRST DAY COVERS SING	LINE PR.	MINT SHEET	LINE PR.	UNUSED F/NH	USED
C82	11¢ Silhouette of Jet .	2.00	3.25	....	.90	.30	.15
C83	13¢ Letter	2.00	3.25	....	1.15	.35	.15

C84

C85

1972-76

SCOTT NO.	DESCRIPTION	FIRST DAY COVERS SING	FIRST DAY COVERS PL. BLK.	MINT SHEET	PLATE BLOCK	UNUSED F/NH	USED
C84-90	**11¢-31¢, 7 varieties, complete . . . .**	**........**	**........**	**........**	**........**	**4.40**	**1.50**

1972

SCOTT NO.	DESCRIPTION	FIRST DAY COVERS SING	FIRST DAY COVERS PL. BLK.	MINT SHEET	PLATE BLOCK	UNUSED F/NH	USED
C84	11¢ City of Refuge . .	2.00	4.25	18.50(50)	1.50	.40	.20
C85	11¢ Olympics	2.00	4.25	18.50(50)	3.10(10)	.40	.20

C86

1973

SCOTT NO.	DESCRIPTION	FIRST DAY COVERS SING	FIRST DAY COVERS PL. BLK.	MINT SHEET	PLATE BLOCK	UNUSED F/NH	USED
C86	11¢ Electronics	2.00	4.25	26.50(50)	2.50	.55	.20

C87

C88

1974

SCOTT NO.	DESCRIPTION	FIRST DAY COVERS SING	FIRST DAY COVERS PL. BLK.	MINT SHEET	PLATE BLOCK	UNUSED F/NH	USED
C87	18¢ Statue of Liberty .	2.00	4.25	27.50(50)	2.50	.60	.40
C88	26¢ Mt. Rushmore . .	2.00	4.25	55.00(50)	5.00	1.25	.20

C89

C90

1976

SCOTT NO.	DESCRIPTION	FIRST DAY COVERS SING	FIRST DAY COVERS PL. BLK.	MINT SHEET	PLATE BLOCK	UNUSED F/NH	USED
C89	25¢ Plane & Globes .	2.00	4.25	35.0050)	3.50	.80	.20
C90	31¢ Plane, Flag & Globes	2.00	4.25	45.00(50)	4.25	1.00	.20

C91

C92

1978-80

SCOTT NO.	DESCRIPTION	FIRST DAY COVERS SING	FIRST DAY COVERS PL. BLK.	MINT SHEET	PLATE BLOCK	UNUSED F/NH	USED
C91-100	**21¢-40¢, 10 varieties, complete**	....	....	....	....	**11.50**	**4.85**
C91-92	Wright Brothers, 2 varieties, attached .	2.40	5.00	95.00(100)	5.00	2.10	1.75
C91	31¢ Wright Brothers & Plane	2.00	....	....	....	1.00	.50
C92	31¢ Wright Brothers & Shed	2.00	....	....	....	1.00	.50

C93

C94

1979

SCOTT NO.	DESCRIPTION	FIRST DAY COVERS SING	FIRST DAY COVERS PL. BLK.	MINT SHEET	PLATE BLOCK	UNUSED F/NH	USED
C93-94	Octave Chanute, 2 varieties, attached .	2.40	5.00	95.00(100)	5.00	2.10	1.75
C93	21¢ Chanute & Plane	2.00	....	....	....	1.00	.50
C94	21¢ Chanute & 2 Planes	2.00	....	....	....	1.00	.50

C95

C96

SCOTT NO.	DESCRIPTION	FIRST DAY COVERS SING	FIRST DAY COVERS PL. BLK.	MINT SHEET	PLATE BLOCK	UNUSED F/NH	USED
C95-96	Wiley Post, 2 varieties, attached .	2.40	5.00	165.00(100)	13.50	3.50	2.75
C95	25¢ Post & Plane . . .	2.00	....	....	....	1.80	1.00
C96	25¢ Plane & Post . . .	2.00	....	....	....	1.80	1.00

C97

SCOTT NO.	DESCRIPTION	FIRST DAY COVERS SING	FIRST DAY COVERS PL. BLK.	MINT SHEET	PLATE BLOCK	UNUSED F/NH	USED
C97	31¢ High Jumper . .	2.00	4.25	44.00(50)	12.00(12)	.95	.40

C98

C99

1980

SCOTT NO.	DESCRIPTION	FIRST DAY COVERS SING	FIRST DAY COVERS PL. BLK.	MINT SHEET	PLATE BLOCK	UNUSED F/NH	USED
C98	40¢ Philip Mazzei . .	2.00	4.25	65.00(50)	15.00(12)	1.40	.25
C99	28¢ Blanche S. Scott	2.00	4.25	42.50(50)	12.50(12)	.90	.25

C100

SCOTT NO.	DESCRIPTION	FIRST DAY COVERS SING	FIRST DAY COVERS PL. BLK.	MINT SHEET	PLATE BLOCK	UNUSED F/NH	USED
C100	35¢ Glenn Curtiss . .	2.00	4.25	45.00(50)	13.00(12)	1.10	.25

C101 C102

C103 C104

1983-85

SCOTT NO.	DESCRIPTION	FIRST DAY COVERS SING	FIRST DAY COVERS PL. BLK.	MINT SHEET	PLATE BLOCK	UNUSED F/NH	USED
C101-16	**28¢-44¢, 16 varieties, complete**	....	....	....	....	**21.50**	**7.50**

1983

SCOTT NO.	DESCRIPTION	FIRST DAY COVERS SING	FIRST DAY COVERS PL. BLK.	MINT SHEET	PLATE BLOCK	UNUSED F/NH	USED
C101-04	Summer Olympics, 4 varieties, attached .	3.50	4.50	64.00(50)	6.50	5.75	4.00
C101	28¢ Women's Gymnastics	2.00	....	....	....	1.50	.50
C102	28¢ Hurdles.	2.00	....	....	....	1.50	.50
C103	28¢ Women's Basketball	2.00	....	....	....	1.50	.50
C104	28¢ Soccer	2.00	....	....	....	1.50	.50

C105 C106

C107 C108

SCOTT NO.	DESCRIPTION	FIRST DAY COVERS SING	FIRST DAY COVERS PL. BLK.	MINT SHEET	PLATE BLOCK	UNUSED F/NH	USED
C105-08	Summer Olympics, 4 varieties, attached	4.50	5.75	60.00(50)	6.75	6.00	4.00
C105	40¢ Shot Put	2.00	....	....	....	1.55	.50
C106	40¢ Men's Gymnastics	2.00	....	....	....	1.55	.50
C107	40¢ Women's Swimming	2.00	....	....	....	1.55	.50
C108	40¢ Weight Lifting . .	2.00	....	....	....	1.55	.50

C109 C110

C111 C112

SCOTT NO.	DESCRIPTION	FIRST DAY COVERS SING	FIRST DAY COVERS PL. BLK.	MINT SHEET	PLATE BLOCK	UNUSED F/NH	USED
C109-12	Summer Olympics, 4 varieties, attached	4.00	5.00	68.00(50)	9.50	6.00	4.00
C109	35¢ Fencing	2.00	....	....	....	1.55	.60
C110	35¢ Cycling	2.00	....	....	....	1.55	.60
C111	35¢ Volleyball	2.00	....	....	....	1.55	.60
C112	35¢ Pole Vault	2.00	....	....	....	1.55	.60

C113

C114

C115

C116

1985

SCOTT NO.	DESCRIPTION	FIRST DAY COVERS SING	PL. BLK.	MINT SHEET	PLATE BLOCK	UNUSED F/NH	USED
C113	33¢ Alfred Verville . .	2.00	4.25	42.00(50)	4.75	1.00	.25
C114	39¢ Lawrence and Elmer Sperry	2.00	4.25	57.50(50)	5.25	1.20	.35
C115	44¢ Transpacific . . .	2.00	4.25	60.00(50)	6.00	1.25	.35
C116	44¢ Junipero Serra .	2.00	4.25	70.00(50)	9.50	1.50	.60

C117

C118

C119

1988

SCOTT NO.	DESCRIPTION	FIRST DAY COVERS SING	PL. BLK.	MINT SHEET	PLATE BLOCK	UNUSED F/NH	USED
C117	44¢ New Sweden . .	2.50	7.50	75.00(50)	10.00	1.60	.90
C118	45¢ Samuel Langley	2.00	4.25	67.50(50)	6.50	1.50	.30
C119	36¢ Igor Sikorsky . .	2.00	4.25	55.00(50)	5.25	1.25	.40

C120

C121

1989

SCOTT NO.	DESCRIPTION	FIRST DAY COVERS SING	PL. BLK.	MINT SHEET	PLATE BLOCK	UNUSED F/NH	USED
C120-25	**6 varieties, complete**	....	....	....	....	**9.00**	**3.00**
C120	45¢ French Revolution	2.00	4.25	37.50(30)	5.50	1.20	.75
C121	45¢ Americas Issue (Key Marco Cat)	2.00	4.25	87.50(50)	8.00	1.85	.45

C122

C123

C124

C125

SCOTT NO.	DESCRIPTION	FIRST DAY COVERS SING	PL. BLK.	MINT SHEET	PLATE BLOCK	UNUSED F/NH	USED
C122-25	Futuristic Mail Delivery, 4 varieties, attached	8.00	10.00	65.00(40)	7.00	6.50	5.00
C122	45¢ Spacecraft	2.00	....	....	....	1.70	.60
C123	45¢ Air Suspended Hover	2.00	....	....	....	1.70	.60
C124	45¢ Moon Rover . . .	2.00	....	....	....	1.70	.60
C125	45¢ Space Shuttle .	2.00	....	....	....	1.70	.60
C126	$1.80 Futuristic Mail Imperf. Souvenir Sheet	6.50	....	....	....	6.50	....

C127

C128

1990-99

SCOTT NO.	DESCRIPTION	FIRST DAY COVERS SING	PL. BLK.	MINT SHEET	PLATE BLOCK	UNUSED F/NH	USED
C127	45¢ Americas Issue (Island Beach)	2.00	4.25	85.00(50)	9.00	1.75	.40
C128	50¢ Harriet Quimby .	2.00	4.25	72.50(50)	7.50	1.60	.50
C128b	50¢ Harriet Quimby, reissue, bullseye perf. (1993)	....	....	85.00(50)	8.50	1.75	.50

C129, C132

C130

SCOTT NO.	DESCRIPTION	FIRST DAY COVERS SING	PL. BLK.	MINT SHEET	PLATE BLOCK	UNUSED F/NH	USED
C129	40¢ William Piper . .	2.00	4.25	65.00(50)	6.25	1.35	.50
C130	50¢ Antarctic Treaty	2.00	4.25	70.00(50)	7.00	1.50	.70

C131

C133

SCOTT NO.	DESCRIPTION	FIRST DAY COVERS SING	PL. BLK.	MINT SHEET	PLATE BLOCK	UNUSED F/NH	USED
C131	50¢ America (Bering Strait) (1991)	2.00	4.25	85.00(50)	8.00	1.75	.65
C132	40¢ William Piper, reissue, bullseye perf. (1993)	....	....	375.00(50)	65.00	6.00	1.00
C133	48¢ Niagara Falls . .	2.25	5.50	25.00(20)	7.50	1.20	.40

C134

C135

SCOTT NO.	DESCRIPTION	FIRST DAY COVERS SING	PL. BLK.	MINT SHEET	PLATE BLOCK	UNUSED F/NH	USED
C134	40¢ Rio Grande	2.10	5.00	20.00(20)	5.00	1.10	.50

2000-06

SCOTT NO.	DESCRIPTION	FIRST DAY COVERS SING	PL. BLK.	MINT SHEET	PLATE BLOCK	UNUSED F/NH	USED
C135	60¢ Grand Canyon .	2.25	5.00	30.00(20)	8.00	1.65	.40
C136	70¢ Nine-Mile Prairie, Nebraska	2.50	6.00	37.50(20)	8.50	1.95	.60

C137

C138, C138a, C138b

C139

C142

SCOTT NO.	DESCRIPTION	FIRST DAY COVERS SING	PL. BLK.	MINT SHEET	PLATE BLOCK	UNUSED F/NH	USED
C137	80¢ Mt. McKinley . .	2.75	6.50	37.50(20)	9.00	1.95	.70
C138	60¢ Acadia National Park	2.50	5.00	28.00(20)	7.00	1.50	.50
C138a	60¢ Acadia National Park die cut 11.5 x 11.75 .	2.75	5.50	40.00(20)	9.00	2.00	.50
C138b	same as above, with "2005" date	2.75	5.50	28.00(20)	7.00	1.50	.50
C139	63¢ Bryce Canyon National Park, self adhesive .	2.25	6.00	28.00(20)	6.00	1.40	.40
C140	75¢ Great Smoky Mountains National Park, self-adhesive	2.25	6.00	33.00(20)	7.00	1.65	.50
C141	84¢ Yosemite National Park, self-adhesive	2.50	6.50	38.00(20)	8.00	1.90	.50
C142	69¢ Okefenokee Swamp, self-adhesive	2.50	6.00	30.00(20)	6.00	1.50	.50
C143	90¢ Hagatna Bay Self-adhesive	2.75	6.50	45.00(20)	9.00	2.25	.70

AIR MAIL SPECIAL DELIVERY STAMPS

771, CE1, CE2

SCOTT NO.	DESCRIPTION	PLATE BLOCK F/NH	PLATE BLOCK F	PLATE BLOCK AVG	UNUSED F/NH	UNUSED F	UNUSED AVG	USED F	USED AVG
CE1	16¢ dark blue (1934)	30.00	18.00	14.50	.80	.70	.55	.70	.55
CE2	16¢ red & blue (1936)	8.00	6.00	4.50	.45	.40	.30	.25	.20
CE2	same, center line block	2.75	2.15	1.75	....	....	....	....	....
CE2	same, arrow block of 4	2.50	1.95	1.50	....	....	....	....	....

SPECIAL DELIVERY STAMPS

E1

E2, E3

E4, E5

(E1-E14 for VF Centering–Fine Price + 35%)

SCOTT NO.	DESCRIPTION	UNUSED NH F	UNUSED NH AVG	UNUSED OG F	UNUSED OG AVG	USED F	USED AVG
	1885 Inscribed "Secures Immediate Delivery at Special Delivery Office" Perf. 12						
E1	10¢ blue.........	750.00	450.00	340.00	220.00	45.00	30.00
	1888 Inscribed "Secures Immediate Delivery at any Post Office"						
E2	10¢ blue.........	550.00	350.00	260.00	170.00	17.50	12.00
	1893						
E3	10¢ orange	420.00	270.00	175.00	125.00	30.00	17.00
	1894 Same type as preceding issue, but with line under "Ten Cents" Unwatermarked						
E4	10¢ blue.........	1300.00	850.00	595.00	400.00	40.00	24.00
	1895 Double Line Watermark						
E5	10¢ blue.........	300.00	195.00	140.00	95.00	5.50	3.25

E6, E8-11

E7

SCOTT NO.	DESCRIPTION	UNUSED NH F	UNUSED NH AVG	UNUSED OG F	UNUSED OG AVG	USED F	USED AVG
	1902						
E6	10¢ ultramarine ...	400.00	250.00	175.00	110.00	6.00	4.00
	1908						
E7	10¢ green	170.00	120.00	80.00	55.00	31.50	22.00
	1911 Single Line Watermark						
E8	10¢ ultramarine ...	275.00	160.00	125.00	75.00	8.00	6.00
	1914 Perf. 10						
E9	10¢ ultramarine ...	500.00	300.00	200.00	130.00	8.00	6.00
	1916 Unwatermarked Perf. 10						
E10	10¢ pale ultra.....	775.00	500.00	350.00	220.00	30.00	22.00
	1917 Perf. 11						
E11	10¢ ultramarine ...	55.00	40.00	30.00	20.00	.65	.50
E11	same, plate block of 6	400.00	300.00	270.00	160.00	....	....

E12, E15

E14, E19

1922-25 Flat Plate Printing Perf. 11

SCOTT NO.	DESCRIPTION	PLATE BLOCK F/NH	PLATE BLOCK F	PLATE BLOCK AVG	UNUSED F/NH	UNUSED F	UNUSED AVG	USED F	USED AVG
E12	10¢ gray violet	(6) 700.00	500.00	400.00	75.00	50.00	30.00	.50	.40
E13	15¢ deep orange (1925)	(6) 550.00	420.00	300.00	60.00	40.00	35.00	1.25	.85
E14	20¢ black (1925)	(6) 70.00	50.00	30.00	4.75	2.75	1.90	1.40	1.00

1927-51 Rotary Press Printing Perf. 11 x 10½

SCOTT NO.	DESCRIPTION	FIRST DAY COVERS SING	FIRST DAY COVERS PL. BLK.	MINT SHEET	PLATE BLOCK	UNUSED F/NH	USED
E15-19	**10¢-20¢, 5 varieties**	....	....	....	**50.00**	**8.50**	**2.60**
E15	10¢ gray violet.....	....	....	45.00(50)	6.75	1.10	.20
E16	15¢ orange (1931) .	....	....	50.00(50)	6.50	1.25	.20
E17	13¢ blue (1944)....	9.00	20.00	42.50(50)	5.00	.95	.20
E18	17¢ orange yellow (1944)	12.00	28.00	175.00(50)	28.00	4.00	2.25
E19	20¢ black (1951) ...	5.00	12.50	97.50(50)	12.00	1.95	.20

E20

E22

SCOTT NO.	DESCRIPTION	FIRST DAY COVERS SING	FIRST DAY COVERS PL. BLK.	MINT SHEET	PLATE BLOCK	UNUSED F/NH	USED
	1954-57						
E20	20¢ deep blue	2.50	6.25	28.00(50)	3.00	.60	.20
E21	30¢ lake (1957)....	2.50	6.25	37.50(50)	4.00	.80	.20
	1969-71						
E22	45¢ carmine & violet blue	2.50	6.25	67.50(50)	7.25	1.40	.35
E23	60¢ violet blue & carmine (1971)	2.75	6.75	67.50(50)	7.00	1.40	.20

REGISTRATION STAMP

F1

1911 Registration

SCOTT NO.	DESCRIPTION	UNUSED NH F	UNUSED NH AVG	UNUSED OG F	UNUSED OG AVG	USED F	USED AVG
F1	10¢ ultramarine ...	125.00	80.00	62.50	40.00	6.50	4.50

U.S. CERTIFIED STAMP

FA1

1955 Certified Mail

SCOTT NO.	DESCRIPTION	FIRST DAY COVERS SING	FIRST DAY COVERS PL. BLK.	MINT SHEET	PLATE BLOCK	UNUSED F/NH	USED
FA1	15¢ red	2.50	6.25	22.50(50)	5.00	.50	.40

J1-J28

J29-J68

SCOTT NO.	DESCRIPTION	UNUSED NH F	UNUSED NH AVG	UNUSED OG F	UNUSED OG AVG	USED F	USED AVG
	1879 Unwatermarked Perf. 12						
J1	1¢ brown	130.00	80.00	55.00	33.00	17.00	11.00
J2	2¢ brown	700.00	400.00	350.00	210.00	14.00	9.00
J3	3¢ brown	95.00	60.00	45.00	27.50	5.00	3.00
J4	5¢ brown	1350.00	800.00	700.00	420.00	38.00	22.00
J5	10¢ brown	1475.00	900.00	775.00	465.00	40.00	25.00
J6	30¢ brown	575.00	350.00	300.00	180.00	70.00	55.00
J7	50¢ brown	925.00	550.00	475.00	285.00	62.50	44.00
	1884-89						
J15	1¢ red brown	105.00	65.00	55.00	33.00	6.00	4.50
J16	2¢ red brown	125.00	75.00	65.00	39.00	4.00	2.25
J17	3¢ red brown	1675.00	1000.00	875.00	525.00	175.00	110.00
J18	5¢ red brown	925.00	550.00	475.00	285.00	27.00	18.00
J19	10¢ red brown	875.00	525.00	450.00	270.00	20.00	12.00
J20	30¢ red brown	325.00	195.00	165.00	99.00	50.00	30.00
J21	50¢ red brown	3000.00	1800.00	1575.00	945.00	210.00	125.00
	1891						
J22	1¢ bright claret....	55.00	35.00	28.00	17.00	1.25	.65
J23	2¢ bright claret....	58.00	35.00	30.00	18.00	1.10	.55
J24	3¢ bright claret....	120.00	75.00	62.50	37.50	12.00	5.50
J25	5¢ bright claret....	155.00	95.00	80.00	48.00	14.00	7.50
J26	10¢ bright claret...	270.00	160.00	140.00	84.00	15.00	9.00
J27	30¢ bright claret...	905.00	545.00	475.00	285.00	150.00	95.00
J28	50¢ bright claret...	905.00	545.00	475.00	285.00	150.00	95.00
	1894 Unwatermarked Perf. 12 (†)						
J29	1¢ pale vermillion .	3135.00	1895.00	1650.00	990.00	400.00	250.00
J30	2¢ dark vermillion .	1235.00	760.00	650.00	400.00	150.00	115.00
J31	1¢ deep claret	95.00	60.00	50.00	30.00	12.00	9.00
J32	2¢ deep claret	75.00	50.00	40.00	24.00	9.00	6.75
J33	3¢ deep claret	335.00	210.00	175.00	110.00	40.00	28.00
J34	5¢ deep claret	525.00	325.00	275.00	170.00	47.50	35.00
J35	10¢ deep claret ...	525.00	325.00	275.00	170.00	31.00	25.00
J36	30¢ deep claret ...	810.00	495.00	425.00	260.00	125.00	75.00
J36b	30¢ pale rose.....	725.00	500.00	350.00	225.00	125.00	75.00
J37	50¢ deep claret ...	2755.00	1710.00	1450.00	900.00	395.00	225.00
	1895 Double Line Watermark Perf. 12 (†)						
J38	1¢ deep claret	20.00	12.50	10.50	6.50	1.00	.75
J39	2¢ deep claret	20.00	13.50	11.00	7.00	.60	.45
J40	3¢ deep claret	125.00	75.00	65.00	39.00	2.75	2.00
J41	5¢ deep claret	135.00	80.00	70.00	42.00	2.25	1.50
J42	10¢ deep claret ...	135.00	80.00	70.00	42.00	5.00	4.00
J43	30¢ deep claret ...	950.00	565.00	495.00	297.00	45.00	35.00
J44	50¢ deep claret ...	725.00	430.00	375.00	225.00	47.50	38.00
	1910-12 Single Line Watermark Perf. 12						
J45	1¢ deep claret	55.00	35.00	30.00	20.00	5.00	3.75
J46	2¢ deep claret	55.00	35.00	30.00	20.00	1.25	1.00
J47	3¢ deep claret	875.00	650.00	495.00	325.00	30.00	18.00
J48	5¢ deep claret	170.00	115.00	90.00	60.00	7.00	4.50
J49	10¢ deep claret ...	200.00	125.00	105.00	65.00	12.50	8.50
J50	50¢ deep claret (1912)	1700.00	1025.00	900.00	550.00	115.00	82.50
	1914 Single Line Watermark Perf. 10						
J52	1¢ carmine lake ...	110.00	67.00	58.00	35.00	10.00	7.00
J53	2¢ carmine lake ...	76.00	47.50	40.00	25.00	.75	.60
J54	3¢ carmine lake ...	1575.00	1000.00	835.00	525.00	40.00	28.00
J55	5¢ carmine lake ...	75.00	45.00	37.50	22.50	5.00	3.50
J56	10¢ carmine lake ..	100.00	60.00	53.00	31.80	2.50	1.50
J57	30¢ carmine lake ..	370.00	225.00	195.00	117.00	27.00	22.00
J58	50¢ carmine lake ..	....	....	14000.00	8500.00	850.00	600.00
	1916 Unwatermarked Perf. 10						
J59	1¢ rose	7000.00	4000.00	3750.00	2250.00	400.00	250.00
J60	2¢ rose	360.00	220.00	180.00	110.00	40.00	28.00

SCOTT NO.	DESCRIPTION	PLATE BLOCK (OG) F/NH	PLATE BLOCK (OG) F	PLATE BLOCK (OG) AVG	UNUSED (OG) F/NH	UNUSED (OG) F	UNUSED (OG) AVG	USED F	USED AVG
	1917 Unwatermarked Perf. 11								
J61	1¢ carmine rose. (6)	85.00	53.00	35.00	7.00	5.00	3.00	.30	.20
J62	2¢ carmine rose. (6)	85.00	53.00	35.00	7.00	5.00	3.00	.30	.20
J63	3¢ carmine rose. (6)	160.00	95.00	70.00	20.00	10.50	6.30	.45	.20
J64	5¢ carmine..... (6)	160.00	95.00	70.00	20.00	10.50	6.30	.30	.20
J65	10¢ carmine rose (6)	225.00	140.00	125.00	31.00	16.00	9.60	.50	.35
J66	30¢ carmine rose	....	....	....	155.00	82.50	49.50	1.50	1.00
J67	50¢ carmine rose	....	....	....	210.00	110.00	66.00	.45	.35
	1925								
J68	1/2¢ dull red.... (6)	20.00	15.00	12.50	2.00	1.25	1.00	.30	.20

J69-J76, J79-J86

J77, J78, J87

J88-J104

SCOTT NO.	DESCRIPTION	PLATE BLOCK (OG) F/NH	PLATE BLOCK (OG) F	PLATE BLOCK (OG) AVG	UNUSED (OG) F/NH	UNUSED (OG) F	UNUSED (OG) AVG	USED F	USED AVG
	1930 Perf. 11								
J69	1/2¢ carmine ... (6)	70.00	50.00	40.00	9.00	6.00	5.00	2.00	1.50
J70	1¢ carmine..... (6)	40.00	32.00	27.00	5.25	2.75	1.75	.30	.20
J71	2¢ carmine..... (6)	55.00	42.00	35.00	6.50	3.75	2.50	.40	.25
J72	3¢ carmine..... (6)	300.00	240.00	190.00	35.00	22.00	15.00	3.00	2.50
J73	5¢ carmine..... (6)	300.00	200.00	145.00	33.00	19.00	13.50	2.80	2.25
J74	10¢ carmine.... (6)	575.00	400.00	300.00	90.00	50.00	30.00	1.10	.80
J75	30¢ carmine....	....	....	....	200.00	125.00	75.00	2.75	2.00
J76	50¢ carmine....	....	....	....	300.00	180.00	125.00	1.10	.80
J77	$1 scarlet...... (6)	325.00	260.00	210.00	52.00	27.50	18.00	.40	.30
J78	$5 scarlet...... (6)	350.00	295.00	220.00	76.00	40.00	28.00	.40	.30
	1931 Rotary Press Printing Perf. 11 x 10½								
J79-86	**1/2¢-50¢, 8 varieties, complete......**	....	....	....	**30.00**	**24.00**	**15.00**	**1.90**	**1.50**
J79	1/2¢ dull carmine	28.00	20.00	14.00	1.75	1.00	.65	.25	.20
J80	1¢ dull carmine .	2.25	1.80	1.25	.30	.25	.20	.25	.20
J81	2¢ dull carmine .	2.25	1.80	1.25	.30	.25	.20	.25	.20
J82	3¢ dull carmine .	3.10	2.50	1.75	.30	.25	.20	.25	.20
J83	5¢ dull carmine .	4.75	3.75	3.00	.40	.35	.25	.25	.20
J84	10¢ dull carmine	9.75	7.50	5.50	1.30	1.00	.70	.25	.20
J85	30¢ dull carmine	60.00	45.00	33.00	10.50	8.00	5.25	.25	.20
J86	50¢ dull carmine	95.00	65.00	50.00	17.00	12.50	8.50	.25	.20
	1956 Rotary Press Printing Perf. 10½ x 11								
J87	$1 scarlet......	260.00	210.00	....	45.00	40.00	....	.30	....

SCOTT NO.	DESCRIPTION	MINT SHEET	PLATE BLOCK F/NH	PLATE BLOCK F	UNUSED F/NH	UNUSED F	USED F
	1959						
J88-101	**1/2¢-$5, 14 varieties, complete**	....	....	....	**20.50**	**14.50**	**3.90**
J88	1/2¢ carmine rose & black	400.00(100)	210.00	175.00	1.70	1.50	1.50
J89	1¢ carmine rose & black	9.50(100)	1.25	.75	.20	.15	.20
J90	2¢ carmine rose & black	10.00(100)	1.25	.75	.20	.15	.20
J91	3¢ carmine rose & black	14.00(100)	1.00	.70	.20	.15	.20
J92	4¢ carmine rose & black	20.00(100)	1.25	.85	.20	.15	.20
J93	5¢ carmine rose & black	20.00(100)	1.00	.70	.20	.15	.20
J94	6¢ carmine rose & black	20.00(100)	1.35	.90	.20	.15	.20
J95	7¢ carmine rose & black	32.00(100)	2.25	1.75	.20	.15	.20
J96	8¢ carmine rose & black	32.00(100)	2.25	1.75	.20	.15	.20
J97	10¢ carmine rose & black	26.00(100)	1.80	1.30	.30	.20	.20
J98	30¢ carmine rose & black	87.00(100)	5.25	4.25	1.00	.60	.20
J99	50¢ carmine rose & black	132.00(100)	7.00	5.75	1.25	1.00	.20
J100	$1 carmine rose & black	280.00(100)	12.50	9.00	2.75	1.95	.20
J101	$5 carmine rose & black	1500.00(100)	60.00	47.50	13.00	9.00	.40
	1978-1985						
J102	11¢ carmine rose & black	37.00(100)	4.00	....	.35	....	.50
J103	13¢ carmine rose & black	38.00(100)	2.95	....	.35	....	.50
J104	17¢ carmine rose & black	125.00(100)	40.00	....	.70	....	.55

OFFICES IN CHINA

SHANGHAI
2¢
CHINA
1919
K1-16: U.S. Postage 498-518 surcharged

SHANGHAI
2 Cts.
CHINA
1922
K17-18: U.S. Postage 498-528B with local surcharge

SCOTT NO.	DESCRIPTION	UNUSED NH F	UNUSED NH AVG	UNUSED OG F	UNUSED OG AVG	USED F	USED AVG
	1919						
K1	2¢ on 1¢ green ...	60.00	40.00	30.00	20.00	30.00	20.00
K2	4¢ on 2¢ rose	60.00	40.00	30.00	20.00	30.00	20.00
K3	6¢ on 3¢ violet	150.00	100.00	70.00	40.00	55.00	35.00
K4	8¢ on 4¢ brown ...	150.00	100.00	70.00	40.00	55.00	35.00
K5	10¢ on 5¢ blue....	150.00	100.00	70.00	40.00	55.00	35.00
K6	12¢ on 6¢ red orange	200.00	130.00	90.00	60.00	82.50	55.00
K7	14¢ on 7¢ black ...	200.00	130.00	90.00	60.00	95.00	62.50
K8	16¢ on 8¢ olive bister	150.00	100.00	70.00	50.00	57.50	35.00
K8a	16¢ on 8¢ olive green	150.00	100.00	70.00	50.00	50.00	32.00
K9	18¢ on 9¢ salmon red	150.00	100.00	70.00	50.00	62.50	37.00
K10	20¢ on 10¢ orange yellow	150.00	100.00	70.00	50.00	50.00	31.00
K11	24¢ on 12¢ brown carmine	150.00	100.00	70.00	50.00	58.00	32.00
K11a	24¢ on 12¢ claret brown	150.00	90.00	75.00	45.00	92.50	55.00
K12	30¢ on 15¢ gray ..	220.00	140.00	100.00	60.00	105.00	67.50
K13	40¢ on 20¢ deep ultra.	300.00	200.00	150.00	90.00	160.00	115.00
K14	60¢ on 30¢ orange red	300.00	200.00	150.00	90.00	140.00	95.00
K15	$1 on 50¢ light violet	1200.00	800.00	600.00	400.00	460.00	340.00
K16	$2 on $1 violet brown	1200.00	800.00	600.00	400.00	400.00	280.00
	1922 LOCAL ISSUES						
K17	2¢ on 1¢ green ...	300.00	200.00	140.00	90.00	100.00	70.00
K18	4¢ on 2¢ carmine..	300.00	200.00	140.00	90.00	90.00	65.00

OFFICIAL STAMPS

O1-O9, O94, O95

O10-O14

O15-O24, O96-O103

O25-O34, O106, O107

Except for the Post Office Department, portraits for the various denominations are the same as on the regular issues of 1870-73

1873 Printed by the Continental Bank Note Co.
Thin hard paper
(OG + 40%)
(O1-O120 for VF Centering–Fine Price + 50%)

DEPARTMENT OF AGRICULTURE

SCOTT NO.	DESCRIPTION	UNUSED F	UNUSED AVG	USED F	USED AVG
O1	1¢ yellow	160.00	100.00	110.00	70.00
O2	2¢ yellow	130.00	80.00	50.00	30.00
O3	3¢ yellow	130.00	80.00	9.00	6.00
O4	6¢ yellow	130.00	80.00	40.00	25.00
O5	10¢ yellow	300.00	170.00	150.00	85.00
O6	12¢ yellow	300.00	170.00	150.00	110.00
O7	15¢ yellow	300.00	170.00	150.00	95.00
O8	24¢ yellow	300.00	170.00	150.00	90.00
O9	30¢ yellow	350.00	200.00	200.00	120.00

EXECUTIVE DEPARTMENT

SCOTT NO.	DESCRIPTION	UNUSED F	UNUSED AVG	USED F	USED AVG
O10	1¢ carmine	600.00	350.00	300.00	195.00
O11	2¢ carmine	400.00	250.00	160.00	95.00
O12	3¢ carmine	400.00	250.00	160.00	90.00
O13	6¢ carmine	550.00	350.00	400.00	235.00
O14	10¢ carmine	550.00	350.00	400.00	280.00

DEPARTMENT OF THE INTERIOR

SCOTT NO.	DESCRIPTION	UNUSED F	UNUSED AVG	USED F	USED AVG
O15	1¢ vermillion	45.00	25.00	6.50	4.50
O16	2¢ vermillion	45.00	25.00	7.25	5.00
O17	3¢ vermillion	45.00	25.00	4.00	2.75
O18	6¢ vermillion	45.00	25.00	5.50	3.25
O19	10¢ vermillion	45.00	25.00	12.00	8.50
O20	12¢ vermillion	45.00	25.00	6.25	4.50
O21	15¢ vermillion	110.00	60.00	13.50	9.50
O22	24¢ vermillion	110.00	60.00	11.25	7.75
O23	30¢ vermillion	110.00	60.00	11.25	7.75
O24	90¢ vermillion	185.00	130.00	30.00	21.00

DEPARTMENT OF JUSTICE

SCOTT NO.	DESCRIPTION	UNUSED F	UNUSED AVG	USED F	USED AVG
O25	1¢ purple	135.00	100.00	65.00	43.50
O26	2¢ purple	175.00	100.00	65.00	43.50
O27	3¢ purple	175.00	100.00	17.00	10.00
O28	6¢ purple	175.00	100.00	25.00	16.00
O29	10¢ purple	175.00	100.00	55.00	35.00
O30	12¢ purple	175.00	100.00	40.00	25.00
O31	15¢ purple	300.00	200.00	120.00	70.00
O32	24¢ purple	700.00	400.00	250.00	155.00
O33	30¢ purple	700.00	400.00	200.00	120.00
O34	90¢ purple	1250.00	700.00	500.00	300.00

O35-O45

O47-O56, O108

O57-O67

O68-O71

NAVY DEPARTMENT
(OG + 30%)

SCOTT NO.	DESCRIPTION	UNUSED F	UNUSED AVG	USED F	USED AVG
O35	1¢ ultramarine	80.00	50.00	30.00	21.00
O36	2¢ ultramarine	80.00	50.00	13.75	9.50
O37	3¢ ultramarine	80.00	50.00	8.00	5.50
O38	6¢ ultramarine	80.00	50.00	13.00	9.00
O39	7¢ ultramarine	400.00	250.00	140.00	85.00
O40	10¢ ultramarine	100.00	60.00	25.00	15.00
O41	12¢ ultramarine	100.00	60.00	25.00	15.00
O42	15¢ ultramarine	200.00	150.00	40.00	28.00
O43	24¢ ultramarine	200.00	150.00	50.00	35.00
O44	30¢ ultramarine	200.00	150.00	28.00	17.00
O45	90¢ ultramarine	700.00	400.00	200.00	120.00

OFFICIAL STAMPS: From 1873 to 1879, Congress authorized the use of Official Stamps to prepay postage on government mail. Separate issues were produced for each department so that mailing costs could be assigned to that department's budget. Penalty envelopes replaced Official Stamps on May 1, 1879.

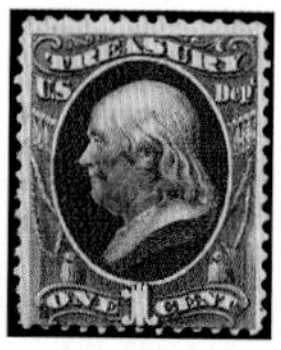

O72-O82, O109-O113

O83-O93, O1140-O120

POST OFFICE DEPARTMENT

SCOTT NO.	DESCRIPTION	UNUSED F	UNUSED AVG	USED F	USED AVG
O47	1¢ black	10.00	7.00	7.00	5.00
O48	2¢ black	12.00	7.00	5.50	3.75
O49	3¢ black	4.00	2.75	.90	.65
O50	6¢ black	12.00	8.00	4.75	3.25
O51	10¢ black	70.00	50.00	32.00	22.50
O52	12¢ black	70.00	50.00	6.75	4.50
O53	15¢ black	70.00	50.00	11.25	7.75
O54	24¢ black	70.00	50.00	14.00	9.50
O55	30¢ black	100.00	60.00	14.00	9.50
O56	90¢ black	100.00	60.00	13.00	7.75

DEPARTMENT OF STATE

SCOTT NO.	DESCRIPTION	UNUSED F	UNUSED AVG	USED F	USED AVG
O57	1¢ dark green	150.00	95.00	40.00	25.00
O58	2¢ dark green	170.00	110.00	65.00	38.00
O59	3¢ bright green	100.00	60.00	14.00	9.50
O60	6¢ bright green	100.00	60.00	18.00	10.50
O61	7¢ dark green	150.00	90.00	40.00	25.00
O62	10¢ dark green	130.00	80.00	30.00	20.00
O63	12¢ dark green	200.00	120.00	90.00	55.00
O64	15¢ dark green	200.00	120.00	55.00	38.00
O65	24¢ dark green	300.00	200.00	140.00	85.00
O66	30¢ dark green	275.00	175.00	110.00	65.00
O67	90¢ dark green	700.00	400.00	225.00	140.00
O68	$2 green & black	700.00	400.00	600.00	365.00
O69	$5 green & black	3500.00	2000.00	3000.00	1900.00
O70	$10 green & black	2800.00	1800.00	2500.00	1500.00
O71	$20 green & black	2250.00	1500.00	1800.00	1050.00

TREASURY DEPARTMENT
(OG + 30%)

SCOTT NO.	DESCRIPTION	UNUSED F	UNUSED AVG	USED F	USED AVG
O72	1¢ brown	55.00	35.00	4.00	2.50
O73	2¢ brown	55.00	35.00	4.00	2.50
O74	3¢ brown	55.00	35.00	1.20	.75
O75	6¢ brown	55.00	35.00	2.25	1.40
O76	7¢ brown	100.00	60.00	20.00	13.00
O77	10¢ brown	100.00	60.00	6.25	4.50
O78	12¢ brown	100.00	60.00	4.75	3.25
O79	15¢ brown	100.00	60.00	6.25	4.50
O80	24¢ brown	400.00	250.00	55.00	36.50
O81	30¢ brown	180.00	100.00	7.25	5.00
O82	90¢ brown	180.00	100.00	8.00	5.50

WAR DEPARTMENT

SCOTT NO.	DESCRIPTION	UNUSED F	UNUSED AVG	USED F	USED AVG
O83	1¢ rose	120.00	70.00	8.00	5.00
O84	2¢ rose	120.00	70.00	8.00	5.00
O85	3¢ rose	120.00	70.00	3.00	1.75
O86	6¢ rose	300.00	180.00	6.00	4.00
O87	7¢ rose	85.00	60.00	58.00	40.50
O88	10¢ rose	34.00	23.75	14.00	8.50
O89	12¢ rose	150.00	100.00	7.25	5.00
O90	15¢ rose	25.00	17.00	8.75	6.25
O91	24¢ rose	25.00	17.00	7.00	5.00
O92	30¢ rose	28.00	20.00	7.00	5.00
O93	90¢ rose	60.00	35.00	32.00	22.50

1879 Printed by American Bank Note Co.
Soft Porous Paper

DEPARTMENT OF AGRICULTURE

SCOTT NO.	DESCRIPTION	UNUSED F	UNUSED AVG	USED F	USED AVG
O94	1¢ yellow	3250.00	2250.00	....	....
O95	3¢ yellow	200.00	125.00	55.00	40.00

DEPARTMENT OF INTERIOR

SCOTT NO.	DESCRIPTION	UNUSED F	UNUSED AVG	USED F	USED AVG
O96	1¢ vermillion	165.00	100.00	175.00	110.00
O97	2¢ vermillion	3.25	2.25	2.00	1.20
O98	3¢ vermillion	2.75	2.00	1.20	.80
O99	6¢ vermillion	4.25	3.00	4.50	3.00
O100	10¢ vermillion	52.00	36.50	48.00	33.50
O101	12¢ vermillion	100.00	70.00	72.00	50.00
O102	15¢ vermillion	220.00	130.00	180.00	125.00
O103	24¢ vermillion	2200.00	1500.00	....	....

DEPARTMENT OF JUSTICE

SCOTT NO.	DESCRIPTION	UNUSED F	UNUSED AVG	USED F	USED AVG
O106	3¢ bluish purple	65.00	45.00	55.00	35.00
O107	6¢ bluish purple	155.00	100.00	145.00	95.00

POST OFFICE DEPARTMENT

SCOTT NO.	DESCRIPTION	UNUSED F	UNUSED AVG	USED F	USED AVG
O108	3¢ black	12.00	8.00	5.00	3.50

TREASURY DEPARTMENT

SCOTT NO.	DESCRIPTION	UNUSED F	UNUSED AVG	USED F	USED AVG
O109	3¢ brown	50.00	30.00	5.50	3.75
O110	6¢ brown	80.00	50.00	28.00	19.50
O111	10¢ brown	150.00	90.00	45.00	28.00
O112	30¢ brown	1200.00	800.00	240.00	150.00
O113	90¢ brown	2000.00	900.00	240.00	150.00

SCOTT NO.	DESCRIPTION	UNUSED F	UNUSED AVG	USED F	USED AVG
	WAR DEPARTMENT				
O114	1¢ rose red	2.75	1.95	2.75	1.75
O115	2¢ rose red	4.00	2.75	2.75	1.75
O116	3¢ rose red	4.00	2.75	1.20	.75
O117	6¢ rose red	3.75	2.50	1.75	1.00
O118	10¢ rose red	28.00	17.00	30.00	21.00
O119	12¢ rose red	20.00	12.00	8.00	5.50
O120	30¢ rose red	70.00	45.00	55.00	37.50

1910-11

SCOTT NO.	DESCRIPTION	UNUSED NH F	UNUSED NH AVG	UNUSED OG F	UNUSED OG AVG	USED F	USED AVG
	Double Line Watermark						
O121	2¢ black	40.00	25.00	20.00	11.00	1.50	1.25
O122	50¢ dark green	350.00	200.00	150.00	100.00	35.00	25.00
O123	$1 ultramarine	350.00	200.00	150.00	100.00	9.50	7.00
	Single Line Watermark						
O124	1¢ dark violet	25.00	15.00	10.00	7.00	1.30	1.00
O125	2¢ black	130.00	75.00	60.00	35.00	4.50	3.00
O126	10¢ carmine	50.00	30.00	20.00	15.00	1.95	1.35

O127-O136

O138-O143

1983-89

SCOTT NO.	DESCRIPTION	FIRST DAY COVERS SING	FIRST DAY COVERS PL. BLK.	MINT SHEET	PLATE BLOCK	UNUSED	USED
O127	1¢ Great Seal	2.00	4.25	11.00(100)	.85	.20	.20
O128	4¢ Great Seal	2.00	4.25	14.00(100)	1.00	.20	.25
O129	13¢ Great Seal	2.00	4.25	40.00(100)	2.50	.50	1.00
O129A	14¢ Great Seal (1985)	2.00	....	40.00(100)	....	.50	.55
O130	17¢ Great Seal	2.00	4.25	60.00(100)	3.50	.60	.50
O132	$1 Great Seal	5.75	14.25	260.00(100)	14.00	2.50	1.25
O133	$5 Great Seal	16.50	41.25	1100.00(100)	55.00	12.50	10.00
			PLATE# STRIP 3		PLATE# STRIP 3		
O135	20¢ Great Seal, coil	2.00	30.00	....	19.50	2.00	2.25
O136	22¢ Seal, coil (1985)	2.00	....	....	....	1.60	2.50
	1985 Non-Denominated Issues						
O138	(14¢) Great Seal, postcard D	2.00	30.00	525.00(100)	45.00	5.50	5.50
O138A	15¢ Great Seal, coil (1988)	2.00	....	....	....	.65	.60
O138B	20¢ Great Seal, coil (1988)	2.00	....	....	....	.80	.75
			PLATE# STRIP 3		PLATE# STRIP 3		
O139	(22¢) Great Seal "D" coil (1985)	2.00	[illegible]	....	[illegible]	5.50	3.25
O140	(25¢) Great Seal "E" coil (1988)	2.00	....	....	....	1.30	2.25
O141	25¢ Great Seal, coil (1988)	2.00	....	....	....	.95	.60
O143	1¢ Great Seal (1989)	2.00	....	10.00(100)	....	.20	.25

O144

O145

O146

O146A

O147

O148

1991-94

SCOTT NO.	DESCRIPTION	FIRST DAY COVERS SING	FIRST DAY COVERS PL. BLK.	MINT SHEET	PLATE BLOCK	UNUSED	USED
O144	(29¢) Great Seal "F" coil	2.00	....	....	....	1.75	.60
O145	29¢ Great Seal, coil	2.00	....	....	....	1.10	.50
O146	4¢ Great Seal	2.00	....	20.00(100)	....	.25	.35
O146A	10¢ Great Seal	2.00	....	35.00(100)	....	.40	.50
O147	19¢ Great Seal	2.00	....	65.00(100)	....	.70	.95
O148	23¢ Great Seal	2.00	....	80.00(100)	....	1.10	1.10

O151

O152

O153

O154

O155

O156

O157, O158, O159, O160, O162

O161

SCOTT NO.	DESCRIPTION	FIRST DAY COVERS SING	FIRST DAY COVERS PL. BLK.	MINT SHEET	PLATE BLOCK	UNUSED	USED
	1993-95						
O151	$1 Great Seal	6.00	....	600.00(100)	....	6.00	4.00
O152	(32¢) Great Seal "G" coil	2.75	....	....	....	1.00	1.25
O153	32¢ Official Mail	1.95	....	....	....	2.00	1.00
O154	1¢ Official Mail	1.95	....	10.00(100)	....	.20	.25
O155	20¢ Official Mail	1.95	....	70.00(100)	....	.80	1.00
O156	23¢ Official Mail	1.95	....	90.00(100)	....	1.00	.85
	1999-2007						
O157	33¢ Great Seal, coil	1.95	....	....	....	1.50	1.35
O158	34¢ Great Seal, coil	1.95	....	....	....	1.35	1.00
O159	37¢ Great Seal, coil	1.95	....	....	....	1.40	1.10
....	same, pl# strip of 5	....	....	....	....	8.00	....
O160	39¢ Great Seal, coil	1.95	....	....	....	.90	.50
....	same, pl# strip of 5	....	....	....	....	6.75	....
O161	$1 Great Seal	2.75	....	45.00(20)	9.00	2.25	1.25
O162	41¢ Great Seal, water-activated, coil	2.25	....	....	....	1.25	.50
....	same, pl# strip of 5	....	....	....	....	7.50	....

PARCEL POST STAMPS

Q1-Q12 Various Designs

SPECIAL HANDLING STAMPS

QE1-QE4

PARCEL POST DUE STAMPS

JQ1-JQ5

(Q1-QE4a for VF Centering–Fine Price + 50%)

SCOTT NO.	DESCRIPTION	UNUSED NH F	UNUSED NH AVG	UNUSED OG F	UNUSED OG AVG	USED F	USED AVG
	1912-13 Parcel Post–All Printed in Carmine Rose						
Q1	1¢ Post Office Clerk	15.00	10.00	7.00	5.00	1.50	1.00
Q2	2¢ City Carrier	20.00	12.00	10.00	7.00	1.25	.90
Q3	3¢ Railway Clerk	45.00	30.00	20.00	15.00	6.00	4.25
Q4	4¢ Rural Carrier	100.00	70.00	50.00	30.00	3.00	1.95
Q5	5¢ Mail Train	100.00	70.00	50.00	50.00	2.50	1.95
Q6	10¢ Steamship	170.00	120.00	80.00	50.00	3.25	2.00
Q7	15¢ Auto Service	170.00	120.00	80.00	45.00	12.50	8.00
Q8	20¢ Airplane	400.00	200.00	200.00	120.00	[illegible]	10.00
Q9	25¢ Manufacturing	200.00	120.00	75.00	50.00	7.00	4.75
Q10	50¢ Dairying	800.00	500.00	350.00	220.00	42.50	27.50
Q11	75¢ Harvesting	270.00	160.00	120.00	70.00	37.50	22.50
Q12	$1 Fruit Growing	1000.00	650.00	420.00	250.00	37.50	22.50
	1912 Parcel Post Due						
JQ1	1¢ dark green	30.00	20.00	12.00	8.00	4.50	3.00
JQ2	2¢ dark green	250.00	150.00	100.00	65.00	16.00	11.00
JQ3	5¢ dark green	45.00	30.00	20.00	12.00	4.50	3.00
JQ4	10¢ dark green	450.00	300.00	200.00	130.00	45.00	30.00
JQ5	25¢ dark green	300.00	200.00	120.00	80.00	4.00	2.75
	1925-29 Special Handling						
QE1	10¢ yellow green	2.25	1.50	1.25	.85	1.50	1.20
QE2	15¢ yellow green	2.50	1.75	1.40	.95	2.00	1.20
QE3	20¢ yellow green	3.50	2.50	2.00	1.40	1.95	1.35
QE4	25¢ yellow green	30.00	20.00	16.50	11.50	8.00	5.00
QE4a	25¢ deep green	45.00	32.50	25.00	17.50	5.00	3.40

POSTAL NOTE STAMPS

PN1-P18

All values printed in black

SCOTT NO.	DESCRIPTION	UNUSED F/NH	UNUSED F/OG	USED F
PN1-18	1¢-90¢, 18 varieties, complete	35.00	24.50	4.00

ENVELOPES

U1-U10
Washington

U19-U24
Franklin

U26, U27
Washington

1853-55

SCOTT NO.	DESCRIPTION	UNUSED ENTIRE	UNUSED CUT SQ.	USED CUT SQ.
U1	3¢ red on white, die 1	2000.00	350.00	30.00
U2	3¢ red on buff, die 1	950.00	100.00	22.50
U3	3¢ red on white, die 2	5800.00	1250.00	50.00
U4	3¢ red on buff, die 2	2450.00	375.00	45.00
U5	3¢ red on white, die 3	......	......	600.00
U6	3¢ red on buff, die 3	......	5000.00	85.00
U7	3¢ red on white, die 4	......	6000.00	125.00
U8	3¢ red on buff, die 4	......	9000.00	140.00
U9	3¢ red on white, die 5	175.00	45.00	5.00
U10	3c red on buff, die 5	75.00	24.00	5.00
U11	6¢ red on white	475.00	300.00	75.00
U12	6¢ red on buff	250.00	175.00	75.00
U13	6¢ green on white	800.00	375.00	135.00
U14	6¢ green on buff	475.00	240.00	95.00
U15	10¢ green on white, die 1	1000.00	575.00	95.00
U16	10¢ green on buff, die 1	475.00	195.00	70.00
U17	10¢ green on white, die 2	850.00	495.00	150.00
U18	10¢ green on buff, die 2	750.00	375.00	95.00

1860-61

SCOTT NO.	DESCRIPTION	UNUSED ENTIRE	UNUSED CUT SQ.	USED CUT SQ.
U19	1¢ blue on buff, die 1	95.00	45.00	16.50
W20	1¢ blue on buff, die 1	115.00	75.00	52.00
W21	1¢ blue on manila, die 1	115.00	65.00	47.00
W22	1¢ blue on orange, die 1	7500.00	4500.00	......
U23	1¢ blue on orange, die 2	950.00	700.00	340.00
U24	1¢ blue on buff, die 3	750.00	400.00	115.00
U26	3¢ red on white	65.00	37.00	22.00
U27	3¢ red on buff	45.00	25.00	14.00
U28	3¢ & 1¢ red & blue on white	850.00	340.00	250.00
U29	3¢ & 1¢ red & blue on buff	800.00	400.00	260.00
U30	6¢ red on white	6000.00	3250.00	1400.00
U31	6¢ red on buff	6500.00	3700.00	1400.00
U32	10¢ green on white	......	1600.00	425.00
U33	10¢ green on buff	4250.00	1600.00	350.00

U34-U37

U40-U41

Washington

1861

SCOTT NO.	DESCRIPTION	UNUSED ENTIRE	UNUSED CUT SQ.	USED CUT SQ.
U34	3¢ pink on white	65.00	30.00	6.00
U35	3¢ pink on buff	65.00	30.00	6.00
U36	3¢ pink on blue (letter sheet)	300.00	82.50	55.00
U37	3¢ pink on orange	7500.00	4950.00	......
U38	6¢ pink on white	200.00	120.00	85.00
U39	6¢ pink on buff	210.00	85.00	62.50
U40	10¢ yellow green on white	85.00	45.00	33.00
U41	10¢ yellow green on buff	85.00	45.00	33.00
U42	12¢ brown & red on buff	500.00	240.00	155.00
U43	20¢ blue & red on buff	550.00	275.00	195.00
U44	24¢ green & red on buff	800.00	225.00	195.00
U45	40¢ red & black on buff	825.00	350.00	325.00

U46-U49

U50-W57

Jackson

1863-64

SCOTT NO.	DESCRIPTION	UNUSED ENTIRE	UNUSED CUT SQ.	USED CUT SQ.
U46	2¢ black on buff, die 1	80.00	55.00	20.00
W47	2¢ black on dark manila, die 1	100.00	75.00	42.00
U48	2¢ black on buff, die 2	6500.00	3000.00	......
U49	2¢ black on orange, die 2	5500.00	2300.00	......
U50	2¢ black on buff, die 3	40.00	18.00	9.60
W51	2¢ black on buff, die 3	650.00	350.00	195.00
U52	2¢ black on orange, die 3	37.00	20.00	10.00
W53	2¢ black on dark manila, die 3	165.00	45.00	35.00
U54	2¢ black on buff, die 4	38.00	18.00	10.00
W55	2¢ black on buff, die 4	150.00	95.00	60.00
U56	2¢ black on orange, die 4	35.00	20.00	8.00
W57	2¢ black on light manila, die 4	35.00	20.00	12.00

U58-U61

U66-U67

Washington

1864-65

SCOTT NO.	DESCRIPTION	UNUSED ENTIRE	UNUSED CUT SQ.	USED CUT SQ.
U58	3¢ pink on white	20.00	10.00	1.80
U59	3¢ pink on buff	15.00	10.00	1.20
U60	3¢ brown on white	150.00	70.00	35.00
U61	3¢ brown on buff	125.00	55.00	30.00
U62	6¢ pink on white	200.00	110.00	28.00
U63	6¢ pink on buff	100.00	50.00	27.00
U64	6¢ purple on white	100.00	70.00	27.00
U65	6¢ purple on buff	75.00	55.00	24.00
U66	9¢ lemon on buff	650.00	420.00	260.00
U67	9¢ orange on buff	220.00	150.00	85.00
U68	12¢ brown on buff	650.00	350.00	250.00
U69	12¢ red brown on buff	210.00	160.00	57.50
U70	18¢ red on buff	210.00	95.00	95.00
U71	24c blue on buff	210.00	90.00	84.00
U72	30¢ green on buff	160.00	110.00	75.00
U73	40¢ rose on buff	330.00	120.00	240.00

U74-W77, U108-U121
Franklin

U78-W81, U122-W158
Jackson

U82-U84, U159-U169
Washington

U172-U180
Taylor

U85-U87, U181-U184
Lincoln

U88, U185, U186
Stanton

U89-U92, U187-U194
Jefferson

U93-U95, U195-U197
Clay

U96-U98, U198-U200
Webster

U99-U101, U201-U203
Scott

U102-U104, U204-U210, U336-U341
Hamilton

U105-U107, U211-U217, U342-U347
Perry

NOTE: For details on die or silmilar appearing varieties of envelopes, please refer to the Scott Specialized Catalogue.

SCOTT NO.	DESCRIPTION	UNUSED ENTIRE	UNUSED CUT SQ.	USED CUT SQ.
	1870-71 REAY ISSUE			
U74	1¢ blue on white	75.00	40.00	30.00
U74a	1¢ ultramarine on white	150.00	75.00	33.00
U75	1¢ blue on amber	60.00	36.00	30.00
U75a	1¢ ultramarine on amber	95.00	70.00	31.00
U76	1¢ blue on orange	30.00	20.00	15.00
W77	1¢ blue on manila	85.00	42.00	36.00
U78	2¢ brown on white	65.00	45.00	15.00
U79	2¢ brown on amber	36.00	18.00	9.00
U80	2¢ brown on orange	17.00	12.00	6.00
W81	2¢ brown on manila	65.00	27.00	21.00
U82	3¢ green on white	18.00	9.00	.90
U83	3¢ green on amber	18.00	8.00	2.00
U84	3¢ green on cream	18.00	10.00	4.00
U85	6¢ dark red on white	55.00	30.00	22.00
U86	6¢ dark red on amber	80.00	45.00	22.00
U87	6¢ dark red on cream	75.00	45.00	16.00
U88	7¢ vermillon on amber	85.00	55.00	200.00
U89	10¢ olive black on white	1300.00	950.00	900.00
U90	10¢ olive black on amber	1300.00	950.00	900.00
U91	10¢ brown on white	150.00	95.00	72.00
U92	10¢ brown on amber	150.00	110.00	54.00
U93	12¢ plum on white	240.00	120.00	84.00
U94	12¢ plum on amber	240.00	120.00	120.00
U95	12¢ plum on cream	350.00	250.00	220.00
U96	15¢ red orange on white	180.00	85.00	75.00
U97	15¢ red orange on amber	395.00	200.00	295.00
U98	15¢ red orange on cream	400.00	340.00	350.00
U99	24¢ purple on white	210.00	150.00	150.00
U100	24¢ purple on amber	400.00	210.00	350.00
U101	24¢ purple on cream	500.00	295.00	575.00
U102	30¢ black on white	290.00	85.00	120.00
U103	30¢ black on amber	600.00	240.00	500.00
U104	30¢ black on cream	380.00	220.00	450.00
U105	90¢ carmine on white	275.00	185.00	375.00
U106	90¢ carmine on amber	800.00	320.00	425.00
U107	90¢ carmine on cream	925.00	300.00	2200.00
	1874-86 PLIMPTON ISSUE			
U108	1¢ dark blue on white, die 1	250.00	195.00	72.00
U109	1¢ dark blue on amber, die 1	200.00	175.00	78.00
U110	1¢ dark blue on cream, die 1	......	1800.00	......
U111	1¢ dark blue on orange, die 1	33.00	24.00	18.00
U111a	1¢ light blue on orange, die 1	33.00	24.00	18.00
W112	1¢ dark blue on manila, die 1	120.00	75.00	45.00
U113	1¢ light blue on white, die 2	3.25	2.00	1.00
U113a	1¢ dark blue on white, die 2	30.00	10.00	7.00
U114	1¢ light blue on amber, die 2	8.00	4.50	4.00
U115	1¢ blue on cream, die 2	10.00	5.00	4.00
U116	1¢ light blue on orange, die 2	1.00	.85	.50
U116a	1¢ dark blue on orange, die 2	15.00	5.00	2.50
U117	1¢ light blue on blue, die 2	13.00	8.00	5.50
U118	1¢ light blue on fawn, die 2	15.00	9.00	5.00
U119	1¢ light blue on manila, die 2	17.00	10.00	3.60
W120	1¢ light blue on manila, die 2	3.00	1.50	1.20
W120a	1¢ dark blue on manila, die 2	17.00	9.50	8.00
U121	1¢ blue on amber manila, die 2	30.00	20.00	11.00
U122	2¢ brown on white, die 1	180.00	150.00	40.00
U123	2¢ brown on amber, die 1	130.00	75.00	48.00
U124	2¢ brown on cream, die 1	......	1200.00	......
W126	2¢ brown on manila, die 1	295.00	160.00	80.00
W127	2¢ vermillon on manila, die 1	4800.00	3200.00	260.00
U128	2¢ brown on white, die 2	100.00	55.00	30.00
U129	2¢ brown on amber, die 2	130.00	90.00	42.00
W131	2¢ brown on manila, die 2	30.00	20.00	16.50
U132	2¢ brown on white, die 3	130.00	90.00	30.00
U133	2¢ brown on amber, die 3	550.00	375.00	75.00
U134	2¢ brown on white, die 4	2200.00	1500.00	160.00
U135	2¢ brown on amber, die 4	675.00	500.00	120.00
U136	2¢ brown on orange, die 4	90.00	55.00	30.00
W137	2¢ brown on manila, die 4	135.00	80.00	40.00
U139	2¢ brown on white, die 5	85.00	65.00	35.00
U140	2¢ brown on amber, die 5	150.00	95.00	64.00
W141	2¢ brown on manila, die 5	42.00	37.00	28.00
U142	2¢ vermillon on white, die 5	10.00	9.00	5.00
U143	2¢ vermillon on amber, die 5	10.00	9.00	4.00
U144	2¢ vermillon on cream, die 5	25.00	20.00	8.00
U146	2¢ vermillon on blue, die 5	195.00	130.00	38.00
U147	2¢ vermillon on fawn, die 5	14.00	9.00	5.00
W148	2¢ vermillon on manila, die 5	9.00	5.00	4.50
U149	2¢ vermillon on white, die 6	100.00	65.00	35.00
U150	2¢ vermillon on amber, die 6	65.00	45.00	18.00
U151	2¢ vermillon on blue, die 6	20.00	13.00	9.50
U152	2¢ vermillon on fawn, die 6	18.00	13.00	5.00
U153	2¢ vermillon on white, die 7	120.00	80.00	30.00
U154	2¢ vermillon on amber, die 7	475.00	400.00	95.00
W155	2¢ vermillon on manila, die 7	50.00	25.00	12.00
U156	2¢ vermillon on white, die 8	2200.00	1600.00	175.00
W158	2¢ vermillon on manila,die 8	200.00	120.00	60.00
U159	3¢ green on white, die 1	65.00	38.00	7.00
U160	3¢ green on amber, die 1	65.00	35.00	10.80
U161	3¢ green on cream, die 1	70.00	45.00	15.00
U163	3¢ green on white, die 2	4.00	1.75	.40
U164	3¢ green on amber, die 2	4.00	1.75	.60
U165	3¢ green on cream, die 2	20.00	10.00	7.00
U166	3¢ green on blue,die 2	18.00	9.00	7.00
U167	3¢ green on fawn, die 2	10.00	6.00	4.00
U168	3¢ green on white, die 3	4750.00	1500.00	95.00
U169	3¢ green on amber, die 3	650.00	350.00	120.00
U172	5¢ blue on white, die 1	22.00	15.00	8.25
U173	5¢ blue on amber, die 1	22.00	15.00	9.00
U174	5¢ blue on cream, die 1	200.00	130.00	40.00
U175	5¢ blue on blue, die 1	60.00	40.00	16.50
U176	5¢ blue on fawn, die 1	295.00	150.00	72.00
U177	5¢ blue on white, die 2	20.00	11.00	7.00
U178	5¢ blue on amber, die 2	20.00	11.00	7.00
U179	5¢ blue on blue, die 2	50.00	35.00	12.00
U180	5¢ blue on fawn, die 2	250.00	150.00	60.00
U181	6¢ red on white	16.00	10.00	7.00
U182	6¢ red on amber	25.00	15.00	7.00
U183	6¢ red on cream	95.00	60.00	18.00
U184	6¢ red on fawn	37.50	25.00	13.00
U185	7¢ vermilion on white	......	2000.00	......
U186	7¢ vermilion on amber	225.00	175.00	75.00
U187	10¢ brown on white,die 1	70.00	50.00	25.00
U188	10¢ brown on amber, die 1	150.00	80.00	38.00
U189	10¢ chocolate on white, die 2	14.00	9.00	4.50
U190	10¢ chocolate on amber, die 2	15.00	10.00	7.00
U191	10¢ brown on buff, die 2	20.00	17.00	8.00
U192	10¢ brown on blue, die 2	20.00	17.00	9.00
U193	10¢ brown on manila, die 2	25.00	20.00	10.00
U194	10¢ brown/amber manila, die 2	28.00	22.00	10.00
U195	12¢ plum on white	750.00	500.00	110.00
U196	12¢ plum on amber	375.00	300.00	195.00
U197	12¢ plum on cream	900.00	240.00	185.00
U198	15¢ orange on white	90.00	50.00	40.00
U199	15¢ orange on amber	325.00	150.00	120.00
U200	15¢ orange on cream	1150.00	600.00	370.00
U201	24¢ purple on white	275.00	170.00	140.00
U202	24¢ purple on amber	275.00	200.00	130.00
U203	24¢ purple on cream	800.00	200.00	130.00
U204	30¢ black on white	85.00	62.00	28.00
U205	30¢ black on amber	140.00	75.00	65.00
U206	30¢ black on cream	750.00	380.00	370.00
U207	30¢ black on oriental buff	150.00	100.00	85.00
U208	30¢ black on blue	130.00	105.00	85.00
U209	30¢ black on manila	150.00	95.00	85.00
U210	30¢ black on amber manila	225.00	180.00	85.00
U211	90¢ carmine on white	160.00	130.00	85.00
U212	90¢ carmine on amber	275.00	210.00	300.00
U213	90¢ carmine on cream	3500.00	1700.00	......
U214	90¢ carmine on oriental buff	280.00	210.00	280.00
U215	90¢ carmine on blue	240.00	195.00	260.00
U216	90¢ carmine on manila	240.00	180.00	260.00
U217	90¢ carmine on amber manila	220.00	150.00	220.00

U218-U221, U582
Pony Express Rider and Train

U222-U226
Garfield

Die 1. Single thick line under "POSTAGE" Die 2. Two thin lines under "POSTAGE"

1876 CENTENNIAL ISSUE

SCOTT NO.	DESCRIPTION	UNUSED ENTIRE	UNUSED CUT SQ.	USED CUT SQ.
U218	3¢ red on white, die 1	80.00	55.00	30.00
U219	3¢ green on white, die 1	60.00	50.00	19.00
U221	3¢ green on white, die 2	80.00	55.00	24.00
	1882-86			
U222	5¢ brown on white	11.00	6.00	3.00
U223	5¢ brown on amber	12.00	6.00	3.50
U224	5¢ brown on oriental buff	210.00	150.00	75.00
U225	5¢ brown on blue	130.00	85.00	40.00
U226	5¢ brown on fawn	500.00	375.00	......

U227-U230
Washington

1883 OCTOBER

SCOTT NO.	DESCRIPTION	UNUSED ENTIRE	UNUSED CUT SQ.	USED CUT SQ.
U227	2¢ red on white	11.00	5.00	2.50
U228	2¢ red on amber	11.00	6.00	3.00
U229	2¢ red on blue	14.00	9.00	5.00
U230	2¢ red on fawn	15.00	9.00	5.50

U231-U249, U260-W292
Washington

U250-U259
Jackson

1883 NOVEMBER
Four Wavy Lines in Oval

SCOTT NO.	DESCRIPTION	UNUSED ENTIRE	UNUSED CUT SQ.	USED CUT SQ.
U231	2¢ red on white	9.50	5.00	2.50
U232	2¢ red on amber	10.00	6.00	4.00
U233	2¢ red on blue	18.00	10.00	7.25
U234	2¢ red on fawn	12.00	7.00	4.50
W235	2¢ red on manila	32.50	22.50	6.50

1884 JUNE

SCOTT NO.	DESCRIPTION	UNUSED ENTIRE	UNUSED CUT SQ.	USED CUT SQ.
U236	2¢ red on white	21.00	13.50	4.50
U237	2¢ red on amber	25.00	17.00	10.00
U238	2¢ red on blue	38.00	27.00	10.00
U239	2¢ red on fawn	23.00	17.00	10.00
U240	2¢ red on white (3-1/2links)	175.00	110.00	50.00
U241	2¢ red on amber (3-1/2links)	2800.00	1000.00	340.00
U243	2¢ red on white (2 links)	180.00	140.00	80.00
U244	2¢ red on amber (2links)	525.00	350.00	78.00
U245	2¢ red on blue (2links)	675.00	500.00	225.00
U246	2¢ red on fawn (2links)	725.00	475.00	160.00
U247	2¢ red on white (round O)	4250.00	3250.00	650.00
U249	2¢ red on fawn (round O)	2200.00	1350.00	450.00

1883-86

SCOTT NO.	DESCRIPTION	UNUSED ENTIRE	UNUSED CUT SQ.	USED CUT SQ.
U250	4¢ green on white, die 1	7.00	4.00	3.50
U251	4¢ green on amber,die 1	8.00	5.50	4.00
U252	4¢ green on buff, die 1	18.00	14.00	10.00
U253	4¢ green on blue, die 1	18.00	14.00	7.00
U254	4¢ green on manila, die 1	22.00	16.00	8.00
U255	4¢ green/amber manila,die 1	33.00	25.00	10.80
U256	4¢ green on white, die 2	20.00	12.00	5.00
U257	4¢ green on amber, die 2	26.00	15.00	7.00
U258	4¢ green on manila, die 2	26.00	16.00	8.00
U259	4¢ green/amber manila,die 2	26.00	16.00	8.00

1884 MAY

SCOTT NO.	DESCRIPTION	UNUSED ENTIRE	UNUSED CUT SQ.	USED CUT SQ.
U260	2¢ brown on white	20.00	17.00	6.00
U261	2¢ brown on amber	20.00	17.00	7.00
U262	2¢ brown on blue	30.00	22.00	10.00
U263	2¢ brown on fawn	20.00	17.00	9.00
W264	2¢ brown on manila	27.00	20.00	12.00

1884 JUNE

SCOTT NO.	DESCRIPTION	UNUSED ENTIRE	UNUSED CUT SQ.	USED CUT SQ.
U265	2¢ brown on white	28.00	20.00	6.50
U266	2¢ brown on amber	77.00	65.00	45.00
U267	2¢ brown on blue	35.00	25.00	10.00
U268	2¢ brown on fawn	23.00	18.00	11.00
W269	2¢ brown on manila	36.00	30.00	14.50
U270	2¢ brown on white (2links)	180.00	150.00	50.00
U271	2¢ brown on amber (2links)	625.00	525.00	120.00
U273	2¢ brown on white (round O)	425.00	325.00	120.00
U274	2¢ brown on amber (round O)	425.00	325.00	100.00
U276	2¢ brown on fawn (round O)	1600.00	1100.00	725.00

1884-86
Two Wavy Lines in Oval

SCOTT NO.	DESCRIPTION	UNUSED ENTIRE	UNUSED CUT SQ.	USED CUT SQ.
U277	2¢ brown on white, die 1	.85	.50	.25
U277a	2¢ brown lake on white, die 1	28.00	21.00	20.00
U278	2¢ brown on amber, die 1	1.50	.75	.50
U279	2¢ brown on buff, die 1	8.00	5.00	2.00
U280	2¢ brown on blue, die 1	5.00	3.00	2.00
U281	2¢ brown on fawn, die 1	6.00	4.00	2.50
U282	2¢ brown on manila, die 1	18.00	12.00	4.00
W283	2¢ brown on manila, die 1	12.00	8.00	5.40
U284	2¢ brown/amber manila, die 1	16.00	10.00	6.00
U285	2¢ red on white, die 1	1700.00	800.00	......
U286	2¢ red on blue, die 1	400.00	325.00	......
W287	2¢ red on manila, die 1	225.00	150.00	......
U288	2¢ brown on white, die 2	900.00	400.00	50.00
U289	2¢ brown on amber, die 2	25.00	19.00	12.00
U290	2¢ brown on blue, die 2	2500.00	1950.00	325.00
U291	2¢ brown on fawn, die 2	47.50	35.00	19.25
W292	2¢ brown on manila, die 2	37.00	25.00	20.00

NOTE: For details on die or silmilar appearing varieties of envelopes, please refer to the Scott Specialized Catalogue.

U293
Grant

1886

SCOTT NO.	DESCRIPTION	UNUSED ENTIRE	UNUSED CUT SQ.	USED CUT SQ.
U293	2¢ green on white	....	....	....
	Entire letter sheet	28.00	....	17.50

U294-U304, U352-W357
Franklin

U305-U323, U358-U370
Washington

U324-U329
Jackson

U330-U335, U377-U378
Grant

1887-94

SCOTT NO.	DESCRIPTION	UNUSED ENTIRE	UNUSED CUT SQ.	USED CUT SQ.
U294	1¢ blue on white	1.10	.60	.25
U295	1¢ dark blue on white	11.40	7.80	3.00
U296	1¢ blue on amber	6.50	4.00	1.50
U297	1¢ dark blue on amber	60.00	48.00	27.00
U300	1¢ blue on manila	1.15	.75	.30
W301	1¢ blue on manila	1.25	.50	.30
U302	1¢ dark blue on manila	33.00	28.00	10.75
W303	1¢ dark blue on manila	22.00	14.50	12.00
U304	1¢ blue on amber manila	18.00	13.00	5.00
U305	2¢ green on white, die 1	37.50	20.00	11.00
U306	2¢ green on amber, die 1	55.00	45.00	17.00
U307	2¢ green on buff, die 1	130.00	95.00	36.00
U308	2¢ green on blue, die 1	......	9500.00	1300.00
U309	2¢ green on manila, die 1	......	......	800.00
U311	2¢ green on white, die 2	.80	.40	.25
U312	2¢ green on amber, die 2	.80	.45	.25
U313	2¢ green on buff, die 2	1.25	.70	.30
U314	2¢ green on blue, die 2	1.25	.70	.30
U315	2¢ green on manila, die 2	3.00	2.00	.60
W316	2¢ green on manila, die 2	12.00	5.00	3.00
U317	2¢ green/amber manila, die 2	6.50	3.00	2.00
U318	2¢ green on white, die 3	210.00	160.00	15.00
U319	2¢ green on amber, die 3	300.00	200.00	25.00
U320	2¢ green on buff, die 3	250.00	180.00	50.00
U321	2¢ green on blue, die 3	325.00	200.00	71.50
U322	2¢ green on manila, die 3	325.00	280.00	70.00
U323	2¢ green/amber manila, die 3	700.00	600.00	80.00
U324	4¢ carmine on white	6.50	3.50	2.25
U325	4¢ carmine on amber	8.00	4.00	3.50
U326	4¢ carmine on oriental buff	17.00	8.00	4.00
U327	4¢ carmine on blue	14.00	7.00	4.25
U328	4¢ carmine on manila	14.00	10.00	7.00
U329	4¢ carmine on amber/manila	14.00	8.00	4.00
U330	5¢ blue on white, die 1	9.00	5.00	5.00
U331	5¢ blue on amber, die 1	11.00	6.00	3.00
U332	5¢ blue on oriental buff, die 1	17.00	7.00	5.00
U333	5¢ blue on blue, die 1	17.00	11.00	6.00
U334	5¢ blue on white, die 2	45.00	30.00	13.00
U335	5¢ blue on amber, die 2	25.00	15.00	8.00
U336	30¢ red brown on white	75.00	65.00	50.00
U337	30¢ red brown on amber	75.00	65.00	50.00
U338	30¢ red brown/oriental buff	75.00	65.00	50.00
U339	30¢ red brown on blue	75.00	65.00	50.00
U340	30¢ red brown on manila	54.00	65.00	50.00
U341	30¢ red brown/amber manila	75.00	65.00	50.00
U342	90¢ purple on white	120.00	80.00	90.00
U343	90¢ purple on amber	150.00	95.00	90.00
U344	90¢ purple on oriental buff	150.00	95.00	90.00
U345	90¢ purple on blue	150.00	95.00	95.00
U346	90¢ purple on manila	150.00	110.00	95.00
U347	90¢ purple on amber manila	150.00	110.00	95.00

U348-U351
Columbus and Liberty, with Shield and Eagle

1893 COLUMBIAN ISSUE

SCOTT NO.	DESCRIPTION	UNUSED ENTIRE	UNUSED CUT SQ.	USED CUT SQ.
U348	1¢ deep blue on white	3.00	2.50	1.25
U349	2¢ violet on white	3.50	2.00	.75
U350	5¢ chocolate on white	15.00	9.60	9.00
U351	10¢ slate brown on white	65.00	35.00	27.50

U371-U373

U374-W376

Lincoln

1899

SCOTT NO.	DESCRIPTION	UNUSED ENTIRE	UNUSED CUT SQ.	USED CUT SQ.
U352	1¢ green on white	3.00	1.20	.25
U353	1¢ green on amber	9.00	6.00	1.80
U354	1¢ green on oriental buff	20.00	15.00	3.00
U355	1¢ green on blue	20.00	15.00	8.00
U356	1¢ green on manila	7.00	2.50	1.10
W357	1¢ green on manila	10.00	3.00	1.10
U358	2¢ carmine on white, die 1	8.00	3.00	2.00
U359	2¢ carmine on amber, die 1	35.00	25.00	15.00
U360	2¢ carmine on buff, die 1	35.00	23.00	13.00
U361	2¢ carmine on blue, die 1	80.00	65.00	38.00
U362	2¢ carmine on white,die 2	.70	.40	.25
U363	2¢ carmine on amber. die 2	3.25	1.50	.25
U364	2¢ carmine on buff, die 2	3.25	1.25	.25
U365	2¢ carmine on blue, die 2	4.00	2.00	.60
W366	2¢ carmine on manila, die 2	11.40	9.00	3.50
U367	2¢ carmine on white, die 3	12.00	7.00	3.00
U368	2¢ carmine on amber, die 3	16.00	10.00	7.00
U369	2¢ carmine on buff, die 3	35.00	25.00	14.00
U370	2¢ carmine on blue, die 3	26.00	13.00	11.00
U371	4¢ brown on white, die 1	32.00	22.00	13.25
U372	4¢ brown on amber, die 1	35.00	22.00	14.00
U373	4¢ brown on white, die 2	......	......	1300.00
U374	4¢ brown on white, die 3	28.00	16.00	9.00
U375	4¢ brown on amber, die 3	85.00	70.00	25.00
W376	4¢ brown on manila, die 3	28.00	18.00	10.00
U377	5¢ blue on white, die 3	18.00	14.00	10.25
U378	5¢ blue on amber, die 3	25.00	18.00	11.50

U379-W384
Franklin

U385-W389, U395-W399
Washington

U390-W392
Grant

U393, U394
Lincoln

U400-W405, U416, U417
Franklin

U406-W415, U418, U419
Washington

1903

SCOTT NO.	DESCRIPTION	UNUSED ENTIRE	UNUSED CUT SQ.	USED CUT SQ.
U379	1¢ green on white	1.25	.80	.25
U380	1¢ green on amber	22.00	16.00	2.25
U381	1¢ green on oriental buff	25.00	19.00	3.00
U382	1¢ green on blue	35.00	24.00	5.00
U383	1¢ green on manila	4.75	3.70	1.00
W384	1¢ green on manila	4.00	3.00	.50
U385	2¢ carmine on white	1.00	.45	.25
U386	2¢ carmine on amber	4.00	2.00	.30
U387	2¢ carmine on oriental buff	3.00	2.00	.35
U388	2¢ carmine on blue	2.75	1.50	.60
W389	2¢ carmine on manila	24.00	20.00	10.00
U390	4¢ chocolate on white	32.00	24.00	12.00
U391	4¢ chocolate on amber	32.00	24.00	12.00
W392	4¢ chocolate on manila	32.00	24.00	13.00
U393	5¢ blue on white	32.00	24.00	13.00
U394	5¢ blue on amber	32.00	24.00	12.00

1904 RECUT DIE

SCOTT NO.	DESCRIPTION	UNUSED ENTIRE	UNUSED CUT SQ.	USED CUT SQ.
U395	2¢ carmine on white	1.15	.65	.25
U396	2¢ carmine on amber	13.00	8.00	1.20
U397	2¢ carmine on oriental buff	8.00	6.00	1.50
U398	2¢ carmine on blue	6.00	4.00	1.10
W399	2¢ carmine on manila	23.00	15.00	10.00

1907-16

SCOTT NO.	DESCRIPTION	UNUSED ENTIRE	UNUSED CUT SQ.	USED CUT SQ.
U400	1¢ green on white	.50	.30	.25
U401	1¢ green on amber	2.75	2.00	.50
U402	1¢ green on oriental buff	13.00	11.00	1.50
U403	1¢ green on blue	13.00	11.00	2.00
U404	1¢ green on manila	5.00	3.30	2.10
W405	1¢ green on manila	1.00	.90	.30
U406	2¢ brown red on white	2.00	1.00	.25
U407	2¢ brown red on amber	9.00	7.00	3.00
U408	2¢ brown red on oriental buff	12.00	9.00	2.00
U409	2¢ brown red on blue	8.00	6.00	2.10
W410	2¢ brown red on manila	60.00	48.00	36.00
U411	2¢ carmine on white	.60	.25	.25
U412	2¢ carmine on amber	.95	.25	.25
U413	2¢ carmine on oriental buff	.70	.50	.25
U414	2¢ carmine on blue	1.25	.50	.25
W415	2¢ carmine on manila	7.80	4.80	2.40
U416	4¢ black on white	10.00	5.00	3.00
U417	4¢ black on amber	12.00	8.00	3.00
U418	5¢ blue on white	13.00	7.20	2.85
U419	5¢ blue on amber	23.00	17.00	13.00

U420-U428, U440-U442
Franklin

U429-U439, U443-U445, U481-U485, U529-U531
Washington

1916-32

SCOTT NO.	DESCRIPTION	UNUSED ENTIRE	UNUSED CUT SQ.	USED CUT SQ.
U420	1¢ green on white	.40	.25	.25
U421	1¢ green on amber	.80	.50	.35
U422	1¢ green on oriental buff	3.00	2.50	1.20
U423	1¢ green on blue	.80	.50	.25
U424	1¢ green on manila	9.00	7.20	4.80
W425	1¢ green on manila	.40	.30	.25
U426	1¢ green on brown (glazed)	60.00	50.00	19.25
W427	1¢ green on brown (glazed)	75.00	62.50	35.00
U428	1¢ green on brown (unglazed)	25.00	17.00	9.00
U429	2¢ carmine on white	.35	.25	.25
U430	2¢ carmine on amber	.50	.30	.25
U431	2¢ carmine on oriental buff	5.00	2.50	.70
U432	2¢ carmine on blue	.50	.30	.25
W433	2¢ carmine on manila	.55	.30	.25
W434	2¢ carmine on brown (glazed)	120.00	100.00	55.00
W435	2¢ carmine/brown (unglazed)	120.00	100.00	55.00
U436	3¢ dark violet on white	.75	.60	.25
U436f	3¢ purple on white (1932)	.55	.40	.25
U436h	3¢ carmine on white (error)	60.00	35.00	33.00
U437	3¢ dark violet on amber	6.00	2.70	1.20
U437a	3¢ purple on amber (1932)	.70	.35	.25
U437g	3¢ carmine on amber (error)	525.00	500.00	325.00
U437h	3¢ black on amber (error)	300.00	200.00	......
U438	3¢ dark violet on buff	30.00	24.00	1.80
U439	3¢ dark violet on blue	10.80	7.20	1.70
U439a	3¢ purple on blue (1932)	.80	.35	.25
U439g	3¢ carmine on blue (error)	500.00	400.00	320.00
U440	4¢ black on white	3.50	1.75	.60
U441	4¢ black on amber	5.00	3.00	.90
U442	4¢ black on blue	6.00	3.00	1.00
U443	5¢ blue on white	6.00	3.20	3.00
U444	5¢ blue on amber	7.00	4.00	1.70
U445	5¢ blue on blue	8.40	4.20	3.50

1920-21 SURCHARGED

Type 1

Type 2

SCOTT NO.	DESCRIPTION	UNUSED ENTIRE	UNUSED CUT SQ.	USED CUT SQ.
U446	2¢ on 3¢ dark violet on white .... (U436)	23.00	15.00	11.75

Surcharge on Envelopes of 1916-21 Type 2

SCOTT NO.	DESCRIPTION	UNUSED ENTIRE	UNUSED CUT SQ.	USED CUT SQ.
U447	2¢ on 3¢ dark violet on white, rose .... (U436)	12.00	9.00	7.70
U448	2¢ on 3¢ dark violet on white .... (U436)	14.00	3.00	2.10
U449	2¢ on 3¢ dark violet on amber .... (U437)	10.00	7.00	6.00
U450	2¢ on 3¢ dark violet on oriental buff .... (U438)	21.40	14.80	14.80
U451	2¢ on 3¢ dark violet on blue .... (U439)	21.00	15.00	11.00

Type 3

Surcharge on Envelopes of 1874-1921 Type 3 bars 2mm apart

SCOTT NO.	DESCRIPTION	UNUSED ENTIRE	UNUSED CUT SQ.	USED CUT SQ.
U454	2¢ on 2¢ carmine on white .... (U429)	210.00	160.00	......
U455	2¢ on 2¢ carmine on amber .... (U430)	4300.00	2300.00	......
U456	2¢ on 2¢ carmine on oriental buff .... (U431)	350.00	295.00	......
U457	2¢ on 2¢ carmine on blue .... (U432)	450.00	400.00	......
U458	2¢ on 3¢ dark violet on white .... (U436)	.75	.55	.40
U459	2¢ on 3¢ dark violet on amber .... (U437)	4.50	3.00	1.20
U460	2¢ on 3¢ dark violet on oriental buff .... (U438)	5.00	4.00	2.00
U461	2¢ on 3¢ dark violet on blue .... (U439)	8.00	6.00	1.20
U462	2¢ on 4¢ chocolate on white .... (U390)	1100.00	650.00	275.00
U463	2¢ on 4¢ chocolate on amber .... (U391)	1750.00	1300.00	375.00
U464	2¢ on 5¢ blue on white .... (U443)	1950.00	1500.00	......

Type 4 like Type 3, but bars 1-1/2 mm apart

SCOTT NO.	DESCRIPTION	UNUSED ENTIRE	UNUSED CUT SQ.	USED CUT SQ.
U465	2¢ on 1¢ green on white .... (U420)	3000.00	1800.00	......
U466A	2¢ on 2¢ carmine on white .... (U429)	1700.00	1000.00	......
U467	2¢ on 3¢ green on white .... (U163)	600.00	450.00	......
U468	2¢ on 3¢ dark violet on white .... (U436)	1.10	.75	.45
U469	2¢ on 3¢ dark violet on amber .... (U437)	5.00	3.75	2.50
U470	2¢ on 3¢ dark violet on oriental buff .... (U438)	10.00	6.00	3.00
U471	2¢ on 3¢ dark violet on blue .... (U439)	13.00	7.00	2.00
U472	2¢ on 4¢ chocolate on white .... (U390)	27.00	14.00	9.60
U473	2¢ on 4¢ chocolate on amber .... (U391)	25.00	17.00	11.00
U474	2¢ on 1¢ on 3¢ dark violet on white .... (U436)	400.00	300.00	......
U475	2¢ on 1¢ on 3¢ dark violet on amber .... (U437)	400.00	300.00	......

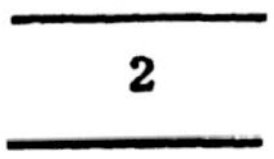

Type 5

Type 6

Type 7

Surcharge on Envelope of 1916-21 Type 5

SCOTT NO.	DESCRIPTION	UNUSED ENTIRE	UNUSED CUT SQ.	USED CUT SQ.
U476	2¢ on 3¢ dark violet on amber .... (U437)	500.00	300.00	......

Surcharge on Envelope of 1916-21 Type 6

SCOTT NO.	DESCRIPTION	UNUSED ENTIRE	UNUSED CUT SQ.	USED CUT SQ.
U477	2¢ on 3¢ dark violet on white .... (U436)	200.00	150.00	......
U478	2¢ on 3¢ dark violet on amber .... (U437)	500.00	375.00	......

Surcharge on Envelope of 1916-21 Type 7

SCOTT NO.	DESCRIPTION	UNUSED ENTIRE	UNUSED CUT SQ.	USED CUT SQ.
U479	2¢ on 3¢ dark violet on white (black) .... (U436)	575.00	475.00	......

1925

SCOTT NO.	DESCRIPTION	UNUSED ENTIRE	UNUSED CUT SQ.	USED CUT SQ.
U481	1-1/2¢ brown on white	.60	.25	.25
U481b	1-1/2¢ purple on white (error)	120.00	105.00	......
U482	1-1/2¢ brown on amber	1.75	1.10	.45
U483	1-1/2¢ brown on blue	2.10	1.80	.90
U484	1-1/2¢ brown on manila	13.25	7.25	3.75
W485	1-1/2¢ brown on manila	1.25	.90	.25

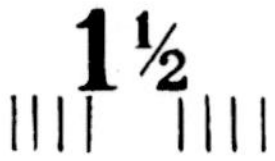

Type 8

Surcharge on Envelopes of 1887 Type 8

SCOTT NO.	DESCRIPTION	UNUSED ENTIRE	UNUSED CUT SQ.	USED CUT SQ.
U486	1-1/2¢ on 2¢ green on white .... (U311)	1350.00	925.00	......
U487	1-1/2¢ on 2¢ green on amber .... (U312)	1900.00	1500.00	......

Surcharge on Envelopes of 1899 Type 8

SCOTT NO.	DESCRIPTION	UNUSED ENTIRE	UNUSED CUT SQ.	USED CUT SQ.
U488	1-1/2¢ on 1¢ green on white .... (U352)	975.00	700.00	......
U489	1-1/2¢ on 1¢ green on amber .... (U353)	200.00	130.00	70.00

Surcharge on Envelopes of 1907-10 Type 8

SCOTT NO.	DESCRIPTION	UNUSED ENTIRE	UNUSED CUT SQ.	USED CUT SQ.
U490	1-1/2¢ on 1¢ green on white .... (U400)	11.00	7.00	4.20
U491	1-1/2¢ on 1¢ green on amber .... (U401)	13.00	9.00	3.00
U492	1-1/2¢ on 1¢ green on oriental buff .... (U402a)	750.00	575.00	145.00
U493	1-1/2¢ on 1¢ green on blue .... (U403c)	170.00	130.00	70.00
U494	1-1/2¢ on 1¢ green on manila .... (U404)	575.00	425.00	110.00

Surcharge on Envelopes of 1916-21 Type 8

SCOTT NO.	DESCRIPTION	UNUSED ENTIRE	UNUSED CUT SQ.	USED CUT SQ.
U495	1-1/2¢ on 1¢ green on white .... (U420)	1.00	.70	.30
U496	1-1/2¢ on 1¢ green on amber .... (U421)	28.00	20.00	14.00
U497	1-1/2¢ on 1¢ green on oriental buff .... (U422)	7.00	5.00	2.50
U498	1-1/2¢ on 1¢ green on blue .... (U423)	2.25	1.50	.90
U499	1-1/2¢ on 1¢ green on manila .... (U424)	20.00	13.00	8.00
U500	1-1/2¢ on 1¢ green on brown (unglazed) .... (U428)	100.00	85.00	40.00
U501	1-1/2¢ on 1¢ green on brown (glazed) .... (U426)	100.00	85.00	36.00
U502	1-1/2¢ on 2¢ carmine on white .... (U429)	475.00	300.00	......
U503	1-1/2¢ on 2¢ carmine on oriental buff...... (U431)	500.00	400.00	......
U504	1-1/2¢ on 2¢ carmine on blue .... (U432)	500.00	475.00	......

Surcharge on Envelopes of 1925 Type 8

SCOTT NO.	DESCRIPTION	UNUSED ENTIRE	UNUSED CUT SQ.	USED CUT SQ.
U505	1-1/2¢ on 1-1/2¢ brown on white .... (U481)	675.00	475.00	.....
U506	1-1/2¢ on 1-1/2¢ brown on blue .... (U483)	675.00	475.00	.....

Type 9

Surcharge on Envelopes of 1899 Type 9

SCOTT NO.	DESCRIPTION	UNUSED ENTIRE	UNUSED CUT SQ.	USED CUT SQ.
U508	1-1/2¢ on 1¢ green on amber .... (U353)	72.00	65.00	.....

Surcharge on Envelopes of 1903 Type 9

SCOTT NO.	DESCRIPTION	UNUSED ENTIRE	UNUSED CUT SQ.	USED CUT SQ.
U508A	1-1/2¢ on 1¢ green on white .... (U379)	7000.00	4800.00	.....
U509	1-1/2¢ on 1¢ green on amber .... (U380)	28.00	15.00	12.00
U509B	1-1/2¢ on 1¢ green on oriental buff .... (U381)	75.00	60.00	50.00

Surcharge on Envelopes of 1907-10 Type 9

SCOTT NO.	DESCRIPTION	UNUSED ENTIRE	UNUSED CUT SQ.	USED CUT SQ.
U510	1-1/2¢ on 1¢ green on white .... (U400)	5.00	3.00	1.50
U511	1-1/2¢ on 1¢ green on amber .... (U401)	400.00	275.00	95.00
U512	1-1/2¢ on 1¢ green on oriental buff .... (U402)	15.00	9.00	4.75
U513	1-1/2¢ on 1¢ green on blue .... (U403)	9.00	6.00	5.00
U514	1-1/2¢ on 1¢ green on manila .... (U404)	45.00	35.00	12.00
U515	1-1/2¢ on 1¢ green on white .... (U420)	.70	.35	.25
U516	1-1/2¢ on 1¢ green on amber .... (U421)	60.00	48.00	32.00
U517	1-1/2¢ on 1¢ green on oriental buff .... (U422)	8.00	6.00	1.50
U518	1-1/2¢ on 1¢ green on blue .... (U423)	8.00	6.00	1.50
U519	1-1/2¢ on 1¢ green on manila .... (U424)	38.00	30.00	12.00
U520	1-1/2¢ on 2¢ carmine on white .... (U429)	525.00	375.00	.....
U521	1-1/2¢ on 1¢ green on white, magenta surcharged .... (U420)	6.50	5.00	4.00

U522

U523-U528

U522: Die 1, "E" of "POSTAGE" has center bar shorter than top bar.

U522a: Die 2, "E" of "POSTAGE" has center and top bars same length.

U525: Die 1 "S" of "POSTAGE" even with "T".

U525a: Die 2 "S" of "POSTAGE" higher than "T".

1926 SESQUICENTENNIAL EXPOSITION

SCOTT NO.	DESCRIPTION	UNUSED ENTIRE	UNUSED CUT SQ.	USED CUT SQ.
U522	2¢ carmine on white, die 1	2.00	1.50	.60
U522a	2¢ carmine on white, die 2	12.50	8.00	4.50

1932 WASHINGTON BICENTENNIAL

SCOTT NO.	DESCRIPTION	UNUSED ENTIRE	UNUSED CUT SQ.	USED CUT SQ.
U523	1¢ olive green on white	2.00	1.25	1.00
U524	1-1/2¢ chocolate on white	3.25	2.00	2.00
U525	2¢ carmine on white, die 1	.75	.50	.25
U525a	2¢ carmine on white, die 2	100.00	85.00	18.00
U526	3¢ violet on white	3.00	2.50	.50
U527	4¢ black on white	27.50	22.00	20.00
U528	5¢ dark blue on white	6.00	5.00	4.00

1932 Designs of 1916-32

SCOTT NO.	DESCRIPTION	UNUSED ENTIRE	UNUSED CUT SQ.	USED CUT SQ.
U529	6¢ orange on white	10.00	5.75	5.00
U530	6¢ orange on amber	17.50	13.00	10.00
U531	6¢ orange on blue	17.00	13.00	11.00

U532 *Franklin* **U533** *Washington* **U535**

1950

SCOTT NO.	DESCRIPTION	FIRST DAY COVER	UNUSED ENTIRE	USED CUT SQ.
U532	1¢ green	2.00	8.50	2.00
U533	2¢ carmine	2.00	1.25	.30
U534	3¢ dark violet	2.00	.50	.25

1952

SCOTT NO.	DESCRIPTION	FIRST DAY COVER	UNUSED ENTIRE	USED CUT SQ.
U535	1-1/2¢ brown	......	6.50	4.00

U537, U538, U552, U556

U539, U540, U545, U553

Surcharge on Envelopes of 1916-32, 1950, 1965, 1971

1958

SCOTT NO.	DESCRIPTION	FIRST DAY COVER	UNUSED ENTIRE	USED CUT SQ.
U536	4¢ red violet	1.75	1.00	.30
U537	2¢ & 2¢ (4¢) carmine (U429)	......	4.00	2.00
U538	2¢ & 2¢ (4¢) carmine (U533)	......	1.00	1.50
U539	3¢ & 1¢ (4¢) purple, die1 (U436a)	......	18.50	12.00
U539a	3¢ & 1¢ (4¢) purple, die 7 (U436e)	......	15.00	10.00
U539b	3¢ & 1¢ (4¢) purple, die 9 (U436f)	......	36.00	16.00
U540	3¢ & 1¢ (4¢) dark violet (U534)	......	.70	1.25

U541
Franklin

U542
Washington

1960

SCOTT NO.	DESCRIPTION	FIRST DAY COVER	UNUSED ENTIRE	USED CUT SQ.
U541	1-1/4¢ turquoise	1.75	1.00	.60
U542	2-1/2¢ dull blue	1.75	1.00	.60

U543

SCOTT NO.	DESCRIPTION	FIRST DAY COVER	UNUSED ENTIRE	USED CUT SQ.
U543	4¢ Pony Express	2.00	.80	.40

U544
Lincoln

U546

1962

SCOTT NO.	DESCRIPTION	FIRST DAY COVER	UNUSED ENTIRE	USED CUT SQ.
U544	5¢ dark blue	1.75	1.20	.25

Surcharge on Envelope of 1958

SCOTT NO.	DESCRIPTION	FIRST DAY COVER	UNUSED ENTIRE	USED CUT SQ.
U545	4¢+1¢ red violet (U536)	......	1.80	1.35

1964

SCOTT NO.	DESCRIPTION	FIRST DAY COVER	UNUSED ENTIRE	USED CUT SQ.
U546	5¢ New York World's Fair	1.75	.75	.45

U547, U548, U548A, U566

U549

U550

U551

1965-69

SCOTT NO.	DESCRIPTION	FIRST DAY COVER	UNUSED ENTIRE	USED CUT SQ.
U547	1-1/4¢ brown	1.75	.95	.25
U548	1-4/10¢ brown (1968)	1.75	1.00	.25
U548A	1-6/10¢ orange (1969)	1.75	.90	.25
U549	4¢ bright blue	1.75	.95	.25
U550	5¢ bright purple	1.75	.90	.25
U551	6¢ light green (1968)	1.75	.85	.25

U554

1968
1958 Type Surcharges on Envelopes of 1965

SCOTT NO.	DESCRIPTION	FIRST DAY COVER	UNUSED ENTIRE	USED CUT SQ.
U552	4¢ & 2¢ (6¢) blue (U549)	9.00	4.75	2.25
U553	5¢ & 1¢ (6¢) purple (U550)	9.00	4.00	2.50

1970

SCOTT NO.	DESCRIPTION	FIRST DAY COVER	UNUSED ENTIRE	USED CUT SQ.
U554	6¢ Moby Dick	1.75	.60	.25

U555

U557

1971

SCOTT NO.	DESCRIPTION	FIRST DAY COVER	UNUSED ENTIRE	USED CUT SQ.
U555	6¢ Conference on Youth	1.75	.90	.25
U556	1-7/10¢ deep lilac	1.75	.40	.25
U557	8¢ ultramarine	1.75	.50	.25

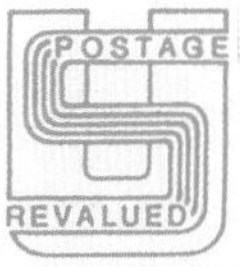

U561 & U562
Surcharge

SCOTT NO.	DESCRIPTION	FIRST DAY COVER	UNUSED ENTIRE	USED CUT SQ.
U561	6¢ & (2¢) (8¢) green (on U551)	4.00	1.25	1.35
U562	6¢ & (2¢) (8¢) blue (on U555)	4.00	3.00	2.75

U563

U564

SCOTT NO.	DESCRIPTION	FIRST DAY COVER	UNUSED ENTIRE	USED CUT SQ.
U563	8¢ Bowling	1.75	.90	.25
U564	8¢ Conference on Aging	1.75	.75	.25

U565

U567

1972

SCOTT NO.	DESCRIPTION	FIRST DAY COVER	UNUSED ENTIRE	USED CUT SQ.
U565	8¢ Transpo '72	1.75	.80	.25

1973

SCOTT NO.	DESCRIPTION	FIRST DAY COVER	UNUSED ENTIRE	USED CUT SQ.
U566	8¢ & 2¢ ultramarine (on U557)	3.00	.55	1.35
U567	10¢ emerald	1.75	.55	.25

U568

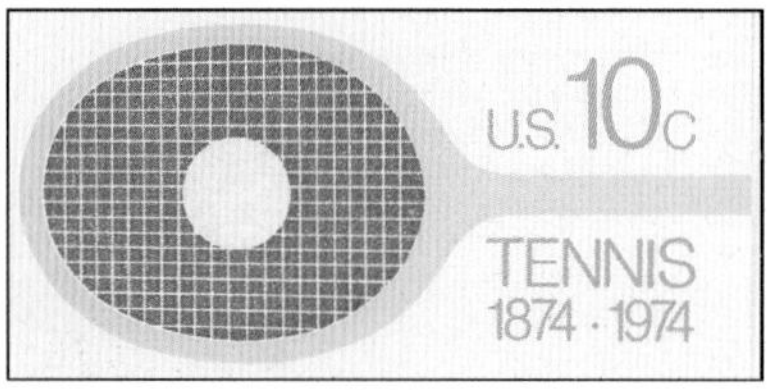

U569

1974

SCOTT NO.	DESCRIPTION	FIRST DAY COVER	UNUSED ENTIRE	USED CUT SQ.
U568	1-8/10¢ blue green	1.75	.35	.25
U569	10¢ Tennis Centenary	2.50	.80	.30

U571

U572

U573

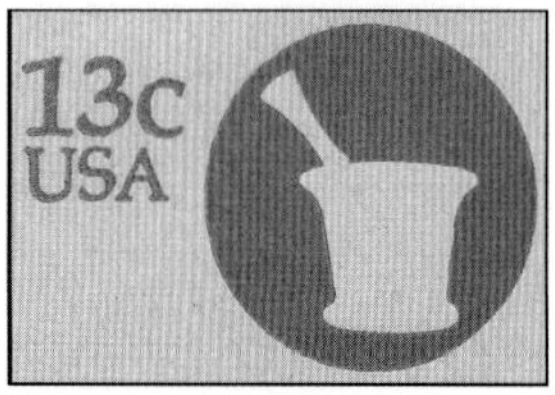

U574

U575

1975-76 BICENTENNIAL ERA

SCOTT NO.	DESCRIPTION	FIRST DAY COVER	UNUSED ENTIRE	USED CUT SQ.
U571	10¢ Seafaring	1.75	.55	.25
U572	13¢ Homemaker (1976)	1.75	.55	.25
U573	13¢ Farmer (1976)	1.75	.55	.25
U574	13¢ Doctor (1976)	1.75	.55	.25
U575	13¢ Craftsman (1976)	1.75	.55	.25

CUT SQUARES: From 1947 to date, Unused Envelope Cut Squares can be supplied at the Unused Entire Price.

U576

1975

SCOTT NO.	DESCRIPTION	FIRST DAY COVER	UNUSED ENTIRE	USED CUT SQ.
U576	13¢ orange brown	1.75	.50	.25

U577

U578

U579

U580

U581

1976-78

SCOTT NO.	DESCRIPTION	FIRST DAY COVER	UNUSED ENTIRE	USED CUT SQ.
U577	2¢ red	1.75	.35	.25
U578	2.1¢ green (1977)	1.75	.35	.25
U579	2.7¢ green (1978)	1.75	.40	.25
U580	(15¢) "A" orange (1978)	1.75	.60	.25
U581	15¢ red & white (1978)	1.75	.60	.25

1976

SCOTT NO.	DESCRIPTION	FIRST DAY COVER	UNUSED ENTIRE	USED CUT SQ.
U582	13¢ Bicentennial (design of U218)	1.75	.55	.25

U583

1977

SCOTT NO.	DESCRIPTION	FIRST DAY COVER	UNUSED ENTIRE	USED CUT SQ.
U583	13¢ Golf	8.00	.80	.25

U584

U585

SCOTT NO.	DESCRIPTION	FIRST DAY COVER	UNUSED ENTIRE	USED CUT SQ.
U584	13¢ Energy Conservation	1.75	.50	.25
U585	13¢ Energy Development	1.75	.50	.25

SCOTT NO.	DESCRIPTION	FIRST DAY COVER	UNUSED ENTIRE	USED CUT SQ.

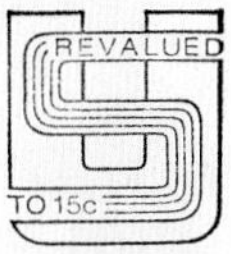

U586, U588

U586

1978

U586	15¢ on 16¢ blue & white	1.75	.55	.25

U587

U587	15¢ Auto Racing	2.00	.75	.25
U588	15¢ on 13¢ white, orange brown (U576)	1.75	.55	.25

U589

U590

1979

U589	3.1¢ ultramarine & white	1.75	.30	.60

1980

U590	3.5¢ purple	1.75	.30	.60

U591

U592

U593

U594

1981-82

U591	5.9¢ brown (1982)	1.85	.30	.60
U592	(18¢) "B" violet & white	1.75	.60	.25
U593	18¢ white & dark blue	1.75	.60	.25
U594	(20¢) "C" brown & white	1.75	60	.15

U595

U596

1979

U595	15¢ Veterinarians	1.75	.60	.25
U596	15¢ Moscow Olympics	1.75	.90	.25

SCOTT NO.	DESCRIPTION	FIRST DAY COVER	UNUSED ENTIRE	USED CUT SQ.

U597

U598

U599

1980

U597	15¢ Bicycle	1.75	.55	.25
U598	15¢ America's Cup	1.75	.55	.25
U599	15¢ Honeybee	1.75	.55	.25

U600

U601

1981

U600	18¢ Blinded Veterans	1.75	.60	.25
U601	20¢ deep magenta & white	1.75	.60	.25

U602

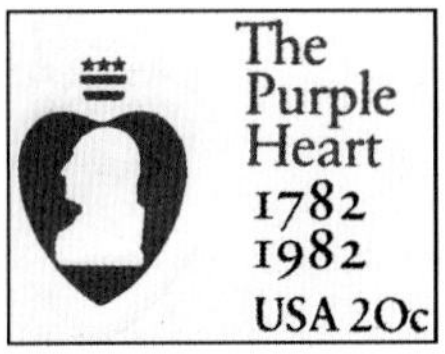

U603

1982

U602	20¢ black, blue & magenta	1.75	.60	.25
U603	20¢ Purple Heart	1.75	.80	.25

U604

U605

U606

1983

U604	5.2¢ orange & white	1.75	.50	.25
U605	20¢ Paralyzed Veterans	1.75	.60	.25

1984

U606	20¢ Small Business	2.00	.60	.25

U607

U608

U609

1985

SCOTT NO.	DESCRIPTION	FIRST DAY COVER	UNUSED ENTIRE	USED CUT SQ.
U607	(22¢) "D"	1.75	.75	.40
U608	22¢ Bison	1.75	.75	.25
U609	6¢ Old Ironsides	1.75	.30	.25

U610

1986

SCOTT NO.	DESCRIPTION	FIRST DAY COVER	UNUSED ENTIRE	USED CUT SQ.
U610	8.5¢ Mayflower	1.75	.30	.25

U611

U612

U613

1988

SCOTT NO.	DESCRIPTION	FIRST DAY COVER	UNUSED ENTIRE	USED CUT SQ.
U611	25¢ Stars	1.75	.80	.25
U612	8.4¢ Constellation	1.75	.30	.25
U613	25¢ Snowflake	1.75	1.00	25.00

U614

U615

U616

U617, U639

1989

SCOTT NO.	DESCRIPTION	FIRST DAY COVER	UNUSED ENTIRE	USED CUT SQ.
U614	25¢ Stamped Return Envelope	1.75	.60	.30
U615	25¢ "USA" and Stars	1.75	.60	.30
U616	25¢ LOVE	1.75	.60	1.00
U617	25¢ Shuttle Docking Hologram	1.75	1.25	.80

U618

U619

1990-91

SCOTT NO.	DESCRIPTION	FIRST DAY COVER	UNUSED ENTIRE	USED CUT SQ.
U618	25¢ Football Hologram	2.75	1.25	.75
U619	29¢ Star	1.75	.75	.30

U620

SCOTT NO.	DESCRIPTION	FIRST DAY COVER	UNUSED ENTIRE	USED CUT SQ.
U620	11.1¢ Birds on Wire	1.75	.60	.55

U621

U622

SCOTT NO.	DESCRIPTION	FIRST DAY COVER	UNUSED ENTIRE	USED CUT SQ.
U621	29¢ Love	1.75	.75	.70
U622	29¢ Magazine Industry	1.75	.75	.60

U623

U624

SCOTT NO.	DESCRIPTION	FIRST DAY COVER	UNUSED ENTIRE	USED CUT SQ.
U623	29¢ Star	1.75	.75	.30
U624	26¢ Country Geese	1.75	.75	.70

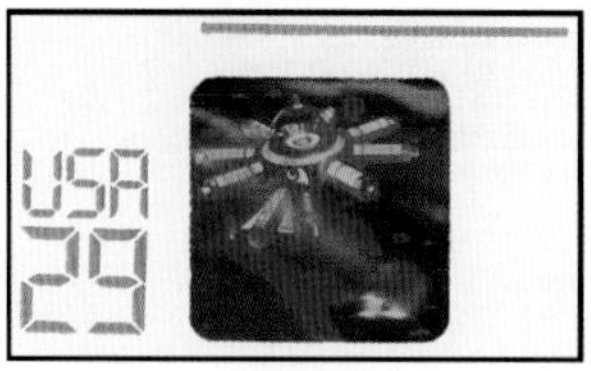

U625

U626

1992

SCOTT NO.	DESCRIPTION	FIRST DAY COVER	UNUSED ENTIRE	USED CUT SQ.
U625	29¢ Space Station	1.75	1.25	.60
U626	29¢ Saddle & Blanket	1.75	.75	.30

U627

U628

SCOTT NO.	DESCRIPTION	FIRST DAY COVER	UNUSED ENTIRE	USED CUT SQ.
U627	29¢ Protect the Environment	1.75	.75	.30
U628	19.8¢ Star	1.75	.60	.30

U629

U630

SCOTT NO.	DESCRIPTION	FIRST DAY COVER	UNUSED ENTIRE	USED CUT SQ.
U629	29¢ Americans With Disabilities	1.75	.75	.30

1993

SCOTT NO.	DESCRIPTION	FIRST DAY COVER	UNUSED ENTIRE	USED CUT SQ.
U630	29¢ Kitten	1.75	1.10	.60

U631

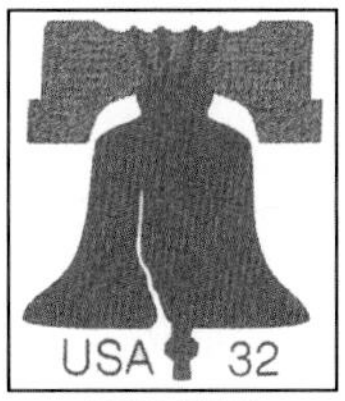

U632, U638

1994

SCOTT NO.	DESCRIPTION	FIRST DAY COVER	UNUSED ENTIRE	USED CUT SQ.
U631	29¢ Football	1.75	.75	.60

U633, U634

U635

1995

SCOTT NO.	DESCRIPTION	FIRST DAY COVER	UNUSED ENTIRE	USED CUT SQ.
U632	32¢ Liberty Bell	1.95	.75	.35
U633	(32¢) "G" Old Glory (Design size 49x38mm)	1.95	.75	.35
U634	(32¢) "G" Old Glory (Design size 53x44mm)	1.95	.75	.35
U635	(5¢) Sheep, Nonprofit	1.95	.60	.55

U636

U637

SCOTT NO.	DESCRIPTION	FIRST DAY COVER	UNUSED ENTIRE	USED CUT SQ.
U636	(10¢) Graphic Eagle, Bulk Rate	1.95	.40	.35
U637	32¢ Spiral Heart	1.95	.75	.35
U638	32¢ Liberty Bell, security	1.95	.75	.35
U639	32¢ Space Station	1.95	.75	.35

U640

U641

1996

SCOTT NO.	DESCRIPTION	FIRST DAY COVER	UNUSED ENTIRE	USED CUT SQ.
U640	32¢ Save our Environment	1.95	.75	.35
U641	32¢ Paralympic Games	1.95	.75	.35

U642, U643

U645

U644

1999-2000

SCOTT NO.	DESCRIPTION	FIRST DAY COVER	UNUSED ENTIRE	USED CUT SQ.
U642	33¢ Flag, yellow, blue & red	1.95	.80	.35
U642a	same, tagging bars to right of design	1.95	.80	.35
U643	33¢ Flag, blue & red	1.95	.80	.35
U644	33¢ Love	1.95	.80	.35
U645	33¢ Lincoln, blue & black	1.95	.80	.35

U646

U647

2001-03

SCOTT NO.	DESCRIPTION	FIRST DAY COVER	UNUSED ENTIRE	USED CUT SQ.
U646	34¢ Eagle, blue gray & gray	1.95	.85	.35
U647	34¢ Lovebirds, rose & dull violet	1.95	.85	.35

U648

U649

U650

SCOTT NO.	DESCRIPTION	FIRST DAY COVER	UNUSED ENTIRE	USED CUT SQ.
U648	34¢ Community Colleges, dark blue & orange brown	1.95	.85	.35
U649	37¢ Ribbon Star, red & blue	1.95	.90	.40
U650	(10¢) Graphic Eagle, Presorted Standard	1.95	.40	.35

U651

U652

SCOTT NO.	DESCRIPTION	FIRST DAY COVER	UNUSED ENTIRE	USED CUT SQ.
U651	37¢ Nurturing Love	1.95	.90	.40
U652	$3.85 Jefferson Memorial, pre-paid flat rate	8.75	8.75	5.00

U653

2004

SCOTT NO.	DESCRIPTION	FIRST DAY COVER	UNUSED ENTIRE	USED CUT SQ.
U653	37¢ Goofy, Mickey Mouse, Donald Duck	3.00	3.00	2.50
U654	37¢ Bambi, Thumper	3.00	3.00	2.50
U655	37¢ Mufasa, Simba	3.00	3.00	2.50
U656	37¢ Jiminy Cricket, Pinocchio	3.00	3.00	2.50

2005

SCOTT NO.	DESCRIPTION	FIRST DAY COVER	UNUSED ENTIRE	USED CUT SQ.
U657	37¢ Wedding Flowers, letter sheet	1.95	3.00	2.50

U658

U659

2006

SCOTT NO.	DESCRIPTION	FIRST DAY COVER	UNUSED ENTIRE	USED CUT SQ.
U658	$4.05 X-Planes, pre-paid flat rate	....	9.25	7.00
U659	39¢ Benjamin Franklin	1.95	.90	.40

U660

U661

2007

SCOTT NO.	DESCRIPTION	FIRST DAY COVER	UNUSED ENTIRE	USED CUT SQ.
U660	$4.60 Air Force One, priority mail, pre-paid flat rate	....	10.00	7.00
U661	$16.25 Marine One, express mail, pre-paid flat rate	....	35.00	30.00

U662

SCOTT NO.	DESCRIPTION	FIRST DAY COVER	UNUSED ENTIRE	USED CUT SQ.
U662	41¢ Horses	2.00	1.00	.50

UC1

UC2-UC7

Airplane in Circle

Die 1. Vertical rudder not semi-circular, but slopes to the left. Tail projects into "G".
Die 2. Vertical rudder is semi-circular. Tail only touches "G" Die 2a. "6" is 6-1/2mm. wide.
Die 2b. "6" is 6mm. wide.
Die 2c. "6" is 5-1/2mm. wide.
Die 3. Vertical rudder leans forward. "S" closer to "O" than to "T" of "POSTAGE" and "E" has short center bar.

1929-44

SCOTT NO.	DESCRIPTION	UNUSED ENTIRE	UNUSED CUT SQ.	USED CUT SQ.
UC1	5¢ blue, die 1	4.50	3.25	2.00
UC2	5¢ blue, die 2	15.00	12.00	6.00
UC3	6¢ orange, die 2a	1.80	1.50	.50
UC3n	6¢, die 2a, no border	3.00	1.50	.50
UC4	6¢, die 2b, with border	55.00	3.00	2.50
UC4n	6¢, die 2b, no border	4.80	3.00	2.50
UC5	6¢, die 2c, no border	1.25	1.00	.40
UC6	6¢ orange on white, die 3	2.00	1.25	.45
UC6n	6¢, die 3, no border	3.00	1.50	.50
UC7	8¢ olive green	18.00	14.50	4.00

AIR 6¢ MAIL

Envelopes of 1916-32 surcharged

1945

SCOTT NO.	DESCRIPTION		UNUSED ENTIRE	UNUSED CUT SQ.	USED CUT SQ.
UC8	6¢ on 2¢ carmine on white	(U429)	1.75	1.40	.75
UC9	6¢ on 2¢ carmine on white	(U525)	120.00	90.00	45.00

REVALUED
5¢
P.O. DEPT.

1946

SCOTT NO.	DESCRIPTION		UNUSED ENTIRE	UNUSED CUT SQ.	USED CUT SQ.
UC10	5¢ on 6¢, die 2a	(UC3n)	4.00	3.00	1.75
UC11	5¢ on 6¢, die 2b	(UC4n)	11.00	10.75	5.50
UC12	5¢ on 6¢, die 2c	(UC5)	1.50	.90	.60
UC13	5¢ on 6¢, die 3	(UC6n)	1.15	.95	.75

UC14, UC15, UC18, UC26
DC-4 Skymaster

UC14: Die 1. Small projection below rudder is rounded.
UC15: Die 2. Small projection below rudder is sharp pointed.

SCOTT NO.	DESCRIPTION	FIRST DAY COVER	UNUSED ENTIRE	USED CUT SQ.
UC14	5¢ carmine, die 1	2.50	1.10	.25
UC15	5¢ carmine, die 2	......	1.10	.30

UC16
DC-4 Skymaster

UC17
Washington and Franklin, Mail-carrying Vehicles

1947

SCOTT NO.	DESCRIPTION	FIRST DAY COVER	UNUSED ENTIRE	USED CUT SQ.
UC16	10¢ red on blue, Entire "Air Letter" on face, 2-line inscription on back	6.00	9.00	6.50
UC16a	Entire, "Air Letter" on face, 4-line inscription on back	......	17.50	15.00
UC16c	Entire "Air Letter" and "Aerogramme" on face, 4-line inscription on back	......	55.00	13.50
UC16d	Entire "Air Letter" and "Aerogramme" on face, 3-line inscription on back	......	9.50	9.00

1947 CIPEX COMMEMORATIVE

SCOTT NO.	DESCRIPTION	FIRST DAY COVER	UNUSED ENTIRE	USED CUT SQ.
UC17	5¢ carmine	3.00	.60	.35

1950 Design of 1946

SCOTT NO.	DESCRIPTION	FIRST DAY COVER	UNUSED ENTIRE	USED CUT SQ.
UC18	6¢ carmine	1.75	.60	.35

ENVELOPE of 1946 Surcharged

ENVELOPE of 1946-47 Surcharged

1951 (Shaded Numeral)

SCOTT NO.	DESCRIPTION	FIRST DAY COVER	UNUSED ENTIRE	USED CUT SQ.
UC19	6¢ on 5¢, die 1 (UC14)	......	1.35	.60
UC20	6¢ on 5¢, die 2 (UC15)	......	1.25	.60

1952 (Solid Numeral)

SCOTT NO.	DESCRIPTION	FIRST DAY COVER	UNUSED ENTIRE	USED CUT SQ.
UC21	6¢ on 5¢, die 1 (UC14)	......	37.50	19.00
UC22	6¢ on 5¢, die 2 (UC15)	......	5.75	2.75
UC23	6¢ on 5¢ (UC17)	......	2450.00	......

UC25

1956 FIPEX COMMEMORATIVE

SCOTT NO.	DESCRIPTION	FIRST DAY COVER	UNUSED ENTIRE	USED CUT SQ.
UC25	6¢ red	1.75	1.10	.60

1958 Design of 1946

SCOTT NO.	DESCRIPTION	FIRST DAY COVER	UNUSED ENTIRE	USED CUT SQ.
UC26	7¢ blue	1.75	1.10	.60

UC27-UC31

Surcharge on Envelopes of 1934 to 1956

1958

SCOTT NO.	DESCRIPTION	FIRST DAY COVER	UNUSED ENTIRE	USED CUT SQ.
UC27	6¢ & 1¢ (7¢) orange, die 2a (UC3n)	......	400.00	......
UC28	6¢ & 1¢ (7¢), die 2b (UC4n)	......	125.00	82.50
UC29	6¢ & 1¢ (7¢) orange, die 2c (UC5)	......	60.00	52.50
UC30	6¢ & 1¢ (7¢) carmine (UC18)	......	1.35	.60
UC31	6¢ & 1¢ (7¢) red (UC25)	......	1.40	.60

UC32

UC33, UC34

UC35

1958-59

SCOTT NO.	DESCRIPTION	FIRST DAY COVER	UNUSED ENTIRE	USED CUT SQ.
UC32	10¢ blue & red Entire letter sheet, 2-line inscription on back (1959)	......	7.00	5.25
UC32a	Entire letter sheet, 3 line inscription on back	2.25	12.00	5.25

1958

SCOTT NO.	DESCRIPTION	FIRST DAY COVER	UNUSED ENTIRE	USED CUT SQ.
UC33	7¢ blue	1.75	.80	.25

1960

SCOTT NO.	DESCRIPTION	FIRST DAY COVER	UNUSED ENTIRE	USED CUT SQ.
UC34	7¢ carmine	1.75	.75	.25

1961

SCOTT NO.	DESCRIPTION	FIRST DAY COVER	UNUSED ENTIRE	USED CUT SQ.
UC35	11¢ red & blue	3.25	3.00	2.50

UC36

1962

SCOTT NO.	DESCRIPTION	FIRST DAY COVER	UNUSED ENTIRE	USED CUT SQ.
UC36	8¢ red	1.75	.85	.25

UC37

UC38, UC39

1965

SCOTT NO.	DESCRIPTION	FIRST DAY COVER	UNUSED ENTIRE	USED CUT SQ.
UC37	8¢ red	1.75	.60	.25
UC38	11¢ J.F. Kennedy	1.75	4.00	3.00

UC40

UC41 (surcharge on UC37)

UC42

1967

SCOTT NO.	DESCRIPTION	FIRST DAY COVER	UNUSED ENTIRE	USED CUT SQ.
UC39	13¢ J.F. Kennedy	1.75	3.50	3.00

1968

SCOTT NO.	DESCRIPTION	FIRST DAY COVER	UNUSED ENTIRE	USED CUT SQ.
UC40	10¢ red	1.75	.85	.25
UC41	8¢ & 2¢ (10¢) red	12.00	.95	.25
UC42	13¢ Human Rights Year	1.75	8.00	4.50

UC43

UC44

1971

SCOTT NO.	DESCRIPTION	FIRST DAY COVER	UNUSED ENTIRE	USED CUT SQ.
UC43	11¢ red & blue	1.75	.70	.25
UC44	15¢ gray, red, white and blue Birds in Flight	1.75	1.60	1.25
UC44a	Aerogramme added	1.75	1.60	1.25

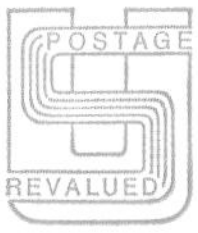

UC45 (surcharge on UC40)

UC47

1971 Revalued

SCOTT NO.	DESCRIPTION	FIRST DAY COVER	UNUSED ENTIRE	USED CUT SQ.
UC45	10 & (1¢) (11¢) red	6.00	2.00	.25

1973

SCOTT NO.	DESCRIPTION	FIRST DAY COVER	UNUSED ENTIRE	USED CUT SQ.
UC46	15¢ Ballooning	1.75	.85	.50
UC47	13¢ rose red	1.75	.75	.25

UC48

UC49

1974

SCOTT NO.	DESCRIPTION	FIRST DAY COVER	UNUSED ENTIRE	USED CUT SQ.
UC48	18¢ red & blue	1.75	1.00	.35
UC49	18¢ NATO 25th Anniversary	1.75	1.00	.50

UC50

UC51

SCOTT NO.	DESCRIPTION	FIRST DAY COVER	UNUSED ENTIRE	USED CUT SQ.
	1976			
UC50	22¢ red, white & blue	1.75	1.00	.50
	1978			
UC51	22¢ blue	1.75	.85	.30

UC52

UC53, UC54

UC55

SCOTT NO.	DESCRIPTION	FIRST DAY COVER	UNUSED ENTIRE	USED CUT SQ.
	1979			
UC52	22¢ Moscow Olympics	1.75	1.70	.30
	1980-81			
UC53	30¢ red, blue & brown	1.75	.85	1.25
UC54	30¢ yellow, magenta, blue & black (1981)	1.75	.85	1.25
	1982			
UC55	30¢ Made in U.S.A.	1.75	.85	1.25

UC56

UC57

SCOTT NO.	DESCRIPTION	FIRST DAY COVER	UNUSED ENTIRE	USED CUT SQ.
	1983			
UC56	30¢ Communications	1.75	.85	1.25
UC57	30¢ Olympics	1.75	.85	2.00

UC58

SCOTT NO.	DESCRIPTION	FIRST DAY COVER	UNUSED ENTIRE	USED CUT SQ.
	1985			
UC58	36¢ Landsat Satellite	1.75	.85	1.25

UC59

SCOTT NO.	DESCRIPTION	FIRST DAY COVER	UNUSED ENTIRE	USED CUT SQ.
UC59	36¢ Travel	1.75	.85	1.25

UC60

SCOTT NO.	DESCRIPTION	FIRST DAY COVER	UNUSED ENTIRE	USED CUT SQ.
UC60	36¢ Mark Twain, Halley's Comet	1.75	1.25	2.00

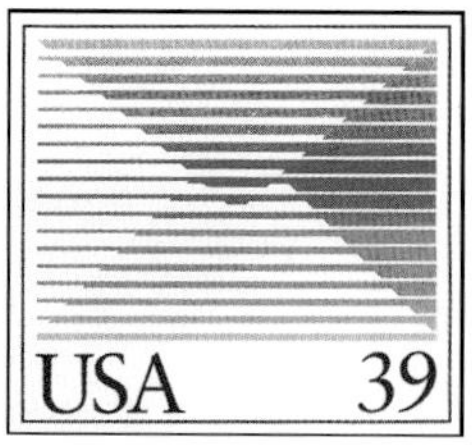

UC61

UC62

SCOTT NO.	DESCRIPTION	FIRST DAY COVER	UNUSED ENTIRE	USED CUT SQ.
	1986			
UC61	39¢ Letters	1.75	1.00	1.25
	1989			
UC62	39¢ Blair & Lincoln	1.75	1.00	1.25

UC63

UC64

SCOTT NO.	DESCRIPTION	FIRST DAY COVER	UNUSED ENTIRE	USED CUT SQ.
	1991			
UC63	45¢ Eagle	1.75	1.00	1.25
	1995			
UC64	50¢ Thaddeus Lowe	1.95	1.25	1.25

UC65

SCOTT NO.	DESCRIPTION	FIRST DAY COVER	UNUSED ENTIRE	USED CUT SQ.
	1999			
UC65	60¢ Voyagers National Park, Minnesota	1.95	1.35	1.25

UO1-UO13

UO14-UO17

UO18-UO69
Washington

OFFICIAL ENVELOPES

NOTE: **For details on similar appearing varieties please refer to the Scott Specialized Catalogue**

POST OFFICE DEPARTMENT

1873 SMALL NUMERALS

SCOTT NO.	DESCRIPTION	UNUSED ENTIRE	UNUSED CUT SQ.	USED CUT SQ.
UO1	2¢ black on lemon	40.00	25.00	11.00
UO2	3¢ black on lemon	30.00	17.00	7.00
UO4	6¢ black on lemon	40.00	28.00	17.00

1874-79 LARGE NUMERALS

SCOTT NO.	DESCRIPTION	UNUSED ENTIRE	UNUSED CUT SQ.	USED CUT SQ.
UO5	2¢ black on lemon	17.00	11.00	5.00
UO6	2¢ black on white	200.00	150.00	40.00
UO7	3¢ black on lemon	5.00	3.50	1.00
UO8	3¢ black on white	6000.00	3250.00	2400.00
UO9	3¢ black on amber	175.00	130.00	40.00
UO12	6¢ black on lemon	28.00	17.00	7.00
UO13	6¢ black on white	6000.00	3250.00	......

1877 POSTAL SERVICE

SCOTT NO.	DESCRIPTION	UNUSED ENTIRE	UNUSED CUT SQ.	USED CUT SQ.
UO14	black on white	12.00	8.00	5.00
UO15	black on amber	950.00	225.00	35.00
UO16	blue on amber	950.00	225.00	38.00
UO17	blue on blue	14.00	10.00	7.00

Portraits for the various denominations are the same as on the regular issue of 1870-73

WAR DEPARTMENT

1873 REAY ISSUE

SCOTT NO.	DESCRIPTION	UNUSED ENTIRE	UNUSED CUT SQ.	USED CUT SQ.
UO18	1¢ dark red on white	1250.00	750.00	325.00
UO19	2¢ dark red on white	3250.00	2500.00	475.00
UO20	3¢ dark red on white	110.00	75.00	48.00
UO22	3¢ dark red on cream	1200.00	950.00	275.00
UO23	6¢ dark red on white	450.00	350.00	95.00
UO24	6¢ dark red on cream	......	8500.00	440.00
UO25	10¢ dark red on white	......	......	2500.00
UO26	12¢ dark red on white	275.00	190.00	65.00
UO27	15¢ dark red on white	225.00	175.00	65.00
UO28	24¢ dark red on white	250.00	200.00	55.00
UO29	30¢ dark red on white	750.00	600.00	165.00
UO30	1¢ vermillion on white	400.00	225.00	......
WO31	1¢ vermillion on manila	38.00	22.00	15.00
UO32	2¢ vermillion on white	......	550.00	......
WO33	2¢ vermillion on manila	400.00	250.00	......
UO34	3¢ vermillion on white	180.00	110.00	45.00
UO35	3¢ vermillion on amber	400.00	140.00	......
UO36	3¢ vermillion on cream	45.00	18.00	14.00
UO37	6¢ vermillion on white	180.00	110.00	......
UO38	6¢ vermillion on cream	......	600.00	......
UO39	10¢ vermillion on white	475.00	375.00	......
UO40	12¢ vermillion on white	240.00	185.00	......
UO41	15¢ vermillion on white	3250.00	275.00	......
UO42	24¢ vermillion on white	675.00	475.00	......
UO43	30¢ vermillion on white	650.00	550.00	......

1875 PLIMPTON ISSUE

SCOTT NO.	DESCRIPTION	UNUSED ENTIRE	UNUSED CUT SQ.	USED CUT SQ.
UO44	1¢ red on white	275.00	210.00	95.00
UO45	1¢ red on amber	......	1200.00	
WO46	1¢ red on manila	10.00	4.50	3.00
UO47	2¢ red on white	200.00	150.00	......
UO48	2¢ red on amber	50.00	40.00	17.00
UO49	2¢ red on orange	75.00	65.00	17.00
WO50	2¢ red on manila	250.00	110.00	60.00
UO51	3¢ red on white	22.00	18.00	11.00
UO52	3¢ red on amber	28.00	22.00	11.00
UO53	3¢ red on cream	10.00	8.00	4.00
UO54	3¢ red on blue	6.00	4.00	3.00
UO55	3¢ red on fawn	12.00	7.00	3.00
UO56	6¢ red on white	110.00	75.00	35.00
UO57	6¢ red on amber	140.00	100.00	50.00
UO58	6¢ red on cream	300.00	250.00	95.00
UO59	10¢ red on white	325.00	275.00	90.00
UO60	10¢ red on amber	1750.00	1320.00	......
UO61	12¢ red on white	200.00	75.00	42.00
UO62	12¢ red on amber	1000.00	850.00	......
UO63	12¢ red on cream	1000.00	800.00	......
UO64	15¢ red on white	325.00	275.00	150.00
UO65	15¢ red on amber	1300.00	1000.00	......
UO66	15¢ red on cream	1200.00	850.00	......
UO67	30¢ red on white	250.00	200.00	150.00
UO68	30¢ red on amber	2500.00	1150.00	......
UO69	30¢ red on cream	1400.00	1100.00	......

UO70-UO72

1911 POSTAL SAVINGS

SCOTT NO.	DESCRIPTION	UNUSED ENTIRE	UNUSED CUT SQ.	USED CUT SQ.
UO70	1¢ green on white	100.00	80.00	25.00
UO71	1¢ green on oriental buff	275.00	210.00	70.00
UO72	2¢ carmine on white	22.00	13.50	4.50

UO73

UO74

UO75

1983

SCOTT NO.	DESCRIPTION	FIRST DAY COVER	UNUSED ENTIRE	USED CUT SQ.
UO73	20¢ blue and white	2.50	1.40	40.00

1985

SCOTT NO.	DESCRIPTION	FIRST DAY COVER	UNUSED ENTIRE	USED CUT SQ.
UO74	22¢ blue and white	2.00	.90	25.00

1987 Design Similar to UO74

SCOTT NO.	DESCRIPTION	FIRST DAY COVER	UNUSED ENTIRE	USED CUT SQ.
UO75	22¢ Savings Bond	3.25	1.40	30.00

UO76

UO77

UO78

UO81

UO83

UO84

1989

SCOTT NO.	DESCRIPTION	FIRST DAY COVER	UNUSED ENTIRE	USED CUT SQ.
UO76	(25¢) "E" black and blue Savings Bonds	2.00	1.40	30.00
UO77	25¢ black and blue	2.00	1.00	25.00
UO78	25¢ black and blue Savings Bonds	2.00	1.00	30.00

1990

SCOTT NO.	DESCRIPTION	FIRST DAY COVER	UNUSED ENTIRE	USED CUT SQ.
UO79	45¢ black & blue seal	2.25	1.40	......
UO80	65¢ black & blue seal	3.00	1.95	......
UO81	45¢ Self-sealing Envelope	2.25	1.40	......
UO82	65¢ Self-sealing Envelope	3.00	1.95	......

UO85

UO86, UO87

UO88, UO89, UO90, UO91, UO92, UO93

1991-92

SCOTT NO.	DESCRIPTION	FIRST DAY COVER	UNUSED ENTIRE	USED CUT SQ.
UO83	(29¢) "F" black and blue Savings Bond	2.00	1.40	30.00
UO84	29¢ black and blue	2.00	1.00	25.00
UO85	29¢ black and blue Savings Bond	2.00	.90	25.00
UO86	52¢ Consular Service	2.50	2.00	......
UO87	75¢ Consular Service	3.00	4.00	......

1995

SCOTT NO.	DESCRIPTION	FIRST DAY COVER	UNUSED ENTIRE	USED CUT SQ.
UO88	32¢ Great Seal, red and blue	2.00	.90	25.00

1999

SCOTT NO.	DESCRIPTION	FIRST DAY COVER	UNUSED ENTIRE	USED CUT SQ.
UO89	33¢ Great Seal, red and blue	2.00	.90	25.00

2001-07

SCOTT NO.	DESCRIPTION	FIRST DAY COVER	UNUSED ENTIRE	USED CUT SQ.
UO90	34¢ Great Seal, red and blue	2.00	1.00	25.00
UO91	37¢ Great Seal, red and blue	2.00	1.00	....
UO92	39¢ Great Seal, red and blue	2.00	1.00	....
UO93	41¢ Great Seal, red and blue	2.00	1.25	....

POSTAL CARDS

Prices Are For Entire Cards

MINT: As Issued, no printing or writing added.
UNUSED: Uncancelled, with printing or writing added.

UX1, UX3, U65

UX4, UX5, UX7
Liberty

UX6, UX13, UX16

1873

SCOTT NO.	DESCRIPTION	MINT	UNUSED	USED
UX1	1¢ brown, large watermark	400.00	60.00	22.50
UX3	1¢ brown, small watermark	90.00	22.00	3.00

1875 Inscribed "Write the Address", etc.

SCOTT NO.	DESCRIPTION	MINT	UNUSED	USED
UX4	1¢ black, watermarked	3250.00	800.00	450.00
UX5	1¢ black, unwatermarked	85.00	7.50	.50

1879

SCOTT NO.	DESCRIPTION	MINT	UNUSED	USED
UX6	2¢ blue on buff	38.00	12.00	27.50

1881 Inscribed "Nothing but the Address", etc.

SCOTT NO.	DESCRIPTION	MINT	UNUSED	USED
UX7	1¢ black on buff	75.00	7.00	.50

UX8

UX9

Jefferson

UX10, UX11
Grant

1885

SCOTT NO.	DESCRIPTION	MINT	UNUSED	USED
UX8	1¢ brown on buff	60.00	10.00	1.50

1886

SCOTT NO.	DESCRIPTION	MINT	UNUSED	USED
UX9	1¢ black on buff	28.00	2.00	.65

1891

SCOTT NO.	DESCRIPTION	MINT	UNUSED	USED
UX10	1¢ black on buff	50.00	6.50	1.75
UX11	1¢ blue on grayish white	25.00	6.00	3.00

UX12

UX14

Jefferson

UX15
John Adams

1894

SCOTT NO.	DESCRIPTION	MINT	UNUSED	USED
UX12	1¢ black on buff Small Wreath	47.50	2.50	.75

1897

SCOTT NO.	DESCRIPTION	MINT	UNUSED	USED
UX13	2¢ blue on cream	200.00	95.00	95.00
UX14	1¢ black on buff Large Wreath	45.00	3.00	.50

1898

SCOTT NO.	DESCRIPTION	MINT	UNUSED	USED
UX15	1¢ black on buff	50.00	12.50	16.00
UX16	2¢ black on buff	15.00	6.25	20.00

UX18

UX19, UX20
McKinley

UX21

1902 Profile Background

SCOTT NO.	DESCRIPTION	MINT	UNUSED	USED
UX18	1¢ black on buff	17.50	1.75	.40

1907

SCOTT NO.	DESCRIPTION	MINT	UNUSED	USED
UX19	1¢ black on buff	50.00	2.50	.60

1908 Correspondence Space at Left

SCOTT NO.	DESCRIPTION	MINT	UNUSED	USED
UX20	1¢ black on buff	60.00	9.00	4.50

1910 Background Shaded

SCOTT NO.	DESCRIPTION	MINT	UNUSED	USED
UX21	1¢ blue on bluish	120.00	18.00	14.00

UX22, UX24
McKinley

UX23, UX26
Lincoln

UX25
Grant

White Portrait Background

SCOTT NO.	DESCRIPTION	MINT	UNUSED	USED
UX22	1¢ blue on bluish	20.00	2.00	.45

1911

SCOTT NO.	DESCRIPTION	MINT	UNUSED	USED
UX23	1¢ red on cream	12.00	4.00	6.00
UX24	1¢ red on cream	10.00	1.50	.35
UX25	2¢ red on cream	1.50	.75	9.00

1913

SCOTT NO.	DESCRIPTION	MINT	UNUSED	USED
UX26	1¢ green on cream	14.00	3.00	9.00

UX27
Jefferson

UX28, UX43
Lincoln

UX29, UX30
Jefferson

UX32, UX33
surcharge

1914

SCOTT NO.	DESCRIPTION	MINT	UNUSED	USED
UX27	1¢ green on buff	.35	.20	.30

1917-18

SCOTT NO.	DESCRIPTION	MINT	UNUSED	USED
UX28	1¢ green on cream	1.00	.40	.40
UX29	2¢ red on buff, die 1	42.00	7.00	2.50
UX30	2¢ red on cream, die 2 (1918)	35.00	5.00	1.80

NOTE: On UX29 end of queue slopes sharply down to right while on UX30 it extends nearly horizontally.

1920 UX29 & UX30 Revalued

SCOTT NO.	DESCRIPTION	MINT	UNUSED	USED
UX32	1¢ on 2¢ red, die 1	55.00	16.50	13.00
UX33	1¢ on 2¢ red, die 2	12.50	2.75	2.25

UX37
McKinley

UX38
Franklin

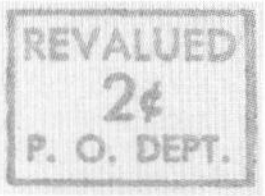

UX39-42
surcharge

1926

SCOTT NO.	DESCRIPTION	MINT	UNUSED	USED
UX37	3¢ red on buff	4.75	2.00	17.50

SCOTT NO.	DESCRIPTION	FIRST DAY COVER	MINT	USED
	1951			
UX38	2¢ carmine rose	1.75	.40	.35
	1952 UX27 & UX28 Surcharged by cancelling machine, light green			
UX39	2¢ on 1¢ green	......	.60	.35
UX40	2¢ on 1¢ green	......	.70	.50
	UX27 & UX28 Surcharge Typographed, dark green			
UX41	2¢ on 1¢ green	......	5.00	2.00
UX42	2¢ on 1¢ green	......	5.25	2.75
	1952 Design of 1917			
UX43	2¢ carmine	1.75	.30	1.00

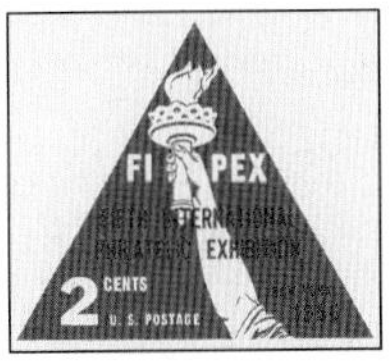

UX44

UX45, UY16

UX46, UY17

SCOTT NO.	DESCRIPTION	FIRST DAY COVER	MINT	USED
	1956 FIPEX COMMEMORATIVE			
UX44	2¢ deep carmine & dark violet	1.75	.35	1.00
	1956 INTERNATIONAL CARD			
UX45	4¢ deep red & ultramarine	1.75	1.75	100.00
	1958			
UX46	3¢ purple	1.75	.50	.25
	As above, but with printed precancel lines			
UX46d	3¢ purple	......	5.00	2.50

ONE CENT
ADDITIONAL
PAID

UX47 surcharge

UX48, UY18
Lincoln

UX49, UX54, UX59, UY19, UY20

SCOTT NO.	DESCRIPTION	FIRST DAY COVER	MINT	USED
	1958 UX38 Surcharged			
UX47	2¢ & 1¢ carmine rose	......	235.00	650.00
Mint *UX47 has advertising				
	1962-66			
UX48	4¢ red violet	1.75	.60	.25
UX48a	4¢ luminescent (1966)	3.00	.60	.25
	1963			
UX49	7¢ Tourism	1.75	4.00	75.00

UX50

UX51

SCOTT NO.	DESCRIPTION	FIRST DAY COVER	MINT	USED
	1964			
UX50	4¢ Customs Service	1.75	.50	1.00
UX51	4¢ Social Security	1.75	.50	1.00

UX52

UX53

SCOTT NO.	DESCRIPTION	FIRST DAY COVER	MINT	USED
	1965			
UX52	4¢ Coast Guard	1.75	.45	1.00
UX53	4¢ Census Bureau	1.75	.45	1.00
	1967 Design of UX49			
UX54	8¢ Tourism	1.75	4.25	75.00

UX55, UY21
Lincoln

UX56

SCOTT NO.	DESCRIPTION	FIRST DAY COVER	MINT	USED
	1968			
UX55	5¢ emerald	1.75	.30	.75
UX56	5¢ Women Marines	1.75	.40	1.00

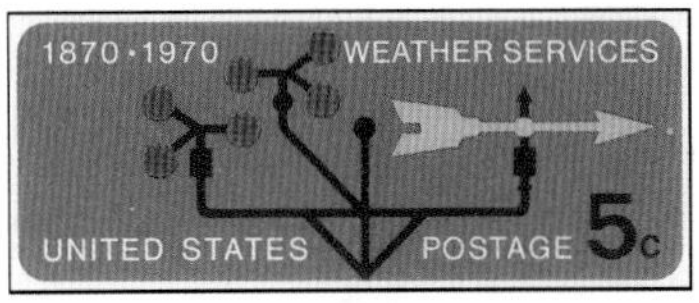

UX57

SCOTT NO.	DESCRIPTION	FIRST DAY COVER	MINT	USED
	1970			
UX57	5¢ Weather Bureau	1.75	.35	1.00

UX58, UY22

SCOTT NO.	DESCRIPTION	FIRST DAY COVER	MINT	USED
	1971			
UX58	6¢ Paul Revere	1.75	.30	1.00
	Design of UX49			
UX59	10¢ Tourism	1.75	4.50	65.00

UX60

SCOTT NO.	DESCRIPTION	FIRST DAY COVER	MINT	USED
	1971			
UX60	6¢ New York Hospital	1.75	.35	1.00

UX61

UX62

UX63

UX64, UY23

SCOTT NO.	DESCRIPTION	FIRST DAY COVER	MINT	USED
	1972			
UX61	6¢ U.S.F. Constellation	1.75	1.00	12.00
UX62	6¢ Monument Valley	1.75	.45	12.00
UX63	6¢ Gloucester, Massachusetts	1.75	.45	7.00
UX64	6¢ John Hanson	1.75	.60	1.00

UX66, UY24

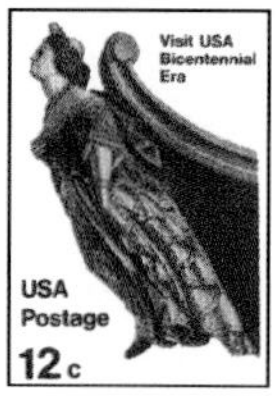

UX67

1973

SCOTT NO.	DESCRIPTION	FIRST DAY COVER	MINT	USED
UX65	6¢ Liberty, magenta, Design of 1873	1.75	.35	1.00
UX66	8¢ Samuel Adams	1.75	.35	1.00

1974

SCOTT NO.	DESCRIPTION	FIRST DAY COVER	MINT	USED
UX67	12¢ Visit USA	1.75	.45	50.00

UX68, UY25

UX69, UY26

UX70, UY27

1975-76

SCOTT NO.	DESCRIPTION	FIRST DAY COVER	MINT	USED
UX68	7¢ Charles Thomson	1.75	.35	12.00
UX69	9¢ J. Witherspoon	1.75	.35	1.00
UX70	9¢ Caesar Rodney	1.75	.35	1.00

UX71

UX72, UY28

1977

SCOTT NO.	DESCRIPTION	FIRST DAY COVER	MINT	USED
UX71	9¢ Federal Court House	1.75	.50	1.00
UX72	9¢ Nathan Hale	1.75	.55	1.00

UX73

UX74, UX75, UY29, UY30

UX76

UX77

1978

SCOTT NO.	DESCRIPTION	FIRST DAY COVER	MINT	USED
UX73	10¢ Music Hall	1.75	.35	1.00
UX74	(10¢) John Hancock	1.75	.35	1.00
UX75	10¢ John Hancock	1.75	.35	1.00
UX76	14¢ "Eagle"	1.75	.50	35.00
UX77	10¢ multicolored	1.75	.50	2.00

UX78

UX79

UX80

1979

SCOTT NO.	DESCRIPTION	FIRST DAY COVER	MINT	USED
UX78	10¢ Fort Sackville	1.75	.35	2.00
UX79	10¢ Casimir Pulaski	1.75	.35	2.00
UX80	10¢ Moscow Olympics	1.75	.60	2.00
UX81	10¢ Iolani Palace	1.75	.35	2.00

UX81

UX82

UX83

UX84

UX85

UX86

1980

SCOTT NO.	DESCRIPTION	FIRST DAY COVER	MINT	USED
UX82	14¢ Winter Olympics	1.75	.60	22.00
UX83	10¢ Salt Lake Temple	1.75	.35	2.00
UX84	10¢ Count Rochambeau	1.75	.35	2.00
UX85	10¢ Kings Mountain	1.75	.35	2.00
UX86	19¢ Sir Francis Drake	1.75	.75	40.00

UX87

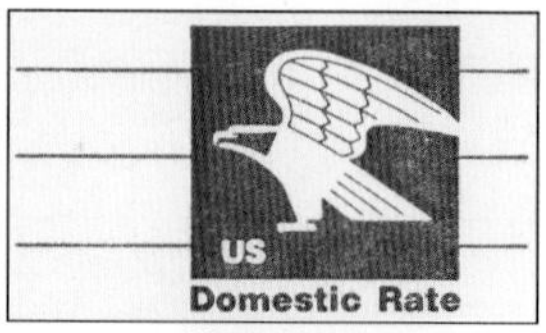

UX88, UY31

UX89, UY32

1981

SCOTT NO.	DESCRIPTION	FIRST DAY COVER	MINT	USED
UX87	10¢ Cowpens	1.75	.35	18.50
UX88	"B" (12¢) violet & white	1.75	.35	.75
UX89	12¢ Isaiah Thomas	1.75	.35	.75

UX90

UX91

UX92, UY33

UX93, UY34

SCOTT NO.	DESCRIPTION	FIRST DAY COVER	MINT	USED
UX90	12¢ Eutaw Springs	1.75	.35	17.50
UX91	12¢ Lewis & Clark	1.75	.35	28.00
UX92	(13¢) Robert Morris	1.75	.35	.75
UX93	13¢ Robert Morris	1.75	.35	.75

UX94

UX95

UX96

UX97

1982

SCOTT NO.	DESCRIPTION	FIRST DAY COVER	MINT	USED
UX94	13¢ Francis Marion	1.75	.35	1.25
UX95	13¢ La Salle	1.75	.35	1.25
UX96	13¢ Academy of Music	1.75	.35	1.25
UX97	13¢ St. Louis Post Office	1.75	.35	1.25

UX98

UX99

UX100

1983

SCOTT NO.	DESCRIPTION	FIRST DAY COVER	MINT	USED
UX98	13¢ General Oglethorpe	1.75	.35	1.25
UX99	13¢ Washington Post Office	1.75	.35	1.25
UX100	13¢ Olympics	1.75	.35	1.25

UX101

UX102

UX103

UX104

1984

SCOTT NO.	DESCRIPTION	FIRST DAY COVER	MINT	USED
UX101	13¢ "Ark" & "Dove"	1.75	.35	1.25
UX102	13¢ Olympics	1.75	.35	1.50
UX103	13¢ Frederic Baraga	1.75	.35	1.25
UX104	13¢ Historic Preservation	1.75	.35	1.25

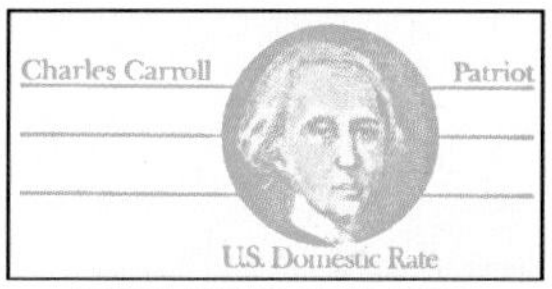

UX105, UX106, UY35, UY36

UX107

UX108

1985

SCOTT NO.	DESCRIPTION	FIRST DAY COVER	MINT	USED
UX105	(14¢) Charles Carroll	1.75	.35	.75
UX106	14¢ Charles Carroll	1.75	.35	.60
UX107	25¢ Flying Cloud	1.75	.65	25.00
UX108	14¢ George Wythe	1.75	.35	.90

UX109

UX110

UX111

UX112

1986

SCOTT NO.	DESCRIPTION	FIRST DAY COVER	MINT	USED
UX109	14¢ Connecticut	1.75	.35	2.00
UX110	14¢ Stamp Collecting	1.75	.35	1.50
UX111	14¢ Francis Vigo	1.75	.35	1.50
UX112	14¢ Rhode Island	1.75	.35	2.00

UX113

UX114

SCOTT NO.	DESCRIPTION	FIRST DAY COVER	MINT	USED
UX113	14¢ Wisconsin	1.75	.35	1.25
UX114	14¢ National Guard	1.75	.35	1.50

UX115

UX116

UX117

1987

SCOTT NO.	DESCRIPTION	FIRST DAY COVER	MINT	USED
UX115	14¢ Steel Plow	1.75	.35	1.50
UX116	14¢ Constitution	1.75	.35	1.00
UX117	14¢ Flag	1.75	.35	.75

SCOTT NO.	DESCRIPTION	FIRST DAY COVER	MINT	USED

UX118

UX119

1987 (continued)

UX118	14¢ Take Pride in America	1.75	.35	1.50
UX119	14¢ Timberline Lodge	1.75	.35	1.50

UX120

UX121

1988

UX120	15¢ America the Beautiful	1.75	.35	.75
UX121	15¢ Blair House	1.75	.35	.85

UX122

UX123

UX122	28¢ Yorkshire	1.75	.65	22.50
UX123	15¢ Iowa Territory	1.75	.35	.85

UX124

UX125

UX124	15¢ Northwest Territory	1.75	.35	.85
UX125	15¢ Hearst Castle	1.75	.35	.85

UX126

UX126	15¢ Federalist Papers	1.75	.35	.85

UX127

UX128

1989

UX127	15¢ The Desert	1.75	.35	.85
UX128	15¢¡ Healy Hall	1.75	.35	.85

SCOTT NO.	DESCRIPTION	FIRST DAY COVER	MINT	USED

UX129

UX130

UX129	15¢ The Wet Lands	1.75	.35	.85
UX130	15¢ Oklahoma Territory	1.75	.35	.85

UX131

UX132

UX131	21¢ The Mountains	1.75	.65	20.00
UX132	15¢ The Seashore	1.75	.35	.85

UX133

UX134

UX133	15¢ The Woodlands	1.75	.35	.85
UX134	15¢ Hull House	1.75	.35	.85

UX135

UX136

UX135	15¢ Philadelphia Cityscape	1.75	.35	.85
UX136	15¢ Baltimore Cityscape	1.75	.35	.85

UX137

UX138

UX137	15¢ New York Cityscape	1.75	.35	.85
UX138	15¢ Washington Cityscape	1.75	.35	.85
UX139-42	15¢ Cityscape sheet of 4 postcards	8.00	20.00	27.50

UX143

UX144

UX143	15¢ White House	1.75	1.50	3.00
UX144	15¢ Jefferson Memorial	1.75	1.50	3.00

UX145

UX146

UX147

UX148

UX150

UX151

UX152

1990

SCOTT NO.	DESCRIPTION	FIRST DAY COVER	MINT	USED
UX145	15¢ Papermaking	1.75	.35	.50
UX146	15¢ Literacy	1.75	.35	.85
UX147	15¢ Bingham	1.75	1.40	3.00
UX148	15¢ Isaac Royall House	1.75	.50	.85
UX150	15¢ Stanford University	1.75	.50	.85
UX151	15¢ DAR Memorial Hall	1.75	1.40	2.50
UX152	15¢ Chicago Orchestra Hall	1.75	.50	.85

UX153

UX154

UX155

1991

SCOTT NO.	DESCRIPTION	FIRST DAY COVER	MINT	USED
UX153	19¢ Flag	1.75	.50	.85
UX154	19¢ Carnegie Hall	1.75	.50	.85
UX155	19¢ Old Red Administration Building	1.75	.50	.50

UX156

UX157

SCOTT NO.	DESCRIPTION	FIRST DAY COVER	MINT	USED
UX156	19¢ Bill of Rights	1.75	.50	.85
UX157	19¢ University of Notre Dame, Administration Building	1.75	.50	.85

UX158

UX159

SCOTT NO.	DESCRIPTION	FIRST DAY COVER	MINT	USED
UX158	30¢ Niagara Falls	1.75	.90	1.50
UX159	19¢ Old Mill University of Vermont	1.75	.45	.50

UX160

UX161

UX162

UX163

UX164

UX165

1992

SCOTT NO.	DESCRIPTION	FIRST DAY COVER	MINT	USED
UX160	19¢ Wadsworth Atheneum	1.75	.50	.85
UX161	19¢ Cobb Hall University of Chicago	1.75	.50	.85
UX162	19¢ Waller Hall	1.75	.50	.85
UX163	19¢ America's Cup	1.75	1.50	4.00
UX164	19¢ Columbia River Gorge	1.75	.50	.85
UX165	19¢ Great Hall, Ellis Island	1.75	.50	.85

UX166

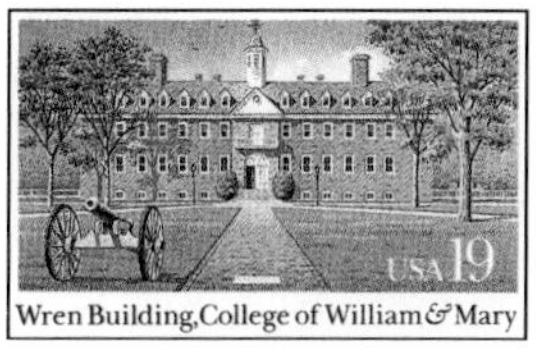

UX167

1993

SCOTT NO.	DESCRIPTION	FIRST DAY COVER	MINT	USED
UX166	19¢ National Cathedral	1.75	.50	.85
UX167	19¢ Wren Building	1.75	.50	.85

UX168

UX169

SCOTT NO.	DESCRIPTION	FIRST DAY COVER	MINT	USED
UX168	19¢ Holocaust Memorial	2.00	1.50	4.00
UX169	19¢ Fort Recovery	1.75	.50	.85

UX170

UX171

SCOTT NO.	DESCRIPTION	FIRST DAY COVER	MINT	USED
UX170	19¢ Playmakers Theatre	1.75	.50	.85
UX171	19¢ O'Kane Hall	1.75	.50	.85

UX172

UX173

1993 (continued)

SCOTT NO.	DESCRIPTION	FIRST DAY COVER	MINT	USED
UX172	19¢ Beecher Hall	1.75	.50	.85
UX173	19¢ Massachusetts Hall	1.75	.50	.85

UX174

UX175

UX176

UX177

1994

SCOTT NO.	DESCRIPTION	FIRST DAY COVER	MINT	USED
UX174	19¢ Abraham Lincoln Home	1.75	.50	.85
UX175	19¢ Myers Hall	1.75	.50	.85
UX176	19¢ Canyon de Chelly	1.75	.50	.85
UX177	19¢ St. Louis Union Station	1.75	.50	.85

UX178

Legends of the West

UX178	*Home on the Range*	**UX188**	*Nellie Cashman*
UX179	*Buffalo Bill*	**UX189**	*Charles Goodnight*
UX180	*Jim Bridger*	**UX190**	*Geronimo*
UX181	*Annie Oakley*	**UX191**	*Kit Carson*
UX182	*Native American Culture*	**UX192**	*Wild Bill Hickok*
UX183	*Chief Joseph*	**UX193**	*Western Wildlife*
UX184	*Bill Pickett*	**UX194**	*Jim Beckwourth*
UX185	*Bat Masterson*	**UX195**	*Bill Tilghman*
UX186	*John Fremont*	**UX196**	*Sacagawea*
UX187	*Wyatt Earp*	**UX197**	*Overland Mail*

SCOTT NO.	DESCRIPTION	FIRST DAY COVER	MINT	USED
UX178-97	19¢ Legends of the West, set of 20	35.00	35.00	65.00

UX198

UX199

UX198

1995

SCOTT NO.	DESCRIPTION	FIRST DAY COVER	MINT	USED
UX198	20¢ Red Barn	1.75	.50	.75
UX199	(20¢) "G" Old Glory	1.75	3.50	3.00

UX201

Civil War

UX200	*Monitor-Virginia*	**UX210**	*Tubman*
UX201	*Lee*	**UX211**	*Watie*
UX202	*Barton*	**UX212**	*Johnston*
UX203	*Grant*	**UX213**	*Hancock*
UX204	*Shiloh*	**UX214**	*Chestnut*
UX205	*Davis*	**UX215**	*Chancellorsville*
UX206	*Farragut*	**UX216**	*Sherman*
UX207	*Douglass*	**UX217**	*Pember*
UX208	*Semmes*	**UX218**	*Jackson*
UX209	*Lincoln*	**UX219**	*Gettysburg*

SCOTT NO.	DESCRIPTION	FIRST DAY COVER	MINT	USED
UX200-19	20¢ Civil War, set of 20	35.00	42.50	65.00

UX220

UX241

SCOTT NO.	DESCRIPTION	FIRST DAY COVER	MINT	USED
UX220	20¢ American Clipper Ships	1.75	.50	.85

UX221

American Comic Strips

UX221	*Yellow Kid*	**UX231**	*Popeye*
UX222	*Katzenjammer Kids*	**UX232**	*Blondie*
UX223	*Little Nemo*	**UX233**	*Dick Tracy*
UX224	*Bring Up Father*	**UX234**	*Alley Oop*
UX225	*Krazy Kat*	**UX235**	*Nancy*
UX226	*Rube Goldberg*	**UX236**	*Flash Gordon*
UX227	*Toonerville Folks*	**UX237**	*Li'l Abner*
UX228	*Gasoline Alley*	**UX238**	*Terry/Pirates*
UX229	*Barney Google*	**UX239**	*Prince Valiant*
UX230	*Little Orphan Annie*	**UX240**	*Brenda Starr*

SCOTT NO.	DESCRIPTION	FIRST DAY COVER	MINT	USED
UX221-40	20¢ American Comic Strips, set of 20	35.00	60.00	65.00

1996

SCOTT NO.	DESCRIPTION	FIRST DAY COVER	MINT	USED
UX241	20¢ Winter Farm Scene	1.75	.50	.50

UX242

Centennial Olympic Games

UX242	*Men's cycling*	**UX252**	*Women's softball*
UX243	*Women's diving*	**UX253**	*Women's swimming*
UX244	*Women's running*	**UX254**	*Men's sprints*
UX245	*Men's canoeing*	**UX255**	*Men's rowing*
UX246	*Decathlon*	**UX256**	*Beach volleyball*
UX247	*Women's soccer*	**UX257**	*Men's basketball*
UX248	*Men's shot put*	**UX258**	*Equestrian*
UX249	*Women's sailboarding*	**UX259**	*Men's gymnastics*
UX250	*Women's gymnastics*	**UX260**	*Men's swimming*
UX251	*Freestyle wrestling*	**UX261**	*Men's hurdles*

SCOTT NO.	DESCRIPTION	FIRST DAY COVER	MINT	USED
UX242-61	20¢ Centennial Olympic Games, set of 20	35.00	50.00	50.00

UX262

UX263

SCOTT NO.	DESCRIPTION	FIRST DAY COVER	MINT	USED
UX262	20¢ McDowell Hall	1.75	.50	.85
UX263	20¢ Alexander Hall	1.75	.50	.85

Engandered Species

UX264

UX264	*Florida panther*
UX265	*Black-footed ferret*
UX266	*American crocodile*
UX267	*Piping plover*
UX268	*Gila trout*
UX269	*Florida manatee*
UX270	*Schaus swallowtail butterfly*
UX271	*Woodland caribou*
UX272	*Thick-billed parrot*
UX273	*San Francisco garter snake*
UX274	*Ocelot*
UX275	*Wyoming toad*
UX276	*California condor*
UX277	*Hawaiian monk seal*
UX278	*Brown pelican*

SCOTT NO.	DESCRIPTION	FIRST DAY COVER	MINT	USED
UX264-78	20¢ Endangered Species, set of 15	26.50	70.00	65.00

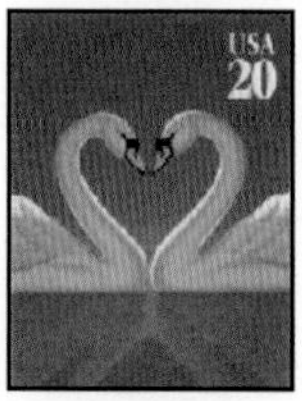

UX279

UX280

1997

SCOTT NO.	DESCRIPTION	FIRST DAY COVER	MINT	USED
UX279	20¢ Swans	2.50	6.00	2.00
UX279a	20¢ Swans, set of 12	20.00(8)	60.00	......
UX280	20¢ Shepard Hall	1.75	.50	.85

UX281

UX282

SCOTT NO.	DESCRIPTION	FIRST DAY COVER	MINT	USED
UX281	20¢ Bugs Bunny	1.75	1.65	2.50
UX282	20¢ Golden Gate Bridge 1.75	.45	1.00	.50

UX283

UX284

SCOTT NO.	DESCRIPTION	FIRST DAY COVER	MINT	USED
UX283	50¢ Golden Gate Bridge at Sunset	1.95	1.40	3.00
UX284	20¢ Fort McHenry	1.75	.50	.85

UX285

Classic Movie Monsters

UX285 *Lon Chaney as The Phantom of the Opera*
UX286 *Bela Lugosi as Dracula*
UX287 *Boris Karloff as Frankenstein's Monster*
UX288 *Boris Karloff as The Mummy*
UX289 *Lon Chaney Jr. as The Wolfman*

UX291

SCOTT NO.	DESCRIPTION	FIRST DAY COVER	MINT	USED
UX285	20¢ Classic Movie Monsters, set of 5	8.75	9.00	7.50
UX289a	same, bklt of 20 (4 of each)	....	35.00	....

UX290

UX292

1998

SCOTT NO.	DESCRIPTION	FIRST DAY COVER	MINT	USED
UX290	20¢ University of Mississippi	1.75	.50	.85
UX291	20¢ Sylvester & Tweety	1.75	1.75	3.00
UX291a	same, bklt of 10	....	17.00	....
UX292	20¢ Girard College, Philadelphia, PA	1.75	.50	.85

UX293

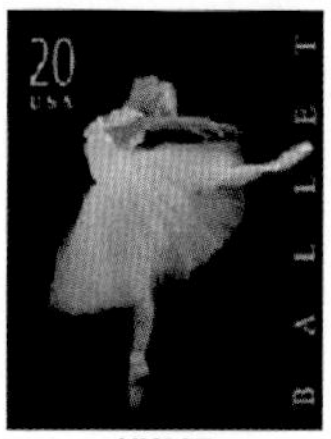

UX297

UX298

SCOTT NO.	DESCRIPTION	FIRST DAY COVER	MINT	USED
UX293-96	20¢ Tropical Birds, set of 4	7.00	5.00	7.50
UX296a	same, bklt of 20 (5 of each)	....	24.00	....
UX297	20¢ Ballet	1.75	1.75	1.50
UX297a	same, bklt of 10	....	17.00	....
UX298	20¢ Kerr Hall, Northeastern University	1.75	.50	.85

UX299

UX300

UX301

SCOTT NO.	DESCRIPTION	FIRST DAY COVER	MINT	USED
UX299	20¢ Usen Castle, Brandeis University	1.75	.50	.85

1999

SCOTT NO.	DESCRIPTION	FIRST DAY COVER	MINT	USED
UX300	20¢ Love, Victorian	1.75	1.40	2.00
UX301	20¢ University of Wisc.-Madison-Bascom Hill	1.75	.50	.60

UX302

UX303

SCOTT NO.	DESCRIPTION	FIRST DAY COVER	MINT	USED
UX302	20¢ Washington and Lee University	1.75	.50	.60
UX303	20¢ Redwood Library & Anthenaum, Newport, RI	1.75	.50	.60

UX304

UX305

SCOTT NO.	DESCRIPTION	FIRST DAY COVER	MINT	USED
UX304	20¢ Daffy Duck	1.75	1.75	1.50
UX304a	same, bklt of 10	....	17.00	....
UX305	20¢ Mount Vernon	1.75	.50	.60

UX306

UX307

Famous Trains

UX307 *Super Chief*
UX308 *Hiawatha*
UX309 *Daylight*
UX310 *Congressional*
UX311 *20th Century Limited*

1999

SCOTT NO.	DESCRIPTION	FIRST DAY COVER	MINT	USED
UX306	20¢ Block Island Lighthouse	1.75	.50	.50
UX307-11	20¢ Famous Trains, set of 5	8.75	7.00	6.00
UX311a	same, bklt of 20 (4 of each)	....	27.50	....

UX312

UX313

UX315

UX316

2000

SCOTT NO.	DESCRIPTION	FIRST DAY COVER	MINT	USED
UX312	20¢ University of Utah	1.75	.50	.60
UX313	20¢ Ryman Auditorium, Nashville, Tennessee	1.75	.50	.60
UX314	20¢ Road Runner & Wile E. Coyote	1.75	1.75	1.50
UX314a	same, bklt of 10	....	17.00	....
UX315	20¢ Adoption	1.75	1.75	1.75
UX315a	same, bklt of 10	....	17.00	....
UX316	20¢ Old Stone Row, Middlebury College, Vermont	1.75	.50	.60

UX336

The Stars and Stripes

UX317	*Sons of Liberty Flag, 1775*	**UX327**	*Star-Spangled Banner, 1814*
UX318	*New England Flag, 1775*	**UX328**	*Bennington Flag, c. 1820*
UX319	*Forster Flag, 1775*	**UX329**	*Great Star Flag, 1837*
UX320	*Continental Colors, 1776*	**UX330**	*29-Star Flag, 1847*
UX321	*Francis Hopkinson Flag, 1777*	**UX331**	*Fort Sumter Flag, 1861*
UX322	*Brandywine Flag, 1777*	**UX332**	*Centennial Flag, 1876*
UX323	*John Paul Jones Flag, 1779*	**UX333**	*38-Star Flag*
UX324	*Pierre L'Enfant Flag, 1783*	**UX334**	*Peace Flag, 1891*
UX325	*Indian Peace Flag, 1803*	**UX335**	*48-Star Flag, 1912*
UX326	*Easton Flag, 1814*	**UX336**	*50-Star Flag, 1960*

SCOTT NO.	DESCRIPTION	FIRST DAY COVER	MINT	USED
UX317-36	The Stars and Stripes, set of 20	35.00	37.50	30.00

UX337

Legends of Baseball

UX337	*Jackie Robinson*	**UX347**	*Lefty Grove*
UX338	*Eddie Collins*	**UX348**	*Tris Speaker*
UX339	*Christy Mathewson*	**UX349**	*Cy Young*
UX340	*Ty Cobb*	**UX350**	*Jimmie Foxx*
UX341	*George Sisler*	**UX351**	*Pie Traynor*
UX342	*Rogers Hornsby*	**UX352**	*Satchel Paige*
UX343	*Mickey Cochrane*	**UX353**	*Honus Wagner*
UX344	*Babe Ruth*	**UX354**	*Josh Gibson*
UX345	*Walter Johnson*	**UX355**	*Dizzy Dean*
UX346	*Roberto Clemente*	**UX356**	*Lou Gehrig*

SCOTT NO.	DESCRIPTION	FIRST DAY COVER	MINT	USED
UX337-56	20¢ Legends of Baseball, set of 20	35.00	30.00	25.00

UX357-60

UX361

SCOTT NO.	DESCRIPTION	FIRST DAY COVER	MINT	USED
UX357-60	20¢ Christmas Deer, set of 4	7.00	6.00	5.00

2001

SCOTT NO.	DESCRIPTION	FIRST DAY COVER	MINT	USED
UX361	20¢ Connecticut Hall, Yale University	1.75	.50	.75

UX362

UX363

UX364

SCOTT NO.	DESCRIPTION	FIRST DAY COVER	MINT	USED
UX362	20¢ University of South Carolina	1.75	.50	.85
UX363	20¢ Northwestern University Sesquicentennial 1851-2001	1.75	.50	.85
UX364	20¢ Waldschmidt Hall, The University of Portland .	1.75	.50	.75

Legendary Playing Fields

UX365	*Ebbets Field*	**UX370**	*Forbes Field*
UX366	*Tiger Stadium*	**UX371**	*Fenway Park*
UX367	*Crosley Field*	**UX372**	*Comiskey Park*
UX368	*Yankee Stadium*	**UX373**	*Shibe Park*
UX369	*Polo Grounds*	**UX374**	*Wrigley Field*

2001

SCOTT NO.	DESCRIPTION	FIRST DAY COVER	MINT	USED
UX365-74	21¢ Legendary Playing Fields, set of 10	35.00	22.50	20.00
UX374a	same, bklt of 10	....	22.50	....

UX375

UX376

UX377

SCOTT NO.	DESCRIPTION	FIRST DAY COVER	MINT	USED
UX375	21¢ White Barn	1.75	.50	.60
UX376	21¢ That's All Folks	2.00	1.75	1.75
UX376a	same, bklt of 10	....	17.00	....
UX377-80	21¢ Santas, set of 4	7.50	6.00	5.00
UX380a	same, complete bklt of 20	......	21.50	......

UX381

UX382

UX386

2002

SCOTT NO.	DESCRIPTION	FIRST DAY COVER	MINT	USED
UX381	23¢ Carlsbad Caverns	1.75	.55	.60
UX382-85	23¢ Teddy Bears, set of 4	7.50	6.00	5.00
UX385a	same, complete bklt of 20	......	27.50	......
UX386-89	23¢ Christmas Snowmen, set of 4	7.50	6.00	5.00
UX389a	same, complete bklt of 20	......	27.50	......

UX390

UX395

UX400

2003

SCOTT NO.	DESCRIPTION	FIRST DAY COVER	MINT	USED
UX390-94	23¢ Old Glory, set of 5	8.75	7.00	6.00
UX394a	same, complete booklet of 20 cards	....	27.50	....
UX395-99	23¢ Southern Lighthouses, set of 5	8.75	7.00	6.00
UX399a	same, complete booklet of 20	....	27.50	....
UX400	23¢ Ohio University, 200th Anniversary	1.75	.55	.60
UX401-04	23¢ Christmas Music Makers, set of 4	7.50	5.00	5.00
UX404a	same, complete bklt of 20	......	21.50	......

UX401

UX405

2004

SCOTT NO.	DESCRIPTION	FIRST DAY COVER	MINT	USED
UX405	23¢ Columbia University, 250th Anniversary	1.75	.55	.60

UX406

UX407

SCOTT NO.	DESCRIPTION	FIRST DAY COVER	MINT	USED
UX406	23¢ Harriton House, 300th Anniversary	1.75	.55	.60
UX407-10	23¢ Art of Disney, set of 4	7.00	5.75	5.00
UX410a	same, complete booklet of 20	....	22.50	....

UX411

UX421

SCOTT NO.	DESCRIPTION	FIRST DAY COVER	MINT	USED
UX411-20	23¢ Art of the American Indian, set of 10	17.50	14.00	13.00
UX420a	same, complete booklet of 20	....	22.50	....
UX421-35	23¢ Cloudscapes, set of 15	26.25	20.00	17.50
UX435a	same, complete booklet of 20	....	22.50	....

UX440

UX449

2005

SCOTT NO.	DESCRIPTION	FIRST DAY COVER	MINT	USED
UX436-39	Disney Characters, set of 4	7.00	5.75	2.00
UX439a	same, complete booklet of 20	....	27.50	....
UX440-44	23¢ Sporty Cars, set of 4	7.00	5.75	2.00
UX444a	same, complete booklet of 20	....	27.50	....
UX445-48	23¢ Let's Dance, set of 4	7.00	5.75	2.00
UX448a	same, complete booklet of 20	....	27.50	....

2006

SCOTT NO.	DESCRIPTION	FIRST DAY COVER	MINT	USED
UX449	24¢ Zebulon Pike Expedition, Bicentennial	1.75	.60	.65

UX450

UX454

SCOTT NO.	DESCRIPTION	FIRST DAY COVER	MINT	USED
UX450-53	24¢ Disney Characters, set of 4	7.00	5.75	2.00
UX453a	same, complete booklet of 20	....	27.50	....
UX454-57	24¢ Baseball Sluggers, set of 4	7.00	5.75	2.00
UX457a	same, complete booklet of 20	....	27.50	....

UX458

D.C. Comics Super Heroes

UX458	*Superman Cover*	**UX468**	*The Flash Cover*
UX459	*Superman*	**UX469**	*The Flash*
UX460	*Batman Cover*	**UX470**	*Plastic Man Cover*
UX461	*Batman*	**UX471**	*Plastic Man*
UX462	*Wonder Woman Cover*	**UX472**	*Aquaman Cover*
UX463	*Wonder Woman*	**UX473**	*Aquaman*
UX464	*Green Lantern Cover*	**UX474**	*Supergirl Cover*
UX465	*Green Lantern*	**UX475**	*Supergirl*
UX466	*Green Arrow Cover*	**UX476**	*Hawkman Cover*
UX467	*Green Arrow*	**UX477**	*Hawkman*

SCOTT NO.	DESCRIPTION	FIRST DAY COVER	MINT	USED
UX458-77	24¢ D.C. Comics Super Heroes, set of 20	40.00	35.00	30.00

Southern Florida Wetlands

UX478	*Snail Kite*	**UX483**	White Ibis
UX479	*Cape Sable Seaside Sparrow*	**UX484**	*American Crocodile*
UX480	*Wood Storks*	**UX485**	*Everglades Mink*
UX481	*Florida Panthers*	**UX486**	*Roseate Spoonbills*
UX482	*Bald Eagle*	**UX487**	*American Alligators*

UX483

SCOTT NO.	DESCRIPTION	FIRST DAY COVER	MINT	USED
UX478-87	39¢ Southern Florida Wetlands, set of 10	....	50.00	....

UX488

2007

SCOTT NO.	DESCRIPTION	FIRST DAY COVER	MINT	USED
UX488	26¢ Pineapple	1.95	.70	.75

UX501

Star Wars

UX489	*Darth Vader*	**UX496**	*Obi-Wan Kenobi*
UX490	*Luke Skywalker*	**UX497**	*Boba Fett*
UX491	*C-3PO*	**UX498**	*Darth Maul*
UX492	*Queen Padme Amidala*	**UX499**	*Yoda*
UX493	*Millennium Falcon*	**UX500**	*Princess Leia and R2-D2*
UX494	*Emperor Palpatine*	**UX501**	*Chewbacca and Han Solo*
UX495	*Anakin Skywalker and Obi-Wan Kenobi*	**UX502**	*X-wing Starfighter*
		UX503	*Stormtroopers*

SCOTT NO.	DESCRIPTION	FIRST DAY COVER	MINT	USED
UX489-503	26¢ Star Wars, set of 15	27.50	21.00	18.00

UX505

SCOTT NO.	DESCRIPTION	FIRST DAY COVER	MINT	USED
UX504-08	26¢ Pacific Coast Lighthouses, set of 5	8.00	6.50	3.00
UX508a	same, complete booklet of 20	....	28.75	....
....	26¢ Marvel Comic Book Heroes, set of 20	40.00	35.00	30.00
....	26¢ Disney Characters, set of 4	7.50	6.00	2.50
....	same, complete booklet of 20	....	28.75	....

SCOTT NO.	DESCRIPTION	FIRST DAY COVER	MINT	USED

AIR POST POSTAL CARDS

UXC1

UXC2, UXC3

1949

SCOTT NO.	DESCRIPTION	FIRST DAY COVER	MINT	USED
UXC1	4¢ orange	2.50	.60	.90

1958 No border on card

SCOTT NO.	DESCRIPTION	FIRST DAY COVER	MINT	USED
UXC2	5¢ red	2.50	2.00	.90

1960
Type of 1958 re-engraved: with border on card

SCOTT NO.	DESCRIPTION	FIRST DAY COVER	MINT	USED
UXC3	5¢ red	2.50	6.25	2.50

UXC4

UXC5, UXC8, UXC11

1963

SCOTT NO.	DESCRIPTION	FIRST DAY COVER	MINT	USED
UXC4	6¢ red	2.50	1.25	3.00

1966

SCOTT NO.	DESCRIPTION	FIRST DAY COVER	MINT	USED
UXC5	11¢ SIPEX	1.75	.75	22.50

UXC6

UXC7

1967

SCOTT NO.	DESCRIPTION	FIRST DAY COVER	MINT	USED
UXC6	6¢ Virgin Islands	1.75	.85	12.50
UXC7	6¢ Boy Scout Jamboree	2.50	.85	18.00
UXC8	13¢ AAM Convention	1.75	1.75	27.50

UXC9, UXC10

1968-71 Precancels

SCOTT NO.	DESCRIPTION	FIRST DAY COVER	MINT	USED
UXC9	8¢ blue & red	1.75	.85	3.00
UXC9at	8¢ luminescent (1969)	20.00	3.00	4.00
UXC10	9¢ red & blue (1971)	1.75	.55	1.50

1971 Inscribed U.S. Air Mail

SCOTT NO.	DESCRIPTION	FIRST DAY COVER	MINT	USED
UXC11	15¢ Travel Service	1.75	2.00	50.00

UXC12

UXC13

1972
Issued with various designs on reverse

SCOTT NO.	DESCRIPTION	FIRST DAY COVER	MINT	USED
UXC12	9¢ Grand Canyon	1.75	.85	165.00
UXC13	15¢ Niagara Falls	1.75	.85	85.00

UXC14

UXC15

1974

SCOTT NO.	DESCRIPTION	FIRST DAY COVER	MINT	USED
UXC14	11¢ red & ultramarine	1.75	1.25	22.50
UXC15	18¢ Visit USA	1.75	1.25	22.50

UXC16

1975

SCOTT NO.	DESCRIPTION	FIRST DAY COVER	MINT	USED
UXC16	21¢ Visit USA	1.75	1.00	22.50

UXC17

UXC18

1978

SCOTT NO.	DESCRIPTION	FIRST DAY COVER	MINT	USED
UXC17	21¢ Curtiss Jenny	1.75	1.25	22.50

1979

SCOTT NO.	DESCRIPTION	FIRST DAY COVER	MINT	USED
UXC18	21¢ Moscow Olympics	1.75	1.25	22.50

UXC19

UXC20

1981

SCOTT NO.	DESCRIPTION	FIRST DAY COVER	MINT	USED
UXC19	28¢ Pacific Flight	1.75	1.25	22.50

1982

SCOTT NO.	DESCRIPTION	FIRST DAY COVER	MINT	USED
UXC20	28¢ Gliders	1.75	1.25	22.50

UXC21

UXC22

SCOTT NO.	DESCRIPTION	FIRST DAY COVER	MINT	USED
	1983			
UXC21	28¢ Olympics	1.75	1.25	22.50
	1985			
UXC22	33¢ China Clipper	1.75	1.25	22.50

UXC23

UXC24

SCOTT NO.	DESCRIPTION	FIRST DAY COVER	MINT	USED
	1986			
UXC23	33¢ Ameripex '86	1.75	1.25	22.50
	1988			
UXC24	36¢ DC-3	1.75	1.00	22.50

UXC25

SCOTT NO.	DESCRIPTION	FIRST DAY COVER	MINT	USED
	1991			
UXC25	40¢ Yankee Clipper	1.75	1.00	22.50

UXC28

UXC26

SCOTT NO.	DESCRIPTION	FIRST DAY COVER	MINT	USED
	1995			
UXC26	50¢ Soaring Eagle	1.75	1.25	22.50

UXC27

SCOTT NO.	DESCRIPTION	FIRST DAY COVER	MINT	USED
	1999			
UXC27	55¢ Mount Rainier, Washington	1.75	1.35	22.50
	2001			
UXC28	70¢ Badlands National Park, South Dakota	2.25	1.60	12.00

PAID REPLY POSTAL CARDS

UY1m, UY3m

UY2m, UY11m

UY4m

UY1r, UY3r

UY2r, UY11r

UY4r

PAID REPLY CARDS: Consist of two halves—one for your message and one for the other party to use to reply.

SCOTT NO.	DESCRIPTION	MINT	UNUSED	USED
	1892 Card Framed			
UY1	1¢ & 1¢ unsevered	40.00	15.00	9.00
UY1m	1¢ black (Message)	6.50	3.25	2.00
UY1r	1¢ black (Reply)	6.50	3.25	2.00
	1893			
UY2	2¢ & 2¢ unsevered	20.00	12.00	22.00
UY2m	2¢ blue (Message)	6.00	3.00	6.50
UY2r	2¢ blue (Reply)	6.00	3.00	6.50
	1898 Designs of 1892 Card Unframed			
UY3	1¢ & 1¢ unsevered	75.00	12.50	15.00
UY3m	1¢ black (Message)	15.50	6.00	3.00
UY3r	1¢ black (Reply)	15.50	6.00	3.00
	1904			
UY4	1¢ & 1¢ unsevered	50.00	10.00	7.00
UY4m	1¢ black (Message)	10.00	4.00	1.20
UY4r	1¢ black (Reply)	10.00	4.00	1.20

UY5m, UY6m, UY7m, UY13m

UY8m

UY12m

UY5r, UY6r, UY7r, UY13r

UY8r

UY12r

SCOTT NO.	DESCRIPTION	MINT	UNUSED	USED
	1910			
UY5	1¢ & 1¢ unsevered	160.00	45.00	24.00
UY5m	1¢ blue (Message)	16.00	10.00	4.00
UY5r	1¢ blue (Reply)	16.00	10.00	4.00
	1911 Double Line Around Instructions			
UY6	1¢ & 1¢ unsevered	160.00	70.00	25.00
UY6m	1¢ green (Message)	25.00	12.00	6.00
UY6r	1¢ green (Reply)	25.00	12.00	6.00
	1915 Single Frame Line Around Instruction			
UY7	1¢ & 1¢ unsevered	1.50	.65	.60
UY7m	1¢ green (Message)	.35	.20	.25
UY7r	1¢ green (Reply)	.35	.20	.25
	1918			
UY8	2¢ & 2¢ unsevered	85.00	30.00	45.00
UY8m	2¢ red (Message)	24.00	9.00	9.00
UY8r	2¢ red (Reply)	24.00	9.00	9.00

SCOTT NO.	DESCRIPTION	MINT	UNUSED	USED
	1920 UY8 Surcharged			
UY9	1¢/2¢ & 1¢/2¢ unsevered	22.50	9.00	10.00
UY9m	1¢ on 2¢ red (Message)	6.00	3.00	4.00
UY9r	1¢ on 2¢ red (Reply)	6.00	3.00	4.00
	1924 Designs of 1893			
UY11	2¢ & 2¢ unsevered	3.00	1.50	32.50
UY11m	2¢ red (Message)	.75	.50	12.00
UY11r	2¢ red (Reply)	.75	.50	12.00
	1926			
UY12	3¢ & 3¢ unsevered	16.50	5.00	30.00
UY12m	3¢ red (Message)	3.25	1.35	7.00
UY12r	3¢ red (Reply)	3.25	1.35	7.00

SCOTT NO.	DESCRIPTION	FIRST DAY COVER	MINT	USED
	1951 Design of 1910 Single Line Frame			
UY13	2¢ & 2¢ unsevered	2.10	1.40	2.25
UY13m	2¢ carmine (Message)	....	.45	1.00
UY13r	2¢ carmine (Reply)	....	.45	1.00
	1952 UY7 Surcharged by cancelling machine, light green			
UY14	2¢/1¢ & 2¢/1¢ unsevered	....	2.00	2.00
UY14m	2¢ on 1¢ green (Message)	....	.50	1.00
UY14r	2¢ on 1¢ green (Reply)	....	.50	1.00
	1952 UY7 Surcharge Typographed, dark green			
UY15	2¢/1¢ & 2¢/1¢ unsevered	....	140.00	50.00
UY15m	2¢ on 1¢ green (Message)	....	20.00	12.00
UY15r	2¢ on 1¢ green (Reply)	....	20.00	12.00
	1956 Design of UX45			
UY16	4¢ & 4¢ unsevered	1.75	1.25	80.00
UY16m	4¢ carmine (Message)	....	.50	40.00
UY16r	4¢ carmine (Reply)	....	.50	40.00
	1958 Design of UX46			
UY17	3¢ & 3¢ purple, unsevered	1.75	4.00	2.50
	1962 Design of UX48			
UY18	4¢ & 4¢ red violet, unsevered	1.75	4.00	2.75
	1963 Design of UX49			
UY19	7¢ & 7¢ unsevered	1.75	3.00	65.00
UY19m	7¢ blue & red (Message)	....	1.00	40.00
UY19r	7¢ blue & red (Reply)	....	1.00	40.00
	1967 Design of UX54			
UY20	8¢ & 8¢ unsevered	1.75	3.00	60.00
UY20m	8¢ blue & red (Message)	....	1.00	40.00
UY20r	8¢ blue & red (Reply)	....	1.00	40.00
	1968 Design of UX55			
UY21	5¢ & 5¢ emerald	1.75	1.75	2.00
	1971 Design of UX58			
UY22	6¢ & 6¢ brown	1.75	1.00	2.00
	1972 Design of UX64			
UY23	6¢ & 6¢ blue	1.75	1.25	2.00
	1973 Design of UX66			
UY24	8¢ & 8¢ orange	1.75	1.00	2.00
	1975			
UY25	7¢ & 7¢ design of UX68	1.75	1.00	9.00
UY26	9¢ & 9¢ design of UX69	1.75	1.00	2.00
	1976			
UY27	9¢ & 9¢ design of UX70	1.75	1.25	2.00
	1977			
UY28	9¢ & 9¢ design of UX72	1.75	1.25	2.00
	1978			
UY29	(10¢ & 10¢) design of UX74	3.00	11.00	10.00
UY30	10¢ & 10¢ design of UX75	1.75	1.25	.40
	1981			
UY31	(12¢ & 12¢) "B" Eagle, design of UX88	1.75	1.25	2.00
UY32	12¢ & 12¢ light blue, design of UX89	1.75	5.00	2.00
UY33	(13¢ & 13¢) buff, design of UX92	1.75	1.85	2.00
UY34	13¢ & 13¢ buff, design of UX93	1.75	1.00	.25
	1985			
UY35	(14¢ & 14¢) Carroll, design of UX105	1.75	2.75	2.00
UY36	14¢ & 14¢ Carroll, design of UX106	1.75	1.25	2.00
UY37	14¢ & 14¢ Wythe, design of UX108	1.75	1.00	2.00
	1987			
UY38	14¢ & 14¢ Flag, design of UX117	1.75	1.00	2.00
	1988			
UY39	15¢ & 15¢ America the Beautiful, design of UX120	1.75	1.00	1.00
	1991			
UY40	19¢ & 19¢ Flag, design of UX153	1.75	1.00	1.005
	1995			
UY41	20¢ & 20¢ Red Barn, design of UX198	1.75	1.00	1.25
	1999			
UY42	20¢ & 20¢ Block Island Lighthouse, design of UX306	1.75	1.00	1.25
	2001-07			
UY43	21¢ & 21¢ White Barn, design of UX375	1.75	1.10	1.50
UY44	23¢ & 23¢ Carlsbad Caverns, design of UX381	1.75	1.10	1.50
UY45	24¢ & 24¢ Zebulon Pike Expedition, design of UX449	1.75	1.35	1.50
UY46	26¢ & 26¢ Pineapple, design of UX488	1.75	1.45	1.50

OFFICIAL POSTAL CARDS

UZ1

SCOTT NO.	DESCRIPTION	FIRST DAY COVER	MINT	USED
	1913			
UZ1	1¢ black (Printed Address)	......	700.00	475.00

UZ2

UZ3

SCOTT NO.	DESCRIPTION	FIRST DAY COVER	MINT	USED
	1983			
UZ2	13¢ Great Seal	1.75	.85	100.00
	1985			
UZ3	14¢ Great Seal	1.75	.85	90.00

UZ4

UZ5

UZ6

SCOTT NO.	DESCRIPTION	FIRST DAY COVER	MINT	USED
	1988			
UZ4	15¢ Great Seal	1.75	.85	100.00
	1991			
UZ5	19¢ Great Seal	1.75	.85	100.00
	1995			
UZ6	20¢ Great Seal	1.75	1.00	100.00

1862-71 First Issue

When ordering from this issue be sure to indicate whether the "a", "b" or "c" variety is wanted. Example: R27c. Prices are for used singles.

R1-R4

R5-R15

R16-R42

SCOTT NO.	DESCRIPTION	IMPERFORATE (a) F	AVG	PART PERF. (b) F	AVG	PERFORATED (c) F	AVG
R1	1¢ Express	60.00	40.00	38.00	25.00	1.25	.85
R2	1¢ Playing Cards	1250.00	800.00	1150.00	750.00	100.00	100.00
R3	1¢ Proprietary	850.00	600.00	200.00	130.00	.60	.40
R4	1¢ Telegraph	500.00	350.00	....	....	13.00	9.00
R5	2¢ Bank Check, blue	.95	.70	2.00	1.35	.30	.20
R6	2¢ Bank Check, orange	....	....	60.00	41.25	.30	.20
R7	2¢ Certificate, blue	14.00	9.00	....	....	27.50	17.50
R8	2¢ Certificate, orange	....	....	....	....	27.50	17.50
R9	2¢ Express, blue	13.00	9.00	22.00	15.00	.40	.25
R10	2¢ Express, orange	....	....	800.00	495.00	8.00	5.00
R11	2¢ Playing Cards, blue	....	....	260.00	175.00	4.00	2.50
R12	2¢ Playing Cards, orange	....	....	....	....	50.00	35.00
R13	2¢ Proprietary, blue	650.00	450.00	235.00	150.00	.50	.35
R14	2¢ Proprietary, orange	....	....	....	....	150.00	95.00
R15	2¢ U.S. Internal Revenue	....	....	....	....	.25	.20
R16	3¢ Foreign Exchange	....	....	425.00	295.00	5.00	3.25
R17	3¢ Playing Cards	....	....	....	....	150.00	95.00
R18	3¢ Proprietary	....	....	425.00	295.00	4.00	2.50
R19	3¢ Telegraph	70.00	48.00	28.00	19.50	2.60	1.80
R20	4¢ Inland Exchange	....	....	....	....	1.65	1.10
R21	4¢ Playing Cards	....	....	....	....	550.00	395.00
R22	4¢ Proprietary	....	....	325.00	225.00	7.00	4.75
R23	5¢ Agreement	....	....	....	....	.50	.35
R24	5¢ Certificate	2.50	1.75	14.00	9.00	.50	.35
R25	5¢ Express	5.50	3.75	8.00	5.50	.50	.35
R26	5¢ Foreign Exchange	....	....	....	....	.50	.35
R27	5¢ Inland Exchange	8.00	5.50	6.00	3.95	.40	.25
R28	5¢ Playing Cards	....	....	....	....	28.00	18.00
R29	5¢ Proprietary	....	....	....	....	28.00	18.00
R30	6¢ Inland Exchange	....	....	....	....	2.00	1.35
R32	10¢ Bill of Lading	55.00	38.00	375.00	250.00	1.25	.85
R33	10¢ Certificate	210.00	150.00	650.00	425.00	.35	.25
R34	10¢ Contract, blue	....	....	375.00	250.00	.35	.25
R35	10¢ Foreign Exchange	....	....	....	....	12.00	8.00
R36	10¢ Inland Exchange	375.00	250.00	5.00	3.25	.25	.20
R37	10¢ Power of Attorney	850.00	525.00	27.00	18.00	1.00	.65
R38	10¢ Proprietary	....	....	....	....	18.00	12.00
R39	15¢ Foreign Exchange	....	....	....	....	17.00	12.00
R40	15¢ Inland Exchange	40.00	27.00	13.00	9.00	1.50	.95
R41	20¢ Foreign Exchange	65.00	40.00	....	....	45.00	27.00
R42	20¢ Inland Exchange	16.00	10.00	18.00	12.00	.40	.25

R43-R53

R54-R65

R66-R76

SCOTT NO.	DESCRIPTION	IMPERFORATE (a) F	AVG	PART PERF. (b) F	AVG	PERFORATED (c) F	AVG
R43	25¢ Bond	275.00	185.00	7.00	5.00	2.75	1.85
R44	25¢ Certificate	11.00	8.00	7.00	5.00	.35	.25
R45	25¢ Entry of Goods	18.00	12.50	90.00	60.00	.85	.60
R46	25¢ Insurance	11.00	8.00	11.00	8.00	.35	.25
R47	25¢ Life Insurance	40.00	27.00	450.00	300.00	7.00	4.75
R48	25¢ Power of Attorney	8.00	5.50	35.00	25.00	.35	.25
R49	25¢ Protest	35.00	25.00	600.00	400.00	7.00	5.00
R50	25¢ Warehouse Receipt	50.00	35.00	450.00	295.00	35.00	24.00
R51	30¢ Foreign Exchange	110.00	75.00	1500.00	950.00	55.00	39.00
R52	30¢ Inland Exchange	65.00	45.00	75.00	50.00	4.00	2.75
R53	40¢ Inland Exchange	1100.00	775.00	8.00	5.50	4.00	2.75
R54	50¢ Conveyance, blue	18.00	12.00	2.00	1.25	.30	.25
R55	50¢ Entry of Goods	....	....	15.00	10.00	.50	.35
R56	50¢ Foreign Exchange	60.00	40.00	90.00	60.00	7.00	5.00
R57	50¢ Lease	30.00	21.00	120.00	80.00	10.00	7.00
R58	50¢ Life Insurance	45.00	30.00	70.00	49.00	1.00	.70
R59	50¢ Mortgage	18.00	12.00	3.00	2.10	.60	.40
R60	50¢ Original Process	4.00	2.75	....	....	.75	.50
R61	50¢ Passage Ticket	80.00	55.00	275.00	185.00	1.40	.95
R62	50¢ Probate of Will	60.00	42.00	130.00	90.00	20.00	13.00
R63	50¢ Surety Bond, blue	275.00	185.00	3.00	2.10	.40	.25
R64	60¢ Inland Exchange	110.00	75.00	65.00	45.00	6.00	4.25
R65	70¢ Foreign Exchange	650.00	450.00	165.00	110.00	12.00	8.00

SCOTT NO.	DESCRIPTION	IMPERFORATE (a) F	AVG	PART PERF. (b) F	AVG	PERFORATED (c) F	AVG
R66	$1 Conveyance	18.00	12.00	550.00	395.00	27.50	18.50
R67	$1 Entry of Goods	40.00	28.00	....	....	2.00	1.40
R68	$1 Foreign Exchange	90.00	60.00	....	....	.75	.50
R69	$1 Inland Exchange	16.00	10.00	475.00	300.00	.55	.40
R70	$1 Lease	40.00	28.00	....	....	4.00	2.75
R71	$1 Life Insurance	185.00	125.00	....	....	7.00	5.00
R72	$1 Manifest	49.50	33.00	....	....	38.00	26.50
R73	$1 Mortgage	28.00	19.00	....	....	225.00	155.00
R74	$1 Passage Ticket	300.00	210.00	....	....	300.00	210.00
R75	$1 Power of Attorney	95.00	65.00	....	....	2.50	1.75
R76	$1 Probate of Will	95.00	65.00	....	....	60.00	42.50

R77-R80

R81-R87

SCOTT NO.	DESCRIPTION	IMPERFORATE (a) F	AVG	PART PERF. (b) F	AVG	PERFORATED (c) F	AVG
R77	$1.30 Foreign Exchange	....	....	....	....	44.00	24.75
R78	$1.50 Inland Exchange	30.00	21.00	....	....	2.90	1.60
R79	$1.60 Foreign Exchange	1350.00	950.00	....	....	88.00	46.75
R80	$1.90 Foreign Exchange	....	....	....	....	60.50	30.25
R81	$2 Conveyance	195.00	135.00	1650.00	1050.00	3.00	2.10
R82	$2 Mortgage	135.00	95.00	....	....	5.00	3.50
R83	$2 Probate of Will	....	....	....	....	70.00	49.00
R84	$2.50 Inland Exchange	....	....	....	....	12.00	8.00
R85	$3 Charter Party	185.00	125.00	....	....	7.00	4.80
R86	$2 Manifest	165.00	105.00	....	....	45.00	30.00
R87	$3.50 Inland Exchange	....	....	....	....	70.00	49.00

R88-R96

R97-R101

SCOTT NO.	DESCRIPTION	IMPERFORATE (a) F	AVG	PART PERF. (b) F	AVG	PERFORATED (c) F	AVG
R88	$5 Charter Party	325.00	225.00	....	....	7.00	4.80
R89	$5 Conveyance	50.00	35.00	....	....	9.00	6.00
R90	$5 Manifest	185.00	125.00	....	....	95.00	65.00
R91	$5 Mortgage	160.00	110.00	....	....	25.00	17.50
R92	$5 Probate of Will	600.00	425.00	....	....	25.00	17.50
R93	$10 Charter Party	800.00	550.00	....	....	35.00	25.00
R94	$10 Conveyance	135.00	95.00	....	....	75.00	50.00
R95	$10 Mortgage	650.00	450.00	....	....	35.00	25.00
R96	$10 Probate of Will	1750.00	1150.00	....	....	35.00	25.00
R97	$15 Mortgage, blue	2400.00	1650.00	....	....	180.00	120.00
R98	$20 Conveyance	150.00	100.00	....	....	95.00	65.00
R99	$20 Probate of Will	2100.00	1500.00	....	....	2100.00	1500.00
R100	$25 Mortgage	1500.00	1050.00	....	....	175.00	115.00
R101	$50 U.S. Internal Revenue	265.00	175.00	....	....	130.00	90.00

R102

SCOTT NO.	DESCRIPTION	IMPERFORATE (a) F	AVG	PART PERF. (b) F	AVG	PERFORATED (c) F	AVG
R102	$200 U.S. Internal Revenue	2350.00	1850.00	....	....	900.00	625.00

R103, R104, R134, R135, R151

R105-R111, R136-R139

R112-R114

R115-R117, R142-R143

1871 SECOND ISSUE

NOTE: **The individual denominations vary in design from the illustrations shown which are more typical of their relative size.**

SCOTT NO.	DESCRIPTION	USED F	USED AVG
R103	1¢ blue and black	55.00	40.00
R104	2¢ blue and black	2.50	1.75
R105	3¢ blue and black	28.00	19.00
R106	4¢ blue and black	90.00	60.00
R107	5¢ blue and black	1.75	1.10
R108	6¢ blue and black	150.00	105.00
R109	10¢ blue and black	1.25	.85
R110	15¢ blue and black	40.00	28.00
R111	20¢ blue and black	7.00	5.00
R112	25¢ blue and black	.80	.55
R113	30¢ blue and black	110.00	75.00
R114	40¢ blue and black	90.00	65.00
R115	50¢ blue and black	.80	.55
R116	60¢ blue and black	150.00	105.00
R117	70¢ blue and black	60.00	42.00

R118-R122, R144

R123-R126, R145-R147

SCOTT NO.	DESCRIPTION	USED F	USED AVG
R118	$1 blue and black	5.00	3.50
R119	$1.30 blue and black	500.00	350.00
R120	$1.50 blue and black	18.00	12.00
R121	$1.60 blue and black	550.00	395.00
R122	$1.90 blue and black	360.00	250.00
R123	$2.00 blue and black	18.00	12.00
R124	$2.50 blue and black	35.00	25.00
R125	$3.00 blue and black	45.00	30.00
R126	$3.50 blue and black	325.00	225.00

R127, R128, R148, R149

R129-R131, R150

SCOTT NO.	DESCRIPTION	USED F	USED AVG
R127	$5 blue and black	27.50	19.00
R128	$10 blue and black	225.00	155.00
R129	$20 blue and black	500.00	350.00
R130	$25 blue and black	625.00	425.00
R131	$50 blue and black	625.00	425.00

1871-72 THIRD ISSUE

SCOTT NO.	DESCRIPTION	USED F	USED AVG
R134	1¢ claret and black	45.00	30.00
R135	2¢ orange and black	.40	.25
R135b	2¢ orange and black (center inverted)	425.00	300.00
R136	4¢ brown and black	60.00	42.00
R137	5¢ orange and black	.40	.20
R138	6¢ orange and black	70.00	49.00
R139	15¢ brown and black	15.00	10.00
R140	30¢ orange and black	20.00	14.00
R141	40¢ brown and black	55.00	40.00
R142	60¢ orange and black	95.00	65.00
R143	70¢ green and black	70.00	49.00
R144	$1 green and black	1.65	1.10
R145	$2 vermillion and black	27.00	18.00
R146	$2.50 claret and black	50.00	35.00
R147	$3 green and black	50.00	35.00
R148	$5 vermillion and black	35.00	24.00
R149	$10 green and black	150.00	100.00
R150	$20 orange and black	650.00	435.00

1874 on greenish paper

SCOTT NO.	DESCRIPTION	USED F	USED AVG
R151	2¢ orange and black	.30	.25
R151a	2¢ orange and black (center inverted)	425.00	300.00

R152 *Liberty*

I. R.

R153 surcharge

I. R.

R154, R155 surcharge

1875-78

SCOTT NO.	DESCRIPTION	UNUSED F	UNUSED AVG	USED F	USED AVG
R152a	2¢ blue on blue silk paper	....	....	.30	.25
R152b	2¢ watermarked ("USIR") paper	....	....	.30	.25
R152c	2¢ watermarked, rouletted	....	....	35.00	24.00

1898 Postage Stamps 279 & 267 Surcharged

SCOTT NO.	DESCRIPTION	UNUSED F	UNUSED AVG	USED F	USED AVG
R153	1¢ green, small I.R.	4.00	2.50	3.00	2.10
R154	1¢ green, large I.R.	.30	.25	.30	.25
R155	2¢ carmine, large I.R.	.30	.25	.30	.25

DOCUMENTARY STAMPS

Newspaper Stamp PR121 Surcharged

INT. REV.
$5.
DOCUMENTARY.

SCOTT NO.	DESCRIPTION	UNUSED F	UNUSED AVG	USED F	USED AVG
R159	$5 dark blue, red surcharge reading down	500.00	350.00	125.00	85.00
R160	$5 dark blue, red surcharge reading up	125.00	85.00	100.00	70.00

R161-R172

R173-R178, R182, R183

1898 Battleships Inscribed "Documentary"

SCOTT NO.	DESCRIPTION	UNUSED F	UNUSED AVG	USED F	USED AVG
R161	1/2¢ orange	3.00	2.10	11.00	8.00
R162	1/2¢ dark gray	.30	.25	.30	.25
R163	1¢ pale blue	.30	.25	.30	.25
R164	2¢ carmine	.30	.25	.30	.25
R165	3¢ dark blue	2.75	1.60	.30	.25
R166	4¢ pale rose	2.00	1.40	.30	.25
R167	5¢ lilac	.65	.45	.30	.25
R168	10¢ dark brown	2.00	1.40	.30	.25
R169	25¢ purple brown	3.50	2.40	.30	.25
R170	40¢ blue lilac (cut cancel .40)	125.00	80.00	1.20	.75
R171	50¢ slate violet	20.00	14.00	.30	.25
R172	80¢ bistre (cut cancel .25)	110.00	80.00	.40	.30
R173	$1 dark green	15.00	10.00	.30	.25
R174	$3 dark brown (cut cancel .25)	40.00	28.00	1.00	.70
R175	$5 orange red (cut cancel .25)	55.00	40.00	2.00	1.40
R176	$10 black (cut cancel .70)	120.00	80.00	4.00	2.75
R177	$30 red (cut cancel 50.00)	400.00	275.00	135.00	95.00
R178	$50 gray brown (cut cancel 2.50)	185.00	125.00	6.00	3.95

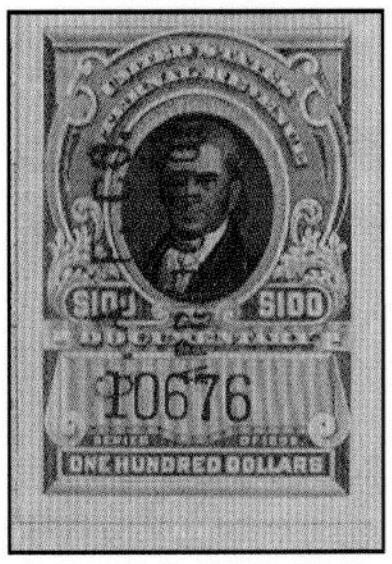
R179, R225, R246, R248

R180, R226, R249

R181, R224, R227, R247, R250

1899 Various Portraits Inscribed "Series of 1898"

SCOTT NO.	DESCRIPTION	UNUSED F	UNUSED AVG	USED F	USED AVG
R179	$100 yellow brown & black.... (cut cancel 20.00)	210.00	150.00	35.00	24.00
R180	$500 carmine lake & black .. (cut cancel 325.00)	1300.00	875.00	850.00	550.00
R181	$1000 green & black .... (cut cancel 150.00)	1000.00	675.00	350.00	265.00

1900

R182	$1 carmine .... (cut cancel .40)	32.50	22.00	.75	.50
R183	$3 lake..................................... (cut cancel 7.50)	200.00	135.00	50.00	35.00

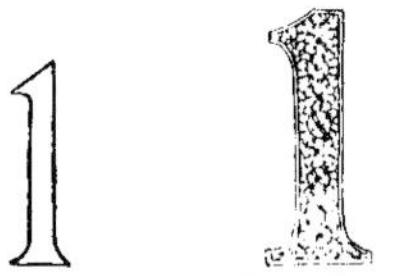
R184-R189 R190-R194

Designs of R173-78 surcharged

R184	$1 gray .... (cut cancel .25)	22.00	15.00	.40	.25
R185	$2 gray .... (cut cancel .25)	22.00	15.00	.40	.25
R186	$3 gray .... (cut cancel 5.00)	100.00	70.00	12.00	8.00
R187	$5 gray .... (cut cancel 1.50)	65.00	45.00	8.00	5.50
R188	$10 gray .... (cut cancel 4.00)	135.00	90.00	22.00	15.00
R189	$50 gray ....(cut cancel 100.00)	1030.00	725.00	500.00	350.00

1902

R190	$1 green .... (cut cancel .35)	35.00	25.00	3.00	2.00
R191	$2 green .... (cut cancel .35)	35.00	25.00	1.50	1.00
R191a	$2 surcharged as R185	125.00	85.00	85.00	60.00
R192	$5 green .... (cut cancel 5.00)	200.00	140.00	28.00	19.00
R192a	$5 surcharge omitted	250.00	170.00	....	....
R193	$10 green .... (cut cancel 50.00)	450.00	300.00	145.00	95.00
R194	$50 green .... (cut cancel 275.00)	1100.00	795.00	850.00	600.00

R195-R216

R217-R223

1914 Inscribed "Series of 1914" Single Line Watermark "USPS"

R195	1/2¢ rose	12.00	8.00	4.00	2.75
R196	1¢ rose	2.50	1.75	.40	.25
R197	2¢ rose	3.00	2.00	.40	.25
R198	3¢ rose	70.00	48.00	35.00	25.00
R199	4¢ rose	20.00	14.00	2.25	1.50
R200	5¢ rose	7.00	4.80	.50	.35
R201	10¢ rose	6.00	4.00	.35	.25
R202	25¢ rose	45.00	30.00	.70	.45
R203	40¢ rose	25.00	17.00	1.50	1.00
R204	50¢ rose	9.00	6.00	.35	.25
R205	80¢ rose	165.00	110.00	11.50	8.00

1914 Double Line Watermark "USIR"

R206	1/2¢ rose	2.00	1.40	.65	.45
R207	1¢ rose	.35	.25	.30	.20
R208	2¢ rose	.40	.25	.30	.25
R209	3¢ rose	2.00	1.40	.35	.25
R210	4¢ rose	4.00	2.50	.60	.40
R211	5¢ rose	2.00	1.40	.40	.25
R212	10¢ rose	.90	.60	.30	.25
R213	25¢ rose	6.00	4.00	1.75	1.20
R214	40¢ rose .... (cut cancel .60)	110.00	75.00	14.00	9.00
R215	50¢ rose	22.00	15.00	.35	.25
R216	80¢ rose .... (cut cancel 1.25)	175.00	115.00	22.00	15.00
R217	$1 green .... (cut cancel .30)	50.00	35.00	.55	.40
R218	$2 carmine .... (cut cancel .25)	75.00	50.00	.85	.60
R219	$3 purple .... (cut cancel .60)	90.00	60.00	4.00	2.75
R220	$5 blue .... (cut cancel .60)	80.00	55.00	4.00	2.75
R221	$10 orange .... (cut cancel 1.00)	180.00	125.00	6.00	4.00
R222	$30 vermillion .... (cut cancel 5.50)	550.00	400.00	18.00	12.00
R223	$50 violet .... (cut cancel 375.00)	1650.00	1050.00	850.00	600.00

1914-15 Various Portraits Inscribed "Series of 1914" or "Series of 1915"

SCOTT NO.	DESCRIPTION	UNUSED F	UNUSED AVG	USED F	USED AVG
R224	$60 brown .... (cut cancel 70.00)	200.00	140.00	150.00	100.00
R225	$100 green .... (cut cancel 17.00)	65.00	45.00	45.00	30.00
R226	$500 blue .... (cut cancel 275.00)	....	....	650.00	450.00
R227	$1000 orange .... (cut cancel 300.00)	....	....	550.00	400.00

R228-239, R251-256, R260-263

1917 Perf. 11

R228	1¢ carmine rose	.30	.25	.25	.20
R229	2¢ carmine rose	.30	.25	.25	.20
R230	3¢ carmine rose	.30	.25	.50	.35
R231	4¢ carmine rose	.30	.25	.30	.25
R232	5¢ carmine rose	.30	.25	.25	.20
R233	8¢ carmine rose	2.25	1.50	.40	.25
R234	10¢ carmine rose	.50	.35	.25	.20
R235	20¢ carmine rose	.80	.55	.30	.25
R236	25¢ carmine rose	1.50	1.00	.30	.25
R237	40¢ carmine rose	2.25	1.50	.50	.35
R238	50¢ carmine rose	2.25	1.50	.25	.20
R239	80¢ carmine rose	6.00	4.00	.30	.25

R240-245, R257-259

Same design as issue of 1914-15 Without dates.

R240	$1 yellow green	7.00	5.00	.30	.25
R241	$2 rose	12.50	8.00	.25	.20
R242	$3 violet .... (cut cancel .30)	40.00	28.00	1.25	.85
R243	$4 yellow brown .... (cut cancel .30)	27.00	18.00	2.00	1.40
R244	$5 dark blue .... (cut cancel .30)	20.00	14.00	.50	.35
R245	$10 orange .... (cut cancel .30)	35.00	24.00	1.50	1.00

Types of 1899 Various Portraits Perf. 12

R246	$30 deep orange, Grant .... (cut cancel 2.50)	50.00	35.00	15.00	10.00
R247	$60 brown, Lincoln .... (cut cancel 1.00)	60.00	40.00	8.00	5.50
R248	$100 green, Washington .... (cut cancel .45)	40.00	27.00	1.25	.80
R249	$500 blue, Hamilton .... (cut cancel 15.00)	375.00	225.00	40.00	28.00
R249a	$500 Numerals in orange	400.00	275.00	60.00	40.00
R250	$1000 orange, Madison (Perf. In. 3.00) .... (cut cancel 3.50)	90.75	52.25	11.00	6.60

1928-29 Perf. 10

R251	1¢ carmine rose	2.25	1.50	1.80	1.20
R252	2¢ carmine rose	.75	.55	.40	.30
R253	4¢ carmine rose	8.00	5.00	5.00	3.50
R254	5¢ carmine rose	1.80	1.20	.75	.50
R255	10¢ carmine rose	2.75	1.85	1.50	1.00
R256	20¢ carmine rose	7.00	5.00	6.00	4.00
R257	$1 green .... (cut cancel 2.00)	175.00	120.00	40.00	27.00
R258	$2 rose	75.00	50.00	3.00	2.00
R259	$10 orange .... (cut cancel 7.00)	250.00	175.00	50.00	35.00

1929-30 Perf. 11 x 10

R260	2¢ carmine rose	4.00	2.75	3.00	2.00
R261	5¢ carmine rose	3.00	2.00	2.25	1.60
R262	10¢ carmine rose	10.50	7.00	8.00	5.00
R263	20¢ carmine rose	17.00	11.00	9.00	6.00

R733, R734

1962 CENTENNIAL INTERNAL REVENUE. Inscribed "Established 1862"

SCOTT NO.	DESCRIPTION	PLATE BLOCK F/NH	UNUSED F/NH	USED F
R733	10¢ violet blue & green	18.00	1.25	.50

1964 Without Inscription Date

R734	10¢ violet blue & green	32.50	3.50	.75

PROPRIETARY STAMPS

RB1-2

RB3-7

1871-74 Perforated 12

SCOTT NO.	DESCRIPTION	VIOLET PAPER (a) F	AVG	GREEN PAPER (b) F	AVG
RB1	1¢ green & black	6.00	4.00	12.00	8.00
RB2	2¢ green & black	7.00	5.00	25.00	17.00
RB3	3¢ green & black	25.00	17.00	65.00	40.00
RB4	4¢ green & black	15.00	10.00	24.00	16.00
RB5	5¢ green & black	160.00	110.00	175.00	120.00
RB6	6¢ green & black	60.00	40.00	125.00	85.00
RB7	10¢ green & black	240.00	165.00	65.00	45.00
RB8	50¢ green & black (large)	750.00	500.00	1100.00	750.00

RB11-12

RB13-19

SCOTT NO.	DESCRIPTION	SILK PAPER (a) F	AVG	WMKD PERF. (b) F	AVG	ROULETTE (c) F	AVG
RB11	1¢ green	2.00	1.40	.50	.35	115.00	80.00
RB12	2¢ brown	2.75	1.85	1.50	1.00	135.00	95.00
RB13	3¢ orange	13.00	9.00	3.50	2.50	110.00	75.00
RB14	4¢ red brown	7.00	5.00	6.00	4.00	....	....
RB15	4¢ red	....	....	5.00	3.50	200.00	140.00
RB16	5¢ black	130.00	90.00	110.00	70.00	....	1200.00
RB17	6¢ violet blue	26.00	17.00	22.00	15.00	400.00	275.00
RB18	6¢ violet	....	....	30.00	21.00	500.00	350.00
RB19	10¢ blue	....	....	350.00	250.00	....	....

RB20-31

RB32-64

RB65-73

1898 Battleship Inscribed "Proprietary"

SCOTT NO.	DESCRIPTION	UNUSED F	AVG	USED F	AVG
RB20	1/8¢ yellow green	.25	.20	.25	.20
RB21	1/4¢ brown	.25	.20	.25	.20
RB22	3/8¢ deep orange	.30	.25	.30	.25
RB23	5/8¢ deep ultramarine	.30	.25	.30	.25
RB24	1¢ dark green	2.25	1.50	.30	.25
RB25	1-1/4¢ violet	.30	.25	.30	.25
RB26	1-7/8¢ dull blue	13.00	9.00	1.75	1.20
RB27	2¢ violet brown	1.25	.85	.30	.25
RB28	2-1/2¢ lake	4.50	3.15	.30	.25
RB29	3-3/4¢ olive gray	45.00	30.00	11.00	7.00
RB30	4¢ purple	14.00	9.00	1.25	.85
RB31	5¢ brown orange	14.00	9.00	1.25	.85

1914 Watermarked "USPS"

SCOTT NO.	DESCRIPTION	UNUSED F	AVG	USED F	AVG
RB32	1/8¢ black	.30	.25	.30	.25
RB33	1/4¢ black	2.40	1.65	1.25	.85
RB34	3/8¢ black	.30	.25	.30	.25
RB35	5/8¢ black	6.00	4.00	2.50	1.75
RB36	1-1/4¢ black	4.00	2.75	1.25	.85
RB37	1-7/8¢ black	48.00	33.00	19.00	13.00
RB38	2-1/2¢ black	12.00	8.00	4.00	2.75
RB39	3-1/8¢ black	110.00	70.00	60.00	40.00
RB40	3-3/4¢ black	50.00	35.00	23.00	16.00
RB41	4¢ black	70.00	48.00	32.00	22.00
RB43	5¢ black	130.00	90.00	85.00	60.00

1914 Watermarked "USIR"

SCOTT NO.	DESCRIPTION	UNUSED F	AVG	USED F	AVG
RB44	1/8¢ black	.30	.25	.30	.25
RB45	1/4¢ black	.30	.25	.30	.25
RB46	3/8¢ black	.70	.50	.40	.28
RB47	1/2¢ black	4.00	2.75	3.50	2.50
RB48	5/8¢ black	.30	.25	.30	.25
RB49	1¢ black	5.00	3.50	4.50	3.00
RB50	1-1/4¢ black	.50	.35	.35	.25
RB51	1-1/2¢ black	3.50	2.50	3.00	2.00
RB52	1-7/8¢ black	1.20	.80	.75	.50
RB53	2¢ black	5.50	4.00	4.50	3.10
RB54	2-1/2¢ black	1.50	1.00	1.20	.80
RB55	3¢ black	5.00	3.50	3.50	2.50
RB56	3-1/8¢ black	6.00	4.00	3.50	2.50
RB57	3-3/4¢ black	12.00	8.00	8.00	5.00
RB58	4¢ black	.40	.30	.30	.25
RB59	4-3/8¢ black	17.00	11.00	9.00	6.00
RB60	5¢ black	3.50	2.50	3.00	2.00
RB61	6¢ black	60.00	48.00	45.00	30.00
RB62	8¢ black	20.00	14.00	12.00	8.00
RB63	10¢ black	12.00	8.00	8.00	5.00
RB64	20¢ black	25.00	17.00	19.00	13.00

1919 Offset Printing

SCOTT NO.	DESCRIPTION	UNUSED F	AVG	USED F	AVG
RB65	1¢ dark blue	.25	.20	.15	.15
RB66	2¢ dark blue	.25	.20	.15	.15
RB67	3¢ dark blue	.95	.55	.55	.35
RB68	4¢ dark blue	.95	.55	.50	.30
RB69	5¢ dark blue	1.10	.65	.55	.35
RB70	8¢ dark blue	9.90	6.05	8.00	4.70
RB71	10¢ dark blue	2.75	1.85	1.95	1.20
RB72	20¢ dark blue	4.40	3.05	2.75	1.65
RB73	40¢ dark blue	21.75	12.95	9.35	5.50

FUTURE DELIVERY STAMPS

FUTURE DELIVERY — Type I

FUTURE DELIVERY — Type II

Documentary Stamps of 1917 Overprinted

1918-34 Perforated 11, Type I Overprint Lines 8mm. Apart

SCOTT NO.	DESCRIPTION	UNUSED F	AVG	USED F	AVG
RC1	2¢ carmine rose	8.00	5.00	.30	.25
RC2	3¢ carmine rose (cut cancel 13.50)	35.00	25.00	22.00	15.00
RC3	4¢ carmine rose	13.00	9.00	.30	.25
RC3A	5¢ carmine rose	95.00	60.00	4.00	2.75
RC4	10¢ carmine rose	22.00	15.00	.30	.25
RC5	20¢ carmine rose	35.00	25.00	.30	.25
RC6	25¢ carmine rose (cut cancel .25)	65.00	45.00	.75	.55
RC7	40¢ carmine rose (cut cancel .25)	75.00	50.00	.75	.55
RC8	50¢ carmine rose	16.00	11.00	.30	.25
RC9	80¢ carmine rose (cut cancel 1.00)	135.00	95.00	10.00	7.00
RC10	$1 green (cut cancel .25)	60.00	45.00	.30	.25
RC11	$2 rose (cut cancel .25)	65.00	45.00	.30	.25
RC12	$3 violet (cut cancel .30)	135.00	95.00	2.00	1.20
RC13	$5 dark blue (cut cancel .25)	110.00	90.00	.50	.35
RC14	$10 orange (cut cancel .35)	135.00	95.00	1.00	.70
RC15	$20 olive bistre (cut cancel .75)	250.00	170.00	5.00	3.50

Perforated 12

SCOTT NO.	DESCRIPTION	UNUSED F	AVG	USED F	AVG
RC16	$30 vermillon (cut cancel 2.00)	85.00	55.00	5.00	3.50
RC17	$50 olive green (cut cancel 2.00)	60.00	42.00	2.00	1.40
RC18	$60 brown (cut cancel 1.25)	85.00	55.00	3.00	2.00
RC19	$100 yellow green (cut cancel 8.00)	150.00	100.00	30.00	20.00
RC20	$500 blue (cut cancel6.00)	100.00	70.00	11.00	7.00
RC21	$1000 orange (cut cancel 1.75)	135.00	95.00	6.00	4.00
RC22	1¢ carmine rose (lines 2mm apart)	1.20	.75	.30	.25
RC23	80¢ carmine rose (lines 2mm apart) (cut cancel .40)	135.00	95.00	2.00	1.40

1925-34 Perforated 11 Type II Overprint

SCOTT NO.	DESCRIPTION	UNUSED F	AVG	USED F	AVG
RC25	$1 green (cut cancel .10)	55.00	40.00	1.00	.70
RC26	$10 orange (cut cancel 5.75)	150.00	100.00	15.00	10.00

STOCK TRANSFER STAMPS

STOCK TRANSFER — Type I

Documentary Stamps Overprinted

STOCK TRANSFER — Type II

1918-22 Perforated 11 Type I Overprint

SCOTT NO.	DESCRIPTION	UNUSED F	AVG	USED F	AVG
RD1	1¢ carmine rose	1.00	.70	.30	.25
RD2	2¢ carmine rose	.30	.25	.30	.25
RD3	4¢ carmine rose	.30	.25	.30	.25
RD4	5¢ carmine rose	.35	.30	.30	.25
RD5	10¢ carmine rose	.35	.30	.30	.25
RD6	20¢ carmine rose	.65	.45	.30	.25
RD7	25¢ carmine rose (cut cancel .25)	1.75	1.10	.30	.25
RD8	40¢ carmine rose	1.50	1.00	.30	.25
RD9	50¢ carmine rose	.80	.50	.30	.25
RD10	80¢ carmine rose (cut cancel .25)	4.00	2.50	.40	.25
RD11	$1 green (red ovverprint) (cut cancel 4.00)	100.00	70.00	22.00	15.00
RD12	$1 green (black overprint)	3.00	2.00	.40	.25
RD13	$2 rose	3.00	2.00	.30	.25
RD14	$3 violet (cut cancel .25)	22.00	15.00	5.00	3.50
RD15	$4 yellow brown (cut cancel .25)	12.00	8.00	.30	.25
RD16	$5 dark blue (cut cancel .25)	8.00	5.00	.30	.25
RD17	$10 orange (cut cancel .25)	18.00	12.00	.40	.35
RD18	$20 olive bistre (cut cancel 3.50)	100.00	70.00	20.00	14.00

Perforated 12

SCOTT NO.	DESCRIPTION	UNUSED F	AVG	USED F	AVG
RD19	$30 vermillion (cut cancel 1.20)	13.50	8.75	4.25	2.75
RD20	$50 olive green (cut cancel 24.00)	70.00	45.00	35.00	35.00
RD21	$60 brown (cut cancel 10.00)	55.00	35.00	16.50	10.75
RD22	$100 green (cut cancel 2.50)	14.75	9.50	4.75	3.00
RD23	$500 blue (cut cancel 70.00)	......	......	110.00	70.00
RD24	$1000 orange (cut cancel 30.00)	......	......	77.50	50.00

1928 Perforated 10 Type I Overprint

SCOTT NO.	DESCRIPTION	UNUSED F	UNUSED AVG	USED F	USED AVG
RD25	2¢ carmine rose	3.00	2.00	.40	.35
RD26	4¢ carmine rose	3.00	2.00	.40	.35
RD27	10¢ carmine rose	2.50	1.75	.40	.35
RD28	20¢ carmine rose	4.00	2.50	.40	.35
RD29	50¢ carmine rose	4.00	2.50	.40	.35
RD30	$1 green	40.00	28.00	.30	.25
RD31	$2 carmine rose	40.00	28.00	.35	.30
RD32	$10 orange (cut cancel .25)	40.00	28.00	.50	.35
RD33	2¢ carmine rose	8.00	5.00	1.00	.70
RD34	10¢ carmine rose	3.00	2.00	.40	.35
RD35	20¢ carmine rose	6.00	4.00	.30	.25
RD36	50¢ carmine rose	4.00	2.50	.30	.25
RD37	$1 green (cut cancel .30)	60.00	40.00	10.00	7.00
RD38	$2 rose (cut cancel .30)	55.00	40.00	9.00	6.00

1920-28 Perforated 10 Type II overprint

SCOTT NO.	DESCRIPTION	UNUSED F	UNUSED AVG	USED F	USED AVG
RD39	2¢ carmine rose	7.00	5.00	1.00	.70
RD40	10¢ carmine rose	2.00	1.40	.60	.40
RD41	20¢ carmine rose	3.00	2.00	.30	.25

SILVER TAX STAMPS

Documentary Stamps of 1917 Overprinted

1934-36

SCOTT NO.	DESCRIPTION	UNUSED F	UNUSED AVG	USED F	USED AVG
RG1	1¢ carmine rose	1.50	1.00	1.00	.70
RG2	2¢ carmine rose	1.75	1.25	.75	.50
RG3	3¢ carmine rose	1.95	1.35	.90	.60
RG4	4¢ carmine rose	2.00	1.40	1.75	1.25
RG5	5¢ carmine rose	3.50	2.50	1.50	1.00
RG6	8¢ carmine rose	4.50	3.00	3.50	2.50
RG7	10¢ carmine rose	5.00	3.50	4.00	2.50
RG8	20¢ carmine rose	7.00	5.00	4.00	2.50
RG9	25¢ carmine rose	6.00	4.00	5.00	3.50
RG10	40¢ carmine rose	7.00	5.00	6.50	4.50
RG11	50¢ carmine rose	10.00	7.00	8.00	5.00
RG12	80¢ carmine rose	18.00	12.00	11.00	7.00
RG13	$1 green	35.00	25.00	18.00	13.00
RG14	$2 rose	40.00	28.00	27.00	18.00
RG15	$3 violet	75.00	50.00	40.00	28.00
RG16	$4 yellow brown	60.00	40.00	25.00	17.00
RG17	$5 dark blue	75.00	50.00	30.00	20.00
RG18	$10 orange	95.00	65.00	25.00	17.00
RG19	$30 vermillion (cut cancel 20.00)	200.00	140.00	60.00	40.00
RG20	$60 brown (cut cancel 30.00)	225.00	150.00	85.00	60.00
RG21	$100 green	275.00	185.00	35.00	22.50
RG22	$500 blue (cut cancel 110.00)	600.00	400.00	235.00	160.00
RG23	$1000 orange (cut cancel 70.00)	......	......	120.00	77.50
RG26	$100 green, 11mm spacing	500.00	350.00	85.00	55.00
RG27	$1000 orange, 11mm spacing	......	......	900.00	600.00

TOBACCO SALE TAX STAMPS

Documentary Stamps of 1917 Overprinted

1934

SCOTT NO.	DESCRIPTION	UNUSED F	UNUSED AVG	USED F	USED AVG
RJ1	1¢ carmine rose	.40	.35	.25	.20
RJ2	2¢ carmine rose	.45	.30	.25	.20
RJ3	5¢ carmine rose	1.40	.90	.45	.30
RJ4	10¢ carmine rose	1.75	1.15	.45	.30
RJ5	25¢ carmine rose	4.75	3.00	1.85	1.20
RJ6	50¢ carmine rose	4.75	3.00	1.85	1.20
RJ7	$1 green	12.00	8.00	1.85	1.20
RJ8	$2 rose	20.00	14.00	2.15	1.40
RJ9	$5 dark blue	25.00	17.00	4.75	3.00
RJ10	$10 orange	40.00	27.00	12.00	7.75
RJ11	$20 olive bistre	100.00	70.00	15.00	9.75

HUNTING PERMIT

RW1

RW2

RW3

RW4

RW5

1934-1938 Inscribed: DEPARTMENT OF AGRICULTURE (NH + 75%)

SCOTT NO.	DESCRIPTION	UNUSED VF	UNUSED F	UNUSED AVG	USED VF	USED F	USED AVG
RW1	1934 $1 Mallards	1000.00	650.00	450.00	160.00	110.00	90.00
RW2	1935 $1 Canvasbacks	900.00	550.00	350.00	200.00	150.00	110.00
RW3	1936 $1 Canada Geese	500.00	300.00	200.00	95.00	65.00	45.00
RW4	1937 $1 Scaup Ducks	450.00	275.00	175.00	65.00	45.00	29.50
RW5	1938 $1 Pintail Drake	700.00	425.00	250.00	75.00	50.00	32.50

RW6

RW7

RW8

RW9

RW10

Note: NH premiums RW6-9 (75%) RW10-16 (50%) RW17-25 (40%)
1939-1958 Inscribed: DEPARTMENT OF INTERIOR

SCOTT NO.	DESCRIPTION	UNUSED VF	UNUSED F	UNUSED AVG	USED VF	USED F	USED AVG
RW6	1939 $1 Green-Winged Teal	300.00	200.00	125.00	55.00	40.00	25.00
RW7	1940 $1 Black Mallards	300.00	200.00	125.00	55.00	40.00	25.00
RW8	1941 $1 Ruddy Ducks .	300.00	200.00	125.00	55.00	40.00	25.00
RW9	1942 $1 Baldpates	300.00	200.00	125.00	55.00	40.00	25.00
RW10	1943 $1 Wood Ducks ..	140.00	85.00	50.00	50.00	40.00	25.00

RW11

RW12

RW13

RW14

RW15

SCOTT NO.	DESCRIPTION	UNUSED VF	UNUSED F	UNUSED AVG	USED VF	USED F	USED AVG
RW11	1944 $1 White Fronted Geese	140.00	85.00	50.00	33.50	24.00	16.00
RW12	1945 $1 Shoveller Ducks	140.00	85.00	50.00	27.00	18.00	14.00
RW13	1946 $1 Redhead Ducks	70.00	45.00	30.00	21.00	15.00	10.50
RW14	1947 $1 Snow Geese ..	70.00	45.00	30.00	21.00	15.00	10.50
RW15	1948 $1 Buffleheads	70.00	45.00	30.00	21.00	15.00	10.50

RW16

RW17

RW18

RW19

RW20

SCOTT NO.	DESCRIPTION	UNUSED VF	UNUSED F	UNUSED AVG	USED VF	USED F	USED AVG
RW16	1949 $2 Goldeneye Ducks	85.00	60.00	30.00	15.50	11.00	7.50
RW17	1950 $2 Trumpeter Swans	120.00	80.00	60.00	14.00	11.00	7.50
RW18	1951 $2 Gadwall Ducks	120.00	80.00	60.00	14.00	11.00	7.50
RW19	1952 $2 Harlequin Ducks	120.00	80.00	60.00	14.00	11.00	7.50
RW20	1953 $2 Blue-Winged Teal	120.00	80.00	60.00	14.00	11.00	7.50

Notes on Hunting Permit Stamps

1. **Unused stamps without gum (uncancelled) are priced at one-half gummed price.**
2. **The date printed on the stamp is one year later than the date of issue listed above.**
3. **#RW1-RW25 and RW31 are plate blocks of 6.**

RW21

RW22

RW23

RW24

RW25

SCOTT NO.	DESCRIPTION	UNUSED VF	UNUSED F	UNUSED AVG	USED VF	USED F	USED AVG
RW21	1954 $2 Ringed-Necked Ducks	110.00	70.00	45.00	11.50	8.25	5.75
RW22	1955 $2 Blue Geese	110.00	70.00	45.00	11.50	8.25	5.75
RW23	1956 $2 American Merganser	110.00	70.00	45.00	11.50	8.25	5.75
RW24	1957 $2 Ameriacn Eider	110.00	70.00	45.00	11.50	8.25	5.75
RW25	1958 $2 Canada Geese	110.00	70.00	45.00	11.50	8.25	5.75

PLATE BLOCKS RW1-RW25

PLATE BLOCKS OF 6

SCOTT NO.	UNUSED NH F	UNUSED NH AVG	UNUSED OG F	UNUSED OG AVG	SCOTT NO.	UNUSED NH F	UNUSED NH AVG	UNUSED OG F	UNUSED OG AVG
RW1	14000.00	10000.00	11000.00	8000.00	RW14	300.00	210.00	225.00	165.00
RW2	10000.00	7000.00	8000.00	6000.00	RW15	325.00	225.00	240.00	180.00
RW3	3250.00	2300.00	2400.00	1700.00	RW16	400.00	280.00	300.00	210.00
RW4	2400.00	1700.00	2000.00	1500.00	RW17	500.00	375.00	400.00	280.00
RW5	3250.00	2300.00	2400.00	1700.00	RW18	500.00	375.00	400.00	280.00
RW6	2200.00	1600.00	1700.00	1200.00	RW19	500.00	375.00	400.00	280.00
RW7	2000.00	1400.00	1500.00	1100.00	RW20	500.00	375.00	400.00	280.00
RW8	2000.00	1400.00	1500.00	1100.00	RW21	500.00	375.00	400.00	280.00
RW9	2000.00	1400.00	1500.00	1100.00	RW22	500.00	375.00	400.00	280.00
RW10	575.00	425.00	475.00	350.00	RW23	500.00	375.00	400.00	280.00
RW11	595.00	450.00	475.00	350.00	RW24	500.00	375.00	400.00	280.00
RW12	400.00	280.00	300.00	210.00	RW25	500.00	375.00	400.00	280.00
RW13	250.00	180.00	200.00	150.00					

RW26

RW27

RW28

RW29

RW30

1959-1971 (NH + 40%)

SCOTT NO.	DESCRIPTION	UNUSED VF	UNUSED F	USED VF	USED F
RW26	1959 $3 Dog & Mallard	160.00	120.00	12.00	9.00
RW27	1960 $3 Redhead Ducks	160.00	120.00	11.50	8.25
RW28	1961 $3 Mallard Hen & Ducklings	160.00	120.00	11.50	8.25
RW29	1962 $3 Pintail Drakes	160.00	120.00	12.00	9.00
RW30	1963 $3 Brant Ducks Landing	160.00	120.00	12.00	9.00

RW31

RW32

RW33

RW34

SCOTT NO.	DESCRIPTION	UNUSED VF	UNUSED F	USED VF	USED F
RW31	1964 $3 Hawaiian Nene Goose	130.00	100.00	12.00	9.00
RW32	1965 $3 Canvasback Drakes	130.00	100.00	12.00	9.00
RW33	1966 $3 Whistling Swans	130.00	100.00	12.00	9.00
RW34	1967 $3 Old Squaw Ducks	130.00	100.00	12.00	9.00

RW35

RW36

RW37

RW38

SCOTT NO.	DESCRIPTION	UNUSED VF	UNUSED F	USED VF	USED F
RW35	1968 $3 Hooded Mergansers	90.00	60.00	12.00	9.00
RW36	1969 $3 White-Winged Scoters	90.00	60.00	9.50	6.75
RW37	1970 $3 Ross's Geese	90.00	60.00	9.50	6.75
RW38	1971 $3 Three Cinnamon Teal	70.00	50.00	9.50	6.75

Notes on Hunting Permit Stamps

1. Unused stamps without gum (uncancelled) are priced at one-half gummed price.
2. The date printed on the stamp is one year later than the date of issue listed above.
3. #RW1-RW25 and RW31 are plate blocks of 6.

RW39

RW40

RW41

RW42

RW43

1972-1978

SCOTT NO.	DESCRIPTION	UNUSED NH VF	UNUSED NH F	USED VF	USED F
RW39	1972 $5 Emperor Geese	40.00	30.00	9.00	7.50
RW40	1973 $5 Steller's Eider	30.00	20.00	9.00	7.50
RW41	1974 $5 Wood Ducks	30.00	20.00	8.00	6.50
RW42	1975 $5 Canvasbacks	30.00	20.00	8.00	6.50
RW43	1976 $5 Canada Geese	30.00	20.00	8.00	6.50

RW44

RW45

SCOTT NO.	DESCRIPTION	UNUSED NH VF	UNUSED NH F	USED VF	USED F
RW44	1977 $5 Pair of Ross's Geese	30.00	20.00	8.00	6.50
RW45	1978 $5 Hooded Merganser Drake	30.00	20.00	8.00	6.50

RW46

RW47

RW48

RW49

1979-1986

SCOTT NO.	DESCRIPTION	UNUSED NH VF	UNUSED NH F	USED VF	USED F
RW46	1979 $7.50 Green-Winged Teal	25.00	15.00	8.00	7.00
RW47	1980 $7.50 Mallards.	25.00	15.00	8.00	7.00
RW48	1981 $7.50 Ruddy Ducks	25.00	15.00	8.00	7.00
RW49	1982 $7.50 Canvasbacks.	25.00	15.00	8.00	7.00

RW50

RW51

RW52

RW53

SCOTT NO.	DESCRIPTION	UNUSED NH VF	UNUSED NH F	USED VF	USED F
RW50	1983 $7.50 Pintails	25.00	15.00	8.00	7.00
RW51	1984 $7.50 Widgeon.	25.00	15.00	8.00	7.00
RW52	1985 $7.50 Cinnamon Teal	25.00	15.00	8.00	7.00
RW53	1986 $7.50 Fulvous Whistling	25.00	15.00	8.00	7.00

RW54

RW55

RW56

RW57

1987-1993

SCOTT NO.	DESCRIPTION	UNUSED NH VF	UNUSED NH F	USED VF	USED F
RW54	1987 $10.00 Redhead Ducks	20.00	16.00	11.00	9.00
RW55	1988 $10.00 Snow Goose	20.00	16.00	12.00	10.00
RW56	1989 $12.50 Lesser Scaup	23.00	18.00	12.00	10.00
RW57	1990 $12.50 Black Bellied Whistling Duck	23.00	18.00	12.00	10.00

RW58

RW59

RW60

SCOTT NO.	DESCRIPTION	UNUSED NH VF	UNUSED NH F	USED VF	USED F
RW58	1991 $15.00 King Eiders	45.00	35.00	18.00	15.00
RW59	1992 $15.00 Spectacled Eider	35.00	30.00	16.50	12.50
RW60	1993 $15.00 Canvasbacks	35.00	30.00	16.50	12.50

RW61

RW62

RW63

RW64

RW65

RW66

1992-1998

SCOTT NO.	DESCRIPTION	UNUSED NH VF	UNUSED NH F	USED VF	USED F
RW61	1994 $15.00 Red-breasted Merganser	35.00	30.00	16.50	12.50
RW62	1995 $15.00 Mallards	35.00	30.00	16.50	12.50
RW63	1996 $15.00 Surf Scoters	35.00	30.00	16.50	12.50
RW64	1997 $15.00 Canada Goose	35.00	30.00	16.50	12.50
RW65	1998 $15.00 Barrow's Goldeneye	55.00	40.00	16.50	12.50
RW65a	1998 $15.00 Barrow's Goldeneye, self-adhesive, pane of 1	35.00	....	18.00	....
RW66	1999 $15.00 Greater Scaup	35.00	30.00	16.50	....
RW66a	1999 $15.00 Greater Scaup, self-adhesive, pane of 1	35.00	....	18.00	....

RW67

RW68

2000-2001

SCOTT NO.	DESCRIPTION	UNUSED NH VF	UNUSED NH F	USED VF	USED F
RW67	2000 $15.00 Mottled Duck	35.00	30.00	16.50	....
RW67a	2000 $15.00 Mottled Duck, self-adhesive, pane of 1	35.00	....	18.00	....
RW68	2001 $15.00 Northern Pintail	35.00	30.00	16.50	....
RW68a	2001 $15.00 Northern Pintail, self-adhesive, pane of 1	35.00	....	18.00	....

RW69

RW70

2002

SCOTT NO.	DESCRIPTION	UNUSED NH VF	UNUSED NH F	USED VF	USED F
RW69	2002 $15.00 Black Scoters	35.00	30.00	16.50	....
RW69a	2002 $15.00 Black Scoters, self-adhesive, pane of 1	35.00	....	18.00	....

RW71

RW72

2003-2005

SCOTT NO.	DESCRIPTION	UNUSED NH VF	UNUSED NH F	USED VF	USED F
RW70	2003 $15.00 Snow Geese	35.00	30.00	16.50	....
RW70a	2003 $15.00 Snow Geese, self-adhesive, pane of 1	35.00	....	18.00	....
RW71	2004 $15.00 Redheads	35.00	30.00	16.50	....
RW71a	2004 $15.00 Redheads, self-adhesive, pane of 1	35.00	....	18.00	....
RW72	2005 $15.00 Hooded Mergansers	35.00	30.00	17.75	....
RW72a	2005 $15.00 Hooded Mergansers, self-adhesive, pane of 1	35.00	....	20.00	....

RW73

RW74

2006-2007

SCOTT NO.	DESCRIPTION	UNUSED NH VF	UNUSED NH F	USED VF	USED F
RW73	2006 $15.00 Ross's Goose	35.00	30.00	18.00	....
RW73a	2006 $15.00 Ross's Goose, self-adhesive, pane of 1	35.00	....	20.00	....
RW74	2007 $15.00 Ringed-Necked Ducks	35.00	30.00	19.00	....
RW74a	2007 $15.00 Ringed-Necked Ducks, self-adhesive, pane of 1	35.00	....	22.00	....

PLATE BLOCKS RW26-RW74

SCOTT NO.		UNUSED NH F	UNUSED OG F
RW26	1959 $3.00 Dog & Mallard	500.00	350.00
RW27	1960 $3.00 Redhead Ducks	400.00	295.00
RW28	1961 $3.00 Mallard Hen &Ducklings	400.00	295.00
RW29	1962 $3.00 Pintail Drakes	500.00	3550.00
RW30	1963 $3.00 Brant Ducks Landing	450.00	300.00
RW31(6)	1964 $3.00 Hawaiian Nene Goose	1975.00	1550.00
RW32	1965 $3.00 Canvasback Drakes	500.00	350.00
RW33	1966 $3.00 Whistling Swans	500.00	350.00
RW34	1967 $3.00 Old Squaw Ducks	550.00	375.00
RW35	1968 $3.00 Hooded Mergansers	280.00	195.00
RW36	1969 $3.00 White-Winged Scoters	250.00	175.00
RW37	1970 $3.00 Ross's Geese	250.00	175.00
RW38	1971 $3.00 Three Cinnamon Teal	175.00	110.00
RW39	1972 $5.00 Emperor Geese	110.00	......
RW40	1973 $5.00 Steller's Eider	100.00	......
RW41	1974 $5.00 Wood Ducks	75.00	......
RW42	1975 $5.00 Canvasbacks	60.00	......
RW43	1976 $5.00 Canada Geese	60.00	......
RW44	1977 $5.00 Pair of Ross's Geese	60.00	......
RW45	1978 $5.00 Hooded Merganser Drake	60.00	......
RW46	1979 $7.50 Green-Winged Teal	72.50	......
RW47	1980 $7.50 Mallards	72.50	......
RW48	1981 $7.50 Ruddy Ducks	72.50	......
RW49	1982 $7.50 Canvasbacks	72.50	......
RW50	1983 $7.50 Pintails	72.50	......
RW51	1984 $7.50 Widgeon	72.50	......
RW52	1985 $7.50 Cinnamon Teal	72.50	......
RW53	1986 $7.50 Fulvous Whistling	72.50	......
RW54	1987 $10.00 Redhead Ducks	82.50	......
RW55	1988 $10.00 Snow Goose	82.50	......
RW56	1989 $12.50 Lesser Scaup	100.00	......
RW57	1990 $12.50 Black Bellied Whistling Duck	100.00	......
RW58	1991 $15.00 King Eiders	150.00	......
RW59	1992 $15.00 Spectacled Eider	150.00	......
RW60	1993 $15.00 Canvasbacks	150.00	......
RW61	1994 $15.00 Red-breasted Merganser	150.00	......
RW62	1995 $15.00 Mallards	150.00	......
RW63	1996 $15.00 Surf Scoters	150.00	......
RW64	1997 $15.00 Canada Goose	150.00	......
RW65	1998 $15.00 Barrow's Goldeneye	150.00	......
RW66	1999 $15.00 Greater Scaup	150.00	......
RW67	2000 $15.00 Mottled Duck	150.00	......
RW68	2001 $15.00 Northern Pintail	150.00	......
RW69	2002 $15.00 Black Scoters	150.00	......
RW70	2003 $15.00 Snow Geese	150.00	......
RW71	2004 $15.00 Redheads	150.00	......
RW72	2005 $15.00 Hooded Mergansers	150.00	......
RW73	2006 $15.00 Ross's Goose	150.00	......
RW74	2007 $15.00 Ringed-Necked Ducks	150.00	......

Note: **#RW1-RW25 and RW31 are plate blocks of six. All others are plate blocks of four.**

STATE HUNTING PERMIT

AL7

ALABAMA

NO.	DESCRIPTION	F-VF NH
AL1	'79 $5 Wood Ducks	10.25
AL2	'80 $5 Mallards	10.25
AL3	'81 $5 Canada Geese	10.25
AL4	'82 $5 Green-Winged Teal	10.25
AL5	'83 $5 Widgeons	11.00
AL6	'84 $5 Buffleheads	20.00
AL7	'85 $5 Wood Ducks	14.00
AL8	'86 $5 Canada Geese	14.00
AL9	'87 $5 Pintails	15.00
AL10	'88 $5 Canvasbacks	11.00
AL11	'89 $5 Hooded Mergansers	10.25
AL12	'90 $5 Wood Ducks	10.25
AL13	'91 $5 Redheads	10.25
AL14	'92 $5 Cinnamon Teal	10.25
AL15	'93 $5 Green-Winged Teal	10.25
AL16	'94 $5 Canvasbacks	10.25
AL17	'95 $5 Canada Geese	10.25
AL18	'96 $5 Wood Ducks	10.25
AL19	'97 $5 Snow Geese	10.25
AL20	'98 $5 Barrows Goldeneye	10.25
AL21	'99 $5 Redheads	10.25
AL22	'00 $5 Buffleheads	10.25
AL23	'01 $5 Ruddy Duck	10.25
AL24	'02 $5 Pintail	10.25
AL25	'03 $5 Wood Duck	10.25
AL26	'04 $5 Ring-Necked Duck	10.25
AL27	'05 $5 Canada Geese	10.25

AK1

ALASKA

NO.	DESCRIPTION	F-VF NH
AK1	'85 $5 Emperor Geese	14.00
AK2	'86 $5 Steller's Eiders	11.00
AK3	'87 $5 Spectacled Eiders	15.00
AK4	'88 $5 Trumpeter Swans	10.00
AK5	'89 $5 Barrow's Goldeneyes	9.25
AK6	'90 $5 Old Squaws	9.25
AK7	'91 $5 Snow Geese	9.25
AK8	'92 $5 Canvasbacks	9.25
AK9	'93 $5 Tule White Front Geese	9.25
AK10	'94 $5 Harlequin Ducks	20.00
AK11	'95 $5 Pacific Brant	20.00
AK12	'96 $5 Aleutian Canada Geese	25.00
AK13	'97 $5 King Eiders	20.00
AK14	'98 $5 Barrows Goldeneye	15.00
AK15	'99 $5 Pintail	15.00
AK16	'00 $5 Common Eiders	15.00
AK17	'01 $5 Buffleheads	15.00
AK18	'02 $5 Black Scoter	9.25
AK19	'03 $5 Canada Geese	9.25
AK20	'04 $5 Lesser Scaup	9.25
AK21	'05 $5 Hooded Merganser	9.25

AZ1

ARIZONA

NO.	DESCRIPTION	F-VF NH
AZ1	'87 $5.50 Pintails	12.00
AZ2	'88 $5.50 Green-Winged Teal	11.25
AZ3	'89 $5.50 Cinnamon Teal	11.25
AZ4	'90 $5.50 Canada Geese	11.25
AZ5	'91 $5.50 Blue-Winged Teal	11.25
AZ6	'92 $5.50 Buffleheads	11.25
AZ7	'93 $5.50 Mexican Ducks	11.25
AZ8	'94 $5.50 Mallards	11.25
AZ9	'95 $5.50 Widgeon	11.25
AZ10	'96 $5.50 Canvasback	11.25
AZ11	'97 $5.50 Gadwall	11.25
AZ12	'98 $5.50 Wood Duck	11.25
AZ13	'99 $5.50 Snow Geese	11.25
AZ14	'00 $7.50 Ruddy Ducks	13.50
AZ15	'01 $7.50 Redheads	13.50
AZ16	'02 $7.50 Ring-necked ducks	13.50
AZ17	'03 $7.50 Northern Shoveler	13.50
AZ18	'04 $7.50 Lesser Scaup	13.50
AZ19	'05 $7.50 Pintails	13.50

AR5

ARKANSAS

NO.	DESCRIPTION	F-VF NH
AR1	'81 $5.50 Mallards	60.00
AR2	'82 $5.50 Wood Ducks	50.00
AR3	'83 $5.50 Green-Winged Teal	70.00
AR4	'84 $5.50 Pintails	26.00
AR5	'85 $5.50 Mallards	14.50
AR6	'86 $5.50 Black Swamp Mallards	12.50
AR7	'87 $7 Wood Ducks	12.50
AR8	'88 $7 Pintails	11.50
AR9	'89 $7 Mallards	11.50
AR10	'90 $7 Black Ducks & Mallards	11.50
AR11	'91 $7 Sulphur River Widgeons	11.50
AR12	'92 $7 Shirey Bay Shovelers	11.50
AR13	'93 $7 Grand Prairie Mallards	11.00
AR14	'94 $7 Canada Goose	11.00
AR15	'95 $7 White River Mallards	11.00
AR16	'96 $7 Black Lab	20.00
AR17	'97 $7 Chocolate Lab	11.00
AR18	'98 $7 Labrador retriever, mallards	11.00
AR19	'99 $7.00 Wood Duck	11.00
AR20	'00 $7 Mallards and Golden Retriever	11.00
AR21	'01 $7 Canvasback	11.00
AR22	'02 $7 Mallards	11.00
AR23	'03 $7 Mallards & Chesapeake Bay Retriever	11.00
AR24	'04 $7 Mallards	11.00
AR25	'04 $20 Mallards	30.00
AR26	'04 $7 Mallards and Labrador Retriever	11.00
AR27	'04 $20 Mallards and Labrador Retriever	30.00

CA16

CALIFORNIA

NO.	DESCRIPTION	F-VF NH
CA1	'71 $1 Pintails	850.00
CA2	'72 $1 Canvasbacks	3,250.00
CA3	'73 $1 Mallards	15.00
CA4	'74 $1 White-Fronted Geese	4.50
CA5	'75 $1 Green-Winged Teal	42.50
CA6	'76 $1 Widgeons	19.00
CA7	'77 $1 Cinnamon Teal	50.00
CA8	'78 $5 Cinnamon Teal	9.00
CA9	'78 $5 Hooded Mergansers	150.00
CA10	'79 $5 Wood Ducks	9.50
CA11	'80 $5 Pintails	9.50
CA12	'81 $5 Canvasbacks	9.75
CA13	'82 $5 Widgeons	9.75
CA14	'83 $5 Green-Winged Teal	9.75
CA15	'84 $7.50 Mallard Decoy	12.50
CA16	'85 $7.50 Ring-Necked Ducks	12.50
CA17	'86 $7.50 Canada Goose	12.50
CA18	'87 $7.50 Redheads	12.50
CA19	'88 $7.50 Mallards	12.50
CA20	'89 $7.50 Cinnamon Teal	12.50
CA21	'90 $7.50 Canada Goose	12.50
CA22	'91 $7.50 Gadwalls	12.50
CA23	'92 $7.90 White-Fronted Goose	12.50
CA24	'93 $10.50 Pintails	15.00
CA25	'94 $10.50 Wood Duck	15.00
CA26	'95 $10.50 Snow Geese	15.00
CA27	'96 $10.50 Mallard	15.00
CA28	'97 $10.50 Pintails	15.00
CA29	'98 $10.50 Green-Winged Teal (pair)	35.00
CA30	'99 $10.50 Wood Duck (pair)	35.00
CA31	'00 $10.50 Canada geese, mallard, widgeon	16.00
CA32	'01 $10.50 Redheads	16.00
CA33	'02 $10.50 Pintails	16.00
CA34	'03 $10.50 Mallards	16.00
CA35	'04 $13.90 Cinnamon Teal	19.50
CA36	'05 $14.20 Pintails	20.00

CO1

COLORADO

NO.	DESCRIPTION	F-VF NH
CO1	'90 $5 Canada Geese	17.00
CO2	'91 $5 Mallards	17.00
CO3	'92 $5 Pintails	12.00
CO4	'93 $5 Green-Winged Teal	12.00
CO5	'94 $5 Wood Ducks	12.00
CO6	'95 $5 Buffleheads	12.00
CO7	'96 $5 Cinnamon Teal	12.00
CO8	'97 $5 Widgeon	12.00
CO9	'98 $5 Redhead	12.00
CO10	'99 $5 Blue-winged Teal	12.00
CO11	'00 $5 Gadwalls	12.00
CO12	'01 $5 Ruddy Duck	12.00
CO13	'02 $5 Common Goldeneyes	12.00
CO14	'03 $5 Canvasbacks	12.00
CO15	'04 $5 Snow Geese	12.00
CO16	'05 $5 Shovelers	9.25

CONNECTICUT

NO.	DESCRIPTION	F-VF NH
CT1	'93 $5 Black Ducks	15.00
CT2	'94 $5 Canvasbacks	15.00
CT3	'95 $5 Mallards	15.00
CT4	'96 $5 Old Squaw	15.00
CT5	'97 $5 Green Winged Teal	15.00
CT6	'98 $5 Mallards	15.00
CT7	'99 $5 Canada Geese	23.00
CT8	'00 $5 Wood Duck	15.00
CT9	'01 Bufflehead	15.00
CT10	'02 Greater Scaups	15.00
CT11	'03 $5 Black Duck	15.00
CT12	'04 $5 Wood Duck	15.00
CT13	'05 $10 Mallards	20.00

DE1

DELAWARE

NO.	DESCRIPTION	F-VF NH
DE1	'80 $5 Black Ducks	95.00
DE2	'81 $5 Snow Geese	85.00
DE3	'82 $5 Canada Geese	80.00
DE4	'83 $5 Canvasbacks	55.00
DE5	'84 $5 Mallards	25.00
DE6	'85 $5 Pintail	14.00
DE7	'86 $5 Widgeons	12.00
DE8	'87 $5 Redheads	12.00
DE9	'88 $5 Wood Ducks	10.50
DE10	'89 $5 Buffleheads	9.75
DE11	'90 $5 Green-Winged Teal	9.75
DE12	'91 $5 Hooded Merganser	9.75
DE13	'92 $5 Blue-Winged Teal	9.75
DE14	'93 $5 Goldeneye	9.75
DE15	'94 $5 Blue Goose	9.75
DE16	'95 $5 Scaup	9.75
DE17	'96 $6 Gadwall	9.75
DE18	'97 $6 White Winged Scoter	9.75
DE19	'98 $6 Blue Winged Teal	9.75
DE20	'99 $6 Tundra Swan	9.75
DE21	'00 $6 American brant	9.75
DE22	'01 $6 Old Squaw	9.75
DE23	'02 $6 Ruddy Ducks	9.75
DE24	'03 $9 Ring Necked Duck	14.00
DE25	'04 $9 Black Scoter	14.00
DE26	'05 $9 Common Merganser and Lighthouse	14.00

FL8

FLORIDA

NO.	DESCRIPTION	F-VF NH
FL1	'79 $3.25 Green-Winged Teal	175.00
FL2	'80 $3.25 Pintails	25.00
FL3	'81 $3.25 Widgeon	25.00
FL4	'82 $3.25 Ring-Necked Ducks	35.00
FL5	'83 $3.25 Buffleheads	60.00
FL6	'84 $3.25 Hooded Merganser	20.00
FL7	'85 $3.25 Wood Ducks	18.00
FL8	'86 $3 Canvasbacks	11.25
FL9	'87 $3.50 Mallards	9.75
FL10	'88 $3.50 Redheads	9.75
FL11	'89 $3.50 Blue-Winged Teal	7.25
FL12	'90 $3.50 Wood Ducks	7.25
FL13	'91 $3.50 Northern Pintails	7.25
FL14	'92 $3.50 Ruddy Duck	7.25
FL15	'93 $3.50 American Widgeon	7.00
FL16	'94 $3.50 Mottled Duck	7.00

NO.	DESCRIPTION	F-VF NH
FL17	'95 $3.50 Fulvous Whistling Duck	10.00
FL18	'96 $3.50 Goldeneyes	15.00
FL19	'97 $3.50 Hooded Merganser	10.00
FL20	'98 $3.50 Shoveler	20.00
FL21	'99 $3 Pintail	12.00
FL22	'00 $3.50 Rin-necked duck	12.00
FL23	'01 $3.50 Canvasback	7.00
FL24	'02 $3.50 Mottled Duck	7.00
FL25	'03 $3.50 Canvasback	....

GA1

GEORGIA

NO.	DESCRIPTION	F-VF NH
GA1	'85 $5.50 Wood Ducks	15.00
GA2	'86 $5.50 Mallards	10.00
GA3	'87 $5.50 Canada Geese	9.00
GA4	'88 $5.50 Ring-Necked Ducks	9.00
GA5	'89 $5.50 Duckling & Golden Retriever Puppy	20.00
GA6	'90 $5.50 Wood Ducks	9.00
GA7	'91 $5.50 Green-Winged Teal	9.00
GA8	'92 $5.50 Buffleheads	9.00
GA9	'93 $5.50 Mallards	9.00
GA10	'94 $5.50 Ring-Necked Ducks	9.00
GA11	'95 $5.50 Widgeons, Labrador Retriever	35.00
GA12	'96 $5.50 Black Ducks	35.00
GA13	'97 $5.50 Lesser Scaup	35.00
GA14	'98 $5.50 Black Lab with Ringnecks	35.00
GA15	'99 $5.50 Pintails	35.00

HAWAII

NO.	DESCRIPTION	F-VF NH
HI1	'96 $5 Nene Geese	9.25
HI2	'97 $5 Hawaiian Duck	9.25
HI3	'98 $5 Wild Turkey	9.25
HI4	'99 $5 Ring-necked Pheasant	15.00
HI5	'00 $5 Erckesls Francolin	15.00
HI6	'01 $5 Japanese Green Pheasant	15.00
HI7	'02 $10 Chukar Partridge	18.00
HI8	'03 $10 Nene Geese	18.00
HI9	'04 $10 Nene Geese	18.00
HI10	'05 $10 California Quail	18.00

ID1

IDAHO

NO.	DESCRIPTION	F-VF NH
ID1	'87 $5.50 Cinnamon Teal	20.00
ID2	'88 $5.50 Green-Winged Teal	13.50
ID3	'89 $6 Blue-Winged Teal	11.50
ID4	'90 $6 Trumpeter Swans	20.00
ID6	'91 $6 Widgeons	10.00
ID7	'92 $6 Canada Geese	10.00
ID8	'93 $6 Common Goldeneye	10.00
ID9	'94 $6 Harlequin Ducks	10.00
ID10	'95 $6 Wood Ducks	20.00
ID11	'96 $6 Mallard	20.00
ID12	'97 $6.50 Shovelers	20.00
ID13	'98 $6.50 Canada Geese	10.00

IL11

ILLINOIS

NO.	DESCRIPTION	F-VF NH
IL1	'75 $5 Mallard	700.00
IL2	'76 $5 Wood Ducks	300.00
IL3	'77 $5 Canada Goose	200.00
IL4	'78 $5 Canvasbacks	150.00
IL5	'79 $5 Pintail	110.00
IL6	'80 $5 Green-Winged Teal	110.00
IL7	'81 $5 Widgeons	110.00
IL8	'82 $5 Black Ducks	80.00
IL9	'83 $5 Lesser Scaup	70.00
IL10	'84 $5 Blue-Winged Teal	70.00
IL11	'85 $5 Redheads	21.00
IL12	'86 $5 Gadwalls	15.50
IL13	'87 $5 Buffleheads	12.50
IL14	'88 $5 Common Goldeneyes	12.50
IL15	'89 $5 Ring-Necked Ducks	10.50
IL16	'90 $10 Lesser Snow Geese	16.00
IL17	'91 $10 Labrador Retriever & Canada Goose	15.50
IL18	'92 $10 Retriever & Mallards	30.00
IL19	'93 $10 Pintail Decoys & Puppy	30.00
IL20	'94 $10 Canvasbacks & Retrievers	30.00
IL21	'95 $10 Retriever, Green-Winged Teal, Decoys	30.00
IL22	'96 $10 Wood Ducks	15.00
IL23	'97 $10 Canvasbacks	15.00
IL24	'98 $10 Canada Geese	15.00
IL25	'99 $10 Canada Geese, black labrador retriever	15.00
IL26	'00 $10 Mallards, golden retriever	25.00
IL27	'01 $10 Canvasback, yellow labrador	25.00
IL28	'02 $10 Canvasbacks, Chesapeake Retriever	25.00
IL29	'03 $10 Chocolate Lab, Green-winged Teal	15.00
IL30	'04 $10 Wood Ducks	15.00
IL31	'05 $10 Green-winged Teal	15.00

IN10

INDIANA

NO.	DESCRIPTION	F-VF NH
IN1	'76 $5 Green-Winged Teal	9.50
IN2	'77 $5 Pintail	9.50
IN3	'78 $5 Canada Geese	9.50
IN4	'79 $5 Canvasbacks	9.50
IN5	'80 $5 Mallard Ducklings	9.50
IN6	'81 $5 Hooded Mergansers	9.50
IN7	'82 $5 Blue-Winged Teal	9.50
IN8	'83 $5 Snow Geese	9.50
IN9	'84 $5 Redheads	9.50
IN10	'85 $5 Pintail	9.50
IN11	'86 $5 Wood Duck	9.50
IN12	'87 $5 Canvasbacks	9.50
IN13	'88 $6.75 Redheads	11.25
IN14	'89 $6.75 Canada Goose	11.25
IN15	'90 $6.75 Blue-Winged Teal	11.25
IN16	'91 $6.75 Mallards	11.25
IN17	'92 $6.75 Green-Winged Teal	11.25
IN18	'93 $6.75 Wood Ducks	11.25
IN19	'94 $6.75 Pintail	11.25
IN20	'95 $6.75 Goldeneyes	11.25
IN21	'96 $6.75 Black Ducks	11.25
IN22	'97 $6.75 Canada Geese	11.25
IN23	'98 $6.75 Widgeon	11.25
IN24	'99 $6.75 Bluebills	11.25
IN25	'00 $6.75 Ring-necked Duck	11.25
IN26	'01 $6.75 Green-winged Teal	11.25
IN27	'02 $6.75 Green-winged Teal	11.25
IN28	'03 $6.75 Shoveler	11.25
IN29	'04 $6.75 Hooded Mergansers	11.25
IN30	'05 $6.75 Buffleheads	11.25

IA14

IOWA

NO.	DESCRIPTION	F-VF NH
IA1	'72 $1 Mallards	200.00
IA2	'73 $1 Pintails	47.50
IA3	'74 $1 Gadwalls	100.00
IA4	'75 $1 Canada Geese	130.00
IA5	'76 $1 Canvasbacks	26.00
IA6	'77 $1 Lesser Scaup	26.00
IA7	'78 $1 Wood Ducks	55.00
IA8	'79 $5 Buffleheads	400.00
IA9	'80 $5 Redheads	40.00
IA10	'81 $5 Green-Winged Teal	35.00
IA11	'82 $5 Snow Geese	19.00
IA12	'83 $5 Widgeons	20.00
IA13	'84 $5 Wood Ducks	42.00
IA14	'85 $5 Mallard & Mallard Decoy	25.00
IA15	'86 $5 Blue-Winged Teal	16.50
IA16	'87 $5 Canada Goose	14.50
IA17	'88 $5 Pintails	12.50
IA18	'89 $5 Blue-Winged Teal	12.50
IA19	'90 $5 Canvasbacks	8.50
IA20	'91 $5 Mallards	8.50
IA21	'92 $5 Labrador Retriever & Ducks	10.00
IA22	'93 $5 Mallards	9.25
IA23	'94 $5 Green-Winged Teal	9.25
IA24	'95 $5 Canada Geese	9.25
IA25	'96 $5 Canvasbacks	9.25
IA 26	'97 $5 Canada Geese	9.25
IA27	'98 $5 Pintails	9.25
IA28	'99 $5 Trumpeter Swan	9.25
IA29	'00 $5.50 Hooded Merganser	9.25
IA30	'01 $6 Snow Geese	10.25
IA31	'02 $8.50 Northern Shoveler	13.00
IA32	'03 $8.50 Ruddy Duck	13.00
IA33	'04 $8.50 Wood Ducks	13.00
IA34	'05 $8.50 Green-winged Teals	13.00

KS1

KANSAS

NO.	DESCRIPTION	F-VF NH
KS1	'87 $3 Green-Winged Teal	9.00
KS2	'88 $3 Canada Geese	7.00
KS3	'89 $3 Mallards	6.50
KS4	'90 $3 Wood Ducks	6.50
KS5	'91 $3 Pintail	6.50
KS6	'92 $3 Canvasbacks	6.50
KS7	'93 $3 Mallards	6.50
KS8	'94 $3 Blue-Winged Teal	6.50
KS9	'95 $3 Barrow's Goldeneye	6.50
KS10	'96 $3 Widgeon	6.50
KS11	'97 $3 Mallard	6.50
KS12	'98 $3 Mallard	6.50
KS13	'99 $3 Mallard (red)	6.50
KS14	'00 $3 Mallard (purple)	6.50
KS15	'01 $3 Mallard (orange)	6.50
KS16	'02 $5 Pintail (blue)	9.00
KS17	'03 $5 Green	9.00
KS18	'04 $5 Red	9.00

KENTUCKY

NO.	DESCRIPTION	F-VF NH
KY1	'85 $5.25 Mallards	15.00
KY2	'86 $5.25 Wood Ducks	10.00
KY3	'87 $5.25 Black Ducks	10.00
KY4	'88 $5.25 Canada Geese	10.00
KY5	'89 $5.25 Retriever & Canvasbacks	10.00
KY6	'90 $5.25 Widgeons	10.00
KY7	'91 $5.25 Pintails	10.00
KY8	'92 $5.25 Green-Winged Teal	12.50
KY9	'93 $5.25 Canvasbacks & Decoy	25.00
KY10	'94 $5.25 Canada Goose	9.75
KY11	'95 $7.50 Retriever, Decoy, Ringnecks	25.00
KY12	'96 $7.50 Blue-Winged Teal	12.00
KY13	'97 $7.50 Shovelers	12.00
KY14	'98 $7.50 Gadwalls	12.00
KY15	'99 $7.50 Common Goldeneyes	12.00
KY16	'00 $7.50 Hooded Merganser	12.00
KY17	'01 $7.50 Mallard	12.00
KY18	'02 $7.50 Pintails	12.00
KY19	'03 $7.50 Snow Goose	12.00
KY20	'04 $7.50 Black Ducks	12.00
KY21	'05 $7.50 Canada Geese	12.00

LA1

LOUISIANA

NO.	DESCRIPTION	F-VF NH
LA1	'89 $5 Blue-Winged Teal	12.50
LA2	'89 $7.50 Blue-Winged Teal	10.00
LA3	'90 $5 Green-Winged Teal	9.25
LA4	'90 $7.50 Green-Winged Teal	13.50
LA5	'91 $5 Wood Ducks	9.75
LA6	'91 $7.50 Wood Ducks	13.50
LA7	'92 $5 Pintails	8.75
LA8	'92 $7.50 Pintails	12.00
LA9	'93 $5 American Widgeon	8.75
LA10	'93 $7.50 American Widgeon	12.00
LA11	'94 $5 Mottled Duck	8.75
LA12	'94 $7.50 Mottled Duck	12.00
LA13	'95 $5 Speckle Bellied Goose	8.75
LA14	'95 $7.50 Speckle Bellied Goose	12.00
LA15	'96 $5 Gadwall	8.75
LA16	'96 $7.50 Gadwell	12.00
LA17	'97 $5.00 Ring Necked Duck	8.75
LA18	'97 $13.50 Ring Necked Duck	18.00
LA19	'98 $5.50 Mallards	8.75
LA20	'98 $13.50 Mallards	18.00
LA21	'99 $5.50 Snow Geese	8.75
LA22	'99 $13.50 Snow Geese	18.00
LA23	'00 $5.50 Lesser Scaup	8.75
LA24	'00 $13.50 Lesser Scaup	18.00
LA25	'01 $5.50 Northern Shoveler	8.75
LA26	'01 $13.50 Northern Shoveler	18.00
LA27	'02 $5.50 Canvasbacks	8.75
LA28	'02 $25 Canvasbacks	32.50
LA29	'03 $5.50 Redhead	8.75
LA30	'03 $25.00 Redhead	32.50
LA31	'04 $5.50 Hooded Merganser	8.75
LA32	'04 $25 Hooded Merganser	32.50
LA33	'05 $5.50 Pintails and Labrador Retriever	8.75
LA34	'05 $25 Pintails and Labrador Retriever	32.50

ME2

MAINE

NO.	DESCRIPTION	F-VF NH
ME1	'84 $2.50 Black Ducks	25.00
ME2	'85 $2.50 Common Eiders	55.00
ME3	'86 $2.50 Wood Ducks	10.00
ME4	'87 $2.50 Buffleheads	8.75
ME5	'88 $2.50 Green-Winged Teal	8.75
ME6	'89 $2.50 Common Goldeneyes	6.50
ME7	'90 $2.50 Canada Geese	6.50
ME8	'91 $2.50 Ring-Necked Duck	6.50
ME9	'92 $2.50 Old Squaw	6.50
ME10	'93 $2.50 Hooded Merganser	6.50
ME11	'94 $2.50 Mallards	6.50
ME12	'95 $2.50 White-Winged Scoters	6.50
ME13	'96 $2.50 Blue-Winged Teal	6.50
ME14	'97 $2.50 Greater Scaup	6.50
ME15	'98 $2.50 Surf Scoters	6.50
ME16	'99 $2.50 Black Duck	6.50
ME17	'00 $2.50 Common Eider	6.50
ME18	'01 $2.50 Wood Duck	6.50
ME19	'02 $2.50 Bufflehead	6.50
ME20	'03 $5.50 Green-winged Teal	11.00
ME21	'04 $5.50 Barrows Goldeneyes	11.00
ME22	'05 $8.50 Canada Goose	16.00

MD1

MARYLAND

NO.	DESCRIPTION	F-VF NH
MD1	'74 $1.10 Mallards	14.00
MD2	'75 $1.10 Canada Geese	12.50
MD3	'76 $1.10 Canvasbacks	12.50
MD4	'77 $1.10 Greater Scaup	12.50
MD5	'78 $1.10 Redheads	12.50
MD6	'79 $1.10 Wood Ducks	12.50
MD7	'80 $1.10 Pintail Decoy	12.50
MD8	'81 $3 Widgeon	7.50
MD9	'82 $3 Canvasback	10.50
MD10	'83 $3 Wood Duck	14.50
MD11	'84 $6 Black Ducks	12.50
MD12	'85 $6 Canada Geese	11.25
MD13	'86 $6 Hooded Mergansers	11.25
MD14	'87 $6 Redheads	11.25
MD15	'88 $6 Ruddy Ducks	11.25
MD16	'89 $6 Blue-Winged Teal	10.25
MD17	'90 $6 Lesser Scaup	10.25
MD18	'91 $6 Shovelers	10.25
MD19	'92 $6 Bufflehead	10.25
MD20	'93 $6 Canvasbacks	10.25
MD21	'94 $6 Redheads	10.25
MD22	'95 $6 Mallards	10.25
MD23	'96 $6 Canada Geese	10.25
MD24	'97 $6 Canvasbacks	10.25
MD25	'98 $6 Pintails	10.25
MD26	'99 $5 Wood Ducks	10.25
MD27	'00 $6 Oldsquaws	10.25
MD28	'01 $6 American Widgeon	10.25
MD29	'02 $9 Black Scoters	13.00
MD30	'03 $9 Lesser Scaup	13.00
MD31	'04 $9 Pintails	13.00
MD32	'05 $9 Ruddy Duck	13.00

MA12

MASSACHUSETTS

NO.	DESCRIPTION	F-VF NH
MA1	'74 $1.25 Wood Duck Decoy	16.50
MA2	'75 $1.25 Pintail Decoy	12.75
MA3	'76 $1.25 Canada Goose Decoy	12.75
MA4	'77 $1.25 Goldeneye Decoy	12.75
MA5	'78 $1.25 Black Duck Decoy	12.75
MA6	'79 $1.25 Ruddy Turnstone Duck Decoy	20.00
MA7	'80 $1.25 Old Squaw Decoy	12.75
MA8	'81 $1.25 Red-Breasted Merganser Decoy	18.00
MA9	'82 $1.25 Greater Yellowlegs Decoy	18.00
MA10	'83 $1.25 Redhead Decoy	18.00
MA11	'84 $1.25 White-Winged Scoter Decoy	18.00
MA12	'85 $1.25 Ruddy Duck Decoy	18.00
MA13	'86 $1.25 Preening Bluebill Decoy	18.00
MA14	'87 $1.25 American Widgeon Decoy	18.00
MA15	'88 $1.25 Mallard Decoy	18.00
MA16	'89 $1.25 Brant Decoy	9.00
MA17	'90 $1.25 Whistler Hen Decoy	9.00
MA18	'91 $5 Canvasback Decoy	9.00
MA19	'92 $5 Black-Bellied Plover Decoy	9.00
MA20	'93 $5 Red-Breasted Merganser Decoy	9.00
MA21	'94 $5 White-Winged Scoter Decoy	9.00
MA22	'95 $5 Female Hooded Merganser Decoy	9.00
MA23	'96 $5 Eider Decoy	9.00
MA24	'97 $5 Curlew Shorebird	10.25
MA25	'98 $5 Canada Goose	10.25
MA26	'99 $5 Oldsquaw Decoy	10.25
MA27	'00 $5 Merganser Hen decoy	10.25
MA28	'01 $5 Black Duck decoy	10.25
MA29	'02 $5 Bufflehead decoy	10.25
MA30	'03 $5 Green-winged Teal decoy	10.25
MA31	'04 $5 Wood Duck Decoy	10.25
MA32	'05 $5 Oldsquaw Drake Decoy	10.25

MI10

MICHIGAN

NO.	DESCRIPTION	F-VF NH
MI1	'76 $2.10 Wood Duck	5.00
MI2	'77 $2.10 Canvasbacks	325.00
MI3	'78 $2.10 Mallards	30.00
MI4	'79 $2.10 Canada Geese	70.00
MI5	'80 $3.75 Lesser Scaup	24.50
MI6	'81 $3.75 Buffleheads	29.00
MI7	'82 $3.75 Redheads	29.00
MI8	'83 $3.75 Wood Ducks	29.00
MI9	'84 $3.75 Pintails	29.00
MI10	'85 $3.75 Ring-Necked Ducks	29.00
MI11	'86 $3.75 Common Goldeneyes	21.50
MI12	'87 $3.85 Green-Winged Teal	11.50
MI13	'88 $3.85 Canada Geese	11.50
MI14	'89 $3.85 Widgeons	8.25
MI15	'90 $3.85 Wood Ducks	8.25
MI16	'91 $3.85 Blue-Winged Teal	7.50
MI17	'92 $3.85 Red-Breasted Merganser	7.50
MI18	'93 $3.85 Hooded Merganser	7.50
MI19	'94 $3.85 Black Duck	7.50
MI20	'95 $4.35 Blue Winged Teal	8.25
MI21	'96 $4.35 Canada Geese	8.25
MI22	'97 $5 Canvasbacks	20.00
MI23	'98 $5 Pintail	8.25
MI24	'99 $5 Shoveler	8.25
MI25	'00 $5 Mallards	25.00
MI26	'01 $5 Ruddy Duck	8.25
MI27	'02 $5 Wigeons	8.25
MI28	'03 $5 Redhead	8.25
MI29	'04 $5 Wood Duck	8.25
MI30	'05 $5 Blue-winged Teals	8.25

MN2

MINNESOTA

NO.	DESCRIPTION	F-VF NH
MN1	'77 $3 Mallards	20.00
MN2	'78 $3 Lesser Scaup	15.00
MN3	'79 $3 Pintails	15.00
MN4	'80 $3 Canvasbacks	15.00
MN5	'81 $3 Canada Geese	15.00
MN6	'82 $3 Redheads	15.00
MN7	'83 $3 Blue Geese & Snow Goose	15.00
MN8	'84 $3 Wood Ducks	15.00
MN9	'85 $3 White-Fronted Geese	11.00
MN10	'86 $5 Lesser Scaup	11.00
MN11	'87 $5 Common Goldeneyes	11.50
MN12	'88 $5 Buffleheads	11.50
MN13	'89 $5 Widgeons	11.50
MN14	'90 $5 Hooded Mergansers	30.00
MN15	'91 $5 Ross's Geese	9.25
MN16	'92 $5 Barrow's Goldeneyes	9.25
MN17	'93 $5 Blue-Winged Teal	9.25
MN18	'94 $5 Ringneck Duck	9.25
MN19	'95 $5 Gadwall	9.25
MN20	'96 $5 Greater Scaup	9.25
MN21	'97 $5 Shoveler with Decoy	9.25
MN22	'98 $5 Harlequin Ducks	9.25
MN23	'99 $5 Green-winged Teal	9.25
MN24	'00 $5 Red-beasted Merganser	9.25
MN25	'01 $5 Black Duck	9.25
MN26	'02 $5 Ruddy Duck	9.25
MN27	'03 $5 Long Tailed Duck	9.25
MN28	'04 $7.50 Common Merganser	11.75
MN29	'05 $7.50 White-winged Scoters and Lighthouse	11.75

MS10

MISSISSIPPI

NO.	DESCRIPTION	F-VF NH
MS1	'76 $2 Wood Duck	24.50
MS2	'77 $2 Mallards	9.25
MS3	'78 $2 Green-Winged Teal	9.25
MS4	'79 $2 Canvasbacks	9.25
MS5	'80 $2 Pintails	9.25
MS6	'81 $2 Redheads	9.25
MS7	'82 $2 Canada Geese	15.00
MS8	'83 $2 Lesser Scaup	9.25
MS9	'84 $2 Black Ducks	9.25
MS10	'85 $2 Mallards	20.00
MS11	'86 $2 Widgeons	9.25
MS12	'87 $2 Ring-Necked Ducks	9.25
MS13	'88 $2 Snow Geese	9.25
MS14	'89 $2 Wood Ducks	7.00
MS15	'90 $2 Snow Geese	14.50
MS16	'91 $2 Labrador Retriever & Canvasbacks	6.00
MS17	'92 $2 Green-Winged Teal	5.25
MS18	'93 $2 Mallards	8.25
MS19	'94 $2 Canvasbacks	15.00
MS20	'95 $5 Blue-Winged Teal	15.00
MS21	'96 $5 Hooded Merganser	15.00
MS22	'97 $5Wood Duck	15.00
MS23	'98 $5 Pintails	9.25
MS24	'99 $5 Ring-necked Duck	9.25
MS25	'00 $5 Mallards	9.25
MS26	'01 $10 Gadwall	14.50
MS27	'02 $10 Wood Duck	14.50
MS28	'03 $10 Pintail	14.50
MS29	'04 $10 Wood Ducks	14.50
MS30	'05 $10 Blue-winged Teal	14.50

MO9

MISSOURI

NO.	DESCRIPTION	F-VF NH
MO1	'79 $3.40 Canada Geese	710.00
MO2	'80 $3.40 Wood Ducks	140.00
MO3	'81 $3 Lesser Scaup	72.50
MO4	'82 $3 Buffleheads	62.50
MO5	'83 $3 Blue-Winged Teal	52.50
MO6	'84 $3 Mallards	42.50
MO7	'85 $3 American Widgeons	25.00
MO8	'86 $3 Hooded Mergansers	16.00
MO9	'87 $3 Pintails	12.50
MO10	'88 $3 Canvasback	11.25
MO11	'89 $3 Ring-Necked Ducks	9.25
MO12	'90 $5 Redheads	8.25
MO13	'91 $5 Snow Geese	8.25
MO14	'92 $5 Gadwalls	8.25
MO15	'93 $5 Green-Winged Teal	8.25
MO16	'94 $5 White-Fronted Goose	8.25
MO17	'95 $5 Goldeneyes	12.00
MO18	'96 $5 Black Duck	12.00

MT34

MONTANA

NO.	DESCRIPTION	F-VF NH
MT34	'86 $5 Canada Geese	17.50
MT35	'87 $5 Redheads	18.00
MT36	'88 $5 Mallards	14.50
MT37	'89 $5 Black Labrador Retriever & Pintail	10.00
MT38	'90 $5 Blue-Winged & CinnamonTeal	9.00

NO.	DESCRIPTION	F-VF NH
MT39	'91 $5 Snow Geese	8.50
MT40	'92 $5 Wood Ducks	8.50
MT41	'93 $5 Harlequin Ducks	9.00
MT42	'94 $5 Widgeons	9.00
MT43	'95 $5 Tundra Swans	9.00
MT44	'96 $5 Canvasbacks	9.00
MT45	'97 $5 Golden Retriever	11.00
MT46	'98 $5 Gadwalls	9.00
MT47	'99 $5 Barrow's Goldeneye	9.00
MT48	'00 $5 Mallard decoy, Chesapeake retriever	9.00
MT49	'01 $5 Canada Geese, Steamboat	9.00
MT50	'02 ($5) Sandhill crane	9.00
MT51	'03 $5 Mallards	9.00

NE1

NEBRASKA

NO.	DESCRIPTION	F-VF NH
NE1	'91 $6 Canada Geese	12.00
NE2	'92 $6 Pintails	12.00
NE3	'93 $6 Canvasbacks	12.00
NE4	'94 $6 Mallards	12.00
NE5	'95 $6 Wood Ducks	12.00

NV7

NEVADA

NO.	DESCRIPTION	F-VF NH
NV1	'79 $2 Canvasbacks & Decoy	55.00
NV2	'80 $2 Cinnamon Teal	10.00
NV3	'81 $2 Whistling Swans	10.00
NV4	'82 $2 Shovelers	10.00
NV5	'83 $2 Gadwalls	12.50
NV6	'84 $2 Pintails	12.50
NV7	'85 $2 Canada Geese	17.50
NV8	'86 $2 Redheads	16.00
NV9	'87 $2 Buffleheads	20.00
NV10	'88 $2 Canvasbacks	12.50
NV11	'89 $2 Ross's Geese	8.25
NV12	'90 $5 Green-Winged Teal	9.25
NV13	'91 $5 White-Faced Ibis	20.00
NV14	'92 $5 American Widgeon	9.00
NV15	'93 $5 Common Goldeneye	9.00
NV16	'94 $5 Mallards	9.00
NV17	'95 $5 Wood Duck	9.00
NV18	'96 $5 Ring Necked Duck	9.00
NV19	'97 $5 Ruddy Duck	9.00
NV20	'98 $5 Hooded Merganser	9.00
NV21	'99 $5 Canvasback Decoy	9.00
NV22	'00 $5 Canvasbacks	9.00
NV23	'01 $5 Lesser Scaup	9.00
NV24	'02 $5 Cinnamon teal	9.00
NV25	'03 $5 Green-winged Teal	9.00
NV26	'04 $10 Redhead	14.00
NV27	'05 $10 Gadwalls	14.00

NH2

NEW HAMPSHIRE

NO.	DESCRIPTION	F-VF NH
NH1	'83 $4 Wood Ducks	150.00
NH2	'84 $4 Mallards	130.00
NH3	'85 $4 Blue-Winged Teal	110.00
NH4	'86 $4 Hooded Mergansers	25.00
NH5	'87 $4 Canada Geese	17.50
NH6	'88 $4 Buffleheads	10.00
NH7	'89 $4 Black Ducks	8.50
NH8	'90 $4 Green-Winged Teal	8.25
NH9	'91 $4 Golden Retriever & Mallards	15.00
NH10	'92 $4 Ring-Necked Ducks	8.25
NH11	'93 $4 Hooded Mergansers	8.25
NH12	'94 $4 Common Goldeneyes	8.25
NH13	'95 $4 Northern Pintails	8.25
NH14	'96 $4 Surf Scoters	8.25
NH15	'97 $4 Old Squaws	8.25
NH16	'98 $4 Canada Goose	8.25
NH17	'99 $4 Mallards	8.25
NH18	'00 $4 Black Ducks	8.25
NH19	'01 $4 Blue-winged Teal	8.25
NH20	'02 $4 Pintails	8.25
NH21	'03 $4 Wood Ducks	8.25
NH22	'04 $4 Wood Ducks	8.25
NH23	'05 $4 Oldsquaw and Lighthouse	8.25

NJ1

NEW JERSEY

NO.	DESCRIPTION	F-VF NH
NJ1	'84 $2.50 Canvasbacks	50.00
NJ2	'84 $5 Canvasbacks	60.00
NJ3	'85 $2.50 Mallards	18.00
NJ4	'85 $5 Mallards	20.00
NJ5	'86 $2.50 Pintails	12.50
NJ6	'86 $5 Pintails	16.00
NJ7	'87 $2.50 Canada Geese	12.50
NJ8	'87 $5 Canada Geese	12.50
NJ9	'88 $2.50 Green-Winged Teal	9.00
NJ10	'88 $5 Green-Winged Teal	10.00
NJ11	'89 $2.50 Snow Geese	12.00
NJ12	'89 $5 Snow Geese	10.50
NJ13	'90 $2.50 Wood Ducks	12.00
NJ14	'90 $5 Wood Ducks	10.00
NJ17	'91 $2.50 Atlantic Brant	15.00
NJ18	'91 $5 Atlantic Brant	10.00
NJ19	'92 $2.50 Bluebills	12.00
NJ20	'92 $5 Bluebills	9.00
NJ21	'93 $2.50 Buffleheads	10.00
NJ22	'93 $5 Buffleheads	9.00
NJ23	'94 $2.50 Black Ducks	10.00
NJ24	'94 $5 Black Ducks	9.00
NJ25	'95 $2.50 Widgeon, Lighthouse	6.50
NJ26	'95 $5 Widgeon, Lighthouse	9.00
NJ27	'96 $2.50 Goldeneyes	8.50
NJ28	'96 $5 Goldeneyes	16.00
NJ29	'97 $5 Oldsquaws	9.00
NJ30	'97 $10 Oldsquaws	16.00
NJ31	'98 $5 Mallards	9.00
NJ32	'98 $10.00 Mallards	16.00
NJ33	'99 $5 Redheads	9.00
NJ34	'99 $10 Redheads	16.00
NJ35	'00 $5 Canvasbacks	9.00
NJ36	'00 $10 Canvasbacks	16.00
NJ37	'01 $5 Tundra Swans	9.00
NJ38	'01 $10 Tundra Swans	16.00
NJ39	'02 $5 Wood Ducks	9.00
NJ40	'02 $10 Wood Ducks	16.00
NJ41	'03 $5 Pintails & Black Lab	9.00
NJ42	'03 $10 Pintails & Black Lab	16.00
NJ43	'04 $5 Merganser/Puppy	9.00
NJ44	'04 $10 Merganser/Puppy	16.00
NJ45	'05 $5 Canvasback Decoys and Retriever	9.00

NM1

NEW MEXICO

NO.	DESCRIPTION	F-VF NH
NM1	'91 $7.50 Pintails	20.00
NM2	'92 $7.50 American Widgeon	20.00
NM3	'93 $7.50 Mallard	20.00
NM4	'94 $7.50 Green-Winged Teal	20.00

NY3

NEW YORK

NO.	DESCRIPTION	F-VF NH
NY1	'85 $5.50 Canada Geese	16.00
NY2	'86 $5.50 Mallards	12.00
NY3	'87 $5.50 Wood Ducks	10.00
NY4	'88 $5.50 Pintails	9.50
NY5	'89 $5.50 Greater Scaup	9.50
NY6	'90 $5.50 Canvasbacks	9.00
NY7	'91 $5.50 Redheads	9.00
NY8	'92 $5.50 Wood Ducks	9.00
NY9	'93 $5.50 Blue-Winged Teal	9.00
NY10	'94 $5.50 Canada Geese	9.00
NY11	'95 $5.50 Common Goldeneye	9.00
NY12	'96 $5.50 Common Loon	9.00
NY13	'97 $5.50 Hooded Merganser	9.00
NY14	'98 $5.50 Osprey	9.00
NY15	'99 $5.50 Buffleheads	12.00
NY16	'00 $5.50 Wood Ducks	9.00
NY17	'01 $5.50 Pintails	9.00
NY18	'02 $5.50 Canvasbacks	9.00

NC1

NORTH CAROLINA

NO.	DESCRIPTION	F-VF NH
NC1	'83 $5.50 Mallards	85.00
NC2	'84 $5.50 Wood Ducks	55.00
NC3	'85 $5.50 Canvasbacks	35.00
NC4	'86 $5.50 Canada Geese	30.00
NC5	'87 $5.50 Pintails	16.00
NC6	'88 $5 Green-Winged Teal	10.50
NC7	'89 $5 Snow Geese	20.00
NC8	'90 $5 Redheads	20.00
NC9	'91 $5 Blue-Winged Teal	20.00
NC10	'92 $5 American Widgeon	20.00
NC11	'93 $5 Tundra Swans	20.00
NC12	'94 $5 Buffleheads	20.00
NC13	'95 $5 Brant, Lighthouse	20.00
NC14	'96 $5 Pintails	20.00
NC15	'97 $5 Wood Ducks	20.00
NC16	'97 $5 Wood Ducks, self-adhesive	15.00
NC17	'98 $5 Canada Geese	15.00
NC18	'98 $5 Canada Geese, self-adhesive	15.00
NC19	'99 $5 Green-winged Teal	15.00
NC20	'99 $5 Green-winged Teal, self-adhesive	15.00
NC21	'00 $10 Green-winged Teal	15.00
NC22	'00 $10 Green-winged Teal, self-adhesive	15.00
NC23	'01 $10 Black Duck, lighthouse	15.00
NC24	'01 $10 Black Duck, lighthouse, self-adhesive	15.00
NC25	'02 $10 Pintails, Hunters, Dog	16.00
NC26	'02 $10 Pintails, Hunters, Dog, self-adhesive	16.00
NC27	'03 $10 Ringneck & Brittney Spaniel	15.00
NC28	'03 $10 Ringneck & Brittney Spaniel, self-adhesive	17.00
NC29	'04 $10 Mallard	15.00
NC30	'04 $10 Mallard, self-adhesive	17.00
NC31	'04 $10 Green-winged Teals	17.00
NC32	'04 $10 Green-winged Teals, self-adhesive	17.00

NORTH DAKOTA

NO.	DESCRIPTION	F-VF NH
ND32	'82 $9 Canada Geese	150.00
ND35	'83 $9 Mallards	80.00
ND38	'84 $9 Canvasbacks	37.50
ND41	'85 $9 Bluebills	25.00
ND44	'86 $9 Pintails	20.00
ND47	'87 $9 Snow Geese	22.00
ND50	'88 $9 White-Winged Scoters	15.00
ND53	'89 $6 Redheads	12.50
ND56	'90 $6 Labrador Retriever & Mallard	12.50
ND59	'91 $6 Green-Winged Teal	12.00
ND62	'92 $6 Blue-Winged Teal	9.50
ND65	'93 $6 Wood Ducks	9.50
ND67	'94 $6 Canada Geese	9.50
ND69	'95 $6 Widgeon	9.50
ND71	'96 $6 Mallards	9.50
ND73	'97 $6 White Fronted Geese	9.50
ND75	'98 $6 Blue Winged Teal	9.50
ND77	'99 $6 Gadwalls	9.50
ND79	'00 $6 Pintails	9.50
ND81	'01 $6 Canada Geese	9.50
ND83	'02 $6 Text, black on green	9.50
ND84	'03 $6 Text, black on green	9.50
ND85	'04 $6 Text, black on green	9.50
ND86	'05 $6 Text, black on green	9.50

OH4

OHIO

NO.	DESCRIPTION	F-VF NH
OH1	'82 $5.75 Wood Ducks	85.00
OH2	'83 $5.75 Mallards	85.00
OH3	'84 $5.75 Green-Winged Teal	75.00
OH4	'85 $5.75 Redheads	50.00
OH5	'86 $5.75 Canvasback	32.50
OH6	'87 $6 Blue-Winged Teal	15.00
OH7	'88 $6 Common Goldeneyes	12.50
OH8	'89 $6 Canada Geese	12.50
OH9	'90 $9 Black Ducks	15.00
OH10	'91 $9 Lesser Scaup	15.00
OH11	'92 $9 Wood Duck	14.00
OH12	'93 $9 Buffleheads	14.00
OH13	'94 $11 Mallards	16.50

NO.	DESCRIPTION	F-VF NH
OH14	'95 $11 Pintails	16.50
OH15	'96 $11 Hooded Mergansers	16.50
OH16	'97 $11 Widgeons	16.50
OH17	'98 $11 Gadwall	16.50
OH18	'99 $11 Mallard	16.50
OH19	'00 $11 Bufflehards	16.50
OH20	'01 $11 Canvasback	16.50
OH21	'02 $11 Ring Neck	16.50
OH22	'03 $11 Hooded Merganser	16.50
OH23	'04 $15 Tundra Swans	21.50
OH24	'05 $15 Wood Duck	21.50

OK4

OKLAHOMA

NO.	DESCRIPTION	F-VF NH
OK1	'80 $4 Pintails	70.00
OK2	'81 $4 Canada Goose	27.50
OK3	'82 $4 Green-Winged Teal	12.00
OK4	'83 $4 Wood Ducks	12.00
OK5	'84 $4 Ring-Necked Ducks	9.50
OK6	'85 $4 Mallards	8.00
OK7	'86 $4 Snow Geese	8.00
OK8	'87 $4 Canvasbacks	8.00
OK9	'88 $4 Widgeons	8.00
OK10	'89 $4 Redheads	8.00
OK11	'90 $4 Hooded Merganser	8.00
OK12	'91 $4 Gadwalls	7.50
OK13	'92 $4 Lesser Scaup	7.50
OK14	'93 $4 White-Fronted Geese	7.50
OK15	'94 $4 Blue-Winged Teal	7.50
OK16	'95 $4 Ruddy Ducks	7.50
OK17	'96 $4 Buffleheads	7.50
OK18	'97 $4 Goldeneyes	7.50
OK19	'98 $4 Shoveler	7.50
OK20	'99 $4 Canvasbacks	7.50
OK21	'00 $4 Pintails	7.50
OK22	'01 $4 Canada Goose	7.50
OK23	'02 $4 Green-winged Teal	7.50
OK24	'03 $10 Wood Duck	14.00
OK25	'04 $10 Mallard	14.00
OK26	'05 $10 Snow Geese	14.00

OR1

OREGON

NO.	DESCRIPTION	F-VF NH
OR1	'84 $5 Canada Geese	35.00
OR2	'85 $5 Lesser Snow Goose	45.00
OR3	'86 $5 Pacific Brant	17.50
OR4	'87 $5 White-Fronted Geese	12.00
OR5	'88 $5 Great Basin Canada Geese	10.00
OR7	'89 $5 Black Labrador Retriever & Pintails	10.00
OR8	'90 $5 Mallards & Golden Retriever	12.50
OR9	'91 $5 Buffleheads & Chesapeake Bay Retriever	11.00
OR10	'92 $5 Green-Winged Teal	11.00
OR11	'93 $5 Mallards	11.00
OR12	'94 $5 Pintails	11.00
OR14	'95 $5 Wood Ducks	11.00
OR16	'96 $5 Mallard/Widgeon/Pintail	11.00
OR18	'97 $5 Canvasbacks	11.00
OR20	'98 $5 Pintail	11.00
OR22	'99 $5 Canada Geese	11.00
OR24	'00 $7.50 Canada Geese, Mallard, Widgeon	13.50
OR25	'01 $7.50 Canvasbacks	13.50
OR26	'02 $7.50 American Wigeon	13.50
OR27	'03 $7.50 Wood Duck	13.50
OR28	'04 $7.50 Ross' Goose	13.50
OR29	'05 $7.50 Hooded Merganser	13.50

PA1

PENNSYLVANIA

NO.	DESCRIPTION	F-VF NH
PA1	'83 $5.50 Wood Ducks	25.00
PA2	'84 $5.50 Canada Geese	22.50
PA3	'85 $5.50 Mallards	12.00
PA4	'86 $5.50 Blue-Winged Teal	10.00
PA5	'87 $5.50 Pintails	10.00
PA6	'88 $5.50 Wood Ducks	10.00
PA7	'89 $5.50 Hooded Mergansers	9.50
PA8	'90 $5.50 Canvasbacks	9.50
PA9	'91 $5.50 Widgeons	9.50
PA10	'92 $5.50 Canada Geese	9.50
PA11	'93 $5.50 Northern Shovelers	9.00
PA12	'94 $5.50 Pintails	9.00
PA13	'95 $5.50 Buffleheads	9.00
PA14	'96 $5.50 Black Ducks	9.00
PA15	'97 $5.50 Hooded Merganser	9.00
PA16	'98 $5.50 Wood Duck	9.00
PA17	'99 $5.50 Ring-necked Ducks	9.00
PA18	'00 $5.50 Green-Winged Teal	9.00
PA19	'01 $5.50 Pintails	9.00
PA20	'02 $5.50 Snow Geese	9.00
PA21	'03 $5.50 Canvasbacks	9.00
PA22	'04 $5.50 Hooded Mergansers	9.00
PA23	'05 $5.50 Red-breasted Mergansers	9.00

RI1

RHODE ISLAND

NO.	DESCRIPTION	F-VF NH
RI1	'89 $7.50 Canvasbacks	12.50
RI2	'90 $7.50 Canada Geese	12.00
RI3	'91 $7.50 Wood Ducks & Labrador Retriever	14.00
RI4	'92 $7.50 Blue-Winged Teal	12.50
RI5	'93 $7.50 Pintails	11.50
RI6	'94 $7.50 Wood Ducks	11.50
RI7	'95 $7.50 Hooded Mergansers	11.50
RI8	'96 $7.50 Harlequin	11.50
RI9	'97 $7.50 Black Ducks	11.50
RI10	'98 $7.50 Black Ducks	11.50
RI11	'99 $7.50 Common Eiders	11.50
RI12	'00 $7.50 Canvasbacks	11.50
RI13	'01 $7.50 Canvasbacks, Mallard, Lighthouse	11.50
RI14	'02 $7.50 White-winged Scoter	11.50
RI15	'03 $7.50 Oldsquaw	11.50
RI16	'04 $7.50 Canvasbacks	11.50
RI17	'05 $7.50 Black Ducks and Lighthouse	11.50

SC5

SOUTH CAROLINA

NO.	DESCRIPTION	F-VF NH
SC1	'81 $5.50 Wood Ducks	75.00
SC2	'82 $5.50 Mallards	110.00
SC3	'83 $5.50 Pintails	110.00
SC4	'84 $5.50 Canada Geese	70.00
SC5	'85 $5.50 Green-Winged Teal	65.00
SC6	'86 $5.50 Canvasbacks	30.00
SC7	'87 $5.50 Black Ducks	20.00
SC8	'88 $5.50 Widgeon & Spaniel	25.00
SC9	'89 $5.50 Blue-Winged Teal	15.00
SC10	'90 $5.50 Wood Ducks	10.00
SC11	'91 $5.50 Labrador Retriever, Pintails & Decoy	15.00
SC12	'92 $5.50 Buffleheads	15.00
SC13	'93 $5.50 Lesser Scaup	15.00
SC14	'94 $5.50 Canvasbacks	15.00
SC15	'95 $5.50 Shovelers, Lighthouse	15.00
SC16	'96 $5.50 Redheads, Lighthouse	15.00
SC17	'97 $5.50 Old Squaws	15.00
SC18	'98 $5.50 Ruddy Ducks	15.00
SC19	'99 $5.50 Barrow's goldeneye	15.00
SC20	'00 $5.50 Wood Ducks, boykin spaniel	15.00
SC21	'01 $5.50 Mallard, yellow labrador,decoy	15.00
SC22	'02 $5.50 Widgeon, Chocolate Labrador	9.00
SC23	'03 $5.50 Green-winged Teal	9.00
SC24	'04 $5.50 Black Labrador	9.00
SC25	'05 $5.50 Canvasbacks	9.00

SD6

SOUTH DAKOTA

NO.	DESCRIPTION	F-VF NH
SD3	'76 $1 Mallards	45.00
SD4	'77 $1 Pintails	85.00
SD5	'78 $1 Canvasbacks	30.00
SD6	'86 $2 Canada Geese	20.00
SD7	'87 $2 Blue Geese	10.00
SD8	'88 $2 White-Fronted Geese	6.00
SD9	'89 $2 Mallards	6.00
SD10	'90 $2 Blue-Winged Teal	5.50
SD11	'91 $2 Pintails	5.50
SD12	'92 $2 Canvasbacks	5.50
SD13	'93 $2 Lesser Scaup	5.50
SD14	'94 $2 Redheads	5.50
SD15	'95 $2 Wood Ducks	5.50
SD16	'96 $2 Canada Goose	5.50
SD17	'97 $2 Widgeons	5.50
SD18	'98 $2 Green Winged Teal	5.50
SD19	'99 $2 Tundra Swam	5.50
SD20	'00 $3 Buffleheads	8.00
SD21	'01 $3 Mallards	8.00
SD22	'02 $3 Canvasbacks	8.00
SD23	'03 $3 Pintail	8.00
SD24	'04 $3 Text, purple	8.00
SD25	'05 $5 Text, magenta	10.00

TN9

TENNESSEE

NO.	DESCRIPTION	F-VF NH
TN1	'79 $2.30 Mallards	175.00
TN2	'79 $5 Mallards, Non-Resident	1,200.00
TN3	'80 $2.30 Canvasbacks	65.00
TN4	'80 $5 Canvasbacks, Non-Resident	525.00
TN5	'81 $2.30 Wood Ducks	50.00
TN6	'82 $6.50 Canada Geese	65.00
TN7	'83 $6.50 Pintails	60.00
TN8	'84 $6.50 Black Ducks	70.00
TN9	'85 $6.50 Blue-Winged Teal	25.00
TN10	'86 $6.50 Mallard	15.00
TN11	'87 $6.50 Canada Geese	15.00
TN12	'88 $6.50 Canvasbacks	20.00
TN13	'89 $6.50 Green-Winged Teal	20.00
TN14	'90 $13 Redheads	20.00
TN15	'91 $13 Mergansers	19.00
TN16	'92 $14 Wood Ducks	19.00
TN17	'93 $14 Pintails & Decoy	19.00
TN18	'94 $16 Mallard	40.00
TN19	'95 $16 Ring-Necked Duck	22.50
TN20	'96 $18 Black Ducks	25.00
TN21	'99 $10 Mallard	18.00
TN22	'00 $10 Bufflehead	18.00
TN23	'01 $10 Wood Ducks	18.00
TN24	'02 $10 Green-winged Teal	18.00
TN25	'03 $10 Canada Geese	18.00
TN26	'04 $10 Wood Ducks	18.00
TN27	'05 $10 Mallards	18.00

TX5

TEXAS

NO.	DESCRIPTION	F-VF NH
TX1	'81 $5 Mallards	55.00
TX2	'82 $5 Pintails	40.00
TX3	'83 $5 Widgeons	190.00
TX4	'84 $5 Wood Ducks	35.00
TX5	'85 $5 Snow Geese	15.00
TX6	'86 $5 Green-Winged Teal	12.00
TX7	'87 $5 White-Fronted Geese	12.00
TX8	'88 $5 Pintails	12.00
TX9	'89 $5 Mallards	12.00
TX10	'90 $5 American Widgeons	12.00
TX11	'91 $7 Wood Duck	12.00
TX12	'92 $7 Canada Geese	12.00
TX13	'93 $7 Blue-Winged Teal	12.00
TX14	'94 $7 Shovelers	12.00
TX15	'95 $7 Buffleheads	12.00
TX16	'96 $3 Gadwalls	85.00
TX17	'97 $3 Cinnamon Teal	85.00
TX18	'98 $3 Pintail, Labrador Retriever	85.00
TX19	'99 $3 Canvasbacks	35.00
TX20	'00 $3 Hooded Merganser	35.00
TX21	'01 $3 Snow Goose	20.00
TX22	'02 $3 Redheads	20.00
TX23	'03 $3 Mottled Duck	20.00
TX24	'04 $3 American Goldeneye	20.00
TX25	'05 $7 Mallards	16.00

UT1

UTAH

NO.	DESCRIPTION	F-VF NH
UT1	'86 $3.30 Whistling Swans	12.00
UT2	'87 $3.30 Pintails	12.00
UT3	'88 $3.30 Mallards	8.50
UT4	'89 $3.30 Canada Geese	7.50
UT5	'90 $3.30 Canvasbacks	7.50
UT6	'91 $3.30 Tundra Swans	7.50
UT7	'92 $3.30 Pintails	7.50
UT8	'93 $3.30 Canvasbacks	7.50
UT9	'94 $3.30 Chesapeake Retriever & Ducks	100.00
UT10	'95 $3.30 Green-Winged Teal	10.00
UT11	'96 $7.50 White-Fronted Goose	14.50
UT12	'97 $7.50 Redheads, pair	50.00

VT1

VERMONT

NO.	DESCRIPTION	F-VF NH
VT1	'86 $5 Wood Ducks	14.00
VT2	'87 $5 Common Goldeneyes	10.00
VT3	'88 $5 Black Ducks	10.00
VT4	'89 $5 Canada Geese	9.50
VT5	'90 $5 Green-Winged Teal	9.50
VT6	'91 $5 Hooded Mergansers	9.50
VT7	'92 $5 Snow Geese	9.50
VT8	'93 $5 Mallards	9.50
VT9	'94 $5 Ring-Necked Duck	8.50
VT10	'95 $5 Bufflehead	8.50
VT11	'96 $5 Bluebills	8.50
VT12	'97 $5 Pintail	8.50
VT13	'98 $5 Blue-Winged Teal	8.50
VT14	'99 $5 Canvasbacks	8.50
VT15	'00 $5 Widgeons	8.50
VT16	'01 $5 Old Squaw	8.50
VT17	'02 $5 Greater Scaups	8.50
VT18	'03 $5 Mallard	8.50
VT19	'04 $5 Pintails	8.50
VT20	'05 $5 Canvasbacks	8.50

VA1

VIRGINIA

NO.	DESCRIPTION	F-VF NH
VA1	'88 $5 Mallards	15.00
VA2	'89 $5 Canada Geese	18.00
VA3	'90 $5 Wood Ducks	9.50
VA4	'91 $5 Canvasbacks	9.50
VA5	'92 $5 Buffleheads	9.50
VA6	'93 $5 Black Ducks	9.00
VA7	'94 $5 Lesser Scaup	9.00
VA8	'95 $5 Snow Geese	9.00
VA9	'96 $5 Hooded Mergansers	9.00
VA10	'97 $5 Pintail, Labrador Retriever	9.00
VA11	'98 $5 Mallards	9.00
VA12	'99 $5 Green-winged Teal	9.00
VA13	'00 $5 Mallards	9.00
VA14	'01 $5 Blue-winged Teal	9.00
VA15	'02 $5 Canvasbacks	9.00
VA16	'03 $5 Mallard	9.00
VA17	'04 $5 Goldeneyes	9.00
VA18	'05 $9.75 Wood Ducks, perforated	19.50
VA19	'05 $9.75 Wood Ducks, rouletted	19.50
VA20	'05 $9.75 Wood Ducks, self-adhesive, die cut	19.50

WA1

WASHINGTON

NO.	DESCRIPTION	F-VF NH
WA1	'86 $5 Mallards	12.50
WA2	'87 $5 Canvasbacks	16.00
WA3	'88 $5 Harlequin	9.50
WA4	'89 $5 American Widgeons	9.50
WA5	'90 $5 Pintails & Sour Duck	9.50
WA6	'91 $5 Wood Duck	9.50
WA8	'92 $6 Labrador Puppy & Canada Geese	9.50
WA9	'93 $6 Snow Geese	9.50
WA10	'94 $6 Black Brant	9.50
WA11	'95 $6 Mallards	9.50
WA12	'96 $6 Redheads	9.50
WA13	'97 $6 Canada Geese	9.50
WA14	'98 $6 Goldeneye	9.50
WA15	'99 $6 Bufflehead	9.50
WA16	'00 $6 Canada Geese, Mallard, Widgeon	14.00
WA17	'01 $6 Mallards	14.00
WA18	'02 $10 Green-winged Teal	14.00
WA19	'03 $10 Pintail	14.00
WA20	'04 $10 Canada Goose	14.00
WA21	'05 $10 Barrow's Goldeneyes	14.00

WV1

WEST VIRGINIA

NO.	DESCRIPTION	F-VF NH
WV1	'87 $5 Canada Geese	15.00
WV2	'87 $5 Canada Geese, Non-Resident	15.00
WV3	'88 $5 Wood Ducks	12.00
WV4	'88 $5 Wood Ducks, Non-Resident	20.00
WV5	'89 $5 Decoys	13.00
WV6	'89 $5 Decoys, Non-Resident	13.00
WV7	'90 $5 Labrador Retriever & Decoy	12.50
WV8	'90 $5 Labrador Retriever & Decoy, Non-Resident	12.50
WV9	'91 $5 Mallards	10.00
WV10	'91 $5 Mallards, Non-Resident	10.00
WV11	'92 $5 Canada Geese	10.00
WV12	'92 $5 Canada Geese, Non-Resident	10.00
WV13	'93 $5 Pintails	10.00
WV14	'93 $5 Pintails, Non-Resident	10.00
WV15	'94 $5 Green-Winged Teal	10.00
WV16	'94 $5 Green-Winged Teal, Non-Resident	10.00
WV17	'95 $5 Mallards	10.00
WV18	'95 $5 Mallards, Non-Resident	10.00
WV19	'96 $5 American Widgeons	10.00
WV20	'96 $5 Widgeon, Non-Resident	10.00

WI3

WISCONSIN

NO.	DESCRIPTION	F-VF NH
WI1	'78 $3.25 Wood Ducks	125.00
WI2	'79 $3.25 Buffleheads	45.00
WI3	'80 $3.25 Widgeons	15.00
WI4	'81 $3.25 Lesser Scaup	11.00
WI5	'82 $3.25 Pintails	8.00
WI6	'83 $3.25 Blue-Winged Teal	9.00
WI7	'84 $3.25 Hooded Merganser	9.00
WI8	'85 $3.25 Lesser Scaup	20.00
WI9	'86 $3.25 Canvasbacks	20.00
WI10	'87 $3.25 Canada Geese	7.00
WI11	'88 $3.25 Hooded Merganser	7.00
WI12	'89 $3.25 Common Goldeneye	7.00
WI13	'90 $3.25 Redheads	7.00
WI14	'91 $5.25 Green-Winged Teal	9.00
WI15	'92 $5.25 Tundra Swans	9.00
WI16	'93 $5.25 Wood Ducks	9.00
WI17	'94 $5.25 Pintails	9.00
WI18	'95 $5.25 Mallards	9.00
WI19	'96 $5.25 Green-Winged Teal	9.00
WI20	'97 $7 Canada Geese	9.00
WI21	'98 $7 Snow Geese	9.00
WI22	'99 $7 Greater Scaups	11.00
WI23	'00 $7 Canvasbacks	11.00
WI24	'01 $7 Common Goldeneye	15.00
WI25	'02 $7 Shovelers	11.00
WI26	'03 $7 Canvasbacks	11.00
WI27	'04 $7 Pintail	11.00
WI28	'05 $7 Wood Ducks	11.00

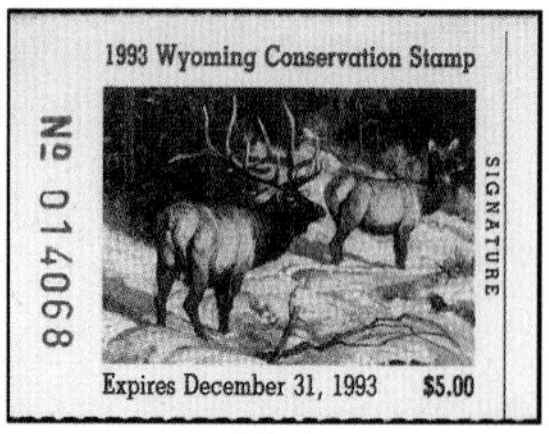

WY10

WYOMING

NO.	DESCRIPTION	F-VF NH
WY1	'84 $5 Meadowlark	60.00
WY2	'85 $5 Canada Geese	60.00
WY3	'86 $5 Antelope	90.00
WY4	'87 $5 Grouse	100.00
WY5	'88 $5 Fish	100.00
WY6	'89 $5 Deer	200.00
WY7	'90 $5 Bear	45.00
WY8	'91 $5 Rams	45.00
WY9	'92 $5 Bald Eagle	40.00
WY10	'93 $5 Elk	20.00
WY11	'94 $5 Bobcat	20.00
WY12	'95 $5 Moose	20.00
WY13	'96 $5 Turkey	20.00
WY14	'97 $5 Rocky Mountain Goats	30.00
WY15	'98 $5 Thunder Swans	30.00
WY16	'99 $5 Brown Trout	30.00
WY17	'00 $5 Buffalo	30.00
WY18	'01 $10 Whitetailed Deer	20.00
WY19	'02 $10 River Otters	20.00
WY20	'03 $10 Mountain Bluebird	20.00
WY21	'04 $10 Cougar	20.00
WY22	'05 $10 Burrowing Owls	20.00

CANAL ZONE

SCOTT NO.	DESCRIPTION	UNUSED NH F	UNUSED NH AVG	UNUSED OG F	UNUSED OG AVG	USED F	USED AVG

CANAL ZONE

PANAMA

1904
U.S. Stamp 300, 319, 304, 306-07 overprinted

SCOTT NO.	DESCRIPTION	UNUSED NH F	UNUSED NH AVG	UNUSED OG F	UNUSED OG AVG	USED F	USED AVG
4	1¢ blue green	100.00	70.00	50.00	30.00	25.00	15.00
5	2¢ carmine	90.00	60.00	40.00	25.00	25.00	15.00
6	5¢ blue	300.00	200.00	150.00	100.00	65.00	40.00
7	8¢ violet black	550.00	350.00	270.00	175.00	95.00	60.00
8	10¢ pale red brown	550.00	350.00	270.00	175.00	100.00	60.00

CANAL

ZONE

1924-25
U.S. Stamps 551-54, 557, 562, 564-66, 569-71 overprinted

Type 1 Flat Tops on Letters "A". Perf. 11

SCOTT NO.	DESCRIPTION	UNUSED NH F	UNUSED NH AVG	UNUSED OG F	UNUSED OG AVG	USED F	USED AVG
70	1/2¢ olive brown	2.50	1.70	1.40	1.00	.75	.55
71	1¢ deep green	2.25	1.35	1.50	.95	1.10	.70
71e	same, bklt pane of 6 ..	300.00	200.00	170.00	100.00	....	....
72	1-1/2¢ yellow brown ...	3.00	2.25	2.10	1.50	1.60	1.10
73	2¢ carmine	20.00	15.00	10.00	7.00	1.75	1.25
73a	same, bklt pane of 6 ..	400.00	300.00	250.00	170.00	....	....
74	5¢ dark blue	50.00	35.00	25.00	20.00	9.00	5.50
75	10¢ orange	100.00	75.00	50.00	40.00	24.00	17.00
76	12¢ brown violet	100.00	75.00	50.00	40.00	27.00	19.50
77	14¢ dark blue	75.00	55.00	40.00	30.00	20.00	14.00
78	15¢ gray	120.00	75.00	50.00	40.00	33.00	22.00
79	30¢ olive brown	100.00	60.00	45.00	30.00	25.00	16.50
80	50¢ lilac	200.00	120.00	100.00	70.00	42.00	25.00
81	$1 violet brown	500.00	380.00	300.00	200.00	100.00	70.00

CANAL

ZONE

1925-28
U.S. Stamps 554-55, 557, 564-66, 623, 567, 569-71, overprinted

Type II Pointed Tops on Letters "A"

SCOTT NO.	DESCRIPTION	UNUSED NH F	UNUSED NH AVG	UNUSED OG F	UNUSED OG AVG	USED F	USED AVG
84	2¢ carmine	80.00	50.00	40.00	30.00	10.00	6.00
84d	same, bklt pane of 6 ..	400.00	300.00	250.00	170.00	....	....
85	3¢ violet	10.00	7.00	5.00	3.00	2.75	1.75
86	5¢ dark blue	10.00	7.00	5.00	3.00	2.75	1.75
87	10¢ orange	90.00	60.00	40.00	30.00	10.00	6.00
88	12¢ brown violet	60.00	40.00	30.00	20.00	14.00	9.00
89	14¢ dark blue	60.00	40.00	30.00	20.00	18.00	11.00
90	15¢ gray	20.00	12.00	10.00	7.00	4.00	2.50
91	17¢ black	10.00	7.00	5.00	3.00	3.00	1.95
92	20¢ carmine rose	20.00	12.00	10.00	7.00	4.00	2.65
93	30¢ olive brown	15.00	10.00	7.00	5.00	4.00	2.50
94	50¢ lilac	600.00	400.00	300.00	210.00	140.00	82.50
95	$1 violet brown	300.00	200.00	180.00	110.00	50.00	31.50

1926
Type II overprint on U.S. Stamp 627

SCOTT NO.	DESCRIPTION	UNUSED NH F	UNUSED NH AVG	UNUSED OG F	UNUSED OG AVG	USED F	USED AVG
96	2¢ carmine rose	10.00	7.00	6.00	4.00	3.75	2.50

1927
Type II overprint on U.S. Stamp 583-84, 591
Rotary Press Printing, Perf. 10

SCOTT NO.	DESCRIPTION	UNUSED NH F	UNUSED NH AVG	UNUSED OG F	UNUSED OG AVG	USED F	USED AVG
97	2¢ carmine	110.00	100.00	75.00	40.00	10.50	6.00
98	3¢ violet	25.00	18.00	10.00	6.00	5.00	3.00
99	10¢ orange	50.00	35.00	30.00	15.00	6.75	4.00

SCOTT NO.	DESCRIPTION	PLATE BLOCK F/NH	PLATE BLOCK F	PLATE BLOCK AVG	UNUSED F/NH	UNUSED F	UNUSED AVG	USED F	USED AVG
100	1¢ green	25.00	20.00	16.00	2.65	1.95	1.35	1.30	.80
101	2¢ carmine	30.00	24.50	19.00	2.75	2.00	1.20	.90	.55
101a	same, bklt pane of 6	....	....	....	200.00	150.00	125.00	....	....
102	3¢ violet (1931) ...	110.00	85.00	68.00	6.50	4.50	2.25	3.50	2.25
103	5¢ dark blue	185.00	155.00	125.00	30.00	22.00	15.00	11.00	7.25
104	10¢ orange (1930)	225.00	180.00	145.00	25.00	17.00	12.00	12.00	8.00

VERY FINE QUALITY: To determine the Very Fine price, add the difference between the Fine and Average prices to the Fine quality price. For example: if the Fine price is $10.00 and the Average price is $6.00, the Very Fine price would be $14.00. From 1935 to date, add 20% to the Fine price to arrive at the Very Fine price.

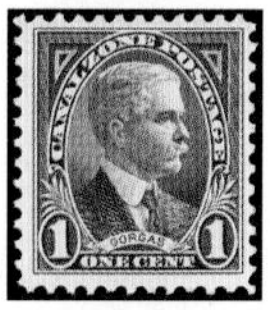

105,160

106

107

108, 161

109

110

111

112

113

114

1928-40 Builders Issue

SCOTT NO.	DESCRIPTION	PLATE BLOCK F/NH	PLATE BLOCK F	PLATE BLOCK AVG	UNUSED F/NH	UNUSED F	UNUSED AVG	USED F	USED AVG
105-14	**1¢-50¢ complete, 10 varieties ....**	....	....	....	**10.40**	**8.05**	**4.95**	**5.70**	**3.45**
105	1¢ Gorgas	3.00	2.00	1.40	.30	.25	.20	.25	.20
106	2¢ Goethals	3.00(6)	2.25	1.30	.30	.25	.20	.25	.20
106a	same, bklt pane of 6	....	....	....	18.00	13.00	8.50	....	....
107	5¢ Gaillard Cut (1929)	15.00(6)	10.00	6.50	1.50	1.20	.85	.50	.40
108	10¢ Hodges (1932)	6.00(6)	4.00	3.50	.40	.30	.20	.25	.20
109	12¢ Gaillard (1929)	14.50(6)	11.00	6.50	1.00	.80	.60	.85	.50
110	14¢ Sibert (1937)	17.00(6)	12.50	9.00	1.10	.90	.70	1.10	.70
111	15¢ Smith (1932)	10.00(6)	6.50	4.00	.65	.50	.30	.50	.30
112	20¢ Rousseau (1932)	11.00(6)	7.50	4.50	.95	.75	.45	.30	.20
113	30¢ Williamson (1940)	13.50(6)	10.00	6.00	1.00	.80	.60	.95	.55
114	50¢ Blackburn (1929)	22.00(6)	16.00	9.50	2.00	1.60	1.10	.85	.50

1933
Type II overprint on U.S. Stamps 720 & 695
Rotary Press Printing, Perf. 11 x 10-1/2

SCOTT NO.	DESCRIPTION	PLATE BLOCK F/NH	PLATE BLOCK F	PLATE BLOCK AVG	UNUSED F/NH	UNUSED F	UNUSED AVG	USED F	USED AVG
115	3¢ Washington	37.50	27.00	16.00	4.00	2.75	1.95	.35	.25
116	14¢ Indian	72.50	50.00	36.00	8.00	6.00	4.00	3.35	2.00

117, 153

1934

SCOTT NO.	DESCRIPTION	PLATE BLOCK F/NH	PLATE BLOCK F	PLATE BLOCK AVG	UNUSED F/NH	UNUSED F	UNUSED AVG	USED F	USED AVG
117	3¢ Goethals	1.50(6)	1.10	.90	.30	.25	.20	.25	.20
117a	same, bklt pane of 6	....	....	....	100.00	60.00	50.00	....	....

1939 U.S. Stamps 803, 805 overprint

SCOTT NO.	DESCRIPTION	PLATE BLOCK F/NH	PLATE BLOCK F/OG	UNUSED F/NH	UNUSED F/OG	USED F
118	1/2¢ red orange	2.75	2.25	.30	.25	.20
119	1-1/2¢ bistre brown	2.75	2.25	.30	.25	.20

FOR CONVENIENCE IN ORDERING, COMPLETE SETS ARE LISTED BEFORE SINGLE STAMP LISTINGS.

SCOTT NO.	DESCRIPTION	PLATE BLOCK F/NH	PLATE BLOCK F/OG	UNUSED F/NH	UNUSED F/OG	USED F

120
Balboa—Before

121
Balboa—After

122	*Gaillard Cut—Before*	123	*After*
124	*Bas Obispo—Before*	125	*After*
126	*Gatun Locks—Before*	127	*After*
128	*Canal Channel—Before*	129	*After*
130	*Gamboa—Before*	131	*After*
132	*Pedro Miguel Locks—Before*	133	*After*
134	*Gatun Spillway—Before*	135	*After*

1939 25th ANNIVERSARY ISSUE

SCOTT NO.	DESCRIPTION	PLATE BLOCK F/NH	PLATE BLOCK F/OG	UNUSED F/NH	UNUSED F/OG	USED F
120-35	**1¢-50¢ complete, 16 varieties ....**	....	....	**118.50**	**85.00**	**70.95**
120	1¢ yellow green	13.00(6)	9.00	.60	.40	.40
121	2¢ rose carmine	12.00(6)	9.00	.70	.50	.50
122	3¢ purple	12.00(6)	9.00	.70	.50	.25
123	5¢ dark blue	20.00(6)	16.00	1.50	1.00	1.20
124	6¢ red orange	40.00(6)	33.00	2.75	1.95	2.50
125	7¢ black	40.00(6)	33.00	2.75	1.95	2.50
126	8¢ green	50.00(6)	41.00	4.00	2.75	3.00
127	10¢ ultramarine	50.00(6)	41.00	4.00	2.75	4.50
128	11¢ blue hreen	120.00(6)	100.00	9.00	6.75	7.00
129	12¢ brown carmine	100.00(6)	75.00	7.25	5.25	7.00
130	14¢ dark violet	120.00(6)	87.50	8.00	5.50	7.00
131	15¢ olive green	170.00(6)	110.00	12.00	8.00	6.00
132	18¢ rose pink	140.00(6)	105.00	11.00	7.25	8.00
133	20¢ brown	180.00(6)	130.00	14.00	10.50	7.00
134	25¢ orange	300.00(6)	220.00	20.00	15.00	16.00
135	50¢ violet brown	360.00(6)	240.00	26.50	19.50	6.00

136

137

138

139

140

1945-49

SCOTT NO.	DESCRIPTION	PLATE BLOCK F/NH	PLATE BLOCK F/OG	UNUSED F/NH	UNUSED F/OG	USED F
136-40	**1/2¢-25¢ complete 5 varieties ....**	....	....	**2.35**	**1.95**	**1.75**
136	1/2¢ Major General Davis (1948)	3.00(6)	2.50	.40	.30	.25
137	1-1/2¢ Gov. Magoon (1948)	3.00(6)	2.50	.40	.30	.25
138	2¢ T. Roosevelt (1948)	.70(6)	.50	.25	.20	.25
139	5¢ Stevens	3.00(6)	2.00	.45	.40	.25
140	25¢ J.F. Wallace (1948)	9.00(6)	7.00	1.00	.85	.85

141

1948 CANAL ZONE BIOLOGICAL AREA

SCOTT NO.	DESCRIPTION	PLATE BLOCK F/NH	PLATE BLOCK F/OG	UNUSED F/NH	UNUSED F/OG	USED F
141	10¢ Map & Coat-mundi	10.00(6)	8.00	1.40	1.00	1.00

142

143

144

145

1949 CALIFORNIA GOLD RUSH

SCOTT NO.	DESCRIPTION	PLATE BLOCK F/NH	PLATE BLOCK F/OG	UNUSED F/NH	UNUSED F/OG	USED F
142-45	**3¢-18¢ complete 4 varieties ....**	....	....	**5.00**	**3.95**	**3.65**
142	3¢ "Forty Niners"	7.00(6)	5.00	.70	.55	.35
143	6¢ Journey–Las Cruces	8.25(6)	6.00	.75	.60	.40
144	12¢ Las Cruces–Panama Trail	19.50(6)	13.75	1.35	1.00	1.10
145	18¢ Departure–San Francisco	25.00(6)	21.00	2.50	2.00	2.00

146

147

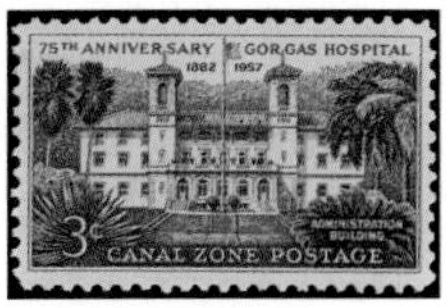

148

149

150

1951-58

SCOTT NO.	DESCRIPTION	PLATE BLOCK F/NH	PLATE BLOCK F/OG	UNUSED F/NH	UNUSED F/OG	USED F
146	10¢ West Indian Labor	25.00(6)	20.00	2.50	2.00	1.70
147	3¢ Panama R.R.(1955)	7.00(6)	5.50	.80	.60	.65
148	3¢ Gorgas Hospital (1957)	5.00	3.50	.60	.50	.45
149	4¢ S.S. Ancon (1958) .	3.50	2.60	.55	.45	.40
150	4¢ T. Roosevelt (1958)	4.00	3.00	.60	.50	.45

151

152, 154

1960-62

SCOTT NO.	DESCRIPTION	PLATE BLOCK F/NH	PLATE BLOCK F/OG	UNUSED F/NH	UNUSED F/OG	USED F
151	4¢ Boy Scout Badge ...	5.00	3.75	.60	.50	.45
152	4¢ Adminstration Building	1.10	.80	.30	.25	.20

LINE PAIR

SCOTT NO.	DESCRIPTION	LINE PAIR F/NH	LINE PAIR F/OG	UNUSED F/NH	UNUSED F/OG	USED F
153	3¢ G.W. Goethals, coil	1.00	.85	.25	.20	.20
154	4¢ Adminstration Building, coil	1.25	1.05	.25	.20	.20
155	5¢ J.F. Stevens, coil (1962)	1.50	1.20	.35	.30	.25

156

157

PLATE BLOCK

SCOTT NO.	DESCRIPTION	PLATE BLOCK F/NH	PLATE BLOCK F/OG	UNUSED F/NH	UNUSED F/OG	USED F
156	4¢ Girl Scout Badge (1962)	3.00	2.20	.45	.40	.35
157	4¢ Thatcher Ferry Bridge (1962)	5.00	4.00	.40	.35	.30
157a	same, silver omitted (bridge)	....	....	8500.00	....	....

158

159

1968-78

SCOTT NO.	DESCRIPTION	PLATE BLOCK F/NH	PLATE BLOCK F/OG	UNUSED F/NH	UNUSED F/OG	USED F
158	6¢ Goethals Memorial	2.50	....	.40	....	.20
159	8¢ Fort San Lorenzo (1971)	3.00	....	.50	....	.25

LINE PAIR

SCOTT NO.	DESCRIPTION	LINE PAIR F/NH	LINE PAIR F/OG	UNUSED F/NH	UNUSED F/OG	USED F
160	1¢ W.C. Gorgas, coil (1975)	1.00	....	.20	....	.20
161	10¢ H.F. Hodges, coil (1975)	5.00	....	.80	....	.45
162	25¢ J.F. Wallace, coil (1975)	24.00	....	3.25	....	3.00

163

165

PLATE BLOCK

SCOTT NO.	DESCRIPTION	PLATE BLOCK F/NH	PLATE BLOCK F/OG	UNUSED F/NH	UNUSED F/OG	USED F
163	13¢ Cascades Dredge (1976)	2.50	....	.50	....	.30
163a	same, bklt pane of 4 ...	....	....	3.50	....	....
164	5¢ J.F. Stevens (#139) Rotary Press (1977) ...	5.00	....	.85	....	1.00
165	15¢ Locomotive (1978)	2.20	....	.50	....	.25

AIR POST

AIR MAIL

105 & 106 Surcharged

25 CENTS 25

1929-31

SCOTT NO.	DESCRIPTION	PLATE BLOCK F/NH	PLATE BLOCK F	PLATE BLOCK AVG	UNUSED F/NH	UNUSED F	UNUSED AVG	USED F	USED AVG
C1	15¢ on 1¢ green, Type I	210.00(6)	150.00	110.00	15.00	12.00	10.00	6.25	4.00
C2	15¢ on 1¢ yellow green, Type II (1931)	....	....	....	170.00	130.00	100.00	75.00	55.00
C3	25¢ on 2¢ carmine	200.00	150.00	140.00	7.00	5.00	4.00	3.00	1.60

AIR MAIL

114 & 106 Surcharged

≡10c

1929

SCOTT NO.	DESCRIPTION	PLATE BLOCK F/NH	PLATE BLOCK F	PLATE BLOCK AVG	UNUSED F/NH	UNUSED F	UNUSED AVG	USED F	USED AVG
C4	10¢ on 50¢ lilac ..	220.00(6)	170.00	150.00	15.00	12.00	9.00	8.00	5.25
C5	20¢ on 2¢ carmine	175.00(6)	135.00	120.00	10.00	7.00	5.00	2.00	1.20

C6-C14

1931-49

SCOTT NO.	DESCRIPTION	PLATE BLOCK F/NH	PLATE BLOCK F	PLATE BLOCK AVG	UNUSED F/NH	UNUSED F	UNUSED AVG	USED F	USED AVG
C6-14	**4¢-$1 complete, 9 varieties ....**	....	....	....	**28.00**	**21.00**	**14.00**	**7.60**	**4.80**
C6	4¢ Gaillard Cut, red violet (1949)	7.00(6)	5.00	3.35	1.00	.75	.55	.85	.55
C7	5¢ yellow green ..	5.50(6)	4.50	2.75	.75	.55	.40	.40	.25
C8	6¢ yellow brown (1946)	7.75(6)	5.50	3.35	1.00	.75	.55	.40	.25
C9	10¢ orange	12.50(6)	9.50	6.00	1.30	1.00	.65	.40	.25
C10	15¢ blue	13.50(6)	10.50	7.00	1.60	1.20	.80	.30	.20
C11	20¢ red violet	21.00(6)	16.00	11.00	2.85	2.20	1.40	.30	.20
C12	30¢ rose lake (1941)	40.00(6)	30.00	20.00	4.50	3.25	2.15	1.30	.80
C13	40¢ yellow	40.00(6)	30.00	20.00	4.50	3.50	2.30	1.30	.80
C14	$1 black	105.00(6)	82.50	55.00	12.00	9.00	6.00	2.75	1.75

C15

C16

C17

C18

C19

C20

1939 25th ANNIVERSARY ISSUE

SCOTT NO.	DESCRIPTION	PLATE BLOCK F/NH	PLATE BLOCK F/OG	UNUSED F/NH	UNUSED F/OG	USED F
C15-20	**5¢-$1 complete 6 varieties ....**	....	....	**74.00**	**54.25**	**48.00**
C15	5¢ Plane over Sosa Hill	45.00(6)	30.00	4.25	3.00	2.75
C16	10¢ Map of Central America	50.00(6)	35.00	4.25	3.00	3.50
C17	15¢ Scene near Fort Amador	55.00(6)	40.00	5.00	3.25	1.30
C18	25¢ Clippper at Cristobal Harbor	275.00(6)	185.00	16.00	12.00	9.00
C19	39¢ Clipper over Gaillard Cut	170.00(6)	110.00	12.50	9.50	8.00
C20	$1 Clipper Alighthing ..	550.00(6)	400.00	36.50	26.50	26.50

C21-31, C34

1951

SCOTT NO.	DESCRIPTION	PLATE BLOCK F/NH	PLATE BLOCK F/OG	UNUSED F/NH	UNUSED F/OG	USED F
C21-26	**4¢-80¢ complete 6 varieties ....**	....	....	**29.25**	**23.25**	**13.00**
C21	4¢ Globe & Wing, red violet	8.00(6)	6.00	1.00	.75	.50
C22	6¢ light brown	6.00(6)	4.50	.80	.55	.40
C23	10¢ light red orange ...	10.50(6)	8.50	1.25	1.00	.50
C24	21¢ light blue	80.00(6)	60.00	10.00	8.00	5.00
C25	31¢ cerise	80.00(6)	60.00	10.00	8.00	5.00
C26	80¢ Light gray black ...	40.00(6)	30.00	6.50	5.00	2.00

1958

SCOTT NO.	DESCRIPTION	PLATE BLOCK F/NH	PLATE BLOCK F/OG	UNUSED F/NH	UNUSED F/OG	USED F
C27-31	**5¢-35¢ complete 5 varieties ....**	....	....	**28.50**	**22.90**	**9.70**
C27	5¢ Globe & Wing, yellow green	8.00	5.50	1.20	1.00	.65
C28	7¢ olive	8.00	5.50	1.20	1.00	.60
C29	15¢ brown violet	33.50	26.50	5.50	4.50	3.00
C30	25¢ orange yellow	90.00	72.50	12.00	9.50	3.00
C31	35¢ dark blue	57.50	45.00	8.00	6.00	3.00

C32

C33

C35

1961-63

SCOTT NO.	DESCRIPTION	PLATE BLOCK F/NH	PLATE BLOCK F/OG	UNUSED F/NH	UNUSED F/OG	USED F
C32	15¢ Emblem Caribbean School	14.00	10.00	1.60	1.25	1.00
C33	7¢ Anti-Malaria (1962)	3.50	2.50	.60	.40	.50
C34	8¢ Globe & Wing carmine (1968)	4.00	2.75	.60	.40	.40
C35	15¢ Alliance for Progress (1963)	13.00	10.00	1.40	1.10	.95

SCOTT NO.	DESCRIPTION	PLATE BLOCK F/NH	F/OG	UNUSED F/NH	F/OG	USED F

C36

C37

C38

C39

C40

C41

1964 50th ANNIVERSARY ISSUE

SCOTT NO.	DESCRIPTION	PLATE BLOCK F/NH	F/OG	UNUSED F/NH	F/OG	USED F
C36-41	**6¢-80¢ complete 6 varieties**	....	....	**11.80**	**8.75**	**9.90**
C36	6¢ Cristobal	3.35	2.75	.60	.45	.45
C37	8¢ Gatun Locks	3.35	2.75	.60	.45	.45
C38	15¢ Madden Dam	8.50	7.00	1.25	.90	.85
C39	20¢ Gaillard Cut	12.50	10.00	2.00	1.40	1.20
C40	30¢ Miraflores Locks	20.00	16.00	3.00	2.00	3.00
C41	80¢ Balboa	25.00	20.00	5.00	4.00	4.50

C42-C53

1965

SCOTT NO.	DESCRIPTION	PLATE BLOCK F/NH	F/OG	UNUSED F/NH	F/OG	USED F
C42-47	**6¢-80¢ complete 6 varieties**	....	....	**5.30**	....	**2.55**
C42	6¢ Gov. Seal, green & black	2.60	....	.45	....	.40
C43	8¢ rose red & black	2.25	....	.40	....	.20
C44	15¢ blue & black	3.00	....	.50	....	.30
C45	20¢ lilac & black	3.50	....	.75	....	.40
C46	30¢ reddish brown & black	5.00	....	1.00	....	.40
C47	80¢ bistre & balck	15.00	....	2.50	....	1.00

1968-76

SCOTT NO.	DESCRIPTION	PLATE BLOCK F/NH	F/OG	UNUSED F/NH	F/OG	USED F
C48-53	**10¢-35¢ complete 6 varieties**	....	....	**4.50**	....	**7.00**
C48	10¢ Gov. Seal, dull orange& black	1.75	....	.35	....	.25
C48a	same, bklt pane of 4	....	....	4.50	....	....
C49	11¢ Seal, olive & black (1971)	1.75	....	.35	....	.30
C49a	same, bklt pane of 4	....	....	3.50	....	....
C50	13¢ Seal, emerald & black (1974)	5.50	....	1.00	....	.35
C50a	same, bklt pane of 4	....	....	6.00	....	....
C51	22¢ Seal, violet & black (1976)	5.00	....	1.00	....	2.50
C52	25¢ Seal, pale yellow green & black	4.00	....	.80	....	.75
C53	35¢ Seal, salmon & black (1976)	6.00	....	1.20	....	2.00

AIR MAIL OFFICIAL STAMPS

C7-14 Overprinted
1941-42 Overprint 19 to 20-1/2 mm. long

OFFICIAL
PANAMA CANAL

SCOTT NO.	DESCRIPTION	PLATE BLOCK F/NH	F/OG	UNUSED F/NH	F/OG	USED F
CO1-7	**5¢-$1 complete 7 varieties**	....	....	**106.00**	**84.00**	**46.00**
CO1	5¢ Gaillard Cut, yellow green (C7)	....	....	6.50	5.00	2.50
CO2	10¢ orange (C9)	....	....	10.00	8.50	3.00
CO3	15¢ blue (C10)	....	....	14.00	11.00	3.00
CO4	20¢ red violet (C11)	....	....	16.00	12.00	5.00
CO5	30¢ rose lake (1942) (C12)	....	....	20.00	16.00	7.00
CO6	40¢ yellow (C13)	....	....	20.00	16.00	10.00
CO7	$1 black (C14)	....	....	40.00	30.00	14.00

1947 Overprint 19 to 20-1/2mm. long

SCOTT NO.	DESCRIPTION	PLATE BLOCK F/NH	F/OG	UNUSED F/NH	F/OG	USED F
CO14	6¢ yellow brown (C8)	....	....	25.00	15.00	6.25

POSTAGE DUE STAMPS

1914
U.S. Postage Due Stamps
J45-46, 49 overprint

CANAL ZONE

SCOTT NO.	DESCRIPTION	UNUSED NH F	AVG	UNUSED OG F	AVG	USED F	AVG
J1	1¢ rose carmine	125.00	105.00	90.00	65.00	17.00	10.00
J2	2¢ rose carmine	410.00	290.00	275.00	200.00	55.00	35.00
J3	10¢ rose carmine	1600.00	1150.00	1200.00	850.00	55.00	35.00

1924
Type I overprint on U.S. Postage Due Stamps J61-62, 65

SCOTT NO.	DESCRIPTION	UNUSED NH F	AVG	UNUSED OG F	AVG	USED F	AVG
J12	1¢ carmine rose	175.00	120.00	120.00	70.00	30.00	20.00
J13	2¢ deep claret	110.00	75.00	65.00	45.00	15.00	9.00
J14	10¢ deep claret	385.00	270.00	260.00	160.00	55.00	40.00

1925
Canal Zone Stamps
71, 73, 75 overprinted

POSTAGE
DUE

SCOTT NO.	DESCRIPTION	UNUSED NH F	AVG	UNUSED OG F	AVG	USED F	AVG
J15	1¢ deep green	200.00	130.00	100.00	55.00	17.00	11.50
J16	2¢ carmine	50.00	35.00	25.00	15.00	7.50	4.50
J17	10¢ orange	85.00	60.00	60.00	40.00	12.50	8.50

1925
Type II overprint on U.S. Postage Due Stamps J61-62, 65

SCOTT NO.	DESCRIPTION	UNUSED NH F	AVG	UNUSED OG F	AVG	USED F	AVG
J18	1¢ carmine rose	14.00	9.25	9.50	6.50	3.00	1.75
J19	2¢ carmine rose	22.00	15.00	15.00	10.00	5.00	3.00
J20	10¢ carmine rose	250.00	160.00	175.00	110.00	20.00	12.00

1929-39
107 Surcharged

POSTAGE DUE
-1-

SCOTT NO.	DESCRIPTION	UNUSED NH F	AVG	UNUSED OG F	AVG	USED F	AVG
J21	1¢ on 5¢ blue	10.00	7.00	5.00	3.50	2.20	1.40
J22	2¢ on 5¢ blue	17.00	12.00	9.00	6.00	3.50	2.00
J23	5¢ on 5¢ blue	17.00	12.00	9.00	6.00	4.00	2.35
J24	10¢ on 5¢ blue	17.00	12.00	9.00	6.00	4.00	2.35

J25

1932-41

SCOTT NO.	DESCRIPTION	UNUSED NH F	AVG	UNUSED OG F	AVG	USED F	AVG
J25-29	**1¢-15¢ complete, 5 varieties**	**5.40**	**3.95**	**4.00**	**3.00**	**3.60**	**2.55**
J25	1¢ claret	.35	.30	.25	.20	.25	.20
J26	2¢ claret	.35	.30	.25	.20	.25	.20
J27	5¢ claret	.55	.45	.45	.35	.25	.20
J28	10¢ claret	2.50	1.75	1.75	1.40	1.75	1.20
J29	15¢ claret (1941)	1.95	1.35	1.50	1.00	1.30	.90

OFFICIAL STAMPS

1941
105, 107, 108, 111, 112, 114, 117, 139 overprinted

OFFICIAL
PANAMA
CANAL

OFFICIAL
PANAMA CANAL

"PANAMA" 10mm. Long

SCOTT NO.	DESCRIPTION	UNUSED F/NH	F	USED F
O1/9	**1¢-50¢ (O1-2, O4-7, O9) 7 varieties**	**132.50**	**96.75**	**21.25**
O1	1¢ yellow green (105)	3.50	2.40	.60
O2	3¢ deep violet (117)	6.00	4.50	1.00
O3	5¢ blue (107)	......	......	40.00
O4	10¢ orange (108)	11.00	8.00	2.25
O5	15¢ gray black (111)	19.00	14.00	3.00
O6	20¢ olive brown (112)	25.00	17.00	3.50
O7	50¢ lilac (114)	60.00	45.00	7.50

1947

SCOTT NO.	DESCRIPTION	UNUSED F/NH	F	USED F
O9	5¢ deep blue (139)	15.00	11.00	4.50

CANAL ZONE MINT POSTAL STATIONERY ENTIRES

ENVELOPES

SCOTT NO.	DESCRIPTION	MINT ENTIRES
U16	1934, 3¢ purple	1.30
U17	1958, 4¢ blue	1.50
U18	1969, 4¢ + 1¢ blue	1.50
U19	1969, 4¢ + 2¢ blue	3.00
U20	1971, 8¢ Gaillard Cut	.90
U21	1974, 8¢ + 2¢ Gaillard Cut	1.25
U22	1976, 13¢ Gaillard Cut	.90
U23	1978, 13¢ + 2¢ Gaillard Cut	.90

AIR MAIL ENVELOPES

SCOTT NO.	DESCRIPTION	MINT ENTIRES
UC3	1949, 6¢ DC-4 Skymaster	4.50
UC4	1958, 7¢ DC-4 Skymaster	5.00
UC5	1963, 3¢ + 5¢ purple	7.00
UC6	1964, 8¢ Tail Assembly	2.75
UC7	1965, 4¢ + 4¢ blue	5.00
UC8	1966, 8¢ Tail Assembly	5.50
UC9	1968, 8¢ + 2¢ Tail Assembly	3.25
UC10	1968, 4¢ + 4¢ + 2¢ Tail Assembly	2.50
UC11	1969, 10¢ Tail Assembly	4.50
UC12	1971, 4¢ + 5¢ + 2¢ blue	4.50
UC13	1971, 10¢ + 1¢ Tail Assembly	4.50
UC14	1971, 11¢ Tail Assembly	1.25
UC15	1974, 11¢ + 2¢ Tail Assembly	1.75
UC16	1975, 8¢ + 2¢ + 3¢ emerald	1.50

POSTAL CARDS

SCOTT NO.	DESCRIPTION	MINT ENTIRES
UX10	1935, 1¢ overprint on U.S. #UX27	2.00
UX11	1952, 2¢ overprint on U.S. #UX38	2.50
UX12	1958, 3¢ Ship in Lock	2.25
UX13	1963, 3¢ + 1¢ Ship in Lock	4.50
UX14	1964, 4¢ Ship in Canal	4.00
UX15	1965, 4¢ Ship in Lock	1.25
UX16	1968, 4¢ + 1¢ Ship in Lock	1.25
UX17	1969, 5¢ Ship in Lock	1.25
UX18	1971, 5¢ + 1¢ Ship in Lock	.95
UX19	1974, 8¢ Ship in Lock	1.00
UX20	1976, 8¢ + 1¢ Ship in Lock	.75
UX21	1978, 8¢ + 2¢ Ship in Lock	.95

AIR MAIL POSTAL CARDS

SCOTT NO.	DESCRIPTION	MINT ENTIRES
UXC1	1958, 5¢ Plane, Flag & Map	4.00
UXC2	1963, 5¢ + 1¢ Plane, Flag & Map	10.50
UXC3	1965, 4¢ + 2¢ Ship in Lock	4.50
UXC4	1968, 4¢ + 4¢ Ship in Lock	3.25
UXC5	1971, 5¢ + 4¢ Ship in Lock	1.25

CONFEDERATE STATES

1, 4
Jefferson Davis

2, 5
Thomas Jefferson

(Confederate States 1-14 + 40% for VF Centering)

1861

SCOTT NO.	DESCRIPTION	UNUSED OG F	UNUSED OG AVG	UNUSED F	UNUSED AVG	USED F	USED AVG
1	5¢ green	275.00	180.00	180.00	120.00	160.00	110.00
2	10¢ blue	300.00	210.00	210.00	150.00	200.00	140.00

3
Andrew Jackson

6, 7
Jefferson Davis
6: Fine Print
7: Coarse Print

1862

SCOTT NO.	DESCRIPTION	UNUSED OG F	UNUSED OG AVG	UNUSED F	UNUSED AVG	USED F	USED AVG
3	2¢ green	800.00	550.00	600.00	400.00	700.00	450.00
4	5¢ blue	200.00	140.00	135.00	95.00	120.00	80.00
5	10¢ rose	1500.00	1000.00	1100.00	650.00	600.00	400.00
6	5¢ light blue, London Print	12.50	9.00	9.00	6.00	30.00	20.00
7	5¢ blue, Local Print	17.50	11.00	13.50	9.00	21.00	15.00

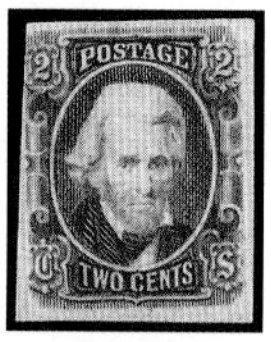

8
Andrew Jackson

1863

SCOTT NO.	DESCRIPTION	UNUSED OG F	UNUSED OG AVG	UNUSED F	UNUSED AVG	USED F	USED AVG
8	2¢ red brown	75.00	50.00	55.00	40.00	400.00	295.00

9

10, 11 (Die A)
Jefferson Davis

12 (Die B)

SCOTT NO.	DESCRIPTION	UNUSED OG F	UNUSED OG AVG	UNUSED F	UNUSED AVG	USED F	USED AVG
9	10¢ blue (TEN)	975.00	675.00	700.00	475.00	550.00	400.00
10	10¢ blue (with frame line)		....	4000.00	2800.00	1750.00	1250.00
11	10¢ blue (no frame)	12.50	8.50	9.00	6.00	16.00	11.00
12	10¢ blue, filled corner	13.50	9.00	9.00	6.00	20.00	14.00

13
George Washington

14
John C. Calhoun

SCOTT NO.	DESCRIPTION	UNUSED OG F	UNUSED OG AVG	UNUSED F	UNUSED AVG	USED F	USED AVG
13	20¢ green	49.00	35.00	35.00	25.00	500.00	400.00

1862

SCOTT NO.	DESCRIPTION	UNUSED OG F	UNUSED OG AVG	UNUSED F	UNUSED AVG	USED F	USED AVG
14	1¢ orange	110.00	80.00	70.00	50.00	......	......

CUBA

U.S. Administration

1899
U.S. Stamps of 267, 279, 279B, 268, 281, 282C surcharged

CUBA

1 c.
de PESO.

SCOTT NO.	DESCRIPTION	UNUSED NH F	UNUSED NH AVG	UNUSED OG F	UNUSED OG AVG	USED F	USED AVG
221	1¢ on 1¢ yellow green	8.50	6.50	5.50	4.00	.65	.40
222	2¢ on 2¢ carmine	16.00	11.00	10.00	7.00	.85	.60
223	2-1/2¢ on 2¢ carmine .	9.00	6.50	5.50	4.00	1.00	.70
224	3¢ on 3¢ purple	23.00	15.00	15.00	10.00	2.00	1.40
225	5¢ on 5¢ blue	23.00	15.00	15.00	10.00	2.50	1.75
226	10¢ on 10¢ brown	45.00	30.00	28.00	19.00	8.00	5.00

227

228

229

230

231

Republic under U.S. Military Rule Watermarked US-C

SCOTT NO.	DESCRIPTION	UNUSED NH F	UNUSED NH AVG	UNUSED OG F	UNUSED OG AVG	USED F	USED AVG
227	1¢ Columbus	5.00	3.50	3.50	2.50	.25	.20
228	2¢ Coconut Palms	5.00	3.50	3.50	2.50	.25	.20
229	3¢ Allegory "Cuba"	5.00	3.50	3.50	2.50	.25	.20
230	5¢ Ocean Liner	7.00	5.00	5.00	3.50	.25	.20
231	10¢ Cane Field	18.00	13.00	13.00	9.00	.75	.55

SPECIAL DELIVERY
1899
Surcharged of 1899 on U.S. E5

SCOTT NO.	DESCRIPTION	UNUSED NH F	UNUSED NH AVG	UNUSED OG F	UNUSED OG AVG	USED F	USED AVG
E1	10¢ on 10¢ blue	190.00	130.00	125.00	85.00	110.00	80.00

E2
Special Delivery Messenger

Republic under U.S. Military Rule
Watermarked US-C Inscribed "Immediate"

SCOTT NO.	DESCRIPTION	UNUSED NH F	UNUSED NH AVG	UNUSED OG F	UNUSED OG AVG	USED F	USED AVG
E2	10¢ orange	90.00	60.00	60.00	40.00	18.00	12.00

POSTAGE DUE STAMPS
1899
Surcharge of 1899 on U.S. J38-39, J41-42

SCOTT NO.	DESCRIPTION	UNUSED NH F	UNUSED NH AVG	UNUSED OG F	UNUSED OG AVG	USED F	USED AVG
J1	1¢ on 1¢ deep claret ..	75.00	50.00	50.00	35.00	7.00	5.00
J2	2¢ on 2¢ deep claret ..	75.00	50.00	50.00	35.00	7.00	5.00
J3	5¢ on 5¢ deep claret ..	75.00	50.00	50.00	35.00	7.00	5.00
J4	10¢ on 10¢ deep claret	50.00	35.00	35.00	25.00	3.00	2.00

GUAM

1899
U.S. Stamps of 279, 267, 268, 272, 280-82C, 284, 275, 276 overprinted

GUAM

SCOTT NO.	DESCRIPTION	UNUSED NH F	UNUSED NH AVG	UNUSED OG F	UNUSED OG AVG	USED F	USED AVG
1	1¢ deep green	40.00	25.00	20.00	13.00	30.00	20.00
2	2¢ red	38.00	25.00	19.00	13.00	29.00	20.00
3	3¢ purple	300.00	200.00	150.00	100.00	190.00	130.00
4	4¢ lilac brown	280.00	190.00	140.00	95.00	190.00	130.00
5	5¢ blue	70.00	50.00	35.00	25.00	50.00	35.00
6	6¢ lake	280.00	190.00	140.00	95.00	225.00	150.00
7	8¢ violet brown	320.00	220.00	160.00	110.00	225.00	150.00
8	10¢ brown (Type I)	110.00	80.00	55.00	40.00	60.00	40.00
10	15¢ olive green	350.00	240.00	175.00	120.00	200.00	140.00
11	50¢ orange	800.00	550.00	400.00	275.00	500.00	350.00
12	$1 black (Type I)	800.00	550.00	400.00	275.00	450.00	300.00

SPECIAL DELIVERY
U.S. Stamp E5 overprint

GUAM

SCOTT NO.	DESCRIPTION	UNUSED NH F	UNUSED NH AVG	UNUSED OG F	UNUSED OG AVG	USED F	USED AVG
E1	10¢ blue	325.00	220.00	165.00	110.00	225.00	160.00

HAWAII

23, 24

25, 26

1864 Laid Paper

SCOTT NO.	DESCRIPTION	UNUSED OG F	UNUSED OG AVG	UNUSED F	UNUSED AVG	USED F	USED AVG
23	1¢ black	....	....	325.00	225.00	....	....
24	2¢ black	....	....	350.00	250.00	....	....

1865 Wove Paper

SCOTT NO.	DESCRIPTION	UNUSED OG F	UNUSED OG AVG	UNUSED F	UNUSED AVG	USED F	USED AVG
25	1¢ dark blue	....	....	350.00	250.00	....	....
26	2¢ dark blue	....	....	350.00	250.00	....	....

27-29, 50-51
King Kamehameha IV

1861-63

SCOTT NO.	DESCRIPTION	UNUSED OG F	UNUSED OG AVG	UNUSED F	UNUSED AVG	USED F	USED AVG
27	2¢ pale rose, horizontal laid paper	400.00	275.00	275.00	185.00	350.00	250.00
28	2¢ pale rose, vertical laid paper	400.00	275.00	275.00	185.00	350.00	250.00

1869 Engraved

SCOTT NO.	DESCRIPTION	UNUSED OG F	UNUSED OG AVG	UNUSED F	UNUSED AVG	USED F	USED AVG
29	2¢ red, thin wove paper	60.00	40.00	40.00	28.00	....	....

30
Princess Kamamalu

31
King Kamehameha IV

32, 39, 52C

33
King Kamehameha V

34
Mataia Kekuanaoa

1864-71 Wove Paper

SCOTT NO.	DESCRIPTION	UNUSED OG F	UNUSED OG AVG	UNUSED F	UNUSED AVG	USED F	USED AVG
30	1¢ purple	10.00	7.00	7.00	5.00	8.50	6.00
31	2¢ rose vermillion	55.00	40.00	40.00	28.00	10.00	7.00
32	5¢ blue	200.00	140.00	140.00	95.00	35.00	25.00
33	6 yellow green	45.00	30.00	30.00	20.00	10.00	7.00
34	18¢ dull rose	105.00	70.00	75.00	50.00	40.00	28.00

35, 38, 43
King David Kalakaua

36, 46
Prince William Pitt Leleichoku

1875

SCOTT NO.	DESCRIPTION	UNUSED OG F	UNUSED OG AVG	UNUSED F	UNUSED AVG	USED F	USED AVG
35	2¢ brown	6.60	4.00	5.50	3.35	2.20	1.40
36	12¢ black	45.00	30.00	37.50	25.00	19.50	12.50

37, 42
Princess Likelike

40, 44, 45
King David Kalakaua

41
Queen Kapiolani

47
Statue of King Kamehameha I

48
King William Lunalilo

49
Queen Emma Kaleleonalani

1882

SCOTT NO.	DESCRIPTION	UNUSED OG F	UNUSED OG AVG	UNUSED F	UNUSED AVG	USED F	USED AVG
37	1¢ blue	20.00	8.00	8.00	5.00	7.00	5.00
38	2¢ lilac rose	280.00	95.00	95.00	65.00	50.00	35.00
39	5¢ ultramarine	30.00	14.00	14.00	10.00	4.00	2.75
40	10¢ black	72.00	50.00	28.00	19.00	22.00	16.00
41	15¢ red brown	100.00	60.00	45.00	32.00	30.00	20.00

1883-86

SCOTT NO.	DESCRIPTION	UNUSED OG F	UNUSED OG AVG	UNUSED F	UNUSED AVG	USED F	USED AVG
42	1¢ green	6.00	4.00	3.00	2.00	2.10	1.50
43	2¢ rose	10.00	6.00	3.50	2.50	1.25	.85
44	10¢ red brown	60.00	40.00	25.00	17.00	11.00	7.00
45	10¢ vermillion	60.00	40.00	25.00	17.00	15.00	10.00
46	12¢ red lilac	150.00	70.00	55.00	40.00	35.00	25.00
47	25¢ dark violet	290.00	180.00	120.00	70.00	70.00	50.00
48	50¢ red	290.00	180.00	120.00	85.00	90.00	60.00
49	$1 rose red	500.00	200.00	150.00	130.00	275.00	185.00
50	2¢ Orange Vermillion	150.00	95.00	....	....	....	....
51	2¢ Carmine	30.00	20.00	....	....	....	....

52
Queen Liliuokalani

1890-91

SCOTT NO.	DESCRIPTION	UNUSED OG F	UNUSED OG AVG	UNUSED F	UNUSED AVG	USED F	USED AVG
52	2¢ dull violet	10.00	6.00	3.00	1.20	2.00	1.40
52C	5¢ deep indigo	220.00	110.00	65.00	40.00	150.00	100.00

Provisional
GOVT.
1893

1893 Provisional Government Red Overprint

SCOTT NO.	DESCRIPTION	UNUSED OG F	UNUSED OG AVG	UNUSED F	UNUSED AVG	USED F	USED AVG
53	1¢ purple	9.00	6.00	6.00	4.25	15.00	10.00
54	1¢ blue	9.00	6.00	6.00	4.25	15.00	10.00
55	1¢ green	2.00	1.40	1.50	1.00	4.00	2.75
56	2¢ brown	12.00	8.00	9.00	6.00	25.00	18.00
57	2¢ dull violet	2.00	1.40	1.50	1.00	1.50	1.00
58	5¢ deep indigo	12.00	8.00	9.00	6.00	30.00	20.00
59	5¢ ultramarine	7.00	5.00	6.00	4.00	3.25	1.95
60	6¢ green	18.00	12.00	13.00	9.00	30.00	20.00
61	10¢ black	11.00	8.00	9.00	6.00	17.00	12.00
62	12¢ black	10.00	7.00	8.00	5.00	18.00	12.00
63	12¢ red lilac	270.00	160.00	110.00	75.00	300.00	200.00
64	25¢ dark violet	50.00	30.00	20.00	15.00	50.00	35.00

Black Overprint

SCOTT NO.	DESCRIPTION	UNUSED OG F	UNUSED OG AVG	UNUSED F	UNUSED AVG	USED F	USED AVG
65	2¢ rose vermillion	130.00	60.00	40.00	30.00	85.00	60.00
66	2¢ rose	1.50	1.00	1.20	.80	3.00	2.00
67	10¢ vermillion	20.00	14.00	15.00	10.00	40.00	28.00
68	10¢ red brown	9.00	6.00	7.00	5.00	15.00	10.00
69	12¢ red lilac	300.00	200.00	210.00	140.00	600.00	395.00
70	15¢ red brown	22.00	15.00	16.00	12.00	35.00	25.00
71	18¢ dull rose	30.00	20.00	22.00	16.00	40.00	28.00
72	50¢ red	75.00	50.00	55.00	40.00	100.00	70.00
73	$1 rose red	120.00	80.00	85.00	60.00	190.00	130.00

74, 80
Coat of Arms

75, 81
View of Honolulu

76
Statue of King Kamehameha I

1894

SCOTT NO.	DESCRIPTION	UNUSED OG F	UNUSED OG AVG	UNUSED F	UNUSED AVG	USED F	USED AVG
74	1¢ yellow	3.00	2.10	2.25	1.55	1.40	1.00
75	2¢ brown	2.75	2.10	2.25	1.55	.80	.55
76	5¢ rose lake	5.00	3.50	4.00	2.75	2.00	1.40

77
Star and Palm

78
S.S."Arawa"

79
Pres. S.B. Dole

SCOTT NO.	DESCRIPTION	UNUSED OG F	UNUSED OG AVG	UNUSED F	UNUSED AVG	USED F	USED AVG
77	10¢ yellow green	7.25	5.00	6.00	4.00	5.00	3.50
78	12¢ blue	16.00	11.00	12.00	8.00	18.00	12.00
79	25¢ deep blue	20.00	14.00	15.00	10.00	15.00	10.00

82
Statue of King Kamehameha I

1899

SCOTT NO.	DESCRIPTION	UNUSED OG F	UNUSED OG AVG	UNUSED F	UNUSED AVG	USED F	USED AVG
80	1¢ dark green	2.00	1.40	1.50	1.00	1.50	1.00
81	2¢ rose	1.80	1.30	1.50	1.00	1.50	1.00
82	5¢ blue	8.00	5.00	6.00	4.00	4.00	2.80

O1
Lorrin A. Thurston

1896 OFFICIAL STAMPS

SCOTT NO.	DESCRIPTION	UNUSED OG F	UNUSED OG AVG	UNUSED F	UNUSED AVG	USED F	USED AVG
O1	2¢ green	50.00	35.00	40.00	28.00	20.00	14.00
O2	5¢ black brown	50.00	35.00	40.00	28.00	20.00	14.00
O3	6¢ deep ultramarine	50.00	35.00	40.00	28.00	20.00	14.00
O4	10¢ bright rose	50.00	35.00	40.00	28.00	20.00	14.00
O5	12¢ orange	50.00	35.00	40.00	28.00	20.00	14.00
O6	25¢ gray violet	50.00	35.00	40.00	28.00	20.00	14.00

MARSHALL ISLANDS

The Marshall Islands are a part of the U.S. administered Trust Territories of the Pacific formed in 1947. They were granted postal autonomy in 1984 on their way to independence.

31

35

1984 COMMEMORATIVES

SCOTT NO.	DESCRIPTION	UNUSED F/NH
31-34	20¢ Postal Independence, attached	2.75

1984-85 MAPS & NAVIGATION

SCOTT NO.	DESCRIPTION	UNUSED F/NH
35-49A	**1¢-$1, 16 varieties**	**14.70**
35	1¢ Mili Atoll	
36	3¢ Likiep Atoll	
37	5¢ Ebon Atoll	
38	10¢ Jaluit Atoll	
39	13¢ Alinginae Atoll	
40	14¢ Wotho Atoll (1985)	
41	20¢ Kwajalein Atoll	
42	22¢ Enewetok (1985)	
43	28¢ Ailinglaplap Atoll	
44	30¢ Majuro Atoll	
45	33¢ Namu Atoll (1985)	
46	37¢ Rongelap Atoll	
47	39¢ Utirik & Taka (1985)	
48	44¢ Ujelang Atoll (1985)	
49	50¢ Maloelap & Aur (1985)	
49A	$1.00 Arno Atoll	

1984-85 BOOKLET PANES

SCOTT NO.	DESCRIPTION	UNUSED F/NH
39a	13¢ Ailingingae (10)	12.40
40a	14¢ Wotho Atoll (10)	12.40
41a	20¢ Kwajalein (10)	13.55
41b	13¢ (5) & 20¢ (5)	14.70
42a	22¢ Eniwetok (10)	13.55
42b	14¢ (5) & 22¢ (5)	14.70

50

54

1984 COMMEMORATIVES

SCOTT NO.	DESCRIPTION	UNUSED F/NH
50-53	40¢ U.P.U.—Hamburg, attached	3.50
54-57	20¢ Dolphins, attached	2.30

58

59

SCOTT NO.	DESCRIPTION	UNUSED F/NH
58	20¢ Christmas, strip of 4	3.20
59-62	20¢ Constitution, attached	2.50

63

65

70

1985 COMMEMORATIVES

SCOTT NO.	DESCRIPTION	UNUSED F/NH
63-64	22¢ Audubon Birds, attached	1.65
65-69	22¢ Seashells, attached	2.75
70-73	22¢ Decade for Women, attached	2.45

74

78

SCOTT NO.	DESCRIPTION	UNUSED F/NH
74-77	22¢ Reef Fish, attached	2.45
78-81	22¢ Youth Year, attached	2.60

82

86

91

SCOTT NO.	DESCRIPTION	UNUSED F/NH
82-85	14¢-44¢ Christmas, 4 varieties	3.20
86-90	22¢ Halley's Comet, strip of 5	6.65
91-94	22¢ Medicinal Plants, attached	2.45

1986-87 MAPS & NAVIGATION

SCOTT NO.	DESCRIPTION	UNUSED F/NH
107	$2 Wotje & Erikub	6.05
108	$5 Bikini Atoll	13.55
109	$10 Stick Chart (1987)	22.50

110

114

1986 COMMEMORATIVES

SCOTT NO.	DESCRIPTION	UNUSED F/NH
110-13	14¢ Marine Invertebrates, attached	2.90
114	$1 AMERIPEX '86 Souvenir Sheet	4.35

115

124

128

SCOTT NO.	DESCRIPTION	UNUSED F/NH
115-18	22¢ Operation Crossroads, Atomic Tests, attached	2.90
119-23	22¢ Seashells, designs as #65-69, attached	3.20
124-27	22¢ Game Fish, attached.	2.60
128-31	22¢ Christmas, Peace, attached	3.20

132

136

1987 COMMEMORATIVES

SCOTT NO.	DESCRIPTION	UNUSED F/NH
132-35	22¢ Whaling Ships, attached	2.90
136-41	33¢, 39¢, 44¢ Historic Aircraft, 3 attached pairs	6.05

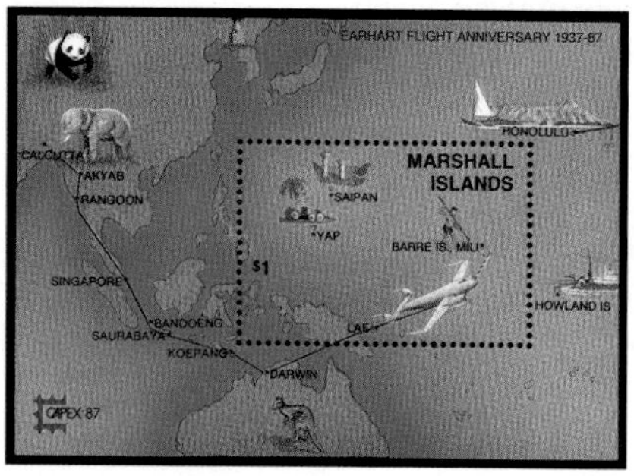

142

SCOTT NO.	DESCRIPTION	UNUSED F/NH
142	$1 CAPEX '87 Souvenir Sheet	3.40

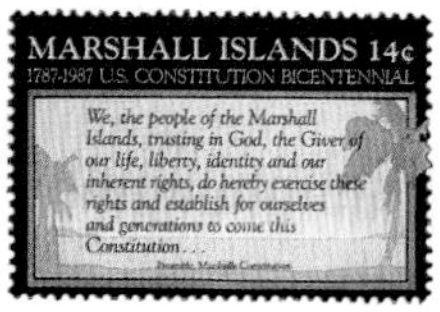

143

152

157

160

SCOTT NO.	DESCRIPTION	UNUSED F/NH
143-51	14¢-44¢ U.S. Constitution, 3 attached strips of 3	6.95
152-56	22¢ Seashells, attached	3.20
157-59	44¢ Copra Industry, attached	3.20
160-63	14¢-44¢ Christmas	2.90

164

168

1988

SCOTT NO.	DESCRIPTION	UNUSED F/NH
164-67	44¢ Marine Birds	4.65

1988-89 Definitives

SCOTT NO.	DESCRIPTION	UNUSED F/NH
168-83	1¢-$5 Fish, 16 singles complete set	28.90
184	$10 Blue Jack (1989)	24.00

Booklet Panes 1987-89

SCOTT NO.	DESCRIPTION	UNUSED F/NH
170a	14¢ Hawkfish pane (10)	6.05
171a	15¢ Balloonfish pane (10)	8.10
173a	22¢ Lyretail wrasse pane (10)	8.65
173b	5 (14¢) & 5 (22¢) pane (10)	6.95
174a	25¢ Parrotfish pane (10)	9.50
174b	5 (15¢) & 5 (25¢) pane (10)	9.50

188

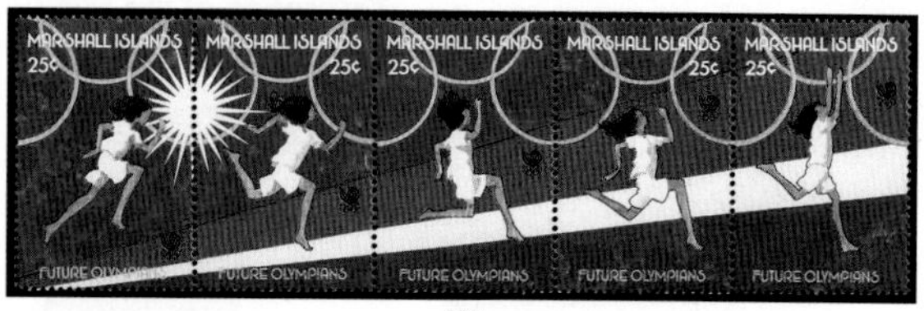

189

SCOTT NO.	DESCRIPTION	UNUSED F/NH
188-89	15¢-25¢ Olympics 2 attached strip of 5	5.50

190a

191

SCOTT NO.	DESCRIPTION	UNUSED F/NH
190	25¢ Stevenson, sheetlet of 9	7.80
191-94	25¢ Ships & Flags, attached	3.20

195

202

SCOTT NO.	DESCRIPTION	UNUSED F/NH
195-99	25¢ Christmas, strip of 5	3.50
200-04	25¢ J.F.K. Tribute, strip of 5	4.35

208a

SCOTT NO.	DESCRIPTION	UNUSED F/NH
205-08	25¢ Space Shuttle, strip of 4	3.20

209

1989 COMMEMORATIVES

SCOTT NO.	DESCRIPTION	UNUSED F/NH
209-12	45¢ Links to Japan, attached	4.65

213

216

SCOTT NO.	DESCRIPTION	UNUSED F/NH
213-15	45¢ Alaska Anniv., strip of 3	3.75
216-20	25¢ Seashells, strip of 5	3.50

221

1989 COMMEMORATIVES (continued)

SCOTT NO.	DESCRIPTION	UNUSED F/NH
221	$1 Japanese Art Souvenir Sheet	2.60

222

226

230a

232

SCOTT NO.	DESCRIPTION	UNUSED F/NH
222-25	45¢ Migrant Birds, attached	4.90
226-29	45¢ Postal Service, attached	5.20
230	$1.50 PHILEX-FRANCE Souv. Sheet	13.55
231	$1.00 Postal Service Centenary Souvenir Sheet	13.55
232-38	25¢-$1 20th Anniversary First Moon Landing	23.00
238a	booklet pane of 232-38	23.50

239

248

1989 WWII Anniversary Issues

SCOTT NO.	DESCRIPTION	UNUSED F/NH
239	25¢ Invasion of Poland	.85
240	45¢ Sinking of HMS Royal Oak	1.65
241	45¢ Invasion of Finland	1.65
242-45	45¢ Battle of River Plate, 4 attached	6.95

1990 WWII Anniversary Issues

SCOTT NO.	DESCRIPTION	UNUSED F/NH
246-47	25¢ Invasion of Denmark and Norway	1.75
248	25¢ Katyn Forest Massacre	.90
249-50	25¢ Bombing of Rotterdam/25¢ Invasion of Belgium	1.75
251	45¢ Winston Churchill	1.65
252-53	45¢ Evacuation at Dunkirk, 2 attached	3.50
254	45¢ Occupation of Paris	1.65
255	25¢ Battle of Mers-el-Kebir	.90
256	25¢ Battles for Burma Road	.90
257-60	45¢ U.S. Destroyers, 4 attached	7.00
261-64	45¢ Battle for Britain, 4 attached	7.00
265	45¢ Tripartite Pact 1940	1.65
266	25¢ Roosevelt Reelected	.90
267-70	25¢ Battle of Taranto, 4 attached	4.40

1991 WWII Anniversary Issues

SCOTT NO.	DESCRIPTION	UNUSED F/NH
271-74	30¢ Roosevelt's Four Freedoms of Speech, 4 attached	4.70
275	30¢ Battle of Beda Fomm	.95
276-77	29¢ Invasion of Greece and Yugoslavia, 2 attached	2.10
278-81	50¢ Sinking of the Bismarck, 4 attached	8.15
282	30¢ Germany Invades Russia	1.15
283-84	29¢ Atlantic Charter, 2 attached	2.15
285	29¢ Siege of Moscow	1.15
286-87	30¢ Sinking of the USS Reuben James, 2 attached	2.15
288-91	50¢ Japanese Attack Pearl Harbor, 4 attached	7.90
288-91b	same, 2nd printing (1 title corrected)	20.50
292	29¢ Japanese Capture Guam	1.20
293	29¢ Fall of Singapore	1.20
294-95	50¢ Flying Tigers, 2 attached	3.90
296	29¢ Fall of Wake Island	1.20

1992 WWII Anniversary Issues

SCOTT NO.	DESCRIPTION	UNUSED F/NH
297	29¢ Arcadia Conference	1.20
298	50¢ Fall of Manila	1.95
299	29¢ Japanese take Rabaul	1.20
300	29¢ Battle of Java Sea	1.20
301	50¢ Fall of Rangoon	1.95
302	29¢ Japanese on New Guinea	1.20
303	29¢ MacArthur evacuated from Corregidor	1.20
304	29¢ Raid on Saint-Nazaire	1.20
305	29¢ Bataan/Death March	1.20
306	50¢ Doolittle Raid on Tokyo	1.95
307	29¢ Fall of Corregidor	1.20
308-11	50¢ Battle of the Coral Sea, 4 attached	8.15
308-11b	same, 2nd printing (4 titles corrected)	26.25
312-15	50¢ Battle of Midway, 4 attached	8.15
316	29¢ Village of Lidice destroyed	1.20
317	29¢ Fall of Sevastopol	1.20
318-19	29¢ Convoy PQ 17 Destroyed, 2 attached	2.35
320	29¢ Marines on Guadalcanal	1.20
321	29¢ Battle of Savo Island	1.20
322	29¢ Dieppe Raid	1.20
323	50¢ Battle of Stalingrad	2.00
324	29¢ Battle of Eastern Solomons	1.20
325	50¢ Battle of Cape Esperance	2.00
326	29¢ Battle of El Alamein	1.20
327-28	29¢ Battle of Barents Sea, 2 attached	2.35

1993 WWII Anniversary Issues

SCOTT NO.	DESCRIPTION	UNUSED F/NH
329	29¢ Casablanca Conference	1.20
330	29¢ Liberation of Kharkov	1.20
331-34	50¢ Battle of Bismarck Sea, 4 attached	8.15
335	50¢ Interception of Admiral Yamamoto	1.95
336-37	29¢ Battle of Kursk, 2 attached	2.45

341

345a

346

1989

SCOTT NO.	DESCRIPTION	UNUSED F/NH
341-44	25¢ Christmas 1989, 4 attached	5.55
345	45¢ Milestones in space (25)	46.00

1990

SCOTT NO.	DESCRIPTION	UNUSED F/NH
346-65A	1¢/$2 Birds (21)	34.35
361a	Essen '90 Germany, miniature sheet of 4 (347, 350, 353, 361)	6.15

366

370

377

SCOTT NO.	DESCRIPTION	UNUSED F/NH
366-69	25¢ Children's Games, 4 attached	5.25
370-76	25¢, $1 Penny Black, singles	20.00
376a	booklet pane of 370-76	20.50
377-80	25¢ Endangered Wildlife, 4 attached	6.70

381

382

383

387

SCOTT NO.	DESCRIPTION	UNUSED F/NH
381	25¢ Joint Issue (US & Micronesia)	1.50
382	45¢ German Reunification	1.75
383-86	25¢ Christmas 1990, 4 attached	4.60
387-90	25¢ Breadfruit, 4 attached	3.90

395

1991

SCOTT NO.	DESCRIPTION	UNUSED F/NH
391-94	50¢ 10th Anniversaary of Space Shuttle, 4 attached	5.55
395-98	52¢ Flowers, 4 attached	6.95
398a	52¢ Phila Nippon, sheet of 4	6.95

399

400

SCOTT NO.	DESCRIPTION	UNUSED F/NH
399	29¢ Operation Desert Storm	1.85
400-06	29¢, $1 Birds, set of 7 singles	31.50
406a	same, booklet pane of 7	32.00

407

411

SCOTT NO.	DESCRIPTION	UNUSED F/NH
407-10	12¢-50¢ Air Marshall Islands Aircraft, set of 4	5.20
411	29¢ Admission to the United Nations	1.15

412

413

SCOTT NO.	DESCRIPTION	UNUSED F/NH
412	30¢ Christmas 1991, Dove	1.30
413	29¢ Peace Corps	1.30

414

418

425

1992

SCOTT NO.	DESCRIPTION	UNUSED F/NH
414-17	29¢ Ships, strip of 4	5.25
418-24	50¢, $1 Columbus, set of 7 singles	21.00
424a	same, booklet pane of 7	21.50
425-28	29¢ Handicrafts, 4 attached	3.75

429

430

SCOTT NO.	DESCRIPTION	UNUSED F/NH
429	29¢ Christmas, 1992	1.05
430-33	9-45¢ Birds, set of 4	5.20

441

466A

478

1993

SCOTT NO.	DESCRIPTION	UNUSED F/NH
434-40	50¢, $1 Reef Life, set of 7 singles	21.00
440a	same, booklet pane of 7	21.50

1993-95

SCOTT NO.	DESCRIPTION	UNUSED F/NH
441-66B	10¢-$10 Ships & Sailing Vessels, 28 varieties.	85.00
466C	"Hong Kong '94" miniature sheet of 4 (#464d-64g)	5.20

1993 WWII Anniversary Issues (continued)

SCOTT NO.	DESCRIPTION	UNUSED F/NH
467-70	52¢ Invasion of Sicily, 4 attached	8.65
471	50¢ Bombing of Schweinfurt	1.95
472	29¢ Liberation of Smolensk	1.15
473	29¢ Landings at Bougainville	1.15
474	50¢ Invasion of Tarawa	1.95
475	52¢ Teheran Conference, 1943	1.95
476-77	29¢ Battle of North Cape, 2 attached	2.60

1994 WWII Anniversary Issues

SCOTT NO.	DESCRIPTION	UNUSED F/NH
478	29¢ Gen. Dwight D. Eisenhower	1.15
479	50¢ Invasion of Anzio	1.95
480	52¢ Siege of Leningrad lifted	1.95
481	29¢ US Liberates Marshall Islands	1.15
482	29¢ Japanese Defeated at Truk	1.15
483	52¢ US Bombs Germany	1.95
484	50¢ Lt. Gen. Mark Clark, Rome Falls to the Allies	1.95
485-88	75¢ D-Day—Allied Landings at Normandy, 4 attached	12.40
485-88b	same, 2nd printing (3 titles corrected)	29.00
489	50¢ V-1 Bombardment of England Begins	1.95
490	29¢ US Marines Land on Saipan	1.15
491	50¢ 1st Battle of Philippine Sea	1.95
492	29¢ US Liberates Guam	1.10
493	50¢ Warsaw Uprising	1.95
494	50¢ Liberation of Paris	1.95
495	29¢ US Marines land on Peliliu	1.95
496	52¢ MacArthur returns to the Philippines	2.00
497	52¢ Battle of Leyte Gulf	2.00
498-99	50¢ Battleship Tirpitz Sunk, 2 attached	4.70
500-03	50¢ Battle of the Bulge, 4 attached	12.25

SCOTT NO.	DESCRIPTION	UNUSED F/NH
	1995 WWII Anniversary Issues	
504	32¢ Yalta Conference Begins	1.40
505	55¢ Bombing of Dresden	4.10
506	$1 Iwo Jima Invaded by US Marines	4.95
507	32¢ Remagen Bridge Taken by US Forces	1.40
508	55¢ Okinawa Invaded by US Forces	2.45
509	50¢ Death of F.D.R.	2.45
510	32¢ US/USSR troops meet at Elbe River	1.65
511	60¢ Russian troops capture Berlin	2.45
512	55¢ Allies liberate concentration camps, 1945	2.45
513-16	75¢ VE Day, 4 attached	20.25
517	32¢ UN Charter signed	1.40
518	55¢ Potsdam Conference convenes	2.60
519	60¢ Churchill resigns	2.60
520	$1 Enola Gay drops atomic bomb on Hiroshima, 1945	5.25
521-24	75¢ VJ Day, 4 attached	19.60
	1994 WWII Anniversary Issues (continued)	
562	$1 MacArthur returns to the Philippines, souvenir sheet	5.20
563	$1 Harry S. Truman/UN Charter souvenir sheet	4.95

567

1993 (continued)

SCOTT NO.	DESCRIPTION	UNUSED F/NH
567-70	29¢ New Capitol	2.90

571

572

576

SCOTT NO.	DESCRIPTION	UNUSED F/NH
571	50¢ Super Tanker "Eagle" souvenir sheet	1.35
572-75	29¢ Life in the 1800s, 4 attached	3.20
576	29¢ Christmas 1993	1.10

577

1994

SCOTT NO.	DESCRIPTION	UNUSED F/NH
577	$2.90 15th Anniversary Constitution souvenir sheet	7.20

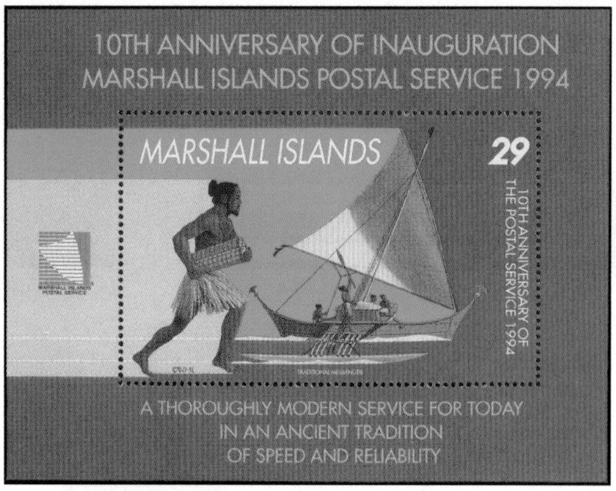

578

SCOTT NO.	DESCRIPTION	UNUSED F/NH
578	29¢ 10th Anniversary Postal Service souvenir sheet	1.05

579

583

582a

SCOTT NO.	DESCRIPTION	UNUSED F/NH
579-80	50¢ World Cup Soccer, 2 attached	6.35
582	50¢ Solar System, Planets, sheetlet of 12	22.75
583-86	75¢ 25th Anniversary of First Moon Landing, 4 attached	8.10
586b	$3 25th Anniversary of First Moon Landing, souvenir sheet	8.10

587a

588

SCOTT NO.	DESCRIPTION	UNUSED F/NH
587	"PHILAKOREA '94" souvenir sheet of 3	5.80
588	29¢ Christmas 1994	1.00

589

1995

SCOTT NO.	DESCRIPTION	UNUSED F/NH
589	50¢ New Year 1995 (Year of the Boar)	2.00

SCOTT NO.	DESCRIPTION	UNUSED F/NH

590a

591a

592a

1995

590	55¢ Marine Life, 4 attached	9.80
591	55¢ John F. Kennedy, strip of 6	8.65
592	75¢ Marilyn Monroe, 4 attached	8.64

593a

594a

593	32¢ Cats, 4 attached	4.35
594	75¢ Space Shuttle, 4 attached	7.50

595a

595	60¢ Pacific Game Fish, 8 attached	19.00

596a

597a

596	32¢ Island Legends, 4 attached, plus 4 labels	3.50
597	32¢ Orchids (Singapore'95), minature sheet of 4	3.50

598

598	50¢ Suzhou Gardens souvenir sheet	1.30

SCOTT NO.	DESCRIPTION	UNUSED F/NH

599

600a

601

599	32¢ Christmas 1995	1.00
600	32¢ Jet Fighter Planes, sheetlet of 25	20.25
601	32¢ Yitzhak Rabin	1.05

603a

604a

1996

602	50¢ New Year 1996 (Year of the Rat)	1.50
603	32¢ Native Birds, 4 attached	8.65
604	55¢ Wild Cats, 4 attached	7.20

605a

606a

607a

608

605	32¢ Sailing Ships, sheetlet of 25	20.50
606	60¢ Olympic Games Centenary, 4 attached	6.70
607	55¢ History of the Marshall Islands, sheetlet of 12	18.15
608	32¢ Elvis Presley First #1 Hit 40th Anniversary	2.30

609

609	50¢ The Palance Museum, Shenyang souvenir sheet	1.75

610

611a

612a

1996 (continued)

SCOTT NO.	DESCRIPTION	UNUSED F/NH
610	32¢ James Dean	1.75
611	60¢ Automobiles, sheet of 8	11.25
612	32¢ Island Legends 1996, 4 attached	3.20

613a

614a

615

SCOTT NO.	DESCRIPTION	UNUSED F/NH
613	55¢ Steam Locomotives, sheet of 12	17.30
614	32¢ Marine Life (Taipei '96), miniature sheet of 4	3.20
615	$3 Stick Chart, Canoe & Flag of the Republic	8.35

616

617a

618a

SCOTT NO.	DESCRIPTION	UNUSED F/NH
616	32¢ Christmas 1996	1.00
617	32¢ World's Legendary Biplanes, sheet of 25	20.50
618	32¢ Native Crafts, 4 attached	3.20

620

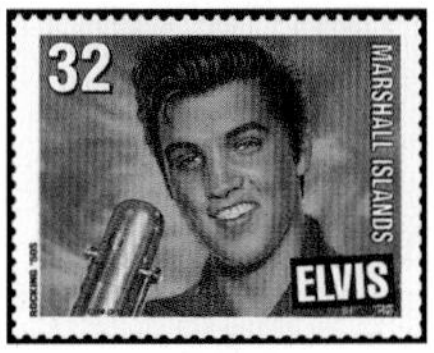

622a

623

1997

SCOTT NO.	DESCRIPTION	UNUSED F/NH
619	60¢ New Year 1997 (Year of the Ox)	1.45
620-21	32¢-60¢ Amata Kabua, President of Marshall Islands, set of 2	2.50
622	32¢ Elvis Presley, strip of 3	3.20
623-24	32¢ Hong Kong '97, 2 sheets of 2	3.50

625a

627a

628

SCOTT NO.	DESCRIPTION	UNUSED F/NH
625	60¢ The Twelve Apostles, sheet of 12	17.30
626	$3 Rubens "The Last Supper", souvenir sheet	7.50
627	60¢ First Decade of the 20th Century, sheet of 15	22.50
628	60¢ Deng Xiaoping (1904-97), Chinese Leader	1.55
629	32¢ Native Crafts (1996), 4 attached, self-adhesive, Die-Cut	4.65
630	32¢ Native Crafts (1996), 4 attached, self-adhesive, perf.	4.65
631-37	50¢-$1 Anniv. 1st US & Marshall Islands Stamps, booklet of 7	12.40

638

640a

641a

SCOTT NO.	DESCRIPTION	UNUSED F/NH
638	16¢ Bristle-Thighed Curlew, strip of 4	1.90
639	50¢ Bank of China, Hong Kong, souvenir sheet	2.15
640	32¢ Canoes, strip of 4	4.05
641	32¢ Legendary Aircraft, sheet of 25	22.75

642a

643a

646a

SCOTT NO.	DESCRIPTION	UNUSED F/NH
642	32¢ "Old Ironsides" Bicentennial	.95
643	32¢ Island Legends, 4 attached	3.50
644	60¢ Marine Life, 4 attached	6.35
645	60¢ Princess Diana, strip of 3	5.20
646	60¢ Events of the 20th Century, 1910-19, sheetlet of 15	25.95

647-48

649a

SCOTT NO.	DESCRIPTION	UNUSED F/NH
647-48	32¢ Christmas, Angel, pair	1.85
649	20¢ US State-Named Warships, sheet of 50	28.80
650	50¢ Treasure Ship, Shanghai '97, souvenir sheet	1.45

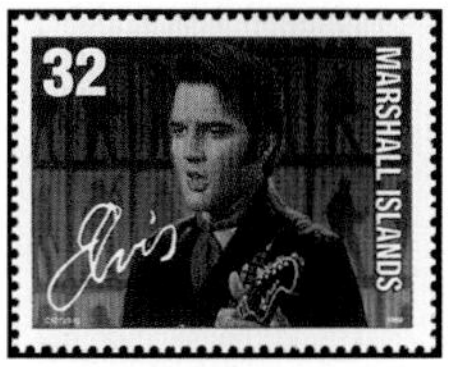

652a

653a

654a

655a

1998

SCOTT NO.	DESCRIPTION	UNUSED F/NH
651	60¢ Year of the Tiger, souvenir sheet	1.75
652	32¢ Elvis Presley's 1968 Television Special, strip of 3	2.90
653	32¢ Sea Shells, strip of 4	3.75
654	60¢ Events of the 20th Century, 1920-29, sheetlet of 15	25.95
655	32¢ Canoes of the Pacific, sheetlet of 8	7.50

665

667a

670

SCOTT NO.	DESCRIPTION	UNUSED F/NH
656	60¢ Berlin Airlift, 4 attached	6.85
657	60¢ Events of the 20th Century, 1930-39, sheetlet of 15	25.95
658-64	60¢-$3 Tsar Nicholas II, bklt of 7 (60¢ x 6, $3 x 1)	19.00
665	32¢ Babe Ruth	.95
666	32¢ Legendary Aircraft of the US Navy, sheetlet of 25	22.50
667	60¢ Chevrolet Automobiles, sheetlet of 8	13.55
668	33¢ Marshalese Language and Alphabet, sheetlet of 24	22.50
669	33¢ New Buildings in Marshall Islands, strip of 3	3.20
670	32¢ Midnight Angel	.95
671-77	60¢-$3 John Glenn's Return to Space, bklt of 7 (60¢ x 6, $3 x 1)	19.00
678	$3.20 Airplane delivering supplies, souvenir sheet	8.65
679	60¢ Events of the 20th Century, 1940-49, sheetlet of 15	25.95
680	33¢ Warships, sheetlet of 25	22.75

682

701a

699a

1999

SCOTT NO.	DESCRIPTION	UNUSED F/NH
681	60¢ Year of the Rabbit, souvenir sheet	2.60
682-89	1¢-¢10 Birds (8)	33.15
690	33¢ Canoes of the Pacific, sheetlet of 8	7.50
691-98	same, self-adhesive, block of 10 (691-97 x 1, 698 x 3)	9.50
699	60¢ Great American Indian Chiefs, sheetlet of 12	20.20
700	33¢ Marshall Islands National Flag	.95
701	33¢ Flowers of the Pacific, 6 attached	5.50
702	60¢ Events of the 20th Century, 1950-59, sheetlet of 15	25.95
703	$1.20 HMAS Australia, souvenir sheet	3.50
704	33¢ Elvis Presley	1.00
705	60¢ IBRA '99 Exhibition, sheetlet of 4	6.65

706

707a

713a

714

SCOTT NO.	DESCRIPTION	UNUSED F/NH
706	33¢ Marshall Islands Constitution, 20th Anniversary	.95
707	33¢ Marshall Islands Postal Service, 15th Anniversary, 4 attached	4.65
708	33¢ Legendary Aircraft, sheetlet of 25	22.50
709	$1 PHILEXFRANCE '99, souvenir sheet	2.80
710	60¢ Tanker Alrehab, souvenir sheet	1.75
711	60¢ Events of the 20th Century, 1960-69, sheetlet of 15	24.80
712	33¢ 1st Manned Moonlanding, 30th Anniversary, sheetlet of 3	2.80
713	33¢ Ships, 4 attached	3.75
714-21	5¢-$5 Birds, set of 8	34.00

722

728a

729a

SCOTT NO.	DESCRIPTION	UNUSED F/NH
722	33¢ Christmas	.95
723	60¢ Events of the 20th Century, 1970-79, sheetlet of 15	24.80
724-25	33¢ Millenium, 2 attached	1.85

2000

SCOTT NO.	DESCRIPTION	UNUSED F/NH
726	60¢ Events of the 20th Century, 1980-89, sheetlet of 15	24.80
727	60¢ New Year 2000 (Year of the Dragon), souvenir sheet	1.75
728	33¢ Legendary Aircraft, sheetlet of 25	22.50
729	33¢ Roses, 6 attached	5.80
730	60¢ Events of the 20th Century, 1990-99, sheetlet of 15	22.50

731a

739a

SCOTT NO.	DESCRIPTION	UNUSED F/NH
731	33¢ Pandas, 6 attached	5.80
732-38	1¢-42¢ American Presidents, 7 sheetlets of 6	22.75
739	33¢ First Zepplin Flight, 4 attached	3.50

740

747a

SCOTT NO.	DESCRIPTION	UNUSED F/NH
740-46	60¢-$1 Sir Winston Churchill, bklt of 7 (60¢ x 6, $1 x 1)	13.55
747	33¢ US Military 225th Anniversary, 3 attached	2.80

748a

750a

SCOTT NO.	DESCRIPTION	UNUSED F/NH
748	33¢ National Government, 4 attached	3.50
749	60¢ Ships, 6 attached	10.10
750	60¢ Queen Mother's 100th birthday, 4 attached	6.65

752a

754a

SCOTT NO.	DESCRIPTION	UNUSED F/NH
751	33¢ Reef Life, sheetlet of 8	6.95
752	60¢ Butterflies, sheetlet of 12	20.20
753	33¢ Reunification of Germany, 10th Anniversary	.95
754	33¢ Submarines, 4 attached	4.35

SCOTT NO.	DESCRIPTION	UNUSED F/NH
755	33¢ Christmas	.80
756	60¢-$1 Sun Yat-sen, bklt of 7 (60¢ x 6, $1 x 1)	10.50

758

2001

SCOTT NO.	DESCRIPTION	UNUSED F/NH
757	80¢ Year of the Snake, souvenir sheet	2.60
758	34¢ Carnations, stamp + label	1.10
759	34¢ Violets, stamp + label	1.10
760	34¢ Jonguil, stamp + label	1.10
761	34¢ Sweet Pea, stamp + label	1.10
762	34¢ Lily of the Valley, stamp + label	1.10
763	34¢ Rose, stamp + label	1.10
764	34¢ Larkspur, stamp + label	1.10
765	34¢ Poppy, stamp + label	1.10
766	34¢ Aster, stamp + label	1.10
767	34¢ Marigold, stamp + label	1.10
768	34¢ Chrysanthemum, stamp + label	1.10
769	34¢ Poinsettia, stamp + label	1.10

770

772

SCOTT NO.	DESCRIPTION	UNUSED F/NH
770-71	$5-$10 Sailing Canoes	43.20
772-75	34¢-$1 Famous People, set of 4	8.65
776	80¢ Butterflies, sheetlet of 12	29.75

777a

778a

SCOTT NO.	DESCRIPTION	UNUSED F/NH
777	34¢ Fairy Tales, 7 varieties attached	8.00
778	34¢ Watercraft Racing, 4 attached	4.20
779	80¢ Manned Spacecraft 40th Anniv, 4 attached	10.35

780a

783a

SCOTT NO.	DESCRIPTION	UNUSED F/NH
780	34¢ Stamp Day	1.10
781	80¢ American Achievements in Space, 4 attached	10.35
782	34¢ Marine Life, 4 attached	4.20
783	34¢ Sports, 4 attached	4.20
784	57¢ Atlan Anien	1.75

785a

788a

798a

SCOTT NO.	DESCRIPTION	UNUSED F/NH
785	34¢ Zodiac Signs, sheetlet of 12	12.70
786	80¢ Phila Nippon 2001, sheetlet of 12	29.70
787	80¢ US Naval Heroes in WWII Pacific Theater, sheetlet of 9	21.60
788	34¢ Classic Cars, 8 attached	8.65
789	34¢-¢1 Remembrance of Victims of Sept. 11, bklt of 7 (34¢ x 6, $1 x 1)	10.10
790	34¢ Christmas, 4 attached	4.20
791	80¢ Airplanes, 10 attached	23.90

2002

SCOTT NO.	DESCRIPTION	UNUSED F/NH
792	80¢ Year of the Horse, souvenir sheet	2.25
793	34¢ Shells, 6 attached	5.80
794	80¢ Reign of Queen Elizabeth, 50th Anniv., souvenir sheet	2.25
795	34¢ United We Stand	1.00
796	34¢ Classic Cars, 8 attached	8.10
797	34¢ Corals, 4 attached	6.50
798	80¢ Butterflies, sheet of 12	28.55

802a

804

SCOTT NO.	DESCRIPTION	UNUSED F/NH
799	34¢ Horses in Art, sheet of 12	11.50
800	80¢ Horses in Art, souvenir sheet	2.25
801	37¢ Russian Fairy Tale The Frog Princess, sheet of 12	12.65
802	80¢ Carousel Figures, 4 attached	9.20
803	37¢ Birds, sheet of 16	17.30
804	80¢ Benjamin Franklin, 2 attached	4.55
805	37¢ Sea Turtles, 4 attached	4.55
806	80¢ Intl. Federation of Stamp Dealers, 50 Anniv., 6 attached	13.85
807	37¢ U.S. Navy Ships, 6 attached	6.35

808a

812a

SCOTT NO.	DESCRIPTION	UNUSED F/NH
808	23¢ Insects and Spiders, sheet of 20	13.25
809	80¢ Classic Cars, 8 attached	18.40
810	80¢ Queen Mother, redrawn, 4 attached	9.50
811	80¢ Regal Princess Cruise Ship, souvenir sheet	2.25
812	80¢ World War I Heroes, 8 attached	18.40
813	37¢ Snowman cookies, 2 attached	2.15

815

817

2003

SCOTT NO.	DESCRIPTION	UNUSED F/NH
814	80¢ Year of the Ram, souvenir sheet	2.25
815	60¢ UN Membership, 12th Anniv.	1.75
816	50¢ Folktales, block of 4	5.70
817-19	37¢-$13.65 Famous People	50.15
820	37¢ Marshallese Culture, block of 8	8.65

821a

SCOTT NO.	DESCRIPTION	UNUSED F/NH
821	80¢ Butterflies, sheetlet of 12	27.40
822	37¢ Powered Flight Centenary, blk of 10	10.35

SCOTT NO.	DESCRIPTION	UNUSED F/NH
823	37¢ Classic Cars, 8 attached	8.65
824	37¢ Marshallese Culture, part 2, 8 attached	8.65
825	37¢ Christmas Ornaments, 4 attached	4.35

827a

833a

2004

SCOTT NO.	DESCRIPTION	UNUSED F/NH
826	$1 Year of the Monkey, souvenir sheet	2.90
827	37¢ Ships, type of 2002, strip of 3	3.20
828	37¢ Classic Cars, type of 2001, 4 attached	8.65
829	37¢ Greetings, sheet of 8	8.65
830-32	37¢ Marshall Islands Postal Service 20th Anniv., set of 3	9.25
833	37¢ Lewis & Clark Expedition, strip of 3	3.20

834a

837a

SCOTT NO.	DESCRIPTION	UNUSED F/NH
834	37¢ D-Day, 60th Anniversary, 4 attached	4.35
835	37¢ Marine Life, 2 attached	2.20
836	60¢ President Ronald Reagan	1.75
837	37¢ First Manned Moon Landing, 35th Anniv., 4 attached	4.35
838	37¢ Festival of the Arts, sheet of 12	12.40
839	23¢ Aircraft, sheet of 50	34.00
840	37¢ Lewis & Clark Expedition, type of 2004, strip of 3	3.20

841

842a

SCOTT NO.	DESCRIPTION	UNUSED F/NH
841	37¢ John Wayne	1.05
842	$1 23rd UPU Congress, Bucharest, Romania, sheet of 4	11.25
843	37¢ Marine Life, sheet of 10	10.40

844a

SCOTT NO.	DESCRIPTION	UNUSED F/NH
844	37¢ Christmas, sheet of 9	9.40
845	37¢ Lewis & Clark Expedition, type of 2004, strip of 3	3.20
846	37¢ Battle of the Bulge, 60th Anniv., block of 4	4.35

847a

849

2005

SCOTT NO.	DESCRIPTION	UNUSED F/NH
847	1¢-$1 United States Presidents, sheet of 45	35.00
848	$1 Year of the Rooster, souvenir sheet	2.50
849	37¢ Rotary International, Centennial	.95
850-53	37¢-$1 Hibiscus Varieties, set of 4	6.85

854a

856

SCOTT NO.	DESCRIPTION	UNUSED F/NH
854	37¢ Hans Christian Anderson, 4 attached	3.75
855	Lewis & Clark Expedition, type of 2004, strip Of 3	2.80
856	37¢ American First Day Cover Society, 50th Anniversary, 4 attached	3.75

857a

860

858a

SCOTT NO.	DESCRIPTION	UNUSED F/NH
857	37¢ VE Day, 60th Anniversary, 4 attached	3.75
858	37¢ Pope John Paul II, 5 attached	4.75
859	37¢-80¢ United Nations, 60th Anniversary, 2 attached	2.90
860-63	1¢-$4 Hibiscus Varieties, set of 4	11.25

864a

865a

SCOTT NO.	DESCRIPTION	UNUSED F/NH
864	37¢ Space Shuttles, 5 attached	4.75
865	37¢ Classic Cars Type of 2001, 8 attached	7.50

866a

867a

SCOTT NO.	DESCRIPTION	UNUSED F/NH
866	37¢ VJ Day, 60th Anniv., 4 attached	3.75
867	37¢ Lewis & Clark Expedition, type of 2004, strip of 3	2.80
868	37¢ Battle of Trafalgar, Bicentennial, sheet of 25	23.75
869	37¢ Battle of Trafalgar, souvenir sheet	4.90

870a

871a

SCOTT NO.	DESCRIPTION	UNUSED F/NH
870	37¢ Christmas, 4 attached	3.75
871	37¢ Lewis & Clark Expedition, type of 2004, strip of 3	2.90

872a

873a

SCOTT NO.	DESCRIPTION	UNUSED F/NH
872	37¢ Marshallese Culture, 5 attached	4.75
873	48¢ Benjamin Franklin, sheet of 9	10.95

875

877

2006

SCOTT NO.	DESCRIPTION	UNUSED F/NH
874	$1 Year of the Dog, souvenir sheet	2.50
875	39¢ Love	1.05
876	84¢ Butterflies, sheet of 12	15.00
877	39¢ First Spaceflight by Yuri Gagarin	1.05

880

883a

SCOTT NO.	DESCRIPTION	UNUSED F/NH
878-81	10¢-$4.05 Hibiscus Varieties, set of 4	12.00
882	1/2¢-50¢ Washington 2006 World Philatelic Exhibition, souvenir sheet of 20	5.00
883	39¢ Sharks, 4 attached	4.00
884	39¢ Operations Crossroads, sheet of 6 stamps + 6 labels	6.00
885	39¢ Lewis and Clark, 2 attached	2.00
886	39¢ Marshallese Culture, 5 attached	5.00
887	39¢ Ships, sheet of 10	11.00
888	39¢ Christmas	1.00

2007

SCOTT NO.	DESCRIPTION	UNUSED F/NH
889	39¢ Greetings, 4 attached	4.00
890	$1 Year of the Pig, souvenir sheet	2.25
891	39¢ Railway Passenger Trains, 6 attached	6.00

SEMI-POSTAL

1996

SCOTT NO.	DESCRIPTION	UNUSED F/NH
B1	32¢+8¢ 50th Anniv. of Nuclear Testing, sheet of 6	7.20

AIR POST

1985

SCOTT NO.	DESCRIPTION	UNUSED F/NH
C1-2	44¢ Audubon Birds, attached	3.40

C8

C9

1986-89

SCOTT NO.	DESCRIPTION	UNUSED F/NH
C3-6	44¢ AMERIPEX '86, attached	5.20
C7	44¢ Operation Crossroads, souvenir sheet	6.05
C8	44¢ Statue of Liberty, Peace	1.40
C9-12	44¢ Girl Scouts, attached	4.65

C13

SCOTT NO.	DESCRIPTION	UNUSED F/NH
C13-16	44¢ Marine Birds, attached	4.90

C17

C22

SCOTT NO.	DESCRIPTION	UNUSED F/NH
C17-20	44¢ CAPEX '87, attached	5.25
C21	45¢ Space Shuttle	1.35
C22-25	12¢-45¢ Aircraft	4.05

Booklet Panes

SCOTT NO.	DESCRIPTION	UNUSED F/NH
C22a	12¢ Dornier DO288, pane (10)	5.50
C23a	36¢ Boeing 737, pane (10)	13.25
C24a	39¢ Hawker 748, pane (10)	14.70
C25a	45¢ Boeing 727, pane (10)	15.85
C25b	5 (36¢) & 5 (45¢), pane (10)	14.40

POSTAL STATIONERY

UX1

SCOTT NO.	DESCRIPTION	UNUSED F/NH
UX1	20¢ Elvis Presley, postal card (1996)	3.75
UX2-5	20¢ Canoes, set of 4	6.00
UX6	20¢ Heavenly Angels, Christmas (1996)	2.00
UX7	32¢ Turtle (1997)	2.00

FEDERATED STATES OF MICRONESIA

Micronesia, formed from the major portion of the Caroline Islands, became postally autonomous in 1984. It forms part of the U.S. administered Trust Territories of the Pacific.

3

5

1984 COMMEMORATIVES

SCOTT NO.	DESCRIPTION	UNUSED F/NH
1-4	20¢ Postal Service, attached	2.90

1984 DEFINITIVES

SCOTT NO.	DESCRIPTION	UNUSED F/NH
5-20	**1¢-$5 16 varieties, singles, complete set**	**28.50**
5	1¢ Pedro de Quiros	
6	2¢ Louis Duperrey	
7	3¢ Fyedor Lutke	
8	4¢ Dumont d'Urville	
9	5¢ Men's House, Yap	
10	10¢ Sleeping Lady Hill	
11	13¢ Lidudhriab Waterfall	
12	17¢ Tonachau Peak	
13	19¢ Pedro de Quiros	
14	20¢ Louis Duperrey	
15	30¢ Fyedor Lutke	
16	37¢ Dumont d'Urville	
17	50¢ Devil Mask, Truk	
18	$1 Sokeh's Rock	
19	$2 Canoes	
20	$5 Stone Money	

21

1984 COMMEMORATIVES

SCOTT NO.	DESCRIPTION	UNUSED F/NH
21 & C4-6	20¢-40¢ AUSIPEX '84, 4 varieties	4.35

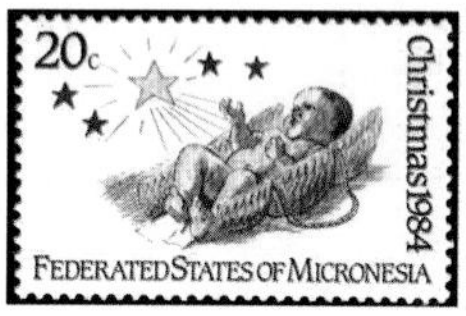

22

SCOTT NO.	DESCRIPTION	UNUSED F/NH
22 & C7-9	20¢-40¢ Christmas '84, 4 varieties	6.05

23

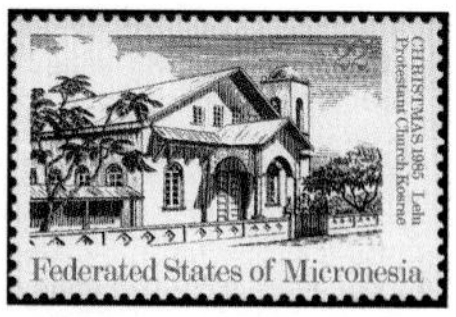

24

1985 COMMEMORATIVES

SCOTT NO.	DESCRIPTION	UNUSED F/NH
23 & C10-12	22¢-44¢ Ships, 4 varieties	4.35
24 & C13-14	22¢-44¢ Christmas '85, 3 varieties	4.35
25-28 & C15	22¢ Audubon, booklet of 4 attached, & 44¢ airmail	4.35

25

SCOTT NO.	DESCRIPTION	UNUSED F/NH
25-28 & C15	22¢ Audubon, booklet of 4 attached, & 44¢ airmail	4.55

31

34

39

1985-88 DEFINITIVES

SCOTT NO.	DESCRIPTION	UNUSED F/NH
31-39 & C34-36	**12 varieties, singles, complete set**	**34.60**
31	3¢ Long-billed	
32	14¢ Truk Monarch	
33	15¢ Waterfall	
34	22¢ Tall Ship Senyavin	
35	22¢ Pohnpei Mountain starling	
36	25¢ Tonachau Peak	
37	36¢ Tall Ship	
38	45¢ Sleeping Lady	
39	$10 National Seal	
C34	33¢ Great truk white-eye	
C35	44¢ Blue-faced parrotfinch	
C36	$1 Yap monarch	

Booklet Panes 1988

SCOTT NO.	DESCRIPTION	UNUSED F/NH
33a	15¢ booklet pane of (10)	10.35
36a	25¢ booklet pane of (10)	11.25
36b	booklet pane of (10), 5—15¢ & 5—25¢	12.70

45

1985 COMMEMORATIVES & AIR MAILS

SCOTT NO.	DESCRIPTION	UNUSED F/NH
45 & C16-18	22¢-44¢ Nan Mandol Ruins, 4 varieties	4.65

46

52

53

1986 COMMEMORATIVES & AIRMAILS

SCOTT NO.	DESCRIPTION	UNUSED F/NH
46 & C19-20	22¢, 44¢ Peace Year	5.50
48-51	22¢ on 20¢ Postal Service, block of 4 attached	2.90
52 & C21-24	22¢-44¢ AMERIPEX '86, 5 varieties	6.05
53	22¢ Passport	.90

54

SCOTT NO.	DESCRIPTION	UNUSED F/NH
54-55 & C26-27	5¢-44¢ Christmas, 4 varieties	4.90

56

58

1987 COMMEMORATIVES & AIR MAILS

SCOTT NO.	DESCRIPTION	UNUSED F/NH
56 & C28-30	22¢-44¢ Shelter for Homeless, 4 varieties	5.20
57	$1 CAPEX '87 souvenir sheet	5.20
58 & C31-33	22¢-44¢ Christmas, 4 varieties	4.35

59

63

67

1988 COMMEMORATIVES & AIR MAILS

SCOTT NO.	DESCRIPTION	UNUSED F/NH
59-62 & C37-38	22¢, 44¢ Colonial Flags, 7 varieties	6.65
63-66	25¢ & 45¢ Summer Olympics, 2 pairs	3.30
67-70	25¢ Christmas, block of 4 attached	2.80
71	25¢ Truk Lagoon, souvenir sheet of 18 varieties	13.25

72

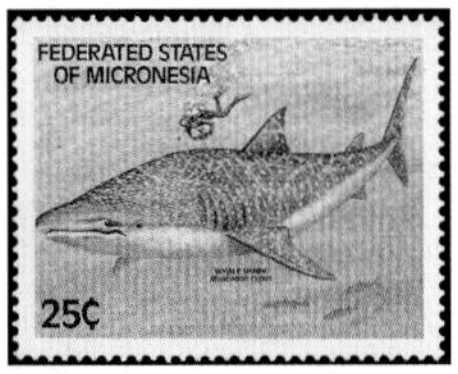

77

1989 COMMEMORATIVES

SCOTT NO.	DESCRIPTION	UNUSED F/NH
72-75	45¢ Flowers, block of 4 attached	5.20
76	$1 Japanese Art souvenir sheet	2.90
77-80	25¢, 45¢ Sharks, attached, 2 pairs	4.05
81	25¢ Space Achievements souvenir sheet of 9	7.80

82

83

SCOTT NO.	DESCRIPTION	UNUSED F/NH
82	$2.40 Priority Mail	6.65
83-102	1¢-$5 Seashells (12)	26.25
85a	15¢ Commercial trochus pane (10)	10.10
88a	25¢ Triton's trumpet pane (10)	15.85
88b	5 (15¢) + 5 (25¢) pane 10	15.85

103a

104

SCOTT NO.	DESCRIPTION	UNUSED F/NH
103	25¢ Fruits & Flowers, sheet of 18	13.55
104-05	Christmas	2.05

106

110

1990 COMMEMORATIVES

SCOTT NO.	DESCRIPTION	UNUSED F/NH
106-09	World Wildlife Fund (4 varieties)	6.35
110-13	45¢ Whaling Ships & Artifacts, 4 attached	5.20
114	$1 Whaling Souvenir Sheet	2.90
115	$1 Penny Black Anniversary Souvenir Sheet	2.90

116

122

SCOTT NO.	DESCRIPTION	UNUSED F/NH
116-20	25¢ P.A.T.S. strip of 5	3.75
121	$1 Expo '90 Souvenir Sheet	2.90
122-23	25¢ & 45¢ Loading Mail	2.60

124

127

SCOTT NO.	DESCRIPTION	UNUSED F/NH
124-26	25¢ Joint Issue, 3 attached	2.60
127-30	45¢ Moths, 4 attached	5.20

131a

SCOTT NO.	DESCRIPTION	UNUSED F/NH
131	25¢ Christmas, sheetlet of 9	6.65

134

138

143a

1991

SCOTT NO.	DESCRIPTION	UNUSED F/NH
132	25¢+45¢ Government bldgs., Souvenir Sheet of 2	2.05
133	$1 New Capitol Souvenir Sheet	2.90
134-37	29¢+50¢ Turtles, 2 pairs	7.20
138-41	29¢ Operation Desert Storm, 4 attached	3.50
142	$2.90 Operation Desert Storm Priority Mail	7.20
142a	$2.90 Operation Desert Storm Souvenir Sheet	7.50
143	29¢ Phila Nippon Souvenir Sheet of 3	2.60
144	50¢ Phila Nippon Souvenir Sheet of 3	4.35
145	$1 Phila Nippon Souvenir Sheet	2.90

SCOTT NO.	DESCRIPTION	UNUSED F/NH

146

149a

1991 (continued)

146-48	29¢ Christmas 1991 set of 3	3.20
149	29¢ Pohnpei Rain Forest, sheetlet of 18	19.00

150a

151a

1992

150	29¢ Peace Corps/Kennedy, strip of 5	4.05
151	29¢ Columbus, strip of 3	6.65

152

154

152-53	29¢, 50¢ UN Membership Anniversary	5.20
153a	same, Souvenir Sheet of 2	5.20
154	29¢ Christmas, 1992	2.60

155a

156

1993

155	29¢ Pioneers of Flight I, 8 attached	6.65

1993-94

156-67	10¢-$2.90, Fish, 16 varieties	27.60

168a

172

173

SCOTT NO.	DESCRIPTION	UNUSED F/NH

177a

179

182

1993

168	29¢ Sailing Ships, sheetlet of 12	21.60
172	29¢ Thomas Jefferson	1.10
173-76	29¢ Canoes, 4 attached	4.35
177	29¢ Local Leaders I, strip of 4	3.50
178	50¢ Pioneers of Flight II, 8 attached	11.25
179-80	29¢, 50¢ Tourist Attractions, Pohnpei	2.90
181	$1 Tourist Attractions, Souvenir Sheet	2.80
182-83	29¢, 50¢ Butterflies, 2 pairs	4.90

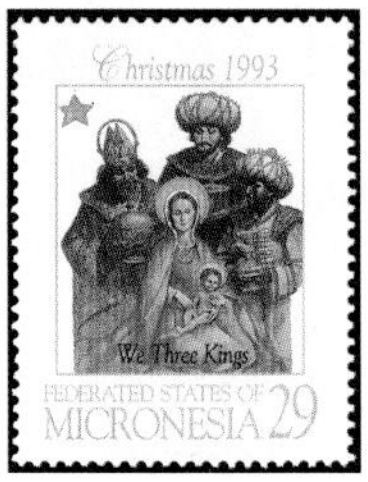

184

186a

184-85	29¢-50¢ Christmas 1993	2.60
186	29¢ Micronesia Culture, sheetlet of 18	18.15

192a

193a

194

1994

187-89	29¢-50¢ Tourist Attractions, Kosrae	3.40
190	"Hong Kong '94" miniature sheet of 4 (#182a, 182b, 183a, 183b)	6.05
191	29¢ Pioneers of Flight III, 8 attached	8.65
192	29¢ 1994 Micronesian Games, 4 attached	4.05
193	29¢ Native Costumes, 4 attached	4.05
194	29¢ Constitution, 15th Anniversary	2.25

195a

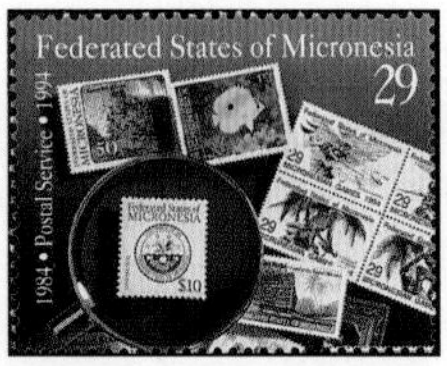

198a

196

195	29¢ Flowers, strip of 4	4.05
196-97	50¢ World Cup Soccer, pair	6.65
198	29¢ 10th Anniv. Inauguration Postal Service, 4 attached	6.85

199a

201a

202

SCOTT NO.	DESCRIPTION	UNUSED F/NH
199	"PHILAKOREA '94" Dinosaur, miniature sheet of 3	7.20
200	50¢ Pioneers of Flight IV, 8 attached	11.50
201	29¢ Migratory Birds, 4 attached	7.20
202-03	29¢, 50¢ Christmas 1994	4.90
204-07	32¢ Local Leaders II, set of 4	7.50

208

1995

SCOTT NO.	DESCRIPTION	UNUSED F/NH
208	50¢ New Year 1995 (Year of the Boar)	1.75

209a

211a

228a

SCOTT NO.	DESCRIPTION	UNUSED F/NH
209	32¢ Chuuk Lagoon, 4 attached	9.25
210	32¢ Pioneers of Flight V, 8 attached	7.20
211	32¢ Dogs, 4 attached	4.35
213-26	32¢-$5.00 Fish, set of 7	31.00
227	32¢ Fish, sheetlet of 25 (1996)	29.70
228	32¢ Flowers II, strip of 4	3.65
229	$1 UN 50th Anniversary Souvenir Sheet	2.80

230a

231a

SCOTT NO.	DESCRIPTION	UNUSED F/NH
230	32¢ Orchids (Singapore '95), min. sheet of 4	3.75
231	60¢ US Warships, 4 attached	6.65
232	50¢ Temple of Heaven Souvenir Sheet	1.45
233	60¢ Pioneers of Flight VI, 8 attached	13.85

234

236

SCOTT NO.	DESCRIPTION	UNUSED F/NH
234-35	32¢-60¢ Christmas Poinsettias	2.55
236	32¢ Yitzhak Rabin	1.30

238a

239a

240a

241a

1996

SCOTT NO.	DESCRIPTION	UNUSED F/NH
237	50¢ New Year 1996 (Year of the Rat)	1.75
238	32¢ Pioneers of Flight VII, 8 attached	9.25
239	32¢ Tourism in Yap, 4 attached	4.35
240	55¢ Sea Stars, 4 attached	6.95
241	60¢ Olympic Games Centenary, 4 attached	8.65
242	50¢ The Tarrying Garden, Suzhou Souvenir Sheet	2.05

243

245a

SCOTT NO.	DESCRIPTION	UNUSED F/NH
243-44	32¢ Marine Vessels, 2 attached	3.30
245	55¢ Automobile, sheet of 8	13.55

247

249a

248a

SCOTT NO.	DESCRIPTION	UNUSED F/NH
247	32¢ Police Drug Enforcement Dog	1.75
248	32¢ Citrus Fruit, strip of 4	8.95
249	60¢ Pioneers of Flight VIII, 8 attached	17.30

250a

251

253

1996 (continued)

SCOTT NO.	DESCRIPTION	UNUSED F/NH
250	32¢ Fish (Taipei '96), miniature sheet of 4	5.20
251-52	32¢-60¢ Christmas 1996, set of 2	3.50
253	$3 Canoe & Flag of Micronesia	9.25

257, 258

1997

SCOTT NO.	DESCRIPTION	UNUSED F/NH
254	60¢ Deng Xiaoping, sheet of 4	8.10
255	$3 Deng Xiaoping, souvenir sheet	9.50
256	$2 Bridge to the Future, salute to Hong Kong, souvenir sheet	7.80
257	32¢ Year of the Ox	1.45
258	$2 Year of the Ox, souvenir sheet	6.35

259

SCOTT NO.	DESCRIPTION	UNUSED F/NH
259	60¢ Return of Hong Kong to China, sheet of 6	11.25
260	$3 Return of Hong Kong to China, souvenir sheet	9.50
261	32¢ Sea Goddesses of the Pacific, sheet of 6	5.50
262-64	20¢-60¢ Hiroshige, 3 sheetlets of 3	12.10
265-66	$2 Hiroshige, souvenir sheets(2)	12.40

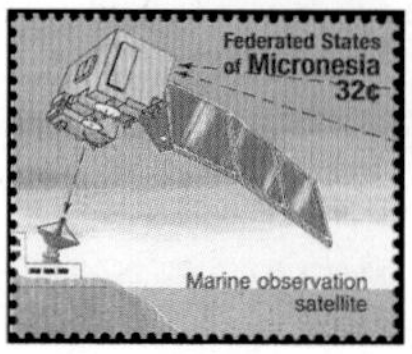

267a 268a 269a

SCOTT NO.	DESCRIPTION	UNUSED F/NH
267	32¢ 2nd Federated States of Micronesia Games, 4 attached	4.35
268	50¢ Elvis Presley, sheetlets of 6	9.25
269	32¢ Undersea Exploration, sheetlet of 9	9.00
270-72	$2 Undersea Exploration, souvenir sheets (3)	18.40

273a 274a

SCOTT NO.	DESCRIPTION	UNUSED F/NH
273	60¢ Princess Diana	1.75
274	50¢ World Wildlife Fund, Butterly Fish, 4 attached	6.35

275-76

SCOTT NO.	DESCRIPTION	UNUSED F/NH
275-76	32¢ Christmas Paintings, Fra Angelico, pair	2.00
277-78	60¢ Christmas Paintings, Simon Marmion, pair	3.75

1998

SCOTT NO.	DESCRIPTION	UNUSED F/NH
279-80	50¢ Year of the Tiger, souvenir sheets (2)	3.30
281	$1 Micronesia's Admission to the UN, sounvenir sheet	3.30
282	32¢ Disney's Winnie the Pooh, sheetlet of 8	10.70
283-84	$1 Disney's Winnie the Pooh, souvenir sheets (2)	14.40

285a

SCOTT NO.	DESCRIPTION	UNUSED F/NH
285	32¢ 1998 World Cup Soccer Championships, sheetlet of 8	8.10
286-87	$2 1998 World Cup, souvenir sheets (2)	12.40
288	$3 Olympics, souvenir sheet	9.80
289-91	32¢-60¢ Old Testament Bible Stories, 3 sheetlets of 3	10.95
292-94	$2 Old Testament Bible Stories, souvenir sheets (3)	16.70

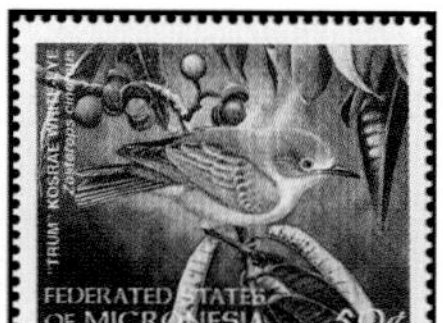

295a 299a

SCOTT NO.	DESCRIPTION	UNUSED F/NH
295	32¢ International Year of the Ocean, sheetlet of 9	8.35
296-98	$2 International Year of the Ocean, souvenir sheets (3)	17.00
299	50¢ Native Birds, 4 attached	5.60
300	$3 Native Birds, souvenir sheet	8.65

319a 320a

SCOTT NO.	DESCRIPTION	UNUSED F/NH
301-19A	1¢-$10.75 Fish, 20 varieties	59.05
320	32¢ Fala, FDR's Dog, sheetlet of 6	5.50
321-22	32¢-60¢ Christmas, 20th Century Art, 2 sheetlets of 3	7.50
323	$2 Christmas, 20th Century Art, souvenir sheet	5.80
324-25	60¢ John Glenn's Return to Space 2 sheets of 6	27.10
326-27	$2 John Glenn's Return to Space 2 souvenir sheets	11.25

SCOTT NO.	DESCRIPTION	UNUSED F/NH

328

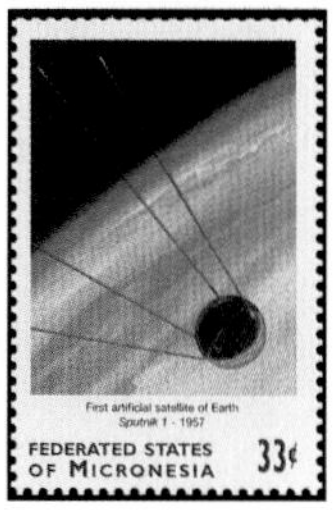

334a

342a

1999

328-33	33¢-$11.75 Fish, 6 varieties	43.20
334	33¢ Russian Space Exploration, sheetlet of 20	17.25
335-36	$2 Russsian Space Exploration 2 souvenir sheets	10.95
337-38	33¢-50¢ "Romance of the 3 Kingdoms" by Lo Kuan-chung, 2 sheetlets of 5	9.25
339	$2 "Romance of the 3 Kingdoms", souvenir sheet	5.50
340-41	55¢ IBRA '99 Exhibition, set of 2	3.05
342	$2 IBRA '99 Exhibition, souvenir sheet	5.50
343	33¢ Voyages of the Pacific, sheetlet of 20	19.00

344a

347a

344	33¢ Space Achievements, sheetlet of 20	19.00
345-46	$2 Space Achievemnets, 2 souvenir sheets	10.95
347	33¢ Earth Day-Endangered Species, sheetlet of 20	19.00
348-49	$2 Earth Day-Endangered Species, 2 souvenir sheets	10.95

356a

358

362a

350-51	33¢ Hokusai Paintings, 2 sheetlets of 6	10.95
352-53	$2 Hokusai Paintings, 2 souvenir sheets	10.95
354	50¢ Flowers, photomosaic of Princess Diana, sheetlet of 8	10.95
355	20¢ Highlights of the 12th Century, sheetlet of 17	10.10
356	33¢ Science & Technology of Ancient China, sheetlet of 17	17.00
357	33¢ Costumes, sheetlet of 20	19.00
358-60	33¢-$2 Christmas-Van Dyck Paintings	8.35
361	$2 Christmas-Van Dyck Paintings, souvenir sheet	5.50
362	33¢ Millenium-Airplanes, sheetlet of 15	14.40
363-64	$2 Millenium-Airplanes, 2 souvenir sheets	10.95

365a

372a

2000

365-67	33¢ Orchids, 3 sheetlets of 6	16.70
368-69	$1 Orchids, 2 souvenir sheets	10.95
370	33¢ Leaders of the 20th Century, sheetlet of 12	10.95
371	$2 New Year 2000 (Year of the Dragon), souvenir sheet	5.50
372-73	20¢-55¢ Butterflies, 2 sheetlets of 6	12.70
374-76	$2 Butterflies, 3 souvenir sheets	16.70
377	20¢ Highlights of the 1920's, sheetlet of 17	9.80

SCOTT NO.	DESCRIPTION	UNUSED F/NH

378

385a

378	33¢ Millennium 2000	.95
379	33¢ Peacemakers, sheetlet of 24	22.75
380	33¢ Philantropists, sheetlet of 16	15.85
381-82	33¢ Mushrooms, 2 sheetlets of 6	10.95
383-34	$2 Mushrooms, 2 souvenir sheets	10.95
385	33¢ Flowers of the Pacific, sheetlet of 6	5.50
386	33¢ Wildflowers, sheetlet of 6	5.50
387	$2 Flowers of the Pacific, souvenir sheet	5.50
388	$2 Wildflowers, souvenir sheet	5.50

389a

390a

389	33¢ 2000 Summer Olympics, Sydney, souvenir sheet of 4	3.50
390	33¢ Zeppelins & Airships, sheetlet of 6	5.50
391-92	$2 Zeppelins & Airships, 2 souvenir sheets	10.95
393	33¢ Queen Mother Flower Photomosaic, sheet of 8	7.20
394	33¢-$1 2000 Summer Olympics, Sydney, souvenir sheet of 3	4.90

395

395-98	33¢ Fish, set of 4	3.50
399-400	33¢ Fish, 2 sheetlets of 9	17.30
401-02	$2 Fish, 2 souvenir sheets	10.95
403	50¢ Pope John Paul II Photomosaic, sheet of 8	10.95

404

408a

404-07	20¢-$3.20 2000 Christmas, set of 4	12.40
408-09	33¢ Dogs & Cats, 2 sheetlets of 6	10.95
410-11	$2 Dogs & Cats, 2 souvenir sheets	10.95

414a

416a

2001

412-13	60¢ Year of the Snake, 2 souvenir sheets	3.40
414	50¢ Pokemon, sheet of 6	8.95
415	$2 Farfetch'd, souvenir sheet	6.05
416-17	50¢-60¢ Whales, 2 sheetlets of 6	18.45
418-19	$2 Whales, 2 souvenir sheets	10.95

420a

424

SCOTT NO.	DESCRIPTION	UNUSED F/NH
420	34¢ Ecology, sheetlet of 6	5.20
421	60¢ Ecology, sheetlet of 4	6.35
422-23	$2 Ecology, 2 souvenir sheets	11.55
424-28	11¢-$3.50 Fish, set of 5	14.40
429	$12.25 Blue-spotted boxfish	32.25
430-35	34¢ Japanese Art, set of 6	5.70
436	34¢ Japanese Art, sheetlet of 6	5.70
437-38	$2 Japanese Art, 2 imperf sheets	10.95
439	60¢ Toulouse-Lautrec Paintings, sheetlets of 3	4.90
440	$2 Toulouse-Lautrec Paintings, souvenir sheet	5.50
441	60¢ Queen Victoria, sheetlet of 6	10.10
442	$2 Queen Victoria, souvenir sheet	5.50
443	60¢ Queen Elizabeth II, 75th Birthday, sheet of 6	10.10
444	$2 Queen Elizabeth II, 75th Birthday, souvenir sheet	5.50

445

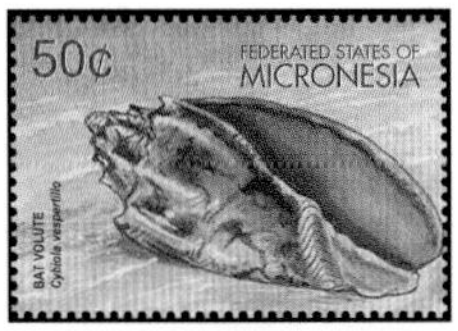

457a

SCOTT NO.	DESCRIPTION	UNUSED F/NH
445-46	60¢ Marine Life, 2 sheetlets of 6	20.20
447-48	$2 Marine Life, 2 souvenir sheets	10.95
449-52	60¢ Prehistoric Animals, set of 4	6.65
453-54	60¢ Prehistoric Animals, 2 sheetlets of 6	20.20
455-56	$2 Prehistoric Animals, 2 souvenir sheets	10.95
457-58	50¢ Shells, 2 sheetlets of 6	16.75
459-60	$2 Sheets, 2 souvenir sheets	10.95

461

469a

473

SCOTT NO.	DESCRIPTION	UNUSED F/NH
461-64	5¢-$2.10 Birds, set of 4	6.95
465-66	60¢ Birds, 2 sheetlets of 6	20.20
467-68	$2 Birds, 2 souvenir sheets	10.95
469-70	60¢ Nobel Prizes Cent., 2 sheetlets of 6	20.20
471-72	$2 Nobel Prizes Cent., 2 souvenir sheets	10.95
473-76	22¢-$1 Christmas, set of 4	5.50
477	$2 Christmas, souvenir sheet	5.50
478-79	60¢ Attack on Pearl Harbor, 60th Anniv., 2 sheetlets of 6	20.20
480-81	$2 Attack on Pearl Harbor, 60th Anniv., 2 souvenir sheets	10.95

485

492a

494a

2002

SCOTT NO.	DESCRIPTION	UNUSED F/NH
482	60¢ Year of the Horse, sheetlet of 5	8.35
483	80¢ Reign of Queen Elizabeth II, 50th Anniv., sheetlet of 4	8.95
484	$2 Reign of Queen Elizabeth II, 50th Anniv., souvenir sheet	5.50
485	$1 United We Stand	2.80
486-87	$1 2002 Winter Olympics, set of 2	5.50
488-89	60¢ Japanese Art, 2 sheetlets of 6	20.20
490-91	$2 Japanese Art, 2 souvenir sheets	10.95
492	80¢ Intl. Year of Mountains, sheet of 4	8.95
493	$2 Intl. Year of Mountains, souvenir sheet	5.50
494	60¢ President John F. Kennedy, sheet of 4	6.65
495	$2 President John F. Kennedy, souvenir sheet	5.50
496	60¢ Princess Diana, sheetlet of 6	9.80
497	$2 Princess Diana, souvenir sheet	5.50

498a

502

504

SCOTT NO.	DESCRIPTION	UNUSED F/NH
498	80¢ International Year of Eco-Tourism, sheet of 6	13.55
499	$2 International Year of Eco-Tourism, souvenir sheet	5.50
500	$1 20th World Boy Scout Jamboree, Thailand, sheet of 3	8.35
501	$2 20th World Boy Scout Jamboree, Thailand, souvenir sheet	5.50
502-03	$1 2002 Winter Olympics, redrawn smaller rings, set of 2	5.50
503a	$2 2002 Winter Olympics, redrawn smaller rings, souvenir sheet	5.50
504	37¢ Xavier High School, 50th Anniversary	1.05
505	80¢ Queen Elizabeth Memorial, souvenir sheet of 4	8.95
506	$2 Queen Elizabeth Memorial, souvenir sheet	5.50

507a

509

525

SCOTT NO.	DESCRIPTION	UNUSED F/NH
507	80¢ Teddy Bear Centennial, sheet of 4	8.95
508	37¢ Elvis Presley (1935-77), sheetlet of 6	6.35
509-13	15¢-$1 Christmas, set of 5	8.10
514	$2 Christmas, souvenir sheet`	5.50
515-19	37¢-80¢ Flora, Fauna & Mushrooms, set of 5 sheets of 6	48.00
520-24	$2 Flora, Fauna & Mushrooms, set of 5 souvenir sheets	27.40
525-37	3¢-$13.65 Bird Definitives, set of 13	72.60

538a

539a

543a

2003

SCOTT NO.	DESCRIPTION	UNUSED F/NH
538	60¢ 1st Non-Stop Solo Transatlantic Flight 75th Anniversary, sheet of 6 ...	9.80
539	37¢ Year of the Ram, sheet of 6	6.05
540	37¢ Astronauts Killed in Shuttle Columbia, In Memorium, sheet of 7	6.95
541	$1 Coronation of Queen Elizabeth II, 50th Anniversary, sheet of 3	8.40
542	$2 Coronation of Queen Elizabeth II, 50th Anniversary, souvenir sheet	5.50
543	$1 Prince Williams, 21st Birthday, sheet of 3	8.35
544	$2 Prince WIlliams, 21st Birthday, souvenir sheet	5.50

545a

551a

SCOTT NO.	DESCRIPTION	UNUSED F/NH
545-46	37¢ Operation Iraqi Freedom, set of 2 sheets of 6	12.30
547	60¢ Tour de France Bicycle Race, Centenary, sheet of 4	6.95
548	$2 Tour de France Bicycle Race, Centenary, souvenir sheet	5.50
549	$1 International Year of Freshwater, sheet of 3	8.35
550	$2 International Year of Freshwater, souvenir sheet	5.50
551	55¢ Powered Flight Centenary, sheet of 6	9.25
552	$2 Powered Flight Centenary, souvenir sheet	5.50
553-54	80¢ Circus Performers, set of 2 sheets of 4	18.15
555	80¢ Paintings of Boy Scouts by Norman Rockwell, sheet of 4	8.95
556	$2 Paintings of Boy Scouts by Norman Rockwell, souvenir sheet, imperf. .	5.50

557a

565

578

SCOTT NO.	DESCRIPTION	UNUSED F/NH
557	80¢ Paintings by Paul Gauguin, sheet of 4	8.95
558	$2 Paintings by Paul Gauguin, souvenir sheet, imperf.	5.50
559-62	37¢-80¢ Paintings by James McNeill Whistler, set of 4	6.35
563	$1 Paintings by James McNeill Whistler, sheet of 3	8.35
564	$2 Paintings by James McNeill Whistler, souvenir sheet, imperf.	5.50
565-68	37¢-80¢ Christmas, set of 4	7.80
569	$2 Christmas, souvenir sheet	5.50
570-73	80¢ Cats, Dogs, Birds & Amphibians, set of 4 sheets of 4	35.75
574-77	$2 Cats, Dogs, Birds & Amphibians, set of 4 souvenir sheets	21.90

2004

SCOTT NO.	DESCRIPTION	UNUSED F/NH
578	37¢ President Bailey Olter	1.05

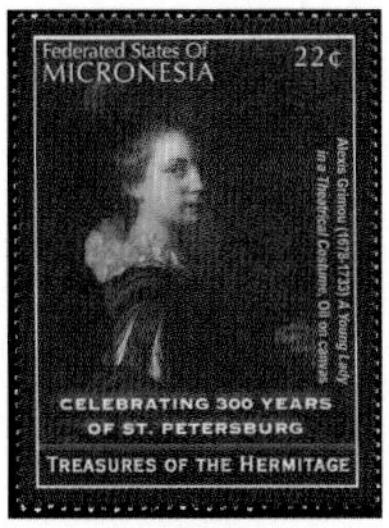

581

586

SCOTT NO.	DESCRIPTION	UNUSED F/NH
579	80¢ Paintings by Pablo Picasso, sheet of 4	8.95
580	$2 Painting by Pablo Picasso, souvenir sheet, imperf.	5.50
581-84	22¢-$1 Paintings in the Hermitage Museum, set of 4	6.65
585	$2 Painting in the Hermitage Museum, souvenir sheet, imperf.	5.50
586	50¢ Year of the Monkey	1.40
587	$1 Year of the Monkey, souvenir sheet	2.80

588a

591a

SCOTT NO.	DESCRIPTION	UNUSED F/NH
588	80¢ Election of Pope John Paul II, 25th Anniv., sheet of 4	8.95
589	80¢ 2004 European Soccer Championships, sheet of 4	8.95
590	$2 2004 European Soccer Championships, souvenir sheet	5.50
591	50¢ D-Day, 60th Anniversary, sheet of 6	8.35
592	$2 D-Day, 60th Anniversary, souvenir sheet	5.50
593	$2 Deng Xiaoping, souvenir seet	5.50

594a

607a

SCOTT NO.	DESCRIPTION	UNUSED F/NH
594-96	80¢ Locomotives, 3 sheets of 4	26.25
597-99	$2 Locomotives, 3 souvenir sheets	16.50

SCOTT NO.	DESCRIPTION	UNUSED F/NH
600-01	2¢-10¢ Birds, Type of 2002, set of 2	.50
602	80¢ International Year of Peace, sheet of 3	6.65
603-06	37¢-$1 2004 Summer Olympics, Athens, set of 4	7.50
607-08	80¢ Elvis Presley's First Recording, 50th Anniv., 2 sheets of 4	17.30
609	55¢ Flowers, sheet of 6	9.20
610	$2 Flowers, souvenir sheet	5.50
611	80¢ FIFA, Centennial, sheet of 4	8.95
612	$2 FIFA, Centennial, souvenir sheet	5.50
613-14	20¢ National Basketball Assoc. Players, set of 2	1.15

615a

625a

623a

SCOTT NO.	DESCRIPTION	UNUSED F/NH
615-17	80¢ Prehistoric Animals, 3 sheets of 4	26.25
618-20	$2 Preshistoric Animals, 3 souvenir sheets	16.75
621	55¢ Fish and Coral, sheet of 6	9.20
622	$2 Fish and Coral, Great barracuda, souvenir sheet	5.50
623	55¢ Reptiles and Amphibians, sheet of 6	9.20
624	$2 Reptiles and Amphibians, Loggerhead turtle, souvenir sheet	5.50
625	Birds of the Pacific, sheet of 6	9.20
626	55¢ Birds of the Pacific, Golden whistler, souvenir sheet	5.50
627-30	37¢-$1 Christmas, set of 4	8.95
631	$2 Chirstmas, souvenir sheet	5.50

632

634a

2005

SCOTT NO.	DESCRIPTION	UNUSED F/NH
632	50¢ Year of the Rooster	1.30
633	20¢ National Basketball Assoc. Player, Luke Walton	.60
634	55¢ Pres. Ronald Reagan, 2 attached	2.80

635a

637a

SCOTT NO.	DESCRIPTION	UNUSED F/NH
635-36	60¢ Elvis Presley, 2 sheets of 6	17.90
637-38	50¢ End of the World War II, 60th Anniv., 2 sheets of 5	15.00

639a

643

SCOTT NO.	DESCRIPTION	UNUSED F/NH
639	$1 Friedrich von Schiller, sheet of 3	7.50
640	$2 Friedrich von Schiller, souvenir sheet	4.90
641-44	37¢-$1 Battle of Trafalgar, Bicent., set of 4	6.85
645	$2 Battle of Trafalgar, Bicent., souvenir sheet	4.75

646

647a

649a

SCOTT NO.	DESCRIPTION	UNUSED F/NH
646	$1 Pope John Paul II	2.60
647	$1 Rotary International, Cent., sheet of 3	7.50
648	$2 Rotary International, Cent., souvenir sheet	4.90
649	$1 Jules Verne, sheet of 3	7.50
650	$2 Jules Verne, souvenir sheet	4.90

651a

652a

SCOTT NO.	DESCRIPTION	UNUSED F/NH
651	80¢ Nature's Wisdom, Expo 2005, Aichi, Japan, sheet of 4	8.00
652	37¢-$1 Boats, sheet of 4	6.85
653	$2 Boats, sovenir sheet	4.90

654

658

SCOTT NO.	DESCRIPTION	UNUSED F/NH
654-57	4¢-37¢ Kosrae Government Building Complex, set of 4	1.85
658	37¢ Vatican City No. 67	.95

659a

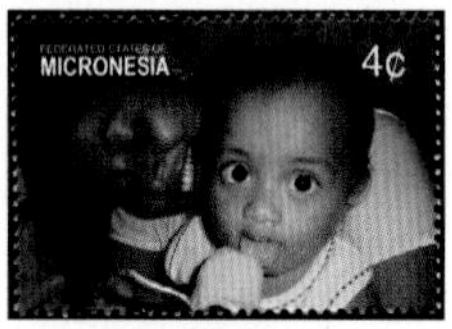

661

SCOTT NO.	DESCRIPTION	UNUSED F/NH
659	50¢ Worldwide Fund for Nature, 4 attached	5.00
660	$1 Albert Einstein, sheet of 4	9.80
661-64	4¢-37¢ Bananas, set of 4	1.95

665a

668

SCOTT NO.	DESCRIPTION	UNUSED F/NH
665	80¢ Hans Christian Anderson, sheet of 3	6.05
666	$2 Hans Christian Anderson, souvenir sheet	4.90
667	80¢ Pope Benedict XVI	2.10
668-71	37¢-$1 Christmas, set of 4	6.85
672	$2 Christmas, souvenir sheet	4.90
673-78	4¢-$1 Flowers, set of 6	6.35
679	80¢ Flowers, sheet of 4	7.00
680-81	$2 Flowers, set of 5 souvenir sheets	8.00

682

2006

SCOTT NO.	DESCRIPTION	UNUSED F/NH
682	50¢ Year of the Dog	1.30
683	$1 Year of the Dog, souvenir sheet	2.50
684-90	24¢-$4.05 Birds, set of 7	14.50
691	39¢ vice President Petrus Tun	1.05
692	$1 Rembrandt, sheet of 4	8.50
693	$2 Rembrandt, souvenir sheet	4.00
694	84¢ Queen Elizabeth II, sheet of 4	8.50
695	$2 Queen Elizabeth II, souvenir sheet	4.90
696	75¢ Space Achievements, sheet of 6	9.00
697-98	$1 Space Achievements, 2 sheets of 4	16.00
699-701	$2 Space Achievements, 3 souvenir sheets	12.00
702-13	1¢-$4.05 Butterflies, set of 12	16.00
716-20	22¢-84¢ Christmas, set of 5	5.50

C1

C39

1984-94 AIR MAIL

SCOTT NO.	DESCRIPTION	UNUSED F/NH
C1-3	28¢-40¢ Aircraft, set of 3	2.50
C25	$1 Ameripex '86 Souvenir Sheet	4.90
C39-42	45¢ State Flags, block of 4 attached	4.90

C43

SCOTT NO.	DESCRIPTION	UNUSED F/NH
C43-46	22¢-45¢ Aircraft Serving Micronesia (4 varieties)	7.50
C47-48	40¢, 50¢ Aircraft and Ships	5.20
C49	$2.90 25th Anniv. First Moon Landing, souvenir sheet	7.50

Postal Stationery

SCOTT NO.	DESCRIPTION	UNUSED F/NH
U1	20¢ National Flag	17.00
U2	22¢ Tail Ship Senyavin	12.00
U3	29¢ on 30¢ New Capitol	5.00

Postal Cards

SCOTT NO.	DESCRIPTION	UNUSED F/NH
UX1-4	20¢ Scenes, set of 4	7.50

REPUBLIC OF PALAU

Palau is a Strategic Trust of the United States; a designation granted by the United Nations after World War II. It is the first Trust Territory to be granted postal independence, which became effective November 1, 1982. The first stamps were issued March 10, 1983.

1

5

1983 COMMEMORATIVES

SCOTT NO.	DESCRIPTION	UNUSED F/NH
1-4	20¢ Art and Preamble, attached	3.50
5-8	20¢ Birds, attached	2.60

9

1983-84 DEFINITIVES

SCOTT NO.	DESCRIPTION	UNUSED F/NH
9-21	**1¢-$5, 13 varieties, singles, complete set**	**28.50**
9	1¢ Sea Fan	
10	3¢ Map Cowrie	
11	5¢ Jellyfish	
12	10¢ Hawksbill Turtle	
13	13¢ Giant Clam	
14	20¢ Parrotfish	
15	28¢ Chambered Nautilus	
16	30¢ Dappled Sea Cucumber	
17	37¢ Sea Urchin	
18	50¢ Starfish	
19	$1 Squid	
20	$2 Dugong (1984)	
21	$5 Pink Sponge (1984)	

1983-84 Booklet Panes

SCOTT NO.	DESCRIPTION	UNUSED F/NH
13a	13¢ Giant Clam (10)	14.75
13b	13¢ (5) & 20¢ (5)	17.00
14b	20¢ Parrotfish (10)	15.85

24

28

33

1983 COMMEMORATIVES

SCOTT NO.	DESCRIPTION	UNUSED F/NH
24-27	20¢ Whales, attached	3.75
28-32	20¢ Christmas, strip of 5	4.05
33-40	20¢ When Different Worlds Meet, attached	5.50

41

51

55

59

1984 COMMEMORATIVES

SCOTT NO.	DESCRIPTION	UNUSED F/NH
41-50	20¢ Seashells, attached	5.75
51-54	40¢ Explorer Ships, attached	4.90
55-58	20¢ Fishing, attached	2.50
59-62	20¢ Christmas, Flowers, attached	2.50

63

67

1985 COMMEMORATIVES

SCOTT NO.	DESCRIPTION	UNUSED F/NH
63-66	22¢ Audubon—Birds, attached	4.65
67-70	22¢ Canoes, attached	2.80

1985 DEFINITIVES

SCOTT NO.	DESCRIPTION	UNUSED F/NH
75-85	14¢-$10, 7 varieties, singles complete set	35.00
75	14¢ Trumpet Triton	....
76	22¢ Parrotfish	....
77	25¢ Damsel Fish	....
79	33¢ Clownfish	....
80	39¢ Sea Turtle	....
81	44¢ Sailfish	....
85	$10 Spinner Dolphins	....

1985 Booklet Panes

SCOTT NO.	DESCRIPTION	UNUSED F/NH
75a	14¢ Trumpet Triton (10)	12.40
76a	22¢ Parrotfish (10)	15.60
76b	14¢ (5) & 22¢ (5)	17.00

86

90

94

95

1985 COMMEMORATIVES

SCOTT NO.	DESCRIPTION	UNUSED F/NH
86-89	44¢ Youth Year, attached	5.20
90-93	14¢-44¢ Christmas, 4 varieties	4.05
94	$1 Trans-Pacific, souvenir sheet	3.75
95-98	44¢ Halley's Comet, attached	4.90

99

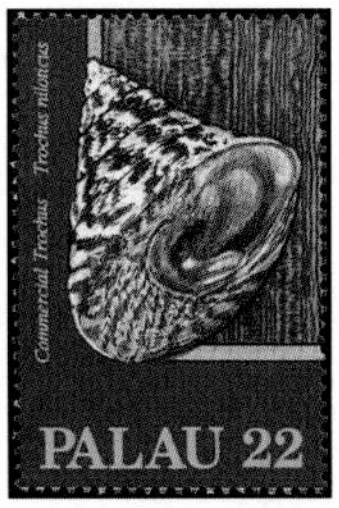

104

1986 COMMEMORATIVES

SCOTT NO.	DESCRIPTION	UNUSED F/NH
99-102	44¢ Songbirds, attached	5.40
103	14¢ World of Sea and Reef, Ameripex '86 sheet of 40	54.75
104-08	22¢ Seashells, strip of 5	4.05

109

113

117

SCOTT NO.	DESCRIPTION	UNUSED F/NH
109-12, C17	22¢ International Peace Year, 4 attached, 44¢ Airmail	6.50
113-16	22¢ Reptiles, attached	3.20
117-21	22¢ Christmas, attached	3.50

121B

122

142

1987 COMMEMORATIVES

SCOTT NO.	DESCRIPTION	UNUSED F/NH
121B-E	44¢ Butterflies, attached	5.50
122-25	44¢ Fruit Bats, attached	5.50

1987-88 FLOWER DEFINITIVES

SCOTT NO.	DESCRIPTION	UNUSED F/NH
126-42	1¢-$5, 17 varieties, single complete set	57.00
126	1¢ Kerdeu	......
127	3¢ Ngemoel	......
128	5¢ Uror	......
129	10¢ Woody Vine	......
130	14¢ Rur	......
131	15¢ Jaml (1988)	......
132	22¢ Denges	......
133	25¢ Ksid (1988)	......
134	36¢ Meldii (1988)	......
135	39¢ Emeridesh	......
136	44¢ Eskeam	......
137	45¢ Shrub (1988)	......
138	50¢ Rriu	......
139	$1 Koranges	......
140	$2 Meliin	......
141	$5 Orchid	......
142	$10 Flower Bouquet (1988)	19.00

1987 Booklet Panes

SCOTT NO.	DESCRIPTION	UNUSED F/NH
130a	14¢ Bikkia Palauensis (10)	5.80
132a	22¢ Bruguiera Gymnorhiza (10)	9.50
132b	14¢ (5) and 22¢ (5)	9.50

1988 Booklet Panes

SCOTT NO.	DESCRIPTION	UNUSED F/NH
131a	15¢ Limnophila (10)	9.50
133a	25¢ Ksid (10)	7.50
133b	15¢ (5) 25¢ (5)	7.20

146

155

1987 COMMEMORATIVES (continued)

SCOTT NO.	DESCRIPTION	UNUSED F/NH
146-49	22¢ Capex '87, attached	2.80
150-54	22¢ Seashells, strip of 5	3.50
155-63	14¢-44¢ U.S. Bicentennial 3 attached, strips of 3	6.65
164-67	12¢-44¢ Japan Links	3.20
168	$1 Japan souvenir sheet	3.20

173

178

SCOTT NO.	DESCRIPTION	UNUSED F/NH
173-77	22¢ Christmas, attached	3.75
178-82	22¢ Marine Species, attached	4.05

187

196a

198

1988 COMMEMORATIVES

SCOTT NO.	DESCRIPTION	UNUSED F/NH
183-86	44¢ Butterflies, attached	4.55
187-90	44¢ Birds, attached	4.55
191-95	25¢ Seashells, strip of 5	4.05
196	25¢ Finlandia sheetlet of 6	4.35
197	45¢ PRAGA '88, sheetlet of 6	7.50
198-202	25¢ Christmas, strip of 5	3.75
203	25¢ Chambered Nautilus, sheetlet of 5	4.35

204

208

1989 COMMEMORATIVES

SCOTT NO.	DESCRIPTION	UNUSED F/NH
204-07	45¢ Endangered Birds, attached	5.20
208-11	45¢ Mushrooms, attached	5.20
212-16	25¢ Seashells, strip of 5	4.05
217	$1 Japanese Art souvenir sheet	3.30
218	25¢ Apollo 11 mission, sheetlet of 25	17.25

SCOTT NO.	DESCRIPTION	UNUSED F/NH

219

220a

222

1989 COMMEMORATIVES (continued)

219	$2.40 Priority Mail	6.65
220	25¢ Literacy (block of 10)	6.90
221	25¢ Stilt Mangrove Fauna, sheetlet of 20	17.00
222-26	25¢ Christmas (strip of 5)	4.05

227

231

1990 COMMEMORATIVES

227-30	25¢ Soft Coral (4 attached)	3.20
231-34	45¢ Forest Birds (4 attached)	5.20

235a

237

235	Prince Boo Visit (sheet of 9)	6.65
236	$1 Penny Black Ann.	2.90
237-41	45¢ Tropical Orchids (strip of 5)	6.65

242

249

254

242-45	45¢ Butterflies II (4 attached)	5.20
246	25¢ Lagoon Life, sheet of 25	18.15
247-48	45¢ Pacifica, pair	4.90
249-53	25¢ Christmas, strip of 5	3.75
254-57	45¢ U.S. Forces in Palau, attached	6.05
258	$1 U.S. Peleliu, souvenir sheet	3.75

SCOTT NO.	DESCRIPTION	UNUSED F/NH

259

263a

267

1991

259-62	30¢ Hard Corals, attached	4.05
263	30¢ Angaur—The Phosphate Island sheet of 16	14.40

1991-92

266-83	1¢-$10 Birds, 18 varieties	63.40

1991 Booklet Panes

269b	19¢ Palau fantail booklet pane (10)	5.80
272a	Booklet pane of 10, 19¢ (5) + 29¢ (5)	7.80
272b	29¢ Palau fruit dove booklet pane (10)	6.65

288a

289a

290a

294a

1991 (continued)

288	29¢ Christianity in Palau, sheetlet of 6	4.90
289	29¢ Marine Life, sheetlet of 20	19.55
290	20¢ Operation Desert Storm, sheetlet of 9	5.50
291	$2.90 Operation Desert Storm Priority Mail	8.35
292	$2.90 Operation Desert Storm Souvenir Sheet	8.35
293	29¢ 10th Anniversary of Independence sheetlet of 8	6.90
294	50¢ Giant Clams, Souvenir Sheet of 5	7.20

295a

297a

295	29¢ Japanese Heritage in Palau, sheet of 6	5.20
296	$1.00 Phila Nippon, Souvenir Sheet	4.35
297	29¢ Peace Corps, sheetlet of 6	5.20

299a

298	29¢ Christmas, 1991, strip of 5	4.05
299	29¢ Pearl Harbor/WWII, sheetlet of 10	12.10

SCOTT NO.	DESCRIPTION	UNUSED F/NH

300a

301a

302a

1992

300	50¢ Butterflies, attached	5.80
301	29¢ Shells, strip of 5	4.35
302	29¢ Columbus & Age of Discovery, sheetlet of 20	17.00
303	29¢ World Environment, sheetlet of 24	19.55
304-09	50¢ Olympians, set of 6 Souvenir Sheets	8.65

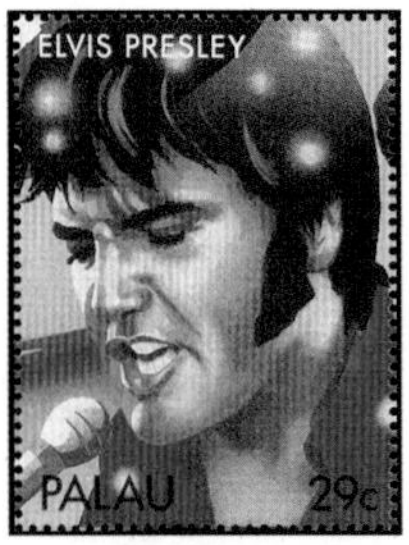

310e

312a

310	29¢ Elvis Presley, sheetlet of 9	9.80
311	50¢ WWII Aircraft, sheet of 10	10.00
312	29¢ Christmas, strip of 5	4.55

313a

314a

1993

313	50¢ Fauna, 4 attached	5.75
314	29¢ Seafood, 4 attached	3.50

315a

316a

315	50¢ Sharks, 4 attached	5.75
316	29¢ WWII in the Pacific, sheetlet of 10	11.25

317a

317	29¢ Christmas 1993, strip of 5	4.25
318	29¢ Prehistoric Sea Creatures, sheet of 25	20.20
319	29¢ International Year of Indigeneous People, sheet of 2	3.40
320	$2.90 Quarrying of Stone Money, souvenir sheet	8.95
321	29¢ Jonah and the Whale, sheet of 25	20.70

SCOTT NO.	DESCRIPTION	UNUSED F/NH

322a

323a

1994

322	40¢ Rays "Hong Kong '94", 4 attached	4.55
323	20¢ Estuarine Crocodile, 4 attached	3.75

324a

327

324	50¢ Large Seabirds, 4 attached	5.80
325	29¢ Action in the Pacific, 1944, sheet of 10	12.40
326	50¢ D-Day, sheet of 10	17.00
327	29¢ Pierre de Coubertin	1.05
328-33	50¢-$2 Winter Olympic medalists, souvenir sheet of 1 (6)	17.00

334a

340a

338a

334	29¢ PHILAKOREA '94 (Fish), sheetlet of 8	8.35
335	40¢ PHILAKOREA '94 (Mammals), sheetlet of 8	11.85
336	50¢ PHILAKOREA '94 (Birds), sheetlet of 8	13.85
337	29¢ 25th Anniversary First Manned Moon Landing, sheet of 20	17.00
338	29¢ Independence Day, strip of 5	4.25
339	$1 50th Anniv. of Invasion of Peleliu, souvenir sheet	3.50
340	29¢ Disney Characters Visit Palau, sheetlet of 9	8.65
341-42	$1 Mickey, Donald visiting Palau, souvenir sheet of 1 (2)	6.95
343	$2.90 Pluto, Mickey in Boat, souvenir sheet	8.65

344a

345a

346a

344	20¢ Int. Year of the Family, sheetlet of 12	6.85
345	29¢ Christmas, strip of 5	4.35
346-48	29¢-50¢ World Cup '94, 3 sheetlets of 12	33.15

351

1995

SCOTT NO.	DESCRIPTION	UNUSED F/NH
350	32¢ Elvis Presley, sheetlet of 9	9.25
351-65	1¢-$10 Palau Fishes, set of 15	59.35

1995 Booklet Panes

SCOTT NO.	DESCRIPTION	UNUSED F/NH
366a	20¢ Magenta dottyback (10)	5.50
367a	32¢ Reef Lizardfish (10)	8.95
367b	same, 20¢ (5) & 32¢ (5)	7.80

368a

369a

370a

372a

1995 (continued)

SCOTT NO.	DESCRIPTION	UNUSED F/NH
368	32¢ WWII Japanese Sunken Ships, sheetlet of 18	17.00
369	32¢ Flying Dinosaurs, sheetlet of 18	17.00
370	50¢ Experimental Aircraft (Jets), sheetlet of 12	17.00
371	$2 Experimental Aircraft (Concorde) souvenir sheet	5.20
372	32¢ Underwater Submersibles, sheetlet of 18	17.30

373a

374a

SCOTT NO.	DESCRIPTION	UNUSED F/NH
373	32¢ Marine Life (Singapore '95), 4 attached	3.75
374	60¢ UN, FAO, 50th Anniversary, 4 attached	6.95
375-76	$2 UN Emblem souvenir sheet (2)	11.25
377-78	20¢-32¢ Independence Anniversary, min. sheet of 4 & single	3.30
379-80	32¢-60¢ 50th End of WWII, sheetlets of 12 & 5	22.25

381

382a

384

SCOTT NO.	DESCRIPTION	UNUSED F/NH
381	$3 B-29 Nose souvenir sheet	8.95
382	32¢ Christmas 1995, strip of 5	4.35
383	32¢ Life Cycle of the Sea Turtle, sheetlet of 12	13.85
384	32¢ John Lennon	1.65

385a

388a

389a

1996

SCOTT NO.	DESCRIPTION	UNUSED F/NH
385	10¢ New Year 1996 (Year of the Rat), strip of 4	2.45
386	60¢ New Year 1996 (Year of the Rat), min. sheet of 2	3.40
387	32¢ UNICEF, 50th Anniversary, 4 attached	3.75
388	32¢ Marine Life, strip of 5	4.65
389-90	32¢-60¢ The Circumnavigators, 2 sheetlets of 9	23.65
391-92	$3 The Circumnavigators, 2 souvenir sheets	17.30
392A-F	1¢-6¢ Disney Sweethearts, set of 6	1.45

393a

396a

SCOTT NO.	DESCRIPTION	UNUSED F/NH
393	60¢ Disney Sweethearts, sheetlet of 9	19.00
394-95	$2 Disney Sweethearts, 2 souvenir sheets	13.85
396	20¢ Jerusalem Bible Studies, sheetlet of 30	17.30

397-98

399-400

SCOTT NO.	DESCRIPTION	UNUSED F/NH
397-98	40¢ 1996 Summer Olympics, pair	2.65
399-400	60¢ 1996 Summer Olympics, pair	4.00

401a

403a

407-08

409a

1996 (continued)

SCOTT NO.	DESCRIPTION	UNUSED F/NH
401	32¢ 1996 Summer Ollympics, sheet of 20	18.15
402	50¢ Birds over the Palau Lagoon, sheet of 20	28.80
403	40¢ Military Spy Aircraft, sheet of 12	14.40
404	60¢ Weird & Wonderful Aircraft, sheet of 12	20.45
405	$3 Stealth Bomber, souvenir sheet	9.50
406	$3 Martin Marietta X-24B, souvenir sheet	9.50
407-08	20¢ Independence, 2nd Anniversary, pair	1.15
409	32¢ Christmas 1996, strip of 5	4.55
410	32¢ Voyage to Mars, sheet of 12	11.25
411-12	$3 Mars rover & Water probe, 2 souvenir sheets	17.30

415

422a

420a

1997

SCOTT NO.	DESCRIPTION	UNUSED F/NH
412A	$2 Year of the Ox, souvenir sheet	6.35
413	$1 50th Anniv. of South Pacific Commission, souvenir sheet	2.90
414-19	1¢-$3 Flowers (Hong Kong '97), set of 6	10.10
420	32¢ Shoreline Plants (Hong Kong '97), 4 attached	3.75
421	50¢ Shoreline Plants (Hong Kong '97), 4 attached	5.80
422-23	32¢-60¢ Bicentennial of the Parachute, sheet of 8	21.60
424-25	$2 Bicentennial of the Parachute, 2 souvenir sheets	14.40
426	20¢ Native Birds & Trees, sheet of 12	6.95

427a

428a

431a

SCOTT NO.	DESCRIPTION	UNUSED F/NH
427-28	32¢-60¢ 50th Anniv. of UNESCO, sheet of 8 & 5	16.75
429-30	$2 50th Anniv. of UNESCO, 2 souvenir sheets	12.70
431	32¢ Prints of Hiroshige, sheet of 5	5.75
432-33	$2 Prints of Hiroshige, 2 souvenir sheets	12.10

–SUPPLIES–

Don't forget that Harris offers a complete line of albums, supplies and accessories for all your stamp collecting needs!

434a

435

SCOTT NO.	DESCRIPTION	UNUSED F/NH
434	32¢ Volcano Goddesses, sheet of 6	6.05
435	32¢ 3rd Anniversary of Independence	.95

436a

440a

450a

SCOTT NO.	DESCRIPTION	UNUSED F/NH
436	32¢ Oceanographic Research, sheetlet of 9	8.65
437-39	$2 Oceanographic Research, souvenir sheets (3)	18.15
440	60¢ Princess Diana	2.05
441-46	1¢-10¢ Disney "Let's Read"	1.45
447	32¢ Disney Characters "Reading", sheetlet of 9	8.10
448	$2 Daisy "The library is for everyone" souvenir sheet	6.95
449	$3 Mickey "Books are magical" souvenir sheet	9.25
450	32¢ Children singing Christmas carol, strip of 5	4.90

453a

457a

458a

1998

SCOTT NO.	DESCRIPTION	UNUSED F/NH
451-52	50¢ Year of the Tiger. souvenir sheets (2)	3.20
453	32¢ Hubble Space Telescope, sheetlet of 6	5.75
454-56	$2 Hubble Space Telescope, souvenir sheets (3)	18.15
457	60¢ Mother Teresa, sheetlet of 4	7.50
458	32¢ Deep Sea Robots, sheetlet of 18	17.30
459-60	$2 Deep Sea Robots, souvenir sheets (2)	12.40

461a

463a

466a

SCOTT NO.	DESCRIPTION	UNUSED F/NH
461	20¢ Israel Stamp Expo ovpt. on Sc. #396, sheetlet of 30	17.30
462	40¢ Legend of Orachel, sheetlet of 12	13.85
463	50¢ 1998 World Cup Soccer, sheetlet of 8	11.25
464	$3 1998 World Cup Soccer, souvenir sheet	8.65
465	32¢ 4th Micronesian Games, sheetlet of 9	8.35
466	32¢ Christmas, Rudolph the Red Nosed Reindeer, strip of 5	4.55
467-70	20¢-60¢ Disney's " A Bug's Life" 4 sheets of 4	20.75
471-74	$2 Disney's "A Bug's Life" 4 souvenir sheets	25.95
475-76	60¢ John Glenn's Return to Space, 2 sheets of 8	27.10
477-78	$2 John Glenn's Return to Space, 2 souvenir sheets	12.40

480a

495a

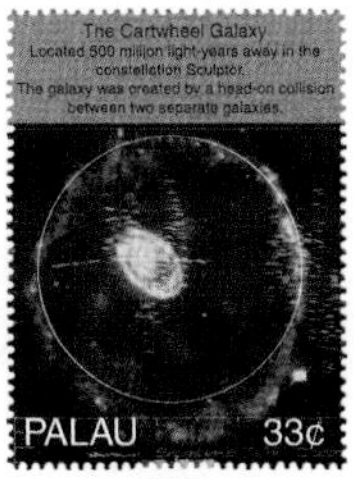

507a

1999

SCOTT NO.	DESCRIPTION	UNUSED F/NH
479	33¢ Environmentalists, sheetlet of 16	15.00
480	33¢ MIR Space Station, sheetlet of 6	5.50
481-84	$2 MIR Space Station, 4 souvenir sheets	22.50
485-94	1¢-$3.20 US & Palau Personalities, set of 10	17.30
495	33¢ Australia '99 World Stamp Expo, sheetlet of 12	10.95
496-97	$2 Australia '99, 2 souvenir sheets	11.25
498-99	55¢ IBRA '99 Exhibition, Caroline Islands Stamps, set of 2	3.10
500	$2 IBRA '99 Exhibition, Caroline Islands Stamps, miniature sheet	5.70
501	33¢ Exploration of Mars, sheetlet of 6	5.70
502-05	$2 Exploration of Mars, 4 souvenir sheets	23.05
506	33¢ Pacific Insects, Earth Day, sheetlet of 20	19.00
507	33¢ International Space Station, sheetlet of 6	5.50
508-11	$2 International Space Station, 4 souvenir sheets	22.50

512a

512	33¢ 20th Century Visionaries, sheetlet of 25	22.50
513-14	33¢ Hokusai Paintings, 2 sheetlets of 6	10.95
515-16	$2 Hokusai Paintings, 2 souvenir sheets	11.25

517a

524a

517	33¢ Apollo 11, 30th Anniversary, sheetlet of 6	5.75
518-21	$2 Apollo 11, 30th Anniversary, 4 souvenir sheets	23.05
522	60¢ Queen Mother (b.1900), sheetlet of 4	6.65
523	$2 Queen Mother (b.1900), souvenir sheet	6.05
524	33¢ Hubble Space Telescope Images, sheetlet of 6	6.05
525-28	$2 Hubble Space Telescope Images, 4 souvenir sheets	23.05
529	20¢ Christmas, Birds and Animals, strip of 5	2.90
530	33¢ Love for Dogs, sheetlet of 10	9.80
531-32	$2 Love for Dogs, 2 souvenir sheets	11.55

553a

557a

2000

533	55¢ Futuristic Space probes, sheetlet of 6	8.65
534-37	$2 Fururistic Space Probes, 4 souvenir sheets	22.50
538-39	20¢ Highlights of 1800-50 and Highlights of 1980-89, 2 Millenium sheetlets of 17	19.00
540	$2 New Year 2000 (Year of the Dragon)	5.75
541-45	$1-$11.75 US Presidents	57.60
546	20¢ 20th Century Discoveries about Prehistoric Life, sheetlet of 20	11.25
547	33¢ 2000 Summer Olympics, Sydney, sheetlet of 4	4.05
548	33¢ Future of Space Exploration, sheetlet of 6	6.05
549-52	$2 Future of Space Exploration, 4 souvenir sheets	21.90
553-54	20¢-33¢ Birds, 2 sheetlets of 6	8.95
555-56	$2 Birds, 2 souvenir sheets	10.95
557	33¢ Visionaries of the 20th Century, sheetlet of 20	19.00
558-61	33¢ 20th Century Science and Medicine Advances, 4 sheetlets of 5	19.30
562-63	$2 20th Century Science and Medicine Advances, 2 souvenir sheets	10.95

564a

568a

SCOTT NO.	DESCRIPTION	UNUSED F/NH
564-65	33¢ Marine Life, 2 sheetlets of 6	10.95
566-67	$2 Marine Life, 2 souvenir sheets	10.95
568	20¢ Millennium, sheetlet of 6	3.20
569	55¢ Millennium, sheetlet of 6	9.50

570a

574a

570-71	33¢ New and Recovering Species, 2 sheetlets of 6	10.95
572-73	$2 New and Recovering Species, 2 souvenir sheets	10.95
574	20¢ Dinosaurs, sheetlet of 6	3.20
575	33¢ Dinosaurs, sheetlet of 6	5.80
576-77	$2 Dinosaurs, 2 souvenir sheets	10.95
578-79	55¢ Queen Mother's 100th birthday, 2 sheetlets of 4	11.55
580	$2 Queen Mother's 100th birthday, souvenir sheet	5.50

581a

584a

581	55¢ First Zeppelin Flight, sheetlet of 6	9.25
582-83	$2 First Zeppelin Flighft, 2 souvenir sheets	10.95
584	33¢ Millennium, sheetlet of 17	19.30
585	50¢ Pope John Paul II, sheetlet of 8	11.55
586-87	60¢ Year of the Snake, 2 souvenir sheets	3.40

589a

592a

588	55¢ Pacific Ocean Marine Life, sheetlet of 6	9.20
589	20¢ Atlantic Ocean Fish, sheetlet of 6	3.40
590-91	$2 Atlantic Ocean Fish, 2 souvenir sheets	10.95
592	33¢ Pacific Arts Festival, sheetlet of 9	8.65
593	33¢ National Museum, 45th anniv., sheetlet of 12	10.95

594

602a

SCOTT NO.	DESCRIPTION	UNUSED F/NH
594-97	33¢ Butterflies, set of 4 singles	4.05
598-99	33¢ Butterflies, 2 sheetlets of 6	11.55
600-01	$2 Butterflies, 2 souvenir sheets	10.95
602-03	33¢ Flora and Fauna, 2 sheetlets of 6	11.55
604-05	$2 Flora and Fauna, 2 souvenir sheets	11.55

616

607

2001

630a

SCOTT NO.	DESCRIPTION	UNUSED F/NH
606	11¢ Lazarus Salil	.35
607-09	70¢-$12.25 Personalities, set of 3	32.85
610-11	60¢ Phila Nippon, Japan, 2 sheetlets of 5	17.00
612	60¢ Phila Nippon, Japan, sheetlet of 6	10.40
613-15	$2 Phila Nippon, Japan, 3 souvenir sheets	16.75
616-19	20¢-$1 Moths, set of 4	6.05
620-21	34¢-70¢ Moths, 2 sheetlets of 6	17.30
622-23	$2 Moths, 2 souvenir sheets	10.95
624-26	34¢-80¢ Nobel Prizes Cent., 3 sheetlets of 6	28.80
627-29	$2 Nobel Prizes Cent., 3 souvenir sheets	16.75
630-31	34¢-80¢ 2002 World Cup Soccer, 2 sheetlets of 6	19.60
632-33	$2 2002 World Cup Soccer, 2 souvenir sheets	10.95

634

638a

639

SCOTT NO.	DESCRIPTION	UNUSED F/NH
634-35	20¢-34¢ Christmas, set of 2	1.65
636	60¢ Queen Mother redrawn, sheet of 4 + label	6.95
637	$2 Queen Mother redrawn, souvenir sheet	5.50
638	60¢ Year of the Horse	1.75
639-40	55¢-60¢ Birds, 2 sheetlets of 6	20.20
641-42	$2 Birds of Palau, 2 souvenir sheets	10.95

645

648

670

2002

SCOTT NO.	DESCRIPTION	UNUSED F/NH
643-44	20¢-30¢ Palau-Japan Friendship Bridge, 2 sheets of 30	43.20
645	$1 United We Stand	2.90
646	80¢ Reign of Queen Elizabeth II, 50th Anniv., sheet of 4	9.20
647	$2 Reign of Queen Elizabeth II, 50th Anniv., souvenir sheet	5.50
648-669	1¢-$10 Birds, set of 22	82.90
670-73	20¢-80¢ Flowers, set of 4	5.50
674-75	60¢ Flowers, 2 sheetlets of 6	20.20
676-77	$2 Flowers, 2 souvenir sheets	10.95

678

680a

SCOTT NO.	DESCRIPTION	UNUSED F/NH
678-79	$1 2002 Winter Olympics, set of 2	5.50
679a	$1 2002 Winter Olympics, souvenir sheet of 2	5.50
680-81	50¢ Cats & Dogs, 2 sheetlets of 6	17.30
682-83	$2 Cats & Dogs, 2 souvenir sheets	10.95
684	80¢ Intl. Year of Mountains, sheet of 4	8.95
685	$2 Intl. Year of Mountains, souvenir sheet	5.50
686	37¢ Flags of Palau and its States, sheet of 17	16.10

696a

688

705a

SCOTT NO.	DESCRIPTION	UNUSED F/NH
687-88	$1 2002 Winter Olympics, redrawn, set of 2	5.50
688a	$1 2002 Winter Olympics, redrawn, souvenir sheet	5.50
689	60¢ Intl. Year of Ecotourism, sheet of 6	10.10
690	$2 Intl. Year of Ecotourism, souvenir sheet	5.50
691	60¢ Japanese Art, sheet of 6	10.10
692-93	80¢ Japanese Art, 2 sheets of 4	18.15
694-95	$2 Japanese Art, 2 souvenir sheets	10.95
696	60¢ Popeye, sheet of 6	10.10
697	$2 Popeye, souvenir sheet	5.50
698	37¢ Elvis Presley, sheet of 6	6.35
699-703	23¢-$1 Christmas, set of 5	8.10
704	$2 Christmas, souvenir sheet	5.50
705	60¢ Teddy Bears, Centenary, sheet of 4	6.65
706	80¢ Queen Mother, sheet of 4	8.95
707	$2 Queen Mother, souvenir sheet	5.50

708a

710a

712a

2003

SCOTT NO.	DESCRIPTION	UNUSED F/NH
708	60¢ 20th World Scout Jamboree, Thailand, sheet of 6	9.80
709	$2 20th World Scout Jamboree, Thailand, souvenir sheet	5.50
710	60¢ Shells, sheet of 6	9.80
711	$2 Shells, souvenir sheet	5.50
712	37¢ Year of the Ram, vert. strip of 3	6.05

714

SCOTT NO.	DESCRIPTION	UNUSED F/NH
713	80¢ President John F. Kennedy, sheet of 4	8.95
714-15	26¢-37¢ Birds, unserifed numerals	1.75
716	37¢ Astronauts, Space Shuttle Columbia, sheet of 7	7.20

717a

723a

SCOTT NO.	DESCRIPTION	UNUSED F/NH
717	60¢ Orchids, sheet of 6	9.80
718	$2 Orchids, souvenir sheet	5.50
719	60¢ Insects, sheet of 6	9.80
720	$2 Insects, souvenir sheet	5.50
721	60¢ 1st Non-Stop Solo Transatlantic Flight, 75th Anniversary, sheet of 6	9.80
722	80¢ President Ronald Reagn, sheet of 4	8.95
723	80¢ Pricess Diana (1961-97), sheet of 4	8.95
724	$1 Coronation of Queen Elizabeth II, 50th Anniversary, sheet of 3	8.40
725	$2 Coronation of Queen Elizabeth II, 50th Anniversary, souvenir sheet	5.50
726	37¢ Operation Iraqi Freedom, sheet of 6	6.05
727	$1 Prince Williams, 21st Birthday, sheet of 3	8.40
728	$2 Prince Williams, 21st Birthday, souvenir sheet	5.50
729	60¢ Tour de France Bicycle Race Centenary, sheet of 4	6.65
730	$2 Tour de France Bicycle Race Centenary, souvenir sheet	5.50
731	55¢ Powered Flight, sheet of 6	9.20
732	$2 Powered Flight, souvenir sheet	5.50
733-36	37¢-$1 Paintings by James McNeil Whistler, set of 4	6.95
737	80¢ Paintings by James McNeil Whistler, sheet of 4	8.95
738	$2 Paintings by James McNeil Whistler, souvenir sheet	5.50
739-40	80¢ Circus Performers, set of 2 sheets of 4	17.30
741-44	37¢-$1 Christmas, set of 4	7.80
745	$2 Christmas, souvenir sheet	5.50

741

748a

2004

SCOTT NO.	DESCRIPTION	UNUSED F/NH
746	60¢ Sea Turtles, sheet of 6	9.80
747	$2 Sea Turtles, souvenir sheet	5.50
748	80¢ Paintings of Norman Rockwell, sheet of 4	8.95
749	$2 Paintings of Norman Rockwell, souvenir sheet	5.50
750	80¢ Paintings by Pablo Picasso, sheet of 4	8.95
751	$2 Painting by Pablo Picasso, souvenir sheet, imperf.	5.50
752-55	37¢-$1 Paintings in the Hermitage Museum, set of 4	7.20
756	$2 Painting in the Hermitage Museum, souvenir sheet, imperf.	5.50

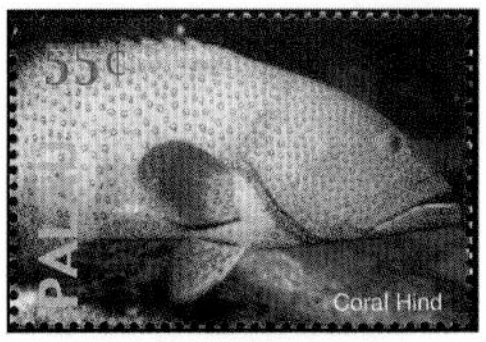

757a

763

SCOTT NO.	DESCRIPTION	UNUSED F/NH
757	55¢ Marine Life, sheet of 6	9.20
758	$2 Marine Life, souvenir sheet	5.50
759	55¢ Minerals, sheet of 6	9.20
760	$2 Minerals, souvenir sheet	5.50
761	50¢ Year of the Monkey	1.45
762	$1 Year of the Monkey, souvenir sheet	2.80
763-64	26¢-37¢ Ninth Festival of Pacific Arts, 2 sheets of 10	17.30

765a

769a

SCOTT NO.	DESCRIPTION	UNUSED F/NH
765-66	26¢-37¢ Marine Life, 2 sheets of 6	10.40
767-68	$2 Marine Life, 2 souvenir sheets	10.95
769	$3 International Year of Peace, sheet of 3	23.95
770	$2 International Year of Peace, souvenir sheet	5.50

771

777a

SCOTT NO.	DESCRIPTION	UNUSED F/NH
771-74	37¢-$1 2004 Summer Olympics, set of 4	7.20
775	80¢ Election of Pope John Paul II, 25th Anniv., Sheet of 4	8.95
776	$2 Deng Xiaoping, Chinese Leader, souvenir sheet	5.50
777	50¢ D-Day, 60th Anniversary, sheet of 6	8.35
778	$2 D-Day, 60th Anniversary, souvenir sheet	5.50

779a

781

SCOTT NO.	DESCRIPTION	UNUSED F/NH
779	80¢ European Soccer Championships, sheet of 4	8.95
780	$2 European Soccer Championships, souvenir sheet	5.50
781-82	37¢ Babe Ruth, set of 2	2.10

783a

787a

SCOTT NO.	DESCRIPTION	UNUSED F/NH
783-84	26¢-37¢ Trains, Bicentennial, 2 sheets of 4	8.35
785-86	$2 Trains, Bicentennial, 2 souvenir sheets	10.95
787-89	80¢ Butterflies, Reptiles, Amphibians, and Birds, 3 sheets of 4	26.80
790-92	$2 Butterflies, Reptiles, Amphibians, and Birds, 3 souvenir sheets	16.45

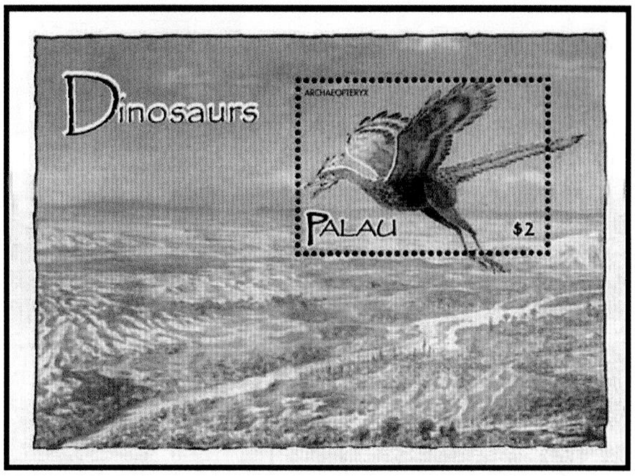

796

SCOTT NO.	DESCRIPTION	UNUSED F/NH
793-95	26¢-80¢ Dinosaurs, 3 sheets of 4	27.10
796-98	$2 Dinosaurs, 3 souvenir sheets	16.15

799a

SCOTT NO.	DESCRIPTION	UNUSED F/NH
799	80¢ FIFA, Centennial, sheet of 4	8.95
800	$2 FIFA, souvenir sheet	5.50

804

801

809a

SCOTT NO.	DESCRIPTION	UNUSED F/NH
801-03	26¢ National Basketball Assoc. Players, set of 3	2.25
804-07	$1 Christmas, set of 4	7.80
808	$2 Christmas, souvenir sheet	5.50
809	80¢ Palau-Rep. of China Diplomatic Relations, 5th Anniv., sheet of 4	8.95

810

2005

SCOTT NO.	DESCRIPTION	UNUSED F/NH
810	50¢ Year of the Rooster, sheet of 4	5.00

811

812

SCOTT NO.	DESCRIPTION	UNUSED F/NH
811	80¢ Rotary International, Centennial, sheet of 4	8.00
812	$1 Friedrich von Schiller, sheet of 3	7.50
813	$2 Friedrich von Schiller, souvenir sheet	4.90

814a

816

SCOTT NO.	DESCRIPTION	UNUSED F/NH
814	$1 Hans Christian Anderson, sheet of 3	7.50
815	$2 Hans Christian Anderson, souvenir sheet	4.90
816-19	37¢-$1 Battle of Trafalgar, Bicent., set of 4	7.50
820	$2 Battle of Trafalgar, Bicent., souvenir sheet	4.90

821a

825a

SCOTT NO.	DESCRIPTION	UNUSED F/NH
821-22	80¢ End of World War II, 60th Anniv., 2 sheets of 4	15.00
823-24	$2 End of World War II, 60th Anniv., 2 souvenir shts	9.80
825	$1 Jules Verne, sheet of 3	7.50
826	$2 Jules Verne, souvenir sheet	4.90

827

830a

SCOTT NO.	DESCRIPTION	UNUSED F/NH
827	$1 Pope John Paul II	2.60
828	80¢ Elvis Presley	2.10
829	80¢ Elvis Presley, sheet of 4	8.00
830	80¢ Trains, sheet of 4	8.00
831	$2 Trains, souvenir sheet	4.90

832a

834a

SCOTT NO.	DESCRIPTION	UNUSED F/NH
832	80¢ VJ Day, 60th Anniv., sheet of 4	8.00
833	$2 VJ Day, 60th Anniv., souvenir sheet	4.90
834	80¢ Expo 2005, Aichi, Japan, sheet of 4	8.00

835a

837a

SCOTT NO.	DESCRIPTION	UNUSED F/NH
835	80¢ Sailing, sheet of 4	7.25
836	$2 Sailing, souvenir sheet	4.90
837-38	$1 World cup Soccer Championships, 75th Anniv., 2 sheets of 3	14.95
839	$1 Sepp Herberger, souvenir sheet	4.95
840	$1 Franz Beckenbauer, souvenir sheet	2.95
841	37¢ Vatican City No. 61	.95

842a

843a

SCOTT NO.	DESCRIPTION	UNUSED F/NH
842	80¢ Taipei 2005 Intl. Stamp Exhibition, sheet of 4	8.00
843	37¢ Items from the National Museum, sheet of 10	9.50

844

845

SCOTT NO.	DESCRIPTION	UNUSED F/NH
844	80¢ Pope Benedict XVI	2.10
845-48	37¢-$1 Christmas, set of 4	6.90
849	$2 Christmas, souvenir sheet	4.90

850

851

2006

SCOTT NO.	DESCRIPTION	UNUSED F/NH
850	50¢ Year of the Dog	1.30
851-52	24¢-39¢ Birds, set of 2	1.75

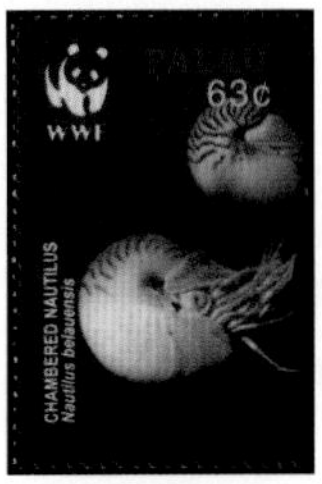

853a

854a

SCOTT NO.	DESCRIPTION	UNUSED F/NH
853	63¢ WWF, 4 attached	6.35
853e	63¢ WWF, souvenir sheet	15.00
854	18¢ World of Sea and Reef, sheet of 40	17.30
855	$2 Mozart, souvenir sheet	5.20

856a

858a

SCOTT NO.	DESCRIPTION	UNUSED F/NH
856	84¢ Queen Elizabeth II, sheet of 4	8.50
857	$2 Queen Elizabeth II, souvenir sheet	4.90
858	$1 Rembrandt, sheet of 4	9.80
859	$2 Rembrandt, souvenir sheet	5.20

860a

861a

SCOTT NO.	DESCRIPTION	UNUSED F/NH
860	$1 International Space Station, sheet of 4	9.00
861-62	75¢ Space Achievements, 2 sheets of 6	20.00
863-85	$2 Space Achievements, 3 souvenir sheets	14.00
867	75¢ Peace Corps, souvenir sheet of 4	7.00
868-69	75¢ Concorde, set of 2	7.00
870	84¢ Christmas, sheet of 4	7.50

B1

C1

C6

1988 SEMI POSTAL

SCOTT NO.	DESCRIPTION	UNUSED F/NH
B1-B4	(25¢ + 5¢) + (45¢ + 5¢) Olympics, 2 pairs	5.25

AIR MAILS

1984 AIR MAILS

SCOTT NO.	DESCRIPTION	UNUSED F/NH
C1-4	40¢ Seabirds, attached	4.55

1985 AIR MAILS

SCOTT NO.	DESCRIPTION	UNUSED F/NH
C5	44¢ Audubon Birds	1.65
C6-9	44¢ German Links, attached	5.50
C10-13	44¢ Transpacific, attached	5.20

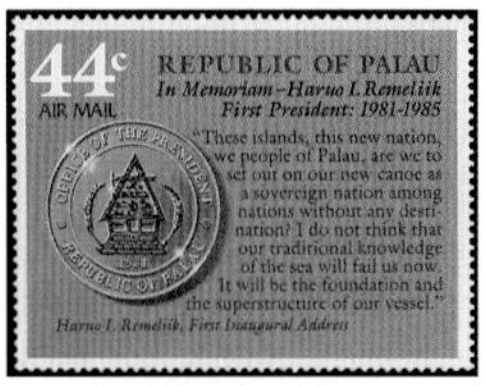

C14

C17

C18

C23a

1986 AIR MAILS

SCOTT NO.	DESCRIPTION	UNUSED F/NH
C14-16	44¢ Remeliik, strip of 3	5.20
C17	44¢ Statue of Liberty	1.30

1989 AIR MAILS

SCOTT NO.	DESCRIPTION	UNUSED F/NH
C18-20	36¢-45¢ Aircraft, complete set of 3	3.75

1991 AIR MAILS

SCOTT NO.	DESCRIPTION	UNUSED F/NH
C21	50¢ 10th Anniv. Airmail, self-adhesive	2.45

1989 BOOKLET PANES

SCOTT NO.	DESCRIPTION	UNUSED F/NH
C18a	36¢ Aircraft pane (10)	10.10
C19a	39¢ Aircraft pane (10)	10.95
C20a	45¢ Aircraft pane (10)	12.10
C20b	5 (36¢) + 5 (45¢) Aircraft pane (10)	11.55

1995

SCOTT NO.	DESCRIPTION	UNUSED F/NH
C22	50¢ World War II, Aircraft, sheetlet of 10	15.85
C23	50¢ Birds (Swallows), 4 attached	5.80

1985 ENVELOPE ENTIRES

SCOTT NO.	DESCRIPTION	UNUSED F/NH
U1	22¢ Marine Life	5.00
U2	22¢ Spear Fishing	8.00
U3	25¢ Chambered Nautilus	2.00
UC1	36¢ Bird, air letter sheet	7.00

1985 POSTAL CARDS

SCOTT NO.	DESCRIPTION	UNUSED F/NH
UX1	14¢ Marine Life	3.50

PHILIPPINES

U.S. Stamps of various issues overprinted

1899
On 260. Unwatermarked

SCOTT NO.	DESCRIPTION	UNUSED NH F	UNUSED NH AVG	UNUSED OG F	UNUSED OG AVG	USED F	USED AVG
212	50¢ orange	650.00	425.00	400.00	280.00	250.00	175.00

On 279, 279d, 267-68, 281, 282C, 283, 284, 275
Double Line Watermarked

SCOTT NO.	DESCRIPTION	UNUSED NH F	UNUSED NH AVG	UNUSED OG F	UNUSED OG AVG	USED F	USED AVG
213	1¢ yellow green	5.75	4.00	3.60	2.50	1.00	.70
214	2¢ orange red	2.50	1.50	1.40	.95	.85	.60
215	3¢ purple	13.00	8.00	8.00	5.00	1.75	1.30
216	5¢ blue	13.00	8.00	8.00	5.00	1.75	1.05
217	10¢ brown (Type I)	50.00	33.00	30.00	20.00	5.00	3.50
217A	10¢ orange brown (Type II)	295.00	195.00	150.00	110.00	35.00	27.50
218	15¢ olive green	75.00	50.00	45.00	30.00	10.00	7.00
219	50¢ orange	295.00	195.00	150.00	110.00	45.00	30.00

1901
On 280, 282, 272, 276-78

SCOTT NO.	DESCRIPTION	UNUSED NH F	UNUSED NH AVG	UNUSED OG F	UNUSED OG AVG	USED F	USED AVG
220	4¢ orange brown	50.00	35.00	30.00	20.00	6.00	4.00
221	6¢ lake	75.00	50.00	45.00	30.00	7.50	5.00
222	8¢ violet brown	75.00	50.00	45.00	30.00	8.00	5.50
223	$1 black (Type I)	800.00	550.00	500.00	350.00	300.00	200.00
223A	$1 black (Type II)	4000.00	2800.00	2500.00	1750.00	900.00	695.00
224	$2 dark blue	900.00	650.00	550.00	400.00	400.00	280.00
225	$5 dark green	1600.00	1100.00	950.00	700.00	1000.00	700.00

1903-04
On 300-313

SCOTT NO.	DESCRIPTION	UNUSED NH F	UNUSED NH AVG	UNUSED OG F	UNUSED OG AVG	USED F	USED AVG
226	1¢ blue green	10.00	7.50	6.00	4.75	.50	.35
227	2¢ carmine	14.00	10.00	9.00	6.00	1.35	.95
228	3¢ bright violet	115.00	80.00	75.00	50.00	17.50	11.50
229	4¢ brown	135.00	100.00	85.00	60.00	27.00	18.00
230	5¢ blue	27.00	18.00	16.00	11.00	1.50	.95
231	6¢ brownish lake	145.00	100.00	90.00	60.00	24.50	15.95
232	8¢ violet black	90.00	65.00	55.00	40.00	15.00	9.75
233	10¢ pale red brown	55.00	40.00	32.00	22.00	3.75	2.25
234	13¢ purple black	75.00	50.00	45.00	30.00	20.00	14.00
235	25¢ olive green	110.00	80.00	70.00	50.00	20.00	14.00
236	50¢ orange	215.00	150.00	135.00	95.00	42.50	30.00
237	$1 black	800.00	550.00	500.00	350.00	300.00	200.00
238	$2 dark blue	1800.00	1400.00	1000.00	800.00	900.00	585.00
239	$5 dark green	2100.00	1600.00	1300.00	1050.00	6000.00	4000.00

On 319

SCOTT NO.	DESCRIPTION	UNUSED NH F	UNUSED NH AVG	UNUSED OG F	UNUSED OG AVG	USED F	USED AVG
240	2¢ carmine	12.00	8.50	7.00	5.00	2.75	1.75

SPECIAL DELIVERY STAMPS

PHILIPPINES

1901
U.S. E5 Surcharged

SCOTT NO.	DESCRIPTION	UNUSED NH F	UNUSED NH AVG	UNUSED OG F	UNUSED OG AVG	USED F	USED AVG
E1	10¢ dark blue	200.00	140.00	120.00	80.00	100.00	75.00

POSTAGE DUE STAMPS

1899
U.S. J38-44 overprinted

SCOTT NO.	DESCRIPTION	UNUSED NH F	UNUSED NH AVG	UNUSED OG F	UNUSED OG AVG	USED F	USED AVG
J1	1¢ deep claret	13.00	9.00	8.50	6.00	3.00	2.00
J2	2¢ deep claret	13.00	9.00	8.50	6.00	3.00	2.00
J3	5¢ deep claret	26.00	18.00	17.00	12.00	3.00	2.00
J4	10¢ deep claret	40.00	30.00	25.00	18.00	7.00	5.00
J5	50¢ deep claret	375.00	260.00	230.00	160.00	125.00	85.00

1901

SCOTT NO.	DESCRIPTION	UNUSED NH F	UNUSED NH AVG	UNUSED OG F	UNUSED OG AVG	USED F	USED AVG
J6	3¢ deep claret	30.00	20.00	19.00	13.00	9.00	6.50
J7	30¢ deep claret	475.00	325.00	300.00	200.00	130.00	90.00

PUERTO RICO

1899
U.S. Stamps 279-79B, 281, 272, 282C overprinted

SCOTT NO.	DESCRIPTION	UNUSED NH F	UNUSED NH AVG	UNUSED OG F	UNUSED OG AVG	USED F	USED AVG
210	1¢ yellow green	11.00	8.50	6.50	4.50	1.75	1.15
211	2¢ carmine	10.00	7.50	6.00	4.00	1.65	1.05
212	5¢ blue	23.00	16.00	14.00	10.00	3.00	2.00
213	8¢ violet brown	70.00	45.00	40.00	28.00	19.00	13.00
214	10¢ brown (I)	50.00	33.00	30.00	20.00	7.00	5.00

1900
U.S. 279, 279B overprinted

SCOTT NO.	DESCRIPTION	UNUSED NH F	UNUSED NH AVG	UNUSED OG F	UNUSED OG AVG	USED F	USED AVG
215	1¢ yellow green	13.00	8.50	8.00	5.50	1.75	1.20
216	2¢ carmine	10.00	7.00	6.00	4.00	3.00	2.00

POSTAGE DUE STAMPS

1899
U.S. Postage Due Stamps J38-39, J41 overprinted

SCOTT NO.	DESCRIPTION	UNUSED NH F	UNUSED NH AVG	UNUSED OG F	UNUSED OG AVG	USED F	USED AVG
J1	1¢ deep claret	45.00	33.00	25.00	18.00	8.00	5.50
J2	2¢ deep claret	40.00	30.00	25.00	18.00	7.00	5.00
J3	10¢ deep claret	350.00	250.00	210.00	150.00	75.00	55.00

The Ryukyu Islands were under U.S. administration from April 1, 1945 until May 15, 1972. Prior to the General Issues of 1948, several Provisional Stamps were used.

RYUKYU ISLANDS

1, 1a, 3, 3a

2, 2a, 5, 5a

4, 4a, 6, 6a

7, 7a

1949 Second Printing

White gum & paper, sharp colors; clean perfs.

SCOTT	DESCRIPTION	F/NH	UNUSED NO. F
1-7	**5s to 1y 7 varieties, complete**	**28.75**	**20.50**
1	5s Cycad	3.00	2.00
2	10s Lily	7.00	5.00
3	20s Cycad	4.50	3.00
4	30s Sailing Ship	2.00	1.50
5	40s Lily	2.00	1.50
6	50s Sailing Ship	5.00	3.50
7	1y Farmer	6.75	5.00

1948 First Printing

Thick yellow gum; gray paper; dull colors; rough perfs.

SCOTT	DESCRIPTION	F/NH	UNUSED NO. F
1a-7a	**5s to 1y, 7 varieties, complete**	**520.00**	**390.00**
1a	5s Cycad	3.75	2.75
2a	10s Lily	2.25	1.50
3a	20s Cycad	2.25	1.50
4a	30s Sailing Ship	3.75	2.75
5a	40s Lily	70.00	50.00
6a	50s Sailing Ship	5.00	30.00
7a	1y Farmer	460.00	350.00

8

9

10

11

12

13

1950

SCOTT	DESCRIPTION	F/NH	UNUSED NO. F
8-13	**50s to 5y, 6 varieties, complete**	**81.50**	**57.65**
8	50s Tile Roof	.30	.20
9	1y Ryukyu Girl	5.00	3.50
10	2y Shun Castle	16.00	11.00
11	3y Dragon Head	35.00	25.00
12	4y Women at Beach	20.00	14.00
13	5y Seashells	9.50	7.00

NOTE: The 1950 printing of #8 is on toned paper and has yellowish gum. A 1958 printing exhibits white paper and colorless gum.

1951

SCOTT	DESCRIPTION	F/NH	UNUSED NO. F
14	3y Ryukyu University	65.00	45.00
15	3y Pine Tree	60.00	40.00
16	10y on 50s (no. 8) Type II	14.00	10.00
16a	same, Type I	50.00	35.00
16b	same, Type III	60.00	40.00
17	100y on 2y (no. 10)	2350.00	1750.00
18	3y Govt. of Ryukyu	135.00	95.00

Type I—Bars are narrow spaced; "10" normal
Type II—Bars are wide spaced; "10" normal
Type III—Bars are wide spaced; "10" wide spaced

14

15

18

19

20

21

1952-53

SCOTT	DESCRIPTION	F/NH	UNUSED NO. F
19-26	**1y to 100y, 8 varieties, complete**		**73.85**
19	1y Mandanbashi Bridge		.35
20	2y Main Hall of Shun Castle		.40
21	3y Shurei Gate		.50
22	6y Stone Gate, Sogenji Temple		4.00
23	10y Benzaiten-do Temple		4.50
24	30y Altar at Shuri Castle		18.00
25	50y Tamaudun Shuri		20.00
26	100y Stone Bridge, Hosho Pond		30.00

28

SCOTT NO.	DESCRIPTION	UNUSED F/NH

29

31

30

1953

27	3y Reception at Shuri Castle	15.00
28	6y Perry and Fleet	1.40
29	4y Chofu Ota and Pencil	13.00

1954

30	4y Shigo Toma & Pen	15.00

1954-55

31	4y Pottery	1.25
32	15y Lacquerware (1955)	6.00
33	20y Textile Design (1955)	4.00

1955

34	4y Noguni Shrine & Sweet Potato Plant	15.00

1956

35	4y Stylized Trees	13.50
36	5y Willow Dance	1.25
37	8y Straw Hat Dance	3.00
38	14y Group Dance	5.00
39	4y Dial Telephone	18.50
40	2y Garland, Bamboo & Plum	2.50

1957

41	4y Map & Pencil Rocket	1.25
42	2y Phoenix	.30

34

35

36

37

38

SCOTT NO.	DESCRIPTION	UNUSED F/NH

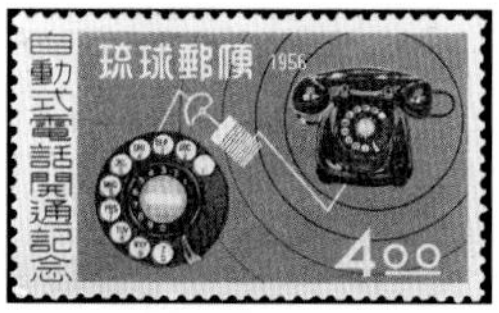

39

40

41

42

43

44-53

1958

43	4y Ryukyu Stamps	1.00
44-53	**1/2¢ to $1.00, 10 varieties, complete, ungummed**	**59.50**
44	1/2¢ Yen, Symbol & Denom., orange	.95
45	1¢ same, yellow green	1.55
46	2¢ same, dark blue	2.50
47	3¢ same, deep carmine	1.95
48	4¢ same, bright green	2.75
49	same, orange	5.00
50	10¢ same, aquamarine	7.00
51	25¢ same, bright violet blue	9.00
51a	25¢ same, bright violet blue (with gum)	12.00
52	50¢ same, gray	18.00
52a	50¢ same, gray (with gum)	13.00
53	$1 same, rose lilac	14.00
54	3¢ Gate of Courtesy	1.40
55	1-1/2¢ Lion Dance	.40

1959

56	3¢ Mountains & Trees	.85
57	3¢ Yonaguni Moth	1.30
58-62	**1/2¢ to 17¢, 5 varieties, complete**	**39.50**
58	1/2¢ Hibiscus	.35
59	3¢ Moorish Idol	1.00
60	8¢ Seashell	12.00
61	13¢ Dead Leaf Butterfly	3.25
62	17¢ Jellyfish	25.00
63	1-1/2¢ Toy (Yakaji)	.80

54

55

56

57

61, 79

63

1960

SCOTT NO.	DESCRIPTION	UNUSED F/NH
64	3¢ University Badge	1.10

DANCES II

SCOTT NO.	DESCRIPTION	UNUSED F/NH
65-68	**1¢-10¢, 4 varieties, complete**	**6.75**
65	1¢ Munsunu	1.75
66	2-1/2¢ Nutwabushi	3.50
67	5¢ Hatomabushi	.90
68	10¢ Hanafubushi	.95

64

65, 81

72

73

74

75

SCOTT NO.	DESCRIPTION	UNUSED F/NH
72	3¢ Torch & Nago Bay	7.50
73	8¢ Runners	1.25
74	3¢ Egret & Sun	6.00
75	1-1/2¢ Bull Fight	1.95

1960-61 REDRAWN INSCRIPTION

SCOTT NO.	DESCRIPTION	UNUSED F/NH
76-80	**1/2¢ to 17¢, 5 varieties, complete**	**20.50**
76	1/2¢ Hibiscus	.50
77	3¢ Moorish Idol	1.25
78	8¢ Seashell	1.25
79	13¢ Dead Leaf Butterfly	1.50
80	17¢ Jellyfish	17.00

88

89

90

91

92

93

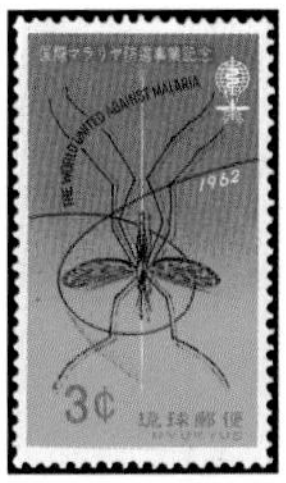
95

97

98

WITH "RYUKYUS" ADDED
1961-64

SCOTT NO.	DESCRIPTION	UNUSED F/NH
81-87	**1¢ to $1.00, 8 varieties, Dancers, complete**	**16.00**
81	1¢ Munsuru	.20
82	2-1/2¢ Nutwabushi (1962)	.25
83	5¢ Hatomabushi (1962)	.45
84	10¢ Hanafubushi (1962)	.65
84A	20¢ Shundun (1964)	4.00
85	25¢ Hanagasabushi (1962)	1.50
86	50¢ Nubui Kuduchi	3.00
87	$1 Kutubushi	7.00

1961

SCOTT NO.	DESCRIPTION	UNUSED F/NH
88	3¢ Pine Tree	1.75
89	3¢ Naha, Steamer & Sailboat	2.25
90	3¢ White Silver Temple	3.00
91	3¢ Books & Bird	1.60
92	1-1/2¢ Eagles & Rising Sun	2.75

1962

SCOTT NO.	DESCRIPTION	UNUSED F/NH
93	1-1/2¢ Steps, Trees & Building	.75
94	3¢ GRI Building	1.00
95	3¢ Malaria Eradication	.70
96	8¢ Eradication Emblem	1.10
97	3¢ Children's Day	1.50

103

104

105

106

107

108

109

110

111

SCOTT NO.	DESCRIPTION	UNUSED F/NH
98-102	**1/2¢ to 17¢ varieties, Flowers, complete**	**3.05**
98	1/2¢ Sea Hibiscus	.25
99	3¢ Indian Coral Tree	.40
100	8¢ Iju	.60
101	13¢ Touch-Me-Not	.75
102	17¢ Shell Flower	1.25
103	3¢ Earthenware	4.00
104	3¢ Japanese Fencing	5.25
105	1-1/2¢ Bingata Cloth	1.25

VERY FINE QUALITY: From 1935 to date, add 20% to the Fine price. Minimum of 3¢ per stamp.

112

113

114

115

116

117

1963

SCOTT NO.	DESCRIPTION	UNUSED F/NH
106	3¢ Stone Relief	1.20
107	1-1/2¢ Gooseneck Cactus	.25
108	3¢ Trees & Hills	1.20
109	3¢ Map of Okinawa	1.50
110	3¢ Hawks & Islands	1.25
111	3¢ Shioya Bridge	1.25
112	3¢ Lacquerware Bowl	3.00
113	3¢ Map of Far East	1.00
114	15¢ Mamaomoto	2.25
115	3¢ Nakagusuku Castle Site	.95
116	3¢ Human Rights	1.00
117	1-1/2¢ Dragon	.70

118

119

120, 120a

121

1964

SCOTT NO.	DESCRIPTION	UNUSED F/NH
118	3¢ Mothers' Day	.50
119	3¢ Agricultural Census	.50
120	3¢ Minsah Obi, rose pink	.65
120a	same, deep carmine	.90
121	3¢ Girl Scout & Emblem	.40
122	3¢ Shuri Relay Station	.90
122a	3¢ same, inverted "1"	40.00
123	8¢ Antenna & map	1.50
124	3¢ Olympic Torch & Emblem	.40

122, 122a

123

124

125

127

126

1964-65

SCOTT NO.	DESCRIPTION	UNUSED F/NH
125	3¢ Karate, "Naihanchi"	.70
126	3¢ Karate, "Makiwara" (1965)	.60
127	3¢ Karate, "Kumite" (1965)	.60

128

129

1964

SCOTT NO.	DESCRIPTION	UNUSED F/NH
128	3¢ Miyara Dunchi	.40
129	1-1/2¢ Snake & Iris	.35

130

131

132

133

134

136

135

139

1965

SCOTT NO.	DESCRIPTION	UNUSED F/NH
130	3¢ Boy Scouts	.60
131	3¢ Onoyama Stadium	.30
132	3¢ Samisen of King Shoko	.60
133	3¢ Kin Power Plant	.30
134	3¢ ICY and United Nations	.25
135	3¢ Naha City Hall	.25

1965-66

SCOTT NO.	DESCRIPTION	UNUSED F/NH
136	3¢ Chinese Box Turtle	.40
137	3¢ Hawksbill Turtle (1966)	.30
138	3¢ Asian Terrapin (1966)	.30

1965

SCOTT NO.	DESCRIPTION	UNUSED F/NH
139	1-1/2¢ Horse	.25

140

141

143

144

145

146

147

148

149

150

1966

SCOTT NO.	DESCRIPTION	UNUSED F/NH
140	3¢ Woodpecker	.30
141	3¢ Sika Deer	.35
142	3¢ Dugong	.35
143	3¢ Swallow	.25
144	3¢ Memorial Day	.20
145	3¢ University of Ryukyus	.20
146	3¢ Lacquerware	.25
147	3¢ UNESCO	.25
148	3¢ Government Museum	.20
149	3¢ Nakasone T. Genga's Tomb	.20
150	1-1/2¢ Ram in Iris Wreath	.20

151

156

SCOTT NO.	DESCRIPTION	UNUSED F/NH

1966-67

151-55	**5 varieties, Fish, complete**	**1.70**
151	3¢ Clown Fish	.30
152	3¢ Young Boxfish (1967)	.30
153	3¢ Forceps Fish (1967)	.45
154	3¢ Spotted Triggerfish (1967)	.35
155	3¢ Saddleback Butterflyfish (1967)	.40

1966

156	3¢ Tsuboya Urn	.25

162 163 164

157

165 166 167 168

1967-68

157-61	**5 varieties, Seashells, complete**	**1.95**
157	3¢ Episcopal Miter	.30
158	3¢ Venus Comb Murex	.30
159	3¢ Chiragra Spider	.35
160	3¢ Green Turban	.35
161	3¢ Euprotomus Bulla	.75
162	3¢ Roofs & ITY Emblem	.25
163	3¢ Mobile TB Clinic	.25
164	3¢ Hojo Bridge, Enkaku Temple	.30
165	1-1/2¢ Monkey	.20
166	3¢ TV Tower & Map	.35

169 170 171 172

173 178 179 180

1968

167	3¢ Dr. Nakachi & Helper	.30
168	3¢ Pill Box	.45
169	3¢ Man, Library, Book & Map	.45
170	3¢ Mailmen's Uniforms & 1948 Stamp	.40
171	3¢ Main Gate, Enkaku Temple	.40
172	3¢ Old Man's Dance	.40

1968-69

173-77	**5 varieties, Crabs, complete**	**2.35**
173	3¢ Mictyris Longicarpus	.40
174	3¢ Uca Dubia Stimpson (1969)	.45
175	3¢ Baptozius Vinosus (1969)	.45
176	3¢ Cardisoma Carnifex (1969)	.60
177	3¢ Ocypode (1969)	.60

1968

178	3¢ Saraswati Pavilion	.40
179	3¢ Tennis Player	.40
180	1-1/2¢ Cock & Iris	.20

1969

181	3¢ Boxer	.40
182	3¢ Ink Slab Screen	.60
183	3¢ Antennas & Map	.30
184	3¢ Gate of Courtesy & Emblems	.30

SCOTT NO.	DESCRIPTION	UNUSED F/NH

181 182 183 184

185 186 187

188 189

1969-70

185-89	**5 varieties, Folklore, complete**	**2.70**
185	3¢ Tug of War Festival	.45
186	3¢ Hari Boat Race	.45
187	3¢ Izaiho Ceremony	.45
188	3¢ Mortardrum Dance (1970)	.75
189	3¢ Sea God Dance	.75

1969

190	1/2¢ on 3¢ (no. 99) Indian Coral Tree	1.25
191	3¢ Nakamura-Ke Farm House	.30
192	3¢ Statue & Maps	.60
193	1-1/2¢ Dog & Flowers	.25
194	3¢ Sake Flask	.35

191 192 193

改 $\frac{1}{2}$¢
(surcharge)
190

194 195 196 197

198 199 200

195-99	**5 varieties, Classic Opera, complete**	**2.85**
195	3¢ "The Bell"	.60
196	3¢ Child & Kidnapper	.60
197	3¢ Robe of Feathers	.60
198	3¢ Vengeance of Two Sons	.60
199	3¢ Virgin & the Dragon	.60
195-99a	**5 varieties, complete, sheets of 4**	**26.00**
195a	3¢ sheet of 4	5.50
196a	3¢ sheet of 4	5.50
197a	3¢ sheet of 4	5.50
198a	3¢ sheet of 4	5.50
199a	3¢ sheet of 4	5.50
200	3¢ Underwater Observatory	.40

201

204

205

206

207

208

212

210

1970-71 Portraits

SCOTT NO.	DESCRIPTION	UNUSED F/NH
201	3¢ Noboru Jahana	.55
202	3¢ Saion Gushichan Bunjaku	1.00
203	3¢ Choho Giwan (1971)	.65

1970

204	3¢ Map & People	.30
205	3¢ Great Cycad of Une	.35
206	3¢ Flag, Diet & Map	1.10
207	1-1/2¢ Boar & Cherry Blossoms	.20

1971

208-12	**5 varieties, Workers, complete**	**2.10**
208	3¢ Low Hand Loom	.40
209	3¢ Filature	.40
210	3¢ Farmer with Raincoat & Hat	.45
211	3¢ Rice Huller	.55
212	3¢ Fisherman's Box & Scoop	.45
213	3¢ Water Carrier	.45
214	3¢ Old & New Naha	.30
215	2¢ Caesalpinia Pulcherrima	.30
216	3¢ Madder	.30

213

214

215

217

218

220

221

223

222

1971-72 Government Parks

217	3¢ View from Mabuni Hill	.30
218	3¢ Mt. Arashi from Haneji Sea	.30
219	4¢ Yabuchi Is. from Yakena Port	.35

1971

220	4¢ Dancer	.30
221	4¢ Deva King	.30
222	2¢ Rat & Chrysanthemums	.30
223	4¢ Student Nurse	.30

224

225

226

227

228

1972

SCOTT NO.	DESCRIPTION	UNUSED F/NH
224	5¢ Birds & Seashore	.55
225	5¢ Coral Reef	.55
226	5¢ Sun Over Islands	.55
227	5¢ Dove & Flags	.95
228	5¢ Antique Sake Pot	.70

AIR MAIL STAMPS

1950

C1	8y Dove & Map, bright blue	160.00
C2	12y same, green	40.00
C3	16y same, rose carmine	25.00

1951-54

C4-8	**13y to 50y, 5 varieties, complete**	**32.25**
C4	13y Heavenly Maiden, blue	3.50
C5	18y same, green	4.50
C6	30y same, cerise	7.00
C7	40y same, red violet (1954)	9.00
C8	50y same, yellow orange (1954)	10.00

C1-3

C4-8

C9-13

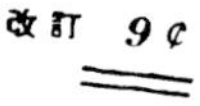

C14-18

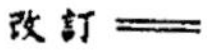

(surcharge)
C19-23

C24

C29

C30

1957

C9-13	**15y to 60y, 5 varieties, complete**	**88.25**
C9	15y Maiden Playing Flute, blue green	10.00
C10	20y same, rose carmine	17.00
C11	35y same, yellow green	19.00
C12	45y same, reddish brown	22.00
C13	60y same, gray	25.00

1959

C14-18	**9¢ to 35¢, 5 varieties, complete**	**51.50**
C14	9¢ on 15y (no. C9)	3.00
C15	14¢ on 20y (no. C10)	4.50
C16	19¢ on 35y (no. C11)	8.50
C17	27¢ on 45y (no. C12)	20.00
C18	35¢ on 60y (no. C13)	18.00

1960

C19-23	**9¢ to 35¢, 5 varieties, complete**	**31.00**
C19	9¢ on 4y (no. 31)	4.00
C20	14¢ on 5y (no. 36)	5.50
C21	19¢ on 15y (no. 32)	4.00
C22	27¢ on 14y (no. 38)	11.00
C23	35¢ on 20y (no. 33)	8.00

1961

C24-28	**9¢ to 35¢, 5 varieties, complete**	**8.75**
C24	9¢ Heavenly Maiden	.45
C25	14¢ Maiden Playing Flute	.80
C26	19¢ Wind God	1.00
C27	27¢ Wind God	4.00
C28	35¢ Maiden Over Tree Tops	3.00

1963

C29	5-1/2¢ Jet & Gate of Courtesy	.25
C30	7¢ Jet Plane	.30

E1

SPECIAL DELIVERY

1950

E1	5y Dragon & Map	40.00

UNITED NATIONS (NEW YORK)

1, 6

2, 10, UX1-2

3, 11

4, 7, 9

5

8

12

13-14

1951

SCOTT NO.	DESCRIPTION	FIRST DAY COVERS SING	INSC. BLK	INSRIP BLK-4	UNUSED F/NH	USED F
1-11	1¢ to $1 Definitives	85.00	150.00	52.00	12.50	8.25

1952-1953

SCOTT NO.	DESCRIPTION	FIRST DAY COVERS SING	INSC. BLK	INSRIP BLK-4	UNUSED F/NH	USED F
12-22	**1952-53 Issues, complete (11)**	......	......	......	**11.50**	......

1952

SCOTT NO.	DESCRIPTION	FIRST DAY COVERS SING	INSC. BLK	INSRIP BLK-4	UNUSED F/NH	USED F
12	5¢ United Nations Day	1.75	3.50	3.00	.65	.30
13-14	3¢ & 5¢ Human Rights Day	2.50	7.00	6.75	1.50	.75

1953

SCOTT NO.	DESCRIPTION	FIRST DAY COVERS SING	INSC. BLK	INSRIP BLK-4	UNUSED F/NH	USED F
15-16	3¢ & 5¢ Refugee Issue	1.80	4.50	9.00	2.25	1.00
17-18	3¢ & 5¢ U.P.U. Issue	3.00	7.50	14.00	3.20	1.50
19-20	3¢ & 5¢ Technical Assistance	1.75	4.40	8.00	1.75	1.05
21-22	3¢ & 5¢ Human Rights Day	7.75	18.50	16.00	3.50	1.55

1954

SCOTT NO.	DESCRIPTION	FIRST DAY COVERS SING	INSC. BLK	INSRIP BLK-4	UNUSED F/NH	USED F
23-30	**1954 Issues, complete (8)**	......	......		**23.00**	......
23-24	3¢ & 8¢ Food & Agriculture	2.05	5.15	9.15	2.00	.75
25-26	3¢ & 8¢ International Labor	2.75	6.85	18.50	4.00	2.15
27-28	3¢ & 8¢ Geneva	4.00	10.00	25.00	5.00	2.25
29-30	3¢ & 8¢ Human Rights Day	7.75	18.50	65.00	15.00	4.00

1955

SCOTT NO.	DESCRIPTION	FIRST DAY COVERS SING	INSC. BLK	INSRIP BLK-4	UNUSED F/NH	USED F
31/40	**1955 Issues, (9) (No #38)**	......	......	......	**12.25**	......
31-32	3¢ & 8¢ Int. Civil Aviation Org.	3.95	10.00	24.50	5.50	3.00
33-34	3¢ & 8¢ UNESCO	2.00	5.00	7.95	1.70	1.10
35-37	3¢ to 8¢ United Nations	3.25	17.50	27.50	6.00	2.25
38	same, souvenir sheet	85.00	......	......`	175.00	55.00
38 var	Second print, retouched	......	......	......	180.00	65.00
39-40	3¢ & 8¢ Human Rights Day	2.00	5.00	6.25	1.30	.90

15-16

17-18

19-20

21-22

23-24

25-26

27-28

57-58

59-60

61-62

63-64

65-66

SETS ONLY: Prices listed are for complete sets as indicated. We regrettably cannot supply individual stamps from sets.

1956

SCOTT NO.	DESCRIPTION	FIRST DAY COVERS SING	INSC. BLK	INSRIP BLK-4	UNUSED F/NH	USED F
41-48	**1956 Issues, complete (8)**	......	......	......	**3.20**	......
41-42	3¢ & 8¢ International Telecommunications	2.00	5.00	6.25	1.30	.90
43-44	3¢ & 8¢ World Health Org.	2.00	5.00	6.25	1.30	.90
45-46	3¢ & 8¢ United Nations Day	1.25	3.15	1.35	.45	.25
47-48	3¢ & 8¢ Human Rights Day	1.25	3.15	1.25	.40	.30

1957

SCOTT NO.	DESCRIPTION	FIRST DAY COVERS SING	INSC. BLK	INSRIP BLK-4	UNUSED F/NH	USED F
49-58	**1957 Issues, complete (10)**	......	......	......	**2.25**	......
49-50	3¢ & 8¢ Meteorological Org.	1.25	3.15	1.35	.35	.25
51-52	3¢ & 8¢ Emergency Force	1.25	3.15	1.35	.35	.25
53-54	same, re-engraved	......	......	3.75	1.10	.30
55-56	3¢ & 8¢ Security Council	1.25	3.15	1.35	.35	.25
57-58	3¢ & 8¢ Human Rights Day	1.25	3.15	1.35	.35	.25

67-68

69-70

71-72

73-74

75-76

77-78

79-80

81-82

83-85

86-87

1958

SCOTT NO.	DESCRIPTION	FIRST DAY COVERS SING	INSC. BLK	INSRIP BLK-4	UNUSED F/NH	USED F
59-68	**1958 Issues, complete (10**	.....	.....	.....	**1.65**	......
59-60	3¢ & 8¢ Atomic Energy Agency	1.25	3.15	1.35	.35	.25
61-62	3¢ & 8¢ Central Hall	1.25	3.15	1.35	.35	.25
63-64	4¢ & 8¢ U.N. Seal	1.25	3.15	1.35	.35	.25
65-66	4¢ & 8¢ Economic & Social Council	1.25	3.15	1.35	.35	.25
67-68	4¢ & 8¢ Human Rights Day	1.21	3.15	1.35	.35	.25

1959

SCOTT NO.	DESCRIPTION	FIRST DAY COVERS SING	INSC. BLK	INSRIP BLK-4	UNUSED F/NH	USED F
69-76	**1959 Issues, complete (8)**	......	......	......	**1.35**	......
69-70	4¢ & 8¢ Flushing Meadows	1.25	3.15	1.40	.35	.25
71-72	4¢ & 8¢ Economic Commission Europe	1.25	3.15	1.40	.35	.25
73-74	4¢ & 8¢ Trusteeship Council	1.25	3.15	1.40	.40	.25
75-76	4¢ & 8¢ World Refugee Year	1.25	3.15	1.40	.35	.25

1960

SCOTT NO.	DESCRIPTION	FIRST DAY COVERS SING	INSC. BLK	INSRIP BLK-4	UNUSED F/NH	USED F
77/87	**1960 Issues, (10) (No #85)**	......	......	......	**1.65**	...
77-78	4¢ & 8¢ Palais de Chaillot	1.25	3.15	1.40	.35	.25
79-80	4¢ & 8¢ Economic Commission Asia	1.25	3.15	1.40	.35	.25
81-82	4¢ & 8¢ 5th World Forestry Congress	1.25	3.15	1.40	.35	.25
83-84	4¢ & 8¢ 15th Anniversary	1.25	3.15	1.40	.35	.25
85	same, souvenir sheet	4.25	......	......	2.10	1.80
85 var	Broken "V" Variety	135.00	......	......	72.50	67.50
86-87	4¢ & 8¢ International Bank	1.25	3.15	1.40	.35	.25

FIRST DAY COVERS: Prices for United Nations First Day Covers are for cacheted, unaddressed covers with each variety in a set mounted on a separate cover. Complete sets mounted on one cover do exist and sell for a slightly lower price.

UNITED NATIONS (NEW YORK)

88-89 90-91 92 93-94

95-96 97-99 100-101 102-103

1961

SCOTT NO.	DESCRIPTION	FIRST DAY COVERS SING	INSC. BLK	INSRIP BLK-4	UNUSED F/NH	USED F
88-99	**1961 Issues, complete (12)**	.....	......	......	**2.65**	......
88-89	4¢ & 8¢ International Court of Justice ...	1.25	3.15	1.35	.35	1.25
90-91	4¢ & 7¢ Int. Monetary Fund	1.25	3.15	1.35	.35	1.25
92	30¢ Abstract Flags	1.25	3.15	2.70	.60	.35
93-94	4¢ & 11¢ Economic Commission Latin America	1.25	3.15	2.70	.60	.35
95-96	4¢ & 11¢ Economic Commission Africa	1.25	3.15	1.40	.35	.25
97-99	3¢, 4¢ & 13¢ Children's Fund	1.25	3.50	2.55	.55	.40

1962

SCOTT NO.	DESCRIPTION	FIRST DAY COVERS SING	INSC. BLK	INSRIP BLK-4	UNUSED F/NH	USED F
100-13	**1962 Issues, complete (14)**	......	......	......	**2.95**	......
100-01	4¢ & 7¢ Housing & Community Development	1.25	3.15	1.40	.35	.25
102-03	4¢ & 11¢ Malaria Eradication	1.25	3.15	2.35	.50	.35
104-07	1¢ to 11¢ Definitives	2.00	4.00	2.75	.65	.35
108-09	5¢ & 15¢ Memorial Issue	1.25	3.15	3.40	.70	.55
110-11	4¢ & 11¢ Operation in the Congo	1.25	3.15	3.25	.65	.55
112-13	4¢ & 11¢ Peaceful Uses of Outer Space	1.25	3.15	1.70	.45	.30

104 105 106 107

108-09 110-11 112-13 114-15 116-17

118 119-20 121-22 123-24

1963

SCOTT NO.	DESCRIPTION	FIRST DAY COVERS SING	INSC. BLK	INSRIP BLK-4	UNUSED F/NH	USED F
114-22	**1963 Issues, complete (9)**	......	......	......	**2.10**	......
114-15	5¢ & 11¢ Science & Technology	1.25	3.15	1.85	.40	.35
116-17	5¢ & 11¢ Freedom From Hunger	1.25	3.15	1.85	.40	.35
118	25¢ UNTEA	1.10	3.00	2.70	.60	.35
119-20	5¢ & 11¢ General Assem. Bldg.	1.25	3.15	1.85	.40	.35
121-22	5¢ & 11¢ Human Rights	1.25	3.15	1.85	.40	.35

1964

SCOTT NO.	DESCRIPTION	FIRST DAY COVERS SING	INSC. BLK	INSRIP BLK-4	UNUSED F/NH	USED F
123-36	**1964 Issues, complete (14)**	......	......	......	**3.05**	......
123-24	5¢ & 11¢ Maritime Organization (IMCO)	1.25	3.15	1.85	.40	.35
125-28	2¢ to 50¢ Definitives	3.25	7.75	6.65	1.30	.85
129-30	5¢ & 11¢ Trade & Development	1.25	3.15	1.85	.40	.35
131-32	5¢ & 11¢ Narcotics Control	1.25	3.45	1.85	.40	.35
133	5¢ Cessation of Nuclear Testing	.60	1.30	.65	.20	.15
134-36	4¢ to 11¢ Education for Progress	1.30	3.25	2.50	.55	.35

125, UX3 126 127 128, U3-4

129-30 131-32 133 134-36

137-38 139-40 141-42 143-45

SCOTT NO.	DESCRIPTION	FIRST DAY COVERS SING	INSC. BLK	INSRIP BLK-4	UNUSED F/NH	USED F
137/53	**1965 Issues, (15) (No #145 or 150)**	.....	.....	......	**2.90**	......
137-38	5¢ & 11¢ United Nations Special Fund ..	1.25	3.15	1.45	.35	.30
139-40	5¢ & 11¢ United Nations Forces in Cyprus	1.25	3.15	1.45	.35	.30
141-42	5¢ & 11¢ I.T.U. Centenary	1.25	3.15	1.45	.35	.30
143-44	5¢ & 15¢ Int'l Cooperation Year	1.25	3.15	1.85	.40	.35
145	same, souvenir sheet	1.75	.....	.....	.60	.50
146-49	1¢ to 25¢ Definitive	3.50	8.75	7.65	1.20	.95

1966

SCOTT NO.	DESCRIPTION	FIRST DAY COVERS SING	INSC. BLK	INSRIP BLK-4	UNUSED F/NH	USED F
150	$1 Definitive	3.10	7.75	9.50	2.25	1.75

1965

SCOTT NO.	DESCRIPTION	FIRST DAY COVERS SING	INSC. BLK	INSRIP BLK-4	UNUSED F/NH	USED F
151-53	4¢ to 11¢ Population Trends	1.60	3.75	1.85	.40	.50

1966

SCOTT NO.	DESCRIPTION	FIRST DAY COVERS SING	INSC. BLK	INSRIP BLK-4	UNUSED F/NH	USED F
154-63	**1966 Issues, complete (10)**	......	......	......	**1.70**	......
154-55	5¢ & 15¢ World Federation (WFUNA) ...	1.25	3.15	1.60	.40	.30
156-57	5¢ & 11¢ World Health Organization	1.25	3.15	1.60	.35	.30
158-59	5¢ & 11¢ Coffee Agreement	1.25	3.15	1.60	.35	.30
160	15¢ Peace Keeping Observers	.60	1.50	1.45	.35	.30
161-63	4¢ to 11¢ UNICEF	1.60	3.75	1.85	.40	.35

1967

SCOTT NO.	DESCRIPTION	FIRST DAY COVERS SING	INSC. BLK	INSRIP BLK-4	UNUSED F/NH	USED F
164/80	**1967 Issues, (16) (No #179)**	......	......	......	**3.20**	......
164-65	5¢ & 11¢ Development	1.25	3.15	1.45	.35	.30
166-67	1-1/2 ¢ & 5¢ Definitives	1.25	3.15	1.10	.35	.30
168-69	5¢ & 11¢ Independence	1.25	3.15	1.45	.35	.30
170-74	4¢ to 15¢ Expo '67 Canada	3.00	7.50	4.20	.90	.85

146 147 148 149 150

151-53 154-55 156-57 158-59

160 161-63 164-65 166

UNITED NATIONS (NEW YORK)

167

168-69

170 171

172

177-78

173

174

175-76

181-82

180

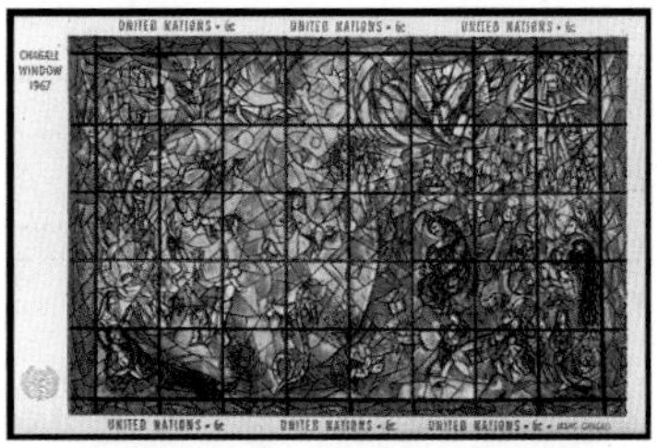
179

197-98

199-200

201-02

203-04

205-06

207-08

209-10

211-12

213-14

215

216-17

218

219

SCOTT NO.	DESCRIPTION	FIRST DAY COVERS SING	FIRST DAY COVERS INSC. BLK	INSRIP BLK-4	UNUSED F/NH	USED F
175-76	5¢ & 15¢ International Tourist Year	1.25	3.15	1.65	.35	.25
177-78	6¢ & 13¢ Towards Disarmament	1.25	3.15	1.90	.40	.35
179	36¢ Chagall Window souvenir sheet	1.25	......	......	.65	.60
180	6¢ Kiss of Peace	.60	......	.65	.25	.15
	1968					
181-91	**1968 Issues, complete (11)**	......	......	......	**4.00**	......
181-82	6¢ & 13 ¢ Secretariat	1.25	3.15	1.80	.40	.35
183-84	6¢ & 75¢ H. Starcke	6.25	15.00	7.50	1.75	1.50
185-86	6¢ & 13¢ Industrial Development	1.25	3.15	1.65	.35	.30
187	6¢ Definitive	.60	1.50	.65	.25	.15
188-89	6¢ & 20¢ Weather Watch	1.25	3.15	2.30	.50	.40
190-91	6¢ & 13¢ International Year—Human Rights	1.25	3.15	2.30	.50	.40
	1969					
192-202	**1969 Issues (11)**	......	......	......	**2.35**	......
192-93	6¢ & 13¢ Institute Training Research	1.25	3.15	1.85	.40	.35
194-95	6¢ & 15¢ U.N. Building—Chile	1.25	3.15	2.15	.45	.40
196	13¢ Definitive	.60	1.50	1.40	.35	.25
197-98	6¢ & 13¢ Peace Through International Law	1.25	3.15	1.85	.40	.35
199-200	6¢ & 20¢ Labor & Development	1.25	3.15	2.35	.50	.45
201-02	6¢ & 13¢ Tunisian Mosaics	1.25	3.15	1.90	.40	.35
	1970					
203/14	**1970 Issues, (11) (No #212)**	......	......	......	**3.25**	......
203-04	6¢ & 25¢ Japanese Peace Bell	1.25	3.15	2.45	.55	.50
205-06	6¢ & 13¢ L. Mekong Delta Devel.	1.25	3.15	1.65	.35	.30
207-08	6¢ & 13¢ Fight Cancer	1.25	3.15	1.65	.35	.30
209-11	6¢ to 25¢ Peace & Progress	1.70	4.25	4.10	.90	.80
212	same, souvenir sheet	1.40	......	......	.90	.85
213-14	6¢ & 13¢ Peace, Justice & Prog.	1.25	3.15	1.65	.35	.30
	1971					
215-25	**1971 Issues (11)**	......	......	......	**3.25**	......
215	6¢ Peaceful Uses Sea-Bed	.60	1.50	.65	.20	.15
216-17	6¢ & 13¢ Support Refugees	1.25	3.15	1.65	.35	.30
218	13¢ World Food Programme	.60	1.50	1.20	.25	.20
219	20¢ Universal Postal Union Building	.70	1.75	1.65	.35	.35
220-21	8¢ & 13¢ Anti-Discrimination	1.25	3.15	1.85	.40	.35
222-23	8¢ & 60¢ Definitives	2.50	6.25	5.70	1.25	1.10
224-25	8¢ & 21¢ International School	1.25	3.15	2.75	.60	.55

183-84

185-86

187, U5

188-89

190-91

192-93

194-95

196

220

221

222

223

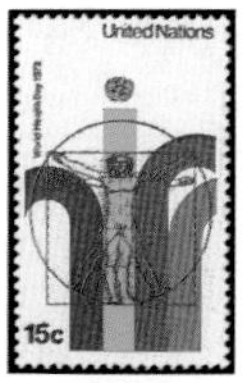

228

227

226

224-25

SETS ONLY: Prices listed are for complete sets as indicated. We regrettably cannot supply individual stamps from sets.

INSCRIPTION BLOCKS: Each corner of United Nations complete sheets contains the U.N. Emblem plus the name of the issue in the selvage. These are offered as Inscription Blocks of Four.

UNITED NATIONS (NEW YORK)

1972

SCOTT NO.	DESCRIPTION	FIRST DAY COVERS SING	INSC. BLK	INSRIP BLK-4	UNUSED F/NH	USED F
226-33	**1972 Issues, complete (8)**	......	......	......	**3.55**	......
226	95¢ Definitive	2.75	6.85	8.65	1.90	1.50
227	8¢ Non-Proliferation	.60	1.50	.80	.20	.15
228	15¢ World Health Org.	.60	1.50	1.40	.30	.25
229-30	8¢ & 15¢ Environment	1.25	3.15	2.15	.45	.40
231	21¢ Economic Commission Europe	.75	1.85	2.10	.45	.40
232-33	8¢ & 15¢ Art—Sert Ceiling	1.25	3.15	2.15	.45	.40

1973

SCOTT NO.	DESCRIPTION	FIRST DAY COVERS SING	INSC. BLK	INSRIP BLK-4	UNUSED F/NH	USED F
234-43	**1973 Issues, complete (10)**	......	......	......	**2.60**	......
234-35	8¢ & 15¢ Disarmament Decade	1.25	3.15	2.15	.45	.40
236-37	8¢ & 15¢ Drug Abuse	1.25	3.15	2.50	.55	.50
238-39	8¢ & 21¢ Volunteers Programme	1.25	3.15	2.75	.60	.55
240-41	8¢ & 15¢ Namibia	1.25	3.15	2.55	.55	.50
242-43	8¢ & 21¢ Human Rights	1.25	3.15	2.75	.60	.55

1974

SCOTT NO.	DESCRIPTION	FIRST DAY COVERS SING	INSC. BLK	INSRIP BLK-4	UNUSED F/NH	USED F
244-55	**1974 Issues, complete (12)**	......	......	......	**3.20**	......
244-45	10¢ & 21¢ ILO Headquarters	1.30	3.25	3.25	.70	.65
246	10¢ Universal Postal Union	.60	1.50	.95	.20	.15
247-48	10¢ & 18¢ Brazil Peace Mural	1.25	3.15	2.55	.55	.50
249-51	2¢ to 18¢ Definitives	1.65	4.15	2.75	.60	.55
252-53	10¢ & 18¢ World Population Year	1.35	3.35	2.55	.55	.50
254-55	10¢ & 26¢ Law of the Sea	1.35	3.35	3.45	1.75	.70

231

232-33

234-35

236-37

238-39

240-41

242-43

244-45

246

1975

SCOTT NO.	DESCRIPTION	FIRST DAY COVERS SING	INSC. BLK	INSRIP BLK-4	UNUSED F/NH	USED F
256/66	**1975 Issues, (10) (No #262)**	......	......	......	**4.05**	......
256-57	10¢ & 26¢ Peaceful Uses of Space	1.35	3.35	3.45	.75	.70
258-59	10¢ & 18¢ Int'l. Women's Year	1.25	3.15	2.55	.55	.50
260-61	10¢ & 26¢ Anniversary	1.30	3.35	3.00	.60	.60
262	same, souvenir sheet	1.55	......	......	1.00	.80
263-64	10¢ & 18¢ Namibia	1.25	3.15	2.55	.55	.50
265-66	13¢ & 26¢ Peacekeeping	1.35	3.35	3.45	.75	.70

1976

SCOTT NO.	DESCRIPTION	FIRST DAY COVERS SING	INSC. BLK	INSRIP BLK-4	UNUSED F/NH	USED F
267-80	**1976 Issues, complete (14)**	......	......	......	**7.90**	......
267-71	3¢ to 50¢ Definitives	3.10	7.75	7.45	1.60	1.35

247-48 249 250, U6 251 252-53

254-55 256-57 258-59 260-62 263-64

265-66

267

268

269

270

271

272-73

274-75

276-77

280

278-79

281-82

283-84

289-90

285-86

287-88

SCOTT NO.	DESCRIPTION	FIRST DAY COVERS SING	INSC. BLK	INSRIP BLK-4	UNUSED F/NH	USED F
272-73	13¢ & 26¢ World Federation	1.50	3.75	3.25	.70	.65
274-75	13¢ & 31¢ Conf. on Trade & Dev.	1.45	3.65	4.70	.85	.75
276-77	13¢ & 25¢ Conference on Human Settlements	1.25	3.15	4.00	.85	.75
278-79	13¢ & 31¢ Postal Admin.	9.50	23.50	18.75	4.00	2.25
280	13¢ World Food Council	.60	1.50	1.40	.30	.25

1977

SCOTT NO.	DESCRIPTION	FIRST DAY COVERS SING	INSC. BLK	INSRIP BLK-4	UNUSED F/NH	USED F
281-90	**Issues, complete (10)**	......	......	......	**3.60**	......
281-82	13¢ & 31¢ WIPO	1.40	3.50	4.20	.90	.80
283-84	13¢ & 25¢ Water Conference	1.35	3.40	3.95	.85	.75
285-86	13¢ & 31¢ Security Council	1.50	3.75	4.05	.65	.60
287-88	13¢ & 25¢ Combat Racism	1.35	3.40	3.50	.75	.70
289-90	13¢ & 10¢ Atomic Energy	1.25	3.15	3.00	.65	.60

1978

SCOTT NO.	DESCRIPTION	FIRST DAY COVERS SING	INSC. BLK	INSRIP BLK-4	UNUSED F/NH	USED F
291-303	**1978 Issues, complete (13)**	......	......	......	**5.65**	......
291-93	1¢, 25¢ & $1 Definitives	4.00	10.00	9.90	2.20	1.90
294-95	13¢ & 31¢ Smallpox Eradication	1.40	3.50	4.40	.95	.85
296-97	13¢ & 18¢ Namibia	1.25	3.15	2.70	.60	.55
298-99	13¢ & 25¢ ICAO	1.30	3.25	3.50	.75	.70
300-01	13¢ & 18¢ General Assembly	1.25	3.15	2.70	.60	.55
302-03	13¢ & 31¢ TCDC	1.50	3.75	4.00	.85	.75

291

292

293

294-95

296-97

298-99

300-01

302-03

304

305

306

307

UNITED NATIONS (NEW YORK)

1979

SCOTT NO.	DESCRIPTION	FIRST DAY COVERS SING	FIRST DAY COVERS INSC. BLK	INSRIP BLK-4	UNUSED F/NH	USED F
304-15	**1979 Issues, complete (12)**	......	......	......	**4.15**	......
304-07	5¢, 14¢, 15¢ & 20¢ Definitives	2.00	5.00	4.40	.95	.85
308-09	15¢ & 20¢ UNDRO	1.35	3.40	3.25	.70	.65
310-11	15¢ & 31¢ I.Y.C.	3.75	9.40	4.95	1.10	.95
312-13	15¢ & 31¢ Namibia	1.55	3.85	4.00	.85	.75
314-15	15¢ & 20¢ Court of Justice	1.40	3.50	3.50	.75	.60

1980 World Flags

- 326 *Luxembourg*
- 327 *Fiji*
- 328 *Viet Nam*
- 329 *Guinea*
- 330 *Surinam*
- 331 *Bangladesh*
- 332 *Mali*
- 333 *Yugoslavia*
- 334 *France*
- 335 *Venezuela*
- 336 *El Salvador*
- 337 *Madagascar*
- 338 *Cameroon*
- 339 *Rwanda*
- 340 *Hungary*

325 308-09 310-11

312-13 314-15 316 317

1980

SCOTT NO.	DESCRIPTION	FIRST DAY COVERS SING	FIRST DAY COVERS INSC. BLK	INSRIP BLK-4	UNUSED F/NH	USED F
316/42	**1980 Issues, (26) (No #324)**	......	......	......	**7.95**	......
316-17	15¢ & 31¢ Economics	1.65	4.15	4.00	.85	.75
318-19	15¢ & 20¢ Decade for Women	1.35	3.40	3.50	.75	.60
320-21	15¢ & 31¢ Peacekeeping	1.60	4.00	4.20	.90	.80
322-23	15¢ & 31¢ Anniversary	1.55	3.90	4.00	.85	.75
324	same, souvenir sheet	1.45	......	......	.95	.90
325-40	15¢ 1980 World Flags, 16 varieties	10.00	......	13.50	3.00	2.75
341-42	15¢ & 20¢ Economic & Social Council	1.30	3.25	3.50	.75	.60

318-19 320 321 322

323 341 342 343

344 345 346-47 348

349 366 367

1981 World Flags

- 350 *Djibouti*
- 351 *Sri Lanka*
- 352 *Bolivia*
- 353 *Equatorial Guinea*
- 354 *Malta*
- 355 *Czechoslovakia*
- 356 *Thailand*
- 357 *Trinidad*
- 358 *Ukraine*
- 359 *Kuwait*
- 360 *Sudan*
- 361 *Egypt*
- 362 *United States*
- 363 *Singapore*
- 364 *Panama*
- 365 *Costa Rica*

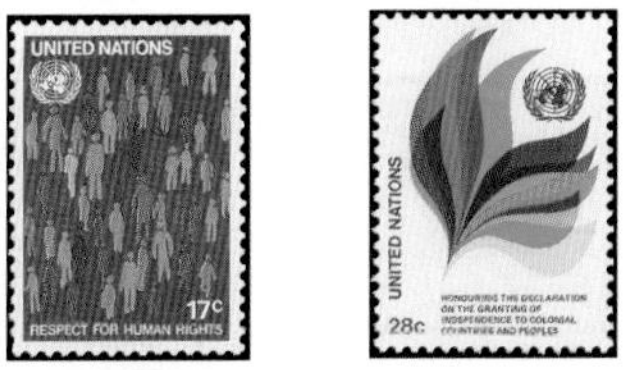

368 369

370 371 372 373 390-91

1981

SCOTT NO.	DESCRIPTION	FIRST DAY COVERS SING	FIRST DAY COVERS INSC. BLK	INSRIP BLK-4	UNUSED F/NH	USED F
343-67	**1981 Issues, complete (25)**	......	......	......	**9.25**	......
343	15¢ Palestinian People	.75	1.85	1.60	.35	.30
344-45	20¢ & 35¢ Disabled Persons	1.70	4.25	4.75	1.00	.90
346-47	20¢ & 31¢ Fresco	1.60	4.00	4.75	1.00	.90
348-49	20¢ & 40¢ Sources of Energy	1.90	4.75	5.45	1.20	1.00
350-65	20¢ 1981 World Flags, 16 varieties	13.50	......	22.00	5.00	4.50
366-67	18¢ & 28¢ Volunteers Program	1.55	3.85	5.50	1.20	.85

1982

SCOTT NO.	DESCRIPTION	FIRST DAY COVERS SING	FIRST DAY COVERS INSC. BLK	INSRIP BLK-4	UNUSED F/NH	USED F
368-91	**1982 Issues, complete (24)**	......	......	......	**9.75**	......
368-70	17¢, 28¢ & 49¢ Definitives	2.50	6.25	9.25	2.00	1.55
371-72	20¢ & 40¢ Human Environment	1.95	4.85	7.00	1.40	1.15
373	20¢ Space Exploration	.90	2.25	3.25	.70	.40
374-89	20¢ World Flags, 16 varieties	13.00	......	22.00	5.00	4.50
390-91	20¢ & 28¢ Nature Conservation	1.75	4.35	5.75	1.20	1.00

1982 World Flags

- 374 *Austria*
- 375 *Malaysia*
- 376 *Seychelles*
- 377 *Ireland*
- 378 *Mozambique*
- 379 *Albania*
- 380 *Dominica*
- 381 *Solomon Islands*
- 382 *Philippines*
- 383 *Swaziland*
- 384 *Nicaragua*
- 385 *Burma*
- 386 *Cape Verde*
- 387 *Guyana*
- 388 *Belgium*
- 389 *Nigeria*

392 393

394 395 396 397 398

1983 World Flags

- 399 *United Kingdom*
- 400 *Barbados*
- 401 *Nepal*
- 402 *Israel*
- 403 *Malawi*
- 404 *Byelorussian SSR*
- 405 *Jamaica*
- 406 *Kenya*
- 407 *China*
- 408 *Peru*
- 409 *Bulgaria*
- 410 *Canada*
- 411 *Somalia*
- 412 *Senegal*
- 413 *Brazil*
- 414 *Sweden*

415 416 417-18

1983

SCOTT NO.	DESCRIPTION	FIRST DAY COVERS SING	FIRST DAY COVERS INSC. BLK	INSRIP BLK-4	UNUSED F/NH	USED F
392-416	**1983 Issues, complete (25)**	......	......	......	**12.50**	......
392-93	20¢ & 40¢ World Communications Year	2.05	5.15	6.75	1.40	1.10
394-95	20¢ & 37¢ Safety at Sea	1.95	4.75	6.75	1.40	1.10
396	20¢ World Food Program	.85	2.10	3.95	.85	.50
397-98	20¢ & 28¢ Trade & Development	1.60	4.00	7.25	1.60	1.00
399-414	20¢ World Flags, 16 varieties	13.00	......	25.00	6.00	7.00
415-16	20¢ & 40¢ Human Rights	2.50	6.25	9.00	2.00	1.50

419 420 421 423

1984 World Flags

- 425 *Burundi*
- 426 *Pakistan*
- 427 *Benin*
- 428 *Italy*
- 429 *Tanzania*
- 430 *United Arab Emirates*
- 431 *Ecuador*
- 432 *Bahamas*
- 433 *Poland*
- 434 *Papua New Guinea*
- 435 *Uruguay*
- 436 *Chile*
- 437 *Paraguay*
- 438 *Bhutan*
- 439 *Central African Republic*
- 440 *Australia*

422 424

UNITED NATIONS (NEW YORK)

SCOTT NO.	DESCRIPTION	FIRST DAY COVERS SING	INSC. BLK	INSRIP BLK-4	UNUSED F/NH	USED F
417-42	**1984 Issues, complete (25)**	......	......	......	20.40	......
417-18	20¢ & 40¢ Population	2.10	5.25	8.50	1.75	1.25
419-20	20¢ & 40¢ Food Day	2.10	5.25	9.50	2.00	1.25
421-22	20¢ & 50¢ Heritage	2.25	5.50	10.50	2.25	1.50
423-24	20¢ & 50¢ Future for Refugees	2.25	5.50	9.00	2.00	1.35
425-40	20¢ 1984 World Flags, 16 varieties	13.00	......	47.50	11.50	10.00
441-42	20¢ & 35¢ Youth Year	2.10	5.25	9.00	2.00	1.25

1985 World Flags

450 *Grenada*
451 *Germany-West*
452 *Saudi Arabia*
453 *Mexico*
454 *Uganda*
455 *Sao Tome & Principie*
456 *U.S.S.R.*
457 *India*
458 *Liberia*
459 *Mauritius*
460 *Chad*
461 *Dominican Republic*
462 *Oman*
463 *Ghana*
464 *Sierra Leone*
465 *Finland*

444

443

445

1985

SCOTT NO.	DESCRIPTION	FIRST DAY COVERS SING	INSC. BLK	INSRIP BLK-4	UNUSED F/NH	USED F
443/67	**1985 Issues, (24) (No #449)**	......	......	......	25.00	......
443	23¢ ILO—Turin Centre	1.00	2.50	3.70	.85	.50
444	50¢ United Nations University in Japan	1.65	4.15	7.75	1.65	1.10
445-46	22¢ & $3 Definitives	8.00	20.00	23.00	5.50	4.50
447-48	22¢ & 45¢ 40th Anniversary	2.30	5.75	8.75	1.75	1.50
449	same, souvenir sheet	2.50	......	......	2.50	1.50
450-65	22¢ 1985 World Flags, 16 varieties	14.00	......	52.50	12.50	10.00
466-67	22¢ & 33¢ Child Survival	2.25	5.65	7.95	1.75	1.10

446

447

1986 World Flags

477 *New Zealand*
478 *Lao PDR*
479 *Burkina Faso*
480 *Gambia*
481 *Maldives*
482 *Ethiopia*
483 *Jordan*
484 *Zambia*
485 *Iceland*
486 *Antigua & Barbuda*
487 *Angola*
488 *Botswana*
489 *Romania*
490 *Togo*
491 *Mauritania*
492 *Colombia*

448

466

441

468

469

473

475

476

1986

SCOTT NO.	DESCRIPTION	FIRST DAY COVERS SING	INSC. BLK	INSRIP BLK-4	UNUSED F/NH	USED F
468-92	**1986 Issues (25)**	......	......	......	24.50	......
468	22¢ African Crisis	1.05	2.60	3.25	.70	.40
469-72	22¢ Development, 4 varieties, attached	2.50	3.25	10.50	9.00	......
473-74	22¢ & 44¢ Philately	2.30	5.75	8.65	1.75	1.00
475-76	22¢ & 33¢ Peace Year	2.25	5.65	8.65	1.90	1.00
477-92	22¢ 1986 World Flags, 16 varieties	14.00	......	52.50	12.50	10.00

493a

494

495

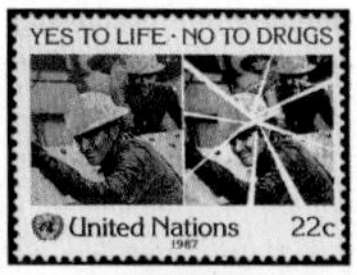

497

1987 World Flags

499 *Comoros*
500 *Democratic Yemen*
501 *Mongolia*
502 *Vanuatu*
503 *Japan*
504 *Gabon*
505 *Zimbabwe*
506 *Iraq*
507 *Argentina*
508 *Congo*
509 *Niger*
510 *St. Lucia*
511 *Bahrain*
512 *Haiti*
513 *Afghanistan*
514 *Greece*

515

517

1986

SCOTT NO.	DESCRIPTION	FIRST DAY COVERS SING	INSC. BLK	INSRIP BLK-4	UNUSED F/NH	USED F
493	22¢ to 44¢ World Federation of United Nations Associations Souvenir sheet of 4	4.00	......	......	5.50	4.00

1987

SCOTT NO.	DESCRIPTION	FIRST DAY COVERS SING	INSC. BLK	INSRIP BLK-4	UNUSED F/NH	USED F
494-518	**1987 Issues (25)**	......	......	......	19.00	......
494	22¢ Trygve Lie	1.05	2.60	5.00	1.00	.75
495-96	22¢ & 44¢ Shelter Homeless	2.25	5.65	8.50	1.75	1.75
497-98	22¢ & 33¢ Anti-Drug Campaign	2.25	5.65	8.25	1.65	1.65
499-514	22¢ 1987 World Flags, 16 varieties	14.00	......	52.50	12.50	10.00
515-16	22¢ & 39¢ United Nations Day	2.30	5.75	7.50	1.50	1.30
517-18	22¢ & 44¢ Child Immunization	2.35	5.70	9.00	2.50	2.00

519

521

524

1988 World Flags

528 *Spain*
529 *St. Vincent & Grenadines*
530 *Ivory Coast*
531 *Lebanon*
532 *Yemen*
533 *Cuba*
534 *Denmark*
535 *Libya*
536 *Qatar*
537 *Zaire*
538 *Norway*
539 *German Democratic Republic*
540 *Iran*
541 *Tunisia*
542 *Samoa*
543 *Belize*

526

544-45

546

548

549

550

1988

SCOTT NO.	DESCRIPTION	FIRST DAY COVERS SING	INSC. BLK	INSRIP BLK-4	UNUSED F/NH	USED F
519/44	**1988 Issues (24) (No #522-23)**	......	......	......	19.25	......
519-20	22¢ & 33¢ World without Hunger	2.25	5.65	10.50	2.35	1.75
521	3¢ For a Better World	.90	2.25	.90	.20	.20
					Sheetlets	
522-23	25¢ & 44¢ Forest Conservation (set of 6, includes Geneva and Vienna)	15.00	40.00	130.00	27.50	25.00
524-25	25¢ & 50¢ Volunteer Day	2.60	6.50	10.50	2.25	2.00
526-27	25¢ & 38¢ Health in Sports	2.30	5.75	12.00	2.75	2.00
528-43	25¢ 1988 World Flags, 16 varieties	14.50	......	52.50	12.50	10.00
544	25¢ Human Rights	1.75	4.25	4.00	.75	.45
545	$1 Human Rights souvenir sheet	2.75	......	......	2.50	2.00

552

553

570-71

1989 World Flags

554 *Indonesia*
555 *Lesotho*
556 *Guatamala*
557 *Netherlands*
558 *South Africa*
559 *Portugal*
560 *Morocco*
561 *Syrian Arab Republic*
562 *Honduras*
563 *Kampuchea*
564 *Guinea-Bissau*
565 *Cyprus*
566 *Algeria*
567 *Brunei*
568 *St. Kitts & Nevis*
569 *United Nations*

572

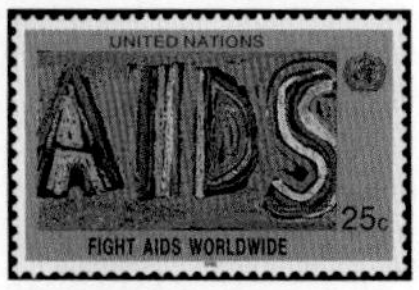

573-74

UNITED NATIONS (NEW YORK)

1989

SCOTT NO.	DESCRIPTION	FIRST DAY COVERS SING	FIRST DAY COVERS INSC. BLK	INSRIP BLK-4	UNUSED F/NH	USED F
546-71	**1989 Issues (26)**	......	......	......	**30.00**	......
546-47	25¢ & 45¢ World Bank	2.60	6.50	12.00	2.75	2.00
548	25¢ Nobel Peace Prize	1.10	1.65	5.75	1.10	.95
549	45¢ United Nations Definitive	1.40	2.10	5.75	1.10	.95
550-51	25¢ & 36¢ Weather Watch	2.30	5.75	15.00	3.50	2.50
552-53	25¢ & 90¢ U.N. Offices in Vienna	3.75	9.25	23.50	5.50	5.00
554-69	25¢ 1989 World Flags, 16 varieties	14.50	......	57.50	13.50	10.00
				Sheetlets (12)		
570-71	25¢ & 45¢ Human Rights 40th Ann. (strips of 3 with tabs)	2.60	6.50	21.00	5.00	....

1990

SCOTT NO.	DESCRIPTION	FIRST DAY COVERS SING	FIRST DAY COVERS INSC. BLK	INSRIP BLK-4	UNUSED F/NH	USED F
572/83	**1990 Issues (11) (No #579)**	......	......	......	**25.50**	......
572	25¢ International Trade Center	1.75	2.95	10.50	2.10	1.80
573-74	25¢ & 40¢ AIDS	2.60	6.50	12.25	2.75	2.25
575-76	25¢ & 90¢ Medicinal Plants	3.75	9.25	16.00	3.50	2.50
577-78	25¢ & 45¢ United Nations 45th Anniversary	2.60	6.50	18.50	4.00	3.50
579	25¢ & 45¢ United Nations 45th Anniversary Souvenir Sheet	2.10	......	......	7.50	7.50
580-81	25¢ & 36¢ Crime Prevention	2.30	5.75	18.00	4.00	3.00
				Sheetlets (12)		
582-83	25¢ & 45¢ Human Rights (strips of 3 with tabs)	2.60	6.50	23.00	5.00	....

575-76

577-78

580-81

584

588

590

591

592

593

595

597

603

605

609

1991

SCOTT NO.	DESCRIPTION	FIRST DAY COVERS SING	FIRST DAY COVERS INSC. BLK	INSRIP BLK-4	UNUSED F/NH	USED F
584-600	**1991 Issues (17)**	......	......	......	**27.50**	......
584-87	30¢ Econ. Comm. for Europe, 4 varieties, attached	4.50	5.50	5.25	4.50	4.00
588-89	30¢ & 50¢ Namibia—A New Nation	3.50	8.75	10.50	2.35	2.00
590-91	30¢ & 50¢ Definitives	4.00	10.00	10.50	2.35	2.00
592	$2 Definitive	5.50	13.50	19.00	4.00	3.00
593-94	30¢ & 70¢ Children's Rights	4.00	10.00	12.50	3.10	2.75
595-96	30¢ & 90¢ Banning of Chemical	4.25	10.50	17.00	3.65	3.00
597-98	30¢ & 40¢ 40th Anniversary of UNPA	3.50	8.75	10.50	2.35	2.25
				Sheetlets (12)		
599-600	30¢ & 50¢ Human Rights (strips of 3 with tabs)	3.00	7.50	31.50	7.00	....

611

613

614

618

620

624

626

629

633

1992

SCOTT NO.	DESCRIPTION	FIRST DAY COVERS SING	FIRST DAY COVERS INSC. BLK	INSRIP BLK-4	UNUSED F/NH	USED F
601-17	**1992 Issues (17)**	......	......	......	**23.00**	......
601-02	29¢-50¢ World Heritage—UNESCO	3.60	9.00	11.25	2.00	1.75
603-04	29¢ Clean Oceans, 2 varieties, attached	2.50	4.95	4.50	1.60	1.50
605-08	29¢ Earth Summit, 4 varieties, attached	3.50	4.25	3.50	2.75	2.50
609-10	29¢ Mission to Planet Earth, 2 varieties, attd	2.50	4.95	14.50	6.00	6.00
611-12	29¢-50¢ Science and Technology	3.60	9.00	8.75	1.95	1.75
613-15	4¢-40¢ Definitives	3.40	8.50	9.75	2.00	1.75
				Sheetlets (12)		
616-17	20¢-50¢ Human Rights (strips of 3 with tabs)	3.00	9.50	22.50	5.50	....

1993

SCOTT NO.	DESCRIPTION	FIRST DAY COVERS SING	FIRST DAY COVERS INSC. BLK	INSRIP BLK-4	UNUSED F/NH	USED F
618-36	**1993 Issues (19)**	......	......	......	**22.75**	......
618-19	29¢-52¢ Aging	3.00	9.50	8.75	2.50	1.75
620-23	29¢ Endangered Species, 4 attached	3.50	4.25	3.50	2.75	2.50
624-25	29¢-50¢ Health Environment	3.60	9.00	8.75	1.95	1.75
626	5¢ Definitive	2.00	4.00	1.00	.20	.20
	Sheetlets (12)					
627-28	29¢-35¢ Human Rights (strips of 3 with tabs)	3.00	9.50	18.50	6.25	....
629-32	29¢ Peace, 4 attached	3.50	8.00	18.00	8.00	7.50
633-36	29¢ Environment—Climate, strip of 4	3.50	7.00	8.00(8)	3.00	2.50

637

643

644

645

646

647

651

653

655

1994

SCOTT NO.	DESCRIPTION	FIRST DAY COVERS SING	FIRST DAY COVERS INSC. BLK	INSRIP BLK-4	UNUSED F/NH	USED F
637-54	**1994 Issues (18)**	....	....	....	**21.50**	....
637-38	29¢-45¢ International Year of the Family	2.25	8.50	8.50	4.25	1.75
639-42	29¢ Endangered Species, 4 attached	3.00	4.25	3.50	2.50	2.25
643	50¢ Refugees	1.75	5.75	5.00	1.50	1.00
644-46	10¢-$1 Definitives (3)	3.50	12.50	12.00	2.75	2.25
647-50	29¢ International Decade for Natural Disaster Reduction, 4 attached	3.00	4.25	9.50	8.50	5.00
651-52	29¢-52¢ Population and Development	2.25	9.00	8.75	1.95	1.50
653-54	29¢-50¢ Development through Partnership	2.25	9.00	8.75	1.75	1.50

UNITED NATIONS (NEW YORK)

656

661

663

1995

SCOTT NO.	DESCRIPTION	FIRST DAY COVERS SING	FIRST DAY COVERS INSC. BLK	INSRIP BLK-4	UNUSED F/NH	USED F
655/69	**1995 Issues (14) (No #665)**	....	....	....	**34.00**	....
655	32¢ 50th Anniversary of the UN	1.75	4.00	3.50	1.60	.65
656	50¢ Social Summit	1.75	5.75	5.00	1.10	.85
657-60	29¢ Endangered Species, 4 attached	3.00	4.25	3.50	2.75	2.25
661-62	32¢-55¢ Youth: Our Future	2.50	11.00	11.00	2.60	1.50
663-64	32¢-50¢ 50th Anniversary of the UN	2.50	11.00	12.00	2.55	1.50

666

668

SCOTT NO.	DESCRIPTION	FIRST DAY COVERS SING	FIRST DAY COVERS INSC. BLK	INSRIP BLK-4	UNUSED F/NH	USED F
665	82¢ 50th Anniversary of the UN, Souvenir Sheet	2.50	....	....	3.50	1.95
666-67	32¢-40¢ 4th World Conference on Women	2.50	9.00	8.00	1.95	1.50
668	20¢ UN Headquarters	1.75	....	1.75	.40	.45

669a

SCOTT NO.	DESCRIPTION	FIRST DAY COVERS SING	FIRST DAY COVERS INSC. BLK	INSRIP BLK-4	UNUSED F/NH	USED F
669	32¢ 50th Anniversary, Miniature Sheet of 12	....	....	....	20.00	....
669a-l	32¢ 50th Anniversary of the UN, booklet single	1.75	....	....	.75	.25
670	same, souvenir booklet of 4 panes of 3	....	....	....	22.00	....

671

672

1996

SCOTT NO.	DESCRIPTION	FIRST DAY COVERS SING	FIRST DAY COVERS INSC. BLK	INSRIP BLK-4	UNUSED F/NH	USED F
671/89	**1996 Issues (18) (No 685)**	....	....	....	**14.20**	....
671	32¢ WFUNA 50th Anniversary	1.75	4.00	3.50	.75	.65
672-73	32¢-60¢ Definitives	2.50	9.00	8.00	2.00	1.60
674-77	32¢ Endangered Species, 4 attached	3.00	4.25	3.50	2.75	2.25
678-82	32¢ City Summit (Habitat II), strip of 5	3.75	5.00	9.00	5.00	3.00
683-84	32¢-50¢ Sport & the Environment	2.50	9.00	8.50	1.95	1.50
685	82¢ Sport & the Environment souvenir sheet	2.50	....	....	2.75	1.95

686

688

SCOTT NO.	DESCRIPTION	FIRST DAY COVERS SING	FIRST DAY COVERS INSC. BLK	INSRIP BLK-4	UNUSED F/NH	USED F
686-87	32¢-60¢ A Plea for Peace	2.50	9.00	9.00	2.00	1.75
688-89	32¢-60¢ UNICEF 50th Anniversary	2.50	9.00	9.00	2.00	1.75

1997 World Flags

690	*Tadjikistan*	**694**	*Liechtenstein*
691	*Georgia*	**695**	*South Korea*
692	*Armenia*	**696**	*Kazakhstan*
693	*Namibia*	**697**	*Latvia*

698

1997

SCOTT NO.	DESCRIPTION	FIRST DAY COVERS SING	FIRST DAY COVERS INSC. BLK	INSRIP BLK-4	UNUSED F/NH	USED F
690/717	**1997 Issues (27) (No. #708, 708A)**	....	....	....	**24.00**	....
690-97	1997 World Flags, 8 varieties	12.50	....	24.50	5.75	5.00
698-99	8¢-55¢ Flowers, UN headquarters	2.25	8.00	8.00	1.85	1.50

700-03

704-07

SCOTT NO.	DESCRIPTION	FIRST DAY COVERS SING	FIRST DAY COVERS INSC. BLK	INSRIP BLK-4	UNUSED F/NH	USED F
700-03	32¢ Endangered Species, 4 attached	3.00	4.25	3.50	2.75	2.25
704-07	32¢ Earth Summit +5, 4 attached	3.00	4.25	4.75	4.35	3.50
708	$1 Earth Summit +5, souvenir sheet	2.50	....	....	3.00	2.25
708a	$1 1997 Pacific '97 overprint on #708	15.00	....	....	19.50	15.00

709-13

SCOTT NO.	DESCRIPTION	FIRST DAY COVERS SING	FIRST DAY COVERS INSC. BLK	INSRIP BLK-4	UNUSED F/NH	USED F
709-13	32¢ Transporation, strip of 5	3.75	5.00	9.00(10)	4.00	3.50

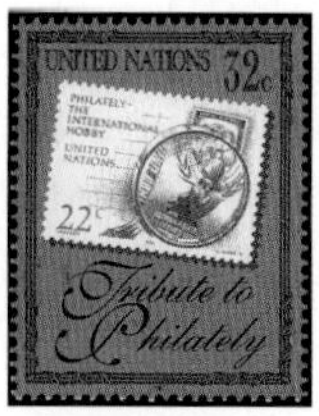

714

716

SCOTT NO.	DESCRIPTION	FIRST DAY COVERS SING	FIRST DAY COVERS INSC. BLK	INSRIP BLK-4	UNUSED F/NH	USED F
714-15	32¢-50¢ Tribute to Philately	2.50	9.00	17.00	4.25	1.50
716-17	32¢-60¢ Terracota Warriors	2.50	9.00	9.50	2.25	1.75
718	same, Souvenir bklt of 6 panes of 4	....	....	....	6.50	....

1998 World Flags

719	*Micronesia*
720	*Slovakia*
721	*Dem. People's Rep. of Korea*
722	*Azerbaijan*
723	*Uzbekistan*
724	*Monaco*
725	*Czeh Republic*
726	*Estonia*

730-33

1998

SCOTT NO.	DESCRIPTION	FIRST DAY COVERS SING	FIRST DAY COVERS INSC. BLK	INSRIP BLK-4	UNUSED F/NH	USED F
719-26	1998 World Flags, 8 varieties	12.50	....	24.50	6.00	5.00
727-29	1¢-21¢ Definitives	4.50	10.00	3.00	.70	.60
730-33	32¢ Endangered Species, 4 attached	3.00	4.25	3.50	3.00	2.25

UNITED NATIONS (NEW YORK)

734a

SCOTT NO.	DESCRIPTION	FIRST DAY COVERS SING	FIRST DAY COVERS INSC. BLK	INSRIP BLK-4	UNUSED F/NH	USED F
734	32¢ Intl. Year of the Ocean, sheetlet of 12	15.00	....	....	8.50	....
735	32¢Rain Forest, Jaguar	1.75	4.25	3.50	.70	.40
736	$2 Rain Forest, Jaguar, souvenir sheet .	7.00	....	....	5.00	4.00
737-38	32¢-40¢ 50 Year of Peacekeeping	3.75	9.00	7.50	1.60	1.40
739-40	32¢-50¢ 50th of the Dec. of Human Rights	4.00	9.50	8.00	1.75	1.60
741-42	32¢-60¢ Schonbrunn Castle	4.25	10.00	8.50	2.00	1.75
743	same, souvenir bklt of 6 panes	....	....	....	10.25	....

1999 World Flags

744	*Lithuania*	**748**	*Moldova*
745	*San Marino*	**749**	*Kyrgyzstan*
746	*Turkmenistan*	**750**	*Bosnia & Herzegovia*
747	*Marshall Islands*	**751**	*Eritrea*

754

1999

SCOTT NO.	DESCRIPTION	FIRST DAY COVERS SING	FIRST DAY COVERS INSC. BLK	INSRIP BLK-4	UNUSED F/NH	USED F
744-51	1999 World Flags, 8 varieties	12.50	....	25.00	6.00	5.00
752-53	33¢-$5 Definitives	12.00	30.00	45.00	11.50	9.50
754-55	33¢-60¢ World Heritage Sites, Australia	4.25	10.00	9.00	2.25	1.75
756	same, souvenir bklt of 6 panes	....	....	....	10.25	....

757-60

SCOTT NO.	DESCRIPTION	FIRST DAY COVERS SING	FIRST DAY COVERS INSC. BLK	INSRIP BLK-4	UNUSED F/NH	USED F
757-60	33¢ Endangered Species, 4 attached ...	3.00	4.25	3.50	3.00	2.25

761-62

764-67

SCOTT NO.	DESCRIPTION	FIRST DAY COVERS SING	FIRST DAY COVERS INSC. BLK	INSRIP BLK-4	UNUSED F/NH	USED F
761-62	33¢ Unispace III Conference	1.75	4.25	6.50	2.00	1.10
763	$2 Unispace III Conference, souvenir sheet	7.00	....	....	5.00	4.00
764-67	33¢ Universal Postal Union	1.75	4.25	3.75	3.00	2.25

770-71

SCOTT NO.	DESCRIPTION	FIRST DAY COVERS SING	FIRST DAY COVERS INSC. BLK	INSRIP BLK-4	UNUSED F/NH	USED F
768	33¢ In Memorium	1.75	4.25	6.75	1.50	.40
769	$1 In Memorium, souvenir sheet	3.25	....	....	2.25	1.10
770-71	33¢-60¢ Education-Keystone to the 21st Century	4.25	10.00	9.00	2.25	1.75

772

773-76

2000

SCOTT NO.	DESCRIPTION	FIRST DAY COVERS SING	FIRST DAY COVERS INSC. BLK	INSRIP BLK-4	UNUSED F/NH	USED F
772	33¢ International Year of Thanksgiving .	1.75	4.25	3.75	.75	.40
773-76	33¢ Endangered Species, 4 attached ...	3.00	4.25	3.75	3.00	2.25

777

787

782

SCOTT NO.	DESCRIPTION	FIRST DAY COVERS SING	FIRST DAY COVERS INSC. BLK	INSRIP BLK-4	UNUSED F/NH	USED F
777-78	33¢-60¢ Our World 2000	4.25	10.00	9.00	2.25	1.75
779-80	33¢-55¢ 55th Anniversary of the UN	4.25	10.00	9.00	2.25	1.75
781	same, 33¢-55¢ souvenir sheet	....	....	....	2.25	1.75
782	33¢ International Flag of Peace	1.75	4.25	3.75	.75	.40
783	33¢ United Nations in the 21st Century .	1.75	4.25	3.75	.75	.40
784-85	33¢-60¢ World Heritage Sites, Spain	4.25	10.00	9.00	2.25	1.75
786	same, souvenir bklt of 6 panes of 4	....	....	....	6.00	....
787	33¢ Respect for Refuges	1.75	4.25	3.75	.75	.40
788	$1 Respect for Refuges,souvenir sheet	3.25	....	....	2.25	1.10

793

789-92

2001

SCOTT NO.	DESCRIPTION	FIRST DAY COVERS SING	FIRST DAY COVERS INSC. BLK	INSRIP BLK-4	UNUSED F/NH	USED F
789-92	34¢ Endangered Species, 4 attached ...	3.00	4.25	3.75	3.00	2.25
793-94	34¢-80¢ Intl. Volunteers Year	4.50	10.00	11.00	2.75	2.00
795-802	2001 World Flags, 8 varieties	12.50	....	25.00	6.00	5.00
803-04	7¢-34¢ Definitives	3.50	8.50	5.00	1.00	.60
805-06	34¢-70¢ World Heritage Sites, Japan	4.50	10.00	10.00	2.50	2.00
807	same, souvenir bklt of 6 panes of 4	....	....	....	8.75	....

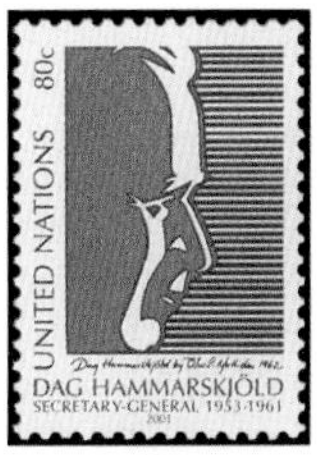

808

816

809

SCOTT NO.	DESCRIPTION	FIRST DAY COVERS SING	FIRST DAY COVERS INSC. BLK	INSRIP BLK-4	UNUSED F/NH	USED F
808	80¢ Dag Hammarskjold	2.50	4.00	8.00	1.95	1.00
809-10	34¢-80¢ 50th Anniv. of the UNPA	4.50	10.00	11.00	2.75	2.00
811	same, $2.40 souvenir sheet	6.50	....	....	6.00	5.00
812-15	34¢ Climate Change, strip of 4	3.00	4.25	3.75	3.00	2.25
816	34¢ Nobel Peace Prize	1.75	4.25	3.75	.75	.40

UNITED NATIONS (NEW YORK)

817

822

2002

SCOTT NO.	DESCRIPTION	FIRST DAY COVERS SING	INSC. BLK	INSRIP BLK-4	UNUSED F/NH	USED F
817	80¢ Children and Stamps	2.50	4.00	8.00	1.95	1.00
818-21	34¢ Endangered Species, 4 attached	3.00	4.25	3.75	3.00	2.25
822-23	34¢-57¢ Independence of East Timor	4.00	9.00	9.00	2.25	1.90
824-27	34¢-80¢ Intl. Year of Mountains, 2 pairs	5.00	11.00	5.50	4.75	4.00
828-31	37¢-60¢ Johannesburg Summit, 2 pairs	4.50	10.00	4.75	4.00	3.00

832

837

SCOTT NO.	DESCRIPTION	FIRST DAY COVERS SING	INSC. BLK	INSRIP BLK-4	UNUSED F/NH	USED F
832-33	34¢-80¢ World Heritage Sites, Italy	4.50	10.00	11.00	2.75	2.00
834	same, souvenir bklt of 6 panes of 4	....	....	....	8.75	....
835	70¢ UNAIDS Awareness, semi postal	2.25	3.75	7.50	1.75	1.00

2003

SCOTT NO.	DESCRIPTION	FIRST DAY COVERS SING	INSC. BLK	INSRIP BLK-4	UNUSED F/NH	USED F
836	37¢ Indigenous Art, sheet of 6	7.00	....	....	5.50	3.50
837-39	23¢-70¢ Definitives	3.50	4.50	12.50	3.00	1.75
840-41	23¢-70¢ Centenary of First Flight, 2 attach.	3.00	4.00	5.50	2.25	1.50

842-45

SCOTT NO.	DESCRIPTION	FIRST DAY COVERS SING	INSC. BLK	INSRIP BLK-4	UNUSED F/NH	USED F
842-45	37¢ Endangered Species, 4 attached	3.50	4.50	4.25	3.50	2.50
846-47	23¢-37¢ Intl. Year of Freshwater, 2 attach.	2.25	3.75	6.00	1.50	1.00
848	37¢ Ralph Bunche	1.75	4.50	4.25	.95	.50
849	60¢ In Memoriam, UN Complex Bombing in Iraq	2.25	4.50	6.00	1.50	.85
850-51	37¢-80¢ World Heritage Sites, United States	4.25	9.50	9.75	2.50	1.75
852	same, souvenir bklt of 6 panes of 4	....	....	....	9.75	....
853-57	37¢ UN Headquarters + labels, vert strip of 5	....	....	....	13.50	....
....	same, sheet of 4 (853-57)	....	....	....	55.00	....

863

865

2004

SCOTT NO.	DESCRIPTION	FIRST DAY COVERS SING	INSC. BLK	INSRIP BLK-4	UNUSED F/NH	USED F
859-61	37¢ Endangered Species, 4 attached	4.00	6.00	4.25	3.50	2.50
862	37¢ Indigenous Art, sheet of 6	7.50	....	....	5.25	4.00
863-64	37¢-70¢ Road Safety	4.50	10.00	10.75	2.75	2.00
865	80¢ Japanese Peace Bell, 50th Anniv.	2.50	5.00	8.00	2.00	1.25

866

SCOTT NO.	DESCRIPTION	FIRST DAY COVERS SING	INSC. BLK	INSRIP BLK-4	UNUSED F/NH	USED F
866-67	37¢-60¢ World Heritage Sites, Greece	4.25	9.50	9.75	2.50	1.75
868	same, souvenir bklt. of 6 panes of 4	....	....	....	16.50	....
869-70	37¢-80¢ My Dream for Peace	4.50	10.00	10.75	2.75	2.00
871-72	37¢-70¢ Human Rights	4.50	10.00	19.50(8)	2.75	2.00
873	37¢ Disarmament	1.75	4.50	4.25	.95	.50

874

876-79

2005

SCOTT NO.	DESCRIPTION	FIRST DAY COVERS SING	INSC. BLK	INSRIP BLK-4	UNUSED F/NH	USED F
874	80¢ U.N. 60th Anniversary	2.50	5.00	8.00	2.00	1.25
875	$1 U.N. 60th Anniv., souvenir sheet	3.25	....	....	2.25	1.25
876-79	37¢ Orchids, 4 attached	4.00	6.00	4.25	3.50	2.50
880-84	80¢ Sculptures-personalized stamps, 5 attached	11.50	25.00	55.00	15.00	6.00
885-86	37¢ Nature's Wisdom	4.50	10.00	10.75	2.75	2.00
887-88	37¢-70¢ International Year of Sports	4.50	10.00	10.75	2.75	2.00
889-90	37¢-80¢ World Heritage Sites, Egypt	4.50	10.00	10.75	2.75	2.00
891	same, souvenir bklt. of 6 panes of 4	....	....	....	17.50	....
892-93	37¢-80¢ My Dream for Peace type of 2004	4.50	10.00	10.75	2.75	2.00
894-95	37¢-80¢ Food for Life	4.50	10.00	10.75	2.75	2.00

896

898

2006

SCOTT NO.	DESCRIPTION	FIRST DAY COVERS SING	INSC. BLK	INSRIP BLK-4	UNUSED F/NH	USED F
896	25¢ Stylized Flags in Heart and Hands	1.75	4.25	3.00	.60	.40
897	37¢ Indigenous Art, sheet of 6	7.50	....	....	5.25	4.00
898-902	39¢ UN Headquarters + labels, strip of 5	7.00	....	....	8.50	....
....	same, sheet of 4	....	....	....	35.00	....

903

908-11

SCOTT NO.	DESCRIPTION	FIRST DAY COVERS SING	INSC. BLK	INSRIP BLK-4	UNUSED F/NH	USED F
903-07	84¢ Sculptures + label, strip of 5	11.00	....	....	10.50	6.00
....	same, sheet of 2	....	....	....	21.00	....
908-11	39¢ Endangered Species, 4 attached	5.00	10.00	4.00	3.50	2.75

UNITED NATIONS (NEW YORK)

913

918

SCOTT NO.	DESCRIPTION	FIRST DAY COVERS SING	INSC. BLK	INSRIP BLK-4	UNUSED F/NH	USED F
912	75¢ Peace personalized stamp	2.25	....	8.00	1.75	1.50
913-914	39¢-84¢ Day of Families	4.50	10.00	10.75	2.75	2.00
915-16	39¢-84¢ World Heritage Sites, France ..	4.50	10.00	10.75	2.75	2.00
917	same, bklt of 6 panes of 4	....	....	....	17.50	....
918-19	39¢-84¢ My Dream of Peace One Day .	4.50	10.00	10.75	2.75	2.00
920	39¢ Flags and Coins, sheet of 8	10.00	....	....	6.75	6.00

925-28

2007

SCOTT NO.	DESCRIPTION	FIRST DAY COVERS SING	INSC. BLK	INSRIP BLK-4	UNUSED F/NH	USED F
921-24	39¢ Flags, 4 varieties	5.00	10.00	4.00	3.50	2.75
925-28	39¢ Endangered Species, 4 attached ...	5.00	10.00	4.00	3.50	2.75
929	84¢ UN Emblem + label	....	....	....	3.00	3.00
....	same, sheet of 10 + 10 labels	....	....	....	30.00	....
930	39¢ Flags and Coins, sheet of 8	10.00	....	....	6.75	6.00
931	84¢ UN Emblem + label	....	....	....	3.00	3.00
....	same, sheet of 10 + 10 labels	....	....	....	30.00	....
932-33	39¢-84¢ Peaceful Vision	4.50	10.00	10.75	2.75	2.00
....	41¢-90¢ World Heritage Sites, South America	5.50	11.00	11.75	3.75	3.00
....	same, bklt panes of 6 panes of 4	....	....	....	20.00	....
....	90¢ UN Peacekeeping Helmet	3.00	4.50	8.50	2.00	1.75
....	90¢ Universal Postal Union, joint issue with Swiss Post Humanitarian Mail	3.00	4.50	8.50	2.00	1.75
....	41¢-90¢ Space for Humanity	5.50	11.00	11.75	4.00	3.00

SEMI-POSTAL

2002

SCOTT NO.	DESCRIPTION	FIRST DAY COVERS SING	INSC. BLK	INSRIP BLK-4	UNUSED F/NH	USED F
B1	37¢ + 6¢ UN AIDS Awareness, souv. sheet	2.00	....	....	1.25	1.00

AIR POST ISSUE

C1-2, UC5

C3-C4, UC1-2

1951-77

SCOTT NO.	DESCRIPTION	FIRST DAY COVERS SING	INSC. BLK	INSRIP BLK-4	UNUSED F/NH	USED F
C1-C23	**AIR MAILS, complete (23)**	......	......	**38.50**	**7.85**	......

C5-6, UXC1, UXC3

C7, UC4

1951-59

SCOTT NO.	DESCRIPTION	FIRST DAY COVERS SING	INSC. BLK	INSRIP BLK-4	UNUSED F/NH	USED F
C1-4	6¢, 10¢, 15¢ & 20¢	24.50	60.00	9.00	2.00	2.00
C5-7	4¢, 5¢ & 7¢ (1957-59)	1.65	4.15	2.25	.55	.45

C8, UXC4

C9, UC6, UC8

C10

C11

C12

1963-77

SCOTT NO.	DESCRIPTION	FIRST DAY COVERS SING	INSC. BLK	INSRIP BLK-4	UNUSED F/NH	USED F
C8-12	6¢, 8¢, 13¢, 15¢, & 25¢ (1963-64)	3.25	8.00	7.50	1.65	1.25

C13

C14

SCOTT NO.	DESCRIPTION	FIRST DAY COVERS SING	INSC. BLK	INSRIP BLK-4	UNUSED F/NH	USED F
C13-14	10¢ & 20¢ (1968-69)	2.00	4.95	3.65	.75	.60

C15, UXC8

C16, UC10

C17, UXC10

C18

SCOTT NO.	DESCRIPTION	FIRST DAY COVERS SING	INSC. BLK	INSRIP BLK-4	UNUSED F/NH	USED F
C15-18	9¢, 11¢, 17¢, & 21¢ (1972)	2.40	6.00	5.25	1.15	.95

C19, UC11

C21

C20, UXC11

SCOTT NO.	DESCRIPTION	FIRST DAY COVERS SING	INSC. BLK	INSRIP BLK-4	UNUSED F/NH	USED F
C19-21	13¢, 18¢, & 26¢ (1974)	2.75	6.95	5.25	1.10	1.00

C22

C23

SCOTT NO.	DESCRIPTION	FIRST DAY COVERS SING	INSC. BLK	INSRIP BLK-4	UNUSED F/NH	USED F
C22-23	25¢ & 31¢ (1977)	2.50	6.25	5.25	1.10	1.05

ENVELOPES AND AIR LETTER SHEETS

U1-U2

U8, U49

U3

U7

(Surcharge)
U9

UC3

(Surcharge)
U12, U13

U10, U11, U12, U13

SCOTT NO.	DESCRIPTION	FIRST DAY COVER	UNUSED ENTIRE
	1953		
U1	3¢ blue	4.50	1.00
	1958		
U2	4¢ ultramarine	.95	.75
	1963		
U3	5¢ multicolored (design #128)	1.00	.35
	1969		
U4	6¢ multicolored (design #128)	.85	.30
	1973		
U5	8¢ multicolored (design #187)	.85	1.00
	1975		
U6	10¢ multicolored (design #250)	.95	.50
	1985		
U7	22¢ Strip Bouquet	2.00	9.50
	1989		
U8	25¢ U.N. Headquarters	2.50	3.00
U9	25¢+4¢ surcharge (U8)	2.00	2.75
U9a	25¢+7¢ surcharge (U8)	7.50	3.25
	1997		
U10	32¢ Cripticandina (79x38mm)	1.35	2.75
U11	32¢ Cripticandina (89x44mm)	1.35	2.25
	1999		
U12	32¢+1¢ surcharge (U10)	1.40	1.75
U13	32¢+1¢ surcharge (U11)	1.40	1.75
	2001		
U14	34¢ NY Headquarters (34x34mm)	1.40	1.75
U15	34¢ NY Headquarters (36x36mm)	1.40	1.75
	2002		
U16	34¢+3¢ surcharge (U14)	1.50	1.95
U17	34¢+3¢ surcharge (U15)	1.50	1.95
	2003		
U18	37¢ U.N. Headquarters (37X47mm)	1.50	1.95
U19	37¢ U.N. Headquarters (40X52mm)	1.50	1.95
	2006		
U20	37¢+2¢ surcharge on #U18	1.50	1.95
U21	37¢+2¢ surcharge on #U19	1.50	1.95
	2007		
....	37¢+4¢ surcharge on #U18	1.75	2.25
....	41¢ UN Emblem	1.75	2.25

AIRMAILS

SCOTT NO.	DESCRIPTION	FIRST DAY COVER	UNUSED ENTIRE
	1952		
UC1	10¢ blue, air letter (design #C3)	8.00	27.50
	1954		
UC2	10¢ royal blue, white borders aerogramme (design of #C3)	......	8.00
	1958		
UC2a	10¢ royal blue, no border (design #C3)	......	7.50
	1959		
UC3	7¢ blue	1.00	2.00
	1960		
UC4	10¢ ultramarine on bluish, letter sheet (design of #C7)	.95	.75
	1961		
UC5	11¢ ultramarine on bluish, letter sheet (design of #C1)	.85	1.00

UC6

UC14, UC15

UC16, UC17

UC7

UC13

UC9, UC22

(surcharge)
UC19, UC24

(surcharge)
UC15, UC17

(surcharge)
UC21

UC18, UC19

UC20, UC21

UC23, UC24

SCOTT NO.	DESCRIPTION	FIRST DAY COVER	UNUSED ENTIRE
	1965		
UC5a	11¢ dark blue on green, letter sheet (design of #C1)	......	2.25
	1963		
UC6	8¢ multicolored (design #C9)	1.00	.75
	1958		
UC7	13¢ shades-blue, letter sheet	.95	.45
	1969		
UC8	10¢ multicolored (design #C9)	.95	.40
	1972-73		
UC9	15¢ shades-blue, letter sheet	.95	.90
UC10	11¢ multicolored (design #C16)	.95	.75
	1975		
UC11	13¢ multicolored (design #C19)	1.00	.55
UC12	18¢ multicolored, aerogramme (design of #222)	1.00	.65
	1977		
UC13	22¢ multicolored, aerogramme	1.25	.90
	1982		
UC14	30¢ black, aerogramme	3.00	2.00
	1988-89		
UC15	30¢+6¢ Surcharge on #UC14	11.50	48.00
UC16	39¢ U.N. Headquarters aerogramme	2.25	5.00
UC17	39¢+6¢ Surcharge on #UC16	2.25	19.00
	1982		
UC18	45¢ Winged Hand	1.95	4.00
	1995		
UC19	45¢+5¢ Surcharge on #UC18	5.00	7.00
	1997/1999		
UC20	50¢ Cherry Blossoms	1.65	2.50
UC21	50¢+10¢ surcharge on #UC20	1.75	2.00
	2001-2007		
UC22	50¢+20¢ on UC9	1.75	2.00
UC23	70¢ Cherry Blossoms	1.75	2.00
UC24	70¢+5¢ surcharge on #UC23	1.75	2.00
....	70¢+20¢ surcharge on #UC23	2.00	1.75
....	90¢ Plane	2.00	1.75

POSTAL CARDS

SCOTT NO.	DESCRIPTION	FIRST DAY COVER	UNUSED ENTIRE
	1952		
UX1	2¢ blue on buff (design of #2)	1.65	.25
	1958		
UX2	3¢ gray olive on buff (design of #2)	.85	.25

UX3

SCOTT NO.	DESCRIPTION	FIRST DAY COVER	UNUSED ENTIRE
	1963		
UX3	4¢ multicolored (design of #125)	.85	.25

UX4

SCOTT NO.	DESCRIPTION	FIRST DAY COVER	UNUSED ENTIRE
	1969		
UX4	5¢ blue & black	.90	.25

UX5-6

SCOTT NO.	DESCRIPTION	FIRST DAY COVER	UNUSED ENTIRE
	1973		
UX5	6¢ multicolored	.85	.25
	1975		
UX6	8¢ multicolored	1.00	.60

UX7

UX8

SCOTT NO.	DESCRIPTION	FIRST DAY COVER	UNUSED ENTIRE
	1977		
UX7	9¢ multicolored	1.00	.75
	1982		
UX8	13¢ multicolored	1.10	.50

UX9

SCOTT NO.	DESCRIPTION	FIRST DAY COVER	UNUSED ENTIRE
	1989		
UX9	15¢ UN Complex	1.10	1.35
UX10	15¢ UN Complex with trees	1.10	1.35
UX11	15¢ Flags	1.10	1.35
UX12	15¢ General Assembly	1.10	1.35
UX13	15¢ UN Complex from East River	1.10	1.35
UX14	36¢ UN Complex and Flags	1.50	1.75
UX15	36¢ Flags	1.50	1.75
UX16	36¢ UN Complex at Dusk	1.50	1.75
UX17	36¢ Security Council	1.50	1.75
UX18	36¢ UN Complex and Sculpture	1.50	1.75
UX19	40¢ UN Headquarters	1.60	4.50
	1998		
UX20	21¢ Secretariat Bldg., Roses	1.75	1.40
UX21	50¢ UN Complex	1.75	1.35
	2001		
UX22	70¢ NY Headquarters	1.75	2.00
	2003		
UX24	23¢ Equestrian Statue	1.75	1.40
UX25	23¢ Lobby	1.75	1.40
UX26	23¢ U.N. Headquarters	1.75	1.40
UX27	23¢ Meeting Room	1.75	1.40
UX28	23¢ Post Office	1.75	1.40
UX29	70¢ Meeting Room	1.75	2.00
UX30	70¢ Peace Bell	1.75	2.00
UX31	70¢ Statue	1.75	2.00
UX32	70¢ U.N. Headquarters	1.75	2.00
UX33	70¢ General Assembly	1.75	2.00

AIR MAILS

SCOTT NO.	DESCRIPTION	FIRST DAY COVER	UNUSED ENTIRE
	1957		
UXC1	4¢ maroon on buff (design of #C5)	.60	.35

(surcharge)
UXC2

SCOTT NO.	DESCRIPTION	FIRST DAY COVER	UNUSED ENTIRE
	1959		
UXC2	4¢ & 1¢ (on UXC1)	......	.75
UXC3	5¢ crimson on buff (design of #C6)	.70	1.00

UXC4

UXC5-6

SCOTT NO.	DESCRIPTION	FIRST DAY COVER	UNUSED ENTIRE
UXC4	6¢ black & blue (design of #C8)	.85	.85
	1965		
UXC5	11¢ multicolored	1.00	.50
	1968		
UXC6	13¢ yellow & green	.95	.50

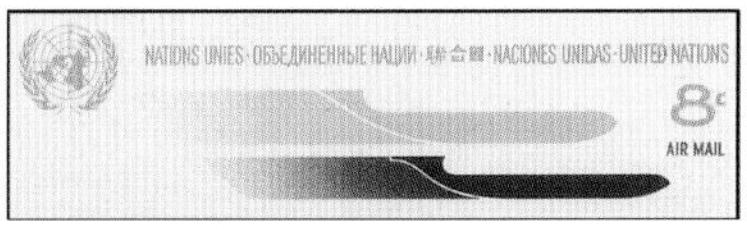

UXC7, UXC9

SCOTT NO.	DESCRIPTION	FIRST DAY COVER	UNUSED ENTIRE
	1969		
UXC7	8¢ multicolored	.90	.65
	1972		
UXC8	9¢ multicolored (design of #C15)	1.00	.50
UXC9	15¢ multicolored	1.00	.55
	1975		
UXC10	11¢ shades—blue (design of #C17)	1.00	.40
UXC11	18¢ multicolored (design of #C20)	1.20	.55

UXC12

SCOTT NO.	DESCRIPTION	FIRST DAY COVER	UNUSED ENTIRE
	1982		
UXC12	28¢ multicolored	1.40	.70

UNITED NATIONS; OFFICES IN GENEVA, SWITZERLAND

Denominations in Swiss Currency

NOTE: Unless illustrated, designs can be assumed to be similar to the equivalent New York or Vienna issues

4

22

61

65

67

69

71

73

74

77

79

82

SCOTT NO.	DESCRIPTION	FIRST DAY COVERS SING	INSC. BLK	INSRIP BLK-4	UNUSED F/NH	USED F
	1969-70					
1-14	5¢ to 10fr Definitives	45.00	110.00	50.00	11.25	10.00
	1971					
15-21	**1971 Issues, complete (7)**	......	......	......	**3.80**	......
15	30¢ Peaceful Uses Sea Bed	.95	2.40	1.40	.30	.25
16	50¢ Support for Refugees	1.10	2.75	1.95	.45	.40
17	50¢ World Food Programme	1.40	3.50	2.65	.55	.45
18	75¢ U.P.U. Building	2.75	6.85	4.00	.80	.80
19-20	30¢ & 50¢ Anti-Discrimination	2.25	5.65	4.25	.90	.60
21	1.10fr International School	3.65	9.00	4.75	1.00	1.15
	1972					
22-29	**1972 Issues, complete (8)**	......	......	......	**5.95**	......
22	40¢ Definitive	1.10	2.75	1.90	.40	.35
23	40¢ Non Proliferation	2.15	5.40	3.50	.75	.75
24	80¢ World Health Day	2.15	5.40	3.75	.85	.85
25-26	40¢ & 80¢ Environment	3.75	9.50	7.95	1.75	1.40
27	1.10fr Economic Committee Europe	3.25	8.15	7.50	1.60	1.35
28-29	40¢ & 80¢ Art—Sert Ceiling	3.50	8.75	8.45	1.85	1.65
	1973					
30-36	**1973 Issues, complete (6)**	......	......	......	**4.60**	......
30-31	60¢ & 1.10fr Disarmament Decade	3.50	8.75	7.00	1.50	1.50
32	60¢ Drug Abuse	2.00	5.00	2.65	.60	.65
33	80¢ Volunteer	2.50	6.25	3.50	.75	.75
34	60¢ Namibia	2.05	5.15	2.75	.60	.75
35-36	40¢ & 80¢ Human Rights	2.65	6.65	6.50	1.40	1.00
	1974					
37-45	**1974 Issues, complete (9)**	......	......	......	**6.05**	......
37-38	60¢ & 80¢ ILO Headquarters	2.75	6.85	4.95	1.10	1.00
39-40	30¢ & 60¢ U.P.U. Centenary	2.25	5.65	4.95	1.10	.90
41-42	60¢ & 1fr Brazil Peace Mural	3.00	7.50	7.00	1.50	1.45
43-44	60¢ & 80¢ World Population Year	2.50	6.25	6.25	1.35	1.25
45	1.30fr Law of the Sea	2.25	5.65	5.95	1.30	1.15
	1975					
46/56	**1975 Issues, (10) (No #52)**	......	......	......	**8.45**	......
46-47	60¢ & 90¢ Peaceful Use of Space	2.40	6.00	6.45	1.40	1.30
48-49	60¢ & 90¢ International Women's Year	2.75	6.85	7.50	1.60	1.40
50-51	60¢ & 90¢ 30th Anniversary	2.25	5.65	6.45	1.40	1.25
52	same, souvenir sheet	2.50		......	1.50	1.40
53-54	50¢ & 1.30fr Namibia	2.50	6.25	7.45	1.60	1.40
55-56	60¢ & 70¢ Peacekeeping	2.10	5.25	6.45	1.40	1.20
	1976					
57-63	**1976 Issues, (7)**	......	......	......	**8.95**	......
57	90¢ World Federation	1.80	4.50	4.45	1.00	.90
58	1.10fr Conference T.& D.	2.10	5.25	4.75	1.05	1.00
59-60	40¢ & 1.50fr Human Settlement	3.00	7.50	7.75	1.65	1.50
61-62	80¢ & 1.10fr Postal Administration	12.00	29.50	22.50	5.00	4.50
63	70¢ World Food Council	1.40	3.50	3.50	.75	.65

SCOTT NO.	DESCRIPTION	FIRST DAY COVERS SING	INSC. BLK	INSRIP BLK-4	UNUSED F/NH	USED F
	1977					
64-72	**1977 Issues, complete (9)**	......	......	......	**6.95**	......
64	80¢ WIPO	1.40	3.50	3.75	.80	.70
65-66	80¢ & 1.10fr Water Conference	3.00	7.50	7.75	1.65	1.45
67-68	80¢ & 1.10fr Security Council	3.00	7.50	7.75	1.65	1.45
69-70	40¢ & 1.10fr Combat Racism	2.50	6.25	7.25	1.50	1.40
71-72	80¢ & 1.10fr Atomic Energy	3.00	7.50	7.75	1.65	1.45
	1978					
73-81	**1978 Issues, complete (9)**	......	......	**30.95**	**6.50**	......
73	35¢ Definitive	.95	2.40	2.20	.45	.40
74-75	80¢ & 1.10fr Smallpox Eradication	2.95	7.50	7.70	1.65	1.45
76	80¢ Namibia	1.50	3.75	4.75	.90	.80
77-78	70¢ & 80¢ ICAO	2.25	5.65	6.25	1.35	1.20
79-80	70¢ & 1.10fr General Assembly	3.00	7.50	7.70	1.65	1.35
81	80¢ TCDC	1.40	3.50	3.95	.85	.75
	1979					
82-88	**1979 Issues, complete (7)**	......	......	......	**6.55**	......
82-83	80¢ & 1.50fr UNDRO	3.10	7.75	9.75	2.15	1.95
84-85	80¢ & 1.10fr I.Y.C.	4.75	11.85	9.50	2.00	1.40
86	1.10fr Namibia	1.90	4.75	4.75	1.05	.95
87-88	80¢ & 1.10fr Court of Justice	3.00	7.50	7.95	1.70	1.55
	1980					
89/97	**1980 Issues, (8) (No #95)**	......	......	......	**5.15**	......
89	80¢ Economics	1.50	3.75	3.95	.85	.75
90-91	40¢ & 70¢ Decade for Women	1.95	4.95	5.25	1.15	1.00
92	1.10fr Peacekeeping	1.85	4.65	5.25	1.15	1.00
93-94	40¢ & 70¢ 35th Anniversary	2.00	5.00	5.15	1.15	1.00
95	Same, Souvenir Sheet	2.75	......	......	1.40	1.25
96-97	40¢ & 70¢ Economic & Social Council	1.85	4.65	5.15	1.15	1.00
	1981					
98-104	**1981 Issues, complete (7)**	......	......	......	**5.50**	......
98	80¢ Palestinian People	1.70	4.25	4.00	.85	.70
99-100	40¢ & 1.50fr Disabled People	2.75	6.85	7.65	1.70	1.45
101	80¢ Fresco	1.50	3.75	4.50	.95	.75
102	1.10fr Sources of Energy	1.50	3.75	5.25	1.15	1.00
103-04	40¢ & 70¢ Conservation	1.75	4.50	5.25	1.25	1.00
	1982					
105-12	**1982 Issues, complete (8)**	......	......	......	**6.45**	......
105-06	30¢ & 1fr Definitives	2.10	5.25	6.50	1.40	1.40
107-08	40¢ & 1.20fr Human Environment	2.40	6.00	7.65	1.70	1.45
109-10	80¢ & 1fr Space Exploration	2.65	6.65	8.50	1.75	1.50
111-12	40¢ & 1.50fr Conservation	2.75	6.95	8.95	1.95	1.50

84

87

90

93

97

104

105

106

110

107

115

118

119

SCOTT NO.	DESCRIPTION	FIRST DAY COVERS SING	INSC. BLK	INSRIP BLK-4	UNUSED F/NH	USED F
	1983					
113-20	**1983 Issues, complete (8)**	......	......	......	**8.35**	......
113	1.20fr World Communications	1.75	4.40	7.25	1.55	1.15
114-15	40¢ & 80¢ Safety at Sea	1.75	4.40	7.25	1.55	1.15
116	1.50fr World Food Program	2.25	5.65	8.00	1.70	1.45
117-18	80¢ & 1.10fr Trade & Development	2.75	6.95	8.95	1.95	1.70
119-20	40¢ & 1.20fr Human Rights	3.50	8.75	10.50	2.05	1.80
	1984					
121-28	**1984 Issues, complete (8)**	......	......	......	**9.20**	......
121	1. 20fr Population	1.75	4.50	10.15	1.50	1.25
122-23	50¢ & 80¢ Food Day	1.75	4.50	8.50	1.75	1.25
124-25	50¢ & 70¢ Heritage	1.75	4.50	10.25	2.25	1.25
126-27	35¢ & 1.50fr Future for Refugees	2.75	6.95	10.50	2.25	1.75
128	1.20fr Youth Year	1.75	4.50	8.95	1.95	1.25
	1985					
129/39	**1985 Issues, (10) (No #137)**	......	......	......	**11.50**	
129-30	80¢-1.20fr Turin Centre	2.75	6.95	12.95	2.75	1.75
131-32	50¢-80¢ U.N. University	2.00	5.00	8.95	1.95	1.25
133-34	20¢-1.20fr Definitives	2.25	5.65	9.75	2.10	1.25
135-36	50¢-70¢ 40th Anniversary	2.00	5.80	8.95	1.95	1.25
137	same, souvenir sheet	2.75	......	......	2.25	1.35
138-39	50¢-1.20fr Child Survival	5.75	14.50	15.25	3.40	2.50
	1986					
140-49	**1986 Issues (10)**	......	......	......	**17.25**	......
140	1.40fr Africa in Crisis	2.00	5.00	11.00	2.50	1.25
141-44	35¢ Development, 4 varieties, attached	2.00	2.75	12.00	10.50	5.00
145	5¢ Definitive	1.10	2.75	.85	.20	.15
146-47	50¢ & 80¢ Philately	1.85	4.65	9.50	2.00	.95
148-49	45¢ & 1.40fr Peace Year	2.75	6.95	13.50	3.00	1.50
150	35¢-70¢ WFUNA, souvenir sheet	2.75	......	......	5.50	2.75
	1987					
151-61	**1987 Issues (11)**	......	......	......	**12.75**	......
151	1.40fr Trygve Lie	2.00	5.00	10.15	2.00	1.75
152-53	90¢-1.40fr Definitive	3.50	8.75	13.00	2.00	1.75
154-55	50¢-90¢ Shelter Homeless	2.00	5.00	9.50	1.95	1.75
156-57	80¢-1.20fr Anti-Drug Campaign	2.75	6.95	13.00	2.00	1.75
158-59	35¢-50¢ United Nations Day	3.50	8.75	8.50	1.50	1.25
160-61	90¢-1.70fr Child Immunization	1.85	4.65	19.50	4.00	3.50

120

122

123

124

125

126

127

128

145

130

133

134

148

149

152

153

164

178

183

184

185

179

201

202

203

204

213

205

206

255

256

SCOTT NO.	DESCRIPTION	FIRST DAY COVERS SING	INSC. BLK	INSRIP BLK-4	UNUSED F/NH	USED F
	1988					
162/172	**1988 Issues, (8) (No #165-66, 172)**	......	......	......	**9.00**	......
162-63	35¢-1.40fr World without Hunger	2.50	6.25	13.00	2.75	2.00
164	50¢ For a Better World	1.25	3.15	4.00	.85	.75
				Sheetlets (12)		
165-66	50¢-1.10fr Forest Conservation (set of 6, includes NY and Vienna)	15.00	40.00	130.00	27.50	25.00
167-68	80¢-90¢ Volunteer Day	2.50	6.25	12.00	2.40	2.00
169-70	50¢-1.40fr Health in Sports	2.75	6.95	13.50	2.25	2.00
171	90¢ Human Rights 40th Anniversary	2.00	5.00	7.00	1.25	1.00
172	2fr Human Rights 40th Anniversary souvenir sheet	2.75	....	....	3.25	3.00
	1989					
173-81	**1989 Issues (9)**	......	......	....	**19.50**	....
173-74	80¢ & 1.40fr. World Bank	2.75	6.95	18.50	4.00	3.00
175	90¢ Nobel Peace Prize	1.50	3.75	8.00	1.40	1.10
176-77	90¢ & 1.10fr World Weather Watch	2.75	6.95	18.50	3.75	2.00
178-79	50¢ & 2fr UN Offices in Vienna	4.00	10.00	20.00	4.50	4.25
				Sheetlets (12)		
180-81	35¢ & 80¢ Human Rights 40th Ann. (strips of 3 w/tabs)	1.85	4.65	24.00	7.00	....
	1990					
182/94	**1990 Issues, No #190 (12)**	......	......	....	**33.50**	......
182	1.50fr International Trade	2.15	5.40	14.00	3.00	2.50
183	5fr Definitive	7.75	19.50	33.50	6.00	5.00
184-85	50¢ & 80¢ SIDA (AIDS)	2.15	5.50	14.00	3.25	2.75
186-87	90¢ & 1.40fr Medicinal Plants	3.60	9.00	18.00	3.50	3.00
188-89	90¢ & 1.10fr Anniversary of U.N	3.00	7.50	18.50	3.50	3.00
190	same, souvenir sheet	3.00	......	......	5.00	4.50
191-92	50¢ & 2fr Crime Prevention	4.15	10.50	19.50	3.75	3.25
				Sheetlets (12)		
193-94	35¢ & 90¢ Human Rights (strips of 3 w/tabs)	1.95	4.95	28.50	7.50	....
	1991					
195-210	**1991 Issues (17)**	......	......	.....	**31.00**	......
195-98	90¢ Econ. Comm. for Europe, 4 varieties, attached	5.75	6.75	7.75	5.50	4.50
199-200	70¢ & 90¢ Namibia—A New Nation	3.85	9.60	15.00	3.25	3.00
201-02	80¢ & 1.50fr Definitives	5.00	12.50	18.50	4.00	3.50
203-04	80¢ & 1.10fr Children's Rights	4.50	11.25	17.50	3.50	3.25
205-06	80¢ & 1.40fr Banning of Chemical Weapons	5.00	12.50	19.50	4.25	3.25
207-08	50¢ & 1.60fr 40th Anniv. of the UNPA	4.75	11.95	19.50	3.75	3.25
				Sheetlets (12)		
209-10	50¢ & 90¢ Human Rights (strips of 3 w/tabs)	2.75	7.50	32.50	8.00	....
	1992					
211-25	**1992 Issues (15)**	......	......	......	**30.00**	......
211-12	50¢-1.10fr. World Heritage—UNESCO	3.60	9.00	18.75	3.75	3.50
213	3fr Definitive	6.00	15.00	21.25	3.75	3.50
214-15	80¢ Clean Oceans, 2 varieties, attached	2.75	5.35	7.50	2.50	2.00
216-19	75¢ Earth Summit, 4 varieties, attached	4.00	4.95	5.50	5.00	4.50
220-21	1.10fr Mission to Planet Earth, 2 varieties, attached	4.00	6.95	12.50	5.00	4.50
222-23	90¢-1.60fr Science and Technology	4.75	11.75	18.00	4.00	3.50
				Sheetlets (12)		
224-25	50¢-90¢ Human Rights (strips of 3 w/tabs	2.75	6.50	32.50	8.00	....
	1993					
226-43	**1993 Issues (18)**	......	......	......	**36.00**	......
226-27	50¢-1.60fr Aging	3.60	9.00	23.50	4.00	3.50
228-31	80¢ Endangered Species, 4 attached	4.00	5.00	6.50	5.00	4.50
232-33	60¢-1fr Healthy Environment	3.00	8.00	11.00	3.50	3.00
				Sheetlets (12)		
234-35	50¢-90¢ Human Rights (strips of 3 w/tabs)	3.00	7.00	33.00	8.00	....
236-39	60¢ Peace, 4 attached	3.50	4.50	10.00	9.00	5.00
240-43	1.10fr Environment—Climate, strip of 4	3.50	8.00	19.00(8)	7.50	6.00

277

279

294

280-83

284-88

1994

SCOTT NO.	DESCRIPTION	FIRST DAY COVERS SING	INSC. BLK	INSRIP BLK-4	UNUSED F/NH	USED F
244-61	**1994 Issues (18)**	....	....	....	**29.00**	....
244-45	80¢-1fr Intl. Year of the Family	3.50	12.50	12.50	3.25	3.00
246-49	80¢ Endangered Species, 4 attached	4.50	5.00	4.75	4.25	4.00
250	1.20fr Refugees	2.50	9.25	12.00	3.00	4.85
251-54	60¢ Intl. Decade for Natural Disaster Reduction, 4 attached	3.50	4.25	10.00	8.00	5.00
255-57	60¢-1.80fr Definitives (3)	5.00	17.50	17.50	4.50	4.00
258-59	60¢-80¢ Population and Development	4.00	10.00	1300	4.00	3.50
260-61	80¢-1fr Development through Partnership	3.50	12.50	13.50	3.50	3.00

1995

SCOTT NO.	DESCRIPTION	FIRST DAY COVERS SING	INSC. BLK	INSRIP BLK-4	UNUSED F/NH	USED F
262/75	**1995 Issues (13) (No #272)**	....	....	....	**51.00**	....
262	80¢ 50th Anniversary of the UN	1.75	6.50	6.00	1.25	1.00
263	1fr Social Summit	2.25	7.50	7.00	1.95	1.75
264-67	80¢ Endangered Species, 4 attached	4.50	5.00	7.00	6.50	6.00
268-69	80¢-1fr Youth: Our Future	3.50	12.50	19.75	4.75	3.50
270-71	60¢-1.80fr 50th Anniversary of the UN	4.75	15.50	19.75	4.75	3.50
272	2.40fr 50th Anniversary of the UN, souvenir sheet	4.50	....	....	4.25	4.00
273-74	60¢-1fr 4th Conference on Women	3.00	10.00	18.00	4.25	2.75
275	30¢ 50th Anniversary, min. sheet of 12	....	....	....	26.00	....
276	same, souvenir booklet of 4 panes of 3	....	....	....	29.00	....

1996

SCOTT NO.	DESCRIPTION	FIRST DAY COVERS SING	INSC. BLK	INSRIP BLK-4	UNUSED F/NH	USED F
277/95	**1996 Issues (18) (No 291)**	....	....	....	**26.35**	....
277	80¢ WFUNA 50th Anniversary	1.75	6.50	6.00	1.50	1.00
278-79	40¢-70¢ Definitives	2.75	10.00	10.50	2.25	2.00
280-83	80¢ Endangered Species, 4 attached	4.50	5.00	7.00	6.50	6.00
284-88	80¢ City Summit (Habitat II), strip of 5	5.00	15.00	17.00	8.00	7.00
289-90	70¢-1.10fr Sport & the Environment	3.50	12.50	13.50	3.25	3.00
291	1.80fr Sport & the Environment souvenir sheet	3.50	....	....	3.75	3.00
292-93	80¢-1fr A Plea for Peace	3.50	12.50	13.50	3.25	3.00
294-95	80¢-1fr UNICEF 50th Anniversary	3.50	12.50	13.50	3.25	3.00

302-05

312

296

314

1997

SCOTT NO.	DESCRIPTION	FIRST DAY COVERS SING	INSC. BLK	INSRIP BLK-4	UNUSED F/NH	USED F
296/315	**1997 Issues (19) (No.# 306)**	....	....	....	**25.00**	....
296-97	10¢-$1 10fr. Definitives	2.75	10.00	11.75	2.75	2.00
298-301	80¢ Endangered Species, 4 attached	4.50	5.00	7.00	6.50	6.00
302-05	45¢ Earth Summit +5, 4 attached	2.50	2.75	6.00	4.50	2.80
306	1.10Fr Earth Summit, souvenir sheet	2.40	....	....	3.00	1.75
307-11	70¢ Transporation, strip of 5	5.50	13.50	11.60(10)	5.50	5.00
312-13	70¢-1.10Fr Tribute to Philately	3.50	12.50	14.50	3.25	3.00
314-15	45¢-70¢ Terracota Warriors	2.75	10.00	14.50	3.50	2.25
316	same, Souvenir bklt of 6 pane of 4	....	....	....	9.25	....

317

322a

318-21

1998

SCOTT NO.	DESCRIPTION	FIRST DAY COVERS SING	INSC. BLK	INSRIP BLK-4	UNUSED F/NH	USED F
317	2fr Definitive	4.00	9.00	14.00	3.00	2.75
318-21	80¢ Endangered Species, 4 attached	4.50	5.00	6.50	5.50	5.00
322	45¢ Intl. Year of the Ocean, sheetlet of 12	15.00	....	....	10.25	....
323	70¢ Rain Forests, Orangutans	2.00	4.50	6.00	1.50	1.40
324	3fr Rain Forests, Orangutans, souvenir sheet	7.00	....	....	5.00	4.00
325-26	70¢-90¢ 50 Years of Peacekeeping	4.00	9.00	13.00	3.25	3.00
327-28	90¢-1.80fr 50th of the Dec. of Human Rights	6.75	15.00	21.00	5.50	5.00
329-30	70¢-1.10fr Schonbrunn Castle	4.50	10.00	14.50	3.65	3.25
331	same, souvenir bklt of 6 panes	....	....	....	10.50	....

332

333

1999

SCOTT NO.	DESCRIPTION	FIRST DAY COVERS SING	INSC. BLK	INSRIP BLK-4	UNUSED F/NH	USED F
332	1.70fr Denfinitive	4.00	9.00	13.00	3.25	2.75
333-34	90¢-1.10fr World Heritage Sites, Australia	4.50	10.00	15.00	3.85	3.25
335	same, souvenir bklt of 6 panes	....	....	....	9.25	....

336-39

347

SCOTT NO.	DESCRIPTION	FIRST DAY COVERS SING	INSC. BLK	INSRIP BLK-4	UNUSED F/NH	USED F
336-39	90¢ Endangered Species, 4 attached	4.50	5.00	7.00	6.00	5.00
340-41	45¢ Unispace III Conference	1.95	4.00	4.25	1.00	.80
342	2fr Unispace III Conference, souvenir sheet	6.00	....	....	4.00	3.00
343-46	70¢ Universal Postal Union	2.00	4.50	6.00	4.00	1.40
347	1.10fr In Memorium	2.40	5.00	8.00	2.00	1.75
348	2fr In Memoriam, souvenir sheet	3.75	....	....	3.50	2.75

349

351

SCOTT NO.	DESCRIPTION	FIRST DAY COVERS SING	INSC. BLK	INSRIP BLK-4	UNUSED F/NH	USED F
349-50	70¢-1.80fr Education-Keystone to the 21st Century	6.50	14.00	19.50	5.00	4.50

2000

SCOTT NO.	DESCRIPTION	FIRST DAY COVERS SING	INSC. BLK	INSRIP BLK-4	UNUSED F/NH	USED F
351	90¢ International Year of Thanksgiving	1.95	4.00	6.60	1.65	1.25
352-55	90¢ Endangered Species, 4 attached	4.50	5.00	7.00	6.00	5.00
356-57	90¢-1.10fr Our World 2000	4.50	10.00	15.00	3.85	3.25
358-59	90¢-1.40fr 55th Anniversary of the UN	4.75	11.00	16.50	4.00	3.25
360	same, 90¢-1.40fr souvenir sheet	....	....	....	4.00	3.25
361	45¢ United Nations in the 21st Century	1.75	3.75	4.50	1.00	.75
362-63	1fr-1.20fr World Heritage Sites, Spain	5.25	11.50	18.00	4.50	4.00
364	same, souvenir bklt of 6 panes	....	....	....	9.25	....
365	80¢ Respect for Regugees	1.75	6.50	6.00	1.25	1.00
366	1.80fr Respect for Refugees, souvenir sheet	3.50	....	....	3.25	2.50

371

384

2001

SCOTT NO.	DESCRIPTION	FIRST DAY COVERS SING	FIRST DAY COVERS INSC. BLK	INSRIP BLK-4	UNUSED F/NH	USED F
367-70	90¢ Endangered Species, 4 attached	4.50	5.00	7.00	6.00	5.00
371-72	90¢-1.10fr Intl. Volunteers Year	4.50	10.00	15.00	3.85	3.25
373-74	1.20fr-1.80fr World Hertiage Sites, Japan	6.00	12.50	22.00	5.50	5.00
375	same, souvenir bklt of 6 panes	....	....	....	10.00	....
376	2fr Dag Hammarskjold	3.50	7.50	14.00	3.50	2.75
377-78	90¢-1.30fr 50th Anniv. of UNPA	4.50	10.00	15.00	3.85	3.25
379	same, 3.50fr souvenir sheet	4.50	....	....	6.00	5.50
380-83	90¢ Climate Change, strip of 4	4.50	5.00	7.00	6.00	5.00
384	90¢ Nobel Peace Prize	1.95	4.00	6.60	1.65	1.25

385

400

2002

SCOTT NO.	DESCRIPTION	FIRST DAY COVERS SING	FIRST DAY COVERS INSC. BLK	INSRIP BLK-4	UNUSED F/NH	USED F
385	1.30fr Palais des Nations	2.75	6.00	10.00	2.50	2.00
386-89	90¢ Endangered Species, 4 attached	4.50	5.00	7.00	6.00	5.00
390-91	90¢-1.30fr Independence of East Timor	4.50	7.50	14.00	3.50	2.75
392-95	70¢-1.20fr Intl. Year of Mountains, 2 pairs	4.50	5.00	7.00	6.00	5.00
396-99	90¢-1.80fr Johannesburg Summit, 2 pairs	6.00	7.00	10.00	8.50	7.00
400-01	90¢-1.30fr World Heritage Sites, Italy	4.50	7.50	14.00	3.50	2.75
402	same, souvenir bklt of 6 panes of 4	....	....	....	22.00	....
403	1.30fr UNAIDS Awareness, semi postal	2.75	6.00	10.00	2.50	2.00
404	3fr Entry of Switzerland into United Nations	7.00	15.00	20.00	5.00	4.00
B1	90¢+30¢ UNAIDS Awareness, souvenir sheet	2.40	....	....	2.25	2.00

406

413

2003

SCOTT NO.	DESCRIPTION	FIRST DAY COVERS SING	FIRST DAY COVERS INSC. BLK	INSRIP BLK-4	UNUSED F/NH	USED F
405	90¢ Indigenous Art, sheet of 6	11.00	....	....	8.50	4.50
406	90¢ Interparliamentary Union	1.95	4.00	6.60	1.65	1.25
407-10	90¢ Endangered Species, 4 attached	4.50	5.00	7.00	6.00	5.00
411-12	70¢-1.30fr Intl. Year of Freshwater, 2 attached	4.25	9.50	14.00	3.50	2.75
413	1.80fr Ralph Bunche	3.75	9.50	12.00	3.00	2.25
415-16	90¢-1.30fr World Heritage Sites, United States	4.50	7.50	14.00	3.50	2.75
417	same, souvenir bklt of 6 panes of 4	....	....	....	10.00	....

429

433

2004

SCOTT NO.	DESCRIPTION	FIRST DAY COVERS SING	FIRST DAY COVERS INSC. BLK	INSRIP BLK-4	UNUSED F/NH	USED F
418-21	1fr Endangered Species, 4 attached	8.00	10.00	8.00	7.50	5.00
422	1fr Indigenous Art, sheet of 6	12.00	....	....	23.00	....
423-24	85¢-1fr Road Safety	4.25	8.00	13.00	3.25	2.50
425	1.30fr Japanese Peace Bell, 50th Anniv.	3.00	7.75	9.00	2.25	1.75
426-27	1fr-1.30fr World Heritage Sites, Greece	4.50	7.50	14.00	3.50	2.75
428	same, souvenir bklt of 6 panes of 4	....	....	....	18.50	....
429-30	85¢-1.20fr My Dream for Peace	4.25	8.00	13.00	3.25	2.50
431-32	85¢-1.30fr Human Rights	5.00	9.00	35.00(8)	4.50	4.00
433	180¢ Sports	4.50	8.50	16.00	4.00	3.50

434

440

2005

SCOTT NO.	DESCRIPTION	FIRST DAY COVERS SING	FIRST DAY COVERS INSC. BLK	INSRIP BLK-4	UNUSED F/NH	USED F
434	1.30fr U.N. 60th Anniv.	3.00	7.75	9.00	2.25	1.75
435	3fr U.N. 60th Anniv., souvenir sheet	7.00	....	....	5.00	4.00
436-39	1fr Orchids, 4 attached	8.00	10.00	8.00	7.50	5.00
440-41	1fr-1.30fr Nature's Wisdom	4.50	7.50	14.00	3.50	2.75
442-43	1fr-1.30fr International Year of Sports	4.50	7.50	14.00	3.50	2.75

444

449

SCOTT NO.	DESCRIPTION	FIRST DAY COVERS SING	FIRST DAY COVERS INSC. BLK	INSRIP BLK-4	UNUSED F/NH	USED F
444-45	1fr-1.30fr World Heritage Sites, Egypt	4.50	7.50	14.00	3.50	2.75
446	same, souvenir bklt of 6 panes	....	....	....	18.50	....
447-48	1fr-1.30fr My Dream for Peace type of 2004	4.50	7.50	14.00	3.50	2.75
449-50	1fr-1.30fr Food for life	4.50	7.50	14.00	3.50	2.75

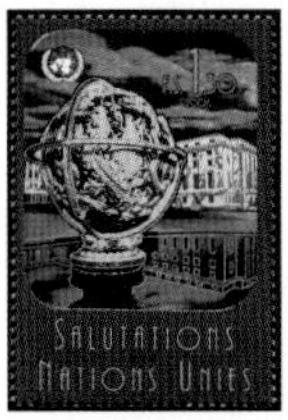
451

453-56

2006

SCOTT NO.	DESCRIPTION	FIRST DAY COVERS SING	FIRST DAY COVERS INSC. BLK	INSRIP BLK-4	UNUSED F/NH	USED F
451	1.30fr Armillary Sphere, Palais des Nations	3.50	6.50	10.00	2.50	2.00
452	1.20fr Indigenous Art, sheet of 6	15.00	....	....	13.00	13.00
453-56	1fr Endangered Species, 4 attached	8.00	10.00	8.00	7.50	5.00

457

462

SCOTT NO.	DESCRIPTION	FIRST DAY COVERS SING	FIRST DAY COVERS INSC. BLK	INSRIP BLK-4	UNUSED F/NH	USED F
457-58	1fr-1.30fr Day of Families	4.50	7.50	14.00	3.50	2.75
459-60	1fr-1.30fr World Heritage Sites, France	4.50	7.50	14.00	3.50	2.75
461	same, 20¢-50¢ souvenir bklt of 6 panes	....	....	....	18.50	....
462-63	85¢-1.20fr My Dream of Peace One Day	4.25	8.00	13.00	3.25	2.50
464	85¢ Flags and Coins, sheet of 8	15.00	....	....	12.00	12.00

465-68

2007

SCOTT NO.	DESCRIPTION	FIRST DAY COVERS SING	FIRST DAY COVERS INSC. BLK	INSRIP BLK-4	UNUSED F/NH	USED F
465-68	1fr Endangered Species, 4 attached	8.00	10.00	8.00	7.50	5.00
469	85¢ Flags and Coins, sheet of 8	15.00	....	....	12.00	12.00
470-71	1.20fr-1.80fr Peaceful Visions	6.00	8.00	15.00	5.00	5.00
....	1fr-1.80fr World Heritage Series, South America	6.00	8.00	15.00	5.00	5.00
....	same, 20¢-50¢ souvenir bklt of 6 panes	....	....	....	22.50	....
....	1.80fr Universal Postal Union, joint issue with Swiss Post Humanitarian Mail	4.00	7.00	11.00	3.50	3.00
....	1.00fr-1.80fr Space for Humanity	5.00	8.00	15.00	4.00	3.00

AIR LETTER SHEETS & POSTAL CARDS

SCOTT NO.	DESCRIPTION	FIRST DAY COVER	UNUSED ENTIRE
	1969		
UC1	65¢ ultramarine & light blue	4.50	1.75
	1969		
UX1	20¢ olive green & black	1.65	.35
UX2	30¢ violet blue, blue, light & dark green	1.65	.50

UX3

UX4

SCOTT NO.	DESCRIPTION	FIRST DAY COVER	UNUSED ENTIRE
	1977		
UX3	40¢ multicolored	1.25	.75
UX4	70¢ multicolored	1.65	1.25

UX5

UX6

SCOTT NO.	DESCRIPTION	FIRST DAY COVER	UNUSED ENTIRE
	1985		
UX5	50¢ Six languages	1.25	4.00
UX6	70¢ Birds & Rainbow	1.65	4.75

UX7

SCOTT NO.	DESCRIPTION	FIRST DAY COVER	UNUSED ENTIRE
	1986		
UX7	70¢+10¢ Surcharge on UX6	8.00	3.25

UX10

SCOTT NO.	DESCRIPTION	FIRST DAY COVER	UNUSED ENTIRE
	1992-93		
UX8	90¢ U.N. Buildings	1.75	3.00
UX9	50¢ + 10¢ Surcharge on UX5	1.75	3.00
UX10	80¢ Postal Card	1.75	3.00

UX11

UX12

SCOTT NO.	DESCRIPTION	FIRST DAY COVER	UNUSED ENTIRE
	1997		
UX11	50¢+20¢ Surcharge on UX5	1.75	3.00
UX12	80¢+30¢ Surcharge on UX10	2.00	3.00

UX13

UX14

SCOTT NO.	DESCRIPTION	FIRST DAY COVER	UNUSED ENTIRE
	1998		
UX13	70¢ Assembly Hall	2.00	2.25
UX14	1.10fr Palais des Nations	2.50	3.00
	2001		
UX15	1.30fr Palais des Nations	2.75	2.50
UX16	70¢+15¢ Surcharge on UX13	2.10	2.25
UX17	90¢+10¢ Surcharge on UX8	2.50	2.25
UX18	1.10fr+10¢ Surcharge on UX14	2.75	2.50

UNITED NATIONS: OFFICES IN VIENNA, AUSTRIA
Denominations in Austrian Currency

NOTE: Unless illustrated, designs can be assumed to be similar to the equivalent New York or Geneva issue

3

5

9

19

24

37

38

40

41

42

43

SCOTT NO.	DESCRIPTION	FIRST DAY COVERS SING	INSC. BLK	INSRIP BLK-4	UNUSED F/NH	USED F
	1979					
1-6	50g to 10s Definitives	6.75	16.95	10.00	2.25	2.50
	1980					
7/16	**1980 Issues, (9) (No #14)**	......	......	......	**6.35**	.....
7	4s International Economic Order	3.75	9.50	11.50	1.25	1.20
8	2.50s International Economic Definitive.85	2.15	(B)1.75	.40	.30	
9-10	4s & 6s Decade for Women	3.10	7.75	6.50	1.25	1.40
11	6s Peacekeeping	1.95	4.85	5.25	1.15	1.05
12-13	4s & 6s 35th Anniversary	3.15	7.85	6.50	1.25	1.40
14	same, souvenir sheet	3.85	......	......	1.40	1.40
15-16	4s & 6s Economic and Social Council2.35	5.85	6.50	1.40	1.20	
	1981					
17-23	**1981 Issues, complete (7)**	......	......	......	**4.90**	......
17	4s Palestinian People	1.55	3.85	3.75	.85	.75
18-19	4s & 6s Disabled Persons	2.40	6.00	5.50	1.25	1.15
20	6s Fresco	1.45	3.65	3.45	.80	.75
21	7.50s Sources of Energy	1.95	4.85	3.95	.85	.70
22-23	5s & 7s Volunteers Program	2.75	6.85	6.75	1.40	1.25
	1982					
24-29	**1982 Issues, complete (6)**	......	......	......	**4.85**	......
24	3s Definitive	.85	2.15	3.00	.65	.45
25-26	5s & 7s Human Environment	2.50	6.25	9.00	1.95	1.40
27	5s Space Exploration	1.25	3.15	3.95	.85	.70
28-29	5s & 7s Nature Conservation	2.50	6.25	7.75	1.65	1.40\
	1983					
30-38	**1983 Issues, complete (9)**	......	......	......	**7.00**	......
30	4s World Communications	.85	2.15	3.95	.85	.55
31-32	4s & 6s Safety at Sea	2.15	5.35	6.15	1.40	1.25
33-34	5s & 7s World Food Program	2.60	6.50	4.45	1.65	1.40
35-36	4s & 8.50s Trade & Develop.	2.75	6.95	8.95	1.95	1.55
37-38	5s & 7s Human Rights	3.15	7.85	8.95	1.95	1.45
	1984					
39-47	**1984 Issues, complete (9)**	....	....	......	**8.55**	....
39	7s Population	1.40	3.50	4.50	1.00	.95
40-41	4.50s & 6s Food Day	1.85	4.65	7.25	1.50	1.50
42-43	3.50s & 15s Heritage	3.50	8.75	10.50	2.25	2.25
44-45	4.50s & 8.50s Future for Refugees	2.25	5.65	10.50	2.25	1.75
46-47	3.50s & 6.50s Youth Year	1.80	4.50	9.00	2.00	1.65
	1985					
48/56	**1985 Issues, (8) (No #54)**	......	......	......	**10.90**	......
48	7.50s I.L.O. Turin Centre	1.25	3.15	6.45	1.40	1.00
49	8.50s U.N. University	1.35	3.40	6.95	1.50	1.10
50-51	4.50s & 15s Definitives	3.15	7.95	13.75	3.25	2.35
52-53	6.50s & 8.50s 40th Anniversary	2.50	6.25	10.00	2.35	2.00
54	Same, Souvenir Sheet	3.25		......	3.00	2.50
55-56	4s-6s Child Survival	2.15	5.40	14.00	3.00	1.70

SCOTT NO.	DESCRIPTION	FIRST DAY COVERS SING	INSC. BLK	INSRIP BLK-4	UNUSED F/NH	USED F
	1986					
57-65	**1986 Issues (9)**	......	......	......	**17.00**	......
57	8s Africa in Crisis	1.35	3.40	7.50	1.50	.90
58-61	4.50s Development, 4 varieties, attached	3.05	7.65	13.00	12.00	2.25
62-63	3.50s & 6.50s Philately	1.95	4.95	9.75	2.00	1.15
64-65	5s & 6s Peace Year	2.25	5.65	12.00	2.50	1.95
66	4s to 7s WFUNA, souvenir sheet	3.05	......	......	5.50	4.00
	1987					
67-77	**1987 Issues (11)**	......	......	......	**13.40**	......
67	8s Trygve Lie	1.35	3.40	7.50	1.10	1.00
68-69	4s & 9.50s Shelter Homeless	2.35	5.95	11.00	2.25	2.00
70-71	5s & 8s Anti-Drug Campaign	2.25	5.65	10.25	2.25	2.00
72-73	2s & 17s Definitives	3.45	8.65	16.00	2.75	2.25
74-75	5s & 6s United Nations Day	2.25	5.65	12.00	2.75	2.00
76-77	4s & 9.50s Child Immunization	2.35	5.95	14.00	3.00	2.50
	1988					
78/86	**1988 Issues, (7) (No #80-81, 87)**	....	....	....	**8.30**	....
78-79	4s & 6s World Without Hunger	2.25	5.65	9.50	2.00	1.50
					Sheetlets	
80-81	4s & 5s Forest Conservation (set of 6, includes NY and Geneva)	22.50	65.00	130.00	35.00	25.00
82-83	6s & 7.50s Volunteer Day	2.35	5.95	14.00	2.75	2.00
84-85	6s & 8s Health in Sports	2.50	6.25	14.50	3.25	2.00
86	5s Human Rights 40th Anniversary	1.00	2.50	7.50	1.50	.60
87	11s Human Rights 40th Anniversary souvenir sheet	1.75	....	....	3.00	2.25
	1989					
88-96	**1989 Issues (9)**	....	....	....	**18.75**	....
88-89	5.50s & 8s World Bank.	2.35	5.95	16.50	3.50	3.00
90	6s Nobel Peace Prize	1.25	3.15	6.75	1.35	1.00
91-92	4s & 9.50s World Weather Watch	2.35	5.95	19.50	4.00	3.50
93-94	5s & 7.50s UN Office in Vienna	2.25	5.65	24.00	5.50	5.00
				Sheetlets(12)		
95-96	4s & 6s Human Rights, 40th Ann. (strips of 3 w/tabs)	2.25	5.65	25.00	5.50	....
	1990					
97/109	**1990 Issues, (12) (No #105)**	....	....	....	**27.95**	....
97	12s Int'l. Trade Center	2.15	5.40	10.50	2.00	1.50
98	1.50s Definitive	.85	2.15	1.80	.40	.30
99-100	5s & 11s AIDS	2.75	6.95	17.00	3.50	3.00
101-02	4.50s & 9.50s Medicinal Plants	2.50	6.25	18.00	3.50	3.00
103-04	7s & 9s 45th Anniv. of U.N.	2.75	6.95	18.00	4.00	3.50
105	same, souvenir sheet	2.75	......	......	5.50	4.00
106-07	6s & 8s Crime Prevention	2.50	6.25	18.00	4.00	3.25
				Sheetlets(12)		
108-09	4.50s & 7s Human Rights (strips of 3 w/tabs)	2.35	5.95	30.00	6.50	....

44

45

46

50

51

64

72

73

93

94

98

116

117

137

118

119

120

138

149

167

168

169

193

194

195

196-99

200-04

1991

SCOTT NO.	DESCRIPTION	FIRST DAY COVERS SING	FIRST DAY COVERS INSC. BLK	INSRIP BLK-4	UNUSED F/NH	USED F
110-24	**1991 Issues, (15)**	....	....	....	**28.95**	....
110-13	5s Econ. Comm. for Europe, 4 varieties, attached	5.50	13.75	6.50	5.00	4.50
114-15	6s & 9.50s Namibia—A New Nation	4.50	11.25	19.50	4.00	3.50
116	20s Definitive Issue	4.75	11.85	19.50	3.75	3.00
117-18	7s & 9s Children's Rights	4.50	11.25	14.50	3.25	3.00
119-20	5s & 10s Chemical Weapons	4.75	11.95	15.00	3.50	3.00
121-22	5s & 8s 40th Anniv. of U.N.P.A.	4.15	10.35	15.00	3.50	3.00
				Sheetlets (12)		
123-24	4.50s & 7s Human Rights (strips of 3 w/tabs)	2.50	6.25	34.50	7.50	....

1992

SCOTT NO.	DESCRIPTION	FIRST DAY COVERS SING	FIRST DAY COVERS INSC. BLK	INSRIP BLK-4	UNUSED F/NH	USED F
125-40	**1992 Issues, (17)**	....	....	....	**31.50**	....
125-26	5s-9s World Heritage—UNESCO	4.25	10.75	15.00	3.25	3.00
127-28	7s Clean Oceans, 2 varieties, attached	4.25	5.50	7.50	3.00	2.50
129-32	5.50s Earth Summit, 4 varieties, attached	4.25	5.25	4.95	6.00	5.00
133-34	10s Mission to Planet Earth, 2 varieties, attached	4.25	5.50	13.00	6.00	5.50
135-36	5.50s-7s Science & Technology	4.00	10.25	13.00	2.75	2.25
137-38	5.50s-7s Definitives	4.00	10.25	13.00	2.75	2.50
				Sheetlets (12)		
139-40	6s-10s Human Rights (strips of 3 w/tabs)	2.75	6.95	38.00	10.00	....

1993

SCOTT NO.	DESCRIPTION	FIRST DAY COVERS SING	FIRST DAY COVERS INSC. BLK	INSRIP BLK-4	UNUSED F/NH	USED F
141-59	**1993 Issues, (19)**	....	....	....	**33.50**	....
141-42	5.50s-7s Aging	4.00	10.25	11.00	2.50	2.25
143-46	7s Endangered Species, 4 attached	5.00	6.00	7.50	6.00	5.00
147-48	6s-10s Healthy Environment	4.00	11.50	13.00	3.50	2.50
149	13s Definitive	4.00	10.25	12.50	3.00	2.50
				Sheetlets (12)		
150-51	5s-6s Human Rights	3.00	7.00	35.00	8.00	....
152-55	5.50s Peace, 4 attached (strips of 3 w/tabs)	2.50	6.00	5.50	4.50	4.00
156-59	7s Environment—Climate, strip of 4	4.00	7.00	12.50(8)	8.25	5.50

1994

SCOTT NO.	DESCRIPTION	FIRST DAY COVERS SING	FIRST DAY COVERS INSC. BLK	INSRIP BLK-4	UNUSED F/NH	USED F
160-77	**1994 Issues (18)**	....	....	....	**30.00**	....
160-61	5.50s-8s Intl. Year of the Family	3.00	10.75	10.50	3.00	2.50
162-65	7s Endangered Species, 4 attached	6.25	7.50	7.50	6.00	5.00
166	12s Refugees	3.50	12.00	11.75	2.25	1.75
167-69	50g-30s Definitives (3)	8.50	33.50	32.50	6.00	5.00
170-73	6s Intl. Decade for Natural Disaster Reduction, 4 attached	5.50	6.50	9.00	7.50	5.00
174-75	5.50s-7s Population and Development	3.00	10.25	14.75	3.25	2.25
176-77	6s-7s Development through Partnership	3.50	10.25	13.50	3.00	2.25

1995

SCOTT NO.	DESCRIPTION	FIRST DAY COVERS SING	FIRST DAY COVERS INSC. BLK	INSRIP BLK-4	UNUSED F/NH	USED F
178/91	**1995 Issues (13) (No #188)**	....	....	....	**53.95**	....
178	7s 50th Anniversary of the UN	2.00	7.25	7.00	1.60	1.25
179	14s Social Summit	3.50	12.50	13.00	3.00	2.25
180-83	7s Endangered Species, 4 attached	6.25	7.50	8.00	7.00	6.00
184-85	6s-7s Youth: Our Future	3.50	10.25	15.00	3.00	2.50
186-87	7s-10s 50th Anniversary of the UN	4.00	11.50	15.00	4.00	3.00
188	17s 50th Anniversary of the UN, souvenir sheet	3.50	....	....	5.00	4.50
189-90	5.50s-6s 4th World Conference on Women	3.25	10.50	15.00	4.00	3.50
191	3s 50thAnniversary, min. sheet of 12	....	....	....	29.00	....
192	same, souvenir booklet of 4 panes of 3	....	....	....	31.00	....

1996

SCOTT NO.	DESCRIPTION	FIRST DAY COVERS SING	FIRST DAY COVERS INSC. BLK	INSRIP BLK-4	UNUSED F/NH	USED F
193/211	**1996 Issues (18) (No 207)**	....	....	....	**27.15**	....
193	7s WFUNA 50th Anniversary	2.00	7.25	7..00	1.60	1.25
194-95	1s-10s Definitives	3.25	10.50	10.50	2.50	2.25
196-99	7s Endangered Species, 4 attached	6.25	7.50	8.00	7.00	6.00
200-04	6s City Summit (Habitat II), strip of 5	6.75	16.50	18.00	8.75	8.00
205-06	6s-7s Sport & the Environment	3.50	10.25	11.50	2.75	2.50
207	13s Sport & theEnvrinronment souvenir sheet	3.25	....	....	3.00	2.75
208-09	7s-10s A Plea for Peace	4.00	11.50	13.50	3.25	3.00
210-11	5.5s-8s UNICEF 50th Anniversary	3.50	10.25	11.50	2.75	2.50

207

208

209

210

211

218-21

214-17

212

228

230

223-27

1997

SCOTT NO.	DESCRIPTION	FIRST DAY COVERS SING	FIRST DAY COVERS INSC. BLK	INSRIP BLK-4	UNUSED F/NH	USED F
212/31	**1997 Issues (19) (No. #222)**	....	....	....	**27.50**	....
212-13	5s-6s Definitives	3.25	10.50	10.50	2.50	2.25
214-17	7s Endangered Species, 4 attached	6.25	7.50	8.00	7.00	6.00
218-21	3.5s Earth Summit +5, 4 attached	3.25	3.75	6.00	4.25	3.00
222	11s Earth Summit +5, souvenir sheet	2.50	....	....	3.00	2.75
223-27	7s Transportation, strip of 5	6.75	9.50	16.00(10)	7.75	7.00
228-29	6.50s-7s Tribute to Philately	3.50	10.25	14.00	2.75	2.50
230-31	3s-6s Terracota Warriors	2.75	8.25	14.00	3.25	2.00
232	same, Souvenir bklt of 6 panes of 4	....	....	....	9.00	....

233

239a

1998

SCOTT NO.	DESCRIPTION	FIRST DAY COVERS SING	FIRST DAY COVERS INSC. BLK	INSRIP BLK-4	UNUSED F/NH	USED F
233-34	6.50-9s Definitives	3.75	8.00	13.50	3.00	2.75
235-38	7s Endangered Species, 4 attached	6.25	7.50	7.00	6.00	5.50
239	3.50s Intl. Year of the Ocean, sheetlet of 12	15.00	....	....	8.50	....
240	6.50s Rain Forest, Ocelot	2.00	4.50	6.75	1.50	1.25
241	22s Rain Forests, Ocelet, souvenir sheet	6.50	....	....	4.50	4.00
242-43	4s-7.50s 50 Years of Peacekeeping	3.25	7.00	11.00	2.50	2.25
244-45	4.50s-7s 50th of the Dec. of Human Rights	3.25	7.00	11.00	2.50	2.25
246-47	3.50s-7s Schonbrunn Castle	3.00	6.50	10.00	2.35	2.10
248	same, souvenir bklt of 6 panes	....	....	....	9.75	....

249

253-56

1999

SCOTT NO.	DESCRIPTION	FIRST DAY COVERS SING	FIRST DAY COVERS INSC. BLK	INSRIP BLK-4	UNUSED F/NH	USED F
249	8s Definitive	2.50	6.75	7.50	2.00	1.50
250-51	4.50s-6.50s World Heritage Sites, Australia	3.00	6.50	10.00	2.35	2.10
252	same, souvenir bklt of 6 panes	....	....	....	7.50	....
253-56	7s Endangered Species, 4 attached	6.25	7.50	7.00	6.00	5.50
257-58	3.50s Unispace III Conference	1.95	4.50	4.00	1.75	.75
259	13s Unispace III Conference, souvenir sheet	3.50	....	....	3.25	3.00
260-63	6.50s Universal Postal Union	2.00	4.50	6.75	4.25	1.25

264

266

SCOTT NO.	DESCRIPTION	FIRST DAY COVERS SING	FIRST DAY COVERS INSC. BLK	INSRIP BLK-4	UNUSED F/NH	USED F
264	3.50s In Memorium	1.95	4.50	4.00	1.25	.75
265	14s In Memoriam	3.50	....	....	2.75	2.00
266-67	7s-13s Education-Keystone to the 21st Century	5.00	11.50	20.00	4.75	4.00

268

273

2000

SCOTT NO.	DESCRIPTION	FIRST DAY COVERS SING	FIRST DAY COVERS INSC. BLK	INSRIP BLK-4	UNUSED F/NH	USED F
268	7s International Year of Thanksgiving	1.95	4.50	5.50	1.25	.95
269-72	7s Endangered Species, 4 attached	6.25	7.50	7.00	6.00	5.50
273-74	7s-8s Our World 2000	4.50	10.50	17.00	4.00	3.00

275

288

SCOTT NO.	DESCRIPTION	FIRST DAY COVERS SING	FIRST DAY COVERS INSC. BLK	INSRIP BLK-4	UNUSED F/NH	USED F
275-76	7s-9s 55th Anniversary of the UN	4.50	10.50	17.00	4.00	3.00
277	same, 7s-9s souvenir sheet	....	....	....	4.00	3.00
278	3.50s United Nations in the 21st Century	1.75	4.50	4.50	4.50	.75
279-80	4.50s-6.50s World Heritage Sites, Spain	3.00	6.50	10.00	2.35	2.10
281	same, souvenir bklt of 6 panes	....	....	....	9.00	....
282	7s Respect for Refugees	1.95	4.50	5.50	1.25	.95
283	25s Respect for Refugees, souvenir sheet	7.00	....	....	5.00	2.45
284-87	7s Endangered Species, 4 attached	6.25	7.50	7.00	6.00	5.50
288-89	10s-12s Intl. Volunteers Year	5.50	12.50	21.00	5.00	4.00
290-91	7s-15s World Hertiage Sites, Japan	4.00	8.00	19.00	4.75	4.00
292	same, souvenir bklt of 6 panes	....	....	....	9.00	....

293

294

2001

SCOTT NO.	DESCRIPTION	FIRST DAY COVERS SING	FIRST DAY COVERS INSC. BLK	INSRIP BLK-4	UNUSED F/NH	USED F
293	7s Dag Hammarskjold	1.95	4.50	5.50	1.25	.95
294-95	7s-8s 50th Anniv. of the UNPA	4.50	10.50	17.00	4.00	3.00
296	same, 28s souvenir sheet	7.50	....	....	5.50	4.50
297-300	7s Climate Change, strip of 4	6.25	7.50	7.00	6.00	5.50
301	7s Nobel Peace Prize	1.95	4.50	5.50	1.25	.95

302

312

2002

SCOTT NO.	DESCRIPTION	FIRST DAY COVERS SING	FIRST DAY COVERS INSC. BLK	INSRIP BLK-4	UNUSED F/NH	USED F
302-07	e0.07-e2.03 Austrian Tourist Attractions	5.50	15.00	35.00	9.00	4.00
308-11	e0.51 Endangered Species, 4 attached	5.00	6.00	5.50	4.75	4.00
312-13	e0.51-1.09 Independence of East Timor	3.50	8.00	16.00	3.75	3.00
314-17	e0.22-0.51 Intl. Year of Mountains, 2 pairs	3.50	4.50	16.00	4.25	3.00
318-21	e0.51-0.58 Johannesburg Summit, 2 pairs	4.50	5.50	6.00	5.00	4.00

322

SCOTT NO.	DESCRIPTION	FIRST DAY COVERS SING	FIRST DAY COVERS INSC. BLK	INSRIP BLK-4	UNUSED F/NH	USED F
322-23	e0.51-0.58 World Heritage Sites, Italy	2.25	7.00	3.00	2.50	2.00
324	same, souvenir bklt of 6 panes of 4	....	....	....	11.00	....
325	e0.51-0.25 UNAIDS Awareness, souvenir sheet	2.25	....	....	2.00	1.50

327

333-34

2003

SCOTT NO.	DESCRIPTION	FIRST DAY COVERS SING	INSC. BLK	INSRIP BLK-4	UNUSED F/NH	USED F
326	e0.51 Indigenous Art, sheet of 6	9.50	....	....	7.50	4.00
327-28	e0.25-e1.00 Austrian Tourist Attractions	2.50	7.50	3.25	2.75	2.25
329-32	e0.51 Endangered Species, 4 attached	5.00	6.00	5.50	4.75	4.00
333-34	e0.55-e0.75 Intl. Year of Freshwater, 2 attach	2.50	7.50	3.25	2.75	2.25

335

341

SCOTT NO.	DESCRIPTION	FIRST DAY COVERS SING	INSC. BLK	INSRIP BLK-4	UNUSED F/NH	USED F
335	e0.04 Schloss Eggenberg, Graz	1.75	4.50	4.50	1.00	.75
336	e2.10 Ralphe Bunche	3.75	9.50	18.00	4.50	3.50
337	e2.10 In Memoriam , UN Complex Bomding in Iraq	3.75	9.50	18.00	4.50	3.50
338-39	e0.51-e0.75 World Heritage Sites, United States	2.50	8.00	11.00	2.75	2.00
340	same, souvenir bklt of 6 panes of 4	....	....	....	11.00	....

353

355

2004

SCOTT NO.	DESCRIPTION	FIRST DAY COVERS SING	INSC. BLK	INSRIP BLK-4	UNUSED F/NH	USED F
341	e0.55 Schloss Schonbrunn, Vienna	2.10	4.00	7.50	1.75	.85
342-45	e0.55 Endangered Species, 4 attached	7.00	9.00	7.00	6.50	4.50
346	e0.55 Indigenous Art, sheet of 6	10.50	....	....	9.75	6.50
347-48	e0.55-e0.75 Road Safety	2.50	8.00	13.00	3.00	2.25
349	e2.10 Japanese Peace Bell, 50th Anniv.	3.75	9.50	20.00	4.75	3.50
350-51	e0.55-e0.75 World Heritage Sites, Greece	2.50	8.00	13.00	3.00	2.00
352	same, souvenir bklt of 6 panes of 4	....	....	....	21.00	....
353-54	e0.55-e1.00 My Dream for Peace	2.75	8.50	16.00	3.50	2.25
355-56	e0.55-e1.25 Human Rights	7.00	25.00	42.50(8)	5.50	5.00

357

359

2005

SCOTT NO.	DESCRIPTION	FIRST DAY COVERS SING	INSC. BLK	INSRIP BLK-4	UNUSED F/NH	USED F
357	e0.55 U.N. 60th Anniv.	2.10	4.00	7.50	1.75	.85
358	e2.10 U.N. 60th Anniv.	3.75	....	....	5.00	3.50
359	e0.75 Definitive	2.35	5.00	9.00	2.00	1.00

360-63

SCOTT NO.	DESCRIPTION	FIRST DAY COVERS SING	INSC. BLK	INSRIP BLK-4	UNUSED F/NH	USED F
360-63	e0.55 Orchids, 4 attached	7.00	9.00	7.00	6.50	4.50
364-65	e0.55-e0.75 Nature's Wisdom	2.50	8.00	13.50	3.00	2.00

366

368

SCOTT NO.	DESCRIPTION	FIRST DAY COVERS SING	INSC. BLK	INSRIP BLK-4	UNUSED F/NH	USED F
366-67	e0.55-e1.10 International Year of Sports	2.75	8.50	17.00	4.00	2.25
368-69	e0.55-e0.75 World Heritage Sites, Egypt	2.50	8.00	13.50	3.00	2.00
370	same, souvenir bklt of 6 panes of 4	....	....	....	21.00	....

371

373

SCOTT NO.	DESCRIPTION	FIRST DAY COVERS SING	INSC. BLK	INSRIP BLK-4	UNUSED F/NH	USED F
371-72	e0.55-e1.00 My Dream for Peace, type of 2004	2.75	8.50	12.00	3.75	2.25
373-74	e0.55-e1.25 Food for Life	2.75	8.50	20.00	4.25	2.25

376-79

2006

SCOTT NO.	DESCRIPTION	FIRST DAY COVERS SING	INSC. BLK	INSRIP BLK-4	UNUSED F/NH	USED F
375	e0.55 Indigenous Art, sheet of 6	11.50	....	....	9.50	9.50
376-79	e0.55 Endangered Species, 4 attached	7.00	9.00	7.00	6.50	4.50

380

382

SCOTT NO.	DESCRIPTION	FIRST DAY COVERS SING	FIRST DAY COVERS INSC. BLK	INSRIP BLK-4	UNUSED F/NH	USED F
380-81	e0.55-e1.25 Day of Families	2.75	8.50	12.00	3.00	2.25
382-83	e0.55-e0.75 World Heritage Sites, France	2.50	8.00	11.00	2.75	2.00
....	same, souvenir bklt of 6 panes of 4	....	....	....	21.00	....

385

387a

SCOTT NO.	DESCRIPTION	FIRST DAY COVERS SING	FIRST DAY COVERS INSC. BLK	INSRIP BLK-4	UNUSED F/NH	USED F
385-86	e0.55-e1.00 My Dream for Peace One Day	2.75	8.50	12.00	3.00	2.25
387	e0.55 Flags and Coins, sheet of 8	15.00	....	....	13.00	13.00

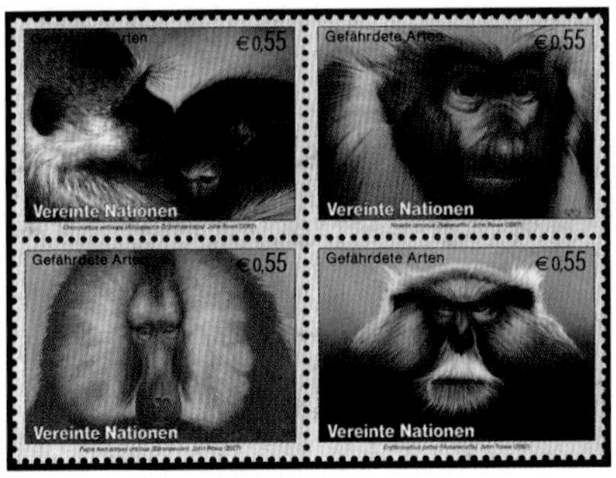

388-91

2007

SCOTT NO.	DESCRIPTION	FIRST DAY COVERS SING	FIRST DAY COVERS INSC. BLK	INSRIP BLK-4	UNUSED F/NH	USED F
388-91	e0.55 Endangered Species, 4 attached	7.00	9.00	7.00	6.50	4.50
392	e0.55 Flags and Coins, sheet of 8	15.00	....	....	13.00	13.00
393-97	e0.55 UN Headquarters + labels, strip of 5	....	....	....	15.00	15.00
....	same, sheet of 2 (393-97)	....	....	....	30.00	....
398-99	e0.55-e1.25 Peaceful Visions	5.00	6.25	15.00	3.75	3.75
....	e0.55-e0.75 World Heritage Sites, South America	2.50	8.00	11.00	2.75	2.00
....	e0.75 Universal Postal Union, joint issue with Swiss Post Humanitarian Mail	2.50	5.00	9.00	2.00	1.00
....	e0.65-e1.15 Space Age for Humanity ...	5.00	6.25	15.00	3.75	3.75

AIR LETTER SHEETS & POSTAL CARDS

U1

1995

SCOTT NO.	DESCRIPTION	FIRST DAY COVER	UNUSED ENTIRE
U1	6s Vienna International Center	1.75	3.50
U2	7s Vienna Landscape	1.75	1.75

1998

SCOTT NO.	DESCRIPTION	FIRST DAY COVER	UNUSED ENTIRE
U3	13s multicolored	4.00	3.00

2002-03

SCOTT NO.	DESCRIPTION	FIRST DAY COVER	UNUSED ENTIRE
U4	e0.51 Vienna International Center	2.50	1.75
U5	e1.09 Vienna International Center	3.75	3.00
U6	e0.51+e0.4 surcharged envelope (U4)	2.50	1.75
U7	e1.09+e0.16 surcharged envelope (U5)	3.75	3.00
U8	e0.55 U.N. Headquarters, Vienna	2.75	1.50
U9	e1.25 U.N. Headquarters, Vienna	4.25	3.25

UC1

UC5

UC3

1962

SCOTT NO.	DESCRIPTION	FIRST DAY COVER	UNUSED ENTIRE
UC1	9s multicolored	4.00	4.00

1967

SCOTT NO.	DESCRIPTION	FIRST DAY COVER	UNUSED ENTIRE
UC2	9s+2s surcharge on UC1	23.50	41.00
UC3	11s Birds in Flight	3.50	3.50
UC4	11s+1s surcharged	9.00	46.00
UC5	12s Vienna Office	4.00	4.00

UX1

UX2

UX3

UX7

1982-85

SCOTT NO.	DESCRIPTION	FIRST DAY COVER	UNUSED ENTIRE
UX1	3s multicolored (1982)	.55	1.50
UX2	5s multicolored (1982)	1.75	1.00
UX3	4s U.N. Emblem (1985)	.85	3.75

1992-94

SCOTT NO.	DESCRIPTION	FIRST DAY COVER	UNUSED ENTIRE
UX4	5s+1s surcharged	......	20.00
UX5	6s Reg Schek Painting	1.75	3.75
UX6	5s Postal Card	1.75	11.00
UX7	6s Postal Card	1.75	3.75
UX8	5s + 50g surcharge on UX6	1.75	4.00

UX11

1997

SCOTT NO.	DESCRIPTION	FIRST DAY COVER	UNUSED ENTIRE
UX9	6s+50s surcharge on UX5	2.50	2.50
UX10	6s+1s surcharge on UX7	2.50	2.75

1998-2003

SCOTT NO.	DESCRIPTION	FIRST DAY COVER	UNUSED ENTIRE
UX11	6.50s multicolored	2.00	1.50
UX12	7s The Gloriette	2.00	1.50
UX13	7s multicolored, type of 1983	2.00	1.50
UX14	e0.51 Clock tower Graz, Austria	1.75	1.50
UX15	e0.51+e0.04 surcharged postal card (UX14)	1.75	1.50
UX16	e0.55 U.N. Headquarters, Vienna	2.75	1.50

CANADA

1, 4, 12
Beaver

2, 5, 10, 13
Prince Albert

7
Jacques Cartier

8, 11

9

14

Queen Victoria

15
Beaver

1851 Laid paper, Imperforate (OG + 75%)

SCOTT NO.	DESCRIPTION	UNUSED VF	UNUSED F	UNUSED AVG	USED VF	USED F	USED AVG
1	3p red	13300.00	9975.00	5900.00	800.00	575.00	350.00
2	6p grayish purple	12750.00	9500.00	5700.00	1500.00	950.00	600.00

1852-55 Wove paper

SCOTT NO.	DESCRIPTION	UNUSED VF	UNUSED F	UNUSED AVG	USED VF	USED F	USED AVG
4	3p red	1275.00	950.00	700.00	200.00	140.00	95.00
4d	3p red (thin paper)	1275.00	950.00	700.00	200.00	140.00	95.00
5	6p slate gray	8800.00	6100.00	3750.00	1100.00	850.00	525.00

1855

SCOTT NO.	DESCRIPTION	UNUSED VF	UNUSED F	UNUSED AVG	USED VF	USED F	USED AVG
7	10p blue	6250.00	4750.00	3200.00	1225.00	875.00	600.00

1857

SCOTT NO.	DESCRIPTION	UNUSED VF	UNUSED F	UNUSED AVG	USED VF	USED F	USED AVG
8	1/2p rose	700.00	475.00	325.00	470.00	325.00	210.00
9	7-1/2p green	6900.00	4800.00	2850.00	1950.00	1350.00	975.00

Very thick soft wove paper

SCOTT NO.	DESCRIPTION	UNUSED VF	UNUSED F	UNUSED AVG	USED VF	USED F	USED AVG
10	6p reddish purple	14400.00	10200.00	6400.00	3100.00	2300.00	1400.00

1858-59 Perf. 12

SCOTT NO.	DESCRIPTION	UNUSED VF	UNUSED F	UNUSED AVG	USED VF	USED F	USED AVG
11	1/2p rose	2200.00	1650.00	1000.00	925.00	650.00	425.00
12	3p red	3400.00	2550.00	1500.00	495.00	335.00	225.00
13	6p brown violet	8200.00	6250.00	4500.00	4350.00	3200.00	2400.00

1859 (OG + 35%)

SCOTT NO.	DESCRIPTION	UNUSED VF	UNUSED F	UNUSED AVG	USED VF	USED F	USED AVG
14	1¢ rose	295.00	210.00	150.00	55.00	35.00	22.00
15	5¢ vermillion	375.00	220.00	145.00	29.00	22.00	15.00
16	10¢ black brown	9200.00	6600.00	3950.00	2750.00	1800.00	1250.00
17	10¢ red lilac	700.00	480.00	325.00	85.00	55.00	33.00
18	12-1/2¢ yellow green	700.00	480.00	325.00	85.00	55.00	33.00
19	17¢ blue	825.00	575.00	400.00	135.00	80.00	50.00

1864

SCOTT NO.	DESCRIPTION	UNUSED VF	UNUSED F	UNUSED AVG	USED VF	USED F	USED AVG
20	2¢ rose	440.00	310.00	195.00	210.00	125.00	70.00

16, 17
Prince Albert

18
Queen Victoria

19
Jacques Cartier

20
Queen Victoria

21

22, 23, 31

24, 32

25, 33

Original Gum: Prior to 1897, the Unused price is for stamps either without gum or with partial gum. If you require full original gum, use the OG premium. Never hinged quality is scarce on those issues. Please write for specific quotations for NH.

1868-75 Wove paper, Perf. 12, unwkd. (OG + 35%)

SCOTT NO.	DESCRIPTION	UNUSED VF	UNUSED F	UNUSED AVG	USED VF	USED F	USED AVG
21	1/2¢ black	70.00	45.00	31.00	41.50	25.00	16.00
22	1¢ brown red	495.00	350.00	245.00	66.00	40.00	28.00
23	1¢ yellow orange	745.00	495.00	325.00	135.00	80.00	50.00
24	2¢ green	495.00	350.00	245.00	55.00	33.00	22.00
25	3¢ red	795.00	525.00	360.00	30.00	17.00	10.00
26	5¢ olive gr. (pf. 11-1/2x12)	925.00	600.00	410.00	185.00	115.00	75.00
27	6¢ dark brown	1300.00	875.00	550.00	80.00	50.00	32.00
28	12-1/2¢ blue	650.00	440.00	275.00	95.00	60.00	40.00
29	15¢ gray violet	67.50	45.00	28.00	35.00	20.00	14.00
29b	15¢ red lilac	740.00	525.00	320.00	90.00	55.00	32.00
30	15¢ gray	70.00	48.00	30.00	35.00	20.00	14.00

26

27

28

29, 30

1873-74 Wove paper. Perf. 11-1/2 x 12, unwatermarked

SCOTT NO.	DESCRIPTION	UNUSED VF	UNUSED F	UNUSED AVG	USED VF	USED F	USED AVG
21a	1/2¢ black	70.00	48.00	30.00	41.50	25.00	16.00
29a	15¢ gray violet	875.00	595.00	360.00	155.00	95.00	57.50
30a	15¢ gray	900.00	620.00	375.00	155.00	95.00	57.50

1868 Wove paper. Perf. 12 watermarked

SCOTT NO.	DESCRIPTION	UNUSED VF	UNUSED F	UNUSED AVG	USED VF	USED F	USED AVG
22a	1¢ brown red	......	1450.00	800.00	......	175.00	115.00
24a	2¢ green	......	2000.00	1250.00	......	240.00	175.00
25a	3¢ red	......	2200.00	1450.00	......	240.00	175.00
27b	6¢ dark brown	......	3600.00	2450.00	......	900.00	650.00
28a	12-1/2¢ blue	......	1250.00	675.00	......	145.00	95.00
29c	15¢ gray violet	......	3600.00	2500.00	......	550.00	375.00

1868 Laid Paper (OG + 20%)

SCOTT NO.	DESCRIPTION	UNUSED VF	UNUSED F	UNUSED AVG	USED VF	USED F	USED AVG
31	1¢ brown red	......	11000.00	6600.00	3400.00	2300.00	1425.00
33	3¢ bright red	......	10000.00	6000.00	......	675.00	495.00

1870-89 Perf. 12

SCOTT NO.	DESCRIPTION	UNUSED VF	UNUSED F	UNUSED AVG	USED VF	USED F	USED AVG
34	1/2¢ black	9.00	6.25	3.75	7.50	4.50	3.00
35	1¢ yellow	28.00	19.00	12.00	1.00	.70	.45
35a	1¢ orange	85.00	57.50	35.00	10.00	6.00	3.50
36	2¢ green	35.00	23.50	14.75	1.75	1.20	.75
36d	2¢ blue green	67.50	45.00	28.50	4.25	2.50	1.50
37	3¢ dull red	74.00	50.00	31.00	2.85	1.75	.90
37c	3¢ orange red	67.50	45.00	25.00	1.75	1.00	.70
37d	3¢ copper red, pf. 12-1/2	......	4725.00	2800.00	1025.00	700.00	425.00
38	5¢ slate green	395.00	275.00	170.00	20.00	12.00	8.25
39	6¢ yellow brown	320.00	225.00	135.00	20.00	12.00	8.25
40	10¢ dull rose lilac	425.00	295.00	175.00	47.50	28.00	19.00

34

35

36

37, 41

38, 42

39, 43

40, 45

44

1873-79 Perf. 11-1/2 x 12 (OG + 20%)

SCOTT NO.	DESCRIPTION	UNUSED VF	UNUSED F	UNUSED AVG	USED VF	USED F	USED AVG
35d	1¢ orange	180.00	125.00	75.00	16.00	9.50	6.00
36e	2¢ green	250.00	170.00	110.00	22.00	13.50	9.00
37e	3¢ red	220.00	150.00	92.50	9.75	5.75	3.75
38a	5¢ slate green	480.00	325.00	200.00	37.00	22.00	15.00
39b	6¢ yellow brown	510.00	345.00	220.00	37.00	22.00	15.00
40c	10¢ pale milky rose lilac	900.00	610.00	380.00	325.00	195.00	130.00

SCOTT NO.	DESCRIPTION	UNUSED VF	F	AVG	USED VF	F	AVG
	1888-93 Perf. 12						
41	3¢ bright vermillion	27.50	18.75	11.50	.75	.45	.25
41a	3¢ rose carmine	340.00	230.00	145.00	10.00	6.00	4.00
42	5¢ gray	77.50	52.00	32.50	5.00	3.00	1.60
43	6¢ red brown	67.50	46.00	28.50	12.50	8.50	5.00
43a	6¢ chocolate	190.00	130.00	80.00	30.00	21.00	12.50
44	8¢ gray	80.00	55.00	33.00	4.50	3.25	1.85
45	10¢ brown red	145.00	98.50	60.00	35.00	22.00	13.75
46	20¢ vermillion	300.00	210.00	125.00	90.00	55.00	35.00
47	50¢ deep blue	305.00	205.00	135.00	80.00	50.00	30.00

46, 47

50-65
Queen Victoria in 1837 & 1897

SCOTT NO.	DESCRIPTION	UNUSED OG VF	F	AVG	USED VF	F	AVG
	1897 Jubilee Issue (NH + 150%)						
50	1/2¢ black	200.00	130.00	75.00	150.00	100.00	75.00
51	1¢ orange	40.00	25.00	20.00	9.00	6.00	4.00
52	2¢ green	50.00	35.00	25.00	12.25	8.25	5.00
53	3¢ bright rose	30.00	20.00	12.00	2.25	1.50	.90
54	5¢ deep blue	120.00	70.00	40.00	22.50	15.00	8.25
55	6¢ yellow brown	500.00	300.00	170.00	150.00	110.00	75.00
56	8¢ dark violet	130.00	80.00	50.00	32.50	19.50	12.00
57	10¢ brown violet	200.00	130.00	75.00	75.00	50.00	28.00
58	15¢ steel blue	500.00	300.00	200.00	150.00	110.00	75.00
59	20¢ vermillion	500.00	300.00	200.00	150.00	110.00	75.00
60	50¢ ultramarine	500.00	300.00	200.00	165.00	110.00	65.00
61	$1 lake	2000.00	1200.00	700.00	500.00	400.00	200.00
62	$2 dark purple	3000.00	2000.00	1400.00	550.00	360.00	220.00
63	$3 yellow bistre	3000.00	2000.00	1400.00	900.00	600.00	450.00
64	$4 purple	3000.00	2000.00	1400.00	900.00	600.00	450.00
65	$5 olive green	3000.00	2000.00	1400.00	900.00	600.00	450.00

66-73

74-84
Queen Victoria

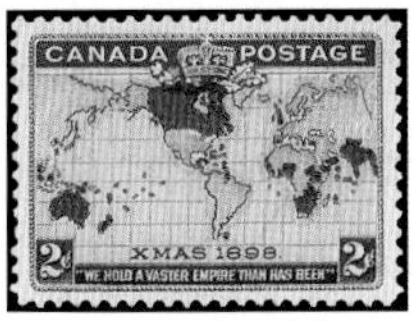

85-86
Map Showing British Empire

77: 2¢ Die I. Frame of four thin lines
77a: 2¢ Die II. Frame of thick line between two thin lines

SCOTT NO.	DESCRIPTION	UNUSED OG VF	F	AVG	USED VF	F	AVG
	1897-98 Maple Leaves (NH + 150%)						
66	1/2¢ black	18.00	12.00	8.00	5.00	3.75	2.20
67	1¢ blue green	60.00	40.00	25.00	1.10	.70	.45
68	2¢ purple	60.00	40.00	25.00	1.65	1.10	.70
69	3¢ carmine (1898)	60.00	40.00	25.00	.45	.30	.25
70	5¢ dark blue, bluish paper	250.00	170.00	120.00	5.75	3.75	2.20
71	6¢ brown	200.00	150.00	100.00	25.00	17.00	11.00
72	8¢ orange	500.00	300.00	170.00	10.00	6.00	3.75
73	10¢ brown violet (1898)	600.00	400.00	250.00	70.00	45.00	30.00
	1898-1902 Numerals (NH + 150%)						
74	1/2¢ black	8.00	5.00	4.00	2.00	1.50	1.00
75	1¢ gray green	45.00	30.00	20.00	.30	.20	.15
76	2¢ purple (I)	45.00	30.00	20.00	.30	.20	.15
77	2¢ carmine (I) (1899)	45.00	30.00	20.00	.30	.20	.15
77a	2¢ carmine (II)	45.00	30.00	20.00	.45	.30	.20
78	3¢ carmine	100.00	70.00	50.00	.50	.40	.30
79	5¢ blue, bluish paper	400.00	250.00	150.00	1.40	1.00	.55
80	6¢ brown	300.00	200.00	120.00	40.00	22.00	11.50
81	7¢ olive yellow (1902)	250.00	150.00	100.00	17.00	10.00	6.50
82	8¢ orange	400.00	250.00	200.00	19.00	11.50	7.50
83	10¢ brown violet	500.00	300.00	220.00	17.00	10.00	6.50
84	20¢ olive green (1900)	900.00	500.00	270.00	80.00	47.00	32.50
	1898 IMPERIAL PENNY POSTAGE COMMEMORATIVE						
85	2¢ black, lavender & carmine	50.00	35.00	25.00	7.25	5.00	3.25
86	2¢ black, blue & carmine	50.00	35.00	25.00	7.25	5.00	3.25
	1899 69 & 78 surcharged						
87	2¢ on 3¢ carmine	30.00	20.00	12.00	5.50	3.50	2.50
88	2¢ on 3¢ carmine	50.00	30.00	20.00	4.00	2.50	1.75s

89-95
King Edward VII

SCOTT NO.	DESCRIPTION	UNUSED NH F	AVG	UNUSED OG F	AVG	USED F	AVG
	1903-08						
89	1¢ green	50.00	35.00	25.00	15.00	.20	.15
90	2¢ carmine	50.00	35.00	25.00	15.00	.20	.15
90a	2¢ carmine, imperf. pair	50.00	35.00	25.00	15.00	......	......
91	5¢ blue, blue paper	350.00	220.00	100.00	80.00	2.00	1.35
92	7¢ olive bistre	350.00	220.00	100.00	80.00	2.00	1.35
93	10¢ brown lilac	600.00	350.00	200.00	150.00	4.50	3.00
94	20¢ olive green	1200.00	650.00	500.00	300.00	25.00	20.00
95	50¢ purple (1908)	1200.00	650.00	500.00	300.00	25.00	20.00

96
Princess and Prince of Wales in 1908

97
Jacques Cartier and Samuel Champlain

98
Queen Alexandra and King Edward

99
Champlain's Home in Quebec

100
Generals Montcalm and Wolfe

101
View of Quebec in 1700

102
Champlain's Departure for the West

103
Arrival of Cartier at Quebec

104-34, 136-38, 184
King George V

Never Hinged: From 1897 to 1949, Unused OG is for stamps with original gum that have been hinged. If you desire Never Hinged stamps, order from the NH listings.

1908 QUEBEC TERCENTENARY ISSUE

SCOTT NO.	DESCRIPTION	UNUSED NH F	AVG	UNUSED OG F	AVG	USED F	AVG
96-103	**1/2¢-20¢ complete, 8 varieties**	**1525.00**	**975.00**	**635.00**	**386.25**	**290.00**	**210.00**
96	1/2¢ black brown	10.00	6.00	4.00	3.00	3.00	1.95
97	1¢ blue green	30.00	20.00	12.00	7.00	3.00	1.95
98	2¢ carmine	50.00	30.00	20.00	12.00	.95	.55
99	5¢ dark blue	100.00	60.00	40.00	25.00	22.50	13.50
100	7¢ olive green	300.00	200.00	120.00	75.00	50.00	40.00
101	10¢ dark violet	300.00	200.00	120.00	75.00	50.00	40.00
102	15¢ red orange	300.00	200.00	130.00	80.00	50.00	40.00
103	20¢ yellow brown	500.00	300.00	200.00	120.00	105.00	75.00
	1912-25						
104-22	**1¢-$1 complete 18 varieties**	**1825.00**	**1100.00**	**730.00**	**450.00**	**31.75**	**19.25**
104	1¢ green	20.00	15.00	10.00	5.00	.20	.15
104a	same, booklet pane of 6	50.00	30.00	20.00	15.00	.....	.....
105	1¢ yellow (1922)	20.00	15.00	10.00	5.00	.20	.15
105a	same, booklet pane of 4	100.00	60.00	40.00	30.00	.....	.....
105b	same, booklet pane of 6	100.00	60.00	40.00	30.00	.....	.....
106	2¢ carmine	20.00	12.00	8.00	5.00	.20	.15
106a	same, booklet pane of 6	70.00	45.00	30.00	20.00	.....	.....
107	2¢ yellow green (1922)	15.00	10.00	7.00	4.00	.20	.15
107b	same, booklet pane of 4	130.00	80.00	70.00	50.00	.....	.....
107c	same, booklet pane of 6	700.00	400.00	350.00	200.00	.....	.....
108	3¢ brown (1918)	30.00	20.00	7.00	4.00	.20	.15
108a	same, booklet pane of 4	190.00	120.00	100.00	60.00	.....	.....

SCOTT NO.	DESCRIPTION	UNUSED NH F	UNUSED NH AVG	UNUSED OG F	UNUSED OG AVG	USED F	USED AVG
109	3¢ carmine (1923)	20.00	15.00	8.00	5.00	.20	.15
109a	same, booklet pane of 4	130.00	75.00	60.00	35.00	.....	.....
110	4¢ olive bistre (1922)	80.00	50.00	30.00	20.00	1.95	1.25
111	5¢ dark blue	200.00	130.00	90.00	60.00	.35	.20
112	5¢ violet (1922)	45.00	30.00	20.00	15.00	.35	.20
113	7¢ yellow ochre	90.00	50.00	30.00	20.00	2.00	1.20
114	7¢ red brown (1924)	40.00	25.00	20.00	12.00	5.50	4.00
115	8¢ blue (1925)	70.00	45.00	35.00	20.00	5.00	4.00
116	10¢ plum	450.00	270.00	170.00	110.00	1.05	.60
117	10¢ blue (1922)	80.00	50.00	40.00	25.00	1.15	.75
118	10¢ bistre brown (1925) .	80.00	50.00	40.00	25.00	1.00	.65
119	20¢ olive green	180.00	100.00	70.00	40.00	.90	.55
120	50¢ black brown (1925) ..	180.00	100.00	70.00	40.00	1.75	1.15
120a	50¢ black	300.00	200.00	130.00	120.00		
122	$1 orange (1923)	220.00	150.00	100.00	60.00	6.00	3.75

1912 Coil Stamps; Perf. 8 Horizontally

SCOTT NO.	DESCRIPTION	UNUSED NH F	UNUSED NH AVG	UNUSED OG F	UNUSED OG AVG	USED F	USED AVG
123	1¢ dark green	170.00	120.00	80.00	50.00	35.00	20.00
124	2¢ carmine	170.00	120.00	80.00	50.00	35.00	20.00

1912-24 Perf. 8 Vertically

SCOTT NO.	DESCRIPTION	UNUSED NH F	UNUSED NH AVG	UNUSED OG F	UNUSED OG AVG	USED F	USED AVG
125-30	**1¢-3¢ complete, 6 varieties ....**	**265.00**	**160.00**	**110.00**	**70.00**	**14.75**	**9.50**
125	1¢ green	35.00	20.00	15.00	10.00	1.00	.65
126	1¢ yellow (1923)	20.00	12.00	10.00	6.00	5.50	3.75
126a	1¢ block of 4	80.00	50.00	45.00	30.00	.....	.....
127	2¢ carmine	40.00	25.00	20.00	12.00	.90	.60
128	2¢ green (1922)	25.00	15.00	12.00	10.00	.90	.60
128a	2¢ block of 4	90.00	50.00	45.00	30.00	.....	.....
129	3¢ brown (1918)	25.00	15.00	12.00	8.00	.90	.60
130	3¢ carmine (1924)	120.00	70.00	45.00	35.00	6.50	4.00
130a	3¢ block of 4	1000.00	700.00	600.00	500.00	.....	.....

1915-24 Perf. 12 Horizontally

SCOTT NO.	DESCRIPTION	UNUSED NH F	UNUSED NH AVG	UNUSED OG F	UNUSED OG AVG	USED F	USED AVG
131	1¢ dark green	12.00	7.00	6.00	4.00	7.00	4.25
132	2¢ carmine	40.00	25.00	20.00	15.00	7.00	5.00
133	2¢ yellow green (1924) .	150.00	85.00	80.00	50.00	45.00	28.00
134	3¢ brown (1921)	15.00	8.00	6.00	4.00	4.50	2.60

135
Quebec Conference of 1867

1917 CONFEDERATION ISSUE

SCOTT NO.	DESCRIPTION	UNUSED NH F	UNUSED NH AVG	UNUSED OG F	UNUSED OG AVG	USED F	USED AVG
135	3¢ brown	100.00	50.00	40.00	20.00	.75	.50

1924 Imperforate

SCOTT NO.	DESCRIPTION	UNUSED NH F	UNUSED NH AVG	UNUSED OG F	UNUSED OG AVG	USED F	USED AVG
136	1¢ yellow	150.00	100.00	75.00	60.00	35.00	23.00
137	2¢ green	70.00	40.00	35.00	30.00	35.00	23.00
138	3¢ carmine	35.00	25.00	20.00	15.00	16.00	12.00

1926
109 Surcharged

SCOTT NO.	DESCRIPTION	UNUSED NH F	UNUSED NH AVG	UNUSED OG F	UNUSED OG AVG	USED F	USED AVG
139	2¢ on 3¢ carmine	90.00	50.00	40.00	30.00	37.00	26.50

109 Surcharged

SCOTT NO.	DESCRIPTION	UNUSED NH F	UNUSED NH AVG	UNUSED OG F	UNUSED OG AVG	USED F	USED AVG
140	2¢ on 3¢ carmine	40.00	28.00	25.00	20.00	16.00	11.00

141
Sir John Macdonald

142
The Quebec Conference of 1867

143
The Parliment Building at Ottawa

144
Sir Wilfred Laurier

145
Map of Canada

1927 CONFEDERATION ISSUE

SCOTT NO.	DESCRIPTION	UNUSED NH F	UNUSED NH AVG	UNUSED OG F	UNUSED OG AVG	USED F	USED AVG
141-45	**1¢-12¢ complete, 5 varieties ....**	**36.25**	**24.75**	**21.75**	**15.25**	**8.25**	**5.10**
141	1¢ orange	3.00	2.25	1.95	1.30	.65	.40
142	2¢ green	2.00	1.25	1.10	.75	.20	.15
143	3¢ brown carmine	8.25	5.50	5.50	3.75	3.50	2.10
144	5¢ violet	5.00	3.25	3.35	2.20	1.80	1.10
145	12¢ dark blue	20.00	14.00	11.00	8.00	3.00	1.85

146
Thomas McGee

147
Sir Wilfred Laurier and Sir John Macdonald

148
Robert Baldwin and L.H. Lafontaine

1927 HISTORICAL ISSUE

SCOTT NO.	DESCRIPTION	UNUSED NH F	UNUSED NH AVG	UNUSED OG F	UNUSED OG AVG	USED F	USED AVG
146-48	**5¢-20¢ complete, 3 varieties ....**	**35.50**	**25.60**	**20.25**	**14.00**	**6.90**	**4.40**
146	5¢ violet	5.00	3.00	2.35	1.75	1.40	.85
147	12¢ green	9.50	7.00	6.00	4.00	3.00	2.00
148	20¢ brown carmine	23.00	17.00	13.00	9.00	3.50	2.20

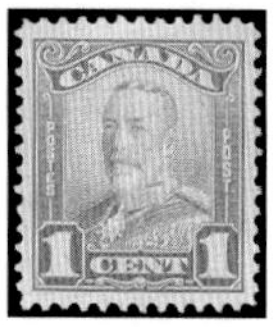

149-154, 160, 161
King George V

155
Mt. Hurd

156
Quebec Bridge

157
Harvesting Wheat

158
Fishing Schooner "Bluenose"

159
The Parliament Building at Ottawa

1928-29

SCOTT NO.	DESCRIPTION	UNUSED NH F	UNUSED NH AVG	UNUSED OG F	UNUSED OG AVG	USED F	USED AVG
149-59	**1¢-$1 complete, 11 varieties ....**	**1035.00**	**640.00**	**525.00**	**355.00**	**130.00**	**95.00**
149-55	**1¢-10¢, 7 varieties ....**	**101.00**	**68.00**	**51.50**	**33.00**	**17.15**	**10.15**
149	1¢ orange	35.00	25.00	20.00	12.00	.25	.20
149a	same, booklet pane of 6	35.00	25.00	20.00	12.00	.....	.....
150	2¢ green	2.00	1.50	1.00	.75	.20	.15
150a	same, booklet pane of 6	30.00	25.00	20.00	12.00	.....	.....
151	3¢ dark carmine	22.00	16.00	12.00	8.00	8.00	4.50
152	4¢ bistre (1929)	30.00	20.00	12.00	10.00	3.50	2.10
153	5¢ deep violet	15.00	12.00	10.00	6.00	2.00	1.30
153a	same, booklet pane of 6	150.00	110.00	90.00	60.00	.....	.....
154	8¢ blue	17.00	10.00	7.00	4.25	4.00	2.30
155	10¢ green	17.00	10.00	7.50	4.50	.80	.50
156	12¢ gray (1929)	40.00	25.00	20.00	15.00	4.50	2.60
157	20¢ dark carmine (1929)	38.00	25.00	18.00	12.00	7.75	5.00
158	50¢ dark blue (1929)	400.00	250.00	200.00	150.00	60.00	45.00
159	$1 olive green (1929)	500.00	300.00	250.00	160.00	50.00	32.50

1929 Coil Stamps. Perf. 8 Vertically

SCOTT NO.	DESCRIPTION	UNUSED NH F	UNUSED NH AVG	UNUSED OG F	UNUSED OG AVG	USED F	USED AVG
160	1¢ orange	50.00	40.00	30.00	20.00	15.50	9.75
161	2¢ green	40.00	30.00	20.00	15.00	2.50	1.75

2¢ Die I. Above "POSTAGE" faint crescent in ball of ornament. Top letter "P" has tiny dot of color.

162-172, 178-183
King George V

173
Parliament Library at Ottawa

2¢ Die II. Stronger and clearer crescent, spot of color in "P" is larger.

174
The Old Citadel at Quebec

175
Harvesting Wheat on the Prairies

176
The Museum at Grand Pre and Monument to Evangeline

177
Mt. Edith Cavell

VERY FINE QUALITY: To determine the Very Fine price, add the difference between the Fine and Average prices to the Fine quality price. For example: if the Fine price is $10.00 and the Average price is $6.00, the Very Fine price would be $14.00. From 1935 to date, add 20% to the Fine price to arrive at the Very Fine price.

1930-31

SCOTT NO.	DESCRIPTION	UNUSED NH F	AVG	UNUSED OG F	AVG	USED F	AVG
162-77	**1¢-$1 complete, 16 varieties ....**	**480.25**	**304.00**	**278.25**	**188.25**	**46.00**	**31.00**
162-72	**1¢-8¢, 11 varieties ....**	**49.80**	**37.35**	**30.25**	**20.10**	**14.00**	**9.30**
162	1¢ orange	1.00	.65	.70	.45	.40	.30
163	1¢ deep green	1.30	.80	.85	.50	.20	.15
163a	same, booklet pane of 4	100.00	70.00	70.00	50.00	.....	.....
163c	same, booklet pane of 6	20.00	13.00	14.00	9.00	.....	.....
164	2¢ dull green	1.10	.65	.55	.40	.20	.15
164a	same, booklet pane of 6	33.00	27.00	20.00	13.00	.....	.....
165	2¢ deep red, die II	1.50	.90	1.00	.60	.20	.15
165a	2¢ deep red, die I	1.40	.85	.95	.55	.20	.15
165b	same, booklet pane of 6	22.00	13.00	15.00	9.50	.....	.....
166	2¢ dark brown, die II (1931)	1.60	1.10	.90	.70	.20	.15
166a	same, booklet pane of 4	95.00	70.00	70.00	50.00	.....	.....
166b	2¢ dark brown, die I (1931)	4.00	2.50	2.75	1.75	2.60	1.75
166c	same, booklet pane of 6	31.00	20.00	21.00	16.00	.....	.....
167	3¢ deep red (1931)	2.25	1.45	1.55	.95	.20	.15
167a	same, booklet pane of 4	35.00	21.00	24.00	17.00	.....	.....
168	4¢ yellow bistre	10.00	6.00	6.50	4.50	3.50	2.20
169	5¢ dull violet	6.00	4.00	3.35	2.20	2.75	1.75
170	5¢ dull blue	3.75	2.00	1.80	1.20	.20	.15
171	8¢ dark blue	18.00	12.00	11.00	7.50	5.00	3.25
172	8¢ red orange	6.00	3.50	3.70	2.50	2.50	1.60
173	10¢ olive green	10.00	7.00	5.50	3.40	.80	.45
174	12¢ gray black	17.00	12.00	9.50	5.50	4.00	2.50
175	20¢ brown red	26.00	18.00	16.00	11.00	.35	.20
176	50¢ dull blue	200.00	125.00	110.00	75.00	10.00	6.00
177	$1 dark olive green	200.00	125.00	120.00	82.00	17.50	10.00

Note: **Coil Pairs for Canada can be supplied at double the single price**

1930-31 Coil Stamps. Perf. 8-1/2 Vertically

SCOTT NO.	DESCRIPTION	UNUSED NH F	AVG	UNUSED OG F	AVG	USED F	AVG
178-83	**1¢-3¢ complete, 6 varieties ....**	**70.25**	**41.75**	**42.75**	**27.00**	**14.20**	**9.00**
178	1¢ orange	13.00	8.00	8.50	5.25	6.50	4.00
179	1¢ deep green	7.00	3.50	4.00	2.50	3.25	2.25
180	2¢ dull green	6.00	3.00	3.50	2.20	2.50	1.40
181	2¢ deep red	20.00	13.00	12.00	7.25	1.80	1.25
182	2¢ dark brown (1931) ...	10.00	5.50	7.00	4.75	.45	.30
183	3¢ deep red (1931)	18.00	11.00	10.25	6.50	.45	.30

1931 Design of 1912-25. Perf. 12x8

SCOTT NO.	DESCRIPTION	UNUSED NH F	AVG	UNUSED OG F	AVG	USED F	AVG
184	3¢ carmine	10.00	7.00	4.00	3.00	2.50	1.00

1931

SCOTT NO.	DESCRIPTION	UNUSED NH F	AVG	UNUSED OG F	AVG	USED F	AVG
190	10¢ dark green	20.00	12.00	9.00	6.00	.20	.15

1932
165 & 165a surcharged

SCOTT NO.	DESCRIPTION	UNUSED NH F	AVG	UNUSED OG F	AVG	USED F	AVG
191	3¢ on 2¢ deep red, die II .	1.00	.70	.75	.40	.20	.15
191a	3¢ on 2¢ deep red, die I ..	2.25	1.55	1.60	.95	1.10	.95

190
Sir George Etienne Cartier

192
King George V

193
Prince of Wales

194
Allegorical Figure of Britannia Surveying the Britsh Empire

1932 OTTAWA CONFERENCE ISSUE

SCOTT NO.	DESCRIPTION	UNUSED NH F	AVG	UNUSED OG F	AVG	USED F	AVG
192-94	**3¢-13¢ complete, 3 varieties ....**	**14.00**	**9.50**	**10.00**	**6.00**	**5.50**	**3.75**
192	3¢ deep red	.80	.55	.55	.35	.20	.15
193	5¢ dull blue	6.00	4.25	4.00	2.70	1.60	1.10
194	13¢ deep green	8.00	5.25	6.00	3.25	4.00	2.70

195-200, 205-207
King George V

201
The Old Citadel at Quebec

1932

SCOTT NO.	DESCRIPTION	UNUSED NH F	AVG	UNUSED OG F	AVG	USED F	AVG
195-201	**1¢-31¢ complete, 7 varieties ....**	**160.00**	**110.00**	**95.00**	**75.00**	**8.65**	**5.70**
195	1¢ dark green	1.20	.80	.70	.50	.20	.15
195a	same, booklet pane of 4	130.00	90.00	80.00	60.00	.....	.....
195b	same, booklet pane of 6	130.00	90.00	80.00	60.00	.....	.....
196	2¢ black brown	1.50	1.00	.75	.50	.20	.15
196a	same, booklet pane of 4	95.00	70.00	65.00	40.00	.....	.....
196b	same, booklet pane of 6	90.00	60.00	50.00	40.00	.....	.....
197	3¢ deep red	2.00	1.50	1.00	.70	.20	.15
197a	same, booklet pane of 4 .	80.00	60.00	50.00	30.00	.....	.....
198	4¢ ochre	60.00	45.00	40.00	30.00	3.95	2.50
199	5¢ dark blue	10.00	8.00	7.00	5.00	.20	.15
200	8¢ red orange	40.00	30.00	25.00	15.00	2.75	1.80
201	13¢ dull violet	60.00	45.00	40.00	30.00	1.95	1.20

202
Parliament Buildings at Ottawa

203

204
S.S. Royal William

208

209

210

1933-34 COMMEMORATIVES

SCOTT NO.	DESCRIPTION	UNUSED NH F	AVG	UNUSED OG F	AVG	USED F	AVG
202/10	**(202-04, 208-10), 6 varieties ....**	**77.00**	**47.25**	**50.65**	**34.20**	**21.25**	**12.95**

1933

SCOTT NO.	DESCRIPTION	UNUSED NH F	AVG	UNUSED OG F	AVG	USED F	AVG
202	5¢ Postal Union	8.00	4.75	5.50	4.00	2.20	1.45
203	20¢ Grain Exhibition	35.00	21.00	25.00	16.00	10.00	5.50
204	5¢ Trans-Atlantic Crossing	9.00	5.25	5.75	4.00	2.20	1.45

1933 Coil Stamps Perf. 8-1/2 Vertically

SCOTT NO.	DESCRIPTION	UNUSED NH F	AVG	UNUSED OG F	AVG	USED F	AVG
205	1¢ dark green	20.00	15.00	10.00	9.00	1.60	1.10
206	2¢ black brown	25.00	20.00	15.00	12.00	.50	.35
207	3¢ deep red	20.00	15.00	10.00	9.00	.25	.15

1934

SCOTT NO.	DESCRIPTION	UNUSED NH F	AVG	UNUSED OG F	AVG	USED F	AVG
208	3¢ Jacques Cartier	6.00	4.00	3.00	2.00	1.00	.60
209	10¢ Loyalists Monument	35.00	25.00	20.00	15.00	5.50	3.75
210	2¢ New Brunswick	4.00	3.00	2.00	1.00	1.40	.80

211

212

213

214

215

216

1935 SILVER JUBILEE ISSUE

SCOTT NO.	DESCRIPTION	PLATE BLOCKS F/NH	PLATE BLOCKS AVG	UNUSED OG F/NH	UNUSED OG AVG	USED F
211-16	**1¢-13¢ complete, 6 varieties**	.....	.....	**21.35**	**15.00**	**8.25**
211	1¢ Princess Elizabeth	4.00	3.00	.40	.30	.25
212	2¢ Duke of York	8.25	6.95	.70	.60	.20
213	3¢ George & Mary	16.00	12.50	1.90	1.40	.20
214	5¢ Prince of Wales	41.00	30.00	5.00	3.60	2.25
215	10¢ Windsor Castle	50.00	36.00	6.00	4.50	2.00
216	13¢ Royal Yacht	62.50	42.50	8.50	5.50	4.00

217-22, 228-30
King George V

223

224

225

226

227

1935

SCOTT NO.	DESCRIPTION	PLATE BLOCKS F/NH	PLATE BLOCKS AVG	UNUSED OG F/NH	UNUSED OG AVG	USED F
217-27	**1¢-$1 complete, 11 varieties**	.....	.....	**165.00**	**110.00**	**13.95**
217	1¢ green	2.75	2.20	.30	.25	.20
217a	same, booklet pane of 4	.....	.....	50.00	33.00	.....
217b	same, booklet pane of 4	.....	.....	25.00	16.50	.....
218	2¢ brown	4.00	3.00	.40	.30	.20
218a	same, booklet pane of 4	.....	.....	50.00	33.00	.....
219	3¢ dark carmine	10.00	7.00	.55	.45	.20
219a	same, booklet pane of 4	.....	.....	16.50	11.00	.....
220	4¢ yellow	45.00	30.00	2.95	2.20	.40
221	5¢ blue	45.00	30.00	2.50	1.95	.20
222	8¢ deep orange	45.00	30.00	2.95	2.20	1.50
223	10¢ Mounted Policeman	70.00	45.00	7.25	5.25	.120
224	13¢ Conference of 1864	70.00	45.00	7.25	5.25	.55
225	20¢ Niagara Falls	195.00	145.00	25.00	16.50	.40
226	50¢ Parliament Building	260.00	175.00	33.00	22.00	4.00
227	$1 Champlain Monument	500.00	325.00	90.00	60.00	7.75

1935 Coil Stamps Perf. 8 Vertically

SCOTT NO.	DESCRIPTION	PLATE BLOCKS F/NH	PLATE BLOCKS AVG	UNUSED OG F/NH	UNUSED OG AVG	USED F
228-30	**1¢-3¢ coils, complete, 3 varieties**	.....	.....	**55.00**	**42.00**	**2.30**
228	1¢ green	.....	.....	20.00	15.00	2.00
229	2¢ brown	.....	.....	20.00	15.00	.70
230	3¢ dark carmine	.....	.....	20.00	15.00	.40

231-236, 238-240
King George VI

237

241

242
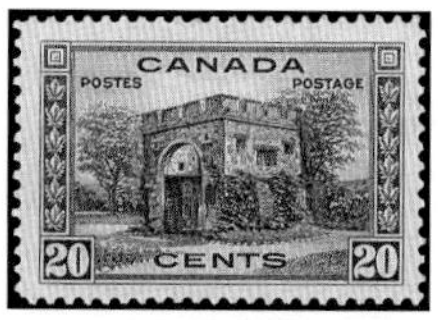
243

244

245

246

247

248

1937

SCOTT NO.	DESCRIPTION	PLATE BLOCKS F/NH	PLATE BLOCKS AVG	UNUSED OG F/NH	UNUSED OG AVG	USED F
231-36	**1¢-8¢ complete, 6 varieties**	.....	.....	**8.30**	**6.40**	**1.30**
231	1¢ green	2.50	2.05	.40	.35	.20
231a	same, booklet pane of 4	.....	.....	11.00	7.50	.....
231b	same, booklet pane of 6	.....	.....	1.65	1.10	.....
232	2¢ brown	3.00	2.50	.55	.40	.20
232a	same, booklet pane of 4	.....	.....	13.00	7.50	.....
232b	same, booklet pane of 6	.....	.....	7.00	5.00	.....
233	3¢ carmine	2.75	2.25	.55	.45	.20
233a	same, booklet pane of 4	.....	.....	2.25	1.65	.....
234	4¢ yellow	12.50	11.00	2.50	1.95	.20
235	5¢ blue	12.00	9.50	2.25	1.65	.20
236	8¢ orange	12.00	9.00	2.50	1.95	.40
237	3¢ Coronation	1.90	1.55	.25	.20	.20

Coil Stamps Perf. 8 Vertically

SCOTT NO.	DESCRIPTION	PLATE BLOCKS F/NH	PLATE BLOCKS AVG	UNUSED OG F/NH	UNUSED OG AVG	USED F
238-40	**1¢-3¢ coils, complete, 3 varieties**	.....	.....	**6.85**	**5.25**	**1.25**
238	1¢ green	.....	.....	1.10	.85	.85
239	2¢ brown	.....	.....	1.95	1.40	.30
240	3¢ carmine	.....	.....	4.15	3.30	.20

1938

SCOTT NO.	DESCRIPTION	PLATE BLOCKS F/NH	PLATE BLOCKS AVG	UNUSED OG F/NH	UNUSED OG AVG	USED F
241-45	**10¢-$1 complete, 5 varieties**	.....	.....	**120.00**	**77.50**	**9.10**
241	10¢ Memorial Hall	23.50	16.50	5.00	3.60	.20
242	13¢ Halifax Harbor	41.50	27.50	8.25	5.50	.40
243	20¢ Fort Garry Gate	82.50	52.50	16.50	11.00	.30
244	50¢ Vancouver Harbor	125.00	77.00	22.00	14.00	3.50
245	$1 Chateau de Ramezay	350.00	230.00	75.00	47.50	5.50

1939 Royal Visit

SCOTT NO.	DESCRIPTION	PLATE BLOCKS F/NH	PLATE BLOCKS AVG	UNUSED OG F/NH	UNUSED OG AVG	USED F
246-48	**1¢-3¢ complete, 3 varieties**	**4.00**	**3.15**	**.70**	**.55**	**.40**
246	1¢ Princess Elizabeth & Margaret	1.40	1.10	.25	.20	.15
247	2¢ War Memorial	1.40	1.10	.25	.20	.15
248	3¢ King George VI & Queen Elizabeth	1.40	1.10	.25	.20	.15

249, 255, 263, 278

250, 254, 264, 267, 279, 281
King George VI

253

256

257

258, 259

260

261

262

1942-43 WAR ISSUE

SCOTT NO.	DESCRIPTION	PLATE BLOCKS F/NH	PLATE BLOCKS AVG	UNUSED OG F/NH	UNUSED OG AVG	USED F
249-62	**1¢-$1 complete, 14 varieties ......**	**.....**	**.....**	**128.50**	**85.25**	**13.75**
249	1¢ green	.95	.75	.25	.20	.15
249a	same, booklet pane of 4	.....	.....	4.50	3.05	.....
249b	same, booklet pane of 6	.....	.....	1.65	1.40	.....
249c	same, booklet pane of 3	.....	.....	1.65	1.10	.....
250	2¢ brown	1.95	1.40	.40	.30	.15
250a	same, booklet pane of 4	.....	.....	4.50	3.05	.....
250b	same, booklet pane of 6	.....	.....	4.50	3.05	.....
251	3¢ dark carmine	2.35	1.85	.40	.30	.15
251a	same, booklet pane of 4	.....	.....	1.95	1.40	.....
252	3¢ rose violet (1943)	1.95	1.40	.40	.30	.15
252a	same, booklet pane of 4	.....	.....	1.65	1.10	.....
252b	same, booklet pane of 3	.....	.....	2.25	1.80	.....
252c	same, booklet pane of 6	.....	.....	4.50	3.05	.....
253	4¢ Grain Elevators	11.00	8.00	1.40	.90	.50
254	4¢ dark carmine (1943)	2.05	1.50	.40	.30	.15
254a	same, booklet pane of 6	.....	.....	1.95	1.40	.....
254b	same, booklet pane of 3	.....	.....	1.95	1.40	.....
255	5¢ deep blue	5.00	3.30	1.00	.65	.15
256	8¢ Farm Scene	10.50	7.25	1.95	1.40	.40
257	10¢ Parliament Buildings	17.50	13.00	3.85	2.75	.15
258	13¢ "Ram" Tank	25.00	18.25	5.00	3.60	3.00
259	14¢ "Ram" Tank (1943)	36.00	27.00	7.75	5.50	.30
260	20¢ Corvette	27.50	21.00	8.00	5.50	.20
261	50¢ Munitions Factory	125.00	80.00	30.00	18.00	1.65
262	$1 Destroyer	345.00	235.00	75.00	50.00	6.50

Coil Stamps Perf. 8 Vertically

SCOTT NO.	DESCRIPTION	PLATE BLOCKS F/NH	PLATE BLOCKS AVG	UNUSED OG F/NH	UNUSED OG AVG	USED F
263-67	**1¢-4¢ complete, 5 varieties ....**	**.....**	**.....**	**9.00**	**6.00**	**1.75**
263	1¢ green	.....	.....	.90	.65	.35
264	2¢ brown	.....	.....	1.30	.95	.75
265	3¢ dark carmine	.....	.....	1.30	.95	.75
266	3¢ rose violet (1943)	.....	.....	2.50	1.65	.25
267	4¢ dark carmine (1943)	.....	.....	3.50	2.20	.20

268

269

270

VERY FINE QUALITY: From 1935 to date, add 20% to the FIne price. Minimum of 3¢ per stamp.

271

272

273

1946 PEACE ISSUE

SCOTT NO.	DESCRIPTION	PLATE BLOCKS F/NH	PLATE BLOCKS AVG	UNUSED OG F/NH	UNUSED OG AVG	USED F
268-73	**8¢-$1 complete, 6 varieties**	**......**	**......**	**60.50**	**41.25**	**5.15**
268	8¢ Farm Scene	5.80	4.40	1.10	.95	.55
269	10¢ Great Bear Lake	6.35	5.50	1.25	1.05	.20
270	14¢ Hydro-Electric Power Station	13.75	11.00	2.75	2.20	.20
271	20¢ Reaper & Harvester	17.60	13.75	3.30	2.75	.20
272	50¢ Lumber Industry	84.15	61.60	16.50	12.10	1.65
273	$1 New Train Ferry	181.50	129.25	38.50	27.50	2.75

274

275

276

277

282

283

1947-49 COMMEMORATIVES

SCOTT NO.	DESCRIPTION	PLATE BLOCKS F/NH	PLATE BLOCKS AVG	UNUSED OG F/NH	UNUSED OG AVG	USED F
274/83	**274-77, 282-83, complete, 6 varieties**	**4.00**	**3.40**	**1.25**	**.85**	**.95**
274	4¢ Alexander G. Bell	.70	.60	.20	.15	.15
275	4¢ Canadian Citizen	.70	.60	.20	.15	.15
	1948					
276	4¢ Princess Elizabeth	.70	.60	.20	.15	.15
277	4¢ Parliament Building	.70	.60	.20	.15	.15

Designs of 1942-43 Coil Stamps Perf. 9-1/2 Vertically

SCOTT NO.	DESCRIPTION	PLATE BLOCKS F/NH	PLATE BLOCKS AVG	UNUSED OG F/NH	UNUSED OG AVG	USED F
278-81	**1¢-4¢ complete, 4 varieties ....**		**......**	**25.00**	**22.50**	**10.50**
278	1¢ green			2.90	2.50	1.65
279	2¢ brown			9.90	9.00	7.00
280	3¢ rose violet			5.25	4.75	1.95
281	4¢ dark carmine			8.25	7.50	2.15
	1949					
282	4¢ Cabot's "Matthew"	.70	.60	.20	.15	.15
283	4¢ Founding of Halifax	.70	.60	.20	.15	.15

COMMEMORATIVES: Commemorative stamps are special issues released to honor or recognize persons, organizations, historical events or landmarks. They are usually issued in the current first class denomination to supplement regular issues.

284, 289, 295, 297 | 285, 290, 298, 305, 309 | 286, 291, 296, 299 | 287, 292, 300, 306, 310 | 288, 293

King George VI

1949 (with "Postes-Postage")

SCOTT NO.	DESCRIPTION	PLATE BLOCK F/NH	UNUSED F/NH	USED F
284-88	**1¢-5¢ complete, 5 varieties**	**10.45**	**2.10**	**.70**
284	1¢ green	.75	.20	.15
284a	same, booklet pane of 3	......	1.25	......
285	2¢ sepia	1.25	.25	.15
286	3¢ rose violet	1.50	.30	.15
286a	same, booklet pane of 3	......	1.50	......
286b	same, booklet pane of 4	......	1.75	......
287	4 dark carmine	2.00	.50	.15
287a	same, booklet pane of 3	......	12.00	......
287b	same, booklet pane of 6	......	13.50	......
288	5¢ deep blue	5.50	1.00	.15

1950 Type of 1949
(without "Postes-Postage")

SCOTT NO.	DESCRIPTION	PLATE BLOCK F/NH	UNUSED F/NH	USED F
289-93	**1¢-5¢ complete, 5 varieties**	**9.50**	**1.65**	**2.05**
289	1¢ green	.65	.20	.15
290	2¢ sepia	1.95	.25	.20
291	3¢ rose violet	.85	.20	.15
292	4¢ dark carmine	1.10	.25	.15
293	5¢ deep blue	5.50	1.05	.75
294	50¢ Oil Wells, Alberta	60.50	12.65	1.05

Coil Stamps Perf. 9-1/2 Vertically

SCOTT NO.	DESCRIPTION	PLATE BLOCK F/NH	UNUSED F/NH	USED F
295-300	**1¢-4¢ complete, 6 vars.**	**......**	**17.00**	**3.30**
	(without "Postes-Postage")			
295	1¢ green	......	.50	.30
296	3¢ rose violet	......	.75	.55
	(with "Postes-Postage")			
297	1¢ green	......	.35	.25
298	2¢ sepia	......	2.25	1.40
299	3¢ rose violet	......	1.50	.20
300	4¢ dark carmine	......	12.65	.75
301	10¢ Fur Resources	4.00	.75	.15
302	$1 Fishing	300.00	65.00	12.00

294

301

302

303

304

311

314

315

1951

1951-52 COMMEMORATIVES

SCOTT NO.	DESCRIPTION	PLATE BLOCK F/NH	UNUSED F/NH	USED F
303/19	**(303-04, 311-15, 317-19) complete, 10 vars.**	**26.10**	**5.25**	**2.90**
303	3¢ Sir Robert L. Borden	1.10	.20	.15
304	4¢ William L.M. King	1.25	.25	.15
	(with "Postes-Postage")			
305	2¢ olive green	.80	.20	.15
306	4¢ orange vermillion	1.00	.20	.15
306a	same, booklet pane of 3	......	2.50	......
306b	same, booklet pane of 6	......	2.75	......
	Coil Stamps Perf. 9-1/2 Vertically			
309	2¢ olive green	......	1.10	.60
310	4¢ orange vermillion	......	2.50	.70
	1951 "CAPEX" Exhibition			
311	4¢ Trains of 1851 & 1951	2.50	.55	.15
312	5¢ Steamships	8.25	1.65	1.35
313	7¢ Stagecoach & Plane	5.00	1.00	.35
314	15¢ "Three Pence Beaver"	5.50	1.00	.30
315	4¢ Royal Visit	.95	.20	.15

317

318

319

316

1952

SCOTT NO.	DESCRIPTION	PLATE BLOCK F/NH	UNUSED F/NH	USED F
316	20¢ Paper Production	7.00	1.35	.15
317	4¢ Red Cross	.95	.20	.15
318	3¢ J.J.C. Abbott	.95	.20	.15
319	4¢ A. Mackenzie	1.10	.25	.10

1952-53

SCOTT NO.	DESCRIPTION	PLATE BLOCK F/NH	UNUSED F/NH	USED F
320	7¢ Canada Goose	1.80	.35	.15
321	$1 Indian House & Totem Pole (1953)	55.00	12.00	.80

1953-54 COMMEMORATIVES

SCOTT NO.	DESCRIPTION	PLATE BLOCK F/NH	UNUSED F/NH	USED F
322/50	**(322-24, 330, 335-36, 349-50) complete, 8 varieties**	**8.95**	**1.90**	**1.15**
322	2¢ Polar Bear	.80	.20	.15
323	3¢ Moose	.90	.20	.15
324	4¢ Bighorn Sheep	1.10	.25	.15

320

321

322

323

324

1953

SCOTT NO.	DESCRIPTION	PLATE BLOCK F/NH	UNUSED F/NH	USED F
325-29	**1¢-5¢ complete, 5 vars.**	**4.50**	**1.10**	**.70**
325	1¢ violet brown	.70	.20	.15
325a	same, booklet pane of 3	.60	......	
326	2¢ green	.70	.20	.15
327	3¢ carmine rose	.85	.20	.15
327a	same, booklet pane of 3	1.40	......	
327b	same, booklet pane of 4	1.40	......	
328	4¢ violet	1.10	.25	.15
328a	same, bklt. pane of 3	......	1.65	......
328b	same, bklt. pane of 6	......	1.95	......
329	5¢ ultramarine	1.40	.30	.15
330	4¢ Queen Elizabeth II	.95	.20	.15

Coil Stamps Perf. 9-1/2 Vertically

SCOTT NO.	DESCRIPTION	PLATE BLOCK F/NH	UNUSED F/NH	USED F
331-33	**2¢-4¢ complete, 3 vars.**	**......**	**4.90**	**3.45**
331	2¢ green	......	1.20	1.00
332	3¢ carmine rose	......	1.20	1.00
333	4¢ violet	......	2.75	1.65
334	50¢ Textile Industry	21.00	4.70	.20

325-29, 331-33

330

334

335

336

337-342, 345-348

343

1954

SCOTT NO.	DESCRIPTION	PLATE BLOCK F/NH	UNUSED F/NH	USED F
335	4¢ Walrus	1.40	.30	.15
336	5¢ Beaver	1.65	.35	.15
336a	same, booklet pane of 5	......	1.95	......
337-43	**1¢-15¢ cpl., 7 vars.**	**10.65**	**2.35**	**1.00**
337	1¢ violet brown	.70	.20	.15
337a	same, booklet pane of 5	......	.75	......
338	2¢ green	.70	.20	.15
338a	mini pane of 25	......	4.40	......
338a	sealed pack of 2	......	8.80	......
339	3¢ carmine rose	.70	.20	.15
340	4¢ violet	.85	.20	.15
340a	same, booklet pane of 5	......	1.65	......
340b	same, booklet pane of 6	......	5.50	......
341	5¢ bright blue	1.10	.20	.15
341a	same, booklet pane of 5	......	1.65	......
341b	mini sheet of 20	......	8.25	......
342	6¢ orange	1.65	.35	.15
343	15¢ Gannet	5.50	1.10	.15

349 350 351 352 353

Coil Stamps Perf. 9-1/2 Vertically

SCOTT NO.	DESCRIPTION	PLATE BLOCK F/NH	UNUSED F/NH	USED F
345-48	**2¢-4¢ complete, 3 vars.**	......	**4.50**	**.60**
345	2¢ green	......	.50	.20
347	4¢ violet	......	1.60	.25
348	5¢ bright blue	......	2.50	.20
349	4¢ J.S.D. Thompson	1.30	.25	.15
350	5¢ M. Bowell	1.30	.25	.15
	1955			
351	10¢ Eskimo in Kayak	1.65	.35	.15

1955-56 COMMEMORATIVES

SCOTT NO.	DESCRIPTION	PLATE BLOCK F/NH	UNUSED F/NH	USED F
352/64	**(352-61, 364 (complete, 11 varieties**	**15.10**	**3.25**	**1.60**
352	4¢ Musk Ox	1.30	.30	.15
353	5¢ Whooping Cranes	1.30	.30	.15
	1955			
354	5¢ Intl. Civil Aviation Org.	1.50	.30	.15
355	5¢ Alberta-Saskatchewan	1.50	.30	.15
356	5¢ Boy Scout Jamboree	1.50	.30	.15
357	4¢ R.B. Bennett	1.50	.30	.15
358	5¢ C. Tupper	1.50	.30	.15
	1956			
359	5¢ Hockey Players	1.50	.30	.15
360	4¢ Caribou	1.50	.35	.15
361	5¢ Mountain Goat	1.50	.35	.15
362	20¢ Paper Industry	6.60	1.35	.15
363	25¢ Chemical Industry	8.25	1.65	.15
364	5¢ Fire Prevention	1.30	.30	.15

354

355

356

357

358

359

360

361

362

363

364

365

1957 COMMEMORATIVES

SCOTT NO.	DESCRIPTION	PLATE BLOCK F/NH	UNUSED F/NH	USED F
365-74	**complete, 10 varieties**	**17.50(7)**	**4.80**	**3.15**
365-68	Recreation, attached	1.90	1.45	1.60
365	5¢ Fishing	......	.40	.20
366	5¢ Swimming	......	.40	.20
367	5¢ Hunting	......	.40	.20
368	5¢ Skiing	......	.40	.20
369	5¢ Loon	1.20	.30	.15
370	5¢ D. Thompson, Explorer	1.20	.30	.15
371	5¢ Parliament Building	1.20	.30	.15
372	15¢ Posthorn & Globe	11.00	2.20	1.75
373	5¢ Coal Miner	1.00	.25	.15
374	5¢ Royal Visit	1.00	.25	.15

1958 COMMEMORATIVES

SCOTT NO.	DESCRIPTION	PLATE BLOCK F/NH	UNUSED F/NH	USED F
375-82	**complete, 8 varieties**	**10.75(6)**	**2.50**	**1.50**
375	5¢ Newspaper	......	.35	.20
376	5¢ Int'l. Geophysical Year	......	.35	.20
377	5¢ Miner Panning Gold	2.00	.35	.20
378	5¢ La Verendrye, Explorer	1.50	.35	.20
379	5¢ S. deChamplain	3.50	.35	.20
380	5¢ National Health	1.50	.35	.20
381	5¢ Petroleum Industry	1.50	.35	.20
382	5¢ Speaker's Chair & Mace	1.50	.35	.20

369

370

371

372

373

374

375

376

377

378

379

380

381

382

1959 COMMEMORATIVES

SCOTT NO.	DESCRIPTION	PLATE BLOCK F/NH	UNUSED F/NH	USED F
383-88	**complete, 6 varieties**	**9.65**	**2.00**	**1.00**
383	5¢ Old & Modern Planes	1.50	.35	.20
384	5¢ NATO Anniversary	1.35	.35	.20
385	5¢ Woman Tending Tree	1.10	.35	.20
386	5¢ Royal Tour	1.10	.35	.20
387	5¢ St. Lawrence Seaway	4.00	.35	.20
387a	same, center inverted	...	9250.00	8500.00
388	5¢ Plains of Abraham	1.10	.35	.20

1960-62 COMMEMORATIVES

SCOTT NO.	DESCRIPTION	PLATE BLOCK F/NH	UNUSED F/NH	USED F
389-400	**complete, 12 varieties**	**17.50**	**4.00**	**2.25**
389	5¢ Girl Guides Emblem	1.50	.35	.20
390	5¢ Battle of Long Sault	1.50	.35	.20
	1961			
391	5¢ Earth Mover	1.50	.35	.20
392	5¢ E.P. Johnson	1.50	.35	.20

383

384

385

386

387

388

389

390

391

392

SCOTT NO.	DESCRIPTION	PLATE BLOCK F/NH	UNUSED F/NH	USED F
393	5¢ A. Meighen	1.50	.35	.20
394	5¢ Colombo Plan	1.50	.35	.20
395	5¢ Natural Resources	1.50	.35	.20
	1962			
396	5¢ Education	1.50	.35	.20
397	5¢ Red River Settlement	1.50	.35	.20
398	5¢ Jean Talon	1.50	.35	.20
399	5¢ Victoria, B.C.	1.50	.35	.20
400	5¢ Trans-Canada	1.50	.35	.20

393

395

396

394

397

398

399

400

401-09

1962-63

SCOTT NO.	DESCRIPTION	PLATE BLOCK F/NH	UNUSED F/NH	USED F
401-05	**1¢-5¢ complete, 5 varieties**	**6.50**	**1.00**	**.70**
401	1¢ deep brown (1963)	.45	.20	.15
401a	same, booklet pane of 5	......	3.30	......
402	2¢ green (1963)	3.60	.20	.15
402a	mini pane of 25	......	4.70	......
402a	same, sealed pack of 2	......	10.50	......
403	3¢ purple (1963)	.70	.20	.15
404	4¢ carmine (1963)	1.00	.20	.15
404a	same, booklet pane of 5	......	3.30	......
404b	mini pane of 25	......	8.00	......
405	5¢ violet blue	1.20	.25	.15
405a	same, booklet pane of 5	......	5.00	......
405b	mini pane of 20	......	12.00	......

1963-64 Coil Stamps, Perf. 9-1/2 Horiz.

SCOTT NO.	DESCRIPTION	PLATE BLOCK F/NH	UNUSED F/NH	USED F
406-09	**2¢-5¢ complete, 4 varieties**	**......**	**13.75**	**4.30**
406	2¢ green	......	4.00	1.55
407	3¢ purple (1964)	......	2.50	1.25
408	4¢ carmine	......	4.00	1.25
409	5¢ violet blue	......	4.00	.50

1963-64 COMMEMORATIVES

SCOTT NO.	DESCRIPTION	PLATE BLOCK F/NH	UNUSED F/NH	USED F
410/35	**(410, 412-13, 416-17, 431-35) 10 varieties**	**10.20**	**2.35**	**1.45**
410	5¢ Sir Casimir S. Gzowski	1.10	.25	.15
411	$1 Export Trade	74.25	15.00	2.50
412	5¢ Sir M. Frobisher, Explorer	1.10	.25	.15
413	5¢ First Mail Routes	1.10	.25	.15
	1963-64			
414	7¢ Jet Takeoff (1964)	1.50	.35	.55
415	15¢ Canada Geese	11.00	2.20	.20
	1964			
416	5¢ World Peace	1.10	.25	.15
417	5¢ Canadian Unity	1.10	.25	.15

410

411

412

413

414, 430, 436

415

416

417

COATS OF ARMS & FLORAL EMBLEMS

419 *Quebec & White Garden Lily*
420 *Nova Scotia & Mayflower*
421 *New Brunswick & Purple Violet (1965)*
422 *Manitoba & Prairie Crocus (1965)*
423 *British Columbia & Dogwood (1965)*
424 *Prince Edward Island & Lady's Slipper (1965)*
425 *Saskatchewan & Prairie Lily (1966)*
426 *Alberta & Wild Rose (1966)*
427 *Newfoundland & Pitcher Plant (1966)*
428 *Yukon & Fireweed (1966)*
429 *Northwest Territories & Mountain Avens (1966)*

418
Ontario & White Trillium

429A
Canada & Maple Leaf

1964-66

SCOTT NO.	DESCRIPTION	PLATE BLOCK F/NH	UNUSED F/NH	USED F
418-29A	**complete, 13 varieties**	**13.60**	**3.10**	**2.00**
418	5¢ red brown, buff & green	1.10	.25	.15
419	5¢ green, yellow & orange	1.10	.25	.20
420	5¢ blue, pink & green	1.10	.25	.15
421	5¢ carmine, green & violet	1.10	.25	.15
422	5¢ red brown, lilac & green	1.10	.25	.15
423	5¢ lilac, green & bistre	1.10	.25	.15
424	5¢ violet, green & deep rose	1.10	.25	.15
425	5¢ sepia, orange & green	1.10	.25	.20
426	5¢ green, yellow & carmine	1.10	.25	.15
427	5¢ black, green & carmine	1.10	.25	.15
428	5¢ dark blue, rose & green	1.10	.25	.15
429	5¢ olive, yellow & green	1.10	.25	.20
429A	5¢ dark blue & red (1966)	1.10	.25	.15
	1964 Surcharged on 414			
430	8¢ on 7¢ Jet Takeoff	1.65	.35	.35
431	5¢ Charlottetown Conference	1.10	.25	.15
432	5¢ Quebec Conference	1.10	.20	.15
433	5¢ Queen Elizabeth's Visit	1.10	.25	.15
434	3¢ Christmas	.85	.20	.15
434a	mini sheet of 25	......	7.50	......
434a	same, sealed pack of 2	......	15.50	......
435	5¢ Christmas	1.10	.25	.15
	Jet Type of 1964			
436	8¢ Jet Takeoff	2.00	.40	.25

1965 COMMEMORATIVES

SCOTT NO.	DESCRIPTION	PLATE BLOCK F/NH	UNUSED F/NH	USED F
437-44	**8 varieties**	**7.80**	**1.85**	**1.15**
437	5¢ I.C.Y.	1.00	.25	.15

431

432

433

434, 435

437

438

439

440

441

442

443-44

SCOTT NO.	DESCRIPTION	PLATE BLOCK F/NH	UNUSED F/NH	USED F
438	5¢ Sir Wilfred Grenfell	1.00	.25	.15
439	5¢ National Flag	1.00	.25	.15
440	5¢ Winston Churchill	1.00	.25	.15
441	5¢ Inter-Parliamentary	1.00	.25	.15
442	5¢ Ottawa, National Capital	1.00	.25	.15
443	3¢ Christmas	.80	.20	.15
443a	mini pane of 25	......	6.50	......
443a	same, sealed pack of 2	......	13.00	......
444	5¢ Christmas	1.40	.25	.15

1966 COMMEMORATIVES

SCOTT NO.	DESCRIPTION	PLATE BLOCK F/NH	UNUSED F/NH	USED F
445-52	**8 varieties**	**7.75**	**1.80**	**1.15**
445	5¢ Alouette II Satellite	1.10	.25	.15
446	5¢ La Salle Arrival	1.10	.25	.15
447	5¢ Highway Safety	1.10	.25	.15
448	5¢ London Conference	1.10	.25	.15
449	5¢ Atomic Reactor	1.10	.25	.15
450	5¢ Parliamentary Library	1.10	.25	.15
451	3¢ Christmas	.70	.20	.15
451a	mini pane of 25	......	4.50	......
451a	same, sealed pack of 2	......	9.00	......
452	5¢ Christmas	.85	.20	.15

445

446

447

448

449

451, 452

450

453

1967 COMMEMORATIVES

SCOTT NO.	DESCRIPTION	PLATE BLOCK F/NH	UNUSED F/NH	USED F
453/77	**(453, 469-77) complete, 10 varieties**	**10.00**	**2.30**	**.45**
453	5¢ National Centennial	1.10	.25	.15

454

455

456, 466

457, 467

458, 468

459-460F, 468A-B, 543-49

461

465B

Regional Views & Art Designs 1967-72 Perf.12 except as noted

SCOTT NO.	DESCRIPTION	PLATE BLOCK F/NH	UNUSED F/NH	USED F
454-65B	**1¢-$1 complete, 14 varieties**	**95.50**	**18.25**	**2.50**
454-64	**1¢-20¢, 11 varieties**	**21.00**	**3.35**	**1.45**
454	1¢ brown	.90	.20	.15
454a	same, booklet pane of 5	......	.90	......
454b	booklet pane, 1¢(1), 6¢(4)	......	3.00	......
454c	booklet pane, 1¢(5), 3¢(5)	......	3.85	......

NOTE: **#454d, 454e, 456a, 457d, 458d, 460g, and 460h are Booklet Singles**

SCOTT NO.	DESCRIPTION	PLATE BLOCK F/NH	UNUSED F/NH	USED F
454d	1¢ perf. 10 (1968)	......	.25	.20
454e	1¢ 12-1/2 x 12 (1969)	......	.45	.15
455	2¢ green	1.40	.20	.15
455a	booklet pane 2¢(4), 3¢(4)	......	1.65	......
456	3¢ dull purple	1.20	.20	.15
456a	3¢ 12-1/2 x 12 (1971)	......	2.20	1.20
457	4¢ carmine rose	1.65	.20	.15
457a	same, booklet pane 5	......	1.50	......
457b	miniature pane of 25	......	20.00	......
457c	same, booklet pane of 25	......	8.00	......
457d	4¢ perf.10 (1968)	......	.70	.30
458	5¢ blue	.85	.20	.15
458a	same, booklet pane of 5	......	6.50	......
458b	miniature pane of 20	......	30.00	......
458c	booklet pane of 20, perf.10	......	7.75	......
458d	5¢ perf. 10 (1968)	......	.70	.30
459	6¢ orange, perf. 10 (1968)	3.85	.35	.15
459a	same, booklet pane of 25	......	10.00	......
459b	6¢ orange 12-1/2x12 (1969)	3.30	.35	.15
460	6¢ black, 12-1/2x12 (1970)	1.95	.25	.15
460a	booklet pane of 25, perf.10	......	15.40	......
460b	booklet pane of 25, 12-1/2x12	......	18.50	......
460c	6¢ black, 12-1/2x12 (1970)	2.20	.30	.15
460d	booklet pane of 4, 12-1/2x12	......	5.50	......
460e	booklet pane of 4, perf.10	......	10.00	......
460f	6¢ black, perf. 12 (1972)	2.50	.50	.15
460g	6¢ black, perf. 10 (I)	......	1.75	.40
460h	6¢ black, perf. 10 (II)	......	4.00	1.25

460, 460a, b,& g: Original Die. Weak shading lines around 6.
460 c, d, e, & h: Reworked plate lines strengthened, darker.
460f: Original Die. Strong shading lines, similar to 468B, but Perf 12x12 .

SCOTT NO.	DESCRIPTION	PLATE BLOCK F/NH	UNUSED F/NH	USED F
461	8¢ "Alaska Highway"	2.00	.35	.20
462	10¢ "The Jack Pine"	1.80	.35	.15
463	15¢ "Bylot Island"	3.30	.55	.15
464	20¢ "The Ferry, Quebec"	3.30	.70	.15
465	25¢ "The Solemn Land"	6.90	1.40	.15
465A	50¢ "Summer Stores"	22.00	4.40	.15
465B	$1 "Imp. Wildcat No. 3"	49.50	9.90	.80

1967-70 Coil Stamps

SCOTT NO.	DESCRIPTION	PLATE BLOCK F/NH	UNUSED F/NH	USED F
466-68B	3¢-6¢ complete, 5 varieties	......	4.50	3.35

Perf. 9-1/2 Horizontally

SCOTT NO.	DESCRIPTION	PLATE BLOCK F/NH	UNUSED F/NH	USED F
466	3¢ dull purple	......	2.50	1.10
467	4¢ carmine rose	......	1.00	.60
468	5¢ blue	......	2.00	.75

Perf. 10 Horizontally

SCOTT NO.	DESCRIPTION	PLATE BLOCK F/NH	UNUSED F/NH	USED F
468A	6¢ orange (1969)	......	.35	.15
468B	6¢ black (1970)	......	.35	.15

NOTE: **See #543-50 for similar issues**

469

470

471

472

473

474

1967

SCOTT NO.	DESCRIPTION	PLATE BLOCK F/NH	UNUSED F/NH	USED F
469	5¢ Expo '67	1.20	.25	.20
470	5¢ Women's Franchise	1.20	.25	.20
471	5¢ Royal Visit	1.20	.25	.20
472	5¢ Pan-American Games	1.20	.25	.20
473	5¢ Canadian Press	1.20	.25	.20
474	5¢ George P. Vanier	1.20	.25	.20
475	5¢ View of Toronto	1.20	.25	.20
476	3¢ Christmas	.90	.20	.15
476a	miniature pane of 25	......	4.25	......
476a	same, sealed pack of 2	......	8.50	......
477	5¢ Christmas	.85	.20	.15

475

476, 477

478

479

480

481

482

483

484

485

486

1968 COMMEMORATIVES

SCOTT NO.	DESCRIPTION	PLATE BLOCK F/NH	UNUSED F/NH	USED F
478-89	**complete, 12 varieties**	**22.00**	**4.30**	**2.70**
478	5¢ Gray Jays	4.15	.45	.20
479	5¢ Weather Map & Inst.	1.20	.25	.20
480	5¢ Narwhal	1.20	.25	.20
481	5¢ Int'l Hydro. Decade	1.20	.25	.20
482	5¢ Voyage of "Nonsuch"	1.20	.25	.20
483	5¢ Lacrosse Players	1.20	.25	.20
484	5¢ G. Brown, Politician	1.20	.25	.20
485	5¢ H. Bourassa, Journalist	1.20	.25	.20
486	15¢ W.W.I Armistice	8.25	1.65	1.20

NOTE: **Beginning with #478, some issues show a printer's inscription with no actual plate number.**

487

488

490

491

492

493

SCOTT NO.	DESCRIPTION	PLATE BLOCK F/NH	UNUSED F/NH	USED F
487	5¢ J. McCrae	1.10	.25	.15
488	5¢ Eskimo Family	.85	.20	.15
488a	same, booklet pane of 10	.....	3.15	.....
489	6¢ Mother & Child	1.10	.25	.15

1969 COMMEMORATIVES

SCOTT NO.	DESCRIPTION	PLATE BLOCK F/NH	UNUSED F/NH	USED F
490-504	**complete, 15 varieties**	**48.25**	**11.25**	**7.15**
490	6¢ Game of Curling	1.10	.25	.15
491	6¢ V. Massey	1.10	.25	.15
492	50¢ A. deSuzor-Cote, Artist	17.60	3.85	2.20
493	6¢ I.L.O.	1.10	.25	.15
494	15¢ Vickers Vimy Over Atlantic	8.80	2.85	1.65
495	6¢ Sir W. Osler	1.10	.25	.15
496	6¢ White Throated Sparrows	1.65	.35	.15
497	10¢ Ipswich Sparrow	3.85	.75	.50
498	25¢ Hermit Thrush	8.25	1.65	1.55
499	6¢ Map of Prince Edward Island	1.10	.25	.15
500	6¢ Canada Games	1.10	.25	.15
501	6¢ Sir Isaac Brock	1.10	.25	.15
502	5¢ Children of Various Races	1.00	.25	.15
502a	booklet pane of 10	......	2.75	......
503	6¢ Children Various Races	1.00	.25	.15
504	6¢ Stephen Leacock	1.20	.25	.15

1970 COMMEMORATIVES

SCOTT NO.	DESCRIPTION	PLATE BLOCK F/NH	UNUSED F/NH	USED F
505/31	**(505-18, 531) 15 varieties**	**24.50**	**11.75**	**11.00**
505	6¢ Manitoba Cent.	.85	.20	.15
506	6¢ N.W. Territory Centenary	.85	.20	.15
507	6¢ International Biological	.85	.20	.15
508-11	Expo '70 attached	9.90	8.80	8.80
508	25¢ Emblems	......	2.15	2.15
509	25¢ Dogwood	......	2.15	2.15
510	25¢ Lily	......	2.15	2.15
511	25¢ Trilium	......	2.15	2.15

494

495

496

500

501

499

502, 503

504

505

506

507

508

509

512

513-514

515

516

517

518

519

524

529

530

SCOTT NO.	DESCRIPTION	PLATE BLOCK F/NH	UNUSED F/NH	USED F
512	6¢ H. Kelsey—Explorer	.85	.20	.15
513	10¢ 25th U.N. Anniversary	3.30	.70	.45
514	15¢ 25th U.N. Anniversary	4.95	1.00	1.10
515	6¢ L. Riel—Metis Leader	1.10	.25	.20
516	6¢ Sir A. Mackenzie-Explorer	1.10	.25	.20
517	6¢ Sir O. Mowat Confederation Father	1.10	.25	.20
518	6¢ Isle of Spruce	1.10	.25	.20
519-30	**5¢-15¢ complete, 12 varieties**	**16.75**	**5.50**	**2.45**
519-23	5¢ Christmas, attached	4.95(10)	2.25	2.00
519	5¢ Santa Claus	......	.40	.15
520	5¢ Sleigh	......	.40	.15
521	5¢ Nativity	......	.40	.15
522	5¢ Skiing	......	.40	.15
523	5¢ Snowman & Tree	......	.40	.15
524-28	6¢ Christmas, attached	6.00(10)	2.50	2.25
524	6¢ Christ Child	......	.45	.15
525	6¢ Tree & Children	......	.45	.15
526	6¢ Toy Store	......	.45	.15
527	6¢ Santa Claus	......	.45	.15
528	6¢ Church	......	.45	.15

NOTE: We cannot supply blocks or pairs of the 5¢ & 6¢ Christmas designs in varying combinations of designs.

SCOTT NO.	DESCRIPTION	PLATE BLOCK F/NH	UNUSED F/NH	USED F
529	10¢ Christ Child	2.20	.40	.20
530	15¢ Snowmobile & Trees	4.50	.85	.90
531	6¢ Sir Donald A. Smith	.85	.20	.15

1971 COMMEMORATIVES

SCOTT NO.	DESCRIPTION	PLATE BLOCK F/NH	UNUSED F/NH	USED F
532/58	**(532-42, 552-58) complete, 18 varieties**	**29.75**	**6.10**	**7.00**
532	6¢ E. Carr—Painter & Writer	.85	.20	.15
533	6¢ Discovery of Insulin	.85	.20	.15
534	6¢ Sir E. Rutherford—Physicist	.85	.20	.15
535-38	6¢-7¢ Maple Leaves	4.00	.90	.50
535	6¢ Maple Seeds	1.10	.25	.15
536	6¢ Summer Leaf	1.10	.25	.15
537	Autumn Leaf	1.10	.25	.15
538	7¢ Winter Leaf	1.10	.25	.15
539	6¢ L. Papineau—Polit. Reform	.85	.20	.15
540	6¢ Copper Mine Expedition	.85	.20	.15
541	15¢ Radio Canada Int'l	7.70	1.65	1.40
542	6¢ Census Centennial	.85	.20	.15

531

532

533

534

535

539

540

541

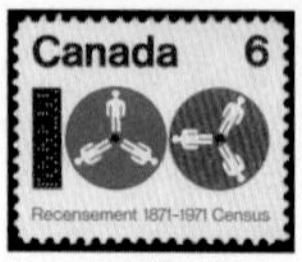
542

543, 549

544, 550

552

553

554-55

556-57

558

559

560

561

SCOTT NO.	DESCRIPTION	PLATE BLOCK F/NH	UNUSED F/NH	USED F
	1971			
543	7¢ Trans. & Communication	3.30	.30	.15
543a	bklt. pane, 7¢(3), 3¢(1), 1¢(1)	......	3.05	......
543b	bklt. pane 7¢(12), 3¢(4), 1¢(4)	......	7.70	......
544	8¢ Parliamentary Library	3.30	.30	.15
544a	bklt. pane 8¢(2), 6¢(1), 1¢(3)		1.95	......
544b	bklt. pane 8¢(11), 6¢(1), 1¢(6)	5.80	......	
544c	bklt. pane 8¢(5), 6¢(1), 1¢(4)	......	2.50	......
	1971 Coil Stamps Perf.10 Horizontally			
549	7¢ Trans. & Communication	......	.40	.15
550	8¢ Parliamentary Library	......	.35	.15
552	7¢ B.C. Centennial	.85	.20	.15
553	7¢ Paul Kane	2.50	.35	.15
554-57	6¢-15¢ Christmas	8.00	1.65	1.50
554	6¢ Snowflake, dark blue	.85	.20	.15
555	7¢ same, bright green	1.10	.25	.15
556	10¢ same, deep carmine & silver	2.20	.45	.40
557	15¢ same, light ultramarine, deep carmine & silver	4.00	.85	.85
558	7¢ P. Laporte	2.65	.25	.15

1972 COMMEMORATIVES

SCOTT NO.	DESCRIPTION	PLATE BLOCK F/NH	UNUSED F/NH	USED F
559/610	**(559-61, 582-85, 606-10) 12 varieties**	**47.85(9)**	**9.75**	**7.55**
559	8¢ Figure Skating	1.10	.25	.20
560	8¢ W.H.O. Heart Disease	1.40	.30	.20
561	8¢ Frontenac & Ft. St. Louis	1.10	.25	.20

VERY FINE QUALITY: From 1935 to date, add 20% to the Fine price. Minimum of 3¢ per stamp.

1972-76 INDIAN PEOPLES OF CANADA

SCOTT NO.	DESCRIPTION	PLATE BLOCK F/NH	UNUSED F/NH	USED F
562-81	**complete, 20 varieties**	**14.00**	**5.90**	**2.85**
562-63	Plains, attached	1.65	.70	.60
562	8¢ Buffalo Chase	......	.30	.15
563	8¢ Indian Artifacts	......	.30	.15
564-65	Plains, attached	1.65	.70	.60
564	8¢ Thunderbird Symbolism	......	.30	.15
565	8¢ Sun Dance Costume	......	.30	.15
566-67	Algonkians, attached (1973)	1.65	.70	.60
566	8¢ Algonkian Artifacts	......	.30	.15
567	8¢ Micmac Indians	......	.30	.15
568-69	Algonkians, attached (1973)	1.65	.70	.60
568	8¢ Thunderbird Symbolism	......	.30	.15
569	8¢ Costume	......	.30	.15
570-71	Pacific, attached (1974)	1.65	.70	.50
570	8¢ Nootka Sound House	......	.30	.15
571	8¢ Artifacts	......	.30	.15
572-73	Pacific, attached (1974)	1.65	.70	.50
572	8¢ Chief in Chilkat Blanket	......	.30	.15
573	8¢ Thunderbird—Kwakiutl	......	.30	.15
574-75	Subarctic, attached (1975)	1.20	.50	.45
574	8¢ Canoe & Artifacts	......	.25	.15
575	8¢ Dance—Kutcha-Kutchin	......	.25	.15
576-77	Subarctic, attached (1975)	1.20	.50	.45
576	8¢ Kutchin Costume	......	.25	.15
577	8¢ Ojibwa Thunderbird	......	.25	.15
578-79	Iroquois, attached (1976)	1.20	.50	.45
578	10¢ Masks	......	.25	.15
579	10¢ Camp	......	.25	.15
580-81	Iroquois, attached (1976)	1.20	.50	.45
580	10¢ Iroquois Thunderbird	......	.25	.15
581	10¢ Man & Woman	......	.25	.15

562

564

582

SCOTT NO.	DESCRIPTION	PLATE BLOCK F/NH	UNUSED F/NH	USED F
	1972 EARTH SCIENCES			
582-85	Sciences, attached	38.50(16)	7.50	7.50
582	15¢ Geology	......	1.80	1.50
583	15¢ Geography	......	1.80	1.50
584	15¢ Photogrammetry	......	1.80	1.50
585	15¢ Cartography	......	1.80	1.50

NOTE: **Plate Block Price is for a miniature pane of 16 Stamps.**

SCOTT NO.	DESCRIPTION	PLATE BLOCK F/NH	UNUSED F/NH	USED F
	1973-76 DEFINITIVE ISSUE PERF. 12 x 12-1/2			
586-93A	**1¢-10¢, 9 varieties**	**6.85**	**1.75**	**1.30**
586	1¢ Sir J. Macdonald	.70	.20	.15
586a	bklt. pane 1¢(3), 6¢(1), 8¢(2)	......	1.00	......
586b	bklt. pane 1¢(6), 6¢(1), 8¢(11)	......	3.00	......
586c	bklt. pane 1¢(2), 2¢(4), 8¢(4)	......	1.30	......
587	2¢ Sir W. Laurier	1.00	.30	.20
588	3¢ Sir R.L. Borden	1.00	.30	.20
589	4¢ W.L. Mackenzie King	1.00	.30	.20
590	5¢ R.B. Bennett	1.00	.30	.20
591	6¢ L.B. Pearson	1.00	.30	.20
592	7¢ L. St. Laurent (1974)	1.00	.30	.20
593	8¢ Queen Elizabeth	1.00	.30	.20
593b	same (pf. 13x13-1/2) (1976)	4.95	1.00	.50
593A	10¢ Queen Elizabeth (perf 13x13-1/2) (1976)	1.10	.25	.50
593c	10¢ same, perf 12x12-1/2 booklet single	......	.35	.50

586

593, 593b, 593A, 604-605

594, 594a, 594B

599, 599a, 600

SCOTT NO.	DESCRIPTION	PLATE BLOCK F/NH	UNUSED F/NH	USED F
	1972-73 Photogravure & Engraved Perf. 12-1/2x12			
594-99	**10¢-$1, 6 varieties**	**23.60**	**5.00**	**1.25**
594	10¢ Forests	1.40	.25	.15
595	15¢ Mountain Sheep	1.75	.35	.15
596	20¢ Prairie Mosaic	2.30	.50	.15
597	25¢ Polar Bears	2.55	.55	.15
598	50¢ Seashore	5.25	1.10	.15
599	$1 Vancouver Skyline(1973)	12.10	2.50	.55

NOTE: **#594-97 exist with 2 types of phosphor tagging. Prices are for Ottawa tagged. Winnipeg tagged are listed on page 320.**

SCOTT NO.	DESCRIPTION	PLATE BLOCK F/NH	UNUSED F/NH	USED F
	1976-77 Perf. 13			
594a	10¢ Forests	1.40	.30	.15
595a	15¢ Mountain Sheep	1.85	.40	.25
596a	20¢ Prairie Mosaic	2.65	.55	.15
597a	25¢ Polar Bears	2.50	.75	.15
598a	50¢ Seashore	8.00	1.65	.15
599a	$1 Vancouver Skyline(1977)	12.10	2.50	.45
	1972 Lithographed & Engraved Perf. 11			
600	$1 Vancouver Skyline	25.00	6.00	2.00
601	$2 Quebec Buildings	25.00	5.00	2.75
	1974-76 Coil Stamps			
604	8¢ Queen Elizabeth	......	.25	.15
605	10¢ Queen Elizabeth (1976)	......	.30	.15
	1972			
606-09	6¢-15¢ Christmas	7.00	1.45	1.25
606	6¢ Five candles	.85	.20	.15
607	8¢ same	1.10	.25	.15
608	10¢ Six candles	1.95	.40	.25
609	15¢ same	3.30	.70	.80
610	8¢ C.Krieghoff—Painter	2.00	.30	.20

606, 607

608, 609

610

611

1973 COMMEMORATIVES

SCOTT NO.	DESCRIPTION	PLATE BLOCK F/NH	UNUSED F/NH	USED F
611-28	**18 varieties, complete**	**27.40**	**6.15**	**4.95**
611	8¢ Monseignor De Laval	1.00	.25	.15
612	8¢ G.A. French & Map	1.35	.30	.15
613	10¢ Spectrograph	1.65	.35	.35
614	15¢ "Musical Ride"	3.30	.70	.60
615	8¢ J. Mance—Nurse	1.00	.25	.15
616	8¢ J. Howe	1.00	.25	.15
617	15¢ "Mist Fantasy" Painting	2.75	.55	.50
618	8¢ P.E.I. Confederation	1.00	.25	.15
619	8¢ Scottish Settlers	1.00	.25	.15
620	8¢ Royal Visit	1.00	.25	.15
621	15¢ same	3.10	.70	.60
622	8¢ Nellie McClung	1.00	.25	.15
623	8¢ 21st Olympic Games	1.00	.25	.15
624	15¢ same	2.75	.55	.60
625-28	6¢ to 15¢ Christmas	5.75	1.20	1.10
625	6¢ Skate	.80	.20	.15
626	8¢ Bird Ornament	1.00	.25	.15
627	10¢ Santa Claus	1.40	.30	.30
628	15¢ Shepherd	2.75	.55	.60

612

615

616

617

618

619

622

623, 624

627

620, 621

625

629

633

634

1974 COMMEMORATIVES

SCOTT NO.	DESCRIPTION	PLATE BLOCK F/NH	UNUSED F/NH	USED F
629-55	**complete, 27 varieties**	**22.40(16)**	**9.15**	**6.25**
629-32	Summer Olympics, attached	1.65	1.40	1.35
629	8¢ Children Diving	......	.35	.20
630	8¢ Jogging	......	.35	.20
631	8¢ Bicycling	......	.35	.20
632	8¢ Hiking	......	.35	.20
633	8¢ Winnipeg Centenary	1.00	.25	.20
634-39	Postal Carriers, attached	3.60(6)	3.00	2.75
634	8¢ Postal Clerk & Client	......	.40	.35
635	8¢ Mail Pick-up	......	.40	.35
636	8¢ Mail Handler	......	.40	.35
637	8¢ Sorting Mail	......	.40	.35
638	8¢ Letter Carrier	......	.40	.35
639	8¢ Rural Delivery	......	.40	.35
640	8¢ Agriculture Symbol	1.00	.25	.15
641	8¢ Antique to Modern Phones	1.00	.25	.15
642	8¢ World Cycling Championship	1.00	.25	.15
643	8¢ Mennonite Settlers	1.00	.25	.15
644-47	Winter Olympics, attached	1.65	1.40	1.20
644	8¢ Snowshoeing	......	.35	.20
645	8¢ Skiing	.....	.35	.20
646	8¢ Skating	.....	.35	.20
647	8¢ Curling	.....	.35	.20
648	8¢ U.P.U. Cent.	1.00	.25	.15
649	15¢ same	2.75	.55	.50
650-53	6¢ to 15¢ Christmas	5.65	1.25	1.10
650	6¢ Nativity	.80	.20	.15
651	8¢ Skaters in Hull	.80	.20	.15
652	10¢ The Ice Cone	1.60	.35	.35
653	15¢ Laurentian Village	2.75	.55	.50
654	8¢ G. Marconi—Radio Inventor	1.00	.25	.15
655	8¢ W.H. Merritt & Welland Canal	1.00	.25	.15

640

641

642

643

644

648, 649

650

651

654

655

656

657

1975 COMMEMORATIVES

SCOTT NO.	DESCRIPTION	PLATE BLOCK F/NH	UNUSED F/NH	USED F
656-80	**complete, 25 varieties**	**67.50(18)**	**16.40**	**12.00**
656	$1 "The Sprinter"	11.00	2.50	1.95
657	$2 "The Plunger"	25.35	5.75	4.40
658-59	Writers, attached	1.05	.45	.40
658	8¢ L.M. Montgomery—Author	......	.20	.15
659	8¢ L. Hemon—Author	......	.20	.15
660	8¢ M. Bourgeoys—Educator	1.00	.25	.15
661	8¢ A. Desjardins—Credit Union	1.00	.25	.15
662-63	Religious, attached	1.05	.45	.45
662	8¢ S Chown & Church	......	.20	.20
663	8¢ J. Cook & Church	......	.20	.20
664	20¢ Pole Vaulter	3.30	.75	.50
665	25¢ Marathon Runner	3.85	.85	.55
666	50¢ Hurdler	6.60	1.50	1.10
667	8¢ Calgary Centenary	1.10	.25	.15
668	8¢ Int'l. Women's Year	1.10	.25	.15
669	8¢ "Justice"	1.10	.25	.15
670-73	Ships, attached	2.75	2.20	1.85
670	8¢ W.D. Lawrence	......	.55	.35
671	8¢ Beaver	......	.55	.35
672	8¢ Neptune	......	.55	.35
673	8¢ Quadra	......	.55	.35
674-79	6¢ to 15¢ Christmas	4.50(4)	1.35	1.25
674-75	Christmas, attached	.85	.40	.35
674	6¢ Santa Claus	......	.20	.15
675	6¢ Skater	......	.20	.15
676-77	Christmas, attached	1.05	.40	.35
676	8¢ Child	......	.20	.15
677	8¢ Family & Tree	......	.20	.15
678	10¢ Gift	1.10	.25	.25
679	15¢ Trees	1.65	.35	.35
680	8¢ Horn & Crest	1.10	.25	.15

658

659

660

661

662-63

664

666

667

668

669

670

674

676

679

680

681

687

689

690

684

691

1976 COMMEMORATIVES

SCOTT NO.	DESCRIPTION	PLATE BLOCK F/NH	UNUSED F/NH	USED F
681-703	**complete, 23 varieties**	**75.00(18)**	**18.15**	**14.25**
681	8¢ Olympic Flame	1.05	.25	.15
682	20¢ Opening Ceremony	2.60	.55	.55
683	25¢ Receiving Medals	3.30	.75	.75
684	20¢ Communication Arts	4.40	1.00	.60
685	25¢ Handicraft Tools	4.95	1.10	.75
686	50¢ Performing Arts	8.25	1.85	1.30
687	$1 Notre Dame & Tower	11.00	2.50	1.95
688	$2 Olympic Stadium	25.85	5.80	4.40
689	20¢ Olympic Winter Games	3.30	.75	.70
690	20¢ "Habitat"	2.20	.50	.45
691	10¢ Benjamin Franklin	1.20	.30	.25
692-93	Military College, attached	1.05	.40	.35
692	8¢ Color Parade	......	.20	.15
693	8¢ Wing Parade	......	.20	.15
694	20¢ Olympiad—Phys. Disabled	3.14	.65	.60
695-96	Authors, attached	1.05	.40	.35
695	8¢ R.W. Service—Author	......	.20	.15
696	8¢ G. Guevremont—Author	......	.20	.15
697	8¢ Nativity Window	.85	.20	.15
698	10¢ same	1.05	.25	.15
699	20¢ same	2.15	.45	.45
700-03	Inland Vessels, attached	1.75	1.40	1.30
700	10¢ Northcote	......	.35	.30
701	10¢ Passport	......	.35	.30
702	10¢ Chicora	......	.35	.30
703	10¢ Athabasca	......	.35	.30

692-93

694

695

696

697

700

704

1977 COMMEMORATIVES

SCOTT NO.	DESCRIPTION	PLATE BLOCK F/NH	UNUSED F/NH	USED F
704/51	**(704, 732-51) complete, 21 varieties**	**20.85(14)**	**6.10**	**4.65**
704	25¢ Silver Jubilee	3.05	.65	.55

705, 781, 781a

713, 713a, 716, 716a , 789, 789a, 791, 792

714, 715, 729, 730, 790, 797, 800, 806

1977-79 Definitives
Perf. 12x12-1/2

SCOTT NO.	DESCRIPTION	PLATE BLOCK F/NH	UNUSED F/NH	USED F
705-27	**1¢ to $2 complete, 22 varieties**	**66.50**	**14.85**	**5.75**
705	1¢ Bottle Gentian	.65	.20	.15
707	2¢ Western Columbine	.65	.20	.15
708	3¢ Canada Lily	.65	.20	.15
709	4¢ Hepatica	.65	.20	.15
710	5¢ Shooting Star	.65	.20	.15
711	10¢ Lady's Slipper	.80	.20	.15
711a	same, perf.13 (1978)	1.10	.25	.15
712	12¢ Jewelweed, perf 13x13-1/2 (1978)	1.45	.30	.15
713	12¢ Queen Elizabeth II, perf.13x13-1/2	1.30	.30	.15
713a	same, perf.12x12-1/2	......	.35	.20
714	12¢ Parliament, perf.13	1.20	.25	.15
715	14¢ same, perf.13 (1978)	1.35	.30	.15
716	14¢ Queen Elizabeth II perf. 13x13-1/2	1.35	.30	.15
716a	14¢ same, perf 12x12-1/2	......	.30	.20
716b	same, booklet pane of 25	......	6.25	......

NOTE: **713a and 716a are from booklet panes. 713a will have one or more straight edges, 716a may or may not have straight edges.**

717

723, 723A

726

Perforated 13-1/2

SCOTT NO.	DESCRIPTION	PLATE BLOCK F/NH	UNUSED F/NH	USED F
717	15¢ Trembling Aspen	1.80	.40	.15
718	20¢ Douglas Fir	1.55	.35	.15
719	25¢ Sugar Maple	2.00	.45	.15
720	30¢ Oak Leaf	2.50	.55	.25
721	35¢ White Pine (1979)	2.75	.60	.35
723	50¢ Main Street (1978)	4.25	.95	.30
723A	50¢ same, 1978 Lic. Plate	4.70	1.00	.25
724	75¢ Row Houses (1978)	6.35	1.40	.50
725	80¢ Maritime (1978)	7.15	1.50	.55
726	$1 Fundy Park (1979)	8.80	1.95	.45
727	$2 Kluane Park (1979)	17.60	3.85	1.30

1977-78 Coil Stamps Perf. 10 Vert.

SCOTT NO.	DESCRIPTION	PLATE BLOCK F/NH	UNUSED F/NH	USED F
729	12¢ Parliament	......	.25	.15
730	14¢ same (1978)	......	.30	.15

732

733

735

736

737

1977 COMMEMORATIVES

SCOTT NO.	DESCRIPTION	PLATE BLOCK F/NH	UNUSED F/NH	USED F
732	12¢ Cougar	1.20	.25	.20
733-34	Thomson, attached	1.20	.50	.45
733	12¢ Algonquin Park	......	.25	.20
734	12¢ Autumn Birches	......	.25	.20
735	12¢ Crown & Lion	1.20	.25	.20
736	12¢ Badge & Ribbon	1.20	.25	.20
737	12¢ Peace Bridge	1.20	.25	.20

738-39

740

741

SCOTT NO.	DESCRIPTION	PLATE BLOCK F/NH	UNUSED F/NH	USED F
738-39	Pioneers, attached	1.20	.50	.45
738	12¢ Bernier & CGS Arctic	......	.25	.15
739	12¢ Fleming & RR Bridge	......	.25	.15
740	25¢ Peace Tower	3.30	.75	.75
741	10¢ Braves & Star	1.05	.25	.15
742	12¢ Angelic Choir	1.20	.25	.15
743	25¢ Christ Child	2.45	.50	.50
744-47	Sailing Ships	1.30	1.00	.95
744	12¢ Pinky	......	.25	.20
745	12¢ Tern	......	.25	.20
746	12¢ Five Masted	......	.25	.20
747	12¢ Mackinaw	......	.25	.20
748-49	Inuit, attached	1.20	.50	.45
748	12¢ Hunting Seal	......	.25	.20
749	12¢ Fishing	......	.25	.20
750-51	Inuit, attached	1.20	.50	.45
750	12¢ Disguised Archer	......	.25	.20
751	12¢ Hunters of Old	......	.25	.20

1978 COMMEMORATIVES

SCOTT NO.	DESCRIPTION	PLATE BLOCK F/NH	UNUSED F/NH	USED F
752/79	**(No #756a)28 varieties**	**33.00(19)**	**9.15**	**6.30**
752	12¢ Peregrine Falcon	1.20	.30	.20
753	12¢ CAPEX Victoria	1.10	.30	.20
754	14¢ CAPEX Cartier	1.35	.30	.20
755	30¢ CAPEX Victoria	2.65	.55	.55
756	$1.25 CAPEX Albert	12.00	2.00	1.40
756a	$1.69 CAPEX sheet of 3	......	3.00	2.15
757	14¢ Games Symbol	1.15	.25	.15
758	30¢ Badminton Players	2.50	.55	.35
759-60	Comm. Games, attached	1.20	.50	.45
759	14¢ Stadium	......	.25	.15
760	14¢ Runners	......	.25	.15
761-62	Comm. Games, attached	2.45	1.05	.95
761	30¢ Edmonton	......	.45	.35
762	30¢ Bowls	......	.45	.35
763-64	Captain Cook, attached	1.15	.50	.45
763	14¢ Captain Cook	......	.25	.15
764	14¢ Nootka Sound	......	.25	.15
765-66	Resources, attached	1.20	.50	.45
765	14¢ Miners	......	.25	.15
766	14¢ Tar Sands	......	.25	.15
767	14¢ CNE 100th Anniversary	1.15	.25	.15
768	14¢ Mere d'Youville	1.15	.25	.15
769-70	Inuit, attached	1.20	.50	.45
769	14¢ Woman Walking	......	.25	.15
770	14¢ Migration	......	.25	.15
771-72	Inuit, attached	1.20	.50	.45
771	14¢ Plane over Village	......	.25	.15
772	14¢ Dog Team & Sled	......	.25	.15

744

748-49

763

752

753

757

764

759

765-66

767

768

769-70

773

780

813

815

SCOTT NO.	DESCRIPTION	PLATE BLOCK F/NH	UNUSED F/NH	USED F
773	12¢ Mary & Child w/pea	1.05	.25	.15
774	14¢ Mary & Child w/apple	1.15	.25	.15
775	30¢ Mary & Child w/goldfinch	2.50	.55	.35
776-79	Ice Vessels, attached	1.20	1.00	.95
776	14¢ Robinson	......	.25	.15
777	14¢ St. Roch	......	.25	.15
778	14¢ Northern Light	......	.25	.15
779	14¢ Labrador	......	.25	.15

1979 COMMEMORATIVES

SCOTT NO.	DESCRIPTION	PLATE BLOCK F/NH	UNUSED F/NH	USED F
780/846	**(780, 813-20, 833-46) complete, 23 varieties**	**27.10(16)**	**8.20**	**4.55**
780	14¢ Quebec Winter Carnival	1.30	.30	.20

1977-83 Definitives Perf 13x131/2

SCOTT NO.	DESCRIPTION	PLATE BLOCK F/NH	UNUSED F/NH	USED F
781-92	**1¢-32¢ complete, 11 varieties**	**13.00**	**3.15**	**1.60**
781	1¢ Gentian (1979)	.65	.20	.15
781a	1¢ same, perf 12x12-1/2	......	.20	.15
781b	booklet pane, 1¢ (2—781a), 12¢ (4—713a)	......	.85	......
782	2¢ Western Columbine (1979)	.65	.20	.15
782a	booklet pane, 2¢ (4—782b), 12¢ (3—716a)	......	.80	......
782b	2¢ same, perf 12x121/2 (1978)	......	.20	.15
783	3¢ Canada Lily (1979)	.65	.20	.15
784	4¢ Hepatica (1979)	.65	.20	.15
785	5¢ Shooting Star (1979)	.65	.20	.15
786	10¢ Lady's-Slipper (1979)	.90	.20	.15
787	15¢ Violet (1979)	1.35	.30	.15
789	17¢ Queen Elizabeth II (1979)	1.50	.35	.15
789a	17¢ same, 12x12-1/2 (1979)	.....	.35	.15
789b	booklet pane of 25	.....	7.45	.....
790	17¢ Parliament Bldg. (1979)	1.50	.30	.15
791	30¢ Queen Elizabeth II (1982)	2.50	.55	.15
792	32¢ Queen Elizabeth II (1983)	2.75	.60	.15

NOTE: **781a, 782b, 797 & 800 are from booklet panes and will have one or more straight edges. 789a may or may not have straight edges.**

1979 Perf 12x12-1/2

SCOTT NO.	DESCRIPTION	PLATE BLOCK F/NH	UNUSED F/NH	USED F
797	1¢ Parliament Building	.....	.70	.30
797a	booklet pane 1¢ (1—797), 5¢ (3—800), 17¢ (2—789a)	.....	1.60	.....
800	5¢ Parliament Building	.....	.30	.25

1979 Coil Stamps Perf 10 Vertical

SCOTT NO.	DESCRIPTION	PLATE BLOCK F/NH	UNUSED F/NH	USED F
806	17¢ Parliament Building, slate green	.....	.50	.15

1979

SCOTT NO.	DESCRIPTION	PLATE BLOCK F/NH	UNUSED F/NH	USED F
813	17¢ Turtle	1.50	.30	.15
814	35¢ Whale	3.05	.65	.35
815-16	Postal Code, attached	1.65	.65	.45
815	17¢ Woman's Finger	......	.30	.15
816	17¢ Man's Finger	......	.30	.15
817-18	Writers, attached	1.65	.65	.45
817	17¢ "Fruits of the Earth"	......	.30	.15
818	17¢ "The Golden Vessel"	......	.30	.15
819-20	Colonels, attached	1.65	.65	.45
819	17¢ Charles de Salaberry	......	.30	.15
820	17¢ John By	......	.30	.15

817-18

819-20

821 *Ontario*

SCOTT NO.	DESCRIPTION	PLATE BLOCK F/NH	UNUSED F/NH	USED F

PROVINCIAL FLAGS

821 *Ontario*	**822** *Quebec*	**823** *Nova Scotia*
824 *New Brunswick*	**825** *Manitoba*	**826** *British Columbia*
827 *Prince Edward Island*	**828** *Saskatchewan*	**829** *Alberta*
830 *Newfoundland*	**831** *Northern Teritories*	**832** *Yukon Territory*

SCOTT NO.	DESCRIPTION	PLATE BLOCK F/NH	UNUSED F/NH	USED F
832a	17¢ Sheet of 12 varieties, attached	......	4.00	......
821-32	set of singles	......	......	3.00
Any	17¢ single	......	.30	.20
833	17¢ Canoe—kayak	1.50	.30	.15
834	17¢ Field Hockey	1.50	.30	.15
835-36	Inuit, attached	1.60	.65	.60
835	17¢ Summer Tent	......	.30	.20
836	17¢ Igloo	......	.30	.20
837-38	Inuit, attached	1.60	.65	.60
837	17¢ The Dance	......	.30	.20
838	17¢ Soapstone Figures	......	.30	.20
839	15¢ Wooden Train	1.00	.25	.15
840	17¢ Horse Pull Toy	1.30	.30	.15
841	35¢ Knitted Doll	2.75	.60	.30
842	17¢ I.Y.C.	1.50	.30	.15
843-44	Flying Boats, attached	1.60	.65	.50
843	17¢ Curtiss, HS2L	......	.30	.20
844	17¢ Canadair CL215	......	.30	.20
845-46	Flying Boats, attached	3.55	1.50	1.40
845	35¢ Vichers Vedette	......	.70	.50
846	35¢ Consolidated Canso	......	.70	.50

833

834

839

835-36

842

843

847

848

1980 COMMEMORATIVES

SCOTT NO.	DESCRIPTION	PLATE BLOCK F/NH	UNUSED F/NH	USED F
847-77	**complete, 31 varieties**	**42.25(23)**	**12.35**	**6.30**
847	17¢ Arctic Islands Map	1.50	.30	.15
848	35¢ Olympic Skiing	2.90	.60	.55
849-50	Artists, attached	1.60	.65	.50
849	17¢ School Trustees	......	.30	.15
850	17¢ Inspiration	......	.30	.15
851-52	Artists, attached	3.05	1.30	1.10
851	35¢ Parliament Bldgs	......	.60	.35
852	35¢ Sunrise on the Saguenay	......	.60	.35
853	17¢ Atlantic Whitefish	1.55	.35	.15
854	17¢ Greater Prairie Chicken	1.55	.35	.15

849

853

855

856

857-58

859

870

860

862

863

865

873

866-67

878

877

SCOTT NO.	DESCRIPTION	PLATE BLOCK F/NH	UNUSED F/NH	USED F
855	17¢ Gardening	1.50	.30	.15
856	17¢ Rehabilitation	1.50	.30	.15
857-58	"O Canada", attached	1.60	.65	.50
857	17¢ Bars of Music	......	.30	.15
858	17¢ Three Musicians	......	.30	.15
859	17¢ John Diefenbaker	1.50	.30	.15
860-61	Musicians, attached	1.60	.65	.50
860	17¢ Emma Albani	......	.30	.15
861	17¢ Healy Willan	......	.30	.15
862	17¢ Ned Hanlan	1.50	.30	.15
863	17¢ Saskatchewan	1.50	.30	.15
864	17¢ Alberta	1.50	.30	.15
865	35¢ Uranium Resources	2.95	.60	.35
866-67	Inuit, attached	1.75	.70	.50
866	17¢ Sedna	......	.35	.15
867	17¢ Sun	......	.35	.15
868-69	Inuit, attached	3.05	1.30	1.10
868	35¢ Bird Spirit	......	.60	.35
869	35¢ Shaman	......	.60	.35
870	15¢ Christmas	1.35	.30	.15
871	17¢ Christmas	1.50	.30	.15
872	35¢ Christmas	2.95	.60	.35
873-74	Aircraft	1.65	.75	.65
873	17¢ Avro Canada CF-100	......	.35	.15
874	17¢ Avro Lancaster	......	.35	.15
875-76	Aircraft, attached	3.25	1.40	1.20
875	35¢ Curtiss JN-4	......	.65	.35
876	35¢ Hawker Hurricane	......	.65	.35
877	17¢ Dr. Lachapelle	1.50	.30	.15

1981 COMMEMORATIVES

SCOTT NO.	DESCRIPTION	PLATE BLOCK F/NH	UNUSED F/NH	USED F
878-906	**complete, 29 varieties**	**32.45(19)**	**10.35**	**5.45**
878	17¢ Antique Instrument	1.50	.30	.15
879-82	Feminists, attached	1.65	1.40	1.10
879	17¢ Emily Stowe	......	.35	.20
880	17¢ Louise McKinney	......	.35	.20
881	17¢ Idola Saint-Jean	......	.35	.20
882	17¢ Henrietta Edwards	......	.35	.20
883	17¢ Marmot	1.50	.30	.15
884	35¢ Bison	3.30	.75	.40
885-86	Women, attached	1.60	.65	.50
885	17¢ Kateri Tekakwitha	......	.30	.15
886	17¢ Marie de L'Incarnation	......	.30	.15
887	17¢ "At Baie Saint-Paul"	1.50	.30	.15
888	17¢ Self-Portrait	1.50	.30	.15
889	35¢ Untitled No. 6	2.95	.60	.40

879

883

885

887

890

894

896

897

898

899

900

903

SCOTT NO.	DESCRIPTION	PLATE BLOCK F/NH	UNUSED F/NH	USED F
890-93	Canada Day, attached	1.65(8)	1.40	1.30
890	17¢ Canada in 1867	......	.35	.20
891	17¢ Canada in 1873	......	.35	.20
892	17¢ Canada in 1905	......	.35	.20
893	17¢ Canada in 1949	......	.35	.20
894-95	Botanists, attached	1.60	.65	.35
894	17¢ Frere Marie Victorin	......	.30	.15
895	17¢ John Macoun	......	.30	.15
896	17¢ Montreal Rose	1.65	.30	.15
897	17¢ Niagara-on-the-Lake	1.65	.30	.15
898	17¢ Acadians	1.65	.30	.15
899	17¢ Aaron Mosher	1.65	.30	.15
900	15¢ Christmas Tree in 1781	1.30	.30	.15
901	15¢ Christmas Tree in 1881	1.30	.30	.15
902	15¢ Christmas Tree in 1981	1.30	.30	.15
903-04	Aircraft, attached	1.65	.75	.50
903	17¢ Canadair CL-41 Tutor	......	.35	.15
904	17¢ de Havilland Tiger Moth	......	.35	.15
905-06	Aircraft, attached	3.25	1.40	1.20
905	35¢ Avro Canada C-102	......	.65	.40
906	35¢ de Havilland Canada Dash-7	......	.65	.40
907	(30¢) "A" Maple Leaf	2.60	1.55	.15
908	(30¢) "A" Maple Leaf, Coil	......	1.90	.15

907, 908

909

914

915

1982 COMMEMORATIVES

SCOTT NO.	DESCRIPTION	PLATE BLOCK F/NH	UNUSED F/NH	USED F
909/75	**(909-16, 954, 967-75) 18 varieties, complete**	**51.25(16)**	**11.95**	**5.00**
909	30¢ 1851 Beaver	2.65	.55	.20
910	30¢ 1908 Champlain	2.65	.55	.20
911	35¢ 1935 Mountie	3.15	.65	.60
912	35¢ 1928 Mt. Hurd	3.15	.65	.60
913	60¢ 1929 Bluenose	6.35	1.30	1.00
913a	$1.90 Phil. Exhib. sheet of 5	......	3.60	......
914	30¢ Jules Leger	2.65	.55	.20
915	30¢ Terry Fox	2.65	.55	.20
916	30¢ Constitution	2.65	.55	.20

916

917

925/952, 1194, 1194A

938

939

926

1982-87 DEFINITIVES

SCOTT NO.	DESCRIPTION	PLATE BLOCK F/NH	UNUSED F/NH	USED F
917-37	**1¢-$5 complete, 23 varieties**	**135.00**	**27.50**	**9.00**
917a-21a	**1¢-10¢, 5 varieties**	**4.10**	**1.00**	**.70**
917	1¢ Decoy	.80	.20	.15
917a	1¢ perf.13x13-1/2 (1985)	.80	.20	.15
918	2¢ Fishing Spear	.80	.20	.15
918a	2¢ perf.13x13-1/2 (1985)	.80	.20	.15
919	3¢ Stable Lantern	.80	.20	.15
919a	3¢ perf.13x13-1/2 (1985)	.80	.20	.15
920	5¢ Bucket	.80	.20	.15
920a	5¢ perf.13x13-1/2 (1984)	.80	.20	.15
921	10¢ Weathercock	1.10	.25	.15
921a	10¢ perf.13x13-1/2 (1985)	1.10	.25	.15
922	20¢ Ice Skates	2.25	.45	.15
923	30¢ Maple Leaf, blue & red, perf.13x13-1/2	2.55	.55	.15
923a	30¢ booklet pane (20) perf 12x12-1/2	......	10.50	......
923b	as above, single	......	.20	.20
924	32¢ Maple Leaf, red & brown, perf.13x13-1/2 (1983)	2.55	.55	.15
924a	32¢ booklet pane (25) perf. 12x12-1/2	......	14.00	......
924b	as above, single	......	.60	.20
925	34¢ Parliament (multicolored, perf.13x13-1/2 (1985)	2.75	.60	.15
925a	34¢ booklet pane (25) perf.13x13-1/2	......	14.00	......
925b	34¢ single, perf 13-1/2x14	......	.75	....
926	34¢ Elizabeth II (1985), perf.13x13-1/2	2.75	.60	.15
926A	36¢ Elizabeth II (1987) perf. 13x13-1/2	20.00	4.00	2.00
926B	36¢ Parliament Library (1987)	3.05	.65	.25
926Bc	as above, booklet pane (10)	......	6.00	......
926Bd	as above, booklet pane (25)	......	15.50	....
926Be	Booklet single (perf. 13-1/2x14)	......	.75	......
927	37¢ Plow (1983)	3.15	.60	.25
928	39¢ Settle bed (1985)	3.30	.75	.25
929	48¢ Cradle (1983)	4.15	.80	.30
930	50¢ Sleigh (1985)	4.40	.85	.30
931	60¢ Ontario Street	4.95	.95	.35
932	64¢ Stove (1983)	5.80	1.00	.40
933	68¢ Spinning Wheel (1985)	1.80	1.10	.40
934	$1 Glacier Park (1984)	8.80	1.75	.55
935	$1.50 Waterton Lakes	12.25	2.50	.80
936	$2 Banff Park (1985)	17.20	3.50	1.10
937	$5 Point Pelee (1983)	41.25	8.50	2.50

1982-87 BOOKLET SINGLES

SCOTT NO.	DESCRIPTION	PLATE BLOCK F/NH	UNUSED F/NH	USED F
938-948	**1¢-36¢ complete, 11 varieties**	**......**	**4.00**	**3.00**
938	1¢ East Block (1987)	......	.20	.15
939	2¢ West Block (1985)	......	.20	.15
940	5¢ Maple Leaf (1982)	......	.20	.15
941	5¢ East Block (1985)	......	.20	.20
942	6¢ West Block (1987)	......	.20	.15
943	8¢ Maple Leaf (1983)	......	.20	.35
944	10¢ Maple Leaf (1982)	......	.25	.35
945	30¢ Maple Leaf, red perf. 12x12-1/2 (1982)	......	.75	.45
945a	booklet pane 2# 940, 1 #944, 1 #945	......	1.20	......
946	32¢ Maple Leaf, brown on white, perf.12x12-1/2 (1983)		......	.65
.35				
946b	booklet pane 2 #941, 1 #943, 1 #946	......	1.10	......
947	34¢ Library, slate blue, perf.12x12-1/2 (1985) .	......	1.00	.70
947a	booklet pane, 3 #939, 2 #941, 1 #947	......	1.40	......
948	36¢ Parliament Library (1987)	......	.75	.45
948a	booklet pane, 2 #938, 2 #942, #948	......	2.00	......

1982-1987 COILS

SCOTT NO.	DESCRIPTION	PLATE BLOCK F/NH	UNUSED F/NH	USED F
950-53	30¢-36¢ complete, 4 varieties	......	2.65	.55
950	30¢ Maple Leaf (1982)	......	.95	.15
951	32¢ Maple Leaf (1983)	......	.60	.15
952	34¢ Parliament (1985)	......	.60	.15
953	36¢ Parliament (1987)	......	.65	.15

954

955 *Yukon Territories*

Paintings

956 *Quebec*
957 *Newfoundland*
958 *Northwest Territories*
959 *Prince Edward Island*
960 *Nova Scotia*
961 *Saskatchewan*
962 *Ontario*
963 *New Brunswick*
964 *Alberta*
965 *British Columbia*
966 *Manitoba*

1982 COMMEMORATIVES

SCOTT NO.	DESCRIPTION	PLATE BLOCK F/NH	UNUSED F/NH	USED F
954	30¢ Salvation Army	2.65	.55	.15
955-66	set of singles	......	8.00	6.50
......	same, any 30¢ single	......	.95	.50
966a	sheet of 12 varieties, attached	......	8.50	......
967	30¢ Regina	2.65	.55	.15
968	30¢ Henley Regatta	2.21	.55	.15
969-70	30¢ Aircraft, attached	2.65	1.00	.90
969	30¢ Fairchild FC-2W1	....	.45	.15

967

968

969

SCOTT NO.	DESCRIPTION	PLATE BLOCK F/NH	UNUSED F/NH	USED F
970	30¢ De Havilland Canada Beaver	......	.45	.15
971-72	Aircraft, attached	6.20	2.20	2.10
971	60¢ Noorduyn Norseman	......	1.00	.50
972	60¢ Fokker Super Universal	......	1.00	.50
973	30¢ Joseph, Mary & Infant	2.65	.55	.15
974	35¢ Shepherds	3.05	.65	.25
975	60¢ Wise Men	5.25	1.10	.45

973

976

978

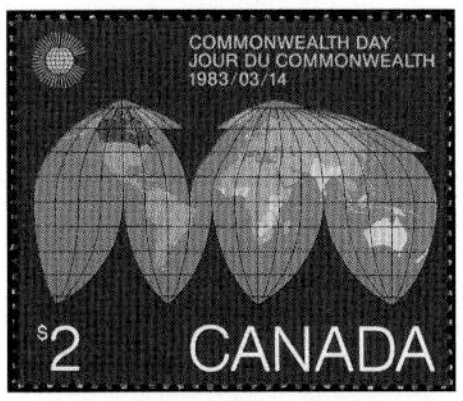

977

1983 COMMEMORATIVES

SCOTT NO.	DESCRIPTION	PLATE BLOCK F/NH	UNUSED F/NH	USED F
976/1008	**(976-82, 993-1008) complete, 23 varieties**	**80.25(20)**	**22.25**	**9.30**
976	32¢ World Comm. Year	2.85	.60	.25
977	$2 Commonwealth Day	35.00	10.00	4.00
978-79	Poet/Author, attached	2.85	1.20	1.10
978	32¢ Laure Conan	......	.55	.25
979	32¢ E.J. Pratt	......	.55	.25
980	32¢ St.John Ambulance	3.10	.60	.25
981	32¢ University Games	3.10	.60	.25
982	64¢ University Games	6.00	1.20	.90

Forts

984 *Ft. William*
985 *Ft. Rodd Hill*
986 *Ft. Wellington*
987 *Fort Prince of Wales*
988 *Halifax Citadel*
989 *Ft. Chambly*
990 *Ft. No. 1 Pt. Levis*
991 *Ft. at Coteau-du-Lac*
992 *Fort Beausejour*

SCOTT NO.	DESCRIPTION	PLATE BLOCK F/NH	UNUSED F/NH	USED F
992a	32¢ Forts, pane of 10	......	7.00	6.50
983-92	set of singles	......	6.50	6.00
......	Any 32¢ single Fort	......	.75	.30
993	32¢ Boy Scouts	2.75	.60	.25
994	32¢ Council of Churches	2.75	.60	.25
995	32¢ Humphrey Gilbert	2.75	.60	.25
996	32¢ Nickel	2.75	.60	.25
997	32¢ Josiah Henson	2.75	.60	.25
998	32¢ Fr. Antoine Labelle	2.75	.60	.25

980

981

983 *Ft. Henry*

993

994

995

996

997

998

999

1003

1004

1007

1009

1010

1011

1012

1013

1014

1015

SCOTT NO.	DESCRIPTION	PLATE BLOCK F/NH	UNUSED F/NH	USED F
999-1000	Steam Trains, attached	2.75	1.10	1.00
999	32¢ Toronto 4-4-0	......	.55	.25
1000	32¢ Dorchester 0-4-0	......	.55	.25
1001	37¢ Samson 0-6-0	3.10	.65	.30
1002	64¢ Adam Brown 4-4-0	5.50	1.10	.52
1003	32¢ Law School	2.75	.60	.25
1004	32¢ City Church	2.75	.60	.25
1005	37¢ Family	3.05	.65	.30
1006	64¢ County Chapel	5.50	1.10	1.00
1007-08	Army Regiment, attached	2.75	1.10	1.00
1007	32¢ Canada & Br.Reg.	.....	.55	.25
1008	32¢ Winn. & Dragoons	.....	.55	.25

1984 COMMEMORATIVES

SCOTT NO.	DESCRIPTION	PLATE BLOCK F/NH	UNUSED F/NH	USED F
1009/44	**(1009-15, 1028-39, 1040-44) complete, 24 varieties**	**60.15(20)**	**14.25**	**6.25**
1009	32¢ Yellowknife	2.75	.60	.25
1010	32¢ Year of the Arts	2.75	.60	.25
1011	32¢ Cartier	2.75	.60	.25
1012	32¢ Tall Ships	2.75	.60	.25
1013	32¢ Canadian Red Cross	2.75	.60	.25
1014	32¢ New Brunswick	2.75	.60	.25
1015	32¢ St. Lawrence Seaway	2.75	.60	.25

PROVINCIAL LANDSCAPES BY JEAN PAUL LEMIEUX

1017 *British Columbia*
1018 *Yukon Territory*
1019 *Quebec*
1020 *Manitoba*
1021 *Alberta*
1022 *Prince Edward Island*
1023 *Saskatchewan*
1024 *Nova Scotia*
1025 *Northwest Territories*
1026 *Newfoundland*
1027 *Ontario*

SCOTT NO.	DESCRIPTION	PLATE BLOCK F/NH	UNUSED F/NH	USED F
1027a	sheet of 12 varieties attached	......	8.50	8.50
1016-27	set of singles	......	8.25	4.75
.....	Any 32¢ single Provinces	......	.75	.30
1028	32¢ Loyalists	2.75	.60	.25
1029	32¢ Catholicism	2.75	.60	.25
1030	32¢ Papal Visit	2.75	.60	.25
1031	64¢ Papal Visit	5.25	1.10	.75

1016 *New Brunswick*

1028

1029

1030

1032

1036

1040

1043

1044

1045

1046

SCOTT NO.	DESCRIPTION	PLATE BLOCK F/NH	UNUSED F/NH	USED F
1032-35	Lighthouses, attached	2.75	2.25	1.75
1032	32¢ Louisbourg	......	.60	.25
1033	32¢ Fisgard	......	.60	.25
1034	32¢ Ile Verte	......	.60	.25
1035	32¢ Gilbraltar Point	......	.60	.25
1036-37	Locomotives, attached	2.75	1.20	1.00
1036	32¢ Scotia 0-6-0	......	.60	.15
1037	32¢ Countess of Dufferin 4-4-0	......	.60	.15
1038	37¢ Grand Trunk 2-6-0	3.15	.65	.30
1039	64¢ Canadian Pacific 4-6-0	5.25	1.10	.52
1039a	Locomotive Souvenir Sheet	......	3.25	2.75
1040	32¢ Christmas	2.75	.60	.25
1041	37¢ Christmas	3.15	.60	.30
1042	64¢ Christmas	5.25	1.10	.52
1043	32¢ Royal Air Force	2.75	1.00	.25
1044	32¢ Newspaper	2.75	1.00	.25

1985 COMMEMORATIVES

SCOTT NO.	DESCRIPTION	PLATE BLOCK F/NH	UNUSED F/NH	USED F
1045/76	**(1045-49, 1060-66, 1067-76) complete, 21 varieties**	**49.40(16)**	**13.75**	**6.00**
1045	32¢ Youth Year	2.75	.60	.25
1046	32¢ Canadian Astronaut	2.75	.60	.25
1047-48	Women, attached	2.75	1.20	1.00
1047	32¢ T. Casgrain	......	.60	.25
1048	32¢ E. Murphy	......	.60	.25
1049	32¢ G. Dumont	2.75	.60	.25
1059a	34¢ Forts pane of 10	......	8.00	8.00
1050-59	set of singles	......	8.50	7.50
......	any Fort single	......	.70	.30
1060	34¢ Louis Hebert	2.75	.60	.20
1061	34¢ Inter-Parliamentary	2.75	.60	.20
1062	34¢ Girl Guides	2.75	.60	.20
1063-66	Lighthouses, attached	2.75	2.50	2.00
1063	34¢ Sisters Islets	......	.60	.20
1064	34¢ Pelee Passage	......	.60	.20
1065	34¢ Haut-fond Prince	......	.60	.20
1066	34¢ Rose Blanche	......	.60	.20
1066b	Lighthouse Souvenir Sheet	......	2.95	2.50
1067	34¢ Christmas	2.75	.60	.20
1068	39¢ Christmas	3.60	.75	.40
1069	68¢ Christmas	6.05	1.35	.60
1070	32¢ Christmas, booklet single	......	.80	......
1070a	same, booklet pane of 10	......	8.00	......
1071-72	Locomotives, attached	2.75	1.25	.75
1071	34¢ GT Class K2	......	.60	.20
1072	34¢ CP Class P2a	......	.60	.20
1073	39¢ CMoR Class 010a	3.30	.75	.40
1074	68¢ CGR Class H4D	6.05	.35	.75
1075	34¢ Royal Navy	2.75	.60	.20
1076	34¢ Montreal Museum	2.75	.60	.20

1047-48

1049

1050

1060

1061

1062

FORTS

1050 *Lower Ft. Garry* **1051** *Fort Anne* **1052** *Fort York*
1053 *Castle Hill* **1054** *Fort Whoop Up* **1055** *Fort Erie*
1056 *Fort Walsh* **1057** *Fort Lennox* **1058** *York Redoubt*
1059 *Fort Frederick*

1063

1067

1075

1076

1077

1078

1986 COMMEMORATIVES

SCOTT NO.	DESCRIPTION	PLATE BLOCK F/NH	UNUSED F/NH	USED F
1077/1121	**(1077-79, 1090-1107,1108-16, 1117-21) complete, 35 varieties**	**70.50**	**22.10**	**11.60**
1077	34¢ Computer Map	2.75	.60	.20
1078	34¢ Expo '86	2.75	.60	.20
1079	39¢ Expo '86	3.30	.75	.32

1987 HERITAGE ARTIFACTS

SCOTT NO.	DESCRIPTION	PLATE BLOCK F/NH	UNUSED F/NH	USED F
1080	25¢ Butter Stamp	2.00	.60	.20
1081	42¢ Linen Chest	3.75	1.00	.35
1082	55¢ Iron Kettle	5.25	1.20	.45
1083	72¢ Hand-drawn Cart	7.75	1.50	.60

1986-87 Definitive

SCOTT NO.	DESCRIPTION	PLATE BLOCK F/NH	UNUSED F/NH	USED F
1084	$5 La Mauricie	39.50	8.50	3.50

1090

1091

1092

1094

1103

1104

1095

1099

1986 COMMEMORATIVES

SCOTT NO.	DESCRIPTION	PLATE BLOCK F/NH	UNUSED F/NH	USED F
1090	34¢ Philippe Aubert de Gaspe	2.75	.60	.20
1091	34¢ Molly Brant	2.75	.60	.20
1092	34¢ Expo '86	2.75	.60	.20
1093	68¢ Expo '86	6.00	1.30	.55
1094	34¢ Canadian Forces Postal Service	2.75	.60	.20
1095-98	Birds, attached	4.75	4.00	3.00
1095	34¢ Great Blue Heron	......	1.10	.45
1096	34¢ Snow Goose	......	1.10	.45
1097	34¢ Great Horned Owl	......	1.10	.45
1098	34¢ Spruce Grouse	......	1.10	.45
1099-1102	Science & Technology, attached	3.00	2.75	2.25
1099	34¢ Rotary Snowplow	......	.75	.30
1100	34¢ Canadarm	......	.75	.30
1101	34¢ Anti-gravity Flight Suit	......	.75	.30
1102	34¢ Variable-pitch Propeller	......	.75	.30
1103	34¢ CBC	2.75	.60	.20
1104-07	Exploration, attached	3.00	2.75	2.25
1104	34¢ Continent	......	.75	.30
1105	34¢ Vikings	......	.75	.30
1106	34¢ John Cabot	......	.75	.30
1107	34¢ Hudson Bay	......	.75	.30
1107b	CAPEX souvenir sheet	......	3.00	2.75

SCOTT NO.	DESCRIPTION	PLATE BLOCK F/NH	UNUSED F/NH	USED F
1108-09	Frontier Peacemakers, attached	2.75	1.25	1.00
1108	34¢ Crowfoot	......	.60	.20
1109	34¢ J.F. Macleod	......	.60	.20
1110	34¢ Peace Year	2.75	.60	.20
1111-12	Calgary, attached	2.75	1.25	1.00
1111	34¢ Ice Hockey	......	.60	.20
1112	34¢ Biathlon	......	.60	.20
1113	34¢ Christmas Angels	2.75	.60	.20
1114	39¢ Christmas Angels	3.30	.75	.32
1115	68¢ Christmas Angels	6.00	1.30	.55
1116	29¢ Christmas Angels, booklet singles	......	.60	.25
1116a	same, booklet pane of 10	......	6.10	......

1108

1110

1111

1113

1117

1122

SCOTT NO.	DESCRIPTION	PLATE BLOCK F/NH	UNUSED F/NH	USED F
1117	34¢ John Molson	2.75	.60	.20
1118-19	Locomotive, attached	3.75	1.25	1.00
1118	34¢ CN V1a	......	.60	.20
1119	34¢ CP T1a	......	.60	.20
1120	39¢ CN U2a	4.25	.95	.75
1121	68¢ CP H1c	6.75	1.50	1.25

1987 COMMEMORATIVES

SCOTT NO.	DESCRIPTION	PLATE BLOCK F/NH	UNUSED F/NH	USED F
1122/54	**(1122-25, 1126-54) complete, 33 varieties ....**	**68.75**	**23.25**	**12.35**
1122	34¢ Toronto P.O.	2.75	.60	.27

1987 CAPEX EXHIBITION

SCOTT NO.	DESCRIPTION	PLATE BLOCK F/NH	UNUSED F/NH	USED F
1123	36¢ Nelson-Miramichi: Post Office	3.00	.60	.30
1124	42¢ Saint Ours P.O.	4.00	.80	.40
1125	72¢ Battleford P.O.	6.50	1.50	1.25
1125A	CAPEX Souvenir Sheet	......	3.00	2.50
1126-29	Exploration, attached	4.00	3.50	3.25
1126	34¢ Brule	......	.95	.45
1127	34¢ Radisson	......	.95	.45
1128	34¢ Jolliet	......	.95	.45
1129	34¢ Wilderness	......	.95	.45
1130	36¢ Calgary Olympics	2.85	.60	.30
1131	42¢ Calgary Olympics	3.30	.80	.40
1132	36¢ Volunteers	4.00	.60	.30
1133	36¢ Charter of Freedom	2.85	.60	.30
1134	36¢ Engineering	2.85	.60	.30

1987 COMMEMORATIVES

SCOTT NO.	DESCRIPTION	PLATE BLOCK F/NH	UNUSED F/NH	USED F
1135-38	Science & Tech., attached	3.00	2.45	2.20
1135	36¢ Reginald A. Fessenden	......	.75	.35
1136	36¢ Charles Fenerty	......	.75	.35
1137	36¢ Desbarats & Leggo	......	.75	.35
1138	36¢ Frederick N. Gisborne	......	.75	.35
1139-40	Steamships, attached	3.00	1.25	1.10
1139	36¢ Segwun	......	.75	.35
1140	36¢ Princess Marguerite	......	.75	.35
1141-44	Historic Shipwrecks, att'd.	3.50	3.00	2.75
1141	36¢ Hamilton & Scourge	......	.85	.35
1142	36¢ San Juan	......	.85	.35
1143	36¢ Breadalbane	......	.85	.35
1144	36¢ Ericsson	......	.85	.35
1145	36¢ Air Canada	2.85	.60	.30

1132

1133

1134

1135

1139

1141

1145

1146

1147

1148

1154

1155

1162

1163

1165

1166

1169

SCOTT NO.	DESCRIPTION	PLATE BLOCK F/NH	UNUSED F/NH	USED F
1146	36¢ Quebec Summit	2.85	.60	.30
1147	36¢ Commonwealth Mtg.	2.85	.60	.30
1148	36¢ Christmas	2.85	.60	.30
1149	42¢ Christmas	3.30	.75	.40
1150	72¢ Christmas	6.35	1.40	1.00
1151	31¢ Christmas booklet single	......	.75	.50
1151a	same, booklet pane of 10	......	6.00	......
1152-53	Calgary Olympics, attached	2.85	1.35	1.10
1152	36¢ Cross-Country Skiing	......	.60	.30
1153	36¢ Ski Jumping	......	.60	.30
1154	36¢ Grey Cup	2.85	.60	.30

1987-91 DEFINITIVE ISSUES

SCOTT NO.	DESCRIPTION	PLATE BLOCK F/NH	UNUSED F/NH	USED F
1155	1¢ Flying Squirrel	.80	.20	.15
1156	2¢ Porcupine	.80	.20	.15
1157	3¢ Muskrat	.80	.20	.15
1158	5¢ Hare	.80	.20	.15
1159	6¢ Red Fox	.80	.20	.15
1160	10¢ Skunk	1.00	.25	.15
1160a	same, perf. 13x12-1/2	35.00	5.00	.50
1161	25¢ Beaver	2.00	.50	.20
1162	37¢ Elizabeth II	3.05	.75	.30
1163	37¢ Parliament	3.05	.75	.30
1163a	same, bklt. pane of 10 (1988)	......	7.50	7.50
1163b	same, bklt. pane of 25 (1988)	......	18.80	15.00
1163c	37¢, perf. 13-1/2x14 (1988)	......	1.20	......
1164	38¢ Elizabeth II (1988)	3.30	.75	.30
1164a	38¢, perf. 13x13-1/2	......	1.50	.75
1164b	same, booklet pane of 10	......	7.50	6.00
1165	38¢ Clock Tower (1988)	3.30	.65	.15
1165a	same, booklet pane of 10	......	8.00	6.00
1165b	same, booklet pane of 25	......	20.00	18.75
1166	39¢ Flag & Clouds	3.30	.75	.15
1166a	same, booklet pane of 10	......	7.50	6.75
1166b	same, booklet pane of 25	......	22.50	18.75
1166c	same, perf. 12-1/2x13	......	15.00	1.00
1167	39¢ Elizabeth II	3.30	.75	.15
1167a	same, booklet pane of 10	......	10.00	6.00
1167b	39¢, perf. 13 (1990)	55.00	16.00	.50
1168	40¢ Elizabeth II (1990)	3.30	.75	.15
1168a	same, booklet pane of 10	......	8.00	6.75
1169	40¢ Flag and Mountains (1990)	3.30	.70	.15
1169a	same, booklet pane of 25	......	26.25	18.75
1169b	same, booklet pane of 10	......	8.00	6.75
1170	43¢ Lynx	4.50	1.00	.30
1171	44¢ Walrus (1989)	4.50	1.00	.20
1171a	44¢, perf. 12-1/2x13	......	3.00	.30
1171b	same, booklet pane of 5	....	12.00	....
1172	45¢ Pronghorn (1990)	4.50	.95	.30
1172b	same, booklet pane of 5	7.50	1.50	.30
1172d	45¢, perf. 13	80.00	18.00	1.20
1172A	46¢, Wolverine (1990)	3.85	1.00	.30
1172Ac	46¢, perf. 12-1/2x13	......	.85	.30
1172Ae	same, booklet pane of 5	......	1.15	.30
1172Ag	same, perf. 14-1/2x14	25.00	5.00	
1173	57¢ Killer Whale	4.90	1.15	.35
1174	59¢ Musk-ox (1989)	4.90	1.15	.35
1174a	same, perf. 13	37.50	10.00	.60
1175	61¢ Timber Wolf (1990)	5.65	1.15	.40
1175a	61¢, perf. 13	325.00	70.00	.50
1176	63¢ Harbor Porpoise	6.00	1.35	.40
1176a	63¢, perf. 13	32.50	6.00	.60
1177	74¢ Wapiti (1988)	7.50	1.50	.60
1178	76¢ Grizzly Bear (1989)	6.00	1.35	.40
1178a	76¢, perf. 12-1/2x13	......	2.50	.35
1178b	same, booklet pane of 5	....	16.00	....
1178c	same, perf. 13	225.00	50.00	2.75
1179	78¢ Beluga (1990)	7.50	1.50	.55
1179a	same, booklet pane of 5	......	12.00	......
1179b	78¢, perf. 13	195.00	40.00	2.65
1179c	same, perf. 12-1/2x13	15.00	3.00	.60
1180	80¢ Peary caribou (1990)	8.50	2.00	.60
1180a	80¢, perf. 12-1/2x13	6.60	2.00	.55
1180b	same, booklet pane of 5	....	17.50	....
1180c	80¢, perf. 14-1/2x14	24.00	6.50	.60

1181

1184

1191, 1192, 1193

1203

SCOTT NO.	DESCRIPTION	PLATE BLOCK F/NH	UNUSED F/NH	USED F
1181	$1 Runnymede Library	7.50	1.50	.80
1182	$2 McAdam Train Station	15.00	3.00	1.50
1183	$5 Bonsecours Market	40.00	8.50	4.00

BOOKLET STAMPS

SCOTT NO.	DESCRIPTION	PLATE BLOCK F/NH	UNUSED F/NH	USED F
1184	1¢ Flag, booklet single (1990)	......	.20	.15
1185	5¢ Flag, booklet single (1990)	......	.20	.15
1186	6¢ Parliament East (1989)	......	.25	.15
1187	37¢ Parliament booklet single	......	.65	.25
1187a	booklet pane (4), 1 #938, 2 #942, 1 #1187	......	1.50	......
1188	38¢ Parliament Library booklet single (1989)	......	.65	.25
1188a	booklet pane (5), 3 #939a, 1 #1186, 1 #1188	......	1.50	......
1189	39¢ Flag booklet single (1990)	......	.75	.30
1189a	booklet pane (4), 1 #1184, 2 #1185, 1 #1189	......	2.00	......
1190	40¢ Flag booklet single (1990)	......	1.50	.50
1190a	booklet pane (4) 2 #1184, 1 #1185, 1 #1190	......	2.50	......

1204

1206

1210

1216

1214

1215

1217-20

1221

SELF-ADHESIVE BOOKLET STAMPS

SCOTT NO.	DESCRIPTION	PLATE BLOCK F/NH	UNUSED F/NH	USED F
1191	38¢ Flag, forest (1989)	......	1.15	.60
1191a	same, booklet pane of 12	......	13.75	......
1192	39¢ Flag field (1990)	......	1.15	.60
1192a	same, booklet pane of 12	......	13.75	......
1193	40¢ Flag, seacoast (1991)	......	1.15	.60
1193a	same, booklet pane of 12	......	13.75	......

COIL STAMPS

SCOTT NO.	DESCRIPTION	PLATE BLOCK F/NH	UNUSED F/NH	USED F
1194	37¢ Parliament Library (1988)	......	.85	.25
1194A	38¢ Parliament Library (1989)	......	.85	.25
1194B	39¢ Flag (1990)	......	.85	.25
1194C	40¢ Flag (1990)	......	.85	.25

1988 COMMEMORATIVES

SCOTT NO.	DESCRIPTION	PLATE BLOCK F/NH	UNUSED F/NH	USED F
1195/1236	**(1195-1225, 1226-36) complete, 39 varieties**	**74.75**	**33.25**	**14.75**
1195-96	Calgary Olympics, att'd.	3.05	1.50	1.15
1195	37¢ Alpine Skiing	......	.65	.30
1196	37¢ Curling	......	.65	.30
1197	43¢ Figure Skating	3.30	.75	.60
1198	74¢ Luge	5.80	1.50	.95
1199-1202	Explorers, attached	3.05	3.00	2.25
1199	37¢ Anthony Henday	......	.65	.30
1200	37¢ George Vancouver	......	.65	.30
1201	37¢ Simon Fraser	......	.65	.30
1202	37¢ John Palliser	......	.65	.30
1203	50¢ Canadian Art	5.00	1.10	.95
1204-05	Wildlife Conservation, att'd.	3.30	1.40	.95
1204	37¢ Ducks Unlimited	......	.65	.30
1205	37¢ Moose	......	.65	.30
1206-09	Science & Technology, att'd.	3.75	3.25	2.50
1206	37¢ Kerosene	......	.85	.35
1207	37¢ Marquis Wheat	......	.85	.35
1208	37¢ Electron Microscope	......	.85	.35
1209	37¢ Cancer Therapy	......	.85	.35
1210-13	Butterflies, attached	4.00	3.50	2.50
1210	37¢ Short-tailed Swallowtail	......	.85	.35
1211	37¢ Northern Blue	......	.85	.35
1212	37¢ Macoun's Arctic	......	.85	.35
1213	37¢ Tiger Swallowtail	......	.85	.35
1214	37¢ Harbor Entrance	3.05	.65	.25
1215	37¢ 4-H Club Anniv.	3.05	.65	.25
1216	37¢ Les Forges Du St. Maurice	3.05	.65	.25

1222

1226

1227

1228

1229-32

SCOTT NO.	DESCRIPTION	PLATE BLOCK F/NH	UNUSED F/NH	USED F
1217-20	Dogs, attached	5.00	4.50	3.00
1217	37¢ Tahltan Bear Dog	......	1.20	.45
1218	37¢ Nova Scotia Retriever	......	1.20	.45
1219	37¢ Canadian Eskimo Dog	......	1.20	.45
1220	37¢ Newfoundland Dog	......	1.20	.45
1221	37¢ Baseball	4.15	.65	.25
1222	37¢ Christmas Nativity	3.50	.75	.25
1223	43¢ Virgin & Child	4.00	.90	.75
1224	74¢ Virgin & Child	6.00	1.15	.95
1225	32¢ Christmas Icons booklet single	......	.75	.30
1225a	same, booklet pane of 10	......	7.00	5.25
1226	37¢ Charles Inglis	3.05	.65	.25
1227	37¢ Ann Hopkins	3.05	.65	.25
1228	37¢ Angus Walters	3.05	.65	.25
1229-32	Small Craft Series, attached	3.30	2.70	2.25
1229	37¢ Chipewyan Canoe	......	.65	.25
1230	37¢ Haida Canoe	......	.65	.25
1231	37¢ Inuit Kayak	......	.65	.25
1232	37¢ Micmac Canoe	......	.65	.25
1233-36	Explorers, attached	3.30	3.00	2.25
1233	38¢ Matonabbee	......	.65	.25
1234	38¢ Sir John Franklin	......	.65	.25
1235	38¢ J.B.Tyrrell	......	.65	.25
1236	38¢ V. Stefansson	......	.65	.25

1237

1243

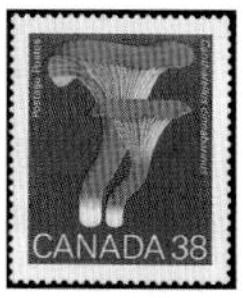

1245

1249

1251

1256, 1256a

1259, 1259a

1260

1252

1989 COMMEMORATIVES

SCOTT NO.	DESCRIPTION	PLATE BLOCK F/NH	UNUSED F/NH	USED F
1237/63	**(1237-56, 1257, 1258, 1259, 1260-63) complete, 26 varieties**	**......**	**18.25**	**7.40**
1237-40	Canadian Photography, att'd.	3.30	3.00	2.25
1237	38¢ W. Notman	......	.65	.25
1238	38¢ W.H. Boorne	......	.65	.25
1239	38¢ A. Henderson	......	.65	.25
1240	38¢ J.E. Livernois	......	.65	.25
1241	50¢ Canadian Art	5.00	1.10	.95
1243-44	19th Century Poets, att'd.	3.30	1.40	.95
1243	38¢ L.H.Frechette	......	.65	.25
1244	38¢ A. Lampman	......	.65	.25
1245-48	Mushrooms, attached	3.30	3.00	2.25
1245	38¢ Cinnabar Chanterelle	......	.85	.30
1246	38¢ Common Morel	......	.85	.30
1247	38¢ Spindell Coral	......	.85	.30
1248	38¢ Admirable Boletus	......	.85	.30
1249-50	Canadian Infantry, attached	195.00	1.50	1.15
1249	38¢ Light Infantry	......	.65	.25
1250	38¢ Royal 22nd Regiment	......	.65	.25
1251	38¢ International Trade	3.30	.65	.25
1252-55	Performing Arts, attached	3.30	2.70	2.25
1252	38¢ Dance	......	.65	.25
1253	38¢ Music	......	.65	.25
1254	38¢ Film	......	.65	.25
1255	38¢ Theatre	......	.65	.25
1256	38¢ Christmas 1989	3.30	.65	.25
1256a	same, booklet single	......	3.75	.75
1256a	same, booklet pane of 10	45.00	....	....
1257	44¢ Christmas 1989	4.60	.85	.40
1257a	same, booklet single	......	4.50	.75
1257a	same, booklet pane of 5	22.50	....	....
1258	76¢ Christmas 1989	7.00	1.40	.70
1258a	same, booklet single	......	5.50	.75
1258a	same, booklet pane of 5	30.00	....	....
1259	33¢ Christmas, booklet single	......	.70	.25
1259a	same, booklet pane of 10	......	12.00	......
1260-63	WWII 50th Anniversary, att'd.	3.30	3.00	2.25
1260	38¢ Declaration of War	......	.80	.20
1261	38¢ Army Mobilization	......	.80	.20
1262	38¢ Navy Convoy System	......	.80	.20
1263	38¢ Commonwealth Training	......	.80	.20

1264

1270

1272-73

1274

1990 COMMEMORATIVES

SCOTT NO.	DESCRIPTION	PLATE BLOCK F/NH	UNUSED F/NH	USED F
1264/1301	**(1264-73, 1274-94, 1295, 1296, 1297, 1298-1301) complete, 38 vars.**	**62.25**	**29.10**	**16.25**
1264-65	Norman Bethune, attached	3.50	2.00	1.50
1264	39¢ Bethune in Canada	.....	1.10	.50
1265	39¢ Bethune in China	.....	1.10	.50
1266-69	Small Craft Series, att'd.	3.50	3.00	2.50
1266	39¢ Dory	.....	.85	.35
1267	39¢ Pointer	.....	.85	.35
1268	39¢ York Boat	.....	.85	.35
1269	39¢ North Canoe	.....	.85	.35
1270	39¢ Multiculturalism	3.30	.70	.25
1271	50¢ Canadian Art,"The West Wind"	5.00	1.10	.95
1272-73	Canada Postal System 39¢ booklet pair	.....	1.50	1.00
1273a	same, booklet pane of 8	.....	7.00	.....
1273b	same, booklet pane of 9	.....	8.00	.....
1274-77	Dolls of Canada, attached	4.00	3.00	2.50
1274	39¢ Native Dolls	.....	.85	.35
1275	39¢ Settlers' Dolls	.....	.85	.35
1276	39¢ Four Commercial Dolls	.....	.85	.35
1277	39¢ Five Commercial Dolls	.....	.85	.35

1278

1279

1283

1287

1288

1289

1293

1294

1297

SCOTT NO.	DESCRIPTION	PLATE BLOCK F/NH	UNUSED F/NH	USED F
1278	39¢ Canada/Flag Day	3.30	.75	.25
1279-82	Prehistoric Life, attached	4.00	3.00	2.50
1279	39¢ Trilobite	.....	.85	.35
1280	39¢ Sea Scorpion	.....	.85	.35
1281	39¢ Fossil Algae	.....	.85	.35
1282	39¢ Soft Invertebrate	.....	.85	.35
1283-86	Canadian Forests, attached	4.00	3.25	2.75
1283	39¢ Acadian	.....	.85	.35
1284	39¢ Great Lakes—St.Lawrence	.....	.85	.35
1285	39¢ Coast	.....	.85	.35
1286	39¢ Boreal	.....	.85	.35
1287	39¢ Climate Observations	3.30	.70	.25
1288	39¢ Int'l. Literacy Year	3.30	.70	.25
1289-92	Can. Lore & Legend, attached	4.00	3.25	2.75
1289	39¢ Sasquatch	.....	.85	.35
1290	39¢ Kraken	.....	.85	.35
1291	39¢ Werewolf	.....	.85	.35
1292	39¢ Ogopogo	.....	.85	.35
1293	39¢ Agnes Macphail	3.30	.70	.25
1294	39¢ Native Mary & Child	3.20	.75	.25
1294a	same, booklet pane of 10	.....	10.00	.....
1295	45¢ Inuit, Mother & Child	5.00	1.10	..75
1295a	same, booklet pane of 5	.....	9.50	.....
1296	78¢ Raven Children	8.00	1.75	1.00
1296a	same, booklet pane of 5	.....	15.00	.....
1297	34¢ Christmas, booklet sgl.	.....	.65	.25
1297a	same, booklet pane of 10	.....	7.00	.....
1298-1301	World War II—1940, att'd.	5.00	4.25	4.00
1298	39¢ Home Front	.....	1.10	.95
1299	39¢ Communal War Efforts	.....	1.10	.95
1300	39¢ Food Production	.....	1.10	.95
1301	39¢ Science and War	.....	1.10	.95

1302

1311

1316

1321

1991 COMMEMORATIVES

SCOTT NO.	DESCRIPTION	PLATE BLOCK F/NH	UNUSED F/NH	USED F
1302-43, 1345-48, 46 varieties		**41.75**	**37.00**	**17.75**
1302-05	Canadian Doctors, att'd.	4.00	3.00	2.25
1302	40¢ Jennie Trout	......	.85	.35
1303	40¢ Wilder Penfield	......	.85	.35
1304	40¢ Sir Frederick Banting	......	.85	.35
1305	40¢ Harold Griffith	......	.85	.35
1306-09	Prehistoric Life, attached	4.00	3.50	2.75
1306	40¢ Microfossils	......	.95	.35
1307	40¢ Early tree	......	.95	.35
1308	40¢ Early fish	......	.95	.35
1309	40¢ Land reptile	......	.95	.35
1310	50¢ Canadian Art, "Forest, British Columbia"	4.50	.95	.75
1311	40¢ The Butchart Gardens, attached booklet single	......	.95	.35
1312	40¢ International Peace Garden, booklet single	......	.95	.35
1313	40¢ Royal Botanical Garden, booklet single	......	.95	.35
1314	40¢ Montreal Botanical Garden, booklet single	......	.95	.35
1315	40¢ Halifax Public Gardens, booklet single	......	.95	.35
1315a	Public Gardens, strip of 5	......	4.00	3.00
1315b	Public Gardens, attached booklet pane of 10	......	8.00	....
1316	40¢ Canada Day	3.50	.75	.25
1317-20	Small Craft Series, attached	3.50	3.00	2.25
1317	40¢ Verchere Rowboat	......	.85	.35
1318	40¢ Touring Kayak	......	.85	.35
1319	40¢ Sailing Dinghy	......	.85	.35
1320	40¢ Cedar Strip Canoe	......	.85	.35
1321	40¢ South Nahanni River	......	.95	.45
1322	40¢ Athabasca River	......	.95	.45
1323	40¢ Voyageur Waterway	......	.95	.45
1324	40¢ Jacques Cartier River	......	.95	.45
1325	40¢ Main River	......	1.95	.45
1325a	Canadian Rivers, strip of 5	......	4.00	3.00
1325b	Canadian Rivers, attached booklet pane of 10	......	8.00	......
1326-29	Arrival of the Ukrainians, attached	4.00	3.00	2.25
1326	40¢ Leaving	....	.85	.35
1327	40¢ Winter in Canada	....	.85	.35
1328	40¢ Clearing Land	....	.85	.35
1329	40¢ Growing Wheat	....	.85	.35
1330-33	Dangerous Public Service Occupations, attached	5.00	4.00	2.50
1330	40¢ Ski Patrol	....	1.10	.35
1331	40¢ Police	....	1.10	.35
1332	40¢ Firefighters	....	1.10	.35
1333	40¢ Search & Rescue	....	1.10	.35
1334-37	Folktales, attached	4.00	3.00	2.25
1334	40¢ Witched Canoe	....	.85	.35
1335	40¢ Orphan Boy	....	.85	.35
1336	40¢ Chinook Wind	....	.85	.35
1337	40¢ Buried Treasure	....	.85	.35
1338	40¢ Queen's University, booklet, single	....	.85	.25
1338a	Same booklet pane of 10	....	8.00	....
1339	40¢ Santa at Fireplace	3.60	.75	.25
1339a	Same, booklet pane of 10	....	8.00	....
1340	46¢ Santa with White horse, tree	4.10	.85	.40
1340a	Same, booklet pane of 5	....	5.00	....
1341	80¢ Sinterklaas, girl	7.00	1.50	1.00
1341a	Same, booklet pane of 5	....	9.00	....
1342	35¢ Santa with Punchbowl, booklet, single	....	.85	.25
1342a	Same, booklet pane of 10	....	8.00	....
1343	40¢ Basketball Centennial	4.00	.85	.25
1344	40¢-80¢ Basketball Souvenir Sheet of 3	....	5.00	....
1345-48	World War II—1941, att'd.	5.00	4.00	3.75
1345	40¢ Women's Armed Forces	....	1.10	.95
1346	40¢ War Industry	....	1.10	.95
1347	40¢ Cadets and Veterans	....	1.10	.95
1348	40¢ Defense of Hong Kong	....	1.10	.95

1326

1330

1334

1338

1343

1349

1339

1342

1991-96 Regular Issue

SCOTT NO.	DESCRIPTION	PLATE BLOCK F/NH	UNUSED F/NH	USED F
1349	1¢ Blueberry (1992)	.80	.20	.15
1350	2¢ Wild Strawberry (1992)	.80	.20	.15
1351	3¢ Black Crowberry (1992)	.80	.20	.15
1352	5¢ Rose Hip (1992)	.80	.20	.15
1353	6¢ Black Raspberry (1992)	.80	.20	.15
1354	10¢ Kinnikinnick (1992)	1.00	.25	.15
1355	25¢ Saskatoon berry (1992)	2.00	.50	.15
1356	42¢ Flag + Rolling Hills	3.20	.75	.20
1356a	Same, booklet pane of 10	....	7.50	6.00
1356b	Same, booklet pane of 50	....	80.00	33.75
1356c	Same, booklet pane of 25	....	18.75	15.00
1357	42¢ Queen Elizabeth II (Karsh)	3.20	.75	.20
1357a	Same, booklet pane of 10	....	7.50	6.00
1358	43¢ Queen Elizabeth II (Karsh) (1992)	4.15	.95	.20
1358a	Same, booklet pane of 10	....	9.40	7.50
1359	43¢ Flag + Prairie (1992)	4.15	.95	.20
1359a	Same, booklet pane of 10	....	7.50	6.00
1359b	Same, booklet pane of 25	....	22.50	18.75
1360	45¢ Queen Elizabeth II (Karsh) (1995)	3.20	.75	.20
1360a	Same, booklet pane of 10	....	8.00	6.00
1361	45¢ Flag & Building (1995)	3.20	.75	.20
1361a	Same, booklet pane of 10	....	9.40	7.50
1361b	Same, booklet pane of 25	....	28.00	22.50
1362	45¢ Flag & Building, perf. 13½ x 13	3.20	.75	.20
1362a	Same, booklet pane of 10	....	8.00	6.00
1362b	Same, booklet pane of 30	....	20.00	15.00
1363	48¢ McIntosh Apple Tree, perf. 13	4.15	.95	.25
1363a	Same, perf. 14½ x 14	....	1.25	.30
1363b	Same, booklet pane of 5	....	7.00	4.50
1364	49¢ Delicious Apple perf.13 (1992)	4.15	.95	.25
1364a	Same, perf. 14½ x 14	3.95	1.25	.30
1364b	Same, booklet pane of 5	....	7.00	4.50
1365	50¢ Snow Apple (1994)	3.95	.95	.30
1365b	Same, perf. 14½ x 14	3.95	1.75	.25
1365a	Same, booklet pane of 5	....	9.00	....
1366	52¢ Gravenstein apple (1995)	3.95	.95	.25
1366a	Same, booklet pane of 5	....	9.00	4.50
1366b	52¢ Gravenstein apple, perf. 14½ x 14	3.95	2.50	.30
1366c	Same, booklet pane of 5	....	12.00	....
1367	65¢ Black Walnut Tree	4.90	1.15	.35
1368	67¢ Beaked Hazelnut (1992)	4.90	1.15	.35
1369	69¢ Shagbark Hickory (1994)	4.90	1.15	.35
1370	71¢ American Chestnut (1995)	4.90	1.10	.35
1371	84¢ Stanley Plum Tree, perf. 13	5.65	1.35	.40
1371a	Same, perf. 14½ x 14	....	2.00	.50
1371b	Same, booklet pane of 5	....	10.00	....
1372	86¢ Bartlett Pear, perf. 13 (1992)	9.00	2.65	.60
1372a	Same, perf. 14½ x 14	13.15	3.00	.60
1372b	Same, booklet pane of 5	....	15.00	....
1373	88¢ Westcot Apricot (1994)	6.40	1.50	.50
1373b	Same, perf. 14½ x 14	6.75	3.00	.60
1363bc	Same, booklet pane of 5	....	15.00	....
1374	90¢ Elberta Peach (1995)	6.00	1.90	.45
1374a	Same, booklet pane of 5	....	10.00	....
1374b	Same, booklet pane of 5, perf. 14½ x 14	....	12.00	....
1375	$1 Yorkton Court House (1994)	6.75	1.50	.55
1376	$2 Provincial Normal School, Nova Scotia (1994)	13.15	3.00	1.05
1378	$5 Carnegie Public Library, Victoria	33.75	8.00	2.25
1388	42¢ Flag and Mountains, quick-stick (1992)	....	.80	.30
1388a	Same, booklet pane of 12	....	10.00	....
1389	43¢ Flag, estuary shore (1993)	....	.80	.30
1394	42¢ Canadian Flag + Rolling Hills, coil	....	.80	.30
1395	43¢ Canadian Flag, coil (1992)	....	.80	.30
1396	45¢ Canadian Flag, coil (1995)	....	.80	.20

1363

1399

1404

1992 COMMEMORATIVES

SCOTT NO.	DESCRIPTION	PLATE BLOCK F/NH	UNUSED F/NH	USED F
1399-1455, 57 varieties		**44.15**	**56.10**	**22.25**
1399	42¢ Ski Jumping	....	.95	.25
1400	42¢ Figure Skating	....	.95	.25
1401	42¢ Hockey	....	.95	.25
1402	42¢ Bobsledding	....	.95	.25
1403	42¢ Alpine Skiing	....	.95	.25
1403a	Olympic Winter Games, Strips of 5	....	4.50	3.00
1403b	Olympic Winter Games, booklet pane of 10	....	8.00	5.00
1404-05	350th Anniversary of Montreal, attached	3.60	1.50	1.00
1404	42¢ Modern Montreal	....	.80	.25
1405	42¢ Early Montreal	....	.80	.25
1406	48¢ Jaques Cartier	3.95	.90	.40
1407	84¢ Columbus	7.65	1.65	.60
1407a	42¢-84¢ Canada '92, Souvenir Sheet of 4	....	4.00	....
1408	42¢ The Margaree River	....	.85	.25
1409	42¢ Eliot or West River	....	.85	.25
1410	42¢ Ottowa River	....	.85	.25
1411	42¢ Niagara River	....	.85	.25
1412	42¢ South Saskatchewan River	....	.85	.25
1412a	Canadian Rivers II, Strip of 5	....	4.00	3.00
1412b	Canadian Rivers II, booklet pane of 10	....	8.00	5.00

1413

1420

SCOTT NO.	DESCRIPTION	PLATE BLOCK F/NH	UNUSED F/NH	USED F
1413	42¢ 50th Anniversary of the Alaska Highway	3.60	.80	.25
1414	42¢ Gymnastics	....	.95	.25
1415	42¢ Track and Field	....	.95	.25
1416	42¢ Diving	....	.95	.25
1417	42¢ Cycling	....	.95	.25
1418	42¢ Swimming	....	.95	.25
1418a	Olympic Summer Games, Strip of 5, attached	....	4.50	3.00
1418b	Olympic Summer Games, booklet pane of 10	....	8.00	5.00
1419	50¢ Canadian Art "Red Nasturtiums"	4.40	1.10	1.00
1420	Nova Scotia	....	2.10	1.00
1421	Ontario	....	2.10	1.00
1422	Prince Edward Island	....	2.10	1.00
1423	New Brunswick	....	2.10	1.00
1424	Quebec	....	2.10	1.00
1425	Saskatchewan	....	2.10	1.00
1426	Manitoba	....	2.10	1.00
1427	Northwest Territories	....	2.10	1.00
1428	Alberta	....	2.10	1.00
1429	British Columbia	....	2.10	1.00
1430	Yukon	....	2.10	1.00
1431	Newfoundland	....	2.10	1.00
1431a	42¢ 125th Anniversary of Canada, 12 various attached	......	24.00	22.00

1432

1436

SCOTT NO.	DESCRIPTION	PLATE BLOCK F/NH	UNUSED F/NH	USED F
1432-35	Canadian Folk Heroes, attached	3.60	3.00	2.25
1432	42¢ Jerry Potts	....	.80	.25
1433	42¢ Capt. William Jackman	....	.80	.25
1434	42¢ Laura Secord	....	.80	.25
1435	42¢ Joseph Montferrand	....	.80	.25
1436	42¢ Copper	....	.85	.25
1437	42¢ Sodalite	....	.85	.25
1438	42¢ Gold	....	.85	.25
1439	42¢ Galena	....	.85	.25
1440	42¢ Grossular	....	.85	.25
1440a	Minerals, Strip of 5	....	4.00	3.00
1440b	Minerals, booklet pane of 10	....	8.00	5.00

1441

1443a

SCOTT NO.	DESCRIPTION	PLATE BLOCK F/NH	UNUSED F/NH	USED F
1441-42	Canadian Space Exploration, attached	3.60	1.50	1.15
1441	42¢ Anik E2 Satellite	....	.80	.25
1442	42¢ Earth, Space Shuttle	....	.80	.25
1443-45	National Hockey League, booklet singles	....	2.40	.75
1443a	Skates, Stick, booklet pane of 8	....	6.40	....
1444a	Team Emblems, booklet pane of 8	....	6.40	....
1445a	Goalie's Mask, booklet pane of 9	....	7.20	....

1446-47

1452

SCOTT NO.	DESCRIPTION	PLATE BLOCK F/NH	UNUSED F/NH	USED F
1446-47	Order of Canada + D. Michener, attached	3.60	1.50	1.15
1446	42¢ Order of Canada	....	.80	.25
1447	42¢ Daniel Roland Michener	....	.80	.25
1448-51	World War II—1942, att'd.	3.60	3.00	2.25
1448	42¢ War Reporting	....	.80	.50
1449	42¢ Newfoundland Air Bases	....	.80	.50
1450	42¢ Raid on Dieppe	....	.80	.50
1451	42¢ U-boats offshore	....	.80	.50
1452	42¢ Jouluvana—Christmas	3.90	.80	.25
1452a	Same, perf. 13¹/2	3.90	.80	.25
1452b	Same, booklet pane of 10	....	7.75	....
1453	48¢ La Befana—Christmas	3.95	.90	.30
1453a	Same, booklet pane of 5	....	4.50	....
1454	84¢ Weihnachtsmann	6.75	1.50	.50
1454a	Same, booklet pane of 5	....	8.00	....
1455	37¢ Santa Claus	....	.70	.25
1455a	Same, booklet pane of 10	....	8.00	....

1455

1456

1460

1993 COMMEMORATIVES

SCOTT NO.	DESCRIPTION	PLATE BLOCK F/NH	UNUSED F/NH	USED F
1456-89, 1491-1506, 50 varieties		**41.00**	**41.50**	**19.50**
1456-59	Canadian Women, attached....	3.60	3.00	2.25
1456	43¢ Adelaide Sophia Hoodless	....	.80	.25
1457	43¢ Marie-Josephine Gerin-Lajoie	...	.80	.25
1458	43¢ Pitseolak Ashoona	....	.80	.25
1459	43¢ Helen Kinnear	....	.80	.25
1460	43¢ Stanley Cup Centennial	3.60	.80	.25

1461

1467

SCOTT NO.	DESCRIPTION	PLATE BLOCK F/NH	UNUSED F/NH	USED F
1461	43¢ Coverlet "Bed Rugg", New Brunswick	....	.85	.25
1462	43¢ Pieced Quilt, Ontario	....	.85	.25
1463	43¢ Doukhobor Bedcover, Saskatchewan	....	.85	.25
1464	43¢ Kwakwaka'wakw ceremonial robe, British Columbia	....	.85	.25
1465	43¢ Boutonne coverlet, Quebec	....	.85	.25
1465a	Handcrafted Textiles, Strip of 5	....	4.00	3.00
1465b	Handcrafted Textiles, booklet pane of 10	....	8.00	5.00
1461-65	Same, set of 5 singles	....	3.90	....
1466	86¢ Canadian Art—"Drawing for the Owl"	6.75	1.50	.95
1467	43¢ Empress Hotel, Victoria, B.C.	....	.85	.25
1468	43¢ Banff Springs Hotel, Banff, Alberta	....	.85	.25
1469	43¢ Royal York Hotel, Toronto, Ontario	....	.85	.25
1470	43¢ Chateau Frontenac, Quebec City, Quebec	....	.85	.25
1471	43¢ Algonquin Hotel, St. Andrews, N.B.	....	.85	.25
1471a	Canadian Pacific Hotels, strip of 5	....	4.00	3.00
1471b	Canadian Pacific Hotels, booklet pane of 10	....	8.00	5.00

1472

1484

1490a

SCOTT NO.	DESCRIPTION	PLATE BLOCK F/NH	UNUSED F/NH	USED F
1472	43¢ Algonquin Park, Ontario	....	1.10	.75
1473	43¢ De la Gaspesie Park,Quebec	....	1.10	.75
1474	43¢ Cedar Dunes Park, P.E.I.	....	1.10	.75
1475	43¢ Cape St. Mary's Reserve, Newfoundland	....	1.10	.75
1476	43¢ Mount Robson Park, B.C..	....	1.10	.75
1477	43¢ Writing-On-Stone Park, Alberta.	....	1.10	.75
1478	43¢ Spruce Woods Park, Manitoba	....	1.10	.75
1479	43¢ Herschel Island Park, Yukon	....	1.10	.75
1480	43¢ Cypress Hills Park, Saskatchewan	....	1.10	.75
1481	43¢ The Rocks Park, New Brunswick	....	1.10	.75
1482	43¢ Blomidon Park, Nova Scotia	....	1.10	.75
1483	43¢ Katannilik Park, Northwest Territories	....	1.10	.75
1483a	100th Anniversary of Territorial Parks, 12 varieties attached	...	12.50	8.00
1484	43¢ Toronto Bicentennial	3.60	.80	.25
1485	43¢ Fraser River	...	.85	.25
1486	43¢ Yukon River	...	.85	.25
1487	43¢ Red River	...	.85	.25
1488	43¢ St. Lawrence River	...	.85	.25
1489	43¢ St. John River	...	.85	.25
1489a	Canadian Rivers III, strip of 5	...	4.00	3.00
1489b	Canadian Rivers III, booklet pane of 10	...	8.00	5.00

1491

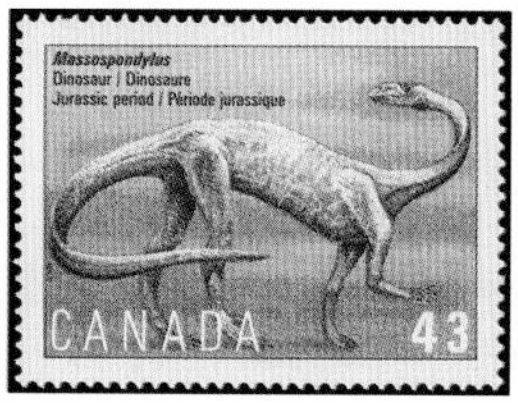

1495

1499

SCOTT NO.	DESCRIPTION	PLATE BLOCK F/NH	UNUSED F/NH	USED F
1490	43¢-86¢ Canadian Motor Vehicles souvenir sheet of 6	...	7.50	6.00
1491-94	Canadian Folklore—Folk Songs, attached....	3.60	3.00	2.25
1491	43¢ The Alberta Homesteader	...	.80	.25
1492	43¢ Les Raftmans	...	.80	.25
1493	43¢ I'se the B'y that Builds the Boat	...	.80	.25
1494	43¢ Bear Song	...	.80	.25

1502

1507

SCOTT NO.	DESCRIPTION	PLATE BLOCK F/NH	UNUSED F/NH	USED F
1495-98	Dinosaurs, attached	4.00	3.50	2.50
1495	43¢ Massospondylus (Jurassic period)	...	.95	.35
1496	43¢ Styracosaurus (Cretaceous period)	...	.95	.35
1497	43¢ Albertosaurus (Cretaceous period)	...	.95	.35
1498	43¢ Platecarpus (Cretaceous period)	...	.95	.35
1499	43¢ Santa Claus—Poland	3.60	.80	.25
1499a	same, booklet pane of 10	...	8.00	...
1500	49¢ Santa Claus—Russia	3.90	.90	.30
1500a	same, booklet pane of 5	...	4.50	...
1501	86¢ Father Christmas, Australia	7.00	1.50	.50
1501a	same, booklet pane of 5	...	7.50	...
1502	38¢ Santa Claus	...	.70	.25
1502a	same, booklet pane of 10	...	7.00	...
1503-06	World War II—1943	3.60	3.00	2.25
1503	43¢ Aid to Allies	...	.80	.50
1504	43¢ Canada's Bomber Force	...	.80	.50
1505	43¢ Battle of the Atlantic	...	.80	.50
1506	43¢ Invasion of Italy	...	.80	.50

1994

SCOTT NO.	DESCRIPTION	PLATE BLOCK F/NH	UNUSED F/NH	USED F
1507-08	43¢ Greeting booklet (10 stamps w/35 stickers)	...	10.00	...

1509

1510

1517

1994 COMMEMORATIVES

SCOTT NO.	DESCRIPTION	PLATE BLOCK F/NH	UNUSED F/NH	USED F
1509-22, 1524-26, 1528-40, 41 varieties		32.50	31.25	13.75
1509	43¢ Jeanne Sauve	3.60	.80	.25
1510	43¢ T. Eaton Prestige	3.60	.80	.25
1510a	43¢ T. Eaton Prestige, booklet of 10	...	8.00	...
1511	43¢ Saguenay River	...	.95	.35
1512	43¢ French River	...	.95	.35
1513	43¢ Mackenzie River	...	.95	.35
1514	43¢ Churchill River	...	.95	.35
1515	43¢ Columbia River	...	.95	.35
1515a	Canadian Rivers IV, strip of 5	...	5.00	4.00
1515b	Canadian Rivers IV, booklet pane of 10	...	10.00	...
1516	88¢ Canadian Art "Vera"	8.00	1.50	1.00

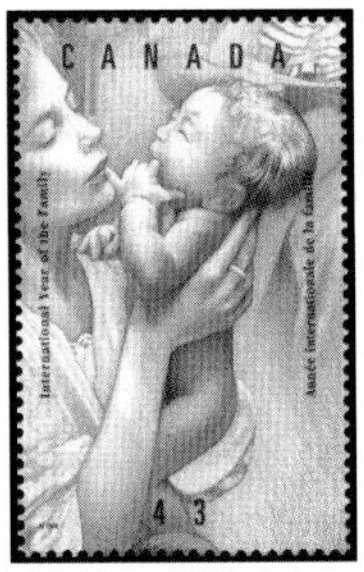

1523a

1524a

1525

SCOTT NO.	DESCRIPTION	PLATE BLOCK F/NH	UNUSED F/NH	USED F
1517-18	Commonwealth Games, attached	3.60	1.50	.60
1517	43¢ Lawn Bowls	...	.80	.25
1518	43¢ Lacrosse	...	.80	.25
1519-20	Commonwealth Games, attached	3.60	1.50	.60
1519	43¢ Wheelchair Marathon	...	.80	.25
1520	43¢ High Jump	...	.80	.25
1521	50¢ Commonwealth Games (Diving)	4.00	.90	.35
1522	88¢ Commonwealth Games (Cycling)	6.75	1.50	.75
1523	43¢ Intl. Year of the Family, souvenir sheet of 5	...	5.00	4.00
1524	Canada Day—Maple Trees, 12 varieties, attached	...	9.00	6.00
1525-26	Famous Canadians, attached	3.60	1.50	1.15
1525	43¢ Billy Bishop, Fighter Ace	...	.80	.25
1526	43¢ Mary Travers, Folk Singer	...	.80	.25
1527	43¢-88¢ Historic Motor Vehicles, souvenir sheet of 6	...	8.00	5.75

1528

1533

1536

SCOTT NO.	DESCRIPTION	PLATE BLOCK F/NH	UNUSED F/NH	USED F
1528	43¢ 50th Anniversary of ICAO	3.60	.80	.25
1529-32	Dinosaurs, attached	3.60	3.00	2.25
1529	43¢ Coryphodon	...	.80	.25
1530	43¢ Megacerops	...	.80	.25
1531	43¢ Short-Faced Bear	...	.80	.25
1532	43¢ Woolly Mammoth	...	.80	.25
1533	43¢ Family Singing Carols	3.60	.80	.25
1533a	same, booklet pane of 10	...	7.75	...
1534	50¢ Choir	3.95	.90	.30
1534a	same, booklet pane of 5	...	4.50	...
1535	88¢ Caroling	6.75	1.50	.75
1535a	same, booklet pane of 5	...	7.50	...
1536	38¢ Caroling Soloist, booklet single	...	.85	.25
1536a	same, booklet pane of 10	...	8.50	...
1537-40	World War II—1944, attached	3.60	3.00	2.25
1537	43¢ D-Day Beachhead	...	.80	.25
1538	43¢ Artillery—Normandy	...	.80	.25
1539	43¢ Tactical Air Forces	...	.80	.25
1540	43¢ Walcheren and Scheldt	...	.80	.25

1995 COMMEMORATIVES

SCOTT NO.	DESCRIPTION	PLATE BLOCK F/NH	UNUSED F/NH	USED F
1541-51, 1553-58, 1562-67, 1570-90, 47 varieties		51.50	33.85	10.40
1541-44	World War II—1945, attached	3.60	3.00	2.25
1541	43¢ Veterans Return Home	....	.80	.25
1542	43¢ Freeing the POW	....	.80	.25
1543	43¢ Libertation of Civilians	....	.80	.25
1544	43¢ Crossing the Rhine	....	.80	.25
1545	88¢ Canadian Art "Floraison"	6.75	1.50	.75
1546	(43¢) Canada Flag over Lake	3.60	.85	.25
1547	(43¢) Louisbourg Harbor, ships near Dauphin Gate	....	.85	.25
1548	(43¢) Walls, streets & buildings of Louisbourg	....	.85	.25
1549	(43¢) Museum behind King's Bastion	....	.85	.25
1550	(43¢) Drawing of King's Garden, Convent, Hospital & barracks	....	.85	.25
1551	(43¢) Partially eroded fortifications	....	.85	.25
1551a	(43¢) Fortress of Louisbourg, strip of 5	....	4.00	3.00
1551b	(43¢) Fortress of Louisbourg, booklet pane of 10	....	8.00	5.00
1552	43¢-88¢ Historic Land Vehicles/Farm and Frontier souvenir sheet of 6	....	6.00	5.75
1553	43¢ Banff Springs Golf Club	....	.85	.25
1554	43¢ Riverside Country Club	....	.85	.25
1555	43¢ Glen Abbey Golf Club	....	.85	.25
1556	43¢ Victoria Golf Club	....	.85	.25
1557	43¢ Royal Montreal Golf Club	....	.85	.25
1557a	43¢ Royal Canadian Golf Assoc., strip of 5	....	4.00	3.00
1557b	43¢ Royal Canadian Golf Assoc., booklet pane of 10	....	8.00	5.00
1558	43¢ Lunenberg Academy Centennial	3.60	.80	.25
1559-61	43¢ Group of Seven 75th Anniv. 3 souv. sheets (2 w/3 stamps and 1 w/4 stamps)	....	8.00	7.50
1562	43¢ Winnipeg, Manitoba 125th Anniversary	3.60	.80	.25
1563-66	Migratory Wildlife, attached	3.60	3.00	2.25
1563, 65-67	Migratory Wildlife, attached (revised inscription)	3.60	3.00	2.25
1563	45¢ Monarch Butterfly	....	.80	.25
1564	45¢ Belted Kingfisher	....	.80	.25
1565	45¢ Northern Pintail	....	.80	.25
1566	45¢ Hoary Bat	....	.80	.25
1568-69	45¢ Canadian Memorial College, Toronto, Greetings Booklet (10 stamps w/15 stickers)	....	10.00	....
1570-73	45¢ Canadian Bridges, attached	3.60	3.00	2.25
1570	45¢ Quebec Bridge, Quebec	....	.80	.25
1571	45¢ Highway 403-401-410 interchange, Ontario	....	.80	.25
1572	45¢ Hartland Covered Wooden Bridge, New Brunswick	....	.80	.25
1573	45¢ Alex Fraser Bridger, British Columbia	....	.80	.25

1546

1547

1553

1558

1559a

1562

1563

1570

1574

SCOTT NO.	DESCRIPTION	PLATE BLOCK F/NH	UNUSED F/NH	USED F
1574	45¢ Polar bear, caribou	....	.80	.40
1575	45¢ Arctic poppy, cargo canoe	....	.80	.40
1576	45¢ Inuk man, igloo, sled dogs	....	.80	.40
1577	45¢ Dog-sled team, ski plane	....	.80	.40
1578	45¢ Children	....	.80	.40
1578a	45¢ Canadian Arctic, strip of 5	....	4.00	3.00
1578b	45¢ Canadian Arctic, booklet pane of 10	....	8.00	5.00
1579	45¢ Superman	....	.80	.40
1580	45¢ Johnny Canuck	....	.80	.40
1581	45¢ Nelvana	....	.80	.40
1582	45¢ Captain Canuck	....	.80	.40
1583	45¢ Fleur de Lys	....	.80	.40
1583a	45¢ Comic Book Characters, strip of 5	....	4.00	3.00
1583b	45¢ Comic Book Characters, booklet pane of 10	....	8.00	5.00
1584	45¢ United Nations, 50th Anniversary	3.60	.80	.40
1585	45¢ The Nativity	3.60	.80	.40
1585a	same, booklet pane of 10	....	8.00	....
1586	52¢ The Annunciation	4.10	.95	.50
1586a	same, booklet pane of 5	....	4.75	....
1587	90¢ Flight to Egypt	6.95	1.70	.70
1587a	same, booklet pane of 5	....	7.75	....
1588	40¢ Holly, booklet single	....	.80	.70
1588a	same, booklet pane of 10	....	7.50	....
1589	45¢ La Francophonie's Agency, 25th Anniversary	3.60	.80	.25
1590	45¢ End of the Holocaust, 50th Anniversary	3.60	.80	.25

1579

1585

1584

1588

1589

1590

1591

1595

1600

1602

SCOTT NO.	DESCRIPTION	PLATE BLOCK F/NH	UNUSED F/NH	USED F
	1996 COMMEMORATIVES			
1591-98, 1602-03, 1606-14, 1617-21, 1622-29, 36 varieties		**41.25**	**32.10**	**13.25**
1591-94	Birds, attached	3.60	3.00	2.00
1591	45¢ American Kestrel	....	.85	.35
1592	45¢ Atlantic Puffin	....	.85	.35
1593	45¢ Pileated Woodpecker	....	.85	.35
1594	45¢ Ruby-throated Hummingbird	....	.85	.35
1595-98	High Technology Industries, attached	3.60	4.00	3.00
1595	45¢ Ocean technology	....	1.10	.45
1596	45¢ Aerospace technology	....	1.10	.45
1597	45¢ Information technology	....	1.10	.45
1598	45¢ Biotechnology	....	1.10	.45
1600-01	45¢ Special Occasions, Greetings Booklet (10 stamps w/35 stickers)	....	10.00	....
1602	90¢ Canadian Art—"The Spirit of Haida Gwaii"	6.95	1.55	.50
1603	45¢ AIDS Awareness	3.60	.80	.25
1604	45¢-90¢ Historic Canadian Industrial & Commercial Vehicles souvenir sheet of 6	....	6.50	5.00
1605	5¢-45¢ CAPEX '96 souvenir pane of 25 vehicle stamps	....	8.00	5.00
1606	45¢ Yukon Gold Rush centennial, strip of 5	....	6.00	5.00
1606a	45¢ Jim Mason's discovery on Rabbit Creek, 1896	....	1.10	.45
1606b	45¢ Miners trekking to gold fields, boats on Lake Laberge	....	1.10	.45
1606c	45¢ Supr. Sam Steele, North West Mounted Police	....	1.10	.45
1606d	45¢ Dawson, boom town, city of entertainment	....	1.10	.45
1606e	45¢ Klondike gold fields	....	1.10	.45
1607	45¢ Canada Day (Maple Leaf), self-adhesive	....	.80	.25
1607a	same, pane of 12	....	12.00	....
1608	45¢ Ethel Catherwood, high jump, 1928	....	1.10	.45
1609	45¢ Etienne Desmarteau, 56 lb. weight throw, 1904	....	1.10	.45
1610	45¢ Fanny Rosenfeld, 100m, 400m relay, 1928	....	1.10	.45
1611	45¢ Gerald Ouellette, smallbore, fifle, prone, 1956	....	1.10	.45
1612	45¢ Percy Williams, 100m, 200m, 1928	....	1.10	.45
1612a	45¢ Canadian Gold Medalists, strip of 5	....	4.00	3.00
1612b	45¢ Canadian Gold Medalists, booklet pane of 10	....	10.00	....
1613	45¢ 125th Anniv. of British Columbia's Entry into Confederation	3.60	.80	.25
1614	45¢ Canadian Heraldy	3.60	.80	.25
1615	45¢ Motion Pictures Centennial, self-adhesive, sheet of 5	....	3.75	2.75
1615a	45¢ L'arrivee d'un train en gate, Lumiere cinematography, 1896	....	.80	.50
1615b	45¢ Back to God's Country, Nell & Ernest Shipman, 1919	....	.80	.50
1615c	45¢ Hen Hop, Norman McLaren, 1942	....	.80	.50
1615d	45¢ Pour la suite du monde, Pierre Perrault, Michel Brault, 1963	....	.80	.50
1615e	45¢ Goin' Down the Road, Don Shebib, 1970	....	.80	.50

1603

1604a

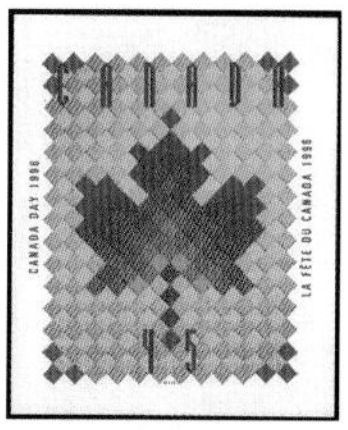

1607

1606a

1608

1613

1614

1615a

1617

1618

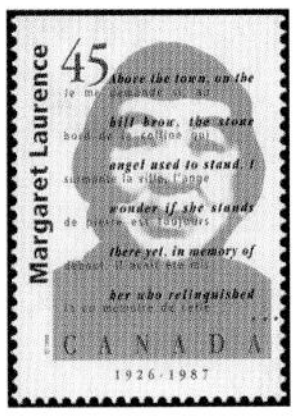

1622

1627

SCOTT NO.	DESCRIPTION	PLATE BLOCK F/NH	UNUSED F/NH	USED F
1616	45¢ Motion Pictures Centennial, . self-adhesive, sheet of 5	....	3.75	2.00
1616a	45¢ Mon oncle Antoine, Claude Jutra, 1971	....	.80	.25
1616b	45¢ The Apprenticeship of Duddy Kravitz, Ted Kotcheff, 1974	....	.80	.25
1616c	45¢ Les Ordres, Michel Brault, 1974	....	.80	.25
1616d	45¢ Les Bons Débarras, Francis Mankiewicz, 1980	....	.80	.25
1616e	45¢ The Grey Fox, Phillip Borsos, 1982	....	.80	.25
1617	45¢ Edouard Montpetit, Educator	3.60	.80	.25
1618-21	Winnie the Pooh, attached	3.60	2.70	1.50
1618	45¢ Winnie, Lt. Colebourne, 1914		.80	.25
1619	45¢ Winnie, Christopher Robin, 1925	....	.80	.25
1620	45¢ Milne and Shepard's Winnie the Pooh, 1926	....	.80	.25
1621	45¢ Winnie the Pooh at Walt Disney World, 1996	....	.80	.25
1621b	same, souvenir sheet of 4 (#1618-21)	....	3.00	2.50
....	same, booklet pane of 8 (2 blocks, #1618-21)	....	5.50	4.50
......	same, 2 booklet panes plus souvenir book	....	10.75	....
1622	45¢ Margaret Laurence (1926-1987)	....	.80	.25
1623	45¢ Donald G. Creighton (1902-1979)	....	.80	.25
1624	45¢ Gabrielle Roy (1909-1983)	....	.80	.25
1625	45¢ Felix-Antoine Savard (1896-1982)	....	.80	.25
1626	45¢ Thomas C. Halliburton (1796-1865)	....	.80	.25
1626a	45¢ Canadian Authors, strip of 5	....	3.75	2.00
1626b	45¢ Canadian Authors, booklet pane of 10	....	7.50	4.00
1627	45¢ Children on snowshoes, sled	3.60	.80	.25
1627a	same, booklet pane of 10	....	7.50	....
1628	52¢ Santa Claus skiing	4.10	.95	.30
1628a	same, booklet pane of 5	....	4.75	....
1629	90¢ Children skating	6.95	1.55	.50
1629a	same, booklet pane of 5	....	7.75	....

1630

1631

1635

1636

1637

1638

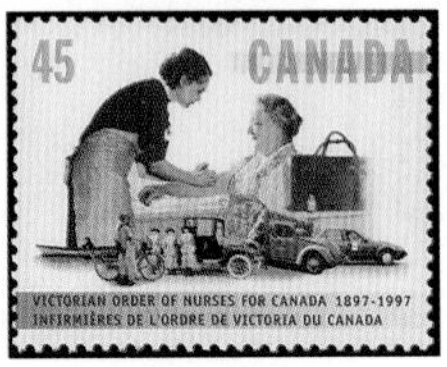

1639

1640

1641

1659

1661

1665

1645

1647

1650

1997 COMMEMORATIVES

SCOTT NO.	DESCRIPTION	PLATE BLOCK F/NH	UNUSED F/NH	USED F
1630, 1631-48, 1649-72, 43 varieties		**90.00**	**34.00**	**11.50**
1630	45¢ New Year 1997 (Year of the Ox)	....	1.10	.60
1630a	same, souvenir sheet of 2	....	2.25	2.10
......	same, souvenir sheet of 2, with Hong Kong '97 overprint	....	6.00	....
1631-34	Birds of Canada, attached	3.75	2.70	1.50
1631	45¢ Mountain bluebird	....	.80	.25
1632	45¢ Western grebe	....	.80	.25
1633	45¢ Northern gannet	....	.80	.25
1634	45¢ Scarlet tanager	....	.80	.25
1635	90¢ Canadian Art "York Boat on Lake Winnipeg"	6.95	1.55	.50
1636	45¢ Canadian Tire, 75th Anniv.	3.75	.80	.25
1637	45¢ Father Charles-Emile Gadbois (1906-1981)	3.75	.80	.25
1638	45¢ Blue poppy	....	.80	.25
1638a	same, booklet pane of 12	....	9.50	....
1639	45¢ Victorian Order of Nurses	3.75	.80	.25
1640	45¢ Law Society of Upper Canada	3.75	.80	.25
1641-44	45¢ Ocean Fish, attached	3.75	3.00	1.75
1641	45¢ Great White Shark		.80	.25
1642	45¢ Pacific Halibut		.80	.25
1643	45¢ Atlantic Sturgeon		.80	.25
1644	45¢ Bluefin Tuna		.80	.25
1645-46	45¢ Confederation Bridge, attached	3.75	1.55	.90
1645	45¢ Lighthouse and Bridge	....	.80	.25
1646	45¢ Bridge and Bird	....	.80	.25
1647	45¢ Gilles Villeneuve, Formula 1 driver	3.75	.80	.25
1648	90¢ Gilles Villeneuve, Formula 1 d iver	7.25	1.60	.80
1648b	45¢-90¢ Gilles Villeneuve, souvenir sheet of 8	....	8.50	....
1649	45¢ John Cabot	3.75	.80	.25
1650-53	45¢ Canada's scenic highways (Canada Day), attached	3.75	3.00	1.75
1650	45¢ Sea to Sky Highway, British Columbia	....	.80	.25
1651	45¢ The Cabot Trail, Nova Scotia	....	.80	.25
1652	45¢ The Wine Route, starting in Ontario	....	.80	.25
1653	45¢ The Big Muddy, Saskatchewan	....	.80	.25
1654	45¢ Industrial Design	3.75	.80	.25
1654v	same, sheet of 24 w/12 different Labels	....	18.75	....
1655	45¢ Highland Games	3.75	.80	.25
1656	45¢ Knights of Columbus in Canada	3.75	.80	.25
1657	45¢ World Congress of the PTT	3.75	.80	.25
1658	45¢ Canada's Year of Asia Pacific	3.60	.80	.25
1659-60	45¢ Ice Hockey "Series of the Century", bklt singles	....	1.60	.70
1660a	same, bklt pane of 10 (5 of each)	....	8.00	....
1661-64	Famous Politicians, attached	3.75	3.00	1.75
1661	45¢ Martha Black	....	.80	.25
1662	45¢ Lionel Chevrier	....	.80	.25
1663	45¢ Judy LaMarsh	....	.80	.25
1664	45¢ Real Caouette	....	.80	.25
1665-68	Supernatural, 4 attached	3.75	3.00	1.75
1665	45¢ Vampire	....	.80	.25
1666	45¢ Werewolf	....	.80	.25
1667	45¢ Ghost	....	.80	.25
1668	45¢ Goblin	....	.80	.25
1669	45¢ Christmas, Stained Glass Window	3.60	.80	.25
1669a	same, bklt pane of 10	....	7.50	....
1670	52¢ Christmas, Stained Glass Window	4.10	.95	.30
1670a	same, bklt pane of 5	....	4.75	....
1671	90¢ Christmas, Stained Glass Window	6.95	1.55	.50
1671a	same, bklt pane of 5	....	7.75	....
1672	45¢ 75th Royal Agriculture Winter Fair, Toronto	3.60	.80	.25

1997-2000 Regular Issues

SCOTT NO.	DESCRIPTION	PLATE BLOCK F/NH	UNUSED F/NH	USED F
1673	1¢ Bookbinding	.80	.20	.15
1674	2¢ Ironwork	.80	.20	.15
1675	3¢ Glass blowing	.80	.20	.15
1676	4¢ Oyster farmer	.80	.20	.15
1677	5¢ Weaving	.80	.20	.15
1678	9¢ Quilting	1.00	.25	.15
1679	10¢ Artistic woodworking	1.10	.25	.15
1680	25¢ Leatherworking	2.00	.50	.15
1682	46¢ Queen Elizabeth II	3.75	.80	.25
1683	47¢ Queen Elizabeth II(2000)	3.75	.85	.25
1687	46¢ Flag over Mountains	3.75	.80	.25
1687a	same, bklt pane of 10	....	8.00	....
1692	55¢ Maple Leaf	4.75	1.10	.35
1692a	same, bklt pane of 5		5.50	....
1694	73¢ Maple Leaf	5.00	1.20	.35
1696	95¢ Maple Leaf	6.25	1.50	.50
1696a	same, bklt pane of 5	....	7.50	....
1697	$1 Loon	7.50	1.50	1.00
1698	$2 Polar Bear	14.50	3.25	2.50
1700	$8 Grizzly Bear	65.00	14.00	6.50
1703	46¢ Flag, coil	....	.80	.25
1705	46¢ Flag over Mountains, self-adhesive	....	.80	.25
1705a	same, bklt pane of 30	....	24.00	....
1706	46¢ Maple Leaf, self-adhesive	....	.80	.25
1706a	same, bklt pane of 18	....	14.50	....
1707	47¢ Flag and Inukshuk, self-adhesive	....	.85	.25
1707a	same, bklt pane of 10	....	8.25	....
1707b	same, bklt pane of 30	....	24.00	....

1708

1709a

1710

1714

1715

1721

1722

1723

1725

1735

1736

1998 COMMEMORATIVES

SCOTT NO.	DESCRIPTION	PLATE BLOCK F/NH	UNUSED F/NH	USED F
1708	45¢ Year of the Tiger	3.60	.80	.25
1708a	same, souvenir sheet of 2	....	1.65	1.30
1709	45¢ Provincial Leaders. sheetlet of 10	....	8.50	7.00
1710-13	Birds, attached	3.75	3.00	1.75
1710	45¢ Hairy Woodpecker	....	.80	.25
1711	45¢ Great Crested Flycatcher	....	.80	.25
1712	45¢ Eastern Screech Owl	....	.80	.25
1713	45¢ Gray Crowned Rosy-Finch	....	.80	.25
1714	45¢ Maple Leaf, self-adhesive, bklt single	....	1.50	.95
1714a	same, bklt pane of 18	....	25.00	....
1714B	45¢ Maple Leaf, self-adhesive, die cut perf. 13	....	.80	.25
1715-20	Fly Fishing, strip of 6, from bklt pane	....	4.75	4.00
1715	45¢ Coquihalla orange, steelhead trout	....	.80	.25
1716	45¢ Steelhead bee, steelhead trout	....	.80	.25
1717	45¢ Dark Montreal, brook trout	....	.80	.25
1718	45¢ Lady Amherst, Atlantic salmon	....	.80	.25
1719	45¢ Coho blue, coho salmon	....	.80	.25
1720	45¢ Cosseboom special, Atlantic salmon	....	.80	.25
1720a	same, bklt pane of 12	....	9.25	....
1721	45¢ Canadian Inst. of Mining Centennial	3.60	.80	.25
1722	45¢ Imperial Penny Post Centennial	3.60	.80	.25
1723-24	Sumo Wrestling Tournament, attached	3.60	1.60	1.50
1723	45¢ Rising sun, Mapleleaf and two wrestlers	....	.80	.25
1724	45¢ Rising sun, Mapleleaf and Sumo champion	....	.80	.25
1724b	45¢ Sumo Wrestling Tournament, souvenir sheet of 2	....	1.75	1.60
1725	45¢ St. Peters Canal, Nova Scotia	....	.80	.60
1726	45¢ St. Ours Canal, Quebec	....	.80	.60
1727	45¢ Port Carling Lock, Ontario	....	.80	.60
1728	45¢ Locks, Rideau Canal, Onrtario	....	.80	.60
1729	45¢ Peterborough lift lock, Trent-Severn Waterway, Ontario		.80	.60
1730	45¢ Chambly Canal, Quebec	....	.80	.60
1731	45¢ Lachine Canal, Quebec	....	.80	.60
1732	45¢ Ice skating on Rideau Canal, Ottawa	....	.80	.60
1733	45¢ Boat on Big Chute Marine Railway, Trent-Severn Waterway	....	.80	.60
1734	45¢ Sault Ste. Marie Canal, Ontario	....	.80	.60
1734a	45¢ Canals of Canada, bklt pane of 10 plus labels	....	8.00	....
1735	45¢ Health Professionals	3.60	.80	.25
1736-37	Royal Canadian Mounted Police 125th Anniv. attd.	3.60	1.60	1.50
1736	45¢ Male mountie, native horse	....	.80	.25
1737	45¢ Female mountie, helicopter, cityscape	....	.80	.25
1737b	same, souvenir sheet of 2	....	3.00	2.75
1737c	same, souvenir sheet of 2 with signature	....	4.00	3.50
1737d	same, souvvenir sheet of 2 with Portugal '98 emblem	....	4.00	3.50
1737e	same, souvenir sheet of 2 with Italia '98 emblem	....	4.00	3.50
1738	45¢ William Roue, designer of Bluenose	3.60	.80	.25

1739

1750

1756

1761

1764

SCOTT NO.	DESCRIPTION	PLATE BLOCK F/NH	UNUSED F/NH	USED F
1739-42	Scenic Highways, 4 attached	3.60	3.00	1.75
1739	45¢ Dempster Highway, Yukon	....	.80	.25
1740	45¢ Dinosaur Trail, Alberta	....	.80	.25
1741	45¢ River Valley, Scenic Drive, New Burnswick	....	.80	.25
1742	45¢ Blue Heron Route, Prince Edward Isalnd	....	.80	.25
1743	45¢ "Peinture", Jean-Paul Riopelle, self-adhesive	....	.80	.25
1744	45¢ "La demiere campagne de Napolean", Fernand Leduc, self-adhesive	....	.80	.25
1745	45¢ "Jet fuligineux sur noir torture", Jean -Paul Monusseau, self-adhesive	....	.80	.25
1746	45¢ "Le fond du garde-robe", Pierre Gauvreau, self-adhesive	....	.80	.25
1747	45¢ "Jean lacustre", Paul-Emile Borduas, self-adhesive	....	.80	.25
1748	45¢ "Syndicat des gens de met", Marcelle Ferron, self-adhesive	....	.80	.25
1749	45¢ "Le tumulte a la machoire crispee", Marcel Barbeau, self-adhesive	....	.80	.25
1749a	45¢ The Automatists, 50th Anniversary, self-adhesive, bklt pane of 7	....	5.75	....
1750-53	Canadian Legendary Heroes, 4 attached	3.60	3.00	1.75
1750	45¢ Napoleon-Alexandre Comeau (1848-1923) outdoorsman	....	.80	.25
1751	45¢ Phyllis Munday (1894-1990), mountaineer	....	.80	.25
1752	45¢ Bill Mason (1929-1988), film maker	....	.80	.25
1753	45¢ Harry "Red" Foster (1905-1985), sports enthusiast	....	.80	.25
1754	90¢ Canadian Art "The Farmer's Family"	6.95	1.55	.50
1755	45¢ Housing in Canada, sheetlet of 9	....	7.50	6.00
1756	45¢ University of Ottawa, 150th Anniversary	3.60	.80	.25
1757	45¢ Elephant, bear performing tricks	....	.80	.25
1758	45¢ Women standing on horse, aerial act	....	.80	.25
1759	45¢ Lion tamer	....	.80	.25
1760	45¢ Contortionists, acrobats	....	.80	.25
1760a	45¢ The Circus, bklt pane of 12	....	9.75	....
1760b	same, souvenir sheet of 4	....	3.00	2.50
1761	45¢ John Peters Humphrey, Human Rights author	3.60	.80	.25
1762-63	Canadian Naval Reserve, 75th Anniversary, attached	3.75	1.55	.90
1762	45¢ HMCS Sackville	....	.80	.25
1763	45¢ HMCS Shawinigan	....	.80	.25
1764	45¢ Christmas, Sculpted wooden angels	3.60	.80	.25
1764a	same, bklt pane of 10	....	7.50	....
1765	52¢ Christmas, Sculpted wooden angels	4.10	.95	.30
1765a	same, bklt pane of 5	....	4.75	....
1766	90¢ Christmas, Sculpted wooden angels	6.95	1.55	.50
1766a	same, bklt pane of 5	....	7.75	....

1767

1770

1999 COMMEMORATIVES

SCOTT NO.	DESCRIPTION	PLATE BLOCK F/NH	UNUSED F/NH	USED F
1767	46¢ New Year 1999, Year of the Rabbit	3.60	.80	.40
1768	same, souvenir sheet of 2	....	1.75	1.25
1769	46¢ Le Theatre du Rideau Vert, 50th Anniversary	3.60	.80	.40
1770-73	Birds, 4 attached	3.60	3.00	1.75
1770	46¢ Northern goshawk	....	.80	.40
1771	46¢ Red-winged blackbird	....	.80	.40
1772	46¢ American goldfinch	....	.80	.40
1773	46¢ Sandhill crane	....	.80	.40
1774	46¢ Northern goshawk, self-adhesive	....	.80	.40
1775	46¢ Red-winged blackbird, self-adhesive	....	.80	.40
1776	46¢ American goldfinch, self-adhesive	....	.80	.40
1777	46¢ Sandhill crane, self-adhesive	....	.80	.40
1777a	same, bklt pane of 6 (1774 x 2, 1775 x 2, 1776 x 2, 1777x 1), self-adhesive	....	4.90	....
1777b	same, bklt pane of 6 (1774 x 1, 1775 x 1, 1776 x 2, 1777 x 2), self-adhesive	....	4.90	....

1778

1779

1999 COMMEMORATIVES (continued)

SCOTT NO.	DESCRIPTION	PLATE BLOCK F/NH	UNUSED F/NH	USED F
1778	46¢ Univ. of British Columbia Museum of Anthropology. 50th Anniversary	3.60	.80	.25
1779	46¢ Sailing Ship Marco Polo	3.60	.80	.25
1779a	same, souvenir sheet of 2 (1779 x 1, Australia 1631 x 1)	....	2.25	....
1780-83	Canada's Scenic Highways, 4 attached	3.60	3.00	1.75
1780	46¢ Gaspe Peninsula, Highway 132, Quebec	....	.80	.25
1781	46¢ Yellowghead Highway (PTH 16), Manitoba	....	.80	.25
1782	46¢ Dempster Highway 8, Northwest Territories	....	.80	.25
1783	46¢ Discovery Trail, Route 230N, Newfoundland	....	.80	.25
1784	46¢ Creation of the Nunavnt Territory	3.60	.80	.25
1785	46¢ International Year of Older Persons	3.60	.80	.25
1786	46¢ Baisakhi, Religious Holiday of Sikh Canadians, 300 th Anniversary	3.60	.80	.25
1787	46¢ Canadian orchid, Arethusa bulbosa, self-adhesive	....	.80	.25
1788	46¢ Canadian orchid, Amerorchis rotundifolia, self-adhesive	....	.80	.25
1789	46¢ Canadian orchid, Platanthera psycodes, self-adhesive	....	.80	.25
1790	46¢ Canadian orchid, Cypripedium pubescens, self-adhesive	....	.80	.25
1790a	same, bklt pane of 12 (1787-90 x 3)	....	9.50	....
1790b	same, souvenir sheet of 4 w/ China '99 emblem	....	4.00	3.50

1791

1799

SCOTT NO.	DESCRIPTION	PLATE BLOCK F/NH	UNUSED F/NH	USED F
1791-94	Horses, 4 attached	3.60	3.00	1.75
1791	46¢ Northern Dancer, thorough-bred race horse	....	.80	.25
1792	46¢ Kingsway Skoal, bucking horse	....	.80	.25
1793	46¢ Big Ben, show horse	....	.80	.25
1794	46¢ Ambro Flight, harness race horse	....	.80	.25
1795	46¢ Northern Dancer, thorough-bred race horse, self-adhesive	....	.80	.25
1796	46¢ Kingsway Skoal, bucking horse, self-adhesive	....	.80	.25
1797	46¢ Big Ben, show horse, self-adhesive	....	.80	.25
1798	46¢ Ambro Flight, harness race horse, self-adhesive	....	.80	.25
1789a	same, bklt of 12 (1795-98 x 3)	....	9.50	....
1799	46¢ Quebec Bar Association, 150th Anniversary	3.60	.80	.25

1800

1801

SCOTT NO.	DESCRIPTION	PLATE BLOCK F/NH	UNUSED F/NH	USED F
1800	95¢ Canadian Art "Unicorn Rooster"	7.25	2.00	1.20
1801-04	46¢ Pan-American Games XIII, 4 attached	3.60	3.00	2.00
1801	46¢ Track & Field	....	1.00	.40
1802	46¢ Cycling, weight lifting, gymnastics	....	1.00	.40
1803	46¢ Swimming, sailboarding, kayaking	....	1.00	.40
1804	46¢ Soccer, tennis, medals winners	....	1.00	.40

1805

1806

SCOTT NO.	DESCRIPTION	PLATE BLOCK F/NH	UNUSED F/NH	USED F
1805	46¢ World Rowing Championships	3.60	.80	.25
1806	46¢ Universal Postal Union	3.60	.80	.25

1807a

1808a

SCOTT NO.	DESCRIPTION	PLATE BLOCK F/NH	UNUSED F/NH	USED F
1807	46¢ Canadian Int. Air Show, 50th Anniv., sheetlet of 4	....	3.25	3.00
1807a	46¢ Fokker DR-1, CT-114 Tutors	....	.80	.50
1807b	46¢ Tutors, H101 Salto sailplane	....	.80	.50
1807c	46¢ De Havilland DH100 Vampire MKIII	....	.80	.50
1807d	46¢ Stearman A-75	....	.80	.50
1808	46¢ Royal Canadian Air Force, 75th Anniv, sheetlet of 6	....	12.75	11.00
1808a	46¢ De Havilland Mosquito FVBI	....	.80	.50
1808b	46¢ Sopwith F1 Camel	....	.80	.50
1808c	46¢ De Havilland Canada DHC-3 Otter	....	.80	.50
1808d	46¢ De Havilland Canada CC-108 Caribou	....	.80	.50
1808e	46¢ Canadair DL-28 Argus MK 2	....	.80	.50
1808f	46¢ North American F86 Sabre 6	....	.80	.50
1808g	46¢ McDonnell Douglas CF-18 Hornet	....	.80	.50
1808h	46¢ Sopwith SF-1 Dolphin	....	.80	.50
1808i	46¢ Armstrong Whitworth Siskin IIIA	....	.80	.50
1808j	46¢ Canadian Vickers (Northrop) Delta II	....	.80	.50
1808k	46¢ Sikorsky CH-124A Sea King Helicopter	....	.80	.50
1808l	46¢ Vickers-Armstrong Wellington MKII	....	.80	.50
1808m	46¢ Avro Anson MKI	....	.80	.50
1808n	46¢ Canadair (Lockheed) CF-104G Starfighter	....	.80	.50
1808o	46¢ Burgess-Dunne seaplane	....	.80	.50
1808p	46¢ Avro 504K	....	.80	.50

1809

1810

SCOTT NO.	DESCRIPTION	PLATE BLOCK F/NH	UNUSED F/NH	USED F
1809	46¢ NATO, 50th Anniversary	3.60	.80	.25
1810	46¢ Frontier College, 100th Anniversary	3.60	.80	.25

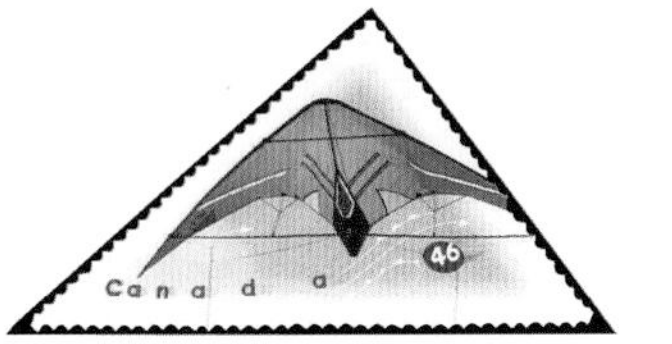

1811a

1813

SCOTT NO.	DESCRIPTION	PLATE BLOCK F/NH	UNUSED F/NH	USED F
1811	33¢ Kites, bklt pane of 8	....	6.50	....
1811a	33¢ Master Control, sport kite by Lam Hoac (triangular)	....	1.00	.40
1811b	33¢ Indian Garden Flying Carpet, edo kite by Skye Morrison (trapezoidal)	....	1.00	.40
1811c	33¢ Gibson Girl, Manufactured box kite (rectangular)	....	1.00	.40
1811d	33¢ Dragon centipede kite by Zhang tian Wei (oval)	....	1.00	.40
1812	Holographic Dove & 2000	....	1.00	.40
....	same, pane of 4	....	3.25	....
1813	55¢ Girl & Dove	....	.95	.70
....	same, pane of 4	....	3.80	....

1814

1815

SCOTT NO.	DESCRIPTION	PLATE BLOCK F/NH	UNUSED F/NH	USED F
1814	95¢ Millenium Dove	....	1.55	1.00
....	same, pane of 4	....	6.25	....
1815	46¢ Christmas, Angel, drum	3.60	.80	.25
1815a	same, bklt pane of 10	....	7.50	....
1816	55¢ Christmas, Angel, toys	4.10	.95	.50
1816a	same, bklt pane of	....	6.00	....
1817	95¢ Christmas, Angel, candle	6.95	1.75	.75
1817a	same, bklt pane of 5	....	8.00	....

1818a

1819a

1820a

SCOTT NO.	DESCRIPTION	PLATE BLOCK F/NH	UNUSED F/NH	USED F
1818	46¢ Millenium Collection-Media Tech. sheet of 4	....	5.00	....
1818a	46¢ IMAX Movies	....	1.00	.75
1818b	46¢ Softimage animation software	....	1.00	.75
1818c	46¢ Ted Rogers Sr. (1900-39) and radio tube	....	1.00	.75
1818d	46¢ Invention of radio facsimile device by Sir William Stephenson (1896-1989)	....	1.00	.75
1819	46¢ Millenium Collection-Canadian Entertainment, sheet of 4	....	5.00	....
1819a	46¢ Calgary Stampede	....	1.00	.75
1819b	46¢ Performers from Cirque du Soleil	....	1.00	.75
1819c	46¢ Hockey Night in Canada	....	1.00	.75
1819d	46¢ La Soiree du Hockey	....	1.00	.75
1820	46¢ Millenium Collection-Entertainers, sheet of 4	....	5.00	....
1820a	46¢ Portia White (1911-68), singer	....	1.00	.75
1820b	46¢ Glenn Gould (1932-82), pianist	....	1.00	.75
1820c	46¢ Guy Lombardo (1902-77), band leader	....	1.00	.75
1820d	46¢ Felix Leclerc (1914-88), singer, guitarist	....	1.00	.75

1821a

1822a

1823a

SCOTT NO.	DESCRIPTION	PLATE BLOCK F/NH	UNUSED F/NH	USED F
1821	46¢ Millenium Collection-Fostering Canadian Talent, sheet of 4	....	5.00	....
1821a	46¢ Royal Canadian Academy of Arts (men viewing painting)	....	1.00	.75
1821b	46¢ Canada Council (sky, musical staff, "A")	....	1.00	.75
1821c	46¢ National Film Board of Canada	....	1.00	.75
1821d	46¢ Canadian Broadcasting Corp.	....	1.00	.75
1822	46¢ Millenium Collection-Medical Innovators, sheet of 4	....	5.00	....
1822a	46¢ Sir Frederic Banting (1891-1941), co-discoverer of insulin, syringe and dog	....	1.00	.75
1822b	46¢ Dr. Armand Frappier (1904-91), microbiologist, holding flask	....	1.00	.75
1822c	46¢ Dr. Hans Selye (1907-82), endocrinologist and molecular diagram	....	1.00	.75
1822d	46¢ Maude Abbott (1869-1940), pathologist, and roses	......	1.00	.75
1823	46¢ Millenium Collection-Social Progress, sheet of 4	....	5.00	....
1823a	46¢ Nun, doctor, hospital	....	1.00	.75
1823b	46¢ Statue of women holding decree	....	1.00	.75
1823c	46¢ Alphonse Desjardins (1854-1920) and wife, credit union founders	....	1.00	.75
1823d	46¢ Father Moses Coady (1882-1959), educator of adults	....	1.00	.75

1824a

1825a

SCOTT NO.	DESCRIPTION	PLATE BLOCK F/NH	UNUSED F/NH	USED F
1824	46¢ Millenium Collection-Charity, sheet of 4	....	5.00	....
1824a	46¢ Canadian Inter. Development Agency (hand and tools)	....	1.00	.75
1824b	46¢ Dr. Lucille Teasdale (1929-96), hospital administrator in Uganda	....	1.00	.75
1824c	46¢ Marathon of Hope inspired by Terry Fox (1958-81)	....	1.00	.75
1824d	46¢ Meals on Wheels program	....	1.00	.75
1825	46¢ Millenium Collection-Humanitarians and Peacekeepers, sheet of 4	....	5.00	....
1825a	46¢ Raoul Dandurand (1861-1942)	....	1.00	.75
1825b	46¢ Pauline Vanier (1898-1991), Elizabeth Smellie (1884-1968) nurses	....	1.00	.75
1825c	46¢ Lester B. Pearson (1897-1972), prime minister and Nobel Peace Prize winner	....	1.00	.75
1825d	46¢ Amputee and shadow (Ottawa Convention on Land Mines)	....	1.00	.75

1826a

1827a

1828a

2000 COMMEMORATIVES

SCOTT NO.	DESCRIPTION	PLATE BLOCK F/NH	UNUSED F/NH	USED F
1826	46¢ Millenium Collection-Canada's First People, sheet of 4	....	5.00	....
1826a	46¢ Chief Pontiac (c.1720-69)	....	1.00	.75
1826b	46¢ Tom Longboat (1887-1949), marathon runner	....	1.00	.75
1826c	46¢ Inuit sculpture of shaman	....	1.00	.75
1826d	46¢ Medicine man	....	1.00	.75
1827	46¢ Millenium Collection-Canada's Cultural Fabric, sheet of 4	....	5.00	....
1827a	46¢ Norse boat, L'Anse aux Meadows	....	1.00	.75
1827b	46¢ Immigrants on Halifax Pier 21	....	1.00	.75
1827c	46¢ Neptune Theater, Halifax (head of Neptune)	....	1.00	.75
1827d	46¢ Stratford Festival (actor and theater)	....	1.00	.75
1828	46¢ Millenium Collection-Literary Legends, sheet of 4	....	5.00	....
1828a	46¢ W.O. Mitchell (1914-98), novelist, and prairie scene	....	1.00	.75
1828b	46¢ Gratien Gelinas (1909-99), actor and playwright, and stars	....	1.00	.75
1828c	46¢ Le Cercle du Livre de France book club	....	1.00	.75
1828d	46¢ Harlequin paperback books	....	1.00	.75

1829a

1830a

1831a

SCOTT NO.	DESCRIPTION	PLATE BLOCK F/NH	UNUSED F/NH	USED F
1829	46¢ Millenium Collection-Great Thinkers, sheet of 4	....	5.00	....
1829a	46¢ Marshall McLuhan (1911-80), philosopher, and television set	....	1.00	.75
1829b	46¢ Northrop Frye (1912-91), literary critic, and word "code"	....	1.00	.75
1829c	46¢ Roger Lemelin (1919-92), novelist, and cast of "The Plouffe Family" TV series	....	1.00	.75
1829d	46¢ Hilda Marion Neatby (1904-75), historian, and farm scene	....	1.00	.75
1830	46¢ Millenium Collection-A Tradition of Generosity, sheet of 4	....	5.00	....
1830a	46¢ Hart Massey (1823-96), Hart House, University of Toronto	....	1.00	.75
1830b	46¢ Dorothy (1899-1965) & Izaak Killam (1885-1955), philantropists	....	1.00	.75
1830c	46¢ Eric Lafferty Harvive (1892-1975), philantropist, and mountain scene	....	1.00	.75
1830d	46¢ Macdonald Stewart Foundation	....	1.00	.75
1831	46¢ Millenium Collection-Engineering and Tech. Marvels, sheet of 4	....	5.00	....
1831a	46¢ Map of Roger Pass, locomotive and tunnel diggers	....	1.00	.75
1831b	46¢ Manic Dams	....	1.00	.75
1831c	46¢ Canadian satellites, Remote Manipulator Arm	....	1.00	.75
1831d	46¢ CN Tower	....	1.00	.75

1832a

1833a

1834a

SCOTT NO.	DESCRIPTION	PLATE BLOCK F/NH	UNUSED F/NH	USED F
1832	46¢ Millenium Collection-Fathers of Invention, sheet of 4	....	5.00	....
1832a	46¢ George Klein (1904-92), gearwheels	....	1.00	.75
1832b	46¢ Abraham Gesner (1797-1864), beaker of kerosene and lamp	....	1.00	.75
1832c	46¢ Alexander Graham Bell (1847-1922), passenger-carrying kite, hydrofoil	....	1.00	.75
1832d	46¢ Joseph-Armand Bombardier (1907-64), snowmobile	....	1.00	.75
1833	46¢ Millenium Collection-Food, sheet of 4	....	5.00	....
1833a	46¢ Sir Charles Saunders (1867-1937), Marquis wheat	....	1.00	.75
1833b	46¢ Pablum	....	1.00	.75
1833c	46¢ Dr. Archibald Gowanlock Huntsman (1883-1973), marketer of frozen fish	....	1.00	.75
1833d	46¢ Products of McCain Foods, Ltd., tractor	....	1.00	.75
1834	46¢ Millenium Collection-Enterprising Giants, sheet of 4	....	5.00	....
1834a	46¢ Hudson's Bay Company (Colonist, Indian, canoe)	....	1.00	.75
1834b	46¢ Bell Canada Enterprises (earth ,satellite, string of binary digits)	....	1.00	.75
1834c	Vachon Co., snack cakes	....	1.00	.75
1834d	46¢ George Weston Limited (Baked Goods, eggs)	....	1.00	.75

1837a

1838a

SCOTT NO.	DESCRIPTION	PLATE BLOCK F/NH	UNUSED F/NH	USED F
1835	46¢ Millenium-2000	3.60	.80	.25
1836	46¢ New Year 2000, Year of the Dragon	3.60	.80	.25
1837	95¢ New Year 2000, Year of the Dragon, souvenir sheet of 1	....	1.75	1.60
1838	46¢ 50th National Hockey League All-Star, sheet 6	....	4.75	3.75
1838a	46¢ Wayne Gretsky (Oilers jersey No. 99)	....	.80	.25
1838b	46¢ Gordie Howe (Red Wings jersey No. 9)	....	.80	.25
1838c	46¢ Maurice Richard (red, white and blue Canadians jersey No. 9)	....	.80	.25
1838d	46¢ Doug Harvey (Canadians jersey No. 2)	....	.80	.25
1838e	46¢ Bobby Orr (Bruins jersey No. 4)	....	.80	.25
1838f	46¢ Jacques Plante (Canadians jersey No. 1)	....	.80	.25

1839

1847

SCOTT NO.	DESCRIPTION	PLATE BLOCK F/NH	UNUSED F/NH	USED F
1839-42	46¢ Birds, 4 attached	3.60	3.00	1.75
1839	46¢ Canada warbler	....	.80	.25
1840	46¢ Osprey	....	.80	.25
1841	46¢ Pacific Loon	....	.80	.25
1842	46¢ Blue Jay	....	.80	.25
1843	46¢ Canada warbler, self-adhesive	....	.80	.25
1844	46¢ Osprey, self-adhesive	....	.80	.25
1845	46¢ Pacific Loon, self-adhesive	....	.80	.25
1846	46¢ Blue Jay, self-adhesive	....	.80	.25
1846a	same, bklt pane of 6 (1843x2, 1844x2, 1845x1, 1846x1)	....	4.75	....
1846b	same, bklt pane of 6 (1843x1, 1844x1, 1845x2, 1846x2)	....	4.75	....
1847	46¢ Supreme Court, 125th Anniversary	3.60	.80	.25

1850

1854a

SCOTT NO.	DESCRIPTION	PLATE BLOCK F/NH	UNUSED F/NH	USED F
1848	46¢ Ritual of the Calling of an Engineer, 75 Anniv.	3.60	.80	.25
1848a	same, tete-beche pair	....	1.60	.50
1849	46¢ Decorated Rural Mailboxes, Ship, fish, house designs	......	.80	.25
1850	same, Flower, cow and church designs	....	.80	.25
1851	same, Tractor design	....	.80	.25
1852	same, Goose head, house designs	....	.80	.25
1852a	same, bklt pane of 12 (1849-52x3)	....	9.50	....
1853	46¢ Picture Frame, self-adhesive	....	.80	.25
1853a	same, bklt pane of 5 plus 5 labels	....	4.00	....
1853b	same, pane of 25	....	20.00	....
1854	55¢ Fresh Waters, bklt pane of 5, self-adhesive	....	4.75	....
1855	95¢ Fresh Waters, bklt pane of 5, self-adhesive	....	8.00	....

1856

1858

SCOTT NO.	DESCRIPTION	PLATE BLOCK F/NH	UNUSED F/NH	USED F
1856	46¢ Queen Mother's 100th Birthday	3.60	.80	.35
1857	46¢ Boys' and Girls' clubs, Centennial	3.60	.80	.35
1858	46¢ Seventh Day Adventists	3.60	.80	.35

1859

1866

SCOTT NO.	DESCRIPTION	PLATE BLOCK F/NH	UNUSED F/NH	USED F
1859-62	46¢ Stampin' the Future, 4 attached	3.60	3.00	1.75
1859	46¢ Rainbow, Spacevechile, astronauts, flag	....	.80	.35
1860	46¢ Children in space vechile, children on ground	....	.80	.35
1861	46¢ Children and map of Canada	....	.80	.35
1862	46¢ Two astronauts in space vechile, planets	....	.80	.35
1863	95¢ Canadian Artists, The Artist at Niagara	7.50	1.75	.50
1864-65	46¢ Tall Ships in Halifax Harbor, 2 attached	3.60	1.60	.95
1865a	same, bklt of 10 (1864-65 x 5)	....	8.25	....
1866	46¢ Department of Labor	3.60	.80	.35
1867	46¢ Petro-Canada, 25th anniversary	....	.80	.35
1867a	same, bklt pane of 12	....	9.50	....
1867b	same, die cut inverted (2 points at TL)	....	3.75	3.75

1868

1873

1876

1877

SCOTT NO.	DESCRIPTION	PLATE BLOCK F/NH	UNUSED F/NH	USED F
1868-71	46¢ Centaceans, 4 attached	3.60	3.00	2.75
1868	46¢ Monodon monoceros	....	.80	.35
1869	46¢ Balaenoptera musculus	....	.80	.35
1870	46¢ Balaena mysticetus	....	.80	.35
1871	46¢ Delphinapterus leucas	....	.80	.35
1872	46¢ Christmas frame	....	.80	.35
1872a	same, bklt pane of 5 + 5 labels	....	4.00	....
1873	46¢ Adoration of the shepherds	3.60	.80	.25
1873a	same, bklt pane of 10	....	7.50	....
1874	55¢ Creche	4.10	.95	.30
1874a	same, bklt pane of 6	....	5.60	....
1875	95¢ Flight into Egypt	6.95	1.55	.50
1875a	same, bklt pane of 6	....	9.25	....
1876-77	46¢ Regiments, 2 attached	3.60	1.60	.95
1876	46¢ Lord Stratchcona's Horse Regiment	....	.80	.35
1877	46¢ Les Voltigeurs de Quebec	....	.80	.35

1879

1880

1881

SCOTT NO.	DESCRIPTION	PLATE BLOCK F/NH	UNUSED F/NH	USED F
1878	47¢ Maple leaves, coil	....	1.00	.30
1879	60¢ Red fox, coil	....	1.50	.50
1879a	same, bklt pane of 6	....	9.00	....
1880	75¢ Gray wolf, coil	....	1.25	.50
1881	$1.05 White-tailed deer, coil	....	1.50	.50
1881a	same, bklt pane of 6	....	9.00	....
1882	47¢ Picture Frame, self-adhesive	....	.85	.25
1882a	same, bklt pane of 5 + 5 labels	....	4.25	....

1883

1885a

SCOTT NO.	DESCRIPTION	PLATE BLOCK F/NH	UNUSED F/NH	USED F
1883	47¢ Year of the Snake	3.75	.85	.30
1884	$1.05 Year of the Snake, souvenir sheet	....	2.00	2.00

1886, 1890

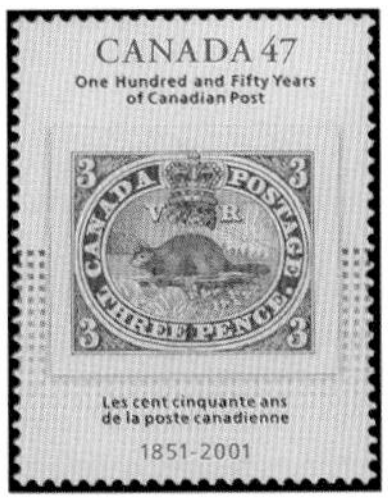

1900

2001 COMMEMORATIVES

SCOTT NO.	DESCRIPTION	PLATE BLOCK F/NH	UNUSED F/NH	USED F
1885	47¢ National Hockey League, sheet of 6 + 3 labels	....	5.00	4.00
1885a	47¢ Jean Beliveau (Canadiens jersey No. 4)	....	.85	....
1885b	47¢ Terry Sawchuk (goalie in Red Wings uniform)	....	.85	....
1885c	47¢ Eddie Shore (Bruins jersey No.2)	....	.85	....
1885d	47¢ Denis Potvin (Islanders jersey No. 5)	....	.85	....
1885e	47¢ Bobby Bull (Black Hawks jersey No.9)	....	.85	....
1885f	47¢ Syl Apps, Sr. (Toronto Maple leafs jersey)	....	.85	....
1886-89	47¢ Birds, 4 attached	3.75	3.25	3.00
1886	47¢ Golden Eagle	....	.85	.30
1887	47¢ Arctic tern	....	.85	.30
1888	47¢ Rock ptarmigan	....	.85	.30
1889	47¢ Lapland longspur	....	.85	.30
1890	47¢ Golden Eagle, self-adhesive	....	.85	.30
1891	47¢ Artic tern, self-adhesive	....	.85	.30
1892	47¢ Rock ptarmigan, self-adhesive	....	.85	.30
1893	47¢ Lapland longspur, self-adhesive	....	.85	.30
1893a	same, bklt pane of 6 (1890 x 2, 1891 x 2, 1892 x 1, 1893 x 1)	....	5.00	....
1893b	same, bklt pane of 6 (1892 x 2, 1893 x 2, 1890 x 1, 1891 x 1)	....	5.00	....

1901

1903a

SCOTT NO.	DESCRIPTION	PLATE BLOCK F/NH	UNUSED F/NH	USED F
1894-95	47¢ Games of La Francophonie, 2 attached	3.75	2.00	1.50
1894	47¢ High jumper	....	1.00	.35
1895	47¢ Dancer	....	1.00	.35
1896-99	47¢ World Figure Skating, 4 attached	3.75	3.25	3.00
1896	47¢ Pairs	....	1.00	.40
1897	47¢ Ice dancing	....	1.00	.40
1898	47¢ Men's singles	....	1.00	.40
1899	47¢ Women's singles	....	1.00	.40
1900	47¢ First Canadian postage stamp	3.75	1.00	.40
1901	47¢ Toronto Blue Jays Baseball Team, 25th anniv.	....	1.00	.40
1901a	same, bklt pane of 8	....	6.75	....
1902	47¢ Summit of the Americans, Quebec	3.75	.85	.40
1903	60¢ Tourist Attractions, bklt pane of 5, self-adhesive	....	6.00	....
1904	$1.05 Tourist Attraction, bklt pane of 5, self-adhesive	....	9.00	....

1905

1906

SCOTT NO.	DESCRIPTION	PLATE BLOCK F/NH	UNUSED F/NH	USED F
1905	47¢ Armemian Apostolic Church	3.75	.85	.30
1906	47¢ Royal Military College	3.75	.85	.30

1909

1911

SCOTT NO.	DESCRIPTION	PLATE BLOCK F/NH	UNUSED F/NH	USED F
1907-08	47¢ Intl. Amateur Athletic Federation World Championship, 2 attached	3.75	1.65	1.00
1907	47¢ Pole Vault	....	.85	.25
1908	47¢ Runner	....	.85	.25
1909	47¢ Pierre Elliot Trudeau	3.75	.85	.25
1909a	same, souvenir sheet of 4	....	3.25	....
1910	47¢ Canadian Roses, souvenir sheet of 4	....	3.25	3.00
1911	47¢ Morden Centennial Rose	....	1.00	.40
1912	47¢ Agnes Rose	....	1.00	.40
1913	47¢ Champion Rose	....	1.00	.40
1914	47¢ Canadian White Star Rose	....	1.00	.40
1914a	same, bklt pane of 4 (1911-14)	....	3.25	....
....	same, complete booklet (1914a x 3)	....	9.50	....

1915

1917

1919-20

SCOTT NO.	DESCRIPTION	PLATE BLOCK F/NH	UNUSED F/NH	USED F
1915	47¢ Great Peace of Montreal	3.75	.85	.25
1916	$1.05 Canadian Artists, "The Space Between Columns"	8.50	1.95	.75
1917	47¢ Shriners	3.75	.85	.25
1918	47¢ Picture Frame, bklt pane of 5 + 5 labels	....	4.25	....
1919-20	47¢ Theater Anniversaries, 2 attached	3.75	1.65	1.00
1919	47¢ Theatre du Nouveau Monde	....	.85	.25
1920	47¢ Grand Theater	....	.85	.25

1921a

1922

SCOTT NO.	DESCRIPTION	PLATE BLOCK F/NH	UNUSED F/NH	USED F
1921	47¢ Hot Air Balloons, self-adhesive, bklt of 8	....	6.75	....
1922	47¢ Horse-drawn sleigh	3.75	.85	.25
1922a	same, bklt pane of 10	....	8.25	....
1923	60¢ Skaters	5.25	1.20	.50
1923a	same, bklt pane of 6	....	7.00	....
1924	$1.05 Children making snowman	8.50	1.95	1.00
1924a	same, bklt pane of 6	....	11.50	....

1927

1931

1928

1929

1930

2002 COMMEMORATIVES

SCOTT NO.	DESCRIPTION	PLATE BLOCK F/NH	UNUSED F/NH	USED F
1927	48¢ Maple Leaves, self-adhesive coil	....	.85	.30
1928	65¢ Jewelry making, coil	....	1.25	.60
1928a	same, bklt pane of 6	....	7.25	....
1929	77¢ Basket weaving, coil	....	1.40	.75
1930	$1.25 Sculpture, coil	....	2.00	.95
1930a	same, bklt pane of 6	....	11.50	....
1931	48¢ Flag & Canada Post Headquarters	....	.85	.30
1931a	same, bklt pane of 10	....	8.25	....
1931b	same, bklt pane of 30	....	24.00	....

1932

1933

1935a

SCOTT NO.	DESCRIPTION	PLATE BLOCK F/NH	UNUSED F/NH	USED F
1932	48¢ Regin of Queen Elizabeth, 50th Anniv.	3.75	.85	.30
1933	48¢ Year of the Horse	3.75	.85	.30
1934	$1.25 Year of the Horse, souvenir sheet	....	2.00	2.00
1935	48¢ National Hockey League Stars, sheet of 6 + 3 labels	....	5.00	4.00
1935a	48¢ Tim Horton	....	.85	.40
1935b	48¢ Guy Lafleur	....	.85	.40
1935c	48¢ Howie Morenz	....	.85	.40
1935d	48¢ Glenn Hall	....	.85	.40
1935e	48¢ Red Kelly	....	.85	.40
1935f	48¢ Phil Esposito	....	.85	.40

1936

1940

SCOTT NO.	DESCRIPTION	PLATE BLOCK F/NH	UNUSED F/NH	USED F
1936-39	48¢ 2002 Winter Olympics, 4 attached	3.75	3.25	3.00
1936	48¢ Short track speed skating	....	.85	.30
1937	48¢ Curling	....	.85	.30
1938	48¢ Freestyle aerial skiing	....	.85	.30
1939	48¢ Women's hockey	....	.85	.30
1940	48¢ Appoint. of First Canadian Governor General	3.75	.85	.30

1941

1942

SCOTT NO.	DESCRIPTION	PLATE BLOCK F/NH	UNUSED F/NH	USED F
1941	48¢ University of Manitoba	....	.85	.30
1941a	same, bklt pane of 8	....	6.75	....
1942	48¢ Laval University	....	.85	.30
1942a	same, bklt pane of 8	....	6.75	....
1943	48¢ University of Trinity College	....	.85	.30
1943a	same, bklt pane of 8	....	6.75	....
1944	48¢ Saint Mary's University, Halifax	....	.85	.30
1944a	same, bklt pane of 8	....	6.75	....

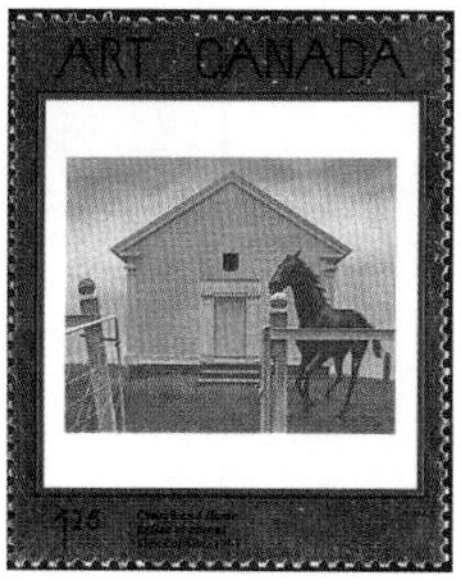

1945

1946a

SCOTT NO.	DESCRIPTION	PLATE BLOCK F/NH	UNUSED F/NH	USED F
1945	$1.25 Canadian Art, Church and Horse	8.50	2.00	.95
1946	48¢ Canadian Tulips, bklt pane of 4, self-adhesive	....	3.25	1.95
1946a	48¢ City of Vancouver tulip	....	1.00	.40
1946b	48¢ Monte Carlo tulip	....	1.00	.40
1946c	48¢ Ottawa tulip	....	1.00	.40
1946d	48¢ The Bishop tulip	....	1.00	.40
1947	48¢ Canadian Tulips, souvenir sheet of 4, perforted	....	3.25	3.00

1948

SCOTT NO.	DESCRIPTION	PLATE BLOCK F/NH	UNUSED F/NH	USED F
1948-51	48¢ Corals, 4 attached	3.75	3.25	3.00
1948	48¢ Dendronepthea Giagantea & Dendronepthea Corals	....	.85	.40
1949	48¢ Tubastrea & Echinogorgia Corals	....	.85	.40
1950	48¢ North Atlantic Pink Tree, Pacific Orange Cup & North Pacific Horn Corals	....	.85	.40
1951	48¢ North Atlantic Giant Orange Tree & Black Coral	....	.85	.40
1951a	same, souvenir sheet of 4	....	3.25	3.00

1954-55

SCOTT NO.	DESCRIPTION	PLATE BLOCK F/NH	UNUSED F/NH	USED F
1952	65¢ Tourists Attractions, bklt pane of 5, self-adhesive	....	6.00	4.00
1952a	65¢ Yukon Quest, Yukon Territory	....	1.25	.60
1952b	65¢ Icefields Parkway, Alberta	....	1.25	.60
1952c	65¢ Agawa Canyon, Ontario	....	1.25	.60
1952d	65¢ Old Port of Montreal, Quebec	....	1.25	.60
1952e	65¢ Kings Landing, New Burnswick	....	1.25	.60
1953	$1.25 Tourists Attractions, bklt pane of 5, self-adhesive	....	9.75	6.50
1953a	$1.25 Northern Lights, Northwest Territories	....	2.00	.95
1953b	$1.25 Stanley Park, Vancouver, British Columbia	....	2.00	.95
1953c	$1.25 Head-Smashed-In Buffalo Jump, Alberta	....	2.00	.95
1953d	$1.25 Saguenay Fjord, Quebec	....	2.00	.95
1953e	$1.25 Peggy's Cove, Nova Scotia	....	2.00	.95
1954-55	48¢ Sculpture, Lumberjacks & Embacle, 2 attached	3.75	1.65	1.00
1954	48¢ Sculpture "Embacle" by Charles Daudelin	....	.85	.30
1955	48¢ Sculpture "Lumberjacks" by Leo Mol	....	.85	.30

1956

1957

SCOTT NO.	DESCRIPTION	PLATE BLOCK F/NH	UNUSED F/NH	USED F
1956	48¢ Canadian Postmasters & Assistants Assoc.	3.75	.85	.30
1957	48¢ World Youth Day, self-adhesive	....	.85	.30
1957a	48¢ World Youth Day, bklt pane of 8, self-adhesive	....	6.75	....

1958

1959

SCOTT NO.	DESCRIPTION	PLATE BLOCK F/NH	UNUSED F/NH	USED F
1958	48¢ Public Services International World Congress	3.75	.85	.30
1959	48¢ Public Pensions, 75th Anniv.	3.75	.85	.30
1960	48¢ Mountains, 8 attached	7.25	6.50	4.00
1960a	48¢ Mt. Logan ,Canada	....	.85	.50
1960b	48¢ Mt. Elbrus, Russia	....	.85	.50
1960c	48¢ Puncak Java, Indonesia	....	.85	.50
1960d	48¢ Mt. Everest, Nepal & China	....	.85	.50
1960e	48¢ Mt. Kilimanjaro, Tanzania	....	.85	.50
1960f	48¢ Vinson Massif, Antarctica	....	.85	.50
1960g	48¢ Mt. Aconcagua, Argentina	....	.85	.50
1960h	48¢ Mt. Mckinley, Alaska	....	.85	.50

1961

1962

SCOTT NO.	DESCRIPTION	PLATE BLOCK F/NH	UNUSED F/NH	USED F
1961	48¢ World Teacher's Day	3.75	.85	.30
1962	48¢ Toronto Stock Exchange	3.75	.85	.30

1963-64

SCOTT NO.	DESCRIPTION	PLATE BLOCK F/NH	UNUSED F/NH	USED F
1963-64	48¢ Communication Technology Centenaries, 2 attach	3.75	1.65	1.00
1963	48¢ Sir Sandford Fleming 91827-1915, cable-laying ship	....	.85	.30
1964	48¢ Guglielmo Marconi 1874-19370, radio and transmission towers	....	.85	.30

1965

1968

SCOTT NO.	DESCRIPTION	PLATE BLOCK F/NH	UNUSED F/NH	USED F
1965	48¢ "Genesis" by Daphne Odjig	3.75	.85	.25
1965a	same, bklt pane of 10	....	8.25	....
1966	65¢ "Winter Travel" by Cecil Youngfox	5.25	1.20	.50
1966a	same, bklt pane of 6	....	7.00	....
1967	$1.25 "Mary and Child" sculpture by Irene Katak Angutitaq	8.50	1.95	.75
1967a	same, bklt pane of 6	....	11.50	....
1968	48¢ Quebec Symphony Orchestra Centenary	3.75	.85	.30

1969

1971a, 1972a

1973

2003 COMMEMORATIVES

SCOTT NO.	DESCRIPTION	PLATE BLOCK F/NH	UNUSED F/NH	USED F
1969	48¢ Year of the Ram	3.75	.85	.30
1970	$1.25 Year of the Ram, souvenir sheet	....	2.00	2.00
1971	48¢ National Hockey League All-Star Game, sheet of 6	....	15.00	15.00
1971a	48¢ Frank Mahovlich	....	2.00	1.50
1971b	48¢ Raymond Bourque	....	2.00	1.50
1971c	48¢ Serge Savard	....	2.00	1.50
1971d	48¢ Stan Mikita	....	2.00	1.50
1971e	48¢ Mike Bossy	....	2.00	1.50
1971f	48¢ Bill Durnan	....	2.00	1.50
1972	48¢ National Hockey League All-Star Game, sheet of 6, self-adhesive	....	40.00	....
1972a	48¢ Frank Mahovlich, self-adhesive	....	5.00	.50
1972b	48¢ Raymond Bourque, self-adhesive	....	5.00	.50
1972c	48¢ Serge Savard, self-adhesive	....	5.00	.50
1972d	48¢ Stan Mikita, self-adhesive	....	5.00	.50
1972e	48¢ Mike Bossy, self-adhesive	....	5.00	.50
1972f	48¢ Bill Durnan, self-adhesive	....	5.00	.50
1973	48¢ Bishop's University, Quebec, 150th Anniv.	....	5.00	.50
1973a	same, bklt pane of 8	....	6.75	....
1974	48¢ University of Western Ontario, 125th Anniv.	....	.85	.30
1974a	same, bklt pane of 8	....	6.75	....
1975	48¢ St. Francis Xavier University, Antigonis, 150th Anniv.	....	.85	.30
1975a	same, bklt pane of 8	....	6.75	....
1976	48¢ Macdonald Institute, Guelph, Ont., Centennial	....	.85	.30
1976a	same, bklt pane of 8	....	6.75	....
1977	48¢ University of Montreal, 125th Anniversary	....	.85	.30
1977a	same, bklt pane of 8	....	6.75	....

1979

1984

SCOTT NO.	DESCRIPTION	PLATE BLOCK F/NH	UNUSED F/NH	USED F
1979-82	Bird paintings by John James Audubon, 4 attached	3.75	3.25	3.00
1979	48¢ Leach's Storm Petrel	....	.85	.40
1980	48¢ Brant	....	.85	.40
1981	48¢ Great Cormorant	....	.85	.40
1982	48¢ Common Murre	....	.85	.40
1983	65¢ Gyfalcon, self-adhesive	....	1.25	.60
1983a	same, bklt pane of 6	....	7.25	....
1984	48¢ Canadian Rangers	3.75	.85	.30
1985	48¢ American Hellenic Educational Progressive Assoc. in Canada, 75th Anniversary	3.75	.85	.30
1986	48¢ Volunteer Firefighters	3.75	.85	.30
1987	48¢ Coronation of Queen Elizabeth II, 50th Anniv.	3.75	.85	.30
1988	48¢ Pedro da Silva, First Courier in New France	3.75	.85	.30

1992

1991

1993

SCOTT NO.	DESCRIPTION	PLATE BLOCK F/NH	UNUSED F/NH	USED F
1989	65¢ Tourist Attractions, bklt pane of 5, self-adhesive	....	8.00	....
1989a	65¢ Wilbeforce Falls, Nunavult	....	1.25	.75
1989b	65¢ Inside Passage, B.C.	....	1.25	.75
1989c	65¢ Royal Canadian Mounted Police Depot Division	....	1.25	.75
1989d	65¢ Casa Loma, Toronto	....	1.25	.75
1989e	65¢ Gatineau Park, Quebec	....	1.25	.75
1990	$1.25 Tourist Attractions, bklt pane of 5, self-adhesive	....	15.00	12.00
1990a	$1.25 Dragon boat races, Vancouver, B.C.	....	2.00	1.00
1990b	$1.25 Polar bear watching, Manitoba	....	2.00	1.00
1990c	$1.25 Nigara Falls, Ontario	....	2.00	1.00
1990d	$1.25 Magdalen Islands, Quebec	....	2.00	1.00
1990e	$1.25 Charlottestown, P.E.I.	....	2.00	1.00
1991	48¢ "Vancouver 2010" overprint	....	1.50	1.00
1991a	same, bklt pane of 10	....	20.00	....
1991b	same, bklt pane of 20	....	35.00	....
1992	48¢ Lutheran World Federation 10th Assem	3.75	.85	.30
1993	48¢ Korean War Armistice, 50th Anniv.	3.75	.85	.30

1994

1998

SCOTT NO.	DESCRIPTION	PLATE BLOCK F/NH	UNUSED F/NH	USED F
1998	48¢ World Road Cycling Championships, Hamilton, Ont.	....	.85	.30
1998a	same, bklt pane of 8	....	6.75	....
1991C-Da	($1.25) Canada-Alaska Cruise Scenes, self-adhesive, 2 attached	....	3.95	2.00
1991C	($1.25) Mountains and Totem Pole	....	1.95	1.00
1991D	($1.25) Mountains and Whale's Tail	....	1.95	1.00
1994-97	48¢ National Library, 50th Anniv. 4 attached	....	3.25	1.95
1994	48¢ Anne Hebert (1916-2000)	....	.85	.30
1995	48¢ Hector de Saint-Denys Garneau (1912-43)	....	.85	.30
1996	48¢ Morley Callaghan (1903-90)	....	.85	.30
1997	48¢ Susanna Moodie (1803-85), Catharine Parr Trail (1802-99)	....	.85	.30
1997b	same, bklt pane of 8 (1994-97 x 2)	....	6.50	....
1999	48¢ Canadian Astronauts, self-adhesive, sheet of 8	....	6.50	....
1999a	48¢ Marc Garneau, self-adhesive	....	.85	.30
1999b	48¢ Roberta Bondar, self-adhesive	....	.85	.30
1999c	48¢ Steve MacLean, self-adhesive	....	.85	.30
1999d	48¢ Chris Hadfield, self-adhesive	....	.85	.30
1999e	48¢ Robert Thrisk, self-adhesive	....	.85	.30
1999f	48¢ Bjarni Tryggvason, self-adhesive	....	.85	.30
1999g	48¢ Dave Williams, self-adhesive	....	.85	.30
1999h	48¢ Julie Payette, self-adhesive	....	.85	.30

2000-01

2002a

SCOTT NO.	DESCRIPTION	PLATE BLOCK F/NH	UNUSED F/NH	USED F
2000-01	48¢ Trees of Canada and Thailand, 2 attached	3.75	1.65	1.00
2000	48¢ Acer Saccharum leaves (Canada)	....	.85	.30
2001	48¢ Cassia fistula (Thailand)	....	.85	.30
2001b	48¢ Trees of Canada and Thailand, souvenir sheet of 2	....	1.65	1.00
2002	48¢ L'Hommage a Rosa Luxemburg by Jean-Paul Riopelle, sheet of 6	....	7.00	7.00
2002a	48¢ Red & Blue dots between birds at LR	....	1.25	1.00
2002b	48¢ Bird with yellow beak at center	....	1.25	1.00
2002c	48¢ Three birds in circle at R	....	1.25	1.00
2002d	48¢ Sun at UR	....	1.25	1.00
2002e	48¢ Birds with purple outlines ar L	....	1.25	1.00
2002f	48¢ Birds with red outline in circle at R	....	1.25	1.00
2003	$1.25 Pink bird in red circle at R, souvenir sheet		....	3.00
3.00				

2004

SCOTT NO.	DESCRIPTION	PLATE BLOCK F/NH	UNUSED F/NH	USED F
2004	48¢ Gift boxes and Ice skates	3.75	.85	.25
2004a	same, bklt pane of 6	....	5.00	....
2005	65¢ Gift boxes and Teddy bear	5.25	1.20	.50
2005a	same, bklt pane of 6	....	7.00	....
2006	$1.25 Gift boxes and Toy duck	8.50	2.50	1.00
2006a	same, bklt pane of 6	....	11.50	....
2007	$5 Moose	37.50	8.50	5.00
2008	49¢ Maple Leaf and Samara, self-adhesive, coil	....	.90	.40
2009	80¢ Maple Leaf on Twig, self-adhesive, coil	....	1.35	.75
2010	$1.40 Maple Leaf on Twig, self-adhesive, coil .	....	2.50	1.25
2011	49¢ Flag over Edmonton, Alberta, self-adhesive	....	.90	.40
2011a	same, bklt pane of 10	....	9.00	....
2012	49¢ Queen Elizabeth II, self-adhesive	....	.90	.40
2012a	same, bklt pane of 10	....	9.00	....
2013	80¢ Maple Leaf on Twig, self-adhesive	....	1.35	.75
2013a	same, bklt pane of 6	....	8.00	....
2014	$1.40 Maple Leaf Twig, self-adhesive	....	2.50	1.25
2014a	same, bklt pane of 6	....	15.00	....

2015

2024

2026

2004 Commemoratives

SCOTT NO.	DESCRIPTION	PLATE BLOCK F/NH	UNUSED F/NH	USED F
2015	49¢ Year of the Monkey	4.00	.90	.40
2016	$1.40 Year of the Monkey souvenir sheet	....	2.75	1.50
2016a	same, with 2004 Hong Kong overprint	....	3.25	1.75
2017	49¢ National Hockey League Stars, sheet of 6	....	5.50	4.00
2017a	49¢ Larry Robinson	....	.90	.40
2017b	49¢ Marcel Dionne	....	.90	.40
2017c	49¢ Ted Lindsay	....	.90	.40
2017d	49¢ Johnny Bower	....	.90	.40
2017e	49¢ Brad Park	....	.90	.40
2017f	49¢ Milt Schmidt	....	.90	.40
2018	49¢ National Hockey League Stars, sheet of 6, self-adhesive	....	5.50	4.00
2018a	49¢ Larry Robinson, self-adhesive	....	.90	.40
2018b	49¢ Marcel Dionne, self-adhesive	....	.90	.40
2018c	49¢ Ted Lindsay, self-adhesive	....	.90	.40
2018d	49¢ Johnny Bower, self-adhesive	....	.90	.40
2018e	49¢ Brad Park, self-adhesive	....	.90	.40
2018f	49¢ Milt Schmidt, self-adhesive	....	.90	.40
2019	49¢ Quebec Winter Carnival, self-adhesive	....	.90	.40
2019a	same, bklt pane of 6	....	5.50	....
2020	49¢ St. Joseph's Oratory, Montreal, self-adhesive	....	.90	.40
2020a	same, bklt pane of 6	....	5.50	....
2024	49¢ Governor General Ramon John Hnatyshyn	4.00	.90	.40
2025	49¢ Royal Canadian Army Cadets, 125th Anniv, self-adhesive	....	.90	.40
2025a	same, bklt pane of 4	....	3.60	....
2026	49¢ The Farm, Ship of Otto Sverdrup, Arctic Explorer	4.00	.90	.40
2027	$1.40 The Farm, Ship of Otto Sverdrup, Arctic Explorer, souvenir sheet	....	2.75	1.50
2028-31	49¢ Urban Transit & Light Rail Systems, 4 attached	4.00	3.60	4.00
2028	49¢ Toronto Transit Commission	....	.90	.40
2029	49¢ Translink Skytrain, Vancouver	....	.90	.40
2030	49¢ Societe de Transport de Montreal	....	.90	.40
2031	49¢ Calgary Transit Light Rail	....	.90	.40

2032

2035

SCOTT NO.	DESCRIPTION	PLATE BLOCK F/NH	UNUSED F/NH	USED F
2032	49¢ Home Hardware, 40th Anniv., self-adhesive	....	.90	.40
2032a	same, bklt pane of 10	....	9.00	....
2033	49¢ University of Sherbrooke, 50th Anniv.	....	.90	.40
2033a	same, bklt pane of 8	....	7.25	....
2034	49¢ University of Prince Edwards Island, Bicenn	....	.90	.40
2034a	same, bklt pane of 8	....	7.25	....
2035	49¢ Montreal Children's Hospital Centenary, self-adhesive	....	.90	.40
2035a	same, bklt pane of 4	....	3.60	....
2036-39	49¢ Bird Paintings by John James Audubon, 4 attache	4.00	3.60	.40
2036	49¢ Ruby-crowned Kinglet	....	.90	.40
2037	49¢ White-winged Crossbill	....	.90	.40
2038	49¢ Bohemian Waxwing	....	.90	.40
2039	49¢ Boreal Chickadee	....	.90	.40
2040	80¢ Lincoln's Sparrow by J.J. Audubon, self-adhesive	....	1.35	.75
2040a	same, bklt pane of 6	....	8.25	....
2041-42	49¢ Pioneers of Trans Mail Service, 2 attached	4.00	1.80	1.00
2041	49¢ Sir Samuel Cunard	....	.90	.40
2042	49¢ Sir Hugh Allan	....	.90	.40

2043

SCOTT NO.	DESCRIPTION	PLATE BLOCK F/NH	UNUSED F/NH	USED F
2043	49¢ D-Day 60th Anniversary	4.00	.90	.40
2044	49¢ Pierre Dugua de Mons, Leader of First French Settlement in Acadia	4.00	.90	.40

SCOTT NO.	DESCRIPTION	PLATE BLOCK F/NH	UNUSED F/NH	USED F
2045	(49¢) Butterfly and Flower, self-adhesive	....	4.25	4.25
2045a	same, bklt pane of 2	....	8.50	....
....	complete bklt, 2045a + phonecard in greeting card	....	10.50	....
2046	(49¢) Children on Beach, self-adhesive	....	4.25	4.25
2046a	same, bklt pane of 2	....	8.50	....
....	complete bklt, 2046a + phonecard in greeting card	....	10.50	....
2047	(49¢) Rose, self-adhesive	....	4.25	4.25
2047a	same, bklt pane of 2	....	8.50	....
....	complete bklt, 2047a + phonecard in greeting card	....	10.50	....
2048	(49¢) Dog, self-adhesive	....	4.25	4.25
2048a	same bklt pane of 2	....	8.50	....
....	complete bklt, 2048a + phonecard in greeting card	....	10.50	....

2026

SCOTT NO.	DESCRIPTION	PLATE BLOCK F/NH	UNUSED F/NH	USED F
2049-50	49¢ 2004 Summer Olympics , Athens, 2 attached	4.00	1.80	1.00
2049	49¢ Spyros Louis 1896 Marathon Gold Medalist	....	.90	.40
2050	49¢ Soccer net inscribed "Canada" girls soccer	....	.90	.40

2051

2056

SCOTT NO.	DESCRIPTION	PLATE BLOCK F/NH	UNUSED F/NH	USED F
2051-52	49¢ Canadian Open Golf Championship, self-adhesive, set of 2	....	1.80	.80
2051	49¢ Canadian Open Golf Championship, 'finishing swing'		.90	.40
2052	49¢ Canadian Open Golf Championship, "ready to putt"........		.90	.40
2053	49¢ Maple Leaf and Samara, self-adhesive, coil	....	.90	.40
2054	80¢ Maple Leaf on Twig, self-adhesive, die-cut 8.25, coil	....	1.35	.75
2055	$1.40 Maple Leaf on Twig, self-adhesive, die-cut 8.25, coil........		2.50	1.25
2056	49¢ Montreal Heart Institute, 50th Anniversary	....	.90	.40
2056a	same, booklet pane of 4	....	3.60	....
2057	49¢ Pets – Fish	....	.90	.40
2058	49¢ Pets – Cats	....	.90	.40
2059	49¢ Pets – Rabbit	....	.90	.40
2060	49¢ Pets – Dog	....	.90	.40
2060a	same, booklet pane of 4	....	3.60	....

2061

2065

SCOTT NO.	DESCRIPTION	PLATE BLOCK F/NH	UNUSED F/NH	USED F
2061-62	49¢ Nobel Laureates in chemistry, 2 attached .	4.00	1.80	1.00
2061	49¢ Gerhard Herzberg, 1971 laureate & molecular structures	....	.90	.40
2062	49¢ Michael Smith, 1993 laureate & DNA double helix	....	.90	.40
2063-64	(49¢) Ribbon Frame & Picture Album Frame, self-adhesive, 2 attached	4.00	1.80	1.00
2063	(49¢) Ribbon Frame, self-adhesive	....	.90	.40
2064	(49¢) Picture Album Frame, self-adhesive	....	.90	.40
2065-66	49¢ Victoria Cross 150th Anniv., 2 attached	4.00	1.80	1.00
2065	49¢ Victoria Cross	....	.90	.40
2066	49¢ Design for Victoria Cross approved w/ QEII's signature........		.90	.40

2068

2069

SCOTT NO.	DESCRIPTION	PLATE BLOCK F/NH	UNUSED F/NH	USED F
2067	47¢ "Self-Portrait" by Jean Paul Lemieux, perf 13 x 13.24	4.00	.90	.40
2068	47¢ – $1.40 Paintings of Jean Paul Lemieux, souvenir sheet of 3	....	4.75	....
2069	49¢ Santa Claus and Sleigh, self-adhesive	....	.90	.40
2069a	same, booklet pane of 6	....	5.50	....
2070	80¢ Santa Claus and Automobile, self-adhesive	....	1.50	.75
2070a	same, booklet pane of 6	....	9.00	....
2071	$1.40 Santa Claus and Train, self-adhesive	....	2.50	1.25
2071a	same, booklet pane of 6	....	15.00	....

2072

2075

2080

SCOTT NO.	DESCRIPTION	PLATE BLOCK F/NH	UNUSED F/NH	USED F
2072	50¢ Red Calla Lilies, self-adhesive, coil	....	.95	.40
2072a	same, serpentine die cut 6.75	....	.95	.40
2072b	same, serpentine die cut 7.25	....	.95	.40
2073	85¢ Yellow Calla Lilies, self-adhesive, coil	....	1.55	.75
2073a	same, serpentine die cut 6.75	....	1.55	.75
2074	$1.45 Iris, self-adhesive, coil	....	2.55	1.25
2074a	same, serpentine die cut 6.75	....	2.55	1.25
2075	50¢ Queen Elizabeth II, self-adhesive	....	.95	.40
2075a	same, booklet pane of 10	....	9.50	....
2076	50¢ Flag and Saskatoon, Saskatchewan, self-adhesive	....	.95	.40
2077	50¢ Flag and Durrell, Newfoundland, self-adhesive	....	.95	.40
2078	50¢ Flag and Shannon Falls, British Columbia, self-adhesive........		.95	.40
2079	50¢ Flag and Mont-Saint-Hillaire, Quebec, self-adhesive	....	.95	.40
2080	50¢ Flag and Toronto, self-adhesive	....	.95	.40
2080a	same, booklet pane of 10 (#2076-80 x 2)	....	9.50	....
2081	85¢ Yellow Calla Lilies, self-adhesive	....	1.55	.40
2081a	same, booklet pane of 6	....	9.25	....
2082	$1.45 Iris, self-adhesive	....	2.55	1.25
2082a	same, booklet pane of 6	....	15.25	....

2083

2086a

2005 Commemoratives

SCOTT NO.	DESCRIPTION	PLATE BLOCK F/NH	UNUSED F/NH	USED F
2083	50¢ Year of the Rooseter	4.25	.95	.40
2084	$1.45 Year of the Rooster, souvenir sheet	....	2.55	1.40
2084a	same, with dates, Canadian and Chinese flags in sheet margin	....	2.55	1.40
2085	50¢ National Hockey League Stars, sheet of 6	....	5.75	5.00
2085a	50¢ Henri Richard	....	.95	.40
2085b	50¢ Grant Fuhr	....	.95	.40
2085c	50¢ Allan Stanley	....	.95	.40
2085d	50¢ Pierre Pilote	....	.95	.40
2085e	50¢ Bryan Trottier	....	.95	.40
2085f	50¢ John Bucyk	....	.95	.40
2086	50¢ National Hockey League Stars, self-adhesive, pane of 6........		5.75	....
2086a	50¢ Henri Richard, self-adhesive	....	.95	.40
2086b	50¢ Grant Fuhr, self-adhesive	....	.95	.40
2086c	50¢ Allen Stanley, self-adhesive	....	.95	.40
2086d	50¢ Pierre Pilote, self-adhesive	....	.95	.40
2086e	50¢ Bryan Trottier, self-adhesive	....	.95	.40
2086f	50¢ John Bucyk, self-adhesive	....	.95	.40

2087a, 2088a

2089

SCOTT NO.	DESCRIPTION	PLATE BLOCK F/NH	UNUSED F/NH	USED F
2087	50¢ Fishing Flies, sheet of 4	....	3.75	3.50
2087a	50¢ Alevin	....	.95	.40
2087b	50¢ Jock Scott	....	.95	.40
2087c	50¢ P.E.I. Fly	....	.95	.40
2087d	50¢ Mickey Finn	....	.95	.40
2088	50¢ Fishing Flies, self-adhesive, bklt pane of 8	....	3.75	3.50
2088a	50¢ Alevin, self-adhesive	....	.95	.40
2088b	50¢ Jock Scott. self-adhesive	....	.95	.40
2088c	50¢ P.E.I. Fly, self-adhesive	....	.95	.40
2088d	50¢ Mickey Finn, self-adhesive	....	.95	.40
2089	50¢ Nova Scotia Agricultural College, self-adhesive	....	.95	.40
2089a	same, booklet pane of 4	....	3.75	....

2090

2092

SCOTT NO.	DESCRIPTION	PLATE BLOCK F/NH	UNUSED F/NH	USED F
2090	50¢ EXPO 2005, Aichi, Japan	4.25	.95	.40
2091	50¢ Daffodils, souvenir sheet of 2	....	1.95	1.25
2092	50¢ Yellow Daffodils, self-adhesive	....	.95	.40
2093	50¢ White Daffodils, self-adhesive	....	.95	.40
2093a	50¢ Daffodils, self-adhesive, bklt pane of 10 ...	....	9.50	....

2094

2099

SCOTT NO.	DESCRIPTION	PLATE BLOCK F/NH	UNUSED F/NH	USED F
2094	50¢ TD Bank Financial Group, 150th Anniv., self-adhesive	....	.95	.40
2094a	same, booklet pane of 10	....	9.50	....
2095-98	50¢ Bird Paintings by John James Audubon, 4 attached	4.25	3.75	3.50
2095	50¢ Horned lark	....	.95	.40
2096	50¢ Piping plover	....	.95	.40
2097	50¢ Stilt sandpiper	....	.95	.40
2098	50¢ Willow ptarmigan	....	.95	.40
2099	85¢ Double-crested Cormorant by John James Audubon, self-adhesive	....	1.40	.75
2099a	same, booklet pane of 6	....	8.50	....

2100

2104

SCOTT NO.	DESCRIPTION	PLATE BLOCK F/NH	UNUSED F/NH	USED F
2100-03	50¢ Bridges, self-adhesive, 4 attached	4.25	3.75	3.50
2100	50¢ Jacques Cartier Bridge, Quebec	....	.95	.40
2101	50¢ Souris Swinging Bridge, Manitoba	....	.95	.40
2102	50¢ Angus L. MacDonald Bridge, Nova Scotia	....	.95	.40
2103	50¢ Canso Causeway, Nova Scotia	....	.95	.40
2104	50¢ Maclean's Magazine	4.25	.95	.40

2105-06

SCOTT NO.	DESCRIPTION	PLATE BLOCK F/NH	UNUSED F/NH	USED F
2105-06	50¢ Biosphere Reserves of Canada and Ireland, 2 attached	4.25	1.90	1.75
2105	50¢ Saskatoon Berries, Waterton Lakes National Park	....	.95	.40
2106	50¢ Deer, Killarney National Park	....	.95	.40

2107

2108

SCOTT NO.	DESCRIPTION	PLATE BLOCK F/NH	UNUSED F/NH	USED F
2107	50¢ Battle of the Atlantic, World War II	4.25	.95	.40
2108	50¢ Opening of Canadian War Museum, Ottawa, self-adhesive	....	.95	.40
2108a	same, booklet pane of 4	....	3.75	....

2109

2112

SCOTT NO.	DESCRIPTION	PLATE BLOCK F/NH	UNUSED F/NH	USED F
2109	50¢ Paintings by Homer Watson	4.25	.95	.40
2110	$1.35 Paintings by Homer Watson, souvenir sheet of 2	....	2.50	2.25
2111	50¢ Search and Rescue, sheet of 8	....	7.60	7.00
2112	50¢ Ellen Fairclough	4.25	.95	.40
2113-14	50¢ 9th FINA World Championships, Montreal, 2 attached	4.25	1.90	1.00
2113	50¢ Diver	....	.95	.40
2114	50¢ Swimmer	....	.95	.40

2115

2117

SCOTT NO.	DESCRIPTION	PLATE BLOCK F/NH	UNUSED F/NH	USED F
2115	50¢ Founding of Port Royal, Nova Scotia, 400th Anniv.	4.25	.95	.40
2116	50¢ Province of Alberta, Centennial, self-adhesive	4.25	.95	.40
2117	50¢ Province of Saskatchewan, Centennial	4.25	.95	.40

2118

2120

SCOTT NO.	DESCRIPTION	PLATE BLOCK F/NH	UNUSED F/NH	USED F
2118	50¢ Oscar Peterson, Pianist, 80th Birthday	....	.95	.40
2118a	same, booklet pane of 4	....	3.75	....
2119	50¢ Acadiaan Deportation, 250th Anniversary .	4.25	.95	.40
2120	50¢ Mass Polio Vaccinations in Canada, 50th Anniv.	4.25	.95	.40
2121	50¢ Youth Sports, self-adhesive, complete booklet of 8 (2121a-d X2)	....	7.50	....
2121a	50¢ Wall Climbing, self-adhesive	....	.95	.40
2121b	50¢ Skateboarding, self-adhesive	....	.95	.40
2121c	50¢ Mountain biking, self-adhesive	....	.95	.40
2121d	50¢ Snowboarding, self-adhesive	....	.95	.40

2122-23

SCOTT NO.	DESCRIPTION	PLATE BLOCK F/NH	UNUSED F/NH	USED F
2122-23	50¢ Wildcats, 2 attached	4.25	1.90	1.00
2122	50¢ Puma concolor	....	.95	.40
2123	50¢ Panthera pardus orientalis	....	.95	.40

2124

2125

SCOTT NO.	DESCRIPTION	PLATE BLOCK F/NH	UNUSED F/NH	USED F
2124	50¢ Snowmen, self-adhesive	....	.95	.40
2124a	same, booklet pane of 6	....	5.75	....
2125	50¢ Creche Figures, St. Joseph Oratory, Montreal, self-adhesive	....	.95	.40
2125a	same, booklet pane of 6	....	5.75	....
2126	85¢ Creche Figures, St. Joseph Oratory, Montreal, self-adhesive	....	1.40	.75
2126a	same, booklet pane of 6	....	8.50	....
2127	$1.45 Creche Figures, St. Joseph Oratory, Montreal, self-adhesive	....	2.55	....
2127a	same, booklet pane of 6	....	15.25	....

2128

2131, 2134

SCOTT NO.	DESCRIPTION	PLATE BLOCK F/NH	UNUSED F/NH	USED F
2128	51¢ Red bergamot flower, self-adhesive, coil	....	.95	.40
2129	89¢ Yellow lady's slipper, self-adhesive, coil	....	1.65	.90
2130	$1.05 Pink fairy slipper, self-adhesive, coil	....	2.00	1.00
2131	$1.49 Himalayan blue poppy, self-adhesive, coil	....	2.70	1.35
2132	89¢ Yellow lady's slipper, self-adhesive	....	1.65	.90
2132a	same, booklet pane of 6	....	10.00	....
2133	$1.05 Pink fairy slipper, self-adhesive	....	2.00	1.00
2133a	same, booklet pane of 6	....	12.00	....
2134	$1.49 Himalayan blue poppy, self-adhesive	....	2.70	1.35
2134a	same, booklet pane of 6	....	16.25	....

2135

SCOTT NO.	DESCRIPTION	PLATE BLOCK F/NH	UNUSED F/NH	USED F
2135	51¢ Flag and Houses, New Glasgow, Prince Edward Island, self-adhesive	....	.95	.40
2136	51¢ Flag and Bridge, Bouctouche, New Brunswick, self-adhesive	....	.95	.40
2137	51¢ Flag and Windmills, Pincher Creek, Alberta self-adhesive	....	.95	.40
2138	51¢ Flag and Lower Fort Garry, Manitoba, self-adhesive	....	.95	.40
2139	51¢ Flag and Dogsled, Yukon Territory, self-adhesive	....	.95	.40
2139a	Flags, booklet pane of 10 (2135-39 x 2)	....	9.50	....

2140

2142

2006 Commemoratives

SCOTT NO.	DESCRIPTION	PLATE BLOCK F/NH	UNUSED F/NH	USED F
2140	51¢ Year of the Dog	4.25	.95	.40
2141	$1.49 Year of the Dog, Dog and pup, souvenir sheet	....	2.70	1.35
2142	51¢ Queen Elizabeth II, 80th Birthday, self-adhesive	....	.95	.40
....	same, bookelt pane of 10	....	9.50	....

2143

2146

SCOTT NO.	DESCRIPTION	PLATE BLOCK F/NH	UNUSED F/NH	USED F
2143-44	51¢ 2006 Winter Olympics, Turin, Italy, 2 attached	4.25	1.90	1.00
2143	51¢ Team pursuit speed skating	....	.95	.40
2144	51¢ Skeleton	....	.95	.40
2145	51¢ Gardens, complete booklet of 8	....	7.60	....
2145a	51¢ Shade garden	....	.95	.40
2145b	51¢ Flower garden	....	.95	.40
2145c	51¢ Water garden	....	.95	.40
2145d	51¢ Rock garden	....	.95	.40
2146	51¢ Party Balloons, self-adhesive	....	.95	.40
2146a	same, booklet pane of 6	....	5.75	....

2147

2149

SCOTT NO.	DESCRIPTION	PLATE BLOCK F/NH	UNUSED F/NH	USED F
2147	51¢ Paintings by Dorothy Knowles	4.25	.95	.40
2147a	same, single from souvenir sheet, perf. 12.75 X 12.5	....	.95	.40
2148	51¢-89¢ Paintings by Dorothy Knowles, souvenir sheet	....	2.60	2.60
2148a	89¢ single from souvenir sheet	....	1.65	.90
2149	51¢ Canadian Labor Congress, 50th Anniversary	4.25	.95	.40
2150	$1.49 Queen Elizabeth 80th Birthday, souvenir sheet of 2	....	5.50	....
2150a	single from souvenir sheet	....	2.75	1.75

2151

2152

SCOTT NO.	DESCRIPTION	PLATE BLOCK F/NH	UNUSED F/NH	USED F
2151	51¢ McClelland & Stewart Publishing, self-adhesive	....	.95	.40
....	same, booklet pane of 8	....	7.60	....
2152	89¢ Canadian Museum of Civilization, self-adhesive	....	1.65	....
....	same, booklet pane of 8	....	13.25	....

2154c

2155, 2156a

SCOTT NO.	DESCRIPTION	PLATE BLOCK F/NH	UNUSED F/NH	USED F
2153	51¢ Canadians in Hollywood, souvenir sheet of 4	....	3.80	....
2154	same, booklet pane of 4	....	3.80	....
2154a	51¢ John Candy, self-adhesive	....	.95	.40
2154b	51¢ Mary Pickford, self-adhesive	....	.95	.40
2154c	51¢ Fay Wray, self adhesive	....	.95	.40
2154d	51¢ Lorne Greene, self-adhesive	....	.95	.40
2154e	same, booklet of 8, Wray on cover	....	7.60	....
2154f	same, booklet of 8, Pickford on cover	....	7.60	....
2154g	same, booklet of 8, Greene on cover	....	7.60	....
2154h	same, booklet of 8, Candy on cover	....	7.60	....
2155	51¢ Champlain Surveys the East Coast	....	.95	.40
2156	2-39¢ and 2-51¢ Champlain, souvenir sheet sheet of 4, joint issue with the U.S.	....	4.50	....
2156a	51¢ single from souvenir sheet	....	.95	.40

2157

2160

SCOTT NO.	DESCRIPTION	PLATE BLOCK F/NH	UNUSED F/NH	USED F
2157	51¢ Vancouver Aquarium, 50th Anniv., self-adhesive	....	.95	.40
2157a	same, booklet pane of 10	....	9.50	....
2158-59	51¢ Canadian Forces Snowbirds, 2 attached	....	1.90	1.00
2158	51¢ view from cockpit	....	.95	.40
2159	51¢ three C-114 Tutor jets	....	.95	.40
2159b	same, souvenir sheet of 2	....	1.90	....
2160	51¢ Atlas of Canada	4.25	.95	.40

2161

2162

SCOTT NO.	DESCRIPTION	PLATE BLOCK F/NH	UNUSED F/NH	USED F
2161	51¢ 2006 World Lacrosse Championship, self-adhesive	....	.95	.40
2161a	same, booklet pane of 8	....	7.60	....
2162	51¢ Mountaineering, self-adhesive	....	.95	.40
2162a	same, booklet pane of 8	....	7.60	....

2163-66

SCOTT NO.	DESCRIPTION	PLATE BLOCK F/NH	UNUSED F/NH	USED F
2163-2166	51¢ Duck decoys	....	3.80	....
2163	51¢ Barrow's Golden Eye decoy	....	.95	.40
2164	51¢ Mallard decoy	....	.95	.40
2165	51¢ Red Breasted Merganser decoy	....	.95	.40
2166	51¢ Black Duck decoy	....	.95	.40
2166b	same, souvenir sheet of 4	....	3.80	....

2167

2168

SCOTT NO.	DESCRIPTION	PLATE BLOCK F/NH	UNUSED F/NH	USED F
2167	51¢ Society of Graphic Designers	....	.95	.40
2168	51¢ Three glasses of wine, self-adhesive	....	.95	.40
2169	51¢ Wine taster, self-adhesive	....	.95	.40
2170	51¢ Various cheeses, self-adhesive	....	.95	.40
2171	51¢ Woman with tray of cheeses, self-adhesive	....	.95	.40
2171a	same, booklet of 8, 2 each 2168-2171	....	7.60	....

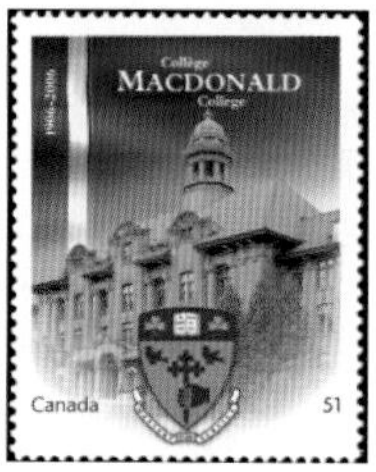

2172

2174

SCOTT NO.	DESCRIPTION	PLATE BLOCK F/NH	UNUSED F/NH	USED F
2172	51¢ MacDonald College, self-adhesive	....	.95	.40
2172a	same, booklet pane of 4	....	3.80	....
2173	51¢ Endangered Species, souvenir sheet of 4 + 4 labels	....	3.80	....
2174	51¢ Newfoundland Marten	....	.95	.40
2175	51¢ Blotched Tiger Salamander	....	.95	.40
2176	51¢ Blue Racer	....	.95	.40
2177	51¢ Swift Fox			
2177b	same, booklet of 8 (2174-2177 x 2)	....	7.60	....

2178

2183

SCOTT NO.	DESCRIPTION	PLATE BLOCK F/NH	UNUSED F/NH	USED F
2178-82	51¢ Opera singers, strip of 5	....	4.75	2.00
2178	51¢ Maureen Forrester	....	.95	.40
2179	51¢ Raorel Jobin	....	.95	.40
2180	51¢ Simoneau and Alarie	....	.95	.40
2181	51¢ Jon Vickers	....	.95	.40
2182	51¢ Edward Johnson	....	.95	.40
2183	51¢ Madonna and Child, self-adhesive	....	.95	.40
2183	same, booklet of pane of 12	....	11.40	....
2184	51¢ Snowman, self-adhesive	....	.95	.40
2184a	same, booklet pane of 12	....	11.40	....
2185	89¢ Winter Joys, self-adhesive	....	1.65	.90
2185a	same, booklet pane of 6	....	5.75	....
2186	$1.49 Contemplation, self-adhesive	....	2.70	1.35
2186a	same, booklet pane of 6	....	16.25	....

2187

2188

SCOTT NO.	DESCRIPTION	PLATE BLOCK F/NH	UNUSED F/NH	USED F
2187	"P" Spotted coalroot flower, self-adhesive, coil	....	.95	.40
2188	Nondenominated "P" Queen Elizabeth II, self-adhesive	....	.95	.40
2188a	same, booklet pane of 10	....	9.50	....

2192

SCOTT NO.	DESCRIPTION	PLATE BLOCK F/NH	UNUSED F/NH	USED F
2189	"P" Flag and Sirmilik National Park Nunaunt, self-adhesive	....	.95	.40
2190	"P" Flag and Cliff near Chemainus, British Columbia self-adhesive	....	.95	.40
2191	"P" Flag and Polar bears near Churchill, Manitoba self-adhesive	....	.95	.40
2192	"P" Flag and Bras d'Or Lake, Nova Scotia, self-adhesive		.95	.40
2193	"P" Flag and Tuktut Nogait National Park, Northwest Territories, self-adhesive	....	.95	.40
2193a	same, booklet pane of 10 (2189-2193 x 2)	....	9.50	....
2193b	same, booklet of 30 (2189-2193 x 6)	....	28.50	....

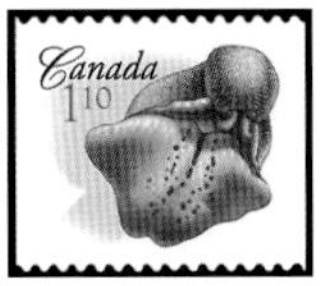

2196

2195

2197

SCOTT NO.	DESCRIPTION	PLATE BLOCK F/NH	UNUSED F/NH	USED F
2194	Flowers souvenir sheet of 4	....	3.80	....
2195	93¢ Flat-leaved Blodderwort, self-adhesive, coil	....	1.75	.75
2196	$1.10 March Skullcap, self-adhesive, coil	....	2.25	.90
2197	$1.55 Little Larkspur, self-adhesive, coil	....	2.80	1.25
2198	93¢ Flat-leaved Blodderwort, self-adhesive	....	1.75	.75
2198a	same, booklet pane of 6	....	10.50	....
2199	$1.10 March Skullcap, self-adhesive	....	2.25	.90
2199a	same, booklet pane of 6	....	13.50	....
2200	$1.55 Little Larkspur, self-adhesive	....	2.80	1.25
2200a	same, booklet pane of 6	....	16.80	....

2201

2203

2007 Commemoratives

SCOTT NO.	DESCRIPTION	PLATE BLOCK F/NH	UNUSED F/NH	USED F
2201	52¢ Year of the Pig	4.25	.95	.40
2202	$1.55 Year of the Pig, souvenir sheet	....	2.70	1.35
2203	52¢ Celebration	....	.95	.40
2203a	same, booklet pane of 6	....	5.75	....

2204-05

SCOTT NO.	DESCRIPTION	PLATE BLOCK F/NH	UNUSED F/NH	USED F
2204-05	52¢ International Polar Year, 2 attached	....	1.90	1.00
2204	52¢ Somateria spectabilis	....	.95	.40
2205	52¢ Crossota millsaeare	....	.95	.40
2205b	52¢ International Polar Year, souvenir sheet of 2	....	5.50	....
2206	52¢ Lilacs, souvenir sheet of 2	....	5.50	....
2207	52¢ White lilacs, self-adhesive	....	.95	.40
2208	52¢ Purple lilacs, self-adhesive	....	.95	.40
2208a	same, booklet pane of 10 (2207-08 x 2)	....	9.50	....

2209

2211

SCOTT NO.	DESCRIPTION	PLATE BLOCK F/NH	UNUSED F/NH	USED F
2209	52¢ HEC Montreal College, self-adhesvie	....	.95	.40
2209a	same, booklet pane of 4	....	3.80	....
2210	52¢ University of Saskotchewan, self-adhesive	....	.95	.40
2210a	same, booklet pane of 4	....	3.80	....
2211	52¢ Jelly Shelf by Mary Pratt	....	.95	.40
2212	52¢-$1.55 Art by Mary Pratt, souvenir sheet	....	3.75	....
2212a	$1.55 Iceberg in North Atlantic by Mary Pratt	....	2.80	1.25

2214

2215

SCOTT NO.	DESCRIPTION	PLATE BLOCK F/NH	UNUSED F/NH	USED F
2213	52¢-$1.55 Ottawa 150th Anniversary souvenir sheet of 2	....	3.75	....
2213a	52¢ Ottawa 150th Anniversary	....	.95	.40
2213b	$1.55 Ottawa 150th Anniversary	....	2.80	1.25
2214	52¢ Ottawa 150th Anniversary, self-adhesive	....	.95	.40
2214a	same, booklet pane of 4	....	3.80	....
2215-18	52¢ Royal Architectural Institute, strip of 4	....	3.80	1.60
2215	52¢ University of Lethbridge	....	.95	.40
2216	52¢ St. Mary's Church	....	.95	.40
2217	52¢ Ontario Science Center	....	.95	.40
2218	52¢ National Gallery of Canada	....	.95	.40

SCOTT NO.	DESCRIPTION	PLATE BLOCK F/NH	UNUSED F/NH	USED F
....	$1.55 Captain George Vancouver	....	2.80	1.25
....	same, souvenir sheet of 1	....	2.80	1.25
....	52¢ FIFA World Youth Championship	....	.95	.40
....	52¢ Canadian Recording Artists, souvenir sheet	....	3.80	....
....	same, booklet of 8	....	7.60	....
....	52¢ Joni Mitchell, self-adhesive	....	.95	.40
....	52¢ Gordon Lightfoot, self-adhesive	....	.95	.40
....	52¢ Paul Anka, self-adhesive	....	.95	.40
....	52¢ Anne Murray, self-adhesive	....	.95	.40

SCOTT NO.	DESCRIPTION	PLATE BLOCK F/NH	UNUSED F/NH	USED F
....	52¢ Terra Nova National Park, self-adhesive	....	.95	.40
....	same, booklet of 10	....	9.50	....
....	52¢ Jasper National Park, self-adhesive	....	.95	.40
....	same, booklet of 10	....	9.50	....
....	52¢ 100 Years of Scouting, self-adhesive	....	.95	.40
....	same, booklet of 8	....	7.60	....

CANADA PHOSPHOR TAGGED ISSUES

Overprinted with barely visible phosphorescent ink

TYPES OF TAGGING

I = Wide Side Bars
II = Wide Bar in Middle
III = Bar at Right or Left
IV = Narrow Bar in Middle
V = Narrow Side Bars

SCOTT NO.	DESCRIPTION			UNUSED F/NH
	1962-63 Queen Elizabeth II			
337-41p	1¢-5¢ Elizabeth	(5)	52.50	10.60
401-5p	1¢-5¢ Elizabeth	(5)	10.75	1.75
404pIV	4¢ Carmine—IV		6.00	1.25
404pII	4¢ Carmine—II		17.50	4.00
405q	5¢ Elizabeth, mini. pane of 25		......	41.25
	1964-67			
434-35p	3¢-5¢ 1964 Christmas	(2)	13.00	2.25
434q	3¢ mini. pane of 25		......	12.10
434q	same, sealed pack of 2		......	25.00
443-44p	3¢-5¢ 1965 Christmas	(2)	3.50	.65
443q	3¢ mini. pane of 25		......	7.70
443q	same, sealed pack of 2		......	15.75
451-52p	3¢-5¢ 1966 Christmas	(2)	3.50	.80
451q	3¢ mini. pane of 25		......	5.15
451q	same, sealed pack of 2		......	10.50
453p	5¢ Centennial		2.25	.45
	1967-72 Queen Elizabeth II			
454-58pI	1¢-5¢—I	(4)	12.50	1.75
454-58pII	1¢-5¢—II	(4)	12.50	1.65
454-57pV	1¢-5¢—V	(4)	7.75	.95
454ep	1¢ booklet single—V		......	.25
457p	4¢ carmine—III		2.75	.35
458q	5¢ mini. pane of 20		......	65.00
459p	6¢ orange, perf.10—I		4.50	.65
459bp	6¢ orange, perf.12-1/2x12—I		4.50	.65
460p	6¢ black, perf 12-1/2x12—I		5.50	.40
460cp	6¢ black, perf 12-1/2x12—II		4.25	.50
460gp	6¢ black, booklet single, perf.10—V		......	.75
460pII	6¢ black, perf. 12—II		4.00	.55
460pV	6¢ black, perf. 12—V		4.00	.50
	1967 Views			
462-65pI	10¢-25¢—I	(4)	45.00	9.00
462-63pV	10¢-15¢—V	(2)	12.50	2.00
	1967-69			
476-77p	3¢-5¢ 1967 Christmas	(2)	3.50	.65
476q	3¢ mini. pane of 25		......	3.30
476q	same, sealed pack of 2		......	7.00
488-89p	5¢-6¢ 1968 Christmas	(2)	3.75	.70
488q	5¢ booklet pane of 10		......	4.15
502-3p	5¢-6¢ 1969 Christmas	(2)	3.50	.60
502q	5¢ booklet pane of 10		......	3.85
	1970-71			
505p	6¢ Manitoba		1.75	.35
508-11p	25¢ Expo '70	(4)	12.50	11.00
513-14p	10¢-15¢ U.N.	(2)	20.00	3.15
519-30p	5¢-15¢ Christmas	(12)	23.50	6.05
541p	15¢ Radio Canada		17.25	3.05
	1971 Queen Elizabeth II			
543-44p	7¢-8¢—I	(2)	9.25	1.05
544q	booklet pane, 8¢(2), 6¢(1), 1¢(3)		......	2.20
544r	booklet pane, 8¢(11), 6¢(1), 1¢(6)		......	6.05
544s	booklet pane, 8¢(5), 6¢(1), 1¢(4)		......	2.75
544pV	8¢ slate—V		4.25	.60
550p	8¢ slate, coil		......	.30
	1971-72			
554-57p	6¢-15¢ Christmas	(4)	11.00	2.50
560p	8¢ World Health Day		3.25	.65
561p	8¢ Frontenac		5.75	.95
562-63p	8¢ Indians	(2)	3.75	1.20
564-65p	8¢ Indians	(2)	3.75	1.20
582-85p	15¢ Sciences	(4)	16.00	13.20
	1972 Pictorials			
594-97	10¢-25¢—V	(4)	10.50	2.25
594-97p I	10¢-25¢—I	(4)	35.00	7.50
	1972			
606-09p	6¢-15¢ Christmas—V	(4)	12.75	2.65
606-09pI	6¢-15¢ Christmas—I	(4)	15.00	3.50
610p	8¢ Krieghoff		3.50	.40

SEMI-POSTAL STAMPS

SCOTT NO.	DESCRIPTION	PLATE BLOCK F/NH	UNUSED F/NH	USED F
	1974-76			
B1-12	**Olympics, 12 varieties**	**28.50**	**5.95**	**5.95**
	1974			
B1-3	Emblems, 3 varieties	7.50	1.75	1.75
B1	8¢ + 2¢ Olympic Emblem	1.75	.55	.55
B2	10¢ + 5¢ same	2.65	.55	.55
B3	15¢ + 5¢ same	3.40	.75	.75
	1975			
B4-6	Water Sports, 3 varieties	7.25	1.50	1.50
B4	8¢ + 2¢ Swimming	1.75	.35	.50
B5	10¢ + 5¢ Rowing	2.65	.55	.55
B6	15¢ + 5¢ Sailing	3.40	.75	.75
B7-9	Combat Sports, 3 varieties	7.25	1.50	1.50
B7	8¢ + 2¢ Fencing	1.75	.35	.35
B8	10¢ + 5¢ Boxing	2.65	.55	.55
B9	15¢ + 5¢ Judo	3.40	.75	.75
	1976			
B10-12	Team Sports, 3 varieties	8.00	1.50	1.50
B10	8¢ + 2¢ Basketball	1.75	.35	.35
B11	10¢ + 5¢ Gymnastics	2.65	.50	.55
B12	20¢ + 5¢ Soccer	3.85	.85	.85
	1997			
B13	45¢ + 5¢ Literacy	....	.90	.40
B13a	same, booklet pane of 10	....	10.00	....

AIR POST STAMPS

C1

C2

C5

SCOTT NO.	DESCRIPTION	UNUSED NH VF	UNUSED NH F	UNUSED NH AVG	UNUSED OG VF	UNUSED OG F	UNUSED OG AVG	USED VF	USED F	USED AVG
	1928									
C1	5¢ brown olive	16.50	11.25	6.95	11.00	7.50	4.75	3.75	2.60	1.75
	1930									
C2	5¢ olive brown	65.00	44.00	27.50	42.00	28.50	17.75	21.00	15.50	10.00
	1932									
C3	6¢ on 5¢ brown olive	11.25	7.75	4.75	8.00	5.50	3.25	3.50	2.60	1.50
C4	6¢ on 5¢ olive brown	28.00	19.00	11.95	18.00	12.25	7.75	11.50	8.75	5.50

C6

C7

C9

SCOTT NO.	DESCRIPTION	PLATE BLOCK F/NH	PLATE BLOCK F/OG	UNUSED F/NH	UNUSED F/OG	USED F
	1935					
C5	6¢ red brown	14.00	11.50	2.40	1.75	.85
	1938					
C6	6¢ blue	16.50	13.25	3.40	2.50	.20
	1942-43					
C7	6¢ deep blue	13.75	11.00	2.75	2.05	.75
C8	7¢ deep blue (1943)	2.75	2.20	.55	.45	.15
	1946					
C9	7¢ deep blue	2.65	2.20	.55	.45	.15
C9a	same, booklet pane of 4	...	2.20	1.80	...	...

AIR POST SPECIAL DELIVERY

CE1

CE3

SCOTT NO.	DESCRIPTION	PLATE BLOCK F/NH	PLATE BLOCK F/OG	UNUSED F/NH	UNUSED F/OG	USED F
	1942-43					
CE1	16¢ bright ultramarine	12.50	9.50	2.20	1.65	1.50
CE2	17¢ bright ultramarine (1943)	14.00	10.75	2.75	2.10	1.95
	1946					
CE3	17¢ bright ultramarine (circumflex "E")	23.10	17.60	5.50	3.75	3.60
	1947					
CE4	17¢ bright ultramarine (grave "E")	23.10	17.60	5.50	3.75	3.60

SPECIAL DELIVERY STAMPS

E1

E2

E3

SCOTT NO.	DESCRIPTION	UNUSED NH VF	UNUSED NH F	UNUSED NH AVG	UNUSED O.G VF	UNUSED O.G F	UNUSED O.G AVG	USED VF	USED F	USED AVG
	1898									
E1	10¢ blue green	180.00	110.00	80.00	70.00	47.50	29.50	11.00	7.50	5.00
	1922									
E2	20¢ carmine	140.00	90.00	65.00	70.00	47.50	29.50	8.75	6.50	4.00
	1927									
E3	20¢ orange	31.00	21.00	13.00	16.50	11.25	6.95	12.50	8.75	5.00
	1930									
E4	20¢ henna brown	90.00	59.50	40.00	48.00	32.50	20.25	16.50	11.25	6.95
	1933									
E5	20¢ henna brown	90.00	61.25	38.00	48.00	32.50	20.25	19.00	13.00	8.25

E4

E6

E7

E10

SCOTT NO.	DESCRIPTION	PLATE BLOCK F/NH	PLATE BLOCK F/OG	UNUSED F/NH	UNUSED F/OG	USED F
	1935					
E6	20¢ dark carmine	72.50	46.50	10.00	6.10	4.50
	1938-39					
E7	10¢ dark green(1939)	24.75	19.25	5.00	3.85	2.75
E8	20¢ dark carmine	247.25	178.25	32.50	22.00	22.50
E9	10¢ on 20¢ dark carmine (#E8) (1939)	36.95	26.50	5.50	3.85	3.85
	1942					
E10	10¢ green	11.50	9.00	2.50	1.95	1.50
	1946					
E11	10¢ green	8.00	6.75	1.65	1.40	.90

WAR TAX STAMPS

MR1

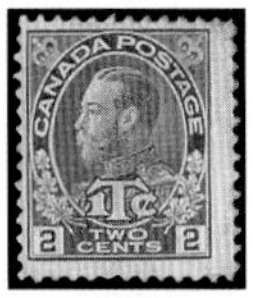

MR3

2¢ + 1¢ Die I. Below large letter "T" there is a clear horizontal line of color. Die II. Right side of line is replaced by two short lines and five dots.

SCOTT NO.	DESCRIPTION	UNUSED NH F	UNUSED NH AVG	UNUSED F	UNUSED AVG	USED F	USED AVG
	1915						
MR1	1¢ green	18.00	12.50	9.00	6.50	.20	.15
MR2	2¢ carmine	18.00	12.50	9.00	6.50	.25	.20
	1916 Perf 12						
MR3	2¢ + 1¢ carmine (I)	23.00	15.00	11.50	8.00	.20	.15
MR3a	2¢ + 1¢ carmine(II)	165.00	110.00	80.00	60.00	4.00	2.50
MR4	2¢ + 1¢ brown (II)	18.00	12.00	10.00	7.00	8.50	5.00
MR4a	2¢ + 1¢ brown(I)	375.00	275.00	195.00	150.00	8.50	6.50
	Perf 12 x 8						
MR5	2¢ + 1¢ carmine	55.00	40.00	27.00	20.00	20.00	14.00
	Coil Stamps Perf. 8 Vertically						
MR6	2¢ + 1¢ carmine (I)	125.00	85.00	75.00	50.00	7.00	5.00
MR7	2¢ + 1¢ brown (II)	27.00	20.00	13.00	9.00	.90	.60
MR7a	2¢ + 1¢ brown (I)	170.00	120.00	85.00	65.00	7.00	5.00

REGISTRATION STAMPS

F2

1875-88 Perf. 12 (NH+50%)

SCOTT NO.	DESCRIPTION	UNUSED O.G. VF	UNUSED O.G. F	UNUSED O.G. AVG	UNUSED VF	UNUSED F	UNUSED AVG	USED VF	USED F	USED AVG
F1	2¢ orange	85.00	56.00	34.00	70.00	46.75	28.50	4.00	2.75	1.55
F1a	2¢ vermillion	100.00	66.00	39.50	82.50	55.00	33.00	9.50	6.35	3.40
F1b	2¢ rose carmine	195.00	130.00	79.50	165.00	110.00	66.00	110.00	72.50	40.00
F1d	2¢ orange, perf 12x11-1/2	365.00	245.00	158.00	305.00	203.50	132.50	88.00	58.85	32.50
F2	5¢ dark green	100.00	66.00	41.50	82.50	55.00	34.50	4.50	3.25	1.95
F2d	5¢ dark green, perf 12x11-1/2	1140.00	960.00	500.00	950.00	800.00	450.00	185.00	125.00	67.50
F3	8¢ blue	550.00	365.00	245.00	455.00	305.00	205.00	410.00	275.00	148.50

POSTAGE DUE STAMPS

J1

J11

J6

J15

J21

SCOTT NO.	DESCRIPTION	UNUSED NH F	UNUSED NH AVG	UNUSED F	UNUSED AVG	USED F	USED AVG
	1906-28						
J1	1¢ violet	14.75	9.25	8.50	5.25	3.50	1.95
J2	2¢ violet	14.75	9.25	8.50	5.25	.75	.50
J3	4¢ violet (1928)	59.50	37.00	34.00	21.00	16.00	10.00
J4	5¢ violet	14.75	9.25	8.50	5.25	1.35	.95
J5	10¢ violet (1928)	38.75	23.75	22.00	13.50	11.00	7.50
	1930-32						
J6	1¢ dark violet	10.25	6.50	5.75	3.50	3.00	1.75
J7	2¢ dark violet	7.50	4.50	4.25	2.50	.75	.50
J8	4¢ dark violet	14.25	8.75	8.50	5.25	3.00	1.75
J9	5¢ dark violet	14.25	8.75	8.50	5.25	5.00	1.65
J10	10¢ dark violet (1932)	88.50	54.50	51.00	31.50	7.00	4.00
	1933-34						
J11	1¢ dark violet (1934)	12.00	7.50	6.75	4.00	5.00	2.95
J12	2¢ dark violet	4.75	2.95	2.75	1.50	.90	.60
J13	4¢ dark violet	11.00	6.75	6.25	3.75	5.00	3.25
J14	10¢ dark violet	20.50	12.75	12.00	7.50	4.00	2.50

SCOTT NO.	DESCRIPTION	UNUSED NH F	UNUSED NH AVG	UNUSED F	UNUSED AVG	USED F
	1935-65					
J15-20	**1¢-10¢ complete, 7 varieties**	**40.00**	**36.50**	**5.50**	**4.95**	**3.35**
J15	1¢ dark violet	.80	.55	.20	.15	.15
J16	2¢ dark violet	.80	.55	.20	.15	.15
J16B	3¢ dark violet (1965)	13.75	9.60	1.95	1.35	1.00
J17	4¢ dark violet	1.35	.95	.20	.15	.15
J18	5¢ dark violet (1948)	2.20	1.55	.35	.25	.25
J19	6¢ dark violet (1957)	13.75	9.60	1.95	1.35	1.00
J20	10¢ dark violet	1.55	1.10	.25	.20	.15

POSTAGE DUES

1967 Perf. 12

Regular Size Design 20mm X 17mm

SCOTT NO.	DESCRIPTION	PLATE BLOCK F/NH	UNUSED F/NH	USED F
J21-27	**1¢-10¢ cpl., 7 vars.**	**18.00**	**3.50**	**3.40**
J21	1¢ carmine rose	1.40	.25	.25
J22	2¢ carmine rose	1.40	.25	.25
J23	3¢ carmine rose	1.40	.25	.25
J24	4¢ carmine rose	2.20	.45	.25
J25	5¢ carmine rose	8.25	1.65	1.35
J26	6¢ carmine rose	2.15	.40	.25
J27	10¢ carmine rose	2.15	.40	.25

1969-78 Perf. 12 (White or Yellow Gum)

Modular Size Design 20mm x 15-3/4 mm

SCOTT NO.	DESCRIPTION	PLATE BLOCK F/NH	UNUSED F/NH	USED F
J28/37	**(J28-31, J33-37) 9 vars.**	**6.50**	**1.95**	**1.60**
J28	1¢ carmine rose (1970)	.65	.20	.15
J29	2¢ carmine rose (1972)	.65	.20	.15
J30	3¢ carmine rose (1974)	.65	.20	.15
J31	4¢ carmine rose (1969)	.65	.20	.15
J32a	5¢ carmine rose (1977)	125.00	24.75	24.75
J33	6¢ carmine rose (1972)	.65	.20	.15
J34	8¢ carmine rose	.80	.20	.15
J35	10¢ carmine rose (1969)	1.00	.20	.20
J36	12¢ carmine rose (1969)	1.10	.25	.25
J37	16¢ carmine rose (1974)	1.65	.40	.35

1977-78

Perf. 12-1/2 X 12

SCOTT NO.	DESCRIPTION	PLATE BLOCK F/NH	UNUSED F/NH	USED F
J28a-40	**1¢-50¢ cpl., 9 vars.**	**24.00**	**5.05**	**4.75**
J28a	1¢ carmine rose	.65	.20	.15
J31a	4¢ carmine rose	.65	.20	.15
J32	5¢ carmine rose	.65	.20	.15
J34a	8¢ carmine rose (1978)	1.95	.40	.25
J35a	10¢ carmine rose	.90	.20	.15
J36a	12¢ carmine rose	11.00	2.25	1.40
J38	20¢ carmine rose	1.95	.40	.35
J39	24¢ carmine rose	2.55	.50	.45
J40	50¢ carmine rose	4.95	1.00	1.95

OFFICIAL STAMPS

1949-50

#249, 250, 252, 254, 269-73 overprinted O.H.M.S.

SCOTT NO.	DESCRIPTION	PLATE BLOCK F/NH	UNUSED F/NH	USED F
O1-10	**1¢-$1 complete, 9 vars.**	......	**290.00**	**165.00**
O1-8	**1¢-20¢, 7 varieties**	......	**47.50**	**18.50**
O1	1¢ green	10.45	2.15	1.65
O2	2¢ brown	110.00	15.40	18.00
O3	3¢ rose violet	10.75	2.20	1.10
O4	4¢ dark carmine	14.85	3.30	.70
O6	10¢ olive	18.70	4.05	.55
O7	14¢ black brown	29.45	6.45	1.85
O8	20¢ slate black	79.75	16.50	2.50
O9	50¢ dark blue green	962.50	203.50	100.00
O10	$1 red violet	247.50	52.25	35.75
	1950 #294 overprinted O.H.M.S.			
O11	50¢ dull green	148.50	30.75	16.50

1950 #284-88 overprinted O.H.M.S.

SCOTT NO.	DESCRIPTION	PLATE BLOCK F/NH	UNUSED F/NH	USED F
O12-15A	**1¢-5¢ cpl., 5 vars.**	**26.75**	**4.90**	**2..50**
O12	1¢ green	3.50	.30	.30
O13	2¢ sepia	3.80	.80	.75
O14	3¢ rose violet	4.95	1.00	.40
O15	4¢ dark carmine	4.95	1.00	.15
O15A	5¢ deep blue	11.00	2.05	1.10

1950 #284-88, 269-71, 294, 273 overprinted G

SCOTT NO.	DESCRIPTION	PLATE BLOCK F/NH	UNUSED F/NH	USED F
O16-25	**1¢-$1 complete, 10 vars.**	......	**115.00**	**60.00**
O16-24	**1¢-50¢, 9 varieties**	......	**37.00**	**8.00**
O16	1¢ green	1.75	.25	.15
O17	2¢ sepia	5.50	1.00	.65
O18	3¢ rose violet	4.95	1.00	.15
O19	4¢ dark carmine	5.25	1.10	.15
O20	5¢ deep blue	11.00	1.20	.75
O21	10¢ olive	12.10	2.60	.40
O22	14¢ black brown	31.35	7.15	1.65
O23	20¢ slate black	74.25	14.85	.90
O24	50¢ dull green	49.50	9.90	3.60
O25	$1 red violet	368.50	82.50	55.00
	1950-51 #301, 302 overprinted G			
O26	10¢ black brown	6.05	1.30	.20
O27	$1 bright ultramarine	395.00	74.25	55.00

SCOTT NO.	DESCRIPTION	PLATE BLOCK F/NH	UNUSED F/NH	USED F
	1951-53 #305-06, 316, 320-21 overprinted G			
O28	2¢ olive green	1.85	.40	.15
O29	4¢ orange vermillion ('52)	3.60	.65	.15
O30	20¢ gray (1952)	9.35	2.10	.15
O31	7¢ blue (1952)	14.60	3.15	.80
O32	$1 gray (1953)	60.50	12.65	7.45
	1953 #325-29, 334 overprinted G			
O33-37	**1¢-5¢ complete, 5vars.**	**8.40**	**1.90**	**.70**
O33	1¢ violet brown	1.35	.30	.15
O34	2¢ green	1.55	.35	.15
O35	3¢ carmine	1.55	.35	.15
O36	4¢ violet	2.20	.50	.15
O37	5¢ ultramarine	2.20	.50	.15
O38	50¢ lightgreen	24.20	5.25	1.00
	1955 #351 overprinted G			
O39	10¢ violet brown	3.55	.80	.15

SCOTT NO.	DESCRIPTION	PLATE BLOCK F/NH	UNUSED F/NH	USED F
	1955-56 #337, 338, 340, 341, 362 overprinted G			
O40-45	**1¢-20¢ cpl., 5vars.**	**17.00**	**3.55**	**.80**
O40	1¢ violet brown(1956)	1.30	.30	.25
O41	2¢ green (1956)	1.65	.35	.15
O43	4¢ violet(1956)	5.35	1.00	.15
O44	5¢ bright blue	2.05	.45	.15
O45	20¢ green(1956)	7.70	1.65	.15
	1963 #401, 402, 404, 405 overprinted G			
O46-49	**1¢-5¢ cpl., 4 vars.**	**14.60**	**2.30**	**2.30**
O46	1¢ deep brown	2.75	.60	.60
O47	2¢ green	2.75	.60	.60
O48	4¢ carmine	7.15	.75	.75
O49	5¢ violet blue	2.75	.45	.45
	1949-50 AIR POST OFFICIAL STAMPS			
CO1	7¢ deep blue, O.H.M.S.(C9)	38.50	8.25	2.65
CO2	7¢ deep blue, G (C9)	88.00	18.15	13.75
	1950 SPECIAL DELIVERY OFFICIAL STAMPS			
EO1	10¢ green, O.H.M.S.(E11)	99.00	20.35	12.25
EO2	10¢ green, G (E11)	130.00	30.00	25.00

1

2

Queen Victoria

4

7

Seal

SCOTT NO.	DESCRIPTION	UNUSED O.G. VF	UNUSED O.G. F	UNUSED O.G. AVG	UNUSED VF	UNUSED F	UNUSED AVG	USED VF	USED F	USED AVG
	1860 Imperforate									
1	2-1/2p dull rose	...	...	...	...	2750.00	1750.00	...	...	...
	1860 Perforated 14									
2	2-1/2p dull rose	895.00	450.00	260.00	475.00	250.00	140.00	300.00	150.00	95.00
	VANCOUVER ISLAND									
	1865 Imperforate									
3	5¢ rose	....	....	....	....	....	....	....	....	....
4	10¢ blue	4500.00	2450.00	1650.00	2450.00	1350.00	900.00	1350.00	725.00	450.00
	Perforated 14									
5	5¢ rose	850.00	450.00	250.00	450.00	240.00	140.00	300.00	150.00	95.00
6	10¢ blue	850.00	450.00	250.00	450.00	240.00	140.00	300.00	150.00	95.00
	BRITISH COLUMBIA									
	1865									
7	3p blue	265.00	140.00	90.00	140.00	75.00	50.00	140.00	75.00	50.00
	New Values surcharged on 1865 design									
	1867-69 Perforated 14									
8	2¢ brown	325.00	175.00	95.00	180.00	95.00	50.00	180.00	95.00	55.00
9	5¢ bright red	550.00	300.00	175.00	325.00	175.00	95.00	300.00	160.00	95.00
10	10¢ lilac rose	4500.00	2450.00	1300.00	2450.00	1300.00	700.00	...	...	...
11	25¢ orange	600.00	325.00	180.00	325.00	170.00	95.00	300.00	160.00	95.00
12	50¢ violet	2000.00	1075.00	650.00	1075.00	575.00	350.00	1075.00	575.00	325.00
13	$1 green	3500.00	1850.00	1050.00	1900.00	1000.00	550.00	...	...	...
	1869 Perforated 12-1/2									
14	5¢ bright red	4500.00	2400.00	1475.00	2400.00	1250.00	775.00	1700.00	900.00	550.00
15	10¢ lilac rose	2500.00	1400.00	800.00	1400.00	750.00	450.00	1450.00	750.00	450.00
16	25¢ orange	1450.00	800.00	400.00	850.00	450.00	250.00	850.00	450.00	250.00
17	50¢ violet	2000.00	1100.00	600.00	1100.00	600.00	350.00	1125.00	600.00	350.00
18	$1 green	4000.00	2250.00	1275.00	2250.00	1175.00	675.00	2250.00	1175.00	675.00

1, 15A, 16

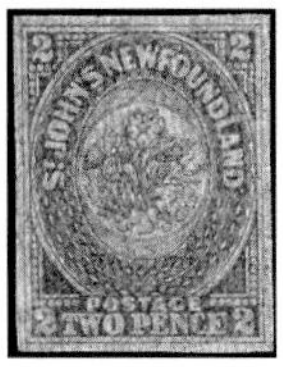
2, 11, 17

3, 11A

4, 12, 18

6, 13, 20

7, 21

8, 22

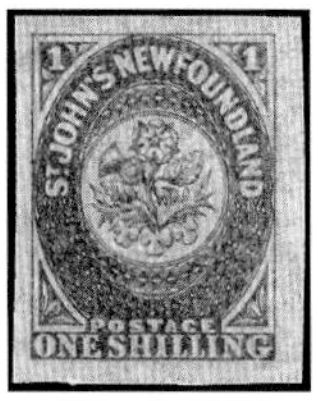
9, 15, 23

24, 38
Codfish

25, 26, 40
Seal

SCOTT NO.	DESCRIPTION	UNUSED O.G. VF	UNUSED O.G. F	UNUSED O.G. AVG	UNUSED VF	UNUSED F	UNUSED AVG	USED VF	USED F	USED AVG
	1857 Imperforate, Thick Paper									
1	1p brown violet	107.50	82.50	57.75	72.50	55.00	38.50	140.00	100.00	70.00
2	2p scarlet vermillion	13000.00	9000.00	6750.00	10000.00	7200.00	5400.00	4400.00	3125.00	2200.00
3	3p green	540.00	410.00	260.00	360.00	275.00	175.00	425.00	300.00	225.00
4	4p scarlet vermillion	8200.00	6150.00	4625.00	7700.00	5750.00	4350.00	3200.00	2000.00	1500.00
5	5p brown violet	250.00	187.50	145.00	200.00	150.00	112.50	325.00	245.00	175.00
6	6p scarlet vermillion	12800.00	9175.00	6500.00	12000.00	9000.00	6750.00	3450.00	2475.00	1750.00
7	6-1/2p scarlet vermillion	3100.00	2325.00	1750.00	2800.00	2100.00	1575.00	2475.00	1775.00	1240.00
8	8p scarlet vermillion	275.00	210.00	155.00	225.00	168.75	125.00	395.00	300.00	205.00
9	1sh scarlet vermillion	15100.00	10750.00	7550.00	14800.00	11100.00	8325.00	5400.00	3800.00	2700.00
	1860 Thin Paper									
11	2p orange	275.00	210.00	155.00	225.00	168.75	125.00	325.00	245.00	185.50
11A	3p green	80.00	62.00	39.50	53.50	41.25	26.40	100.00	83.00	55.00
12	4p orange	2600.00	1950.00	1475.00	2400.00	1800.00	1350.00	1200.00	900.00	675.00
12A	5p violet brown	127.50	100.00	49.50	85.00	66.00	33.00	180.00	138.00	88.00
13	6p orange	3900.00	3000.00	2250.00	2600.00	2000.00	1500.00	715.00	550.00	385.00
	1861-62 Thin Paper									
15	1sh orange	27000.00	19250.00	12500.00	21500.00	15450.00	10900.00	8050.00	5750.00	4600.00
15A	1p violet brown	195.00	150.00	100.00	130.00	100.00	66.00	175.00	138.00	105.00
16	1p reddish brown	4725.00	3375.00	2375.00	3775.00	2700.00	1950.00	...	...	...
17	2p rose	195.00	150.00	100.00	130.00	100.00	66.00	175.00	138.00	83.00
18	4p rose	58.75	45.00	25.50	39.25	30.25	17.00	65.00	50.00	24.00
19	5p reddish brown	64.50	44.50	33.00	43.00	33.00	22.00	71.50	55.00	34.65
20	6p rose	32.25	24.75	13.20	21.50	16.50	8.80	69.00	53.00	35.75
21	6-1/2p rose	96.75	74.25	39.60	64.50	49.50	26.40	320.00	240.00	180.00
22	8p rose	82.50	63.50	33.00	55.00	42.35	22.00	320.00	240.00	180.00
23	1sh rose	48.50	37.00	19.75	32.00	24.75	13.20	320.00	240.00	180.00

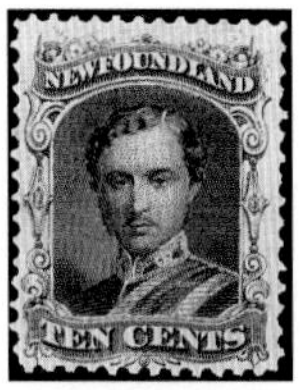
27
Prince Albert

28, 29
Queen Victoria

30
Fishing Ship

31
Queen Victoria

32, 32A, 37
Prince of Wales

35, 36
Queen Victoria

SCOTT NO.	DESCRIPTION	UNUSED O.G. VF	UNUSED O.G. F	UNUSED O.G. AVG	UNUSED VF	UNUSED F	UNUSED AVG	USED VF	USED F	USED AVG
	1865-94 Perforate 12 Yellow Paper									
24	2¢ green	74.50	57.25	39.25	57.25	44.00	30.25	32.00	24.75	13.75
24a	2¢ green (white paper)	56.00	43.00	26.50	43.00	33.00	20.35	22.75	17.60	9.90
25	5¢ brown	560.00	430.00	300.00	430.00	330.00	230.00	285.00	220.00	148.00
26	5¢ black (1868)	280.00	215.00	143.00	215.00	165.00	110.00	120.00	93.00	60.50
27	10¢ black	280.00	215.00	143.00	215.00	165.00	110.00	71.50	55.00	38.50
27a	10¢ black (white paper)	130.00	100.00	64.50	100.00	77.00	49.50	43.00	33.00	18.15
28	12¢ pale red brown	345.00	265.00	175.00	265.00	204.00	137.50	165.00	126.50	87.50
28a	12¢ pale red brown (white paper)	45.50	35.00	18.50	35.00	26.95	14.30	35.00	26.95	14.30
29	12¢ brown (1894)	45.50	35.00	18.50	35.00	26.95	14.30	32.00	24.75	13.20
30	13¢ orange	110.00	85.00	57.25	85.75	66.00	44.00	57.25	44.00	30.25
31	24¢ blue	37.50	28.50	20.00	28.75	22.00	15.40	26.50	20.35	13.75
	1868-94									
32	1¢ violet	37.00	28.50	18.50	28.50	22.00	14.30	28.50	22.00	11.00
32A	1¢ brown lilac, re-engraved (1871)	56.00	43.00	23.00	43.00	33.00	17.60	43.00	33.00	17.60
33	3¢ vermillion (1870)	345.00	265.00	180.00	265.00	203.50	137.50	165.00	26.50	71.50
34	3¢ blue (1873)	280.00	215.00	143.00	215.00	165.00	110.00	23.00	17.60	9.90
35	6¢ dull rose (1870)	16.00	12.15	7.15	12.15	9.35	5.50	12.25	9.35	5.50
36	6¢ carmine lake (1894)	18.50	14.25	10.00	14.25	11.00	7.70	14.25	11.00	7.70
	1876-79 Rouletted									
37	1¢ brown lilac (1877)	52.00	40.00	40.00	40.00	30.25	30.75	21.50	16.50	11.00
38	2¢ green (1879)	63.00	48.50	48.50	48.50	37.40	37.40	35.75	27.50	17.60
39	3¢ blue (1877)	170.00	130.00	100.00	130.00	99.00	99.00	10.00	770	5.25
40	5¢ blue	110.00	85.75	85.75	85.75	66.00	66.00	10.00	7.70	5.25

41-45
Prince of Wales

46-48
Codfish

53-55
Seal

56-58
Newfoundland Dog

SCOTT NO.	DESCRIPTION	UNUSED O.G. VF	UNUSED O.G. F	UNUSED O.G. AVG	UNUSED VF	UNUSED F	UNUSED AVG	USED VF	USED F	USED AVG
	1880-96 Perforate 12									
41	1¢ violet brown	15.50	10.50	5.65	13.00	8.80	4.70	9.25	7.15	3.60
42	1¢ gray brown	15.50	10.50	5.65	13.00	8.80	4.70	9.25	7.15	3.60
43	1¢ brown (Reissue) (1896)	35.00	23.75	13.25	29.50	19.80	11.00	23.50	18.15	10.20
44	1¢ deep green (1887)	9.90	6.60	3.95	8.25	5.50	3.30	3.60	2.75	1.65
45	1¢ green (Reissue) (1897)	10.75	7.25	4.50	9.00	6.05	3.85	6.50	4.95	2.75
46	2¢ yellow green	19.75	13.25	7.95	16.50	11.00	6.60	13.50	10.45	5.50
47	2¢ green (Reissue) (1896)	44.50	29.50	15.85	37.00	24.75	13.20	19.25	14.85	8.25
48	2¢ red orange (1887)	16.75	11.25	5.95	14.00	9.35	4.95	7.50	5.80	3.30
49	3¢ blue	24.00	16.50	9.95	20.00	13.75	8.25	4.25	3.30	1.85
51	3¢ umber brown (1887)	19.75	13.25	8.50	16.50	11.00	7.15	4.25	3.30	1.85
52	3¢ violet brown (Reissue) (1896)	52.50	35.00	18.50	43.75	29.15	15.40	38.00	29.15	15.40
53	5¢ pale blue	290.00	198.00	120.00	245.00	165.00	99.00	11.25	8.80	4.95
54	5¢ dark blue (1887)	120.00	79.00	46.25	100.00	66.00	38.50	8.50	6.60	3.60
55	5¢ bright blue (1894)	24.50	16.50	9.95	20.50	13.75	8.25	6.50	4.95	2.50

59
Schooner

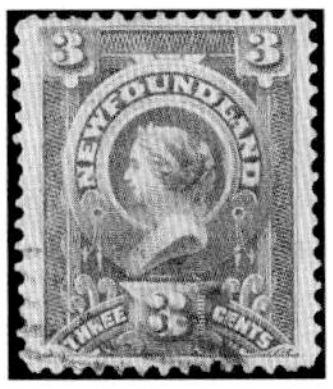

60
Queen Victoria

ONE CENT
ONE CENT
ONE CENT

1897
60a surcharged in black

61
Queen Victoria

62
John Cabot

63
Cape Bonavista

SCOTT NO.	DESCRIPTION	UNUSED O.G. VF	UNUSED O.G. F	UNUSED O.G. AVG	UNUSED VF	UNUSED F	UNUSED AVG	USED VF	USED F	USED AVG
	1887-96									
56	1/2¢ rose red	7.25	5.65	3.30	6.10	4.70	2.75	5.75	4.40	2.50
57	1/2¢ orange red (1896) 38.50	29.75	15.85	32.00	24.75	13.20	34.00	26.40	15.40	
58	1/2¢ black (1894)	6.00	4.60	2.45	5.00	3.85	2.05	5.00	3.85	2.05
59	10¢ black	55.75	43.00	26.50	46.50	35.75	22.00	43.00	33.00	17.60
	1890									
60	3¢ slate	9.40	7.25	3.95	7.85	6.05	3.30	.85	.65	.40

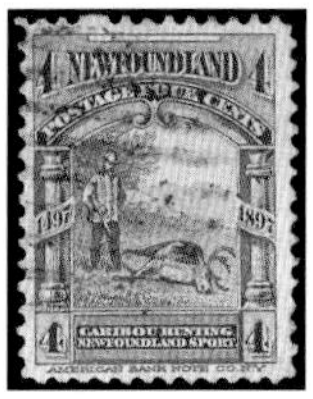
64
Caribou Hunting

65
Mining

66
Logging

67
Fishing

68
Cabot's Ship

69
Ptarmigan

70
Seals

71
Salmon Fishing

72
Seal of Colony

73
Coast Scene

74
King Henry VII

1897 CABOT ISSUE

SCOTT NO.	DESCRIPTION	UNUSED O.G. VF	UNUSED O.G. F	UNUSED O.G. AVG	UNUSED VF	UNUSED F	UNUSED AVG	USED VF	USED F	USED AVG
61-74	**1¢-60¢ complete, 14 varieties**	**360.00**	**275.00**	**170.00**	**206.00**	**149.00**	**97.50**	**153.50**	**118.00**	**64.75**
61	1¢ deep green	2.70	2.10	1.40	1.55	1.20	.80	1.55	1.20	.65
62	2¢ carmine lake	3.40	2.60	1.75	1.95	1.50	1.00	1.55	1.20	.65
63	3¢ ultramarine	5.00	3.85	2.50	2.85	2.20	1.45	1.45	1.10	.60
64	4¢ olive green	8.15	6.30	4.00	4.65	3.60	2.30	3.55	2.75	1.65
65	5¢ violet	8.15	6.30	4.00	4.65	3.60	2.30	3.55	2.75	1.65
66	6¢ red brown	7.45	5.75	3.85	4.25	3.30	2.20	4.30	3.30	2.00
67	8¢ red orange	16.20	12.50	7.70	9.25	7.15	4.40	6.45	4.95	2.75
68	10¢ black brown	22.50	17.25	10.50	12.85	9.90	6.05	6.10	4.70	2.60
69	12¢ dark blue	23.50	18.25	11.50	13.50	10.45	6.60	7.50	5.80	3.15
70	15¢ scarlet	23.50	18.25	11.50	13.50	10.45	6.60	8.25	6.35	3.50
71	24¢ gray violet	23.50	18.25	11.50	13.50	10.45	6.60	8.50	6.60	3.60
72	30¢ slate	68.25	53.00	31.75	39.00	30.25	18.15	35.75	27.50	15.40
73	35¢ red	150.00	115.00	70.00	85.75	66.00	40.15	64.75	49.50	26.40
74	60¢ black	16.85	12.50	7.70	9.65	7.15	4.40	8.50	6.60	3.60

1897

SCOTT NO.	DESCRIPTION	UNUSED O.G. VF	UNUSED O.G. F	UNUSED O.G. AVG	UNUSED VF	UNUSED F	UNUSED AVG	USED VF	USED F	USED AVG
75	1¢ on 3¢ gray lilac, Type a	35.00	26.25	19.75	30.00	22.50	15.00	18.00	13.50	10.00
76	1¢ on 3¢ gray lilac, Type b	140.00	105.00	78.75	120.00	90.00	67.50	140.00	105.00	78.75
77	1¢ on 3¢ gray lilac, Type c	525.00	395.00	295.00	450.00	337.50	255.00	480.00	360.00	270.00

78
Edward, Prince of Wales

79, 80
Queen Victoria

81, 82
King Edward VII

83
Queen Alexandria

84
Queen Mary

85
King George V

1897-1901 ROYAL FAMILY ISSUE

SCOTT NO.	DESCRIPTION	UNUSED O.G. VF	UNUSED O.G. F	UNUSED O.G. AVG	UNUSED VF	UNUSED F	UNUSED AVG	USED VF	USED F	USED AVG
78-85	**1/2¢-5¢ complete, 8 varieties**	**105.00**	**80.50**	**52.50**	**58.00**	**44.75**	**29.00**	**18.40**	**14.00**	**8.10**
78	1/2¢ olive green	3.85	3.00	2.00	2.15	1.65	1.10	2.65	2.05	1.10
79	1¢ carmine rose	5.40	4.10	2.80	3.00	2.30	1.55	3.55	2.75	1.55
80	1¢ yellow green (1898) 3.25	2.50	1.70	1.80	1.40	.95	.25	.20	.15	
81	2¢ orange	6.40	4.95	3.15	3.55	2.75	1.75	4.30	3.30	2.00
82	2¢ vermillion (1898) 11.60	8.90	5.95	6.45	4.95	3.30	.75	.55	.35	
83	3¢ orange (1898)	20.60	15.85	10.00	11.45	8.80	5.60	.75	.55	.35
84	4¢ violet (1901)	27.00	20.75	13.85	15.00	11.55	7.70	4.30	3.30	1.85
85	5¢ blue (1899)	32.00	24.75	15.85	17.85	13.75	8.60	2.85	2.20	1.20

86
Map of Newfoundland

87
King James I

88
Arms of the London & Bristol Company

89
John Guy

90
Guy's Ship the "Endeavour"

91
View of the Town of Cupids

92, 92A, 98
Lord Bacon

93, 99
View of Mosquito Bay

94, 100
Logging Camp

95, 101
Paper Mills

96, 102
King Edward VII

SCOTT NO.	DESCRIPTION	UNUSED O.G. VF	UNUSED O.G. F	UNUSED O.G. AVG	UNUSED VF	UNUSED F	UNUSED AVG	USED VF	USED F	USED AVG
					1908					
86	2¢ rose carmine	25.75	19.75	13.85	14.30	11.00	7.70	1.45	1.10	.70

1910 JOHN GUY ISSUE—Lithographed Perf.12

SCOTT NO.	DESCRIPTION	UNUSED O.G. VF	UNUSED O.G. F	UNUSED O.G. AVG	UNUSED VF	UNUSED F	UNUSED AVG	USED VF	USED F	USED AVG
87/97	**(87-92, 92A, 93-97) 12 varieties**	**475.00**	**350.00**	**195.00**	**285.00**	**219.00**	**145.00**	**320.00**	**245.00**	**129.00**
87	1¢ deep green, perf. 12x11	2.30	1.75	1.25	1.45	1.10	.80	1.10	.85	.50
87a	1¢ deep green	5.25	4.00	2.65	6.80	2.50	1.65	2.15	1.65	1.00
87b	1¢ deep green, perf. 12x14	4.00	3.10	1.90	2.55	1.95	1.20	1.95	1.50	.95
88	2¢ carmine	8.00	6.15	4.25	5.00	3.85	2.65	.85	.65	.40
88a	2¢ carmine, perf. 12x14	5.75	4.40	2.95	3.55	2.75	1.85	.85	.65	.40
88c	2¢ carmine, perf. 12x11-1/2	210.00	160.00	105.00	129.00	99.00	66.00	85.00	66.00	35.75
89	3¢ brown olive	13.65	10.50	7.00	8.55	6.60	4.40	10.75	8.25	4.40
90	4¢ dull violet	22.75	17.60	11.45	14.25	11.00	7.15	9.30	7.15	3.60
91	5¢ ultramarine, perf. 14x12	9.00	7.00	4.75	5.75	4.40	2.95	3.50	2.75	1.50
91a	5¢ ultramarine	20.50	15.85	11.45	12.85	9.90	7.15	4.30	3.30	1.85
92	6¢ claret (I)	91.00	70.00	46.50	57.25	44.00	29.15	57.25	44.00	23.60
92A	6¢ claret (II)	34.50	26.50	17.60	21.45	16.50	11.00	25.75	19.80	11.00
93	8¢ pale brown	57.25	44.00	29.00	35.75	27.50	18.15	45.00	34.65	17.60
94	9¢ olive green	57.25	44.00	29.00	35.75	27.50	18.15	45.00	34.65	17.60
95	10¢ violet black	57.25	44.00	29.00	35.75	27.50	18.15	40.00	30.25	15.95
96	12¢ lilac brown	57.25	44.00	29.00	35.75	27.50	18.15	45.00	34.65	17.60
97	15¢ gray black	68.50	52.75	35.00	43.00	33.00	22.00	55.75	42.90	22.00

#92 Type I. "Z" of "COLONIZATION" is reversed. #92A Type II. "Z" is normal

97, 103
King George V

104
Queen Mary

105
King George

106
Prince of Wales

107
Prince Albert

108
Princess Mary

109
Prince Henry

1911 Engraved. Perf. 14

SCOTT NO.	DESCRIPTION	UNUSED O.G. VF	UNUSED O.G. F	UNUSED O.G. AVG	UNUSED VF	UNUSED F	UNUSED AVG	USED VF	USED F	USED AVG
98-103	**6¢-15¢ complete, 6 varieties**	**450.00**	**345.00**	**310.00**	**285.00**	**216.00**	**132.00**	**280.00**	**216.00**	**117.50**
98	6¢ brown violet	27.95	21.50	14.95	21.50	13.45	9.35	17.15	13.20	8.80
99	8¢ bistre brown	68.50	52.75	34.25	43.00	33.00	21.45	43.00	33.00	21.45
100	9¢ olive green	57.25	44.00	28.00	35.75	27.50	17.60	35.25	27.50	17.60
101	10¢ violet black	115.00	88.00	52.00	71.50	55.00	32.50	71.50	55.00	17.60
102	12¢ red brown	103.00	79.25	46.50	64.50	49.50	29.15	64.50	49.50	29.15
103	15¢ slate brown	103.00	79.25	46.50	64.50	49.50	29.15	64.50	49.50	29.15

110
Prince George

111
Prince John

112
Queen Alexandria

113
Duke of Connaught

114
Seal of Colony

1911 ROYAL FAMILY ISSUE

SCOTT NO.	DESCRIPTION	UNUSED O.G. VF	UNUSED O.G. F	UNUSED O.G. AVG	UNUSED VF	UNUSED F	UNUSED AVG	USED VF	USED F	USED AVG
104-14	**1¢-15¢ complete, 11 varieties**	**347.00**	**268.00**	**175.00**	**178.00**	**137.00**	**91.25**	**170.00**	**130.00**	**85.00**
104	1¢ yellow green	2.95	2.25	1.60	1.45	1.10	.80	.25	.20	.15
105	2¢ carmine	3.60	2.75	1.75	1.80	1.40	.90	.25	.20	.15
106	3¢ red brown	33.75	26.00	16.50	17.15	13.20	8.80	17.15	13.20	8.80
107	4¢ violet	25.00	19.50	13.50	12.85	9.90	7.15	11.45	8.80	6.05
108	5¢ ultramarine	14.25	11.00	7.50	7.15	5.50	3.60	1.80	1.40	.75
109	6¢ black	25.00	19.50	13.50	12.85	9.90	7.15	12.85	9.90	7.15
110	8¢ blue (paper colored)	94.25	72.50	44.00	47.95	36.85	23.65	47.95	36.85	23.65
110a	8¢ peacock blue (white paper)	99.50	76.50	48.00	50.00	38.50	24.75	50.00	38.50	24.75
111	9¢ blue violet	35.00	27.00	18.00	17.85	13.75	8.80	17.85	13.75	8.80
112	10¢ dark green	45.00	35.00	24.00	23.50	18.15	12.10	23.50	18.15	12.10
113	12¢ plum	45.00	35.00	24.00	23.50	18.15	12.10	23.50	18.15	12.10
114	50¢ magenta	41.50	32.00	21.50	21.45	16.50	11.00	21.45	16.50	11.00

115

116

TWO
CENTS
72
surcharged

THREE
CENTS
70 & 73
surcharged

131

132

133

134

135

136

137

138

139

140

1919 TRAIL OF THE CARIBOU ISSUE

SCOTT NO.	DESCRIPTION	UNUSED O.G. VF	UNUSED O.G. F	UNUSED O.G. AVG	UNUSED VF	UNUSED F	UNUSED AVG	USED VF	USED F	USED AVG
115-26	**1¢ -36¢ complete, 12 varieties**	**240.00**	**186.00**	**120.00**	**138.00**	**106.50**	**69.50**	**123.50**	**94.50**	**61.35**
115	1¢ green	2.30	1. 75	1.15	1.30	1.00	.65	.40	.30	.20
116	2¢ scarlet	2.55	1.95	1.45	1.45	1.10	.80	.55	.40	.25
117	3¢ red brown	3.20	2.45	1.65	1.80	1.40	.90	.35	.25	.15
118	4¢ violet	5.00	3.85	2.50	2.85	2.20	1.45	1.45	1.10	.65
119	5¢ ultramarine	5.75	4.40	2.70	3.25	2.50	1.55	1.45	1.10	.65
120	6¢ gray	26.00	20.25	13.50	15.00	11.55	7.70	15.00	11.55	7.70
121	8¢ magenta	20.00	15.50	10.50	11.45	8.80	6.05	10.75	8.25	5.50
122	10¢ dark green	15.00	11.55	6.75	8.50	6.60	3.85	3.50	2.75	1.65
123	12¢ orange	50.00	38.50	25.00	28.50	22.00	14.30	25.00	19.25	12.65
124	15¢ dark blue	41.25	31.75	20.25	23.50	18.15	11.55	23.50	18.15	11.00
125	24¢ bistre	46.00	35.50	23.00	26.50	20.35	13.20	26.50	20.35	13.20
126	36¢ olive green	37.35	28.75	19.25	21.45	16.50	11.00	21.50	16.50	11.00

SCOTT NO.	DESCRIPTION	UNUSED O.G. F	UNUSED O.G. AVG	UNUSED F	UNUSED AVG	USED F	USED AVG
	1920						
127	2¢ on 30¢ slate	6.90	4.25	4.95	3.05	4.95	3.05
	Bars 10-1/2mm apart						
128	3¢ on 15¢ scarlet	247.50	150.00	165.00	104.50	181.50	104.50
	Bars 13-1/2mm apart						
129	3¢ on 15¢ scarlet	11.55	6.95	8.25	6.05	8.25	6.05
130	3¢ on 35¢ red	11.55	6.95	8.25	6.05	8.25	6.05

141

142

143

144

145, 163, 172
Map of Newfoundland

146, 164, 173
S.S. Caribou

1923-24 PICTORIAL ISSUE

SCOTT NO.	DESCRIPTION	UNUSED O.G. F	UNUSED O.G. AVG	UNUSED F	UNUSED AVG	USED F	USED AVG
131-44	**1¢-24¢ complete, 14 varieties**	**121.00**	**73.00**	**85.00**	**50.95**	**77.00**	**47.00**
131	1¢ gray green	2.65	1.60	1.95	1.05	.25	.15
132	2¢ carmine	1.75	1.05	1.30	.65	.20	.15
133	3¢ brown	2.65	1.60	1.95	1.05	.20	.15
134	4¢ brown violet	2.20	1.35	1.65	.90	1.55	.95
135	5¢ ultramarine	3.85	2.30	2.75	1.50	1.75	1.10
136	6¢ gray black	4.80	2.85	3.30	1.75	3.30	1.75
137	8¢ dull violet	3.85	2.30	2.75	1.50	2.60	1.40
138	9¢ slate green	24.75	14.85	16.50	10.45	16.50	10.45
139	10¢ dark violet	4.25	2.55	3.05	1.65	1.75	1.10
140	11¢ olive green	7.70	4.60	5.50	3.05	5.50	3.05
141	12¢ lake	8.00	4.80	5.80	3.15	5.80	3.15
142	15¢ deep blue	9.10	5.45	6.60	3.85	6.35	3.60
143	20¢ red brown (1924)	8.80	5.25	6.35	3.30	4.95	2.75
144	24¢ black brown (1924)	44.00	26.50	30.25	19.80	30.25	19.80

147, 165, 174
Queen Mary and King George

148, 166, 175
Prince of Wales

149, 167, 176
Express Train

150, 168, 177
Newfoundland Hotel, St. John's

151, 178
Town of Heart's Content

152
Cabot Tower, St. John's

153, 169, 179
War Memorial, St. John's

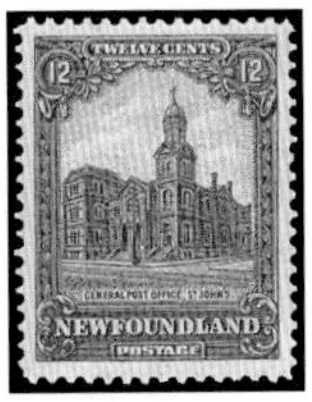

154
Post Office, St. John's

156, 170, 180
First Airplane to Cross Atlantic Non-Stop

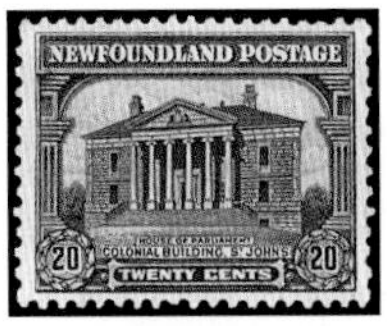

157, 171, 181
House of Parliament, St. John's

159, 182
Grand Falls, Labrador

1928 Tourist Publicity Issue

Unwatermarked. Thin paper, dull colors

SCOTT NO.	DESCRIPTION	UNUSED O.G. F	UNUSED O.G. AVG	UNUSED F	UNUSED AVG	USED F	USED AVG
145-59	**1¢-30¢ complete, 15 varieties**	**97.85**	**58.75**	**67.25**	**38.25**	**51.00**	**30.25**
145	1¢ deep green	1.65	1.00	1.05	.55	.55	.35
146	2¢ deep carmine	2.15	1.30	1.50	.85	.55	.35
147	3¢ brown	2.75	1.65	1.85	1.00	.35	.20
148	4¢ lilac rose	3.30	2.00	2.10	1.40	1.65	1.00
149	5¢ slate green	6.35	3.80	4.40	2.50	3.05	1.85
150	6¢ ultramarine	4.70	2.80	3.30	1.95	2.75	1.50
151	8¢ light red brown	6.35	3.80	4.40	2.50	3.60	1.95
152	9¢ myrtle green	7.45	4.50	5.50	2.75	4.40	2.50
153	10¢ dark violet	7.45	4.50	5.50	2.75	3.85	2.20
154	12¢ brown carmine	5.50	3.30	3.85	2.20	3.05	1.65
155	14¢ red brown	7.45	4.50	5.50	2.75	3.05	2.20
156	15¢ dark blue	8.00	4.80	6.05	3.05	4.95	2.65
157	20¢ gray black	7.45	4.50	5.50	3.05	3.30	1.85
158	28¢ gray green	24.75	14.85	14.85	9.90	13.75	8.80
159	30¢ olive brown	7.70	4.50	5.50	3.05	4.95	2.65

1929

SCOTT NO.	DESCRIPTION	UNUSED O.G. F	UNUSED O.G. AVG	UNUSED F	UNUSED AVG	USED F	USED AVG
160	3¢ on 6¢ gray black	3.50	2.10	2.95	1.75	2.95	1.75

1929-31 Tourist Publicity Issue

Types of 1928 re-engraved
Unwatermarked. Thicker paper, brighter colors

SCOTT NO.	DESCRIPTION	UNUSED O.G. F	UNUSED O.G. AVG	UNUSED F	UNUSED AVG	USED F	USED AVG
163-71	**1¢-20¢ complete, 9 varieties**	**123.00**	**73.95**	**78.00**	**44.00**	**50.25**	**27.00**
163	1¢ green	1.75	1.05	1.30	.65	.45	.30
164	2¢ deep carmine	1.75	1.05	1.30	.65	.20	.15
165	3¢ deep red brown	2.00	1.20	1.45	.80	.20	.15
166	4¢ magenta	2.95	1.75	2.10	1.10	1.00	.60
167	5¢ slate green	4.40	2.65	3.15	1.75	1.00	.60
168	6¢ ultramarine	11.55	6.95	8.25	4.40	6.60	3.60
169	10¢ dark violet	6.05	3.65	4.40	2.50	1.65	1.00
170	15¢ deep blue (1930)	41.25	24.95	24.75	14.30	23.10	12.10
171	20¢ gray black (1931)	57.75	34.75	35.75	20.35	18.70	9.90

1931 Tourist Publicity Issue

Types of 1928 re-engraved, watermarked, coat of arms
Thicker paper, brighter colors

SCOTT NO.	DESCRIPTION	UNUSED O.G. F	UNUSED O.G. AVG	UNUSED F	UNUSED AVG	USED F	USED AVG
172-82	**1¢-30¢ complete, 11 varieties**	**195.00**	**114.00**	**130.00**	**71.50**	**93.50**	**50.50**
172	1¢ green	2.50	1.40	1.65	.95	.90	.55
173	2¢ red	3.85	2.30	2.50	1.40	1.20	.75
174	3¢ red brown	3.85	2.30	2.50	1.40	.90	.55
175	4¢ rose	4.95	3.00	3.35	1.85	1.35	.85
176	5¢ greenish gray	9.90	5.95	7.15	3.85	6.05	3.30
177	6¢ ultramarine	22.00	13.25	15.40	8.80	13.75	7.70
178	8¢ light red brown	22.00	13.25	15.40	8.80	13.75	7.70
179	10¢ dark violet	11.55	6.95	8.25	4.40	6.05	3.30
180	15¢ deep blue	41.25	24.75	27.50	14.85	24.75	13.20
181	20¢ gray black	44.00	26.00	29.15	15.40	8.80	4.40
182	30¢ olive brown	38.50	21.00	24.75	13.20	20.90	11.00

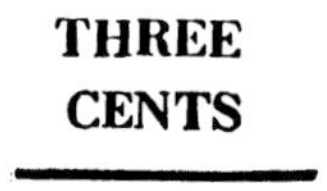

160
136 surcharged in red

183, 253
Codfish

185, 186
King George

187
Queen Mary

188, 189
Prince of Wales

190, 191, 257
Caribou

192
Princess Elizabeth

193, 260
Salmon

194, 261
Newfoundland Dog

195, 262
Northern Seal

196, 263
Trans-Atlantic Beacon

1932-37 RESOURCES ISSUE Perf. 13-1/2

SCOTT NO.	DESCRIPTION	UNUSED O.G. F	UNUSED O.G. AVG	UNUSED F	UNUSED AVG	USED F	USED AVG
183-99	**1¢-48¢ complete, 17 varieties**	**93.50**	**56.00**	**57.00**	**36.50**	**37.95**	**25.75**
183	1¢ green	1.50	.95	1.05	.65	.35	.25
184	1¢ gray black	.35	.20	.25	.20	.20	.15
185	2¢ rose	1.50	.90	1.05	.65	.20	.15
186	2¢ green	1.50	.90	1.00	.65	.20	.15
187	3¢ orange brown	1.20	.75	.85	.55	.20	.15
188	4¢ deep violet	4.95	2.90	3.60	2.30	1.40	.90
189	4¢ rose lake	.55	.35	.40	.30	.20	.15
190	5¢ violet brown (I)	6.60	3.95	4.40	2.75	.90	.55
191	5¢ deep violet (II)	1.00	.60	.65	.50	.20	.15
191a	5¢ deep violet (I)	10.45	6.25	7.00	5.25	.60	.40
192	6¢ dull blue	11.00	6.60	7.15	5.35	7.15	5.35
193	10¢ olive black	1.40	.85	.95	.60	.60	.40
194	14¢ black	2.75	1.65	1.95	1.30	1.65	1.10
195	15¢ magenta	2.75	1.65	1.95	1.30	1.65	1.10
196	20¢ gray green	2.75	1.65	2.95	1.30	.85	.55
197	25¢ gray	3.05	1.85	2.10	1.40	1.75	1.15
198	30¢ ultramarine	30.25	18.15	20.35	12.10	18.15	12.10
199	48¢ red brown (1937)	14.85	8.95	10.45	6.60	4.25	2.75

197, 265
Sealing Fleet

198, 266
Fishing Fleet

208
The Duchess of York

209, 259
Corner Brook Paper Mills

210, 264
Loading Iron Ore, Bell Island

1932 Perf. 13-1/2

SCOTT NO.	DESCRIPTION	UNUSED O.G. F	UNUSED O.G. AVG	UNUSED F	UNUSED AVG	USED F	USED AVG
208-10	7¢-24¢ complete, 3 varieties	6.60	4.00	4.70	3.15	4.50	3.10
208	7¢ red brown	1.55	.95	1.10	.75	1.10	.75
209	8¢ orange red	1.55	.95	1.10	.75	1.00	.65
210	24¢ light blue	3.85	2.30	2.75	1.85	2.65	1.85

1933 LAND & SEA OVERPRINT

SCOTT NO.	DESCRIPTION	UNUSED O.G. F	UNUSED O.G. AVG	UNUSED F	UNUSED AVG	USED F	USED AVG
211	15¢ brown	10.00	6.00	7.15	4.40	5.75	3.55

L. & S. Post.
211
No. C9 with Overprint and Bars

212
Sir Humphrey Gilbert

213
Compton Castle, Devon

214
The Gilbert Arms

216
Token to Gilbert from Queen Elizabeth

215
Eton College

217
Gilbert Commissioned by Queen Elizabeth

218
Gilbert's Fleet Leaving Plymouth

219
The Fleet Arriving at St. John's

220
Annexation of Newfoundland

221
Coat of Arms of England

1933 SIR HUMPHREY GILBERT ISSUE

SCOTT NO.	DESCRIPTION	UNUSED O.G. F	UNUSED O.G. AVG	UNUSED F	UNUSED AVG	USED F	USED AVG
212-25	**1¢-32¢ complete, 14 varieties**	**144.00**	**86.75**	**98.75**	**65.95**	**94.75**	**67.50**
212	1¢ gray black	.95	.60	.75	.50	.55	.40
213	2¢ green	1.20	.75	.95	.60	.55	.40
214	3¢ yellow brown	1.65	1.00	1.30	.85	.95	.65
215	4¢ carmine	1.65	1.00	1.30	.85	.40	.30
216	5¢ dull violet	2.10	1.30	1.65	1.10	.95	.65
217	7¢ blue	15.95	9.50	10.45	6.60	12.65	8.25
218	8¢ orange red	8.25	5.00	5.80	3.85	5.80	4.15
219	9¢ ultramarine	9.35	5.60	6.35	4.15	6.30	4.40
220	10¢ red brown	8.25	5.00	5.80	3.85	4.95	3.60
221	14¢ black	18.15	10.95	12.65	8.25	11.55	8.25
222	15¢ claret	18.15	10.95	12.40	8.00	11.00	8.25
223	20¢ deep green	11.00	6.60	8.25	5.50	7.70	5.25
224	24¢ violet brown	27.50	16.50	18.15	12.65	18.15	13.20
225	32¢ gray	27.50	16.50	18.15	12.65	18.15	13.20

222
Gilbert on the "Squirrel"

223
1624 Map of Newfoundland

224
Queen Elizabeth I

225
Gilbert Statue at Truro

226
Windsor Castle and King George

1935 SILVER JUBILEE

SCOTT NO.	DESCRIPTION	UNUSED F/NH	UNUSED F	USED F
226-29	**4¢-24¢ complete, 4 varieties**	**11.00**	**8.40**	**8.00**
226	4¢ bright rose	1.10	.85	.60
227	5¢ violet	1.10	.85	.75
228	7¢ dark blue	2.75	2.20	2.20
229	24¢ olive green	6.60	4.95	4.95

1937 CORONATION ISSUE

SCOTT NO.	DESCRIPTION	UNUSED F/NH	UNUSED F	USED F
230-32	**2¢-5¢ complete, 3 varieties**	**1.90**	**1.55**	**1.40**
230	2¢ deep green	.55	.45	.40
231	4¢ carmine rose	.55	.45	.35
232	5¢ dark violet	.90	.75	.75

230
King George VI and Queen Elizabeth

233

234
Die I: Fine Impression
Die II: Coarse Impression

235

236

237

238

239

240

241

242

245, 254
King George VI

243

1937 LONG CORONATION ISSUE

SCOTT NO.	DESCRIPTION	UNUSED F/NH	UNUSED F	USED F
233-43	**1¢-48¢ complete, 11 varieties**	**30.25**	**20.95**	**17.85**
233	1¢ Codfish	.50	.35	.25
234	3¢ Map, die I	2.05	1.40	.60
234a	3¢ same, die II	1.85	1.20	.45
235	7¢ Caribou	2.20	1.55	1.35
236	8¢ Paper Mills	2.20	1.55	1.50
237	10¢ Salmon	4.15	2.75	2.50
238	14¢ Newfoundland Dog	3.30	2.30	2.05
239	15¢ Northern Seal	3.30	2.30	2.05
240	20¢ Cape Race	2.75	1.95	1.65
241	24¢ Bell Island	3.60	2.55	2.30
242	25¢ Sealing Fleet	3.60	2.55	2.20
243	48¢ Fishing Fleet	4.15	2.75	2.50

249

2
▲ CENTS ▲
250
249 surcharged

1938 ROYAL FAMILY Perf. 13-1/2

SCOTT NO.	DESCRIPTION	UNUSED F/NH	UNUSED F	USED F
245-48	**2¢-7¢ complete, 4 varieties**	**6.55**	**4.45**	**1.65**
245	2¢ green	1.65	1.10	.15
246	3¢ dark carmine	1.85	1.10	.15
247	4¢ light blue	1.95	1.40	.15
248	7¢ dark ultramarine	1.65	1.10	1.20
249	5¢ violet blue	.85	.60	.60

249 SURCHARGED

SCOTT NO.	DESCRIPTION	UNUSED F/NH	UNUSED F	USED F
250	2¢ on 5¢ violet blue	1.30	.95	.95
251	4¢ on 5¢ violet blue	1.00	.75	.75

252

267

1941 GRENFELL ISSUE

SCOTT NO.	DESCRIPTION	UNUSED F/NH	UNUSED F	USED F
252	5¢ dull blue	.45	.35	.35

1941-44 RESOURCES ISSUE

Designs of 1931-38. Perf. 12-1/2

SCOTT NO.	DESCRIPTION	UNUSED F/NH	UNUSED F	USED F
253-66	**1¢-48¢ complete, 14 varieties**	**16.25**	**10.25**	**10.30**
253	1¢ dark gray	.30	.20	.15
254	2¢ deep green	.30	.20	.15
255	3¢ rose carmine	.30	.25	.15
256	4¢ blue	.65	.45	.15
257	5¢ violet	.65	.50	.15
258	7¢ violet blue (1942)	1.00	.65	.85
259	8¢ red	.85	.65	.60
260	10¢ brownish black	.85	.55	.55
261	14¢ black	1.65	1.10	1.20
262	15¢ pale rose violet	1.65	1.10	1.20
263	20¢ green	1.65	1.10	1.20
264	24¢ deep blue	1.95	1.35	1.55
265	25¢ slate	1.95	1.35	1.55
266	48¢ red brown (1944)	3.30	2.20	1.40

TWO

CENTS

268
267 surcharged

269

270

1943-47

SCOTT NO.	DESCRIPTION	UNUSED F/NH	UNUSED F	USED F
267	30¢ Memorial University	1.45	1.05	.95
268	2¢ on 30¢ University (1946)	.35	.30	.30
269	4¢ Princess Elizabeth (1947)	.35	.30	.15
270	5¢ Cabot (1947)	.35	.30	.15

AIR POST STAMPS

Trans-Atlantic
AIR POST,
1919.
ONE DOLLAR.

C2
70 surcharged

AIR MAIL
to Halifax, N.S.
1921

C3
73 overprinted

Air Mail
DE PINEDO
1927

C4
74 overprinted

Trans-Atlantic
AIR MAIL
By B. M.
"Columbia"
September
1930
Fifty Cents

C5
126 surcharged

C6, C9
Airplane and Dog Team

1919

SCOTT NO.	DESCRIPTION	UNUSED O.G. VF	UNUSED O.G. F	UNUSED O.G. AVG	UNUSED VF	UNUSED F	UNUSED AVG	USED VF	USED F	USED AVG
C2	$1 on 15¢ scarlet	200.00	150.00	112.50	175.00	131.25	98.00	180.00	135.00	105.00
C2a	same without comma after "POST"	240.00	180.00	135.00	210.00	157.50	120.00	225.00	170.00	125.00

1921

SCOTT NO.	DESCRIPTION	UNUSED O.G. VF	UNUSED O.G. F	UNUSED O.G. AVG	UNUSED VF	UNUSED F	UNUSED AVG	USED VF	USED F	USED AVG
C3	35¢ red	180.00	135.00	105.00	140.00	105.00	78.75	140.00	105.00	78.75
C3a	same with period after "1921"	200.00	150.00	112.50	175.00	131.25	98.00	180.00	135.00	105.00

C7, C10
First Trans-atlantic Airmail

C8, C11
Routes of Historic Trans-atlantic Flights

TRANS-ATLANTIC
WEST TO EAST
Per Dornier DO-X
May, 1932.
One Dollar and Fifty Cents

C12
C11 surcharged

C13

1931 Unwatermarked

SCOTT NO.	DESCRIPTION	UNUSED O.G. VF	UNUSED O.G. F	UNUSED O.G. AVG	UNUSED VF	UNUSED F	UNUSED AVG	USED VF	USED F	USED AVG
C6	15¢ brown	12.85	9.90	5.95	8.50	6.60	4.40	8.50	6.60	4.40
C7	50¢ green	32.15	24.75	15.00	21.50	16.50	11.00	23.50	18.15	12.65
C8	$1 blue	85.75	66.00	39.50	57.25	44.00	30.25	60.00	46.75	31.35

Watermarked Coat of Arms

SCOTT NO.	DESCRIPTION	UNUSED O.G. VF	UNUSED O.G. F	UNUSED O.G. AVG	UNUSED VF	UNUSED F	UNUSED AVG	USED VF	USED F	USED AVG
C9	15¢ brown	10.00	7.70	4.56	7.15	5.50	3.30	7.15	5.50	3.30
C10	50¢ green	50.00	38.50	23.00	32.15	24.75	16.50	30.75	23.65	15.95
C11	$1 blue	120.00	93.50	56.00	78.50	60.50	42.35	75.00	57.75	38.50

1932 TRANS-ATLANTIC FLIGHT

SCOTT NO.	DESCRIPTION	UNUSED O.G. VF	UNUSED O.G. F	UNUSED O.G. AVG	UNUSED VF	UNUSED F	UNUSED AVG	USED VF	USED F	USED AVG
C12	$1.50 on $1 blue	470.00	360.00	225.00	360.00	275.00	181.50	360.00	275.00	181.50

SCOTT NO.	DESCRIPTION	UNUSED O.G. VF	UNUSED O.G. F	UNUSED O.G. AVG	UNUSED VF	UNUSED F	UNUSED AVG	USED VF	USED F	USED AVG

C14

C15

1933 LABRADOR ISSUE

SCOTT NO.	DESCRIPTION	UNUSED O.G. VF	UNUSED O.G. F	UNUSED O.G. AVG	UNUSED VF	UNUSED F	UNUSED AVG	USED VF	USED F	USED AVG
C13-17	**5¢-75¢ complete, 5 varieties**	**206.00**	**172.50**	**103.50**	**135.00**	**112.50**	**75.00**	**135.00**	**112.50**	**75.00**
C13	5¢ "Put to Flight"	15.85	13.20	7.95	9.90	8.25	5.75	9.90	8.25	5.80
C14	10¢ "Land of Heart's Delight"	23.75	19.80	11.85	13.75	11.55	8.00	13.75	11.55	8.00
C15	30¢ "Spotting the Herd"	39.50	33.00	19.75	26.50	22.00	14.85	26.50	22.00	14.85
C16	60¢ "News from Home"	69.25	57.75	34.75	46.25	38.50	24.75	46.25	38.50	24.75
C17	75¢ "Labrador, The Land of Gold"	69.25	57.75	34.75	46.25	38.00	25.85	46.25	38.00	25.85

C16

C17

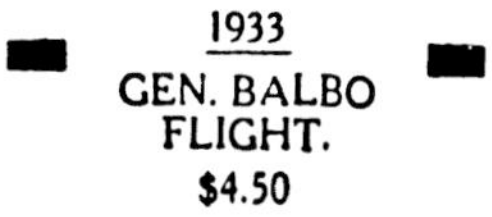

C18
C17 Surcharged

C19

1933 BALBOA FLIGHT ISSUE

SCOTT NO.	DESCRIPTION	UNUSED O.G. VF	UNUSED O.G. F	UNUSED O.G. AVG	UNUSED VF	UNUSED F	UNUSED AVG	USED VF	USED F	USED AVG
C18	$4.50 on 75¢ bistre	650.00	545.00	330.00	460.00	385.00	302.50	460.00	385.00	302.50

1943

SCOTT NO.	DESCRIPTION	UNUSED O.G. VF	UNUSED O.G. F	UNUSED O.G. AVG	UNUSED VF	UNUSED F	UNUSED AVG	USED VF	USED F	USED AVG
C19	7¢ St. John's	.55	.45	.40	.50	.40	.35	.30	.25	.15

POSTAGE DUE STAMPS

J1

1939 Unwatermarked, Perf. 10-1/2x10

SCOTT NO.	DESCRIPTION	UNUSED F/NH	UNUSED F	USED F
J1	1¢ yellow green	2.50	1.65	1.65
J2	2¢ vermillion	3.85	2.50	2.50
J3	3¢ ultramarine	4.95	3.30	3.30
J4	4¢ yellow orange	6.05	4.15	4.15
J5	5¢ pale brown	4.15	2.75	2.75
J6	10¢ dark violet	3.85	2.65	2.65

1946-49
Unwatermarked, Perf. 11

SCOTT NO.	DESCRIPTION	UNUSED F/NH	UNUSED F	USED F
J1a	1¢ yellow green	4.95	3.30	3.30

Unwatermarked, Perf. 11x9

SCOTT NO.	DESCRIPTION	UNUSED F/NH	UNUSED F	USED F
J2a	2¢ vermillion	4.95	3.30	3.30
J3a	3¢ ultramarine	5.50	3.85	3.85
J4a	4¢ yellow orange	7.15	4.95	4.95

Watermarked, Perf. 11

SCOTT NO.	DESCRIPTION	UNUSED F/NH	UNUSED F	USED F
J7	10¢ dark violet	9.35	6.35	6.35

1
Crown of Great Britain surrounded by Heraldic Flowers of the United Kingdom

6

7

8

9

10

11

1851 PENCE ISSUE. Imperforate

SCOTT NO.	DESCRIPTION	UNUSED O.G. VF	UNUSED O.G. F	UNUSED O.G. AVG	UNUSED VF	UNUSED F	UNUSED AVG	USED VF	USED F	USED AVG
1	3p red	2025.00	1565.00	865.00	1350.00	1045.00	577.50	425.00	320.00	240.00
2	6p olive yellow	4800.00	3700.00	2250.00	3200.00	2475.00	1495.00	775.00	580.00	440.00
3	1sh bright red violet	16750.00	11200.00	8000.00	10000.00	8000.00	5000.00	3800.00	2850.00	2150.00
4	1sh dull violet	14000.00	10500.00	7700.00	10000.00	7700.00	4800.00	4800.00	3600.00	2700.00

1860-63 CENTS ISSUE
(NH + 50%)

SCOTT NO.	DESCRIPTION	UNUSED O.G. VF	UNUSED O.G. F	UNUSED O.G. AVG	UNUSED VF	UNUSED F	UNUSED AVG	USED VF	USED F	USED AVG
6	1¢ Locomotive	40.00	30.00	22.50	30.00	22.50	17.00	28.00	21.00	15.50
7	2¢ Queen Victoria, orange (1863)	15.00	11.25	8.50	12.50	9.50	7.00	14.00	10.50	7.75
8	5¢ same, yellow green	15.00	11.25	8.50	12.50	9.50	7.00	14.00	10.50	7.75
9	10¢ same, vermillion	45.00	33.75	25.25	42.00	31.50	23.75	45.00	33.75	25.00
10	12-1/2¢ Ships	70.00	52.50	39.50	60.00	45.00	33.75	70.00	52.50	39.50
11	17¢ Prince of Wales	45.00	33.75	25.25	42.00	31.50	23.75	45.00	33.75	25.00

Nova Scotia #1-13

1

2, 3
Royal Crown and Heraldic Flowers of the United Kingdom

1851-53 PENCE ISSUE
Imperf. Blue Paper

SCOTT NO.	DESCRIPTION	UNUSED O.G. VF	UNUSED O.G. F	UNUSED O.G. AVG	UNUSED VF	UNUSED F	UNUSED AVG	USED VF	USED F	USED AVG
1	1p Queen Victoria	2600.00	1950.00	1450.00	2200.00	1650.00	1250.00	500.00	375.00	280.00
2	3p blue	725.00	550.00	400.00	575.00	430.00	300.00	140.00	105.00	73.50
3	3p dark blue	950.00	715.00	500.00	800.00	600.00	420.00	190.00	142.50	100.00
4	6p yellow green	3485.00	2675.00	2050.00	3000.00	2200.00	1500.00	430.00	330.00	220.00
5	6p dark green	7650.00	5885.00	4535.00	6200.00	4650.00	3250.00	850.00	637.50	450.00
6	1sh reddish violet	18000.00	13500.00	9450.00	14000.00	10500.00	7350.00	3550.00	2675.00	1850.00
7	1sh dull violet	18500.00	13875.00	9725.00	15000.00	11250.00	7875.00	3900.00	2925.00	2050.00

8

11
Queen Victoria

12

1860-63 CENTS ISSUE
White or Yellowish Paper, Perf. 12
(NH + 50%)

SCOTT NO.	DESCRIPTION	UNUSED O.G. VF	UNUSED O.G. F	UNUSED O.G. AVG	UNUSED VF	UNUSED F	UNUSED AVG	USED VF	USED F	USED AVG
8	1¢ black	6.50	4.30	2.65	5.40	3.60	2.20	4.95	3.30	2.20
9	2¢ lilac	8.85	5.95	3.95	7.40	4.95	3.30	7.40	4.95	3.30
10	5¢ blue	340.00	230.00	150.00	285.00	192.50	126.50	11.50	7.70	4.25
11	8-1/2¢ green	5.95	3.95	2.65	4.95	3.30	2.20	19.75	13.20	8.25
12	10¢ vermillion	8.85	5.95	3.95	7.40	4.95	3.30	7.40	4.95	3.30
13	12-1/2¢ black	29.75	19.75	15.00	24.75	16.50	12.65	24.75	16.50	11.55

1, 5

2, 6

3, 7

Queen Victoria

1861 PENCE ISSUE, Perf. 9

SCOTT NO.	DESCRIPTION	UNUSED O.G. VF	UNUSED O.G. F	UNUSED O.G. AVG	UNUSED VF	UNUSED F	UNUSED AVG	USED VF	USED F	USED AVG
1	2p dull rose	375.00	280.00	197.50	325.00	245.00	170.00	190.00	142.50	100.00
2	3p blue	855.00	660.00	130.00	700.00	525.00	370.00	400.00	300.00	210.00
3	6p yellow green	1375.00	1025.00	725.00	1200.00	900.00	625.00	800.00	600.00	425.00

4

8

9

10

1862-65 PENCE ISSUE, Perf. 11 to 12
(NH + 50%)

SCOTT NO.	DESCRIPTION	UNUSED O.G. VF	UNUSED O.G. F	UNUSED O.G. AVG	UNUSED VF	UNUSED F	UNUSED AVG	USED VF	USED F	USED AVG
4	1p yellow orange	25.00	19.25	13.50	19.25	14.85	10.45	26.00	19.50	13.75
5	2p rose	7.50	5.75	3.60	5.75	4.40	2.75	5.75	4.40	2.75
6	3p blue	12.00	7.85	4.30	9.30	6.05	3.30	12.00	9.00	6.25
7	6p yellow green	90.00	53.50	35.75	69.50	41.25	27.50	70.00	52.50	36.75
8	9p violet	60.50	35.75	23.50	46.50	27.50	18.15	58.00	43.50	30.00

1868-70 PENCE ISSUE
(NH + 50%)

SCOTT NO.	DESCRIPTION	UNUSED O.G. VF	UNUSED O.G. F	UNUSED O.G. AVG	UNUSED VF	UNUSED F	UNUSED AVG	USED VF	USED F	USED AVG
9	4p black	10.25	7.85	5.40	7.85	6.05	4.15	19.25	14.85	9.35
10	4-1/2p brown (1870)	46.50	35.75	25.00	35.75	27.50	19.25	43.00	33.00	22.00

11

12

13

14

15

16
Queen Victoria

1872 CENTS ISSUE
(NH + 40%)

SCOTT NO.	DESCRIPTION	UNUSED O.G. VF	UNUSED O.G. F	UNUSED O.G. AVG	UNUSED VF	UNUSED F	UNUSED AVG	USED VF	USED F	USED AVG
11	1¢ brown orange	6.00	4.60	3.00	5.00	3.85	2.50	9.30	7.15	4.70
12	2¢ ultramarine	12.90	9.90	6.60	10.75	8.25	5.50	23.50	18.15	12.10
13	3¢ rose	20.75	15.85	10.55	17.25	13.20	8.80	15.00	11.55	7.70
14	4¢ green	6.90	5.25	3.65	5.75	4.40	3.05	26.50	20.35	13.75
15	6¢ black	5.75	4.30	3.30	4.75	3.60	2.75	23.50	18.15	12.10
16	12¢ violet	6.50	5.00	3.30	5.40	4.15	2.75	35.75	27.50	20.35

NOTES

HOW TO WRITE YOUR ORDER

Please use order form

1. Print all requested information (name, address, etc.)
2. Indicate quantity, country (U.S, UN, CAN or province), catalog number, item description (sgle., pt. block, F.D. cover, etc.)
3. Specify condition (F, VF, NH etc.) and check whether mint or used.
4. Enter price as listed in this catalog.
5. Total all purchases, adding shipping/handling charge from table below. Alabama and Georgia residents (only) also add sales tax.
6. Payment may be made by check, money order, or credit card (VISA, Discover or MasterCard accepted). ORDERS FROM OUTSIDE THE U.S. MUST BE PAID BY CREDIT CARD, and all payment must be in U.S. funds.

SHIPPING AND HANDLING CHARGES*
Safe delivery is guaranteed. We assume all losses.

If ordering STAMPS ONLY Orders under $150.00	add $3.95
If order includes supply items and totals	
Orders under $50.00	add $4.95
Orders over $50.00	add $6.95
Orders over $150.00	add $8.95
Orders over $300	add $11.95

*The following charges may not fully cover the actual postage or freight, insurance and handling cost for foreign orders, and additional charges may be added.

H.E. HARRIS PERFORMANCE PLEDGE

- All stamps are genuine, exactly as described, and have been inspected by our staff experts.
- H.E. Harris & Co. upholds the standards set forth by the American Philatelic Society and the American Stamp Dealers Association.
- If you have any problem with your order, phone us at 1-800-546-2995. We will handle it to your complete satisfaction.
- 30 day return privilege on all merchandise.

Catalog or Stock No.	Qty.	Description	Mint	Used	Unit Price	Total Price
					TOTAL THIS SIDE	

H.E. Harris & Co.®

Serving the Collector Since 1916

4001 Helton Drive, Bldg. A • Florence, AL 35630

www.whitmanbooks.com

You may also order by phone 1-800-546-2995 or Fax 1-256-246-1116

30 day Money-back Guarantee on every item.

Sorry, no CODs.

Make payment in U.S. dollars by personal check, money order, Visa, Master Card, Discover or American Express. Please do not send cash.

Orders for shipment outside the U.S. must be paid by credit card and shipping charges will be added.

We Thank You For Your Order!

RUSH SHIPMENT TO:

Name ______________________________

Address ______________________________

City/State/Zip ______________________________

Phone *(in case of question about your order)* ______________________________

FAST CREDIT CARD ORDERING

☐ VISA ☐ MasterCard ☐ DISCOVER ☐ AMERICAN EXPRESS

Card # ______________________________

Expiration Date ______________________________

Signature ______________________________

Catalog or Stock No.	Qty.	Description	Mint	Used	Unit Price	Total Price

Shipping & Handling

If ordering STAMPS ONLY Orders under $150.00 .... add $3.95

If order includes supply items and totals

Orders under $50.00 .... add $4.95

Orders over $50.00 .... add $6.95

Orders over $150.00 .... add $8.95

Orders over $300 .... add $11.95

Foreign orders: S&H will be added separately.

TOTAL FRONT	
TOTAL REVERSE	
DISCOUNTS–If applicable	
SUBTOTAL	
SHIPPING CHARGE	
AL & GA RESIDENTS ADD SALES TAX	
TOTAL PURCHASE	

For Office Use Only

2008USBNA

Catalog or Stock No.	Qty.	Description	Mint	Used	Unit Price	Total Price
TOTAL THIS SIDE						

Catalog or Stock No.	Qty.	Description	Mint	Used	Unit Price	Total Price
					TOTAL THIS SIDE	